Cost Accounting

Second Edition

Cost Accounting

Second Edition

M Y Khan
Former Professor of Finance
Department of Financial Studies
University of Delhi
Delhi

P K Jain
Emeritus Professor of Finance, Department of Management Studies
Indian Institute of Technology Delhi

McGraw Hill Education (India) Private Limited

Published by McGraw Hill Education (India) Private Limited,
444/1, Sri Ekambara Naicker Industrial Estate, Alapakkam, Porur, Chennai 600116, Tamil Nadu, India.

Cost Accounting, 2/e

Sixth reprint 2019
RLBZCDDTDZCCC

ISBN (13 digits): 978-93-392-0344-3
ISBN (10 digits): 93-392-0344-5

07 08 09 10 11 RAJ 23 22 21 20 19

Managing Director: *Lalit Singh*
Senior Portfolio Manager: *Hemant K Jha*
Assistant Manager—Production Services: *Atul Gupta*
General Manager—Production: *Rajender P Ghansela*
Manager—Production: *Reji Kumar*

Typeset at The Composers, 260, C.A Apt., Paschim Vihar, New Delhi 110063, and,
Printed and Bound in India at Rajkamal Electric Press, Plot No.2, Phase – IV, Kundli, Sonepat, Haryana.

Visit us at: www.mheducation.co.in ; (Toll free in India): **1800 103 5875**
Write to us at: info.india@mheducation.com

CIN: U80302TN2010PTC111532

Preface

We are pleased to place in the hands of the readers this new edition of our book *Cost Accounting*. The main focus of this revised edition is on providing to the readers an in-depth analysis of how to ascertain cost, and use cost accounting information for profit planning, cost control and decision-making. It is primarily designed for teachers and students of cost accounting in the commerce, management and related disciplines, as well as in courses like chartered accountancy.

Thoroughly enriched content and pedagogy sets apart this second edition from the previous one.

Enriched content

All the chapters have been revised and updated. Apart from this, a new chapter on Activity Based Costing System has been included. It also includes a section on Quality Costs in Chapter 16.

Enriched pedagogy

Learning Objectives Each chapter begins with a number of learning objectives to ensure broad understanding of the concepts, theories and techniques of cost accounting.

Margin Notes Throughout the text, margin notes in side bars define the important concepts and key terms when they are first introduced. They would enable the readers to re-inforce their learning.

Chapter Summary Chapter-end comprehensive summaries would provide a bird's eye view of the main points by way of recapitulation.

Cases Yet another distinctive feature is the inclusion of selective cases. These chapter-end cases can be used by the readers to synthesise and apply related concepts, theories and techniques.

Solution Manual The revised edition contains the solution manual on the companion website: ***http://www.mhhe.com/khan_jain_cost2e*** having detailed solutions to all the chapter-end numerical review questions in the book.

Acknowledgements

We would like to express our intellectual debt of gratitude to the numerous authors who have enriched the stream of literature in cost accounting on which we have liberally drawn. Some of the more specific references are indicated in the text itself. The authors also record a word of appreciation for Prof. Surendra S Yadav's contribution.

We gratefully acknowledge contribution of our Ph.D. students Ms Vandana Bhama and Ms Sadaf Anwar. We have a word of appreciation for the excellent support from Ms Vibha Mahajan, Mr. Tapas K Maji, Mr. Hemant K Jha, Ms Silvi Dua, Mr. Manohar Lal and Mr. Atul Gupta of MHEI for the speedy and excellent publication of the book.

M Y Khan
P K Jain

Preface to the First Edition

The book *Cost Accounting* is devoted to a discussion of concepts, theories, techniques of cost ascertainment and their application for planning, control, performance evaluation and decision making. The objective is to provide to the readers an in-depth insight into these aspects of cost accounting in a simple, logical, lucid, and comprehensive manner. It is primarily addressed to the students and teachers of cost accounting, chartered accountancy, commerce, management and related disciplines. It would also be useful to the practicing chartered accountants, cost accountants, company secretaries and professional executives.

Organisation

To ensure a logical presentation of the theme, the book is divided into three parts: (i) Introduction, (ii) Product Costing/Cost Ascertainment, and (iii) Profit Planning, Cost Control, Performance Evaluation and Decision Making.

Part one consists of two chapters. Chapter 1, which is devoted to an overview of cost accounting, discusses its objectives, relationships between cost accounting and financial accounting, and between cost accounting and management accounting; and also cost ascertainment, and installation of costing system. The cost concepts related to managerial needs are examined in Chapter 2.

The subject matter covered in part two is the ascertainment of cost in different jobs, processes, activities, and so on. The chapters 3 to 6 dwell on the elements of costs, namely, costing and control of materials (Chapter 3), labour (Chapter 4), factory/manufacturing overheads (Chapter 5), and non-manufacturing overheads (Chapter 6). Chapters 7 to 12 of this part examine the system and procedure of product costing in various situations: Chapter 7 (Job-order, Batch and Contract Costing); Chapter 8 (Process, Joint and By-product Costing); Chapter 9 (Unit and Operating Costing); Chapter 10 (Variable and Absorption Costing); Chapter 11 (Uniform Costing and Inter-firm Comparison); and Chapter 12 (Reconciliation and Integration).

The application of cost data in planning, controlling, evaluating performance and decision making are described and comprehensively illustrated in the last part of the book. As a tool of profit planning, cost-volume-profit analysis and budgeting are illustrated in Chapters 13 and 14 respectively. Chapter 15 (Standard Costs), Chapter 16 (Cost Variances) and Chapter 17 (Revenue Variances) discuss the application of cost data for cost control purposes. The relevant aspects of performance evaluation are examined in Chapter 18 (Responsibility Accounting). The last chapter analyses the various short-term product and pricing decisions based on costing data.

Pedagogical Features

The pedagogy of the book is tailored to the requirement of the readers to improve their understanding and comprehension of the subject matter. The main pedagogical features are:

Organisation The treatment of the subject-matter is structured around cost ascertainment/ product costing and the uses of cost accounting information for planning, controlling, performance evaluation, and decision making. Our approach is to describe a concept followed by an illustration with the help of numerous step-by-step examples and their solutions, to make it easier to understand. We have followed a concise and simple writing style so that the text is easy to read. In short, we have adopted a lucid, non-mathematical, problem and solution approach to explain the concepts and theories of cost accounting.

Solved Problems Our experience has shown that the intricacies of concepts/theories are best learnt by numerical illustrations. Several real-life illustrative problems with solutions have, therefore, been included in each chapter. This is, in fact, one of the unique features of our text.

Exercises A comprehensive set of questions and real-life class-tested problems at the end of all the chapters serve as a means by which students may test their grasp of the material presented within the chapters. Numerous problems are included to provide multiple self-testing opportunities to the readers. Answers to end-of-chapter problems are given to cross-check their performance in preparing detailed problems-solutions.

Support Items The detailed bibliography and index are intended to guide those who may be interested in a more detailed study of the subject.

Complementary Volumes Related titles are our following books published by Tata McGraw-Hill Publishing Company Ltd.

— *Theory and Problems in Cost Accounting*
— *Basic Financial Management*
— *Management Accounting* (third edition)

We hope that the readers would find our new volume useful. Suggestions for its improvement are welcome.

AUTHORS

Contents

Cost Accounting— An Overview

Learning Objectives

1. Understand the nature of cost accounting.
2. Explain basic cost concepts, their definitions and classifications as a conceptual foundation.
3. Analyse the main elements of costs.
4. Illustrate the installation of cost accounting system.

INTRODUCTION

The primary purpose of accounting is to provide financial information relating to an economic/ business activity. It is concerned with measuring, recording, and reporting financial information by the management to plan and control the activities of a business as well as by other stakeholders who provide funds or who have various interests in the operations of an entity. The accounting system that provides the information to measure product costs and performance, and control the operations of a firm is called cost accounting. An overview of this system of accounting is the focus of this chapter, which is a background to a detailed account of its features in the subsequent chapters of this book. Section 1 of the chapter dwells on the nature of cost accounting in terms of its objectives, and the relationship between financial, cost and management accounting. The cost concepts and their classifications are briefly outlined in Section 2 to provide a conceptual foundation for the subject-matter covered subsequently. The framework of cost ascertainment/product costing is presented in Section 3. While the considerations in the installation of a costing system in an organisation are highlighted in Section 4, the last Section summarises the main points.

Accounting system that provides the information to measure product costs and performance, and control the operations of a firm is called cost accounting.

NATURE OF COST ACCOUNTING

This section dwells on the nature of cost accounting. It is illustrated with reference to (i) Meaning and objectives of cost accounting and (ii) The relationship between cost, financial and management accounting.

Meaning and Objectives

Meaning Financial accounting results in reports to external parties on the status of assets, liabilities and equity; results of operations; changes in owner's equity and changes in the sources and uses of funds for an accounting period. Cost data are/must be accumulated both for external financial accounting and internal management purposes. It accumulates, classifies and interprets information concerning the cost of materials, labour and other costs of manufacturing and marketing. Thus, it communicates financial information to management for planning, evaluating and controlling resources.

One of the primary objectives of financial accounting is the income determination. While calculating income, cost data are also used. Cost accounting provides an important input to financial accounting to the extent it provides cost data for determining income and financial position.

Thus, cost accounting is that part of accounting which identifies, defines, measures, reports and analyses the various elements of direct and indirect costs associated with manufacturing and providing goods/services. In the process of accumulating costs for inventory valuation and income determination, the needs of external users and management are fulfilled. It also provides management with an accurate, timely information for planning, controlling, and company operations.

Objectives The information needs of management and cost accounting objectives are closely related. The main objectives of cost accounting are: (i) Product costing (Cost ascertainment); (ii) Planning, performance evaluation and control and (iii) Decision making.

Product Costing Ascertainment of cost is one primary objective of cost accounting. The determination of total product cost and cost per unit are important for inventory valuation, product pricing and managerial decision making. Product costing covers the entire cycle of accumulating manufacturing and other costs and subsequently assigning them to work-in-process, finished goods, and so on.

Planning and Control The creation of useful cost data and information for planning and control by management is another important objective of cost accounting. The tools of managerial planning and control are budgeting and standard costing. The different plans/budgets are evaluated in relation to associated costs and benefits. The control technique compares the actual and budgeted performances. The variances between budgets/standard costs and actuals/actual costs are analysed by causes and, in that light, corrective actions are taken.

Decision Making Yet another objective of cost accounting is to provide information for both short- and long-term decisions. Decision-making primarily involves choice out of available alternatives.

Financial, Cost and Management Accounting

Accounting is a system of collecting, summarising, analysing and reporting information about a business enterprise, in financial (monetary) terms. The business accounting system consists of three parts: (i) Financial accounting, (ii) Cost accounting, and (iii) Management accounting. The inter-relationship between them is discussed below.

Financial and Cost Accounting: Similarities Financial accounting and cost accounting represent the two parts of the accounting information system of a business enterprise. These are similar on two counts. *Firstly*, operating information is used in the preparation of financial as well as cost accounts. If an enterprise has two completely different systems for collecting information for two purposes, it would involve, among other things, the incurrence of extra costs. The use of financial accounting information for cost accounting is, therefore, economical. This implies that financial accounting has a significant influence on cost accounting. *Secondly*, the considerations which make *Generally Accepted Accounting Principles* (GAAP) useful in financial accounting, are equally relevant in cost accounting also. For example, management cannot base its reporting system on non-verifiable, subjective estimates of costs because cost and revenue concepts in financial accounting are based on the idea of objectivity.

Differences Nevertheless, the two systems of accounting differ from each other in several respects. One basic difference between financial accounting and cost accounting relates to the structure or format of presenting information. Financial accounting has a single unified structure in the sense that the information relating to the operations of various enterprises is presented on a more or less uniform basis. It may be recalled that the end-products of financial accounting are the three financial statements: (i) Balance sheet, (ii) Statement of profit and loss/Income statement and (iii) Cash flow statement. The preparation of various financial statements on the basis of a specified model implies that, while preparing accounts, all firms arrange the information in a uniform manner. *In other words, financial accounting has a unified structure.*

Financial accounting has a single unified structure in the sense that the information relating to the operations of various enterprises is presented on a more or less uniform basis.

Why is the structure of financial accounting uniform? The primary objective of financial accounting is to provide information to outside parties, namely, shareholders, creditors, Government, investors, lenders, and so on. These outside-users of the financial statements are interested in information from many different perspectives. In order to enable an inter-firm comparison, there is a distinct need to present financial accounting on a uniform basis, and within a unified structure. The unified structure of financial accounts, therefore, facilitates communication between a business and the outside stakeholders interested in it.

In contrast, cost accounting concerns itself with the accounting information that is useful to the management only. As this type of accounting is undertaken for internal use, its structure varies with the requirements and circumstances of each case. In other words, cost accounting is tailored to meet the needs of the management of a specific business, and therefore, it lacks a single unified structure. A related aspect is the impact of the GAAP on the preparation of the two types of accounting. Financial accounting is prepared in accordance with the GAAP. Accounting is the 'language of business', as it is the principal means by which information about a business is communicated to those interested in it. If, therefore, the information is to be communicated effectively and understood properly, it should be prepared in accordance with a mutually understood set of rules. These ground rules are referred to as GAAP. They represent laws or rules to be used as guideline in the preparation of financial accounts. In other words, GAAP provides a specified framework for the preparation of financial accounts which has evolved over the years and is based on experience, reason, usage, convention and necessity. Thus, they ensure that financial accounts are prepared in accordance with certain norms and standards for better comprehension and reliability. On the other hand, cost accounting is for the exclusive use of the management of a firm. Outsiders do not need such accounts and have no access to them either. Therefore, there is a scope for flexibility in its preparation. It can be tailored to the specific needs of the management. The criterion for inclusion of any information in cost accounting is the *utility*. In short, financial accounting, which essentially caters to the needs of outsiders, is prepared according to the norms set by the GAAP, whereas cost accounting, as an aid to managerial decision making, is dependent on, and largely influenced by, the internal requirements of the management.

The third difference between financial accounting and cost accounting relates to the need for preparing such accounts. The preparation of financial accounts is a statutory obligation. In fact, the corporate laws and regulations that govern the functioning of a corporate enterprise not only make it mandatory to prepare such accounts, but also lay down the model/format in which such accounts are to be prepared. The corporate laws also prescribe independent audit by professional auditors to ensure that the accounts reflect a *true and fair view* of the firms' affairs. Apart from this, tax regulations also require the maintenance of records by business establishments. In sharp contrast, cost accounting was entirely *optional* till 2010-11. It was prepared only if it was deemed useful to the management. There were no external compulsions for its preparation. The format, as also the items to be included, were exclusively dependent on the management's discretion.

However, with effect from 2011-12, the Ministry of Corporate Affairs issued various cost audit orders wherein maximum industries were brought under cost audit net. The scope has been extended further (vide Cost Audit Order November 6, 2012); the cost audit has been made compulsory (from the financial year commencing on or after January 1, 2013) for the companies which are engaged in production, processing, manufacturing or mining of the products/activities and fulfill the following criteria: (i) the company's equity or debt securities are listed or are in the process of listing on any stock exchange (whether in India or outside India), (ii) the turnover of company exceeds ₹20 crore (for products/services covered under Table 1 of Cost Accounting Record Rules) and exceeds ₹100 crore (for products/services covered under Table 2) in the immediate preceding financial year and, (iii) the net worth of the company exceeds ₹5 crore in the immediate preceding financial year. In operational terms, the cost records are compulsory for the firms which satisfy the above mentioned criteria; cost accounting is *optional* only for firms which are outside the stated criteria.

The end-products of financial accounting are the three financial statements, namely, balance sheet, statement of profit and loss, and cash flow statement. The balance sheet and the statement of profit and loss report the financial position on a particular date, and the results of the operation of the firm during an accounting period respectively. The cash flow statement reports the inflow and outflow of cash during a given period of time. These are essentially, records of what has happened in the past. Therefore, these are aptly called *historical accounts.* On the other hand, cost accounting does not record the financial history of an enterprise. Though past data is included in cost accounting, a major part of its contents is related to the future plans. It is, therefore, *future-oriented.* It aims at providing data for budgeting, planning, and so on. Thus, cost accounting lays more emphasis on the future.

Moreover, financial accounting relates to the business as a *whole.* While some firms do prepare financial accounts on a segmented basis for the main lines of business, the emphasis is on the entire business. Cost accounting focuses on parts of the business. In cost accounting, the business is divided into different responsibility centres—cost, profit and investment. The term, responsibility centre, refers to the division of an enterprise into sections, departments, products, individual activities, and so on. In brief, financial accounting deals with the business as a whole, whereas cost accounting focuses on its different parts.

Finally, financial accounting and cost accounting also differ in relation to their ultimate objectives. Financial accounting is prepared to serve the purpose of external reporting. Therefore, from the viewpoint of the management, the purpose of financial accounting is accomplished when it is reflected in the above mentioned three financial statements. In a way, it is an *end* in itself, whereas cost accounting is only a *means to an end.* In other words, cost accounting is designed to serve as an aid to managerial decision making. With the help of cost accounting, the management can discharge its planning, directing and controlling functions. In *planning,* the manager decides what actions should be taken to help the organisation achieve its goals. In *directing,* the manager oversees the conduct of day-to-day operations. And in *controlling,* steps are taken to ensure that the responsibility centres are operating in the best possible manner.

Cost and Management Accounting Cost accounting is that branch of the accounting information system which records, measures and reports information about costs. *A cost is a sacrifice of resources.* The costs are reflected in the accounting system by outlays of cash, promises to pay cash at a future date, and the expiration of the value of an asset. The primary purpose of cost accounting is cost ascertainment and its use in decision making and performance evaluation. A cost accounting system provides data for both financial accounting and management accounting. When costs are used by outsiders, such as shareholders or creditors, to evaluate the performance of the management and make investment decisions, they are said to be used for financial accounting purposes. On the other hand, when cost data are used inside the organisation to evaluate the performance of operations, activities, personnel, and so on, as the basis of decision making, they are said to be used for management accounting purposes. For instance, in a manufacturing business, the costs of products sold, and stock on hand, include the total expenditure on materials, labour, and all the other production costs. Each of these costs must first be measured, then accumulated and, finally, distributed to the work-in-process, finished goods and cost of goods sold. Consequently, the amount of profit reported by a manufacturing company depends on the *accuracy of its cost calculations.* Thus, cost accounting is useful for performance appraisal.

Cost accounting also helps in planning. Planning is a process of setting goals and allocating resources to achieve these goals. The expected financial outcome of planning is expressed in terms of budgets. A firms can increase its profits in two ways: (i) By increasing unit sale price/sales volume, and (ii) By reducing costs.

While the first cannot always be under the control of the management, the second falls well within the managerial domain. A detailed cost accounting system is an important requirement for a systematic cost control. For this reason, the management must understand the nature and behaviour of different elements of cost, know when and where they are incurred, and who is responsible for them. The actual cost/profit should be compared with the planned estimates. The differences between these should be analysed to identify the reasons for deviations, and corrective action should be taken to eliminate them. Thus, cost accounting is very useful to management for profit planning.

Cost accounting is also useful for the purpose of control. Control comprises managerial action to correct conditions that cause deviation between the actual and planned performance. Comparison between the actual and budgeted cost will highlight a poor or good performance, as well as the operations that have gone out of control and warrant corrective action. Thus, cost accounting provides the basis for cost/managerial control.

COST CONCEPT/DEFINITION, AND CLASSIFICATIONS[2]

This section presents the basic cost concepts, their definitions and classifications to provide a conceptual foundation for the subject matter to be covered in the remainder of this book.

Basic Cost Concept

Cost is defined as the 'value' of the sacrifice made to acquire goods/services, measured in monetary terms by the acquisition of assets or incurrence of liabilities at the time the benefits are acquired. At the time of acquisition, the cost incurred is for the present or future benefits. When these benefits are utilised, the costs become expense. An expense is defined as a cost that has given a benefit and is now *expired. Unexpired costs* that can give future benefits are classified as *assets.* Expenses are matched against revenues to determine net income/loss for a period. *Revenue* is defined as the price of products sold/services rendered.

An expense is defined as a cost that has given a benefit and is now *expired. Unexpired costs* that can give future benefits are classified as *assets.*

Cost Classifications

Cost data/cost accounting information is routinely accessed by management for the purpose of (a) product costing, (b) performance evaluation and (c) managerial decision making. It consists of past revenues and costs necessary for product costing and performance evaluation, as well as projected revenues and costs necessary for managerial decision making. The cost data are classified into various categories according to:

— Elements of a product (product cost);
— Relationship to production;
— Relationship to volume;
— Ability to trace;
— Department where incurred;
— Functional areas/Activities performed;
— Period charged to income; and
— Relationship to planning, controlling and decision making.

Elements of a Product/Product Cost/Cost Elements This classification provides management with information necessary for product pricing and income measurement. The cost elements of a product (its integral components) are (i) Materials, (ii) Direct labour and (iii) Factory overheads.

Materials These are the principal substances used in production and are transformed into finished goods by the addition of direct labour and factory overheads. The cost of materials may be divided into direct and indirect materials.

Direct Materials All materials (a) that can be identified with the production of a finished item/ product, (b) that can be easily traced to the product and (c) that represent a major material cost of producing that product are called direct materials.

Indirect Materials These are materials involved in the production of a product (say, consumables, oil, lubricants, etc.) but are not direct materials. These are included as a part of factory overheads.

Labour It is the physical/mental effort expended in the production of a product. Labour costs are divided into (a) direct and (b) indirect.

Direct Labour All labour directly involved in the production of a finished product (a) that can be easily traced to the product and (b) that represents a major labour cost of producing that product is known as direct labour.

Indirect Labour It is the labour involved in the production of a product that is not considered direct labour. It is included as part of factory overheads.

Factory Overheads They include indirect materials, indirect labour, and all other indirect manufacturing costs which cannot be directly identified with any specific product. They can be further classified as fixed, variable, and mixed which are explained later.

Relationship to Production This classification is closely related to the cost elements of a product, namely, direct materials, direct labour and factory overheads, and the major objective of planning and control. Based on relationship to production, the two categories of costs are: (i) Prime costs and (ii) Conversion costs.

Prime Costs These are direct materials and direct labour. These are directly related to production.

Conversion Costs These are concerned with transforming direct material into finished goods. These include direct labour and factory overheads.

Relationship to Volume Costs vary with changes in volume of production. Understanding their behaviour is vital in almost all aspects of product costing, performance evaluation and managerial decision making. On the basis of relationship to volume, costs are classified as variable, fixed and mixed. These cost behaviour patterns are applicable *only* within the relevant range defined as that interval of activity within which the total fixed costs and per unit variable costs remain constant.

Variable Costs These costs are those in which the total cost are assumed to change in direct proportion to changes in volume/output within the relevant range, while the unit cost remains constant. Their implication for the management in planning and controlling of variable costs is that with all other factors held constant (for example, unit sale price and total fixed cost), each desired per unit expansion of productive activity triggers an incremental change in total variable costs equal to a constant amount per unit. As long as the unit sale price exceeds the unit variable cost, productive activity should be expanded. The variable costs are controlled by the departmental head responsible for incurring them.

Fixed Costs Such costs are those in which the total fixed costs remain constant over a relevant range of volume/output, while the unit fixed cost varies with output. Beyond the relevant range of output, fixed costs will vary. The higher management controls the volume of production and is, therefore, responsible for fixed costs. The implication for management in planning and controlling fixed cost is that with all other factors such as unit sale price and variable cost remaining constant, productive activity should be expanded as far as possible, which will reduce the fixed costs per unit to its lowest level.

Mixed Costs These contain both fixed and variable characteristics over various relevant ranges of operation. These are of two types: (i) Semi-variable costs and (ii) Step costs.

Semi-variable Costs The fixed part of a semi-variable cost usually represents a minimum fee for making a particular item/service available. The variable portion is the cost charges for actually using the service. For example, most telephone service charges are made up of two elements: (i) A fixed charge for allowing to make/receive a call, (ii) Plus an additional variable charge for each call actually made. Other examples of such costs are truck rentals, equipment rentals and utilities.

Step Costs The fixed part of step costs changes abruptly at various levels of activity because these costs are acquired in indivisible portions. A typical example of such costs is supervisors' salary. If one supervisor is needed for every 20 workers, two supervisors would be required, if, for instance, 30 workers are employed. If two additional workers are hired, still only two supervisors would be needed. If the number, however, increases to 42, three supervisors would be required. A step cost is similar to a fixed cost within a very small relevant range. Another example of step costs is inspection cost. The nature of such cost is that it gives the appearance of increase in series of steps and, hence, the name step costs.

Although mixed costs are neither wholly fixed nor wholly variable in nature, these must ultimately be segregated into their fixed and variable components for planning and control purposes.

Ability to Trace From the viewpoint of ability to trace it to specific jobs/ departments/sales territories, and so on, cost may be (i) Direct, and (ii) Indirect.

Direct Costs These are costs that are traceable conveniently and wholly by management to specific items/areas. The examples of such costs are direct material and direct labour for a specific product.

Indirect Costs These are common to many items and cannot be traced to any one item /area. These are usually charged to items/areas on the basis of allocation techniques. For example, indirect manufacturing costs are allocated as a part of factory overheads.

Department Where Incurred A department-wise costing is helpful to management in controlling overhead cost and in income measurement. A department is a major functional division of a business. A manufacturing company has typically two departments: (i) Production and (ii) Service.

Production Departments These directly contribute to production of goods. These include departments in which conversion/production processes take place, including manual/machine operations directly performed on the goods manufactured.

Service Departments These are not directly related to production. These provide services for other departments. Their costs are usually allocated to production departments benefiting from the services. The examples of service departments are payroll, factory office, personnel, cafeteria, and security of factory.

Functional Areas Function-wise costs are accumulated on the basis of activity performed. In the case of a manufacturing company, cost classification by functions relates to manufacturing, marketing, administrative and financing.

Manufacturing Costs These are related to production of items and consist of direct materials, direct labour, and factory overhead costs.

Marketing Costs These are incurred in promoting products/service.

Administrative Costs These are incurred in directing, controlling, and operating a company. Such costs include salaries to management and officers working in office.

Financing Costs These relate to acquiring funds for the operations of the company. These include interest on loans and cost of credit to customers.

Period Charged to Income Costs can also be classified on the basis of when they are charged to income/revenues. Such a classification helps management in (i) income measurement, (ii) preparation of financial statements and (iii) matching expenses to income properly in appropriate period. Based on period charged to income, cost are classified into product and period costs.

Product Costs These are directly/indirectly identifiable with the product and include direct materials, direct labour, and factory overheads. Upon completion of the product, they are inventoried (included in inventory) as they provide benefit/ income only after sale. The product costs are recorded as expense after sale of the product, known as cost of goods sold and are matched against income/revenue for the period in which the products are sold.

Period Costs These are not at all related to production. The examples of such costs are accountants' salary (administrative expense), depreciation on a salesmans' car (marketing expense) and interest on bonds (financing expense). Period costs are not inventoried but are charged to revenue immediately as there is no relationship between cost and revenue.

Relationship to Planning, Controlling and Decision Making The costs related to planning, controlling and decision-making are as follows.

Standard and Budgeted Costs The standard costs are those which should be incurred in a particular production process under normal conditions. A budget is a quantitative expression of objectives and a means of monitoring progress towards achievement of those objectives. Standard costing is usually concerned with per unit costs. It serves the same purpose as a budget. Budgets, however, usually provide forecasted activity on a total basis rather than on a unit cost basis. Both standard costs and budgets are used, first, to set standards/goals of performance and, second, to control actual performance through variance analysis in terms of the difference between the expected and actual.

Controllable and Non-controllable Costs The controllable costs are those which may be directly influenced by divisional managers in a given time period. Where, for instance, managers have authority to acquire and use, the cost may be considered controllable by them. On the other hand, non-controllable costs are those which are not directly administered/acquired and used at a given level of management.

Committed and Discretionary Fixed Costs A committed fixed cost arises from the necessity to have a basic organisational structure in terms of essential property, plan, equipment, personnel, and so on. It is long-term cost and cannot be reduced without adversely affecting the ability of the company to operate at a minimum level of productive capacity.

A discretionary fixed cost is a short-run cost and can be reduced to operate at any desired level of activity warranted by the committed fixed costs. It arises from decision for repairs and maintenance costs, advertising costs, training of personnel, and so on.

Relevant and Irrelevant Costs Relevant costs are expected future costs that differ among alternative courses of action. They may be eliminated if some activity is changed/dropped.

Irrelevant costs are not affected by management action. An example of irrelevant costs is sunk cost that is irrevocable such as insurance and property taxes. When confronted with a choice, they are not relevant and should not be considered for decision-making analysis.

However, relevancy is not an attribute of any particular cost. An identical cost may be relevant in one situation but irrelevant in another. Which costs are relevant and which are irrelevant would depend upon the specific facts of a given situation.

Differential Costs The difference between the costs associated with alternative courses of action on an item by item basis is differential cost. If the differential cost is increasing, it is called incremental cost; it is known as decremental cost when the differential cost is decreasing.

The differential cost is the key to a specific decision. Frequently, incremental costs equal variable costs. But in case of production beyond the relevant range, fixed cost would also increase along with variable cost. For decision-making in such special situation, incremental analysis should consider the differential both in fixed cost and variable cost.

Opportunity Costs When a decision to pursue one alternative is made, the benefits of other options are foregone. Benefits lost from rejecting the next best alternative are the opportunity costs of the chosen option.

Although opportunity costs are not shown in accounting records as they are not actually incurred, they are relevant costs for decision-making and must be considered in evaluating a proposed alternative.

Shut-down Costs These are those fixed costs which would be incurred even if there was no production. Examples of such costs are rent, storage costs, insurance, salary, and so on. In a seasonal industry, management has to decide whether to suspend operations or to remain open during the 'off-season'. In the short run, it is advantageous to remain open as long as sufficient sales can be generated to cover variable cost and contribute to the recovery of fixed costs.

COST ASCERTAINMENT/PRODUCT COSTING

An important objective of cost accounting is product costing. Cost ascertainment is the process of determining costs on the basis of actual data. The cost ascertainment involves: (i) Collection and classification of cost/expenditure according to cost elements; (ii) Its allocation /apportionment to cost centres/units; (iii) Choice of an appropriate method of costing; and (iv) Selection of an appropriate costing technique.

Elements of Cost

There are three broad elements of cost: direct material, direct labour, and overheads.

Direct Material The substance from which the product is made is known as material. All materials which become an integral part of the finished product and which can be conveniently assigned to specific physical units are direct material.

Direct Labour Human efforts, both physical and mental, used for conversion of materials into finished products is labour. Labour cost which can be wholly, conveniently identified with a specific physical unit of product is direct labour cost. Such costs are specifically and conveniently traceable to a specific product.

Overheads These include (i) Indirect material cost (ii) Indirect labour cost, and (iii) Indirect expenses.

Indirect Material Cost It is the cost of materials which cannot be conveniently assigned to a specific physical units of production. The examples of such a cost are consumable stores, oil and waste, and so on.

Indirect Labour Cost It cannot be conveniently traced to a specific unit of product/output. It includes, wages of storekeepers, foremen, time-keepers, directors fee, salary of salesmen, and so on.

Indirect Expenses The expenses which cannot be directly, conveniently and wholly allocated to specific cost units/centres are treated as indirect expenses. They consist of: (i) Factory/manufacturing/workers/production expenses, (ii) Office and administrative expenses, and (iii) Selling and distribution expenses.

Indirect Manufacturing Expenses These are incurred in the factory. Included in these are expenses relating to production management, such as rent, rates and insurance of factory premises, power used in factory, depreciation of plant and machinery, and so on.

Office and Administrative Expenses These pertain to management of business and include office rent, lighting and heating, postage, telephone, fax and other charges, depreciation of office furnitures and equipments, legal charges, audit fee, and so on.

Selling and Distribution Charges These are incurred for marketing of products, dispatching goods sold, and so on and include (i) advertisement expenses, cost of preparing tenders, travelling expenses, bad debts, collection charges, (ii) warehouse charges, packing and loading charges and carriage outwards, and so on.

The various elements of cost are depicted in Figures 1.1 and 1.2.

Cost Centres and Cost Units

The second element in cost ascertainment is allocation/apportionment of cost/expenses to cost centres/units.

Cost Centres While ascertaining cost, various cost elements are accumulated cost centre-wise. A cost centre means "*a location, person, or item of equipment (or a group of these) for which costs*

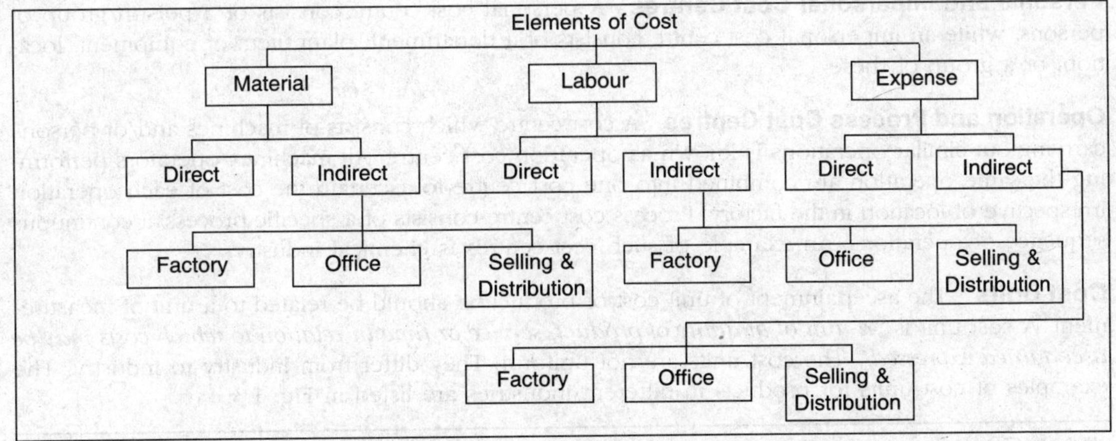

Figure 1.1 *Elements of Cost*

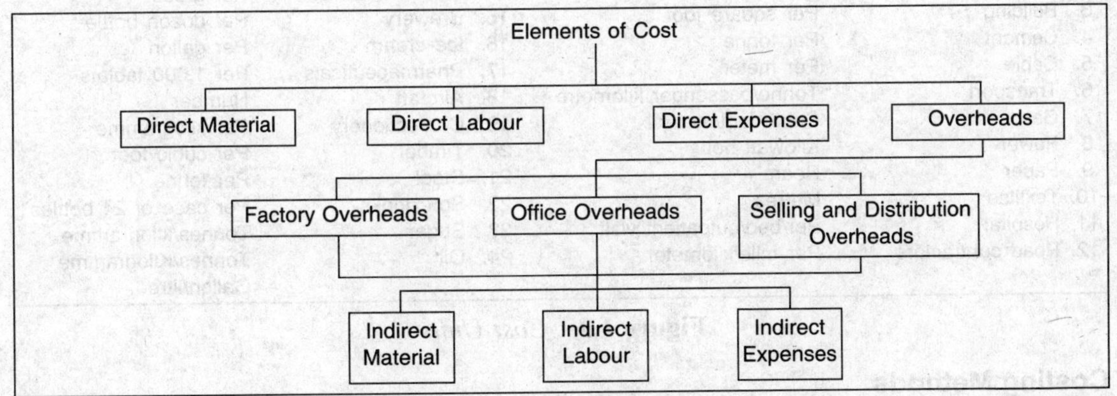

Figure 1.2 *Elements of Cost*

may be ascertained and used for the purpose of cost control'. It is an organisational segment/area of activity to accumulate costs. In other words, a cost centre refers to a convenient segment into which the organisation is appropriately divided for product costing. For instance, in a laundry, various activities such as collecting, sorting, marking and washing are performed. For purposes of cost accumulation, each of these activities may be treated as cost centre. All costs relating to particular activity (cost centre) would be separately accumulated to compute the cost of production of that cost centre. Cost centres can be classified into:(i) Productive, unproductive/service and mixed, (ii) Personal and impersonal, and (iii) Operation and process.

Productive, Unproductive/Service and Mixed Cost Centres A productive cost centre is actually engaged in manufacturing a product. An unproductive centre does not directly make products but provides essential service/aid to the productive centre and includes administration, repairs and maintenance, stores and drawing office. Mixed cost centres produce as well as provide services. A typical example of a mixed cost centre is a tool shop. The manufacture of dyes and jigs in the tool shop for specific jobs/orders is illustrative of productive cost centre, while its repair service for the factory represents service cost centre.

Personal and Impersonal Cost Centres A personal cost centre consists of a person/group of persons, while an impersonal cost centre consists of a department, plant, item of equipment, location, or a group of these.

Operation and Process Cost Centres A cost centre which consists of machines and/or persons carrying out similar operations is known as operation cost centre. All machines/operators performing the same operation are combined into one cost centre to ascertain the cost of each operation irrespective of location in the factory. Process cost centre consists of a specific process/a continuous sequence of operations. An example of such cost centres is chemical industry.

Cost Units The ascertainment of unit cost of production should be related to a unit of measurement. A cost unit is "*a unit of quantity of product, service or time in relation to which costs may be ascertained/expressed.*" The cost units are not uniform. They differ from industry to industry. The examples of cost units for products in different industries are listed in Fig. 1.3.

Industry/Enterprise	*Cost Unit*	*Industry*	*Cost Unit*
1. Automobile	Number	13. Bicycle	Number
2. Brickworks	Per 1,000 bricks	14. Nuts and bolts	Per gross
3. Building	Per square foot	15. Brewery	Per dozen bottle
4. Cement	Per tonne	16. Ice cream	Per gallon
5. Cable	Per meter	17. Pharmaceuticals	Per 1,000 tablets
6. Transport	Tonne/passenger kilometre	18. Aircraft	Number
7. Gas	Cubic foot/meter	19. Confectionery	Per kilogramme
8. Power	Kilowatt hour	20. Timber	Per cubic foot
9. Paper	Ream	21. Steel	Per tonne
10. Textiles	Metres	22. Soft drinks	Per case of 24 bottles
11. Hospital	Per/bed/outpatient visit	23. Sugar	Tonnes/kilogramme
12. Road contractors	Per mile/kilometer	24. Oil	Tonnes/Kilogramme Gallon/litre

Figure 1.3 *Cost Units*

Costing Methods

As observed earlier, costing is the process and technique of ascertaining costs. Different methods can be applied to ascertain costs. The method to be used differs from industry to industry and according to nature of business. It primarily depends on the manufacturing process and the method of measuring the departmental and finished products. Basically, there are two methods of costing, namely, specific order costing or job/ terminal costing and operations/process/ period costing.

Specific Order/Job/Terminal Costing This category of basic costing methods is applicable where the work consists of separate jobs/batches/contracts as per specific orders and customer specifications and includes: (i) Job costing, (ii) Batch costing, and (iii) Contract costing.

Job Costing According to this method, costs are collected for each job/work/project separately. Where production is not repetitive, and consists of distinct jobs/ lots with which costs can be identified, job costing method is used. It is applicable to enterprises engaged in printing, machine tool manufacturing, foundaries and forging shops, general engineering workshops, house-building, and ship building. The cost unit is the specific job.

Batch Costing It is an extension of job costing. A batch consists of a number of similar products. The cost of a group of products constituting the batch and not the single item within the batch is ascertained. It is applicable for the production of nuts and bolts, medicines, biscuits, garments, and spare parts and components and so on. Each batch constitutes the cost unit.

Contract Costing A contract is a big job and is spread over a period of time. Contract costing is applicable to builders, civil engineering contractors, construction and mechanical engineering firms. The contract is the cost unit.

Operations/Process/Period Costing This basic method of costing is applicable where standardised products result from a sequence of repetitive and, more or less, continuous operations/processes to which costs are charged. The costs cannot be traced to specific units and are averaged for the number of units manufactured. This method includes: (i) Process costing, (ii) Unit/output costing, and (iii) Service/ operating costing.

Process Costing Where (i) production is continuous, (ii) manufacturing is carried on by distinct and well defined processes, (iii) the finished product of one process (stage) becomes the raw material of the subsequent process, (iv) different products with/without byproducts are produced simultaneously of the same process, and (v) products are exactly identical, the costing method is called process costing. Cost has to be computed (a) for each process and (b) for each unit at each process by averaging the total process cost. The industries in which this method is applicable are textiles, chemicals, paper, tanneries, paints, food, explosives, soaps, and so on.

Unit/Output/Single Costing Where a single item is produced and the final product is homogeneous, the costing method is known as unit/output/single costing. The per unit cost is computed, dividing the total cost by the number of units manufactured. Industries in which this method is applicable are brick making, collieries, flour mills, paper mills, cement manufacturing, oil drilling, and so on.

Operating (Service) Costing This method is suitable for enterprises/industries which provide services and do not manufacture any physical goods. Examples are transport undertakings, electricity companies, hospitals, hotels, railways, and so on. The cost units differ among these service organisations depending on the nature of service being provided. There is usually a composite cost unit such as tonne-passenger kilometer (transport undertakings), kilowatt-hour (power companies), patient-day (hospitals), and so on.

Costing Techniques/Types

The various costing methods outlined above can be used under different costing techniques. These techniques/types refer to the manner of ascertaining cost for cost control and decision-making purposes and include uniform costing, variable costing, absorption costing, historical costing, and standard costing.

Uniform Costing It is the use of standarised principles, practices and methods of cost accounting by several undertakings for a common control or comparison of costs. It includes methods of costing, accounting classification, methods of defining costs and charging depreciation, allocation/ apportionment of overheads to cost centres/cost units, and so on.

Variable Costing It is a technique of cost ascertainment in which all variable costs only which arise due to a change in volume of production, are charged to products/operations/processes. The fixed costs are accounted for in the profits of the period in which they arise. This technique is employed to ascertain the effect of change in volume/product mix and so on profit.

Absorption Costing This technique charges all costs, that is, all variable as well as all fixed, to operations/products/processes.

Historical Costing It is a system of costing in which costs are determined after they have been incurred. It ascertains actual cost incurred in the past.

Standard Costing Standard costs are predetermined in conformity with the most efficient operation and use of resources. The standard costing technique compares actual cost with standard cost. The variances between them, if any, are analysed and, in the light of the analysis of the probable causes, remedial actions are initiated by the management.

INSTALLATION OF A COST ACCOUNTING SYSTEM

A cost accounting system is a system of accounting that accumulates cost, ascertains cost of products/jobs, and prepares cost information reports using some procedures and principles for recording cost data. This section briefly describes the installation of a costing system.

Features/Characteristics/Factors

The main characteristics of an ideal cost accounting system/factors having a bearing on the installation of such a system are as detailed below:

Suitability A costing system should be devised to suit the nature, conditions, requirements, manufacturing processes/methods, nature and number of products, and size of the company. It should serve the purpose of the company by supplying the necessary information for product costing, planning and control, and decision making.

Simplicity The system should be simple and amenable to easy understanding. The information should be presented in the appropriate format at the right time to make it meaningful to users.

Flexibility The system should be flexible to accommodate changes in conditions and circumstances. It must be capable of expansion/contraction in consonance with emerging requirements.

Economical A costing system should be economical taking into account the requirements of the business in terms of cost benefit analysis. It should reflect the financial capacity of the business.

Comparability The information provided by the cost accounting system must be comparable with (i) past figures, (ii) figures of other concerns/industry as a whole, and/or (iii) other departments. This would enable a more reliable basis of performance evaluation.

Timeliness The information must be timely to enable management take suitable action for cost control and decision making.

Organisational Set-up The system must correspond to the organisational set-up/authority to ensure accountability for costs incurred in various departments.

Uniformity All forms/proformas in the accounting system should be uniform in size and quality. Different forms should be in different colours to improve efficiency. Printed forms should be suitably designed for collection and dissemination of cost data. They should also contain instructions as to their use and disposal. The filling of forms should involve as little clerical work as possible.

Efficient Material Control System Materials constitute a significant proportion of total cost. An efficient system of materials control is a pre-requisite for an ideal cost accounting system. An appropriate method of pricing material issues also deserves consideration.

Adequate Wage Procedure A well-defined wage system helps control labour costs. There should be a well-defined wage procedure for time recording, preparation of wage sheets, and payment of wages.

Departmentalisation of Expenses To ascertain cost accurately, there should be a good system of collection/apportionment/absorption of overheads.

Reconciliation The cost and financial accounts should preferably be integrated. If not, the cost accounting system should be devised in a way to ensure easy reconciliation between them.

Duties and Responsibilities The duties and responsibilities of the cost accountant(s) should be clearly laid down.

External Factors Though the installation of the costing system depends primarily on internal factors and situation within the organisation, external factors may also have a bearing on the structure of the system. For instance, cost accounting rules applicable to manufacturing companies in India require certain cost information to be developed and submitted to the Government.

Steps/Procedures

The steps involved in installing a cost accounting system are listed below:

Objectives The objectives to be achieved through the costing system should be laid down. If the objective is cost determination only, the system would be simple, but it would have to be elaborate to provide information for the objective of planning and control and managerial decision making.

Study of Existing Organisation/Routine This should be with reference, *inter alia,* to the following:

- Nature of business/operation/process carried;
- Extent of responsibility/authority of various functionaries;
- Factory layout with particular reference to the manufacturing departments;
- Treatment of wastage of materials;
- Time recording, computing and paying wages;
- System of issuing orders for production; and
- Fixed/semi-variable and variable overheads.

Structure of Cost Accounts A suitable system of cost accounting should be tailored to the manufacturing process. The structure of cost accounts should be in tune with the natural production line. The system should be designed in such a way that there is a gradual build up of the cost at each stage of production till completion stage.

Determination of Cost Rates This would entail a thorough study of factory conditions. Decisions would have to be made regarding (i) classification of costs into direct and indirect, (ii) grouping of indirect costs into production, selling and administration, (iii) treatment of wastes, (iv) method of pricing issues, (v) method of recovering overheads, and (vi) calculation of overheads rates. A complete cost accounting code should be drawn up so that expenses can be quickly classified as to both source and cause.

Introduction of the System To ensure effective cooperation, before putting the system in place, its implications should be explained to all the functionaries. The system should be introduced gradually only by stages and the existing routines/practices should be utilised as far as possible.

Organisation of Cost Office The cost office should preferably be situated adjacent to the factory to avoid delays in routing out documents/clearing up discrepancies. The duties of the cost office fall into the following four categories:

Stores Accounts Posting of receipt of materials and issues of stores in stores ledger and preparing material abstracts.

Labour Accounting Evaluation of time sheets and job cards; preparing labour abstracts and preparation of payrolls.

Cost Accounts Posting of all cost accounts.

Cost Control Posting cost control accounts from data supplied from the above three sections; preparation of special statistical and other information for management for carrying out special investigation.

Relationship with other Departments The costing department should function independently, reporting directly to the top management. It should be structured to serve management at all levels. There should be a whole system of records and reports.

Authority and Responsibility These should be clearly defined to make the cost accounting successful.

SUMMARY

- Cost accounting is that part of accounting which identifies, defines, measures, reports and analyses the various elements of direct and indirect costs associated with manufacturing and providing goods/services. The main objectives of cost accounting are product costing/cost ascertainment, planning, performance evaluation, cost control and decision making.
- Cost accounting, as a part of accounting system of a firm, although closely related to financial accounting, differs in important respects. The main points of distinction between them are: (i) Structure/format or presentation and the related aspects of the impact of GAPP on their preparation, (ii) Need for their preparation, (iii) Historical versus future orientation, (iv) Whole versus segment, and (v) Objectives.
- The cost data/cost accounting information is classified into various categories according to:
  - Elements of a product;
  - Relationship to production;
  - Relationship to volume;
  - Ability to trace;
  - Department where incurred;
  - Functional areas/activities performed;
  - Period charged to incomes; and
  - Relationship to planning, control and decision making.
- An important objective of cost accounting is product costing/cost ascertainment. Cost ascertainment is the process of determining costs on the basis of actual data. It involves: (i) Collection and classification of costs according to cost elements, (ii) Its allocation to cost centres/units, (iii) Choice of an appropriate method and costing technique.
- There are three broad elements of costs: direct material, direct labour, and overheads.

- A cost centre refers to a convenient segment into which the organisation is appropriately divided for product costing. The cost unit is a unit of quantity of product/service/time in relation to which costs may be ascertained/expressed.
- Different methods can be applied to ascertain costs according to the nature of industry/business. The various costing methods are: (i) Job costing, Batch costing and Contract costing, (ii) Process costing, (iii) Unit/output/single costing/operating costing.
- The cost accounting techniques refer to the manner of ascertaining costs and include uniform costing, variable costing, absorption costing, historical costing, and standard costing.
- The main elements of a sound costing system are suitability, simplicity, flexibility, comparability, timeliness, organisation set-up, uniformity, efficient control material system, adequate wage procedures, departmentalisation of expenses, reconciliation, and duties and responsibilities. The steps involved in installing a costing system include, laying down the objectives, study of existing organisation, structure of cost accounts, determination of cost rates, and the organisation of cost office.

REFERENCES

1. N.K. Prasad, *Principles and Practices of Cost Accounting* (Book Syndicate Pvt. Ltd., Calcutta, 1985)
2. Polimeni, et al, *Cost Accounting*, 3rd Edition (McGraw-Hill, New York, 1991)

EXERCISES

1.1 Indicate whether the following statements are true or false:

(i) Cost Accounting is a part of financial accounting.
(ii) Cost Accounting has a single unified format of presenting information.
(iii) Prime cost is sum of material and labour costs.
(iv) Fixed costs do not change with changes in the level of activity.
(v) Conversion costs are costs of converting direct materials into finished goods.
(vi) Mixed costs vary in direct proportion to the level of activity.
(vii) Period costs are related to production.
(viii) Shut-down costs are to be incurred even if there is no production.
(ix) Factory overheads include indirect labour costs and indirect manufacturing expenses.
(x) Cost centre is a convenient segment into which the organization is divided for product costing.
(xi) Cost units are uniform for all industries.

(**Answers: (i)** False, **(ii)** False, **(iii)** False, **(iv)** False, **(v)** True, **(vi)** False, **(vii)** False, **(viii)** True, **(ix)** False, **(x)** True, **(xi)** False)

1.2(a) What is cost accounting? Discus briefly its important objectives in a business firm.

1.2(b) State and explain the major differences between financial accounting and cost accounting.

1.3 Explain the importance of cost accounting as a managerial tool.

1.4 Enumerate the steps that you would take for installation of a costing system in an organisation. What are the essentials of an effective costing system?

1.5 "Cost accounting is an unnecessary luxury for business establishments". Do you agree with the statement? Discuss.

1.6 Examine the matters, which you will investigate, and the problems which you expect to face before installing a costing system in a manufacturing company.

1.7 How does cost accounting help in the planning and control of operations of a business enterprise?

1.8 Explain why is it necessary to devise different methods of costing for different industries and list the several methods employed.

1.9 A factory makes only one product in one quality and size. The owner says that his financial accounts easily give him the material, labour and other cost per unit. Write a brief letter to convince him that he still needs a costing system.

1.10 Define 'cost unit' and 'cost centre'. Also give a few suitable examples of each.

1.11 "Costs may be classified in a variety of ways according to their name and information needs of management". Explain and discuss this statement giving examples of classification required for different purposes.

1.12 "A sound costing system must place the same emphasis on cost control as on cost ascertainment". Comment on the statement.

1.13 You have been asked to install a costing system in a manufacturing business. Apart from technical costing problems, what practical difficulties would you expect to meet and how would you propose to obviate or overcome them?

2 Chapter

Cost Concepts

Learning Objectives

1. Explain cost concepts relating management needs to income measurement
2. Illustrate cost concepts relating to profit planning
3. Discuss cost concepts relating to control
4. Analyse cost concepts relating to decision-making.

INTRODUCTION

One of the important inputs in managerial decision-making is cost data. There is, however, no single concept of cost, which can cater to all management needs. The "*needs concept*" of cost depends on the conditions under which the costs are required to be measured and the purpose for which measurement is required. In other words, cost data which are relevant and useful in one situation may be quite irrelevant and useless in another. Developing the data on the required lines can be designated as "the concept of cost relevancy."[1] The concept implies the need of different sets of cost data for different objectives, purposes and situations. The object of the present chapter is to describe the various concepts of cost related to managerial needs. Management needs can be classified into four broad groups:

1. Income measurement
2. Profit planning
3. Costs control
4. Special situations requiring special decisions.

COST CONCEPTS RELATING TO INCOME MEASUREMENT

There are four cost concepts which pertain to income measurement. These are: **(i)** Product costs and Period costs; **(ii)** Absorbed costs and Unabsorbed costs; **(iii)** Expired costs and Unexpired costs; and **(iv)** Joint product costs and Separable costs.

Product Costs and Periods Costs

Product costs are costs which can be identified with goods produced for resale.

Product Costs The distinction between product costs and period costs assumes significance in the income determination process. In a variable costing system, only variable costs are recognised as product costs. The rationale is that it is only these costs which are affected by the production volume. If there is no production, there will be no material and direct labour cost (elements of variable costs) and, hence, no production cost. Therefore, variable costs are often called product costs. Thus, production costs can be defined as *those costs, which can be identified with goods produced or purchased for resale.* They vary with production. Raw material and direct labour are the examples of product costs.

Period costs are costs which are matched against the revenue of the current period.

Period Costs In contrast, period costs are costs which vary with the passage of time and not with volume of production. Rent, insurance, salary of a works manager and general manager, and so on. will vary *pari passu* with the time period. For instance, factory rent may be paid per month. Every month, this sum is to be paid irrespective of the volume of production. Likewise, insurance instalment of a quarter is to be paid whether there is production or no production. Logically, therefore, they should be considered expenses of the year in which they have been incurred and not be carried forward to the next year as part of the inventory costs. In brief, period cost may be defined as *costs which are matched against the revenue of the current period,* that is, the sum of period costs is deducted as expenses from the revenue of the current period only.

Absorbed Costs and Unabsorbed Cost

Absorbed costs are costs absorbed by the revenues of the period in which product has been sold.

The importance of this classification in the income determination process emanates from the fact that variable production costs are not the only true costs. Product costs should include some proportion of fixed costs. This can best be understood by an example. Let us assume that the management decides that product manufactured on an operator-controlled machine be henceforth manufactured on an automated process involving high cost machinery. Assume further, that as a result of the change in the production process, there will be no variation in material costs or variable manufacturing costs per unit. There will be a change only in direct labour cost which henceforth will become part of the fixed cost associated with the machine. According to the definition of product costs (as per variable costing), the cost of production will be reduced by the direct labour cost, simply because of a change in the method of manufacture. Certainly, this is not a logical viewpoint. Therefore, the argument that the benefits of fixed costs lapse with the passage of time and, hence, must be absorbed by the revenues of that period only to which they relate ignores the point that facilities represented by those costs are value-creating[2].

From the above it follows that fixed costs add value to the product and this value is well taken account of in determining the selling price. Therefore, such costs must be absorbed by the revenues of the period in which the products have been sold and not necessarily in the year in which they have been incurred. The fact that goods are held as inventories so that they can be sold in future further reinforces the above contention. Therefore, fixed costs are relevant and inventoriable. This argument is in line with another cost concept, namely, expired and unexpired cost.

Expired and Unexpired Cost

An expired cost is one which cannot contribute to the production of future revenues. In contrast, an unexpired cost is one which has the capacity of contributing to the production of revenue in the future. Inventory constitutes a good example of unexpired cost, as it can be sold in subsequent years and will influence total future revenues. These arguments, then, constitute the rationale of the concept of the absorbed and unabsorbed costs, the problem of allocating fixed costs notwithstanding. Fixed factory or production costs are related to capacity to produce. They are necessary to be spent to create infrastructure facilities so that the manufacturing process can set in. Therefore, they are as necessary costs of production as the variable costs. Accordingly, production should absorb fixed costs at a certain pre-fixed standard rate, which normally is determined with reference to the budgeted fixed cost and the normal capacity to produce. Suppose that fixed costs are ₹30,000 and the normal production is 15,000 units. The standard fixed overhead rate (SFOR) of recovery is ₹2 per unit (₹30,000 ÷ 15,000 units). In other words, every unit of production absorbs ₹2 of fixed costs. If the company produces 10,000 units, the total absorbed costs will be ₹20,000 (10,000 units × ₹2, SFOR). Obviously, ₹10,000 constitutes unabsorbed costs (₹30,000, actual cost – ₹20,000, absorbed costs). Thus, absorbed costs may be defined as those costs, which have been charged to production. Costs, which remain uncharged to production are referred to as unabsorbed costs. In contrast, overabsorbed costs represent the positive difference of fixed costs charged to production and actual fixed costs. Such a situation will arise if actual production is more than the normal production. In the above example, if the company produces 16,250 units, the costs charged to production will be ₹32,500 (16,250 units × ₹2, SFOR). The overabsorbed cost will be ₹2,500 [₹30,000, actual fixed costs (AFC) – ₹32,500 charged to production]. Figure 2.1 portrays these relationships.

Expired cost is a cost which cannot contribute to the production of future revenues.

Unexpired cost has the capacity to contribute to the production of revenue in the future.

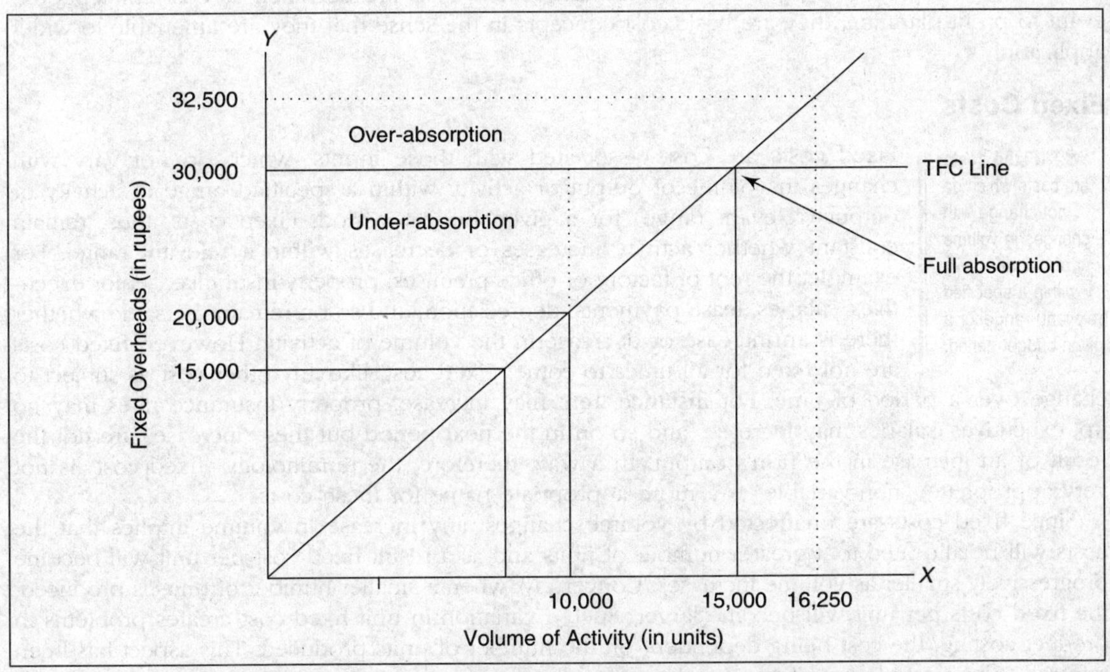

Figure 2.1 *Absorbed and Unabsorbed Costs*

Symbolically,

$$\text{Absorbed costs} = \text{Units produced} \times \text{SFOR} \quad \textbf{(2.1)}$$

$$\text{Unabsorbed costs} = [\text{AFC} - (\text{Units produced} \times \text{SFOR})] \quad \textbf{(2.2)}$$

$$\text{Overabsorbed costs} = [\text{Units produced} \times \text{SFOR}) - \text{AFC}] \quad \textbf{(2.3)}$$

Joint Product Costs and Separable Costs

Joint product costs are the costs of a single process, or a series of processes that simultaneously produce two or more products of significant sales value. Such costs are not attributable to different individual products until after a certain stage of production known as the split-off point.[3]

Separable cost, in contrast, refers to any cost that can be attributed exclusively and wholly to a particular product, process, division or department.

The above cost concepts are helpful in the determination of the true costs of a particular segment of the business and, hence, the correct income.

COST CONCEPTS RELATING TO PROFIT PLANNING

Profit planning is concerned with taking a series of decisions where alternatives are available. Planning deals with the future. Therefore, future costs are relevant costs in the profit planning function. Cost volume profit relationship is an integral part of profit planning, that is, how the costs and profits vary with sales volume. The relevant cost concept are:

1. Fixed, Variable and Semi-variable/Mixed costs,
2. Future costs and Budgeted costs.

Although the fixed, variable and semi-variable/mixed costs are classified as cost concepts relevant to profit planning, they are basic cost concepts in the sense that they are amenable to wider application.

Fixed Costs

Fixed costs are costs which do not change with changes in volume of output/activity within a specified (relevant) range for a given budget period.

Fixed costs are costs associated with those inputs, which do not vary with changes in volume of output or activity within a specified range of activity or output (relevant range) for a given budget period. Fixed costs, thus, remain constant whether activity increases or decreases within a relevant range. For example, the rent of factory or office premises, property insurance, senior executives' salaries, lease payments, depreciation, and so on remain the same whether there is an increase or decrease in the volume of activity. However, fixed costs are not fixed for all times to come. Fixed cost, like any other cost, is subject to change over a period of time. For instance, rent may increase, property insurance rates may go up, executives' salaries may increase, and so on in the next period but these increases are not the result of an increase in the firm's output. In a way, therefore, the terminology "fixed cost" is not very appropriate; "non-variable" is a more appropriate name for these costs.

Since fixed costs are unaffected by volume changes, any increase in volume implies that the costs will be allocated to a greater number of units and as a result fixed cost per unit will become progressively smaller as volume increases. Conversely, when a smaller number of units is produced, the fixed costs per unit will become larger. Such a variation in unit fixed cost creates problems in product costing, the cost being dependent on the number of units produced. This aspect has been referred to as "troublesome fixed costs."[4]

Table 2.1 illustrates the nature of fixed costs.

Table 2.1 Production Volume and Fixed Costs

Production (in units)	*Total fixed cost (TFC)*	*Average fixed cost per unit*
1,000	₹10,000	₹10
2,000	10,000	5
5,000	10,000	2
10,000	10,000	1

Figure 2.2 portrays the relationship between volume and total fixed costs. The relationship between volume and fixed costs per unit is exhibited by Figure 2.3. While fixed cost remain constant at ₹10,000 in total, cost per unit starts decreasing as the volume increases. Thus, there is an inverse relationship between production volume and average fixed cost (AFC) per unit (Figure 2.3). Hence, fixed costs are constant on an aggregative basis but are variable on a unit basis.

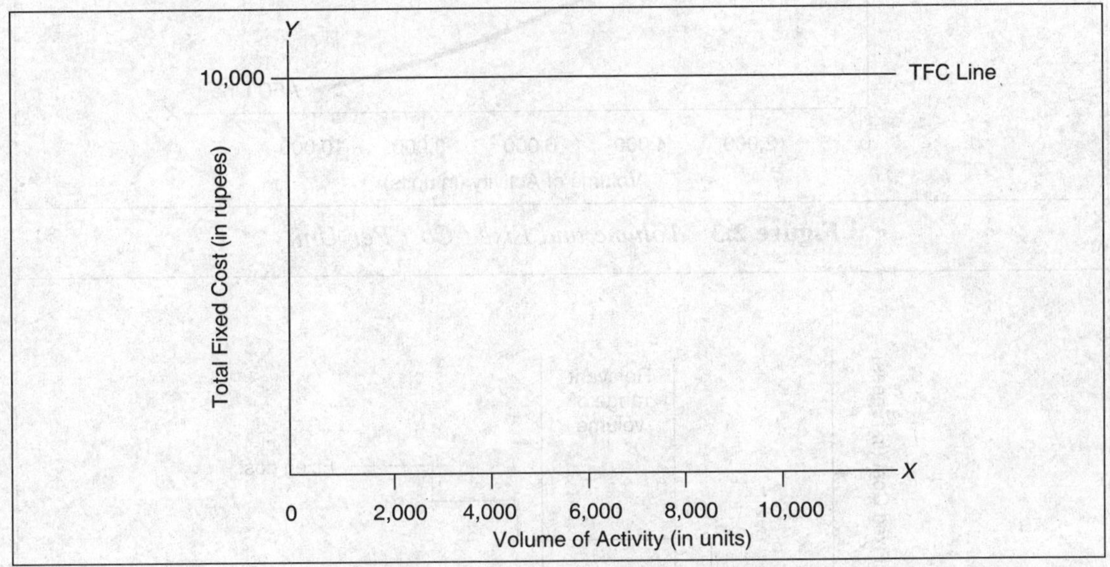

Figure 2.2 *Volume and Total Fixed Costs*

As stated earlier, fixed costs will not change over a wide range of volume (the relevant range). They will fluctuate before and beyond that range. For example, prolonged strike or lockout may cause fixed costs to be reduced if executives or employees are laid off. Likewise, an expansion of activity beyond the present capacity will require purchase of new plant and equipment, engaging additional foremen and supervisors and, hence, additional fixed costs will result from these new inputs.[5] Such costs behaviour is shown in Figure 2.4. It is for this reason that fixed costs are sometimes called "capacity costs" as they measure the capacity for manufacturing, sales, administration and research. They reflect the capability for sustaining a planned volume of activity.[6]

It is useful to sub-divide fixed costs into "committed" fixed costs and "discretionary" fixed costs from the point of view of profit planning and control.

Committed Fixed Costs Fixed costs caused by the purchase of capacity producing assets such as plant and equipment are called committed costs. These costs are on an increase in a growing firm as usually such a firm switches over to automatic plant operation from a manual one, resulting

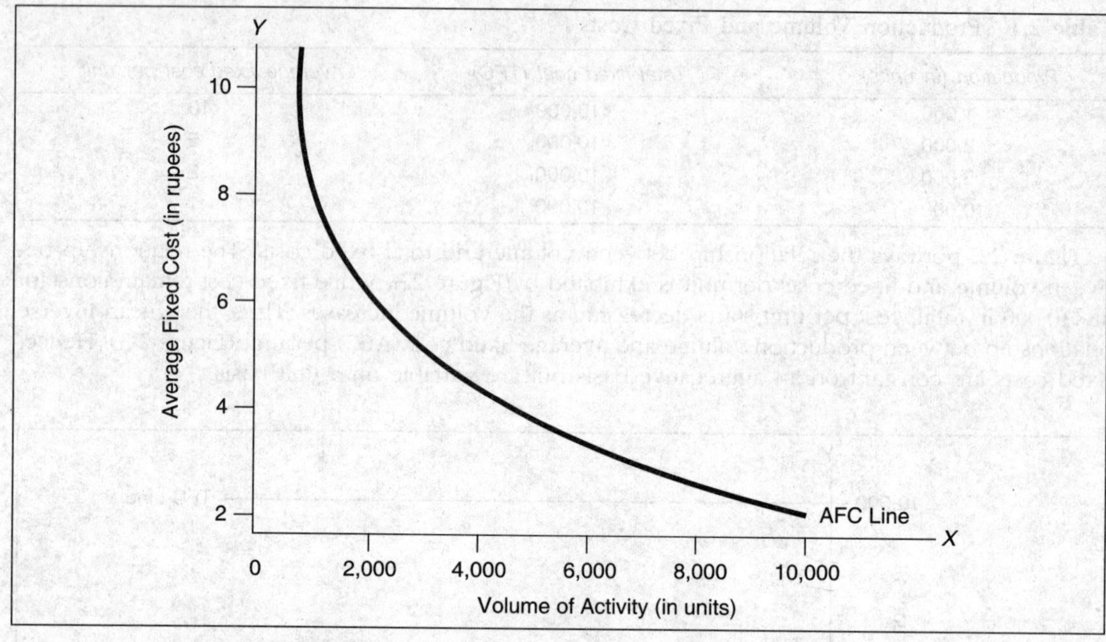

Figure 2.3 *Volume and Fixed Cost Per Unit*

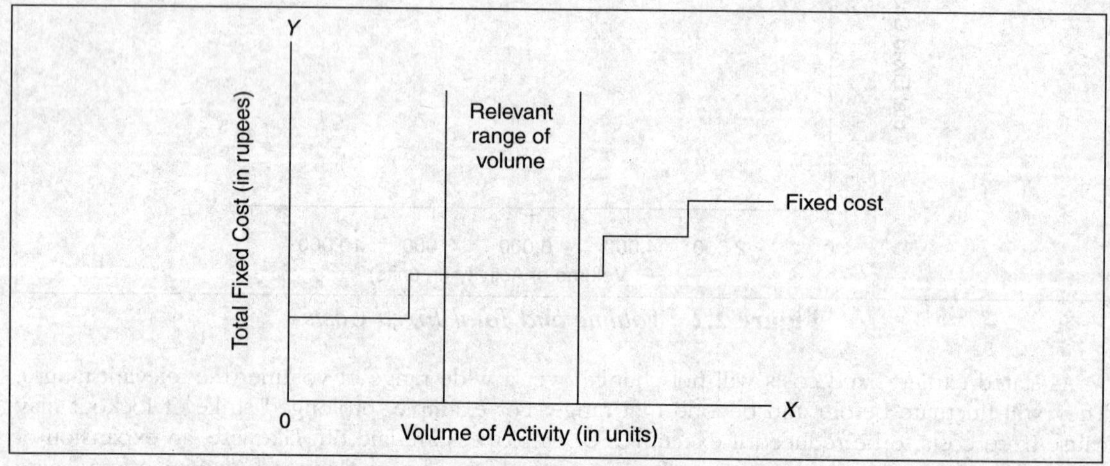

Figure 2.4 *Behaviour of Fixed Costs*

Committed fixed costs are costs caused by the acquisition of capacity-producing assets.

in higher expenditure on plant and equipment. Depreciation, rent, property taxes, salaries of key personnel, insurance, and so on are examples of committed fixed costs. These costs are known as committed fixed costs because the company has committed itself to incur such costs by making long range decisions which will extend several years into the future. Such costs cannot be reduced substantially without impairing the organisation's competence to meet long range goals. The committed fixed costs are the least responsive of the fixed costs, because they tend to be less affected by month-to-month and year-to-year decisions. For instance, once buildings are constructed and machinery is installed, little can be done in day-do-day operations to affect the total level of committed costs. From the point of view of the management, therefore, the stress should be to increase current utilisation of these facilities so as to augment income. It is for this reason that fixed costs are ignored for short-term decisions, that is, the management decides to sell a product at a price below the total cost but higher than variable cost. In such situations, the concept of the contribution margin as a decision-criterion becomes important. Contribution margin per unit is the difference between the selling price and the variable cost per unit.

Discretionary Fixed Costs These costs are also known as *programmed costs or managed costs.* The costs caused by management policy decisions to undertake activities such as research and development, training programmes for its employees, advertising and sales promotion, charitable and/or political donations, management consulting services, and so on, are called discretionary fixed costs. Such costs can be reduced substantially (and in extreme cases almost entirely) for a given year in difficult times at the discretion of management. For instance, the management may decide not go give any donations, may stop making advertisements in newspapers or other media and, thus, eliminate these costs.

Discretionary fixed costs are costs caused by management policy decisions.

The amount/size of discretionary fixed costs is decided by the top management at the beginning of the budget period, specifying the allocation for each of the expenditure items listed above. For example, the management may decide to allocate ₹2 lakh for market research and development, ₹1 lakh for sales promotion and advertising, and so on. These expenditures are allocated in the light of the long-term goals of the company. The advantages accruing from such expenditures cannot be expected in the same budget period in which they have been incurred. For example, even a technological break-through that could shorten production time appreciably would have no effect until it was properly tested, installed and checked—a process that would most likely extend into some future budgeted period.[7] Therefore, discretionary fixed costs are not subject to ordinary engineering input-output analysis which holds true for most other costs.[8]

Variable Costs

Costs that tend to vary in direct proportion or in a one-to-one relationship to changes in production activity, sales activity or some other measure of volume within relevant range for a given budget period are referred to as variable costs.[9] Material costs, direct labour costs and supplies are examples of variable cost. The cost of these inputs increases/ decreases in proportion to increase/decrease in volume. It is so because these inputs are used in the exact quantities needed. Table 2.2 portrays relationship between direct material, direct labour and total variable costs and production volume.

Variable costs are costs that tend to vary in direct proportion to change in production in relevant range.

Table 2.2 Production Volume and Variable Costs

Production (units)	*Direct Material costs (@ ₹8 per unit)*	*Direct Labour costs (@ ₹2 per unit)*	*Total variable costs (@ ₹10 per unit)*
8,000	64,000	16,000	80,000
8,100	64,800	16,200	81,000
8,300	66,400	16,600	83,000
8,500	68,000	17,000	85,000

Table 2.2 shows that each change of one unit of product causes a change of ₹10 of variable cost (₹8 materials and ₹2 labour). As output increases, so do the variable costs increase in the same proportion. For instance, at 8,000 units production level, variable costs are ₹80,000; at 8,500 units,

such costs become ₹85,000. Expressed mathematically, there is a linear relationship between volume and variable costs. Thus, total variable costs vary in direct proportion to volume and, consequently, are constant per unit of volume. Figures 2.5 and 2.6 illustrate this relationship. In view of their behaviour, variable costs are sometimes called "engineered costs". An engineered costs is any cost that has an explicit, specified, physical relationship with a selected measure of activity. Most variable costs are of this type. An "engineered" variable cost is said to exist when work measurement techniques (material standards with the help of production engineers, labour standards through time and motion study) have carefully established an optimum relationship between input and output.[10] Direct material and direct labour are a prime example of engineered costs. Like fixed costs, some of the variable costs are discretionary in nature, that is, they are dependent upon management policy. As an illustration, let us suppose that the management has pre-determined that *X* per cent of the sales revenue will be spent for items such as market research and advertising. These costs will, obviously, vary in direct proportion to the sales revenue but the reasons for variability are not the same as in case of direct materials or direct labour.

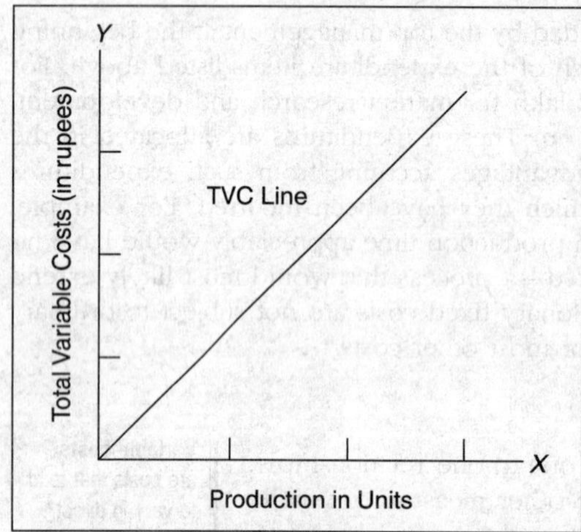

Figure 2.5 *Total Variable Cost*

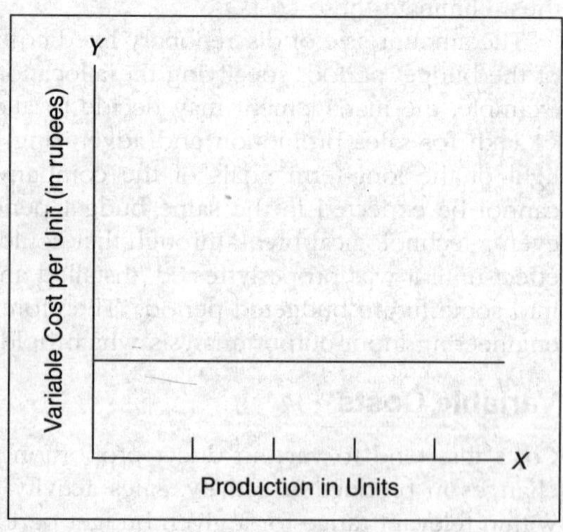

Figure 2.6 *Variable Cost per Unit*

Semi-Variable Costs (Mixed Costs)

Mixed costs are costs which consist of partly fixed costs and partly variable costs.

All costs which are neither perfectly variable nor absolutely fixed in relation to volume changes are called semi-variable costs. Semi-variable costs are also known as mixed costs as they consist both of fixed costs and variable costs. The fixed component of mixed costs represents the cost of providing capacity, whereas the variable component is caused by using the capacity. The first part is not affected by the changes in activity (and is thus like the fixed cost), while the latter part is influenced by the changes in activity (and is, thus, like the variable cost). Thus, semi-variable costs change in the same direction as volume but not in direct proportion thereto. Figure 2.7 exhibits such a relationship.

Telephone, power, repairs and maintenance costs are some of the examples of mixed costs. For example, a telephone bill involves the twin elements of cost: fixed charge consisting of basic cost for telephone service (telephone rent) irrespective of the calls made; and variable charge consisting of actual number of telephone calls made. In the case of power expenses, meter rent is a fixed charge and power usage is a variable charge.

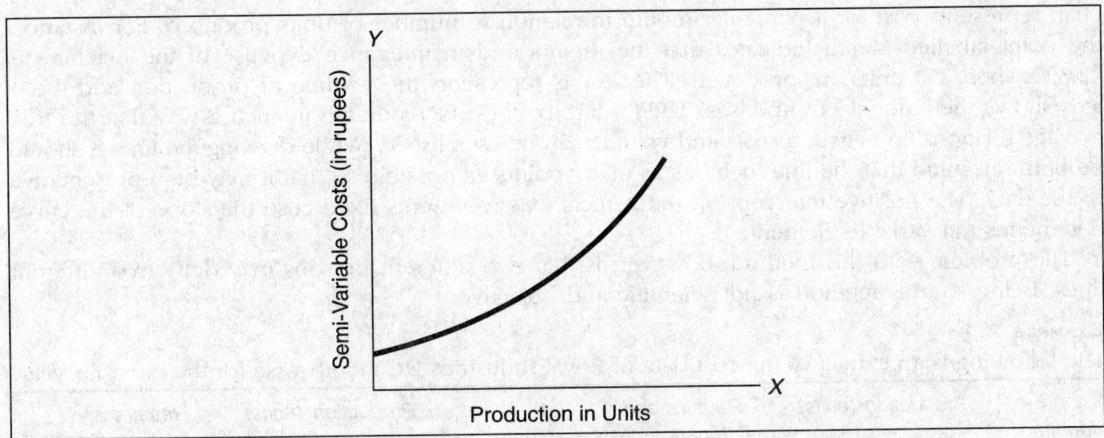

Figure 2.7 *Semi-Variable Costs*

Ideally, semi-variable costs should be bifurcated into fixed and variable elements as the functions of profit planning, cost control and decision-making assume that costs are either variable or fixed.

Methods of Mixed Cost Segregation There are four methods to bifurcate mixed costs:

1. Graphic Method (Scatter Diagram)
2. Two Point Method (High-Low Method)
3. Analytical Approach
4. Method of Least Squares.

Graphic Method The graphic method of dividing mixed costs into their fixed and variable components makes use of all relevant past data pertaining to cost-volume relationships. The data are plotted on a scatter graph, as shown in Figure 2.8, on the basis of Example 2.1. Each point on a

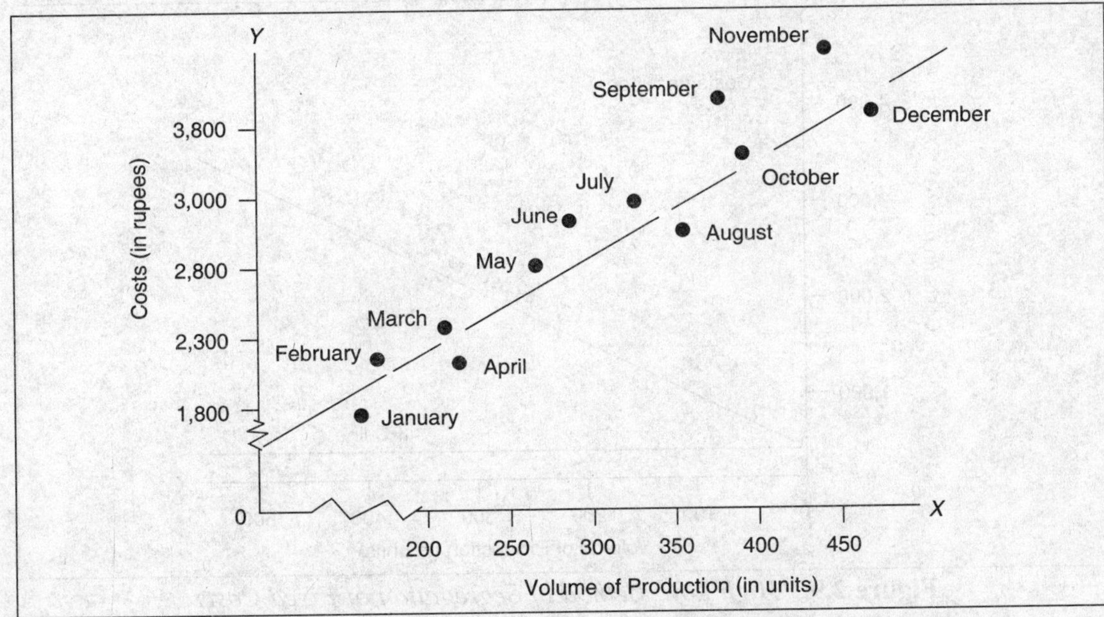

Figure 2.8 *Graphic Method of Segregation of Fixed Costs*

chart represents cost for a particular month in relation to number of units produced. For instance, the point labelled March indicates that the repairs and maintenance expense of the machine is ₹2,300 when 250 units are produced. The *X* axis represents the volume of production and the *Y* axis shows the amount of expenses. Then a line of "best fit" is drawn in such a way that the true average relationship between costs and volume can be established. While drawing the line, it should be borne in mind that the line includes as many points as possible so that it may be representative of the data. The positive intercept on the vertical axis represents fixed cost: the slope of the curve determines the variable element.

The problem with this method, however, is that two different persons may draw two different lines. Being so, this method is not scientific and objective.

Example 2.1

The following is an extract of the cost data of Royal Industries Ltd month-wise for the previous year:

Month	*Production (units)*	*Repairs and maintenance costs*	*Month*	*Production (units)*	*Repairs and maintenance costs*
January	200	₹1,800	July	350	₹3,000
February	200	1,900	August	350	2,950
March	250	2,300	September	400	3,350
April	250	2,250	October	400	3,300
May	300	2,650	November	450	3,750
June	300	2,750	December	450	3,650

High-Low Method As the name suggests, this method makes use of two observations rather than all the observations for drawing the cost line. The two points chosen are: (i) The high cost point; and (ii) The low cost point corresponding g to some specific volume (may be number of units produced as in Example 2.1 or any other measure of volume such as, labour-hours, machine-hours, telephone calls made, power consumed, and so on). Figure 2.9 shows the relationship on the basis of data contained in Example 2.1. The relevant data are plotted as follows.

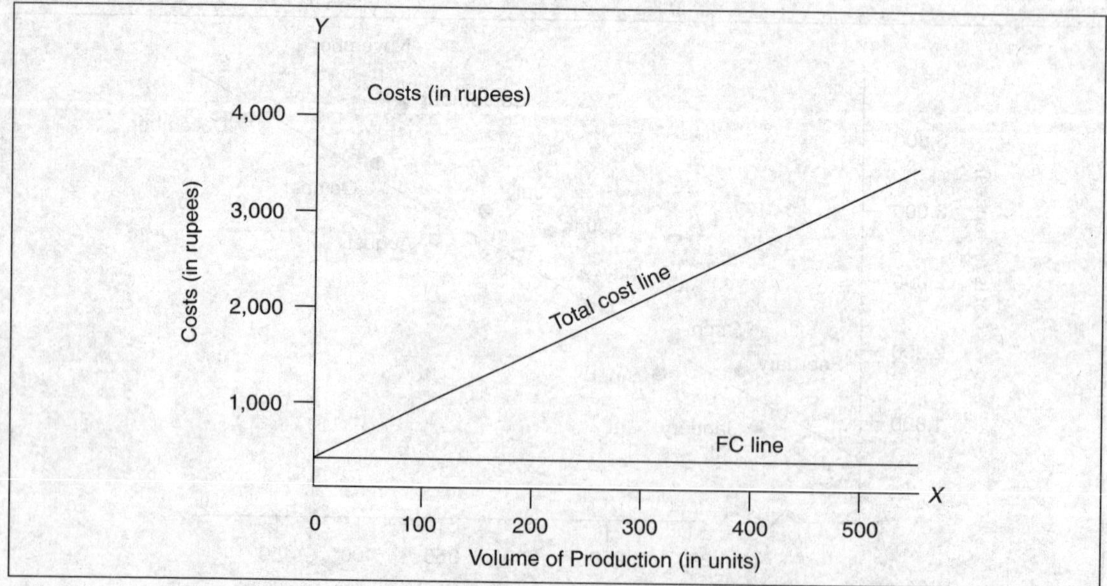

Figure 2.9 *High Low Method of Segregation of Fixed Costs*

The intercept on the vertical axis represents fixed cost and the slope of the cost line represents the variable element of the cost.

Month	*Production (in units)*	*Costs*
January	200 (P_l) (lower production)	₹ 1,800 (Low cost point, C_L)
November	450 (P_H) (higher production)	3,750 (High cost point, C_H)

The algebraic method will yield identical results as shown below:

Variable rate = Difference in cost ($C_H - C_L$) ÷ Difference in production ($P_H - P_L$) = ₹1,950 ÷ 250 units = ₹7.8 per unit

Fixed overhead component at P_L = ₹1,800 – (₹7.8 × 200) = ₹240

P_H = ₹3,750 – (₹7.8 × 450) = ₹240

Thus, mixed cost = ₹240 + ₹7.8X

In statistical terms, total cost (Y) is a function of (i) fixed element, a, and (ii) variable element, b, multiplied by number of units produced, X:

$$Y = a + bX$$

In Example 2.1, the cost equation (flexible budget cost line)

$$Y = ₹240 + ₹7.8\ X$$

The high-low method is statistically not desirable as its results are based only on two extreme observations. Because of the danger of relying on extreme points, which may not be representative of normal situations, the high-low method is not recommended.[11] From the point of view of obtaining reliable and representative results, all data points should be used and not just two, as a basis of cost estimation. Therefore, the method is unscientific and inaccurate.

Analytical Method This method is also called the "degree of variability" technique because the genesis of this method lies in measuring the extent of variability of costs with volume. In other words, the technique is based on a careful analysis of each item to determine how far the cost varies with volume.[12] Some of the mixed cost may have a 40 per cent degree of variability while others may have only 20 per cent. The virtue of this method, apart from easy understanding, is that it closely examines each constituent of the mixed costs, and therefore, is likely to give most accurate figures of fixed and variable elements. But it may be emphasised again that this method also suffers from subjectivity in that the degree of variability associated with each part of semi-variable costs is to be determined by the accountant/some other person entrusted with the job. Obviously, two different persons will assign two different percentages to the degree of variability attached with an element of semi-variable cost. But then there is no accurate method of apportioning the mixed cost into fixed and variable components. One can only approximate. Such an analysis is of particular significance in making flexible budgets.

EXAMPLE 2.2

The analysis of factory overheads of Hypothetical Ltd reveals that on an average there is a 40 per cent degree of variability at 100 per cent level of activity. Budgeted mixed overheads are ₹10,000. What would they be at 50, 70 and 90 per cent levels of activity?

SOLUTION

Variable overheads = (Budgeted mixed overheads × Degree of variability) = ₹10,000 × 0.40 = ₹4,000

Fixed overheads at 100 per cent capacity = (₹10,000 – ₹4,000) = ₹6,000

Variable overheads at 1 per cent capacity = Total variable overheads ÷ 100 = ₹4,000 ÷ 100 = ₹40

Flexible Budget (Overheads Costs)

Particulars	Level of capacity (per cent)		
	50	70	90
Fixed overheads	₹6,000	₹6,000	₹6,000
Variable overheads (level of capacity × ₹40)	2,000	2,800	3,600
Total	8,000	8,800	9,600

Method of Least Squares This method is perhaps the most accurate and scientific to apportion mixed costs. The line is not plotted arbitrarily like the scatter diagram method. It is located by means of solving the two linear equations based on the formula for drawing a straight line regression equation. The basic equation is:

$$Y = a + bX \tag{2.4}$$

Where Y = Total cost
a = Fixed element of mixed cost
b = Variable cost to volume ratio
X = Any measure of volume (production, hours, and so on)

From Equation 2.4 follows the two simultaneous linear equations:

$$\Sigma Y = na + b\,\Sigma X \tag{2.5}$$

$$\Sigma XY = a\,\Sigma X + b\,\Sigma X^2 \tag{2.6}$$

EXAMPLE 2.3

ABC Ltd furnishes the following overhead cost behaviour of mixed cost for the first 6 months of the current year. You are required to segregate these costs into fixed and variable.

Month	Units produced	Cost		
	(X)	(Y)	XY	X^2
January	20	₹900	₹18,000	₹400
February	10	700	7,000	100
March	30	1,100	33,000	900
April	20	900	18,000	400
May	00	500	00	00
June	30	1,300	39,000	900
	110	5,400	1,15,000	2,700

SOLUTION

Substituting the values in Equations 2.5 and 2.6

$$5{,}400 = 6a + 110b \tag{1}$$

$$1{,}15{,}000 = 110a + 2{,}700b \tag{2}$$

Multiplying Equation 1 by 110 and 2 by 6, we have

$$5{,}94{,}000 = 660a + 12{,}100b$$

$$6{,}90{,}000 = 660a + 16{,}200b$$

Subtracting Equation 1 from Equation 2,

$$96{,}000 = 4{,}100b$$

$$\therefore \quad b = 23.41$$

Substituting b in Equation 1 we have $6a = 2{,}824.39$ or $a = 470.73$.
Thus, the least squares equation is

$$Y = 470.73 + 23.41\,X$$

The equation indicates that fixed costs are ₹470.73, when volume X is zero and for each unit of production beyond zero costs will increase by ₹23.41 (variable costs). The results of this equation

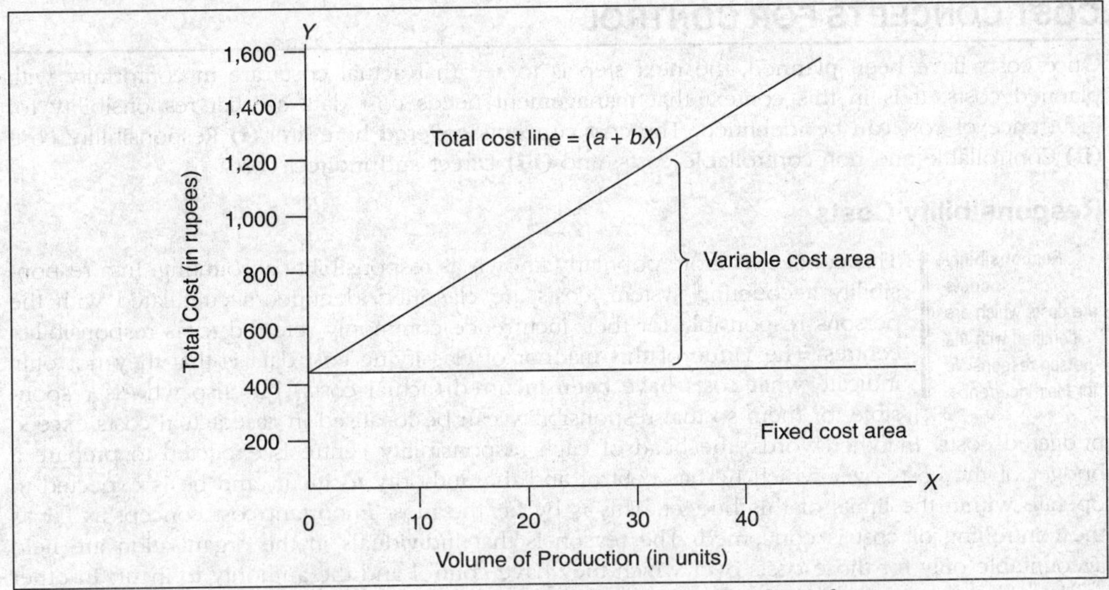

Figure 2.10 *Total Cost at Various Levels of Production*

can be used to estimate total costs for any volume within the relevant range. Figure 2.10 exhibits this relationship.

This method is by far the best among the four methods of segregating mixed costs.

Future Costs

Future costs are relevant costs in the profit planning function of management. Those costs which are reasonably expected to be incurred at some future date as a result of a current decision are called future costs. Since they deal with a future period, they are estimated costs based on expectations, Such costs are of paramount importance to the management as they are the only costs over which it can exercise any control. In the case of historical costs, there can only be retrospection and nothing much can be done about them if they are more than the budgeted cost, for the simple reason that they have already been incurred. However, future costs can be planned for and planned to be reduced. If they are too high, resources can be planned to meet the high costs and efforts can be made, if possible, to reduce them. Thus, the measurement of future costs is critically associated with the active management functions of planning and control.[13]

Future costs are costs reasonably expected to be incurred at some future date as a result of a current decision.

Budgeted Costs

When an operating plan involving future costs is accepted, and incorporated formally in the budget for a specific period, such costs get converted to what may be referred to as budgeted costs. Budgeted costs are important elements in that they provide the basis for measuring the actual performance of different cost centres and, therefore, constitute an important input of responsibility accounting.

Budgeted costs are costs which are incorporated formally in the budget of a specific period.

COST CONCEPTS FOR CONTROL

Once costs have been planned, the next step is to see that actual costs are in conformity with planned costs. It is in this context that management needs cost data so that responsibility for incurrence of cost can be identified. The cost concepts covered here are: **(i)** Responsibility cost; **(ii)** Controllable and non-controllable costs; and **(iii)** Direct and indirect costs.

Responsibility Costs

Responsibility costs are costs which are identified with the person responsible for their incurrence.

This concept is more popularly known as responsibility accounting. In a responsibility accounting system, costs are classified/identified/accumulated with the persons responsible for their incurrence commonly referred to as responsibility centres. The virtue of this manner of classifying cost data is that they not only indicate what costs have been incurred (actual costs) but also who is responsible for them so that responsibility can be localised in case actual costs exceed budgeted costs. In other words, the head of each responsibility centre is expected to prepare a budget of the costs over which he has control and the authority to incur, and he is expected to operate within the limits of this budget. This is by far the most important cost concept as far as the controlling of cost is concerned. The reason is that individuals in the organisation are held accountable only for those costs over which they have control and the authority to incur. In other words, they are not accountable for costs which they cannot control. For example, a foreman is not held liable for excess price paid by the purchase manager; he can be held liable only for the excessive usage of materials, if any. This gives rise to another concept of cost: controllable and non-controllable costs.

Controllable costs are costs the amount of which is significantly influenced by the action of the manager of the responsibility centre.

Controllable and Non-controllable Costs "An item of cost is controllable if the amount of cost incurred in (or assigned to) a responsibility centre is significantly influenced by the actions of the manager of the responsibility centre. Otherwise, it is non-controllable."[14]

The important characteristics of controllable costs are: **(i)** They are in relation to a particular responsibility centre (or the managerial area of responsibility involved); **(ii)** The head of the responsibility centre has *significant* influence but *not complete* influence on its controllability; **(iii)** They are relevant for the time period under review. For instance, the purchase manager has entered into a price contract, say for three months, with a supplier of raw materials used in production. Then price is not controllable by him for the relevant period of contract (three months) but is possibly controllable after the expiry of the contract period. Likewise, the sales manager may have entered into a contract for making advertisements for a certain period at an agreed amount.

The first characteristic indicates that the concept of controllable costs is a relative concept in the sense that when a company is viewed as a single entity, all costs are controllable at one level or another level of management. For instance, the top management may decide to close down one of the departments/divisions/segments of the business and, thus, reduce its cost to zero. The management may also decide to purchase a component from an outside supplier, hitherto manufactured by the company itself. These examples indicate that costs are uncontrollable only at intermediate and lower levels of management. For instance, a departmental supervisor has no control over the fixed costs allocated to his department, a sales manager has no control over the price/cost at which goods have been transferred to his department by the production manager. Thus, allocated costs are not controllable by the responsibility centre to which the allocation is made.

Since all costs are controllable at the higher echelons of management, the management control system should focus on those costs which are controllable at lower/intermediate levels of management. It is important to stress here that cost controllability does not involve eliminating costs, but its endeavour is to keep them as close as possible to some desirable and reasonably attainable levels or standards.[15]

Direct and Indirect Costs The various items of cost in a responsibility centre may be classified as either direct or indirect. Those costs which can be identified logically and practically in their entirety to a particular department or a product are called direct costs. Those costs which are not practically identifiable exclusively and wholly to a particular product, division or segment are called indirect cost. Indirect costs are frequently called "common costs" as they are allocated between two or more products/departments/divisions of a business. The salary of the chief executive who looks after the entire business, is an example of indirect cost. A divisional manager's salary is a direct cost if that division happens to be one specific responsibility centre. However, within divisions, if there are a number of products to be manufactured, then for each product unit (which is a separate responsibility centre), the divisional manager's salary will be the indirect cost. Thus, the distinction between a direct cost and an indirect cost depends upon the unit under consideration. If a cost can be directly and wholly traced to a particular responsibility centre under consideration, it is direct cost and if it is allocated to it from somewhere else in the organisation, it is an indirect cost.

Direct costs are costs which can be identified logically and practically in their entirety to a particular department/product.

This distinction is important as only direct costs are controllable costs for various responsibility centres. Indirect costs are not controllable.

COST CONCEPTS FOR DECISION-MAKING

Management is concerned with two types of decisions: (i) Long-range (capacity decisions) which cover a long time span and take into account the time value of money, (ii) Short-range or operating decisions cover a short span of time and, therefore, time value of money is not considered to be significant. Decisions involving production, output, pricing of special orders, addition or dropping of a product line, make or buy, processing further or sell, temporary shutdown and so on are examples of short-range decisions. To have correct decision, management requires estimates of all future benefits and costs concerning a particular decision. The relevant cost concepts affecting the latter type of decisions are: **(i)** Relevant and irrelevant costs; **(ii)** Incremental cost/differential cost; **(iii)** Out of pocket costs and sunk costs; **(iv)** Opportunity costs and imputed costs.

Relevant and Irrelevant Costs

Cost which is influenced by a decision is a relevant cost and, hence, is important for decision-makers. Cost which is not affected by a decision is irrelevant cost, that is, it will be the same regardless of the choice that is made. As a result, such a cost is of no relevance to decision-makers. Therefore, it should be ignored while taking decisions. Committed fixed costs are irrelevant costs. However, it should not be taken to mean that relevant costs are equivalent to variable costs. In situations where additional fixed costs are to be incurred as a result of a decision, fixed costs are as much the relevant costs as the variable costs are. As an illustration, if the company wants to make a component hitherto purchased from the outside suppliers, the relevant costs will be: **(i)** Cost of material and direct labour (variable cost) and **(ii)** Fixed costs (required for creating new facilities so that the manufacturing process of making a component can start). Thus, relevant costs, truly speaking, are incremental costs, fixed and variable classification notwithstanding.

Relevant costs are costs which are influenced by a decision.

Incremental Cost/Differential Cost

Incremental costs are additional costs caused by a particular decision.

Differential cost is the difference in cost between any two acceptable alternatives.

This is by far the most important concept of cost in the decision-making process. Incremental costs are the additional costs which will be incurred if management chooses one course of action as opposed to another. They are the extra, or incremental costs, caused by a particular decision.

A differential cost is the difference in cost between any two available, acceptable alternatives. This approach compares the two alternatives directly by looking at the differences between them.[16] The difference in cost between buying a component from outside and making it in the company is a differential cost, relevant for decision-making. Furthermore, differential costs always relate to a specific time period. What it implies is that with the passage of time and change of situation, the amount of differential costs will vary. It is a broader concept than variable cost as it also takes into account additional fixed costs caused by a management decision.

Out of Pocket Costs and Sunk Costs

Sunk costs are costs which have already been incurred and would not require current cash expenditure.

A cost which requires current or future cash expenditures as a result of a decision is labelled as an out of pocket cost. In situations where funds/cash resources available are limited, such costs become very decisive in the decision-making process. In contrast, those costs which have already been incurred in the past and will not require current cash expenditure are called sunk costs.

Thus, the two cost concepts are the opposites of each other. In the case of the sunk cost a prior investment of cash resources has been made, while cash will be required currently or in the near future period in the cash of out of pocket costs.

Depreciation, depletion and amortisation of intangible assets (like preliminary expenses, cost of issue of shares and debentures) are some of the examples of sunk costs. Since sunk costs are the results of past commitments, they should be ignored/disregarded for purposes of decision-making. "*Do not cry over spilt milk*" should be the management's attitude towards such costs.

From the above it will be erroneous to infer that all variable costs are out of pocket costs and that all fixed costs are sunk costs. The chief executive's salary may be fixed but is very much an out of pocket cost as it requires current cash outlay. Similarly, in certain situations, variable costs may not be affected by the decision and, therefore, will be sunk costs. For example, assume that a company is considering a change in the manufacturing process with no change in production volume; the variable costs will remain unchanged and, therefore, will be labelled as sunk costs with respect to the decision. Consider the facts in Table 2.3.

Table 2.3 Differential Cost

Particulars	*Present manufacturing process*	*Proposed manufacturing process*
Direct material	₹2,00,000	₹2,00,000
Direct labour	3,00,000	3,00,000
Factory overheads	3,50,000	2,50,000
Total costs	8,50,000	7,50,000

The materials and labour costs are estimated at ₹5,00,000 under both the manufacturing processes. They are sunk costs in this situation. The decrease of factory overheads in the proposed manufacturing process is the differential cost relevant for decision-making, though it is largely in the nature of a fixed cost.

The above illustration highlights the fact that variable costs are not always relevant costs and fixed costs are not always irrelevant costs from the points of view of decision-making. Included in the category of relevant costs for decision-making are all those costs which differ among the alternatives at hand. It is not significant whether the cost belongs to the fixed or variable category. Therefore, differential costs (incremental costs) are the only "material" costs for effective and efficient decision-making. It is this concept of differential costing, also known as incremental analysis, which is used for short-term non-recurring decision-making.

Opportunity Costs and Imputed Costs

Opportunity costs represent the benefits foregone by not choosing the second best alternative in favour of the best one. When we decide to follow one alternative, we are also deciding not to follow another. As a result, all the benefits that would have accrued are given up. To the extent they can be quantified/measured, they are opportunity costs of the decision and relevant costs for a decision. Assume that a company owns a building; it could be either used for business purposes or be rented to others. If a decision is taken to use the building, the amount of rent foregone constitutes the opportunity cost. Opportunity costs are associated only with feasible alternatives. The lost rent is an opportunity cost only if there are potential tenants willing to hire the building. Since they are hypothetical/theoretical costs, they are not entered in the accounting records. But the cost of the second best alternative must be taken into account before taking a decision.

Opportunity costs represent benefits foregone by not choosing the second best alternative in favour of the best one.

Imputed costs are similar to the opportunity costs in that they are not recorded in the accounting books. However, they are hypothetical costs that must be taken into account if a correct decision is to be arrived at. Interest is the principal example of imputed costs.

SUMMARY

- From the viewpoint of managerial needs, cost concepts fall into four broad categories—income measurement, profit planning, cost control, and special situations.
- There are four cost concepts pertaining to income measurement. These are Product and period costs; Absorbed and unabsorbed costs; Expired and unexpired costs; and Joint and separable costs.
- Production costs are costs which can be identified with goods produced/purchased for resale. Period costs are costs which are matched against the revenue of the current period.
- Absorbed costs are costs which must be absorbed by the revenue of the period in which the products have been sold and not necessarily in the year in which they have been incurred.
- An expired cost is one which can not contribute to the production of future revenues. An unexpired cost has the capacity to contribute to the production of revenue in future, for example, inventory.
- Joint product costs are the costs of a single process/series of processes that simultaneously produce two or more products of significant sale value. Separable costs refer to any cost that can be attributed exclusively and wholly to a particular product/process/division/department.
- The cost concepts relevant to profit planning are: **(i)** Fixed, variable and semi-variable/mixed costs, and **(ii)** Future and budgeted costs.
- Fixed (non-variable) costs do not change with changes in volume of output or activity within a specified range of activity/output (relevant range) for a given budget period. Fixed costs caused by the purchase of capacity producing assets such as plants are called committed fixed costs. The discretionary fixed (managed) costs are caused by management policy decision to undertake activities such as research and development, training programme for employees, advertising and sales promotion and so on.

- Costs that tend to vary in total in direct proportion or in one-to-one relationship to changes in production/sales/some other measure of volume are variable costs.
- All costs which are neither perfectly variable nor absolutely fixed in relation to volume changes are called semi-variable (mixed) costs. They consist of both fixed costs and variable costs.
- The methods of segregating of mixed costs are the graphic method, the high-low method, the analytical method and the method of least squares.
- The concepts relating to cost control are Responsibility costs, Controllable and non-controllable costs, and Direct and indirect costs.
- Responsibility costs are costs which are classified/identified/accumulated with the person(s) responsible for their incurrence.
- An item of cost is controllable if the amount of cost incurred in (assigned to) a responsibility centre is significantly influenced by the actions of the manager of the responsibility centre. Otherwise, it is non-controllable.
- Those costs which can be identified logically and practically in their entirety to a particular department/product are called direct costs. Those costs which are not practically identifiable exclusively and wholly to a particular product/division/segment are called indirect (common) costs.
- The cost concepts affecting decision-making are Relevant and irrelevant costs, Differential costs, out-of-pocket costs and sunk costs, and Opportunity costs and imputed costs.
- Costs which are influenced by a decision are a relevant cost and cost which is not affected by a decision is irrelevant cost.
- Differential/incremental costs are the differential/additional costs which would be incurred if the management chooses one course of action as opposed to another. They are incremental costs caused by a particular decision.
- A cost which requires a current/future cash expenditure as a result of a decision is an out of pocket cost. Costs which have already been incurred in the past are sunk costs.
- Opportunity cost represents the benefits foregone by not choosing the second best alternative in favour of the best one. Imputed costs are hypothetical costs that must be considered for correct decision, for example, interest cost.

REFERENCES

1. P.F. Bourke in D.L. Anderson and Donald L. Raun, *Information Analysis in Management Accounting*, (Santa Barbara, New York, 1978), p. 6.
2. *Ibid.*, p 9.
3. C.T. Horngren, *Introduction to Management Accounting*, (Prentice-Hall, New Jersey, 1978), p. 118.
4. C.L. Moore and R.K. Jaedicke, *Managerial Accounting*, (South Western Publishing Company, Chicago, 1972), pp. 263-64.
5. R.M. Copeland and P.E. Dascher, *Managerial Accounting*, (John Wiley, New York, 1978), p. 75
6. Horngren, C.T., and G.L. Sundlem, *Introduction to Management Accounting*, (Prentice Hall, New Delhi, 1990), p. 206.
7. Copeland and Dascher, *op.cit.*, p. 76.
8. Horngren, *op.cit.*, p. 208.

9. The phrase 'relevant range' is important. It can be explained with reference to direct material cost (the most important constituent of variable costs). Assume purchase cost of 1 kg of materials is ₹10; for 10 kgs it would be ₹100; if purchases are of 100 kgs, the material cost per kg may be less than ₹10 (say, it is ₹9.5 per kg); extending the purchase size to 1,000 kg, the cost per kg may further decrease (say to ₹8.5 per kg), as the quantity purchased is substantially higher at 1,000 kgs compared to 100 kgs earlier). Given the fact of having trade discounts on bulk purchases, the per unit cost of material would depend on quantity of materials to be purchased. In real situation, the firm (based on its budgeted production) would have its budgeted requirement of direct materials.

Based on the likely quantity of direct materials to be purchased (say 10,000 kg for ₹80,000) per kg material cost would be ₹8; the direct material cost at the rate of ₹8 per kg would be valid only if the quantity purchased are in the vicinity of 8,000 kg; in case, there is substantial decrease/increase in the purchased quantity, per unit cost may increase/decrease. This then constitutes the rationale of having relevant range as a part of definition of VC.

10. *Ibid.*, p. 208.
11. *Ibid.*, p. 224.
12. J.L. Brown and L.R. Howard, *Principles and Practice of Management Accounting*, (Macdonald and Evans Ltd, London, 1969), p. 249
13. Fremgen, *Accounting for Managerial Analysis*, (Illinois, Irwin, 1976), p. 17.
14. R.N. Anthony and G.A. Welsh, *Fundamentals of Management Accounting*, (Richard D. Irwin, Homewood, Illinois, 1977, p. 451).
15. Fremgen, *op.cit.*, p. 28.
16. D.T. Decoster, *Management Accounting: A Decision Emphasis*, (John Wiley and Sons, New York, 1979)), p. 10.

REVIEW QUESTIONS

RQ.2.1 In the following multiple choice questions, select the correct answers.

(i) A company undertakes job-works. Which one of the following is likely to be a variable cost? (a) the wages of workers paid on monthly basis, (b) the salary of the factory manager, (c) the wages of shop floor workers paid by piece rate, (d) the rent of the factory.

(ii) A company makes plastic windows and doors. Which one of the following is likely to be a fixed cost?
(a) the cost of heating the factory, (b) the cost of the plastic, (c) sales commission, (d) none of these.

(iii) When units produced increase, total variable costs ________
(a) increase in proportion to the units produced, (b) increase at a greater rate than units produced, (c) increase at a lesser rate than units produced, (d) do not change.

(iv) As production increases (within relevant range), total fixed costs ________
(a) increase in proportion to the units produced, (b) increase at a greater rate than units produced, (c) increase at a lesser rate than units produced, (d) do not change.

(v) When units produced increase (within relevant range), variable cost per unit ________
(a) increase in proportion to the units produced, (b) increase at a greater rate than units produced, (c) increase at a lesser rate than units produced, (d) do not change.

(vi) As production increases, fixed cost per unit ________
(a) decreases, (b) increases, (c) we can't tell, (d) do not change.

(vii) The line equation expressing the total costs (y) might be expressed (based on the following information: total fixed costs = ₹10,000; and variable cost per unit = ₹5) as follows:
(a) x = 5y – 10,000, (b) x = 10,000y – 5, (c) y = 5x + 10,000, (d) y = 10,000x + 5

(viii) The Scattergraph method ________
(a) is a more accurate method of analysing mixed costs than the high-low method, (b) is a less accurate method of analysing mixed costs than the high-low method, (c) is as accurate method of analyzing mixed costs as the high-low method, (d) is more accurate than method of least squares.

(ix) All opportunity costs are
(a) relevant costs, (b) irrelevant costs, (c) increment costs, (d) none of these

(x) Most of the historical costs are
(a) relevant costs, (b) irrelevant costs, (c) increment costs, (d) none of these

[Answers: (i) c (ii) a (iii) a (iv) d (v) d (vi) a (vii) c (viii) a (ix) a (x) b]

RQ.2.2 Fill in the following blanks.

(i) The volume range over which cost relationships are valid is termed as ________.

(ii) Future costs that differ under proposed alternatives are ________.

(iii) Costs that are important to decision-makers, but are not recorded in financial accounting records are ________.

(iv) Costs which increase with increase in production volume are ________.

(v) The vertical axis intercept of total cost function represents ________.

(vi) Fixed costs like rent, insurance, salaries etc. are also known as ________.

(vii) Incremental and opportunity costs are ________ for decision-making.

(viii) The synonymous term for existing fixed costs is ________ from the perspective of decision-making.

(ix) ________ the most scientific method of segregating mixed costs into fixed and variable components.

(x) Indirect costs are ________ from the perspective of cost control.

[Answers: (i) relevant range, (ii) relevant costs, (iii) opportunity costs, (iv) incremental costs, (v) fixed costs, (vi) period costs, (vii) relevant costs, (viii) sunk costs, (ix) method of least squares, (x) non-controllable costs.]

RQ.2.3 (a) Are all fixed costs sunk costs? Explain.

(b) What are opportunity costs? Are opportunity costs relevant in decision-making? Give examples in support of your answer.

RQ.2.4 (a) "Certain costs are controllable and certain other costs are non-controllable." This is a meaningless statement unless we define what portion of the organisation is being discussed. Explain.

(b) Write short notes on controllable and uncontrollable costs.

RQ.2.5 What are the various methods by which you would split semi-variable costs in its fixed and variable elements?

RQ.2.6 (a) The classification of costs as controllable and non-controllable depends upon a point of reference. Explain.

(b) Direct costs and controllable costs are not necessarily the same. Comment.

(c) Why are sunk costs not relevant in decision-making?

RQ.2.7 (a) "All future costs are relevant." Do you agree? Why?

(b) "Fixed costs are really variable. The more you produce the less they become." Do you agree? Explain.

RQ.2.8 (a) "All controllable costs are direct costs. Not all direct costs are controllable." Explain with the help of suitable examples.

(b) Distinguish between (i) engineered, (ii) discretionary, and (iii) committed costs. Give suitable examples. Are all these costs controllable?

CASE

2.C.1 (Cost Concepts) Sycon Technology Inc (STI) is a NRI-owned company headquartered in Silicon Valley, California, U.S.A. The STI provides software services and software products in the area of telecom and networking technologies. The main line of work is in turnkey software projects in those areas. It has been growing phenomenally in the past two years. Yet, it has to refuse projects since it is unable to handle more business. Anupam Singh, the CEO, STI, is concerned about the state of affairs since refusing business is not in the long-term interest of the company. Due to non-availability of experienced persons, he is seriously constrained in expanding his business.

The Chief Operating Officer (COO) of STI, N.K. Singh, has suggested to the CEO that a possible solution could be to set up a development centre in India. Since a lot of talented software engineers are available there and the cost of operating the centre would be much lower than expanding the company in the USA itself. To carry a feasibility study of setting up the new development centre, Anupam Singh hires the services of Delhi-based consultant - ABC Consultants.

ABC Consultants identified three locations for setting up the development centre: Delhi, Noida and Gurgaon. The major cost elements associated with these three locations identified by ABC after wide-ranging consultations/survey are summarised below:

- Rental of office space: Delhi office, ₹3,000 per square feet per annum; Noida office, ₹700; and Gurgaon office, ₹900. The development centre would require the office for 50 engineers. On an average, 100 square feet per engineer would be required after taking into account all service areas also.
- Setup costs including architect's fee: Delhi office, ₹12,00,000; Noida office, ₹35,00,000; and Gurgaon office, ₹17,00,000
- Cost of 64kpbs STP Internet link shared with other companies through Software Technology Park (STP): Delhi site, ₹10,00,000; Noida site, ₹8,00,000; and Gurgaon site ₹12,00,000. However, the running costs for all the three sites would be ₹3,00,000 per annum.
- Average price of personal computers, ₹60,000 and workstation cost to buy additional equipment to set up the office such as UPS, LAN hubs, routers and ethernet switch and so on, ₹85,000 per work station at all the sites.
- Employee compensation:
  - (i) Annual salary, ₹2,00,000
  - (ii) Housing facility/Monthly rent of a two-bed room apartment: Delhi, ₹9,500; Noida, ₹5,000; and Gurgaon, ₹4,500.
  - (iii) Transport facility/hiring of buses (monthly charges): Delhi, ₹17,000; Noida and Gurgaon ₹22,000 each.
- Cost of running offices:
  - (i) Electricity charges (annual): Delhi, ₹6,00,000; Noida, ₹7,00,000; and Gurgaon, ₹5,50,000
  - (ii) Annual water charges: Delhi, ₹25,000; Noida, ₹28,000 and Gurgaon, ₹38,000.
  - (iii) Telephone charges, ₹20,000 monthly irrespective of the location.
- Consultants fee/charges: ₹3,00,000.

Based on the above facts, ABC Consultants prepared a report (cost schedule) for consideration of the CEO, as given in Exhibit 1:

Exhibit 1 Cost Schedule/Report (Annual Costs) Relating to Development Centres

Cost Elements	*Location*		
	Delhi	*Gurgaon*	*Noida*
Fixed Costs*: (A)			
Space rental	₹1,50,00,000@	₹45,00,000@@	₹35,00,000@@
Setup costs	12,00,000	17,00,000	35,00,000
STP link costs	10,00,000	12,00,000	8,00,000
Equipment costs	42,50,000	42,50,000	42,50,000
Consultant's fee	3,00,000	3,00,000	3,00,000
	2,17,50,000	1,19,50,000	1,23,50,000

(Contd.)

(*Contd.*)

Variable Costs** (B)			
Salary	1,00,00,000	1,00,00,000	1,00,00,000
Employee housing	57,00,000[1]	27,00,000[2]	30,00,000[3]
Employee transport	6,12,000[4]	7,92,000[5]	7,92,000[6]
Electricity charges	6,00,000	4,50,000	7,00,000
Water charges	25,000	38,000	28,000
Telephone charges	2,40,000[7]	2,40,000	2,40,000
STP link usage charges	3,00,000	3,00,000	3,00,000
	1,74,77,000	1,46,20,000	1,50,60,000
Total (A + B)	3,92,27,000	2,65,70,000	2,74,10,000

@(50 × 100 × ₹3,000) @@(50 × 100 × ₹900) @@@(50 × 100 × ₹700)
[1](₹9,500 × 12 × 50) [2](₹4,500 × 12 × 50) [3](₹5,000 × 12 × 50)
[4](3 × ₹17,000 × 12) [5](3 × ₹22,000 × 12) [6](3 × ₹22,000 × 12)
[7](₹20,000 × 12)
*Costs which do not vary with a change in number of employees
**Costs which change directly with the change in number of employees.

On the basis of the above cost analysis, ABC consultants has recommended that the STI's development centre in India should be located in Gurgaon.

REQUIRED: Should the Consultant's recommendation be accepted?

Before taking a final decision, the CEO referred the Consultants' report to the CFO, Nipon Shah for review. His findings/comments on the report are summarised below:

- Fixed costs are non-time cost and should be recovered over the life of the asset. The setup costs and STP link costs are fixed costs, having 4-year lives. They should be assumed to have been incurred throughout the 4-year period.
- The Consultant fee is sunk cost.
- Equipment costs, salary and telephone charges are the same for all the locations and, therefore, irrelevant cost with respect to the decision to locate the development centre.

In the light of these, the CFO prepared the following cost report.

Cost Elements	*Delhi*	*Noida*	*Gurgaon*
(A) Fixed Costs			
Space rental	₹1,50,00,000	₹45,00,000	₹35,00,000
Setup costs (total ÷ 4)	3,00,000	42,50,000	8,75,000
STP link costs (total ÷ 4)	10,00,000	12,00,000	8,00,000
	1,55,00,000	52,25,000	45,75,000
(B) Variable Costs			
Employee housing	57,00,000	27,00,000	30,00,000
Employee transport	6,12,000	7,92,000	7,92,000
Electricity charges	6,00,000	4,50,000	7,00,000
Water charges	25,000	38,000	28,000
	69,37,000	40,80,000	45,20,000
Total (A + B)	2,24,87,000	93,05,000	90,95,000

RECOMMENDATION: The CFO has recommended the setting of the development centre at Gurgaon.

Costing and Control of Materials

Learning Objectives

1. Discuss the prerequisites to an effective control system for materials
2. Explain the purchase and issue procedures for materials, system of accounting for materials issued and inventory control techniques
3. Understand the cost of inventory
4. Illustrate methods of pricing of materials issued/inventory costing
5. Choose an appropriate inventory valuation method.
6. Discuss just-in time inventory/production.

INTRODUCTION

Raw materials constitute an essential element of production. After raw materials are purchased and temporarily placed in store, they are processed/transformed into finished goods. This chapter explores the costing and control of materials. Section 1 analyses the control of materials. The costing of materials is examined in Section 2. Section 3 describes just-in time inventory/production. The main points are summarised in the last section.

CONTROL OF MATERIALS

Rigid control over materials are necessary not only to guard against theft, but also to minimise waste and misuse from causes such as excessive inventories, overissue, deterioration, spoilage, and obsolescence. There are certain prerequisites to an effective control system for materials:[1]

- Materials of the desired quantity will be available when needed;
- Materials will be purchased only when a need exists and in economical qualities;
- Purchases of materials will be made at most favourable prices;
- Vouchers for the payments of materials purchased will be approved only if the materials have been received in good condition;
- Materials will be protected against loss by proper physical control;

- Issue of materials will be properly authorised and accounted for; and
- All materials, at all times, will be charged, as the responsibility of some individual.

The control of materials, as an element of cost of production, is illustrated with reference to the purchase and issues procedures, inventory systems, and inventory control techniques.

Organisation for Control: Purchase and Issues Procedures

Control is achieved in part through an organisational structure that allows specialisation, and at the same time it defines authority, fixes responsibility and provides a system of checks and balances. To secure the advantage of specialisation, the function related to material acquisition (purchase) and handling, are usually subdivided. A centralised purchasing department is charged with the responsibility of planning orders for materials with reliable vendors at the right time and at the right price. A receiving department inspects incoming shipments/purchased goods and verifies the quantities received on orders. A stores department is held responsible for protecting materials against physical deterioration and ensuring that it is properly issued. Record-keeping is centralised in the accounting department where transactions are entered in the accounts only after documentary evidence has been supplied by other departments. Invoices are paid in the finance/credit department after approval by the accounting department. Checks and balances (that is, effective internal controls) are provided by making each department independent of the others.

Accounting for materials usually involves two activities: **(i)** Purchase of materials and **(ii)** Issue of materials.

Purchase of Materials Generally, there is a purchasing department whose function is to order/purchase materials and supplies for production. The purchase manager is responsible for ensuring that the items ordered: **(a)** Meet the quality standards, **(b)** Are acquired at the lowest price and **(c)** Are delivered on a timely basis. A typical purchase procedure involves three steps: **(1)** Purchase requisition, **(2)** Purchase order, and **(3)** Receipt of materials.

Purchase Requisition Purchase is initiated through a purchase requisition. It is a written request, sent to inform the purchasing department of a need for materials and supplies. The purchase requisition serves two purposes:

1. It notifies the purchasing department that a need exists for materials to start the purchase process in motion;
2. It fixes responsibility for the purchase request.

Although a purchase requisition is usually preprinted according to the specifications of a particular company, most forms include the requisition (serially numbered); name of the department/individual making the request; quantity of the items requested; identifying the catalogue number; description of the item; unit price; total price; shipping, handling, insurance and related costs; total cost of entire requisition; order date; required delivery date, and authorised signature. Figure 3.1 shows a purchase requisition.

Two copies of purchase requisition are customarily made, the original going to the purchasing department (to place the order), and the copy remaining with the stores clerk who requested the purchase order (to keep track of orders placed).

Purchase Order After the requisition has been approved, the purchasing department places order. For routine purchases, the order is usually sent through established sources of supply; in other cases, the purchasing department may ask for bids or send out requests for quotations before placing the order. A purchase order is a written request to a supplier for specified goods at

Avon Company Ltd
Purchase Requisition

Number

Department/Individual making request...............................
Order date.............................Delivery date requested.............................

Quantity	Catalogue number	Description	Unit price	Total
Approved by.......................................			Total cost	

Figure 3.1 *Purchase Requisition*

an agreed price. The request also stipulates terms of delivery and terms of payment. The purchase order authorises the supplier to deliver goods and submit a bill. To provide control over issuance of purchase orders, they are serially numbered. The items commonly included in a purchase ordered are: preprinted name and address of the company placing the order; purchase order number; name and address of supplier; order date; date delivery requested, delivery and payment terms; quantity of items ordered; catalogue number; description, unit and total price; shipping, handling, insurance and related costs; total cost of entire order; and authorised signature. Figure 3.2 shows a purchase order.

Avon Company Ltd
(full address)
Purchase Order

Number

Supplier.................................. Order date...............................
Address.................................. Date delivery requested by ....
Delivery terms........................ Payment terms................................

Quantity	Catalogue number	Description	Unit price	Total
Approved by...			Total cost	

Figure 3.2 *Purchase Order*

The original order is sent to the supplier (to place the order). Copies of the purchase order usually go to the: **(i)** Accounting department (to be used in checking the supplier's invoice when a voucher is being prepared for payment, and for future recording in the purchase journal and the general and subsidiary ledgers); **(ii)** Receiving department (to alert them to expect a delivery), and **(iii)** Credit/finance department (for eventual payment within the discount period). A copy is retained by the purchasing department to maintain a file of all purchase orders issued.

Receiving Materials When the goods that were ordered are delivered, the receving department unpacks and counts them. In order to ensure that the goods delivered are actually counted, the copy of the purchase order sent to the receiving department does not show/deliberately omit the quantity ordered. The supplier sends a packing slip giving details of the goods supplied/shipped. To ensure that the goods are not damaged and that they meet the specifications of the purchase order and the packing list, they are checked by the receiving department. Quantities and condition on receipt of goods are noted by the receiving department on a Receiving Report as shown in Figure 3.3. The report includes the suppliers' name, purchase order number; date, delivery was received; quantity received; description of goods, discrepancies, if any, from the purchae order (or mention of damaged goods), and authorised signature. While the original report is kept with the receiving department, copies are sent to:

- Purchasing department, to indicate that the material was received, as well as to supply information about the goods received that might be useful in evaluating the suppliers'/vendors' performance in sending the materials on schedule;
- Credit/finance department, to be matched against the purchase order and the suppliers' bill. If the receiving report, purchase order and suppliers' bill tally, payment is authorised;
- Accounting department, to record in journal and ledger together with the related liability; and
- Stores, to infom that the goods have arrived.

Avon Company Ltd
Receiving Report

Number

Supplier....................................
Purchase order number...
Date received..

Quantity	Catalogue number	Description	Unit price	Total

Authorised signature.....................................

Figure 3.3 *Receiving Report*

In brief, for purposes of internal control over materials, the purchase order, receiving report, and the suppliers'/vendors' invoice should be matched/approved by an independent party. The accounting department should be responsible for checking and approving payment since they would not have a conflict of interest. Figure 3.4 illustrates the use of the three forms, namely purchase requisition, purchase order, and receiving reports together with the vendors' invoice.

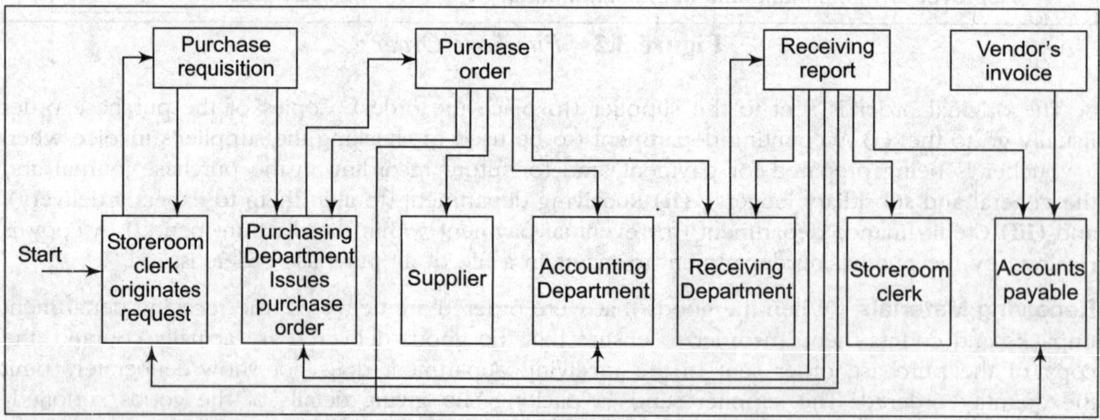

Figure 3.4 *Purchase Requisition, Purchase Order, Receiving Report and Vendors' Invoice*

Storing and Issuance of Materials Materials are transferred from the receiving department to the stores. The person in charge of the stores is responsible for proper storage, protection and issue of all materials. Efficient storing is another important step in materials control system. The basic accounting records of any inventory system are the documents required to authorise and record materials movements in/out of the store, namely, stocks/stores/materials ledger cards, bin cards and materials requisition note.

Stock/Stores/Materials Ledger Cards They show quantities on order, expected delivery dates and quantities reserved/required for work to be processed. They show the account number; description/type of material; location; unit measurement; minimum and maximum quantities to carry; details about the materials received; issued and balance. This is the basis of stock control as it is used to determine when additional stock needs to be acquired.

Bin Card This usually shows quantities of each type of material received, issued and on hand. It is placed in the bin/shelf or is hung over the almirah/rack otherwise known as bin. Separate bin cards are prepared for each item of stores. A bin card is shown in Figure 3.5.

Bin card shows quantities of each type of material received, issued and on hand.

Avon Company Ltd
Bin Card

Description........................... Bin card.......................
Stores ledger number.......................... Code number.......................
Minimum level........................ Unit number.......................

Date	Received		Issue		Balance quantity	Check
	Reference	Quantity	Reference	Quantity		

Figure 3.5 *Bin Card*

Materials Requisition Note/Form As an element of material control system, no materials can be issued from the store without proper authorisation by competent authority. The insurance of materials is authorised by means of a materials requisition form prepared by the production manager/departmental supervisor. It shows the job number/department requesting the goods; their quantity and description and the unit cost and total cost of the materials issued. Figure 3.6 shows a material requisition note/form.

Materials Requisition Form

Date requested .... Approved by ....
Department requesting .... Date issued ....
Requisition number .... Issued to ....

Quantity	Description	Job number	Unit cost	Total

Figure 3.6 *Materials Requisition Note*

The note is prepared generally in triplicate. One copy is retained by the requesting department and two are sent to the stores. The signature of the recipient is obtained on both. The issue is recorded in the bin card and one copy is sent for accounting.

Materials Returned to Stores Materials requisitioned from store, and not needed, or found to be defective are returned to the stores. A returned material report is prepared, either by the person returning the material or by the incharge of the store upon receipt of the material. The original is used as a basis for crediting the accounts charged, while the duplicate copy is filed in the department returning the materials.

When summary of materials is prepared, the quantity and value of goods returned to the stores are deducted from the total materials issued. Similarly, the amount is deducted from the total amount charged to each department. Alternatively, returned materials may be recorded in the receipts section while putting a symbol/notation in red ink to indicate that it is not a receipt of new materials. The entry in red is helpful in insolating department consistently over requisitioning materials.

Some of the departments may prefer to use the excess materials on the next job instead of returning them to the store. A materials transfer note is prepared to transfer costs from one original job to the new job and also, the transfer is noted in the stock records.

System of Accounting for Materials Issued/Inventory Systems

Either the periodic inventory system or the perpetual inventory system may be used to account for materials issued to production and ending materials inventory.

Periodical inventory system involves physical count of materials on hand at periodical intervals to arrive at the ending inventory.

Periodic Inventory System Under the periodic inventory system, the purchase of materials is recorded in Purchase of Raw Materials Account. The opening/beginning inventory, if any, is recorded in a separate Materials Inventory-Opening Account. The materials available for use during a period equal purchases plus opening inventory. A physical count is made of the materials on hand at the end of the period to arrive at the closing/ending materials inventory. The cost of materials for the period is determined as shown in Exhibit 3.1.

Exhibit 3.1 Cost of Materials Issued

Materials inventory-opening
+ Purchases
= Materials available for use
− Materials inventory-closing (based on physical count)
= Cost of materials issued

The entire book inventory is verified at a given date by an actual count of materials on hand. This physical inventory is usually taken near the end of the accounting year/period. This method provides for the recording of the purchases on a daily basis but does not provide for a continuous inventory-taking. Neither does it provide for a daily/continous computation of cost of goods sold. At the end of each accounting year, a physical count is made of the quantity of goods on hand, and the value of the inventory is determined by using an appropriate pricing method and attaching costs to units counted. It is assumed that goods not on hand at the end of the period have been sold. There is no system and accounting for shrinkage, losses, theft and wastage throughout the accounting period, and they can be discovered only at the end.

Perpetual inventory system shows both cost of materials issued and ending materials inventory directly.

Perpetual Inventory System The purchase of materials is recorded under the perpetual inventory system in Materials Inventory Account rather than in a Purchase of Raw Materials Account. The opening/beginning materials inventory, if any, is also shown on the debit side of the Materials Inventory Account. The Materials Inventory Account is credited for the cost of materials issued, with a corresponding debit to Work-in-Process Inventory Account. The effect is that the cost of materials issued is charged to production at the time when the materials are issued and the balance in the Material Inventory Account shows the cost of materials still available for use/issue. Therefore, both the cost of materials issued and the ending materials inventory can be directly ascertained after each transaction.

The perpetual inventory system is superior to the periodic inventory system. It provides better inventory/materials control and more information than the periodic inventory system. The recording and accounting of material cost is, therefore, illustrated below, using perpetual inventory system.

Recording/Accounting for Material Cost When a perpetual inventory system is used to account for materials inventory, a subsidiary ledger records card is maintained. Its total must equal the amount/balance in the Materials Inventory Control Account in the general ledger. The materials subsidiary ledger has a separate inventory record card for each item of inventory. Figure 3.7 shows an inventory record card. It shows the date, quantity and amount of materials received (debit) and issued (credit), and the resulting balance (debit).

Inventory Record Card

Item.......................... Description................................

Received			Issued			Balance		
Date	Quantity	Amount	Date	Quantity	Amount	Date	Quantity	Amount

Figure 3.7 *Inventory Record Card*

The use of perpetual inventory system also involves physical count of materials on hand, at least once a year, in order to check for possible loss or shrinkage due to theft or spoilage. If the physical count does not match with the balance in the inventory record cards, the book figures are adjusted upward/downward to reflected the actual count.

Journal Entries The purchase and issue of materials (direct as well indirect) are journalised as follows:

(i) When materials are purchased:
Direct Materials Inventory A/c Dr
    To Cash/Accounts Payable (credit purchases)
Indirect Material Inventory A/c Dr
    To Cash/Accounts Payable A/c (credit purchase)

(ii) Issue of direct materials for production:
Work-in-process Inventory A/c Dr
    To Materials Inventory A/c

(iii) Issue of indirect materials for production:
Factory Overhead Control A/c Dr
    To Materials Inventory A/c

Direct materials are debited to work-in-process inventory because they represent a major element of production cost and, therefore, require separate recognition to provide better control. On the other hand, indirect materials represent insignificant amounts and/or are not directly traceable to a product and are, therefore, charged to factory overhead control account. The factory overhead control account accumulates all indirect cost of production such as indirect materials, indirect labour, factory depreciation, and so on. Factory overheads are discussed in detail in Chapter 5.

EXAMPLE 3.1

The following data relate to wood pulp inventory of Premier Supply Company Ltd for the month of April.

April	1	Opening inventory, 10,000 kilos of wood pulp costing ₹50 per kilo
	10	Purchases: 3,000 kilos @ ₹55/Kilo
	16	Issued: 3,000 kilos
	26	Issued: 7,500 kilos
	28	Purchases: 4,000 kilos @ ₹60/Kilo
	30	Issued: 3,500 kilos

All purchases are cash purchases. Journalise the above transactions under a perpetual inventory system. Also, compute the cost of materials issued and ending materials inventory. The company uses FIFO (first-in-first-out) method to value ending inventory.

SOLUTION

Journal Entries:

April	10	Materials inventory (3,000 × ₹55)	Dr	₹1,65,000	
		To Cash			₹1,65,000
	16	Works-in-process inventory	Dr	1,50,000	
		To Materials inventory (3,000 × ₹50)			1,50,000
	26	Work-in-process inventory	Dr	3,77,500	
		To Materials inventory [(7,000 × ₹50) + (500 × ₹55)]		3,77,500	
	28	Materials inventory (4,000 × ₹60)	Dr	2,40,000	
		To Cash			2,40,000
	30	Work-in-process inventory	Dr	1,97,500	
		To Materials inventory [(2,500 × ₹55) + (1,000 × ₹60)]		1,97,500	

Computation of Cost:

Materials Inventory A/c

April	1	To opening stock	₹5,00,000	April	16	By work-in process	₹1,50,000
	10	To cash	1,65,000		26	By work-in process	3,77,500
	28	To cash	2,40,000		30	By work-in process	1,97,500
					30	By balance c/d	1,80,000
			9,05,000				9,05,000

Work-in-Process A/c

April	16	To materials inventory	₹1,50,000
	26	To materials inventory	3,77,500
	30	To materials inventory	1,97,500
			7,25,000

Summary:

Cost of materials issued	₹7,25,000
Ending materials inventory	1,80,000

Adjustment for Discrepancies As observed earlier, physical count of materials under the perpetual inventory system may not tally with the inventory record cards (stores ledger). The discrepancy may result from: (a) Unavoidable reasons such as evaporation; absorption/moisture; temperature changes affecting the volume of stock; shrinkage; deterioration in quality, for example, through rust; and loss due to breaking bulk or cutting up and (b) Avoidable reasons such as pilferage, unsuitable storage, careless handling, under and over issues, and materials unused but not returned to stores. The stores ledger records should be corrected to tally with the physical units in inventory irrespective of the reasons for inventory shortage. The following adjusting entries are made in different situations.

(a) When book inventory is more than the physical inventory and the shortage is normal:
Factory Overheads Control A/c Dr
To Stores Ledger Control A/c

(b) When the shortage in physical inventory is due to non-recording of inventory shortage:
Work-in-process Control A/c Dr
To Stores Ledger Control A/c

In both the above situations, in the stores ledger, an entry for both quantity and value is recorded in the Issue Column and a reduction is made in the Balance Column.

(c) In case of inventory gain, that is, when the stores ledger balance is less than the physical inventory (inventory overages), reverse adjusting entries of (a) and (b) above are passed. In the stores ledger, an entry for quantity and value both is recorded in the Received Column and addition is made in the Balance Column.

(d) The above adjustments are made when the inventory shortage/overage is normal and is expected in the normal course of business operations. If the loss is abnormal/due to unusual circumstances such as fire, theft, sabotage, the proper treatment is to transfer it to costing profit and loss account:
Costing Profit and Loss A/c Dr
To Stores Ledger Control A/c

Abnormal loss is considered a non-manufacturing loss, and is taken as a period charge against income of the current accounting period.

(e) If the discrepancies are slight, the balance of the stores ledger may be accepted for inventory verification and accounting purposes. No adjustment is required in such a situation.

Inventory Control Techniques

The important techniques covered here are: **(i)** ABC analysis, **(ii)** Economic order quantity (EOQ), **(iii)** Reorder-point and **(iv)** Safety stock.

ABC System: Classification Problem The first step in the inventory control process is classification of different types of inventories to determine the type and degree of control required for each. The ABC System is a widely-used classification technique to identify various items of inventory for purposes of inventory control. This technique is based on the assumption that a firm should not exercise the *same* degree of control on *all* items of inventory. It should rather keep more rigorous control on items that are: **(1)** Most costly, and/or **(2)** Slowest-turning, while items that are less expensive should be given less control effort.

ABC system assumes different degrees of control on different items of inventory.

On the basis of the cost involved, the various inventory items are, according to this system, categorised into three classes: A, B and C. The items included in group A involve the largest investment. Therefore, inventory control should be the most rigorous and intensive, and the most sophisticated inventory control techniques should be applied to these items. The C group consists of items of inventory which involve relatively small investments, although the number of items is fairly large. These items warrant the minimum attention. The B group stands midway. It deserves less attention than A but more than C. It can be controlled by employing less sophisticated techniques.

The task of inventory planning is to properly classify all the inventory items into one of these three categories. The typical breakdown of inventory items looks approximately as shown in Table 3.1.[2]

Table 3.1 Inventory Breakdown Between Number of Items and Inventory Value

Group	*Number of items (per cent)*	*Inventory value (per cent)*
A	15	70
B	30	20
C	55	10
Total	100	100

Some points emerge from Table 3.1. While group A is the least important in terms of the number of items, it is by far the most important in terms of the investments involved. With only 15 per cent of the number, it accounts for as much as 70 per cent of the total value of inventory. The firm should direct most of its inventory control efforts to the items included in this group. The items comprising the B group account for 20 per cent of the investments in the inventory. They deserve less attention than A but more than C which involves only 10 per cent of the total value although, number-wise its share is as high as 55 per cent. The A B C analysis is illustrated in Example 3.2.

Example 3.2

A firm has seven different items in its inventory. The average number of each of these items held, along with their unit costs, is listed below.

Items number	*Average number of units in inventory*	*Average cost per unit*
1	20,000	₹60.80
2	10,000	102.40
3	32,000	11.00
4	28,000	10.28
5	60,000	3.40
6	30,000	3.00
7	20,000	1.30

The firm wishes to introduce an A B C inventory system. Suggest a breakdown of the items into A, B and C classifications.

Solution

The ABC analysis is presented in Table 3.2.

Table 3.2 ABC Analysis

Item (1)	*Units* (2)	*Per cent of Total* (3)		*Unit Cost* (4)	*Total Cost* (5)	*Per cent of Total* (6)	
1	20,000	10	15	₹ 60.80	₹ 12,16,000	₹ 38.00	70
2	10,000	5		102.40	10,24,000	32.00	
3	32,000	16	30	11.00	3,52,000	11.00	20
4	28,000	14		10.28	2,88,000	9.00	
5	60,000	30		3.40	2,04,000	6.4	
6	30,000	15	55	3.00	90,000	2.8	10
7	20,000	10		1.30	26,000	0.8	
Total	2,00,000	100	100		32,00,000	100.00	100

The A B C system of classification of various items of inventory for determining degree of inventory control effort is a very useful technique. It should, however, be used with caution. For example, an item of inventory may be very inexpensive. Under the A B C system, it would be classified into C category. But it may be very critical to the production process and may not be easily available. It, therefore, deserves the special attention of management. But in terms of the A B C framework, it would be included in the category which requires the least attention. This is a limitation of the A B C analysis.

Economic Order Quantity Model (EOQ): Order Quantity Problem After various inventory items are classified on the basis of the A B C analysis, the management becomes aware of the type of control that would be appropriate for each of the three categories of the inventory items. The A group of items warrant the maximum attention and the most rigorous control. A key inventory problem particularly in respect of group A items relate to the determination of the size or quantity in which inventory should be acquired. In other words, while purchasing raw materials or finished goods, the questions to be answered are: *How much inventory should be bought in one lot under one order on each replenishment? Should the quantity to be purchased be large or small? Or should the requirements of material during a given period (say six months or one year) be acquired in one lot or should it be acquired in instalments or in several small lots?* Such inventory problems are called order quantity problems.

The determination of the appropriate quantity to be purchased in each lot to replenish stock as a solution to the order quantity problem necessitates a resolution of conflicting goals. Buying in large quantities implies higher average inventory level, which will assure: (i) Smooth production/sale operations, and (ii) Lower ordering or set-up costs. But it will involve higher carrying costs. On the other hand, small orders would reduce the carrying costs of inventory by reducing the average inventory level but the ordering costs would increase, as also there is a likely interruption in operations due to stock-outs. A firm should place neither too large nor too small orders. On the basis of a trade-off between benefits derived from the availability of inventory and the cost of carrying that level of inventory, the appropriate or optimum level of the order to be placed should be determined. The optimum level of inventory is popularly referred to as the Economic Order Quantity (EOQ). It is also known as the Economic Lot Size. *The economic order quantity may be defined as that level of inventory order that minimises the total cost associated with inventory management.* Stated with reference to the cost perspectives, EOQ refers to the level of inventory at which the total cost of inventory comprising acquisition/ordering/set-up costs and carrying costs is the minimum.

EOQ is the level of inventory order that minimises the total cost associated with inventory management.

For analysing the EOQ as an inventory management technique, several sophisticated and mathematical models are available.[3] These are, however, outside the scope of this book. We illustrate here the analysis of EOQ on the basis of a simple non-mathematical approach. Nevertheless, the main elements of the order quantity problem are covered by the analytical method followed here.

Assumptions The EOQ model, as a technique to determine the economic order quantity, illustrated by us, is based on three restrictive assumptions, namely:

(i) The firms knows with certainty the annual usage (consumption) of a particular item of inventory.

(ii) The rate at which the firm uses inventory is steady over time,

(iii) The orders placed to replenish inventory stocks are received at exactly the point in time when inventories reach zero.

In addition, it may also be assumed that ordering and carrying costs are constant over the range of possible inventory levels being considered.

Approaches The EOQ model can be illustrated: **(i)** By long/analytical approach or trial and error approach, and **(ii)** By the shortcut or simple mathematical approach.

Trial and Error Approach Given the total requirements of inventory during a given period of time depending upon the inventory planning horizon, a firm has different alternatives to purchase its inventories. For instance, it can buy its entire requirements in one single lot at the beginning of the inventory planning period. Alternatively, the inventories may be procured in small lots periodically, say, weekly, monthly, quarterly, six-monthly, and so on. If the purchases are made in one big lot, the firm's average inventory holdings would be relatively large, whereas, it would be relatively small in case of acquisition of inventory in small lots. The smaller the lot, the lower the average inventory and *vice-versa.* The high average inventory would involve high carrying costs. On the other hand, low inventory holdings are associated with high ordering cost. The trial and error or long analytical approach to determine EOQ uses different permutations and combinations of lots of inventory purchases so as to find out the least ordering and carrying cost combination. In other words, according to this approach, the carrying and acquisition costs for different sizes of orders to purchase inventories are computed, and the order-size with the lowest total cost (ordering plus carrying) of inventory is the economic order quantity. The mechanics of the computation of EOQ with the trial and error approach is illustrated in Example 3.3.

Carrying costs are cost associated with the maintenance/ holding of inventory.

Ordering costs are costs associated with acquisition of/ placing order for inventory.

EXAMPLE 3.3

A firm's inventory planning period is one year. Its inventory requirement for this period is 1,600 units. Assume that its acquisition costs are ₹50 per order. The carrying costs are expected to be ₹1 per unit per year for an item. The firm can procure inventories in various lots as follows: **(i)** 1,600 units, **(ii)** 800 units, **(iii)** 400 units, **(iv)** 200 units, and **(v)** 100 units. Which of these order quantities is the economic order quantity?

SOLUTION

The calculations of the inventory costs for the data in Example 3.3 for different order quantities are shown in Table 3.3.

Table 3.3 Inventory Cost for Different Order Quantities

1.	Size of order (units)	1,600	800	400	200	100
2.	Number of orders	1	2	4	8	16
3.	Cost per order	₹50	₹50	₹50	₹50	₹50
4.	Total ordering cost (2 × 3)	50	100	200	400	800
5.	Carrying cost per unit	1	1	1	1	1
6.	Average inventory (units)	800	400	200	100	50
7.	Total carrying cost (5 × 6)	₹800	₹400	₹200	₹100	₹50
8.	Total cost (4 + 7)	₹850	₹500	₹400	₹500	₹850

WORKING NOTES

(i) Number of orders = Total inventory requirement/ Order size

(ii) Average inventory = Order size/2

It can be seen from Table 3.3 that the carrying and ordering costs taken together are the lowest for the order size of 400 units. This, therefore, is the economic order quantity.

The calculation of EOQ is further developed in Example 3.4.

EXAMPLE 3.4

The following details are available in respect of a firm:

1. Inventory requirement per year, 6,000 units
2. Cost per unit (other than carrying and ordering costs), ₹5
3. Carrying costs per item for one year, ₹1
4. Cost of placing each order, ₹60
5. Alternative order size (units): 6,000, 3,000, 2,000, 1,200, 1,000, 600 and 200.

Determine the EOQ.

SOLUTION

The EOQ is determined in Table 3.4.

Table 3.4 Determination of Economic Order Quantity

1. Cost of items purchased each year	₹30,000	₹30,000	₹30,000	₹30,000	₹30,000	₹30,000	₹30,000
2. Order size (units)	6,000	3,000	2,000	1,200	1,000	600	200
3. Number of orders	1	2	3	5	6	10	30
4. Average inventory (units)	3,000	1,500	1,000	600	500	300	100
5. Total carrying cost	₹3,000	₹1,500	₹1,000	₹600	₹500	₹300	₹100
6. Total ordering costs	60	120	180	300	360	600	1,800
7. Total cost (carrying plus ordering cost)	3,060	1,620	1,180	900	860	900	1,900

Clearly, the EOQ is 1,000 units.

WORKING NOTES

(i) Total carrying costs = Average inventory × Carrying cost per unit

(ii) Total ordering costs = Number of orders × Cost per order

Mathematical (Short-cut) Approach The economic order quantity can, using a short-cut method, be calculated by the following equation:

$$\text{EOQ} = \sqrt{2\,AB/C} \tag{3.1}$$

Where A = Usage unit for the inventory planning period (total inventory requirement in units)
B = Ordering cost per buying order*
C = Carrying cost per unit

EXAMPLE 3.5

Using the facts in Example 3.3, find out the EOQ by applying the short-cut mathematical approach.

SOLUTION

$$\text{EOQ} = \sqrt{\frac{2 \times 1{,}600 \times 50}{1}} = 400 \text{ units}$$

Limitations While using the EOQ model, it should be noted that it suffers from shortcomings which arise mainly due to the restrictive nature of the assumptions on which it is based. The important limitations are:

1. The assumption of a constant consumption/usage and the instantaneous replenishment of inventory are of doubtful validity. As discussed subsequently, deliveries from suppliers may be slower than expected for reasons beyond control. It is also possible that there may be unusual and unexpected demand for the stocks. To meet such contingencies, firms have to make provision by keeping additional inventories which are known as safety stocks.

2. Another weakness of the EOQ model is that the assumption of a known annual demand for inventories is open to question. There is the likelihood of a discrepancy between the actual and the expected demand leading to a wrong estimate of the economic order quantity.
3. In addition to the above, there are some computational problems involved. For instance, Equation 3.1 may give the EOQ in fractional figures, say, 232.5 units. A more difficult situation may occur with the use of the model in that the number of orders to be may turn out to be a fraction.

Reorder point is that level of inventory which is equal to the consumption during the lead time.

Reorder Point: Order Point Problem The EOQ technique determines the size of an order to acquire inventory so as to minimise the carrying as well as the ordering` costs. In other words, the EOQ provides an answer to the question: How much inventory should be ordered in one lot? Another important question pertaining to efficient inventory management is: When should the order to procure inventory be placed? This aspect of inventory management is covered under the order point problem.

The reorder point is stated in terms of the level of inventory at which an order should be placed for replenishing the current stock of inventory. In other words, reorder point may be defined as that level of inventory when a fresh order should be placed with the suppliers for procuring additional inventory equal to the economic order quantity. Although some sophisticated reorder point formulae are available, they are outside the scope of this book We have, therefore, used a simple formula to calculate the reorder point. It is based on the following assumptions: (i) Constant daily usage of inventory and (ii) Fixed lead time. In other words, the formula assumes a condition of certainty.

The reorder point = Lead time in days × Average daily usage of inventory (3.2)

The term, "lead time" refers to the time normally taken in receiving the delivery of inventory after placing orders with the suppliers. It covers the time span from the point when a decision to place an order for the procurement of inventory is made to the actual receipt of the inventory by the firm. In other words, the lead time consists of the number of days required by the suppliers to receive and process the order as well as the number of days during which the goods will be in transit from the supplier. The lead time may also be called the procurement time of inventory.

The average usage means the quantity of inventory consumed daily. We can, therefore, define reorder point *as that inventory level which should be equal to the consumption during the lead time.*

EXAMPLE 3.6

Suppose the average consumption (daily usage) of inventory of a firm is 5,000 units. The number of days required to receive the delivery of inventory after placing the order (lead, that is, processing and transit time) is 15 days. The reorder point = 5,000 units × 15 days = 75,000 units. The implication is that the firm should place an order for replenishing the stock of inventory as soon as the level reaches 75,000 units. The size of the order would obviously be equal to the EOQ.

Safety stock is the minimum additional inventory to serve as a safety margin to meet unanticipated increase in usage.

Safety Stock The economic order quantity and the reorder point, as inventory management techniques, have been explained so as to keep the discussion simple, on the assumption of certainty conditions. That is, we had assumed: **(i)** Constant/fixed usage/requirement of inventory and **(ii)** Instantaneous replenishment of inventory. The assumptions are, however, of questionable validity in real world situations, that is, under conditions of uncertainty. For instance, the demand for inventory is likely to fluctuate from time to time. In particular, at certain points of time the demand may exceed the anticipated level. In other words, a discrepancy between the assumed (anticipated/expected) and the actual usage rate of inventory is likely to occur in practice. Similarly, the receipt of the inventory from the suppliers may be delayed beyond the expected lead time. The delay may result from factors beyond control such as strikes, floods, transportation, and other bottlenecks. Thus, a firm would come across situations in which the actual usage of inventory is higher than the anticipated level, and/or the delivery of the inventory from the suppliers is delayed. Another way of saying the same thing is that the demand for inventory cannot be anticipated with certainty, that is, the likely demand for inventory is uncertain.

The effect of increased usage and/or slower delivery would be shortage of inventory. That is, the firm would disrupt production schedule and alienate the customers. The firm would, therefore, be well advised to keep a sufficient safety margin by having additional inventory to guard against stock-out situations. Such stocks are called safety stocks. This would act as a buffer/cushion against a possible shortage of inventory caused by either increased usage or delayed delivery of inventory. The safety stock may, thus, be defined as ***minimum additional inventory to serve as safety margin/ buffer/cushion to meet unanticipated increase in usage resulting from unusually high demand and/ or uncontrollable late receipt of incoming inventory.***

Figure 3.8 has been drawn to show clearly the interrelationship that exists among various concepts of inventory discussed so far. It serves the useful purpose of presenting an integrated picture at one place. In the Figure, inventory of 400 units is delivered on Day 0. The company has the policy of maintaining a safety stock of 200 units. With the receipt of 400 units inventory on Day 0, the inventory level reaches 600 units (the maximum level). With the withdrawal of raw material inventory from the store at the rate of 40 units per day, the balance of inventory stock declines to 360 units after 6 days [600 units — (40 units × 6 days)]. This level is the reorder point. If delivery

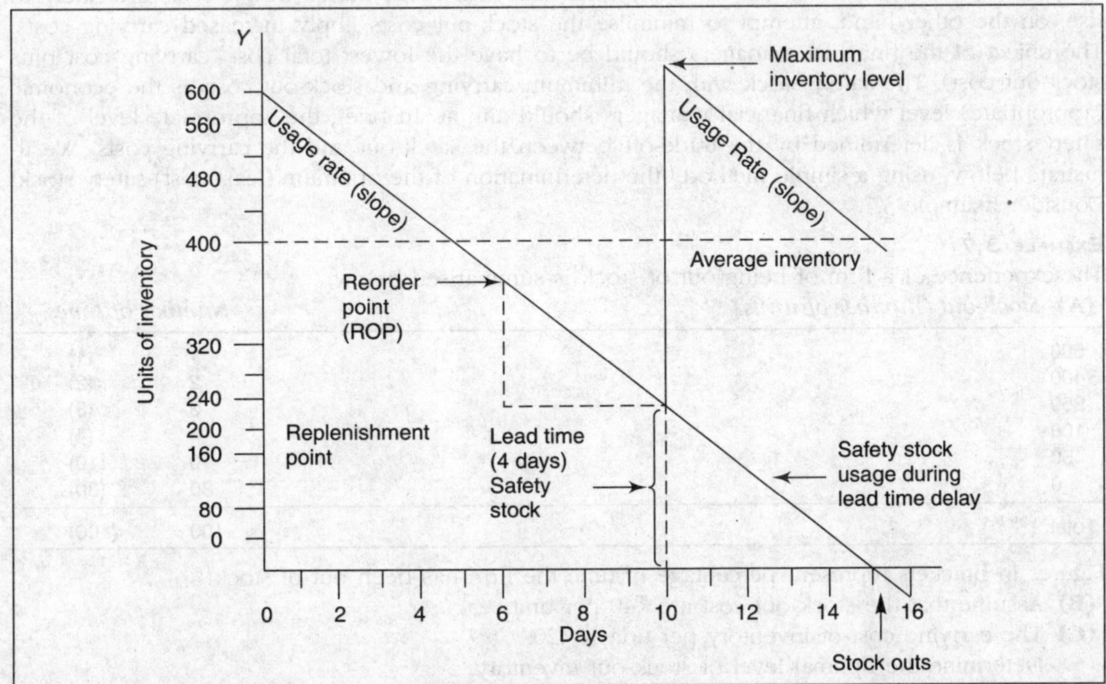

Figure 3.8 *Reorder Point, Replenishment Point, Maximum Inventory Level, Average Inventory and Safety Stock*

is on time, the next replenishment point is reached at Day 10. On the 10th day the company has a maximum level of stock of 600 units. If, however, inventory is not received in time, the company has a safety stock of five days to fall back upon.

How can the decision-maker determine the safety stock? What is his responsibility? The safety stock involves two types of costs: **(i)** Stockout and **(ii)** Carrying costs. The job of the financial manager is to determine the appropriate level of safety stock on the basis of a trade-off between these two types of conflicting costs.

Stock-out costs are costs associated with the shortage (stock-out) of inventory.

The term, 'stock-out-costs' refers to the cost associated with the shortage (stock-out) of inventory. It is, in fact, an opportunity cost in the sense that due to shortage of inventory the firm would be deprived of certain benefits. The denial of the benefits which would otherwise be available to the firm are the stock-out costs. The first, and the most obvious, of these costs is the loss of profits which the firm could have earned from increased sales if there was no shortage of inventory. Another category of stock-out costs is in terms of damage to relations with customers.[4] Since, due to shortage of inventory the firm would not be able to meet customer's requirements, the latter may turn to the firm's competitors. Of course, this type of cost cannot be easily and precisely quantified. The shortage of inventory may also disrupt the production schedule of the firm. The production process would grind to a halt, involving idle time.

The carrying costs are the costs associated with the maintenance of inventory. Since the firm is required to maintain additional inventory, in excess of the normal usage, additional carrying costs are involved.

The stock-out and the carrying costs are counterbalancing. The larger the safety stock, the larger the carrying costs and *vice versa.* Conversely, the larger the safety stock, the smaller the stock-out costs. In other words, if the firm minimises the carrying costs, the stock-out costs are likely to rise; on the other hand, attempt to minimise the stock-out costs imply increased carrying costs. The object of the financial managers should be to have the lowest total cost (carrying cost plus stock-out cost). The safety stock with the minimum carrying and stock-out costs is the economic (appropriate) level which financial managers should aim at. In brief, the appropriate level of the safety stock is determined by the trade-off between the stock-out and the carrying costs. We illustrate below, using a simple method,[5] the determination of the optimum (least cost) safety stock. Consider Example 3.7.

Example 3.7

The experience of a firm of being out of stock is summarised below:

(A) *Stock-out (number of units)* — *Number of times*

Stock-out (number of units)	Number of times	
500	1	(1)
400	2	(2)
250	3	(3)
100	4	(4)
50	10	(10)
0	80	(80)
Total	100	(100)

Figures in brackets represent percentage of time the firm has been out of stock.

(B) Assume that the stock-out cost are ₹40 per unit.

(C) The carrying cost of inventory per unit is ₹20.

Determine the optimal level of stock-out inventory.

SOLUTION

Table 3.5 Computation of Expected Stock-out Costs

Safety stock level (units) (1)	*Stock-out (units)* (2)	*Stock-out costs (₹40 per unit)* (3)	*Probability of stock-out* (4)	*Expected stock-out cost [(3) × (4)]* (5)	*Total expected stock-out cost* (6)
500	0	0	0	0	0
400	100	₹4,000	0.01	₹40	₹40
250	250	10,000	0.01	100	
	150	6,000	0.02	120	220
100	400	16,000	0.01	160	
	300	12,000	0.02	240	
	150	6,000	0.03	180	580
50	450	18,000	0.01	180	
	350	14,000	0.02	280	
	200	8,000	0.03	240	
	50	2,000	0.04	80	780
0	500	20,000	0.01	200	
	400	16,000	0.02	320	
	250	10,000	0.03	300	
	100	4,000	0.04	160	
	50	2,000	0.10	200	1,180

WORKING NOTES

(i) The determination of the optimum safety stock involves dealing with uncertain demand. The first step, therefore, is to estimate the size of stock-out in terms of the shortage of inventory at different levels of safety stock as well as the probability of being out of stock.

Size of stock-out (units): The shortage of inventory at different levels of safety stock can be computed as follows:

(a) Assuming the firm's experience has been that it has been short of inventory by 500 units only once in 100 times. If, therefore, the level of safety stock is 500 units, it will never be short of inventory. It means that with 500 units of safety stock, the size of stock-out would be zero.

(b) When the firm has a safety stock of 400 units, it could be short by 100 units.

(c) Further, with 250 units of safety stock, the firm could be short by 250 units if the actual demand turns out to be 500 units greater than expected; 150 units short, if the demand turns out to be 400 units greater than the expected. Thus, the size of stock-out could be 250 units or 150 units depending upon the level of actual demand.

(d) It should be obvious that the size of stock-out increases with a decrease in the level of safety stock. The size of the stock-out for safety stock levels of 100 units, 50 units and 0 units can be computed on the lines of step (c) above.

The stock-out size at a different safety stock levels is computed in column (2) of Table 3.5.

Probability of stock-out: The probability of stock-out at different levels of safety stock can be computed as follows:

(a) If the safety stock of the firm is 500 units, there is no chance of the firm being out of stock. The probability of stock-out is, therefore, zero.

(b) When the safety stock is 400 units, there is 1 per cent chance that the firm will be short of inventory. The probability of stock-out is, therefore, 0.01.

(c) The probability of stock-out for other levels of safety stock is similarly computed in column 4 of Table 3.5.

(ii) After the determination of the size and probability of stock-out, the next step is the calculation of the stock-out cost. The stock-out cost can be found out by multiplying the stock-out by the stock-out cost per unit and the probability of stock-out cost.

When the stock-out is expected to be 100 units (safety stock being 400 units), the stock-out cost would be 100 × ₹40 = ₹4,000. But the probability of stock-out of this size is only 0.01. Therefore, the expected stock out cost would be ₹4,000 × 0.01 = ₹40. For other levels of safety stock, the stock-out cost can be similarly computed (column 5 of Table 3.5).

(iii) The next step is to compute the total expected stock-out costs (column 6 of Table 3.5).

(iv) Then, the carrying costs should be calculated. The carrying costs are equal to the safety stock multiplied by the carrying costs per unit (column 3 of Table 3.5).

(v) Finally, the carrying costs and the expected stock-out costs at each safety stock level should be added (column 4 of Table 3.5). The optimum safety stock would be that level of inventory at which the total of these two costs is the lowest. This is shown in Table 3.6.

Table 3.6 Computation of Total Safety Stock Costs

Safety stock level (units) (1)	*Expected stock-out costs** (2)	*Carrying costs (₹20 per unit)* (3)	*Total safety stock cost (2+3)* (4)
0	₹1,180	₹0	₹1,180
50	780	1,000	1,780
100	580	2,000	2,580
250	220	5,000	5,220
400	40	8,000	8,040
500	0	10,000	10,000

*From Table 3.5 column 6.

Thus, the optimum safety stock is zero unit.

COST OF INVENTORY AND COSTING METHODS

This section presents and evaluates the alternative practices and policies to measure the cost of inventory. We first discuss what is included in the cost of inventory. This is followed by a discussion of the inventory costing methods. In the light of the requirements of management, an evaluation of these methods is also presented.

Cost of Inventory

The cost of inventory may be said to be composed of two elements: **(i)** Inventory quantities determined on the basis of either physical count or perpetual inventory records and **(ii)** Unit cost. In other words, inventory value/cost can be found out by multiplying physical quantity of inventory by unit cost/cost per unit. The physical quantity can be determined from the cost accounting records. The term *unit* cost merits some elaboration.

In general, the basis of inventory valuation is the "lower of cost or market" or more appropriately "the lower of actual cost or replacement cost." Although replacement costs can be estimated for interim periods, and adjustments made later on to reflect the conditions at the close of the year, the market value can be known with certainty only at the close of the accounting period.

As regards the actual cost, there are several elements associated with it. They are: **(i)** Invoice cost, **(ii)** Freight charges and costs of buying, receiving and storing, and **(iii)** Discounts-trade/quantity as well as cash. In valuing inventory, management has to decide which of these should be included to determine the actual cost.

In theory, all the costs which are necessary to acquire the materials and to put them in a position where they are ready to be used should be considered in valuing inventory. It can, therefore, be argued on theoretical grounds that in addition to the invoice cost, the other two components are also relevant. In other words, the value of inventory should consist of invoice cost net of all discounts plus appropriate portions of the cost of freight, buying, receiving, and storing.

However, there are practical difficulties in computing unit cost on the basis of the theoretical ideal. For instance, appropriate portions of the cost of buying, receiving, and storing are exceedingly difficult to determine. Similar difficulties may sometimes be countered with identifying the relevant freight costs. On the contrary, the inclusion of discounts also does not seem to be very appropriate. The trade and quantity discounts exist for the purpose of defining the true invoice cost of the material. Cash discounts are considered as a reward for early payment (absence of such discounts may signify as penalty for late payment). The reward can be interpreted as income while the penalty can be interpreted as a loss rather than a part of unit cost.

Thus, items like freight, cost of storing, and discount are amenable to different treatments depending on facts and circumstances. However, whichever way they are treated, the firm should consistently follow the practice.

Methods of Inventory Costing/Pricing of Materials Issued

There are a number of generally accepted methods of determining the cost of inventories at the close of the accounting period. As already observed, our interest in discussing these methods is to identify a suitable method as a basis of inventory valuation. The selection of a suitable method assumes significance in view of the fact that it has a direct bearing on the cost of goods sold and consequently on profit. Therefore, the method should be selected in the light of the probable effects on profits over a period of years.[6] The discussion here of the methods to value inventory should, therefore, be viewed in this perspective.

First In First Out (FIFO) Method The calculation of inventory according to the FIFO method is illustrated in Table 3.7.

Table 3.7 Inventory Valuation (FIFO Method)

Date	*Receipts*			*Issues*			*Inventory*		
	Quantity (1)	*Cost (2)*	*Value (3)*	*Quantity (4)*	*Cost (5)*	*Value (6)*	*Quantity (7)*	*Cost (8)*	*Value (9)*
January									
1							10,000	₹21	₹2,10,000
9	1,000	₹22.1	₹22,100				11,000	—	2,32,100
12				2,000	₹21	₹42,000	9,000	—	1,90,100
27	1,000	23.10	23,100				10,000	—	2,13,200
February									
10				4,000	21	84,000	6,000	—	1,29,200
16	2,000	24.10	48,200				8,000	—	1,77,400
March									
3	2,000	24.10	48,200				10,000	—	2,25,600

(Contd.)

(Contd.)

17				4,000	21	84,000	6,000	—	1,41,600
29	4,000	22.90	91,600				10,000	—	2,33,200
April									
4	2,000	21.40	42,800				12,000	—	2,76,000
18				4,000	@	93,400	8,000	—	1,82,600
23	2,000	20.40	40,800				10,000	—	2,23,400
May									
12				1,000	24.10	24,100	9,000	—	1,99,300
24	3,000	20.00	60,000				12,000	—	2,59,300
June									
10				1,000	24.10	24,100	11,000	—	2,35,200
30	2,000	20.20	40,400				13,000	—	2,75,600
Total	19,000		4,17,200	16,000		3,51,600			

@ 1,000	₹22.10	₹22,100
1,000	23.10	23,100
2,000	24.10	48,200
4,000	—	93,400

FIFO method assumes that the inventory is consumed in chronological order, that is, those received first are issued/consumed first and value fixed accordingly.

The FIFO method of valuation of inventory is based on the assumption that the inventory is consumed in chronological order, that is, those received first are deemed to have been issued/consumed first and priced accordingly.[7] It can be seen from Table 3.7 that with an opening inventory of 10,000 units at ₹21, the first 10,000 units issued/consumed are charged to the cost of goods sold at this opening inventory rate (₹21). The April 18 issue or consignment of 4,000 units is costed on the basis of the first receipts of the year: January 9, 1,000 units at ₹22.10, January 27, 1,000 units at ₹23.10, and February 16, 2,000 units at ₹24.10. The 1,000 each issued on May 12 and June 10 are costed on the basis of the 2,000 received on March 3. Therefore, the cost of the 13,000 inventory on June 30 is composed of the receipts of March 29, April 4 and 23, May 24 and June 30 and the value is the sum of the costs of these receipts.

Average Cost Method According to the average cost method, each purchase is added to inventory and an average cost determined. Materials are charged into cost of sales at this average until another lot is received, when a new average unit inventory cost is calculated. Using the basic data contained in Table 3.7, the average cost of inventroy is calculated in Table 3.8.

Table 3.8 Inventory Valuation (Average Cost Method)

Date	*Receipts*			*Issues*			*Inventory*		
	Quantity (1)	*Cost* (2)*	*Value (3)*	*Quantity (4)*	*Cost** (5)*	*Value (6)*	*Quantity (7)*	*Cost** (8)*	*Value (9)*
January									
1							10,000	₹21.00	₹2,10,000
9	1,000	₹22.10	₹22,100				11,000	21.10	2,32,100
12				2,000	₹21.10	₹42,200	9,000	21.10	1,89,900
27	1,000	23.10	23,100				10,000	21.30	2,13,000
February									
10				4,000	21.30	85,200	6,000	21.30	1,27,800
16	2,000	24.10	48,200				8,000	22.00	1,76,000

(Contd.)

(Contd.)

March									
3	2,000	24.10	48,200				10,000	22.42	2,24,200
17				4,000	22.42	89,680	6,000	22.42	1,34,520
29	4,000	22.90	91,600				10,000	22.612	2,26,120
April									
4	2,000	21.40	42,800				12,000	22.41	2,68,920
18				4,000	22.41	89,640	8,000	22.41	1,79,280
23	2,000	20.40	40,800				10,000	22.008	2,20,080
May									
12				1,000	22.008	22,008	9,000	22.008	1,98,072
24	3,000	20.00	60,000				12,000	21.506	2,58,072
June									
10				1,000	21.506	21,506	11,000	21.506	2,36,566
30	2,000	20.20	40,400				13,000	21.30	2,76,966
Total	19,000		4,17,200	16,000		3,50,234			

* Actual
** Average

LIFO method assumes valuation of inventory on the basis of inverse sequence of receipts.

Last In First Out (LIFO) Method As discussed above, under the FIFO as well as the average cost methods, it is possible to calculate the cost of sales each month, and at the same time determine a known inventory cost rate for the succeeding period(s). Under the LIFO method, on the other hand, the cost of goods sold and the value of closing inventory can be determined only after the final lot of the year has been received. This is because of the assumption underlying the valuation of inventory, according to this method. As the name LIFO suggests, the use of inventory is valued on the basis of the inverse sequence of receipts. Materials received last are deemed to have been issued first and priced accordingly; physical movement of materials need not be in that order. The calculations of the value of inventory on the basis of this method are illustrated in Table 3.9.

Table 3.9 Inventory Valuation (LIFO Method)

		Quantity	*Cost*		*Value*
PART A					
Straight LIFO:					
Inventory (Janaury 1)		10,000	₹21.0	—	₹2,10,000
Receipts		19,000	—	—	4,17,200
Total		29,000	—	—	6,27,200
Inventory (June 30)		13,000			
Inventory (Janaury 1)	10,000	—	21.0	2,10,000	
Receipts (Janaury 9)	1,000	—	22.10	22,100	
(Janaury 27)	1,000	—	23.10	23,100	
(February 16)	1,000	—	24.10	24,100	
	13,000				2,79,300
Cost of inventory issued		16,000			3,47,900
PART B					
Additions at average cost:					
Inventory (January 1)		10,000	21.0		2,10,000
Receipts		19,000	21.958 app.		4,17,200
Total		29,000			6,27,200

(Contd.)

(Contd.)

Inventory (June 30)		13,000			
Inventory (January 1)	10,000	—	21.00	2,10,000	
Added Inventory	3,000	—	22.322	66,966	
	13,000	—			2,76,966
Cost of inventory issued		16,000			3,50,234
PART C					
Additional at FIFO cost:					
Inventory (Janaury 1)	—	10,000	21.0		2,10,000
Receipts	—	19,000	—		4,17,200
Total		29,000	—		6,27,200
Inventory (June 30)	—	13,000			
March 29	4,000	—	22.90	91,600	
April 4	2,000	—	21.40	42,800	
April 23	2,000	—	20.40	40,800	
May 24	3,000	—	20.00	60,000	
June 30	2,000	—	20.20	40,400	
	13,000	—	—	—	2,75,600
Cost of inventory issued		16,000			3,51,600

As can be seen from Table 3.9, LIFO method has three variations which are shown in parts A, B, and C respectively of the table. Under the first of these, namely, the straight LIFO method (Part A), the costs to addition to inventory in any year are the cost of the first equivalent quantity of purchases of the year. Under the second (Part B), the costs of the additions in taken at the average cost of the year. Under the third variations (Part C), the costs of the additions in any year are the costs of the last equivalent quantity or purchases in the year. In other words, additions to a LIFO inventory can be valued at FIFO cost, average cost, or LIFO cost.

However, regardless of the variation of the LIFO method used for costing additions to inventory in any one year, the years are on a straight LIFO basis regarding additions and reductions. Thus, the cost used for valuation in the first year in the LIFO method is the cost used for that quantity in every year so long as the quantity at the close of any year is not less than the original quantity. Cost of additions in a year as determined by the method selected (FIFO, Average, or LIFO for the year), is also used year after year so long as that quantity plus the original quantity remain on inventory. Reductions in inventory result in the elimination of the additions of the most recent year, and from there on back into the original quantity, if the inventory drops that far. Table 3.10 shows closing inventories for six years. As the quantities on hand at the close of the year increased in the first and second years, they were costed at the applicable rate for the respective year. In the third year, the reduciton in quantities removed the additions of the second year and 1,000 those of the first year. In the fourth year, quantities increased, and the increase was costed on the basis of the cost of that year. In the fifth year, a substantial reduction in quantities took out the fourth and the first year's additions and 1,000 of the original quantity. LIFO costs of these passed out of the picture with this reduction, and in the sixth year the increase over the fifth year was costed on the basis of acquisitons in the sixth year.

Table 3.10 Inventory Valuation (LIFO Method—6 Years)

Particulars	*Quantity*	*Rate*	*Value*
Opening inventory at cost—first year'	10,000	₹21.00	₹2,10,000
Closing inventory:			
First year—opening inventory	10,000	21.00	2,10,000
First year's additions	3,000	23.10	69,300
Total	13,000	—	2,79,300
Second year—first year's opening	10,000	21.00	2,10,000
First year's additions	3,000	23.10	69,300
Second year's additions	2,000	22.00	44,000
Total	15,000	—	3,23,300
Third year—first year's opening	10,000	21.00	2,10,000
First year's additions	2,000	23.10	46,200
Total	12,000	—	2,56,200
Fourth year—first year's opening	10,000	21.00	2,10,000
First year's additions	2,000	23.10	46,200
Fourth year's additions	1,000	25.00	25,000
Total	13,000	—	2,81,200
Fifth year—remainder of first year's opening	9,000	21.00	1,89,000
Sixth year—remainder of first year's opening	9,000	21.00	1,89,000
Sixth year's additions	1,000	26.00	26,000
Total	10,000	—	2,15,000

Specific Identification/Actual Cost Method Under this method, the materials issued are priced at their actual cost which involves identification of each lot purchased. It is the simplest but also the most time-consuming method of determining cost of materials used and cost of the ending inventory. It entails keeping a record of the purchase price of each specific unit and the quantity of specific units used. Cost of material used is computed by multiplying the quantity used by the specific price of each material. In many cases, when materials are purchased, a tag showing the price is attached in order to identify them. This method may be usefully applied if purchase prices are fairly stable and material is readily identifiable.

Base Stock Prices Method The base stock refers to the minimum quantity of stock of materials that a firm has to maintain at all times. Under this method, it is assumed that the minimum stock which must always be carried is in the nature of fixed assets, and is never realised while the business continues. The minimum stock is carried at original cost of acquisition. The quantity of materials in excess of the base stock is available for production, while the base stock is used only in case of emergency. The excess is priced in conjunction with one of the other methods such as FIFO or LIFO. Thus, this method cannot be used idependently. Moreover, estimation of base stock may be difficult. It can be used in industries having relatively long processing period, and where the cost of finished product is largely made up of basic raw materials such as crude oil, hides and so on.

Base stock is the minimum quantity of stock of materials that a firm has to maintain all times.

Standard Price Method This method of pricing issues is based on a standard price for a specified period. A standard price is fixed for each class of materials in advance after proper investigation. The method is suitable where standard costing is relevant. The difference between actual price and standad price is transferred to purchase price variance which reveals to what extent actual costs are different from standard material cost. This method is simple to operate and provides stability in costing system. However, standard price/cost does not often reflect actual/expected cost but only a notional cost/generalised target. The stock value does not show actual cost incurrence and, therefore, does not necessarily conform to acceptable principles of stock valuation.

Replacement price is the market price prevailing on the date of issue of materials.

Replacement/Market Price Method Under this method, materials are issued at the price at which they can be replaced, that is, at the market price prevailing on the date of issue. This method could be applied principally to materials purchased in advance for use in large quantities, in anticipation of economic/profitable use, or in such items of stores which are either obsolete or are lying unused for a long time in store. It reflects current cost of production and may be useful in such cases where quotations based on competitive market prices of materials are sent. However, it may be difficult to ascertain current price of each item of material at the time of issue. It is also not based on actual cost incurred and, therefore, may add confusion and complications in cost accounting.

Choice of a Method We now attempt to select an appropriate method. First, the implications of the different methods from the viewpoint of cost, and consequently their impact on profits, are analysed. The factors which are responsible for the differences among the methods in so far as their impact on cost flows and profits is concerned, are then ideitnfied. Finally, the suitability of the different methods to value inventory is examined. The Institute of Chartered Accountants of India issued in 1999 fresh accounting standad for inventory valuation. Our focus here is, therefore on the relative suitability of FIFO, LIFO, and Average methods.

Implications of Different Inventory Valuation Methods As stated earlier, inventory is, from the accounting point of view, included in the profit and loss account/income statement as cost of goods sold, and in the balance sheet as inventory on the assets side. The different methods of valuing inventory will have their impact on the flow of cost through the balance sheet into the profit and loss account. If, therefore, different methods to value inventory produce differing inventory values, they will also show differing amounts of cost of goods sold which will inevitably affect the profits. The implications of different methods of valuing inventory, in other words, is that depending upon the method selected, the amount of profit as shown by the profit and loss account will be different. From the viewpoint of income determination, thus, the choice of an appropriate method assumes significance. The impact of the various methods on profits through threir impact on the flow of cost for the data contained in Tables 3.7 through 3.10 is illustrated in Table 3.11.

Table 3.11 Impact of Inventory Valuation on Cost Flows/Profits

	FIFO	*Average cost*	*LIFO*
Beginning inventory	₹2,10,000	₹2,10,000	₹2,10,000
Add: Receipts	4,17,200	4,17,200	4,17,200
Total	6,27,200	6,27,200	6,27,200
Deduct: Ending inventory	2,75,600	2,76,966	2,75,600
Materials put into process	3,51,600	3,50,234	3,51,600

It is clear from the table that each method produces a different figure for the transfer of raw materials to work-in-process. Ultimately, when the goods are sold, the varying methods of inventory valuation will have their impact on cost of goods sold and, thus, on profits.

Causes of Differences The exclusive reason for the difference in cost and profit according to the different inventory valuation methods is the changing purchase price or unit cost. If the purchase prices do not change at all or remain stable, all the inventory valuation methods will produce identical cost and profit figures. To elaborate, let us assume the following facts about the purchase of materials by a hypothetical firm.

Date of purchase		Units acquired	Unit cost (stable price)	Unit cost (rising price)	Unit cost (falling price)
(1)		(2)	(3)	(4)	(5)
January	1	2	₹10	₹10.00	₹10.00
	15	4	10	10.20	9.70
	31	3	10	10.50	9.40

If the inventory on January 31 consists of two units, the inventory values and cost flows for each-inventory method, assuming no beginning inventory, are presented in Table 3.12.

Table 3.12 Cost Flows Under Different Assumptions of Price Levels

	FIFO	Average	LIFO
(A) *Stable price level*			
Ending inventory (2 units)	₹20.00	₹20.00	₹20.00
Materials put in process (7 units)	70.00	70.00	70.00
(B) *Rising price level*:			
Ending inventory (2 units)	21.00	20.50	20.00
Materials in process (7 units)	71.30	71.80	72.30
(C) *Falling price level*			
Ending inventory (2 units)	18.80	19.40	20.00
Materials in process (7 units)	68.20	67.60	67.00

The conclusions emerging from Table 3.12 are:

1. When prices are stable, all inventory valuation methods give the same figure of cost.

2. When prices are rising, the LIFO produces the highest cost flow and the lowest inventory. The FIFO has exactly the opposite effect.

3. When prices are falling, the LIFO method produces the lowest cost and the highest inventory. The impact of FIFO is exactly opposite.

4. Thus, the LIFO and the FIFO methods are extremes and the average methods falls in between.

Evaluation There is no one best method of inventory valuation. The three methods–FIFO, Average and LIFO–are suitable under different circumstances. As already observed, different methods affect the income determination (profit and loss account) and asset measurement (balance sheet). The discussion of the choice of a suitable method here is accordingly divided into two parts: The implications **(i)** On income determination and **(ii)** On asset measurement.

Income Determination: *FIFO Method* The FIFO method is based on an assumption regarding the physical flow of materials. As observed earlier, the implicit physical flow is the chronological order, that is, materials which are purchased/received first are consumed/issued/sold first. This assumption of the pattern of flow of materials closely approximates a theoretically sound method of inventory valuation, namely, *specific identification.* The term, "specific identification," means that the units in inventory should be identified with the specific unit costs to which they apply. The merit of the FIFO method is that the physical flow of materials match the flow of cost.[8]

LIFO Method The LIFO method cannot be justified on the basis of the physical flow of materials. The justification of this method is based on *cost flow.* Under conditions of changing prices, the LIFO method matches costs and revenues. Since the LIFO method assumes that the latest item in, is the first item out, the current cost of materials are matched with the current selling price/current revenues. *This matching of current costs with current revenues is the essence of the argument for the LIFO method.*

Average Method The average method is mid-way between FIFO and LIFO. The justification for the average method has two aspects. First, it differs from the FIFO and LIFO methods in respect of the physical flow of the materials. While the FIFO fits a first-in-first-out system and the LIFO fits a last-in-first-out (current cost) system, the average method fits a system, which has no specific pattern of physical flow. Therefore, where the units in inventory are identical, interchangeable and do not follow any specific pattern of physical flow, the average cost system would be appropriate. But such a situation is more imaginary than real. It provides no justification for the appropriateness of the average cost method. The second aspect is that it is a statistical technique. As an averaging technique, it can balance the effect of changes in purchase price on inventories and cost of materials put into prices, and ultimately in the cost of goods sold.

In brief, there is not one best method to value inventories. The method chosen should fit a particular situation. In case of a physical flow pattern, the FIFO method may be appropriate. The lack of a clearly identifiable physical flow pattern may justify the use of the Average method. The relevance of cost flows, as distinct from physical flows, particularly in periods of changing prices, would warrant the use of the LIFO method.

Asset Measurement We now highlight the effect of these methods on the inventory value to be shown in the balance sheet.

FIFO Method Under this method, as noted earlier, inventory is valued on the assumption of chronological cost flow. This implies that the unused/unsold inventory consists of the most recent purchases and, therefore, can be assumed to be valued at current cost. The value of inventory as shown in the balance sheet would reflect the *current cost,* if the FIFO method is used.

LIFO Method According to this method, obviously, the inventory figure would *not* appear in the balance sheet at the *current cost.* It will reflect rather the cost of raw materials purchased in the past year. Assuming rising prices, the inventory value based on the LIFO method would tend to be *undervalued* (Table 3.10). It can be seen from the table that inventory (not in physical terms but for purposes of costing) may consist of inventory purchased as early as six years or more. In that situation, the inventory figure included in the balance sheet would be actually the price paid on the purchase of inventory six years ago. In a period of rising prices, this value would naturally be grossly out of line with the currently prevailing price. This would imply that the balance sheet will not reflect the current worth of the inventory. That the inventory value will not be correct is another way of saying that the balance sheet will present a distorted picture of the affairs of the firms.

A possible solution to correct the above distortion in the balance sheet implicit in the *undervaluation* of inventory with the LIFO method is a modified/adjusted LIFO method. According to the latter, inventory should be shown in the balance sheet in two parts: **(i)** As usual and **(ii)** The current cost should be shown in the *inner* column. To illustrate, the inventory data contained in Table 3.10 would appear in the balance sheet (sixth year) as follows:

Balance Sheet

	Inventory(Current cost, ₹2,60,000)	₹2,15,000

The modified LIFO method will, thus, serve the needs of correct income determination as well as correct asset measurement. However, this is subject to a qualification, namely, the current year's purchases (units) should exceed the current year's consumption (units). If for reasons such as strike/lockouts, transportation problems, and so on, the current consumption exceeds the current purchases, profits will rise. The increase will depend upon the extent of liquidation of the previous years' inventory. This increase in profit is termed as *liquidation profit*,[9] which is equal to the difference between the current cost of the inventory and the cost of the inventory purchased in the past. Assume 2 lakh units of the previous years' inventory has been used in the current year (2013), the difference in the current cost of the inventory and the cost of the inventory purchased is ₹25 per unit. The liquidation profit is ₹50 lakh (2 lakh units × ₹25).

The reporting of the liquidation profit separately from the operating profit would be found useful by management for a comparison of profits over a period of time. An additional advantage of such a policy would be that tax payment would be deferred by the firm, which will ultimately result in lower tax incidence due to time value of money.

JUST-IN TIME INVENTORY/PRODUCTION

The level of inventories by retailers are influenced by the demand patterns of their customers and supply relationship with their distributors and manufacturers, the suppliers to their manufacturers and so on. Supply chain describes the flow of goods/services/information from the initial source of materials and services to the delivery of products to consumers regardless of whether those activities occur in the same organisation or in other organisations. There are significant gains to companies in the supply chain from coordinating their activities and sharing information. There would be (a) fewer stock outs at the retail level, (b) reduced manufacture of goods not immediately needed by retailers, (c) fewer manufacturing orders that have to be "rushed" or "expedited" and (d) lower inventories held by each company in the supply chain. Of the numerous systems developed by manufacturing companies to plan and implement production and inventory activities within their plants, just-in-time (JIT) production/inventory is a widely used system.

Just-in-time refers to acquiring materials and manufacturing goods only as needed to fill customer orders.

Concept

The JIT is an innovative manufacturing system. It refers to acquiring materials and manufacturing goods only as needed to fill customer orders. The JIT production, also called *lean production,* is a **demand-pull**[10] manufacturing system because each component in a production line is produced as soon as and only when needed by the next step in the production line. Demand triggers each step of the production process, starting with customer demand for a finished product at the end of the process and working all the way back to the demand for direct materials at the beginning of the process. In this way, demand pulls an order through the production line. The JIT production systems aim to simultaneously (i) meet customer demand in a timely way, (ii) with high quality products and (iii) at the lowest possible total cost.[11]

As a demand-pull manufacturing system, JIT contrasts with more traditional *supply push* system in which manufacturers simply produce as many goods as possible. The JIT system is characterised by extremely small/non-existent inventories of material, work-in-process, and finished goods. Materials are scheduled to arrive only as needed, and products flow quickly from one production process to the next without having to move into temporary storage facilities. Finished goods in excess of existing customer orders are not produced.

Non-value added activities refers to those functions that do not directly increase the worth of a product to a customer.

The JIT is, however, more than an approach to inventory management. It is a philosophy of eliminating *non-value-added activities* and increasing product quality throughout the manufacturing process. Non-value-added activities refer to those functions that do not directly increase the worth of a product to a customer. Examples of such activities are: storing direct materials, setting up machinery and time during which machinery/employees stand idle. Cost savings through the reduction/elimination of such activities usually do not influence customer satisfaction. In contrast, value-added-activities do increase the value of the product to the customers. Included in such activities are product design, all manufacturing processes, manufacturing to customer specifications and convenient channels of distribution.

Value added activities do increase the value of a product to the customers.'

Financial Benefits of JIT and Relevant Costs

In computing the relevant benefits and costs of reducing inventories in JIT production systems, account should be taken of all benefits. In addition to lower carrying costs of inventory, other benefits of lower inventory are[12]: **(i)** greater transparency of the production process, **(ii)** heightened emphasis on eliminating the specific causes of rework, scrap and waste, and **(iii)** lower manufacturing to lead times.

Illustration To illustrate, Hindustan Tools Corporation (HTC), manufacturer of brass fittings, is considering implementing a JIT production system. The HTC would have to incur ₹10,00,000 in annual tooling costs to reduce setup times. It is expected that JIT will reduce average inventory by ₹50,00,000. The relevant costs of insurance, storage, materials handling and setup are likely to decline by ₹3,00,000. The HTC's required rate of return on inventory investment is 10 per cent.

The other benefits associated with low inventories in JIT production system of HTC are: (i) improved quality and reduced rework on 500 units each year would result in a saving of ₹500 per unit; and (ii) better quality and faster delivery will enable HTC to charge ₹20 more per unit on the 20,000 units that it sells every year.

Based on the cost savings in carrying costs of inventory only, HTC would not find the implementation of JIT system feasible as the additional tooling cost (₹10,00,000) exceeds the annual cost savings in carrying costs of ₹8,00,000 [(0.10 × ₹50,00,000) + ₹3,00,000]. However, on the basis of the total benefits in terms of cost savings in carrying costs plus the annual relevant quality and delivery benefits, HTC would be well advised to implement the JIT systems as the total benefits exceed the annual implementation costs of ₹10,00,000 as shown below.

1. Cost savings in carrying cost of inventory		₹8,00,000
2. Plus quality and delivery benefits:		
• Rework savings (₹500 × 500 units)	₹2,50,000	
• Additional contribution margin (₹20 × 20,000)	4,00,000	6,50,000
		14,50,000

Performance Measure

The measures that managers can use to evaluate and control JIT production are discussed below.

Personal Observation The production layout in a JIT plant is streamlined and operations are not obscured by piles of inventory/rework. For this reason, personal observation is more effective in JIT plants compared to traditional plants.

Financial Performance Measure The financial measure that is widely used is inventory turnover ratio, that is, cost of goods sold ÷ inventory. This ratio would increase in a JIT system.

Non-financial Performance Measures Included in this category of measures are:

- Decrease in manufacturing lead time
- Increase in units produced per hour
- Decrease in number of days inventory on hand
- Decrease in total setup time for machines ÷ total manufacturing time
- Decrease in number of units requiring rework or scrap ÷ total number of units started and completed.

Effect on Costing System

The JIT system has effect on the costing systems. In the first place, by reducing material handling, warehousing and inspection, it reduces overhead costs. Second, it facilitates direct tracing of some costs usually classified as indirect, for example, material handling, and machine operating costs. Finally, the use of multi-skilled workers allows the costs of setup, maintenance and quality inspection to be traced as direct costs.

SUMMARY

- Materials are the basic input that are transformed into finished goods in the production process. Materials costs based on relationship with finished goods, can be broken down into direct and indirect costs.
- Accounting for materials in a manufacturing company usually involves two activities: purchase of materials (requiring a purchase requisition, purchase order, and receiving report) and the issue of materials requiring a materials requisition form.
- Materials may be entered into accounting records under either the periodic or the perpetual system. The periodic system is relatively simple and does not maintain a continuous record of the large volume of materials issued. In contrast, under the perpetual system, the cost of materials is determined as the material are placed in production.
- The first step in the inventory planning/control process is the classification of different types of inventory to determine the type and degree of control required for each. The ABC system is a widely-used classification technique for the purpose. On the basis of the cost involved, the various items are classified into three categories: **(i) A**, consisting of items with the largest investment, **(ii) C**, with relatively small investments, but fairly large number of items, and **(iii) B**, which stands mid-way between category A and C. Category A needs the most rigorous control, C requires minimum attention, and B deserves less attention than A but more than C.
- The second key inventory problem relates to determination of the size/quantity of inventory which would be acquired. This is the order quantity problem. The economic order quantity, or economic lot size (EOQ) is that level of inventory order which minimises the total cost associated with inventory management. Stated with reference to cost perspective, EOQ refers to the level of inventory at which the total cost of inventory comprising (i) order/setup cost, and (ii) carrying costs is the minimum.

  Symbolically,

  $$EOQ = \sqrt{2AB/C}$$

  where A = Annual usage of inventory in units, B = Buying cost per order, C = Carrying cost per unit per year
- Yet another important question relating to inventory planning and control is: When should the order to procure inventory be placed? It is what is called the order point problem. The re-order point is that level of inventory when a fresh order should be placed with suppliers to procure

additional inventory equal to the EOQ. It is that inventory level which is equal to the consumption during the lead time or procurement time.

Re-order level = (Daily usage × Lead time) + Safety stock

Minimum level = Re-order level – (Normal usage × Average delivery time)

Maximum level = Reorder level – (Minimum usage × Maximum delivery time) + Re-order quantity

Average stock level = Minimum level + (Re-order quantity)/2

Danger level = (Average consumption per day × Lead time in days for emergency purchases)

➢ The safety stocks are the minimum additional inventory which serve as a safety margin to meet an unanticipated increase in usage. This increase may be due to an usually high demand or because of uncontrollable late receipt of incoming inventory. The following steps are involved in determining the level of safety stocks:

(i) The first step is to estimate the probability of being out of stock, as well as the size of stock-out in terms of the shortage of inventory at different levels of safety stock.

(ii) After the determination of the size and probability of stock-out, the next step is the calculation of the stock-out cost. The stock-out cost can be found out by multiplying the stock-out by the cost per unit, and the probability of stock-out.

(iii) Then, the carrying cost should be calculated. The carrying cost are equal to the safety stock multiplied by the carrying costs per unit.

(iv) Finally, the carrying costs and the expected stock-out costs at each safety level should be added. The optimum safety stock would be that level of inventory at which the total of these two costs is the lowest.

➢ The proper costing of inventory is important from the point of view of the income determination and asset measurement. The important inventory costing methods are: FIFO, Weighted Average, LIFO and Inflated Cost Method. The FIFO method *assumes* that the inventory is consumed in chronological order, that is, items received first are deemed to have been issued/consumed first and priced accordingly. The LIFO method is based on the *assumption* that the cost of inventory is computed on the basis of the inverse sequence of receipts. According to the Weighted Average Method, the weighted average price of purchases and inventory is taken as the basis for determining the cost of the inventory. The Inflated Cost Method takes into account normal material losses caused due to transportation, material handling and storage losses.

➢ The implication of different inventory costing method is: **(i)** When prices are stable, all inventory valuation methods give the same figure of cost, **(ii)** when prices are rising, the LIFO produces the highest cost flow and the lowest inventory, **(iii)** When prices are falling, the LIFO method produces the lowest cost and the highest inventory. The impact of FIFO is exactly opposite, and **(iv)** the LIFO and the FIFO methods are extremes and the weighted average method falls in between.

➢ JIT, as an innovative manufacturing system, refers to acquiring materials and manufacturing goods only as needed to fill customer orders. Also called lean production system, it is a demand-pull manufacturing system because each component in a production line is produced as soon as and only when needed by the next step in the production line.

➢ However, it is more than an approach to inventory management. It is a philosophy of eliminating non-value-added activities.

➢ The benefits of JIT are in addition to lower carrying cost of inventory, improved quality, reduced rework, faster delivery and so on.

➢ The measures of performance that managers use to evaluate and control JIT are personal observations, financial, and non-financial measures.

➢ The effects of JIT on costing system are reduced overheads and direct tracing of some indirect costs.

REFERENCES

1. Polimeni, R.S., Fabozzi, F.J., Adelberg, A.H., Kole, M.A., *Cost Accounting,* (McGraw-Hill, 1991, New York), p. 90.
2. Based on studies By A. Synder, "*Principles of Inventory Management*", Financial Executive, April, 1964, pp 13-21.
3. For instance, for a detailed development and discussion of such models refer to R.I. Levin and C.A. Kirkpatrick, *Quantitative Approaches to Management,* (McGraw-Hill), New York, 1975).
4. S.E. Bolten, *Managerial Financial,* (Houghton Mifflin Co., Boston, 1976), p. 392.
5. For a more comprehensive and sophisticated treatment refer to M.C. Findlay, and E.E. Williams, *An Integrated Analysis for Managerial Finance,* (Prentice-Hall. Englewood Cliffs, 1970), p. 87.
6. It may not be out of place to mention that once a method is selected, it must be used consistently and cannot be changed from year to year.
7. In practice, the physical movement of materials may not follow the chronological order; in fact, in many situations, materials received last may be issued first as the strict adherence to the chronological order needs the removal of materials received in the 'last' so that the materials received 'first'/'earlier' can be issued. This obviously adds to the logistic inconvenience (which is avoidable). The chronological movement is desired when materials are perishable in nature.
8. I.W. Keller and W.L. Ferrara, *Management Accounting for Control,* (Tata McGraw-Hill Publishing Company Ltd., New Delhi, 1979), p. 81.
9. M.J. Gordon and G. Shillinglow, *Accounting: A Management Approach,* (Richard D. Irwin, Homewood, Illinois, 1974), p. 286.
10. Williams, J. R., *Financial and Management Accounting,* TMH, 2004, p. 788.
11. Horngren, C.T., *Cost Accounting,* Pearson, 2004, p. 697.
12. *Ibid,* pp. 697-698.

SOLVED PROBLEMS

P.3.1 If the price of the material is ₹15 per unit and the annual consumption is 4,000 units, the interest and store-keeping charges are 20 per cent of the value and the cost of placing of an order and receiving the goods is ₹60, how much material should be ordered at one time?

SOLUTION

$$\text{EOQ} = \sqrt{\frac{2\text{ AB}}{\text{C}}}$$

Where A = Annual usage of inventory (in units)

B = Ordering cost per buying order

C = Carrying cost per unit

$$\text{EOQ} = \sqrt{\frac{2 \times 4{,}000 \times 60}{3}} = 400 \text{ units.}$$

400 units should be ordered at one time.

WORKING NOTES

$$\text{Total carrying cost} = \frac{4{,}000 \times ₹15 \times 20}{100} = ₹12{,}000$$

$$\text{Carrying cost per unit} = \frac{₹12{,}000}{4{,}000 \text{ units}} = ₹3$$

P.3.2 Two components, A and B are used as follows:

Normal usage	:	50 units each per week
Minimum usage	:	25 units each per week
Maximum usage	:	75 units each per week
Re-order quantity	:	A: 300 units; B: 500 units
Re-order period	:	A: 4 to 6 weeks; B: 2 to 4 weeks

Calculate for each component: **(a)** Re-order level, **(b)** Minimum level, **(c)** Maximum level, and **(d)** Average stock level.

SOLUTION

(a) *Re-order level* = (Maximum usage × Maximum delivery time)

A = 75 × 6 weeks = 450 units

B = 75 × 4 weeks = 300 units

(b) *Minimum level* = Re-order level — (Normal usage × Average delivery time in weeks)

A = 450 units — (50 units × 5 weeks) = 200 units

B = 300 units — (50 units × 3 weeks) = 150 units

(c) *Maximum level* = Re-order level — (Minimum usage × Minimum delivery time) + Re-order quantity

A = 450 units — (25 × 4) + 300 units = 650 units

B = 300 units — (25 × 2) + 500 units = 750 units

(d) (i) Average stock level = Minimum level + (Re-order quantity)/2

A = 200 + (300)/2 = 350 units

B = 150 + (500/2) = 400 units

(ii) (Minimum level + Maximum level)/2

A = (200 + 650)/2 = 425 units

B = (150 + 500)/2 = 325 units

P.3.3 The following information pertaining to a firm are available:

Annual consumption	12,000 units (360 days)
Cost per unit	₹1
Cost per order	12
Inventory carrying cost (%)	20
Lead time (maximum, normal and minimum) (days)	30-15-5
Daily consumption: (maximum, normal and minimum) (units)	45-33-15

Calculate inventory levels.

SOLUTION

(a) *Economic-order quantity* = $\sqrt{\dfrac{2AB}{C}} = \sqrt{\dfrac{2 \times 12{,}000 \times \text{Rs } 12}{0.20}}$ = 1,200 units

Carrying cost per unit = $\left(\dfrac{\text{Rs } 12{,}000 \times 0.2}{12000 \text{ units}}\right)$ = ₹0.20

(b) Re-order level = (Maximum usage × Maximum delivery time) = 45 units × 30 days = 1,350 units

(c) Minimum level = Re-order level — (Normal usage × Average delivery time in days)

= 1,350 units — (33 units × 15 days) = 855 units

(d) Maximum Level = Re-order level — (Minimum usage × Minimum delivery time) + Re-order quantity

= 1,350 units — (15 units × 5 days) + 1,200 units

= 1,350 units — 75 units + 1,200 units = 2,475 units

(e) (i) Average stock level = Minimum level + (Re-order quantity)/2 = 855 units + 600 = 1,455 units
(ii) (Minimum level + Maximum level)/2 = (855 units + 2,475 units)/2 = 1,665 units

P.3.4 Peekay Company Ltd has been buying a given item in lots of 1,200 units which is a six months' supply, the cost per unit is ₹12, order cost is ₹8 per order, and carrying cost is 25 per cent. You are required to calculate the savings per year by buying in economical lot quantities.

SOLUTION

EOQ = $\sqrt{2\ AB/C}$ $\sqrt{(2 \times 2{,}400 \times 8)/3}$ = 114 units

Total carrying cost = 2,400 × ₹12 × 25/100 = ₹7,200

Carrying cost per unit (C) = 7,200 ÷ 2,400 units = ₹3

Savings due to EOQ:

Particulars	*Present*	*With EOQ*
1. Size of order (units)	1,200	114
2. Number of order	2	22
3. Cost per order	₹8	₹8
4. Total ordering cost (2 × 3)	16	176
5. Carrying cost per unit	3	3
6. Average inventory (units)	600 (1,200 ÷ 2)	57 (114 ÷ 2)
7. Total carrying cost (5 × 6)	1,800	171
8. Total cost (4 + 7)	1,816	347
Differential costs (savings)	₹1,469	

P.3.5 Ganges Pump Company Ltd. uses about 75,000 valves per year and the usage is fairly constant at 6,250 per month. The valve cost of ₹1.50 per unit when bought in large quantities, and the carrying cost is estimated to be 20 per cent of average inventory investment on an annual basis. The cost to place an order and process the delivery is ₹18.

It takes 45 days to receive delivery from the date of an order and a safety stock of 3,250 valves is desired.

You are required to determine: **(i)** The most economical order quantity and frequency of orders, **(ii)** The order point, and **(iii)** The most economical order quantity if the valves cost ₹4.50 each instead of ₹1.50 each.

SOLUTION

EOQ = $\sqrt{2\ AB/C} = \sqrt{(2 \times 75{,}000 \times 18)/0.30}$ = 3,000 units

WORKING NOTES

(i) *Total carrying cost* = (75,000 × ₹1.50 × 20) ÷ 100 = ₹22,500
Carrying cost per unit = ₹22,500/75,000 = ₹0.30 per unit

(ii) Order point (Lead time × normal usage during lead time) + safety stock
(1.5 months × 6,250 units per month) + 3,250 units = 12,625 units.

(iii) *EOQ when cost per valve is ₹4.50:* = $\sqrt{2\ AB/C} = \sqrt{(2 \times 75{,}000 \times \text{Rs } 18)/\text{Rs } 0.90}$ =1,733 units
Total carrying cost = (75,000 × ₹4.50 × 20) ÷ 100 = ₹67,500
Carrying cost per unit = ₹67,500/75,000 = ₹0.90

P.3.6 Precision Engineering Factory Ltd consumes 50,000 units of a component per year. The ordering, receiving and handling cost are ₹3 per order while the trucking costs are ₹12 per order. Further details are as follows: deterioration and obsolescence cost, ₹0.004 per unit per year; storage cost, ₹1,000 per year for 50,000 units. Interest cost is ₹0.06 per unit per year. Calculate the economic order quantity.

SOLUTION

EOQ = $\sqrt{2\ AB/C} = \sqrt{2 \times 50{,}000 \times 15/0.084}$ = 4,226 units

Carrying cost per unit: Interest cost, ₹0.060 + Deterioration and obsolescence cost, ₹0.004 + Storage, ₹0.020 (₹1,000/50,000) = ₹0.084.

P.3.7 A customer has been ordering 5,000 special design metal columns at the rate of 1,000 per order during the past year. The production cost is ₹12 a unit–₹8 for materials and labour and ₹4 for overheads (fixed) cost. It costs ₹1,500 to set up for one run of 1,000 columns, and inventory carrying cost is 20 per cent. Since this customers may buy at least 5,000 columns this year, the company would like to avoid making five different production runs. Find the most economic production run.

SOLUTION

Economic production run is given by the formula of EOQ in which B is setting up costs for one production run in place of buying cost per order. Accordingly economic production run = $\sqrt{(2 \times 50{,}000 \times 1{,}500)/\text{Rs } 2.40}$ = 2,500 units

P.3.8 Royal Industries Ltd manufacturers plastic lunch boxes in a moulding process. On an annual basis, the industry manufacturers 1,000 plastic lunch boxes at a cost of ₹4 per unit. The industry's differential costs of carrying the item in the finished goods inventory are 20 per cent of the inventory value per year, and the set-up costs per production run is ₹200. What is the optimum production-run?

SOLUTION

Optimum production = $\sqrt{2\text{ AB/C}} = \sqrt{2 \times 1{,}000 \times \text{Rs } 200/0.080}$ = 707 units

P.3.9 M/s Tubes Ltd are the manufacturers of picture tubes for T.V. The following are the details of the operation during the current year:

Average monthly market demand (tubes)	2,000
Ordering cost (per order)	₹100
Inventory carrying cost (per cent per annum)	20
Cost of tubes (per tube)	500
Normal usage (tubes per week)	100
Minimum usage (tubes per week)	50
Maximum usage (tubes per week)	200
Lead time to supply (weeks)	6-8

Compute from the above:

1. Economic order quantity. If the supplier is willing to supply quarterly 1,500 units at a discount of 5 per cent, is it worth accepting?
2. Maximum level of stock
3. Minimum level of stock
4. Reorder level.

SOLUTION

1. *Economic order quantity*

Annual demand (A) = Normal usage per week × 52 weeks = 100 tubes × 52 = 5,200 tubes. Ordering cost per order (B) = ₹100 per order

Inventory carrying cost per unit per annum(C) = ₹500 × 0.20 = ₹100 per unit per annum

EOQ = $\sqrt{2\text{ AB/C}} = \sqrt{(2 \times 5{,}200 \text{ units} \times \text{Rs } 100) \div \text{Rs } 100}$ = 102 tubes

If supplier is willing to supply 1,500 units at a discount of 5 per cent:

Total cost (When order size is 1,500 units) = Cost of 5,200 units + Ordering cost + Carrying cost

= [5,200 × (500 × 0.95)) + [(5,200/1,500) × ₹100) + ($\frac{1}{2}$ × 1,500 × 0.20 × 475)]

= ₹24, 70,000 + ₹346.67 + ₹71, 250 = ₹25, 41,596.67

Total cost (when order size is 102 units) = (5,200 × 500) + (5,200/102 × ₹100)
+ (1/2 × 102 × 0.20 × 500)
= ₹26,00,000 + ₹5,098.03 + ₹5,100 = ₹26, 10,198.03

Since the total cost under quarterly supply of 1,500 units with 5 per cent discount is lower than when order size is 102 units, the offer should be accepted. While accepting this offer, consideration of capital blocked on order size of 1,500 units per quarter has been ignored.

2. Maximum level of stock = Reorder level+Reorder quantity—(Minimum usage × Minimum reorder period)

= 1,600 units + 102 units — (50 units × 6 weeks) = 1,402 units

3. Maximum level of stock = Reorder level—(Normal usage × Average reorder period)

= 1,600 units—(100 units × 7 weeks) = 900 units

4. Reorder level = Maximum consumption × Maximum reorder period = 200 units × 8 weeks = 1,600 units.

P.3.10 IPL Limited uses a small casting in one of its finished products. The castings are purchased from a foundry. IPL Limited purchases 54,000 castings per year at a cost of ₹800 per casting.

The castings are used evenly throughout the year in the production process on a 360-day-per-year basis. The company estimates that it costs ₹9,000 to place a single purchase order and about ₹300 to carry one casting in inventory for a year. The high carrying costs result from the need to keep the castings in carefully controlled temperature and humidity conditions, and from the high cost of insurance.

Delivery from the foundry generally takes 6 days, but it can take as much as 10 days. The days of delivery time and percentage of their occurrence are shown in the following tabulation:

Delivery time (days)	6	7	8	9	10
Percentage of occurrence	75	10	5	5	5

REQUIRED: **(i)** Compute the economic order quantity (EOQ). **(ii)** Assume the company is willing to assume a 15 per cent risk of being out of stock. What would be the safety stock? The re-order point? **(iii)** Assume the company is willing to assume a 5 per cent risk of being out of stock. What would be the safety stock? The re-order point? **(iv)** Assume 5 per cent stock-out risk. What would be the total cost of ordering and carrying inventory for one year? **(v)** Refer to the original data. Assume that using process re-engineering the company reduces its cost of placing a purchase order to only ₹600. In addition, the company estimates that when the waste and inefficiency caused by inventories are considered, the true cost of carrying a unit in stock is ₹720 per year.

(a) Compute the new EOQ.

(b) How frequently would the company be placing an order, as compared to the old purchasing policy?

SOLUTION

(i) *Computation of economic order quantity (EOQ):*

$$\text{EOQ} = \sqrt{\frac{2AB}{C}} = \sqrt{\frac{2 \times 54{,}000 \times \text{Rs } 9{,}000}{\text{Rs } 300}} = 1.800 \text{ castings}$$

(ii) *Safety stock:* (Assuming a 15 per cent risk of being out of stock)

Safety stock for one day = 54,000/360 days = 150 castings

Reorder point = Minimum stock level + Average consumption

= 150 + (6 × 150) = 1,050 castings

(iii) *Safety stocks:* (Assuming a 5 per cent risk of being out of stock)

Safety stock for three days = 150 × 3 days = 450 castings

Reorder point = 450 castings + 900 castings = 1,350 castings.

(iv) Total cost of ordering = (54,000/1,800) × ₹9,000 = ₹2,70,000

Total cost of carrying = (450 +1/2 × 1,800) × ₹300 = ₹4,05,000

(v) (a) Computation of new EOQ:

$$\text{EOQ} = \sqrt{\frac{2 \times 54{,}000 \times 600}{720}} = 300 \text{ castings}$$

(b) Under the new purchasing policy, the order will be placed more frequently. In fact, each order is to be placed after 2 days (1 year = 360 days). Under old purchasing policy each order was placed after 12 days.

P.3.11 RST Limited has received an offer of quantity discount on its order of materials as under:

Price per tonne	*Tonnes number*
₹9,600	Less than 50
9,360	50 and less than 100
9,120	100 and less than 200
8,880	200 and less than 300
8,640	300 and above

The annual requirement for the material is 500 tonnes. The ordering cost per order is ₹12,500 and the stock holding cost is estimated at 25 per cent of the material cost per annum.
Required: (i) Compute the most economical purchase level. (ii) Compute EOQ if there are no quantity discounts and the price per tonne is ₹10,500.

SOLUTION

(1) *Calculation of Most Economical Purchase Level:*

(1) Order size (Q) (Units)	40	50	100	200	300
(2) No. of orders (Units) [A/Q]	12.5	10	5	2.5	1.67
(3) Cost of purchase (A) × Per unit cost	₹48,00,000 (500 × 9,600)	₹46,80,000 (500 × 9,360)	₹45,60,000 (500 × 9,120)	₹44,40,000 (500 × 8,880)	₹43,20,000 (500 × 8,640)
(4) Ordering cost [(A/Q) × ₹12,500]	1,56,250	1,25,000	62,500	31,250	20,875
(5) Carrying cost [(Q/2) × c × 25%]	48,000 [(40/2) × 9,600 × 0.25)	58,000 [(50/2) × 9,360 × 0.25)	1,14,000 [(100/2) × 9,120 × 0.25)	2,22,000 [(200/2) × 8,880 × 0.25]	3,24,000 [(300/2) × 8,640 × 0.25)]
Total cost (3 + 4 + 5)	₹50,04,250	₹48,63,500	₹47,36,500	₹46,93,250	₹46,64,875

Total cost is minimum (₹46,64,875) when the order size is 300 units. Hence, the most economical purchase level is 300 units.

(2) $$\text{EOQ} = \sqrt{\frac{2AB}{C}} = \sqrt{\frac{2 \times 500 \times \text{Rs } 12{,}500}{10{,}500 \times 0.25}} = 69 \text{ tonnes}$$

P.3.12 SK Enterprise manufactures a special product "ZE". The following particulars were collected for the year 2004:

Annual consumption	12,000 units (360 days)
Cost per unit	₹1
Ordering cost	₹12 per order
Inventory carrying cost	24%
Normal lead time	15 days
Safety stock	30 days consumption

REQUIRED: (i) Re-order quantity (ii) Re-order level (iii) What should be the inventory level (ideally) immediately before the material order is received?

SOLUTION

(i) Re-order quantity/EOQ = $\sqrt{2\,AB/C} = \sqrt{(2 \times 12{,}000 \times \text{Rs } 12) \div \text{Re } 0.24} = 1{,}095$ units

Carrying cost per unit (c) = (12,000 units × 0.24)/12,000 units = ₹0.24 per unit

(ii) Re-order level = (Normal lead time × Daily consumption) + Safety stock
= (15 days × 33.33 units) + (30 days × 33.33 units) = 1,500 units

(iii) Minimum ideal level = Re-order level — (Normal usage per day × Average delivery time in days)
= 1,500 units — (33.33 units × 15 days) = 1,000 units

P.3.13 G. Ltd. produces a product which has a monthly demand of 4,000 units. The product requires a component X which is purchased at ₹20. For every finished product, one unit of component is required. The ordering cost is ₹120 per order and the holding cost is 10 per cent per annum.

You are required to calculate:

(i) Economic order quantity.

(ii) If the minimum lot size to be supplied is 4,000 units, what is the extra cost, the company has to incur?

(iii) What is the minimum carrying cost, the company has to incur?

SOLUTION

(i) *Determination of EOQ*

$$\text{EOQ} = \sqrt{\frac{2\,AB}{C}} = \sqrt{\frac{2 \times 48{,}000 \text{ units} \times \text{Rs } 120}{\text{Rs } 2}} = 2{,}400 \text{ units}$$

A = 4,000 units per month × 12 months = 48,000 units
C = ₹20 cost per unit × 0.10 = ₹2 per unit per annum

(ii) *Determination of Extra Cost when Lot Size is 4,000 Units*

Particulars	*Cost when lot size is*	
	4,000 units	*2,400 units*
1. Annual usage (units)	48,000	48,000
2. Size of order	4,000	2,400
3. Number of orders (1 ÷ 2)	12	20
4. Cost per order	₹120	₹120
5. Total ordering costs (3 × 4)	1,440	2,400
6. Carrying cost per unit per annum	2	2
7. Average inventory (size of order/2)	2,000	1,200
8. Total carrying cost (6 × 7)	₹4,000	₹2,400
9. Total costs (5 + 8)	₹5,400	₹4,800

Extra costs to be incurred is ₹640 (₹5,440 — ₹4,800), when the order size is 4,000 units.

(iii) *There is a positive relationship between the total carrying cost the firm incurs and the size of the average inventory it carries; this average size of inventory, in turn, is positively related to the size of order. In view of these facts, the minimum carrying costs, the firm is to incur is ₹2,400 (corresponding to EOQ of 2,400 units and the average inventory level of 1,200 units)*

P.3.14 A company manufactures a product from a raw material, which is purchased at ₹60 per kg. The company incurs a handling cost of ₹360 plus freight of ₹390 per order. The incremental carrying cost of inventory of raw material is ₹0.50 per kg. per month. In addition, the cost of working capital finance on the investment in inventory of raw material is ₹9 per kg per annum. The annual production of the product is 1,00,000 units and 2.5 units are obtained from one kg of raw material.

REQUIRED:

(i) Calculate the economic order quantity of raw materials.

(ii) Advise, how frequently should orders for procurement be placed.

(iii) If the company proposes to rationalise placement of orders on quarterly basis, what percentage of discount in the price of raw materials should be negotiated?

SOLUTION

(i) $EOQ = \sqrt{\frac{2AB}{C}} = \sqrt{\frac{2 \times 40{,}000 \text{ kgs} \times \text{Rs } 750}{\text{Rs } 15}}$ = 2,000 kgs

Annual usage in kgs (A) = 1,00,000 units/2.5 units = 40,000 kgs

Ordering cost per order (B) = ₹360 + ₹390 = ₹750

Carrying cost per kg per annum (C) = (₹0.50 per kg per month ×12 months) + ₹9 per kg cost of working capital finance per annum = ₹15

(ii) *Frequency of placing an order in a year*

Annual usage (in kgs)	40,000
EOQ (in kgs)	2,000
Number of orders placed in a year (40,000 kgs/2,000 kgs)	20*

* Frequency of placing an order is 18 days (360 days/20)

(iii) (a) *Incremental Total Cost to be Incurred when Orders are Placed on quarterly basis i.e., 10,000 kgs (40,000 Annual usage/4 Quarters)*

Particulars	*On EOQ Basis*	*On Quarterly Basis*
1. Annual usage (kgs)	40,000	40,000
2. Size of orders	2,000	10,000
3. Number of orders (1 ÷ 2)	20	4
4. Cost per order	₹750	₹750
5. Total orderings costs (3 × 4)	15,000	3,000
6. Carrying cost per unit	15	15
7. Average inventory (size of order/2) (kgs)	1,000	5,000
8. Total carrying cost (6 × 7)	₹15,000	₹75,000
9. Total cost (5 + 8)	30,000	78,000
Incremental costs (₹78,000 – ₹30,000) per year = ₹48,000		

(b) The firm should be able to earn discount of ₹48,000 on its total annual purchases of 40,000 kgs (40,000 kgs × ₹60 per kg = ₹24,00,000). The negotiated discount sum will be: (₹48,000/₹24,00,000) × 100 = 2 per cent.

P.3.15 The Complete Gardener is deciding on the economic order quantity for two brands of lawn fertilizer: Super Grow and Nature's Own. The following information is collected:

Particulars	*Fertilizer*	
	Super Grow	*Nature's Own*
Annual demand	2,000 Bags	1,280 Bags
Relevant ordering cost per purchase order	₹1,200	₹1,400
Annual relevant carrying cost per bag	480	560

Required:

(i) Compute EOQ for Super Grow and Nature's Own.

(ii) For the EOQ, what is the sum of the total annual relevant ordering costs and total annual relevant carrying costs for Super Grow and Nature's Own?

(iii) For the EOQ, compute the number of deliveries per year for Super Grow and Nature's Own.

SOLUTION

(i) $EOQ = \sqrt{\frac{2AB}{C}} = \sqrt{\frac{2 \times 2{,}000 \times 1{,}200}{480}}$ = 100 bags (Super Grow)

$= \sqrt{\frac{2 \times 1{,}280 \times 1{,}400}{560}}$ = 80 bags (Nature's Own)

(ii) and **(iii)** Statement showing Total Relevant Costs for Super Grow and Nature's Own Fertilizer

Particulars	*Super Grow*	*Nature's Own*
Annual demand (bags)	2,000	1,280
EOQ (bags)	100	80
Number of orders/deliveries	20	16
Multiplied by ordering cost per order	₹1,200	₹1,400
(a) Total ordering cost	24,000	22,400
Average inventory (1/2 × EOQ) of bags	50	40
Multiplied by carrying cost per bag	480	560
(b) Total carrying cost	24,000	22,400
(c) Total cost (a) + (b)	48,000	44,800

P.3.16 A Company has the option to procure a particular material from two sources:
Source I assures that defectives will not be more than 2 per cent of supplied quantity.
Source II does not give any assurance, but on the basis of past experience of supplies received from it, it is observed that defective percentage is 2.8 per cent.

The material is supplied in lots of 1,000 units. Source II supplies the lot at a price, which is lower by ₹100 as compared to source 1. The defective units of material can be rectified for use at a cost of ₹5 per unit.

You are required to find out which of the two sources is more economical.

SOLUTION

Statement showing Comparative Costs Associated with two Sources of Material Supplies

Particulars	*Material source I*	*Material source II*
1. Material supplied (in units)	1,000	1,000
2. Defective units (in percentage)	2	2.8
3. Total defective units (I × 2)	20	28
4. Rectification cost per unit	₹5	₹5
5. Total rectification (3 × 4)	100	140
6. Additional price paid in Source I	100	—
7. Total additional costs (5 + 6)	200	140

Material Source II is more economical as it entails lower costs. The company is advised to buy materials from Source II.

P.3.17 A factory uses 4,000 varieties of inventory. In terms of inventory holding and inventory usage, the following information is compiled.

Number of varieties of inventory	*Percentage*	*% value of inventory holding (average)*	*% of inventory usage (in end-product)*
3,875	96.875	20	5
110	2.750	30	10
15	0.375	50	85
4,000	100.00	100	100

Classify the items of inventory as per ABC analysis with reasons.

SOLUTION

(i) 15 number of varieties of inventory items should be classified as 'A' category (as per ABC analysis) as, while they constitute less than one per cent (0.375 per cent) of total number of inventory items handled by the store, their value is 50 per cent. Besides, these varieties (15) account for 85 per cent of total inventory usage (in end-product). Thus, this group is the most important.

(ii) 3,875 number of inventory items should be classified as 'C' category as they constitute 96.875 per cent of total varieties of inventory items handled by the store; such inventories account for only for 20 per cent of total value and 5 per cent of total inventory usage (in-end product). Thus, this group is the least important.

(iii) 10 number of inventory items should be classified as 'B' category as they occupy intermediate position between A category (15 items) and C category (3,875 items). These items (110) require more attention than C category items but less attention than A category items as per ABC analysis. In financial terms also, these items require 30 per cent investment (less than A category but more than C category) with 2.75 per cent of total number of varieties of inventory handled by store; such number is much higher for C category (96.875 per cent) and lower for A category (0.375 per cent).

P.3.18 From the following informations prepare a stores ledger account under FIFO method:

1-1-X6	Opening stock, 1,000 units at ₹5 each
5-1-X6	Purchased, 900 units at ₹6 each
10-1-X6	Issued, 1,200 units
12-1-X6	Purchased, 800 units at ₹6.20 each
15-1-X6	Purchased, 300 units at ₹6.40 each
19-1-X6	Issued, 400 units
22-1-X6	Issued, 600 units
27-1-X6	Purchased, 200 units at ₹6.50 each
31-1-X6	Issued, 600 units

SOLUTION

Stores Ledger (FIFO Method)

Date		*Receipts*			*Issues*			*Balance*		
		Quantity	*Rate*	*Amount*	*Quantity*	*Rate*	*Amount*	*Quantity*	*Rate*	*Amount*
January	1							1,000	₹5	5,000
	5	900	₹6	₹5,400				1,900	—	10,400
	10				1,000	₹5	₹5,000			
					200	6	1,200	700	—	4,200
	12	800	6.20	4,960				1,500		9,160
	15	300	6.40	1,920				1,800		11,080
	19				400	6	2,400	1,400		8,680
	22				300	6	1,800			
					300	6.20	1,860	800		5,020
	27	200	6.50	1,300				1,000		6,320
	31				500	6.20	3,100			
					100	6.40	640	400		2,580

P.3.19 The following is a summary of receipts and issues of materials in a factory during January, current year:

January	1	Opening balance, 500 units @ ₹25 per unit
	3	Issue, 70 units
	4	Issue, 100 units
	8	Issue, 80 units
	13	Received from supplier, 200 units @ ₹24.50 per unit
	14	Returned to store, 15 units @ ₹24 per unit
	16	Issue, 180 units
	20	Received from supplier, 240 units @ ₹24.75 per unit
	24	Issue, 304 units
	25	Received from supplier, 320 units @ ₹24.50 per unit
	26	Issue, 112 units
	27	Returned to store, 12 units @ ₹24.50 per unit
	31	Received from supplier, 100 units @ ₹25 per unit.

Work out on the basis of First-in-First-Out price at which materials are to be issued and the value of stock as on January, 31. The physical verification revealed that on January, 15 there was a shortage of 5 units and another of 8 units on January 28.

SOLUTION

Cost of Inventory Used and its Valuation (FIFO Method)

Date	Receipts			Issues			Balance		
	Quantity	*Rate*	*Amount*	*Quantity*	*Rate*	*Amount*	*Quantity*	*Rate*	*Amount*
January 1							500	₹25	₹12,500
3				70	25	1,750	430		10,750
4				100	25	2,500	330	—	8,250
8				80	25	2,000	250	—	6,250
13	200	₹24.5	₹4,900				450	—	11,150
14	15[1]	24.0	360				465	—	11,510
15				5[2]	25	125	460	—	11,385
16				180	25	4,500	280	—	6,885
20	240	24.75	5,940				520	—	12,825
24									
				65	25	1,625			
				200	24.5	4,900			
				15	24.0	360			
				24	24.75	594	216	—	5,346
25	320	24.50	7,840			2,772	536	—	13,186
26				112	24.75	424	—	10,414	
27	12[1]	24.50	294				436	—	10,708
28				8[2]	24.75	198	428	—	10,510
31	100	25.0	2,500				528	—	13,010

1. Returned to stores; 2. Shortage (deemed to be an issue and priced accoridngly)
   Value of material on January 31, ₹13,010.

P.3.20 Assume everything to be the same as provided in **P. 3.19**, work out on the basis of LIFO, the price at which materials are to be issued and the value of stock as on January 31.

SOLUTION

Cost of Inventory Used and its Valuation (LIFO Method)

Date	Receipts			Issues			Balance		
	Quantity	*Rate*	*Amount*	*Quantity*	*Rate*	*Amount*	*Quantity*	*Rate*	*Amount*
January 1							500	₹25	₹12,500
3				70	25	₹1,750	430	—	10,750
4				100	25	2,500	330	—	8,250
8				80	25	2,000	250	—	6,250
13	200	₹24.5	₹4,900				450	—	11,150
14	15[1]	24.0	360				465	—	11,510
15				5[2]	24	120	460	—	11,390
16				10	24	240			
				170	24.5	4,165	280	—	6,985
20	240	24.75	5,940				520	—	12,925
24				240	24.75	5,940			
				30	24.50	735			
				34	25.00	850	216		5,400
25	320	24.50	7,840				536	—	13,240

(Contd.)

(Contd.)

26				112	24.50	2,744	424	—	10,496
27	12[1]	24.50	294				436	—	10,790
28				8[2]	24.50	196	428	—	10,594
31	100	25.00	2,500				528	—	13,094

1. Returned to stores; 2. shortage

Value of materials on January 31, ₹13,094

P.3.21 The following are the transactions in respect of purchase and issue of components forming a part of an assembly of a product manufactured by a firm which required to update its cost of production, very often for bidding tenders and finalising cost plus contracts:

January	5	1,000 units purchased @ ₹12 each
	11	Issued 2,000 units to production
February	1	1,500 units purchased @ ₹13 each
	18	Issued 2,400 units to production
	26	Issued 1,000 units to production
March	8	1,000 units purchased @ ₹14 each
	17	1,500 units purchased @ ₹15 each
	28	2,000 units issued to production

Stock on January, 1 was 5,000 units valued at ₹11 each. State the method you would adopt in pricing the issue of components, giving reasons. What value would you place on stocks as on March 31, which happens to be financial year-end?

Solution

The LIFO method is ideal under conditions of rising prices (as is in the present question), as it matches current costs (higher costs) with current revenues, leading to correct income determination. Stores ledger, based on LIFO is given below.

Stores Ledger (LIFO Method)

Date		Receipts			Issues			Balance		
		Quantity	Rate	Amount	Quantity	Rate	Amount	Quantity	Rate	Amount
January	1							5,000	₹11	₹55,000
	5	1,000	12	₹12,000				6,000	—	67,000
	11				1,000 1,000	12 11	₹12,000 11,000	4,000	—	44,000
								5,500		63,500
February	1	1,500	13	19,500						
	18				1,500 900	13 11	19,500 9,900	3,100 2,100		34,100 23,100
	26				1,000	11	11,000			
March	8	1,000	14	14,000				3,100		37,100
	17	1,500	15	22,500				4,600		59,600
	28				1,500 500	15 14		22,500 7,000		30,100

Stock on March, 31 = ₹30,100.

P.3.22 From the following details of store receipts and issues of material "Exe" in a manufacturing unit, prepare the store ledger using weighted average method of valuing the issues.

November	1	Opening stock, 2,000 units @ ₹5 each
	3	Issued, 1,500 units to production

(Contd.)

(Contd.)

4	Received, 4,500 units @ ₹6 each
8	Issued, 1,600 units to production
9	Returned to stores, 100 units by production department (from the issues of November 3)
16	Received, 2,400 units @ ₹6.50 each
19	Returned to supplier, 200 units out of the quantity received on November 4
20	Received, 1,000 units @ ₹7.00 each
24	Issued to production, 2,100 units
27	Received, 1,200 units @ ₹7.50 each
29	Issued to production, 2,800 units.

Note: Use rates up to two decimal places.

SOLUTION

Stores Ledger (Weighted Average Method)

Date	Receipts			Issues			Balance		
	Quantity	*Rate*	*Amount*	*Quantity*	*Rate*	*Amount*	*Quantity*	*Rate*	*Amount*
November 1							2,000	₹5	₹10,000
3				1,500	₹5	₹7,500	500	5	2,500
4	4,500	₹6	₹27,000	1,600	5.9	9,440	5,000	5.9	29,500
8							3,400	5.9	20,060
9	100[1]	5	500				3,500	5.87	20,560
16	2,400	6.50	15,600				5,900	6.13	36,160
19				200[2]	6.0'	1,200	5,700	6.13	34,960
20	1,000	7.00	7,000				6,700	6.26	41,960
24				2,100	6.26	13,146	4,600	6.26	28,814
27	1,200		9,000				5,800	6.52	37,814
29		7.50		2,800	6.52	18,256	3,000	6.52	19,558

1. Returned to stores; 2. Returned to supplier.

P.3.23 The following information is provided by Sunrise Industries Ltd for the fortnight of April, current year in respect of material Exe:

Stock on April	1	100 units @ ₹5 per unit
Purchases:		
	5	300 units @ ₹6 per unit
	8	500 units @ ₹7 per unit
	12	600 units @ ₹8 per unit
Issues:		
	6	250 units
	10	400 units
	14	500 units

REQUIRED: (a) Calculate using FIFO and LIFO methods of pricing issues (i) the value of materials consumed during the period and (ii) the value of stock materials on April 15, current year; (b) Explain why the figures in (i) and (ii) in part (a) of this question are different under the two methods of pricing of materials issued/used. You need not draw up the stores ledgers.

SOLUTION

(a) *(i) Value of Materials Exe Consumed during April (FIFO Basis)*

Date		Receipts			Issues			Balance		
		Quantity	Rate	Amount	Quantity	Rate	Amount	Quantity	Rate	Amount
April	1							100	₹5	₹500
	5	300	₹6	₹1,800				400	—	2,300
	6				100 150	₹5 6	₹500 900	150	—	900
	8	500	7	3,500				650	—	4,400
	10				150 250	6 7	900 1,750	250 850		1,750 6,550
	12	600	8	4,800	250 250	7 8	1,750 2,000			
	14							350		2,800

(ii) *Value of Materials Exe Consumed during April (LIFO Basis)*

Date		Receipts			Issues			Balance		
		Quantity	Rate	Amount	Quantity	Rate	Amount	Quantity	Rate	Amount
April	1							100	₹5	₹500
	5	300	₹6	₹1,800				400	—	2,300
	6				250	₹6	₹1,500	150	—	800
	8	500	7	3,500				650		4,300
	10				400	7	2,800	250		1,500
	12	600	8	4,800				850		6,300
	14				500	8	4,000	350		2,300

Cost of materials consumed		*FIFO*	*LIFO*
April	6	₹1,400	₹1,500
	10	2,650	2,800
	14	3,750	4,000
Total cost of materials used		7,800	8,300
Value of stock			
Balance, opening		₹500	₹500
Add purchases		10,100	10,100
Less value of materials consumed		(7,800)	(8,300)
Closing stock		2,800	2,300

(b) Cost of materials issued under LIFO method is higher by ₹500 (₹8,300, LIFO-₹7,800, FIFO), therefore, value of stock in LIFO method is lower by ₹500 (₹2,800—₹2,300).

P.3.24 The following transactions occur in the purchase and issue of a material.

January	2	Purchased, 4,000 units at ₹4 per unit.
	20	Purchased, 500 units at ₹5 per unit
February	5	Issued, 2,000 units
	10	Purchased, 6,000 units at ₹6 per unit
	12	Issued, 4,000 units
March	2	Issued, 1,000 units
	5	Issued, 2,000 units
	15	Purchased, 4500 units at ₹5.50 per unit
	20	Issued, 3,000 units

Prepare stores ledger account using (a) Simple Average Method, (b) Weighted Average Method.

SOLUTION

(a) *Stores Ledger (Simple Average Method)*

Date		Receipts			Issues			Balance		
		Quantity	Rate	Amount	Quantity	Rate	Amount	Quantity	Rate	Amount
January	2	4,000	₹4	₹16,000				4,000	₹4	₹16,000
	20	500	5	2,500				4,500	—	18,500
February	5				2,000	4.5[1]	9,000	2,500	—	9,500
	10	6,000	6	36,000				8,500	—	45,500
	12				4,000	5.0[2]	20,000	4,500	—	25,500
March	2				1,000	6.0[3]	6,000	3,500	—	19,500
	5				2,000	6.0	12,000	1,500	—	7,500
	15	4,500	5.50	24,750				6,000	—	32,250
	20				3,000	5.75[4]	17,250	3,000	—	15,000

Note: (1) (₹4 + ₹5)/2 = ₹4.50; (2) (₹4 + ₹5 + ₹6)/3 = ₹5; (3) ₹6; (4) (₹6 + ₹5.50)/2 = ₹5.75

(b) *Stores ledger (Weighted Average Method)*

Date		Receipts			Issues			Balance		
		Quantity	Rate	Amount	Quantity	Rate	Amount	Quantity	Rate	Amount
January	2	4000	₹4	₹16,000				4,000	₹4	₹16,000
	20	500	5	2,500				4,500	4.11	18,500
February	5				2,000	₹4.11	₹8,220	2,500	4.11	10,280
	10	6,000	6	36,000				8,500	5.44	46,280
	12				4,000	5.44	21,760	4,500	5.45	24,520
March	2				1,000	5.45	5,450	3,500	5.45	19,070
	5				2,000	5.45	10,900	1,500	5.45	8,170
	15	4,500	5.50	24,750				6,000	5.49	32,920
	20				3,000	5.49	16,470	3,000	5.49	16,470

P.3.25 The following information is extracted from the stores ledger:

Material X

Opening Stock		Nil
Purchases:		
January	1	100 @ ₹1 per unit
	20	100 @ ₹2 per unit
Issues:		
	22	60 for job W-16
	23	60 for job W-17

Complete the receipts and issues valuation by adopting the First-in-first-out, Last-in-last-out and the Weighted Average Method.

SOLUTION

Stores Ledger Account (FIFO, LIFO, Weighted Average Cost Method)

Date		Receipts			Issues			Balance		
		Quantity	Rate	Amount	Quantity	Rate	Amount	Quantity	Rate	Amount
(a) FIFO										
January	1	100	₹1	₹100				100	₹1	₹100
	20	100	2	200				200	—	300
	22				60	₹1	₹60	140	—	240
	23				40 }	1	40 }			
					20 }	2	40 }	80	—	160

(Contd.)

(*Contd.*)

(b) LIFO										
January	1	100	1	100				100	1	100
	20	100	2	200				200	—	300
	22				60	2	120	140	—	180
	23				40 20	2 1	80 20	80		80
(c) Weighted Average Cost Method										
January	1	100	1	100				100	1	100
	20	100	2	200				200	1.5	300
	22				60	1.5	90	140	1.5	210
	23				60	1.5	90	80	1.5	120

P.3.26 A manufacturer of Surat purchased three chemicals, A, B and C from Bombay. The invoice gave the following information:

Chemical A:	3,000 kgs @ ₹42 per kg	₹1,26,000
Chemical B:	5,000 kgs @ ₹38 per kg	1,90,000
Chemical C:	2,000 kgs @ ₹47.50 per kg	95,000
Sales tax		20,550
Railway freight		10,000
Total cost		4,41,550

A shortage of 200 kgs in chemical A, of 280 kgs in chemical B and of 100 kgs in chemical C was noticed due to breakages. At Surat, the manufacturer paid octroi duty @ ₹1 per kg. He also paid cartage, ₹2,000 for chemical A, ₹6,000 for chemical B and ₹3,000 for chemical C. Calculate the stock rate that you would suggest for pricing issue of chemicals assuming a provision of 5 per cent towards further deterioration.

SOLUTION

Statement showing Determination of Issue Price of Materials

Particulars	*Chemical A*	*Chemical B*	*Chemical C*
Purchase price	₹1,26,000	₹1,90,000	₹95,000
Add sales tax (0.05[1] × purchase price)	6,300	9,500	4,750
Add railway freight (apportioned in the ratio of quantity, 3:5:2)	3,000	5,000	2,000
Add octroi @ ₹1 per kg of material received	2,800	4,720	1,900
Add cartage charges	2,000	6,000	3,000
Total cost	1,40,100	2,15,220	1,06,650
Divided by expected quantity available for issue (kgs)	2,660	4,484	1,805
Issue price per kg	52.67	48.00	59.09

WORKING NOTES

1. Sales tax = (Total sales tax/Total purchase price) × 100 = (₹20,550/₹4,11,000) × 100 = 5 per cent
2. Statement showing the quantity (kgs) of chemicals available for issue

Particulars	*Chemical A*	*Chemical B*	*Chemical C*
Quantity purchased	3,000	5,000	2,000
Less shortage*	200	280	100
Quantity received at store	2,800	4,720	1,900
Less provision for further loss (5 per cent)*	140	236	95
Quantity available for issue	2,660	4,484	1,805

*It is assumed that both shortages due to breakage and deterioration in quantity of materials are normal losses.

P.3.27 A Ltd furnishes the following stores transactions for September of current year:

September 1	Opening balance, 25 units; value, ₹162.50
4	Issues (Requisition 85), 8 units
6	Receipts from B and Co. (GNR 26), 50 units @ ₹5.75 per unit
7	Issues (Requisition 97), 12 units
10	Returns to B and Co., 10 units
12	Issues (Requisition 10), 15 units
13	Issues (Requisition 110), 20 units
15	Receipts from M and Co. (GNR 33), 25 units @ ₹6.10 per unit
17	Issues (Requisition 121). 10 units
19	Received replacement from B and Co. (GRN 38), 10 units
20	Returned from department material of B and Co. (MRR 4), 5 units
22	Transfer from Job 182 to Job 187 in department (MTR 6), 5 units
26	Issue (Requisition 146), 10 units
29	Transfer from Department A to Department B (MTR 10), 5 units
30	Shortage in stock-taking, 2 units

Write up the stores ledger under FIFO method and LIFO method.

SOLUTION

Stores Ledger (FIFO Method)

Date	*Receipts*			*Issues*			*Balance*		
	Quantity	*Rate*	*Amount*	*Quantity*	*Rate*	*Amount*	*Quantity*	*Rate*	*Amount*
September 1							25	₹6.5	₹162.5
4				8	₹6.50	₹52	17	—	110.5
6	50	₹5.75	₹287.50				67		398.0
7				12	6.50	78	55	—	320.0
10				10[1]	5.75	57.5	45	—	262.5
12				5	6.50	32.5			
				10	5.75	57.5	30	—	172.5
13				20	5.75	115.0	10	—	57.5
15	25	6.10	152.50				35	—	210.0
17				10	5.75	57.5	25	—	152.50
19	10	5.75[2]	57.50				35	—	210.00
20	5	5.75[3]	28.75				40		238.75
26				5[4]	5.75	28.75			
				5	6.10	30.50	30		179.50
30				2[5]	6.10	12.20	28		167.30

Note: (1) Returned to supplier; (2) Replacement from supplier (obviously at initial sale price of ₹5.75 per unit; (3) Returned to stores; (4) The material received as replacement from vendor has been treated as a fresh supply and hence will be used after supplies purchased on September 15 are exhausted. Since, materials returned (5 units) on September 20 (from within) relate to purchases of September 6, these units have been priced at ₹5.75 per unit; (5) Shortage (deemed to be am issue and priced accordingly); (6) The transfer from one job to another (September, 22) and from one department to another (September, 29) are book entries for adjusting the cost of respective jobs and, therefore, have not been taken into account in stores ledger account.

Stores Ledger (LIFO Method)

Date	Receipts			Issues			Balance		
	Quantity	Rate	Amount	Quantity	Rate	Amount	Quantity	Rate	Amount
September 1							25	₹6.5	₹162.5
4				8	₹6.50	₹52	17	—	110.5
6	50	₹5.75	₹287.50				67	—	398
7				12	5.75	69	55		329
10				10	5.75	57.50	45		271.5
12				15	5.75	86.25	30		185.25
13				13	5.75	74.75			
				7	6.50	45.50	10		65
15	25	6.10	152.50				35		217.50
17				10	6.10	61.00	25		156.50
19	10	5.75	57.50				35		214
20	5	5.75	28.75				40		242.75
26				10	5.75	57.50	30		185.25
30				2	6.10	12.20	28@		173.05

@ Closing stock consists of

10 units @ ₹6.50	=	₹65
5 units @ ₹5.75	=	28.75
13 units @ ₹6.10	=	79.30
		173.05

P.3.28 With help of the following information, prepare the store ledger based on the weighted average method of pricing issues.

September 1	Opening balance	24,000 kgs @ ₹7.5 per kg
1	Purchased	44,000 kgs @ ₹7.6 per kg
2	Issued	10,000 kgs
5	Issued	16,000 kgs
12	Issued	24,000 kgs
13	Purchased	10,000 kgs @ ₹8 per kg
18	Issued	24,000 kgs
22	Purchased	50,000 kgs @ ₹8 per kg
28	Issued	30,000 kgs
30	Issued	22,000 kgs

Note: Use rates up to two decimals.

SOLUTION

Store Ledger (Weighted Average Method)

Date	Receipts			Issues			Balance		
	Quantity	Rate	Amount	Quantity	Rate	Amount	Quantity	Rate	Amount
September 1							24,000	₹7.5	₹1,80,000
1	44,000	₹7.6	₹3,34,400				68,000	7.56	5,14,400
2				10,000	₹7.56	₹75,600	58,000	7.56	4,38,800
5				16,000	7.56	1,20,960	42,000	7.56	3,17,840
12		24,000	7.561,81,440	18,000		7.56	1,36,400		

(*Contd.*)

(*Contd.*)

13	10,000	8.0	80,000				28,000	7.73	2,16,400
18				24,000	7.73	1,85,520	4,000	7.73	30,880
22	50,000	8.0	4,00,000				54,000	7.98	4,30,880
28				30,000	7.98	2,39,378	24,000	7.98	1,91,502
30				22,000	7.98	1,75,560	2,000	7.97	15,942

REVIEW QUESTIONS

RQ.3.1 Indicate whether the following statements are 'true' or 'false'.

(i) It is desired that the company should exercise same degree of control on all items of inventory.
(ii) ABC analysis classifies all the material in the organization into three categories, namely, X, Y and Z.
(iii) In ABC analysis, A category of materials warrants maximum attention followed by B and C category of materials.
(iv) Economic order quantity (EOQ) helps in determining the order size that should be placed in order to minimize the total costs associated with inventory management.
(v) EOQ assumes that the rate of consumption of inventory is constant over a period of time.
(vi) The higher is the EOQ, the higher are the ordering costs.
(vii) The lower is the EOQ, the lower are the carrying costs.
(viii) Re-order point signifies that level of inventory which is expected to be consumed during the lead time period.
(ix) Safety stock is the amount of inventory that needs to be maintained to meet the unforeseenable condition, say, increase in daily usage, increase in lead time, etc.
(x) The FIFO method assumes that materials received first are issued first.
(xi) Liquidation profits occur at the time of winding-up of a business firm

[Answers: (i) False, (ii) False, (iii) True, (iv) True, (v) True, (vi) False, (vii) True, (viii) True, (ix) True, (x) False, (xi) False.]

RQ.3.2 Fill in the blanks:

(i) _________ appropriate costing method when prices of raw materials are increasing.
(ii) _________ costing method serves the needs of correct income determination as well as correct asset measurement.
(iii) _________ is the formula used to determine EOQ.
(iv) In EOQ, average inventory is determined dividing _________.
(v) Minimum level = _________.
(vi) _________ form is the basis of issuing materials from the store.
(vii) Purchase of materials is initiated through _________.
(viii) _________ card is hung over the rack or shelf where material is stored.

[Answers: (i) LIFO, (ii) Modified LIFO method, (iii) ($\sqrt{2AB/C}$), (iv) Order size/2, (v) Reorder level — (Normal usage per day × Average delivery time in days), (vi) Material requisition, (vii) Purchase requisition form, (viii) Bin.]

RQ.3.3 Describe the functions and responsibilities of the purchasing department.

RQ.3.4 Identify the three forms commonly used to purchase goods. What items are usually included in them?

RQ.3.5 How is the cost of materials issued determined?

RQ.3.6 Write notes on:

(i) Periodic inventory system
(ii) Perpetual inventory system.

RQ.3.7 Compare LIFO with FIFO methods of inventory valuation

RQ.3.8 Explain with the help of a suitable example how current costs can be shown on both the income statement and the balance sheet under the LIFO inventory method.

RQ.3.9 "Management makes policy decision, at one time or another, regarding methods of inventory valuation. These decisions are important because they directly affect the way income will be computed." Discuss.

RQ.3.10 Explain and contrast the use of FIFO and LIFO methods of inventory pricing on income determination and asset valuation in a period of inflation. Illustrate your answer with respect to the following data:

January	1	Inventory	1,000 units at ₹3 each
	31	Purchases	1,200 units at ₹4 each
February	28	Purchases	1,100 units at ₹5 each
March	28	Purchases	1,400 units at ₹6 each
	31	Sales	4,000 units at ₹8 each

RQ.3.11 "LIFO is acceptable, because it makes use of historical cost; replacement cost is not acceptable because it adjusts cost figures to a value that is not related to the amount paid for them." Examine this point of view for dealing with the problem of changes in the purchasing power of money. How would you match the cost of non-current assets with current revenue?

RQ.3.12 Purchases of a certain product during March are set out below:

March	1	100 units @ ₹10.00
	12	100 units @ ₹9.80
	15	50 units @ ₹9.60
	20	100 units @ ₹9.40

Units sold during the month were as follows: March 10, 80 units; March 14, 100 units; March 30, 90 units. There were no opening inventories.

You are required to determine the cost of goods sold for March under three different valuation methods: FIFO, LIFO, and Weighted average cost.

RQ.3.13 In what manner do the various methods of inventory valuation affect reporting profits? Which method of inventory valuation would you recommend in an inflationary situation?

RQ.3.14 What are the methods of pricing materials issues? When do you advocate pricing the issues at cost price based on Last-In-First-Out method?

RQ.3.15 What is meant by the ABC inventory control system? On what key premise is this system based? What are its limitations?

RQ.3.16 Define economic order quantity (EOQ). How can it be computed? What are the limitations of the EOQ model?

RQ.3.17 In connection with inventory ordering and control, certain terms are basic. Explain the meaning of each of the following:

1. Economic order quantity
2. Re-order point
3. Lead time
4. Safety stock

RQ.3.18 Define JIT. Explain its features.

RQ.3.19 What are the benefits of JIT? What measures can managers take to control and evaluate JIT?

RQ.3.20 After the annual stock-taking you come to know of some significant discrepancies between book stock and physical stock. You gather the following information:

Items	Stock card (units)	Store ledger (units)	Physical check (units)	Cost/unit
A	600	600	560	₹60
B	380	380	385	40
C	750	780	720	10

What action should be taken to record the information shown above, assuming discrepancies are to be treated as abnormal?

RQ.3.21 From the following data, determine the EOQ.

(a) List price of product X is ₹800 per gross.
(b) 40 per cent trade discount is allowed on list price on purchases in gross lots.
(c) Freight cost is ₹20 per gross from the transport company to the factory premises.
(d) Annual usage or product X: 36 gross per year.
(e) Cost of placing an order is ₹10, the cost of receiving an order is ₹20.
(f) Carrying cost is 20 per cent of the effective purchase price of goods per year.
(g) Insurance and taxes are approximately 12 per cent of the net delivered cost of inventory.
 (i) Determine the total annual cost of inventory based on uniform order lot sizes of 1, 2, 3, 4, 5 and 6 gross of product X.
 (ii) Determine the minimum stock re-order point of product X, given the following: (a) working days: 240; (b) normal delivery time to receive an order: 20 working days from the date of purchase request is initiated; (c) safety stock: 1 gross.

RQ.3.22 JP Limited manufacturers of a special product, follows the policy of EOQ for one of its components. The component's details are as follows:

Purchase price per component, ₹200
Cost of an order, ₹100
Annual cost of carrying one unit in inventory, 10 per cent of purchase price
Annual usage of components, 4,000

The company has been offered a discount of 2 per cent on the price of the component provided the lot size is 2,000 components at a time. You are required to (i) compute the EOQ, (ii) advise whether the quantity discount offer can be accepted (assume that the inventory carrying cost does not vary according to discount policy) and (iii) would your advise differ if the company is offered 5 per cent discount on a single order?

RQ.3.23 ABC Ltd. has several items of inventory. The average number of each of these as well as their unit costs is listed below:

Item	Average inventory (units)	Average cost per unit	Item	Average inventory (units)	Average cost per unit
1	4,000	₹19.6	11	1,800	₹250
2	200	100	12	130	27
3	440	24	13	4,400	95
4	2,000	168	14	3,200	26
5	20	1,650	15	1,920	20
6	300	60	16	800	12
7	160	760	17	3,400	22
8	3,000	30	18	2,400	100
9	1,200	19	19	120	210
10	6,000	5	20	320	40

The company wishes to adopt an ABC inventory system. How should the items be classified into A, B and C?

RQ.3.24 The following information is available relating to the stockout of a firm:

Stockout (units)	*Number of times*
800	2
600	3
400	5
200	10
0	30
	50

The selling price of each unit is ₹200. The carrying costs are ₹19 per unit. The stockout costs are ₹50 per unit.

(i) If the firm wishes to never miss a sale, what should be its safety stock? What is the total cost associated with this level of safety stock? What are the associated costs with safety stock of 600, 400 and 200 units, respectively?

(ii) What is the optimal safety stock level?

RQ.3.25 The store ledger account for Material X in a manufacturing concern reveals the following data for the quarter ended September 30:

Date		*Receipts*		*Issues*	
		Quantity	*Price*	*Quantity*	*Price*
July 1	Balance b/d	1,600	₹20	—	—
9		3,000	22	—	—
13		—	—	1,200	₹25,560
August 5		—	—	900	19,170
17		3,600	24	—	—
24		—	—	1,800	41,220
September 11		2,500	25	—	—
27		—	—	2,100	49,710
29		—	—	700	16,560

Physical verification on September 30 revealed an actual stock of 3,800 units. You are required to:

(a) Indicate the method of pricing employed in the above.

(b) Complete the above account by making entries you would consider necessary including adjustments, if any, and giving explanations for such adjustments.

ANSWERS

[Comprehensive solutions to all numerical review questions are available on the companion website: http://www.mhhe.com/khan_jain_cost2e]

RQ.3.20 For items A and C, there is shortage of ₹3,000. For item B, there is abnormal gain of ₹200. These amounts will be transferred to costing profit and loss account.

RQ.3.21 **(i)** EOQ 4 gross (as purchases are allowed in gross lots) Annual cost of inventory ₹1,136 (1 gross), ₹652 (2 gross), ₹528 (3 gross), ₹494 (4 gross), ₹496 (5 gross), ₹516 (6 gross)
(ii) 4 gross

RQ.3.22 **(i)** 200 units
(ii) Quantity discount offer of 2 per cent should be accepted
(iii) Advised to avail 5 per cent trade discount.

RQ.3.23 Items 11, 13, 4, 18 are to be classified as A category (% value 68.24). Items 7, 8, 14, 1 are to be classified as B category (% value 21.17). The remaining items are to be classified as C category (% value 10.56).

RQ.3.24 **(i)** 800 units safety stock (costs are ₹15,200); 600 units (₹11,800), 400 units (₹9,000), 200 units (₹7,200) **(ii)** 200 units

RQ.3.25 **(a)** weighted average cost method **(b)** closing stock: 3,800 units @ ₹23.7 = ₹90,060; shortage of 200 units to be charged at ₹23.7 per unit.

4

Chapter

Costing and Control of Labour

Learning Objectives

1. Illustrate accounting for labour in terms of time-keeping, computation of payroll and allocation of payroll
2. Discuss special problems relating to accounting for labour in terms of taxes, fringe benefits, shift premiums, overtime, idle time and minimum guaranteed wages and incentive plans
3. Explain labour turnover in terms of its measurement, causes, costs and their treatment
4. Examine two interrelated efficiency rating procedures, that is, job evaluation and merit rating.

INTRODUCTION

Manufacturing is a process by which raw materials are converted into finished products. The two elements of conversion costs are direct labour, and factory overheads. If the manufacturing process is labour-intensive, labour costs constitute a significant component in the conversion process. This chapter explores the costing and control of labour. The costing and control of factory overheads follow in Chapter 5.

The compensation paid to the employees engaged in production related activities represents factory labour cost. The principal labour cost is *wages* paid to production workers made on hourly, daily, monthly, or price work basis. Included in labour costs are not only the regular earnings of the workers but also supplementary costs such as pensions, vocation and holiday pays, insurance benefits and other fringe benefit costs. Labour costs are direct or indirect.

Direct labour cost consists of the wages paid to labourers who work on a product directly, either manually or using a machine. It comprises wages which can be identified with, and allocated to, cost units. Direct labour, in other words, is the labour that: **(i)** Is directly involved in the production of a finished product, **(ii)** Can be easily traced to a product, and **(iii)** Represents a major labour cost of manufacturing that product.[1] Examples are assembly-line workers, machine operators, moulders, samplers, and finishers.

Indirect labour is a factory labour which is not engaged in production. It is not directly traceable to a product. It cannot be allocated but can be apportioned to/absorbed by cost centres/units. Examples of indirect labour who are indirectly related to production are product designers, job supervisors, product inspectors, and so on. Indirect labour is included in factory overhead cost.

Section 1 illustrates accounting for labour. Some problems relating to accounting for labour and labour turnover are discussed in Sections 2 and 3 respectively. The efficiency rating procedures, namely, job evaluation and merit rating are briefly examined in Section 4. The main points are summarised in the last Section.

ACCOUNTING FOR LABOUR

Accounting for labour by a manufacturing organisation usually involves three activities: **(i)** Timekeeping, **(ii)** Computation of total payroll (wages), and **(iii)** Allocation of total payroll costs.

Timekeeping

The timekeeping function involves two major activities in labour costing and control: **(i)** It accumulates the total number of hours worked by each worker so as to calculate his earnings and **(ii)** It determines how the labour-hours were spent so that proper distribution can be made in the cost records.

Timekeeping is usually centred in a separate time-keeping section of the personnel department. In small plants, however, timekeeping is mostly taken care of by each department head or, in some cases, by the workers themselves. The two source-documents commonly used in time keeping are: **(a)** Time or clock card and **(b)** Labour job ticket.

Time/Clock Card It is inserted in a time clock by the workers several times each day, that is: **(i)** Upon arrival, **(ii)** Going for lunch, **(iii)** Taking a break, and **(iv)** Leaving for the day. This provides a reliable source for computing and recording total payroll costs. Figure 4.1 shows a time card.

Time Card

Employee name....................
Employee/clock number............................
Shift............................

Department.............................
Week...........................

Day	Regular (time)				Overtime		Hours	
	In	Out	In	Out	In	Out	Regular	Overtime
						Total		

Figure 4.1 *Time Card*

Labour Job Tickets They are prepared daily by workers for each job worked on. They indicate the number of hours worked, a description of the work performed and the workers' wage rate (inserted by the payroll department). The total of the labour cost and hours for different jobs as shown on labour job tickets should equal the total labour cost and labour-hours for the period as shown on time cards. Figure 4.2 shows a labour job ticket.

Labour Job Ticket

Employee............................ Nature of work........................
Shift................................ Units completed........................
Job number................................ Department........................
Date................................

Time started	Time stopped	Hours worked	Rate	Amount

Approved by............

Figure 4.2 *Labour Job Payroll*

Computation of Total Payroll

The payroll department computes the total payroll including the gross amount earned and the net amount payable to employees after deduction of taxes and so on. It distributes the payroll and maintains records of employees' earnings, wage rate and job classification. The procedure is that the time cards are entered on the payroll sheet/summary. Figure 4.3 shows a payroll sheet. It forms the basis for the preparation of payroll vouchers authorising disbursements for the net amount payable to workers.

Payroll Sheet

Week.......

Employee	Hours worked	Rate	Gross pay	Deduction	Net pay

Figure 4.3 *Payroll Summary*

Allocation of Payroll Costs

On the basis of the time cards and job tickets, the cost accounting departments allocate the total payroll costs to individual jobs/departments/products. Alternatively, the payroll department itself prepares the allocation and sends it to cost accounting department for accounting in the form of appropriate journal entries. The total payroll cost must equal the sum of labour costs allocated to the individual jobs/departments/products.

Journal Entries to Record Labour Costs Payrolls are generally prepared weekly, fortnightly or monthly. Gross wages for an individual worker are determined by multiplying the hours shown on time cards by the hourly rate, plus any bonus or overtime. The payroll and related liabilities for deductions are journalised for each payroll period. The employee payroll expenses and payroll cost distribution are usually journalised at the end of the month. The basic journal entries to record factory labour costs are as follows:

(A) To record the payroll:

Work-in-process Inventory (direct labour)	Dr
Factory Overhead Control (indirect labour)	Dr
To Payroll Payable	

(B) To record deductions and payment of payroll (wages):	
Payroll Payable	Dr
To Employee Deductions Payable	
To Cash (to employees)	
(C) To record fringe benefits costs (pension, insurance, and so on):	
Factory Overhead Control	Dr
To Employee Benefits Payable	

SPECIAL PROBLEMS RELATING TO ACCOUNTING FOR LABOUR

The accounting for labour involves special problems that are not encountered in the accounting for materials. The problem areas discussed in this section are:

- Workers/employees taxes
- Employer taxes and fringe benefits
- Shifts premiums
- Overtime
- Idle time
- Minimum guaranteed wages and incentive plans.

Workers Taxes

Employers are required to deduct income taxes as well as social security payments, such as provident fund/pension contributions, which are remitted to government/social security organisations on a monthly/quarterly basis.

Fringe Benefit Costs

Employers are required to pay a matching contribution towards provident/pension funds of workers. They also bear the cost of workman's compensation insurance to provide funds to employees who are injured on the job.

EXAMPLE 4.1

Journalise the following payroll cost for the week ending April 15:

Factory payroll:		
Direct labour-Job 10	₹1,80,000	
Indirect labour	1,44,000	₹3,24,000
Other payroll:		
Salesmen's salaries	1,45,800	
Administrative salaries	70,200	2,16,000
Gross payroll		5,40,000
Social security contribution payable (employees contribution)		37,800
Social security contributions payable (employers contribution)		37,800
Income-tax deducted at source		1,35,000
Employees pension fund (paid by employer)		39,960

SOLUTION

Assuming all employers contribution and fringe benefits are recorded on a weekly basis, the following journal entries would be made on April 15:

(a) To record the payroll:			
Work-in-process Inventory—Job 10	Dr	₹1,80,000	
Factory Overhead Control (indirect labour)	Dr	1,44,000	
Selling Expenses Control	Dr	1,45,800	
Administrative Expenses Control	Dr	70,020	
To Payroll Payable			₹5,40,000
(b) To record employee taxes and pay the payroll:			
Payroll Payable	Dr	₹5,40,000	
To Employee Income Taxes Payable			₹1,35,000
To Employee Social Security Contribution Payable			37,800
To Cash (to employees – residual balance)			3,67,200
(c) To record employer contribution and fringe benefit costs:			
Factory Overhead Control (₹3,24,000 × 14.4 %*)	Dr	₹46,656	
Selling Expenses Control (₹1,45,800 × 14.4%)	Dr	20,995	
Administrative Expenses Control (₹70,200 × 14.4%)	Dr	10,109	
To Employer Social Security Contribution payable			₹37,800
To Employers Pension Fund			39,960
(d) To pay on a periodic basis all taxes/contribution and fringe benefit liabilities:			
Employee Income Taxes Payable	Dr	₹1,35,000	
Employee Social Security Contribution Payable	Dr	37,800	
Employer Social Security Contribution Payable	Dr	37,800	
Employer Pension Fund Contribution Payable	Dr	39,960	
To Cash/Bank			₹2,50,560

* (₹37,800 + ₹39,960)/₹5,40,000 = 14.4%

Shift Premiums

The shift premium/differential refers to the payment of higher hourly rates for working in less desirable evening/night shift(s). It is charged to factory overhead control rather than work-in-process, and spread over all units produced because they are not caused by specific units. If day shift rate is ₹65 per hour and the night shift rate for the same job is ₹70, for a worker working 50-hours week in the night shift, the entry would be:

Shift premium is the payment of higher hourly rates for working in less desirable (night) shifts.

Work-in-process Inventory (50 hours × ₹65)	Dr	₹3,250	
Factory Overhead Control-Shift Premium (50 hours × ₹5/hour)	Dr	250	
To Payroll Payable (50 hours × ₹70/hour)			₹3,500

Overtime Premium

Regular earnings represent the total hours worked, including overtime hours multiplied by the regular pay rate. But a higher rate may be paid for overtime work. This is called overtime premium and represents the overtime hours multiplied by the premium rate. The premium rate is usually a fraction of the regular rate.

Accounting Treatment Depending on the underlying cause of overtime, overtime premium is treated in three ways when overtime results from: **(i)** Random scheduling of jobs, **(ii)** Requirements of a specific job, and **(iii)** Negligence or poor workmanship.

Random Scheduling of Jobs Overtime premium should be treated like shift premium and charged to factory overhead control. The entry to record overtime premium is:

Work-in-process Inventory—Job No. (Total hours worked × Normal hourly rate) Dr
Factory Overhead Control-Overtime Premium (Overtime hours × Overtime premium rate) Dr
To Payroll Payable

Requirements of a Specific Job The overtime premium should be charged to the specific job that caused the overtime. If a rush order caused overtime for which the customer agrees to pay as a special service, the entry would be:

Work-in-process—Job No. Dr
To Payroll Payable

Negligence/Poor Workmanship The overtime premium should be charged to as a loss and the entry would be:

Work-in-process Inventory—Job No. Dr
Loss from Overtime Premium Dr
To Payroll Payable

The treatment accorded to overtime premium would determine action to be taken by management in planning and control of labour costs. The recording of loss, for example, would call for closer supervision/better on-the-job training.

Idle Time

Idle time results from payment when workers have no work.

When workers have no work to perform but are still paid for their time, idle time results. The accounting treatment from the point of view of labour cost control depends upon the reason for idle time. It could be normal or due to negligence/inefficiency.

If idle time is normal for the production process and is unavoidable, the cost of idle time is charged to factory overhead control and the entry is:

Work-in-process Inventory—Job No. (Hours worked × Rate per hour) Dr
Factory Overhead Control-Idle Time (Hours × Hourly rate) Dr
To Payroll Payable

If idle time is caused by negligence/inefficiency, it is charged to a loss account and the entry would be:

Work-in-process Inventory Dr
Loss from Idle Time Dr
To Payroll Payable

Minimum Guaranteed Wage and Incentive Plans

Under the piecework rate system of wage payment, employees earnings is equal to the number of units produced multiplied by the piecework rate. Several manufacturing organisations have a system of wage payment under which employees are paid a minimum guaranteed wage with a stipulation that they can earn more if they produce more. If the output multiplied by the piece rate results in an amount less than the guaranteed wage, the difference is charged to the factory overhead control; if the former exceeds the latter, it should be charged to the work-in-process inventory. Thus, under this system of wage payment, an average employee is expected to earn not only the minimum wage but a bonus as well. Employees who produce more than a specified number of units (piecework) receive a bonus.

The incentive (bonus) plans vary in format and application. They fall into two categories: **(1)** Differential piece rates schemes and **(2)** Premium bonus plans.

Differential Piece Rates Schemes Included in this category are **(i)** Taylor Differential Piece Rate System, **(ii)** Merrick Differential Piece Rate System, and **(iii)** Gantt Task and Bonus Plan.

Taylors Differential Piece Rate System Under this system, there are two price wage rates: a low rate for output below standard performance, and a higher rate applicable to workers whose production is above standard. The efficiency of a worker may be determined as a percentage of: **(i)** Time allowed for a job to the actual time taken or **(ii)** Actual output to standard output within a specified time. For example, if standard time allowed for a job is 15 hours, while the actual time taken is 20 hours, workers efficiency/performance is (15 × 100) ÷ 20 = 75 per cent. Similarly, if standard output is 5 units per hour, and the actual output is 6 units per hour, efficiency = (6 × 100) ÷ 5 = 120 per cent. The merit of this system is that it provides a strong incentive to the efficient workers. The slow worker is penalised while the efficient worker is duly rewarded.

EXAMPLE 4.2

The standard production in Hypothetical Ltd is 20 units per hour. For the first week of April, a workers' record (working 8 hours per day) is as follows:

Monday	140 units	Wednesday	175 units
Tuesday	160 units	Thursday	180 units
Friday	200 units		

Compute the workers daily earnings. The effective hourly rate and the labour cost per unit under the Taylor Differential Piece Rate System with piece rates are as specified below: ₹2 per unit below standard; ₹2.40 at standard and upto 20 per cent above standard; and ₹3 per unit when daily output exceeds 20 per cent above standard.

SOLUTION

Taylor Differential Piece Rate System

Days	Standard output	Actual output	Efficiency (%)	Piece rate ₹2	Piece rate ₹2.40	Piece rate ₹3	Effective hourly rate	Cost per unit
Monday	160	140	87.5	280	—	—	₹35.0	₹2
Tuesday	160	160	100.0	—	384	—	48.0	2.4
Wednesday	160	175	109.4	—	420		52.5	2.4
Thursday	160	180	112.5	—	432		54.0	2.4
Friday	160	200	125.0	—	—	600	75.0	3.0

EXAMPLE 4.3

Assuming the following facts, calculate the earnings of workers under Taylor Differential Piece Rate System:

- Standard time per piece; 20 minutes
- Normal rate per hour, ₹27
- In a 9-hour day, A produces 25 units and B produces 30 units.
- Differential to be applied: 80 per cent of piece rate below standard and 120 per cent above standard.

SOLUTION

Efficiency of A = 92.6 per cent = (25/27) × 100
B = 111 per cent = (30/27) × 100

Piece rate of A = 0.80 × ₹9 = ₹7.2
B = 1.2 × ₹9 = ₹10.8

Earnings of A = 25 × ₹7.2 = ₹180

B = 30 × ₹10.8 = ₹324

Merrick Differential Piece Rate System This is a modification of/improvement over the Taylor Differential Piece Rate System. It uses three piece rates. Normal piece rates are paid when output is upto 83 per cent of the standard output; 110 per cent of normal piece rates are paid for output between 83 - 100 per cent; and 120 per cent is paid if the output exceeds 100 per cent. While it rewards efficient workers, it does not penalise less efficient workers as minimum upto 83 per cent could possibly be achievable by all workers.

EXAMPLE 4.4

From the under-mentioned facts, calculate the earnings of A, B and C under the Merrick Differential Piece Rate System:

- Normal piece rate (upto 83 per cent of high task output), ₹30 per unit;
- High task, 40 units per week
- Output for the week: A, 32 units; B, 37 units; C, 42 units.

SOLUTION

Efficiency of A = (32 × 100) ÷ 40 = 80 per cent
B = (37 × 100) ÷ 40 = 92.5 per cent
C = (42 × 100) ÷ 40 = 105 per cent

Wages of A = (32 × ₹30) = ₹960
B = (37 × ₹30 × 110) ÷ 100 = ₹1,221
C = (42 × ₹30 × 120) ÷ 100 = ₹1,516

Gantt Task and Bonus Plan This system is a mixture of a guaranteed time rate with a bonus and piece rate plan using the differential principle. When output is below standard/high task (efficiency below 100 per cent), time rate is guaranteed. In case of output at standard level (100 per cent efficiency), bonus @ 20 per cent on time rate is payable, while higher price rate on whole output is paid if output exceeds standards. At the same time, it provides security/encouragement to less efficient workers.

EXAMPLE 4.5

Calculate the wages of workers A, B and C under the Gantt Task and Bonus Plan from the facts given below:

- Time rate, ₹30 per hour for 40-hours week
- Standard production, 40 units per week
- Piece rate above standard output, ₹36
- Weekly output: A, 32 units; B, 37 units; C, 42 units

SOLUTION

Wages: A = ₹1,200 (40 × ₹30): output below standard (32 units)
B = ₹1,200 (40 × ₹30): output below standard (37 units)
C = ₹1,512 (42 × ₹36): output above standard (42 units)

Premium Bonus Plans Under the time rate basis of wage payment, additional production beyond normal level benefits the employers, whereas, with piece rate system the benefit goes to the employees. Bonus plans are a mid-way in the sense that savings are shared between them. The plans included in premium bonus plans are Halsey Premium Plan, Halsey-Weir Plan, Rowan Plan, and Bedaux Point Plan.

Halsey Premium Plan Under this system, time rate is guaranteed and if a worker completes his jobs within/in more than standard time, he is paid the standard rate. But if the job is completed in less than the standard time, he is given wages for actual hours taken plus bonus equal to normally 50 per cent of the wages of the time saved; the remaining portion represents the share of the employer. The earning of a worker is computed according to Equation 4.1.

Workers earnings = (Time taken × Rate) + [0.50 × (Standard time – Time taken) × Rate] (4.1)

Halsey-Weir Premium Plan This plan is similar to the Halsey Plan with the only difference that the bonus/premium is usually applied on 33.33: 66.67 basis.

EXAMPLE 4.6

The standard time to complete the work is 10 hours. The wage rate is ₹40 per hour. If the job is completed in 8 hours, compute the earnings per hour using Halsey Premium and Halsey-Weir Premium plans.

SOLUTION

Computation of Wages and Earnings per Hour

Halsey premium			*Halsey-Weir plan*	
Total wages	(8 × ₹40) + 0.50 × (2 × ₹40) =	₹360	(8 × ₹40) + 0.333 × (2 × ₹40) =	₹346.67
Earnings per hour	(₹360 ÷ 8) =	45	(₹346.67 ÷ 8) =	43.33

Rowan Plan This scheme is similar to the Halsey Plan in that a standard time is fixed for the completion of a job and bonus is paid in respect of the time saved. But a ceiling is applied to the size of the bonus. The bonus hours are computed as a proportion of the time taken, while time saved bears to the time allowed and is paid for at time rate.

The bonus = (Time taken ÷ Time allowed) × Time saved × Time rate (4.2)

The earnings are calculated according to Equation 4.3.

Earnings (Time taken × Rate per hour) + [(Standard time – Time taken) ÷ Standard time] × Time taken × Rate per hour (4.3)

EXAMPLE 4.7

From the undermentioned facts, calculate bonus, total earnings, and rate of earnings per hour under the Rowan plan:

- Time allowed, 6 hours
- Time taken, 4 hours
- Hourly rate, ₹30

SOLUTION

Bonus = [(4/6) × 2 × ₹30 = ₹40*

Earnings = (4 × ₹30) + ₹40* or 40* [(6 – 4) ÷ 6] × 4 × ₹30

Earnings per hour = ₹160 ÷ 4 = ₹40

Bedaux Point Plan Under this plan, a guaranteed hourly rate is paid until standard production is achieved, and a premium or additional wage is paid for units in excess of standard. Instead of being paid as piece rate, an hour's production is converted into points by dividing a standard hour's production in units into 60 minutes. A minute of standard time is termed as Bedaux Point (B), 60 units making one hour's work and the number of B points determined accordingly for each job. For instance, if 10 units are standard, each unit is 6 points (B). At standard performance, a worker produces a point per minute and for the first 60 points produced in an hour, he gets the hourly rate. For additional production, a bonus of 75 per cent of the rate is given to the workers; the remaining 25 per cent is paid to the supervisory staff and other indirect labour. Thus, under the Bedaux Point Plan, the guaranteed daily wage would apply for production upto standard. In excess of 60 points in an hour, bonus is paid equal to 75 per cent.

EXAMPLE 4.8

From the information given below, compute bonus and total earnings according to Bedaux Point Plan:

Standard production for 8 hours daily = 100 (number)
Actual production for hours daily = 120 (number)
Hourly wage rate = ₹30

SOLUTION

Standard points = 8 × 60 = 480 (B)
Actual points = (120 × 480) ÷ 100 = 576 (B)
Points saved = 576 – 480 = 96 × 0.75 = 72
Bonus earned = (72 × ₹30) ÷ 60 = ₹36
Total earnings = (8 × ₹30) + ₹36 (bonus) = ₹276

While incentive plans of wage payments are intended to improve labour performance/efficiency, their possible negative effects must be examined by management. They involve increased clerical cost due to additional record keeping. Moreover, quantity may become the main consideration to the detriment of quality of production. Therefore, incentive plans should be introduced only if increase in total payroll costs is offset by increase in production/sales, as well as reduction in labour cost per unit and/or labour-related costs per unit.

Labour turnover is the rate at which employees leave employment at a factory.

LABOUR TURNOVER

Labour turnover may be defined as the rate of change in the composition of the labour force in an organisation. It is the rate at which employees leave employment at a factory. Labour turnover has important implications for labour cost, efficiency and productivity. The objective should be to keep labour turnover at minimal.

Measurement of Labour Turnover

There are three methods to measure labour turnover: (i) Separation method, (ii) Flux/Separation-cum-replacement method, and (iii) Replacement/Net labour turnover method.

Separation Method Labour turnover is measured according to Equation 4.4.

Labour turnover = [(Employees leaving (number of separations) in a period ÷ Average number of workers employed)] × 100 (4.4)

Flux or Separation-cum-Replacement Method Labour turnover is measured according to Equation 4.5.

Labour turnover = [(Number of separations (employees leaving) + Number of replacements (new employees, excluding those recruited for expansion)] ÷ (Average number employed) × 100 (4.5)

Replacement/Net Labour Turnover Method Labour turnover is computed according to Equation 4.6.

Labour turnover = (Number of workers replaced in a period ÷ Average number employed) × 100 (4.6)

EXAMPLE 4.9

The information relating to the workforce of Premier Industries Ltd during the latest month is listed below:

- Number of workers in the beginning and end of the month 19,000 and 21,000 respectively;
- During the month workers discharged, 600 and left on their own, 200;
- During the month workers engaged, 2,000 out of which workers appointed against vacancies caused by separation, 400 and on account of expansion, the remaining 1,600.

Compute the monthly labour turnover rate and the equivalent annual rates under the three methods of labour turnover measurement.

SOLUTION

1. Separation Method:
   Labour turnover rate = (800 × 100) ÷ 20,000* = 4 per cent *(19,000 + 21,000) ÷ 2
   Equivalent annual turnover = (4 × 365 days) ÷ 30 days = 48.67 per cent
2. Flux Method:
   Labour turnover rate = (800 + 400) ÷ 20,000* = 6 per cent
   Equivalent annual rate = (6 × 365) ÷ 30 = 73 per cent
3. Replacement Method:
   Labour turnover rate = (400 × 100) ÷ 20,000* = 2 per cent
   Equivalent annual rate = (2 × 365) ÷ 30 = 24.33 per cent

Of the three, separation method is a better indicator of the labour turnover in a factory organisation.

Causes of Labour Turnover

The causes of labour turnover may be avoidable and unavoidable.

Avoidable Causes Such causes are avoidable in the sense that with suitable measures they can be eliminated. They include:

- Low wage rates and earnings
- Dissatisfaction with job/Unsatisfactory working conditions
- Unsatisfactory relationship with supervisors/fellow workers
- Lack of conveyance, accommodations, medical, educational, recreational and housing facilities
- Unfair methods of promotion/lack of promotional avenues
- Seasonal nature of job.

Unavoidable Causes They include

- Change for better jobs
- Retirement and death
- Domestic/family responsibilities/constraints
- Dismissal/discharge due to insubordination, negligence, inefficiency and
- Retrenchment/lay off.

Costs of Labour Turnover

The cost of labour turnover consists of two elements; preventive and replacements.

Preventive Costs This include all those costs which are incurred to keep the labour turnover rate as low as possible to prevent workers from leaving the organisation and keeping them satisfied. High preventive costs would result in low labour turnover. The preventive costs, *inter alia*, include costs of providing to workers/families:

- Medical, housing and recreational facilities

- Benefits like pension, gratuity and bonus
- Educational facilities to children of employees
- Good working conditions
- Other welfare facilities.

Replacement Costs These costs arise on account of labour turnover and consequent replacement of employees. They include costs which are incurred for recruitment/training of new workers as well as those which result from wastages, losses, lower production due to less competent and inexperienced new employees:

Personnel Department Expenses This is for recruitment/training new employees and loss of production time during training period.

Inefficiency of New Workers This has an adverse effect on production.

Delay in Recruitment of New Workers Recruitment of new workers is time-consuming, necessitating overtime payment to existing employees and the consequent burden on the organisation.

Cost of Abnormal Breakages This pertains to tools, equipments by new/inexperienced workers as well as machine break-down and the consequent interruption of production.

Cost of Spoilage and Defectives More spoilage/defectives are likely to occur due to mishandling/carelessness of new workers. The greater the spoilage/defectives, the larger is the production costs.

The replacement cost of labour turnover can be computed in two ways: **(i)** By separation and replacement method and **(ii)** By profit forgone method.

Separation and Replacement Method Under this method, the specific costs associated with separation (turnover) and replacements (recruitment/training) are accumulated. The separation costs include terminal pay, gratuity and other benefits. The replacement costs include costs associated with selection/training of new employees. Another relevant cost is the lost contribution in terms of sales less additional variable cost due to labour cost of lost hours due to replacement, and increase in material and variable overhead due to increase in potential sales.

EXAMPLE 4.10

From the information given below, calculate the cost of labour turnover, using separation and replacement method:

Income Statement for the Year Ended March 31, Current Year

Sales		₹40,00,000
Variable costs:		
Materials	₹10,00,000	
Direct labour	8,00,000	
Variable overheads	8,00,000	26,00,000
Contribution		14,00,000
Less fixed overheads		9,00,000
Profit before tax		5,00,000

The direct labour-hours worked during the period were 20,300 of which 500 hours pertained to new workers on training. Only 40 per cent of trainee's time was productive. As replacement of workers left was delayed for some time, 600 productive hours were lost.

The company incurred direct costs as a consequence of separation/replacements detailed below: Separation, ₹40,000; Selection, ₹60,000, and Training, ₹1,00,000.

SOLUTION

Cost of Labour Turnover

Direct labour-hours worked		20,300
Less unproductive time of new workers (0.60 × 500)		300
Productive hours		20,000
Loss labour hours:		
Replacement	600	
Training	300	900
Unit sales per productive labour hour (₹40,00,000 ÷ 20,000)		₹200
(i) Loss of potential sales (900 hours × ₹200)		1,80,000
Direct labour cost per hour worked (₹8,00,000 ÷ 20,300)		39.41
(ii) Increase in direct labour cost of lost hours due to replacement (600* hours × ₹39.41)		23,646
* (300 hours already included while calculating hourly rate)		
(iii) Increase in material and variable overheads due to increase in potential sales (₹18,00,000 ÷ ₹40,00,000) × ₹1,80,000		81,000
(iv) Total increase in cost [(ii) + (iii)]		1,04,646
Contribution foregone [(i) – (iv)]		75,354
Add separation, selection and training costs (₹40,000 + ₹60,000 + ₹1,00,000)		2,00,000
Cost of labour turnover		2,75,354

Profit Forgone Method According to this method, the cost of labour turnover equals the profit foregone in terms of the difference between the actual profit for the period and the estimated profit that would have been earned had no labour turnover occurred. Alternatively, contribution lost due to labour turnover and costs incurred consequent on labour turnover equal profit foregone.

EXAMPLE 4.11

The sales of Premier Industries Ltd in the previous year aggregated ₹1,66,06,600 and the P/V (profit – volume) ratio was 20 per cent. The actual hours worked was 4.45 lakh. The actual direct hours included 30,000 hours attributable to training of new recruits of which 50 per cent represented unproductive hours. As a result of delays in filling vacancies caused by labour turnover, 1,00,000 potentially productive hours were lost.

The cost associated with labour turnover were: **(i)** Settlement cost due to leaving, ₹87,640; **(ii)** Recruitments cost, ₹53,480; **(iii)** Selection costs, ₹25,500, and **(iv)** Training costs, ₹60,980.

Assuming the potential production loss consequent upon labour turnover could have been sold at the prevailing price, find the profit foregone in the previous year on account of labour turnover.

SOLUTION

Determination of Profit Foregone

Contribution foregone (working note)	₹7,72,400
Settlement cost	87,640
Recruitment cost	53,480
Selection cost	25,500
Training cost	60,980
Total	10,00,000

WORKING NOTE

Determination of contribution foregone:

Actual hours worked	4,45,000
Less unproductive hours (0.50 × 30,000)	15,000
Actual productive hours	4,30,000
Sales lost (₹1,66,06,600 ÷ 4,30,000 hours) × 1,00,000 hours	₹38,62,000
Contribution lost (₹38,62,000 × 0.20, P/V ratio)	7,72,400

Treatment of Labour Turnover Costs Labour turnover costs are usually treated as factory overhead. The preventive costs are distributed among different departments on the basis of workers in each department. The replacement costs are shared by the departments affected by the labour turnover on the basis of number of workers replaced.

Control of Labour Turnover Costs: Labour Turnover Report This report is prepared by the personnel department periodically with a view to minimising labour turnover costs by taking appropriate measures. It contains turnover statistics, turnover rate and reasons for turnover divided into avoidable and unavoidable. It shows whether workers are leaving through dissatisfaction or are being dismissed because of unsuitability/bad relations. A specimen of labour turnover report is given in Figure 4.4.

Labour Turnover Report Date..............

	Month	Cumulative since beginning of year	Last year
Number of employees			
Employees leaving			
Labour turnover (%)			
Reasons for leaving:			
Avoidable:			
....			
....			
....			
Total			
Percentage			
Unavoidable:			
....			
....			
....			
Total			
Percentage			
Number of replacements			
Percentages			

Figure 4.4 *Labour Turnover Report*

EFFICIENCY RATING PROCEDURES

This Section examines the two interrelated efficiency rating procedures, namely, job evaluation and merit rating.

Job Evaluation

Meaning Job evaluation is the systematic technique of analysis and assessment of jobs to ascertain their comparative labour/job worth. Every job has its own characteristics. Depending upon these, jobs demand varying degrees of qualifications, skill, experience and soon on the part of the operators performing them. For instance, some jobs may require physical ability, others may need a high degree of mental ability, yet others may need skill, experience and high educational qualification. Thus, job evaluation is the process of review, analysis and systematic classification of a job in accordance with its characteristics in terms of the varying factors it demands from the employees/workers. In other words, it grades all jobs with reference to their main characteristics so that the relative merit of each job in terms of work value/worth may be ascertained. Its focus is on the job and it has nothing to do with the rating of the employees.

Job evaluation is the systematic technique of analysis and assessment of jobs to ascertain their comparative worth.

Objectives/Importance/Uses The uses to which job evaluation may be put to, and the advantages acccruing from it, are specified below:

Fixation of Wage Structure The main aim/utility of job evaluation relates to fixation of a systematic, rational and equitable basis for differential wages/salaries in an organization. Fixation of wages on an impersonal basis, solely based on the job requirements, eliminates personal biases and errors. This results in simplified and balanced wage structure which are fair both for the employees as well as the employers. A related dimension is that anomalies in the wages of employees can be identified by comparing the actual wages *vis-a-vis* the job evaluation.

Help in Recruitment of New Workers The job evaluation technique generates useful information for recruitment of new workers. Since the exact requirement of each job is known, the personnel department can select only those workers who satisfy the requirements of the specific job. Likewise, promotions, transfers and so on can be made on a rational basis for different employees in the organisation.

Improvement of Labour Relations Job evaluation improves labour relations as it obviates scope for unfairness, favouritism, nepotism and so on.

Methods of Evaluation The job evaluation methods may be **(i)** qualitative or **(ii)** quantitative. The qualitative/non-qualitative methods include **(1)** job ranking method, and **(2)** job grading/grade description method. The quantitative method is primarily a point rating method.

Job Ranking Method According to this method, different jobs are evaluated and ranked on the basis of relative difficulty in performance and responsibilities. As a first step, all jobs are properly studied in terms of job requirements, qualification, responsibilities, hazards, working conditions and so on. On the basis of comparison of the job with the same components of another job, jobs are ranked in ascending/descending order. It is a method of informal arrangement of a hierarchy of jobs from the lowest to the highest or *vice versa*. After ranking, each job is put in ranked scale of jobs.

Job ranking is the evaluation and ranking of jobs on the basis of relative difficulty in performance and responsibilities

The ranking method of job evaluation is simple to use, easy to understand and less costly to operate. But it is less accurate. It could be usefully employed by small organisations only where jobs are few and well defined. Where jobs are complex in large organisations, the usefulness of this method would be rather limited.

Job grading is ranking of jobs on the basis of predetermined standard/scale.

Job Grading/Grade Description Method This method is a variant of the job ranking method. It is also an improvement over the ranking method. Under the job grading method, a predetermined/hypothetical scale/standard of job values is determined on the basis of education, experience, skill, responsibilities and so on and each job is placed in suitable grades/classes. The jobs within each grade are approximately of similar nature. The method is simple, less costly and administratively feasible. It attempts applying a rational basis for grading jobs. But like the ranking method, it is less accurate and is not suitable for large/complex organisations.

Factor ranking is the analysis of job factors such as skills, efforts, responsibilities and working conditions.

Point/Factor Ranking Method According to this method, each job is analysed in terms of job factors consisting of elements like basic skills and knowledge, mental and physical efforts, responsibilities, working conditions and so on. As a first step, depending upon its nature and the extent to which it requires the various factors for its performance, each job is assigned points/weightage. A job requiring a large number of these factors would rank high in the process of job evaluation compared to those requiring smaller number of these factors. Moreover, two dissimilar jobs may have the same gradation if each has the same number of points. An illustrative/list of characteristic which may be taken into account for job evaluation and hypothetical points allotted against each is summarised in Figure 4.5.

Basic Factors;		Main Factors:			
Background skill and knowledge	400	Education	100		
		Training	150		
		Experience	150	Sub-factors:	
				Education:	100
			400	Non-matriculate	10
				High School	20
				Intermediate	30
				Degree	40
					100
Skill and efforts	400	Mental:			
		Reasoning	100		
		Observation	60		
		Initiation	20		
		Physical:			
		Mascular	100		
		Stamina	100		
		Dexterity	20	Training:	75
			400		
Responsibilities	300	Degree of supervision	100		
		Responsibility for material	100		
		Safety for others	50		
		Confidential information	50		
			300		
Working condition	200	Hazard	60	Physical:	
		Risk and safety	80	Mascular:	
		Disagreeableness	60	High	50
			200	Medium	30
				Ordinary	20
		Total	1,300		100

Figure 4.5 *Job Characteristics/Factors*

The second step is to review the specification of a job, analyse it into various factors/characteristics and evaluate each job in terms of assigning points. This is illustrated below:

Job Factors

Job	*Background skill and knowledge*	*Skill and efforts required for job performance*	*Responsibility*	*Working conditions*	*Total point*
A	40	80	100	80	300
B	120	20	70	140	350
C	50	160	200	20	430
D	300	40	60	100	500
E	400	200	10	180	790

Finally, jobs are ranked in the order of points and are placed in a number of arbitrary grades for each of which wages scales/ranges of pay are fixed. The gradation/fixation of wages for the various grades are shown below:

Wages Scales/Grades

Points Value	*Grade*	*Pay Scale (per month)*
100-198	I	₹6,000-7,000
200-398	II	7,000-8,000
400-498	III	8,000-10,000
500-598	IV	10,000-12,000
600-898	V	12,000-13,800
900-1.098	VI	13,800-16,000
1,100-1,198	VII	16,000-20,000
1,200-1,300	VIII	20,000-24,000

This method is theoretically sound and objective but it is difficult to operate. The relative points/weights of different job factors need to be developed very carefully and in an objective manner.

Merit Rating

Meaning As a systematic method of determining the relative worth of employees, merit rating is the comparative appraisal of the individual merits of an employee. It is a technique to rate an employees' performance through some norms/standards. The factors/characteristics that are considered in merit appraisal of the employees are:

Merit rating is the comparative appraisal of the individual merit of an employee through some performance standards.

- Quantity of work done
- Quality of work done
- Sense of responsibility
- Initiative
- Reliability and integrity
- knowledge, skill, experience and aptitude for work
- Cooperation and discipline
- Sense of judgement
- Attendance and punctuality and so on.

Each of these factors is assigned a point rating/value and each employee is rated according to the extent of the point value he possesses. The employees may be ranked individually in order of the points they score. Alternatively, they may be arranged in groups according to their common ratings. The individual/group rating may also be expressed as a ratio of the normal/standard rating.

Comparison With Job Evaluation While job evaluation is the process of analysis and classification of jobs according to their characteristics, merit rating refers to the evaluation of the merits of employees and their classification into groups on that basis. Merit rating differs from job evaluation in several respects. In the first place, job evaluation is the assessment of the relative worth of jobs in an organisations; merit rating in the assessment of the relative worth of an employee with respect to a job. In other words, while job evaluation rates jobs, merit rating rates employees on their jobs. Secondly, job evaluation helps in establishing a rational wage/salary structure. In contrast, merit rating provides a scientific basis for determining fair wages for each employee based on his ability/competence and performance. Finally, job evaluation simplifies wage/salaries administration by rationalising and bringing uniformity in the wage/salary rates. But merit rating helps in determining a fair rate of pay for different employees on the basis of their relative performance.

Objectives The main objectives of merit rating are the following:

- To find out the suitability of an employee for a particular job
- To assess an employee's merit for promotion, grant of increment, payment of reward for good work and so on.
- To serve as a basis for incentive payment and for simplification of wage structure and
- To analyse the employee's defects/bring out their strength and special abilities.

Shortcomings/Limitations Merit rating improves labour relations, reduces labour turnover and stimulates competition among employees and, thus, contributes to increased production, improved productivity and so on. Nevertheless, it suffers from certain limitations/shortcomings. Being a matter of mostly opinion/subjective, the rating may be erroneous and may result in unrest/dissatisfaction among the employees. Moreover, raters may be influenced by past ratings of an employee. This may vitiate their judgement. The employee(s) may have improved in course of time. Further, irrelevant factors may be given prominence by the raters. For example, raters may be highly influenced by one specific/strong good/adverse factor. If merit rating is inaccurate/unreliable/subjective, it may not serve the intended purpose.

SUMMARY

- ➢ Labour is the physical/mental effort expended in the production of a product. Labour costs can be broken down into direct and indirect, based on the employees' relationship with the finished product. Total labour costs are based on elements other than just gross wages. The additional costs include bonus payments, vacation pay, pension costs and other fringe benefits including employees contribution to health, life and other insurance.
- ➢ The accounting for labour in a manufacturing organisation generally involves three activities: timekeeping, computation of total payroll and allocation of payroll costs. Journal entries to record the payroll (wages) payments and associated liabilities for amounts withheld are made for each period.
- ➢ The accounting for labour involves special problems that are not encountered in the accounting for materials. They are: taxes and fringe benefit costs, shift premiums, overtime, idle time, and minimum guaranteed wage and incentive plans. The incentive/bonus plans vary in format and applications. They fall into two categories: differential price rate schemes and premium bonus plans. Included in the first category are **(1)** Taylor Differential Piece Rate **(2)** Merrick Differential Piece Rate, and **(3)** Gantt Task and Bonus Plan.
- ➢ Under the Taylor Differential Piece Rate System, there are two piece wage rates: a low rate for output below standard performance and a higher rate applicable to workers where production is above standard. The efficiency of a worker may be determined as a percentage of **(i)** time allowed for a job to the actual time taken or **(ii)** actual output to standard output within a specified time.

- Merrick Differential Piece Rate System is a modification of/improvement over the Taylor Differential Piece Rate System. It uses three piece rates. Normal piece rates are paid when output is upto 83 per cent of the standard output; 110 per cent of normal piece rates are paid for output between 83–100 per cent; 120 per cent is paid if the output exceeds 100 per cent.
- Gantt Task and Bonus Plan is a mixture of a guaranteed time rate with a bonus and piece rate plan using the differential plan when output is below standard (efficiency below 100 per cent), time rate is guaranteed. In case of output at standard level (100 per cent efficiency) bonus at the rate of 20 per cent on time rate is payable while a higher piece rate on the whole output is paid if output exceeds standard.
- Under the time rate basis of wage payment, additional production beyond normal level benefits the employer(s); with piece rate system, the benefit goes to the employee(s). Bonus plans are a mid-way in the sense that the savings are shared between them. These plans include **(i)** Halsey/Halsey-Weir Plan and **(ii)** Rowan Plan.
- Under the Halsey Premium Plan the earnings and bonus of a worker is computed as below:
  Earnings = (Time taken × rate) + [0.50 × (Standard time – Time taken) × Rate]
  Bonus = [0.50 × (Standard time – Time taken) × Rate]
- Halsey-Weir Premium Plan is similar to Halsey Plan with the difference that the bonus/premium is usually applied on 33.33 : 66.67 basis.
- According to the Rowan Plan earnings and bonus are computed as below:]
  Workers earnings = (Time taken × Rate per hour) + [(Standard time – Time taken) ÷ Standard time] × Time taken × Rate Per hour
  Bonus = (Time taken ÷ Time allowed) × Time saved × Time rate
- Labour turnover is the rate at which employees leave employment. It has implications for labour cost. The objective should be to keep the labour turnover at minimal. Labour turnover can be measured in three ways: by Separation method, Flux method and Replacement method.
- According to the separation method, labour turnover = [Employees leaving (number of separations) in a period ÷ Average number of workers employed] × 100
- According to flux/separation-cum-replacement method, labour turnover = [(Number of employees leaving) + Number of employees joining/replacements against vacancies of those leaving (new employees) ÷ Average number employed)] × 100
- According to replacement/net labour turnover method, labour turnover = (Number of workers replaced in a period ÷ Average number employed) × 100
- The causes of labour turnover may be avoidable in the sense that with suitable measures they can be eliminated or unavoidable. The labour turnover cost consists of two elements, that is, preventive cost and replacement. The replacement can be computed in either of two ways: **(i)** Separation and replacement method and **(ii)** Profit forgone method.
- Under separation and replacement method, the specific costs associated with separation (turnover) and replacements (recruitment/training) are accumulated. The separation costs include terminal pay, gratuity and other benefits. The replacament costs include costs associated with selection/training of new employees. Another relevant cost is the lost contribution in terms of sales less additional variable cost due to labour cost of lost hours due to replacement, and increase in material and variable overhead costs due to increase in potential sales.
- According to profit foregone method, the cost of labour turnover equals the profit foregone in terms of the difference between the actual profit for the period and the estimated profit that would have been earned had no labour turnover occurred. Alternatively, contribution lost due to labour turnover and costs incurred consequent on labour turnover equal profit foregone.
- Labour turnover costs are usually treated as factory overhead. While the preventive costs are distributed among different departments, the replacements costs are shared by the department(s) affected by the labour turnover. The personnel department prepares a labour turnover report periodically to minimise turnover by taking appropriate measures.

- ➢ Job evaluation is the systematic technique of analysis and assessment of jobs to ascertain their comparative labour/job worth. It grades all jobs with reference to their main characteristics so that the relative merit of each job in terms of work value may be ascertained. Its focus is on jobs and it has nothing to do with the rating of the employees. The job evaluation methods are: **(i)** job ranking method, **(ii)** job grading/grade description method and **(iii)** point rating method.
- ➢ According to the job ranking method, different jobs are evaluated and ranked on the basis of relative difficulty in performance and responsibilities.
- ➢ Under the job grading method, a predetermined/hypothetical scale/standard of job value is determined on the basis of education, experience, skill, responsibilities and so on and each job is placed in suitable grade(s)/class(es).
- ➢ According to the point/factor ranking method, each job is analysed in terms of job factors consisting of elements like basic skills and knowledge, mental and physical efforts, responsibilities, working conditions and so on. Each job is assigned points/weightage.
- ➢ As a systematic method of determining the relative worth of employees, merit rating is the comparative appraisal of the individual merits of an employee. It rates an employees' performance through some norms/standards.

REFERENCE

1. Polimeni, Fabbozi and Adelberg, *op. cit.*, p. 100.

SOLVED PROBLEMS

P. 4.1 Calculate the earnings of a worker under **(1)** Halsey Plan and **(2)** Rowan Plan from the following particulars: **(i)** Hourly rate of wages guaranteed, ₹50 per hour; **(ii)** Standard time for producing one dozen articles—3 hours; **(iii)** Actual time taken by the worker to produce 20 dozen articles—48 hours.

SOLUTION

Determination of Earnings of a Worker

(i) Halsey plan: (Hours worked × Rate per hour) + [(50% Time saved (Hours) × Rate per hour)] = (48 × ₹50) + (0.5 × 12 × ₹50) = ₹2,700

(ii) Rowan plan: (Hours worked × Rate per hour) + (Time saved/Time allowed) × Time taken × Rate per hour) = (48 × ₹50) + [(12/60) × 48 × ₹50] = ₹2,880.

P. 4.2 During a week a worker produced 300 units, working for 48 hours. The hourly rate is ₹40. The estimated time to produce a unit is 10 minutes. Under incentive scheme, 20 per cent additional time is allowed. Calculate his gross earnings under Halsey and Rowan Plans.

SOLUTION

Determination of Earnings of a Worker

(i) *Halsey Plan* : (Hours worked × Rate per hour) + (50% Time saved × Rate per hour)
: (48 hours × ₹40) + [0.5 (60 hours[1] – 48 hours) × ₹40]
: ₹1,920 + (6 × ₹40) = ₹2,160

(1) Normal time allowed (10 minutes × 300 units) =	3,000 minutes
Plus 20 per cent additional time (0.2 × 3,000) =	600
Standard time allowed (60 hours)	3,600 minutes

(ii) *Rowan Plan* : (Hours worked × Rate per hour) + (Time saved/Time allowed) × Time taken × Rate per hour
: (48 hours × ₹40) + (12 hours/60 hours) × 48 hours × ₹40
: ₹1,920 + (1/5 × 48 × ₹40) = ₹2,304

P. 4.3 A workman's wages for a guaranteed 44 hours week is ₹75 per hour. The estimated time to produce one article is 30 minutes and under an incentive plan, the time allowed is increased by 20 per cent.

During a week, a worker produced 100 articles. Calculate the wages under: (a) Time rate, (b) Rowan system and (c) Halsey system.

SOLUTION

Determination of Earnings of a Worker

(i) Time Rate	: (44 hours × ₹75) = ₹3,300
(ii) Rowan System	: (44 hours × ₹75) + (16 hours/60 hours)[1] × 44 hours × ₹75
	: ₹3,300 + ₹880 = ₹4,180
(iii) Halsey Plan	: (44 hours × ₹75) + (8 hours × ₹75) = ₹3,300 + ₹600 = ₹3,900

1 Normal time per article (minutes)	30
Plus 20 per cent extra time allowed	6
Standard time per article (minutes)	36
Standard time for 100 articles (60 hours)	
Time saved (60 hours – 44 hours worked) (hours)	16

P. 4.4 An employee working under a bonus scheme saves 10 hours in a job for which the standard time is 60 hours. Calculate the rate per hour worked and wages payable to him if incentive bonus of 10 per cen on the hourly rate is payable when standard time (namely, 100 per cent efficiency) is achieved, and a further incentive bonus of 1 per cent on hourly rate for each 1 per cent excess of that 100 per cent efficiency is payable. Assume that the normal rate of payment is ₹50 per hour.

SOLUTION

Determination of Total Wages and Effective Rate per Hour

Wages (50 hours × ₹50)	₹2,500
Plus bonus (0.10 × ₹2,500)	250
Plus incentive (1% for efficiency in excess of 100%)	
Efficiency (60 actual hours/50 standard hours) = 120%	
Plus incentive (120% – 100%) × 2,500	500
Total wages	3,250
Effective rate per hour (₹3,250/50 hours)	65

P. 4.5 Calculate the earnings of workers A, B and C under Straight Piece Rate System and Merrick's Multiple Piece Rate System from the following particulars:

Normal rate per hour	₹54
Standard time per unit	1 minute

Output per day is as follows:

Worker A—390 units

Worker B—450 units

Worker C—600 units

Working hours per day are 8.

SOLUTION

Earnings of Workers Under Straight Piece Rate System

Worker A = (390 units × ₹0.90@) =	₹351
Worker B = (450 units × ₹0.90@) =	405
Worker C = (600 units × ₹0.90@) =	540

@ ₹54/60 units = ₹0.90

Earnings of Workers under Merrick's Multiple Piece Rate System

Particulars/Workers	A	B	C
1. Actual output per day	390	450	600
2. Standard output per day (8 hours)	480	480	480
3. Efficiency level (1 ÷ 2) × 100 (%)	81.25	93.75	125
4. Revised wage rate per unit	₹0.90*	₹0.99**	₹1.08***
5. Earnings (1 × 4)	351	445.50	648

* Normal rate; ** 10 per cent above normal rate; *** 20 per cent above normal rate.

P. 4.6 A job can be executed either through workman A or B. A takes 32 hours to complete the job while B finishes it in 30 hours. The standard time to finish the job is 40 hours.

The hourly wage rate is same for both the workers. In addition, workman A is entitled to receive bonus according to Halsey Plan (50 per cent sharing) while B is paid bonus as per Rowan Plan. The works overheads are absorbed on the job at ₹7.50 per labour-hour worked. The factory cost of the job comes to ₹2,600 irrespective of the workman engaged. Find out the hourly wage rate and cost of raw materials input. Also, show cost against each element of cost included in factory cost.

Solution

Statement of Factory Cost of Jobs A and B

Particulars/Workman	Job A	Job B
Material cost	₹X	₹X
Wages (workmen)	36 Y	37.5 Y
Work overheads @ ₹7.50 per hour worked	240	225
Factory cost	2,600	2,600
Standard time (hours)	40	40
Actual time taken (hours)	32	30
Time saved (hours)	8	10
Bonus	4 Y(1)	7.5Y(2)
Wages paid	32 Y	30 Y
Total wages paid	36 Y	37.5Y

1. Bonus for A under Halsey Plan: Time saved × 0.50 × Hourly rate = 8 × 0.50 × ₹Y = 4 Y
2. Bonus for B under Rowan Plan: (Time saved ÷ Standard time) × Time taken × Hourly rate) = (10 × 40) ÷ 30 × ₹Y = 7.5 Y

Now, from the above we can deduce that:

₹X + ₹36 Y + ₹240 = ₹2,600

₹X + ₹37.5 Y + ₹225 = ₹2,600

Solving above equations, we get:

X = ₹2,000

Y = ₹10 per hour.

Therefore, material cost (X) is ₹2,000, and hourly wage rate (Y) is ₹10 per hour.

P. 4.7 Supreme Industries Ltd recently adopted an incentive plan. Factory workers are paid at ₹3.75 per unit with a guaranteed minimum wages of ₹1,000 per week. Following is a report on employees' productivity for the week ending March, current year. All employees had worked the full 40-hour week. Weekly summary is as follows:

Workers' name	Units produced
A	240
B	275
C	250
D	280
E	220
F	300

Required (a) Compute each employee's gross wages per week, (b) What amount should be charged to work-in-process charged to factory overheads?

SOLUTION

(a) *Statement showing Determination of Gross Wages*

Name	*Units produced*	*Piece rate*	*Piecework earnings*	*Below minimum*	*Total earnings*
A	240	₹3.75	₹900.00	₹100	₹1,000.00
B	275	3.75	1,031.25	—	1,031.25
C	250	3.75	937.50	62.50	1,000.00
D	280	3.75	1,050.00	—	1,050.00
E	220	3.75	825.00	175.00	1,000.00
F	300	3.75	1,125.00	—	1,125.00
			5,868.75	337.50	6,206.25

(b) Amount to be charged to work-in-process (WIP) inventory is ₹5,868.75

(c) Amount to be charged to factory overheads is ₹337.50.

P. 4.8 In an engineering concern, the employees are paid incentive bonus in addition to their normal wages at hourly rates. Incentive bonus is calculated in proportion of time taken to time allowed, of the time saved. The following details are made available in respect of employees X, Y and Z for a particular week:

	X	*Y*	*Z*
Normal wages (per hour)	₹40	₹50	₹60
Completed units of production	6,000	3,000	4,800
Time allowed per 100 units (hour)	0.8	1.5	1.0
Actual time taken (hours)	42	40	48

You are required to work out for each employee: **(i)** The amount of bonus earned, **(ii)** The total amount of wags received, and **(iii)** The total wages cost per 100 units of output.

SOLUTION

Statement showing the amount of Bonus Earned, Wages Received, and Wages Cost per 100 units of Output

	X	*Y*	*Z*
Completed units of production	6,000	3,000	4,800
Time allowed for units produced	48	45	48
Actual time taken (hours)	42	40	48
Time saved (hours)	6	5	—
Normal wages (per hour)	₹40	₹50	₹60
Basic wages (Actual hours × Normal rate)	1,680	2,000	2,880
(i) Bonus earned (Time taken/Time allowed) × Time saved × Wage rate	210	222.20	—
(ii) Total wages cost	1,890	2,222.20	2,880
(iii) Wages cost per 100 units	31.50	74.10	60

P. 4.9 The time allowed for a job is 8 hours. The hourly rate is ₹8. Prepare a statement showing: **(i)** The bonus earned, **(ii)** The total earnings of labour, and **(iii)** Hourly earnings under the Halsey System with 50 per cent bonus for time saved, and Rowan System for each hour saved respectively.

SOLUTION

Determination of Bonus, Total Earnings of Labour and Hourly Earnings as per Halsey and Rowan Systems

Time allowed (hours)	Time taken (hours)	Time saved (hours)	Basic wages at ₹8 per hour	Bonus		Total earnings		Hourly earnings	
				Halsey System@	Rowan System@@	Halsey System (Col. 4 + Col. 5)	Rowan System (Col. 4 + Col. 6)	Halsey System (Col. 7 ÷ Col. 2)	Rowan System (Col. 8 ÷ Col. 2)
1	2	3	4	5	6	7	8	9	10
8	8	Nil	₹64	—	—	₹64	₹64	₹8	₹8.0
8	7	1	56	₹4	₹7	60	63	8.57	9.0
8	6	2	48	8	12	56	60	9.33	10.0
8	5	3	40	12	15	52	55	10.40	11.0
8	4	4	32	16	16	48	48	12.00	12.0
8	3	5	24	20	15	44	39	14.67	13.0
8	2	6	16	24	12	40	28	20.0	14.0
8	1	7	8	28	7	36	15	36.0	15.0

@ Standard wage rate × 0.5 × Time saved

@@ Standard wage rate × (Time saved/Time allowed) × Time taken

P.4.10 A skilled worker in XYZ Ltd is paid a guaranteed wage rate of ₹30 per hour. The standard time per unit for a particular product is 4 hours. P, a machineman, has been paid wages under the Rowan Incentive Plan and he had earned an effective hourly rate of ₹37.50 on the manufacture of that particular product.

What could have been his total earnings and effective hourly rate, had he been put on Halsey Incentive Scheme (50 per cent)?

SOLUTION

(i) Total Earnings of Machineman, P as per Haley Incentive Scheme (50 per cent)
= (Time taken× Rate per hour) + [0.50 × (Standard time – Time taken) × Rate per hour
= (3 hours × ₹30) + [0.5(4 Hours – 3 Hours) × ₹30]
= ₹90 + ₹15 = ₹105

(ii) *Effective Hourly Rate = Total earnings/Number of hours = ₹105/3 = ₹35*

WORKING NOTES

Detemination of Time Taken by a Machineman

Earnings as per Rowan Incentive Plan are = (Time taken × Rate per hour) + [(Standard time – Time taken) ÷ Standard time] × Time taken × Rate per hour

Let time taken by x

$$₹37.50 = ₹30x + [(4 - x) \div 4] \times x ₹30$$

Let both sides be divided be $1/x$

$$= ₹37.50 = ₹30 + \left[\frac{4-x}{4}\right] \times ₹30 = ₹37.50 = ₹30 + \left[\frac{₹120 - 30x}{4}\right]$$

$$₹7.5 = ₹30 - 7.5\,x$$

$$7.5x = ₹225 \quad \text{or} \quad x = ₹22.5/7.5 = 3 \text{ hours}$$

P.4.11. Calculate the earnings of workers A, B and C under Straight Piece Rate System and Merrick's Multiple Piece Rate System from the following particulars:

Normal rate per hour	₹54
Standard time per unit (minutes)	1

Output (units) per day is as follows:

Worker A	390
Worker B	450
Worker C	600

Working hours per day are 8.

SOLUTION

Determination of Wages under Straight Piece Rate System

Worker	(Output per day × Rate per unit)	Amount
A	(390 Units × ₹0.90)[1]	₹351
B	(450 Units × ₹0.90)	405
C	(600 Units × ₹0.90)	540

1. Normal rate per hour ₹54 ÷ Standard output per hour 60 = ₹0.90

(i) *Determination of Wages under Merrick's Multiple Piece Rate System*

Worker	Efficiency ratio (Actual production /Standard production i.e., 60 × 8 = 480 units) (%)	Rate per unit*	Actual units produced	Wages payable
A	(390/480) = 81.25	₹0.90	390	₹351
B	(450/480) = 93.75	0.99	450	445.50
C	(600/480) = 125.00	1.08	600	648

*Normal piece rate is paid when output is upto 83 per cent of the standard output (and hence ₹0.90 per unit for worker A); 110 per cent of normal piece rate when output is between 83-100 per cent (and hence ₹0.99 per unit for worker B); and 120 per cent is paid when output exceeds 100 per cent (and hence ₹1.08 per unit for worker C).

P.4.12 From the following information, calculate labour turnover rate and labour flux rate:
Number of workers as on January 1 = 7,600
Number of workers on December 31 = 8,400
During the year, 80 workers left while 320 workers were discharged. 1,500 workers recruited during the year; of these 300 workers were recruited because of exits and the rest were recruited in accordance with expansion plans.

SOLUTION

(i) *Separation Method* = [(Number of workers leaving i.e., (left + discharged in a period) ÷ Average number of workers employed] × 100
= [(80 + 320)/ (7,600 + 8,400) ÷ 2] = 5 per cent

(ii) *Replacement Method* = (Number of workers replaced in a period) ÷ (Average number of workers employed) × 100
= (300/8,000) × 100 = 3.75 per cent

(iii) *Labour Flux Rate* = [(Number of workers leaving + Number of workers replaced excluding those who were recruited for expansion) ÷ (Average number of workers employed)] × 100
= [(400 + 300)/8000] × 100 = 8.75 per cent

P. 4.13 The cost accountant of Y Ltd has computed labour turnover rates for the quarter ended March 31, current year as 10 per cent, 5 per cent, and 3 per cent respectively under Flux Method. Replacement Method and Separation Method. If the number of workers replaced during that quarter is 30, find out the number of **(1)** workers recruited and joined and **(2)** workers left and discharged.

SOLUTION

Average number of workers on roll: Labour turnover rate (replacement method) = [Number of replacement ÷ Average number of workers on roll]
(N) × 100
0.05 = 30/N
Therefore, average number of workers on roll (N) is 600.

1. Labour turnover rate (Separation Method) = (Number of separation (s) ÷ Average number of workers on roll) × 100
   0.03 = S/600
   S = 18
   Therefore, number of workers left and discharged is 18.

2. Number of workers recruited and joined

Labour turnover rate (Flux Method) = [Number of separation (S) + Number of replacement (R)] ÷ Average number of workers (N) × 100

0.10 = (18 + R)/600

R = 42

Therefore, workers recruited and joined are 42.

P. 4.14 The management of In and Out Limited are worried about their increasing labour turnover in the factory, and before analysing the causes and taking remedial steps, they want to have an idea of the profit forgone as a result of labor turnover in the last year.

Last year, sales amounted to ₹8,30,33,000 and the profit-volume ratio was 20 per cent. The total number of actual hours worked by the direct labour force was 4.45 lakh. As a result of the delays by the Personnel Department in filling vacancies due to labour turnover, 1,00,000 potentially productive hours were lost. The actual direct labour-hours included 30,000 hours attributable to training new recruits, out of which half of the hours were unproductive.

The cost incurred consequent to labour turnover revealed on analysis the following:

Settlement costs due to leaving	₹4,38,200
Recruitment costs	2,67,400
Selection costs	1,27,500
Training costs	3,04,900

Assuming the potential production lost as a consequence of labour turnover could have been sold at prevailing prices, find the profit forgone last year on account of labour turnover.

SOLUTION

Statement showing Profit Foregone due to Labour Turnover Last year

Settlement costs due to leaving	₹4,38,200
Recruitment costs	2,67,400
Selection costs	1,27,500
Training costs	3,04,900
Contribution lost due to lost sales	38,62,000
Total loss	50,00,000

WORKING NOTES

Direct labour-hours paid for	4,45,000
Less unproductive direct labour-hours	15,000
Actual direct labour-hours (productive)	4,30,000
Sales lost for 1,00,000 hours (₹8,30,33,000/4,30,000) × 1,00,000 hours	₹1,93,10,000
Contribution lost (₹1,93,10,000 × 0.20)	38,62,000

P. 4.15 The Managing Director of All Found Limited is very much perturbed to see that labour turnover is increasing every year. Before taking an appropriate action, he desires to know the profit forgone on account of labour turnover. You are required to calculate the profit forgone on account of labour turnover from the following:

Income statement for the current year ended March, 31

Sales		₹20,00,000
Variable costs:		
Material	₹5,00,000	
Direct labour	4,00,000	
Variable overheads	4,00,000	13,00,000
Contribution		7,00,000
Less fixed overheads		2,00,000
Profit before taxes		5,00,000

The direct labour-hours worked in the concern during the period were 20,300, of which 500 hours pertained to the new workers on training. Only 40 per cent of the trainees time was productive. As replacement for the worker left was delayed for some time, 600 productive hours were lost.

The direct costs incurred by the company as a consequence of labour separation and replacement were as follows:

Separation costs	₹20,000
Selection costs	30,000
Training costs	50,000

Solution

Statement showing Determination of Profit Forgone due to Labour Turnover

Separation costs	₹20,000
Selection costs	30,000
Training costs	50,000
Contribution forgone	37,680
	1,37,680

Working Notes

(i) Direct labour hours paid for	20,300
Less unproductive time of new workers (0.6 × 500)	300
Productive hours	20,000
Total labour hours lost including 600 for replacement	900
Unit sales per productive labour-hour (₹20,00,000/20,000)	₹100
Loss of potential sales (900 hours × ₹100)	90,000
Less variable costs:	
Material costs (₹5,00,000/₹20,00,000) × ₹90,000	22,500
Variable overheads (₹4,00,000/₹20,00,000) × ₹90,000	18,000
Increase in direct labour cost (600 hours) (₹4,00,000/20,300 hours)	11,820
Contribution foregone	37,680

P. 4.16 A company is undecided as to what kind of wage scheme should be introduced. The following particulars have been compiled in respect of three systems, which are under consideration of the management:

Particulars	Workers		
	A	*B*	*C*
Actual hours worked in a week	38	40	34
Hourly rate of wages	₹60	₹50	₹72
Production in units:			
Product P	21	—	60
Product Q	36	—	135
Product R	46	25	—
Standard time allowed per unit of each product is:			
	P	**Q**	**R**
Minutes	12	18	30

For the purpose of piece rate, each minute is valued at ₹1.

You are required to calculate the wages of each worker under:

(i) Guaranteed hourly rates basis

(ii) Piece work earnings basis, but guaranteed 75 per cent of basic pay (guaranteed hourly rate) if his earnings are less than 50 per cent of basic pay.

(iii) Premium bonus where the worker receives bonus based on Rowan scheme.

SOLUTION

(i) *Computation of Wages of Workers under Guaranteed Hourly Rate Basis*

Particulars	Workers		
	A	B	C
1. Actual hours worked in a week	38	40	34
2. Multiply by hourly rate of wages	₹60	₹50	₹72
3. Guaranteed wages per week	₹2,280	₹2,000	₹2,448

(ii) *Computation of Wages of Workers under Piece Work Earnings Basis*

Product	Piece rate per unit	Units produced by workers			Wages of workers		
		A	B	C	A	B	C
1	2		3			4 (2 × 3)	
P	(12 minutes × ₹1) = ₹12	21	—	60	₹252	—	₹720
Q	(18 minutes × ₹1) = 18	36	—	135	648	—	2,430
R	(30 minutes × ₹1) = 30	46	25	—	1,380	750	—
					2,280	150@	3,150

@ Since ₹750 is less than 50% of basic pay (of ₹2,000), he would be paid 75 per cent × ₹2,000 = ₹1,500.

(iii) *Rowan scheme provides the following basis of computing bonus.*

Bonus = (Time taken/Time allowed) × Time saved × Time rate

(a) *Determination of Time Allowed to Workers*

Product	Standard time allowed per unit (in minutes)	Units produced by workers			Total standard time allowed to workers (in hours)		
		A	B	C	A	B	C
P	12	21	—	60	252	—	720
Q	18	36	—	135	648	—	2,430
R	30	46	25	—	1,380	750	—
					2,280	750	3,150

(b) Determination of Bonus Payable under Rowan Scheme

Workers	Time (in hours)			Wage rate per hour	Earnings	Bonus	Total earnings + bonus
	Taken	Allowed	Saved				
A	38	38	—	₹60	₹2,280	—	₹2,280
B	40	12.5	NA	50	2,000	—	2,000
C	34	52.5	18.5	72	2,448	862.6[1]	3,310.60

1 = (34/52.5) × 18.5 × ₹72 = ₹862.60

P. 4.17 ZED Ltd is working by employing 50 skilled workers. It is considering the introduction of incentive scheme-either Halsey scheme (with 50 per cent bonus) or Rowan scheme of wage payment for increasing the labour productivity to cope up the increasing demand for the product by 40 per cent. It is believed that proposed incentive scheme could bring about an average 20 per cent increase over the present earnings of the workers; it could act as sufficient incentive for them to produce more.

Because of assurance, the increase in productivity has been observed as revealed by the figures for the month of April.

Hourly rate of wages (guaranteed)	₹30
Average time for producing one unit by one worker at the previous performance (This may be taken as time allowed)	1.975 hours
Number of working days in the month	24
Number of working hours per day of each worker	8
Actual production during the month	6,120 units

REQUIRED: **(i)** Calculate the effective rate of earnings under the Halsey scheme and the Rowan scheme. **(ii)** Calculate the savings to the ZED Ltd in terms of direct labour cost per piece. **(iii)** Advise ZED Ltd about the selection of the scheme to fulfill their assurance.

SOLUTION

(i) *Determination of Effective Rate of Earnings*

Halsey Scheme: (Hours worked in a month × Rate per hour) + (0.50 of time saved × Rate per hour)
= (24 days × 8 hours per day × 50 workers = 9,600 hours × ₹30 per hour) + [0.50 × (Time allowed 6,120 units × 1.975 hours = 12,087 hours - 9,600 hours) × ₹30)]
= ₹2,88,000 + 37,305 = ₹3,25,305
Effective earnings per hour = (₹3,25,305/9,600 hours) = ₹33.89
Rowan Scheme: (Hours worked in a month × Rate per hour) + [(Time saved/Time allowed) × Time taken × Rate per hour]
= (9,600 hours × ₹30) + [(2,487/12,087) × 9,600 × ₹30]
= ₹2,88,000 + ₹59,258 = ₹3,47,258
Effective earnings per hour (₹3,47,258/9,600) = ₹36.17

(ii) *Computation of Savings in Direct Labour Cost per Unit/Piece*

Halsey Scheme:	
Current production cost per unit (1.975 hours x ₹30 per hour)	₹59.25
Less production cost under Halsey scheme (₹3,25,305/6,120 units)	53.15
Savings per unit	6.10
Rowan Scheme:	
Current production cost	₹59.25
Less production cost under Rowan Scheme (₹3,47,258/6,120 units)	56.74
Savings per unit	2.51

(iii) Zed Ltd. has assured workers the increase in wages by 20 per cent (i.e. from present level of ₹2,88,000 to 3,45,600); this assurance can be fulfilled only under Rowan scheme as only under this scheme, the wage payable is ₹3,47,258. The total wage amount under Halsey scheme is ₹3,25,305 only (increase of 13 per cent only). Therefore, Zed Ltd is advised to adopt Rowan scheme.

REVIEW QUESTIONS

RQ.4.1 (a) Indicate whether the following statements are true or false.

(i) Piece work system of wage payment is good for quality-conscious organizations producing aesthetic products or decorative items.
(ii) Taylor piece rate system has differential piece rates.
(iii) Merrick differential piece rate system has two wage rates: a lower rate for output below standard performance and higher rate for output above standard performance.
(iv) Gantt task and bonus plan is a mixture of guaranteed time rate with bonus and piece rate plan using the differential principle.
(v) Cost of labour turnover includes preventive and replacements costs.

(b) In the following multiple choice questions select the correct answers.

(vi) Which of the following are earnings of workers A and B under Taylor differential piece rate system, given the following data?
- Standard time per piece; 20 minutes
- Normal rate per hour, ₹9
- In a 9-hour day, A produces 25 units and B produces 30 units.
- Differential to be applied: 80 per cent of piece rate below standard and 120 per cent above standard.

(a) ₹50, ₹90, (b) ₹60, ₹108, (c) ₹75, ₹90, (d) ₹50, ₹188.

(vii) Which of the following are the earnings of A, B and C under Merrick differential piece rate system, given the following data?
- Normal piece rate (upto 83% of high task output), ₹10 per unit
- High task, 40 units per week
- Weekly output: A, 32 units; B, 37 units; C, 42 units

(a) ₹320, ₹407, ₹504, (b) ₹352, ₹407, ₹504, (c) ₹320, ₹444, ₹504, (d) ₹300, ₹407, ₹504.

(viii) Which of the following are the earning of A, B and C under Gantt task and bonus plan given the following data?
- Time rate ₹10 per hour for 48 hours week.
- Standard production, 48 units per week.
- Piece rate above standard output, ₹12.
- Weekly output A, 38 units; B, 45 units; C, 50 units.

(a) ₹480, ₹480, ₹600, (b) ₹480, ₹480, ₹500, (c) ₹380, ₹450, ₹500, (d) ₹480, ₹450, ₹600.

(ix) Which is the earning (per hour) payable to A under Halsey premium plan given the following data?
- Time given to complete the work- 8 hours
- Wage rate ₹4 per hour
- Job completed in 6 hours

(a) ₹4.67 per hour., (b) ₹4 per hour, (c) ₹3.5 per hour, (d) ₹4.5 per hour.

(x) Which of the following is the earning of A (as per data given in Question No ix), under Halsey-Weir premium plan?

(a) ₹26.67, (b) ₹24, (c) ₹28, (d) ₹29.33.

(xi) Which of the following is the earning (per hour) of A (as per data given in Question No ix), under Rowan plan?

(a) ₹30 or ₹5/hour, (b) ₹30 or ₹3.75/hour, (c) ₹30 or ₹4/hour, (d) ₹30 or ₹3/hour.

(xii) Under the Bedaux point plan which is the amount of bonus and earnings given the information below?
- Standard production – 8 hours daily = 100 (units).
- Actual production for hours daily = 125 (units).
- Hourly wage rate = ₹3.

(a) ₹4.5 and ₹28.5, (b) ₹4 and ₹28, (c) Nil and ₹24, (d) ₹4.8 and ₹28.8.

[Answers: (i) False, (ii) True, (iii) False, (iv) True, (v) True, (vi) b (vii) a (viii) a (ix) a (x) a (xi) a (xii) a.]

RQ.4.2 What are the costs included in total labour cost besides gross wages?

RQ.4.3 Explain timekeeping and book keeping and state the detailed records normally maintained under them.

RQ.4.4 What is idle time? How is it treated in costing of labour?

RQ.4.5 What is overtime premium? Discuss its treatment in cost accounting and suggest a procedure for its control.

RQ.4.6 What is labour turnover? How is it measured? What are its costs? How can they be reduced?

RQ.4.7 What are incentive plans? Describe the main types of incentives plans.

RQ.4.8 Explain and illustrate the differential price rate schemes type of incentive/bonus plans.

RQ.4.9 Write notes on the different types of premium bonus plans. Illustrate your answer with examples.

RQ.4.10 The time taken for a particular operation for operator X in the Process Division of a manufacturing concern on three different counts was 24, 22 and 27 minutes while that of operator Y was 20, 23 and 26 minutes. It has been ascertained that the rating of 'X' is 70/60 and that of 'Y' is 55/60. Allowance for fatigue, personal needs are assumed at 15 per cent. Calculate, using the above information as a base, for that particular operation, (i) the standard time, and (ii) the time allowed under an incentive allowance of 30 per cent of standard time.

RQ.4.11 A skilled worker is allowed to take 9 hours to complete a job on daily wages and 6 hours on a scheme of payment by results. His daily rate is ₹75 per hour. The material cost is ₹400 and the overheads are recovered at 150 per cent of the total direct wages. Calculate the factory cost of the product under (i) piece-work plan, (ii) Halsey Plan and (iii) Rowan Plan, assuming work is completed in 6 hours.

RQ.4.12 Mr. A is working by employing 10 skilled workers. He is considering the introduction of some incentive scheme — either Halsey Scheme (with 50 per cent bonus) or Rowan Scheme — of wage payment for increasing the labour productivity to cope with the increased demand for the product. He feels that if the proposed incentive scheme could bring about an average 20 per cent increase over the present earnings of the workers, it could act as sufficient incentive for them to produce more and he has accordingly given this assurance to the workers. As a result of the assurance, the increase in productivity observed as revealed by the following figures for the current month:

Hourly rate of wages (guaranteed)	₹20
Average time for producing 1 piece by one worker at the previous performance (This may be taken as time allowed) (hours)	2
Number of working days in the month	25
Number of working hours per day for each worker	8
Actual production during the month (units)	1,250

REQUIRED:

(a) Calculate effective rate of earnings per hour under Halsey Scheme and Rowan Scheme.

(b) Calculate the savings to Mr. A in terms of direct labour cost per piece under the schemes.

(c) Advise Mr. A about the selection of the scheme to fulfill assurance.

RQ.4.13 From the following data provided to you, find out the labour turnover rate by applying (a) Flux method, (b) Replacement method, and (c) Separation method.

Number of workers on the payroll: At the beginning of the month, 500; At the end of the month, 600. During the month, 5 workers left, 20 persons were discharged and 75 workers were recruited. Of these, 10 workers were recruited in the vacancies of those leaving, while the rest were engaged for an expansion scheme.

RQ.4.14 Your organisation is experiencing a high labour turnover in recent years and management would like you to submit a report on the loss suffered by the Company due to such labour turnover. Following figures are available for your consideration:

Sales (₹lakhs)	₹600
Direct materials	150
Direct labour (4,80,000 man-hours)	48
Other variable expenses	60
Fixed overheads	80

The direct man-hours include 9,000 man-hours spent on trainees and replacement, only 50 per cent of which were productive. Further, during the year, 12,000 man-hours of potential work could not be availed of because of delayed replacement. The cost incurred due to separations and replacements amounted to ₹1 lakh.

On the basis of above data, prepare comparative statement showing actual profit *vis-à-vis* the profit which would have been realised had there been no labour turnover.

ANSWERS **[Comprehensive solutions to all numerical review questions are available on the companion website: http://www.mhhe.com/khan_jain_cost2e]**

RQ. 4.10 (i) 28.45 minutes **(ii)** 37 minutes
RQ. 4.11 (a) (i) ₹450, **(ii)** ₹562.50, **(iii)** ₹675 wages; **(b)** Factory cost **(i)** ₹1,525, **(ii)** ₹1,806.25, **(iii)** ₹2,087.50
RQ. 4.12 (a) Halsey Scheme, ₹22.50; Rowan Scheme ₹24, **(b)** Halsey Scheme, ₹4.0; Rowan Scheme ₹1.60; **(c)** The Rowan plans is advised to be adopted.
RQ. 4.13 (a) Flux method (6.36 per cent), **(b)** Replacement method (1.82 per cent), **(c)** Separation method (4.55 per cent)
RQ. 4.14 Loss of profit due to labour turnover ₹13,33,312

Costing and Control of Factory (Manufacturing) Overheads

Learning Objectives

1. Explain how factory overheads are determined
2. Discuss and illustrate the factory overheads application/absorption rate
3. Analyse the methods/procedures of allocating costs of service departments to production departments
4. Explain the methods of absorption of factory overheads
5. Illustrate the treatment of under/over-absorption of factory overheads

INTRODUCTION

The previous two chapters discussed costing and control of direct material costs (Chapter 3) and direct labour costs (Chapter 4) that are incurred in manufacturing of products. The third element of production costs, namely, factory overheads is the subject matter of this Chapter. Section 1 deals with determination of factory overheads. It also deals with determination of factory overheads application/absorption rate. The methods/procedure of allocating costs of service departments to production departments are discussed in Section 2. Section 3 explains the methods of absorption of factory overheads. Section 4 illustrates the treatment of the difference between actual factory overheads incurred and factory overheads absorbed, that is, under-absorption/over-absorption of factory overheads. The main points are summarised in the last Section.

FACTORY OVERHEAD COSTS

Factory overhead costs refer to all indirect manufacturing costs which cannot be identified with particular orders or units of product. These costs include the following:

- Indirect materials and indirect labour.
- Factory rent, rates, lighting, power, and fuel.
- Depreciation on factory plant and equipments and factory building.

Factory overhead costs refer to all indirect manufacturing costs which cannot be identified with a particular order/unit/product.

- Insurance, repairs and maintenance of factory plant and equipments and building.
- Storekeeping, toolroom costs.

Factory Overhead Application/Absorption Rate

Cost allocation is the allotment of whole items of costs to cost centres/units.

Cost apportionment is the allotment of common costs to cost centres on the basis of benefits received

Overhead absorption is the allotment of factory overheads to cost units objects by means of overhead application rate.

Direct costs normally can be conveniently identified/allocated to specific jobs. Material requisitions and workers' time sheets provide sufficient indication where these costs are to be charged. The same is, however, not true for the indirect manufacturing costs as they are incurred for the factory as a whole. Being *common costs,* they are divided/shared/charged among various *cost centres* and/or *cost units.*

The procedure for allotting factory overheads to cost centres/objects/units cover cost allocation, cost apportionment, and overhead absorption. While the allotment of whole items of cost to cost centres or cost units is referred to as *cost allocation,* the allotment of common costs to two or more cost centres on the estimated basis of benefits received is known as cost *apportionment.* The allotment of factory overheads to cost units/objects by means of predetermined factory overhead application rate is called *overhead absorption.*

The factory overhead absorption rate can either be *actual* overhead rate or a *predetermined* overhead rate. Normally, a predetermined overhead rate is preferred, the reason being: **(a)** It is useful in 'bidding' cases to determine quotation prices; **(b)** It enables individual jobs to be costed immediately on their completion; and **(c)** Such a rate levels out the fluctuations which may be caused by variations in actual factory overhead costs and/or actual level of activity.

The two key factors to determine the factory overhead application rate for a period are: **(a)** To select a volume/level of production (more commonly referred to as capacity) to be used as a base for applying factory overheads to production (denominators) and **(b)** To budget factory overheads at the capacity selected (numerator).

Concepts of Capacity Choice of the capacity to be used as a base in applying factory overheads often raises a difficult question. The reason is that there are more than one basis of determining capacity. For instance, capacity can be based on the physical facilities that have been installed, or productive capacity that can be utilised (giving due allowance for unavoidable lost hours both in respect of machines and workers), or actual capacity used in relation to the expected sales volume. While one capacity level relates to the level of production (determined by engineers, with no regard to the expected sales volume) the other is the expected product sales. The choice (by and large *subjective* in nature) is to be made from one of the following four possibilities: **(i)** Maximum/Theoretical idle capacity, **(ii)** Practical capacity **(iii)** Normal/Long-term production capacity, and **(iv)** Expected/Short-term actual capacity.

Maximum or Theoretical Idle Capacity It refers to the volume of production that a particular production department or factory is capable of producing if the plant were in continuous operation at *peak efficiency at all times.* In other words, such a capacity base does not have any provision for either a lack of sales orders or interruptions in production (due to machine break-down, machine downtime for repairs and maintenance, set-up time, holidays, weekends, and so on). At this capacity level, the plant is assumed to function 24 hours a day, 7 days a week, 52 weeks a year without any interruptions, in order to yield the highest physical output possible, that is, 100 per cent of plant capacity.[1]

Practical Capacity Unlike theoretical capacity measure, practical capacity does not expect full utilisation of the plant; it makes due allowances for unavoidable idleness of workers and machinery caused by repairs and maintenance, machine set-up, fatigue, and time lost through vacations and holidays. However, this measure does not take into consideration plant and personnel made idle due to the lack of sales orders. In *operational* terms, it is the maximum capacity expected when the plant operates at *a planned level of efficiency.*

Practical capacity is the maximum capacity expected when the plant operates at a planned level of efficiency

Normal or Long-run Productive Capacity Unlike practical capacity, normal capacity allows for idleness both of plant and personnel caused due to a lack of sales orders. Normally, capacity is equal to, or less than, practical production capacity depending upon the volume of expected sales. More often, normal capacity is less than practical capacity. Further, normal capacity is not based just on one year's sales; it is the average annual volume of production needed to meet ordinary and usual sales demand over a cycle of years long enough (say 5 years) to even out seasonal , cyclical, and other variations in customer demand.

Normal capacity is equal to, or less than, practical capacity depending on the volume of expected sales.

Expected or Short-run Actual Capacity It is the volume of production required to meet the estimated/projected demand for the next period/year (that is in a single year only). Thus, expected actual capacity differs from normal capacity in the length of time to determine capacity base; this measure does not smoothen out cyclical variations in sales that are likely to occur over a period of time as it is guided by one year projections only. Such a measure may appeal to those firms which are interested more in short-term planning and control.

Example 5.1 illustrates these 4 concepts of capacity.

EXAMPLE 5.1

The Hypothetical Manufacturing Company Ltd wishes to determine various capacity levels both in terms of production units and machine-hours. One machine-hour produces 10 units of finished product. The production department in which the machine is located normally operates 6 days a week (except Sunday) on a single, eight-hour shift. The plant is closed for 10 working days each year for holidays.

Plant is closed for 200 hours each year for its repairs and maintenance. Normal sales demand averages 20,000 units a year over a 5-year period (extensive product changes are made every five years). The expected sales volume for the next year is 19,000 units. Show the machine-hours and production capacity at the four levels.

SOLUTION

Machine-hours and production capacity at 4 levels of capacity are shown in Table 5.1.

Table 5.1 Capacity at Various Levels

Details of computation		Capacity: Machine-hours	Capacity: Production units @ 10 units per hour
1. Maximum capacity (365 days × 8 hours per day)		2,920	29,200
2. Practical capacity			
Maximum capacity (in hours)	2,920		
Less idle capacity:			
Sundays (52 days × 8 hours)	416		
Holidays (10 days × 8 hours)	80		
Plant maintenance	200	2,224	22,240
3. Normal capacity		2,000	20,000
4. Expected capacity		1,900	19,000

Table 5.1 shows that factory overhead applied rate will markedly vary among 4 capacity measures and thereby affect production costs, inventory costs, and profits. Therefore, it is important to select an appropriate capacity level to determine reliable and correct factory overhead application rate.

The first measure based on theoretical ideal/maximum capacity is more of academic significance rather than of practical relevance, as it is practically infeasible for plant to operate at such a capacity (for instance, in Example 5.1, it is not always possible for the firm to produce 29,200 units).

Likewise, practical capacity level suffers from lack of realism in that it focuses more on production than sales it can achieve. In practice, it is not a tenable assumption that the firm will produce without taking into account its sales level. However, this measure can be fruitfully applied if a manufacturing firm has captive market, that is, it can sell *all* it produces. But, in practice, this is rarely the case for the majority of the firms; most firms are expected to produce only as much as they can sell.

From the foregoing, it follows that sales projections are a vital factor in the planning process and must be considered while estimating production levels. For most manufacturing firms, either normal productive capacity or expected productive capacity is used to determine factory overhead application rate as both these bases explicitly recognise expected product sales.

Between the two, the normal long-run productive capacity base should be preferred. Such a measure, assuming all other factors remain constant, **(i)** Yields uniform product costs per unit across different time periods; **(ii)** Eliminates the possibility of manipulation of unit product cost by varying production levels intentionally. The latter situation is likely to arise in firms selling products which exhibit pronounced variations in their demand pattern across different time periods (over a cycle of years, say 5 years).

In sum, therefore, normal capacity level is conceptually correct measure to determine factory overhead application rate.

Budgeted Factory Overhead Costs Once the estimated level of production (capacity) has been decided, a manufacturing firm prepares a budget of expected production/factory overheads likely to be incurred in the next year. For estimating budgeted factory overheads, past historical cost data are normally taken as the base and adjustments are made for likely changes in prices/rates of various cost constituents of factory overheads. These overhead costs are classified based on their behaviour in relation to production into three categories: fixed, variable, and mixed costs; mixed costs, in turn, are segregated into fixed and variable.[3] Budgeted factory overheads are computed as shown in Format 5.1.

Format 5.1 Determination of Budgeted Factory Overhead Costs

Total budgeted fixed factory overheads	____
Add variable factory overheads (Budgeted capacity level × Budgeted variable overhead rate)	____
Total	____

EXAMPLE 5.2

For Hypothetical Ltd in Example 5.1, assume further that the budgeted fixed overhead costs are estimated at ₹6 lakh and variable overhead costs at ₹100 per unit as the basis of determining factory overhead application rate. Compute the factory overhead application rate.

SOLUTION

Table 5.2 Determination of Factory Overhead Application Rate

(a)	*Total budgeted fixed overheads*	
	Fixed overhead costs	₹6,00,000
	Variable overhead costs (2,000 hours × ₹100)	2,00,000
		8,00,000
(b)	Normal capacity (machine-hours)	2,000
(c)	(i) Factory overhead application rate (₹8,00,000/2,000) per hour	₹400
	(ii) Factory overhead application rate (₹8,00,000/20,000 units) per unit	40

COST ALLOCATION

When a company produces more than one product, it is important that the factory overhead costs (as determined above) are allocated to various production departments or cost centres. These departments, in turn, assign these costs to product(s) on some equitable basis. Thus, when multiple products are produced, a single factorywide factory overhead application rate is not appropriate for allocating factory overheads. On grounds of equity, the production departments receiving greater benefits should be charged a higher share of these overheads and *vice-versa*. This process of assigning direct and indirect manufacturing costs to various cost centres is referred to as *cost allocation.* Proper cost allocation is of crucial significance as wrong cost allocation can distort income determination, asset valuation, performance evaluation, and decision-making in a firm.

The cost allocation process is comprised of three basic activities.[4]

1. Accumulating the costs on the basis of department or division or product.
2. Identifying the cost objects or recipients of the allocated costs, say, a unit of product or a department.
3. Selecting a method for relating the costs so accumulated to the cost objects.

The third aspect is the most difficult as common costs cannot be directly associated with a single unit, or production department, or division. Some meaningful base needs to be developed to relate costs and cost objects.

While no allocation base can be hundred per cent foolproof (in terms of precision and accuracy), following bases are commonly used for allotting fixed overheads:

Labour-related Factory Overheads

(Say supervisor's salaries, canteen expenses) are usually allocated on the basis of number of employees, direct labour-hours, wages paid or similar other labour related criteria.

Machine-related Factory Overheads

(Say insurance, maintenance, depreciation) are normally allocated on the basis of machine-hours, current book value of machinery, number of machines, or similar other machine-related criteria.

Space-related Factory Overheads

(Say factory building rent and insurance, lighting, maintenance of building) are usually allocated on the basis of space occupied or similar other space-related criteria.

Service-related Costs

(Say materials handling, utility) are normally allocated on the basis of value, quantity, time and similar other service related criteria.

While the principle of cost allocation, in theory, appears to be easy, it is not so simple when it is put to practice. Methods used in practice are often somewhat arbitrary. As far as possible, each factory overhead cost item should be analysed on its own merit to arrive at the most suitable/equitable base.

Departmental Rates

It is common for manufacturing firms to have several departments that are involved either directly or indirectly in production. The discussion that follows dwells on determination of departmental rates related to factory overheads.

Direct Departmental Costs These are the costs which can be easily traced to specific departments. For instance, indirect materials used in production department (say X) can be traced through requisitions on store and can wholly be allocated to department X; likewise, indirect labour (foreman's and supervisor's salaries) wholly engaged in department X can be traced through payroll records; the same applies for depreciation on machines and plants exclusively used in the department X and annual maintenance contact payment for these machines.

Indirect Departmental Costs These are the costs which are common to more than one department and, hence, need to be shared/apportioned among the departments receiving benefits. Building occupancy costs (such as rent, maintenance and light); factory insurance premium, power charges for machine operations (where there are no separate metres for departments) are the major costs included in this category.

Charging Cost of Service Departments

It is a important to take into account costs incurred on service departments to compute factory overheads application rate of production departments.

A service department is a department which provides benefits to producing departments and/or service departments. For instance, maintenance department (responsible for the upkeep of the machinery and building), utility department (responsible for providing power and electricity for a factory), personnel department (responsible for keeping records of personnel employed), are the examples of service departments. Since the output of such service departments is not sold to outside customers, their costs must be covered by production departments, receiving their services.

Accordingly, apportioned service department costs to production departments (in which material conversion or production takes place) can be construed similar to indirect manufacturing costs. The following methods are used to apportion total budgeted costs of service department to production departments (also known as secondary distribution of factory overheads; allocation of indirect manufacturing costs like indirect labour and indirect materials to production departments is referred as primary distribution): **(i)** Direct method, **(ii)** Step method, **(iii)** Repeated distribution method, and **(iv)** Algebraic method.

Direct Method Total budgeted costs of service departments are apportioned between/among production departments only, ignoring any services provided by service departments to each other. This method is the most appropriate when there is virtually no provision of rendering services on reciprocal basis among the service departments. This method has the virtue of simplicity as far as its use in assigning costs to production departments is concerned.

Example 5.3 illustrates how total budgeted costs of five service departments in a manufacturing company are apportioned between its two production departments. It also shows the *modus operandi* of determining factory overhead application/absorption rate for each of the two production departments (after taking into account the share of service departments).

EXAMPLE 5.3

A manufacturing company has 5 service departments and 2 production departments. The total budgeted costs for the period for each department were as follows:

Service Departments:	
Building and grounds	₹1,00,000
Personnel	10,000
General factory and administration	2,60,900
Cafeteria	16,400
Storeroom	26,700
Production Departments:	
Machinery	3,47,000
Assembly	4,89,000

The following schedule was prepared to assist in allocating service department costs:

Department	*Direct labour-hours*	*Number of employees*	*Square feet*	*Total labour-hours*	*Number of requisitions*
Building and grounds	—	—	—	—	—
Personnel	—	—	2,000	—	—
General factory administration	—	35	7,000	—	—
Cafeteria	—	10	4,000	1,000	—
Storeroom	—	5	7,000	1,000	—
Machinery	5,000	50	30,000	8,000	2,000
Assembly	15,000	100	50,000	17,000	1,000
	20,000	200	1,00,000	27,000	3,000

The company management decided that the appropriate bases used by each service department would be the following:

Building and grounds	Square feet
Personnel department	Employees
General factory administration	Total labour-hours
Cafeteria	Employees
Storeroom	Requisitions

Direct labour-hours are used as the basis for computing the production dapartment's factory overhead application rates.

You are required to allocate the total budgeted costs of the service departments by using direct method. Also, determine the factory overhead absorption rates for the production departments.

SOLUTION

Table 5.3 Determination of Factory Overhead Absorption Rates for Production Departments (Machinery and Assembly)

Items	*Basis of charge*	*Service Departments*					*Production Departments*	
		Building and grounds	*Personnel*	*General factory administration*	*Cafeteria*	*Storeroom*	*Machinery*	*Assembly*
Budgeted costs	Allocation	₹1,00,000	₹10,000	₹2,60,900	₹16,400	₹26,700	₹3,47,000	₹4,89,000
Cost of service departments apportioned to production departments:								
Building and grounds	Square feet ratio (3:5)	(1,00,000)					37,500	62,500
Personnel	Employees (1:2)		(10,000)				3,333	6,667
General factory administration	Total labour-hours (8:17)			(2,60,900)			83,488	1,77,412
Cafeteria	Employees (1:2)				(16,400)		5,467	10,933
Storeroom	Requisitions (2:1)					(26,700)	17,800	8,900
Total cost		—	—	—	—	—	4,94,588	7,55,412
Direct labour-hours							5,000	15,000
Factory overhead absorption rate (Total cost/Direct labour-hours)							98.92	50.36

Step Method In situations, when one service department renders services to another (that is reciprocity exists), the step method is more appropriate than the direct method. This method takes into consideration the *total/true* cost of each service department (and not partial) in assigning them to production departments.

The following is a list of steps used for the purpose of apportioning budgeted costs of service departments:[5]

(i) It is usual to apportion first the cost of that service department which renders services to the largest number of other service departments.

(ii) The budgeted costs of the service department that renders services to the next largest number of service departments are then apportioned. Obviously, any apportioned costs added to this service department from step 1 are included. The sum of budgeted service cost, so arrived at, is then apportioned among the remaining service departments (whose costs are yet to be assigned). The service department whose budgeted costs were apportioned as per the step 1 will not receive any cost share from the second department.

(iii) This sequence is continued, step-by-step, until all the budgeted service department costs have been apportioned to production departments.

Using the facts given in Example 5.3, cost apportionment of service departments as per Step method is shown in Table 5.4.

Table 5.4 Determination of Factory Overhead Absorption Rates for Production Departments (Machinery and Assembly)

Items	*Basis of charge*	*Service Departments*					*Production Departments*	
		Building and grounds	*Personnel*	*General factory administration*	*Cafeteria*	*Storeroom*	*Machinery*	*Assembly*
Budgeted costs	Allocation	₹1,00,000	₹10,000	₹2,60,900	₹16,400	₹26,700	₹3,47,000	₹4,89,000
Distribution of factory overheads of:								
Building and grounds	Square feet ratio	(1,00,000)	2,000	7,000	4,000	7,000	30,000	50,000
Personnel	Employees		(12,000)	2,100	600	300	3,000	6,000
General factory administration	Total labour-hours			(2,70,000)	10,000	10,000	80,000	1,70,000
Cafeteria	Employees				(31,000)	1,000	10,000	20,000
Storeroom	Requisition					(45,000)	30,000	15,000
Total cost		—	—	—	—	—	5,00,000	7,50,000
Direct labour-hours (DLH)							5,000	15,000
Factory overhead absorption rate (Total cost/DLH)							100	50

The allocation of 5 service departments (SD) is made in the following order: **(a)** Building and grounds (shared with 4 SD), **(b)** Personnel department (shared with 3 SD), **(c)** General factory administration (shared with 2 SD), **(d)** Cafeteria (with one SD), and **(e)** Service departments costs of storeroom is apportioned only with 2 production departments and not with any service department.

It may be noted that under direct method, budgeted costs of each of the five service departments were apportioned between 2 production departments only; service departments had not been apportioned any costs, at any stage.

Repeated Distribution Method The process of apportioning service departments overhead is continued until the figures of unapportioned sum(s) of service department(s) become negligible: The following steps are involved in its application:

(i) The first service department's (to be identified on the basis of the order in which their names are stated) budgeted costs are to be apportioned. As a result, the balance of the first service department becomes nil; its costs are apportioned among other departments (on the basis of their percentage share or some other base stated).

(ii) The budgeted costs of the second service department (consisting of original amount plus the apportioned sum from the first service department) is to be apportioned among other departments including the first service department.

(iii) This process continues for all the remaining/other service departments. The steps shown as per (i) to (iii) refer to the first phase.

(iv) The second phase of cycle starts once again with the first service department; it will consist only of apportioned amounts from other service departments. As a result, the total costs of service departments become less and less with each phase of apportionment.

(v) The process comes to an end when it is found that the residual sum (to be apportioned) has been either exhausted or has become virtually insignificant.

Consider Example 5.4.

EXAMPLE 5.4

A small company has three production departments and two service departments. Distribution summary of overheads (per week) is as follows:

Production departments:	
A	₹13,600
B	14,700
C	12,800
Service departments:	
X	9,000
Y	3,000

The expenses of service departments are charged on a percentage basis, which is as follows:

Department	*A*	*B*	*C*	*X*	*Y*
X	40	30	20	—	10
Y	30	30	20	20	—

Apportion the cost of service departments by using the repeated distribution method.

SOLUTION

Table 5.5 Apportionment of Cost of Service Departments to Production Departments

Particulars	*Production departments*			*Service departments*	
	A	*B*	*C*	*X*	*Y*
Primary apportionment	₹13,600	₹14,700	₹12,800	₹9,000	₹3,000
Department X overheads apportioned in ratio of (4:3:2:1)	3,600	2,700	1,800	(9,000)	900
Department Y overheads (₹3,900) apportioned in the ratio of (3:3:2:2)	1,170	1,170	780	780	(3,900)
Department X overheads (₹780) apportioned in the ratio of 4:3:2:1	312	234	156	(780)	78
Department Y overheads (₹78) apportioned in the ratio of 3:3:2:2	23	23	16	16	(78)
Department X overheads (₹16) apportioned in the ratio of 4:3:2:1	6	5	3	(16)	2
Department Y overheads (₹2) apportioned in the ratio of 3:3:2:2	1	1	—	—	(2)
Total	18,712	18,833	15,555	—	—

Algebraic Method This method is the most appropriate of all the four methods when reciprocal services exist between service departments. It is also called the reciprocal services method as it takes into account cost flows in both directions between service departments that render services to each other. Typically, the service departments provide services to each other in most of the manufacturing firms in practice. This method provides conceptually the most correct budget cost estimates of service departments and their subsequent apportionment.

Example 5.5 illustrates its application.

EXAMPLE 5.5

Tiny Industries Ltd has 2 service (SD) and 2 production departments (PD). It employs the algebraic method to allocate budgeted service department costs. The following information is available:

Department	*Budgeted costs*	*Services provided by*	
		Department A	*Department B*
Total costs:			
SD A	₹1,00,000	—	20 %
SD B	2,00,000	35 %	—
Factory overhead costs:			
PD_1	1,40,000	15	45
PD_2	60,000	50	35
	5,00,000	100 %	100 %
Direct labour-hours (DLH):			
PD_1	20,000		
PD_2	10,000		

From the above information, you are required to: **(a)** Allocate the service departments costs to production departments. Use algebraic equation method, **(b)** Compute factory overhead absorption rate, based on direct labour-hours.

SOLUTION

(a) Let X be the total overhead costs of SD A and Y be of SD B

X = ₹1,00,000 + 0.20Y

Y = ₹2,00,000 + 0.35X

Substituting,

X = ₹1,00,000 + 0.20 × (₹2,00,000 + 0.35X) = ₹1,00,000 + ₹40,000 + 0.07X

= ₹1,40,000/0.93 = ₹1,50,538

Y = ₹2,00,000 + 0.35 × (₹1,50,538) = ₹2,52,688

Allocation of Overheads Among Production Departments

Items	*Production Departments*		*Total*
	P_1	P_2	
Direct overheads	₹1,40,000	₹60,000	₹2,00,000
SD A (15:50)	22,581	75,269	97,850
SD B (45:35)	1,13,709	88,441	2,02,150
Total	2,76,290	2,23,710	5,00,000

WORKING NOTES

1. Total expenses of SD A	₹1,50,538
Less share of SD B (0.35 × ₹1,50,538)	52,688
Amount to be divided between production departments	97,850
2. Total expenses of SD B	2,52,688
Less share of SD A (0.20 × ₹2,52,688)	50,538
Amount to be divided between production departments	2,02,150

(b) *Factory Overhead Absorption Rate (based on DLH) for Production Departments*

For P_1 (₹2,76,290/20,000, DLH)	₹13.8145
For P_2 (₹2,23,710/10,000, DLH)	22.3710

ABSORPTION OF FACTORY OVERHEADS

Absorption rate is the equitable allotment of factory overheads to cost units/objects.

If in production cost centre/department, all units produced are identical, the total factory overheads of production department could be shared equally among the units produced. For instance, if the total budgeted production department costs (inclusive of apportioned share from service departments) are ₹1,50,000 per month, budgeted production units are 15,000; factory overhead (predetermined) rate would be ₹10 per unit.

However, when the units are not normally identical and different facilities are used in their production, if a unit rate were used, some units would be over-charged and others under-charged. This will cause wrong cost estimation of various products and, hence, incorrect income reporting of these products to the management. On the basis of income reporting, the management may like to encourage more profitable products (in terms of expansion) in future; it may be possible that these products, in effect, may not be more profitable as they have been charged lower share of factory overheads than their due. Further, the management may like to discontinue products (which appear to be less profitable or loss-incurring) due to overcharge of factory overheads.

Thus, it is imperative to have an equitable allotment of factory overheads to cost units. This allotment of factory overheads to cost units/cost objects is referred to as *absorption*. The absorption rate is usually expressed in terms of rupee(s) per unit of estimated activity base (called denominator activity).

There are no definitive rules for determining which base to use as the denominator activity. However, a close nexus between the denominator activity base and factory overhead costs should be ensured. This will facilitate determination of equitable and fair absorption rate. Besides, the method used should be simple and economical; as far as possible, denominator activity base "must be a factor that is common to all jobs, has a high correlation with the incurrence of overhead costs, and is easy to measure."[6]

Some common bases for absorption of factory overhead are: **(i)** Units of production **(ii)** Direct materials cost, **(iii)** Direct labour cost **(iv)** Prime cost method **(v)** Direct labour-hours and **(vi)** Machine-hours.

Units of Production Method

Under this method, factory overheads are absorbed at a uniform rate for each unit produced. This method is suitable when a production department manufacturers only one type of product. The factory overhead absorption rate is computed using Equation 5.1.

Estimated factory overhead costs ÷ Estimated units of production **(5.1)**

Direct Material Cost Method

Direct material cost method the overhead recovery rate is given by dividing estimated overhead costs by the estimated direct material cost.

This method is an appropriate basis of charging fixed overheads to production when overhead costs are closely related to direct materials cost. In an assembly area, where many of the costs correspond to the quantity of materials used, it may be equitable to assign factory overhead costs on the basis of direct materials costs. The overhead recovery rate (in terms of percentage of direct materials cost) is computed, using Equation 5.2.

(Estimated factory overhead costs ÷ Estimated direct materials cost) × 100 **(5.2)**

However, in practice, this method should not be normally followed (except in situation when factory overhead costs are significantly correlated to direct material costs) for the following reasons:

(a) While cost of materials is often subject to considerable fluctuations, factory overhead costs are not normally accompained by similar fluctuations.

(b) For firms using job costing, this method may give very distorted results. The mere fact that a job uses materials of a very expensive nature is no justification for the assumption that the factory overhead appropriate to that job will be proportionately heavier.[7]

(c) Overheads attributable to jobs tend to vary more in tune with time spent on them rather than on the value of materials used by them as most factory overheads, say, rent, rates insurance and salaries accrue on time basis. For this reason, time should be reckoned the key factor in charging factory overhead costs to production.

Direct Labour Costs Basis/Method

This method is suggested for the following reasons:

(a) There is built-in mechanism to consider time factor; it is reasonable to assume that the greater the direct labour costs attributed to a job, the longer is likely to be the time spent on that job.

(b) Labour rates are usually more stable than material prices.

(c) Variable factory overhead costs are likely to vary, to some extent, with the number of employees and, thus, with direct labour costs.

Direct labour cost basis computes the factory overhead rate as a percentage of direct labour cost.

However, this method may not provide correct results in situations when different types of labour personnel (obviously subject to different wage rates) are used in different jobs. For instance, assume in Job A, skilled labour is used (which is paid at ₹20 per hour); unskilled labour is used in Job B, paid @ ₹10 per hour. As per this method, factory overheads will be charged twice in Job A compared to Job B, assuming both jobs use the same hours. Thus, the wages incurred on different jobs may not be necessarily in the same ratio as the hours spent and, hence, distortion in absorption of overheads. The question of overtime further compounds the problem.

(d) This method will also be inappropriate if the major share of factory overhead costs consists of depreciation, repairs and maintenance, and other machine-related costs. In such a situation, there is likely to be a little relationship between factory overhead costs and direct labour costs.

The factory overhead rate in terms of percentage of direct labour cost is computed, using Equation 5.3.

(Estimated factory overhead costs ÷ Estimated direct labour costs) × 100 **(5.3)**

Prime Cost Method

Since both direct materials and direct labour give rise to factory overheads, both these costs (prime cost) should be the basis to arrive at factory overhead absorption rate. Equation 5.4 provides the computation basis (in terms of percentage of prime cost).

(Estimated factory overhead costs ÷ Estimated prime costs) × 100 **(5.4)**

This method is an ideal in the most unlikely situation (or rare situation) when the same material and the same type of labour (drawing uniform wages) is engaged in production/jobs carried out by the manufacturing firms. Conversely, this method has the drawback of giving very distorted results if different types of materials as well as different types of labour is used in production/jobs.

Direct Labour-hours

This method is an appropriate absorption base when there is a direct relationship between factory overhead costs and direct labour-hours. It is likely to be so for businesses where most of the work is accomplished by labour. The results under this method are not distorted even when there is a marked difference among hourly wage rates as this method takes into account *hours* used on the job and not *the labour cost.* As stated earlier, factory overheads are likely to vary more in tune with time and not with labour cost; therefore this method is more logical than direct labour cost method. The factory overhead absorption rate per direct labour-hour is computed using Equation 5.5.

Estimated factory overhead costs ÷ Estimated direct labour-hours **(5.5)**

This method, however, will be inappropriate if factory overhead costs are primarily based on machine-related activity.

Machine-hour Rate

Machine-hour rate is calculated by dividing the etimated factory overhead costs by the estimated machine- hours.

This method is the most ideal method of absorbing factory overheads of those production departments in which machinery represents the predominant factor of production, that is, where most of the work is done through machines. This generally occurs in those production departments which are largely automated; as a result, the major share of factory overhead costs consist of depreciation on plant and machinery installed/used in that department. Firms, providing computer services, normally charge their costs based on computer time used. The factory overhead absorption rate per machine-hour (MHR) is computed according to Equation 5.6.

Estimated factory overhead costs ÷ Estimated machine-hours **(5.6)**

Since most of the work is done through machines, machine-hour rate is normally adopted to absorb factory overheads.

In cases where production department has several machines (serving different needs), the factory overheads among different machines (each machine/block of machine constitutes a cost centre) should be apportioned on equitable basis. For instance, **(i)** rent and rates, lighting and heating costs can be apportioned on the basis of *effective* floor space occupied (that is, allowing for reasonable space to operate the machine; **(ii)** insurance may be apportioned on the basis of book value of machines; **(iii)** depreciation may be computed on the basis of effective cost of the machine and its effective useful life in hours; **(iv)** power costs should be charged on the basis of actual units consumed; **(v)** supervision costs are to be apportioned on the basis of the degree of supervision required by each machine. Similarly, other production department costs are to be apportioned on the most equitable basis. The estimated productive machine-hours should be based on effective hours for which the machine works. It should exclude time lost due to setting-up of the machine and its maintenance.

Further, total overheads related to machine should be segregated in two categories, normally: fixed costs (commonly called standing charges), and variable costs (referred to as machine expenses) for cost control purposes, as also for decision-making purposes. Included in machine expenses are depreciation, power, repairs and maintenance; standing charges include rent and rates, general lighting, insurance, and supervisor's salary.

Where the work performed by direct labour personnel is identifiable with a particular machine group, their direct wages should be included as part of the machine group cost. Thus production/ job will be charged with a machine-hour rate which is inclusive of direct wages.[8] Such a rate is known as *comprehensive* machine-hour rate.

Examples 5.6 and 5.7 illustrate the computation of machine-hour rate and comprehensive machine-hour rate respectively.

EXAMPLE 5.6

Compute the machine-hour rate from the following data:

Cost of machine	₹30,00,000
Estimated scrap value after the expiry of its useful life (5 years)	5,00,000
Rent and rates for the shop per month	10,000
General lighting for the shop per month	6,000
Insurance premium for the machine per annum	48,000
Repairs and maintenance expenses per annum	50,000
Power consumption — 10 units per hour @ ₹6 per unit	60
Estimated working hours per annum 2,200 (including setting-up time of 200 hours; no power is required during setting-up time)	
Shop supervisor's salary per month	30,000

The machine occupies one-fourth of the total area of the shop. The supervisor is expected to devote one-fifth of his time for supervising the machine.

Determine machine-hour rate.

SOLUTION

Determination of Machine-hour Rate

Particulars		*Rate per hour*
Standing charges:		
Rent and rates (₹10,000 per month × 12)/4	₹30,000	
General lighting (₹6,000 per month × 12)/4	18,000	
Insurance premium per annum	48,000	
Shop supervisor's salary (₹30,000 per month × 12)/5	72,000	
Total standing charges	1,68,000	
Productive working machine-hours (2,200 – 200, setting-up time)	2,000	
Standing charges per hour (₹1,68,000/2,000)		₹84.00
*Machine expenses**:		
Repairs and maintenance expenses (₹50,000/2,000 hours)	25.0	
Depreciation [(₹30 lakh – ₹5 lakh)/5years] ÷ 2,000 hours	250.0	
Power consumption per hour	60.0	335.00
Machine-hour rate per hour		419.00

*are in the nature of mixed and variable costs.

EXAMPLE 5.7

A machine costs ₹9 lakh and is deemed to have a scrap value of 10 per cent at the end of its effective life (9 years). Ordinarily, the machine is expected to run for 2,400 hours per annum but it is estimated that 150 hours will be lost for normal repairs and maintenance and further 750 hours will be lost due to staggering. The other details in respect of machine shop are:

Wages, bonus and provident fund contribution of each of two operators (each operator is in charge of two machines) (per year)	₹1,80,000
Rent of the shop (per year)	1,20,000
General lighting of the shop (per month)	10,000
Insurance premium for one machine (per year)	32,000
Cost of repairs and maintenance per machine (per month)	10,000
Shop supervisor's salary (per month)	20,000
Power consumption of machine per hour 20 units @ ₹6 per unit	
Other factory overheads attributable to the shop (per annum)	1,60,000

There are four identical machines in the shop. The supervisor is expected to devote one-fifth of time for supervising the machine. Compute a comprehensive machine-hour rate from the above details.

SOLUTION

Determination of Comprehensive Machine-hour Rate per Hour (per machine)

Particulars		Amount per hour
Standing charges per annum		
Rent and rates (₹1,20,000/4 machines)	₹30,000	
General lighting (₹10,000 × 12)/4 machines	30,000	
Insurance premium	32,000	
Supervisor's salary (₹20,000 × 12)/5	48,000	
Other factory overheads (₹1,60,000/4 machines)	40,000	
Total standing charges	1,80,000	
Standing charges per hour (₹1,80,000/1,500[1] machine-hours)		₹120
Machine charges per hour		
Wages, bonus and provident fund (₹1,80,000/2 machines) = ₹90,000/1,500 machine-hours	60	
Repairs and maintenance (₹10,000 × 12)/1,500	80	
Power (20 units × ₹6 per unit)	120	
Depreciation [(₹9 lakh – ₹0.90 lakh)/9 years] ÷ 1,500	60	320
Machine-hour rate		440

Note: Productive machine–hours (2,400 – 150 – 750) = 1,500

There is no absorption method which is the best to charge factory overheads in all situations. Selection of the method that best serves a firm's needs can be made only after the factory overheads have been carefully analyzed and their incurrence has been observed to exhibit direct/close association with the method (say machine-hours, labour-hours, direct wage cost, direct material cost) chosen for absorption of factory overheads.

UNDERABSORPTION AND OVERABSORPTION OF FACTORY OVERHEADS

Once the factory overhead absorption/application rate has been determined, it is used as the basis to charge factory overhead costs to actual production. The rate is applied to production on an ongoing basis as goods are manufactured according to the method used (say, direct labour-hours, machine-hours, units produced). For instance, assume that factory overhead absorption rate is ₹50 per machine-hour, using machine-hour as a base and that, 10,000 machine-hours were used, ₹5,00,000 (10,000 machine-hours × ₹50) of factory overheads will be charged to production. If the actual factory overheads are ₹6,00,000, it implies they are underabsorbed/underapplied by ₹1,00,000 (₹6,00,000 – ₹5,00,000). Alternatively, if the actual factory overheads are ₹4,50,000, it is the case of overabsorption/overapplied factory overheads by ₹50,000 (₹5,00,000 – ₹4,50,000).

The under-absorption and overabsorption of factory overheads are computed as per Equations 5.7 and 5.8.

Overhead variance is the difference between the actual factory overhead costs and the absorbed factory overheads.

Under-absorption of factory overheads = Actual factory overheads – Overheads charged to production **(5.7)**

Overabsorption of factory overheads = Overheads charged to production – Production overheads **(5.8)**

The difference between the actual factory overhead costs and absorbed factory overheads is referred to as overhead variance.[9] Overhead variances may be disposed of by following either of the two methods:

First, they may be treated as a period costs and, therefore, assigned to the income statement of current period. The adjustment is made through cost of goods sold account. Journal entries will be as follows:

Cost of Goods Sold A/c . . . . Dr To Factory Overhead Control A/c (For charging under-absorbed factory overheads)	
Factory Overhead Control A/c . . . . Dr To Cost of Goods Sold A/c (For adjusting over-absorbed factory overheads)	

This method is normally used when variance is insignificant in amount.

In the second method, it may be considered as the cost of production of the current period and the amount is pro-rated to work-in-process inventory, finished goods inventory, and cost of goods sold in proportion to the unadjusted factory overhead balance in each account. This method is normally used when the variance is significant in amount. The objective is to allocate the under-or overabsorbed factory overhead costs to those accounts which were distorted by using incorrect absorption rate and to bring their ending balances close to what they would have been if the correct application rate had been used. Journal entries would be as follows:

Work-in-process Inventory A/c	Dr
Finished Goods Inventory A/c	Dr
Cost of Goods Sold A/c	Dr
To Factory Overhead Control A/c	
(For charging under-applied factory overheads)	
Factory Overhead Control A/c	Dr
To Work-in-process Inventory A/c	
To Cost of Goods Sold A/c	
(For adjusting over-applied factory overheads)	

Apart from the magnitude of variance, the treatment would also depend on the nature of such variances. If the variance has been an outcome of abnormal factors/unusual events (say, defective planning), it should be considered as period costs and taken to current year's cost of goods sold account. On the contrary, if such a variance has been caused by errors in estimation (either of budgeted factory overhead or activity base), it should be pro-rated to work-in-process inventory, finished goods inventory and cost of goods sold.

EXAMPLE 5.8

In a manufacturing unit, factory overhead was recovered at a predetermined rate of ₹25 per manday. The total factory overhead expenses incurred and the mandays actually worked were ₹41.50 lakh and 1.5 lakh, respectively. Out of the 40,000 units produced during a period, 30,000 were sold.

On analysing the reasons, it was found that 60 per cent of the unabsorbed overheads were due to defective planning and the rest were attributable to increase in overhead costs.

How would unabsorbed overheads be treated in cost accounts?

SOLUTION

Determination of Unabsorbed Factory Overheads

Factory overhead expenses incurred	₹41,50,000
Less factory overheads absorbed (1,50,000 mandays × ₹25 per manday)	37,50,000
Unabsorbed factory overheads	4,00,000

Treatment of Unabsorbed Factory Overheads:

(1) 60 per cent of unabsorbed overheads are attributed to defective planning. Being abnormal in nature, ₹2,40,000 (0.60 × ₹4 lakh) is charged to costing profit and loss account		₹2,40,000
(2) ₹1,60,000 is to be pro-rated between cost of goods sold (30,000 units) and finished goods inventory (10,000 units):		
— Cost of goods sold (₹1,60,000 × 3/4)	₹1,20,000	
— Finished goods inventory (₹1,60,000 × 1/4)	40,000	1,60,000
		4,00,000

EXAMPLE 5.9

The XYZ Ltd has the following information relating to applied and actual factory overheads for the current month:

Factory overheads, incurred	₹1,52,500
Applied factory overheads	1,98,500

Applied factory overhead costs are in the following accounts:

Cost of goods sold	1,60,000
Ending work-in-process inventory	17,500
Ending finished goods inventory	21,000

You are required to allocate the under or overapplied factory overheads to relevant accounts and pass necessary journal entries at the month-end.

SOLUTION

Overapplied/Overabsorbed Factory Overheads:

Applied factory overheads	₹1,98,500
Less factory overheads incurred	1,52,500
	46,000
Over-absorbed factory overheads will be pro-rated in the following accounts:	
Cost of goods sold (₹1,60,000/₹1,98,500) × ₹46,000	37,078
Ending work-in-process inventory (₹17,500/₹1,98,500) × ₹46,000	4,055
Ending finished goods inventory (₹21,000/₹1,98,500) × ₹46,000	4,867
	46,000

Journal Entries:

Factory Overhead Applied A/c. . . . . . .Dr	₹1,98,500	
To Over-applied Factory Overhead A/c		₹46,000
To Factory Overhead Control A/c		1,52,500
Overapplied Factory Overhead A/c. . . . . . .Dr	46,000	
To Cost of Goods Sold A/c		37,078
To Ending Work-in-process Inventory A/c		4,055
To Ending Finished Goods Inventory A/c		4,867

SUMMARY

- Factory overheads represent all indirect manufacturing costs. Unlike direct costs, these costs cannot be conveniently and wholly charged to product cost centres. All of the factory overhead costs find their way into production costs through a somewhat difficult method of allocations and apportionments and reallocations and reapportionments. Allotment of common costs/factory overheads to cost centres/cost objects/cost units is often made on a somewhat arbitrary basis. Cost allocation procedures are costly as they use the time of cost accountants and decision-makers. Therefore, cost allocation should be justified on the basis of cost-benefit considerations. Yet, cost allocation is necessary to determine the true cost of products, particularly in the case of multi-product firms.

➢ Costing and control of factory overheads involves **(i)** Determination of factory overheads application role, **(ii)** Allocation of overheads, **(iii)** Absorption of overheads and **(iv)** Under/over absorption of overheads.

➢ Factory overheads costs are normally allocated at a predetermined factory overhead application rate. It is determined dividing budgeted factory overhead costs (consisting of fixed costs, variable costs and mixed costs) for the coming period/year by capacity level. Among four capacity measures, normal capacity and expected capacity levels (theoretical capacity, practical capacity), normal capacity (based on long-run productive capacity) is considered as the best denominator measure.

➢ Cost common to more than one department are to be allocated among the production departments receiving benefits, and service department costs are to be distributed among producing departments. Cost incurred in service departments are apportioned by **(i)** Direct method, **(ii)** Step method, **(iii)** Repeated dstribution method, and **(iv)** Algebraic method, among production departments as part of factory overhead costs.

➢ According to direct method, total budgeted costs of service departments are apportioned between/among production departments, ignoring any services provided by service departments to each other.

➢ In situations when one service department renders services to another (that is reciprocity exits), the step method is more appropriate than the direct method. This method takes into consideration the *total/true* cost of each service department (and not partial) in assigning them to production departments.

The following is a list of steps used for the purpose of apportioning budgeted costs of service departments.

(i) It is usual to apportion first the cost of that service department which renders services to the largest number of other service departments.

(ii) The budgeted costs of the service department that renders services to the next largest number of service departments are then apportioned. Obviously, any apportioned costs added to this service department from step 1 are included. The sum of budgeted service cost, so arrived at, is then apportioned to note that the service department (whose costs are yet to be assigned). It is important to note that the service department whose budgeted costs were apportioned as per the step 1 will not receive any cost share from the second department.

(iii) This sequence is continued, step-by-step, until all the budgeted service department costs have been apportioned departments.

➢ The process of apportioning service departments overhead according to repeated distribution method is continued until the figures of unapportioned sum(s) of service department(s) become negligible: The following steps are involved in its application:

(i) The first service department's (to be identified on the basis of the order in which their names are stated) budgeted costs are to be apportioned. As a result, the balance of the first service department becomes nil; its costs are apportioned among other departments (on the basis of their percentage share or some other stated base).

(ii) The budgeted costs of the second service department (consisting of original amount plus the apportioned sum from the first service department) is to be apportioned among other departments including the first service department.

(iii) This process continues for all the remaining/other service departments. The steps shown as per (i) to (iii) refer to the first phase.

(iv) The second phase of cycle starts once again with the first service department; it will consist only of apportioned amounts from other service departments. As a result, the total costs of service departments becomes less and less with each phase of apportionment.

(v) The process comes to an end when it is found that the residual sum (to be apportioned) has been either exhausted or has become virtually insignificant.

- The algebraic method is the most appropriate of all the four methods when reciprocal services exist between service departments. This method is also called the reciprocal services method as it takes into account cost flows in both directions between service departments that render services to each other. This is typical for the service departments to provide services to each other in most of the manufacturing firms in practice. This method provides conceptually the most correct budget cost estimates of service departments and their subsequent apportionment.
- Factory overheads of production departments (inclusive of appropriate apportioned share from other services departments) are to be applied to production/jobs. Some common bases of absorption of factory overheads are: **(i)** Units of production, **(ii)** Direct materials cost, **(iii)** Direct labour cost, **(iv)** Prime cost method, **(v)** Direct labour-hours, and **(vi)** Machine-hours.
- According to units of production method, the factory overhead absorption rate = Estimated/bugeted factory overhead costs ÷ Estimated/budgeted units of production
- According to the direct material cost method, the overhead recovery rate in terms of percentage of direct material cost = (Estimated/budgeted factory overhead cost/Estimated direct material cost) × 100
- The factory overhead rate according to direct labour cost method = (Estimated factory overhead cost/Estimated direct labour cost) × 100
- According to prime cost method the factory overhead rate = (Estimated factory overhead cost/Estimated prime cost) × 100
- The factory overhead absorpation rate per direct labour hour = Estimated factory overhead costs ÷ Estimated direct labour-hours
- According to the machine-hour rate, the factory overhead absorption rate per machine-hour (MHR) = Estimated factory overhead costs ÷ Estimated machine-hours
- Since most of the work is done through machines, machine-hour rate is normally adopted to absorb factory overheads.
- In cases where prodution department has several machine (serving different needs), the factory overheads among different machines (each machine/block of machine constitutes a cost centre) should be apportioned on equitable basis. For instance, **(i)** rent and rates, lighting and heating costs can be apportioned on the basis of *effective* floor space occupied (that is, allowing for reasonable space to operate the machine); **(ii)** insurance may be apportioned on the basis of book value of machines; **(iii)** depreciation may be computed on the basis of effective cost of the machine and its effective useful life in hours; **(iv)** power costs should be charged on the basis of actual units consumed; **(v)** supervision costs are to be apportioned on the basis of the degree of supervision required by each machine. Similarly, other production departments costs are to be apportioned on the most equitable basis. The estimated productive machine-hours should be based on effective hours for which the machine works. It should exclude time lost due to setting-up of the machine and its maintenance.
- Further, total overheads related to machine should be normally segregated in two categories: fixed costs (commonly called standing charges), and variable costs (referred to as machine expenses) for cost control purposes, as also for decision-making purposes. Included in machine expenses are depreciation, power, repairs and maintenance; standing charges include rent and rates, general lighting, insurance, and supervisor's salary.

- Where the work performed by direct labour personnel is identifiable with a particular machine group, their direct wages should be included as part of the machine group cost. Thus production/job will be charged with a machine-hour rate which is inclusive of direct wages. Such a rate is known as *comprehensive* machine-hour rate.
- Direct labour-hour rate (where factory overhead costs consist primarily of labour activity) and machine-hour rate (where indirect manufacturing costs predominantly comprise of machine-related activity) are the two suitable methods. Further, for cost control and decision-making purposes, factory overhead absorption rate should be computed separately both for fixed costs and variable costs.
- When predetermined factory overhead applied rate is used as the basis of absorption of indirect manufacturing costs, it is seldom that the total factory overhead costs applied to production (or jobs) in a given period are equal to the total factory overhead costs incurred in that period. When the absorbed factory overheads exceed the actual, it is a situation of overabsorption; under-absorption results when the actual factory overhead costs exceed the factory overheads charged to production. At the end of accounting period, if the over/under-applied overhead balance is insignificant, it is normally closed by transferring to cost of goods sold; if it is being sizeable, it is pro-rated to work-in-process inventory, finished goods inventory and cost of goods sold.

REFERENCES

1. Polimeni, R.S., *et. al., Cost Accounting: Concepts and Application for Managerial Decision Making* (New York, McGraw-Hill), 1991, p. 143.
2. *Ibid.*, 143-44.
3. For methods of segregating mixed costs, please refer to Chapter 7.
4. Deakin, E.B. and M.W. Maher, *Cost Accounting,* (Illinois, Irwin), 1984, p. 89.
5. Polimeni, R.S., *et. al., op. cit.*, p. 160.
6. Morse, W.J., *Cost Accounting,* (Massachusetts, Addison-Wesley Publishing Co.), 1978, p. 66
7. Wald, J., *Bigg's Cost Accounts,* (London, Macdonald & Grans Limited), 1978, p. 118
8. *Ibid.*, p. 124
9. For details of overhead variances, please refer to Chapter 16 of this book.

SOLVED PROBLEMS

P.5.1 Atlas Engineering Limited accepts a variety of jobs which require both manual and machine operations. The budgeted profit and loss account for the current period is as follows: (₹in lakh)

Sales		75
Cost:		
Direct materials	10	
Direct labour	5	
Prime cost	15	
Production overheads	30	
Production cost	45	
Administrative, selling and distribution overheads	15	60
Profit		15

Other budgeted data:

Labour-hours for the period	25,000
Machine-hours for the period	15,000
Number of jobs for the period	300

An enquiry has been received recently from a customer and the production department has prepared the following estimate of the prime cost required for the job.

Direct material	₹2,500
Direct labour	2,000
Prime cost	4,500
Labour-hours required	80
Machine-hours required	50

You are required to:

(a) Calculate by different methods, six overhead absorption rates for absorption of production overhead and comment on the suitability of each.

(b) Calculate the production overhead cost of the order based on each of the above rates.

(c) Give your recommendation to the company.

SOLUTION

(a) *Statement showing Determination of Production Overhead Rate under various Methods of Absorption.*

Method of absorption	*Production overhead absorption rate*
1. Percentage of direct material cost (₹30 lakh/₹10 lakh) × 100	300 per cent (3 times) of direct material cost
2. Percentage of direct labour cost (₹30 lakh/₹5 lakh) × 100	600 per cent (6 times) of direct labour cost
3. Percentage of prime cost (₹30 lakh/₹15 lakh) × 100	200 per cent (twice) of prime cost
4. Machine-hour rate (₹30 lakh/15,000 hours)	₹200 per machine-hour
5. Direct labour-hour rate (₹30 lakh/25,000 hours)	₹120 per labour-hour
6. Production unit method (₹30 lakh/300 Jobs)	₹10,000 per job

(b) *Statement showing Determination of Production Overhead Cost of a Job under various Methods of Absorption.*

Method	*Production overhead cost*
1. Percentage of direct material cost	₹2500 × 3 = ₹7,500
2. Percentage of direct labour cost	₹2,000 × 6 = ₹12,000
3. Percentage of prime cost	₹4,500 × 2 = ₹9,000
4. Machine-hour rate	50 hours × ₹200 = ₹10,000
5. Direct labour-hour rate	80 hours × ₹120 = ₹9,600
6. Production unit method	1 × ₹10,000 = ₹10,000

(c) RECOMMENDATION The company is advised to apply machine-hour rate to compute production overhead cost as mechanisation is high.

P.5.2 A company's production costs for the current ending March 31 are given below:

Item	*Production departments*			*Service departments*			*Total*
	P_1	P_2	P_3	*Office*	*Stores*	*Workshop*	
Direct wages	₹2,00,000	₹2,50,000	₹3,00,000	—	—	—	₹7,50,000
Direct materials	3,00,000	3,50,000	4,50,000	—	—	—	11,00,000
Indirect materials	20,000	30,000	30,000	₹10,000	₹20,000	₹20,000	1,30,000
Indirect wages	30,000	30,000	40,000	1,00,000	1,00,000	50,000	3,50,000
Area (sq. metres)	200	250	300	150	100	250	1,250
Book value of machinery	3,00,000	3,50,000	2,50,000	—	—	1,50,000	10,50,000

(*Contd.*)

(Contd.)

Total horse power (H.P.) of machines	15	20	25	—	—	5	65
Machine-hours worked	10,000	20,000	15,000	—	—	5,000	50,000

The other expenses are as follows:

Rent	₹1,25,000
Insurance	10,500
Depreciation (per cent of value of machinery)	15
Power	38,000
Light	12,500

You are required to prepare an overhead analysis sheet for the departments showing clearly the basis of apportionment where necessary.

SOLUTION

Overhead Analysis Sheet

Item	*Basis*	*Production departments*			*Service departments*			*Total*
		P_1	P_2	P_3	*Office*	*Stores*	*Workshop*	
Indirect materials	Allocation	₹20,000	₹30,000	₹30,000	₹10,000	₹20,000	₹20,000	₹1,30,000
Indirect wages	Allocation	30,000	30,000	40,000	1,00,000	1,00,000	50,000	3,50,000
Rent	Area	20,000	25,000	30,000	15,000	10,000	25,000	1,25,000
Insurance	Value of machine	3,000	3,500	2,500	—	—	1,500	10,500
Depreciation	Value of machine	45,000	52,500	37,500	—	—	22,500	1,57,500
Power	Horse power	8,770	11,690	14,620	—	—	2,920	38,000
Light	Area	2,000	2,500	3,000	1,500	1,000	2,500	12,500
Total		1,28,770	1,55,190	1,57,620	1,26,500	1,31,000	1,24,420	8,23,500
office overheads	Direct wages	33,730	42,170	50,600	(1,26,500)	—	—	—
Stores overheads	Direct materials	35,730	41,680	53,590	—	(1,31,000)	—	—
Workshop overheads	Machine-hours	27,650	55,300	41,470	—	—	(1,24,420)	—
Total overheads		2,25,880	2,94,340	3,03,280	—	—	—	8,23,500

P.5.3 Deccan Manufacturing Limited has three departments which are regarded as production departments. Service department's costs are distributed to these production departments using the "Step Ladder Method" of distribution. Estimates of factory overhead costs to be incurred by each department in the forthcoming quarter are as follows. Data required for distribution is also shown against each department.

Department	*Factory overheads*	*Direct labour-hours*	*Number of employees*	*Area in square metres*
Production				
X	₹1,93,000	4,000	100	3,000
Y	64,000	3,000	125	1,500
Z	83,000	4,000	85	1,500

(Contd.)

(Contd.)

Service				
P	45,000	1,000	10	500
Q	75,000	5,000	50	1,500
R	1,05,000	6,000	40	1,000
S	30,000	3,000	50	1,000

The overhead costs of the 4 service departments are distributed in the same order, namely, P,Q,R and S respectively on the following basis:

Departments	*Basis*
P	Number of employees
Q	Direct labour-hours
R	Area in square metres
S	Direct labour-hours

You are required to: **(a)** Prepare a schedule showing the distribution of overhead costs of the four service departments to the three production departments; and **(b)** Calculate the overhead recovery rate per direct labour-hour for each of the three production departments.

SOLUTION

(a) *Statement showing Distribution of Factory Overhead Costs of Service Department among Production Departments as per Step Ladder Method*

Particulars	*Service departments*				*Production departments*		
	P	*Q*	*R*	*S*	*X*	*Y*	*Z*
Factory overhead costs	₹45,000	₹75,000	₹1,05,000	₹30,000	₹1,93,000	₹64,000	₹83,000
Distribution of factory overhead of Department P (in the ratio of number of employees)	(45,000)	5,000	4,000	5,000	10,000	12,500	8,500
Distribution of factory overhead of Department Q, ₹80,000 (in the ratio of direct labour-hours)	—	(80,000)	24,000	12,000	16,000	12,000	16,000
Distribution of factory overheads of Department R, ₹1,33,000 (in the ratio of area used)	—	—	(1,33,000)	19,000	57,000	28,500	28,500
Distribution of factory overheads of Department S, ₹66,000 (in the ratio of direct labour-hours)	—	—	—	(66,000)	24,000	18,000	24,000
Total cost					3,00,000	1,35,000	1,60,000
(b) Divided by direct labour-hours					4,000	3,000	4,000
Overhead recovery rate per hour (Total cost/DLH)					75	45	40

P.5.4 Modern Machines Limited has three production departments (A, B and C) and two service departments (D and E). From the following figures extracted from the records of the company, calculate the overhead rate per labour-hour of production departments. Total direct labour hours of departments A, B and C are 5,000, 5,000 and 2,000 respectively.

Indirect materials	₹1,50,000
Indirect wages	1,00,000
Depreciation on machinery	2,50,000
Depreciation on buildings	50,000
Rent, rates and taxes	1,00,000
Electric power for machinery	1,50,000
Electric power for lighting	5,000
General expenses	1,50,000

Items	*Total*	*A*	*B*	*C*	*D*	*E*
Drect materials (₹)	6,00,000	2,00,000	1,00,000	1,90,000	60,000	50,000
Direct wages (₹)	4,00,000	1,50,000	1,50,000	40,000	20,000	40,000
Value of machinery (₹)	25,00,000	6,00,000	10,00,000	4,00,000	2,50,000	2,50,000
Floor area (sq. feet)	50,000	15,000	10,000	10,000	5,000	10,000
Horse power of machines	150	50	60	30	5	5
Number of light points	50	15	10	10	5	10
General expenses	1,50,000	50,000	50,000	20,000	10,000	20,000

The expenses of service departments D and E are to be apportioned as follows:

	A	*B*	*C*	*D*	*E*
Department D (%)	40	20	30	—	10
Department E (%)	30	30	40	—	—

SOLUTION

Determination of Departmental Overhead Rates of Production

Item	*Basis of charge*	*Total*	*Production departments*			*Service departments*	
			A	*B*	*C*	*D*	*E*
Direct materials	Allocation	₹1,10,000	—	—	—	₹60,000	₹50,000
Direct wages	Allocation	60,000	—	—	—	20,000	40,000
Indirect materials	Direct materials usage ratio	1,50,000	₹50,000	₹25,000	47,500	15,000	12,500
Indirect wages	Direct wages usage ratio[1]	1,00,000	37,500	37,500	10,000	5,000	10,000
Depreciation (machinery)	Value of machinery	2,50,000	60,000	1,00,000	40,000	25,000	25,000
Depreciation (building)	Floor area	50,000	15,000	10,000	10,000	5,000	10,000
Rent, rates and taxes	Floor area	1,00,000	30,000	20,000	20,000	10,000	20,000
Electric power (machinery)	Horse power	1,50,000	50,000	60,000	30,000	5,000	5,000
Electric power (lighting)	Light points	5,000	1,500	1,000	1,000	500	1,000
General expenses	Labour-hours	1,50,000	50,000	50,000	20,000	10,000	20,000
Total		11,25,000	2,94,000	3,03,500	1,78,500	1,55,500	1,93,500
Cost of service Department D apportioned			62,200	31,100	46,650	(1,55,500)	15,550
Cost of service Department E apportioned		—	62,720	62,710	83,620	—	(2,09,050)
Total overheads		11,25,000	4,18,920	3,97,310	3,08,770	—	—
Labour-hours		—	5,000	5,000	2,000	—	—
Overhead rate per direct labour-hour			83.78	79.46	154.39	—	—

1. May also be based on the basis of direct labour-hours.

P.5.5 A factory is having three production departments: A, B and C, and two service departments, namely, Boiler House (BH) and Pump Room (PR). The Boiler House is to depend upon the Pump Room for supply of water and Pump Room, in turn, is dependent on the Boiler House for supply of power for driving the pump. The expenses incurred by the production departments during a period are: A, ₹8,00,000; B, ₹7,00,000; and C, ₹5,00,000. The expenses for Boiler House are ₹2,34,000 and the Pump Room are ₹3,00,000.

The expenses of the Boiler House and Pump Room are apportioned to the production departments on the following basis:

	A	B	C	B.H.	P.R.
Expenses of Boiler House (%)	20	40	30	—	10
Expenses of Pump Room (%)	40	20	20	20	—

Show clearly as to how the expenses of Boiler House and Pump Room would be apportioned to A, B and C departments. Use algebraic equation method.

SOLUTION

Let X be total overhead costs of Boiler House, and

Y be total overhead costs of Pump Room

X = ₹2,34,000 + $0.2Y$

Y = ₹3,00,000 + $0.1X$

Or, X = ₹2,34,000 + 0.2 × (₹3,00,000 + $0.1X$) = ₹2,34,000 + ₹60,000 + 0.02 X = ₹2,94,000/0.98

= ₹3,00,000

Y = ₹3,00,000 + 0.1 × (₹3,00,000) = ₹3,30,000

Allocation of Overheads among Production Departments

Particulars	Production departments			Total
	A	B	C	
Direct overheads	₹8,00,000	₹7,00,000	₹5,00,000	₹20,00,000
Boiler House (2:4:3)	60,000	1,20,000	90,000	2,70,000 [1]
Pump Room (4:2:2)	1,32,000	66,000	66,000	2,64,000 [2]
Total	9,92,000	8,86,000	6,56,000	25,34,000

WORKING NOTES

1. Total expenses of Boiler House	₹3,00,000
Less share of Pump Room (0.10 × ₹3,00,000)	30,000
Amount to be apportioned among production departments	2,70,000
2. Total expenses of Pump Room	3,30,000
Less share of Boiler House (0.20 × ₹3,30,000)	66,000
Amount to be apportioned among production departments	2,64,000

P.5.6 A factory has three production departments (P_1, P_2 and P_3) and two service departments (S_1 and S_2). Budgeted overheads for the next year have been allocated/apportioned by the cost department among the five departments. The secondary distribution of service department overheads is pending and the following details are given to you:

Department	Overheads apportioned/allocated	Estimated level of activity
P_1	₹48,000	500 labour-hours
P_2	1,12,000	1,200 machine-hours
P_3	52,000	600 labour-hours

(Contd.)

(Contd.)

Apportionment of service department costs		
S_1	16,000	P_1 (20 per cent), P_2, (40 per cent), P_3 (20 per cent), S_2 (20 per cent)
S_2	24,000	P_1 (10 per cent), P_2 (60 per cent), P_3 (20 per cent), S_1 (10 per cent)

Calculate the overhead rate of each production department after completing the distribution of service department costs.

SOLUTION

Let, X be total overhead costs of S_1

Y be total overhead costs of S_2

We get simultaneous equations,

X = ₹16,000 + 0.1Y

Y = ₹24,000 + 0.2X

Or, X = ₹16,000 + 0.10 × (₹24,000 + 0.2X) or 0.98X = ₹18,400

X = ₹18,775

Y = ₹24,000 + 0.20 (₹18,775) = ₹27,755

Allocation of Overheads among Production Departments

Particulars	*Production departments*		
	P_1	P_2	P_3
Direct overheads	₹48,000	₹1,12,000	52,000
Allocation of overheads			
Department S_1 (₹18,775)	3,755 (0.20)	7,510 (0.40)	3,755 (0.20)
Department S_2 (₹27,755)	2,776 (0.10)	16,653 (0.60)	5,551 (0.20)
Total cost	54,531	1,36,163	61,306
Estimated capacity	500 (labour-hours)	1,200 (machine-hours)	600 (labour-hours)
Overhead cost per hour	₹109.10	₹113.50	₹102.20

P.5.7 Alpha limited has decided to analyse the profitability of its five new customers. It buys bottled water at ₹90 per case and sells to retail customers at a list price of ₹108 per case. The data pertaining to five customers are:

	Customers				
	A	*B*	*C*	*D*	*E*
Cases sold	4,680	19,688	1,36,90	71,550	8,775
List selling price	₹108	108	108	108	108
Actual selling price	108	106.20	99	104.40	97.20
Number of purchase orders	15	25	30	25	30
Number of customer visits	2	3	6	2	3
Number of deliveries	10	30	60	40	20
Kilometers travelled per delivery	20	6	5	10	30
Number of expedited deliveries	0	0	0	0	1

Its five activities and their cost drivers are:

Activity	*Cost driver rate*
Order taking	₹750 per purchase order
Customer visits	₹600 per customer visit
Deliveries	₹5.75 per delivery km travelled
Product handling	₹3.75 per case sold
Expedited deliveries	₹2,250 per expedited delivery

REQUIRED:

(i) Compute the customer-level operating income of each of five retail customers now being examined (A,B,C,D and E). Comment on the results. **(ii)** What insights are gained by reporting both the list selling price and the actual selling price for each customer? **(iii)** What factors should Alpha Limited consider in deciding whether to drop one or more of five customers?

SOLUTION

(i) *Statement showing Operating Income of Customers A to E*

Particulars	*Customers*				
	A	*B*	*C*	*D*	*E*
Cases sold	4,680	19,688	1,36,800	71,550	8,775
Revenues (at listed price)	₹5,05,440	₹21,26,304	₹1,47,74,400	₹77,27,400	₹9,47,700
Less costs:					
Cost of goods sold					
(cases sold x ₹90)	4,21,200	17,71,920	1,23,12,000	64,39,500	7,89,750
Discount	—	35,438	12,31,200	2,57,580	94,770
		(19,688 × ₹1.80)	(1,36,800 × ₹9)	(71,550 × ₹3.60)	(8,775 × ₹10.80)
Order taking costs	11,250	18,750	22,500	18,750	22,500
(No. of purchase orders × ₹750)					
Customer visits costs:					
(No. of customer visits × ₹600)	1,200	1,800	3,600	1,200	1,800
Delivery vehicles travel costs					
(₹5.75 per km)	1,150	1,035	1,725	2,300	3,450
Product handling costs					
(cases sold × ₹3.75)	17,550	73,830	5,13,000	2,68,313	32,906
Cost of expediting deliveries	—	—	—	—	2,250
Operating income	53,090	2,23,531	6,90,375	7,39,757	274

COMMENT: Although the number of cases sold is maximum in the case of customer C, the most profitable customer is D. The primary reason is that customer C gets 2.5 times discount *vis-à-vis* customer D, the respective discount rates being ₹9 per case and ₹3.60. Further, customer E is the least profitable as he gets the maximum discount of ₹10.80 per case, places orders more frequently, requires more customer visits as well as more traveling costs compared to other customers.

(ii) *Insights gained by reporting the two sets of prices, i.e., the listed selling price (LSP) and the actual selling price (ASP) for each customer*

The difference between the LSP and the ASP represents discount. The discount amount offered to customers enables Alpha Limited to examine whether the discount offered to various customers has bearing on the sales made to them. In general, the expectation is the higher is the amount of discount, the higher is the likely sales volume. The relevant data showing the relationship between the two is contained in the following table:

Discount per case	*Sales volume in cases (customer)*
₹0.00	4,680 (Customer A)
1.80	19,688 (Customer B)
3.60	71,550 (Customer D)
9.00	1,36,800 (Customer C)
10.80	8,775 (Customer E)

There is direct relationship between discount amount and sales, except in the case of customer E. There is need to examine (a) the reason for higher discount (of ₹10.80) in the case of customer E and (b) whether it will be profitable to offer discount to customer A also.

(iii) *Factors to be considered in dropping one or more customers*

Since there is profit from each customer, the decision of dropping the customers should be the last option/resort. The major factors to be considered are: (a) To determine the projected profitability in respect of each customer. In particular, the company should examine profitability in respect of customers E (the least profitable) and A (low profitable). (b) There is need to segregate cost data into avoidable costs and unavoidable costs. Based on such data, profitability for each customer should be determined. (c) The company should explore to ascertain whether it is possible to have more profits by offering different discount rate structure to different customers (in particular between customers C and D).

P. 5.8 E-books is an online book retailer. The company has four departments. The two sales departments are corporate sales and consumer sales. The two support-departments are Administrative (Human resources, Accounting), and Information systems. Each of the sales departments conducts merchandising and marketing operations independently.

The following data are available for October, 2013:

Departments	*Revenues*	*Number of employees*	*Processing time used (in minutes)*
Corporate sales	₹16,67,750	42	2,400
Consumer sales	8,33,875	28	2,000
Administrative	—	14	400
Information systems	—	21	1,400

Cost incurred in each of four departments for October, 2013 are as follows:

Corporate sales	₹12,97,751
Consumer sales	6,36,818
Administrative	94,510
(Information systems)	3,04,720

The company uses number of employees as a basis to allocate administrative costs and processing time as a basis to allocate information systems costs.

REQUIRED:

(i) Allocate the support department costs to the sales departments using the direct method. **(ii)** Rank the support departments based on percentage of their services rendered to other support departments. Use this ranking to allocate support costs based on the step-down allocation method. **(iii)** How could you have ranked the support departments differently? **(iv)** Allocate the support department costs to two sales departments using the reciprocal allocation method.

SOLUTION

(i) *Statement showing the Allocation of Support Department Costs to the Sales Departments (using Direct Method)*

Particulars	Basis of allocation	Sales department		Support department	
		Corporate sales	Consumer sales	Administrative	Information systems
Cost incurred	No. of employees	₹12,97,751	₹6,36,818	₹94,510	₹3,04,720
Administrative cost	(6:4)	56,706	37,804	(94,510)	—
Information systems cost	Processing time (6:5)	1,66,211	1,38,509	—	(3,04,720)
		15,20,668	8,13,131	—	—

(ii) *Ranking of Support Departments based on Percentage of their Services Rendered to other Support Departments*

(a) Administrative support department provides 23.077 per cent [21/(42 + 28 + 21) × 100] of its services to information systems support department. Thus, 23.077 per cent of ₹94,510 = ₹21,810.

(b) Information system support department provides [400/(2,400 + 2,000 + 400) × 100] 8.33 per cent of its services to administration support department. Thus 8.33 per cent of ₹3,04,720 = ₹25,383.

Statement showing Allocation of Support Costs (using Step-down Allocation Method)

Particulars	Basis of allocation	Support department		Sales department	
		Administrative	Information systems	Corporate sales	Consumer sales
Cost		₹94,510	₹3,04,720	₹12,97,751	₹6,36,818
Reallocation of administrative department cost	No. of employees (6:4:3)	(94,510)	21,810	43,620	29,080
			3,26,530		
Reallocation of information system department cost	Processing time (6:5)	—	(3,26,530)	1,78,107	1,48,423
				15,19,478	8,14,321

(iii) *An alternative ranking is based on the rupee amount (figures obtained under requirement (ii) of services rendered to other service departments. This approach would use the following sequence of ranking:*

— Allocation of information systems overheads as first (₹25,383 provided to administrative department)

— Allocated administrative overheads as second (₹21,810 provided to information systems).

(iv) *Statement showing Allocation of Support Department Costs to the Sales Departments (using Reciprocal Allocation Method)*

Particulars	Sales department	
	Corporate sales	Consumer sales
Costs	₹12,97,751	₹6,36,818
Reallocation of cost of administrative department (46.16% and 30.77% of ₹1,22,243)	56,427	37,614
Reallocation of cost of information systems department (50% and 41.67% of ₹3,32,922)	1,66,461	1,38,729
	15,20,639	8,13,161

WORKING NOTES

(i) *Percentage of Services Provided by Service Department between themselves and Sales Departments.*

Particulars	Service departments		Sales departments	
	Administrative	Information system	Corporate sales	Consumer sales
Administrative	—	23.07%	46.16%	30.77%
Information systems	8.33%	—	50%	41.67%

(ii) *Determination of Total Cost of Support Department: (using Simultaneous Equation Method)*

Let X and Y be the total costs of support departments Administrative overheads and Information systems respectively.

X = ₹94,510 + 0.0833Y

Y = ₹3,04,720 + 0.2307X

Or X = ₹94,510 + 0.0833 (₹3,04,720 + 0.2307X)

Or X = ₹94,510 + ₹25,383 + 0.01922X

Or X – 0.01922 X = ₹1,19,893

Or 0.98078X = ₹1,19,893

X = ₹1,19,893/0.98078 = ₹1,22,243

Y = ₹3,04,720 + 0.2307 (₹1,22,243)

Y = ₹3,04,720 + 28,202 = ₹3,32,922

P.5.9 A machine was purchased on January 1, in the current year. The following information relate to the machine:

Cost of machine	₹4,20,000
Estimated life	10 years of 2,000 hours per year
Estimated scrap value	₹20,000
Estimated repairs for whole life	₹1,05,000
Power consumed per hour	5 units @ ₹5 per unit
Insurance (on original cost)	0.75% per month
Consumable stores	₹300 per month

The machine is installed in a department whose monthly rent is ₹5,000 and this machine occupies 1/5 of the area. Total monthly lighting expenses is ₹4,000 for 10 light points, of which 3 relate to the machine. A supervisor with monthly salary of ₹16,000, devotes 1/4 of his time to this machine. Calculate machine hour rate.

SOLUTION

Determination of Machine-hour Rate

	Per year	Per hour
Standing charges:		
Insurance (0.75% per month × 12 × ₹4,20,000)	₹37,800	
Rent (₹5,000 per month × 12 months × 1/5)	12,000	
Lighting charges (₹400 per point per month × 12 months × 3 points)	14,400	
Supervisor's salary (₹16,000 per month × 12 months × 1/4)	48,000	
Total standing charges	1,12,200	
Standing charges per hour (₹1,12,200/2,000 hours)		₹56.10
Machine expenses:		
Depreciation per hour (₹4,20,000 – ₹20,000)/10 years = ₹40,000/2,000		20.00
Consumable stores (₹300 per month × 12 months)/2,000		1.80
Power consumed (5 units × ₹5)		25.00
Repairs (₹1,05,000/10 years) = ₹10,500/2,000		5.25
Machine-hour rate per hour		108.15

P.5.10 A machine was purchased on April 1 in the current year for ₹5 lakh. The total cost of all machinery inclusive of the new machine was ₹75 lakh. The following particulars are further available:

Expected life of machine, 10 years
Scrap value at the end of 10 years, ₹5,000
Repairs and maintenance for the machine during the year, ₹20,000
Expected number of working hours of machine per year, 4,000
Insurance premium annually for all the machines, ₹45,000
Electricity consumption for the machine per hour (@ ₹5 per unit), 10 units
Area occupied by the machine, 100 sq. feet
Area occupied by other machines, 1,500 sq. feet
Rent per month of the department, ₹8,000
Lighting charges for 20 points for the whole department, out of which 3 points are for the machine, ₹1,200 per month.

Compute the machine-hour rate for the new machine on the basis of the data given above.

SOLUTION

Computation of Machine-hour Rate of New Machine

	Per annum	*Per hour*
Standing charges:		
Insurance premium (₹45,000 × ₹5 lakh)/₹75 lakh	₹ 3,000	
Rent (₹96,000 per year × 100 sq. feet)/1,600 sq. feet	6,000	
Lighting charges (₹14,400 per year × 3 points)/20 points	2,160	
Total standing charges	11,160	
Standing charges per hour (₹11,160 ÷ 4,000 hours)		₹2.790
Machines expenses:		
Depreciation per hour (₹5 lakh – ₹5,000)/40,000 hours		12.375
Power charges (10 units × ₹5)		50.000
Repairs and maintenance (₹20,000/4,000 hours)		5.000
Machine-hour rate		70.165

P.5.11 X Ltd, having fifteen different types of automatic machines furnishes information as under for current year.

(i) Overhead expenses: Factory rent, ₹9,60,000 (floor area 80,000 sq. ft.); Heat and gas, ₹4,50,000, and Supervision, ₹12,00,000.

(ii) Wages of the operator are ₹480 per day of 8 hours. He attends to one machine when it is under set-up and two machines while they are under operation.

(iii) Cost of machine ₹4,50,000; Life of machine, 10 years, and scrap value at the end of its life, ₹50,000.

(iv) Annual expenses on special equipment attached to the machine are estimated at ₹30,000.

(v) Estimated operation time of the machine is 3,600 hours while set-up time is 400 hours per annum.

(vi) The machine occupies 5,000 sq. ft. floor area.

(vii) Power costs ₹25 per hour while machine is in operation.

Find out the comprehensive machine-hour rate of machine B. Also find out machine costs to be absorbed in respect of use of machine B on the following two work orders:

	Work order 31	*Work order 32*
Machine set-up time (hours)	10	20
Machine operation time (hours)	90	180

SOLUTION

Statement showing Comprehensive Machine-hour Rate of Machine B of X Ltd

Particulars		Amount
Standing charges:		
Factory rent (₹9,60,000/80,000 sq. ft.) × 5,000 sq. ft.		₹60,000
Heat and gas (₹4,50,000/15 machines)		30,000
Supervision (₹12,00,000/15 machines)		80,000
Depreciation [(₹4,50,000 – ₹50,000)/10 years]		40,000
Annual expenses on special equipment		30,000
Total		2,40,000
Machine-hours		4,000
Fixed cost per hour		60
	Set up rate per hour	*Operation rate per hour*
Fixed cost	₹60	₹60
Power	—	25
Wages	60	30
Comprehensive machine-hour rate	120	115

Statement of Machines B Costs to be Absorbed on the Two Work Orders

Particulars	Work order 31			Work order 32		
	Hours	Rate	Amount	Hours	Rate	Amount
Set up time cost	10	₹120	₹1,200	20	₹120	₹2,400
Operation time cost	90	115	10,350	180	115	20,700
Total cost			11,550			23,100

P.5.12 A machine shop cost centre contains 6 machines of equivalent capacities. Three operators are employed on each machine: one at ₹50 per hour and two at ₹25 per hour each. The factory works a 40-hour week which includes 4 hours for setup time. The work is jointly done by the operators. The operators are paid fully for the 40 hours. In addition, they are paid a bonus of 10 per cent on productive time. Costs are reported for this company on the basis of 13 four-week periods.

The company for the purposes of computing machine-hour rate includes direct wages of the operators and also recoups the factory overheads allocated to the machines. The following details of factory overheads applicable to the cost centre are available:

1. Setup time as described above.
2. Depreciation, 10 per cent per annum on original cost on each machine (original cost of each machine is ₹1,30,000)
3. Maintenance and repairs per week per machine is ₹2,500
4. Consumable stores per week per machine is ₹3,600
5. Power, 20 units per hour per machine at ₹5 per unit
6. Apportionment to the cost centre:

Rent per annum	₹1,44,000
Heat and light per annum	5,40,000
Foreman's salary (2 in number)	7,20,000
Total expenses for 6 machines	14,04,000

From the above, you are required to compute: (a) The cost of running one machine for a 4-week period and (b) The machine-hour rate.

SOLUTION

(a) *Determination of Cost of Running one Machine for a 4-week period.*

Standing charges:		
Rent per annum (₹1,44,000/6 machines)	₹24,000	
Heat and light per annum (₹5,40,000/6)	90,000	
Foreman's salary per annum (₹7,20,000/6)	1,20,000	
Total expenses for one machine per annum	2,34,000	
Expenses for a 4-week period (₹2,34,000/13)		₹18,000
Wages for a 4-week period		17,440[1]
Total standing charges		35,440
Machine expenses		
Depreciation (₹1,30,000 × 0.10 × 1/13)		1,000
Repairs an maintenance (₹2,500 × 4 weeks)		10,000
Consumable stores (₹3,600 × 4 weeks)		14,400
Power (144 Hours × 20 units × ₹5 per unit)		14,400[2]
Total machine expenses		39,800
Total cost (₹35,440 + ₹39,800)		75,240

(b) *Machine-hour rate* = ₹75,240/144 (36 hours × 4) productive hours = ₹522.50.

WORKING NOTES

(1) Determination of wages:

Hours for 4 weeks	160
Rate per hour [(1 operator × ₹50) + (2 operators × ₹25)]	₹100
Wages for 4 weeks (160 × ₹100)	16,000
Add bonus for productive time (36 hours per week × 4 weeks × ₹100 per hour) × 0.1	1,440
	₹17,440

(2) It is assumed that no power is used during setup time of the machine.

P.5.13 A machine shop has 8 identical drilling machines manned by 6 operators. The machines cannot be worked without an operator wholly engaged on it. The original cost of all these 8 machines, works out to ₹80 lakh. These particulars are furnished for a 6-month period:

Normal available hours per month	208
Absenteeism with pay (hours)	18
Leave with pay (hours)	20
Normal idle time unavoidable (hours)	10
Average rate of wages per day of 8 hours	₹200
Production bonus estimated (per cent on wages)	15
Value of power consumed	80,500
Supervision and indirect labour	33,000
Lighting and electricity	12,000

These particulars are for a year:

Repairs and maintenance including consumables, 3 per cent on value of machines. Insurance, ₹4,00,000

Depreciation, 10 per cent on original cost

Other sundry works expenses, ₹1,20,000

General management expenses allocated, ₹5,45,300

You are required to work out a comprehensive machine-hour rate.

SOLUTION

Determination of Comprehensive Machine-hour Rate of Machine Shop

		Amount (6 months)
Standing charges:		
Supervision and indirect labour	₹33,000	
Lighting and electricity	12,000	
Insurance (₹4,00,000 × 6/12)	2,00,000	
Other sundry works expenses (₹20,000 × 6/12)	60,000	
General management expenses (₹5,45,300 × 6/12)	2,72,650	₹5,77,650
Machine charges:		
Power	80,500	
Repairs and maintenance including consumables (0.03 × ₹80 lakh × 0.5 year)	1,20,000	
Depreciation (.10 × ₹80 lakh × 0.5 year)	4,00,000	
Operators wages	1,71,000[1]	
Production bonus (0.15 × ₹1,71,000)	25,650	7,97,150
Total		13,74,800
Machine-hour rate (₹13,74,800/5,760 hours[2])		238.70

WORKING NOTES

1. Determination of wages payable to operators:

Normal available hours per month	208
Less absenteeism hours per month (without pay)	18
Number of hours for which wages are to be paid	190
Wages paid for 6 operators for 6 months @ ₹25 per hour (₹200/8 hours) = 190 hours × ₹25 × 6 months × 6 operators)	₹1,71,000

2. Determination of machine-hours available for work (for 6 months):

Normal available hours per operator (per month)	208
Less absenteeism hours	18
Less leave hours	20
Less normal idle time hours	10
Effective hours available per operator per month	160
Total effective hours for 6 operators for 6 months (160 × 6 × 6)	5,760

P.5.14 Gemini Enterprise Ltd undertakes three different jobs: A, B, and C. All of them require the use of a special machine and also the use of computer. The computer is hired and the hire charges work out to be ₹4,20,000 per annum. The expenses regarding the machine are estimated as follows:

Rent for the quarter	₹ 17,500
Depreciation per annum	2,00,000
Indirect charges per annum	1,50,000

During the first month of operation, the following details were taken from the job register:

Job	*A*	*B*	*C*
Number of hours the machine was used			
(a) Without the use of the computer	600	900	—
(b) With the use of computer	400	600	1,000

You are required to compute the machine-hour rate (a) for the firm as a whole for the month when the computer was used and when the computer was not used, (b) for the individual jobs: A,B and C.

SOLUTION

(a) *Determination of Machine-hour rate when the Computer was not used:*

Total overheads of machine per month:	
Rent (₹17,500/3 months) per month	₹5,833
Depreciation (₹2,00,000/12 months) per month	16,667
Indirect charges (₹1,50,000/12 months) per month	12,500
	35,000
Total machine-hours in a month:	
Without the use of computer	1,500
With the use of computer	2,000
	3,500
Machine-hour rate (without use of computer) ₹35,000/3,500 hours)	10
When computer is used:	
Machine-hour rate per hour (determined above)	10
Add computer charges per hour(₹4,20,000/12 months) = ₹35,000 per month/2,000 hours	17.50
	27.50

(b) *Determination of Machine-hour Rate (MHR) for Jobs A, B and C*

Particulars	Jobs					
	A		B		C	
	Hours	Amount	Hours	Amount	Hours	Amount
MHR, without computer @ ₹10 per hour	600	₹6,000	900	₹9,000	—	—
MHR with use of computer @ ₹27.50 per hour	400	11,000	600	16,500	1,000	₹27,500
Total	1,000	17,000	1,500	25,500	1,000	27,500
MHR		17		17		27.50

P.5.15 In a machine shop, the machine-hour rate is worked out at the beginning of a year on the basis of a 13-week period which is equal to three calendar months. The following estimates for operating a machine are relevant.

Total working hours available per week	48
Maintenance time included in the above	2
Setting up time included in the above	2
Cost details:	
Operator's wages per month	₹13,000
Supervisor's salary per month	20,000
Written down value of machine (depreciation at 12 per cent)	18,00,000
Repairs and maintenance per annum	1,60,000
Consumable stores per annum	3,00,000
Rent, rates and taxes (for the quarter apportioned)	48,108

Power consumed is 10 units per hour @ ₹5 per unit. Power is required for productive hours only. Setting-up time is part of productive time but no power is required for setting-up jobs.

The operator and supervisor are permanent. Repairs and maintenance and consumable stores are variable.

You are required to:

(a) Work out the machine-hour rate

(b) Work out the rate for quoting to the outside party for utilising the idle capacity in the machine shop assuming a profit of 20 per cent above variable cost.

SOLUTION

(a) *Determination of Machine-hour Rate*

Standing charges:		
Operator's wages (₹13,000 × 3 months)		₹39,000
Supervisors' salary (₹20,000 × 3 months)		60,000
Rent, rates and taxes		48,108
Total standing fixed charges		1,47,108
Standing charges per hour (₹1,47,108/598 productive hours, that is, 46 hours × 13 weeks)		₹246.00
Variable cost per hour:		
Power (10 units × ₹5 per unit × 44/46 hours)	₹47.83	
Repairs and maintenance (₹40,000/598)	66.89	
Consumable stores (₹75,000/598)	125.42	
Depreciation [(₹18 lakh × 0.12)/4] ÷ 598 hours	90.30	330.44
Machine-hour rate		576.44

(b) *Determination of Quotation Price:*

Variable cost per machine-hour	₹330.44
Add 20 per cent profit	66.09
Quotation price per hour	396.53

ASSUMPTION Depreciation is treated as machine charges and, hence, is more close to variable cost category.

P.5.16 The budgeted working conditions for a cost centre are as follows:

Normal working week, 40 hours
Number of machines, 10
Normal weekly loss of hours on maintenance, and so on, 5 hours per machine
Estimated annual factory overheads, ₹50,40,000
Estimated direct wages rate, ₹30 per hour
Number of weeks worked per year, 48

Actual results in respect of a 4 week period are:

Factory overheads incurred, ₹5,80,000
Wages incurred, ₹49,200
Machine-hours produced, 2,000

You are required to calculate: **(a)** The overhead rate per machine-hour and **(b)** The amount of under or over-absorption of both factory overheads and wages.

SOLUTION

(a) Machine-hour rate = ₹50,40,000/16,800[1] hours = ₹300

(b) *Determination of Overheads Under-or Overabsorbed:*

Factory overheads incurred	₹5,80,000
Overheads absorbed (2,000 hours × ₹300)	6,00,000
Overheads overabsorbed (₹6,00,000 – ₹5,80,000)	20,000

Determination of Wages Under or Overabsorbed:

Wages incurred	₹49,200
Wages absorbed (10 machines × 40 hours per week × 4 weeks × ₹30 per hour)	48,000
Wages underabsorbed (₹49,200 – ₹48,000)	1,200

WORKING NOTES

(1) Normal working hours per year for 10 machines (40 hours × 10 machines × 48 weeks)	19,200
Less hours lost due to maintenance in a year (5 hours × 10 machines × 48 weeks)	2,400
	16,800

P.5.17 In a small factory, overheads of a particular department are recovered on the basis of ₹50 per machine-hour. The total expenses incurred and the actual machine-hours for the department for the month of August were ₹8,00,000 and 10,000 respectively. Of the amount of ₹8,00,000, ₹1,50,000 became payable due to an award of the Labour Court and ₹50,000 was in respect of expenses of the previous year booked in the current month (August). Actual production was 40,000 units, of which 30,000 units were sold. On analysing the reasons, it was found that 60 per cent of the under-absorbed overhead was due to defective planning and the rest was attributed to normal cost increase. How would you treat the under-absorbed overhead in the cost accounts?

SOLUTION

Determination of Underabsorbed Overhead Expenses

Total expenses incurred in August	₹8,00,000
Less amount paid as per Labour Court award (assumed to be abnormal expense)	1,50,000
Less expenses paid related to previous year	50,000
Overhead expenses relating to current month	6,00,000
Less overheads recovered (10,000 machine-hours × ₹50)	5,00,000
Underabsorbed factory overheads	1,00,000

Treatment of underabsorbed overheads in cost accounts

1. 60 per cent of underabsorbed factory overheads (₹1,00,000) is attributed to defective planning. Being abnormal in nature, the amount of ₹60,000 is to be charged to costing profit and loss account

2. Balance 40 per cent of underabsorbed factory overheads is prorated between cost of sales (30,000 units) and finished goods inventory (10,000 units).

Accordingly, ₹40,000 distribution between the two is as follows:

Cost of sales	₹30,000	
Finished goods	10,000	₹40,000
Total unabsorbed overheads (₹60,000 + ₹40,000)		1,00,000

P.5.18 ABC Ltd manufactures a single product and absorbs the production overheads at a predetermined rate of ₹100 per machine-hour.

At the end of current financial year, it has been found that actual production overheads incurred were ₹6,00,000. It included ₹45,000 on account of 'written off' obsolete stores and ₹30,000 being the wages paid for the strike period under an award.

The production and sales data for the current year is as under:

Production:	
Finished goods (units)	20,000
Work-in-progress (50% complete in all respects) (units)	8,000
Sales:	
Finished goods (units)	18,000

The actual machine-hours worked during the period were 4,800. It has been found that one-third of the under-absorption of production overheads was due to lack of production planning and the rest was attributable to normal increase in costs.

You are required to:

(i) Calculate the amount of under-absorption of production overheads during the current year; and
(ii) Show the accounting treatment of under-absorption of production overheads.

SOLUTION

(i) *Determination of Unabsorbed Production Overheads*

Production overhead expenses incurred (gross)		₹6,00,000
Less "written off" obsolete stores	₹45,000	
Less wages paid for the strike period	30,000	75,000
Net relevant production overheads expenses		5,25,000
Less production overheads absorbed (4,800 machine-hours × ₹100 per machine-hour)		4,80,000
Unabsorbed production overheads		45,000

(ii) *Treatment of Unabsorbed Production Overheads:*

(1) One-third of unabsorbed overheads are attributed to lack of production planning. Being abnormal in nature ₹15,000 (₹45,000 × 1/3) is charged to costing profit and loss account ₹15,000

(2) The balance sum of ₹30,000 is to be pro-rated among Cost of goods sold (18,000 units), work-in-progress(4,000 units i.e., 8,000 units × 50 per cent completion) and finished goods inventory 2,000 units) as follows:

Cost of goods sold (₹30,000 × 18/24)	₹22,500	
Work-in-progress (₹30,000 × 4/24)	5,000	
Finished goods inventory (₹30,000 × 2/24)	2,500	30,000
		45,000

Journal entry will be as follows:

Cost of goods sold A/c	.... Dr	₹22,500	
Work-in-progress A/c	.... Dr	5,000	
Finished goods inventory A/c	.... Dr	2,500	
To Factory overhead control A/c			₹30,000

REVIEW QUESTIONS

RQ.5.1 (a) Indicate whether the following statements are 'True' or 'False'.

(i) Factory overheads are direct manufacturing costs.
(ii) Indirect labour and indirect materials form part of factory overheads.
(iii) Factory overheads are common costs and are shared among various cost centres.
(iv) Allotment of whole items of cost to cost centres is referred to as cost apportionment.
(v) Allotment of factory overheads to cost units by means of predetermined factory overhead application rate is called overhead absorption.
(vi) Normal capacity is less than theoretical capacity.

(b) In the following multiple choice questions, select the correct answers:

(vii) Which of the following is correct factory overheads application rate given:
Budgeted fixed overhead costs – ₹6 lakh; Variable overhead cost ₹100 per unit; Theoretical capacity – 3,000 units; and Normal capacity – 2,000 units.
(a) ₹400 per unit, (b) ₹300 per unit, (c) ₹350 per unit, (d) None of these.

(viii) Compute the machine hour rate from the data below:
Cost of machine ₹3,00,000; Estimated scrap value after expiry of its useful life (5 years) ₹50,000. Assume machine is subject to straight line method of depreciation; Rent and rates per month ₹2,000; Insurance premium/annum ₹6,000; and Estimated working hours/annum 2,000.
(a) ₹40 per machine hour, (b) ₹30 per machine hour, (c) ₹35 per machine hour, (d) None of these.

(ix) Following data is available: Factory overhead absorption rate is 50 per machine-hour; 10,000 machine-hours were used; If actual factory overheads are ₹6,00,000. This implies that firm has (a) Under-absorption, (b) Over-absorption, (c) Under-allocation, (d) Over-allocation.

[Answers: (i) False, (ii) True, (iii) True, (iv) False, (v) True, (vi) True, (vii) a, (viii) a, (ix) a.]

RQ.5.2 What do you understand by fixed overheads? Why are they called 'burdens'?

RQ.5.3 What two key factors determine the factory overhead application rate for a period? Why are these factors important?

RQ.5.4 What do you understand by classification, allocation, apportionment, and absorption in relation to overhead expenses? Explain with examples.

RQ.5.5 What do you understand by the terms production department and service department? Explain the rationale for allocating the service department costs to production departments. Using your own figures, illustrate how the expenses are absorbed over the production department? Consider at least three service departments that are to be absorbed by production departments.

RQ.5.6 (a) Distinguish between cost allocation, cost apportionment and cost absorption, (b) Explain in brief various methods for apportionment of service department's cost over production departments.

RQ.5.7 Describe how costs are allocated under the direct method, the step method, and the algebraic method.

RQ.5.8 What are the requisites of a good method of absorption of factory overheads?

RQ.5.9 What information is necessary to calculate machine-hour rate for overhead absorption? State the conditions in which this method is most effective.

RQ.5.10 What are the five bases commonly used to compute the factory overhead absorption rate and when is each one appropriate to use?

RQ.5.11 What is meant by absorbed overhead? Under what circumstances will a difference arise between absorbed and actual overheads? How would you dispose of the balance?

RQ.5.12 What is meant by under/overabsorption of factory overheads? How will you account for them in cost accounts? Does it bear any impact while submitting quotations?

RQ.5.13 A company has three production cost centres A, B, and C and two service cost centres X and Y. Costs allocated to service centres are required to be apportioned to the production centres to find out cost of production of different products.

It is found that benefit of service cost centres is also received by each other along with the production cost centres. Overhead costs as allocated to the five cost centres and estimates of benefit of service cost centres received by each of them are as under:

Cost centres	*Overhead costs as allocated*	*Estimates of benefits received from service centres (%)*	
		X	*Y*
A	₹80,000	20	20
B	40,000	30	25
C	20,000	40	50
X	20,000	—	5
Y	10,000	10	—

Required: Work out final overhead costs of each of the production departments including reapportioned cost of service centres using (a) continuous distribution method and (b) simultaneous equation method.

RQ.5.14 XYZ Ltd. has three production departments (P, Q, and R) and two service departments (X and Y). The following data relate to these departments:

Particulars	*P*	*Q*	*R*	*X*	*Y*
Direct wages	₹30,000	₹20,000	₹30,000	₹15,000	₹1,950
Worked hours	3,070	4,475	2,419	—	—
Value of machine	6,00,000	8,00,000	10,00,000	50,000	50,000
HP of machines	60	30	50	10	—
Light points	10	15	20	10	5
Floor space (square feet)	2,000	2,500	3,000	2,000	500

Additional information

Rent	₹50,000
Lighting	6,000
Power	15,000
Indirect wages	19,390
Depreciation on machines	1,00,000
Sundries	96,950

Determine overhead recovery rate per hour for production departments, if X's expenses are distributed to P, Q, R, and Y in the ratio of 2 : 3 : 4 : 1 and Y's expenses are distributed in the ratio of 4 : 2 : 3 : 1 to P, Q, R, and X respectively.

RQ.5.15 A company has two production departments and two service departments. The data relating to a period are as under:

	Production Departments		*Service Departments*	
	PD_1	*PD_2*	*SD_1*	*SD_2*
Direct Materials	₹8,00,000	₹4,00,000	₹1,00,000	₹2,00,000
Direct Wages	9,50,000	5,00,000	2,00,000	1,00,000
Overheads	8,00,000	5,00,000	3,00,000	2,00,000
Power requirement at normal capacity operations (Kwh)	20,000	35,000	12,500	17,500
Actual Power consumption during the period (Kwh)	13,000	23,000	10,250	10,000

The power requirement of these departments are met by a power generation plant. The said plant incurred an expenditure, which is not included above, of ₹12,18,750 out of which a sum of ₹8,43,750 was variable and the rest fixed.

After apportionment of power generation plant costs to the four departments, the service department overheads are to be redistributed on the following bases:

	PD_1	*PD_2*	*SD_1*	*SD_2*
SD_1	50 per cent	40 per cent	—	10 per cent
SD_2	60 per cent	20 per cent	20 per cent	—

You are required to:

(i) Apportion the power generation plant costs to the four departments.

(ii) Re-apportion service department cost to production departments.

(iii) Calculate the overhead rates per direct labour hour of production departments, given that the direct wage rates of PD_1 and PD_2 are ₹50 and ₹40 per hour respectively.

RQ.5.16 A manufacturing unit has added a new machine to its fleet of five existing machines. The total cost of purchase and installation of the machine is ₹7,50,000. The machine has an estimated life of 5 years and is expected to realise ₹30,000 as scrap at the end of its working-life.

Other relevant data are as follows:

(i) Budgeted working-hours is 2,400 based on 8 hours per day for 300 days. This includes 400 hours for plant maintenance.

(ii) Power used by the machine is 5 units per hour at a cost of ₹6 per unit. No current is drawn during maintenance.
(iii) The machine requires special oil for heating which is replaced once in every month at a cost of ₹2,500 on each occasion.
(iv) Estimated cost of maintenance of the machine is ₹1,000 per week of 6 working days.
(v) 3 operators control the operations of the entire battery of six machines and the average wages per person amounts to ₹4,500 per week *plus* 40 per cent fringe benefits.
(vi) Departmental and general works overheads allocated to the operation during the last year was ₹6,00,000. During the current year, it is estimated that there will be an increase of 12.5 per cent of this amount. No incremental overhead is envisaged for the installation of the new machine.

You are required to compute the machine-hour rate for recovery of the running cost of the machine.

RQ.5.17 The following data pertains to the machine shop of an engineering company, relating to the current year. The machine shop has 3 cost centres A, B, and C, each having 3 distinct set of machines.

Particulars	*A*	*B*	*C*	*Total*
Number of workers	400	400	800	1,600
Number of machine-hours	50,000	50,000	60,000	1,60,000
Percentage of HP	40	25	35	100
Value of assets	₹20,00,000	₹35,00,000	₹30,00,000	₹85,00,000
Direct wages	16,00,000	20,00,000	24,00,000	60,00,000
Indirect wages				18,00,000
Supervisory salaries				7,00,000
Depreciation				8,50,000
Insurance				4,25,000
Electricity charges				12,00,000
Welfare expenses				9,00,000
Office and other expenses				16,00,000

Work out a composite machine-hour rate for each of the cost centres, showing the basis of apportionment of expenses amongst the cost centres.

RQ.5.18 From the following particulars calculate labour cost per hour:
(a) Basic salary, ₹200 per working day
(b) Dearness allowance per month, ₹5 per/ every point over 100 cost of living index (current cost of living index is 700 points)
(c) Leave salary, 10 per cent of [(a) + (b)]
(d) Employer's contribution to provident fund, 8 per cent of [(a) + (b) + (c)]
(e) Employer's contribution to state insurance, 2.5 per cent of [(a) + (b) + (c)]
(f) Expenditure on amenities to labour, ₹1,000 per head per month
(g) Number of working days in a month, 25 days of 8 hours each.

ANSWERS

[Comprehensive solutions to all numerical review questions are available on the companion website: http://www.mhhe.com/khan_jain_cost2e]

RQ.5.13 **(a)** Final overhead costs ₹86,523 **(A)**, ₹49,196 **(B)**, ₹34,271 **(C)**
(b) ₹86,533 **(A)**, ₹49,196 **(B)**, ₹34,271 **(C)**
RQ.5.14 Overhead recovery rate ₹30.10 **(P)**, ₹20.20 **(Q)**, ₹50.30 **(R)**
RQ.5.15 **(i)** ₹10,83,240 **(PD_1)**, ₹9,99,410 **(PD_2)**, ₹2,08,900 **(SD_1)**, ₹2,27,200 **(SD_2)** **(ii)** ₹20,64,898 **(PD_1)**, ₹15,53,852 **(PD_2)** **(iii)** ₹108.70 **(PD_1)**, ₹124.30 **(PD_2)**
RQ.5.16 Machine hour rate ₹377
RQ.5.17 Machine hour rate ₹75.20 **(A)**, ₹86.50 **(B)**, ₹89.83 **(C)**.
RQ.5.18 Labour hour rate, ₹53.60.

Costing and Control of Non-Manufacturing Overheads

Learning Objectives

1. Discuss the nature, accounting and control of administrative overheads
2. Explain the nature of selling and distribution overheads, their accounting treatment and control and the related aspect of analysis of sales
3. Illustrate the treatment of special items of cost

INTRODUCTION

The previous chapter has illustrated the costing and control of factory (manufacturing) overheads. Though the control techniques used in manufacturing costs/overheads are by and large applicable to non-manufacturing costs/overheads, due to difficulty in cost-benefit analysis as the benefits are not easily measurable, such overheads require accounting and control treatment different from that of the factory overheads. The non-manufacturing overheads fall into two groups: **(i)** Administrative costs and **(ii)** Selling and distribution costs. Sections 1 and 2 respectively discuss the costing and control of these two categories of non-manufacturing costs. The main points are summarised in Section 3.

ADMINISTRATIVE OVERHEADS/COSTS

This section discusses the meaning/nature, accounting, and control of administration overheads.

Meaning and Nature

Administrative overheads are incurred for planning, general management and control of an organisation.

The administrative overheads are those costs which are incurred for formulating policy to be followed, directing the organisation in a manner that these policies are effectively carried out, and controlling its operations. They are, in other words, incurred for planning, general management and control of organisation. They have, therefore, some special features which distinguish them from other overheads, namely, factory/manufacturing and selling and distribution. In most cases, the amount of such costs is relatively small. Moreover, due to the nature of most of the items of expenses, it is difficult to fix suitable norms/standards for comparison with the actual costs. Such overheads are, therefore, not susceptible to the same degree of control as are other overheads. The methods of absorption of administrative overheads in product costing are, in addition, mostly arbitrary as a result of which it is not possible to have an accurate/equitable cost ascertainment. They, however, do not show wide fluctuations as they are not related to output/sales.

Depending on the organisational structure, two types of administrative costs are typically incurred in a large manufacturing organisation: **(i)** Those incurred within the plant/factory in terms of provision of staff and other administrative support to the factory. The associated costs are controllable at the factory level; **(ii)** Those incurred centrally in the head office and allocated to various plants on an equitable basis. The associated costs are controllable at the head office level.

The administrative overheads include, *inter alia*, the following costs items:

- **Indirect material: (i)** Printing and stationery used in office and **(ii)** Other office supplies.
- **Indirect labour: (i)** Salary and allowances/fee of office and administrative staff including Board of Directors, Managing Director, Chairman, accounting and secretarial staff; **(ii)** Salary/allowances/fee of legal advisor/public relations officer and staff, and internal and statutory auditors.
- **Indirect expenses: (i)** Office rent, rates, and insurance; **(ii)** Office lighting, heating, and cleaning; **(iii)** Depreciation and repairs of office building, furniture and fittings; **(iv)** Legal charges; **(v)** Bank charges; **(vi)** Trade subscriptions and donations and **(vii)** Miscellaneous office expenses.

Accounting for Administrative Overheads

The procedures for the primary accounting and analysis of administrative overheads, namely, classification, allocation and departmentalisation follow the same patterns as in the case of factory overheads described in the preceding chapter. In brief, as a first step, they are classified according to the nature and purpose of cost. Each type of cost is allotted a separate Control Account Number for this purpose. A control account, namely, Administrative Overhead Control Account, is opened in the cost books to record the total administrative overheads incurred in an accounting period. The next step, similar to the procedure adopted for factory overhead, is to departmentalise the cost. These administrative departments serve as cost centres for the purpose of collection and control of these overheads. A typical list of such departments is given in Exhibit 6.1.

Exhibit 6.1 Departmentalisation of Administrative Overheads

1. Accounts Department	4. Legal Department
2. Factory Estate Department	5. Personnel Departmen
3. General Office	6. Secretarial Department

The expenses that can be identified with specific departments are allocated directly. Those that cannot be so identified are apportioned to the various departments on a suitable basis in a manner similar to that for manufacturing overheads.

Accounting Methods There are three methods of accounting of administrative overheads: **(i)** Transfer to costing profit and loss account; **(ii)** Apportionment to manufacturing, selling and distribution divisions/functions, and **(iii)** Addition as a separate item of cost.

Transfer to Costing Profit and Loss Account According to this method, administrative overheads are treated as period costs to be excluded from product costs for two reasons: **(i)** They are mainly fixed costs which do not vary with production/sales and **(ii)** There is no equitable basis to charge them to other products/divisions/functions/departments. The accounting treatment is simple.

At the end of the accounting period, as a step in closing the books, Profit and Loss Account is debited and the Administrative Overhead Control Accounts credited. However, non-inclusion of administrative overheads results in understatement of product costs.

Apportionment to Manufacturing and Selling, and Distribution Divisions This method recognises only two basic functions of a manufacturing organisation, namely, **(i)** manufacturing and **(ii)** selling and distribution. As administrative overheads are incurred for manufacturing as well as selling and distribution, these suitably are apportioned between production and selling and distribution expenses. As a result, they lose their identity and are merged with manufacturing and selling and distribution costs.

The expenses apportioned to manufacturing and selling and distribution overheads respectively are treated in the same way as other items of such overheads. Each item is first allocated to service cost and production centres. The cost of the service centre is then apportioned to the production cost centres and ultimately absorbed in cost units. These overheads incurred are debited to Administrative Overhead Control Account. On apportionment, the amount pertaining to manufacturing is transferred to Works/Manufacturing/Factory Overhead Control Account/Work-in-Process Account, and those pertaining to selling and distribution are debited to Selling and Distribution Control Account.

The main problem with this method of accounting of administrative overheads is the selection of a suitable/equitable basis for their apportionment. As the nature of the various items of these overheads is different from each other, each item is analysed separately for the purpose. Some of the items can be allocated directly on the basis of the amount spent. In the case of most items, however, equitable bases have to be adopted for apportionment of each item of expenditure. The bases adopted for apportionment of factory overheads would be useful here also. An illustrative list of items and the basis of their apportionment is given in Exhibit 6.2.

Exhibit 6.2 Apportionment of Administrative Overheads

Item/Expense	*Basis of Apportionment*
1. Office rent and rates	Floor area
2. Depreciation of office building	Floor area or capital value
3. Legal expenses	Number of employees
4. Personnel department expenses	Number of employee
5. Filing	Number of items handled
6. Typing	Number of letters typed
7. Invoicing	Number of invoices
8. Correspondence	Number of letters drafted

Addition as a Separate Item of Cost Under this method, administrative overhead is added as a separate cost element to the cost units sold. It is apportioned to the cost of product/goods sold on the basis of an equitable administrative overhead rate much in the same way as is done for the determination of factory overhead rate. Depending upon the suitability and equitability under the given circumstances, the administrative overhead rate can be computed using one of the following bases: **(i)** Sales value/quantity; **(ii)** Cost of sales/selling cost; **(iii)** Works/manufacturing cost; **(iv)** Conversion costs; **(v)** Production units, and **(vi)** Gross profit.

Control of Administrative Overheads

As administrative overheads typically relate to the general and financial management of an organisation, their major portion represents policy costs that are mostly fixed in nature and, therefore, largely non-controllable. Moreover, fixation of norm/standard to measure the effectiveness of such costs is beset with serious difficulties, coupled with the fact that the amount involved is rather small. The introduction and operation of a control system is difficult as well as not very worthwhile. Nonetheless, the normal methods of controlling costs may, with suitable adjustments, be applied to such costs as well, as explained below.

Comparison with Past Performance The administrative overheads allocated to various administrative/service departments/cost centres may be compared periodically with the corresponding expenditure in a previous period. The effectiveness of this method would depend upon the level of activity during the period of comparison. Alternatively, the cost of a department may be compared with the cost of similar services from outside. Similarly, the administrative overhead absorption rate my also be compared over a period of time and the relative efficiency of a department would be reflected in the extent of under/over absorption.

Budgetary Control The technique of budgetary control can be used and periodic comparison with actuals would reveal relative efficiency.

Standard Costing Although standards cannot be set with the same degree of precision as in case of manufacturing costs, standards for certain types of administrative work with standard units of measurement can be established. The examples of such types of work are clerical, typing, posting, filing and billing, and so on. The standard costing techniques, however, cannot be applied to fixed administrative costs such as depreciation of office buildings/machines/equipments, and so on. They may be included in a separate fixed cost budget for the information of the top management.

SELLING AND DISTRIBUTION OVERHEADS

This section discusses the nature of selling and distribution oveheads, their accounting treatment, and control, and the related aspect of analysis of sales.

Nature

Although the selling and distribution functions are separate but as *after-production costs*, there is overlapping between the two. They are, therefore, dealt with together for accounting and control purposes. As most of the items of such costs are not identifiable with specific products, they are in the nature of indirect costs/overheads.

Selling overheads are costs incurred in selling to existing customers, retaining customers and in promoting sales to potential customers.

Selling Overheads Selling overheads/costs include the costs incurred in selling to existing customers, retaining customers and in promoting sales to potential customers. They consist of the following items.

Direct Selling Costs Such costs are incurred for soliciting/obtaining orders, market research, and supply of goods to customers. They are paid to sales executives/staff/office.

Advertising and Sales Promotion Costs The major items of expenditure are:

- Advertising;
- Sales promotion: exhibitions, displays, posters, films, distribution of samples and free gifts/ diaries/calendars

Credit and Collection Costs These include expenses relating to collection of receivables and bad debts.

Financial and General Administration Costs Included in this category are **(i)** royalty on sales, **(ii)** discounts and allowances, **(iii)** sales invoicing, and **(iv)** accounts.

Distribution Overheads Distribution overheads begin when a order has been obtained, and generally end when goods are to be despatched. They include the following.

Transportation Costs Such costs consist of expenditure on different modes of transport, comprising salary of staff, maintenance/depreciation/insurance of vehicles, demurrage and wharfage and dispatch of goods, and so on.

Warehousing and Storage Costs The main items of such costs are the cost of storage such as warehouse rent, salary of warehouse staff, warehouse office expenses, depreciation, and insurance.

Financial and General Administration The distribution expenses covered under this head are **(i)** cost of carrying stock and **(ii)** financial/cost accounting costs, and so on.

Accounting of Selling and Distribution Overheads

The accounting of selling and distribution overheads involves three-stage analysis: **(i)** By nature/object, **(ii)** By function/cost centre, and **(iii)** By product/cost units.

Analysis by Nature/Object The selling and distribution costs are analysed according to the nature/object of different items of such costs. An illustrative list of such cost items nature-wise includes: **(i)** advertising, **(ii)** commission/remuneration, **(iii)** customs excise/duty, **(iv)** depreciation, **(v)** discounts and allowances, **(vi)** fees, **(vii)** freight, **(viii)** heating, **(ix)** insurance, **(x)** lighting/power **(xi)** materials and consumable stores/supplies, **(xii)** packing, **(xiii)** postage, **(xiv)** rent, **(xv)** repairs, **(xvi)** services, and so on. Like the manufacturing costs, selling and distribution overheads may be fixed, variable, and semi-variable.

Functional Analysis The functional analysis of selling and distribution costs is similar to departmentalisation and apportionment of manufacturing overheads to cost centres. The main operational functions with reference to such costs my be further classified into **(i)** direct selling, **(ii)** advertising and sales promotion, **(iii)** transportation, **(iv)** warehousing and storage, **(v)** credit and collection, **(vi)** financial, **(vii)** general administration, **(viii)** warranty claims, and **(ix)** miscellaneous. The functional analysis can be extended to locations, namely, territories/sales offices/customers/salesmen. Each function and location constitutes a cost centre for accounting and control of selling and distribution costs. Such costs are allocated to functions/locations to which they relate, for example, freight charges, packing materials, remuneration of salesmen, postage and stationery, and so on. The items/expenses which cannot be allocated may be apportioned on some suitable basis. An illustrative list of bases for such apportionment is given in Exhibit 6.3.

Exhibit 6.3 Apportionment of Selling and Distribution Overheads

Expense item	*Basis*
1. Advertising	Sales vale/physical units
2. Credit control	Number of orders
3. Depreciation	Value of assets
4. Insurance	Property value
5. Rent	Floor space
6. Warehousing	Sales volume
7. Transport	Weight/number of packages/distance carried

Analysis by Products/Groups of Products Selling and distribution costs can also be analysed by products/groups of products, for example, products A and B and location-wise, that is, Territory/

Zone 1 (East), 2 (South), 3 (West), and 4 (North). This type of analysis is somewhat similar to absorption of manufacturing overheads to cost units. Such an analysis can also be made for a group of products based on some common factors such as prices, sales order, and salesmen. There are two other related methods of analysis of such overheads, namely, by channels of distribution/methods of sale and by customers.

Apportionment of Functional Costs The direct functional costs are allocated to cost units. The indirect functional costs which cannot be allocated directly are apportioned to cost units on the basis of following methods: **(i)** Rate per article based on number/other physical unit of the product (i.e. advertisement, transportation and warehousing expenses); **(ii)** Percentage of turnover (i.e. direct selling costs, general administration/finance cost); **(iii)** Percentage of cash collected (bad debts and credit collection expenses); **(iv)** Percentage of works cost (e.g. fixed selling and distribution costs); **(v)** Percentage of stock of finished goods; **(vi)** Number of orders; **(vii)** Number of invoices, and **(viii)** Percentage of value added (i.e. total sales less cost of materials). Each item of such expenses should be analysed and allocated to different products (cost centres) on the basis of services rendered.

EXAMPLE 6.1

Following data is available relating to ABC Ltd. for a certain month:

	Territory I	*Territory II*	*Territory III*
Selling expenses	₹76,000	₹42,000	₹62,400
Distribution costs	40,000	18,000	20,000
Number of units sold	16,000	6,000	10,000
Sales	7,60,000	2,80,000	5,20,000

The company adopts sales basis and quantity basis for application of selling and distribution costs respectively. Compute **(a)** the territory-wise overhead recovery rates separately for selling and distribution costs and **(b)** the amount of selling and distribution costs chargeable to a consignment of 2,000 units of a product, sold in each territory at ₹45 per unit.

SOLUTION

(a) *Statement Showing Determination of Overhead Recovery Rates for Selling and Distribution Costs*

(i) *Selling cost recovery rate:* (Selling expenses/Sales) × 100
Territory I (₹76,000/₹7,60,000) × 100 = 10 per cent of sales
Territory II (₹42,000/₹2,80,000) × 100 = 15 per cent of sales
Territory III (₹62,400/₹5,20,000) × 100 = 12 per cent of sales

(ii) *Distribution cost recovery rate per unit sold:* (Distribution costs/Number of units sold)
Territory I (₹40,000/16,000 units) = ₹2.50 per unit sold
Territory II (₹18,000/6,000 units) = ₹3
Territory III (₹20,000/10,000 units) = ₹2

(b) *Statement Showing Determination of Selling and Distribution Costs Charged to Consignment of 2,000 units*

Particulars	*Territory I*	*Territory II*	*Territory III*
Number of units sold	2,000	2,000	2,000
Sales revenue	₹90,000	₹90,000	₹90,000
Selling cost	9,000	13,500	10,800
Distribution cost	5,000	6,000	4,000
Total cost	14,000	19,500	14,800

EXAMPLE 6.2

The Hypothetical Ltd. is making a study of the relative profitability of two products—A and B. In addition to direct costs, indirect selling and distribution costs to be allocated between the two products are as under:

Insurance charge for inventory (finished)	₹78,000
Storage costs	1,40,000
Packing and forwarding charges	7,20,000
Salesman salaries	8,50,000
Invoicing costs	4,50,000

Other details are:

	Product A	*Product B*
Selling price per unit	₹500	₹1,000
Cost per unit (exclusive of indirect selling and distribution cost)	300	600
Annuals sales (in units)	10,000	8,000
Average inventory (in units)	1,000	800
Number of invoices	2,500	2,000

One unit of product A requires a storage space twice as much as product B. The cost to pack and forward is the same for both the products. The salesmen are paid salary plus commission @ 5 per cent on sales and equal amount of efforts are put forth on the sales of each of the products.

REQUIRED: **(i)** Set up a schedule sharing the apportionment of the indirect selling and distribution costs between the two products, **(ii)** Prepare a statement sharing the relative profitability of two products.

SOLUTION

(i) *Schedule Showing Apportionment of Indirect Selling and Distribution Costs Between Products A and B*

Particulars	*Basis of apportionment*	*Products*		
		A	*B*	*Total*
Insurance charges	Value of average inventory (₹500 × 1,000): (₹1,000 × 800) = 5:8	₹30,000	₹48,000	₹78,000
Storage costs	Storage space occupied by inventory (1000 × 2): (800 × 1) = 20:8	1,00,000	40,000	1,40,000
Packing and forwarding	Annual sales (units) = 10:8	4,00,000	3,20,000	7,20,000
Salesmen's salaries	Efforts of salesmen (1:1)	4,25,000	4,25,000	8,50,000
Salesmen's commission	Sales value (₹500 × 1,000) : (₹1,000 × 800)	2,50,000	4,00,000	6,50,000
Invoicing costs	Number of invoices (2500:2000) = 5:4	2,50,000	2,00,000	4,50,00
Total cost		14,55,000	14,33,000	28,88,000

(ii) *Statement Showing Relative Profitability of Two Products—A and B*

Particulars	*Product A*	*Product B*
Annual sales revenue	₹50,00,000	₹80,00,000
Loss cost of goods sold	30,00,000	48,00,000
Gross profit	20,00,000	32,00,000
Less indirect selling and distribution costs	14,55,000	14,33,000
Profit	5,45,000	17,67,000
Profit as percentage of sales	10.9	22.09

Control of Selling and Distribution Overheads

The control of selling and distribution costs is comparatively difficult due to the special nature of such costs. The incidence of such costs is dependent upon various external factors such as distance of market, sales terms and extent of competition, and so on. The problems associated with their control are: **(i)** Absence of control over customers/competitors; **(ii)** Lack of proper definition of capacity of a sales organisation; **(iii)** Absence of control/direct supervision over staff/representatives employed outside, necessitating the use of incentive plans of remuneration for them; **(iv)** Fixation of market prices without reference to cost of production; **(v)** Difficulty in obtaining data regarding market operations; and **(vi)** Difficulty in accurately determining the market capacity. Most of the items of selling and distribution overheads are in the nature of policy/discretionary costs which are largely uncontrollable at lower levels of management. Nevertheless, control of such costs may be effected by comparison with past performance (actual) or with the help of budgets and standards like the administrative and factory overheads.

A contributory factor to effective planning and control is the analysis of sales.

Sales Analysis Sales may be analysed in a number of ways according to market segments. The methods of analysis, according to different market segments and the purpose served by each are discussed below.

Salesmen-wise The turnover by each salesman is ascertained for comparison of **(a)** actual sales with past/budgeted sales/sales quota or inter-salesmen comparison for corrective action, and **(b)** sales volume *vis-à-vis* selling costs for control of cost and fixing up commission/bonus payable to salesmen.

Performance Evaluation of Salesmen As much of the success of marketing strategy of a company depends on the efficiency of its salesmen including selling agents/offices, their performance evaluation is an important element in sales analysis. Such evaluation is made on the basis of performance in relation to one/more standards/targets specified below:

- Sales turnover
- Gross profit/contribution on sales
- Percentage of sales quota achieved
- Number/volume of new business obtained/lost
- Number of calls made.

Sales Territory The analysis of sales by territory enables **(i)** comparison with budgets/potential sales, **(ii)** determination of each territory's contribution to net profits, **(iii)** control of selling and distribution costs through correlation with sales volume, **(iv)** assessment of the extent of penetration of competitors, and so on.

Product/Product Lines-wise The usefulness of such analysis is based on **(i)** ascertainment of profit of each product/product line and comparison with past data for control purposes, **(ii)** product planning in terms of choice of product mix based on profitability, **(iii)** ascertainment of sales trends for each product, and **(iv)** control of selling and distribution costs in relation to sales volume of each product.

Customer-wise This analysis of sales is useful to:

- Ascertain profit by each type of customer,
- Maintain a reasonable balance between the types of customers and the extent of discount allowed to each

- Ascertain by type of customers the potential for future sales
- Determine their preferences in respect of quality/type of products.

Distribution Channel-wise Sales Such analysis is useful to ascertain profits of various channels of distribution and to assess their relative viability. The distribution channels refer to the series of middlemen/intermediary agencies through whom the products of a manufacturer reach the consumers. They include wholesalers, retailers, selling agents, commission agents, distributors, and so on. The choice of a channel of distribution is related to improvement in sales and provision of more effective customer service. Each distribution system produces different level of sales/profits and incurs different distribution costs. The main objective of evaluation of distribution alternatives is to determine/select the one which would bring in the highest sales/profits through the least cost. The evaluation process is based on a consideration of the relationship between sales value and the related costs for each alternative.

By Size of Order The analysis of sales on the basis of size of orders would enable comparison of cost of handling and transportation with the sales volume of various sizes as well as decision regarding trade discount for sales of various sizes.

Unit Price-wise This analysis of sales provides information relating to price trends which may be useful in the formulation of a price policy for products.

Period-wise A comparison of sales over a period of time would reveal trends, periodic/cyclical movements, seasonal/fluctuating characteristics of the product and assist in formulating sales policy on long-term basis.

SUMMARY

- The non-manufacturing overheads consist of administrative and selling and distribution costs. The administrative costs are incurred for policy formulation, direction, organisation and control of operations of an organisation.
- Their special features are that their amount is relatively small, fixation of standards for them is difficult and their absorption in product costing is arbitrary. There are three methods of accounting of administrative overheads: **(i)** transfer to costing profit and loss account, **(ii)** apportionment to manufacturing, selling and distribution functions, and **(iii)** addition as a separate item of cost.
- Though the introduction and operation of a control system is both difficult as well as not very useful, the normal methods of controlling cost, namely, comparison with past record, budgeting control and standard costing, may with suitable adjustments, be applied to such cost as well.
- Although the selling and distribution functions are separate but as after-production costs, there is overlapping between the two. These are, therefore, dealt with together for costing and control purposes. The selling overheads are incurred for selling to existing customers/retaining customers and for promoting sales to potential customers.
- The distribution overheads begin when an order is obtained and generally ends when goods are despatched. The accounting of selling and distribution overheads involves three-stage analysis: **(i)** by nature, **(ii)** by function, and **(iii)** by product. The control of such costs is comparatively difficult due to their special nature.
- An important factor in their control is sales analysis. Sales may be analysed in a number of ways and according to market segments. The methods of analysis are:
  - — By salesmen
  - — By territories
  - — By product
  - — By customer
  - — By distribution channel
  - — By size of order
  - — By period.

SOLVED PROBLEMS

P.6.1 A company is producing three types of products A, B and C. The sales territory of the company is divided into three areas X, Y and Z. The estimated sales for the year are as under:

Product	Territories X	Y	Z
A	₹5,00,000	₹2,00,000	—
B	3,00,000	—	₹8,00,000
C	—	7,00,000	4,00,000

Budgeted advertising cost is as under:

Product	Territories X	Y	Z	Total
Local cost	₹32,000	₹45,000	₹42,000	₹1,19,000
Common cost				58,000

You are required to prepare the statement showing cost (per cent on sales) for each product and territory.

SOLUTION

Statement showing Determination of Product-wise Advertising Cost

Particulars of Cost	*Products* *Product A*	*Product B*	*Product C*	*Total*
Local cost:				
Territory X[1]	₹20,000	₹12,000	—	₹32,000
Territory Y[2]	10,000	—	35,000	45,000
Territory Z[3]		28,000	14,000	42,000
Common cost: (apportioned as % of sales)[4]	14,000	22,000	22,000	58,000
Total apportioned cost	44,000	62,000	71,000	1,77,000
Sales	7,00,000	11,00,000	11,00,000	29,00,000
Per cent on sales	6.29	5.64	6.45	6.10

Statement showing Determination of Territory-wise Advertising Cost

Particulars	*Territory X*	*Territory Y*	*Territory Z*	*Total*
Local cost (direct allocation)	₹32,000	₹45,000	₹42,000	₹1,19,000
Common cost (apportionment as % of sales, territory-wise)[5]	16,000	18,000	24,000	58,000
Total apportioned costs	48,000	63,000	66,000	1,77,000
Total sales	8,00,000	9,00,000	12,00,000	29,00,000
Per cent on sales	6.00	7.00	5.50	6.10

WORKING NOTES

Local/territory costs are apportioned to products on the basis of their sales value.

1. Local cost of territory X (₹32,000) has been apportioned in the ratio of 5:3, i.e.
   Product A (₹32,000 × 5/8) = ₹20,000
   Product B (₹32,000 × 3/8) = 12,000
2. Local cost of territory Y (₹45,000) is apportioned in the ratio of 2:7:
   Product A (₹45,000 × 2/9) = ₹10,000 Product C (₹45,000 (7/9) = 35,000
3. Costs of Territory Z (₹42,000) are apportioned in the ratio of 8:4:
   Product B (₹42,000 × 8/12) = ₹28,000
   Product C (₹42,000 × 4/12) = 14,000

4. (₹58,000/₹29,00,000) × ₹7,00,000 = ₹14,000 (Product A)
   (₹58,000/₹29,00,000) × ₹11,00,000 = 22,000 (Product B)
   (₹58,000/₹29,00,000) × ₹11,00,000 = 22,000 (Product C)
5. ₹5,800 common costs are apportioned in territories X, Y, Z in proportion of sales made in each of these territories, i.e. (8:9:12)
   (₹58,000/₹29,00,000) × ₹8,00,000 = ₹16,000 (Territory X)
   (₹58,000/₹29,00,000) × ₹9,00,000 = ₹18,000 (Territory Y)
   (₹58,000/₹29,00,000) × ₹12,00,000 = ₹24,000 (Territory Z)

P.6.2 XYZ Ltd., having an extensive marketing network throughout the country, sells its products throughout four zonal sales offices, namely, A, B, C and D. The budgeted expenditure for the year are given below:

Sales manager's salary			₹12,00,000
Expenses relating to sales manager's office			8,00,000
Travelling salesmen's salaries			32,00,000
Travelling expenses			3,60,000
Advertisements			3,00,000
Godown rent: Zone	A	₹1,50,000	
	B	2,52,000	
	C	98,000	
	D	1,80,000	6,80,000
Insurance on inventories			2,00,000
Commision on sales @ 5% on sales			60,00,000

The following further particulars are also available:

Zone	*Sales (₹lakh)*	*Number of salesmen*	*Total mileage covered*	*Allocation of advertisement (%)*	*Average stock in ₹lakh*
A	360	5	6,000	30	60
B	480	6	14,000	30	80
C	160	2	4,500	20	40
D	200	3	5,500	20	20

Based on the above details, compute zone-wise selling overheads, as a percentage to sales.

SOLUTION

Statement showing Determination of Zone-wise Selling Overhead Rates

Particulars	*Basis of apportionment*	*Zones A*	*B*	*C*	*D*	*Total*
Sales manager salary	Sales ratio	₹3,60,000	₹4,80,000	₹1,60,000	₹2,00,000	₹12,00,000
Office expenses of sales	Sales ratio	2,40,000	3,20,000	1,00,667	1,33,330	8,00,000
Travelling salesman's salaries	No. of salesmen	10,00,000	12,00,000	4,00,000	6,00,000	32,00,000
Travelling expenses	Mileage covered	72,000	1,68,000	54,000	66,000	3,60,000
Advertisement	(3:3:2:2)	90,000	90,000	60,000	60,000	3,00,000
Godown rent	Actual	1,50,000	2,52,000	98,000	1,80,000	6,80,000
Insurance (stock)	(6:8:4:2)	60,000	80,000	40,000	20,000	2,00,000
Commission	(5% of sales)	18,00,000	24,00,000	8,00,000	10,00,000	60,00,000
Total overheads		37,72,000	49,90,000	17,18,670	22,59,330	1,27,40,000
Sales revenue		3,60,00,000	4,80,00,000	1,60,00,000	2,00,00,000	12,00,00,000
Selling overheads as % of sales		10.48	10.40	10.74	11.30	10.62

P.6.3 A manufacturing concern sells its sale product in three sizes of packages—small, medium, and large—each package containing one, two and three dozen units of the product respectively. Sales for the year were:

	Number of packages sold	*Sales rate*
Small size	20,000	₹10
Medium size	5,00,000	15
Large size	5,00,000	20

The factory cost was 30 paise per unit of product and the administration overhead was added at 2% of sales. The following selling and distribution expenses were incurred:

Advertising:	
Small	₹30,000
Medium	6,00,000
Large	15,00,000
Packages:	
Small	5,000
Medium	5,00,000
Large	5,00,000
General advertising (as % of sales)	1
Commission (as % of sales)	10
Sales office expenses (as % of sales)	2
Travelling expenses:	
Small	1,000
Medium	80,000
Large	30,000

Prepare a comparative income statement for each size of package.

SOLUTION

Income Statement, Package-wise

Particulars		*Packages*	
	Small	*Medium*	*Large*
Number of units	₹2,40,000	₹120,00,000	₹18,00,00,000
Sales revenue	2,00,000	75,00,000	1,00,00,000
Factory cost (₹0.3 per unit)	72,000	36,00,000	54,00,000
Administration overheads	4,000	1,50,000	2,00,000
Advertising	30,000	6,00,000	15,00,000
Packaging expenses	5,000	5,00,000	5,00,000
General advertising	2,000	75,000	1,00,000
Commission	20,000	7,50,000	10,00,000
Sales office expenses	4,000	1,50,000	2,00,000
Traveling expenses	1,000	80,000	30,000
Total cost of sales	1,38,000	59,05,000	89,30,000
Profit (Sales-Cost of sales)	62,000	15,95,000	10,70,000

REVIEW QUESTIONS

RQ.6.1 Indicate whether the following statements are 'true' or 'false'.

(i) Apportionment of office rent and rates is done on the basis of floor area.

(ii) Selling and distribution expenses form part of selling and administrative overheads.

(iii) Selling and distribution expenses are exclusively indirect costs.

(iv) Warehousing and storage costs are part of selling overheads.
(v) Selling overheads generally include indirect selling cost, advertising and sales promotion costs and credit and collection costs.
(vi) Distribution expenses primarily include transportation cost, warehousing and storage costs.
(vii) Huge advertisement cost, which would yield benefits over a period of time in future, should still be charged to profit and loss account in which it is incurred.
(viii) Sales analysis has only on two bases, namely, product and territory.
(ix) Warehousing costs are apportioned on the basis of sales volume.

[Answers: (i) True, (ii) False, (iii) False, (iv) False, (v) True, (vi) True, (vii) False, (viii) False, (ix) True.]

RQ.6.2 Explain the term administrative overheads and briefly discuss three methods of treatment thereof in cost accounts.

RQ.6.3 What, according to you, are the steps to be followed in controlling administrative overheads?

RQ.6.4 What problems are encountered in applying administrative costs partly to the manufacturing and partly to the selling department of a business firm?

RQ.6.5 What are non-manufacturing costs? Give a few examples of such costs.

RQ.6.6 What are selling and distribution overheads? Give four examples of such costs. How can such costs be controlled?

RQ.6.7 Distinguish between selling costs and distribution costs. What is the relevance of such a distinction?

RQ.6.8 For purposes of product costing, explain how would you allocate or apportion each of the following items of overhead:

(a) Traveler's salaries, commissions and expenses
(b) After-sales services costs
(c) Warehousing costs
(d) Market research costs

RQ.6.9 How would you deal with the following items in the cost accounts of a manufacturing concern?

(a) Packing expenses
(b) Sales promotion expenses
(c) Director's fees and salaries
(d) Bad debts

RQ.6.10 A company is making a study of the relative profitability of the two products A and B. In addition to direct costs, indirect selling and distribution costs to be allocated between the two products are as under:

Insurance charges for inventory (finished)	₹78,000
Storage costs	1,40,000
Packing and forwarding charges	7,20,000
Salesmen salaries	8,50,000
Invoicing costs	4,50,000

Other details are:

	Product A	*Product B*
Selling price per unit	₹500	₹1,000
Cost per unit (exclusive of indirect selling and distribution costs)	300	600
Annual sales in units	10,000	8,000
Average inventory (units)	1,000	800
Number of invoices	2,500	2,000

One unit of product A requires a storage space twice as much as product B. The cost to pack and forward one unit is the same for both the products. Sales men are paid salary *plus* commission @ 5 per cent on sales and equal amount of efforts are put forth on the sales of each of the products.

Required:

(i) Set up a schedule showing the apportionment of the indirect selling and distribution costs between the two products.

(ii) Prepare a statement showing the relative profitability of the two products.

RQ.6.11 Marketing Division of company wishes to discontinue the sale of one of the products in view of unprofitable operations. Following details are available with regard to turnover, costs, and activity for the current year ending 31st March.

	Products			
	P	*Q*	*R*	*S*
Sales turnover	₹6,00,000	₹10,00,000	₹5,00,000	₹9,00,000
Cost of sales	3,50,000	8,00,000	3,70,000	4,80,000
Storage area (square metres)	40,000	60,000	70,000	30,000
Number of cartons sold	2,00,000	3,00,000	1,50,000	3,50,000
Number of bills raised	1,00,000	1,20,000	80,000	1,00,000

Overhead costs and basis of apportionment are:

Fixed expenses

		Basis of apportionment
Administrative wages and salaries	₹1,00,000	Number of bills raised
Salesmen's salaries and expenses	1,20,000	Sales turnover
Rent and insurance	60,000	Storage area
Depreciation	20,000	Number of cartons

Variable costs

Commission	4 per cent of sales
Packing materials and wages	₹0.50 per carton
Stationery	₹0.20 per bill

Based on the above data, you are required to:

(i) prepare a statement showing summary of Selling and Distribution Costs to the products, and

(ii) prepare a Profit and Loss Statement showing contribution and profit or loss on sale of each of the products to enable the marketing department and take an appropriate decision on discontinuance of the sale of a product.

ANSWERS **[Comprehensive solutions to all numerical review questions are available on the companion website: http://www.mhhe.com/khan_jain_cost2e]**

RQ.6.10 (i) Product A, ₹14,55,000; Product B, ₹14,33,000
(ii) Net profit Product A, ₹5,45,000; Product B, ₹17,67,000
RQ.6.11 (i) Product A, ₹10,00,000; B, ₹2,09,000; C, ₹3,08,000; D, ₹1,75,000; Product E, ₹3,06,000
(ii) Product Q may be discontinued as it has maximum loss of ₹1,08,000

7 Chapter

Activity Based Costing System

Learning Objectives

1. Understand how traditional cost systems, using only volume-related allocation basis (i.e. unit level drivers), distort product and customer costs
2. Design an activity-based cost system, using activities the organisation performs for accumulating/allocating costs
3. Determine the appropriate activity cost drivers when tracing activity costs to products and customers
4. Use activity-based cost information to make strategic and operational control decisions
5. Understand the importance of measuring the practical capacity of resources and the cost of unused capacity
6. Assign marketing, distribution, and selling expenses to customers
7. Analyse and manage customer profitability
8. Discuss the role of activity-based cost systems for service companies
9. Examine the pros and cons of activity-based costing system.

INTRODUCTION

The focus of traditional cost accounting is on product costing by tracing costs to the product and allocating indirect costs through cost centres. While the direct costs are in proportion to the volume of production, the indirect costs (i.e. the production/administration/selling/distribution overheads) are apportioned to the individual products on the basis of volume-related methods such as machine-hour rate, labour-hour rate, percentage of direct cost/labour, and so on. These (normal) methods of apportionment/allocation are inadequate to prorate common costs of different functions/activities to the product costs. The activity-based costing system provides a solution to the inadequacies of the traditional method of overhead absorption/allocation. Sections 1–5, respectively, focus on **(i)** traditional (manufacturing) costing system, its limitations and activity-based cost (ABC) management **(ii)** measuring the cost of resource capacity **(iii)** marketing, selling and distribution expenses and managing customer profitability **(iv)** service companies and **(v)** pros and cons of ABC system. The main points are summarised in the last section.

TRADITIONAL MANUFACTURING COSTING SYSTEM

The traditional costing system (TCS), as discussed in Chapter 5, assigns direct (material and labour) costs to products. The indirect costs/overheads [e.g. machine expenses, scheduling, quality control, purchasing, maintenance, supervision and general factory expenses (for building depreciation, insurance, utilities and housekeeping)] are accumulated as support department expenses. These expenses, in turn, are allocated, first, to production departments (cost centres). Second, the accumulated indirect costs in production departments are assigned to individual jobs/products on the basis of pre-determined overhead allocation rates. These are based on/in proportion to some measure of volume such as direct labour cost, directly labour-hour rate, machine-hour rate and so on. An illustrative cost allocation process for Montex Pen Manufacturing Company Ltd. is shown in Exhibit 7.1.

Exhibit 7.1 Montex Pen Total and Product Profitability

	Blue Pens (1)	*Black Pens* (2)	*Red Pens* (3)	*Purple Pens* (4)	*Total* (5)
Production/Sales volume	25,000	20,000	4,500	500	50,000
Unit sale price	₹45	₹45	₹46.5	₹49.5	
Sales (a)	11,25,000	9,00,000	2,09,250	24,750	₹22,59,000
Material costs	3,75,000	3,00,000	70,200	8,250	7,53,450
Direct labour costs	1,50,000	1,20,000	27,000	3,000	3,00,000
Overheads (300% of direct labour)	4,50,000	3,60,000	81,000	9,000	9,00,000*
Total costs (b)	9,75,000	7,80,000	1,78,200	20,250	19,53,450
Total operating income [(a) – (b)]	1,50,000	1,20,000	31,050	4,500	3,05,550
Return on sales (%)	13.3	13.3	14.8	18.2	13.5

Limitations/Inadequacies of Traditional Costing System

The TCS, using only the measure of production as allocation base, has the merit of being simple, easy to use and understand, and applied consistently from year to year. It is adequate for financial reporting of inventory valuation. The problem with the TCS is that it assumes that all overheads costs are proportionate to production volume, for example, when volume increase by 20 per cent, overheads increase by 20 per cent, when volume increases by 50 per cent, overheads increase by 50 per cent, and so on. However, many overhead costs (such as the cost of setting up equipment for a production run, the cost of inspecting raw materials, and the cost of handling materials) are not proportionate to volume. In fact, many overhead costs are affected by product complexity rather than volume. The result is that simple high volume products would be overcosted whereas complex low-volume products would be undercosted. To illustrate, consider the overhead costs associated with starting a production line. Both a high-volume product (which is associated with a large number of labour and machine-time) and a low-volume product (which is associated with a small amount of labour and machine-time) many require the same amount of set up time/cost. However, since setup costs (along with all other overheads) are allocated only on the basis of production volume, the high-volume product would receive a larger **allocation** of set up cost. Thus, it would be overcosted. The low-volume product would obviously receive a smaller **allocation** of setup cost, and, thus, would be undercosted.

The use of volume-related allocation base for allocating overheads/production cost centre expenses to products/jobs would, thus, lead to product **cost distortion** in an environment of complex and high product variety. **Cost distortion results from overcosting of high-volume products and**

undercosting of low-volume products. To illustrate the nature of the distortion, consider the case of two pen manufacturers: **(i)** Montex Pen Manufacturing Company Ltd. and **(ii)** Luxor Pen Manufacturing Company Ltd.

Cost distortion results from overcosting of high-volume products and undercosting of low-volume products.

Assume Luxor makes one-model one-colour (black) 5,00,000 pens. Montex also makes 5,00,000 pens, but of different colours, sizes, varieties ranging between specialty pens with annual production as low as 50 pens per year to high volume standard (blue and black) pens whose annual production volume are each about 50,000 per year. Even though both Luxor and Montex make the same product and physical output, Montex has a highly varied mix. It would have about the same cost of materials, require the same number of labour/machine-hours for actual production but it would also require much higher indirect and support costs because of its more varied product mix and complex production task as compared to Luxor. The requirement of much larger production support staff of Montex would be to **(i)** schedule machine and production runs, **(ii)** perform setups, **(iii)** inspect produced items after setup, **(iv)** move materials, **(v)** ship orders, **(vi)** expedite orders, **(vii)** rework defective items, **(viii)** design new products, **(ix)** improve existing products, **(x)** negotiate with vendors, **(xi)** schedule material receipts, **(xii)** order, receive and inspecting materials and parts, and **(xii)** update and maintain the much larger computer-based information system. It would also operate with considerably higher levels of idle time, setup time, overtime, inventory, rework and scrap.[1] Montex would naturally require many more resources to support its highly varied mix.

Based on the TCS, the overhead costs would be allocated/applied on the basis of their respective production volumes. The black and blue pens (50,000 each) represent about 10 per cent of Montex's output (5,00,000 units). About 10 per cent of its overhead would be applied to each of them. A low volume specialty product (50 pens per year) represents only 0.1 per cent of its output. Obviously, 0.1 per cent of its overhead would be allocated to the low-volume product. The TCS would, therefore, report essentially identical product costs for **all** products (standard/high-volume as well as specialty/low-volume) irrespective of their relative production volumes. However, considerably more of Montex's per unit indirect and support costs are required for the low-volume specialty pens than for the high-volume black and blue pens. Thus, the TCS would systematically and grossly underestimate the cost of resources for low-volume pens and would overestimate the cost of high-volume/standard black and blue pens (products). **The activity-based costing (ABC) system eliminates this major source of cost distortion**. The next section illustrates how the ABC system provides a solution to the inadequacies of the TCS in terms of these cost distortions.

ACTIVITY BASED COSTING/MANAGEMENT (ABC/ABM) SYSTEM

The traditional costing system uses actual departments or cost centres for accumulating and redistributing/allocating costs. The ABC system, instead of using **cost centres**, uses **activities** for accumulating costs. The focus shifts from what the money was being spent on (e.g. labour, equipment, supplies and so on) to what the resources required by the spending were actually doing. The resource expenses are assigned to activities based on how much of the resource expenses are required or used to perform the activities. **The ABC system is a system based on activities linking spending on resources to the products/services produced/ delivered to customers.**

ABC System is a system based on activities linking spending on resources to the products/services produced/ delivered to customers.

The ABC system first accumulates indirect resource costs for each of the activities of a particular plant, department, value-chain function or organisation and then assigns the costs of activities to the products, services or other costs objects that require the activity. One of the most important difference between the TCS and the ABC system is the extent of allocation across the value chain.

The TCS generally allocates only indirect production costs to the products. These are the only costs that can be added to the inventory value of a product for financial reporting purpose and the TCS often focuses on simply measuring such inventory values. It normally does not allocate the costs of other value chain functions because these are not appropriate costs to include in inventory. The ABC system, in contrast, focuses on the costs that are important to decision-makers. It often expands allocation of costs beyond production to processes such as design, marketing, order processing and customer services. As a result, though more complex, ABC generates more accurate and useful costs to aid decision-making.

The basic idea of ABC is that costs are grouped accordingly to what drives (causes) them to be incurred. These cost drivers are used as the absorption base. **Cost drivers** are defined as those activities/transactions that are significant determinants of cost. In other words, the cost driver is an activity that generates cost. It is a structural determinant of cost-related activity. Since activities are presumed to cause costs, a link should be made between activities and products by assigning costs of activities to products based on an individual products demand for each activity. Costs are grouped into pools according to the activities which derive them. For example, a cost pool may be procurement of goods. All the costs associated with procurement, namely, ordering, inspection, storing and so on would be included in this cost pool and cost driver identified. The procurement cost per acquisition is then calculated. This provides a means to trace the cost of procurement to individual products. Thus, ABC focuses on different costs for different purposes and the identification of only those costs that are relevant to a particular decision.

Cost Allocation

The ABC system uses a two-stage approach, similar to but more general than traditional cost system: **(i)** tracing costs to activities and **(ii)** tracing costs from activities to products.

Tracing Costs to Activities The first step in cost allocation under the ABC system is to identify major activities that cause overhead costs to be incurred. Some of the activities are related to production volume but others are not. The costs of resources consumed performing these activities are grouped into costs pools. Some common activities and associated costs are listed in Exhibit 7.2 (Columns 1 and 2).

Exhibit 7.2 Common Activities and Associated Costs/Cost Drivers

Major Activities (1)	*Associated Costs (2)*	*Cost Driver (3)*
Processing purchase orders for materials and parts	Labour costs for workers deter-mining order quantities, contact-ing vendors, and preparing purchase orders	Number of purchase orders processed
Handling material and parts	Labour costs for workers handling material and parts, depreciation of equipment used to move material and parts	Number of material requisitions
Inspecting incoming material and parts	Labour costs for workers performing inspections, depreciation of equipment used to test strength of materials, tolerances, etc.	Number of receipts

(Contd.)

(*Contd.*)

Setting up equipment	Labour costs for workers involved in setups, depreciation of equipment used to adjust equipment	Number of setups
Producing goods using manu-facturing equipment	Depreciation on manufacturing equipment	Number of machine-hours
Supervising assembly workers	Salary of assembly supervisors	Number of assembly labour-hours
Inspecting finished goods	Labour cost for finished goods inspections, depreciation of equipment used to test whether finished goods meet customer specifications, etc.	Number of inspections
Packing customer orders	Labour cost for packing workers, cost of packing materials, etc.	Number of boxes packed

Tracing Costs from Activities to Products The next step is to assign costs to products using cost driver as a measure of activity. Activity cost drivers represent the quantity of activities used to produce individual products. ***Activity cost drivers are measures that identify the linkage between activities and cost objects; they serve as quantitative measures of the output of activities***. Cost drivers associated with some activities are listed in Exhibit 7.3 (Column 3).

Activity cost drivers are measures that identify the linkage between activities and cost objects; they serve as quantitative measures of the output of activities.

It may be noted that some of the cost drivers are volume-related, for example, machine-hours and assembly labour-hours. One example of costs not related to production volume is number of inspections. Some low-volume products that involve complex/ fragile parts may need a large number of inspections, whereas some high-volume products that involve simple/rugged parts may need relatively few inspections. Similarly, number of setups is another cost driver that may not be related to volume. Both low-volume and high-volume products may require the same number of setups.

Selecting Activity Cost Drivers Activity cost drivers are the central innovation of ABC system. They are also the most difficult to measure, particularly the quantity of each activity cost driver used by each product. Each firm must decide how many separate activities and related cost pools and cost drivers to identify. If too many activities are identified, the system will be unnecessarily costly and confusing. For example, if a company produces 200 products and identifies 100 key activities, it must account for 20,000 (200 × 100) product-activity relations. On the other hand, if too few activities are used, ABC system is not likely to produce accurate data. The selection of an activity cost driver reflects a subjective trade-off between accuracy and cost of measurement.

A firm can choose from three types of activity cost drivers: **(i)** Transaction, **(ii)** Duration, and **(iii)** Intensity (direct charging).

Transaction Drivers **Transaction drivers are used to count the frequency of an activity/the number of times an activity is performed**. They assume that the same quantity of resources is required every time an activity is performed. An example of transaction driver is the number of setups. If the variation in the quantity of resources used by each activity is small, that is, all setup times are between, say, 40 and 50 minutes, a transaction driver would be fine for assigning activity expenses to the cost object. If, however, the amount of resources required to perform the activity varies considerably, that is, the setup times range from 40 minutes to 7 hours, transaction driver would be the least expensive as well as the least accurate. The use

Transaction drivers are used to count the frequency of an activity/number of times an activity is performed.

of a transaction driver will overcost simple products and undercost complex products. Duration drivers avoid this distortion.

Duration drivers represent the amount of time required to perform an activity.

Duration Drivers **Duration drivers represents the amount of time required to perform an activity**. Example of duration drivers are setup-hours, inspection-hours, direct labour-hours. They are more accurate than transaction drivers but more expensive to implement.

Intensity drivers are used to charge directly for the resources used each time an activity is performed.

Intensity Drivers **Intensity drivers are used to charge directly for the resources used each time an activity is performed**. In cases where a particularly complex product may require special setup and quality control personnel, as well as special gauging and test equipment each time the machine is setup to produce the product, activity costs should be charged directly to the output based on work orders or other records that accumulate the activity expenses incurred for that output. Intensity drivers are the most accurate but the most expensive to implement.

Activity cost driver rate is the amount determined by dividing the activity expenses by the total quantity of the activity cost driver.

The choice of an appropriate cost driver involves balancing the benefits of increased accuracy against the cost of increased measurement. The goal of the ABC system should be to have the best cost system—not the most accurate.

Activity Cost Driver Rate The next step is to compute the Activity Cost Driver Rate (ACDR). **The ACDR is the amount determined by dividing the activity expenses by the total quantity of the activity cost driver.** This rate is used to assign activity costs to individual products.

Activity-Based Costing Products Profitability Report Finally, ABC Products Profitability Report is prepared. It combines activity expenses assigned to each product with their direct (labour and material) costs. The activity expenses assigned to a product is arrived at by multiplying the ACDR by the quantity of each activity cost driver used by each product.

Illustration We will now illustrate the step-wise cost allocation of overhead costs and the preparation of the ABC Products Profitability Report for the Montex Pen Manufacturing Company in Exhibit 7.1.

(A) The total overheads (aggregating ₹9,00,000) were comprised of the following:

Expense category	*Expenses*
Indirect labour	₹3,00,000
Fringe benefits	2,40,000
Computer system expenses	1,50,000
Machinery	1,20,000
Maintenance	60,000
Energy	30,000
Total	9,00,000

(B) The activities and activity expenses of the Montex Pen Manufacturing Company are summarised below:

Overhead Cost Items	*Cost Driver*				*Total Expenses*
	Handle Production Runs	*Set up*	*Support Machines*	*Run Machine Products*	
1 Indirect labour and 1/2 fringe benefits	50%	40%	10%	—	₹4,20,000
2 Computer expenses	80%	—	20%	—	1,50,000

(Contd.)

(Contd.)

3 Machine depreciation	—	—	—	100%	1,20,000
4 Maintenance	—	—	—	100%	60,000
5 Energy	—	—	—	100%	30,000
Activity Expenses	₹3,30,000*	₹1,68,000†	₹72,000□	₹2,10,000Δ	7,80,000

*(₹4,20,000 × 0.50) + (₹1,50,000 × 0.80) = ₹2,10,000 + ₹1,20,000 = ₹3,30,000
†(₹4,20,000 × 0.40) = ₹1,68,000
□(₹4,20,000 × 0.10) + (₹1,50,000 × 0.20) = ₹42,000 + ₹30,000 = ₹72,000
Δ(₹1,20,000 + ₹60,000 + ₹30,000) × 1.00 = ₹2,10,000

Activity Cost Driver	*Products*				
	Blue Pens	*Black Pens*	*Red Pens*	*Purple Pens*	*Total@*
Direct labour-hour/unit	0.02	0.02	0.02	0.02	2,000
Machine-hour/unit	0.10	0.10	0.10	0.10	10,000
Production runs	70.00	65.00	50.00	15.00	200
Setup time/run	4.00	2.40	5.60	5.60	—
Total setup time (hour)	280.00	156.00	280.00	84.00	800
Number of products	1.00	1.00	1.00	1.00	4

@Total labour and machine-hours are obtained by multiplying the unit amounts by the quantity of each type of pen sold (from Exhibit 7.1), that is, 25,000 blue, 20,000 black, 4,500 red and 500 purple pens.

(C) The activity cost driver rates and the activity expenses assigned to products are shown below:

Activity	*Activity Expense*	*Activity Cost Driver*	*Activity Cost Driver*	*Activity Cost Driver Rate Quantity*
Handle production runs	₹3,30,000	Number of production runs	200	₹1,650 per run
Set up machines	1,68,000	Number of setup hours	800	210 per setup hour
Support products	72,000	Number of products	4	18,000 per product
Run machines	2,10,000	Number of machine-hours	10,000	2.10 per machine-hour
Total	7,80,000			

Activity Expenses Assigned to Products

Activity	*ACDR*	*ACDQ for Blue*	*Activity Expenses: Blue*	*ACDQ for Black*	*Activity Expenses: Black*	*ACDQ For Red*	*Activity Expenses: Red*	*ACDQ for Purple*	*Activity Expenses: Purple*
(1)	*(2)*	*(3)*	*(4)*	*(5)*	*(6)*	*(7)*	*(8)*	*(9)*	*(10)*
Handle Production Run	₹1,650	70	₹1,15,500	65	₹1,07,250	50	₹82,500	15	₹24,750
Setup Machines	210	280	58,800	156	32,760	280	58,800	84	17,640
Support Products	18,000	1	18,000	1	18,000	1	18,000	1	18,000
Run Machines	2.10	5,000	1,05,000	4,000	84,000	900	18,900	100	210

Note: ACDR = Activity Cost Driver Rate; ACDQ = Activity Cost Driver Quantity

(D) The ABC product profitability report for the Montex Pen Manufacturing Company is shown in Exhibit 7.3.

Exhibit 7.3 Activity-Based Costing Products Profitability Report

	Blue Pens	*Black Pens*	*Red Pens*	*Purple Pens*	*Total*
Sales revenues	₹11,25,000	₹9,00,000	₹2,09,250	₹24,750	₹22,59,000
Material cost	3,75,000	3,00,000	70,200	8,250	7,53,450
Direct labour cost	1,50,000	1,20,000	27,000	3,000	3,00,000
Gross Margin	6,00,000	4,80,000	1,12,050	13,500	12,05,550
Overheads:					
— 50% fringe benefit on direct labour	60,000	48,000	10,800	1,200	1,20,000
— Handle production runs	1,15,500	1,07,250	82,500	24,250	3,30,000
— Setup machines	58,800	32,760	58,800	17,640	1,68,000
— Support products	18,000	18,000	18,000	18,000	72,000
— Run machines	1,05,000	84,000	18,900	2,100	2,10,000
Total	3,57,300	2,90,010	1,89,000	63,690	9,00,000
Operating income	**2,42,700**	**1,89,990**	**(76,950)**	**(50,190)**	**3,05,550**
Return on sales (%)	21.7	21.1	(36.8)	(202.8)	13.5

COMMENT: First, the return on sale (as a measure of profitability) according to the ABC system (Exhibit 7.3) is quite different from the return on sale according to the TCS (Exhibit 7.1). The two specialty pens (red and purple) are the most profitable according to the TCS. In sharp contrast, the blue and black pens are the only profitable pens according to the ABC systems and the red and purple pens are the most unprofitable. The reason for these differences is that incremental revenues from sale of red and purple pens are not able to cover the additional expenses caused by increase in overhead resources cost to support a large computer system and more indirect and support employees. The TCS, allocating overhead costs proportional to direct labour cost has assigned too much costs to the high-volume, simple products (black and blue pens) and too little cost to the low-volume and more complex products (red and purple pens). The production of complex, low-volume products creates disproportionate demands for resources that perform setups, handle production runs and support products. Secondly, the ABC profitability report contains far more information than the highly aggregated TCS-based report. In a single item (overheads), it aggregates a complex set of activities performed by the indirect and support resources for the four types of pens. The ABC-based report shows the cost of all the activities performed for each type of pen.

Activity-Based Management (ABM)

The ABM is a management tool that involves analysing and costing activities with the goal of improving efficiency and effectiveness. It is closely related to the ABC but it differs from the **ABC** in its primary goal. While ABC focuses on activities with the object of measuring costs of products/activities produced by them, the focus of ABM is on activities with a view to managing the activities themselves. In other words, resources are traced in ABC to activities to facilitate costing of products/services; resources are traced in ABM to activities to facilitate evaluation of activities. To clarify the difference, consider activity involved in setting up equipment for a production run. The ABC seeks to measure the cost of setup and then assign a cost to product based on how many setups each product requires. The ABM would focus on ways to improve the setup process and ways to eliminate the demand for setup activity (thus reducing setup costs).

Activity-based management refers to a set of actions that management can take, based on information from an ABC study to increase/improve profitability.

The ABM refers to a set of actions that management can take, based on information from an ABC study/system, to increase/improve profitability. The information contained in Exhibit 7.3 provides numerous insights about how to increase the profitability of Montex pens. To be able to compete in both the high-volume (blue and black pens) and the low-volume, specialty (red and purple pens), the profitability of the Montex pens can be significantly increased by a combination of a set of actions, namely, **(i)** repricing, **(ii)** increase in sales volume, **(iii)** process improvement and **(iv)** engineering and design improvements.

Repricing of Unprofitable Products One set of actions to improve profitability of Montex pens involves repricing of the two unprofitable pens—red and purple so as to cover their production costs. The red and purple pens can also be made profitable by **(i)** modifying distribution arrangements, **(ii)** changing their product design so that they can be built with simpler and fewer parts and **(iii)** imposing minimum order sizes to eliminate short, unprofitable production runs.

Increase in Sales Volume A simultaneous set of actions to improve profitability of Montex pens is to increase the sales volume of the highly profitable pens, namely, blue and black to generate incremental revenues in excess of their incremental costs.

Process Improvement Yet another ABC-based management action to improve profitability of Montex pens may relate to improving processes. For example, the Montex Pen Manufacturing Company may focus on how to reduce setup times so that the low-volume red and purple pens would require less resources and, therefore, less cost to produce, rather than try to run their production equipment faster.

Engineering and Design Improvements This set of actions would focus on seeking ways to design products that would be easier to produce and would require fewer modifications once introduced. This would reduce the resource demands by a product-sustaining activity.

The combined effect of the above set of actions would be that Montex Pen Company would produce the same volume and mix of products with fewer resources.

COST OF RESOURCE CAPACITY[2]

For the computation of the activity cost driver rates (ACDRs) in the preceding section, the expenses of each activity were divided by the output form that activity (such as number of production runs, number of setup-hours, number of products and number of machine-hours) to obtain the average cost. It is, however, possible that resources supplied exceeded the used resources. For example, in the Montex Pen case in the preceding section, although only 200 production runs were scheduled during the quarter, the indirect labour supplied could have performed 240 production runs. The unit cost per production was (₹3,30,000 ÷ 200 runs) ₹1,650. The ₹3,30,000 of resources could actually have handled 240 productions runs. There was, in other words, overestimation of the cost of handling each production run. A better estimate for the cost of resources to handle each production can, therefore, be obtained by dividing the capacity expenses by the practical capacity of work the resources could perform.

Practical Capacity

Practical capacity is the maximum amount of work that can be performed by resources supplied for production/services. It is expressed as a predetermined percentage of theoretical capacity. **Theoretical capacity means the normal working hours of a machine/worker (employee).** If the theoretical capacity is 50 hours per week and the practical capacity is 80 per cent of the theoretical capacity, the practical capacity would be 40 hours (50 × 0.80) per week per employee. The practical capacity of 80 per cent (40 hours per week) is based on the assumption that 20 per cent time of

Practical capacity is the maximum amount of work that can be performed by resources supplied for production/services.

Theoretical capacity means the normal working hours of a machine/worker/employee.

employees is utilised for breaks, arrival and departure and so on, which are not related to actual work performance. Similarly, 20 per cent represents allowance for downtime of machines due to maintenance, repair and rescheduling fluctuations and so on. The unit cost per production run = cost of capacity supplied ÷ practical cost of resources supplied, that is, ₹3,30,000 ÷ 240 runs = ₹1,375. Compared to the cost per production run based on actual work performed (₹1,650), the unit cost based on practical capacity is considerably lower (₹1,375).

Unused Capacity

Cost of unused capacity is the amount/ expense of resources unused during production.

The cost per production run based on the actual work performed (i.e. 200 production runs) of ₹1,650, thus, includes, in effect, two types of costs: **(i)** the cost of resources used for actual production runs handled and **(ii)** cost of unused capacity. **The cost of unused capacity is the amount/expense of resources unused during production** (240 – 200 = 40 production runs).

The unused capacity should not be treated as general cost to be shared across all production lines. Such a cost should not be assigned to products produced/ customers served during a period. It should also not be ignored. In order to ensure that the activity cost driver rate reflects the efficiency of allocation of cost to each production run, the cost of supply resources capacity to do work (₹3,30,000) should be related to the quantity of work the resources **can** perform rather than that actually performed (i.e. 240 production runs and not 200 production runs).

The cost of unused capacity should be assigned to the person/department/customer/market segment concerned with/responsible for it. For example, if the unused capacity was intended to meet anticipated demands from a particular customer/market segment, such cost caused by lower-than-expected demand can be assigned to the person/organisational unit responsible for that customer/ segment on a lump-sum basis. Similarly, the cost of unused capacity related to a particular product line should be assigned to the product line concerned due to non-materialistion of demand. In brief, in assigning costs of unused capacity, the costs should be traced at the level where decisions affecting supply of capacity resources and the demand for these resources are made in the organisation/company.

ABC FOR MARKETING, SELLING AND DISTRIBUTION EXPENSES

In the preceding section, we have illustrated the ABC system for allocation of manufacturing overheads. With focus on customer satisfaction and market-oriented strategies, expenses related to marketing, selling and distribution have become significant components of the overheads costs of companies. Many of these expenses do not relate to individual products/product lines but are associated with individual customers, market segments and distribution channels. This section illustrates activity-based costing for marketing, selling, distribution and administration costs.

Tracing Costs to Customers

The focus of ABC system is on tracing marketing, selling and distribution costs to customer segments. To illustrate, consider two customers, Simple and Complex, of Avon Industries Ltd. Avon Ltd. currently uses the traditional/conventional cost accounting system and distributes the marketing, selling and distribution to customers based on sales revenue, that is, approximately one-third of total sales. The traditional costing-based profitability of Simple and Complex (customers) is summarised in Exhibit 7.4:

Exhibit 7.4 Traditional Costing Based Customer Profitability Analysis

Particulars	*Simple*	*Complex*
Sales revenue	₹12,80,000	₹12,60,000
Costs of goods sold	6,16,000	6,24,000
Gross margin	6,64,000	6,36,000
Marketing, selling, distribution and administrative expenses (0.33 × sales)	4,22,000	4,15,800
Operating profit	2,41,600	2,20,200
Profit (as percentage of sale)	18.8	17.5

Identification of Activities and Cost Drivers The first step in the ABC system for marketing, selling and distribution overheads is identifying the activities performed by the resources and selecting activity cost drivers linking each activity to individual customers. The activity, activity cost description and activity cost driver are listed below:[3]

Activity	*Activity Cost Driver*
1 Marketing and technical support	1 Estimated proportion of time spent on each customer
2 Travel to customers	2 Actual expenditure
3 Distribution of sales catalogue	3 Number of mailings
4 Servicing of customers	4 Estimated proportion of time spent on each customer and supplies used by them
5 Handle customer orders	5 Number or orders
6 Warehouse inventory for customers	6 Quality of inventory and space required by customer
7 Shipping/despatch to customers	7 Actual records

Identify Resource Spending The next step is to identify the resource spending in the various accounts. The customer profile of Simple and Complex is as follows. Simple orders only a few products in large quantities, places order predictably and with long lead times, and requires little sales and technical support. But Complex requires a great deal of handholding and continuously inquires whether products could be modified to meet his specific needs. In addition to marketing resources, many technical resources are required to service Complex. Complex also places many small orders for special products, requires expeditious delivery and pays slowly, increasing the demands on order processing, invoicing and accounts receivable process of Avon Ltd. Suppose the following marketing, selling, distribution and administrative costs are identified for the two customers.

Activity	*Simple*	*Complex*
1 Marketing and technical support	₹28,000	₹2,16,000
2 Travel to customers	4,800	28,800
3 Distribution of sales catalogue	400	400
4 Servicing of customers	16,000	1,68,000
5 Handling customer orders	2,000	72,000
6 Warehouse inventory	3,200	35,200
7 Ship/despatch to customers	50,400	168,000
Total activity expenses	1,04,800	6,88,400

Customer Profitability Analysis Report The next step is to prepare a customer profitability analysis as shown in Exhibit 7.5.

Exhibit 7.5 Activity-Based Costing Customer Profitability Analysis

Particulars	*Simple*	*Complex*
Sales revenue	₹12,80,000	₹12,60,000
Cost of goods sold	6,16,000	6,24,000
Gross margin	6,64,000	6,36,000
Marketing, selling and distribution expenses:		
Marketing and technical support	28,000	2,16,000
Travel to customers	4,800	28,000
Distribution of sales catalogue	400	400
Servicing of customers	16,000	1,68,000
Handling customer orders	2,000	72,000
Warehouse inventory	3,200	35,000
Ship/despatch to customers	50,400	1,68,000
Total activity expenses	1,04,800	6,88,400
Operating profit	5,59,200	(–52,400)
Profits as percentage of sales (operating margin)	43.7	(–4.2)

COMMENT: Both customers—Simple and Complex—are profitable according to the traditional customer profitability analysis (Exhibit 7.4). But according to the ABC customer profitability analysis (Exhibit 7.5), Simple is a highly profitable customer while Complex is a very unprofitable customer. The reason is that ordering and support activities of Simple places few demands on the Avon's marketing, selling, distribution and administrative resource as a result of which its operating margin is much higher.

Managing Customer Profitability[4]

Managing customer profitability is the use of ABC customer profitability analysis to manage profitable and unprofitable customers.

The ABC customer profitability analysis of Avon Ltd. can be used to manage its profitable and unprofitable customers.

Profitable Customers Such customers are low-cost ones to serve and also offer high margin. Avon Ltd should, if necessary, offer discounts, incentives and special services to retain such valuable customers to protect them from competitors.

Unprofitable Customers These customers drag down the profitability of companies due to low margin and high cost of servicing which can be caused by **(i)** unpredictable order patterns, **(ii)** small order size, **(iii)** large demand on technical and sales personnel and so on. The unprofitable customers can be transformed into profitable ones through a whole range of actions, such as, process improvement, activity-based pricing and managing customer relationships.

Process Improvement One set of actions to make unprofitable customers profitable is to improve the internal operations to reduce/lower the costs of servicing customers. For example, the problem associated with smaller order sizes could be resolved by reducing the batch-related costs, namely, setups and order handling. This would enable accommodation of customer preferences without increasing overall prices. Electronic systems greatly reduce the cost of processing larger quantities of small orders. Similarly, companies can customise their products at the latest possible stage to meet customer preferences for large variety of products. They can also use information technology to increase the linkages from design to manufacturing so as to be able to offer greater variety and customisation without additional costs.

Activity-Based Pricing Activity-based pricing prices orders and not products. When prices are based on valid cost information, customers would shift their ordering, shipping/despatching and distribution patterns in a way so as to lower total supply-chain costs for the benefit of customers as well as suppliers.

Pricing is the most powerful tool to transform unprofitable customers into profitable customers. Activity-based pricing sets a base price for a standard quantity for each standard product. For any special services, the company may provide several options with associated prices. The prices for special services may recover the activity-based cost-to-serve and allow the customer to choose from the features of services it wishes at a price to cover the cost of providing those features/services for the customers.

Another option for the Avon Ltd. may be to earn a margin on special services by pricing them above the cost of services. Price surcharges could be imposed after designing and producing special variants for a customer's particular needs. Discounts could be offered when the ordering pattern lowers the cost of supplying it.

Managing Relationships Finally, companies can convert unpredictable customers into profitable customers by persuading them to increase the scope of the purchases of their other products/services. The margin from increased purchases of other products/services would contribute to cover customer-sustaining costs.

ABC FOR SERVICE COMPANIES

The ABC system is as much applicable and useful to a service company as it is to a manufacturing company. Service organisations include companies in **(a)** financial services (i.e. banks, insurance organisations, money managers), **(b)** transportation (i.e. airlines, roads and railways), **(c)** telecommunications, **(d)** wholesale and retail, **(e)** healthcare and so on. This section illustrates the ABC model for a service company with particular reference to a telecommunication company.

Cost Structure of Service Companies

As shown in an earlier section, the ABC system in a manufacturing company focuses on the service component and not on the direct (material and labour) costs of manufacturing operations. It addresses the support resources for the manufacturing process, such as, purchasing, scheduling, inspecting, designing, supporting products and processes and handling customers and orders. The direct costs are traced to individual products.

Service companies have a unique cost structure. Virtually all the costs of a service company are indirect/fixed. A service company has little or no direct material—its personnel provide indirect support to products/customers—and, hence the company does not have direct/traceable costs to serve as allocation base. The variable cost (i.e. the increase in spending due to an incremental transaction/customer) is practically zero. For example, for a telecommunication company, handling one more phone call from a customer/one more data transfer involves no incremental spending. Therefore, the cost to provide a service based on variable costs by a service company may be close to zero.

Customer Costs

Customer costs Basic operating costs of service companies are determined by customer behaviour.

In contrast to manufacturing companies, customer behaviour determines the basic operating costs of products/services of service companies. For example, customers of a telecommunications company can order a basic service in several ways, namely, through a phone call, a letter, or a visit to a local unit. A customer may order two/one phone line(s). An engineer may have to go there to install a new line or may make a change at the local switching centre. A customer may make only one request or several and can pay either by direct debit over the Internet, a telephone banking transfer, a mailed cheque or in person. The cost of each option is obviously quite different. Therefore, far more relevant and useful information would be available to the telecom company by measuring revenues/costs at the customer level rather than at the product level. Service companies should, therefore, identify the differential profitability of individual customers as they determine the quantity of demands for the operating activities.

In addition, a customer may have more than one relationship with a service company. For example, a customer of a telecom company may have, in addition to the basic phone line, a high speed data line, a long distance account, a service contract, equipment rentals and so on. The service company should act on total relationship profitability of a customer and not on the profitability of just a single service.

ABC Model Illustrated

The structure/construction of the ABC system in a service company is almost identical to that of a manufacturing company, that is, **(i)** identify activities, **(ii)** assign resources expenses to activities, **(iii)** determine activity cost drivers, **(iv)** calculate activity cost driver rate and **(v)** compute product/customer cost. We illustrate below the ABC model for a service company with reference to IBM-Daksh.

The billing department of IBM-Daksh customer care centre requires accurate and useful information about the cost of providing account inquiry and bill printing services for its 1,20,000 residential and 20,000 commercial customer accounts. A local service centre has offered to provide all the functions currently performed by IBM-Daksh's billing department at ₹21.5 per residential account and ₹40 per commercial account.

All costs in the billing department are indirect. There are no direct or unallocated costs. The resources used to support the billing department of IBM-Daksh in the previous month are summarised below:

Expense	*Expense amount*
Telecommunications	₹2,92,600
Computer expenses	8,90,000
Supervisors	1,68,000
Paper	36,000
Occupancy	2,35,000
Account inquiry labour	8,67,300
Printing machines	2,75,000
Billing labour	2,81,750
Verification labour	56,250
Other resources	3,35,000
	34,37,500

The billing department of IBM-Daksh uses a traditional costing system that allocates all indirect costs based on (i) the number of account inquiries, namely, 20,000 (80 per cent) for residential customers and 5,000 (20 per cent) for commercial customers.

Suppose IBM-Daksh wants to introduce ABC system for its billing department. They have identified the following activities and the related cost drivers:

Activity	*Cost driver*
Account billing	Number of printed pages
Bill verification	Number of accounts verified
Account inquiry	Number of inquiries
Correspondence	Number of letters
Other activities	Number of printed pages

The resources used to perform the activities and the activities performed are shown here:

Resources Used to Perform Activity	*Activity Performed (%)*					
	Account Inquiry	*Correspondence*	*Billing*	*Verification*	*Others*	*Total*
Supervisor	40	10	30	—	20	100
Account inquiry labour	90	10	—	—	—	100
Billing labour	—	—	30	70	—	100
Verification labour	—	—	—	100	—	100
Paper	—	—	100	—	—	100
Computer	45	5	35	10	5	100
Telecommunications	90	—	—	—	10	100
Occupancy	65	—	15	—	20	100
Printing machines	—	5	90	—	5	100
All other resources	—	—	—	—	100	100

The number of cost driver units for the billing department of IBM-Daksh is shown below:

Activity	*Cost driver units*	*Number of cost driver units*		
		Residential	*Commercial*	*Total*
1 Account inquiry	Number of inquiries	20,000	5,000	25,000
2 Correspondence	Number of letters	1,800	1,000	2,800
3 Bill printing	Number of printed pages	1,20,000	40,000	1,60,000
4 Verification	Number of accounts verified	—	20,000	20,000
5 Other activities	Number of printed pages	1,20,000	40,000	1,60,000

REQUIRED:

(a) Using the traditional costing system, should the IBM-Daksh accept the offer of the local service centre to perform all the functions?

(b) Would the decision be different with ABC system?

SOLUTION

(a) Cost Computation for Billing Department (Traditional Costing System)

Particulars	*Residential*		*Commercial*	
1 Cost	₹27,50,000@		₹6,87,500@@	
2 Number of inquiries	20,000	(0.80)	5,000	(0.20)
3 Number of accounts	1,20,000		20,000	
4 Cost per account (1 ÷ 3)	22.9		34.4	

@₹34,37,5000 × (0.80) @@₹34,37,500 × (0.20)

Decision: The billing department should accept the offer of the local service centre to service residential accounts as there is a saving of ₹1.4 per account (₹22.9 – ₹21.5). But it should continue to service the commercial accounts because of lower cost of ₹5.6 (₹40 – ₹34.4).

(b) The computation of activity-based cost per account for each customer class (residential and commercial is illustrated below).

(b) (i) Total Traceable Costs

Resource	Cost	Activity Cost Pool				
		Account Inquiry	Corres-pondence	Billing	Verification	Others
1 Supervisors	₹1,68,000	₹67,200[a]	₹16,800[b]	₹50,400[c]	—	₹33,600[d]
2 Account inquiry labour	8,67,300	7,80,570	86,730	—	—	—
3 Billing labour	2,81,250	—	—	84,375	₹1,96,875	—
4 Verification labour	56,250	—	—	—	56,250	—
5 Paper	36,600	—	—	36,600	—	—
6 Computer	8,90,000	4,00,500	44,500	3,11,500	89,000	44,500
7 Telecommunications	2,92,600	2,63,340	—	—	—	29,260
8 Occupancy	2,35,000	1,52,750	—	35,250	—	47,000
9 Printing machines	2,75,000	—	13,750	2,47,500	—	13,750
10 Others	3,35,000	—	—	—	—	3,35,500
Total traceable cost	34,37,500	16,64,360	1,61,780	7,65,625	3,42,125	5,03,610

[a](₹16,8,000 × 0.40) [b](₹16,8,000 × 0.10) [c](₹1,68,000 × 0.30) [d](₹16,8,000 × 0.20)

(b) (ii) Costs Driver

Activity	Traceable costs (1)	Number of Driver Units (2)	Cost per Driver Units [(1) ÷ (2)]
Account inquiry	₹16,64,360	25,000 inquiries	₹66.5744
Correspondence	1,61,780	2,800 letters	57.7786
Account billing	7,65,625	1,60,000 printed pages	4.7852
Bill verification	3,42,125	20,000 accounts verified	17.1062
Other activities	5,03,610	1,60,000 printed pages	3.1476

(b) (iii) Cost per Customer Class

Activity	Cost Per Driver Unit	Residential Customer Accounts		Commercial Customer Accounts	
		Number of Driver Units	Cost	Number of Driver Units	Cost
(1)	(2)	(3)	(4)	(5)	(6)
Account inquiry	₹66.5744	20,000 inquiries	₹13,31,490	5,000 inquiries	₹3,32,870
Correspondence	57.7786	2,800 letters	1,04,001	1,000 letters	57,779
Account billing	4.7852	1,20,000 pages	5,74,224	40,000 pages	1,91,408
Billing verification	17.1062	—	—	20,000 accounts	3,42,124
Other activities	3.1476	1,20,000 pages	3,77,712	40,000 pages	1,25,904
Total Costs			23,87,415		10,50,085
Number of accounts			1,20,000		20,000
Cost per account			₹19.90		₹52.50
Cost per account (traditional system)			22.90		34.40

COMMENTS: The traditional costing system overcosts the high-volume residential accounts (₹22.9) and substantially undercosts the low-volume complex commercial accounts (₹34.40). The cost per account for residential accounts using ABC system (₹19.9) is 13 per cent less than the cost generated by the traditional system [₹22.9 – ₹19.9 = (₹3 ÷ ₹22.9) × 100]. The cost per account of commercial accounts, using ABC system, is similarly more than the cost from the traditional system [₹52.50 – ₹34.10 = (₹16.42 ÷ ₹24.10) × 100 = 53%].

Decision: The ABC system gives a diametrically opposite decision. The billing department of IBM-Daksh should accept the offer of the local service centre to service commercial accounts as there is a saving of ₹12.10 (₹52.50 – ₹40). But it should continue to service the residential accounts because of lower cost of ₹1.6 (₹21.5 – ₹19.9).

PROS AND CONS

The ABC system offers some real advantages but it also suffers from some major limitations. This section briefly describes the pros and cons of ABC system.

Advantages

A major benefit of ABC system is that, in contrast to the traditional costing system, it is not likely to undercost complex low-volume products and overcost high-volume simple products. This is so because the cost drivers used by the ABC system to assign costs are unrelated to volume and many more cost drivers are used.

The second benefit of the ABC system is that it may result in improved cost control. This is so because costs are broken into a number of activities rather than into a few cost pools. The managers know the costs of setups, inspections, order taking, stocking, moving inventory, and other key activities so that they see a need to improve efficiency and reduce costs.

Disadvantages

A major disadvantage of ABC system is that it is more expensive/costly to develop and maintain compared to a traditional costing system. For example, consider an ABC system with 25 cost pools applied to 100 different products. Assigning cost to 25 pools will be costly and 2,500 (25 pools × 100 products) allocations will have to be made to assign costs to products.

The most serious limitation of ABC system is that, in practice, it is used to develop the **full cost** of products. Since full costs include allocation of costs that are fixed (e.g. depreciation and supervisory salaries), the cost per unit generated by the ABC system does not measure the incremental costs needed to produce an item. An incremental information is required for decision-making. The fixed costs are sunk costs and sunk costs are not relevant for decisions since they are not incremental.

To conclude, for companies which do not use the information generated by the ABC system in an overly simplistic way (i.e. treat the full cost information as if it were full cost information), an ABC is likely to be, on the whole, quite beneficial.

REFERENCES

1. Anthony A.A., Kaplan, R.S. and Young,S.M., *Management Accounting*, Pearson (London, 2004), p.126.
2. Ibid, p.137.
3. Ibid, p.144.
4. Ibid, p.145.

SUMMARY

➢ The traditional costing system (TCS) assigns indirect costs/overheads to job/products in two stages: first, the accumulated cost are allocated to production departments (cost centers), second, the accumulated costs in cost centres are assigned to individual job/products on the basis of an overhead allocation rate based on/in proportion to some measure of volume of production such as direct labour cost, direct labour-hour rate, machine-hour rate and so on. It has the merit of being simple, easy to use and understand, and applied consistently from year to year. It is adequate for financial reporting of inventory valuation.

➢ It has, however, serious limitations/inadequacies due to its assumption that all overheads are proportionate to volume of production. Many overheads costs are, actually, not proportionate to volume. Examples of such costs are setup costs of machines/equipment, cost of inspection/handling of materials and so on. They are affected by complexity rather than volume. As a result, simple high-volume products would be overcosted (i.e. receive a larger allocation of overheads) and low-volume complex products would be undercosted (i.e. receive a smaller allocation of overheads). The use of volume-related allocation base of TCS for allocating overheads would result in product cost distortion in an environment of complex and high product variety. The ABC system eliminates this source of cost distortion.

➢ The ABC system also uses a two-stage overhead allocation: **(i)** tracing costs to activities and **(ii)** tracing costs from activities to products/jobs.

➢ The first step is to identify major activities that cause/drive overhead costs to be incurred. Some of the activities are related to production volume (such as production runs, salary of supervisors and so on) but others are not (such as inspection/handling of materials, setting up equipment and so on). The cost of resources consumed in performing these activities are grouped into cost pools.

➢ The next step is to assign costs to products/jobs using cost drivers as a measure of activity. Cost drivers represent the quantity of activities used to produce individual products. They identify the linkage between activities and cost objects and serve as quantitative measures of the output of activities. In fact, they are the central innovation of ABC system. A firm can choose from three types of cost drivers: **(i)** transaction, **(ii)** duration and **(iii)** intensity (direct charging).

➢ Transaction cost drivers are used to count the frequency of an activity/number of times an activity is performed. It is the least expensive as well as the least accurate. Duration drivers represent the amount of time required to perform an activity (e.g. inspection-hours). They are more accurate than transaction drivers, but more expensive to implement. Intensity drivers are used to charge directly for the resources used each time an activity is performed. They are the most accurate but the most expensive to implement. The choice of an appropriate activity cost driver involves balancing the benefits of increased accuracy against the cost of increased measurement.

➢ The activity costs are assigned to individual jobs/products on the basis of activity cost driver rate (ACDR). The ACDR = activity expenses 4 total quantity of the activity cost driver. The activity expenses assigned to a product = ACDR 3 quantity of each activity cost driver used by the product concerned.

➢ The activity-based management (ABM) refers to a set of actions that management can take, based on information from an ABC study, to increase/improve profitability. These include a combination of **(i)** repricing of unprofitable products, **(ii)** increasing sales volume of highly profitable products, **(iii)** process improvement (e.g. how to reduce setup times in contrast to faster run of production, equipment and **(iv)** engineering and design improvements. Their combined effect would be production of the same volume and mix of products with fewer resources.

➢ Practical capacity is a better measure of cost of resources to handle each production (i.e. capacity expenses 4 practical capacity). It is the maximum amount of work that can be performed by resources supplied for production/services and is expressed as a percentage of theoretical capacity. Theoretical capacity means the normal working hours of a machine/working employee. The difference between theoretical capacity and practical capacity is the time utilised by the employees for breaks, arrivals, departures and so on, which are not related to actual work performance. It may also represent allowances for downtimes of machines due to maintenance, repair and rescheduling fluctuations and so on. The expenses of resources unused during the production (difference between theoretical capacity and practical capacity) is the cost of unused capacity. Such a cost should be assigned to the person/customer/department/market segment concerned with/responsible for it.

- Marketing, selling and distribution expenses are significant components of overhead costs of companies. Most of these costs are associated with customers, market segments and distribution channels rather than to individual products. The ABC is applicable to such costs also. Its focus is on tracing these costs to customer segments. The activities performed by these services are first identified together with activity cost drivers linking each activity to individual customers. The resource spending in the various customer accounts are then identified. The final stage is preparation of customer profitability analysis.
- The ABC customer profitability analysis can be used to manage its profitable and unprofitable customers. To protect them from competitive inroads profitable customers may be offered discounts/incentives and special services to retain them. The unprofitable customers can be transformed into profitable customers through a number of actions: **(i)** process improvement, **(ii)** activity-based pricing and **(iii)** managing customer relationships.
- The ABC system is as much applicable to service companies as it is to a manufacturing company. Service companies have a unique cost structure. Virtually all their costs are indirect/fixed. In contrast to manufacturing companies, customer behaviour determines the basic operating costs of products/services of service companies. They should, therefore, identify the differential profitability of individual customers as they determine the quantity of demands for their operating activities. Moreover, service companies should act on total relationship profitability of a customer and not on the profitability of just a single customer. The structure/construction of the ABC system of a service company is identical to that of a manufacturing company.
- The ABC system has advantages as well as limitations. Its major benefits are: **(i)** it does not undercost complex low-volume products and overcost high-volume simple products, **(ii)** it may result in improved cost control. The limitations of ABC system are two-fold: **(a)** it is costly to develop and maintain and **(b)** it is used to develop full costs and does not measure the incremental costs needed to produce an item.

SOLVED PROBLEMS

P.7.1 Image Furnishing Ltd. manufacturers a variety of premium board room chairs. Its job-costing system is designed using an activity-based approach. There are two direct cost categories consisting of direct materials and direct manufacturing labour and three indirect costs pools representing three activity areas at the plant:

Manufacturing activity area	*Budgeted costs*	*Cost driver used as allocation base*	*Cost allocation rate*
Material handling	₹2,00,000	Parts	₹0.25
Cutting	21,60,000	Parts	2.50
Assembly	20,00,000	Direct manufacturing labour-hours	25.00

Two styles of chairs were produced in March: executive chair and chairman chair. Their quantities, direct material costs and other data for March are as follows:

Type of chair	*Units produced*	*Direct material costs*	*Number of parts*	*Direct manufacturing labour-hours*
Executive	5,000	₹6,00,000	1,00,000	7,500
Chairman	100	25,000	3,500	500

The direct manufacturing labour rate is ₹20 per hour. Assuming no beginning/ending inventory, compute the total manufacturing costs and units costs of the two types of chairs.

SOLUTION

(a) Manufacturing Costs with Activity-based Costing

Particulars	*Executive chair*	*Chairman chair*
Direct manufacturing costs:		
Direct material costs	₹6,00,000	₹25,000
Direct manufacturing labour [(executive chair 7,500 labour-hours, chairman chair, 500 labour-hours) × ₹20]	1,50,000	10,000
	7,50,000	35,000
Indirect manufacturing costs:		
Material handling [(Executive chair, 1,00,000 parts; Chairman chair, 3,500 parts) × ₹0.25]	25,000	875
Cutting [(Executive chair, 1,00,000 parts; Chairman chair, 3,500 parts) × ₹2.50]	2,50,000	8,750
Assembly [(Executive chair, direct manufacturing labour-hours, 7,500; Chairman chair, direct manufacturing labour-hours, 500) × ₹25]	1,87,500	12,500
	4,62,500	22,125
Total manufacturing costs	12,12,500	57,125

P.7.2 The Aeronautical Ltd. has production facility specialising in jobs for the aircraft components market. The traditional costing system has two direct-cost categories, namely, direct materials and direct manufacturing labour and a single direct cost pool, that is, manufacturing overhead allocated on the basis of direct labour-hours. The indirect cost allocation rate would have been ₹115 direct manufacturing labour-hour.

The company has now decided to replace the single indirect cost pool with five indirect cost pools, representing five activity areas each with its own supervising and budget responsibility. The relevant data are as follows:

Activity area	*Cost driver used as an allocation base*	*Cost allocation rate*
Material handling	Parts	₹0.40
Lathe work	Turns	0.20
Milling	Machine-hours	20.00
Grinding	Parts	0.80
Testing	Units tested	15.00

Two representative jobs processed under the new system of the facility at the most recent period had the following features:

Particulars	*Job 101*	*Job 102*
Direct material costs per job	₹9,700	₹59,900
Direct manufacturing labour cost per job	750	11,250
Direct manufacturing labour-hours per job	25	375
Parts per job	500	2,000
Turns per job	20,000	60,000
Machine-hours per job	150	1,050
Units per job	10	200

REQUIRED:

(a) Compute the per unit manufacturing costs of each job under the traditional job-cutting system.

(b) Compute the per unit manufacturing costs of each job under the activity-based costing system.

SOLUTION

(a) Manufacturing Costs with Traditional Job Costing System

Particulars	*Job 101*	*Job 102*
Direct manufacturing costs per job:		
Direct materials per job	₹9,700	₹59,900
Direct manufacturing labour per job	750	11,250
	10,450	71,150
Indirect manufacturing costs per job: (Job 101, 25 labour-hours; job 102, 375 labour-hours) × ₹115	2,875	43,125
Total manufacturing costs per job	13,325	1,14,275

(b) Manufacturing Costs with Activity-based Costing System

Particulars	*Job 101*	*Job 102*
Direct manufacturing costs per job:		
Direct materials per job	₹9,700	₹59,900
Direct manufacturing labour per job	750	11,250
	10,450	71,150
Indirect manufacturing costs:		
Material handling [(Job 101, 500 parts; Job 102, 2,000 parts) × ₹0.40]	200	800
Lathe work [(Job 101, 20,000 turns; Job 102, 60,000 turns) × ₹0.20]	4,000	12,000
Milling [(Job 101,150 machine-hours; Job 102, 1050 machine-hours) × ₹20]	3,000	21,000
Grinding [(Job 101, 500 parts; Job 102, 2,000 parts) × ₹0.80]	400	1,600
Testing [(Job 101, 10 units; Job 102, 200 units) × ₹15]	150	3,000
	7,750	38,400
Total manufacturing costs	18,200	1,09,550

P.7.3 A company manufacturing two products furnishes the following data for a year:

Product	*Annual output (Units)*	*Total machine-hours*	*Total number of purchase orders*	*Total number of set-ups*
A	5,000	20,000	160	20
B	60,000	1,20,000	384	44

The annual overheads are as under:

Volume-related activity costs	₹5,50,000
Setup-related costs	8,20,000
Purchase-related costs	6,18,000

You are required to calculate the cost per unit of each product A and B based on:

(i) Traditional method of charging overheads

(ii) Activity based costing method.

Solution

(i) Statement showing Cost per unit of Products: (A and B based on Traditional Method of Charging Overheads)

Total annual overheads (₹5,50,000 + 8,20,000 + 6,18,000)	₹19,88,000

Total machine hours	1,40,000
Machine-hour rate (₹19,88,000/1,40,000 hours)	14.2

Particulars	*Products*	
	A	*B*
Annual output (units)	5,000	60,000
Total machine-hours	20,000	1,20,000
Overhead cost	₹2,84,000*	₹17,04,000**
Overhead cost per unit	₹56.80@	₹28.40@@

*(20,000 × ₹14.20) **(1,20,000 × ₹14.20)
@(₹2,84,000/5,000 units) @@(₹17,04,000/60,000 units)

(ii) Statement showing Cost per unit Products (A and B based on Activity based Costing Method)

Machine-hour rate (₹5,50,000/1,40,000 hours)	₹3.93
Cost of one setup (₹8,20,000/64 setups)	12,812.50
Cost of purchase order (₹6,18,000/544 orders)	1,136.03

Particulars	*Products*	
	Product A	*Product B*
Total machine-hours	20,000.00	1,20,000.00
Cost related to volume activities	₹78,600.00@	4,71,600.00@@
Cost related to purchases	₹1,81,764.80*	₹4,36,235.52**
Cost related to setups	2,56,250.00$	₹5,63,750.00$$
Total costs	5,16,614.80	14,71,585.52
Annual output (units)	(÷) 5,000.00	(÷) 60,000.00
Cost per unit	₹103.32	₹24.53

@(20,000 hours × ₹3.93) @@(1,20,000 hours × ₹3.93)
*(160 orders × ₹1,136.03) **(384 orders × ₹1,136.03)
$(20 setups × ₹12,812.50) $$(44 set-ups × ₹12,812.50)

P.7.4 Family Store wants information about the profitability of individual product lines: soft drinks, fresh produce and packaged food. The store provides the following data for the current year for each product line:

	Soft drinks	*Fresh produce*	*Packaged food*
Revenues	₹7,93,500	₹21,00,600	₹12,09,000
Cost of goods sold	6,00,000	15,00,000	9,00,000
Cost of bottles returned	12,000	0	0
Number of purchase orders placed	360	840	360
Number of deliveries received	300	2,190	660
Hours of shelf-stocking time	540	5,400	2,700
Items sold	1,26,000	11,04,000	3,06,000

Family Store also provides the following information for the current year:

Activity	Description of activity	Total cost	Cost-allocation base
Bottle returns	Returning of empty bottles	₹12,000	Direct tracing of soft drink line
Ordering	Placing of orders for purchases	1,56,000	1,560 purchase orders
Delivery	Physical delivery and receipt of goods	2,52,000	3,150 deliveries
Shelf-stocking	Stocking of goods on store shelves and on-going restocking	1,72,800	8,640 hours of shelf-stocking time
Customer support	Assistance provided to customers including checkout	3,07,200	15,36,000 items sold

REQUIRED:

(i) Family Store currently allocates support cost (all costs other than cost of goods sold) to product lines on the basis of cost of goods sold of each product line. Calculate the operating income and operating income as a % of revenues for each product line. **(ii)** If Family Store allocates support costs (other than cost of goods sold) to product lines using an activity-based costing system, calculate the operating income and operating income as a % of revenues for each product line. **(iii)** Comment on your answers in requirements **(i)** and **(ii)**.

SOLUTION

(i) Statement showing Operating Income and Operating Income as a Percentage of Revenues for 3 Products of Family Store

Particulars	Soft drinks	Fresh produce	Packaged food	Total
Revenues	₹7,93,000	₹21,00,600	₹12,09,000	₹41,04,000
Cost of goods sold (COGS)	6,00,000	15,00,000	9,00,000	30,00,000
Support cost (30% of COGS)	1,80,000	4,50,000	2,70,000	9,00,000
Total cost	7,80,000	19,50,000	11,70,000	39,00,000
Operating income	13,500	1,50,600	39,900	2,04,000
Operating income as a % of revenue	1.70	7.17	3.30	4.97

WORKING NOTES

1. Total Support Cost:

Bottle returns	₹12,000
Ordering	1,56,000
Delivery	2,52,000
Shelf-stocking	1,72,800
Customer support	3,07,200
Total support cost	9,00,000

2. Percentage of Support Cost of Goods Sold (COGS)

= (₹9,00,000/30,00,000) × 100 = 30%

(ii) Statement showing Operating Income and Operating Income as a Percentage of Revenues for 3 Products of Family Store

Particulars	Soft drinks	Fresh produce	Packaged foods	Total
Revenues	₹7,93,500	₹21,06,000	₹12,09,900	₹41,04,000
Cost of goods sold	6,00,000	15,00,000	9,00,000	30,00,000
Cost of bottles returned	12,000	—	—	12,000
Ordering cost [360:840:360]	36,000	84,000	36,000	1,56,000
Delivery cost [300:2,190:660]	24,000	1,75,200	52,800	2,52,000

(*Contd.*)

(*Contd.*)

Shelf-stocking cost [540:5,400:2,700]	10,800	1,08,000	54,000	1,72,800
Customer support cost [1,26,000:11,04,000:3,06,000]	25,200	2,20,800	61,200	3,07,200
Total cost	7,08,000	20,88,000	11,04,000	39,00,000
Operating income	85,500	12,600	1,05,900	2,04,000
Operating income as % of revenues	10.78	0.60	8.75	4.97

WORKING NOTE

Computation of Cost for each Cost Activity:

Activity	*Total cost*	*Cost allocation base*	*Cost activity rate*
Ordering	₹1,56,000	1,560 purchase orders	₹100 per purchase order
Delivery	2,52,000	3,150 deliveries	80 per delivery
Shelf-stocking	1,72,800	8,640 hours	20 per stocking hours
Customer support	3,07,200	15,36,000 items sold	0.20 per items sold

(iii) COMMENT: The operating income margins are more credible and authentic under the ABC costing system *vis-à-vis* the traditional costing system. The reason is that the ABC method provides more equitable basis of allocation of costs among user units.

P.7.5 RST Limited specialises in the distribution of pharmaceutical products. It buys from the pharmaceutical companies and resells to each of the three different markets:

(i) General supermarket chains
(ii) Drugstore chains
(iii) Chemist shops

The following data for the month of April current year in respect of RST Limited has been reported:

	General supermarket chains	*Drugstore chains*	*Chemist shops*
Average revenue per delivery	₹84,975	₹28,875	₹5,445
Average cost of goods sold per delivery	82,500	27,500	4,950
Number of deliveries	300	825	2,750

In the past, RST Limited has used gross margin percentage to evaluate the relative profitability of its distribution channel.

The company plans to use activity-based costing for analysing the profitability of its distribution channels. The activity analysis of RST Limited is as under:

Activity area	*Cost driver*
Customer purchase order processing	Purchase orders by customers
Line-item ordering	Line-items per purchase order
Store delivery	Store deliveries
Cartons dispatched to stores	Cartons despatched to a store per delivery
Shelf-stocking at customer store	Hours of shelf-stocking

The April, current year operating costs (other than cost of goods sold) of RST Limited are ₹8,27,970. These operating costs are assigned to five activity areas. The cost in each area and the quantity of the cost allocation basis used in that area for April, current year, are as follows:

Activity area	*Total cost in April, current year*	*Total unit of cost allocation base used in April, current year*
Customer purchase order processing	₹2,20,000	5,500 orders
Line-item ordering	1,75,560	58,520 line items
Store delivery	1,95,250	3,905 store deliveries
Cartons despatched to store	2,09,000	2,09,000 cartons
Shelf-stocking at customer store	28,160	1,760 hours

Other data for April, current year include the following:

	General supermarket chains	*Drugstore chains*	*Chemist shops*
Total number of orders	385	990	4,125
Average number of line items per order	14	12	10
Total number of store deliveries	330	825	2,750
Average number of cartons shipped per store delivery	300	80	16
Average number of hours of shelf-stocking per store delivery	3	0.6	0.1

REQUIRED:

(i) Compute for April, current year, gross-margin percentage for each of its three distribution channels and compute RST Limited's operating income.

(ii) Compute the April, current year rate per unit of the cost-allocation base for each of the five activity areas.

(iii) Compute the operating income of each distribution channel in April, current year using the activity-based costing information. Comment on the results. What new insights are available with activity-based cost information?

(iv) Describe four challenges one would face in assigning the total April, current year operating costs of ₹8,27,970 to five activity areas.

SOLUTION

(i) Statement showing Operating Income and Gross Margin Percentage of three Distribution Channels of RST Limited

Particulars	*General super market chains*	*Drugstore chains*	*Chemist shops*	*Total*
Revenues	₹2,80,41,750 (330 × ₹84,975)	₹2,38,21,875 (825 × ₹28,875)	₹1,49,73,750 (2,750 × ₹5,445)	₹6,68,37,375
Less cost of goods sold	2,72,25,000 (330 × ₹82,500)	2,26,87,500 (825 × ₹27,500)	1,36,12,500 (2,750 × ₹4,950)	6,35,25,000
Gross margin	8,16,750	11,34,375	13,61,250	33,12,375
Less operating costs				8,27,970
Operating income				24,84,405
Gross margin (%)	2.91	4.76	9.09	4.96
Operating income (%)				3.72

(ii) Computation of rate per unit of cost allocation for five activity areas for April current year

1 Customer purchase order processing (₹2,20,000/5,500 orders)	₹40 per order
2 Line-item ordering (₹1,75,560/58,520 line items)	3 per line item hours
3 Store delivery (₹1,95,250/3,905 store deliveries)	50 per delivery
4 Cartons despatched (₹2,09,000/2,09,000 deliveries)	1 per despatch
5 Shelf-stocking at customer store (₹28,160/1,760 hours)	16 per hour

(iii) Statement showing Operating Income Statement of Distribution Channels in April, current year (using Activity Based Costing Information)

Particulars	General supermarket chains	Drugstore chains	Chemist shops
Gross margin	₹8,16,750	₹11,34,375	₹13,61,250
Less operating costs:			
Customer purchase	15,400	39,600	1,65,000
Order processing	(₹40 × 385 orders)	(₹40 × 990 orders)	(₹40 × 4,125 orders)
Line-item ordering	16,170 (₹3 × 14 × 385 orders)	35,640 (₹3 × 12 × 990 orders)	1,23,750 (₹3 × 10 × 4,125 orders)
Store delivery	16,500 (₹50 × 330 deliveries)	41,250 (₹50 × 825 deliveries)	1,37,500 (₹50 × 2,750 deliveries)
Cartons dispatched	99,000 (₹1 × 300 cartons × 330 deliveries)	66,000 (₹1 × 80 cartons × 825 deliveries)	44,000 (₹1 × 16 cartons × 2,750 deliveries)
Shelf-stocking	15,840 (₹16 × 330 deliveries × 3 Activity hours)	7,920 (₹16 × 825 deliveries × 0.6 Activity hours)	4,400 (₹16 × 2,750 deliveries × 0.1 Activity hours)
Operating income	6,53,840	9,43,965	8,86,600
Operating income (%)	2.33	3.96	5.92

COMMENT: The activity based costing technique focuses on different costs for different purposes and identifies only those costs which are relevant to a particular decision.

It highlights the distribution channel, namely, chemist shops which use larger amount RST Limited's resources per rupee of revenue earned *vis-à-vis* the other two distribution channels. Ratio of operating costs of revenues for 3 channels is as follows:

General supermarket chains	0.58%
Drugstore chains	0.80%
Chemist shops	3.17%

(iv) Challenges faced in assigning total operating cost of ₹8,27,970:

— Selection of an appropriate cost-allocation base
— Development of a reliable data base for the chosen cost base
— Developing the rate per unit of each cost allocation base
— Behavioural factors

P.7.6 MST Limited has collected the following data for its two activities. It calculates activity cost rates based on cost driver capacity.

Activity	Cost driver	Capacity	Cost
Power	Kilowatt-hours	50,000 hours	₹2,00,000
Quality inspections	Number of inspections	10,000 inspections	₹3,00,000

The company makes three products, M, S and T. For the year ended March 31, current year, the following consumption of cost drivers was reported:

Product	Kilowatt-hours	Quality inspections
M	10,000	3,500
S	20,000	2,500
T	15,000	3,000

REQUIRED:

(i) Compute the costs allocated to each product from each activity, (ii) Calculate the cost of unused capacity for each activity.

SOLUTION

(i) Statement showing Cost Allocation to each Product from each Activity:

Product	Power		Quality inspections	
M	(10,000 hours × ₹4)	₹40,000	(3,500 inspections × ₹30)	₹1,05,000
S	(20,000 hours × ₹4)	80,000	(2,500 inspections × ₹30)	75,000
T	(15,000 hours × ₹4)	60,000	(3,000 inspections × ₹30)	90,000
		1,80,000		2,70,000

WORKING NOTE

(i) Computation of rate per unit of cost driver:
Power (₹2,00,000/50,000 hours) = ₹4 per hour
Quality inspection (₹3,00,000/10,000 inspections) = ₹30 per inspection

(ii) Cost computation of unused capacity for each activity

Power (₹2,00,000 – ₹1,80,000)	₹20,000
Quality inspections (₹3,00,000 – ₹2,70,000)	30,000
Total cost of unused capacity	50,000

P.7.7 MNP Suits is a ready-to-wear suit manufacturer. It has four customers: two wholesale-channel customers and two retail-channel customers. MNP Suits has developed the following activity-based costing system:

Activity	Cost driver	Rate in next year
Order processing	Number of purchase orders	₹1,225 per order
Sales visits	Number of customer visits	7,150 per visit
Delivery-regular	Number of regular deliveries	1,500 per delivery
Delivery-rushed	Number of rushed deliveries	4,250 per delivery

List selling price per suit is ₹1,000 and average cost per suit is ₹550. The CEO of MNP Suits wants to revaluate the profitability of each of the four customers in the current year to explore opportunities for increasing the profitability of his company in next year. The following data are available for the current year:

Item	Wholesale customers		Retail customers	
	W	H	R	T
Total number of orders	44	62	212	250
Total number of sales visits	8	12	22	20
Regular deliveries	41	48	166	190
Rush deliveries	3	14	46	60
Average number of suits per order	400	200	30	25
Average selling price per suit	₹700	₹800	₹850	₹900

REQUIRED:

(i) Calculate the customer-level operating income, current year. (ii) What do you recommend to the CEO of MNP Suits to do to increase the company's operating income next year? (iii) Assume MNP Suits' distribution channel cost are ₹17,50,000 for its wholesale customers and ₹10,50,000 for the retail customers. Also, assume that its corporate sustaining costs are ₹12,50,000. Prepare the income statement of MNP Suits for the current year.

SOLUTION

(i) Statement showing Computation of Customer-level Operating Income in the Current Year.

Particulars	*Wholesale customers*		*Retail customers*	
	W	*H*	*R*	*T*
Revenue at list price	₹1,76,00,000 (44 × 400 × 1,000)	₹1,24,00,000 (62 × 200 × 1,000)	₹63,60,000 (212 × 30 × 1,000)	₹62,50,000 (250 × 25 × 1,000)
Less discount	52,80,000 (44 × 400 × 300)	24,80,000 (62,200 × 200)	9,54,000 (212 × 30 × 150)	6,25,000 (250 × 25 × 100)
Revenue at actual prices	1,23,20,000	99,20,000	54,06,000	56,25,000
Less cost of goods sold	96,80,000 (44 × 400 × 550)	68,20,000 (62,200 × 550)	34,98,000 (212 × 30 × 550)	34,37,500 (250 × 25,550)
Gross margin	26,40,000	31,00,000	19,08,000	21,87,500
Customer level operating costs:				
Order processing (44,62,212,250) ÷ (₹1,225)	53,900	75,950	2,59,700	3,06,250
Sales visits (8,12,22,20) ÷ (₹7,150)	57,200	85,800	1,57,300	1,43,000
Delivery regular (41,48,166,190) ÷ (₹1,500)	61,500	72,000	2,49,000	2,85,000
Delivery rushed (3,14,46,60) ÷ (₹4,250)	12,750	59,500	1,95,500	2,55,000
Customer-level operating income	24,54,650	28,06,750	10,46,500	11,98,250
Customer level operating income as percentage on revenues at actual prices	19.92	28.29	19.35	21.30

(ii) The activity based costing (ABC) system is a far more refined costing system and reports costs that better measure the way jobs/products/customers use the resources of the company.

The ABC cost system reveals areas where R and T (retail customers) cause more costs to the company. The identified areas are high number of orders, high number of customer visits and high number of rushed deliveries.

The CEO needs to explore if this high level of activity can be reduced without reducing customer revenues.

(iii) Income Statement of MNP Suits for the Current Year

Particulars	*Wholesale customers*	*Retail customers*	*Total*
Operating income	₹52,61,400	₹22,44,750	₹75,06,150
Less distribution channel cost	17,50,000	10,50,000	28,00,000
Distribution channel level operating income	35,11,400	11,94,750	47,06,150
Less corporate sustaining costs			12,50,000
Operating income			34,56,150

P.7.8 Garden Tools Manufactures Ltd. (GTML) produces garden tools and lawn maintenance products that are sold through an All-India chain of stores. The GTML manufactures more than 50 products and approximately 20 per cent of its revenue comes from selling small home garden tools such as rakes, pruners and spades. It also manufacturers high-quality lawn movers, edgers and blowers for professional lawn service companies. Sales of these products, however, have not been a major source of revenue.

The CFO of GTML, Harsha Desai, is concerned about the apparent profitability of two of its products, namely, **(i)** a high-volume product Model-300 spade and **(ii)** a low-volume product, Model-800 mowers.

At the beginning of current year, the total estimated manufacturing overhead was ₹20,00,00,000 and the estimated total labour cost was ₹4,00,00,000. For the current year, the expected sales revenues from sale of Model-300 spade and Model-800 mowers are summarised below:

Particulars	Model-300 Spade	Model-800 Mower
1 Number of units sold	42,500	400
2 Sales revenue	₹38,25,000	₹12,00,000
3 Direct labour cost	4,59,000	60,000
4 Direct material cost	7,65,000	2,40,000

The GTML allocates manufacturing overheads to products based on direct labour cost. The product process for spades is fairly simple. The GTML uses one supplier for the metal handle and blade. It produces shafts on an automatic lathe and the handles, blades and shafts are assembled by hand at single workstation.

The production process for mowers is much more complicated. Twenty suppliers are used to supply the 50 components involved in producing the Model-800. Moreover, assembly of mowers makes uses of 15 separate assembly workstations.

The estimated total manufacturing overhead (₹20,00,00,000) is related to four cost drivers as shown below:

Overhead cost item/pool	Annual cost	Cost driver	Estimated annual value	Cost per driver unit
(1)	(2)	(3)	(4)	(5)
1 Set up costs	₹2,00,00,000	Number of setups	1,000	₹20,000
2 Material handling cost	1,00,00,000	Number of material requisitions	2,000	5,000 per requisition
3 Depreciation of equipment	5,00,00,000	Number of requisition	20,000	2,500 per machine-hour
4 Others 12,00,000		Number of work-stations used in production of product	3,000 work-stations across all products	40,000 per workstation

The production information for 42,500 spades (Model-300) and 400 Mowers (Model-800) is summarised below:

Particulars	Model-300 spade	Model-800 mower
1 Number of setups	2	5
2 Number of material requisitions	3	50
3 Number of machine-hours	40	100
4 Number of workstations	1	15

REQUIRED:

From the above information, compute the profitability of the two products: M-300 spade and M-800 mowers, using **(a)** traditional costing approach/system and **(b)** ABC system/approach to allocate manufacturing overheads. Comment on the differences in **(a)** and **(b)**.

SOLUTION

(a) Profitability of Models 300 and 800 (Traditional/Production Volume based Approach)

Particulars	Model-300 spade (42,500 units)		Model-800 mower (400 units)
1 Sales revenue (42,500 × ₹90)	₹38,25,000	(400 × ₹3,000)	₹12,00,000
2 Direct labour cost	4,59,000		60,000
3 Direct material cost	7,65,000		2,40,000
4 Overheads	22,95,000@		3,00,000@@
5 Total cost (2 + 3 + 4)	35,19,000		6,00,000
6 Gross profit (1 – 5)	3,06,000		6,00,000
7 Cost per unit [(5) ÷ 42,500]	82.8	[(5) ÷ 400]	–1,500
8 Gross profit per unit [(6) ÷ 42,500]	7.2	[(6) ÷ 400]	1,500
9 Gross profit as % of sales (%) (6 ÷ 1)	8.0		50

@Direct labour cost, ₹4,59,000 × 5 (manufacturing cost, ₹20,00,00,000 ÷ ₹4,00,00,000, labour cost) = ₹22,95,000

@@₹60,000 × 5 = ₹3,00,000

(b) Profitability of Model-300 and Model-800 (ABC Approach)

Particulars		*Model-300 spade (42,500 units)*	*Model-800 mower (400 units)*
1 Direct labour cost		₹4,59,000	₹60,000
2 Direct material cost		7,65,000	2,40,000
3 Overheads:			
(i) Setup costs	(₹20,000 × 2)	40,000	
	(₹20,000 × 5)		1,00,000
(ii) Material handling cost			
	(₹5,000 × 3)	15,000	
	(₹5,000 × 50)		2,50,00
(iii) Depreciation of equipment			
	(₹2,500 × 40)	1,00,000	
	(₹2,500 × 100)		2,50,000
(iv) Others			
	(₹40,000 × 1)	40,000	
	(₹40,000 × 15)		6,00,000
Total overheads		1,95,000	12,00,000
4 Total cost		14,19,000	15,00,000
5 Cost per unit		33.4	3,750
6 Selling price per unit		90.0	3,000
7 Gross profit per unit		56.6	(–750)
8 Gross profit as % of sales (%)		63.0	(25)

(c) Comparison of Profitability of Model-300 and Model-800

Particulars	*Traditional approach*		*ABC approach*	
	Model-300	*Model-800*	*Model-300*	*Model-800*
1 Cost per unit	₹82.8	₹1,500	₹33.4	₹3,750
2 Gross profit as % of sales	8.0	50	63.0	(25)

COMMENT: The cost of Model 300-drops from ₹82 in the traditional approach to ₹33.4 per unit in the ABC approach and the cost of Model-800 increases from ₹1,500 to ₹3,750. The ABC approach reveals that the high-volume product (Model-300 spades) is very profitable as reflected in the gross profit margin (63%) while the selling price (₹3,000) does not cover even the full cost (₹3,750) of the low-volume product (Model-800) with a negative (–25%) gross margin.

P.7.9 Bajaj Electric Company (BEC) produces electric motors used by manufacturing companies such as those of home appliances. Each motor is made to customer specifications. The BEC has an activity-based costing system with the following overhead costs and cost drivers:

Cost pool	*Annual amount*	*Annual cost driver*
Direct labour-related	₹20,00,000	₹50,00,000 direct labour cost
Material ordering	5,00,000	25,000 purchase orders
Material inspection	30,00,000	20,000 receiving reports
Equipment setup	10,00,000	5,000 setups
Quality control	20,00,000	10,000 inspection of motors
Machine-related	40,00,000	20,000 machine-hours
Miscellaneous	20,00,000	₹2,00,00,000 of product costs other than
Total overheads	1,45,00,000	miscellaneous overheads

The BEC has received an order from Prakash Electronics Store (PES) for 5 identical motors. The BEC estimated the following costs (total) and activities related to the order:

- Material cost, ₹5,000
- Labour cost, ₹2,000
- Purchase order, 2
- Receiving reports, 2
- Setups, 1
- Inspections, 1
- Machine-hours 10

REQUIRED:

(a) Calculate the cost of PES job, assuming the BEC uses a traditional costing system with labour cost as the allocation base.

(b) Calculate the cost using the ABC system.

(c) Comment on the differences in (a) and (b).

SOLUTION

(a) Calculation of Cost of PES Job (Traditional Costing)

Material		₹5,000
Labour		2,000
Overheads (₹2.9[@] × ₹2,000)		5,800
		12,800
[@]Total overheads	₹1,45,00,000	
Total labour cost	₹50,00,000	
Overhead rate per rupee of labour cost (₹1,45,00,000 ÷ ₹50,00,000)	2.9	

(b) Calculation of Cost of PES job (ABC Approach)

Material cost		₹5,000
Labour cost		2,000
Overheads:		
• Labour-related (0.40 × ₹2,000)	₹800	
• Material ordering (₹200 × 2)	400	
• Material inspection (₹1,500 × 2)	3,000	
• Setups (₹2,000 × 1)	2,000	
• Quality control (₹2,000 × 2)	4,000	
• Machine-related (₹200 × 10)	2,000	
• Miscellaneous (0.10 × cost other than Miscellaneous, ₹17,200)	1,720	
Total		13,920
Total cost		20,920

WORKING NOTES

Cost pool	*Overhead rate (annual amount ÷ annual driver)*
1 Direct labour-related (₹20,00,000 ÷ ₹50,00,000 direct labour cost)	₹0.40 per direct labour cost
2 Material ordering (₹5,00,000 ÷ 25,000 purchase orders)	200 per purchase order
3 Material inspection (₹30,00,000 ÷ 20,000 receiving reports)	1,500 per receiving report
4 Equipment setup (₹10,00,000 ÷ 5,000 setups)	2,000 per setup
5 Quality control (₹20,00,000 ÷ 10,000 inspections)	2,000 per inspection
6 Machine-related (₹40,00,000 ÷ 20,000 machine-hours)	200 per machine-hour
7 Miscellaneous (₹20,00,000 ÷ 2,00,00,000 product costs other than miscellaneous overheads)	0.10 per rupee of product other than miscellaneous overheads

COMMENT: Costs are higher in the ABC system as the PES job is relatively small and makes use of a number of activities whose costs are not proportionate to volume.

P.7.10 The management of Reliance Telecom Gurgaon area customer care centre is contemplating the implementation of the ABC system. The centre has 1,96,000 residential customers and 50,000 commercial customers. The relevant data are summarised below:

Resource	*Monthly cost*	*Percentage of resource used in activity (%)*				
		Billing	*Account inquiry*	*Correspondence*	*Verification*	*Others*
1 Supervisors	₹1,22,000	40	35	8	—	17
2 Account inquiry labour	4,08,000	—	85	15	—	—
3 Billing labour	1,80,000	70	—	—	30	—
4 Paper	23,200	100	—	—	—	—
5 Computers	5,72,000	30	48	7	10	5
6 Telecommunications	1,98,400	—	85	—	—	15
7 Occupancy	2,24,000	15	70	—	—	15
8 Printers	3,00,000	80	—	5	—	15
9 Others	2,36,000	—	—	—	—	100
	22,63,680					

Activity	*Cost driver*	*Monthly number of cost driver units*		
		Residential	*Commercial*	*Total*
1 Printing	Lines	23,52,000	25,00,000	48,52,000
2 Account inquiry	Inquiries	19,600	15,000	34,600
3 Correspondence	Letters	3,920	5,000	8,920
4 Verification	Accounts	98,000	25,000	1,23,000

The management of Reliance Telecom has decided not to allocate the other resource costs.

REQUIRED:

(a) Prepare schedules to determine the cost per driver unit for each activity and the activity-based cost per account for each customer type.

(b) Consider the verification activity. Suppose the cost per account verified is ₹0.90. The centre verifies 50 per cent of residential and accommodation bills. Given that there are, on an average, 50 lines on each commercial bill and only 12 lines on each residential bill, comment on the use of accounts verified as a cost driver. What could be a more plausible and reliable cost driver?

SOLUTION

(a) (i) Traceable Cost of Activities of Billing Department of Reliance Telecom

Resource	*Cost*	*Activity*				
		Billing inquiry	*Account*	*Correspondence*	*Verification*	*Others*
(1)	*(2)*	*(3)*	*(4)*	*(5)*	*(6)*	*(7)*
1 Supervisors	₹1,22,000	₹48,800[a]	₹42,700[b]	₹9,760[c]	—	₹20,740[d]
2 Account inquiry labour	4,08,000	—	3,46,800	61,200	—	—
3 Billing labour	1,80,000	1,26,000	—	—	₹54,000	—
4 Paper	23,200	23,200	—	—	—	—
5 Computers	5,72,000	1,71,600	3,43,200	50,050	57,200	28,600
6 Telecommunications	1,98,400	—	1,68,708	—	—	29,772
7 Occupancy	2,24,000	33,600	1,56,800	—	—	33,600

(Contd.)

(Contd.)

8 Printers	3,00,000	2,40,000	—	15,000	—	45,000
9 Others resources	2,36,000	—	—	—	—	2,36,000
Total traceable cost	22,63,680	6,43,200	9,89,568	1,26,000	1,11,200	3,93,712

[a](₹1,22,000 × 0.40) [b](₹1,22,000 × 0.35) [c](₹1,22,000 × 0.08) [d](₹1,22,000 × 0.17)

(ii) Cost per Driver Unit

Activity (driver units)	*Driver costs*		
	Traceable costs	*Total number of driver units*	*Cost per driver unit*
	(1)	*(2)*	*(3) [(1) ÷ (2)]*
Account inquiry (inquiries)	₹9,89,568	34,600 inquiries	₹28.600231
Correspondence (letters)	1,26,000	8,920 letters	14.12556
Account billing (lines)	6,43,200	48,52,000 lines	0.13256
Bill verification (accounts verified)	1,11,200	1,23,000 accounts verified	0.90406

(iii) Cost per Customer Class

Activity	*Cost per Driver Unit*	*Customer Class*			
		Residential		*Commercial*	
		Number of Driver Units	*Cost*	*Number of Driver Units*	*Cost*
Account inquiry	₹28.600231	19,600 inquiries	₹5,60,564	15,000 inquiries	₹4,29,004
Correspondence	14.12556	3,920 letters	55,372	5,000 letters	70,628
Account billing	0.13256	23,52,000 lines	3,11,788	25,00,000 lines	3,31,412
Bill verification	0.90406	98,000 accounts	88,596	25,000 accounts	22,600
Total cost			10,16,324		8,53,644
Number of accounts			1,96,000		50,000
Cost per account			5.18		17.08

(b) The ABC system allocates 79.7 per cent [98,000 ÷ 1,23,000 (98,000 + 25,000)] of verification costs to residential accounts based on the number of accounts verified. However, the work performed to verify a bill is rather closely related to the number of lines on the bill. The amount of effort of employees would depend on the number of lines in each account rather than on the number of accounts. The lines verified is, therefore, a more reliable cost driver.

The number of lines verified for residential accounts are: 12 lines per account × 98,000 accounts = 11,76,000 lines. The number of lines verified for commercial accounts are: 50 lines per account × 25,000 accounts verified = 12,50,000 lines. Therefore, 48.5 per cent [11,76,000 ÷ 24,26,000 (11,76,000 + 12,50,000)] of verification costs should be allocated to residential accounts based on lines verified.

P.7.11 The new Controller of Bharti Telecom (BT) has discovered that BT's customers differ greatly in their ordering pattern and interaction with BT's sales force. He feels that BT's costing system does not accurately assign marketing, distribution and selling expenses to customer. He has developed an ABC system to assign these expenses to customers. He has identified the following marketing, selling and distribution costs for two customers, Alpha and Beta.

	Alpha	*Beta*
1 Travelling by sales representatives	₹36,000	₹1,68,000
2 Servicing customers	60,000	4,40,000
3 Handling customer orders	4,000	48,000
4 Shipping to customers	96,000	2,88,000
	196,00	9,44,000

(Contd.)

(Contd.)

The following additional information is available:		
1 Sales	17,20,000	14,00,000
2 Cost of goods sold	8,80,000	6,20,000

REQUIRED:

(a) Using the current costing approach of assigning marketing, selling and distribution expenses to customers using 33 per cent of sales revenue, determine the operating profit of the two customers.

(b) Using the ABC information provided, determine their operating profits.

(c) Which of the two methods produces more accurate assignment of marketing, selling and distribution expenses to customers? Explain.

SOLUTION

(a) Customer Profitability Analysis (Current Costing Approach)

Particulars	*Alpha*	*Beta*
Sales revenue	₹17,20,000	₹14,00,000
Cost of goods sold	8,80,000	6,20,000
Gross margin	8,40,000	7,80,000
Marketing, selling and distribution expenses (0.33 × sales revenue)	5,67,600	4,62,000
Operating profit	2,72,400	3,18,000
Profit (as percentage of sales)	15.8	22.7

(b) Customer Profitability Analysis (ABC Approach)

Particulars	*Alpha*	*Beta*
Sales revenue	₹17,20,000	₹14,00,000
Cost of goods sold	8,80,000	6,20,000
Gross margin	8,40,000	7,80,000
Marketing, selling and distribution expenses:		
— Travelling by sales representatives	36,000	1,68,000
— Servicing customer	60,000	4,40,000
— Handling customer orders	4,000	48,000
— Shipping to customers	96,000	2,88,000
Total activity expenses	1,96,000	9,44,000
Operating profit	6,44,000	(–1,64,000)
Profit (as percentage of sales)	37.4	(–11.7)

(c) Beta customer is more profitable than Alpha customer according to the current costing system. Moreover, both the customers are profitable. But customer Alpha emerges as highly profitable and Beta emerges as the most unfavourable customer according to the ABC approach. The ABC obviously produces more accurate assignment of marketing, selling and distribution expenses. As can be seen from the computations, travel, customer services and shipping to customers, have huge demands on Beta's marketing, selling and distribution resource in contrast to Alpha's. But the current costing system fails to make this distinction between them.

P.7.12 Hinduja Health Centre (HHC) runs three programmes: **(1)** alcoholic rehabilitation, **(2)** drug addict rehabilitation, and **(3)** aftercare (counseling and support of patients after release from a mental hospital). The HHC's budget for current year follows:

Professional salaries:		
4 physicians × ₹3,00,000	₹12,00,000	
18 psychologists × ₹1,50,000	27,00,000	
20 nurses × ₹60,000	12,00,000	₹51,00,000
Medical supplies		3,00,000
General overhead (administrative salaries, rent, utilities, etc.)		8,80,000
		62,80,000

Dr. Anupam Verma, the Director of the HHC, is keen on determining the cost of each programme. He has compiled the following data describing employees allocations to individual programmes:

	Alcohol	*Drug*	*Aftercare*	*Total employees*
Physicians		4		4
Psychologists	6	4	8	18
Nurses	4	6	10	20

Eight patients are in residence in the alcohol programme, each staying for about six months. Thus, the clinic provides 40 patient-years of service in the alcohol programme. Similarly, 100 patients are involved in the drug programme for about six months each. Thus, the clinic provides 50 patient-years of service in the drug programme.

Dr Verma has recently become aware of activity-based costing as a method to refine costing systems. He asks his accountant, Kulkarni, how he should apply this new technique. Kulkarni obtains the following information:

(a) Consumption of medical supplies depends on the number of patient-years.

(b) General Overhead Costs consist of

Rent and clinic maintenance	₹1,80,000
Administrative costs to manage patient charts, food, laundry	6,00,000
Laboratory services	1,00,000
Total	8,80,000

(c) Other Information about Individual Departments:

	Alcohol	*Drug*	*Aftercare*	*Total employee*
Square feet of space occupied by each programme	9,000	9,000	12,000	30,000
Patient-years of service	40	50	60	150
Number of laboratory tests	400	1,400	70	2,500

REQUIRED:

1. Using an activity-based costing approach to cost analysis, calculate the cost of each programme and the cost per patient-year of the alcohol and drug programmes. What benefits can HHC obtain by implementing the ABC system?
2. What factors, other than cost, do you think HHC should consider in allocating resources to its programmes?

SOLUTION

1. Activity-based Costs for each Programme and Cost per Patient-year of the Alcohol and Drug programmes:

	Alcohol	*Drug*	*Aftercare*
Direct labour:			
Physicians [₹3,00,000 × (0;4;0)]	—	₹12,00,000	—
Psychologists [₹1,50,000 (× 6;4;8)]	₹9,00,000	6,00,000	₹12,00,000
Nurses labour costs	2,40,000	3,60,000	6,00,000
Direct labour costs	11,40,000	21,60,000	18,00,000
Medical supplies[1] [₹2,000 × (40; 50; 60)]	80,000	1,00,000	1,20,000
Rent and clinic maintenance[2] [₹6 × (9,000; 9,000; 12,000)]	54,000	54,000	72,000
Administrative costs to manage patient charts, food, and laundry[3] [₹4,000 × (40; 50; 60)]	1,60,000	2,00,000	2,40,000
Laboratory services[4] [₹40 × (400; 1,400; 7,000]	16,000	56,000	28,000
Total costs	14,50,000	25,70,000	22,60,000

Cost per patient = ₹14,50,000/40 = ₹ 36,250 (alcohol)
= 25,70,000 ÷ 50 = 56,400 (drug).

[1]Allocated using patient-years
[2]Allocated using square feet of space
[3]Allocated using patient-years
[4]Allocated using number of laboratory tests

The ABC system allocates costs more accurately because it identifies better cost drivers. It chooses cost driers for overhead costs that have a cause-and-effect relationship between the cost drivers and the costs.

By implementing the ABC system, Dr Verma can gain a more detailed understanding of costs and cost drivers. This is valuable information from a cost management perspective. The system can yield insight into the efficiencies with which various activities are performed. Dr Verma can then examine if redundant activities are performed. He can study trends and work toward improving the efficiency of the activities.

In addition, the ABC system will help Dr Verma detrmine which programmes are the most costly to operate. This will be useful in making long-run decisions as to which programme to offer or emphasise on. The ABC system will also assist Dr Verma in setting up those prices for the programmes that reflect their costs more accurately.

2. The concern with using costs per patient-year as the rule to allocate resources among its programmes is that it emphasises "input" to the exclusion of "outputs" or effectiveness of the programmes. After-all, the goal is to cure patients while controlling costs, not to minimise costs per-patient year. The problem, of course, is measuring outputs.

Unlike many manufacturing companies, where the outputs are obvious because they are tangible and measurable, the outputs of service organisations are more difficult to measure. Examples are "cured" patients as distinguished from "processed" or "discharged" patients, "educated" as distinguished from "partially educated" students, and so on.

REVIEW QUESTIONS

RQ.7.1 Indicate whether the followings statements are 'True' or 'False'.

(i) Activity based costing (ABC) system is applicable only for allocation of manufacturing overheads.

(ii) ABC system has the potential of eliminating cost distortion.

(iii) Higher-volume products would have higher share of indirect costs in ABC system.

(iv) ABC system uses cost centres for accumulating costs.
(v) Cost drivers are significant determinants of costs in ABC system.
(vi) Duration drivers represent the number of times an activity is performed.
(vii) Transaction drivers represent the amount of time required to perform an activity.
(viii) Intensity drivers are used to charge directly for the resources used each time an activity is performed.
(ix) Practical capacity is higher than theoretical capacity.
(x) Activity based costing prices products.
(xi) ABC system is appropriate only for manufacturing firms.
(xii) ABC based costing systems are more costly than traditional costing systems.

[Answers: (i) False, (ii) True, (iii) False, (iv) False, (v) True, (vi) False, (vii) False, (viii) True, (ix) False, (x) False, (xi) False, (xii) True.]

RQ.7.2 Fill in the following blanks:

(i) In traditional costing system, the accumulated costs, first, are allocated to __________ and then such costs are assigned to __________.
(ii) ABC system first traces costs to __________ and then to __________.
(iii) Costs are assigned to products/jobs using __________ as a measure of activity.
(iv) In ABC system, a firm can choose from three types of cost drivers, namely, __________
(v) Among three types of cost drivers, __________ is the least accurate in ABC system.
(vi) __________ are the most accurate cost drivers.
(vii) Activity costs are assigned to individual jobs/products on the basis of __________
(viii) Activity cost driver rate = __________ divided by total quantity of activity cost driver.
(ix) Activity expenses assigned to a product = __________ (X) Quantity of each activity cost driver used by the product/job.
(x) Cost incurred in performing activities are grouped into __________

[Answers: (i) Production/cost centres; (iv) Transaction, duration and intensity, (v) Transaction cost drivers, (vi) Intensity drivers, (vii) Activity cost driver rate, (viii) Activity expenses, (ix) Activity cost driver rate, (x) Cost pools.]

RQ.7.3 Briefly explain how traditional methods of allocation of overheads to products may underallocate costs to low-production-volume products and overallocate costs to high-volume products.

RQ.7.4 How does ABC differ from the traditional costing approach?

RQ.7.5 When would ABC give more accurate costs than traditional costing system?

RQ.7.6 How does ABC differ from activity-based management?

RQ.7.7 What are the benefits and limitations of ABC?

RQ.7.8 Explain the two-stage allocation of overheads in activity-based costing.

RQ.7.9 "Conventional product costing systems are likely to overcost high-volume products". Do you agree with this statement? Explain.

RQ.7.10 What do the terms 'activity cost driver' and 'activity cost driver rates' mean?

RQ.7.11 How do activity-based costing systems avoid distortions in tracing costs to products?

RQ.7.12 How are cost driver rates selected in activity-based costing system?

RQ.7.13 In ABC, what are the trade-offs made in choosing among transaction, duration and intensity activity cost drivers.

RQ.7.14 How can the information from an ABC systems guide improvement in operations and decisions about products/customers?

RQ.7.15 Why should practical capacity be used in calculating activity cost drivers?

RQ.7.16 Discuss some of the special considerations in designing a cost accounting system for service organisations.

RQ.7.17 Aptech Computers manufactures mouse devices for computers. They make 12 different models of mouse devices as well as several other types of computer components. They use activity-based costing to assign manufacturing overheads to products. The data relating to one of their products–wireless remote mouse–and the ABC cost pools are given below.

(a) Wireless Remote Mouse: Annual production, 20,000 units; Direct materials per unit, ₹310; Direct labour per unit, ₹60.

(b) Manufacturing overhead cost pools

Cost pool	*Cost*	*Cost driver*
1 Materials ordering	₹80,00,000	Number of purchase orders
2 Materials inspection	40,00,000	Number of receiving reports
3 Equipment setup	2,00,00,000	Number of setups
4 Quality control	90,00,000	Number of inspections
5 Others	15,00,00,000	Direct labour cost
Total manufacturing overheads	19,10,00,000	

(c) Activity information related to cost drivers

Cost pool	*Annual activity*	
	All products	*Remote Mouse*
1 Materials ordering	10,00,000 orders	10,000 orders
2 Materials inspection	20,000 receiving reports	3,000 reports
3 Equipment setup	1,000 setups	10 setups
4 Quality control	40,000 inspections	4,000 inspections
5 Others	10,00,000 direct labour hours	1,20,000 direct labour hours

REQUIRED:

(a) Calculate the overhead rate per unit of activity for each of the 5 cost pools.
(b) Calculate the total overhead assigned to the production of the remote mouse.
(c) Calculate the overhead cost per unit for the remote mouse.
(d) Calculate the total unit cost for the remote mouse.

RQ.7.18 The Sports Manufacturers Ltd. produces two products: (i) a recreational whitewater play boat and (ii) a high performance competition boat. The recreation boat is uniform in style and dimensions. The competition boat is customer designed to fit the individual requirement. The data related to the two products for the most recent year are summarised below:

		Recreation boat		*Competition boat*
1 Sales and production (number)		900		100
2 Sales price (per boat)		₹3,000		₹3,300
3 Unit costs:				
Direct material	₹750		₹1,000	
Direct labour	500		500	
Overheads[@]	675	1,925	675	2,175
Gross profit (2 – 3)		1,075		1,125

[@]Overheads (total):

- Depreciation of building ₹1,25,000
- Depreciation of equipment 1,25,000
- Materials ordering 75,000
- Quality control 50,000
- Maintenance and security 50,000
- Setup and drafting 1,00,000
- Supervision 1,50,000

Total: 6,75,000

Overhead rate based on direct labour cost:

Total overhead	6,75,000
Total labour (₹500 × 900) + (₹500 × 100)	5,00,000
Rate (overhead labour) per direct labour cost	1.35

REQUIRED:

(a) The traditional costing system that Sports Manufacturers is using, assigns the total overheads on the basis of direct labour cost. Discuss why this is not an accurate way to assign overheads to the two products.

(b) Assume that a consultant to create an ABC system for Sports Manufactures develops the following data:

Cost pool	*Amount*	*Driver*	*Driver activity*	
			Recreation boat	*Competition boat*
Building	₹1,25,000	Square footage	6,000	1,000
Equipment	1,25,000	Machine-hours	3,400	600
Material ordering	75,000	Number of orders	200	150
Quality control	50,000	Number of inspections	300	150
Maintenance and security	50,000	Square footage	6,000	1,000
Setup and drafting	1,00,000	Number of setups	20	40
Supervision	1,50,000	Direct labour cost	₹4,50,000	₹50,000

Determine the overhead allocation to each line of boats using an ABC approach and compute the total unit cost for each model.

(c) Discuss why activity-based allocations are different from those generated by the traditional method.

RQ.7.19 The HDFC Bank Ltd. is contemplating to implement an ABC system for its teller department. The activities identified and the associated cost drivers for its New Friends Colony Branch are summarised below:

Support activity	*Estimated cost*	*Activity cost driver*	*Quantity*
1 Process deposits	₹1,48,150	Number of deposits processed	1,66,250
2 Process withdrawals	1,30,400	Number of withdrawals processed	1,13,750
3 Answer inquiries	1,24,000	Number of customer inquiries	2,25,000
4 Negotiable instruments' selling	24,300	Number of negotiable instruments sold	5,500
5 Balance drawers	21,450	Number of drawers balanced	6,500

REQUIRED:

(a) Compute the activity cost driver rates for each of the support facilities.

(b) Estimate in total monthly support costs for a typical amount from the information given below:

Support activity	*Average monthly volume*
1 Process deposits	11,500
2 Process withdrawals	30,000
3 Answer customer inquiries	10,500
4 Sell negotiable instruments	2,500

RQ.7.20 The Delhi Manufacturers Ltd. (DML) manufactures two products. Their estimated unit cost and production data are summarised below:

Item	Product	
	D1	D2
Direct material cost	₹120	₹180
Direct labour cost (₹48 per hour)	96	240
Estimated production (units)	4,00,000	1,50,000

The manufacturing support costs are estimated to be ₹2,61,40,000 for the current year. The activity cost pools and cost drivers are as given below:

Activity	Costs	Activity cost driver	Practical capacity	Cost driver units required by	
				D1	D2
1 Machine setups	₹17,00,000	Setup hours	13,000	4,000	8,400
2 Purchase ordering	40,000	Number of orders	200	50	100
3 Machining	2,40,00,000	Number of machine-hours	1,50,000	80,000	30,000
4 Inspection	1,44,000	Number of batches	2,400	800	1,200
5 Packing and despatch	2,56,000	Number of despatches	3,200	160	3,000
Total	2,61,40,000				

REQUIRED:

(a) Estimate the manufacturing cost per unit of each product if support costs are assigned to products using activity-based cost driver rates based on practical capacity.

(b) Compute the variance/difference between the estimated manufacturing support costs and the support costs assigned to DML's products in (a).

RQ.7.21 Reliable Automative Manufacturers Ltd. (RAML) is an automatic components/parts supplier. The Hyundai Motors has approached the RAML to expand its production part P-808 to a total annual quantity of 4,000 units. P-808 is a low-volume, complex product with a high gross margin that is based on a proposed/quoted unit sale price of ₹15. The RAML uses the traditional costing system, allocating indirect manufacturing costs currently at 400 per cent of direct labour cost (i.e. ₹1,32,00,000 annual factory overhead ÷ ₹33,00,000 annual direct labour cost). Producing 4,000 units of part P-808 requires ₹20,000 of direct materials and ₹4,000 of direct labour. The unit cost and gross margin percentage of P-808 according to the traditional costing system are computed below:

Particulars	Total cost (1)	Per unit cost (2) [(1) ÷ 4,000]
Direct materials	₹20,000	₹5.00
Direct labour	4,000	1.00
Indirect manufacturing (400 × direct labour)	16,000	4.00
Total cost	40,000	10.00
Sales price quoted		15.00
Gross margin		5.00
Gross margin percentage		33.00

The management of RAML has decided to examine the effectiveness of their traditional costing system versus an activity-based costing system. The following data have been collected by a team of accounting and engineering analysts:

Activity	Traceable factory overhead costs (annual)	Cost drivers	Annual cost-driver quantity	Cost-driver consumption (4,000 units of P-808)
1 Quality	₹32,00,000	Number of pieces scrapped	20,000	240
2 Production scheduling and setups	26,00,000	Number of setups	1,000	8
3 Shipping	12,00,000	Number of containers shipped	1,20,000	20
4 Shipping administration	2,00,000	Number of shipments	2,000	10
5 Production	60,00,000	Number of machine-hours	20,000	30

REQUIRED:

(a) Calculate the unit cost and gross margin of part P-808 using the ABC approach.

(b) Based on (a) which course of action would you recommend regarding the Hyundai's proposal?

ANSWERS

[Comprehensive solutions to all numerical review questions are available on the companion website: http://www.mhhe.com/khan_jain_cost2e]

RQ.7.17(a) Material ordering ₹80 per order, Material inspection ₹200 per report, Equipment set up ₹20,000 per set up, Quality control ₹225 per inspection, Others ₹150 per direct labour hour

(b) ₹1,97,80,000

(c) ₹989

(d) ₹1,359

RQ.7.18 (a) Major share of factory overhead costs consists of depreciation, supervision, maintenance and other related costs. In such a situation, there is likely to be a little relationship between factory overhead costs and direct labour costs.

(b) (i) Recreation boat ₹1,806.41, (ii) ₹3,242.27

(c) The ABC system allocates more accurately as it identifies better cost drivers. It chooses cost drivers that have a cause and effect relationship between the cost drivers and overhead costs. In contrast, all overhead costs are allocated on the basis of direct labour costs.

RQ.7.19(a) Process deposits ₹0.891 per deposit processed, ₹1.146 per withdrawal processed, ₹0.55 per customer enquiry, ₹4.41 per negotiable instrument sold ₹3.3 per drawer balanced.

(b) ₹61,426.50

RQ.7.20(a) D_1 ₹249.48, D_2 ₹461.54

(b) Costs under the ABC system ₹1,96,24,336, Costs under traditional costing system ₹2,61,40,000; difference is ₹65,15,664.

RQ.7.21(a) Unit cost ₹23.35, Gross margin (₹8.35) per unit.

(b) Since there is negative gross margin, proposal should not be accepted.

CASES

7.C.1 ABC and Customer Profitability

To increase its share of deposits accounts, the UTI Bank Ltd (UBL) took two actions recently: first, to respond to depositor-customers inquiries about account balances, clearance of cheques and fee charged, it set up a call centre; second, it paid year-end bonuses to branch managers who met the target in terms of additional customers. Inspite of the fact that 75 per cent of the branch managers met the target increase in the number of customers, the profits of the UTI Bank Ltd (UBL) continued to decline. It was not clear to the CEO, Pulin Naik, why inspite of serving more customers, profits of the UBL were declining. The branch manager of

Cannaught Circle Branch, Dinesh Parekh, noticed that retail customers were increasing but there was a decline in the number of business customers.

The costing system of the UBL was developed in 1996 when it was setup. It is still in operation. According to current practice, no costs are traced directly to customers. The total indirect costs are assigned simply to customer lines (i.e. retail customers and business customers) in terms of the total number of cheques processed.

Dinesh suspected that the current costing system of UBL was responsible for the state of affairs. He wondered if an ABC system, with customer-line as the primary cost object, could be introduced in UBL.

The top management of UBL was initially skeptical about any such move in view of the decline in its profit. Dinesh Parekh finally succeeded in pursuading the CEO, Pulin Naik, to allow a pilot ABC study for the five branches of UBL located in Delhi. An implementation team including Dinesh and the managers of the other four branches of UBL was constituted for the purpose.

As a first step, the implementation team identified three activities: **(i)** cheque payments, **(ii)** tellers withdrawals and deposits and **(iii)** customer service call centre.

The second step was to scrutinise the total indirect costs of all the New Delhi branches. The implementation team of the pilot study classified the components of the indirect cost into appropriate activity pools as summarised below:

Cost	*Activity cost pool to which cost is assigned*	*Estimated total cost for New Delhi Branches*
1 Salary of cheque-processing personnel	Cheque payments	₹22,00,000
2 Depreciation on cheque-processing equipment	Cheque payments	35,00,000
3 Teller salary	Teller withdrawals/deposits	60,00,000
4 Salary at call centre	Customer service call centre	22,50,000
5 Toll free phone lines at call centre	Customer service call centre	3,00,000
Total indirect costs		1,42,50,000

The implementation team also identified the following cost drivers:

Activity cost pool	*Activity cost driver*
1 Cheque payments	Number of cheques processed
2 Teller withdrawals/deposits	Number of teller transactions
3 Customer service call centre	Number of calls

The ABC team then identified the retail customer lines and business customer lines listed below:

Activity cost driver	*Number of units of activity cost driver by retail customers*	*Number of units of activity cost driver used by business customers*	*Total*
(1)	*(2)*	*(3)*	*(4)*
1 Cheques processed	57,00,000	2,28,00,000	2,85,00,000
2 Teller transactions	16,00,000	4,00,000	20,00,000
3 Customer call centres	4,75,000	25,000	5,00,000
4 Deposit accounts	7,50,000	2,50,000	10,00,000

The average revenues (from interest earned on account balances) from each type of account earned by the UBL is: **(i)** per retail customer account, ₹50 and **(ii)** per business customer account, ₹200.

REQUIRED:

(A) Using the current cost accounting practices of UBL:

1. compute the indirect cost allocation rate,
2. determine the total indirect cost assigned to the retail customer lines and business customer lines,
3. compute the proportion of the total indirect cost assigned to the retail customer line and business customer line,
4. determine the indirect cost per retail and business account,
5. assuming that there are no direct costs, compute the average profit per account for retail and business customers.

(B) Using the proposed ABC System:

1. compute the indirect cost allocation rate for each of the three activities: cheque payments, teller withdrawal/deposits and customer call centre,
2. calculate the activity-wise total indirect costs allocated to each retail and business customer lines,
3. compute the proportion of each activity's resources used by the retail and business customer lines,
4. compute the indirect cost per retail and business customer account,
5. compute the average profit per account of both retail and business customers.

(C) Was UBL's bonus-based incentive plan to increase the number of deposit accounts a sound strategy? In the light of the ABC analysis, what changes would you suggest in the strategy? What benefits can UBL get from the ABC analysis?

SOLUTION

(A) (1) Computation of indirect cost allocation rate

Total indirect cost	₹1,42,50,000
Total number of cheques processed	2,85,00,000
Indirect cost per cheque processed (₹1,42,50,000/2,85,00,000)	Re. 0.50

(2) Computation of total indirect cost assigned to retail and business customer lines

Particulars	*Retail customer lines*	*Business customer lines*
Number of cheques processed	57,00,000	2,28,00,000
Indirect cost allocated @ Re.0.50 per cheque processed	₹28,50,000	₹1,14,00,000

(3) Computation of the proportion of the total indirect cost assigned to retail and business customer lines

Total indirect cost allocated	₹1,42,50,000
Proportion of indirect cost allocated to retail customer lines (28,50,000/1,42,50,000)	0.20
Proportion of indirect cost allocated to business customer lines (1,14,00,000/1,42,50,000)	0.80

(4) Computation of indirect cost per retail and business account

Particulars	*Retail account*	*Business account*
Total indirect cost allocated	₹28,50,000	₹1,14,00,000
Number of deposit accounts	7,50,000	2,50,000
Indirect cost per account	₹3.8	₹45.6

(5) Statement showing average profit per retail and business account

Particulars	Retail account	Business account
Average revenue per account	₹50	₹200
Indirect cost per account	3.8	45.6
Average profit per account	46.2	154.4

(B) (1) Computation of indirect cost allocation rate under ABC system

Activity	Total cost	Activity cost driver	Number of units of activity cost	Cost allocation rate driver
Cheque payments	₹57,00,000	Cheques Processed	2,85,00,000	Re. 0.20 per cheque processed
Teller withdrawal/deposits	60,00,000	Teller transactions	20,00,000	₹3.00 per teller transaction
Customer call centre	25,50,000	Customer calls	5,00,000	₹5.10 per customer call

(2) Computation of activity-wise total indirect cost assigned to retail and business customer lines under ABC system

Particulars	Retail customer lines	Business customer lines
Cheque payments	₹11,40,000	₹45,60,000
Teller withdrawal/deposits	48,00,000	12,00,000
Customer call centre	24,22,500	1,27,500
Total	83,62,500	58,87,500

(3) Computation of the proportion of activity resources used by retail and business customer lines under ABC system

Activity	Proportion used by retail customer lines	Proportion used by business customer lines
Cheque payments	0.20	0.80
Teller withdrawal/deposits	0.80	0.20
Customer call centre	0.95	0.05

(4) Computation of indirect cost per retail and business account under ABC system

Particulars	Retail account	Business account
Total indirect cost allocated	₹83,62,500	₹58,87,500
Number of deposit accounts	7,50,000	2,50,000
Indirect cost per account	₹11.15	₹23.55

(5) Statement showing average profit per retail and business account under ABC system

Particulars	Retail account	Business account
Average revenue per account	₹50	₹200
Indirect cost per account	11.15	23.55
Average profit per account	38.85	176.45

(C) UBL's bonus-based incentive plan to increase the number of deposit accounts was not a sound strategy as it resulted in increase in the number of retail customers and decrease in the number of business customers.

The ABC analysis reveals that retail customers place greater demands on UBL's resources. Retail customers account for 80 per cent of teller withdrawls/deposit transactions and 95 per cent of customer calls while the revenue per retails customer is only 25 percent of that of a business customer. As a result, the indirect cost per retail customer account is approximately 22 per cent of revenue compared to 12 per cent for a business customer account. As business coustomers are more profitable, UBL should adopt a strategy that will increase the number of business customers.

Based on the ABC analysis, UBL can work towards making its retail customer accounts more profitable by either imposing restrictions on number of withdrawls/deposits and customer calls for retail customers or by increasing the revenue per retail customer.

7.C.2 ABC and Distribution Channel Profitability In January, current year, the top management of Color Plus Ltd. was debating the relative profitability of its three distribution channels: (a) catalogue sales, (b) corporate sales and (c) retail sales. They asked Deepak Parekh, a financial analyst, to conduct a channel profitability analysis. The results of his analysis would have a significant bearing on the company's distribution strategy.

Color Plus Ltd. sells garments. It contracts out the manufacturing of all products to outside supplies. Its employees maintain a large catalogue mailing list. The catalogue buyers, mostly individuals, place generally small quantity orders by phone or over the Internet.

The corporate sales orders are generally large-quantity orders and are brought in through the field sales force of Colur Plus. About three-quarters of corporate orders involve time-consuming order specification and/or price negotiation by the salesman and usually some design experts.

Most of the retail orders are also procured by the field sales force through personal visits to retail outlets. The buyers generally purchase medium quantities of goods at wholesale prices. Some of the retailers require special product labelling and packaging.

Currently all the three distribution channels look profitable as shown in Exhibit 1.

Exhibit 1 Gross Margin Levels of Distribution Channels

	Distribution Channels (Amount ₹thousands)			
	Catalogue	*Corporate*	*Retail*	*Total*
Sales	₹1,50,000	₹50,000	₹1,00,000	₹3,00,000
Cost of sales	75,000	32,500	70,000	1,77,500
Gross margin	75,000	17,500	30,000	1,22,500

The CFO of Color Plus believes that the gross margin-level measure may be a misleading performance indicator. He noted that the selling, general and administrative (SGA) expenses were "below" the gross margin line. His institution was that if the SGA costs were allocated to distribution channels, quite a different performance picture may result. To address his concern, Deepak Parekh was assigned the responsibility of looking into the SGA costs.

During the course of the study to identify the relevant SGA expenses, Deepak noticed that direct sales force was paid a 10 per cent commission on the sales brought in by them. The other SGA expenses for current year were found by Deepak as given below:

Item	Amount (₹thousand)
1 Marketing and sales support	₹30,000
2 Design	4,500
3 Information system	10,000
4 General administration	15,000
	59,500

After identifying the relevant SGA expenses, Deepak proceeded to identify the major activities that were the cause of SGA expenses. Exhibit 2 shows Deepak Parkeh's estimate of the proportion of each of the SGA expense items caused by each of the activities identified by him.

Exhibit 2 Activity-wise SGA Expenses

SGA Items	*Activities*						
	Customer mailing	*Take phone or internet order*	*Take field order*	*Special negotiation field order*	*Process customer invoice*	*Others*	*Total*
1 Marketing and sales support	10%	10%	30%	50%	—	—	100%
2 Design	—	—	—	90%	—	10%	100%
3 Information system	—	10%	—	—	10%	80%	100%
4 General administration	—	—	—	10%	10%	80%	

Deepak Parekh's next task was to assign the costs of each of the activities to the distribution channels. The information collected by him is given in Exhibit 3.

Exhibit 3 Channel-wise Cost of Activities

Activity	*Channels*			
	Catalogue	*Corporate*	*Retail*	*Total*
1 Customer mailings	1,96,000	2,000	2,000	2,00,000
2 Number of phone orders	6,000	60	120	6,180
3 Number of field orders	—	800	800	1,600
5 Number of field orders requiring special negotiation	—	600	200	800
5 Total number of orders (2 + 3)	6,000	860	920	7,780

REQUIRED:

(a) Calculate the profitability of each of the three distribution channels both in terms of total amount and return on sales.

(b) What are the implications of these for the distribution strategy of Color Plus?

SOLUTION

(a) Statement showing Profitability of Distribution Channels

Particulars	*Catalogue*	*Corporate*	*Retail*	*Total*
Sales	₹1,50,000	₹50,000	₹1,00,000	₹3,00,000
Cost of sales	75,000	32,500	70,000	1,77,500
Gross margin	75,000	17,500	30,000	1,22,500
SGA expenses				
Sales commission		5,000	10,000	15,000
Customer mailing	2,940	30	30	3,000
Take phone/internet orders	3,882	39	79	4,000
Take field orders		4,500	4,500	9,000
Special negotiation field order		15,412	5,138	20,550
Process customer invoices	1,927	277	296	2,500
Others	15,771	2,261	2,418	20,450
Net margin/(loss)	50,480	(10,019)	7,539	48,000
Return on sales (%)	67.3	(57.3)	25.1	39.2

WORKING NOTE

1. Computation of Activity costs

	Expense Head				
	Marketing and sales support	*Design*	*Information system*	*General administration*	*Total*
Activity					
Customer mailing	₹3,000	—	—	—	₹3,000
Take phone/Internet orders	3,000	—	₹1,000	—	4,000
Take field orders	9,000	—	—	—	9,000
Special Negotiation	15,000	₹4,050	—	₹1,500	20,550
Processing Invoices	—	—	1,000	1,500	2,500
Others	—	450	8,000	12,000	20,450
Total	30,000	4,500	10,000	15,000	59,500

2. Computation of activity cost driver rates

Activity	*Total activity cost*	*Activity cost driver*	*Number of units of activity cost driver*	*Activity cost driver rate*
Customer mailing	₹3,000	Customer Mailings	2,00,000	Re. 0.015 per customer mailing
Take phone/internet orders	4,000	Number of phone/ internetorders	6,180	Re. 0.647 per phone/ internet/order
Take field orders	9,000	Number of field Orders	1,600	₹5.625 per field order
Special negotiations	20,550	Number of special negotiation orders	800	₹25.688 per special negotiation order
Processing invoices	2,500	Total number of orders	7,780	Re. 0.3213 per order
Others	20,450	Total number of	7,780	₹2.6285 per order

(b) The analysis carried out in part (a) shows that the corporate distribution channel is incurring a loss. This channel incurs an expense of nearly 40% of its sales revenue on taking field orders and negotiating special orders. Almost the entire design costs are incurred on special negotiation corporate orders. The order size is small and is not sufficient to absorb the design and sales support costs. To make the channel profitable, the company may fix the minimum size of a special order and also exhort its sales force to increase sales from the corporate channel.

7.C.3 ABC and Product Pricing Jay Engineering manufacturers electronic testing and measurement instruments. Many products are customr designed with recent orders for function generators, harmonic analysers, logic analysers, temperature measurement instruments and data logging instruments. Jay prices its instruments at 33 per cent over estimated cost (excluding administrative and selling costs).

It has come to the notice of the CEO of Jay that its sales-mix has changed. It is receiving fewer larger orders for simple instruments and more small orders for complex instruments. The CEO intuitively feels that the reason for Jay not being price competitive for simple products may the current cost accounting system. On the suggestion of Director (operations), he hires Jain Consultants to conduct a study to switch to ABC system.

Jain Consultants have selected two recent orders for study: (i) a 1,600 unit order for a temperature monitoring instrument and (ii) an order for 2 harmonic analysers. The costs and price data relating to them are given in Exhibit 1.

Exhibit 1 Cost and Price Data

	Temperature Monitor	*Harmonic Analyser*
1 Component cost per unit	₹800	₹8,000
2 Direct labor per unit	80	1,600
3 Overhead per unit	400	8,000
4 Cost per unit	1,280	17,600
5 Markup (30%)	384	5,280
6 Price per unit	1,664	22,880
7 Number of units	1,600	2
8 Value or order	26,62,400	45,760

Currently, the overhead (₹16,00,00,000 annually) is applied based on direct labour cost (₹3,20,00,000). Jain Consultants have broken down the annual overheads into six cost pools and identified the related cost driver as given in Exhibit 2.

Exhibit 2 Cost Pools and Cost Drivers

Cost Pools	*Annual Cost*	*Annual Cost Driver*
1 Production design	₹2,40,00,000	2,40,000 design-hours
2 Material ordering and handling	3,20,00,000	2,00,000 unique part numbers
3 Inspection	1,00,00,000	8,00,000 inspections
4 Setup	60,00,000	1,00,000 setups
5 Labour-related overheads	2,40,00,000	₹3,20,00,000 direct labour cost
5 Depreciation of plant and equipment	6,40,00,000	4,00,00,000 machine-hours
Total	16,00,00,000	

Jain Consultants have also estimated that the temperature monitoring instrument and the harmonic analyser make use of the cost drivers as shown in Exhibit 3.

Exhibit 3 Use of Cost Drivers by the Monitor and Analyser

	For 1,600 Monitors	*For 2 Analysers*
Number of design-hours	84	200
Number of unique parts	30	40
Number of inspections	400	30
Number of setups	1	1
Machine-hours	200	10

REQUIRED:

(a) Based on Jain Consultants data, compute the cost per unit of each product using the ABC approach.

(b) Based on Jain Consultants work, Jay Engineering has introduced an ABC system (as per Exhibit 2). Recently, Jay has received order from Amity International for a unique data logging device, requiring ₹32,000 of components and ₹8,000 of direct labour together with the following requirements:

- Number of design-hours 50
- Number of unique parts 30
- Number of inspections 20
- Number of setups 1
- Machine-hours 16

Amity International has indicated that they already have a quote from another supplier for ₹38,000. Calculate the cost of data logging device, using the ABC approach. How does it stand in relation to the competitors quote?

SOLUTION

(a) Statement showing cost per unit using the ABC approach

	Temperature Monitor	*Harmonic Analyser*
Component cost per unit	₹800	₹8,000
Direct labour per unit	80	1,600
Overhead per unit	72	14,626
Cost per unit	952	24,226

WORKING NOTES

1. Computation of cost driver rate using the ABC approach

Activity	*Annual cost*	*Cost driver*	*Number of units of cost driver per annum*	*Cost driver rate*
Production design	₹2,40,00,000	design hours	2,40,000	₹100 per design hour
Material ordering and handling	3,20,00,000	unique part numbers	2,00,000	₹160 per unique part
Inspection	1,00,00,000	inspections	8,00,000	₹12.5 per Inspection
Setup	60,00,000	setups	1,00,000	₹60 per setup
Labour-related overheads	2,40,00,000	direct-labour cost	₹3,20,00,000	75% of direct labour cost
Depreciation of plant and equipment	6,40,00,000	machine-hours	4,00,00,000	₹1.60 per machine hour

2. Computation of overhead cost per unit using the ABC approach

Activity	Cost driver rate	For 1,600 Monitors: Units of cost driver	For 1,600 Monitors: Cost	For 2 Analysers: Units of cost driver	For 2 Analysers: Cost
Production design	₹100	84	₹8,400	200	₹20,000
Material ordering and handling	160	30	4,800	40	6,400
Inspection	12.5	400	5,000	30	375
Setup	60	1	60	1	60
Labour related overhead	75% of direct labour cost	₹1,28,000	96,000	₹3,200	2,400
Depreciation of plant	1.6	200	320	10	16
Total overhead cost			1,14,580		29,251
Overhead cost per unit (rounded off)			72		14,626

(b) Statement showing the cost of data logging device using the ABC approach

Component cost	₹32,000
Direct labour cost	8,000
Overhead cost	16,136
	56,136
Mark-up (30%)	16,841
Price per unit	72,977

WORKING NOTE

Computation of overhead cost per unit using the ABC approach

Activity	Cost driver rate	Units of cost driver	Cost
Production design	₹100	50	₹5,000
Material ordering and handling	160	30	4,800
Inspection	12.5	20	250
Setup	60	1	60
Labour related overhead	75% of direct labour cost	₹8,000	6,000
Depreciation of plant	1.6	16	26
Total overhead cost per unit			16,136

The cost of the company for a unit of the data logging device is nearly 48% higher than the quoted price of the other supplier.

Job-order, Batch and Contract Costing

Learning Objectives

1. Describe and illustrate job/order costing
2. Describe and illustrate batch costing
3. Describe and illustrate contract costing

INTRODUCTION

This chapter describes and illustrates the systems of job/order, batch and contract costing. It is accordingly divided into four sections. Section 1 is devoted to job costing. Sections 2 describes and illustrate batch costing. Contract costing constitutes subject matter of Section 3. The main points are summarised in the last Section.

JOB/ORDER COSTING

This Section illustrates job costing as a method of cost accumulation. As the system of costing depends upon the operating environment/production procedure, we first outline the nature of job costing in terms of the situations/manufacturing processes in which such a costing method is appropriate. This is followed by the cost accounting cycle for jobs. The cost recording procedure under job costing is dependent on whether the firm maintains both the general and factory ledgers or only the general ledger. The cost accumulation in job costing is illustrated here in both situations.

Job order costing is the procedure to accumulate cost when work is performed pursuant to an order to meet individual customer's specifications.

Nature and Suitability

As the name implies, job-order costing refers to a costing system that determines the production cost of individual orders/jobs. Under this system, costs are assigned to, and accumulated for, each job. Such a system of cost accumulation is related to the flow of production in which a firm has to work on a job in pursuance of an order received from a customer. The order may be for a single item or a number of identical items manufactured as a group, that is, a batch. For instance, a book publishing company prints performed pursuant to an order, and when products are manufactured or services rendered to meet individual customers' specifications.

The essence of job costing is that as all jobs/orders are not necessarily alike, they do not pass through the same manufacturing process. In other words, since each job requires varying amounts of materials and labour and different levels of skills or attention, the cost of one job would differ from another. Thus, the cost should be recorded separately for each job. Therefore, the job-order costing system traces costs with individual production orders/jobs. In other words, in the case of certain manufacturing processes/situations, whether dealing with a product or service, is the relative uniqueness of the work (specific identity) performed for each job/client/order. Therefore, in this system of costing, each job or batch is regarded as a cost unit from the viewpoint of cost accumulation. Thus, the distinguishing feature of job-order costing is the ability to identify costs with a specific project/job/order or group of units.[1]

It follows from the above that job-order costing is, in general, appropriate in situations when each job (work) is unique, easily identifiable, and can serve as a cost objective.[2] Such a system can be appropriately applied to accumulate costs in the following situations:

1. Auto-repair shops, where each repair job requires varying amounts of material and labour. The mechanic will charge the cost of any replaced parts and the number of labour-hours spent in repairing.
2. Automobile assembly, where each car includes a variety of different options.
3. Printing shops, where each print order requires a different type of paper, ink, design and so on.
4. Foundries, where special parts are to be manufactured as per order.
5. Hospitals, where the costs of services provided to each patient are billed separately.
6. Contractors, shipbuilders and motion picture companies.
7. Machine shops, tool shops and design engineers.
8. Public accounting firms and other similar professions, where each audit, tax return, or management services engagement needs varying amounts of professional time and attention.
9. Furniture making firms, where they may produce a batch of similar chairs, tables, sofas, and so on. Each batch may be treated as a job.

Cost Accounting Cycle/Job Cost Sheet

This section discusses the work flow and cost recording procedure in job costing. The backbone of the job costing system is the *job cost sheet.*

On receipt of an order by a firm employing job costing, a job cost sheet is prepared. Every job order is given a specific number. For identification, a job cost sheet bearing the alloted number is maintained for each job put into production. General information in respect of the job order is recorded at the top of the job sheet. As regards specific information, the job cost sheet enumerates the appropriate inputs required in three basic categories: direct material, direct labour and overhead to carry out the order. Depending on data requirements for planning, controlling costs and evaluating performance, additional information such as labour-hours, machine-hours, quantity and quality of the materials to be used may also be recorded in the job sheet. Besides, it also contains information regarding the quantum and quality of the final output and the date by which the supply is to be made; it may also provide reference of the customer. In some job cost situations, the job sheet follows the job physically through the production process, serving not only to accumulate costs, but also providing the appropriate routing for the job.[3] The labour and materials used by each production department on the job are recorded on the job sheet. A reference of the overhead criterion such as, direct material, direct labour, machine-hour rate or labour-hour rate used is also recorded on the job sheet. On completion of the work in one department, the goods are transferred to the next relevant department along with the job sheet. This process is repeated till the job is completed. At the final stage, the job sheet contains all the materials, labour and overhead costs that were incurred on each job, as the work on an order progresses through various stages of production. As a result, profit earned or loss suffered on the job can be easily determined. The job sheet also provides room for comparing the actual total costs with estimated costs. The reasons for variance in these costs are determined so as to prevent their future occurrence. All this information is vital to the management for evaluating employee performance and controlling the costs. Thus, the job cost sheet constitutes the backbone of the job-order system. In fact, it is a vital document for subsequent accounting records. The format of the cost sheet varies from firm to firm depending on their individual requirements. Exhibit 8.1 is the commonly used cost-sheet format. Columns may be added or deleted as circumstances warrant.

Exhibit 8.1 Job Cost Sheet

Job No.

Customer name	______	Date started	______
and address	______	Date promised	______
Description	______	Date finished	______
Quantity	______	Special remarks, if any	______

	Materials			*Labour*			*Overheads*		
	Quantity	Rate	Amount	Hours	Rate	Amount	Hours	Rate	Amount
Department 1									
Department 2									
Department 3									

Cost Summary

	Materials	*Labour*	*Overheads*	*Total*	
				Actual	*Estimate*
Department 1					
Department 2					
Department 3					
Job order price					
Profit (Loss)					

Discrepancies between actual and estimated costs are explained below:
1.
2.
3.

Recording Job Costs in Accounts

The accounting system of recording job costs will depend on whether the general ledger records all cost transactions or a special ledger called factory ledger is *separately* maintained for the purpose. It is ideal/preferable if the cost accountant is concerned with recording the costs in respect of the use of material and labour closer to the scene of production operations in the factory ledger, and the financial accountant is concerned with paying the bills and the records are maintained in the general ledger. Such a system of record keeping also rules out duplication of clerical effort.

The *modus operandi* is that a factory ledger account is opened in the general ledger to substitute for the accounts, which have been recorded in the factory ledger. Likewise, a general ledger account is provided in the factory ledger. Such cost recording can be said to be on a *self-balancing basis* as the general ledger and the factory ledger are independent of each other. The balances in these accounts are kept equal at all times. When an entry is made in the factory ledger accounts at the general office, it is offsetted by an entry made in the general ledger account at the factory office. In view of the usefulness of keeping a separate cost record in the factory ledger, it is commended for adoption. The accounting procedure to be adopted if both the factory and general ledgers are maintained is explained first. The accounting procedure when no separate ledger is kept and all transactions are recorded in a general ledger is illustrated subsequently. We have first explained the procedure relating to the: **(i)** Accounting for materials, **(ii)** Accounting for labour, **(iii)** Accounting for overheads, and **(iv)** Accounting for completed jobs. A comprehensive illustration follows the theoretical discussion.

Accounting for Materials Certain raw materials may be purchased to cater to the specifications of particular jobs. Typically, more basic materials of common use on a number of jobs are acquired and held in the materials inventory. For each type of raw material held by the manufacturing firm, a separate materials ledger card is prepared which indicates the quantity and cost of materials held for future use. When the materials are needed for a job, the job supervisor or any other authorised person, requisitions them through a *materials requisition slip/form* which forms the basis for the entry transferring materials from materials inventory (materials and supplies) account to the concerned job account. This form identifies the job order number and lists the type and quantity of materials drawn from the inventory. Any material not used in the job for which it was requisitioned would be returned. The relevant accounting entries in the factory and general ledgers to record the **(i)** purchase, **(ii)** issue, and **(iii)** return of materials would be as follows:

Factory ledger:

1. Debit materials inventory/materials and supplies A/c, and Credit general ledger.
2. Debit work-in-process A/c, and Credit materials inventory/materials and supplies A/c.
3. Reversal of entry (2)

General ledger:

1. Debit factory ledger, and Credit accounts payable/cash or bank.
2. No entry
3. No entry

Materials inventory is also used for indirect materials and supplies. Often, it is not worthwhile to assign the costs of these materials directly to the jobs in which they are used, as their value is insignificant compared to the total cost of the job. Hence, they are charged to the indirect manufacturing overhead account *(indirect manufacturing costs control account)*. The journal entry for the acquisition of indirect materials is the same as that for the purchase of direct materials in both sets of ledgers. However, the issue of such materials to production is considered as an addition to indirect manufacturing cost and is charged to the manufacturing overhead cost control account. Subsequently, indirect material costs are allocated to jobs on the basis of some predetermined rate of absorption of indirect overheads.

Accounting for Labour In job-order costing, direct labour costs are payments for the services of employees directly engaged in manufacturing activities on jobs in progress—for example, wages paid to machinists, drill press operators, welders, and assemblers.

It is usual for manufacturing firms to pay wages to production workers on the basis of time; moreover, they are also usually provided with *a job time card* on which they record the number of hours spent on each job on a working day. The direct labour cost of any job is ascertained by the product of the number of hours spent on that job and the worker's hourly wage rate. In determining true hourly wage rate, calculations should not be limited to only the wage amount paid to him, but should also include the employer's contribution to the provident fund, pension and insurance plans, and other fringe benefits that are paid to him by the firm.

It is important to recognise here the element of indirect labour cost in the aggregate payments made to production workers. Indirect labour includes the costs of supervisors, foremen, maintenance, security and time keeping personnel; it also includes the costs of idle time, machine setup time, rework time and overtime wages paid to direct labourers. The justification in including overtime premium in indirect overhead is the fact that overtime is the result of overall activity. If the overall level of activity were lower, the job worked on during overtime hours would be worked on during regular hours. Accordingly, overtime premiums are allocated to all jobs through the overhead account.[4] However, if overtime premium accrues on account of a "*rush*" job where the customer is willing to pay for shorter than normal delivery time, the premium amount can be charged directly to a specific job.

The following journal entries would be recorded in respect of the labour cost:

Factory ledger:
Debit work-in-process A/c (for direct labour) and Debit factory overhead control (A/c (for indirect labour) and *Credit general ledger.*
General ledger:
Debit factory ledger A/c, and Credit wages payable A/c /cash or bank.

Accounting for Manufacturing Overheads Unlike direct material and labour costs which can wholly and exclusively be identified with specific jobs, costs relating to manufacturing overheads cannot be conveniently traced to a particular job as overhead costs are indirect in nature and pertain to the factory or organisation as a whole. In other words, they are not caused by a specific job. Nevertheless, each job requires the services of indirect overheads. This gives rise to the need for charging each job with its fair share of indirect overheads to determine its true cost.

Manufacturing overheads can be charged to various jobs either at the actual overhead rate or a *predetermined* overhead rate. The merits of a predetermined overhead rate are: **(a)** It is useful in 'bidding' cases to determine the tender/quotation price; **(b)** It enables individual jobs to be costed as soon as they are completed and, thus, helps in providing more rapid product cost information to the management; and **(c)** Such a rate levels out the fluctuations which may be caused by variations in actual overhead costs and actual activity. For these reasons, manufacturing overheads are often applied to jobs at a predetermined overhead rate:

Predetermined overhead rate is budgeted manufacturing overheads divided by budgeted activity

Predetermined overhead rate = Budgeted manufacturing overheads/Budgeted activity **(8.1)**

For estimating budgeted manufacturing overheads, past historical cost data are taken as the base and adjustments are made for likely changes in prices/rates of various elements of overheads. The overheads are segregated into two categories: variable (for example, power and heating, indirect materials, repairs and maintenance) and fixed (for example, insurance, rent, property taxes, work manager's salary). Thus,

Budgeted manufacturing overheads =

[Total budgeted fixed overheads + Budgeted variable overhead rate] × Budgeted activity **(8.2)**

The budgeted activity measure "must be a factor that is common to all jobs, has a high correlation with the incurrence of overhead costs, and is easy to measure.[5] Where most of the work is done by machines, the machine-hour rate is often used to charge indirect overheads to jobs. The labour-hour rate or direct labour cost is useful in situations where most of the work is accomplished by labour.

Like manufacturing overheads, one reasonable way of estimating budgeted activity can be to make adjustments in the previous year's activity level on the basis of the management's expectation for the coming year.

Consider Example 8.1.

EXAMPLE 8.1 *(DETERMINING PREDETERMINED OVERHEADS RATE)*

Hypothetical Ltd employs job-order costing. It uses an annual predetermined rate for applying manufacturing overheads to jobs. The company furnishes you with the following information regarding its overheads for the coming year at normal activity: Fixed overheads, ₹20,00,000; and Variable overheads, ₹15,00,000.

The estimates of the direct labour cost, direct labour hours and machine-hours at normal activity along with a set of correlation coefficients between overheads and various measures of activity, as compiled from past records, are also given:

	Normal level of activity	*Correlation coefficient with overheads*
Direct labour cost	₹10,00,000	0.7
Direct labour hours	20,000	0.8
Machine hours	10,000	0.6

Determine the predetermined (i) fixed, (ii) variable, and (iii) total overhead rates.

SOLUTION

Predetermined overhead rates should be based on direct labour-hours (DLH):

(i) Predetermined fixed overhead rate = ₹20,00,000 ÷ 20,000 = ₹100
(ii) Predetermined variable overhead rate = ₹15,00,000 ÷ 20,000 = ₹75
(iii) Total predetermined overhead rate = ₹35,00,000 ÷ 20,000 = ₹175

Further assume that Hypothetical Ltd during the first quarter received an invitation from a regular customer to bid on a job. The job was estimated to require ₹1,00,000 of direct materials and the following: Direct labour cost, ₹50,000; Direct labour-hours, 1,500; and Machine-hours, 500

Determine the bid price the company should quote assuming its normal practice of charging 20 per cent on factory cost to cover other administrative overheads and profit. Assume further that the company uses a predetermined factory overhead rate to assign factory overheads to jobs.

SOLUTION

Job Cost Sheet to Determine the Bid Price

Particulars	*Amount*
Direct materials	₹1,00,000
Direct labour cost	50,000
Prime cost	1,50,000
Add factory overheads (1,500 direct labour-hours @ ₹175 per hour)	2,62,500
Factory cost	4,12,500
Add 20 per cent for administrative overheads and profit	82,500
Bid price	4,95,000

Over-applied or Under-applied Manufacturing Overheads When predetermined overhead rate is used as the basis of absorption of overheads, it is seldom that the total overhead costs applied to jobs in a given period are equal to the total overhead costs of that period. When the applied overhead exceeds the actual, it is referred to as over-applied/absorbed overhead. It is known as under-applied/absorbed in case the applied is less than the actual. The difference between the actual and applied manufacturing overhead costs is designated as the *variance.*

Suppose in Example 8.1, the company's actual overheads were ₹9,00,000 and total direct labour-hours used were 4,500 in the first quarter. The applied overheads would amount to ₹7,87,500 [4,500 DLH × ₹175 (Total predetermined overhead rate per hour)]; overhead is under-applied by ₹1,12,500 (₹9,00,000 – ₹7,87,500).

Disposition of Variance Overhead variances may be disposed of by following either of the two methods: **(i)** They may be assigned to the income statement of the current period by charging the entire amount to the cost of goods sold account; or **(ii)** They may be considered as the cost of production of the current period and accordingly may be pro-rated to work-in-process, finished goods and cost of goods sold. The treatment would depend on the nature of such variance.

If the variance has been an outcome of unusual events of the current period, it should be charged to the cost of goods sold. But if such a variance has been caused by errors in estimation or fundamental changes in cost structure, it should be pro-rated over work-in-process, finished goods and cost of goods sold. For the firm in Example 8.1, consider the following additional information:

Job No.	*Direct costs*	*Overheads charged In quarter*	*Status of job at the end of the quarter*
50	₹11,00,000	₹3,60,000	Cost of goods sold
51	9,00,000	2,25,000	Finished goods inventory
52	6,50,000	2,02,500	Work-in-process inventory
	26,50,000	7,87,500	

Show the process of adjusting under-applied overheads.

SOLUTION

Manufacturing/Factory Overhead Adjustment

Account	*Overhead-charged in quarter*	*Percentage of overhead applied in quarter*	*Under-applied overheads (₹1,12,500) × (percentage)*	*Total costs assigned to jobs after adjustment*
Cost of goods sold	₹3,60,000	45.7	₹51,412.50	₹4,11,412.50
Finished goods inventory	2,25,000	28.6	32,175.00	2,57,175.00
Work-in-process inventory	2,02,500	25.7	28,912.50	2,31,412.50
	7,87,500	100.00	1,12,500.00	9,00,000.00

The following journal entries would be required to give effect to manufacturing overheads.

Factory ledger

1. Debit Factory Overhead Control A/c, and Credit General Ledger
   (For indirect manufacturing costs incurred).
2. Debit Work-in-Process/Individual Jobs A/c, and Credit Factory Overhead Control A/c
   (For charging indirect overheads to jobs).
3. Debit Cost of Goods Sold A/c, and Credit Factory Overhead Control A/c
   (For charging under-applied overheads to cost of goods sold account under first method).
   Entry number (3) would be reversed in the case of over-applied overheads.
4. Debit Work-in-Process/Individual Jobs
   Debit Finished Goods inventory
   Debit Cost of Goods Sold, and
   Credit Factory Overhead Control A/c
   (For charging under-applied overheads under pro-rating method).
   Entries (3) and (4) would be reversed in the case of over-applied overheads.

General ledger

1. Debit Factory Ledger A/c, and Credit Various Credits (Accounts Payable), Credit Accumulated Depreciation, and so on.
   (For indirect manufacturing costs incurred).

For subsequent transactions no entry is required in the general ledger as these transactions do not affect the general ledger accounts.

Accounting for Completed Jobs Normally, in a job costing system when work on a job is completed, it would be available for delivery to a customer. At the time of completion, all work-in-process account balances pertaining to that job are transferred directly to cost of goods sold account. In case, production is made in anticipation of future sale, relevant costs from work-in-process will be transferred to the finished goods inventory account. The journal entries in the factory ledger would be as follows:

1. *Production is as per order*
   Debit Cost of Goods Sold A/c, and
   Credit Work-in-process A/c
   (Transfer of cost on completion of the job).
2. *Production is for future sale*
   (a) Debit Finished Goods Inventory A/c, and
   Credit Work-in-process A/c
   (b) *At the time of sale*
   Debit Costs of Goods Sold A/c, and
   Credit finished goods inventory.

Accounting for Non-manufacturing Costs Costs such as sales commissions, freight and delivery charges, can sometimes be related directly to particular jobs. Since these costs are incurred subsequent to the completion of the job, they cannot be classified as the cost of production. They should be separately shown as the direct costs of selling, distributing, and servicing particular jobs in job cost sheets which can be modified to add non-manufacturing costs. This information is useful in estimating future job costs and in bidding on prices.

We now illustrate the cost recording procedure in job costing with a comprehensive example.

EXAMPLE 8.2 *(JOB COSTING SYSTEM: FACTORY LEDGER AND GENERAL LEDGER METHOD)*

Jay Engineering Company Ltd uses a job-order cost system. The following is a summary of its operations during January:

1. Purchases of raw materials and supplies, ₹37,500.
2. Materials and supplies were requisitioned and issued as follows:
   Direct materials:

Job No.	101	₹6,000	
	102	9,000	
	103	1,400	₹16,400
Indirect materials			400

3. Factory payroll sent to the general office for payment was distributed as follows:
   Direct labour:

Job No.	101	₹5,400	
	102	6,000	
	103	600	
			₹12,000
Indirect labour			4,000

4. Indirect miscellaneous manufacturing costs incurred, ₹5,200.
5. Indirect manufacturing costs were applied using a rate of 70 per cent of direct labour cost.
6. Job No. 101 (100 units) and Job No. 102 (50 units) were completed and transferred to finished goods.
7. Goods despatched to customers were as follows: From Job No. 101, 50 units; From Job No. 102, 100 units.

Prepare the required ledger accounts to record the above transactions in the factory ledger.

SOLUTION

Job Ledger

Particulars	*Job No. 101*	*Job No. 102*	*Job No. 103*
Raw materials and supplies	₹6,000	₹9,000	₹1,400
Direct labour	5,400	6,000	600
Indirect manufacturing costs applied	3,780	4,200	420
	15,180	19,200	2,420

Factory Ledger Accounts

Raw Materials and Supplies A/c

To general ledger (purchase of inventory)	₹37,500	By work-in-process	₹16,400
		By factory overhead control A/c	400

Work-in-Process A/c

To raw materials and supplies	₹16,400	By finished goods (cost of Job Nos. 101 and 102	₹34,380
To general ledger (direct labour payment)	12,000		
To factory overhead control (applied A/c)	8,400		

Finished Goods Inventory A/c

To work-in-process	₹34,380	By cost of goods sold (₹7,590 + ₹12,800)	₹20,390

Cost of Goods Sold A/c

To finished goods inventory	₹20,390		

Factory Overhead Control A/c

To raw materials and supplies	₹400		
To general ledger (indirect labour payment)	4,000		
To general ledger (miscellaneous expenses)	5,200		

Factory Overhead Control Applied A/c

		By work-in-process	₹8,400

General Ledger Accounts

		By raw materials and supplies	₹37,500
		By work-in-process	12,000
		By factory overhead control A/c	4,000
		By factory overhead control A/c	5,200

Note: Ledger accounts are not balanced as the transactions pertain to only a month's period.

General Ledger Accounts

Factory Ledger (A/c)

To accounts payable	₹37,500		
To wages payable	16,000		
To miscellaneous credits	5,200		

Accounts Payable A/c*

By factory ledger A/c	₹37,500

Wages Payable A/c*

By factory ledger A/c	₹16,000

Miscellaneous Credits A/c*

By factory ledger A/c	₹5,200

*Debits in these accounts would be made when payments are made.

The above cost recording procedure is valid when a *separate* factory ledger is maintained. We now enumerate the accounting system when the general ledger records *all* transactions and no separate factory ledger is maintained. A comprehensive illustration (Example 8.3) demonstrates the actual recording procedure.

EXAMPLE 8.3 *(JOB ORDER COSTING: GENERAL LEDGER METHOD)*

The following transactions occurred at the Small Machine Manufacturing Company Ltd:

1. Issued ₹1,000 in supplies from the materials inventory.
2. Purchased materials worth ₹20,000.
3. Purchased materials costing ₹15,800 on cash basis.
4. Paid for the materials purchased.
5. Issued materials worth ₹17,000 to the production department.
6. Incurred wages of ₹42,000 which were debited to a temporary account called the wages payable account. Of this amount, ₹8,000 was withheld for taxes; the balance was paid in cash to the employees.
7. Analysis of the wage accounts reveals that 60 per cent was direct labour, 30 per cent indirect manufacturing labour and 10 per cent administrative and selling costs.
8. Paid cash for utilities, power, equipment maintenance, and other miscellaneous items for the manufacturing plant. The total amount was ₹21,600.
9. Applied overhead on the basis of 175 per cent of direct labour costs.
10. Depreciation on plant and equipment is to be charged at ₹10,500.
11. The following balances appeared in the accounts of company:

	Opening	*Closing*
Materials inventory	₹37,050	—
Work-in-process inventory	8,250	—
Finished goods inventory	41,500	₹33,200
Cost of goods sold		65,850

You are required to prepare T accounts to show the costs during the period.

SOLUTION

Ledger Accounts

Materials Inventory A/c

To balance b/d	₹37,050	By factory overhead control A/c	₹1,000
To accounts payable	20,000	By work-in-process inventory	17,000
To cash (purchases)	15,800	By balance c/d	54,850
	72,850		72,850
To balance b/d	54,850		

Work-in-Process Inventory A/c

To balance b/d	₹8,250	By finished goods inventory A/c	₹57,550
To raw materials inventory	17,000	By balance c/d	37,000
To factory overhead control A/c	44,100		
To wages control A/c (₹42,000 × 0.60)	25,200		
	94,550		94,550
To balance b/d	37,000		

Finished Goods Inventory A/c

To balance b/d	₹41,500	By cost of goods sold	₹65,850
To work-in-process inventory (balancing figure)	57,550	By balance c/d	33,200
To balance b/d	33,200		
	99,050		99,050

Factory Overhead Control A/c

To raw materials inventory	₹1,000	By work-in-process A/c (₹25,200 × 1.75)	₹44,100
To wages control A/c (₹42,000 × 0.30)	12,600	By factory-overhead control applied A/c (under-absorbed)	1,600
To cash (for various overheads)	21,600		
To accumulated depreciation on plant	10,500		
	45,700		45,700

Apart from the manufacturing firms, service organisations such as engineering, consulting and accounting, firms can also usefully apply the job-order costing system. The job-order costing procedure is basically the same in both service and manufacturing organisations, except that the former do not make use of any direct materials. Instead of having an indirect manufacturing overhead account, service firms can have the title of service overhead account, to represent and accumulate costs in respect of indirect materials, indirect labour and other overheads.

Evaluation

Job order costing is useful in the following ways:

1. Job costing data can be utilised for estimating the production costs of specific jobs or lots of production. If, for example, a customer places an order with the firm to manufacture a sepcific type of product that has unique characteristics different from the other products manufactured by the company, a job-order cost system should be utilized to accumulate the production costs associated with this product. In other words, job costing system provides the basis for determining the 'bidding' price for similar jobs that will be considered in the future.
2. Estimates of future job costs serve not only as a basis for bidding and price setting but also as a standard for measuring efficiency and evaluating the performance through comparisons with the actual costs incurred. Since under this system, all costs such as direct materials, direct labour and other expenses which can be traced directly to particular or specific jobs must be forecast as separate identifiable amounts, subsequent comparisons between actual job costs incurred and estimated job costs can be made on an item-by-item basis. This process helps the management in assigning responsibilities for variance in costs to different responsibility centres that worked on the job. Thus, this process assists the management in discharging its control function.

3. From the point of view of accounting also, the system is easy to operate as the costs are recorded order or job-wise.
4. Finally, job cost sheets which are the focal point of job order system can be utilised by the management to segregate jobs on the basis of contributions/profits made by them. This information, in turn, will help the management in deciding which types of jobs should be accorded priority.

The only drawback visualised in the system is that it requires detailed record-keeping for each of the jobs, and, therefore, may prove to be more expensive to use.

BATCH COSTING

This Section illustrates batch costing, as a system of cost accumulation. As mentioned earlier, batch costing is a variant of job costing. It is a natural type of system to be utliised in situations when a firm manufactures products in readily identifiable batches or definite lots.

The I.C.M.A. London has defined batch costing as "that form of specific order costing which applies where similar articles are manufactured in batches either for sale or for use within the company". In most cases, this costing is similar to job-costing. "A batch is a cost unit which consists of a group of similar articles, which maintain its identity throughout one or more stages of production:" In such a system, each batch can serve as a cost objective for identification of costs as each job is a cost objective in the job-order costing system. Hence, the cost recording procedure in the batch costing system is similar to that of the job costing system.

For identification purposes, each batch is required to be numbered in batch costing as each job is numbered in the job costing system. Similarly, direct material, direct labour and any other direct costs which can be traced directly to a specific batch are charged to it and indirect manufacturing overheads are applied at the predetermined rate. Thus, the normal principles of job-order costing system apply to batch costing also. However, there are some points of distinction between the two.

The unique feature which distinguishes job costing from batch costing is that, while in the former production is tailored to meet the customers' specifications, in the latter, in general, goods are produced to inventory them for future sale to customers. The situations in which batch costing might gainfully be applied include, furniture making, small tool making, manufacture of fabric, clothing and toys, as well as certain food processing undertakings.

The determination of batch/quantity to be produced in each job is another salient feature which distinguishes it from job costing. The determination of the appropriate size of the batch produced necessitates a resolution of conflicting goals. Production in large quantities implies lower *setting-up* costs as such costs are normally fixed per batch. Thus, the unit cost falls with an increase in size of the batch. But an increase in size of the batch produced would involve higher carrying costs of holding inventory in stock. These costs include the cost of storage, risk of pilferage, spoilage and obsolescence and loss interest on the investment blocked in inventories. Therefore, the size of batch produced should neither be too small nor too large. On the basis of a trade-off between benefits derived from setting-up costs and the costs of carrying the inventory, an appropriate production level of the batch should be determined. Stated with reference to the cost perspective, the economic batch quantity (EBQ), can be determined by Equation 8.3. This is similar to the method of determining the economic order quantity (EOQ):

$$EBQ = \sqrt{2\ AS/C} \qquad \textbf{(8.3)}$$

Where A = annual requirements of the product

S = setting-up costs per batch

C = carrying cost per unit of inventory per annum

EXAMPLE 8.4 The following details are available in respect of a small tool manufacturing firm:

Annual estimated demand per year (units)	1,600
Cost of production per unit	₹5
Carrying costs per unit for one year	1
Setting up cost per batch	50

Determine EBQ.

SOLUTION

Using Equation 8.3,

$$\text{EBQ} = \sqrt{\frac{2 \times 1{,}600 \times ₹50}{₹1}} = 400 \text{ units}$$

CONTRACT COSTING

Contract costing is also a variant of job costing. It is a specialized costing system, which applies to construction works. This section outlines and illustrates contract costing. It first discusses the cost accumulation process in contracts, which are completed in one accounting year. It is followed by a discussion of determination of profit on incomplete contracts. *Cost plus* contracts are covered in the last part.

Contract Accounts

A separate account is kept for each individual *contract* for the purpose of cost accumulation and profit determination. Each contract account constitutes the *cost unit* as well as the *cost centre.* Generally, under other costing systems, cost is allocated first to the cost centre (may be a department or process) and then to the individual jobs (cost units). The nature of contract work is such that most of the costs (material, labour and overheads) are directly traceable to the contract. All direct costs are debited to the contract account; indirect/overhead costs relating to the overall administration and other central services are apportioned to each contract on some predetermined equitable basis. On completion of the contract, the contract price is credited to the contract account; excess credit and excess debit respectively represent profit and loss from the contract. Exhibit 8.2 summarises the contract account when the contract is complete within an accounting year.

EXHIBIT 8.2 *Proforma Contract Account*

Particulars	*Amount*	*Particulars*	*Amount*
To materials (direct)		By materials returned to store	
To materials (issued from the store)		By materials transferred to another contract site	
To wages and salaries		By materials sold	
To sub-contract payments[1]		By abnormal loss (theft of materials, loss of plant due to fire, and so on.)	
To other direct expenses[2]			
To indirect expenses (apportioned share of overheads)		By closing stock of materials	
To plant and equipment (purchase price/book value)		By plant and equipment (closing balance)	
To profit and loss A/c (surplus)		By profit and loss A/c (deficiency)	

[1]Payment for specialised character jobs such as lifts, steel work, heating installation, and so on.

[2]Include architects' and consultants' fees, hire charges of plant and equipment, insurance of contract site, and so on.

Profit Determination on Incomplete Contracts

The determination of profit in case of contracts which are not completed in one accounting year is an important aspect of contract accounting.

The actual profits will be known only on completion of the contract, but a contractor would be interested in determining the profits periodically to even out fluctuations in the profits of the firm. When a part/proportion of profits is not taken into account each year, the contractor's annual accounts may show low profits (or even a loss) for each year in which no major contract(s) is/are completed and exceptionally high profits in a year in which a large contract(s) is/are completed. Thus, there would be wide fluctuations in the contractor's annual profits, making inter-year profits incomparable. The profits to be accounted for in different years will depend on the following considerations:

1. No profit is accounted for in the early stages of the contract. Conventionally, a contract is deemed to be in early stages if less that one-fourth of the job has been completed. In other words, no profit should be considered unless one-fourth of the contract is complete. However, if any loss is anticipated, it should always be provided for.
2. Profit should be considered only on that part of the work which is certified by the contractee's architect and no profit should be reckoned on work completed but not certified.
3. Adequate provision should be made for contingencies likely to affect the completion of the work. For instance, conventionally, one-third of the expected profits are taken into account if the contract, as certified by the architect, is between one-fourth and one-half complete, and two-thirds are considered when the job is half or more than half complete.
4. The profit to be considered should be in the proportion of cash received from the contractee to the amount of certified work.

   Based on the foregoing conventions, the determination of profit on incomplete contracts to be credited to profit and loss account can be summarised as follows:

   (a) When work certified is 25 per cent or more but less than 50 per cent of the total contract

   $$\text{Estimated (notional) profit} \times \frac{1}{3} \times \frac{\text{Cash received}}{\text{Work certified}} \tag{8.4}$$

   (b) When work certified is 50 per cent or more

   $$\text{Estimated (notional) profit} \times \frac{2}{3} \times \frac{\text{Cash received}}{\text{Work certified}} \tag{8.5}$$

   The difference between the estimated and transferred profits represents the *reserve for future contingencies* left in the contract account to be carried forward to the following year(s).
5. To show the *pari passu* relationships between work certified and the amount of profit to be transferred to the current year's profit and loss account, the estimated profit can be computed on the basis of Equation 8.6. However, this equation should be applied when at least 25 per cent of the work is complete.

$$\text{Estimated profit} \times \frac{\text{Work certified}}{\text{Contract price}} \times \frac{\text{Cash received}}{\text{Work certified}}$$

$$\text{Or} \quad \text{Estimated profit} \times \frac{\text{Cash received}}{\text{Work certified}} \tag{8.6}$$

Estimated Profit

When a contract is nearing completion, the contractor would be in a better position to estimate future profits with a greater degree of accuracy. Since the contract has reached on advanced stage, he would find himself in a position where he can estimate the likely future costs to be incurred to get the contract completed and a margin for contingencies. These costs can be added to the costs already incurred on the contract. The *total cost* so arrived at can be deducted from the contract price to arrive at the profit figure. Even in this case, the profit to be carried to the profit and loss account is generally required to be adjusted both for future contingencies and cash received:

$$\text{Estimated total profit} \times \frac{\text{Value of work certified}}{\text{Contract price}} \times \frac{\text{Cash received}}{\text{Work certified}} \quad (8.7)$$

$$\text{Estimated profit} \times \frac{\text{Value of work certified}}{\text{Contract price}} \quad (8.8^*)$$

*When cash position is satisfactory.

Estimated total profit means: [Contract price – Costs already incurred + Estimated future costs + Margin for contingencies] (8.9)

In case of non-availability of information about work certified, profit

$$= \text{Estimated total profit} \times \frac{\text{Cost of work to date}}{\text{Estimated total cost}} \quad (8.10)$$

Exhibit 8.3 provides the format of contract account, Exhibit 8.4 presents information in the balance sheet and Exhibit 8.5 contractee account.

EXHIBIT 8.3 *Proforma Contract Account*

(When the Work is in Process)	
To materials (direct)	By materials returned to store
To materials (ex-store)	By materials transferred to contract site
To wages and salaries	(specify number)
To sub-contract payments	By materials sold
To other direct expenses	By abnormal loss
To plant (purchased)	By closing stock of materials
To profit and loss A/c (transfer part of	By closing value of plant
realised profits)	By work-in-progress
To reserve for future contingencies	Certified
	Uncertified
(When the Work is Completed)	
To work-in-progress (opening)	By reserve for future contingencies
Work certified	By materials returned
Work uncertified	By plant returned
To plant	By any other item to be credited
Opening balance	By contractee (with the contract price)
Purchase	
To other items of expenses	
To profit and loss A/c (profit)	

EXHIBIT 8.4 *Skeleton Balance Sheet*

Liabilities	*Assets*
Profit and loss A/c [will include profit on contract)	Work-in-progress
(specify the contract number)]	Work certified
Less loss on contract (specify the contract number)	Work uncertified

(*Contd.*)

Sundry creditors	Less reserve for contigencies
Wages accrued	Less contractee (payment received)
Direct expenses accrued	Materials in hand
Any other expenses(specify)	Materials at site

EXHIBIT 8.5 *Contract A/c*

To balance c/d	By bank (amount received)
	By balance b/d

Cost Plus Contracts

Cost plus contracts are the contracts in which the contractor is reimbursed not only the costs incurred by him in executing the contract, but also, remunerated a stipulated profit for rendering his services. The stipulated profit may either be a fixed amount decided in advance or determined subsequently with reference to certain percentage of costs to be incurred by him. The latter approach is more commonly employed as such contacts are generally undertaken when the cost of a contract cannot be computed with a reasonable degree of accuracy at the time of undertaking the job. A few examples of such contracts are construction of a newly designed building, aircraft, ship, machine; or any urgent construction work; or work which is spread over a long period of time during which the expected prices of basic inputs are liable to fluctuate, that is, contracts which require a significant part of materials to be imported from other countries at foreign exchange rates likely to be subject to considerable fluctuations.

Cost plus contracts are useful from both the points of view of the contractor/manufacturer and contractee/customer. The manufacturer is assured of recovering all his costs and is, therefore, protected against possible losses which may arise due to upward revision of material prices, wages and other items of cost. In other words, there is a built-in *escalation clause* to protect his interests in such contracts. They are equally beneficial to the clients, especially those who are particular about the quality of work and cost is relatively of less concern for them. However, such contracts are not without drawbacks. For instance, there is no incentive for the contractor to economize specially in terms of the costs incurred. For a reduction in costs implies less remuneration for him, if his share is based on the percentage of costs, which is most likely in such contracts.

To overcome these problems, the following principles may be followed:

1. Certain broad limits regarding the type of materials to be used and the prices to be paid for them should be agreed upon in advance.
2. Likewise, rates of allowable wastage and spoilage should also be agreed upon at the time of undertaking the contract. By such agreements, the client will not be penalised for inefficiencies of the contractor in terms of abnormal wastage, high costs of material and so on.
3. Again, the broad limits of the category of labour force and the rate which is payable for each category should be laid down specifically in advance. As far as possible, the agreement should provide that overtime payments will normally not be allowed without the sanction and approval of the contractee.
4. After completion of the contract, the mode of valuation of the plant, which had been specially purchased for the contract, should be decided in advance. Likewise, depreciation rates of existing plants should be predetermined. The basis of overhead charges should also be outlined to avoid controversy later on.

In a nutshell, there is an obvious need for establishing clear-cut parameters for every probable item of cost as part of the agreement between the contractor and the contractee at the contract initiation stage. Above all, the agreement should provide for a fair return to the contractor so that his interest and motivation in the contract are sustained.

SUMMARY

- In this chapter we have discussed the determination of cost of a job defined as the work done in pursuance of an order from a customer for the supply of a specific type of product to suit his needs.
- The job costing system is applicable in the case of a single item or batch. It is also applicable both to manufacturing and service activities.
- The procedure of determining cost according to this method is to trace/attach costs of the specific job by means of a cost sheet set up for each job. Direct materials and direct labour costs are traced directly to the specific jobs; indirect manufacturing costs are applied to jobs by means of a predetermined overhead application rate.
- At the end of the accounting period, there will be an over or under-applied overhead balance. If this balance is insignificant in nature, it is usually closed to the cost of goods sold, but significant amounts may need to be *pro-rated* to appropriate accounts, that is, work-in-process, finished goods and cost of goods sold.
- The procedure of recording cost depends on whether a firm maintains only a general ledger or whether it records transactions in a general as well as a factory ledger.
- A variant of job costing is contract costing. The cost accumulation in this system of costing is done through a contract account. The difference between the contract price and various direct and indirect costs incurred in completing the contract is the profit or loss.
- Although the profit on a contract can be known only when the contract is fully complete, conventionally, profits are estimated for intervening years also for contracts which extend beyond one year.
- The variables having a bearing on the determination of profits on incomplete contracts are: (i) The extent of completion of the work; (ii) The extent of work certified by the architect of the contractee; and (iii) Cash received from the contractee. The difference between the profit estimated and transferred represents reserve for future contingencies.

REFERENCES

1. Morse, W.J., *Cost Accounting*, (Addison-Wesley Publishing Co., Massachusetts), 1978, p. 55.
2. Chatfield, M. and Weilson, D., *Cost Accounting*, (Harcourt Brance Joyanvich, New York), 1983, p. 115.
3. Moriarity, S. and Allen, C.P. *Cost Accounting*, (Harper and Row Publishers, New York), p. 516.
4. Morse, W.J., *op. cit.*, p. 58.
5. *Ibid.*, p. 66.

SOLVED PROBLEMS

P. 8.1 The normal expenses attributable to machine No. III and the normal hours for which the machine is expected to be utilized in the current year are indicated below:

Fixed		₹20,000
Variable:		
Power	₹15,000	
Repairs	9,000	
Lubricants	6,000	30,000
		50,000

Predetermined normal hours of working:	
To make ready	200
Running on jobs	800
Total	1,000

From the data furnished below, compute the cost of job No. 8237:

Materials consumed (10 units of ₹50 per unit)	₹500
Direct labour cost:	
To make ready: 2 machine-hours at ₹10	20
Running on job: 8 machine-hours at ₹10	80
	600

Note: Whenever a job is to be put on the machine, the machine is cleaned, any tools or jigs already on the machine are removed, and new tools and so on. suitable for the particular job are fitted before commissioning the machine for the job and the time involved is to be charged to the job as 'Make ready' time.

Solution

Job Cost Sheet

Customer name	Job No. 8237................................
Description and quantity	Date started................................
Special remarks	Date promised ....
(Machine III is used on job)........................	Date finished................................

Particulars	*Rate*	*Hours/units*	*Amount*
Materials (Requisition No....)	₹50	10	₹500
Wages: (To make ready)	10	2	20
(Running on job)	10	8	80
Prime cost			600
Factory overheads:			
To make ready	20	2	40
Running on job (see working note)	57.50	8	460
Cost of production			1,100

Working Notes

Determination of factory overheads: Total normal machine-hours are 1,000; of which setting-up time (to make ready) is 200 hours. Fixed expenses will be pro-rated on the basis of 1,000 hours and variable expenses on the basis of 800 hours the machine worked. The rates, so determined would be:

Fixed overhead rate to make ready (₹20,000, total expenses ÷ 1,000)	₹20.00
Variable (₹30,000, total expenses ÷ 800)	37.50
Overhead rate to make ready	20.00
Overhead rate for running time would be the sum of the two rates, (₹20 + ₹37.50)	57.50

P. 8.2 A shop-floor supervisor of a small factory presents the following per unit cost for Job No. 421 to determine the selling price:

Materials	₹70
Direct wages (1.8 hours @ ₹25) (Department X, 0.8 hour; Department Y, 0.6 hour; Department Z, 0.4 hour)	45
Chargeable expenses (special stores items)	5
Prime cost	120
Add 33.33 per cent for expenses	40
Total	160

Analysis of the profit and loss A/c for the current quarter shows the following:

Materials used		₹1,50,000	Sales less returns	₹2,50,000
Direct wages:				
Department X	₹10,000			
Department Y	12,000			
Department Z	8,000	30,000		

(*Contd.*)

(Contd.)

Special stores items		4,000		
Overheads:				
Department X	5,000			
Department Y	9,000			
Department Z	2,000	16,000		
Gross profit c/d		50,000		
		2,50,000		2,50,000
Selling expenses		20,000	Gross profits b/d	50,000
Net profit		30,000		
		50,000		50,000

It is also noted that average hourly wage rates for the 3 departments, X, Y, and Z are similar. Direct labour-hour method is followed to absorb overheads.

You are required to: **(i)** Draw up a job cost sheet; **(ii)** Calculate revised cost for the current year, using actual figures as basis; and **(iii)** Add 20 per cent to total costs to determine selling price.

Solution

Job Cost Sheet

Customer name .... Job No. 421

Description and quantity .... Date started..

Special remarks .... Date promised

Date finished ....

Particulars	*Rate*	*Hours/quantity*	*Amount*
Materials used			₹70.00
Direct wages:			
Department X	₹25	0.8	20.00
Department Y	25	0.6	15.00
Department Z	25	0.4	10.00
Direct expenses			5.00
Prime cost			120.00
Indirect overheads: (see working note)			
Department X	12.50	0.8	10.00
Department Y	18.75	0.6	11.25
Department Z	6.25	0.4	2.50
Cost of production (total cost)			143.75
Add 20 per cent profit margin on cost			28.75
Selling price			172.50

Working Notes

Determination of Overhead Rate

Department	*Overheads*	*Direct labour-hours (Total wages ÷ hourly rates)*	*Rate per hour*
X	₹5,000	400	₹12.50
Y	9,000	480	18.75
Z	2,000	320	6.25

P. 8.3 The Rathi Engineering Company Ltd manufactures special-purpose small machines to order. In the beginning of the year, there were two jobs in process, namely, Job No. 100 and Job No. 101. The following costs were applied to these jobs in the previous year:

	Job 100	Job 101
Direct materials	₹25,000	₹40,000
Direct labour	20,000	15,000
Overheads	22,200	16,650
	67,200	71,650

During January of the current year, the following transactions took place:

1. Raw materials costing ₹2,00,000 were purchased on account.
2. Supplies costing ₹40,000 were purchased for cash.
3. Jobs 102, 103 and 104 were started and the following costs applied to them:

	Job 102	Job 103	Job 104
Direct materials	₹15,000	₹50,000	₹35,000
Direct labour	25,000	30,000	20,000

4. Jobs 100 and 101 were completed; additional direct labour costs incurred on them were ₹10,000 and ₹20,000 respectively.
5. Wages paid to production employees during January totalled ₹1,25,000, of which accrued wages of the previous year were ₹25,000; wages payable at the end of the current month were ₹20,000.
6. Depreciation for the month totalled ₹50,000.
7. Utilities bills totalling ₹60,000 were received for the January operations.
8. Supplies costing ₹10,000 were used.
9. Miscellaneous overhead expenses totalled ₹12,000 for January.

Actual overhead is applied for individual jobs at the end of each month using a rate based on actual direct-labour costs. You are required to

(a) Determine the overhead rate for the month of January.
(b) Pass the necessary journal entries for each of the transactions that book place during January.
(c) Specify all subsidiary records affected by each transaction.
(d) Determine the amount of profit earned on Jobs 100 and 101, assuming job prices of ₹1,10,000 and ₹1,70,000 respectively.
(e) Prepare a statement of cost of goods manufactured.

SOLUTION

(a) *Determination of Overhead Rate (January)*

Indirect labour:			
Wages paid		₹1,25,000	
Less wages outstanding of previous year		(25,000)	
Add wages outstanding of current month		20,000	
		1,20,000	
Less direct labour			
Job 100	₹10,000		
101	20,000		
102	25,000		
103	30,000		
104	20,000	(1,05,000)	₹15,000
Depreciation			50,000
Utilities			60,000
Supplies			10,000
Miscellaneous overhead			12,000
Total overheads			1,47,000
Actual direct labour cost			1,05,000
Overhead rate (₹1,47,000 ÷ ₹1,05,000) × 100 (per cent)			140

(b) *and* **(c)** *Subsidiary Records Affected by the Transactions are shown along with Journal Entry.*

Particulars		*Dr Amount*	*Cr Amount*
Stores control A/c	Dr	₹2,00,000	
To accounts payable			₹2,00,000
(Inventory ledger cards, payable ledger)			
Supplies inventory A/c	Dr	40,000	
To bank			40,000
(Supplies inventory may have separate records and accordingly subsidiary ledgers would be affected)			
Work-in-process A/c	Dr	1,00,000	
To stores control			1,00,000
(Job cost sheets and inventory ledger cards)			
Factory overhead control A/c (individual labour)	Dr	15,000	
Work-in-process	Dr	1,05,000	
To wages payable			1,20,000
(Overhead ledger cards, job cost sheets and payable ledger)			
Wages payable A/c	Dr	1,25,000	
To bank/cash			
(Payables ledger)			1,25,000
Factory overhead control A/c	Dr	1,32,000	
To accumulated depreciation			50,000
To accounts payable (utilities)			60,000
To supplies inventory			10,000
To sundry accounts			12,000
(overheads ledger *cards payables ledger and fixed assets ledger)*			
Accounts payable (utilities)	Dr	50,000	
To bank/cash			50,000
(Accounts payable ledger)			
Work-in-process A/c	Dr	1,47,000	
To factory overhead control			1,47,000
(Job cost sheets and overhead ledger cards)			
Finished stock inventory	Dr	2,10,850	
To work-in-process			2,10,850

(d) *Job Cost Sheet (for jobs 100 and 101)*

Particulars	*Job 100*	*Job 101*
Opening work-in-process		
Direct materials	₹25,000	₹40,000
Direct labour	20,000	15,000
Overhead	22,200	16,650
	67,200	71,650
Add current month cost		
Direct labour	10,000	20,000
Overhead (140 per cent)	14,000	28,000
Total cost	91,200	1,19,650
Profit (balancing figure)	18,800	50,350
Job prices	1,10,000	1,70,000

(e) *Statement of Cost of Goods Manufactured for the month of January*

Particulars		*Amount*
Direct materials		₹1,00,000
Direct labour		1,05,000
Prime cost		2,05,000
Add factory overheads		
Indirect labour	₹15,000	
Depreciation	50,000	
Utilities	60,000	
Supplies	10,000	
Miscellaneous overheads	12,000	1,47,000
Gross factory cost		3,52,000
Add work-in-process (opening)		
Job 100	67,200	
Job 101	71,650	1,38,850
Less closing work-in-process		
Job 102 (₹15,000 + ₹25,000 + ₹35,000)	75,000	
Job 103 (₹50,000 + ₹30,000 + ₹42,000)	1,22,000	
Job 104 (₹35,000 + ₹20,000 + ₹28,000)	83,000	(2,80,000)
Cost of goods manufactured		2,10,850

P.8.4 The Philips Company Ltd produces gramophone records and has several different recording companies as clients. Since each order is separately identifiable, a job order accounting system is in use. Two departments are utilized, and the following overhead budget data at normal activity are available for the whole current year as well as the actual overhead cost for the first month (January):

Particulars	*Overhead budget for the current year at normal level of activity*	*Actual overheads(January)*
Department X		
Fixed	₹7,20,000	₹66,000
Variable	6,00,000	63,000
Department Y		
Fixed	10,80,000	87,000
Variable	9,00,000	51,000

During January, 2 jobs were in production (209 and 210). The following is a summary of some of the data from their respective job cost sheets.

Items	*Job 209*		*Job 210*	
	Departments		*Departments*	
	X	Y	X	Y
Direct labour	₹1,08,000	₹15,000	₹36,000	₹42,000
Direct labour-hours	24,000	3,000	6,000	9,000
Machine-hours	4,800	24,000	3,000	12,000

The estimates of the departments' direct-labour cost, direct labour-hours, and machine-hours at normal activity are also provided in the following table, along with a set of correlation coefficients between overheads and the various measure of activity that have been compiled from past production and cost data.

	Department X		Department Y	
	Normal level of activity	Correlation co-efficient with overheads	Normal level of activity	Correlation co-efficient with overheads
Direct labour cost	₹15,00,000	0.8	₹7,20,000	0.6
Direct labour-hours	30,000	0.9	15,000	0.8
Machine-hours	9,000	0.5	6,000	0.9

During January, the company received an invitation from a regular customer to bid on a job which, if won, would be executed in February. The job was estimated to require ₹1,50,000 of materials and to involve:

	Department X	Department Y
Direct labour cost	₹75,000	₹33,000
Direct labour-hours	1,500	600
Machine-hours	300	210

How much overhead would you include in the bid? Estimate the bid price, the company should quote, assuming the company's normal practice of charging 20 per cent on cost price as profit.

Solution

Job Cost Sheet to Determine the Tender Price

Particulars	Amount		Amount
Direct materials			₹1,50,000
Direct labour cost:			
Department X	₹75,000		
Department Y	33,000		1,08,000
Prime cost			2,58,000
Add overhead costs			
Department X:			
Fixed (1,500 × ₹24)	36,000		
Variable (1,500 × ₹20)	30,000	₹66,000	
Department Y:			
Fixed (210 × ₹180)	37,800		
Variable (210 × ₹150)	31,500	69,300	1,35,300
Factory cost			3,93,300
Add estimated profit @ 20 per cent on cost			78,660
Bid price			4,71,960

Working Notes

Determination of overhead rates:

Department X [Direct labour hours (DLH) has been taken as basis. The reason is there is the highest correlation between DLH and overhead incurred]

Fixed = ₹7,20,000 ÷ 30,000 DLH = ₹24

Variable = ₹6,00,000 ÷ 30,000 DLH = ₹20

Department Y [Machine-hour rate (MHR) has been taken as the basis. The reason there exists the highest correlation between MHR and overhead]:

Fixed = ₹10,80,000 ÷ 6,000 = ₹180

Variable = ₹9,00,000 ÷ 6,000 = ₹150

P.8.5 A jobbing factory has undertaken to supply 200 pieces of a component per month for the ensuing 6 months. Every month a batch order is opened against which materials and labour-hours are booked at actuals; overheads are levied at a per/labour hour rate. The selling price contracted for is ₹8 per piece. From the following data, present the cost and profit per piece of each batch order and overall position of the order for 1,200 pieces:

Months	Batch output	Material cost	Direct wages	Direct labour-hours
January	210	₹650	₹120	24
February	200	640	140	28
March	220	680	150	28
April	180	630	140	27
May	200	700	150	30
June	220	720	160	32

The other details are:

Month	Chargeable expenses	Direct labour-hours
January	₹12,000	480
February	10,560	440
March	12,000	500
April	10,580	460
May	13,000	500
June	12,000	480

Solution

Batch Cost Sheet for six months (January to June)

Month	Material	Cost of production			Batch output (units)	Cost per unit (5 × 6)	Selling price per unit	Profit (loss) per unit
		Direct wages	Overheads*	Total				
(1)	(2)	(3)	(4)	(5)	(6)	(7)	(8)	(9)
January	₹650	₹120	₹600	₹1,370	₹210	₹6.52	₹8	₹1.48
February	640	140	672	1,452	200	7.26	8	0.74
March	680	150	672	1,502	220	6.83	8	1.17
April	630	140	621	1,391	180	7.73	8	0.27
May	700	150	780	1,630	200	8.15	8	(0.15)
June	720	160	800	1,680	220	7.64	8	0.36
	4,020	860	4,145	9,025	1,230			

*Overheads = (Direct labour-hours × Labour-hour rate)

Labour-hour rate = (Chargeable expenses ÷ Direct labour-hours)

Overall position of the order of 1,200 units

Sale revenue (1,200 × ₹8)	₹9,600
Less cost of production (₹9,025/1,230) × 1,200	8,805
Profit	795

P.8.6 You are required to prepare a cost-sheet of an engineering work showing the actual and estimated cost of a batch of 100 units from the following information:

The batch passes through 3 departments, A, B and C. Materials used for the batch:

Department A—600 units @ ₹10 per unit

Department B—50 units @ ₹20 per unit

Direct labour

Department A—10 hours @ ₹20 per hour

Department B—2 hours @ ₹25 per hour

Department C—10 hours @ ₹15 per hour

Factory overhead

Department A—150 per cent on direct wages

Department B—₹10 per labour hour

Department C—66.67 per cent on direct wages.

After the batch is complete, 100 units of raw materials issued to department A are found to be surplus and are returned to stores.

A comparison of the actual costs with the estimated costs of the direct materials and the factory overhead has shown that the actual costs exceed the respective estimated costs by 20 per cent, whereas the actual labour costs is 25 per cent lower than the estimated costs.

You are required to show in the cost sheet, the costs of the batch and the difference between the estimated costs and the actual costs. Show detailed workings separately.

SOLUTION

Batch Cost Sheet (100 units)

Special remarks .... Batch no. ....

Date started. .... Date finished ....

Particulars			Cost		
			Actual	Estimated	Adverse (A) Favourable (F)
Materials: (Requisition no....)					
Department A (600 units × ₹10)		₹6,000			
Less returns (100 units × ₹10)		1,000	₹5,000	₹4,167	₹833A
Department B (50 units × ₹20)			1,000	833	167A
Direct labour:					
Department	A (10 hours × ₹20)		200	250	50F
	B (2 hours × ₹25)		50	62	12F
	C (10 hours × ₹15)		150	188	38F
Factory overhead:					
Department	A (200 × ₹150%)		300	250	50A
	B (20 × ₹10)		200	167	33A
	C (150 × ₹66.67%)		100	83	17A
Total			7,000	6,000	1,000A

Summary of Variances: Department-wise

Particulars		Actual	Estimated	Variance
Department A:	Materials	₹5,000	₹4,167	₹833A
	Labour	200	250	50F
	Overheads	300	250	50A
Total		5,500	4,667	833A
Department B:	Materials	1,000	833	167A
	Labour	50	62	12F
	Overheads	200	167	33A
Total		1,250	1,062	188A
Department C:	Materials	150	188	38F
	Labour	100	83	17A
Total		250	271	21F

P.8.7 The following is the trial balance of Premier Construction Company Ltd engaged in the execution of Contract 747 for the year ending March 31 of the current year:

Particulars	Dr Amount	Cr Amount
Amount received (contractor's account)		₹30,00,000
Buildings	₹16,00,000	
Creditors		7,20,000
Bank balance	3,50,000	
Capital account		50,00,000

(Contd.)

(*Contd.*)

Materials	20,00,000	
Wages	18,00,000	
Expenses	4,70,000	
Plant	25,00,000	
Total	87,20,000	87,20,000

The work on Contract 747 had commenced on April 1 of the current year. Materials costing ₹17,00,000 were sent to the site of the contract but those costing ₹60,000 were destroyed in an accident. Wages amounting to ₹18,00,000 were paid during the year. Plant costing ₹5,00,000 was used on the contract all through the year. Plant with a cost of ₹20,00,000 was used from April 1 to December 31 and was then returned to the stores. Materials of the cost of ₹40,000 were at site on March 31.

The contract was for ₹60,00,000 and the work certified was 80 per cent of the total contract work at the end of the year. Uncertified work was estimated at ₹1,50,000 on March 31. Expenses are charged to contract at 25 per cent of wages. Plant is to be depreciated at 10 per cent for the entire year.

Prepare Contract 747 account for the current year ending March 31 and make out the balance sheet as on that date in the books of Premier Construction Company Ltd. Also prepare contractee's account.

SOLUTION

Contract A/c (747) for the Year Ending March 31

Particulars	*Dr Amount*	*Particulars*	*Cr Amount*
To materials	₹17,00,000	By profit and loss A/c (abnormal loss due to materials destroyed in an accident)	₹60,000
To wages	18,00,000	By plant at site (₹5,00,000 – ₹50,000, depreciation @ 10 per cent for the full year)	4,50,000
To plant (₹5,00,000 + ₹20,00,000)	25,00,000	By plant returned to store (₹20,00,000 – ₹1,50,000, depreciation @ 10 per cent for 9 months)	18,50,000
To expenses allocated to contract (0.25 × ₹18,00,000)	4,50,000	By materials at site	40,000
To profit c/d	9,00,000	By *work-in-process:*	
		Work certified (0.80 × ₹60,00,000)	48,00,000
		Work uncertified	1,50,000
	73,50,000		73,50,000
To profit and loss A/c[1]	3,75,000	By profit b/d	9,00,000
To reserve for unforeseen contingencies[2]	5,25,000		
	9,00,000		9,00,000

[1]Determination of profit (to be transferred to profit and loss account)

$$\text{Estimated profit} \times \frac{2}{3} \times \frac{\text{Cash received}}{\text{Work certified}}$$

$$\text{or } ₹9{,}00{,}000 \times \frac{2}{3} \times \frac{₹30{,}00{,}000}{₹48{,}00{,}000} = ₹3{,}75{,}000$$

[2]Reserve for unforeseen contingencies = ₹9,00,000 – ₹3,75,000 = ₹5,25,000

General Profit and Loss Account

To abnormal loss	₹60,000	By contract A/c (747)	₹3,75,000
To absorbed expenses (₹4,70,000 – ₹4,50,000)	20,000		
To depreciation on plant (₹20,00,000 for 3 months @ 10 per cent)	50,000		
To net profit	2,45,000		
	3,75,000		3,75,000

Contractee's Account

To balance c/d	₹30,00,000	By bank	₹30,00,000
		By balance b/d	30,00,000

Balance Sheet as on March 31

Liabilities	*Amount*	*Assets*		*Amount*
Capital	₹50,00,000	Buildings		₹16,00,000
Profit and loss A/c	2,45,000	Plant in store		
Creditors	7,20,000	(₹20,00,000 – ₹2,00,000)		18,00,000
		Plant at site (₹5,00,000 – ₹50,000)		4,50,000
		Materials in store		
		(₹20,00,000 – ₹17,00,000)		3,00,000
		Materials at site		40,000
		Work-in-process:		
		Work certified	₹48,00,000	
		Work uncertified	1,50,000	
		Less reserve for unforeseen contingencies	(5,25,000)	
		Less cash received from contractee	(30,00,000)	14,25,000
		Bank balance		3,50,000
	59,65,000			59,65,000

P. 8.8 The following information relates to a building contract for ₹30,00,000.

Particulars	*Year 1*	*Year 2*
Materials issued	₹9,00,000	₹2,52,000
Direct wages	6,90,000	3,15,000
Direct expenses	66,000	30,000
Indirect expenses	18,000	4,200
Work certified	22,50,000	30,00,000
Work uncertified	24,000	–
Materials at site	15,000	21,000
Plant issued	42,000	6,000
Cash received from contractee	18,00,000	30,00,000

The value of the plant at the end of years 1 and 2 was ₹21,000 and ₹15,000 respectively. Prepare: (i) The contract account; (ii) The contractee account; and (iii) Show how the various relevant figures would appear in the assets side of the balance sheet.

SOLUTION

Contract A/c for the End of Year 1

Particulars	Dr Amount	Particulars	Cr Amount
To materials	₹9,00,000	By materials at site	₹15,000
To direct wages	6,90,000	By plant at site	21,000
To direct expenses	66,000	By work-in-progress:	
To indirect expenses	18,000	Work certified	22,50,000
To plant	42,000	Work uncertified	24,000
To profit c/d	5,94,000		
	23,10,000		23,10,000
To profit and loss account (₹5,94,000 × 2/3 × ₹18,00,000) ÷ ₹22,50,000	3,16,800	By profit b/d	5,94,000
To reserve for unforeseen contingencies	2,77,200		
	5,94,000		5,94,000

Contract Account for the End of Year 2

Particulars	Dr Amount	Particulars	Cr Amount
To work-in-progress b/d	₹22,74,000	By reserve for unforeseen contingencies	₹2,77,200
To materials at site	15,000	By materials at site	21,000
To plant at site	21,000	By plant at site	15,000
To materials	2,52,000	By contractee's A/c	30,00,000
To direct wages	3,15,000		
To direct expenses	30,000		
To indirect expenses	4,200		
To plant issued	6,000		
To profit and loss A/c	3,96,000		
	33,13,200		33,13,200

Contractee's Account

Year end 1	To balance c/d	18,00,000	Year end 1	By bank	18,00,000
		18,00,000			18,00,000
Year end 2	To contract A/c	30,00,000	Beginning year 2	By balance b/d	18,00,000
			Year end 2	By bank (balance received)	12,00,000
		30,00,000			30,00,000

Balance Sheet (skeleton) as at the End of Year 1

Liabilities	Amount	Assets		Amount
		Materials at site		₹15,000
		Plant at site		21,000
		Work-in-process:		
		Work certified	₹22,50,000	
		Work uncertified	24,000	
		Less reserve for unforeseen contingencies	(2,77,200)	
		Less cash received	(18,00,000)	1,96,800

Balance Sheet as at the End of Year 2

	Materials at site	₹21,000
	Plant at site	15,000

P.8.9 As on March 31, of the current year, ₹4,89,000 has been expended upon a contract and certificates of value of work certified have been received to date of the value of ₹6,00,000. The cost of work uncertified on the date was estimated at ₹15,000. Upto the end of the previous year, profit of ₹30,000 had been taken on the contract. It is estimated that the contract will take a further 4 months to complete and that it will necessitate an additional expenditure of ₹1,00,000. The total estimated expenditure upon the contract is to include a provision of 5 per cent for contingencies. The contract price is ₹7,20,000 and ₹5,40,000 has been received in cash to date. Determine the amount of profit to be credited to profit and loss account.

SOLUTION

Computation of Profit

Particulars	*Amount*
Total expenditure upto March 31	₹4,89,000
Add additional estimated expenditure	1,00,000
	5,89,000
Add provision for contingencies (5 per cent on total estimated expenditure $\frac{5}{95}$ × ₹5,89,000)	31,000
Total estimated expenditure on contract	6,20,000
Contract price	7,20,000
Estimated total profit (₹7,20,000 – ₹6,20,000)	1,00,000
Cumulative profit to be taken to profit and loss account $\left(₹1{,}00{,}000 \times \frac{₹6{,}00{,}000}{₹7{,}20{,}000} \times \frac{₹5{,}40{,}000}{₹6{,}00{,}000}\right)$	75,000
Less already credited to the profit and loss account of the previous year	30,000
Profit to be credited to current year profit and loss account	45,000

P.8.10 A contractor enters into a contract to construct a building for ₹8,00,000. Work began in April of the current year and it is estimated that the contract will take 16 months to complete. Work is proceeding on schedule and the costs charged to the contract at the end of the current year are as follows:

Materials used	₹2,00,000
Materials returned	10,000
Wages	2,60,000
Plant hire and other expenses	65,000
Establishment charges	50,000

Additional information

Materials at site	₹ 5,000
Work certified upto date	6,50,000
Cash received on account	6,00,000
Work not certified	15,000

It is estimated that the following further expenditure will be incurred to complete the work:

Materials	₹15,000
Labour	20,000
Sub-contractors	50,000
Plant hire and other expenses	15,000
Establishment charges	10,000

Prepare the contract account indicating the amount to be credited to the profit and loss account of the current year, assuming provision for contingencies amounting to 5 per cent of the total cost is to be made and the contractor's cash position is satisfactory.

SOLUTION

Contract Account for the Year Ending March 31

Particulars	Dr Amount	Particulars	Cr Amount
To materials	₹2,00,000	By materials returned	₹10,000
To wages	2,60,000	By materials at site	5,000
To plant hire and other expenses	65,000	By *work-in-process:*	
To establishment expenses	50,000	Work certified	6,50,000
To profit c/d	1,05,000	Work uncertified	15,000
	6,80,000		6,80,000
To profit and loss account	72,698	By profit b/d	1,05,000
To reserve for contingencies	32,302		
	1,05,000		1,05,000

Computation of Estimated Profit

Expenditure upto March 31			₹5,60,000
Add estimated expenditure to complete the contract:			
Materials at site	₹5,000		
Add required	15,000	₹20,000	
Labour		20,000	
Sub-contractors		50,000	
Plant hire and other expenses		15,000	
Establishment charges		10,000	1,15,000
			6,75,000
Add provision for contingencies (5 × ₹6,75,000) ÷ 95			35,526
Total estimated cost			7,10,526
Contract price			8,00,000
Estimated profit			89,474

Proportion of profit to be carried to current year profit and loss account = (₹89,474 × ₹6,50,000) ÷ ₹8,00,000 = ₹72,698

P.8.11 Kapoor Engineering Company Ltd undertakes a long-term contract which involves the fabrication of pre-stressed concrete blocks and the erection of the same on consumer's site.

The following information is supplied regarding the contract which is incomplete on March 31 of the current year:

Fabrication costs to date:	
Direct materials	₹2,80,000
Direct Labour	90,000
Overheads	75,000
	4,45,000

(*Contd.*)

(*Contd.*)

Erection costs to date		15,000
Total cost incurred		4,60,000
Contract price		8,19,000
Cash received on account		6,00,000
Technical estimate of work completed to date:		
Fabrication		
Direct price	80 per cent	
Direct labour and overheads	75 per cent	
Erection	25 per cent	

You are required to prepare a statement for submission to the management indicating:

1. The estimated profit on the completion of the contract, and
2. The estimated profit-to-date on the contract.

SOLUTION

1. *Statement Showing Estimated Profit to be Carried to Profit and Loss Account for the Current Year Ended March 31*

Expenditure upto March 31:		
Direct materials	₹2,80,000	
Direct labour	90,000	
Overheads	75,000	
Erection costs to date	15,000	₹4,60,000
Add estimated expenditure to complete the contract::		
Direct materials (₹2,80,000 × 20) ÷ 80	70,000	
Direct labour and overheads (₹1,65,000 × 25) ÷ 75	55,000	
Erection cost (₹15,000 × 75) ÷ 25	45,000	1,70,000
Total estimated cost		6,30,000
Contract price		8,19,000
Estimated profit		1,89,000

2. Proportion of profit to be carried to current year's profit and loss account:

$$\text{Estimated total profit} \times \frac{\text{Cost of work to date}}{\text{Estimated total cost}} = ₹1,89,000 \times \left(\frac{₹4,60,000}{₹6,30,000}\right) = ₹1,38,000$$

P.8.12 M/s Bhagwandas Associates undertook a contract for ₹15,00,000 on an arrangement that 80 per cent of the value of the work done, as certified by the architect of the contractee, should be paid for immediately and that the remaining 20 per cent be retained until the contract was completed.

In year 1, the amounts expended were: Materials, ₹1,80,000; Wages, ₹1,70,000; Carriage, ₹6,000; Cartage, ₹1,000; Sundry expenses, ₹3,000. The work was certified for ₹3,75,000 and 80 per cent of this was paid as agreed.

In year 2, the amounts expended were: Materials, ₹2,20,000; Wages, ₹2,30,000; Carriage, ₹23,000; Cartage, ₹2,000; Sundry expenses, ₹4,000. Three-fourths of the contract was certified as done by March 31, and 80 per cent of this was received accordingly. The value of unused stock and work-in-process uncertified was ascertained at ₹20,000.

In year 3, the amounts expended were: Materials, ₹1,26,000; Wages, ₹1,70,000; Cartage, ₹6,000; Sundry expenses, ₹3,000 and on September 30, the whole contract was completed. Show how the contract account and also the contractee's account would appear in each of these years in the books of the contactor, assuming that the balance due to him was paid on completion of the contract.

SOLUTION

Contract Account for the Year Ending 1

Particulars	Dr Amount	Particulars	Cr Amount
To materials	₹1,80,000	By work-in-process	
To wages	1,70,000	Work certified	₹3,75,000
To carriage	6,000		
To cartage	1,000		
To sundry expenses	3,000		
To profit c/d	15,000		
	3,75,000		3,75,000
To profit and loss account (₹15,000 × 1/3 × 80/100)	4,000	By profit b/d	15,000
To reserve for unforeseen contingencies	11,000		
	15,000		15,000

Contract Account for the Year Ending 2

Particulars	Dr Amount	Particulars	Cr Amount
To work-in-process	₹3,75,000	By reserve for unforeseen contingencies	₹11,000
To materials	2,20,000	By *work-in-process:*	
To carriage	23,000	Work certified	
To wage	2,30,000	($^3/_4$ × ₹15,00,000)	11,25,000
To cartage	2,000	Work uncertified	20,000
To sundry expenses	4,000		
To profit c/d	3,02,000		
	11,56,000		11,56,000
To profit and loss A/c (₹3,02,000 × 2/3 × 80/100)	1,61,067	By profit b/d	3,02,000
To reserve for unforeseen contingencies	1,40,933		
	3,02,000		3,02,000

Contract Account for the Year Ending 3

Particulars	Dr Amount	Particulars	Cr Amount
To work-in-process b/d	₹11,45,000	By reserve for unforeseen contingencies	₹1,40,933
To materials	1,26,000	By contractee's A/c	15,00,000
To wages	1,70,000		
To cartage	6,000		
To sundry expenses	3,000		
To profit and loss A/c	1,90,933		
	16,40,933		16,40,933

Contractee's Account

		Amount			Amount
Year end 1	To balance c/d	₹3,00,000	Year end 1	By bank A/c	₹3,00,000
		3,00,000			3,00,000
Year end 2	To balance c/d	9,00,000	Year 2 beginning	By balance c/d	3,00,000
			Year 2 end	By bank	6,00,000
		9,00,000			9,00,000
Year end 3	To contract A/c	15,00,000	Year 3 beginning	By balance b/d	9,00,000
			Year 3 end	By bank (balance received)	6,00,000
		15,00,000			15,00,000

P.8.13 The following particulars are obtained from the books of Vinak Construction Limited as on March 31 of the current year:

Plant and equipment at cost	₹4,90,000
Vehicles at cost	2,00,000

Details of contract which remain uncompleted as on March 31:

Particulars	Contract numbers V. 20	V. 24	V. 25
Estimated final sales value	₹8,00,000	₹5,60,000	₹16,00,000
Estimated final cost	6,40,000	7,00,000	12,00,000
Wages	2,40,000	2,00,000	1,20,000
Materials	1,00,000	1,10,000	44,000
Overheads (excluding depreciation)	1,44,000	1,46,000	58,000
Total costs to date	4,84,000	4,56,000	2,22,000
Value certified by architects	7,20,000	4,20,000	2,40,000
Progress payments received	5,00,000	3,20,000	2,00,000

Depreciation of plant and equipment and vehicles should be charged at 20 per cent to the three contracts in proportion to work certified. You are required to prepare statements to show contract-wise and over-all:

(i) profit/loss to be taken to the profit and loss account for the year ended March 31.
(ii) work-in-process as would appear in the balance sheet as March 31.

SOLUTION

Statement of Profit/loss to be taken to Profit and Loss A/c for the year Ending March 31

	Contract numbers V. 20	V. 24	V. 25	Total
(A) 1. Estimated final contract price	₹8,00,000	₹5,60,000	₹16,00,000	—
2. Work certified by architects	7,20,000	4,20,000	2,40,000	—
3. Percentage of completion [(2) as per cent (1)]	90	75	15	—
(B) 1. Estimated final contract price	8,00,000	5,60,000	16,00,000	—
2. *Less* estimated final costs	6,40,000	7,00,000	12,00,000	—
3. Estimated profit (loss)	1,60,000	(1,40,000)	4,00,000	—
(C) 1. Work certified	7,20,000	4,20,000	2,40,000	13,80,000
2. *Less cost incurred:*				
Wages	2,40,000	2,00,000	1,20,000	5,60,000
Materials	1,00,000	1,10,000	44,000	2,54,000
Overheads (excluding depreciation)	1,44,000	1,46,000	58,000	3,48,000
Depreciation (working note 1)	72,000	42,000	24,000	1,38,000
Notional profit (loss) [(1)-(2)]	1,64,000	(78,000)	(6,000)	80,000
Profit/(loss) to be taken to profit and loss A/c	1,00,000	(1,40,000)@	(6,000)	(46,000)
Reserve for future contingencies	64,000	62,000	—	1,26,000

@₹7,00,000, estimated financial cost – ₹5,60,000, estimated sales value.

Statement of Work-in-process as Would Appear in the Balance Sheet as on March 31

Particulars	*V. 20*	*V. 24*	*V. 25*	*Total*
Work certified	₹7,20,000	₹4,20,000	₹2,40,000	₹13,80,000
Less reserve for future contingenies	64,000	62,000	—	1,26,000
Less payments received	5,00,000	3,20,000	2,00,000	10,20,000
Work-in-process	1,56,000	38,000	40,000	2,34,000

WORKING NOTES

1. Total depreciation [0.20 × (₹4,90,000 + ₹2,00,000)] = ₹1,38,000
   Depreciation is apportioned to three contracts in proportion to work certified: ₹7,20,000; ₹4,20,000; and ₹2,40,000:

   Contract V. 20: $\frac{₹7,20,000}{₹13,80,000} \times ₹1,38,000 = ₹72,000$

   Contract V. 24: $\frac{₹4,20,000}{₹13,80,000} \times ₹1,38,000 = ₹42,000$

   Contract V. 25: $\frac{₹2,40,000}{₹13,80,000} \times ₹1,38,000 = ₹24,000$

2. Profit to be estimated: Estimated total cost $\times \frac{\text{Value of work certified}}{\text{Contract price}} \times \frac{\text{Cash received}}{\text{Work certified}}$

   $₹1,60,000 \times \frac{₹7,20,000}{₹8,00,000} \times \frac{₹5,00,000}{₹7,20,000} = ₹1,00,000$

3. Loss transferred:

Contract	Amount
V. 24	₹1,40,000
V. 25	6,000

P.8.14 Compute a conservative estimate of profit on contract (which has been 80 per cent complete) from the following particulars. Illustrate your methods of computing the profit.

Total expenditure to date	₹1,70,000
Estimated further expenditure to complete the contract (including contingencies)	34,000
Contract price	3,06,000
Work certified	2,00,000
Work not certified	17,000
Cash received	1,63,200

SOLUTION

Methods of computing the conservative estimates of profit (80 per cent contract complete):

(i) (Estimated profit × Work certified) ÷ Contract price =(₹1,02,000 × ₹2,00,000) ÷ ₹3,06,000 = ₹66,667

(ii) (Estimated profit × Work certified × Cash received) ÷ (Contract price × Work certified) = (₹1,02,000 × ₹2,00,000) × ₹1,63,200) ÷ (₹3,06,000 × ₹2,00,000) = ₹54,400

(iii) (Notional profit × Work certified) ÷ Contract price = (₹47,000 × ₹2,00,000)/₹3,06,000 = ₹30,719

(iv) (Notional profit × Cash received × 2/3) ÷ Work certified = (₹47,000 × ₹1,63,200 × 2/3) ÷ ₹2,00,000 = ₹25,568

WORKING NOTES

1. *Notional profit*

Value of work certified		₹2,00,000
Less: cost of work certified (Total expenditure till date – Work not certified) (₹1,70,000 – 17,000)		1,53,000
		47,000

2. *Estimated profit*

Contract price		*3,06,000*
Less total expenditure till date	₹1,70,000	
Estimated further expenditure to complete the contract	34,000	2,04,000
		1,02,000

P.8.15 Deluxe Limited undertook a contract for ₹5,00,000 on July 1, year 1. On June 30, year 2, when accounts were closed, the following details about the contract were gathered:

Materials purchases	₹1,00,000
Wages paid	45,000
General expenses	10,000
Plant purchased	50,000
Materials on hand (June 30, year 2)	25,000
Wages accrued (June 30, year 2)	5,000
Work certified	2,00,000
Cash received	1,50,000
Work uncertified	15,000
Depreciation of plant	5,000

The above contract contained an escalation clause which read as follows:

"In the event of prices of materials and rates of wages increasing by more than 5 per cent, the contract price will be increased accordingly by 25 per cent of the rise in the cost of materials and wages beyond 5 per cent in each case."

It was found that since the date of signing the agreement, the prices of the materials and wage rates increased by 25 per cent. The value of the work certified does not take into account the effect of the above clause.

Prepare the contract account. Workings should form part of the answer.

SOLUTION

Contract Account of Deluxe Ltd. for the Year Ending June 30, Year 2

To materials	₹1,00,000	By work-in progress:	
To wages paid and accrued (₹45,000 + ₹5,000)	50,000	Work certified	₹2,00,000
		Work uncertified	15,000
To general expenses	10,000	By contract escalation[1]	5,000
To depreciation on plant	5,000	By materials in hand	25,000
To profit and loss a/c[2]	20,000		
To work-in-process reserve	60,000		
	2,45,000		2,45,000

WORKING NOTES

(a) *Contract Escalation Charges*

	Total increase		Upto 5 per cent		Beyond 5 per cent
1 Materials	(₹75,000 × 25÷125) =	₹15,000	(₹75,000 × 5 ÷ 125) =	₹3,000	₹12,000
2 Wages	(₹50,000 × 25÷125) =	10,000	(₹50,000 × 5 ÷ 125) =	2,000	8,000
		25,000		5,000	20,000

Therefore, increase in contract price = 0.25 × ₹20,000 = ₹5,000.

(b) Since more than 25 per cent but less than 50 per cent of contract has been completed, one-third of the notional profit as reduced by proportion of cash received is transferred to P&L A/c: Notional profit × 1/3 × Cash received/Work certified = ₹80,000 × 1/3 × (₹1,50,000/₹2,00,000) = ₹20,000

P.8.16 A contractor, who prepares his accounts on March 31 every year, commenced a contract on April 1, of the current year. The costing records concerning the said contract reveal the following information on March 31, of the current year-end:

Materials charged to site	₹2,58,100
Labour engaged	5,60,500
Foremen's salary	79,300

Plants costing ₹2,60,000 had been on site for 146 days. Their working life is estimated at 7 years and their final scrap value at ₹15,000. A supervisor, who is paid ₹4,000 per month, has devoted approximately three-fourths of his time to this contract. The administrative and other expenses amount to ₹1,40,000. Materials in hand at site on March 31, of the current year cost ₹25,400. Some of the material costing ₹4,500 was found unsuitable and was sold for ₹4,000 and a part of the plant costing ₹5,500 (on March 31 of the current year) unsuited to the contract was sold at a profit of ₹1,000.

The contract price was ₹22,00,000 but it was accepted by the contractor for ₹20,00,000. On March 31, of the current year, two-thirds of the contract was completed. Architects certificate had been issued covering 50 per cent of the contract price and ₹7,50,000 so far has been paid on account.

Prepare contract account and state how much profit or loss should have been included in the financial accounts of the current year; workings should be clearly given. Depreciation is charged on time basis.

Also prepare the contractee's account and show how these accounts would appear in the balance sheet as on March 31, of the current year.

SOLUTION

Contract Account from April 1 to March 31, Current Year

To materials	₹2,58,100	By materials at site	₹25,400
To labour costs	5,60,500	By materials sold	4,000
To foremen's salary	79,300	By P/L A/c (loss on sales of materials)	500
To depreciation on plant[1]	14,000	By cost of work done c/d	10,49,000
To supervisor's salary[2]	27,000		
To administrative and other expenses	1,40,000		
	10,78,900		10,78,900
To cost of work done b/d	10,49,000	By work-in-progress	
To profit c/d	2,13,250	Work certified[3]	10,00,000
		Work uncertified[3]	2,62,250
	12,62,250		12,62,250
To profit and loss A/c[4]	1,06,625	By profit b/d	2,13,250
To work-in-progress reserve A/c	1,06,625		
	2,13,250		2,13,250

Contractee's Account

To balance c/d	₹7,50,000	By bank	₹7,50,000

Extracts from Balance Sheet as on March 31, Current Year

Liabilities	*Amount*	*Assets*		*Amount*
Profit and loss A/c[(6)]	₹1,07,125	Plant at site[(5)]		₹2,40,500
		Work-in-progress		
		Work certified	₹10,00,000	

(*Contd.*)

(*Contd.*)

	Work uncertified	2,62,250	
		12,62,250	
	Less reserve	1,06,625	
		11,55,625	
	Less cash received	7,50,000	4,05,625
	Materials at site		25,400

WORKING NOTES

1. Depreciation on plant =(₹2,60,000–₹15,000)÷7 years × (146 days ÷365 days) = ₹14,000
2. *Supervisor's salary:* ₹4,000 × 9 months × 3/4 = ₹27,000
3. Work *certified and work uncertified:* Work certified: 0.50 × ₹20,00,000 = ₹10,00,000. Since the cost of two-third of the contract is ₹10,49,000, the total estimated cost of completed contract is ₹15,73,500 (₹10,49,000 × 3/2). Accordingly, cost apportioned to 50 per cent of contract = ₹7,86,750 (0.50 × ₹15,73,500). Therefore, work uncertified = Total cost incurred till date-Cost apportioned to work certified = ₹10,49,000 – ₹7,86,750 = ₹2,62,250.
4. ₹2,13,250 × 2/3 × ₹7,50,000/₹10,00,000 = ₹1,06,625.
5. *Plant A/c*

To balance b/d	₹2,60,000	By contract a/c (depreciation)	₹14,000
To profit and loss A/c (profit on sale of plant)	1,000	By bank (sale consideration)	6,500
		By balance c/d	2,40,500
	2,61,000		2,61,000

6. *Profit and Loss A/c*

To contract a/c	₹500	By plant a/c	₹1,000
To balance c/d	1,07,125	By contract a/c	1,06,625
	1,07,625		1,07,625

EXERCISES

8.1 Indicate whether the followings statements are 'True' or 'False'.

(i) In job order system of costing, each order is regarded as cost unit from the point of view of cost accumulation.

(ii) Process costing is appropriate when each job (work) is unique and easily identifiable.

(iii) A job cost-sheet is the backbone of job costing.

(iv) A job-cost sheet does not enumerate the appropriate inputs required, say, direct materials, direct labour and overheads.

(v) A job cost sheet does not contain date of starting the work and the delivery date.

(vi) A job-cost sheet does not help out in comparing the actual cost of job with the standard cost already set.

(vii) Under-absorption of overheads implies that overheads charged to various jobs are higher than actual overheads.

(viii) When an organization deals in such products that all the time it gets orders which are totally different from last served ones, the job order costing should not be applied as it may result into biased bidding rates.

(ix) Job costing data may be used for estimating the production cost of specific jobs or job of production.

(x) Manufacturing overheads can be identified with specific jobs.

(xi) Direct materials and direct labour cost are traced to jobs by means of materials requisition forms and job time card.

(xii) In an oil refinery, job costing is more appropriate.
(xiii) Contract costing is appropriate for construction works.
(xiv) In contracting costing, profit is reckoned only on work certified.
(xv) When work certified is 50 per cent or more, two-third of estimated profit is reckoned as profit earned.
(xvi) There is built-in escalation clause in cost plus contracts.
(xvii) Cost plus contracts are not beneficial for contractee/customers.

[Answer: (i) True, **(ii)** False, **(iii)** True, **(iv)** False, **(v)** False, **(vi)** False, **(vii)** False, **(viii)** False, **(ix)** True, **(x)** False, **(xi)** True, **(xii)** False, **(xiii)** True, **(xiv)** True, **(xv)** False, **(xvi)** True, **(xvii)** False]

8.2 What are the characteristics of companies that are likely to be using job order cost system? Specify five concrete situations when use of job order cost system is most appropriate. What is a job-cost sheet?

8.3 Enumerate, in brief, the cost recording procedure in a job-order cost system. Illustrate your answer with examples.

8.4 Why is it difficult to identify manufacturing overheads with products manufactured? Also, state the difference between the manufacturing overheads control account and manufacturing overhead applied account.

8.5 How is job costing in service organisations different from job costing in manufacturing organisations?

8.6 Explain the meaning of batch costing. How does such a costing differ from job costing?

8.7 A firm is engaged in manufacturing jobs of long duration. Examine the detailed procedure suitable for costing purposes.

8.8 Discuss the method of ascertaining profit on the following contracts: (i) When the contract is completed, (ii) When the contract is not complete, and (iii) When the contract is nearing completion.

8.9 Indicate how would you deal with the following items:

1. Plant and machinery purchased and used on contract work.
2. Amounts received from contractee.
3. Materials lying unused at site.

8.10 (i) Discuss the implications of cost-plus contracts from the view point of (a) manufacturer, (b) customer.

(ii) What is the relevance of the escalation clause if provided in a contract?

8.11 A factory engaged in making non-standard products to customers' specifications processes all production through three departments. The cost figures of the factory for the month of September of the current year are furnished as follows:

Nature of expenses	*Total expenses*	*Departments*		
		A	B	C
Direct materials	₹18,600	₹7,500	₹6,400	₹4,700
Labour	15,000	6,000	5,000	4,000
Total overhead expenses	7,500	3,000	2,500	2,000
	41,100	16,500	13,900	10,700

Prepare a simple cost sheet for products X and Y on the basis of data furnished below:

Product	*Cost elements*	*Expenses incurred in department*		
		A	B	C
X	Direct material	₹100	₹200	₹300
	Direct labour	50	60	70
Y	Direct material	50	90	140
	Direct labour	70	60	80

8.12 A Ltd. employs a job-order costing system. The factory expenses incurred in the month of March of the current year (as shown by the factory overhead control account) are as follows:

Cutting shop	₹3,62,500
Assembly shop	47,550
Spraying shop	6,700
Finishing shop	79,000

Overheads have been debited to jobs as follows:

Cutting–₹130 per machine-hour for 2,200 hours.

Assembly–140 per cent of direct labour cost. Direct labour cost is ₹33,000.

Spraying–₹6 per piece for 925 pieces.

Finishing–₹75 per direct labour-hour for 1,100 hours.

All expenses are charged to a factory overhead control account and are transferred from this account at the end of each month to the departmental overhead account.

You are required to (a) record the necessary journal entries for factory overheads incurred and absorbed, and (b) state the amount of over- or under-absorption of overheads in each department. Assume that the company maintains both factory ledger and general ledger.

8.13 A small factory can produce 60,000 units per annum at its optimum capacity. The estimated unit costs of production are as under:

Direct material	₹3
Direct labour	2
Indirect expenses	
Fixed (per annum)	1,57,000
Variable (per unit)	5
Semi-variable per annum up to 50 per cent capacity and an extra ₹10,000 for every 25 per cent increase in capacity or part thereof.	50,000

The factory produces only against orders (and not for stock). The production programme of the factory is as indicated below. The management desires to ensure a profit of ₹1,00,000 for the year. Work out the average selling price at which each unit should be quoted.

First 3 months of the year : 50 per cent of the capacity

Remaining 9 months : 80 per cent of the capacity

Ignore selling and administration overheads.

8.14 A job shop commenced its operations on January 1 of the current year. During the first quarter, the following transactions took place:

(i) Materials costing ₹4,00,000 were purchased on account.

(ii) Materials purchased were placed in process.

(iii) A total of 2,000 direct labour-hours were charged to individual jobs at the rate of ₹50 per hour.

(iv) The fixed manufacturing overhead totalled ₹1,60,000.

(v) The variable manufacturing overhead totalled ₹40,000.

(vi) Only job 10, with material charges of 40,000, direct labour charges of ₹20,000, and applied overhead rate, was in process at the end of the period.

Additional information:

(i) The firm uses an actual job-order cost system.

(ii) The variable manufacturing overhead is a function of direct labour-hours.

(iii) All overheads are allocated to individual jobs on the basis of a single rate based on direct labour-hours.

You are required to record journal entries for the current quarter assuming only general ledger is maintained.

8.15 A building contractor, having undertaken construction work at a contract price of ₹5,00,000 begins the execution of the work on January 1. The following are the particulars of the contract upto December 31:

Machinery installed at site	₹30,000
Materials sent to site	1,70,698
Wages paid at site	1,48,750
Direct expenses	6,334
Overhead charges allocated	8,252
Materials returned from site	1,098
Work certified by architect	3,90,000
Cash received	3,60,000
Cost of work not yet certified	9,000
Materials in hand as on December 31	3,766
Wages accrued due on December 31	5,380
Value of machinery as on December 31	22,000

Prepare the contract account.

8.16 A building contractor took a contract for the construction of a certain building on January 31. The agreed contract price was ₹16,00,000. The contractor had made the following expenditure during the year:

Direct materials purchased	₹40,000
Materials issued from stores	60,000
Direct labour	60,000
Plant	1,60,000
Direct expenses	40,000
	3,60,000

From the following information prepare a contract account for the year. Also show the amount of work-in-process which will be shown in the balance-sheet of the contractor:

Value of plant on December 31	₹1,20,000
Stock of materials at site on December 31	20,000
Materials returned to stores	4,000
Work certified by the architect	3,00,000
Cash received from contractee	2,80,000
Cost of work not yet certified	16,000

8.17 Pioneer Construction Company Limited obtained a contract for the erection of a multi-storey building. Building operations started in July last year. The contract price was ₹9,00,000. On June 30, the end of the current financial year, the cash received on account was ₹3,60,000, being 80 per cent of the amount on the surveyor's certificate. The following additional information is given.

Materials issued to contractor	₹1,80,000
Materials on hand at site as on June 30	7,500
Wages	2,46,600
Plant purchased specially for contract and to be depreciated at 10 per cent per annum	30,000
Direct expenses incurred	12,900
General overhead allocated to contract	7,600
Work finished but not yet certified cost	15,000

You are required to prepare the contract account and statement showing the profit on the contract till the end of the current year ending June indicating what proportion of the profit the company would be justified in taking to the credit of the profit and loss account, and to show what entries in respect of the contract would appear in the balance sheet.

8.18 The Construction Company Ltd is engaged on two contracts during the year. The following information relates to these contracts, which commenced on January 1 and July 1, respectively.

Particulars	*Contracts* A	B
Contract price	₹3,00,000	₹4,00,000
Direct materials issued	55,000	44,000
Materials returned to store	500	1,000
Direct labour payments	48,000	32,000
Wages accrued, December 31	2,000	2,500
Plant installed at cost	30,000	45,000
Establishment charges	25,000	15,000
Direct expenses	15,000	10,000
Direct expenses accrued, December 31	1,000	500
Work certified by architect	1,60,000	80,000
Cost of work not yet certified	10,000	15,000
Materials at site, December 31	5,500	4,000
Cash received from contractees	1,50,000	60,000
Depreciation of plant per annum (per cent)	33.33	10

Show the accounts for these contracts and for the contractees.

8.19 A public works contractor secured a contract at a price of ₹5,00,000. Work began on July 1 and the contract ledger account showed the following items debited upto March 31, in the following year:

Materials		₹90,000
Wages		1,05,000
Direct charges		5,000
Plant		16,000
The measurement at March 31, reads as follows:		
Total work done certified to date		2,40,000
Total work done for last measurement		2,10,000
Total work done for month		30,000
Less retention money, (10 per cent)		3,000
		27,000
Material on site	₹5,000	
Less 20 per cent	1,000	4,000
		31,000

Prepare a proforma account for the contract showing the profit earned to date, and indicate by means of a note the basis on which you arrive at the amount which may be carried to profit and loss account. Allow for depreciation on the plant at 10 per cent per annum.

8.20 An expenditure of ₹1,94,000 has been incurred on a contract to the end of March 31 of the current year. The value of work certified is ₹2,20,000. The cost of work done but not yet certified is ₹6,000. It is estimated that the contract will be completed by June 30 of the current year and an additional expenditure of ₹40,000 will have to be incurred to complete the contract. The total estimated expenditure on the contract is to include a provision of 2.5 per cent for contingencies. The contract price is ₹2,80,000, and ₹2,00,000 has been realised in cash upto March 31. Calculate the proportion of profit to be taken to the profit and loss account as on March 31 under different methods.

8.21 The following is the trial balance of Cosmos Construction Ltd, engaged in the execution of contract number 303, for the current year ending December 31:

Contractee's account: (75 per cent of work certified)		₹3,60,000
Accumulated depreciation account		50,000
Creditors		12,000
Buildings	₹2,00,000	
Bank balance	45,000	
Share capital		5,00,000
Materials	2,00,000	
Wages	1,80,000	
Expenses	47,000	
Plant	2,50,000	
	9,22,000	9,22,000

The work on contract number 303 commenced on January 1.

Materials costing ₹1,70,000 were sent to the site of the contract but those costing ₹6,000 were destroyed in an accident. Plant costing ₹50,000 was used on the contract all through the year. Plant costing ₹2,00,000 was used from January 1 to September 30 and was then returned to the stores.

The contract was for ₹6,00,000 and the contractee paid 75 per cent of the work certified. The cost of work uncertified was estimated to be ₹15,000 on December 31 on which date materials costing ₹4,000 were at the site of the contract.

Expenses are charged to the contract @ 25 per cent of wages. Plant is to be depreciated at 10 per cent according to the straight line method for the entire year.

Prepare contract number 303 account for the current year ending December 31 and the balance sheet of Cosmos Construction Limited as on that date.

ANSWERS

8.11 Total cost of production: product X, ₹870, product Y, ₹595.

8.12 (a) Under absorption ₹76,500 (cutting shop), ₹1,350 (Assembly shop), ₹1,150 (spraying shop).
(b) Overabsorption ₹3,500 (Finishing shop).

8.13 Average selling price ₹22.

8.14 Cost of goods completed and transferred ₹6,00,000; Overhead rate per hour ₹100.

8.15 Profit, ₹56,450 (to be credited to the current year's profit and loss A/c, ₹34,738; Reserve for unforeseen contingencies, ₹21,712).

8.16 Work-in-process, ₹3,16,000; No profit as work completed is less than one-fourth of total contract.

8.17 Profit, ₹22,400 (to be credited to Profit and loss A/c, ₹11,947, to be taken to reserve for unforeseen contingencies, ₹10,453).

8.18 Contract A: Profit, ₹20,000 (to be credited to the current year's Profit and loss A/c ₹12,500; Reserve for unforeseen contingencies, ₹7,500). Contract B: Loss, ₹4,500.

8.19 Profit, ₹42,800 (to be carried to current year's Profit and loss A/c, ₹12,840; Reserve for unforeseen contingencies, ₹29,960); Loss in material is normal. The firm has a policy of receiving 90 per cent in cash.

8.20 Profit, ₹28,571.

8.21 Profit on contract number 303, ₹45,000; Profit of the firm, ₹32,000; Balance sheet total (net basis), ₹5,44,000.

Process, Joint and By-product Costing

Learning Objectives

1. Understand the nature of process costing, its comparison with job costing and its suitability
2. Illustrate the accounting procedure involved in computing cost for completed, partially completed units and spoilage and inter-process profits
3. Discuss accounting procedure for joint products
4. Analyse the costing treatment of by-products
5. Explain the costing for selling at split-off point or processing further

INTRODUCTION

The purpose of this chapter is to discuss and illustrate process costing–a system of costing applicable to organisations whose products pass through different processes. Section 1 examines the nature of process costing in terms of its comparison with job costing and the types of organisations for which it is suitable. The accounting procedure involved in computing the cost under this system of costing is illustrated in Section 2 with reference to: **(a)** Completed units, **(b)** Partially completed/incomplete units, **(c)** Spoilage, and **(d)** Inter-process profits. Sections 3 and 4 deal respectively with the related aspects of joint products and by-products. The costing for selling at split-off point or processing further is discussed in Section 5. The major points are summarised in the last Section.

> **Process costing** is used when identical units are produced through an on-going series of production steps (processes).

NATURE AND SUITABILITY

The process costing system refers to the procedure of determining the average unit cost in situations in which the product passes through more than one stage of the manufacturing process. In other words, it is used when identical units are produced through an on-going series of uniform production steps. The process costing system, as a cost accumulation procedure, can be applied when: **(i)** The output is homogeneous, that is, the units produced are alike in all respects,

(ii) Production is continuous, **(iii)** Production precedes sales, and **(iv)** There is feasibility of segmentation of the manufacturing operations into clearly identifiable processes or departments. In view of these features, process costing is appropriate for industries such as chemicals, food processing, breweries, petroleum refining, glass, metal manufacturing, steel making, paper, and so on.

The process costing system can be distinguished from the job costing system in several respects. In the first place, in job costing, jobs receive varying degrees of skill and attention from each production department or operation; in process costing, units of output produced receive identical attention from each production department or operation. Secondly, the job-order cost system identifies costs essentially with a specific job, while the process cost system identifies costs with units of work performed during a period of time. Thirdly, in job costing, unit costs are determined continuously as each job is completed, whereas in process costing, unit costs are determined periodically. Fourthly, in job costing, production is for a specific order to meet an individual customer's specifications; therefore, sales normally precede production. In process costing, production is for building up inventories for future sales and, therefore, production precedes sales. Further, the materials needed for jobs would depend on the receipt of specific job-order, and therefore, the materials inventory/stock held is small/minimum in job costing. In process costing, the materials needed for output are known and, hence, the materials inventory kept on hand tends to be higher *vis-à-vis* job costing. In addition, in job costing most of the costs are directly traceable to the jobs and, therefore, a major part of the total costs normally consists of direct costs; overheads form a relatively low proportion of these costs. In process costing, automation/mechanisation is feasible to a greater extent entailing higher overhead costs, but in job costing production runs are relatively short since the number of units produced each time depends on specific orders received. In marked contrast, in process costing, production being on a mass scale, production runs are long and often continuous. Finally, job cost sheets for each job are the backbone of the job/order costing system. Cost-of-production reports for each production process, department or operation constitute the focal points of the process costing system.

The foregoing differences notwithstanding, job and process costing systems are not mutually exclusive, that is, a firm need not limit itself to the adoption of either of the two systems. For, the same firm can use both the methods to serve cost information needs. For instance, automobile manufacturing firms may employ job costing in their engineering departments and process costing in their main assembly lines. Similarly, heavy equipment manufacturing firms often use job costing to determine the total cost of a large machine but the costs of mass produced machine components like switches, valves, and so on, are first determined by the process cost method.

COST ACCUMULATION IN PROCESS COSTING

The process cost system accumulates production costs according to departments or processes. Each department/process constitutes a *responsibility centre* from the point of view of cost control and performance evaluation through techniques such as standard costing, responsibility accounting, budgeting, and so on, It provides unit cost measures that are helpful in establishing selling price particularly when the firm employs 'cost plus' or some other type of cost-based product pricing.

Process costing assumes a sequential flow of cost from one process to another as units of output pass through a number of specified production processes.

Process costing assumes a sequential flow of costs from one process to another as units of output pass through a number of specified production processes. That is, the units leave the first process and take their costs with them to the second process, the units leave the second process and take their costs with them to the third process, and this process continues till the last process, when output is finally completed. Each process performs part of the total operation and transfers its 'finished' output to the next process, in which it is the input/raw material for further processing. The finished product of the last process is transferred to the finished goods inventory. Thus, the cost becomes cumulative as production moves along, the final process determining the total cost.

In process costing, a work-in-process account (process account) is set up for each production process, and the material, labour and indirect manufacturing overhead costs are recorded as the work progresses. Direct materials and direct labour costs are assigned to the respective process accounts using materials requisition forms and payroll records. Likewise, indirect manufacturing overhead costs are often allocated to the units of each process on the basis of a predetermined departmental overhead application rate.

The procedure to determine the cost under process costing will depend on the stage of completion of the product in each process. From the point of view of the level of completion, a product may be fully or partially complete. During the production process, some units may be wasted. Moreover, the output of one process may be transferred at cost price or market/inflated price. We, therefore, elaborate the computation of unit costs in each of these situations in the discussions that follow.

Completed Units

Example 9.1 shows the calculation of costs when units are fully complete.

EXAMPLE 9.1

A product passes through two processes, A and B. During the month ended June 30, 1,500 units were produced. The detailed cost break-up is as follows:

	Process A	*Process B*
Direct materials	₹90,000	₹75,000
Direct labour	75,000	1,50,000
Direct expenses	15,000	18,000

Indirect overhead costs during the period were ₹60,000 apportioned to the processes on the basis of direct labour cost. No work-in-progress existed at the beginning and end of the period.

Prepare relevant process accounts.

SOLUTION

Process A Account

To direct materials	₹90,000	By cost of output transferred to process B	₹2,00,000
To direct labour	75,000		
To direct expenses	15,000		
To indirect overheads (₹60,000 × 1/3)	20,000		
	2,00,000		2,00,000

Process B Account

To process A (cost transferred)	₹2,00,000	By cost of output transferred to finished goods inventory	₹4,83,000
To direct material	75,000		
To direct labour	1,50,000		
To direct expenses	18,000		
To indirect overheads (₹60,000 × 2/3)	40,000		
	4,83,000		4,83,000

Finished Goods Inventory

To process B (cost of output)	₹4,83,000		

Incomplete Units

Given the nature of the production process, some units may remain incomplete at the time of accounting for the total cost of production. In such a situation, some units are complete while others are incomplete/partially complete. For the purpose of cost accumulation, the units of production are to be converted into comparable units. They are referred to as *equivalent units.* For instance, 100 units of inventory estimated to be 40 per cent complete are considered equivalent to 40 completed units. Therefore, for cost determination purposes, 100 partially completed units will be considered equal to 40 units of equivalent production. Symbolically:

Equivalent units = Actual number of partially completed units × Stage of completion **(9.1)**

The computation of equivalent units is illustrated in Examples 9.2 and 9.3, assuming that the stage of completion is uniform in respect of all items of cost and it is different in respect of raw materials and conversion costs (labour and overheads) respectively.

EXAMPLE 9.2

From the following information of ABC Manufacturers Limited, prepare a statement of equivalent units.

Opening inventory: Partially completed units (40 per cent complete)	600
Units introduced during the period	10,000
Closing inventory (partially completed units: 70 per cent complete)	2,000

SOLUTION

Statement of Equivalent Units

1. Work necessary to complete opening inventory (600 × 0.60)	360
2. Work necessary to start and finish units introduced during the current year (10,000 – 2,000 partially completed units)	8,000
3. Work performed on closing inventory (2,000 × 0.70)	1,400
Total number of equivalent units	9,760

EXAMPLE 9.3

From the following production record of XYZ Manufacturing Company Ltd, prepare a statement of equivalent units:

Units in process-opening		2,000
Stage of completion (%):	material	100
	labour	60
	overheads	50
New units introduced		20,000
Units completed		18,000
Units in process-closing		4,000
Stage of completion (%):	material	100
	labour	50
	overheads	40

SOLUTION

Table 9.1 Statement of Equivalent Units

Input	*Particulars*	*Number of units (completed or otherwise)*	*Work performed during the current period [stage of completion (per cent)]*			*Equivalent produced units: input units × stage completion in respect of*		
			Material	*Labour*	*Overheads*	*Material*	*Labour*	*Overheads*
Opening inventory 2,000 units	Work expended on opening inventories (100 per cent stage of completion)	2,000	Nil	40	50	—	800	1,000
+ 20,000 units introduced during the current period	Units started and completed during the current period (18,000 total units completed inventory)	16,000	100	100	100	16,000	16,000	16,000
	Closing inventory (work-in-process)	4,000	100	50	40	4,000	2,000	1,600
22,000		22,000				20,000	18,800	18,600

Process Accounts/Production Cost Report

Under the process costing system, the cost of production can be shown in form of production cost reports and/or process cost accounts.

Production Cost Report The cost of production report forms the backbone of the process cost records. It provides the summary of the production activity and costs of each process or department. On the basis of information regarding production activity in the report, it is possible to determine the number of equivalent units processed, unit costs per equivalent unit, and the quantity and cost of ending work-in-process inventories and of units completed and transferred to subsequent processing departments/finished goods inventory account. Cost of production report provides production and cost information, generally, in the following sequence of steps for a given period:

Equivalent units are incomplete units expressed in terms of completed units.

1. It accounts for physical flow of *all* units irrespective of their stage of completion during the period under reference.
2. It shows the computation of *equivalent* units of materials, labour and overheads; often the last two items are clubbed together and shown under the head of conversion costs.
3. It provides information for the total costs to be accounted for, consisting of the cost of opening work-in-process plus the costs of material, labour and factory overhead that were assigned to these units during the current period.
4. It shows very explicitly the procedure of determining the cost per equivalent unit of output processed.
5. Finally, it indicates the manner of allocating the cost of processing to ending work-in-process and to units completed and transferred.

The total cost of production of each process is split into: **(i)** Cost of output and **(ii)** Closing inventory. The distribution between these two elements would depend on the method of valuation of work-in-process (closing inventory), namely, weighted average method and first-in-first-out (FIFO) method.

Weighted Average Cost Method Under this method, total costs in process are divided by *equivalent* units produced by the process to ascertain the cost per equivalent unit. Total cost in process is the sum of the current production costs and the costs of opening work-in-process. Total equivalent units produced by the process are determined by adding units completed during the current period and equivalent units of work performed on opening and closing inventories.

FIFO Method Unlike the weighted average cost method, this method is based on the assumption that units in process at the beginning of the period are the first to be completed and accordingly the first costs incurred in the current period should be attached to the units of the opening work-in-process inventory. Therefore, under this method, the cost of the units that are completed from the opening inventory is separated from the cost of the units that have been introduced and completed during the current period. As a result, under the FIFO method, closing work-in-process inventory is based on the cost pertaining to the current period only *vis-à-vis* average cost under the weighted average cost method.

Exhibits 9.1 and 9.2 show the process accounts prepared as per the weighted average cost and FIFO methods respectively.

Exhibit 9.1 Process Account (Weighted Average Cost Method)

Dr.	Cr.
To work-in-process (opening inventory)	By cost of completed units transferred to next process/finished goods inventory A/c
To current costs	By closing work-in-process
Material	
Labour	
Overheads	
To closing work-in-process inventory to be carried to the next period	

Exhibit 9.2 Process Account (FIFO Method)

Dr.	Cr.
To work-in-process opening inventory during the current period (units partially completed in earlier period)	By units completed
To current costs	1. Units started in earlier period and completed during the current period
1. To complete opening inventory units	2. Units started and completed during the current period
2. To work initiated on new units in the current period in this process:	3. Units started but not completed during the current period
(a) Some of which are completed and transferred	
(b) Some of which are not yet completed and carried as opening inventory for next period	
To closing work-in-process inventory to be carried forward to the next period	

The effect of the two methods of valuation is that a larger share of the total cost will be allocated to the closing inventory according to the FIFO method, whereas with the weighted average cost method the current output will be charged at a relatively higher amount. Example 9.4 illustrates the process costs using both these methods.

EXAMPLE 9.4

For the firm in Example 9.3, assume the following:

Cost of 2,000 units in process (opening):	
Materials	₹6,000
Labour	3,600
Overheads	2,400
Processing costs during the current period	
Materials	69,900
Labour	56,560
Overheads	58,360

Prepare a cost of production report for the current period using **(a)** weighted average and **(b)** FIFO costing methods.

SOLUTION

Cost of Production Report of Process A (Weighted average cost method)

Flow of completed or partially completed units:				
Opening	2,000			
Introduced	20,000			
Total in process	22,000			
Less completed	18,000			
In process	4,000			
Equivalent units in process:				
		Conversion costs		
	Material	*Labour*	*Overhead*	
Units completed	18,000	18,000	18,000	
Equivalent units in ending inventory	4,000	2,000	1,600	
	22,000	20,000	19,600	
Total cost to be accounted for:				
	Material	*Labour*	*Overheads*	*Total*
Work-in-process (opening)	₹6,000	₹3,600	₹2,400	₹12,000
Current costs	69,900	56,560	58,360	1,84,820
Total cost in process	75,900	60,160	60,760	1,96,820
Equivalent units (EU) in process	22,000	20,000	19,600	—
Cost per equivalent unit in process (Total cost ÷ EU)	3.45	3.008	3.1	9.558
Costs accounted for:				
Transferred to finished goods inventory (18,000 × ₹9.558)				1,72,044
Work-in-process (closing inventory)				
Materials (4,000 × 100 per cent × ₹3.45)		₹13,800		
Labour (4,000 × 0.50 × ₹3.008)		6,016		
Overheads (4,000 × 0.40 × ₹3.1)		4,960		24,776
Total costs accounted for				1,96,820

Cost of Production Report of Process A (FIFO method)

Flow of completed or partially completed units:	
Opening	2,000
Introduced	20,000
Total in process	22,000
Less completed	18,000
In process	4,000

(*Contd.*)

(Contd.)

Equivalent units manufactured:

		Conversion costs	
	Material	Labour	Overheads
Units completed	18,000	18,000	18,000
Equivalent units in ending inventory	4,000	2,000	1,600
Equivalent units in process	22,000	20,000	19,600
Less equivalent units in opening inventory	2,000	1,200	1,000
Equivalent units manufactured	20,000	18,800	18,600

Total costs to account for:

	Material	Labour	Overheads	Total
Opening work-in-process	—	—	—	₹12,000
Current costs	₹69,900	₹56,560	₹58,360	1,84,820
Total costs in process				1,96,820
Equivalent units manufactured	20,000	18,800	18,600	—
Cost per equivalent unit manufactured	3.495	3.0085	3.1376	9.6411

Costs accounted for:

Transferred to finished goods inventory		
First batch:		
Work-in-process opening inventory	₹12,000	
Add conversion costs:		
Labour (2,000 × 0.40 × ₹3.0085)	2,406.8	
Overheads (2,000 × 0.50 × ₹3.1376)	3,137.6	₹17,544.4
Second batch:		
Started and completed (16,000 × ₹9.6411)		1,54,257.6
Work-in-process (closing):		
Materials (4,000 × 100 per cent × ₹3.495)	13,980	
Labour (4,000 × 0.50 × ₹3.0085)	6,017	
Overheads (4,000 × 0.40 × ₹3.1376)	5,020.16	25,017.16
		1,96,819.16

Comparison For comparison of the two costing methods, summary results of important items are listed below:

	FIFO		Weighted average cost
(A) Cost of output transferred from			
(i) Opening inventory	₹17,544.40		₹1,72,044
(ii) Current production	1,54,257.60	₹1,71,802	
(B) Closing work-in-process		25,017.16	24,776
		1,96,819.16	1,96,820

Spoilage

In the case of firms whose output passes through several stages, some wastage/spoilage of units takes place for a variety of reasons, such as breakdown of machines, use of substandard material, poor workmanship, evaporation, shrinkage, and so on. The effect of wastage is that the actual units produced are less than the units introduced initially.

Spoilage is wastage of units due to breakdown of machines, use of sub-standard material, poor workmanship, evaporation, shrinkage and so on.

The treatment of spoiled units depends on the nature of the spoilage/wastage/loss. The wastage may be normal or abnormal. *Normal loss* may be defined as the loss of units which is an inherent part of the production process caused by natural or unavoidable causes such as milling, drying, breaking, weighing, evaporating, processing, loading, unloading, and so on. Any loss in excess of the normal spoilage is called *abnormal loss.* It is a controllable loss. It involves consumption of resources without accruing corresponding benefits to the firm. On the other hand, if the number of units actually lost are less than the number of units normally expected to get lost, the difference would represent an abnormal gain/effectiveness.

Normal spoilage forms part of the product cost. Since it is inherent in the production process, it occurs even under efficient operating conditions. Therefore, the cost of production of spoiled units is recovered from the good units. Abnormal loss is treated as a period cost and is written off as a loss of the period in which it occurs. It is relevant for determining the process cost. Likewise, abnormal gain is transferred to the profit and loss account of the period.

Normal spoilage is the loss of units which is an inherent part of the production process caused by natural/unavoidable causes.

It is likely that the wasted units (normal as well as abnormal) may have salvage value. The sale proceeds of the units in normal waste would reduce the cost of production. The loss on abnormal wastage charged against the costing profit and loss account will be lower to the extent of the revenue received from their sale.

The unit cost with normal spoilage and with salvage value is computed as per Equation 9.2 and the amount of loss on account of abnormal spoilage to be transferred to profit and loss account is determined as in Equation 9.3.

Cost per unit = (Total process cost — Salvage value of normal spoilage) ÷ (Total units introduced — Normal loss in units) **(9.2)**

Abnormal loss = [Abnormal loss in units × Unit production cost] — Salvage value of abnormal spoilage **(9.3)**

The treatment of spoilage is illustrated in Example 9.5.

Example 9.5

Six hundred kgs of material was charged to process I at the rate of ₹40 per kg. The direct labour accounted for ₹2,000 and the other departmental expenses amounted to ₹7,600. The normal loss is 10 per cent of input. During the period, the actual production was 500 kgs and 100 kgs was scrap. Assuming that the scrap is saleable at ₹20 per kg, prepare a ledger account of process I, showing the values of normal and abnormal losses.

Solution

Process I Account

Particulars	Units (kgs)	Amount	Particulars	Units (kgs)	Amount
To materials	600	₹24,000	By normal loss (600 × 0.10)	60	₹1,200
To wages		2,000	By abnormal loss	40	2,400
To departmental expenses		7,600	By process II (500 units transferred at ₹60 each)	500	30,000
	600	33,600		600	33,600

Working Notes

Cost per unit = (₹33,600 - ₹1,200)/ 540 units = ₹60

Amount of abnormal loss

Units introduced	600
Less normal loss (10 per cent)	60
Normal output expected	540
Less actual output achieved	500
Abnormal loss (units)	40
(×) Cost per unit	₹60
Total loss	₹2,400
Less sale value of scrap (40 × ₹20)	800
Effective loss	1,600

We now take comprehensive examples (14.6 to 14.10) to illustrate the preparation of process accounts under different situations.

EXAMPLE 9.6 *(CLOSING WORK-IN-PROCESS WITH PROCESS LOSS OR GAIN)*
AB Ltd is engaged in the process engineering industry. During the month of April, 2,000 units were introduced in process X, the normal loss was estimated at 5 per cent of input. At the end of the month, 1,400 units had been produced and transferred to process Y; 460 units were incomplete and 140 units had to be scrapped during the process. The incomplete units had reached the following stages of completion: Material, 75 per cent; Labour, 50 per cent; Overhead, 50 per cent. Further information on process X:

Cost of the 2,000 units	₹58,000
Additional direct material	14,400
Direct labour	33,400
Direct overhead	16,700

Scrapped units realised ₹10 each.

Prepare a statement of equivalent production, statement of cost, statement of apportionment of cost and process X account.

SOLUTION

Statement of Equivalent Production

Input	Particulars	Number of units (completed or otherwise)	Stage completion (per cent)			Equivalent units (units × stage of completion)		
			Material	Labour	Over-heads	Material	Labour	Over-heads
2,000	Units introduced		100	100	100	1,400	1,400	1,400
	Units produced	1,400						
	Normal loss (0.5 × 2,000)	100	—	—	—	—	—	—
	Abnormal loss (140 units – 100, normal)	40	100	100	100	40	40	40
	Closing inventory	460	75	50	50	345	230	230
		2,000				1,785	1,670	1,670

Statement of Cost

Particulars	Total cost	Equivalent production (units)	Cost per unit
Materials			
Cost of units introduced	₹58,000		
Additional direct material	14,400		
	72,400		
Less sale proceeds of scrap material (100 units × ₹10)	1,000		
	71,400	1,785	₹40
Direct labour	33,400	1,670	20
Direct overheads	16,700	1,670	10
	1,21,500		70

Statement of Apportionment of Cost

Particulars	Element of cost	Equivalent production	Cost per unit	Cost	Total cost
Finished production	Material	1,400	₹40	₹56,000	
	Labour	1,400	20	28,000	
	Overhead	1,400	10	14,000	₹98,000

(Contd.)

(Contd.)

Abnormal loss	Material	40	40	1,600	
	Labour	40	20	800	
	Overhead	40	10	400	2,800
Work-in-process	Material	345	40	13,800	
	Labour	230	20	4,600	
	Overhead	230	10	2,300	20,700
					1,21,500

Process X Account

Particulars	Units	Amount	Particulars	Units	Amount
To raw material	2,000	₹58,000	By normal loss	100	₹1,000
To other direct materials		14,400	By abnormal loss	40	2,800
To direct labour		33,400	By process Y (transferred @ ₹70)	1,400	98,000
To direct overheads		16,700	By work-in-process	460	20,700
	2,000	1,22,500		2,000	1,22,500

EXAMPLE 9.7 *(OPENING AND CLOSING WORK-IN-PROCESS WITH PROCESS LOSS/GAINS)*

The finished output of a factory passes through two processes, the entire material being introduced at the beginning of the first process. From the following production and cost data relating to the first process, work out the value of closing inventory and the value of materials transferred to the second process. Also prepare process I account.

Process I: Opening stock, 10,000 units at ₹50,000

Stage of completion of opening inventory: Materials, 100 per cent; Labour, 60 per cent; Overheads; 50 per cent.

Units introduced during the process: 50,000 units at ₹1,44,000; Direct labour, ₹81,000; Overheads, ₹80,000.

Units transferred to next process, 38,000

Spoilage during the process (units), 7,000

Stage of completion of closing inventory, 15,000 units: Material, 100 per cent; Labour, 50 per cent; Overheads, 40 per cent.

Normal loss, 10 per cent of input.

Sale value of spoilage, ₹2 per unit.

SOLUTION

Statement of Cost

Particulars	Total cost	Equivalent production (units)	Cost per unit
Materials	₹1,44,000		
Less sale value of normal scrap (6,000 × ₹2)	12,000		
	1,32,000	44,000	₹3
Direct labour	81,000	40,500	2
Overheads	80,000	40,000	2
	2,93,000		7

Statement of Equivalent Production

Input units	Particulars	Number of units (completed or otherwise)	Stage completion (per cent)			Equivalent units (units × stage of completion)		
			Material	Labour	Overheads	Material	Labour	Overheads
10,000	Opening stock (100 per cent stage of completion)	10,000	Nil	40	50	—	4,000	5,000
50,000	Units started and completed (38,000 – 10,000, opening inventory)	28,000	100	100	100	28,000	28,000	28,000
	Normal loss (0.10 × 60,000)	6,000	—	—	—	—	—	—
	Abnormal loss (7,000-6,000)	1,000	100	100	100	1,000	1,000	1,000
	Closing work-in-process	15,000	100	50	40	15,000	7,500	6,000
60,000		60,000				44,000	40,500	40,000

Note: FIFO method of cost flow has been assumed.

Statement of Apportionment of Cost

Particulars	Element of cost	Equivalent production	Cost per unit	Total cost	
Opening inventory (combined)	—	—	—	₹50,000	—
	Material	—	—	—	—
	Labour	4,000	₹2	8,000	
	Overheads	5,000	2	10,000	₹68,000
Units introduced and completed	Material	28,000	3	84,000	
	Labour	28,000	2	56,000	
	Overheads	28,000	2	56,000	1,96,000
Abnormal loss	Material	1,000	3	3,000	
	Labour	1,000	2	2,000	
	Overheads	1,000	2	2,000	7,000
Closing work-in-process	Material	15,000	3	45,000	
	Labour	7,500	2	15,000	
	Overheads	6,000	2	12,000	72,000

Process I Account

Particulars	Units	Amount	Particulars	Units	Amount
To opening work-in-process	10,000	₹50,000	By normal loss	6,000	12,000
			By abnormal loss	1,000	7,000
To direct material costs	50,000	1,44,000	By process II (₹68,000 + ₹1,96,000)	38,000	2,64,000
To direct labour		81,000			
To overheads		80,000	By work-in-process	15,000	72,000
	60,000	3,55,000		60,000	3,55,000

EXAMPLE 9.8 *(DETERMINATION OF ABNORMAL LOSS WHEN UNITS ARE SCRAPPED AND SPOILED UNITS ARE AT DIFFERENT STAGES OF COMPLETION)*

In **Example 9.7**, assume the stages of completion in respect of 7,000 spoiled units are as follows: Material, 100 per cent; Labour, 50 per cent; Overheads, 60 per cent.
Determine the abnormal loss.

SOLUTION

Determination of Abnormal Loss

Cost element	Number of units	Stage of completion (per cent)	Equivalent units	Cost per unit	Total cost
Material	1,000	100	1,000	₹3.000	₹3,000.00
Labour	1,000	50	500	2.025	1,012.50
Overheads	1,000	60	600	2.020	1,212.00
					5,224.50

Material cost	(₹1,32,000 ÷ 44,000)	=	₹ 3.00 per unit
Labour cost	(₹81,000 ÷ 40,000)	=	2.025 per unit
Overhead costs	(₹80,000 ÷ 39,600)	=	2.02 per unit

EXAMPLE 9.9 *(ABNORMAL LOSS AND ABNORMAL GAIN WITH NO WORK-IN-PROCESS INVENTORY)*

XYZ Chemical Ltd processes a range of products including a detergent, 'Washo', which passes through 3 processes before completion and transfer to the finished goods warehouse. During April, data relating to this product were as follows:

Particulars	Process I	Process II	Process III	Total
Basic raw material (1,000 units)	₹6,000	—	—	₹6,000
Direct raw material added in process	8,500	9,500	5,500	23,500
Direct wages	4,000	6,000	12,000	22,000
Direct expenses	1,200	930	1,340	3,470
Production overhead				16,500
Output (units)	920	870	790	
Normal loss in process of input (per cent)	10	5	10	
Scrap value per unit	2	5	10	

The production overhead is absorbed as a percentage of direct wages. There was no stock at the start or at the end of any process.

You are required to prepare the following accounts: **(i)** Process I; **(ii)** Process II; **(iii)** Process III; **(iv)** Abnormal loss; and **(v)** Abnormal gain.

SOLUTION

Process I Account

Particulars	Units	Amount	Particulars	Units	Amount
To raw materials	1,000	₹6,000	By normal loss (0.10 × 1,000)	100	₹200
To other direct raw materials		8,500	By process II (transferred @ ₹25 per unit: ₹22,500 ÷ 900)	920	23,000
To direct wages		4,000			
To direct expenses		1,200			
To manufacturing overheads [0.75 × (₹16,500 ÷ ₹22,000) of wages]		3,000			
To abnormal gain (920 – 900, normal output)	20	500			
	1,020	23,200		1,020	23,200

Process II Account

Particulars	Units	Amount	Particulars	Units	Amount
To output transferred from process I	920	₹23,000	By normal loss (0.05 × 920)	46	₹230
To direct raw materials		9,500	By process III (transferred @ ₹50: ₹43,700 ÷ 874)	870	43,500
To direct wages		6,000	By abnormal loss (8,74 normal output – 8,70)	4	200
To direct expenses		930			
To manufacturing overheads (0.75 × ₹6,000)		4,500			
	920	43,930		920	43,930

Process III Account

Particulars	Units	Amount	Particulars	Units	Amount
To output transferred from process II	870	₹43,500	By normal loss (870 × 0.10)	87	₹870
To direct material		5,500	By finished stock A/c (final output transferred @ ₹90 per unit)	790	71,100
To direct wages		12,000			
To direct expenses.		1,340			
To manufactured overhead (0.75 × ₹12,000)		9,000			
To abnormal gain (790 – 783, normal output)	7	630			
	877	71,970		877	71,970

Abnormal Loss Account

Particulars	Units	Amount	Particulars	Units	Amount
To process II	4	200	By sale proceeds of scrap @ ₹5 per unit	4	20
			By profit @ loss A/c (loss transferred)		180
	4	200		4	200

Abnormal Gain Account

Particulars	Units	Amount	Particulars	Units	Amount
To normal loss			By process I A/c	20	500
Process I	20	40	By process III A/c	7	630
Process II	7	70			
To profit and loss account (profit transferred)		1,020			
	27	1,130		27	1,130

EXAMPLE 9.10 *(INTERMEDIATE PROCESS OUTPUT IS PARTIALLY SOLD AND PARTIALLY TRANSFERRED)*

A chemical company processes a patent material used in buildings. The material is produced in three consecutive grades: soft, medium and hard. The details of its operations are as follows:

	Process I	*Process II*	*Process III*
Raw material used (kgs.)	1,000		
Cost per kg.	₹200		
Total manufacturing expenses	87,500	₹39,500	₹10,710
Weight lost (per cent of input of the process)	5	10	20
Scrap (Sale price ₹50 per kg.) (kgs.)	50	30	51
Sale price per kg.	350	500	800

Management expenses were ₹7,500 and selling expenses, ₹5,000. Two-thirds of the output of process I and one-half of the output of process II is passed on to the next process and the balance is sold. The entire output of process III is sold.

Prepare relevant process accounts.

SOLUTION

Process I Account

Particulars	*kgs.*	*Amount*	*Particulars*	*kgs.*	*Amount*
To direct raw materials	1,000	₹2,00,000	By weight lost	50	—
To manufacturing expenses		87,500	By scrap sales	50	₹2,500
To profit		10,000	By sales (900 × 1/3)	300	1,05,000
			By Process II	600	
			(₹2,85,000 × 2/3)	—	1,90,000
	1,000	2,97,500		1,000	2,97,500

Process II Account

Particulars	*kgs.*	*Amount*	*Particulars*	*kgs.*	*Amount*
To process I			By weight lost	60	—
(transferred from)	600	₹1,90,000	By scrap sales	30	₹1,500
To manufacturing expenses		39,500	By sales (510 × 1/2)	255	1,27,500
To profit		13,500	By process III (transferred)		
			(₹2,28,000 × 1/2)	255	1,14,000
	600	2,43,000		600	2,43,000

Process III Account

Particulars	*kgs.*	*Amount*	*Particulars*	*kgs.*	*Amount*
To process II			By weight loss	51	—
(transferred from)	255	₹1,14,000	By scrap sales	51	₹2,550
To manufacturing expenses		10,710	By sales	153	1,22,400
To profit		240			
	255	1,24,950		255	1,24,950

Statement of Profit

Profit from			
Process	I	₹10,000	
	II	13,500	
	III	240	
Total			₹23,740
Less: management expenses		7,500	
selling expenses		5,000	12,500
Net profit			11,240

Note: Weight lost as well as scrap material is assumed to be normal loss.

Inter-Process Profits

The transfer of the output of one process to another can either be at the cost or at the market/inflated price. The cost basis of inter-process transfer of output has a serious limitation in that the efficiency or inefficiency of one process is passed on to the next. The market price basis overcomes this weakness.

The efficiency of process operations can be judged by comparing the value of output of a process with the price which would be paid for purchasing material from the market. If the market

Inter-process profit is the profit arising out of transfer of the product of one process to the other on the basis of market/inflated price.

price is lower, the process operations are clearly not efficient. Conversely, if the market price is higher, efficiency of the process operations should be recognised in terms of profits contributed by the process equal to the excess of market price over its cost. Naturally, for true comparison of efficiency of, say, process II, the output of process I should be transferred at market price and not at the cost price. '*Market/inflated price transfer formula*' has an additional advantage in that the final process account is not artificially distorted by inclusion of a figure of profit which has, in fact, accrued throughout the sequence of prior processes. Each process is, thus, made to stand by itself. The determination of the true cost of each process independent of others is of utmost significance particularly for those process industries where there are clear-cut possibilities of getting the intermediate supplies form the market. Therefore, the '*economy cost*' of performing such operations should be determined. For these reasons, inter-process transfer should be at the current market value or by the addition of an arbitrary percentage to cost. Such transfers would involve inter-process profits.

One important consequence of inflated transfer price (for inter-processes output) would be on valuation of closing stock. The inter-processes profit should be deducted from the closing inventory to show the inventory at cost price. This is illustrated in Examples 9.11 and 9.12.

EXAMPLE 9.11 (*INTER-PROCESS PROFITS*)

A product passes through three processes, A, B, and C. The output of process A and B is charged to the next process at a price calculated to give a profit of 16.67 per cent on transfer price while the output of process C is charged to the finished stock account at a profit of 13.33 per cent on the transfer price. From the following particulars, prepare the process cost accounts and calculate the amount of reserve that should be made in respect of the stock in hand.

	Process A	*Process B*	*Process C*
Materials and labour	₹7,000	₹2,800	₹4,800
Closing stock	2,000	2,800	2,000

There was no stock in hand at the beginning of the period. The closing stocks are valued at prime cost in each process.

SOLUTION

Process A Account

Particulars	*Amount*	*Particulars*	*Amount*
To materials and labour	₹7,000	By closing stock	₹2,000
To profit (₹6,000 × 0.1667)	1,000	By process B (₹5,000 × 120/100)	6,000
	8,000		8,000

Process B Account

Particulars	*Amount*	*Particulars*	*Amount*
To process A	₹6,000	By closing stock	₹2,800
To material and labour	2,800	By process C (₹6,000 × 120/100)	7,200
To profit (₹7,200 × 0.1667)	1,200		
	10,000		10,000

Process C Account

Particulars	*Amount*	*Particulars*	*Amount*
To process B	₹7,200	By closing stock	₹2,000
To materials and labour	4,800	By finished goods (10,000 × 115.38/100)	11,538
To profit (₹11,538 × 0.1333)	1,538		
	13,538		13,538

WORKING NOTES

1. Profit of 16.67 per cent on transfer means 20 per cent on cost price.
2. Likewise, profit of 13.33 per cent on transfer price means 15.38 per cent on cost.
3. Provision for unrealised profit:

Process A: Nil

Process B: (₹1,000 × 2,800)/8,800 = ₹318

Process C: Closing stock of process C of ₹2,000 is made up of respective cost proportions of C: B, that is, 2:3 (₹4,800: ₹7,200).

Process C's share is = ₹2,000 × 2/5 = ₹800

Process B's share is = ₹2,000 × 3/5 = ₹1,200

Profit included in ₹1,200 (process B's cost) is = ₹1200 × 20/120 = ₹200 (i)

Profit included in ₹1,000. This includes part of process A's costs: ₹1,000 × 60/88= ₹682.

₹682 includes profit element of = ₹682 × 20/120 = ₹113 (ii)

Total profit included in process C = ₹313 (200 + 113) (i + ii)

Statement of Profit

Process A		₹1,000
Process B	₹1,200	
Less provision for unrealised profit	318	882
Process C	1,538	
Less provision for unrealised profit	313	1,225
Profit realised		3,107

Alternatively

Process A Account

Particulars	Total	Cost	Profit	Particulars	Total	Cost	Profit
To materials and labour	₹7,000	₹7,000	—	By closing stock	₹2,000	₹2,000	—
To profit (₹5,000 × 50/3 × 3/250)	1,000	—	₹1,000	By process B (transferred)	6,000	5,000	₹1,000
	8,000	7,000	1,000		8,000	7,000	1,000

Process B Account

	Total	Cost	Profit		Total	Cost	Profit
To process A	₹6,000	₹5,000	₹1,000	By Closing stock (2,800 × 1,000) ÷ 8,800	₹2,800	₹2,482	₹318
To materials and labour	2,800	2,800	—	By process C (transferred)	7,200	5,318	1,882
To profit and loss A/c (₹6,000 × (50 × 3) ÷ (3 × 250))	1,200	—	1,200				
	10,000	7,800	2,200		10,000	7,800	2,200

Process C Account

To process B	₹7,200	₹5,318	₹1,882	By closing stock	₹2,000	₹1,687	₹313
To materials and labour	4,800	4,800	—	By finished			

(Contd.)

(*Contd.*)

To profit and loss A/c (0.1333 × ₹11,538)	1,538	—	1,538	goods A/c (at 115.38 per cent of cost)	11,538	8,431	3,107
	13,538	10,118	3,420		13,538	10,118	3,420

EXAMPLE 9.12 (*INTER-PROCESS PROFIT WHEN OPENING INVENTORY OF PROCESSES IS GIVEN*)

A Ltd makes a product which passes through two processes before it is completed and transferred to finished stock. The following data related to the month of December:

Particulars	*Process I*	*Process II*	*Finished stock*
Opening stock	₹7,500	₹9,000	₹22,500
Direct materials	15,000	15,750	
Direct wages	11,200	11,250	
Factory overheads	10,500	4,500	
Closing stock	3,700	4,500	11,250
Inter-process profit included in opening stock		1,500	8,250

Output of process I is transferred to process II at 25 per cent profit on the transfer price. Output of process II is transferred to finished stock at 20 per cent profit on the transfer price. Stocks in process are valued at prime cost. Finished stock is valued at the price at which it is received from process II. Sales during the period were ₹1,40,000.

Prepare process cost account and finished goods account showing the profit element at each stage.

SOLUTION

Process I Account

Particulars	*Total*	*Cost*	*Profit*	*Particulars*	*Total*	*Cost*	*Profit*
To opening stock	₹7,500	₹7,500	—	By process II (₹40,500 × 133.33/100)	₹54,000	₹40,500	₹13,500
To direct materials	15,000	15,000	—				
To direct wages	11,200	11,200	—				
Less closing stock	(3,700)	(3,700)					
Prime cost	30,000	30,000					
To factory overheads/ process cost	10,500	10,500					
Process cost	40,500	40,500					
To profit & loss A/c(0.25 × ₹54,000)	13,500		₹13,500				
	54,000	40,500	13,500		54,000	40,500	13,500

Process II Account

Particulars	*Total*	*Cost*	*Profit*	*Particulars*	*Total*	*Cost*	*Profit*
To opening stock	₹9,000	₹7,500	₹1,500	By finished stock			
To process I							

(*Contd.*)

(Contd.)

(transferred from)	54,000	40,500	13,500	(₹90,000 × 125/100)	₹1,12,500	₹75,750	₹36,750
To direct materials	15,750	15,750	—				
To direct wages	11,250	11,250	—				
Less closing stock	(4,500)	(3,750)	(750)				
Prime cost	85,500	71,250	14,250				
To factory overheads	4,500	4,500	—				
Process cost	90,000	75,750	—				
To profit & loss A/c	22,500	—	22,500				
	1,12,500	75,750	36,750		1,12,500	75,750	36,750

Finished Stock Account

To opening stock	₹22,500	₹14,250	₹8,250	By closing stock	₹11,250	₹7,500	₹3,750
To Process II (transferred from)	1,12,500	75,750	36,750	By sales	1,40,000	82,500	57,500
To profit & loss A/c (profit transferred)	16,250	—	16,250				
	1,51,250	90,000	61,250		1,51,250	90,000	61,250

WORKING NOTES

1. If ₹90,000 prime cost includes ₹15,000 profit, then ₹4,500 closing stock would include: ₹15,000 × ₹4,500)/₹90,000 = ₹750

2. *Statement of Profit*

Particulars		*Amount*
Process I:		₹13,500
Process II:	₹22,500	
Adjustment: provision for unrealised profit		
Add for opening stock	1,500	
Less for closing stock	750	23,250
Finished stock account	16,250	
Adjustment of provision for unrealised profit		
Add for opening stock	8,250	
Less for closing stock	3,750	20,750
		57,500

3. If ₹1,35,000 includes ₹45,000 profit, then ₹11,250 closing stock would include: (₹45,000 × ₹11,250) ÷ ₹1,35,000 = ₹3,750

The process accounts prepared in columnar form are more informative and useful as they provide classified information regarding cost and profit. This information shows inter-process profits included in the value of output (stock) transferred from one process to another, while such profits are to be computed separately in non-columnar form of process accounts.

JOINT PRODUCTS

Joint products are a feature of industries which process natural raw materials such as petroleum, chemicals, dairy products, wood products, mining and extractive industries. Two or more products produced simultaneously from a common set of inputs through a single manufacturing process (joint process), are called joint products.

Since joint products are the result of the use of some common items of cost, these items of cost are known as common/joint costs. The joint/multiple products resulting from common costs can be either sold at this stage of production or they can be processed further. Therefore, this stage of the joint production process is known as the *split-off point*. *Split-off point* is that stage in the manufacturing process where the joint products are separately identifiable. Prior to the point of split-off/ separation, products are not subject to identification nor are the costs. Therefore, production costs incurred prior to the split-off point are called *joint costs*, and those incurred after the split-off point are called *separable costs*. Being so, separable costs can be directly traced to specific products and, therefore, do not entail any problem of cost allocation while the same is not true of joint costs.

Split-off point is that stage in the manufacturing process where the joint products are separately identifiable.

Allocation of Joint Costs

The critical problem in accounting for joint products is that of allocating common process costs among the separate/multiple outputs that emerge from the joint process. The allocation method used will determine the amount of common processing cost allocated to each of the joint outputs. The commonly-used methods for allocating joint processing costs include:

Joint cost are the costs incurred prior to the split-off point.

1. Physical quantities method/Unit method.
2. Relative sales value method/Net realisable value method.
3. Net realisable value less normal profit method.
4. Weighted averages cost method.

Physical quantity method allocates joint costs in proportion to the physical measurement of the output, e.g., volume, weight, surface area.

Physical Quantities Method/Unit Method Under this method, the total costs (material, labour and overhead) incurred in the joint production process are allocated to various products in proportion to the physical measurement of the output. The physical measure might be volume, weight, surface area or any other common measure of the physical characteristics. Thus, under this method, the common attribute is aggregated and the joint costs are allocated on the basis of each product's relative share of it. This is illustrated in Example 9.13.

EXAMPLE 9.13 *(ALLOCATION OF JOINT COSTS UNDER UNIT METHOD)*

Royal Industries Ltd manufactures products X, Y and Z by processing a specific raw material in Department 1. The production process is such that every 1,100 kgs of raw materials that is put into Department 1 yields 400 kgs of X, 250 kgs of Y and 350 kgs of Z. The total cost of processing a batch of 1,100 kgs of raw materials through Department 1 is ₹22,000. Allocate the joint costs to the three products using the physical quantity method.

SOLUTION

Joint Cost Allocation Using Unit Method

Product	*Output (kgs)*	*Rates (per cent)*	*Allocated joint cost*	*Cost per unit*
X	400	40	₹8,800	₹22
Y	250	25	5,500	22
Z	350	35	7,700	22
	1,000	100	22,000	22

This method results in identical unit costs for each product. Identical benefits exist only if the products are homogeneous. It will, therefore, provide a satisfactory basis of allocating joint cost if the different products are homogeneous and their sale prices are relatively close to each other.

Otherwise, it may lead to misleading results in that there will be wide divergence in the gross margin of the different products as shown in Table 9.2.

Table 9.2 Gross Margin of Different Products

	Product X	*Product Y*	*Product Z*
Sales price	₹33	₹44	₹66
Less cost of production	22	22	22
Cross margin	11	22	44
Gross margin percentage	33.33	50	66.67

Relative Sales Value/Net Realisable Value (NRV) Method As per this method, joint costs are *prorated* among multiple products on the basis of the market value of the products manufactured. This method is based on the premise that if a product has a higher sale price, it costs more to produce and, hence, the market value basis to allocate join costs.

Net realisable value is the sale value after further processing less further processing cost.

If the joint products can be sold at the split-off point, sales price measure can *directly and conveniently* be applied for joint costs allocation. In case the products are not readily marketable at the split-off point, but require further processing, it is necessary to estimate the sales value at the split-off-point. This is usually estimated by taking the sale value after further processing and deducting the additional processing costs.

Net realisable value = Sales value after further process — Further processing cost (9.4)

From the facts in **Example 9.13 and Table 9.2** and assuming all products are sold at the split-off point, joint cost allocation under the relative sale value method would be, as shown in Table 9.3.

Table 9.3 Joint Cost Allocation Using Sales Value Method

Product	*Output (kgs)*	*Market price*	*Market value*	*Rates*	*Allocated joint cost*	*Cost per unit*
X	400	₹33	₹13,200	132/473	₹6,140	₹15.35
Y	250	44	11,000	110/473	5,116	20.46
Z	350	66	23,100	231/473	10,744	30.70
	1,000		47,300		22,000	22.00

Thus, the costs per unit are in proportion to the sale prices. The relative sale price method generates the same margin percentage (53.48 per cent) for all products. Thus, this approach implies a matching of input costs with revenues generated by each output.

In practice, however, it may so happen that the joint products may not be in a condition to be sold at the split-off point; they may need further processing to become marketable. In such cases, a hypothetical sales value needs to be estimated at the split-off point to allocate joint costs. The resulting hypothetical sales value/net realisable value is used for joint cost allocation in the same way as actual market value at the split-off point. Assuming that for the firm in Example 9.13, the additional processing for products X, Y and Z is done in departments 2, 3 and 4 respectively. Following are the costs incurred in these departments to process the batch of 1,100 kgs of materials:

Product	*Output (kgs)*	*Department*	*Further processing/ separable cost*	*Unit cost*
X	400	2	₹6,000	₹15
Y	250	3	4,500	18
Z	350	4	7,000	20

Assuming no change in market price, joint costs of Royal Industries Ltd would be allocated as shown in Table 9.4.

Table 9.4 Allocation of Joint Costs [Net Realisable Value (NRV) Method]

Product	*Output (kgs)*	*Market price*	*Market value*	*Separable cost*	*Net realisable value*	*Rates*	*Allocated joint costs*	*Joint cost per unit*
X	400	₹33	₹13,200	₹6,000	₹7,200	72/298	₹5,315	₹13.28
Y	250	44	11,000	4,500	6,500	65/298	4,799	19.19
Z	350	66	23,100	7,000	16,100	161/298	11,886	33.96
	1,000		47,300	17,500	29,800		22,000	22.00

The gross margin rates for each product according to this method are shown in Table 9.5.

Table 9.5 Gross Margin Rates

	Product X	*Product Y*	*Product Z*
Sales price	₹33.00	₹44.00	₹66.00
Less cost of production:			
Joint cost	13.28	19.19	33.96
Separable cost	15.00	18.00	20.00
	28.28	37.19	53.96
Gross margin	4.72	6.81	12.04
Gross margin rate (percentage)	14.3	15.5	18.21

The NRV method is based on the assumption that the processing costs incurred subsequent to the split-off point contribute nothing to profit; the increase in the product's sales value is equal to the separable costs. This supposition is fundamentally wrong as it implies that the firm would be willing to process its products further even if they do not contribute to profits. This is not likely to be true in practice for manufacturing firms. Therefore, it may be more logical to argue that profit is earned over the entire span of production rather than just during the joint span. Thus, this method of allocating joint costs ignores the profits from further processing of the product beyond the split-off point.

Net Realisable Value Less Normal Profit Method This method is based on the fundamental axiom that profits are earned on total cost incurred, and not on joint costs only. The following are the steps required to apply this method:

(i) Determine the ratio of the total production cost (joint and separable) to total final market value. This ratio is an average cost ratio per rupee of sales.
(ii) Subtract the average cost ratio form 100 per cent to find an average/normal profit ratio.
(iii) Finally, subtract the sum of the separable costs and normal profit from the market value. The amount so arrived at would be allocated joint costs corresponding to each product. Table 9.6 shows the cost allocation.

Table 9.6 Joint Cost Allocation Using NRV Less Normal Profit Method

Product	*Output (kgs)*	*Market value*	*Normal profit*	*Separable costs*	*Joint cost allocation*	*Joint cost per unit*
X	400	₹13,200	₹2,177	₹6,000	₹5,023	₹12.557
Y	250	11,000	1,814	4,500	4,686	22.744
Z	350	23,100	3,809	7,000	12,291	35.117
	1,000	47,300	7,800	17,500	22,000	

WORKING NOTES

Normal profit ratio = 100 per cent — [Total costs — (Joint + Separable) × 100] ÷ Total market value = 100 per cent — [(₹22,000 + ₹17,500) × 100 ÷ ₹47,300, 83.5 per cent = 16.5 per cent]

It may be noted that gross profit margin is uniform (16.5 per cent) for all the products as per this method which may not be a desirable characteristic. Therefore, this method should again not be taken as a perfect measure of allocating joint costs but, certainly, it is one, which is logically superior to others discussed so far.

Weighted Average Method Where the products are heterogeneous, the weighted average method can provide a reasonable basis for allocating joint costs. This method is theoretically superior to the physical quantity method as this method, by assigning different weights to different products, recognises some significant characteristics of the output. As the weight factors can reflect the varying amounts of time required to process the units, the difficulty of the processing procedure, the amount of material and labour used and other significant factors, there would be a positive correlation between these factors and the assigned value of weights. The sale price is one of the widely-used weight factors in practice.

According to this method, the volume of output for each product is multiplied by a weight that reflects the collective differences among the products. In order to have reliable results from the method, weights should be assigned after giving due and careful consideration to all the relevant characteristics of the product.

Continuing with the example of Royal Industries Ltd, assume that the following are the weights assigned to products X, Y and Z after taking into consideration a variety of factors: X, 1; Y, 2; Z, 4. Using the weighted average method, the joint costs are allocated in Table 9.7.

Table 9.7 . Joint Cost Allocation Using Weighted Average Method

Product	*Output (kgs)*	*Weight*	*Weighted output*	*Ratio*	*Allocated joint cost*	*Cost per unit*
X	400	1	400	4/23	₹3,826	₹9.56
Y	250	2	500	5/23	4,783	19.13
Z	350	4	1,400	14/23	13,391	38.26
	1,000		2,300		22,000	

Thus, according to this method, joint cost per unit is in direct proportion to the weights assigned to various products. The major limitation of the method is the problem of establishment of the weights. These weights are frequently the result of individual judgement and, therefore, may not be objective. In all fairness, this method would be an ideal one if weights could be objectively determined.

BY-PRODUCTS

A by-product is incidental to the process of manufacturing the main/joint products. It is an output whose value does not contribute materially to the revenues of the firm. Its amount, relative to the value of the main product, is small. Chemical residues, sawdust and shavings, and slag are typical by-products of the chemicals, timber and steel processing industries respectively. By-products differ from scrap. For instance, scrap is sold as it is while by-products may have to undergo additional processing before sale. Moreover, it may so happen that the disposal of scrap may involve some expenses instead of yielding any revenue, whereas a by-product always generates some revenue.

By-products is incidental to the process of manufacturing the main/joint products.

The accounting treatment of by-products will depend on whether the by-product is sold at the split-off point or processed further. The former is discussed here while the latter is covered in the next section. The two most commonly used methods of accounting for by-products are: **(1)** Miscellaneous income method, and **(2)** Net realisable value method (NRV).

Miscellaneous Income Method

Under this method, sales revenue contributed by the by-products is considered as miscellaneous income of the firm. All costs are assigned to only the main products and not to the by-products. This method is considered as the most appropriate when the value of the by-product is uncertain or so trivial that it is not likely to have any significant/noticeable effect on inventory or profit.

Net Realisable Value Method

In case the value of a by-product is large enough to have a significant effect on inventory or profits, the by-product should be valued at its net realisable value/sale value. This treatment would cause *reduction in the cost of production of the main products.* The cost of the joint process is assigned to the joint products as well as to by-products. Therefore, the cost of production of the main output would be lower by the proportionate charge to the by-product. There are two variants of this method: **(i)** Recognisation of no profit on the sale of by-products **(ii)** Recognition of some normal profit.

Recognisation of No Profit on the Sale of By-products As per this variant, the sale price of the by-product would be considered to consist of two elements, namely, **(i)** Production cost assigned to it out of joint costs, and **(ii)** Selling and distribution cost. Accordingly, the share of joint costs allocated to by-products would be:

Sale price of by-products — Selling and distribution cost of by-products = Joint process cost allocated to by-products **(9.5)**

Recognisation of Some Normal Profit on the Sale of By-products A second variant is to recognise some normal profit from the sales of by-products. Accordingly, the sale price of by-product would be considered consisting of three elements, namely, **(i)** Production cost (share of joint costs) allocated to it; **(ii)** Selling and distribution cost; and **(iii)** Normal profit. The share of joint costs allocated to by-products would be determined as follows (Equation 9.6).

Sale price of by-products — Normal profit — Selling and distribution cost of by-products **(9.6)**

Example 9.14

For the facts contained in **Example 9.13**, let as assume further that joint production process also yields by-product (70 kgs) in addition to three main products X, Y, Z. Its selling price is ₹2 per kg and selling costs are ₹0.50 per kg. Determine the share of joint costs **(i)** if firm does not recognize profit on the sale of its by-product; and **(ii)** if it recognizes 10 per cent profit on such sales.

Solution

Share of Joint Costs

(i) When no profits are recognized:	
Sales revenue (70 kgs × ₹2)	₹140
Less selling costs (70 kgs × ₹0.50)	35
Share of joint costs (70 kgs × ₹1.50)	105
(ii) When 10 per cent profits are recognised:	
Sales revenue (70 kgs × ₹2)	140
Less normal profit (₹140 × 0.10)	14
Less selling costs (70 kgs × ₹0.50)	35
Share of joint costs (70 kgs × ₹1.30)	91

SELL NOW (AT SPLIT-OFF POINT) OR PROCESS FURTHER

As mentioned in the preceding section, a joint product can be sold at the split-off point or processed further and sold later as a completed production unit. This section explains the accounting for the sale or further processing of the main products as well as the by-products. This exercise will be helpful to the management in arriving at a decision, whether the product should be sold at the split-off point or processed further. From the point of view of managerial decision-making, incremental costs of further processing should be compared with the incremental revenue. This aspect is comprehensively elaborated in a subsequent chapter dealing with short-term decisions.

Main Products Requiring Further Processing

Examples 9.15 and 9.16 illustrate the application of process costing to the main products.

EXAMPLE 9.15 *(SELL NOW OR PROCESS FURTHER: SINGLE PRODUCT)*

A B C Ltd manufactures a single product which it sells to firms which process it further before sale. The normal quarterly operating volume for the company is 50,000 units produced and sold. The relevant cost data are as follows:

Selling price		₹10.00
Less standard costs:		
Direct materials	₹3.00	
Direct labour	1.50	
Variable manufacturing overheads	1.00	
Fixed manufacturing overheads (₹25,000 per quarter)	0.50	
Variable selling overheads	1.00	
Fixed selling expenses (₹12,500 per quarter)	0.25	7.25
Standard (budgeted) profit per unit		2.75

The company's management is considering the possibility of further processing the product and selling it directly to the customers. The management estimates that the product can be sold @ ₹14 per unit after further processing. The following are the estimates of the *additional (per unit/quarter)* costs of processing 50,000 units:

Direct labour	₹1.00
Variable manufacturing overheads	0.50
Variable selling costs	0.20
Additional fixed manufacturing overheads (per quarter)	10,000
Additional sales expenses (per quarter)	5,000

You are required to compute the cost (i) without, and (ii) with further processing. Is further processing advisable?

SOLUTION

Cost Comparison: Incremental Analysis

Particulars	*Without further processing*		*With further processing*		*Difference from further processing*	
	Per unit	*Total*	*Per unit*	*Total*	*Per unit*	*Total*
Sales	₹10.00	₹5,00,000	₹14.00	₹7,00,000	₹4.00	₹2,00,000
Less variables costs:						
Direct material	3.00	1,50,000	3.00	1,50,000	0.00	—
Direct labour	1.50	75,000	2.50	1,25,000	1.00	50,000

(*Contd.*)

(*Contd.*)

Manufacturing overheads	1.00	50,000	1.50	75,000	0.50	25,000
Selling overheads	1.00	50,000	1.20	60,000	0.20	10,000
Total	6.50	3,25,000	8.20	4,10,000	1.70	85,000
Contribution	3.50	1,75,000	5.80	2,90,000	2.30	1,15,000
Less separable identifiable fixed costs:						
Manufacturing		—		10,000		10,000
Sales		—		5,000		5,000
Product margin		1,75,000		2,75,000		1,00,000
Less common fixed costs:						
Manufacturing		25,000		25,000		—
Sales		12,500		12,500		—
Net income		1,37,500		2,37,500		1,00,000

Since further processing would result in a greater product margin and net income, the new proposal is acceptable.

EXAMPLE 9.16 (*SELL NOW OR PROCESS FURTHER: MULTIPLE PRODUCTS*)

XYZ Ltd produces three products, A, B and C. One type of a raw material is used for all these products. Raw material enters the process in department 1 of the factory. Department 1 separates material for products A, B and C. During the last quarter, ₹4,00,000 of material was issued to Department 1. Other direct costs of operating Department 1 were ₹2,00,000. The output of products A, B and C from Department 1 was: A, 10,000 units; B, 5,000 units; C, 2,000 units.

Products A, B and C can be sold after being processed from Department 1 (split-off point) at prices of ₹60, ₹30 and ₹20 respectively. After the split off, product A could be processed further in Department 2. With additional processing, product A can be sold at ₹70 per unit. After the split-off, product B could be processed further in Department 3 for ₹30,000 additional cost, and will fetch ₹35 per unit after processing. Product C is not suitable for further processing and has to be sold at the point of split-off. What action should be management take?

SOLUTION

Sell or Process Further: Decision Analysis

Particulars	*Product A*			*Product B*		
	Sell now	*Process further*	*Difference from further processing*	*Sell now*	*Process further*	*Dfferences from further processing*
Sales	₹6,00,000	₹7,00,000	₹1,00,000	₹1,50,000	₹1,75,000	₹25,000
Less separable costs	—	50,000	50,000	—	30,000	30,000
Joint cost of ₹6,00,000 from Department 1	Irrelevant as costs not affected by the decision					
Contribution (decrease)	₹6,00,000	6,50,000	50,000	1,50,000	1,45,000	(5,000)

Thus, it is profitable to process product A further because it yields an incremental profit of ₹50,000, (additional revenue being ₹1,00,000 and additional cost, ₹50,000). The decision is based on the assumption that there is no other opportunity cost for using the facilities of Departments 2 and 3.

By-Products Processed Further

There are several methods of accounting for costs of further processing: **(i)** Recognition of no profit on sale of by-products; **(ii)** Recognition of normal profit on by-products; and **(iii)** Separate cost records for by-products.

Recognition of No Profit on Sale of By-products Method Under this method, share of joint costs allocated to by-products would be determined by subtracting both selling and further processing costs from the sale price of by-products.

Sale price of by-products — Further processing cost beyond split-off point — Selling cost = Joint costs **(9.7)**

Recognition of Normal Profit on Sale of By-Products/Reversal Cost Method The share of joint costs assigned to by-products is given by Equation 9.8.

Sale-price-Further processing cost beyond shift off point-Selling cost-Estimated normal profit. **(9.8)**

This method is also known as the reversal cost/replacement/opportunity cost method and is most appropriate when by-products are used/utilised in the firm itself as material for manufacturing/processing some other products. Under this method, by-products are valued at the price which would have been paid by the firm in making outside purchases for these products.

Separate Cost Record for By-products This method is most appropriate in situations when the joint manufacturing process yields by-products which are relatively of high value and/or of large quantity; they also require further processing after separation from the joint manufacturing process. In such situations, the by-products cease to be by-products; they become as significant as the main products. Accordingly, they must normally be treated as main products and the cost allocated on some equitable and rational basis.

EXAMPLE 9.17 *(REVERSAL COST METHOD)*

In manufacturing the main product, Hypothetical Ltd processes the incidental waste into two products, A and B. From the following data relating to the products, you are required to prepare a comparative profit and loss statement showing the individual costs and other details. The total costs upto separation point were ₹3,10,400.

	Main product	*By-product A*	*By-product B*
Sales	₹8,00,000	₹64,000	₹96,000
Costs after separation	80,000	12,800	14,400
Estimated net profit (per cent to sales value)		20	30
Estimated selling expenses (as per cent to sales value)	20	10	15

SOLUTION

Statement Showing Allocation of Joint Costs

Particulars	*By-product A*	*By-product B*
Sales	₹64,000	₹96,000
Less: estimated net profit on sale (20 per cent, A; and 30 per cent, B)	12,800	28,800
estimated selling expenses (10 per cent, A, and 15 per cent, B)	6,400	14,400
separable costs	12,800	14,400
Share of joint costs allocated	32,000	38,400

Share of main products in joint costs, therefore, would be: ₹3,10,400 — (₹32,000 + ₹38,400) = ₹2,40,000.

Comparative Profit and Loss Account

Particulars	*Main product*	*By-product A*	*By-product B*
Sales revenue	₹8,00,000	₹64,000	₹96,000
Less cost of production:			
Joints costs	2,40,000	32,000	38,400
Separable costs	80,000	12,800	14,400
Gross profit	4,80,000	19,200	43,200
Less selling expenses	1,60,000	6,400	14,400
Net profit	3,20,000	12,800	28,800

SUMMARY

- The process costing system measures the cost of products under conditions of continuous production, sequential processing and homogeneous output. The procedure under such a system of costing essentially involves averaging the total costs of a process or a department. It is used in industries such as chemicals, food processing, breweries, petroleum refining, paper, glass, metal manufacturing and so on.
- The procedure to determine the cost will depend on, firstly, the stage of completion of the product, in each process, secondly, the extent of wastage, spoilage of units in the process and, thirdly, the inter-process profits.
- In cases where some units are complete, while others are incomplete or partially complete, for the purpose of cost accumulation, the partially completed units are to be converted into comparable equivalent units. Equivalent units = [Actual number of partially completed units × Stage of completion]
- The cost of production is shown in the form of a production cost report and/or process cost account. The total cost of production of each process is split into the cost of output and the closing inventory/work-in-process. The distribution between these two elements depends on the method of valuation of work-in-process, namely, weighted average method and first-in-first-out (FIFO) method.
- The spoilage of units under process costing may take place due to a variety of reasons, like use of sub-standard material, poor workmanship, evaporation, shrinkage, break-down of machines, and so on. The effect of spoilage is that the number of actual units produced is less than the units introduced initially. The spoilage or wastage may be normal or abnormal. The unit cost with normal spoilage

$$= \left(\frac{\text{Total process costs} - \text{Salvage value of normal spoilage}}{\text{Total units introduced} - \text{Normal loss in units}}\right)$$

- Abnormal loss = [(Abnormal loss in units × Unit production cost) – Salvage value of abnormal spoilage]
- The transfer of output of one process to the other can either be at cost or the inflated/market price. Transfers at the latter price involve inter-process profits. These profits should be deducted from closing inventory to determine true profits.
- Two or more products produced simultaneously from a common set of inputs through a single manufacturing (joint) process are called joint products. The joint products can be sold either at the stage of production (split-off point) itself or they can be processed further. The costs incurred before the split-off point are called joint/common/inseparable costs and the costs incurred beyond that point are known as separable costs. The crucial factor in accounting for joint products is the allocation of joint costs among the joint/multiple products from the joint process.

- The commonly used methods of allocating joint process costs are: **(i)** Physical quantities method/ unit method, **(ii)** Relative sales value method/net realisable value method, **(iii)** Net realisable value less normal profit method, and **(iv)** Weighted average cost method.
- Under the physical quantities method, the total joint costs are allocated to the joint products in proportion to the physical measurement of output.
- In the net realisable value method, joint costs are pro-rated on the basis of the market value of the joint products.
- The net realisable value less normal profit method differs from the net realisable value method to the extent the joint costs less normal profits are pro-rated.
- Where the joint products are heterogeneous, the weighted average cost method provides a reasonable basis for allocating the joint costs.
- A by-product is incidental to the process of manufacturing the main/joint product. The accounting treatment depends on whether the by-product is sold at the split-off point or is processed further. The two most commonly-used methods of accounting for by-products are: **(i)** Miscellaneous income method, and **(ii)** Net realisable value method, *(NRV)*.
- Under the miscellaneous income method, the income generated by the by-products is treated as a miscellaneous income and all the associated costs are charged to the main product.
- According to the NRV method, the by-product is valued at its net realisable value and the joint costs are pro-rated between the main product and the by-product. Joint process cost allocated to by-product = (Sale price of by-products – Selling and distribution costs of by-products)
- A variation of this is to recognise some normal profit from the sale of by-products.
- Joint cost allocated to by-products = (Sale price of by-products – Normal profit – Selling and distribution costs of by-product)

SOLVED PROBLEMS

P.9.1 The product of ABC Ltd passes through three distinct processes for completion. From past experience, it is ascertained that normal wastage in each process is as under:

Process	Wastage (%)	Sale value of wastage per unit
A	2	₹0.25
B	4	0.50
C	2.5	0.60

The expenses were as follows:

	Process A	*Process B*	*Process C*
Materials	₹12,000	₹10,000	₹9,000
Direct labour	16,000	5,000	4,900
Manufacturing expenses	2,000	3,400	3,590
Other factory expenses	3,500	2,005	2,004

4,000 units were initially introduced in process at a cost of ₹13,560. The output of each process was as under: A, 3,850 units; B, 3,600 units; and C, 3,500 units.

Prepare process accounts and also work out the sale price per unit of finished stock so as to realise 20 per cent profit on selling price.

SOLUTION

Process A Account

Particulars	*Units*	*Amount*	*Particulars*	*Units*	*Amount*
To units introduced	4,000	₹13,560	By normal wastage	80	₹20
To materials		12,000	By abnormal wastage@	70	840

(Contd.)

(*Contd.*)

To direct labour		16,000	₹12 per unit		
To manufacturing expenses		2,000	By process B (output		
To other factory expenses		3,500	transferred @ ₹12		
			per unit, ₹47,040 ÷		
			3,920, normal output)	3,850	46,200
	4,000	47,060		4,000	47,060

Process B Account

Particulars	*Units*	*Amount*	*Particulars*	*Units*	*Amount*
To process A	3,850	₹46,200	By normal wastage	154	₹77
(transferred from)			By abnormal loss @		
To materials		10,000	₹18 per unit	96	1,728
To direct labour		5,000	By process C (output	3,600	64,800
To manufacturing expenses		3,400	transferred @ ₹18		
To other factory expenses		2,005	per unit, ₹66,528÷		
			3,696, normal output)		
	3,850	66,605		3,850	66,605

Process C Account

To process B	3,600	₹64,800	By normal wastage	90	₹54
(transferred from)			By abnormal loss		
To materials		9,000	@ ₹24 per unit	10	240
To direct labour		4,900	By finished stock	3,500	84,000
To manufacturing expenses		3,590	(output transferred @		
To other factory expenses		2,004	₹24 per unit,		
			₹84,240 ÷ 3,510 units)		
	3,600	84,294		3,600	84,294

Selling price per unit = ₹30 (₹24 + ₹6, profit)

P.9.2 A product passes through two consecutive processes having relative standard output of 80 per cent and 90 per cent of inputs. In addition, standard yield is obtained by giving scrap allowances of 10 per cent and 5 per cent of outputs of process I and II respectively. Scraps of each process are sold at ₹1,000 per tonne.

There was no work-in-process at any stage, all materials were issued in process I as follows and all scraps arising from the processes were sold, except closing stock of 10 tonnes (opening stock was nil). Material issued: 'A'; 100 tonnes @ ₹2,000 per tonne; 'B'; 400 tonnes @ ₹1,500 per tonne; and 'C'; 500 tonnes @ ₹1,200 per tonne.

The actual outputs and scraps were 85-per cent and 8 per cent in process I and 80 per cent and 10 per cent in process II. Assume that there was no price variance.

You are required to find out the standard cost and actual cost per tonne of a product.

SOLUTION

(a) *Value of Materials Used*

Type of materials	*Quantity (tonnes)*	*Rate*	*Amount*
A	100	₹2,000	₹2,00,000
B	400	1,500	6,00,000
C	500	1,200	6,00,000
	1,000		14,00,000

(b) *Statement of Production–Standard and Actual*

Particulars	Standard Percentage	Standard Quantity (tonnes)	Actual Percentage	Actual Quantity (tonnes)
(i) Process I				
Input in process I	100	1,000	100	1,000
Output of process I	80	800	85	850
Less scrap	10	80	8	68
Finished output of process transferred to process II		720		782
(ii) Process II				
Inputs to process II	100	720	100	782
Output of process II	90	648	80	625.60
Less scrap	5	32.40	10	62.56
Finished output (yield) of process II		615.60		563.04

(c) *Cost of Finished Product per Tonne*

	Standard	Actual
Value of materials used	₹14,00,000	₹14,00,000
Less scrap sale value		
Standard: (102.4 tonnes @ ₹1,000)		
Less closing stock of 10 tonnes @ ₹1,000	10,000	
102.4 tonnes sold @ ₹1,000 per tonne	1,02,400**	
Actual: (120.56 tonnes@ ₹1,000)		
Less closing stock of 10 tonnes @ ₹1,000		10,000
120.56 tonnes sold @ 1,000 per tonne		1,20,560***
Net cost	12,87,600	12,69,440
Finished output in tonnes	615.60	563.04
Cost of finished output per tonne	2,092	2,255

** (Process I 80 tonnes + Process II 32.4 tonnes-closing stock 10 tonnes) = 1,02,400

*** (Process I 68 tonnes + Process II 62.56 tonnes-closing stock 10 tonnes) = 1,20,560

P.9.3 A product passes through two processes. The output of Process 1 becomes the input of Process II and the output of Process II is transferred to warehouse. The quantity of raw materials introduced into Process I is 20,000 kgs at ₹10 per kg. The cost and output data for the month under review are as under:

Particulars	Process I	Process II
Direct materials	₹60,000	₹40,000
Direct labour	40,000	30,000
Production overheads	39,000	40,250
Normal loss	8%	5%
Output	18,000	17,400
Loss realisation of ₹/Units	2.00	3.00

The company's policy is to fix the selling price of the end product in such a way as to yield a profit of 20 per cent on selling price.

REQUIRED:

(i) Prepare the process accounts **(ii)** Determine the selling price per unit of the end product.

SOLUTION

(i)

Process I Account

Particulars	Kgs	Amount	Particulars	Kgs	Amount
To raw materials	20,000	₹2,00,000	By normal loss	1,600	₹3,200
To direct materials		60,000	By abnormal loss @ ₹18.25 per kg	400[1]	7,300[2]
To direct labour		40,000	By process II (output transferred @ ₹18.25 per kg)	18,000	3,28,500
To production overheads		39,000			
	20,000	3,39,000		20,000	3,39,000

Process II Account

Particulars	Kgs	Amount	Particulars	Kgs	Amount
To process I account	18,000	₹3,28,500	By normal loss	900	₹2,700
To direct materials		40,000	By finished stock (output transferred @ ₹25.50 per kg)	17,400	4,43,700
To direct labour		30,000			
To production overheads		40,250			
To abnormal gain @ ₹25.50 per kg.	300	7,650[3]			
	18,300	4,46,400		18,300	4,46,400

WORKING NOTES

1. *Abnormal Loss in Process I Account*

Normal output expected (20,000 kgs. – 8% Normal loss)	18,400 kgs
Less actual output	18,000
Abnormal loss	400

2. *Value of Abnormal Loss in Process I*

Total cost of process I	₹3,39,000
Less sales value of normal loss (1,600 kgs × ₹2)	3,200
Normal cost of normal output (20,000 kgs – 1,600 kgs)	3,35,800
Normal cost per kg (₹3,35,800/18,400 kgs)	18.25
Value of abnormal loss (400 kgs × ₹18.25)	7,300

3. *Abnormal Gain in Process II Account*

Normal output expected (18,000 kgs – 5% normal loss)	17,100 kgs
Actual output	17,400
Abnormal gain	300

4. *Value of Abnormal Gain in Process II Account*

Normal cost of normal output (17,100 kgs) (i.e., ₹4,38,750 – ₹2,700)	₹4,36,050
Normal cost per kg (₹4,36,050/17,100 kgs)	25.50
Value of abnormal gain (300 kgs × ₹25.50)	7,650

(ii) *Determination of Selling Price per Kg*

Cost per kg	₹25.50
Add desired profit @ 20% of selling price [₹20 on selling price of ₹100 or 20 on cost of ₹80 cost i.e., 25% on cost price (₹25.50 × 0.25)]	6.375
Selling price per kg	31.875

P.9.4 S.M. Limited furnishes you the following information relating to process B for the month of October:

1. Opening work-in-process, Nil
2. Units introduced, 10,000 units @ ₹3 per unit
3. *Expenses debited to the process*
   Direct materials, ₹14,650
   Labour, ₹21,148
   Overheads, ₹42,000
4. Normal loss in process, 1 per cent of input
5. Closing work-in-process, 350 units
   Degree of completion
   Material, 100 per cent
   Labour and overheads, 50 per cent
6. Finished output, 9,500 units
7. Degree of completion of abnormal loss:
   Material, 100 per cent
   Labour and overheads, 80 per cent
8. Units scrapped as normal loss were sold at ₹1 per unit.
9. All the units of abnormal loss were sold at ₹2.50 per unit.

Prepare: **(a)** Statement of equivalent production, **(b)** Statement of cost, **(c)** Process B account, and **(d)** Abnormal loss account.

SOLUTION

(a) *Statement of Equivalent Production in Process B*

Input	*Particulars*	*Units completed or otherwise*	*Stage of completion (per cent)*		*Equivalent units*	
			Material	*Conversion cost*	*Material*	*Conversion cost*
10,000	Units introduced					
	Units produced	9,500	100	100	9,500	9,500
	Normal loss (10,000 × 0.01)	100	—	—	—	—
	Abnormal loss (150 units – 100 normal)	50	100	80	50	40
	Work-in-process	350	100	50	350	175
10,000		10,000			9,900	9,715

(b) *Statement of Cost*

Particulars	*Total cost*	*Equivalent production in units*	*Cost per unit*
Cost of units introduced	₹30,000		
Additional direct materials	14,650		
	44,650		
Less sale proceeds of normal loss units (100 units × ₹1)	100		
Total material cost	44,550	9,900	₹4.5
Conversion costs			
Direct labour	21,148		
Overheads	42,000		
Total conversion costs	63,148	9,715	6.5
Total cost	1,07,698		11.00

(*Contd.*)

(Contd.)

Value of work-in-process	
Material (350 units × ₹4.50)	₹1,575.00
Conversion costs (175 units × ₹6.50)	1,137.50
	2,712.50
Value of abnormal loss	
Materials (50 units × ₹4.50)	225
Conversion costs (40 units × ₹6.50)	260
	485

(c) *Process B Account*

Particulars	Units	Amount	Particulars	Units	Amount
To materials	10,000	₹30,000	By normal loss	100	₹100
To direct materials		14,650	By abnormal loss	50	485
To labour		21,148	By finished stock		
To overheads		42,000	@ ₹11 per unit	9,500	1,04,500
			By work-in-process		
			inventory	350	2,713
	10,000	1,07,798		10,000	1,07,798

(d) *Abnormal Loss Account*

Particulars	Units	Amount	Particulars	Units	Amount
To process B	50	₹485	By sales	50	₹125
			By costing profit and loss A/c	—	360
	50	485		50	485

P.9.5 A company within the food industry mixes ingredients in two different processes to produce one product. The output of process I becomes the input of process II and the output of process II is transferred to the packing department. From the information given below, you are required to open accounts for process I, process II, abnormal loss and packing department and to record the transactions for the week ended May.

Process I	
Input:	
Material A	600 kgs at ₹5 per kg
Material B	400 kgs at ₹10 per kg
Mixing labour	43 hours at ₹20 per kg
Normal loss	5 per cent of weight input, disposed of at ₹1.60 per kg
Output	920 kgs
Process II	
Input:	
Material C	660 kgs at ₹12.50 per kg
Material D	420 kgs at ₹7.50 per kg
Flavouring essence	₹330
Mixing labour	37 hours at ₹20 per hour
Normal waste	5 per cent of weight input with no disposal value
Output	1,800 kgs

No work-in-process at the beginning of the week but 100 kgs in process at the end of the week and estimated to be only 50 per cent complete so far as labour and overheads were concerned.

Overhead of ₹3,200 incurred by the two processes to be absorbed on the basis of mixing labour-hours.

SOLUTION

Process I Account

Particulars	Quantity	Amount	Particulars	Quantity	Amount
To material A	600	₹3,000	By normal loss	50	₹80
To material B	400	4,000	By abnormal loss	30	300
To mixing labour (43 hours @ ₹20 per hour)		860	By transfer to process II @ ₹10 per kg	920	9,200
To overhead (@ ₹40 per hour)		1,720			
	1,000	9,580		1,000	9,580

Process II Account

Particulars	Quantity	Amount	Particulars	Quantity	Amount
To Process I	920	₹9,200	By normal waste	100	
To material C	660	8,250	By work-in-process	100	₹1,160
To material D	420	3,150	By packing department (1,800 kgs × ₹12.20)	1,800	21,960
To flavouring essence		300			
To mixing labour		740			
To overhead		1,480			
	2,000	23,120		2,000	23,120

Abnormal Loss Account

Particulars	Quantity	Amount	Particulars	Quantity	Amount
To process A/c	30	₹300	By sale	30	₹48
			By balance to P/L A/c		252
	30	300		30	300

Packing Department Account

Particulars	Quantity	Amount	Particulars	Quantity	Amount
To Process II	1,800	₹21,960	By balance c/d		₹21,960
		21,960			21,960

WORKING NOTES

(i) *Statement of Equivalent Production (Process II)*

Input	Particulars	Units completed or otherwise	Stage of completion		Equivalent units produced	
			Material	Conversion cost	Material	Conversion cost
920 kgs (output from process I) + 1,080 kgs introduced during process II 2,000	Kgs output completed	1,800	100	100	1,800	1,800
	Normal loss (0.05 × 2,000 kgs)	100	—	—	—	—
	Work-in-process	100	100	50	100	50
		2,000			1,900	1,850

(ii) *Statement of Cost*

Particulars	Total cost	Equivalent production (kg)	Cost per unit/kg
Materials transferred from Process I	₹9,200		
Add current process costs:			
Material C	8,250		
Material D	3,150		
Flavouring essence	300		
Total material cost	20,900	1,900	₹11
Conversion cost			
Mixing labour	740		
Overhead	1,480		
	2,220	1,850	1.2

(iii) *Statement of Apportionment of Cost*

Particulars	*Element of cost*	*Equivalent production*	*Cost per kg*	*Cost*	*Total*
Finished input	Material	1,800	₹11	₹19,800	
	Conversion costs	1,800	1.2	2,160	₹21,960
Work-in-process	Material	100	11.0	1,100	
	Conversion costs	50	1.2	60	1,160
					23,120

(iv) *Determination of overhead absorption rate* = ₹3,200 (Total labour-hours (43 + 37) = ₹40 per labour-hour

(v) *Cost per kg of output* = (₹9,580 — ₹80) ÷ 950 = ₹10

P.9.6 Product B passes through two processes before it is completed and transferred to finished stock. The following data are available for the month of March of the current year:

Particulars	*Process I*	*Process II*
Opening stock (at prime cost)	₹5,000	₹8,000
Direct materials	40,000	12,000
Direct labour	35,000	40,000
Production overheads	20,000	24,000
Closing stock (at prime cost)	10,000	4,000

Output of processes are transferred to the next ones at the following transfer prices:

Process I–@ 25 per cent on the transfer price to Process I

Process II–@ 25 per cent on the transfer price to finished stock.

Finished stocks are valued at the price at which they are received from Process II, and are as follows: Opening stock, ₹20,000; Closing stock, ₹30,000. Sales for the month amounted to ₹3,00,000. Provision for internal process profits as on March 1 were as follows:

Included in work-in-process of Process II, ₹1,500; Included in finished stock, ₹6,500

Calculate: **(a)** Process costs, **(b)** Gross profit, and **(c)** Write up the provision for inter-process profit account.

Solution

(a)

Process I Account

Particulars	*Total*	*Cost*	*Profit*	*Particulars*	*Total*	*Cost*	*Profit*
To opening stock	₹5,000	₹5,000	—	By Process III			
To direct materials	40,000	40,000	—	(output transferred			
To direct labour	35,000	35,000	—	at $133\frac{1}{3}$% of cost			
Less closing stock	(10,000)	(10,000)	—	(₹90,000 ×			
Prime cost	70,000	70,000	—	$133\frac{1}{3}$%)	₹1,20,000	₹90,000	₹30,000
To factory overheads	20,000	20,000					
Process costs	90,000	90,000					
To profit and loss A/c (profit at 25% on transfer price or $33\frac{1}{3}$ % on cost)	30,000	—	30,000				
	1,20,000	90,000	30,000		1,20,000	90,000	30,000

Process II Account

To opening stock	₹8,000	₹6,500	₹1,500	By finished stock A/c (output transferred)	₹2,50,000	₹1,69,200	₹80,800
To Process I (transferred from)	1,20,000	90,000	30,000				

(Contd.)

(*Contd.*)

Particulars	Total	Cost	Profit	Particulars	Total	Cost	Profit
To direct materials	12,000	12,000	—				
To direct labour	40,000	40,000	—				
Less closing stock@	(4,000)	(3,300)	(700)				
Prime cost	1,76,000	1,45,200	30,800				
To factory overheads	24,000	24,000	—				
Process cost	2,00,000	1,69,200	30,800				
To profit and loss A/c (profit at 20% on transfer price or 25% on cost)	50,000	—	50,000				
	2,50,000	1,69,200	80,800		2,50,000	1,69,200	80,800

@Cost of closing stock is worked out proportionately: (₹1,48,500 × ₹4,000) ÷ ₹1,80,000 = ₹3,300
Profit = ₹4,000 — ₹3,300, cost = ₹700

Finished Stock Account

Particulars	Total	Cost	Profit	Particulars	Total	Cost	Profit
To balance b/d	₹20,000	₹13,500	₹6,500	By closing stock	₹30,000	₹20,300@	₹9,700
To Process I (transferred from)	2,50,000	1,69,200	80,800	By sales	3,00,000	1,62,400	1,37,600
To profit and loss A/c (profit transferred)	60,000	—	60,000				
	3,30,000	1,82,700	1,47,300		3,30,000	1,82,700	1,47,300

@Cost of closing stock = (₹1,82,700 × ₹30,000) ÷ ₹2,70,000 = ₹20,300

(b) *and* **(c)** *Statement of profit*

Process I		₹30,000
Process II	₹50,000	
Adjustment of provision for unrealised profit		
Add on opening stock	1,500	
Less on closing stock	(700)	50,800
Finished stock account	60,000	
Adjustment of provision for unrealised profit		
Add on opening stock	6,500	
Less on closing stock	(9,700)	56,800
		1,37,600

P.9.7 The Food Specialists Ltd has two cost centres: **(i)** Cooking and **(ii)** Mix-pack. Material is added at the beginning of production in each cost centre, and labour is added equally during production in each cost centre. The FIFO method is used in the Cooking department and the weighted average method in the Mix-pack department.

The following information is available for the month of January:

Particulars	*Cooking*	*Mix-Pack*
Work-in-process opening, January 1		
Materials	₹4,980	₹570
Labour	500	300
Overhead	400	240
Prior department cost	—	2,130
Current month's cost		
Materials	1,98,000	76,380
Labour	50,250	80,000
Overhead	40,200	64,000

Inventory and production records show that Cooking had 500 litres, 40 per cent processed in the beginning of the month and 400 litres, 50 per cent processed at the end of the month; Mix-pack had 300 litres, 50 per cent processed in the beginning of the month and 400 litres, 30 per cent processed at the end of the month.

Production reports for the month show that 'Cooking' started 20,000 litres into production and completed and transferred 20,100 litres to Mix-pack; Mix-pack completed and transferred 20,000 one-litre containers of the finished product to the warehouse.

You are required to prepare a process cost report for the Cooking department as well as for Mix-pack department. Also prepare relevant process accounts.

SOLUTION

Production Cost Report of Cooking Centre for the month of January (FIFO basis)

1. *Units schedule*		
Opening inventory (40 per cent)		500
Add introduced during the month		20,000
Total		20,500
Less closing work-in-process inventory (50 per cent)		400
Units completed and transferred		20,100
2. *Cost to be accounted for*		
Opening inventory (₹4,980 + ₹500 + ₹400)		₹5,880
Materials		1,98,000
Conversion costs:		
Labour	₹50,250	
Overhead	40,200	90,450
		2,94,330

3. *Equivalent units and unit cost*	*Material*	*Conversion cost*
Opening inventory	Nil	300
Units introduced and completed (20,000 – 400)	19,600	19,600
Closing inventory	400	200
Equivalent units produced	20,000	20,100
Costs	₹1,98,000	₹90,450
Cost per unit	9.90	4.50

4. *Accounting for total costs transferred to Mix-pack*		
Opening inventory	₹5,880	
Costs to complete (300 × ₹4.50)	1,350	₹7,230
Started and completed 19,600 × (₹9.90 + ₹4.50)		2,82,240
Closing work-in-process inventory		
Materials (400 × ₹9.90)	3,960	
Conversion costs (200 × ₹4.50)	900	4,860
Total costs accounted for		2,94,330

Cooking Process Account

Particulars	Unit (litres)	Amount	Particulars	Unit (litres)	Amount
To opening inventory	500	₹5,880	By Mix-pack	20,100	₹2,89,470
To material	20,000	1,98,000	By closing work-in-process	400	4,860
To labour		50,250			
To overheads		40,200			
	20,500	2,94,330		20,500	2,94,330

Cost of Production Report of Mix-pack Department for the month of January (Weighted Average Cost basis)

1. *Units schedule*

Opening inventory (50 per cent)	300
Add units transferred from Cooking centre	20,100
Total	20,400
Less closing work-in-process inventory	400
Units completed and transferred	20,000

2. *Cost to be accounted for*

	Cooking centre	Mix-pack		Total costs
		Material	Conversion costs	
Opening inventory	₹2,130	₹570	₹540	₹3,240
Current period costs	2,89,470	76,380	1,44,000	5,09,850
	2,91,600	76,950	1,44,540	5,13,090

3. *Equivalent units and unit cost*

	Cooking centre	Mix-pack	
		Material	Conversion costs
Units completed	20,000	20,000	20,000
Plus closing work-in-process	400	400	120
	20,400	20,400	20,120
Cost per equivalent unit	₹14.2941	₹3.772	₹7.184

4. *Accounting for total costs*

Transferred to finished goods inventory [20,000 × ₹25.2501 (₹14.2941 + ₹3.772 + ₹7.184)]		₹5,05,002
Work-in-process (closing)		
Cooking centre (400 × ₹14.294)	₹5,717.60	
Material (400 × ₹3.772)	1,508.80	
Conversion costs (120 × ₹7.184)	862.08	8,088.48
Total costs accounted for		5,13,090.48

Mix-pack Process Account

Particulars	Unit (litres)	Amount	Particulars	Unit (litres)	Amount
To opening work-in-process inventory	300	₹3,240	By finished goods inventory account (transferred to)	20,000	₹5,05,002
To cooking process A/c (transferred from)	20,100	2,89,470	By work-in-process	400	8,088
To materials		76,380			
To labour		80,000			
To overheads		64,000			
	20,400	5,13,090		20,400	5,13,090

P.9.8 RST Ltd. manufactures plastic moulded chairs (for kids). Three models of moulded chairs, all variation of the same design are standard, deluxe and executive. The company uses an operation costing system.

RST Ltd. has extrusion, form, trim and finish operations. Plastic sheets are produced by the extrusion operation. During the forming operation, the plastic sheets are moulded into chair seats and the legs are added. The standard model is sold after this operation. During the trim operation, the arms are added to the deluxe and executive models and the chair edges are smoothed. Only the executive model enters the finish operation, in which padding is added. All of the units produced received the same steps within each operation. In April, units of production direct material cost incurred are as follows:

	Units produced	Extrusion materials	Form materials	Trim materials	Finish materials
Standard model	10,500	₹1,26,000	₹42,000	₹0	₹0
Deluxe model	5,250	63,000	21,000	15,750	0
Executive model	3,500	42,000	14,000	10,500	21,000
	19,250	2,31,000	77,000	26,250	21,000

The total conversion costs for the month of April, are:

	Extrusion operation	Form operation	Trim operation	Finish operations
Total conversion costs	₹6,06,375	₹2,97,000	₹1,55,250	₹94,500

REQUIRED:

(i) For each product produced by RST Ltd. during April, determine the unit cost and the total cost.

(ii) Now consider the following information for May. All unit costs in May are identical to the April unit costs calculated as above in (i). At the end of May, 1,500 units of the Deluxe model remain in work-in-progress. These units are 100 per cent complete as to materials and 65 per cent complete in the trim operation. Determine the cost of the Deluxe model work-in-process inventory at the end of May.

SOLUTION

Statement showing Unit Cost and Total Cost of three models of Chairs

Particulars	Standard model cost	Deluxe model cost	Executive model cost
Extrusion material	₹12	₹12	₹12
Form material	4	4	4
Trim material	—	3	3
Finish material		—	6
Extrusion operation	31.50	31.50	31.50
Form operation	15.43	15.43	15.43
Trim operation	—	17.74	17.74
Finish operation	—	—	27.00
Total unit cost	62.93	83.67	116.67
Units produced	10,500	5,250	3,500
Total cost	6,60,765	4,39,267.5	4,08,345

WORKING NOTES

(i) *Statement of Material and Conversion Cost per Equivalent Unit:*

Particulars	Extrusion	Form	Trim	Finish
Equivalent units (1)	19,250*	19,250*	8,750**	3,500
Material cost (2)	₹2,31,000	₹77,000	₹26,250	₹21,000
Conversion cost (3)	6,06,375	2,97,000	1,55,250	94,500
Material cost per equivalent unit (2/1)	12	4	3	6
Conversion cost per equivalent unit (3/1)	31.50	15.43	17.74	27

*(10,500 + 5,250 + 3,500)

**(5,250 + 3,500)

(ii) *Statement showing Cost of 1,500 units of Deluxe Model of Chairs (Work-in-process inventory) at the end of May*

Particulars	Equivalent (1)	Unit cost (2)	Total cost (3) = (1) × (2)
Extrusion materials	1,500	₹12	₹18,000
Form materials	1,500	4	6,000

(Contd.)

(Contd.)

Trim materials	1,500	3	4,500
Extrusion operation	1,500	31.50	47,250
Form operation	1,500	15.43	23,145
Trim operation (1,500 x 65%)	975	17.74	17,296.50
Total cost			1,16,191.5

P.9.9 Following information is available regarding process A for the month of February, related to the current year.

Production record:	
Units in process as on February 1	
(All materials used, 25 per cent complete for labour and overheads)	4,000
New units introduced	16,000
Units completed	14,000
Units in process as on February 28	
(All materials used, 33-1/3 per cent complete for labour and overheads)	6,000
Cost records:	
Work-in-process as on February 1	
Materials	₹6,000
Labour	1,000
Overheads	1,000
	8,000
Cost during the month	
Materials	25,600
Labour	15,000
Overheads	15,000
	55,600

Presuming that average method of inventory is used, prepare:

(i) Statement of equivalent production.
(ii) Statement showing cost for each element
(iii) Statement of apportionment of cost.
(iv) Process cost account for process A.

Solution

(i) *Statement of Equivalent Production (Average Cost Method)*

Flow of completed or partially completed units:	
Opening (at the beginning of month)	4,000
Introduced during the month	16,000
Total in process	20,000
Less units completed	14,000
Units in process	6,000

Particulars	*Number of units completed or otherwise*	*Stage of completion (per cent)*			*Equivalent units*		
		Materials	*Labour*	*Overheads*	*Materials*	*Labour*	*Overheads*
Units completed	14,000	100	100	100	14,000	14,000	14,000
Units in process	6,000	100	$33\frac{1}{3}$	$33\frac{1}{3}$	6,000	2,000	2,000
					20,000	16,000	16,000

(ii) *Statement showing Cost for each Element*

Particulars	Materials	Labour	Overheads	Total
Opening work-in-process	₹6,000	₹1,000	₹1,000	₹8,000
Cost incurred during February	25,600	15,000	15,000	55,600
Total cost	31,600	16,000	16,000	63,600
Equivalent units	20,000	16,000	16,000	—
Cost per equivalent unit	₹1.58	₹1	₹1	₹3.58

(iii) *Statement of Apportionment of Cost*

Particulars	Element of cost	Equivalent production (in units)	Cost per unit	Total cost	
Finished production	Materials	14,000	₹1.58	₹22,120	
	Labour	14,000	1.00	14,000	
	Overheads	14,000	1.00	14,000	₹50,120
Work-in-process	Materials	6,000	1.58	₹9,480	
	Labour	2,000	1.00	2,000	
	Overheads	2,000	1.00	2,000	13,480
					63,600

(iv) *Process A Account*

Particulars	Units	Amount	Particulars	Units	Amount
To Opening Work-in-process	4,000	₹8,000	By Completed units	14,000	₹50,120
To Materials	16,000	25,600	By Closing work-in-process	6,000	13,480
To Labour		15,000			
To Overheads		15,000			
	20,000	63,600		20,000	63,600

P.9.10 The following information is given in respect of Process 3 for the month of January, current year.

Opening stock – 2,000 units made-up of:	
Direct materials-I	₹12,350
Direct materials-II	13,200
Direct labour	17,500
Overheads	11,000
Transferred from Process 2: 20,000 units @ ₹6 per unit.	
Transferred to Process 4: 17,000 units	
Expenditure incurred in Process 3:	
Direct materials	30,000
Direct labour	60,000
Overheads	60,000

Scrap: 1,000 units – Direct materials, 100 per cent; Direct labour, 60 per cent; Overheads, 40 per cent
Normal loss: 10 per cent of production.
Scrapped units realised: ₹4 per unit
Closing Stock: 4,000 units – Degree of completion: Direct materials, 80 per cent, Direct labour, 60 per cent and Overheads, 40 per cent

Prepare Process 3 Account using average price method, along with necessary supporting statements.

SOLUTION

Statement of Equivalent Production (Average Cost Method)

Particulars	Total units to be accounted for	Stage of completion(%)				Equivalent units			
		Materials I	Materials II	Labour	Over -heads	Materials I	Materials II	Labour	Over -heads
Units completed	17,000	100	100	100	100	17,000	17,000	17,000	17,000
Normal loss (10%) (2,000 units + 20,000 units – 4,000 units)	1,800	—	—	—	—	—	—	—	—
Closing stock (work-in-process)	4,000	100	80	60	40	4,000	3,200	2,400	1,600
Abnormal gain (balancing figure)	(800)*	100	100	100	100	(800)	(800)	(800)	(800)
Total	22,000	—	—	—	—	20,200	19,400	18,600	17,800

* 22,800 — 22,000 (total units to be accounted for i.e., 2,000 opening stock units + 20,000 transferred from Process No. 2). It may be noted that units completed include units due to abnormal gain also.

Statement of Cost

Particulars	Total cost	Equivalent units	Equivalent per unit cost
Direct materials-I:			
Opening stock	₹12,350		
Add cost of 20,000 units transferred form process 2@ ₹6 per unit	1,20,000		
	1,32,350		
Less scrap value of normal loss units (1,800 x ₹4)	7,200		
	1,25,150	20,200	₹6.2
Direct materials-II:			
Opening stock	₹13,200		
Introduced in process 3	30,000		
	43,200	19,400	2.2268
Direct labour:			
Included in opening stock	17,500		
Costs incurred as per process 3	60,000		
	77,500	18,600	4.1667
Overheads:			
Included in opening stock	11,000		
Costs incurred as per process 3	60,000		
	71,000	17,800	3.9888
Total cost per unit			16.5778

Statement showing Apportionment of Costs

Cost of completed units	(17,000 units × ₹16.5778)		₹2,81,822.60
Valuation of abnormal gain	(800 units × ₹16.5778)		13,262.24
Valuation of closing stock (Work-in-process):			
Direct materials I	(4000 Units × ₹6.1955)	₹24,782	
Direct Materials II	(3,200 Units × 2.2268)	7,125.76	
Direct Labour	(2,400 Units × 4.1667)	10,000.08	
Overheads	(1,600 Units × 3.9888)	6,382.08	48,289.92

Process 3 Account

Particulars	Units	Amount	Particulars	Units	Amount
To opening work-in-process	2,000	₹54,050	By Normal loss	1,800	₹7,200
To Process 2	20,000	1,20,000	By Finished goods	17,000	2,81,822
To Direct materials II		30,000	By Closing work-in-process	4,000	48,290
To Direct labour		60,000			
To Overheads		60,000			
To Abnormal gain	800	13,262			
	22,800	3,37,312		22,800	3,37,312

P.9.11 A factory producing P also produces a by-product Q which is further processed into a finished product. The joint cost of manufacture is given below: Material, ₹5,000; Labour, ₹3,000; and Overheads, ₹2,000.

Subsequent costs are as under:

	P	Q
Material	₹3,000	₹1,500
Labour	1,400	1,000
Overheads	600	500
	5,000	3,000

Selling prices are: P, ₹16,000; Q, ₹8,000.

Estimated profits on selling prices are 25 per cent for P and 20 per cent for Q.

Assume that selling and distribution expenses are in proportion of sales price.

Show how you would apportion joint costs of manufacture, and prepare a statement showing cost of production of P and Q.

SOLUTION

Apportionment of Joint Costs

Particulars	P	Q
Selling price	₹16,000	₹8,000
Less profits @ 25 per cent (P) and 20 per cent (Q) on selling price	4,000	1,600
Less selling and distribution expenses (2:1)	267	133
Cost of production	11,733	6,267
Less separable costs subsequent to split-off point	5,000	3,000
Share of joint costs (6,733: 3,267 for P and Q)	6,733	3,267

Statement showing Cost of Production of P and Q

Elements of cost	Joint costs		Separable costs		Total cost	
	P	Q	P	Q	P	Q
Materials	₹3,367	₹1,633	₹3,000	₹1,500	₹6,367	₹3,133
Labour	2,020	980	1,400	1,000	3,420	1,980
Overheads	1,346	654	600	500	1,946	1,154
	6,733	3,267	5,000	3,000	11,733	6,267

WORKING NOTES

Determination of Selling and Distribution Expenses

Sales revenue (P and Q)		₹24,000
Less profit (P and Q)		5,600
Cost of sales		18,400
Less cost of production		
Joint costs	₹10,000	
Separable costs [₹5,000 (P) + ₹3,000 (Q)]	8,000	18,000
Selling and distribution expenses		400

P.9.12 X Ltd manufactures product A which yields two by-products, B and C. In a period the amount spent upto the point of separation was ₹20,600. Subsequent expenses were:

	A	B	C
Materials	₹300	₹200	₹250
Direct wages	400	300	200
Overhead	300	270	180
	1,000	770	630

Gross sales value of products A, B and C was ₹15,000, ₹10,000, and ₹5,000 respectively. It was estimated that the net profit as a percentage of sales in case of products B and C would be 25 per cent and 20 per cent respectively. Ascertain the profit earned on A.

SOLUTION

Statement showing the Allocation of Joint Costs between Products B and C (NRV less Normal Profit Method)

Products	*Sales value*	*Profit*	*Separable costs*	*NRV/Joint costs*
B	₹10,000	₹2,500	₹770	₹6,730
C	5,000	1,000	630	3,370

Joint cost to be allocated to A would be: ₹20,600 — (₹6,730 + ₹3,370) = ₹10,500

Statement showing Profit Earned by Product A

Sales revenue			₹15,000
Less cost of production			
Joint cost		₹10,500	
Separable costs:			
Material	₹300		
Direct wages	400		
Overheads	300	1,000	11,500
Profit			3,500

P.9.13 From the following information, find the profit made by each product apportioning joint costs on sales-value basis:

Joint costs		
Direct material		₹1,26,000
Power		25,000
Petrol, oil, lubricants		5,000
Labour		7,500
Other charges		4,100
		1,67,600
	Product X	*Product Y*
Selling costs	₹20,000	₹80,000
Sales	1,52,000	1,68,000

SOLUTION

Statement showing Profit after Apportionment of Joint Costs

Particulars	*Product X*	*Product Y*	*Total*
Sales	₹1,52,000	₹1,68,000	₹3,20,000
Less cost of production			
(In the ratio of sales: 19:21)			
Direct material	59,850	66,150	1,26,000
Power	11,875	13,125	25,000
Petrol, oil, lubricants	2,375	2,625	5,000
Labour	3,562.50	3,937.50	7,500

(Contd.)

(*Contd.*)

Other charges	1,947.50	2,152.50	4,100
Gross profit	72,390	80,010	1,52,400
Less selling costs	20,000	80,000	1,00,000
Profit	52,390	10	52,400

P.9.14 XYZ Chemicals Manufacturing Company Ltd buys a particular raw material at ₹4 per litre. At the end of the processing in department 1, this raw material splits-off into products, X, Y and Z. Product X is sold at the split-off point, with no further processing. Products Y and Z require further processing before they can be sold. Product Y is processed in department 2, and product Z is processed in department 3. Following is a summary of costs and other related data for the end of the current year.

	Department		
	1	2	3
Cost of raw material	₹2,40,000	—	—
Direct labour	35,000	₹2,25,000	₹3,25,000
Manufacturing overhead	24,000	1,05,000	2,25,000
		Products	
	X	Y	Z
Litres sold	10,000	15,000	22,500
Closing inventory	5,000	—	7,500
Sales	₹1,50,000	₹4,80,000	₹7,50,000
Sale price per litre	15	32	25

There were no opening and closing inventories of basic raw materials at the beginning as well as at the end of the year. All finished goods inventory of litres was complete as to processing. The company uses the relative sales value method of allocating joint costs.

You are required to prepare: **(i)** Schedule showing the allocation of joint cost; **(ii)** Cost of sales of each product, the cost of each ending inventory; and **(iii)** A comparative statement of profit.

SOLUTION

(i) *Schedule showing Allocation of Joint Cost*

Product	*Output (litres)*	*Market price*	*Total market price*	*Separable costs*	*Net realisable value*	*Joint cost*	*Total cost*	*Cost per unit*
X	15,000	₹15	₹2,25,000	—	₹2,25,000	₹1,17,000	₹1,17,000	₹7.8
Y	15,000	32	4,80,000	₹3,30,000	1,50,000	78,000	4,08,000	27.2
Z	30,000	25	7,50,000	5,50,000	2,00,000	1,04,000	6,54,000	21.8
				8,80,000		2,99,000	11,79,000	

Joint cost = [₹2,40,000 + ₹35,000 + ₹24,000] = ₹2,99,000 of Department 1 allocated in the ratio of 9:6:8 among products X, Y, and Z respectively.

(ii) *Schedule showing Cost of Sales and Ending Inventory of each Product*

Product	*Cost per unit*	*Units sold (litres)*	*Cost of sales*	*Inventory units (litres)*	*Inventory cost*
X	₹7.8	₹10,000	₹78,000	5,000	₹39,000
Y	27.2	15,000	4,08,000	—	—
Z	21.8	22,500	4,90,500	7,500	1,63,500

(iii) *Comparative Statement of Profit*

Particulars	*Product X*	*Product Y*	*Product Z*
(a) Sales revenue	₹1,50,000	₹4,80,000	₹5,62,500
Less cost of sales			
Production cost			
(i) Joint cost	1,17,000	78,000	1,04,000
(ii) Separable cost	—	3,30,000	5,50,000
Total cost	1,17,000	4,08,000	6,54,000
Less closing inventory	39,000	—	1,63,500
(b) Cost of goods sold	78,000	4,08,000	4,90,500
(c) Gross profit [(a) – (b)]	72,000	72,000	72,000

P.9.15 The ABC Ltd makes three products from one common input. Process I is the joint process and every 100 kgs of input yields: 60 kgs of product A; 30 kgs of product B; and 5 kgs of product C and the remaining 5 kgs is a waste product with no market value.

Product A requires further processing in process II at an average cost of ₹10 per kg. It is then sold at ₹100 per kg. Product B is sold at split-off point at ₹50 per kg. Product C after further processing in process III (at ₹2.5 per kg), is sold at ₹5 per kg. The selling expenses associated with C are negligible, and the company desires the cost of product C to be such as to earn a profit of 10 per cent on sales.

During the current period, 1,00,000 kgs of input was processed through process I (assume no inventories), and the total operating costs in Process I were ₹51,85,000.

You are required: **(i)** To determine the amount of Process I cost assigned to by-product C; **(ii)** To determine the amount of joint costs to be assigned to A and B using the relative sales value approach; **(iii)** To determine the amount of joint costs to be assigned to A and B, using the net realisable value less normal profit approach.

SOLUTION

(i) *Determination of Cost of By-product C*

Sales revenue (₹5 × 5,000 kgs, that is, 1,00,000 kgs × 0.5)	₹25,000
Less separable costs in Process III (₹2.5 × 5,000 kgs)	12,500
Less profit [10 per cent of selling price (0.10 × ₹25,000)]	2,500
Cost of Process I (joint costs) assigned to product C	10,000

(ii) *Statement showing Allocation of Joint Cost between Products A and B (Relative Sales Value Approach)*

Product	*Output (kgs)*	*Sales price*	*Total market value*	*Separable costs*	*NRV*	*Joint cost*
A	60,000	₹100	₹60,00,000	₹6,00,000	₹54,00,000	₹40,50,000
B	30,000	50	15,00,000	—	15,00,000	11,25,000
			75,00,000		69,00,000	51,75,000

(iii) *Statement showing the Allocation of Joint Cost between Products A and B (NRV Less Normal Profit Approach)*

Product	*Market value*	*Normal profit*	*Separable cost*	*NRV*	*Joint cost*
A	₹60,00,000	₹13,80,000	₹6,00,000	₹40,20,000	₹40,20,000
B	15,00,000	3,45,000	—	11,55,000	11,55,000

Normal profit ratio = 100 per cent — (₹51,75,000+₹6,00,000) ÷ ₹75,00,000 = 100 —77 = 23 per cent

P.9.16 The XYZ Chemical Company Ltd produces chemicals X and Y from material Z. 10 litres of raw material Z yield 8 litres of X and 2 litres of Y as a result of processing it in department I. Product X requires furhter processing in department II and then is sold at ₹150 per litre. Product Y is sold at the split-off point for ₹112.50 per litre. The following additional data are available for the current period.

Department I	
Inventory (in litres)	100
Percentage completion of conversion costs	50
Cost of material Z added in current period (1,100 litres)	₹22,000
Conversion costs in current period	31,500
Department II	
Inventory (in litres)	200
Percentage completion of conversion costs	25
Conversion costs in current period	₹52,000
Finished goods inventories	
Product X	100
Product Y	50

Prepare a statement apportioning the joint costs of Department I between Products X and Y using the net realisable value less normal profit method.

SOLUTION

Department I

Total cost (₹22,000 + ₹31,500)		₹53,500
Less cost of closing inventory (work-in-process):		
Material cost (100 litres × ₹20)	₹2,000	
Conversion cost [100 × 0.50 × ₹31.500 ÷ 1,050)]	1,500	3,500
Cost to be allocated between products X and Y		50,000

WORKING NOTES

(i) 1,050 are equivalent units: (1,000, completed units + 100 units, work in process × 0.50 complete).

(ii) Litres produced, 1,000

Product X (0.80 × 1,000) = 800 litres

Product Y (0.20 × 1,000) = 200 litres

Department II (Product X)

Equivalent units started and finished (800 litres from Department I - 200 litres, closing inventory)	600
Add closing equivalent units inventory (200 × 0.25)	50
Equivalent units produced	650
Conversion costs	₹52,000
Cost per equivalent unit (₹52,000 ÷ 650)	80

Statement Apportioning Joint Cost of Department I between Products X and Y (NRV Less Normal Profit Method)

Product	Output (litres)	Selling price	Total market value	Normal profit	Separable costs	Joint costs
X	800	₹150	₹1,20,000	₹24,000	₹64,000	₹32,000
Y	200	112.50	22,500	4,500	—	18,000

Normal profit rate = 100 —[₹50,000 + (₹80 × 800)] ÷ ₹1,42,500 = 100 — 80 = 20 per cent

Separable costs for completed 800 units @ ₹80 per equivalent unit = (₹80 × 800) = ₹64,000.

P.9.17 X Ltd is in the food processing industry. In one of its processes, three joint products are manufactured. Traditionally, the company apportions costs incurred upto the joint products' pre-separation point on the basis of weight of output of the product.

You are required to prepare statements for the management to express:

(a) The profit or loss of each product as ascertained, using weight basis of apportioning pre-separation joint cost.

(b) The optimal contribution which could be obtained from the manufacture of these products.

The following process data for December are given. Costs incurred upto separation point are ₹96,000.

	Product A	Product B	Product C
Cost incurred after separation point	₹20,000	₹12,000	₹8,000
Selling price per tonne:			
Completed product	500	800	600
Estimated, if sold at separation point	250	700	450
Output (tonnes)	100	60	80

The cost of any unused capacity after the separation point should be ignored.

SOLUTION

Comparative Profit and Loss Account for Products, A, B and C

Particulars	Products			
	A	B	C	Total
Sales revenue	₹50,000	₹48,000	₹48,000	₹1,46,000
Less cost of production:				
Joint costs (allocated in of proportion output 10:6:8)	40,000	24,000	32,000	96,000
Separable costs	20,000	12,000	8,000	40,000
Profit/(loss)	(10,000)	12,000	8,000	10,000

(b) In order to ascertain whether the firm is following a sound policy regarding processing all products beyond the split-off point, we should adopt the incremental analysis which compares incremental revenue from further processing with incremental costs (separable costs) incurred by the firm.

Particulars	Product A	Product B	Product C
(i) Number of units (tonnes)	100	60	80
(ii) Incremental revenue from further processing per unit	₹250	₹100	₹150
(iii) Total incremental revenue (i) × (ii)	25,000	6,000	12,000
(iv) Incremental cost from further processing	20,000	12,000	8,000
(v) Incremental profit/loss [(iii) – (iv)]	5,000	(6,000)	4,000

The incremental analysis suggests that products A and C should be processed further beyond the split-off point as they yield positive contributions. Product B should be sold at split-off point because further processing cost is more than the incremental revenue it fetches. Accordingly, contributions would be maximum and optimal when products A and C are processed further and product B is sold at the split-off point. This is shown in the following statement:

Statement Showing Optimal Contribution

Particulars	Product A	Product B	Product C	Total
Sales revenue	₹50,000	₹42,000	₹48,000	₹1,40,000
Less variable costs for further processing	20,000	—	8,000	28,000
Contribution	30,000	42,000	40,000	1,12,000
Less joint costs		Not required		96,000
Profit				16,000

P.9.18 Two products P and Q are obtained in a crude form and require processing at a cost of ₹5 for P and ₹4 for Q per unit before sale. Assuming a net margin of 25 per cent on cost, their sale prices are fixed at ₹13.75 and ₹8.75 per unit respectively. During the period, the joint cost was ₹88,000 and the outputs were: P, 8,000 units; Q, 6,000 units. Ascertain the joint cost per unit

SOLUTION

Statement for Ascertaining Joint Cost per Unit

Product	*P*	*Q*
Output (units)	*8,000*	*6,000*
Selling price per unit	₹13.75	8.75
Less, profit margin @ 25 per cent on cost or 20 per cent on sales	(2.75)	(1.75)
	11	7
Less post split off cost	(5)	(4)
Pre-split off net joint cost per unit	6	3
Share in joint cost of units of P and Q can be obtained by apportioning in ratio of 8:3[1]	64,000	24,000
Joint cost per unit	8@	4@@

@(₹64,000/8000 units) @@(₹24,000/6,000 units)

WORKING NOTES

1. *Calculation of Ratio of Apportionment of Joint Cost*

Products	*P*	*Q*
Units	8,000	6,000
Pre-split off net joint cost per unit	₹6	₹3
Total output cost	48,000	18,000
Ratio	8 :	3

P.9.19 A company purchases raw materials worth ₹11.04 lakh and processes them into four products P, Q, R and S, which have a unit sale price of ₹3, ₹9, ₹16, and ₹60, respectively at split-off point, as they could be sold as such to other processors. However, during year, the company decided to further process and sell products P, Q and S, while product R would be sold at split-off point to other processes. The processing of raw materials into the four products cost ₹28 lakh to the company. The other data for the year were as under (amount in ₹lakh):

Product	*Output (units)*	*Sales*	*Additional processing (variable) cost after split-off*
P	10,00,000	46.00	12.00
Q	20,000	4.00	2.40
R	10,000	1.60	—
S	18,000	12.00	0.40

You are required to work out the company's annual income If the joint costs are allocated amongst the four products on the basis of 'net realisable value' at split-off point, what would be the compan's annual income?

SOLUTION

Statement showing Annual Income for four Products (₹in lakh):

Products	*Sales*	*Joint cost (working note 1)*	*Additional processing cost after split-off*	*Total cost (3+4)*	*Net income (2–5)*
(1)	*(2)*	*(3)*	*(4)*	*(5)*	*(6)*
P	46.00	27.20	12.00	39.20	6.80
Q	4.00	1.28	2.40	3.68	0.32
R	1.60	1.28	—	1.28	0.32
S	12.00	9.28	0.40	9.68	2.32
Total	63.60	39.04	14.80	53.84	9.76

WORKING NOTES

1. Statement showing Allocation of Joint Cost amongst the Products P, Q, R and S (under Net Realisable Values at Split-off Point Method) (₹in lakh)

Products	Sales value	Less additional processing cost	Net realisation value beyond split-off point	Computation	Joint costs
(1)	(2)	(3)	(4)	(5)	(6)
P	46.00	12.00	34.00	$\frac{39.04 \times 34.00}{48.80}$	27.20
Q	4.00	2.40	1.60	$\frac{39.04 \times 1.60}{48.80}$	1.28
R	1.60	—	1.60	$\frac{39.04 \times 1.60}{48.80}$	1.28
S	12.00	0.40	11.60	$\frac{39.04 \times 11.60}{48.80}$	9.28
Total:	63.60	14.80	48.80		39.04

P.9.20 JKL Ltd produces two products — J and K together with a by-product L from a single main process (process I). Product J is sold at the point of separation for ₹55 per kg, whereas product K is sold for ₹77 per kg after further processing into product k2. By-product L is sold without further processing for ₹19.25 per kg.

Process I is closely monitored by a team of chemists, who planned the output per 1,000 kg of input materials to be as follows:

Product J	500 kgs
Product K	350 kgs
Product L	100 kgs
Toxic waste	50 kgs

The toxic waste is disposed at a cost of ₹16.50 per kg, and arises at the end of processing. Process II which is used for further processing of product K into product K2, has the following cost structure:

Fixed costs	₹2,64,000 per week
Variable cost	16.50 per kg processed

The following actual data relate to the first week of the month:

Process I	
Opening work-in-progress	Nil
Material input	40,000 kgs costing ₹6,60,000
Direct labour	4,40,00
Variable overheads	1,76,000
Fixed overheads	2,64,000
Outputs:	
Product J	19,200 kgs
Product K	14,400 kgs
Product L	4,000 kgs
Toxic waste	2,400 kgs
Closing work-in-progress	Nil
Process II	
Opening work-in-progress	Nil
Input of product K	14,400 kgs
Output of product K2	13,200 kgs
Closing work-in-progress (50% converted and conversion costs were incurred in accordance with the planned cost structure)	1,200 kgs

REQUIRED:

(i) Prepare process I account for the first week of the month using the final sales value method of attribute the pre-separation costs to join products. **(ii)** Prepare the toxic waste account and process I account for the first week of the month. **(iii)** Comment on the method used by the JKL limited to attribute the pre-separation costs to joint products. **(iv)** Advise the management of JKL limited whether or not, on purely financial grounds, it should continue to process product K into product K2:

(a) If product k could be sold at the point of separation for ₹47.30 per kg; and

(b) If the 60 per cent of the weekly fixed costs of process II were avoided by not processing product K further.

SOLUTION

(i) *Process I Account*

Particular	Units in Kg	Rate per kg	Amount	Particulars	Units in Kg	Rate per kg	Amount
To material	40,000	₹16.50	₹6,60,000	By sales (product L)	4,000	₹19.25	₹77,000
To direct labour			4,40,000	By normal loss	2,000	(16.50)	(33,000)*
To variable overheads			1,76,000	By abnormal loss	400	44	17,600
To fixed overheads			2,64,000	By product J	19,200		7,21,171
				By product K	14,400		7,57,229
	40,000		15,40,000		40,000		15,40,000

*Disposal costs and, therefore, deducted.

WORKING NOTES

1. *Valuation of Abnormal Loss per kg:*
   = (₹15,40,000 — ₹77,000 + ₹33,000)/(40,000kgs × 0.85 excluding product L and waste)
   = ₹14,96,000/34,000 kgs = ₹44 per kg
2. *Calculation of Joint Cost of the Output (J and K):*
   = ₹15,40,000 + Disposal cost, [₹33,000 — ₹77,000 — ₹17,600] = ₹14,78,400
3. *Allocation of Joint Cost between Joint Products J and K (using Final Sales Value Method)*

Products	Quantity (kgs)	Sales value	Joint cost
J	19,200	₹10,56,000 (19,200 kgs × ₹55)	₹7,21,171
K	14,400	11,08,800 (14,400 kgs × ₹77)	7,57,229
		21,64,800	14,78,400

(ii) *Toxic Waste Account*

Particulars	Units in kg	Rate per kg	Amount	Particulars	Units in kg	Rate per kg	Amount
To process I A/c	2,000	16.50	(₹33,000)	By balance c/d		16.50	(₹33,000)

Process II Account

Particulars	Units in kg	Rate per kg	Amount	Particulars	Units in kg	Rate per kg	Amount
To process I A/c ₹11,73,917 (product K)	14,400	₹52.585	₹7,57,229	By product K2	13,200	—	
To variable overheads			2,37,600	By closing work-in-process	1,200	—	84,912
To fixed overheads		16.50	2,64,000				
			12,58,829				12,58,829

WORKING NOTES

1. *Valuation of 1,200 kgs of Closing Work-in-process*

Material 100% complete (1,200 kgs × ₹52.585)	₹63,103
Fixed and variable overheads	
[(₹2,37,600 + ₹2,64,000)/(13,800 units [14,200 – 600])] × 600 units	21,809
	84,912

(iii) *Comment on the Method used by JKL Ltd:*

JKL Ltd has used the commonly used method of final sales value for allocating joint costs between products J and K. Other methods used are: (a) Physical measure method, (b) Constant gross margin percentage method and (c) Net realisable value method.

(iv) *Whether Further Processing of Product K to K_2 should be undertaken or not:*

Incremental sales revenue per kg from further processing (₹77 – ₹47.30)	₹29.70
Less incremental variable cost per kg of further processing	16.50
Incremental contribution per kg from further processing	13.20
Total incremental contribution (14,400 kgs × ₹13.20)	1,90,080
Less avoidable fixed cost (60% × ₹2,64,000)	1,58,400
Incremental profit	31,680.00

Break-even point = Avoidable fixed costs/Incremental contribution per kg = ₹1,58,400/13.20 = 12,000 kgs

The company should opt for further processing in case the output is expected to exceed 12,000 kgs per week.

P.9.21 Pokemon Chocolates manufactures and distributes chocolate products. It purchases Cocoa beans and processes them into two intermediate products:

Chocolate powder liquor base

Milk-chocolate liquor base.

These two intermediate products become separately identifiable at a single split off point. Every 500 pounds of cocoa beans yields 20 gallons of chocolate — powder liquor base and 30 gallons of milk-chocolate liquor base.

The chocolate power liquor base is further processed into chocolate powder. The milk-chocolate liquor base is further processed into milk-chocolate. Every 30 gallons of milk-chocolate liquor based yields 340 pounds of milk chocolate.

Production and sales data for October, current year are:

Cocoa beans processed 7,500 pounds

Costs of processing Cocoa beans to split off point (including purchase of beans) = ₹7,12,500

	Production	*Sales*	*Selling price*
Chocolate powder	3,000 pounds	3,000 pounds	₹190 per pound
Milk chocolate	5,100	5,100	₹237.50 per pound

The October, separable costs of processing chocolate-powder liquor into chocolate powder are ₹3,02,812.50. The October, 2004 separable costs of processing milk-chocolate liquor base into milk-chocolate are ₹6,23,437.50.

Pokemon could have sold the chocolate powder liquor based for ₹997.50 a gallon and the milk-chocolate liquor base for ₹1,235 a gallon.

REQUIRED:

(i) Calculate how the joint cost of ₹7,12,500 would be allocated between the chocolate powder and milk-chocolate liquor bases under the following methods:

(a) Sales value at split off point **(b)** Physical measure (gallons) **(c)** Estimated net realizable value, (NRV) and **(d)** Constant gross-margin percentage NRV.

(ii) What is the gross-margin percentage of the chocolate powder and milk-chocolate liquor bases under each of the methods in requirements (i)? **(iii)** Could Pokemon have increased its operating income by a change in its decision to fully process both of its intermediate products? Show your computation.

SOLUTION

(i) *Allocation of Joint Cost under Various Methods*

Particulars	*Chocolate powder liquor base*	*Milk chocolate liquor base*	*Total*
(a) Sales value at split of point method:			
Sales value of products at split off	₹2,99,250 (300 × ₹997.50)	₹5,55,750 (450 gallons × ₹1,235)	₹8,55,000
Weights (in proportion of sale value)	0.35	0.65	1.00
Joint cost allocated	(₹7,12,500 × 0.35) ₹2,49,375	(₹7,12,500 × 0.65) ₹4,63,125	7,12,500
(b) Physical measure method:			
Output	300 gallons	450 gallons	750 gallons
Weights (300:450)	(300/750) = 0.40	(450/750) = 0.60	1.00
Joint cost allocated (in proportion of output)	(₹7,12,500 × 0.40) = ₹2,85,000	(₹7,12,500 × 0.60) = ₹4,27,500	₹7,12,500
(c) Net realisable value (NRV) method:			
Final sales value of production	(3,000 pounds × ₹190) = ₹5,70,000	(5,100 pounds × ₹237.50) = ₹12,11,250	₹17,81,250
Less separable costs	3,02,812.50	6,23,437.50	9,26,250
Net realizable value at split off point	2,67,187.50	5,87,812.50	8,55,000
Weights (in proportion of NRV)	0.3125	0.6875	1.00
Joint cost allocated	(₹7,12,500 × 0.3125) = ₹2,22,656.25	(₹7,12,500 × 0.6875) = ₹4,89,843.75	₹7,12,500
(d) Constant gross margin percentage NRV method:			
Final sales value of production	₹5,70,000	₹12,11,250	₹17,81,250
Less gross margin (8%)	45,600	96,900	1,42,500
Cost of goods available for sale	5,24,400	11,14,350	16,38,750
Less separable costs	3,02,812,50	623,437.50	9,26,250
Joint cost allocated	2,21,587.50	4,90,912.50	7,12,500

WORKING NOTES

Computation of Gross Margin

Final sales value of total production	₹17,81,250
Less joint and separable cost	16,38,750
Gross margin	1,42,500
Gross margin (%) (₹1,42,500/₹17,81,250)/ × 100	8

(ii) *Computation of Gross Margin of Chocolate Powder and Milk Chocolate Liquor Bases under various Methods*

Particulars	*Sales value at split off*	*Physical measure*	*Net realizable value*	*Constant gross margin NRV*
Chocolate powder liquor base:				
Final sales value	₹5,70,000	₹5,70,000	₹5,70,000	₹5,70,000
Less separable costs	3,02,812.50	3,02,812.50	3,02,812.50	3,02,812.50
Less joint costs	2,49,375.00	2,85,000.00	2,22,656.25	2,21,587.50
Gross margin	17,812.50	(17,812.50)	44.531.25	45,600.00
Gross margin (%)	3.125	(3.125)	7.8125	8
Milk chocolate liquor base:				
Final sales value	₹12,11,250	₹12,11,250	₹12,11,250	₹12,11,250
Less separable costs	6,23,437.50	6,23,437.50	6,23,437.50	6,23,437.50

(Contd.)

(*Contd.*)

Less joint costs	4,63,125	4,27,500	4,89,843.75	4,90,912
Gross margin	1,24,687.50	1,60,312,50	97,968.75	96,900.50
Gross margin (%)	10.29	13.23	8.08	8

(iii) *Further Processing of Chocolate Powder Liquor Base into Chocolate Powder*

Particulars	*Amount*
Incremental revenue [₹5,70,000 – (₹997.50 × 300)]	₹ 2,70,750
Less incremental costs	3,02,812,50
Incremental operating income	(32,062.50)

Further Processing of Milk Chocolate Liquor Base into Milk Chocolate

Particulars	*Amount*
Incremental revenue [₹12,11,250 – (450 × ₹1,235)]	₹ 6,55,500
Less incremental cost	6,23,437,50
Incremental operating income	32,062.50

From the above, it is clear that Pokemon Chocolates could increase operating income (by ₹32,062.50) by processing further milk chocolate liquor base into milk chocolate and selling chocolate liquor base at split off point itself.

P.9.22 The Sunshine Oil Company purchases crude vegetable oil. It does refining of the same. The refining process results in four products at the split-off point: M,N,O and P.

Product O is fully processed at the split-off point. Product M,N and P can be individually further refined into 'Super M', 'Super N' and 'Super p'. In the most recent month (October), related to current year the output (in gallons) at split-off point was:

Product M	3,00,000
Product N	1,00,000
Product O	50,000
Product P	50,000

The joint cost of purchasing the crude vegetable oil and processing it were ₹40,00,000.

Sunshine had no beginning or ending inventories. Sales of Product O in October were ₹20,00,000. Total output of products M, N and P was further refined and then sold. Data related to October are as follows:

Particulars	*Further processing costs to make Super Products*	*Sales*
'Super M'	₹80,00,000	₹1,20,00,000
'Super N'	32,00,000	40,00,000
'Super P'	36,00,000	48,00,000

Sunshine had the option of selling products M, N and P at the split-off point. This alternative would have yielded the following sales for October:

Product M	₹20,00,000
Product N	12,00,000
Product P	28,00,000

You are required to answer:

(i) How would the joint cost of ₹40,00,000 be allocated between each product under each of the following methods (a) sales value at split-off: (b) physical output (gallons): and (c) estimated net realizable value?

(ii) Could Sunshine have increased its October operating profits by making different decisions about the further refining of product M, N or P? Show the effect of any change you recommend on operating profits.

SOLUTION

(i) *(a) Joint Cost Allocation using Sales Value at Split-off Method*

Products (1)	Sales value at split-off point (2)	Basis of joint cost allocation (3)	Joint cost allocated (Col 3 × ₹40 lakh) (4)
M	₹20,00,000	20/80	₹10,00,000
N	12,00,000	12/80	6,00,000
O	20,00,000	20/80	10,00,000
P	28,00,000	28/80	14,00,000
	80,00,000		40,00,000

* assumed sales value at split-off point.

(b) Joint Cost Allocation using Physical Output Method

Products (1)	Output (gallons) (2)	Basis of joint cost allocation (3)	Joint cost allocated (Col 3 × ₹40 lakh) (4)
M	₹3,00,000	3/5	₹24,00,000
N	1,00,000	1/5	8,00,000
O	50,000	1/10	4,00,000
P	50,000	1/10	4,00,000
	5,00,000		40,00,000

(c) Joint Cost Allocation using Estimated Net Realisable Value Method

Products (1)	Sales value after further processing (2)	Further processing costs (3)	Net realisable value (Col.2 - Col. 3) (4)	Basis of joint cost allocation (5)	Joint cost allocated (Col. 5 x 40 lakh) (6)
M	₹1,20,00,000	₹80,00,000	₹40,00,000	40/80	₹20,00,000
N	40,00,000	32,00,000	8,00,000	8/80	4,00,000
O	—	—	20,00,000	20/80	10,00,000
P	48,00,000	36,00,000	12,00,000	12/80	6,00,000
			80,00,000		40,00,000

(ii) *Sell or Process Further: Decision Analysis*

Particulars	Products M	N	P
Sales value after further processing	₹1,20,00,000	₹40,00,000	₹48,00,000
Less sales value before further processing	20,00,000	12,00,000	28,00,000
Incremental sales revenue	1,00,00,000	28,00,000	20,00,000
Less further processing costs	80,00,000	32,00,000	36,00,000
Incremental profit (loss) from further processing	20,00,000	(4,00,000)	(16,00,000)

Sunshine would have increased profits by ₹20 lakh if it had processed Product M further; further processing of products N and P would have caused losses.

P.9.23 Two products P and Q are obtained in a crude form and require further processing at a cost of ₹5 for P and ₹4 for Q per unit before sale. Assuming a net margin of 25 per cent on cost, their sale prices are fixed at ₹13.75 and ₹8.75 per unit respectively. During the period, the joint cost was ₹88,000 and the outputs were: P, 8,000 units; Q, 6,000 units
Ascertain the joint cost per unit.

SOLUTION

Statement showing Allocation of Joint Costs

Particulars	Products	
	P	*Q*
Selling price per unit	₹13.75	₹8.75
Less estimated net profit (25 per cent on cost or 20 per cent on sales)	2.75	1.75
Less separable post split-off cost	5.00	4.00
Pre-split/joint cost per unit	6.00	3.00
Multiplied by output (in units)	8,000	6,000
Joint costs are to be shared between products P and Q in the ratio of 48000: 18,000 i.e., 8:3 respectively	48,000	18,000
Share of joint costs (P: ₹88,000 × 8/11 and Q: ₹88,000 × 3/11	64,000	24,000

P.9.24 ABC Ltd operates a simple chemical process to convert a single material into three separate items, referred to here as X, Y an Z. All three end products are separated simultaneously at a single split-off point.

Product X and Y are ready for sale immediately upon split-off without further processing or any other additional costs. Product Z, however, is processed further before being sold. There is no available market price for Z at the split-off point.

The selling prices quoted here are expected to remain the same in the coming year. During 2002-03, the selling prices of the items and the total amounts sold were:

X—186 tons sold for ₹1,500 per ton
Y—527 tons sold for ₹1,125 per ton
Z—736 tons sold for ₹750 per ton

The total joint manufacturing costs for the year were ₹6,25,000. An additional ₹3,10,000 was spent to finished product Z.

There were no opening inventories of X, Y or Z. At the end of the year, the following inventories of complete units are on hand:

X—180 tons
Y—60 tons
Z—25 tons

There was no opening or closing work-in-progress.

Required:

(i) Compute the cost of inventories of X, Y and Z for balance sheet purposes and cost of goods sold for income statement purposes as of March 31, 2003, using:

(a) Net realisable value (NRV) method of joint cost allocation.

(b) Constant gross-margin percentage NRV method of joint-cost allocation.

(ii) Compare the gross-margin percentages for X, Y and Z using two methods given in requirement (i).

SOLUTION (I) (A)

Statement showing Joint Cost Allocation among Products X, Y and Z (Net Realizable Value Method)

Particulars	Products			
	X	*Y*	*Z*	*Total*
Final sales value of total production	₹5,49,000[@]	₹6,60,375[£]	₹5,70,750*	₹17,80,125
Less further processing costs	—	—	3,10,000	3,10,000
Net realisable value	5,49,000	6,60,375	2,60,750	14,70,125
Joint cost allocated[1]	2,33,398	2,80,748	1,10,854	6,25,000

[@](366 tons × ₹1,500) [£](587 tons × ₹1,125) *(761 tons × ₹750)

WORKING NOTES

1. *Apportionment of joint cost:*

X = (₹6,25,000/₹14,70,125) × ₹5,49,000 = ₹2,33,398

Y = (₹6,25,000/14,70,125) × ₹6,60,375 = ₹2,80,748
Z = (₹6,25,000/14,70,125) × ₹2,60,750 = ₹1,10,854

(i) (a) *Cost of Goods Sold for the year and Cost of Closing Inventory as of March 31, 2003 (NRV Method)*

Products (1)	Allocated joint cost (2)	Further processing cost (3)	Cost of goods available for sale (4) = (2) + (3)	Cost of ending inventory[2] (5)	Cost of goods sold (6) = (4) − (5)
X	₹2,33,378	—	₹2,33,398	₹1,14,785	₹1,18,613
Y	2,80,748	—	2,80,748	28,692	2,52,056
Z	1,10,854	3,10,000	4,20,854	13,846	4,07,008
Total	6,25,000	3,10,000	9,35,000	(1,57,323)	7,77,677

2. *Computation of Total Production:*

Products (1)	Quantity sold in tons (2)	Quantity of ending inventory in tons (3)	Total production (4) (2) + (3)	Ending inventory percentage (5) = (3)/(4)
X	186	180	366	49.18%
Y	527	60	587	10.22
Z	736	25	761	3.29

Income Statement (based on Net Realisable Value Method)

Products	Sales revenue	Cost of goods sold	Gross margin	Gross margin %
X	₹2,79,000@	₹1,18,613	₹1,60,387	57.49%
Y	5,92,875*	2,52,056	3,40,819	57.49
Z	5,52,000£	4,07,008	1,44,992	26.26
Total	14,23,875	7,77,677	6,46,198	

@(186 tons × ₹1,500)
£(527 tons × ₹1,125)
*(736 tons × ₹750)

(i) (b) *Statement showing Joint Cost Allocation among Products X, Y and Z (Gross Margin Percentage Net Realisable Value Method)*

Particulars	Products X	Y	Z	Total
Final sales value of total production	₹5,49,000	₹6,60,375	₹5,70,750	₹17,80,125
Less gross margin[3] (refer to working note)	2,60,641	3,13,517	2,70,967	8,45,125
	2,88,359	3,46,858	2,99,783	9,35,000
Less additional cost			3,10,000	3,10,000
Joint cost allocated	2,88,359	3,46,858	(10,217)	6,25,000

3. *Gross Margin Percentage*

Final sales value of production	₹17,80,125
Less joint costs and additional costs	9,35,000
Gross margin	8,45,125
Gross margin %(₹8,45,125/17,80,125) × 100	47.4756%

Cost of Goods Sold for the year and Cost of Closing Inventory as of March 31, 2003 (using Constant Gross Margin percentage NRV method)

Particulars	Products X	Y	Z	Total
Allocated joint cost	₹2,88,359	₹3,46,858	(₹10,217)	₹6,25,000
Add additional cost			3,10,000	3,10,000
Cost of goods available for sale (CGAS)	2,88,359	3,46,858	2,99,783	9,35,000
Less cost of ending inventory	1,41,815*	35,449@	9,863£	1,87,127
Cost of goods sold	1,46,544	3,11,409	2,89,920	7,47,873

*(49.18% × 2,88,359)
@(10.22% × 3,46,858)
£(3.29% × 2,99,783)

Income statement (based on constant gross margin percentage NRV method)

Particulars	Products X	Y	Z	Total
Sales revenue	₹2,79,000	₹5,92,875	₹5,52,000	₹14,23,875
Less cost of goods sold	1,46,544	3,11,409	2,89,920	7,47,873
Gross margin	1,32,456	2,81,466	2,62,080	6,76,002
Gross margin (%)	47.48	47.48	47.48	47.48

Comparative statement of gross margin percentage for X, Y and Z (using net realizable value and constant gross margin percentage NRV methods)

Method	Product gross margin percentage X	Y	Z
Net realisable value	57.49	57.49	26.26
Constant gross margin percentage NRV	47.48	47.48	47.48

REVIEW QUESTIONS

RQ.9.1(a) Indicate whether the followings statements are 'True' or 'False'.

(i) Process costing is appropriate when the output is heterogeneous and/or the production process is generally intermittent.
(ii) In process costing, unit cost is determined periodically.
(iii) Less amount of inventory needs to be maintained in process costing as compared to job costing.
(iv) Job costing and process costing are mutually exclusive systems of costing.
(v) Process costing usually does not include a work-in-process account.
(vi) In process costing, the units of production in process need to be converted into equivalent units.
(vii) 100 units of inventory estimated to be 40 per cent complete are considered equivalent to 60 per cent completed units.
(viii) The split of production cost into (a) cost of output, and (b) closing inventory would remain same in FIFO as well as weighted average method of valuing work-in-process closing inventory.
(ix) In process costing, both normal and abnormal losses are controllable losses.
(x) Normal spoilage and abnormal spoilage are treated as product cost in process costing.
(xi) Abnormal spoilage cost is treated as a period cost and is written off as a loss in the period in which it occurs.
(xii) Transfer of output from one process to another can be either at cost or at market/inflated prices.
(xiii) The cost basis of inter-process transfer of output is better than market price basis.
(xiv) In process costing, production normally precedes sales.
(xv) Normal spoilage forms part of product costs.
(xvi) Normal loss is a controllable loss.
(xvii) Production costs incurred after the split-off point are joint costs.

(xviii) Physical quantities method results in identical unit costs for each product.

(b) In the following multiple choice questions, select the correct answers.

The following data of ABC Ltd. is given below.

Process I

— Raw material charged — 600 kg @ ₹4/kg.

— Direct labour ₹200.

— Departmental expenses ₹760.

— Normal loss is 10 per cent of input.

— During the period actual production was 500 kg and 100 kg was scrap. The scrap is sellable at ₹2/kg.

(xix) Calculate cost per unit which is cost per unit for ABC Ltd.

(a) ₹6 per unit, **(b)** ₹5.6 per unit, **(c)** ₹5 per unit, **(d)** None of these.

(xx) What is the amount of effective abnormal loss for ABC Ltd.?

(a) ₹240, **(b)** ₹160, **(c)** ₹200, **(d)** None of these.

[Answers: (i) False, (ii) True, (iii) False, (iv) False, (v) False, (vi) True, (vii) False, (viii) False, (ix) False, (x) False, (xi) True, (xii) True, (xiii) False, (xiv) True, (xv) True, (xvi) False, (xvii) True, (xviii) True, (xix) a (xx) b.]

RQ.9.2 Fill in the following blanks

(i) ____________ report forms the backbone of the process cost records (Cost of production/Job cost sheet).

(ii) Loss in excess of the normal spoilage is ____________ (abnormal loss/normal waste).

(iii) Production costs incurred prior to split-off point are called ____________ (joint costs/seperable costs).

(iv) Another name of unit method used for allocating joint costs is ____________ (physical quantities method/relative sales value).

(v) Where the joint products are heterogeneous, it is appropriate to use ____________ method (weighted average cost/net reliable value).

[Answers: (i) cost of production, (ii) abnormal loss, (iii) joint costs, (iv) physical quantities method, (v) weighted average cost.]

RQ.9.3 Specify the production situations that are more suitable to the process costing system.

RQ.9.4 Distinguish between process costing and job costing. Why is cost accumulation easier under the process costing system than under the job costing system?

RQ.9.5 Specify the important elements of a production report.

RQ.9.6 Explain clearly the difference between scrap, by-products, and joint products. Give the cost accounting treatment for each.

RQ.9.7 What is meant by 'equivalent units?' Discuss its importance in valuing work-in-process.

RQ.9.8 Explain normal and abnormal wastage and state how they should be dealt with in process cost accounts.

RQ.9.9 Under what circumstances are identical results obtained under weighted average and FIFO process costing?

RQ.9.10 Compare the weighted average method with the FIFO method in calculating unit costs.

RQ.9.11 An accountant has described cost allocations to joint products as a "necessary evil"? Comment.

RQ.9.12 Define joint products and by-products. Explain the various methods available for apportionment of joint costs to joint products.

RQ.9.13 What is meant by the split-off point? What is its significance in product costing?

RQ.9.14 When is the sales value method preferable to the quantity method as a means of allocating joint costs? In many manufacturing processes, waste products and by-products are produced. What problems do these present in costing the main product and how are they overcome?

RQ.9.15 A manufacturer can sell part of the output of process 1 as it is or process it further in process 2. What cost are relevant in a decision to sell it as it is or to process it further? What costs are irrelevant?

RQ.9.16 What are inter-process profits? How are such profits taken into account while valuing closing stock from the point of view of the balance sheet? Do you subscribe to the view that the output of one process should be transferred to another at a profit?

RQ.9.17 A product passes through two processes, A and B. The output of A passes on to B and that of B becomes the finished product. From the following information, prepare the process accounts:

	Process A	*Process B*
Materials consumed	₹24,000	₹12,000
Direct labour	28,000	16,000
Manufacturing expenses	8,010	8,000
Input in process A (units)	20,000	
Input in process A	20,000	
Output (units)	18,000	16,600
Normal wastage of input (%)	5	10
Value of normal wastage per 100 units	16	20

RQ.9.18 From the following data, prepare process accounts for a single product:

	Process I	*Process II*
(i) Period: December of the current year		
(ii) Work-in-process at the beginning	Nil	Nil
(iii) *Cost incurred in the period*		
Direct materials	₹60,000	—
Labour	12,000	₹16,000
Factory overheads	24,000	20,000
(iv) *Units of production*		
Received in process	40,000	36,000
Completed and transferred	36,000	32,000
Remaining in process at the end of the period	2,000	2,500
Loss-in-process (normal loss)	2,000	1,500
(v) *Production remaining in process should be valued at:*		
Material, 100 per cent		
Labour and overheads, 50 per cent.		

RQ.9.19 The following information is available from the records of a company engaged in manufacturing a single product.

Opening work-in-process	Quantity (units)	16,000
	Material	₹1,48,000
	Wages	33,000
	Overhead	29,000
Added during the year	Quantity (units)	69,000
	Material	5,62,000
	Labour	1,67,000
	Overhead	1,51,000
Finished during the year	Quantity (units)	56,000
Closing work-in-progress	Quantity (units)	24,000
	Material: 100% complete	
	Labour and overhead: 1/3 complete	

Tabulate the production and cost figures to give quantities, units values and total value for completed output and value of each element of cost for closing work-in-progress. Weighted average method of valuation may be used.

RQ.9.20 A manufacturing company makes a product using two processes. For the month of June, the information recorded for the second process is: A work-in-progress balance of 400 units brought forward from May was valued at ₹5,760. During June, 17,040 units were transferred from the first to the second process at a cost of ₹1,32,320. Costs incurred by the second process were:

Direct material issued	₹64,288
Direct wages	31,696
Overheads	15,848

The transfer of finished goods to the stock was 15,120 units. Number of units scrapped during the period was 880; 1,440 units were in work-in-progress at the end of the month.

There was a normal loss of 5 per cent of production. Units scrapped were sold at ₹3 each. The particulars relating to degree of completion are as follows:

	Degree of completion (%)		
	Opening stock	*Closing stock*	*Scrap*
Direct material	70	80	100
Direct wages	50	60	80
Overheads	50	60	80

Prepare the necessary accounts.

RQ.9.21 G.H. & Company Ltd. manufactures a product in the process costing and its work-in-progress stock at the end of each month is valued at FIFO basis.

At the beginning of the month of June, the inventory of work-in-progress showed 400 units, 40 per cent complete, valued as follows:

Material	₹3,600
Labour	3,400
Overheads	1,000
	8,000

In the month of June, materials were purchased for ₹75,000. Wages and overheads amounted to ₹79,800 and ₹21,285, respectively. Actual issue of material to production was ₹68,500. Finished stock was 2,500 units. There was no loss in process.

At the end of month, the work-in-progress inventory was 500 units, 60 per cent complete as to labour and overheads, and 80 per cent complete as to the material.

Prepare a process account for recording the month's transactions and a process cost sheet showing the total unit costs.

RQ.9.22 A product passes through two processes, A and B. Output of process A is transferred to process B at cost plus 25 per cent and finished output of B is similarly transferred to finished stock at cost plus 25 per cent. There is no work-in-progress in any process on December 31. At this date, the following information is further available:

	Process A	*Process B*
Materials consumed	₹8,000	₹24,000
Wages	12,000	16,000
Closing stock (valued at prime cost)	4,000	12,000

Out of the finished stock, a portion remained at hand valued at ₹11,000 and the balance was sold for ₹58,000.

Prepare process accounts and the finished stock account. Question of overheads and opening stock is to be ignored. Also show how much reserves will be created for the unrealised profit.

RQ.9.23 In manufacturing the main product A, a company processes the resulting waste material into two by-products, M_1 and M_2. Using the method of working backwards from the sales value to an estimated cost, prepare a comparative profit and loss statement of the three products from the following data:

(i) Total costs upto separation point was ₹1,36,000.

	A	M_1	M_2
(ii) Sale (all production)	₹3,28,000	₹32,000	₹48,000
(iii) Cost after separation	—	9,600	14,400
(iv) Estimated net profit percentage to sales values	—	20	30
(v) Estimated selling expenses as percentage of sales values	20	20	20

RQ.9.24 Product Z yields by-products X and Y. The joint manufacturing expenses are ₹65,500. From the following information, show how you would apportion the joint expenses of manufacture.

	X	Y	Z
(i) Sales	₹1,00,000	₹40,000	₹25,000
(ii) Manufacturing costs after separation	20,000	5,000	4,000
(iii) Estimated selling expenses on sales (%)	20	20	20
(iv) Estimated profit on sales (%)	20	25	30

RQ.9.25 The Assam Oil Company Ltd. processes crude oil in Department 1. During the current period, the following costs were incurred in Department 1 to obtain 20,000 barrels of product A and 30,000 barrels of product B:

Direct materials	₹50,000
Direct labour	1,50,000
Variable overheads	75,000
Fixed overheads	53,000
	3,28,000

Product A could be sold at the split-off point for ₹5 per barrel or processed in Department 2 at an additional cost of ₹4 per barrel and then sold for ₹10 per barrel. During the current period, all 20,000 barrels of A were processed in the Department. There was an ending inventory of 5,000 barrels of product A.

Product B must be processed further in Department 3. The following information from the current period is available about Department 3: Barrels processed, 31,000; Costs, ₹3,10,000.

The figure of 31,000 barrels includes 1000 barrels from the previous period's production of Department 1 processed in this period. There is an ending inventory of 1,000 barrels of B. The selling price of B is ₹20 per barrel.

You are required to determine to cost of ending finished inventories, using the net realisable value method to allocate the joint costs.

RQ.9.26 Calculate the estimated cost of production of by-products X and Y at the point of separation from the main product.

	By-product X	By-product Y
Selling price per unit	₹12	₹24
Cost per unit after separation from the main product	3	5
Units produced	500	200

Selling expenses amount to 25 per cent of the total works cost, that is, including both pre-separation and post-separation works cost.

Selling prices are arrived at by adding 20 per cent of the total of all costs, that is, the sum of work costs and selling expenses.

RQ.9.27 Alfa Ltd. uses a chemical process to convert a single raw material into three separate products, A, B, and C which are separated at a single split-off point. A and B are ready for sale immediately after split-off point without further processing or any additional costs. Product C is processed further before being sold. During the year ending December 31, the quantities sold and the realisations were:

Product	*Quantity (M_t)*	*Sales value (₹lakh)*
A	600	19.20
B	1,700	34.00
C	875	14.00

There were no opening inventories of A, B, and C. Total manufacturing costs for the year were ₹50.50 lakh. Costs after split-off point to process product C were ₹3 lakh. On December 31, the closing stocks were:

A	900 M_t
B	300 M_t
C	125 M_t

Prepare a statement of the 'cost' of inventories of A, B, and C. Your presentation should include a summary of the cost of goods sold by product-line and unit costs.

ANSWERS [Comprehensive solutions to all numerical review questions are available on the companion website: http://www.mhhe.com/khan_jain_cost2e]

RQ.9.17 Abnormal loss 1,000 units in process A; cost per unit of process A, ₹3.15; process B: cost per unit, ₹5.7; abnormal gain, 400 units.

RQ.9.18 Process A: Cost of completed (36,000) units, ₹91,870, work-in-process (2,000 units), ₹4130; Process B: cost of completed (32,000) units, ₹1,19,860. Work-in-process (2,500 units), ₹8,010.

RQ.9.19 Equivalent units produced, 80,000 in terms of material, 64,000 in terms of labour and overhead; cost of finished output (56,000 units), ₹8,29,500; work-in-process (24,000 units), ₹2,60,500.

RQ.9.20 Cost of production transferred to next process, ₹2,27,640; work-in-process, ₹6,840; abnormal loss, ₹1,152.

RQ.9.21 Transfer to finished stock ₹1,56,095, work-in-process ₹21,485, Equivalent cost: materials ₹25, Labour ₹33,000, Overheads ₹8.06

RQ.9.22 Total profit, ₹21,413; Reserve for unrealised profit-finished stock, ₹2,787, Process B: ₹800.

RQ.9.23 Share of joint costs for products A, M^1 and M^2 is ₹1,16,800, ₹9,600, respectively; Net profit for these products is ₹1,45,600 (A), ₹6,400 (M^2) and ₹14,400 (M^2).

RQ.9.24 Joint expenses should be apportioned among X, Y and Z is the ratio of 40 : 17 : 8.5. (₹40,000, ₹17,000, ₹8,500).

RQ.9.25 Share of joint costs: ₹93,714 (product A), ₹2,34,286 (product B): Closing inventories, ₹43,450 (product A), ₹17,810 (Product B).

RQ.9.26 Estimated cost of production at the point of separation: By-product X, ₹5 per unit (Total ₹2,500); By-product Y, ₹11 per unit (Total ₹2,200).

RQ.9.27 Cost of inventories: A, ₹14,40,000; B, ₹3,00,000; C, ₹1,18,750.

Unit/Single/Output and Operating Costing

Learning Objectives

1. Explain and illustrate unit/single/output costing.
2. Examine and illustrate operating/service costing.

INTRODUCTION

The objective of this chapter is to describe unit and operating costing. While unit costing, like job and process costing, is applicable to manufacturing organisations, operating costing is suitable for cost determination in service organisations. The nature of service organsiations differs widely depending on the nature of service. Our focus in this chapter is, on elucidating the general procedure with special reference to transport costing. Section 1 of the chapter illustrates unit costing, and operating costing is the subject matter of Section 2. The main points are summarised in the last section.

UNIT/SINGLE/OUTPUT COSTING

Unit cost is a method of costing used in those industries, which are engaged in manufacturing *exclusively one* homogeneous product or a few grades of the same product. It is also referred to as *single/output costing*. The examples of industries in which this type of costing is applicable are cement, paper, sugar, steel, quarries, brickworks and breweries. The *unit* cost is the average cost, that is, the total cost divided by the number of units produced. The cost units may be expressed in terms of number, weight, volume and time. The following is a list of some industries and the corresponding cost units adopted by them.

Type of industry	*Cost unit*
Brick making	1,000 bricks made
Steel manufacturing	Per tonne
Cement, coal, collieries, quarries	Per tonne
Paper	Per kg-tonne
Bolts, nuts	Gross or per 1,000
Paint manufacturing	Per litre
Gas works	Per 1,000 cubic metres produced
Electricity undertakings	Per kilowatt-hour

The computation of cost in unit costing is done in the form of cost sheet/production statement and production account.

Cost Sheet/Production Statement

A *cost sheet* or production statement is the statement that provides a logical, detailed and systematic presentation of various elements of cost information obtained through the cost records. It also includes the figures of sales revenue and profits. The term production statement may signify statement of units produced. Such a statement may more aptly be designated as a statement of costs and profits.

Production Account

Production account is an accounting presentation (ledger account shape) of the information contained in the production statement. In financial accounting, it is known by the name of *manufacturing account.* Whatever the mode of cost presentation, such a compilation is made at periodic intervals, say every month, every quarter. For the sake of comparison and cost control, wherever possible, the corresponding figure for the past period or standard cost figure may also be provided in the cost sheet or production statement.

In preparing the cost sheet/production account, the following items need special attention.

Salvage Value of Scrap Material Cost of production should be reduced by the sale proceeds of scrap. In case material is not processed, sale proceeds of such materials should be deducted from the cost of materials issued. Where materials have undergone manufacturing process, the sale proceeds from such scrap should be deducted from the factory cost.

Defective Product Defective products can sometimes be made saleable after incurring extra expenditure. When such defects are caused by normal reasons, the additional expenditure on salvaging these products is included as a part of factory cost; but in the case of abnormal reasons, the cost of rectification of these products is transferred to the costing profit and loss account.

By-Product The sale proceeds realised from by-products is deducted from the factory cost.

Work-in-Process The adjustment for opening and closing work-in-process should be carried out at the appropriate stage (prime cost or work cost) in preparing the statement of cost of production.

The formats of cost sheet/production statement and production account are given in Exhibits 10.1 and 10.2.

Exhibit 10.1 *Cost Sheet/Production Statement for the Period......*

(Units produced)

Particulars	Last Period		Current Period	
	Total cost	Unit cost	Total cost	Unit cost
Direct materials consumed				
Direct wages				
Other direct/chargeable expenses	—	—		
Prime Cost				
Add factory or works overheads (specify each item)	—	—	—	—
Factory Cost, (gross)				
Add opening work-in-process				
Less closing work-in-process	—	—	—	—

(Contd.)

(*Contd.*)

Factory Cost (net)				
Add administrative overheads				
Cost of Production				
Add opening stock of finished goods				
Less closing stock of finished goods	—	—	—	—
Cost of Goods Sold				
Add selling overheads (specify each item)	—	—	—	—
Cost of Sales				
Add profit as per cent of cost price or selling price	—	—	—	—
Sales Revenue (Total)	—	—	—	—

Exhibit 10.2 *Production Account for the Period.....*

Particulars	*Dr Amount*	*Particulars*	*Cr Amount*
To direct materials:	—	By prime cost c/d	—
Opening stock			
Add purchases			
Add carriage on purchase			
Less closing stock			
To direct labour			
To other direct/chargeable expenses			
To prime cost b/d		By closing stock of work-in-process	
To factory overheads (specify each item)		By factory cost c/d	
To opening stock of work-in-process			
To factory cost b/d		By cost of production c/d	
To administrative overheads (specify each item)			
To opening stock of finished goods		By closing stock of finished goods	
To cost of production b/d		By cost of goods sold c/d	
To cost of goods sold b/d		By cost of sales c/d	
To selling overheads (specify each item)			
To cost of sales b/d		By sales	
To profit (balancing figure)			

EXAMPLE 10.1

Work out, in cost sheet form, the unit cost of production per tonne of special paper, manufactured by a paper mill in March of the current year from the following data:

Direct materials:	
	Paper pulp—500 tonnes @ ₹5,000 per tonne
	Other materials—100 tonnes @ ₹3,000 per tonne
Direct labour:	
	80 skilled men @ ₹300 per day for 25 days
	40 unskilled men @ ₹200 per day for 25 days
Direct expenses:	
	Special equipment—₹3,00,000
	Special dyes—₹1,00,000
Works/factory overheads:	
	Variable @ 100 per cent and fixed @ 60 per cent on direct wages
	Administrative overhead @ 10 per cent of factory cost
	Selling and distribution overhead @ 15 per cent on work cost.

400 tonnes of special paper was manufactured and sold @ ₹20,000 per tonne and ₹80,000 was realised by the sale of waste material during the course of manufacture. The scrap value of the special equipment and dyes after utilisation in manufacture is nil.

Prepare the production account also.

SOLUTION

Cost Sheet for the Period Ending March, Current Year

Particulars	Total cost (400 tonnes)	Cost per tonne
Direct materials used:		
Paper pulp	₹25,00,000	₹6,250
Other materials	3,00,000	750
Direct labour cost:		
Skilled men (80 men × ₹300 × 25 days)	6,00,000	1,500
Unskilled men (40 men × ₹200 × 25 days)	2,00,000	500
Other direct expenses:		
Special equipment	3,00,000	750
Special dyes	1,00,000	250
Prime cost	40,00,000	10,000
Add factory overheads:		
Variable (100 per cent on direct wages)	8,00,000	2,000
Fixed (₹8,00,000 × 0.60)	4,80,000	1,200
Less sale proceeds of waste material	(80,000)	(200)
Factory/Works cost	52,00,000	13,000
Add administrative overheads:		
10 per cent of factory cost	5,20,000	1,300
Cost of production	57,20,000	14,300
Add selling and distribution overheads: (₹52,00,000 × 0.15)	7,80,000	1,950
Cost of sales	65,00,000	16,250
Profit	15,00,000	3,750
Sales	80,00,000	20,000

Note Sale proceeds of waste materials have been deducted at the stage of factory overheads since materials have undergone manufacturing process.

Production Account for the Period Ending March Current Year

Particulars	Dr Amount	Particulars	Cr Amount
To direct materials:		By prime cost c/d	₹40,00,000
Paper pulp			
(500 tonnes × ₹5,000)	₹25,00,000		
Other materials			
(100 tonnes × ₹3,000)	3,00,000		
To direct labour:			
Skilled men (80 × ₹300 × 25)	6,00,000		
Unskilled men (40 × ₹200 × 25)	2,00,000		
To other direct expenses:			
Special equipment	3,00,000		
Special dyes	1,00,000		
	40,00,000		40,00,000
To prime cost b/d	40,00,000	By sale proceeds of waste material	80,000
To factory overheads:			
Variable	8,00,000	By factory cost c/d	52,00,000
Fixed	4,80,000		
	52,80,000		52,80,000
To factory cost b/d	52,00,000	By cost of production c/d	57,20,000
To administrative overheads	5,20,000		
	57,20,000		57,20,000
To cost of production b/d	57,20,000	By cost of sales c/d	65,00,000
To selling and distribution overheads	7,80,000		
	65,00,000		65,00,000
To cost of sales b/d	65,00,000	By sales	80,00,000
To profit	15,00,000		
	80,00,000		80,00,000

Example 10.2

The following extracts of costing information related to commodity Y for the half year ending September 30 of the current year:

Purchases of raw materials	₹1,32,000
Direct wages	1,10,000
Rent, rates, insurance and works overhead	44,000
Carriage inwards	1,584
Stock, April 1 of the current year:	
Raw materials	22,000
Finished products (1,600 units)	17,600
Stock, September 30 of the current year:	
Raw materials	24,464
Finished products (3,200 units)	35,200
Work-in-process, April 1	5,280
Work-in-process, September 30	17,600
Cost of factory supervision	8,800
Sales of finished product	3,30,000

Advertising, discounts allowed and selling costs amounted to Re 0.75 per unit sold and 25,600 units of commodity were produced during the period.

You are required to ascertain (a) the value of raw materials used; (b) prime cost; (c) the cost of turnover of the period; (d) net profit for the period; and (e) net profit per tonne of the commodity sold.

SOLUTION

Production Statement/Cost Sheet for the Half-Year Ending September 30

Particulars	*Total cost*		*Cost per unit*
Direct materials consumed:			
Opening stock	₹22,000		
Add purchases	1,32,000		
Add carriage on purchases	1,584		
Less closing stock	(24,464)	₹1,31,120	
Direct wages		1,10,000	
Prime cost (25,600 units)		2,41,120	₹9.41875
Add factory overheads:			
Rent, rates, insurance and works overheads	44,000		
Cost of factory supervision	8,800	52,800	
Gross works cost		2,93,920	
Add opening work-in-process inventory		5,280	
Less closing work-in-process inventory		(17,600)	1.58125@
Net works cost (cost of production)		2,81,600	11.00
Add opening finished goods inventory (1,600 units)		17,600	
Less closing finished goods inventory (3,200 units)		(35,200)	—
Cost of goods sold (24,000 units) (25,600 + 1,600 – 3,200)		2,64,000	11.00
Add selling and distribution overheads		18,000	0.75
Cost of sales		2,82,000	11.75
Add profit (balancing figure)		48,000	2.00
Sales revenue (24,000 units)		3,30,000	13.75

@Factory overheads per unit of output is ₹1.58125, that is, cost of goods sold, ₹11–prime cost, ₹9.41875.

Note It is assumed that the firm is using the average costing method of valuing work-in-process.

EXAMPLE 10.3 (***PRODUCTION ACCOUNT***)

From the following cost records of Small Paints Limited, you are required to prepare production account with maximum possible break-up of costs and profits for the month ending March 31 of the current year:

Opening raw materials inventory	₹1,50,000
Closing raw materials inventory	1,80,000
Direct wages	1,00,000
Indirect wages	10,000
Opening work-in-process inventory	55,000
Closing work-in-process inventory	70,000
Sales	4,00,000
Purchase of raw materials	1,30,000
Carriage on purchases of materials	5,000
Factory rent, rates and power	30,000
Depreciation of plant and machinery	7,000
Repairs of machinery	3,000
Advertising	12,000
Office rent and taxes	5,000
Salesmen salaries and commission	15,000
Opening stock of finished goods inventory	1,00,000
Closing stock of finished goods inventory	65,000
Sale of scrap	2,000

SOLUTION

Production Account for the Month Ending March 31......

Particulars		Dr Amount	Particulars	Cr Amount
To direct materials:				
Opening stock	₹1,50,000		By prime cost c/d	₹2,05,000
Add: purchases	1,30,000			
carriage	5,000			
Less closing stock	(1,80,000)	₹1,05,000		
To direct wages		1,00,000		
		2,05,000		2,05,000
To prime cost b/d		2,05,000		
To indirect wages		10,000	By factory cost c/d	2,38,000
To factory rent, rates and power		30,000		
To depreciation of plant and machinery		7,000		
To repairs of machinery		3,000		
		2,55,000		
Add opening work-in-process		55,000		
Less closing work-in-process		(70,000)		
Less sale of scrap		(2,000)		
		2,38,000		2,38,000
To factory cost b/d		2,38,000	By cost of production c/d	2,43,000
To office rent and taxes		5,000		
		2,43,000		2,43,000
To cost of production b/d		2,43,000	By closing stock	65,000
To opening stock		1,00,000	By cost of goods sold c/d	2,78,000
		3,43,000		3,43,000
To cost of goods sold b/d		2,78,000	By cost of sales c/d	3,05,000
To advertising		12,000		
To salesman salaries and commission		15,000		
		3,05,000		3,05,000
To cost of sales b/d		3,05,000	By sales	4,00,000
To profit		95,000		
		4,00,000		4,00,000

EXAMPLE 10.4 *(PROJECTED COST SHEET)*

Electronics Ltd furnishes the following information for 10,000 TV valves manufactured during the previous year:

Material	₹9,00,000
Direct wages	6,00,000
Power and consumable stores	1,20,000
Factory indirect wages	1,50,000
Lighting of factory	55,000
Defective work (cost of rectification)	30,000
Clerical salaries and management expenses	3,35,000
Selling expenses	55,000
Sale proceeds of scrap	20,000
Plant repairs, maintenance and depreciation	1,15,000

Last year, the net selling price was ₹316 per unit and all the units were sold. As from April 1 of the current year, the selling price was reduced to ₹310 per unit. It was estimated that production could be increased in the current year by 50 per cent due to spare capacity. Rates for materials and direct wages would increase by 10 per cent.

You are required to prepare a statement of cost and profit for the current year, assuming that 15,000 units will be produced and sold during the year and that factory overheads will be recovered as a percentage of direct wages, and office and selling expenses as a percentage of the works cost.

Solution

Project Statement of Cost and Profit for the Current Year (Output 15,000 Units)

Particulars	*Total cost*	*Cost per unit*
Material cost @ ₹99 per unit	₹14,85,000	₹99
Direct wages @ ₹66 per unit	9,90,000	66
Prime cost	24,75,000	165
Add factory overheads (0.75 × direct wages)*	7,42,500	49.50
Work cost	32,17,500	214.50
Add office and selling overheads (0.20 × works cost)**	6,43,500	42.90
Cost of sales	38,61,000	257.40
Estimated profit (balancing figure sales price-cost of sales)	7,89,000	52.60
Sales revenue	46,50,000	310.00

Working Notes

**Determination of Factory Overheads:*

Factory overheads (previous year):	
Power and consumable stores	₹1,20,000
Factory indirect wages	1,50,000
Lighting of factory	55,000
Cost of rectification of defective work (assumed to be normal)	30,000
Plant repairs, maintenance and depreciations	1,15,000
Less sale of scrap	(20,000)
Total	4,50,000
Direct wages	6,00,000
Factory overheads as per cent of direct wages	75

***Determination of Office and Selling Overheads:*

Works cost (previous year):	
Material cost	₹9,00,000
Direct wages	6,00,000
Factory overheads as above	4,50,000
	19,50,000
Selling and office overheads (₹3,35,000 + ₹55,000)	3,90,000
Office and selling overheads as per cent of works cost	20

Bid Price

Cost sheet or statement of cost of production and profit is a useful means of determining the bid price to be quoted for a specific tender. In preparing such a statement, probable changes in the input prices/rates should be taken into account. Moreover, fixed costs should be ignored if the tender output can be met out of the existing plant capacity of the firm. Consider Example 10.5.

Example 10.5 *(Determination of Tender Price)*

From the following data, prepare a production statement of Torch Manufacturing Company Ltd for the current year ending March 31:

Opening materials inventory	₹70,000
Closing materials inventory	9,800
Purchase of materials	1,05,000
Factory wages	1,90,000
Factory expenses	35,000
Establishment expenses	20,000
Opening finished inventory	Nil
Closing finished inventory	70,000
Sales	3,78,000

The number of torches manufactured during the year was 8,000. The company wants to quote for the supply of 2,000 torches for the coming year. The torches to be quoted are similar to those in the current year but cost of materials is expected to increase by 10 per cent and factory labour by 20 per cent.

Prepare a statement showing the price to be quoted so as to give the same percentage of profit on turnover as was realised during the current year assuming that other costs will be the same as in the previous year.

SOLUTION

Statement of Cost of Production and Profit to Quote Prices

Particulars	*Total cost (2,000 units)*	*Cost per unit*
Materials cost	₹45,430[1]	₹22.715
Direct wages	57,000[2]	28.500
Prime cost	1,02,430	51.215
Add factory expenses @ ₹4.375(₹35,000 ÷ 8,000 units)	8,750	4.375
Factory cost	1,11,180	55.590
Add establishment expenses @ ₹2.50 (₹20,000 ÷ 8,000 units)	5,000	2.500
Cost of production	1,16,180	58.090
Add margin of profit (0.10 × sales or 1/9 of cost price)	12,908	6.454
Quotation price	1,29,088	64.544

WORKING NOTES

[1]*Determination of Material Cost:*

Opening inventory	₹70,000
Add purchases	1,05,000
Less closing inventory	(9,800)
Cost of material consumed	1,65,200
÷ Number of torches manufactured	8,000
Material cost per unit	20.650
Add 10 per cent cost (increase)	2.065
Material cost (current) per unit	22.715

[2]*Determination of Labour Cost:* (₹1,90,000 ÷ 8,000)	23.75
Add 20 per cent increase	4.75
Current labour cost per unit	28.50

[3]*Determination of Margin of Profit on Sales of Previous Year:*

Sales revenue		₹3,78,000
Less cost of production:		
Cost of materials consumed	₹1,65,200	
Factory wages	1,90,000	
Factory expenses	35,000	
Establishment expenses	20,000	
	4,10,200	
Less closing inventory of finished product	(70,000)	3,40,200
Profit		37,800
Profit as per cent of sales revenue = (₹37,800 ÷ ₹3,78,000) = 10 per cent		

EXAMPLE 10.6 *(Cost Sheet with By-product)*

From the following particulars make out a weekly cost sheet showing profit on the main product of Mini Petroleum Company Ltd:

Crude oil used	5,00,000 litres @	₹20
Petrol produced (main product)	1,50,000 litres	50
By-products:		
(i) Lubricating oil produced	50,000 litres	40
(ii) Fuel oil produced	2,50,000 litres	20
(iii) Kerosene produced	30,000 litres	25
Raw materials consumed		4,00,000
Wages paid		8,00,000
Repairs and renewals		6,00,000
Salaries and general charges		12,00,000

Show the percentage of each product to the weight of crude oil used.

SOLUTION

Cost Sheet For the Week Ending (Units in Litres)

Particulars	*Quantity (litres)*	*Total cost*	*Cost per unit*
Crude oil used (input)	5,00,000	₹1,00,00,000	
Raw materials		4,00,000	
Wages		8,00,000	
Repairs and renewals		6,00,000	
Salaries and general charges		12,00,000	
Total cost of production of main product and by-products (joint cost)		1,30,00,000	
Less sale proceeds from by-products (output)			
Lubricating oil	(50,000)	(20,00,000)	
Fuel oil	(2,50,000)	(50,00,000)	
Kerosene	(30,000)	(7,50,000)	
Wastage (assumed to be normal)	(20,000)	Nil	
Cost of production of main product (petroleum)	1,50,000	52,50,000	₹35
Profit (balancing figure)		22,50,000	15
Sales revenue		75,00,000	50

Statement Showing the Percentage of Each Product to be Weight of Crude Used

Input (litres)	Particulars	Output (litres)	Percentage
5,00,000	Crude oil		
	Petrol	1,50,000	30
	Lubricating oil	50,000	10
	Fuel oil	2,50,000	50
	Kerosene	30,000	6
	Wastage	20,000	4
5,00,000	Total	5,00,000	100

OPERATING (SERVICE) COSTING

The term operating costing is applied to unit costing of services as opposed to that of products. It is applicable where standardised services are provided, either by an undertaking or by a service cost centre within an undertaking. Thus, operating (also known as service) costing is suitable for public utility undertakings providing services to the community at large, such as road and rail transport companies, electricity undertakings, hospitals and theatres. It is also suitable for cost ascertainment by ancillary services departments of manufacturing units such as power house, boiler house, hospital, internal transport and canteen for the benefit of employees.

Operating (Service) Costing applicable where standardised services are provided by an undertaking or by service cost culture within it.

The cost per unit in service costing is based on average cost. Example of units to express average cost are as follows:

Organisation	Cost unit
Transport undertakings	Passenger–km (passenger traffic) or Tonne–km (goods transport)
Electricity boards/Organisation	Kilowatt– hours
Hospitals	Patient– days, outpatients treated, cost per major or minor surgical operation
Boiler houses	Quantity (kg or lb) of steam generated
Canteens	Meals served; cups of tea sold.

The unit costs in service organisations are ascertained in the form of operating cost sheet. It is a statement of operating costs (and sometimes profit also) in operating costing. Corresponding to the fixed costs, variable costs and semi-variable costs in manufacturing organisations, the operating costs in service organisations are generally categorised into three groups, namely, standing charges, running costs, and repairs and maintenance. The repairs and maintenance is often clubbed with running costs. The main elements of these categories of costs in the case of a transport undertaking are detailed as follows:

Standing Charges

Standing charges are those, which are incurred irrespective of the mileage run. They are like fixed costs. Included in this category are the following expenses:

1. License fees
2. Insurance premium
3. Road tax
4. Garage costs and administration
5. Drivers' wages (gross) including provident fund contribution of employers

6. Attendant-cum-cleaner's wages
7. Interest on capital (if considered as a part of cost).

Running Costs

Running costs are those which vary more or less in direct proportion to the mileage run. The following is a list of such expenses:

1. Cost of fuel (diesel, petrol etc.)
2. Lubricants, grease and oil
3. Repairs and maintenance (strictly semi–variable)
4. Cost of tyres, tubes and other spare parts
5. Depreciation.

In costing transport undertakings, the cost unit is normally passenger–km (in the case of passenger traffic) and tonne–km (in the case of goods transport). However, passenger–km/tonne–km unit may not be applicable in all situations. For instance, where the material is bulky but of small weight, say, empty containers (drums and tins), a certain maximum volume is often considered as equivalent to one tonne. For example, in sea freight, a maximum volume of 40 cubic feet is considered equivalent to one tonne for freight purposes. Likewise, some other standard freight measure is adopted for items such as cars, televisions, refrigerators, and so on.

In transport, the total operating cost should be determined with reference to each vehicle under suitable cost headings, namely, standing charges, running charges and maintenance charges. The passenger–km or tonne–km can be conceived as a function of the following variables:

1. The number of vehicles (fleet)
2. The carrying capacity of the vehicle in terms of number of passengers/freight
3. Distance travelled
4. Number of days on an average for which the vehicle is likely to be in operation
5. Number of trips in a day; going and coming should be considered as two trips
6. Passenger/weight actually carried on an average.

Example 10.7

DHT Ltd. is running 4 buses between two towns which are 100 kms apart: the seating capacity of each bus is 50 passengers and 80 per cent of this capacity is actually used. Each vehicle makes 2 round trips daily and the vehicles are working on an average of 25 days a month. Determine the passenger–kms. Also, determine cost per passenger–km, if the total operating costs for 4 buses are ₹160,00,000.

Solution

Passenger–km = Number of buses × Distance × Capacity × Trips × 2 × Days × Percentage of the capacity used = (4 × 100 × 50 × 2 × 2 × 25) × 0.80 = 16,00,000

Cost per passenger–km =Total costs/ Total passenger–kms = ₹160,00,000/16,00,000 = ₹10

When the transport undertaking owns vehicles having different capacities, cost unit should be determined with reference to varying capacities.

Example 10.8

(Determination of Cost Unit When Vehicle Have Different Rated Capacities)

A transport company operates the following fleet: 20 trucks of 10 tonne capacity, 10 trucks of 5 tonne capacity, 5 mini-trucks of 2 tonne capacity.

The first two types of trucks are used for long distances and the mini-truck is utilised for local transport only. In a week, the following distances were covered by each of the trucks: 10 tonne capacity truck 600 kms, 5 tonne capacity truck; 500 kms; 2 tonne capacity truck, 300 kms.

If the total cost is ₹14,80,000, determine the cost per tonne–km, assuming that all vehicles worked to their full capacity during the period.

SOLUTION

Determination of Total Tonne – Kilometres (Kms)

Number of vehicles	Capacity in tonnes	Distance in kms	Tonne–kms
20	10	600	1,20,000
10	5	500	25,000
5	2	100	3,000
			1,48,000

Cost per tonne – kilometre = ₹17,76,000/ 1,48,000 = ₹10

Each vehicle, in a way, is a *cost centre* in operating costing. Therefore, a separate cost sheet is maintained for each vehicle in the cost accounting department. Detailed information to be incorporated in the cost sheet is available from the *daily log sheet* maintained by the bus operators. The daily log sheet provides complete information in respect of each journey. For instance, it records kilometers travelled, weight or passengers carried, the time when the journey commenced and when it was completed. Apart from the journey, the log sheet also records the supplies of petrol, diesel or other materials made to the vehicle. Cost in respect of road tax, insurance, tyres and spares are entered directly in the records already maintained. Wages of the drivers and assistants are recorded from the payroll register.

When a transport company maintains its own repairs and maintenance department, the vehicle can be charged for the cost and the time mechanics spend on its repairs and maintenance. For this purpose, they maintain *time sheets* to record time spent by them on each vehicle. Subsequently, these time sheets are the guiding reference to apportion cost of this department among various vehicles. Likewise, the materials issued (tyres, tubes, and other spares) from the central store are classified and the relevant costs of such materials transferred to the concerned cost sheet of each vehicle.

At suitable periodical intervals, the costs are transferred from the vehicle cost sheets to the summary statement of the operating cost of the fleet as a whole. Costs are recorded under suitable headings of running costs and standing costs. The cost classification enables a comparison of each vehicle's performance. The total costs so determined are averaged out to determine cost per km or cost per tonne–km or cost per passenger–km as applicable. Comparison can be made with operating cost of other transport companies/ undertakings operating in that region to judge the operating efficiency of the firm.

Apart from inter-firm comparisons, certain ratios can also be determined and used for the purpose. One such ratio can be the *capacity utilisation ratio.* This ratio would measure the relationship between the capacity used (tonne–km/passenger–km) and the capacity available. The higher the ratio, the better it is. This ratio can be compared with the corresponding ratio of earlier years also. Another important ratio in this regard can be the *cost revenue ratio.* This ratio would establish the relationship between cost per tonne–km incurred and revenue per tonne–km realised; the lower the ratio, the better it is. The ratio of more than 1 (or 100 per cent) signals unprofitability and very high ratios point to deteriorating profitability.

Finally, for control purposes, the following data may be compiled for each vehicle at periodical intervals: **(i)** the mileage run, **(ii)** fuel consumed and the km per litre, **(iii)** lubricants consumed, and **(iv)** working days analysis in respect of **(a)** running under load, **(b)** under repair, **(c)** loses through abnormal causes such as driver's absence or breakdown of vehicle. This exercise also helps in assessing whether it is profitable to operate a particular vehicle on a certain route or not.

SUMMARY

- Unit/single/output costing is a method of costing used in those industries which are engaged in the manufacture of a homogeneous product or a few grades of the same product such as cement, paper, sugar, steel, brick works, breweries. The cost units are expressed in terms of number, weight, volume and time. Examples of cost unit are per kg, per tonne, per litre, per gross and per 1,000 units.
- The computation of costs in unit costing is recorded in a cost sheet/production statement or production account. The various elements of cost are arranged in a way so as to calculate prime cost, works cost, cost of production, cost of goods sold and cost of sales. In preparing these, items like salvage value of scrap, defective products and work-in-process merit special attention.
- Operating (service) costing is applied to service organisations as well as to service departments of manufacturing organsiations. The basic principles of cost determination are similar to those in unit costing, but the unit of measurement is composite such as passenger-km, tonne-km and kilowatt-hours. Another distinguishing feature of this type of costing is the basis of cost classification. The major elements of cost are standing charges (fixed costs) and running cost (variable costs).

PRACTICAL PROBLEMS

P.10.1 A mini factory is engaged in making standard products which pass through three departments. The cost figures of the factory for the week of November of the current year are furnished below:

Particulars	*Total*	*Departments*		
		A	*B*	*C*
Direct materials	₹18,600	₹7,500	₹6,400	₹4,700
Labour cost	15,000	6,000	5,000	4,000
Total overhead expenditure	7,500	3,000	2,500	2,000
	41,100	16,500	13,900	10,700

Prepare a simple cost sheet for products X and Y on the basis of data furnished below:

Particulars	*Departments*		
	A	*B*	*C*
Product X — Material	₹100	₹200	₹300
— Labour	50	60	70
Product Y — Material	50	90	140
— Labour	70	60	80

SOLUTION

Cost Sheet of Products X and Y for the Month of November

Particulars	*Total cost*		*Percentage of total cost*	
	X	*Y*	*X*	*Y*
Department A				
Direct materials	₹100	₹50	₹11.50	₹8.40
Direct labour	50	70	5.74	11.77
Overheads (0.50 × direct wages)	25	35	2.87	5.88
(a) *Total*	175	155	20.11	26.05

(Contd.)

(Contd.)

Department B				
Direct materials	200	90	22.99	15.13
Direct labour	60	60	6.90	10.09
Overhead (0.50 × direct wages)	30	30	3.45	5.04
(b) *Total*	290	180	33.34	30.26
Department C				
Direct materials	300	140	34.48	23.53
Direct labour	70	80	8.05	13.45
Overhead (0.50 × direct wages)	35	40	4.02	6.72
(c) *Total*	405	260	46.55	43.70
Total (a+b+c)	870	595	100.00	100.00

Note It is obvious from the cost figures of November that the firm is following the percentage of labour cost method as the basis of recovering overheads.

P.10.2 In a long established mini factory a plant installed 20 years ago at a cost of ₹3,00,000 is still in use though its book value has been brought down to ₹1 (nominal). The cost figures of its output per month are given below:

Electrical power	₹3,000
Repairs and maintenance	4,500
Consumable stores	500
Wages of 3 workers (gross)	18,000
Raw materials (production)	2,60,000
Overheads allocated	24,000
	3,10,000

Units produced: 20,000, sold at ₹20 per unit, selling expenses being ₹30,000 per month.

The management scrapped this plant and installed a more efficient modern plant and particulars of its workings are given below:

Cost of new plant installed (subject to 10 per cent depreciation per annum)	₹13,50,000
Electric power	7,500
Repairs and maintenance	6,500
Consumable stores	1,000
Wages of 2 workers (new)	27,000
Salary of 1 new mechanic	14,000
Overheads allocated	36,000

The new plant utilises raw materials costing ₹8 lakh per month and produces 70,000 units which are sold at ₹21 each. The selling expenses increased to ₹70,000 per month. The plant cost and additional capital outlay involved in increasing stock of raw materials and extended credit to customers was financed by a 9% loan for ₹30,00,000, which was wholly utilised on the change-over from old to new plant. This change also involved lay-off of workers and the wages paid to them during the period and other losses due to non-working of the plant for a period of two months amounted to ₹2,40,000 and it was decided by the management that the loss should be absorbed in production accounts in the remaining period of eight months in the current financial year.

You are required to prepare a comparative cost sheet for the last month of working of the old plant and the first month's working of the new plant indicating the monthly profit and loss on account of the change-over.

Assume that realisation on the sale of old plant is adjusted in the estimated loss of ₹2,40,000 and ignore interest on extended credit to customer for which no indication has been given.

SOLUTION

Comparative Cost Sheet Showing the Effect of Change of the Existing Plant to the New One on the Profits of the Firm

Particulars	Old plant (20,000 units)			New plant (70,000 units)		
	Total cost	*Unit cost*	*Per cent to sale price*	*Total cost*	*Unit cost*	*Per cent to total sale price*
Raw materials	₹2,60,000	₹13	₹65.0	₹8,00,000	₹11.4	₹54.28
Wages	18,000	0.90	4.5	27,000		
Salary of new mechanic/				14,000	0.58	2.77
Prime cost	2,78,000	13.90	69.5	8,41,000	11.98	57.05
Add factory overheads						
Electric power	3,000			7,500		
Repairs and maintenance	4,500	0.4	2.0	6,500	0.20	0.95
Consumable stores	500			1,000		
Depreciation for 1 month:						
Old plant (book value)	—	—	—			
New plant (0.10 × ₹13,50,000)/ 12 months				11,250	0.16	0.76
Factory cost	2,86,000	14.3	71.5	8,67,250	12.34	58.76
Add other miscellaneous overheads:						
Allocated overheads	24,000	1.2	6.00	36,000	0.45	2.14
Interest on loan for one month (₹30,00,000 × 0.09 × 1/12)				22,500	0.32	1.52
Loss due to change-over of the plant to be spread over 8 months (₹2,40,000 ÷ 8)				30,000	0.43	2.05
Cost of production	3,10,000	15.5	77.5	9,55,750	13.54	64.47
Add selling overheads	30,000	1.5	7.5	70,000	1.0	4.76
Cost of sales	3,40,000	17	85.0	10,25,750	14.54	69.23
Profit (balancing figure)	60,000	3	15.0	4,44,250	6.46	30.77
Sales revenue	4,00,000	20	100.0	14,70,000	21.00	100.00

NOTES

1. Since expenses related to factory are separately given, allocated overheads are assumed to be administrative overheads.
2. Interest normally should not form part of cost sheet. But it has been taken into account here as the purpose of the exercise is to ascertain the comparative cost of production; the interest is clubbed with general overheads and not shown separately as a financial charge. Likewise, loss due to change-over is dealt with. Alternatively, both these expenses could have been shown as direct expenses.

P.10.3 A company manufacture four sizes of toy chairs, A, B, C and D in its workshop and transfers them to the sales department at a profit of 50 per cent on transfer price. The workers are paid piece rates of ₹2, ₹4, ₹6 and ₹8 per board for sizes A, B, C and D respectively. Dearness allowance at flat rate of ₹10 per direct labour day is distributed among workers. Miscellaneous direct payments to workers are 25 per cent of the basic wages. From the following information for the month of July, you are required to find out the total cost per toy chain of each size and its transfer price:

Sizes	*A*	*B*	*C*	*D*
Direct labour day	100	200	300	200
Number of toy chairs manufactured	4,000	2,500	2,000	1,500
Direct materials	₹25,000	₹15,000	₹20,000	₹20,000
Workshops' overhead				
Indirect materials		₹4,800		
Indirect labour		4,000		
Indirect expenses		8,000		

Indirect materials are to be apportioned on the basis of direct material cost and remaining expenses are to be allocated on the basis of direct labour days.

SOLUTION

Statement of Cost of Production and Profit of Toy Chairs (A,B,C and D) for the Month Ending July

Particulars	*Total cost*				*Cost per unit*			
	A	*B*	*C*	*D*	*A*	*B*	*C*	*D*
Direct materials	₹25,000	₹15,000	₹20,000	₹20,000	₹6.25	₹6.00	₹10.00	₹13.34
Direct wages[@]	11,000	14,500	18,000	17,000	2.75	5.80	9.00	11.33
Prime cost	36,000	29,500	38,000	37,000	9.00	11.80	19.00	24.67
Add factory overheads								
Indirect materials (0.10 × direct material cost): (₹8,000 ÷ 80,000)	2,500	1,500	2,000	2,000	0.63	0.60	1.00	1.33
Indirect labour (in proportion of number of labour days: (1:2:3:2)	500	1,000	1,500	1,000	0.12	0.40	0.75	0.67
Indirect expenses (1:2:3:2)	1,000	2,000	3,000	2,000	0.25	0.80	1.50	1.33
Factory cost/cost of production	40,000	34,000	44,500	42,000	10.00	13.60	22.25	28.00
Add 50 per cent of transfer price	40,000	34,000	44,500	42,000	10.00	13.60	22.25	28.00
Transfer price	80,000	68,000	89,000	84,000	20.00	27.20	44.50	56.00

[@] *Determination of Direct Wages*

	A	*B*	*C*	*D*
Piece wages (number of toy chairs × wage rate)	₹8,000	₹10,000	₹12,000	₹12,000
Dearness allowance (labour days × ₹10)	1,000	2,000	3,000	2,000
Miscellaneous payments (0.25 × piece wages)	2,000	2,500	3,000	3,000
	11,000	14,500	18,000	17,000

P.10.4 An ancillary unit supplies a forge component to an automobile manufacturer. The existing forging machine has been in use for 6 years. An improved forge is available in the market. The comparative features of both are given below:

Particulars	*Existing forge*	*New forge*
Original cost	₹12,00,000	₹24,00,000
Life (years)	10	10
Labour cost per annum	1,20,000	1.80,000
Fuel	2,40,000	3,60,000
Power	1,00,000	1,40,000
Consumables	1,20,000	2,00,000
Repairs and maintenance	1,20,000	1,80,000
Tooling	80,000	2,00,000
Production per hour (numbers)	10	20
Number of hours working per year (on two-shift basis)	4,000	4,000
Rejection on inspection (per cent)	6	2

Work out a comparative cost of production statement for the two machines. Assume there is no salvage value for both the machines. Use straight line method of depreciation and ignore interest and taxation.

SOLUTION

Comparative Conversion Cost of Production Statement for Two Machines, Namely, Existing Forge and New Forge

Particulars	*Total cost*		*Cost per unit*	
	Existing forge	*New forge*	*Existing forge*	*New forge*
Number of working hours per year	4,000	4,000	—	—
(x) Production per hour	10	20	—	—
Production units (gross)	40,000	80,000	—	—
Less rejection on inspection	(2,400)	(1,600)	—	—
Good units produced	37,600	78,400	—	—
Conversion costs[@]				
Labour cost	₹1,20,000	₹1,80,000	₹3.191	₹2.296
Fuel	2,40,000	3,60,000	6.383	4.592
Power	1,00,000	1,40,000	2.660	1.786
Consumables	1,20,000	2,00,000	3.191	2.551
Repairs and maintenance	1,20,000	1,80,000	3.191	2.296
Tooling	80,000	2,00,000	2.128	2.551
Depreciation (original)	1,20,000	2,40,000	3.191	3.061
Total cost	9,00,000	15,00,000	23.935	19.133

[@]Since raw materials cost is not given in the present problem, statement of cost of production is confined only to conversion costs.

P.10.5 A toy manufacturer earns an average net profit of ₹3 per piece on a selling price of ₹15 by producing and selling 60,000 pieces at 60 per cent of the potential capacity. The composition of cost of sales is:

Direct material	:	₹4	
Direct wages	:	1	
Works overheads	:	6	(50 per cent fixed)
Sales overheads	:	1	(25 per cent variable)

During the current year, he intends to produce the same number but anticipates that:

1. His fixed charges will go up by 10 per cent.
2. Rates of direct labour will increase by 20 per cent.
3. Rates of direct material will increase by 5 per cent.
4. Selling price cannot be increased.

Under these circumstances, he obtains an order for a further 20 per cent of his capacity. What minimum price will you recommended for accepting an order to ensure the manufacturer an overall profit of ₹1,83,500?

SOLUTION

Statement Showing the Cost of Production and Profit at 60,000 Units

Particulars	*Total cost*	*Cost per unit*
Direct materials (₹4 × 105 × 60,000) ÷ 100	₹2,52,000	₹4.20
Direct labour (₹1 × 120 × 60,000) ÷ 100	72,000	1.20
Prime cost	3,24,000	5.40
Add factory overheads:		
Variable (60,000 × ₹3)	1,80,000	3.00
Fixed (₹3 × 60,000) = ₹1,80,000+10 per cent	1,98,000	3.30
Factory cost/cost of production	7,02,000	11.70

(*Contd.*

(*Contd.*

Add selling and distribution overheads:		
Variable (60,000 × ₹0.25)	15,000	0.25
Fixed (60,000 × ₹0.75) = ₹45,000+10 per cent	49,500	0.825
Cost of sales	7,66,500	12.775
Profit (balancing figure)	1,33,500	2.225
Sales revenue (60,000 × ₹15)	9,00,000	15.000

Statement Showing Determination of Minimum Price to be Quoted for Special Order of 20,000 Units

Particulars	*Total cost*	*Cost per unit*
Relevant cost of production:		
Direct materials	₹84,000	₹4.20
Direct labour	24,000	1.20
Variable works overhead	60,000	3.00
Variable sales overhead	5,000	0.25
Total incremental cost of production	1,73,000	8.65
Add profit expected from special order(₹1,83,500–₹1,33,500)	50,000	2.50
Minimum price	2,23,000	11.15

P.10.6 A small manufacturer produces 8,000 units per month, per unit split-up cost and sales value of which are given below:

Direct materials	₹30
Direct labour	20
Fixed overheads (₹2,00,000)	25
Variable overheads	40
	115
Selling and distribution expenses:	
Fixed (₹80,000)	10
Variable	15
	140
General administration (fixed ₹2,40,000)	30
Margin of profit (subject to taxation)	5
Sales value	175

Due to increase in demand and consequent extension of delivery dates and dissatisfaction among customers, the management decided to provide for an output of 12,000 units per month in the next year (against anticipated demand of 15,000 units), which would involve a capital outlay of ₹6,00,000 on which interest and financial charge would amount to 10 per cent per annum.

Prepare a comparative consolidated cost statement showing anticipated margin of profit for the present output (of 8,000 units) and the proposed output (of 12,000 units).

Assume that in the coming year, there will be an all-round increase of 5 per cent in the different items of expenses except fixed expenses.

If the proposal is adopted, due to the proposed increase in output, there will be an increase of 25 per cent in fixed overheads, 20 per cent in fixed selling and distribution expenses and 10 per cent in general administration, apart from the interest and financial charges.

If it is decided to maintain the present level of sales, an increase of 2 per cent in sales price is possible and this figure should be taken for the level of production at 8,000 units per month.

SOLUTION

Consolidated Cost Statement Showing Margin of Profit at Present and Proposed (8,000 and 12,000) Output Levels

Particulars	Total cost 8,000 units	Total cost 12,000 units	Cost per unit 8,000 units	Cost per unit 12,000 units
Direct materials	₹2,52,000	₹3,78,000	₹31.5	₹31.5
Direct labour	1,68,000	2,52,000	21.0	21.0
Prime cost	4,20,000	6,30,000	52.5	52.5
Add factory overheads:				
Fixed	2,00,000	2,50,000	25.0	20.83
Variable overheads	3,36,000	5,04,000	42.0	42.00
Factory cost	9,56,000	13,84,000	119.5	115.33
Add general overheads:				
Fixed	2,40,000	2,64,000	30.0	22.00
Interest charges (₹6,00,000 × 0.10 × 1/12)	—	5,000	—	0.42
Cost of production	11,96,000	16,53,000	149.5	137.75
Add selling and distribution overheads:				
Fixed	80,000	96,000	10.0	8.00
Variable	1,26,000	1,89,000	15.75	15.75
Cost of sales	14,02,000	19,38,000	175.25	161.50
Margin of profit	26,000	1,62,000	3.25	13.50
Sales revenue	14,28,000	21,00,000	178.50@	175.00@@

@Sale price would increase by 2 per cent (₹175 + ₹3.50). @@Sale price would remain unchanged.

P.10.7 The following figures are extracted from the books of an iron foundry for January of the current year:

Raw materials opening stock	₹14,000
Purchases during the year	1,00,000
Closing inventory	10,000
Direct wages	20,000
Works overhead (50 per cent on direct wages)	

Stores overhead on materials, 10 per cent on the cost of materials, 10 per cent of the casting were rejected being not upto specification and a sum of ₹800 was realised from sale of scrap; 10 per cent of the finished casting were found to be defective in manufacture and were rectified by expenditure of additional works overhead charges to the extent of 20 per cent on the proportionate direct wages. The total gross output of casting during the year was 2,000 tonnes.

Find out the manufacturing cost of the saleable casting per tonne.

SOLUTION

Cost Sheet Determining Manufacturing Cost of the Saleable Casting (for January)

Particulars		Total cost	Cost per unit
Direct materials consumed:			
Opening stock	₹14,000		
Add purchases	1,00,000		
Less closing stock	(10,000)	₹1,04,000	₹57.778
Direct wages		20,000	11.111
Prime cost		1,24,000	68.889
Add works overheads			
Factory overheads (0.50 × direct wages)		10,000	5.556
Stores overhead (0.10 × ₹1,04,000)		10,400	5.778
Less scrap realised (0.10 × 2,000 tonnes)		(800)	(0.444)
Rectification cost of 10 per cent of good castings (2,000 tonnes – 200 tonnes) = 1800 tonnes × 0.10 = 180 tonnes) (₹20,000 × 180 × 20) ÷ (2,000 × 100)		360	0.200
Manufacturing cost of good castings (1,800 tonnes)		1,43,960	79.98

P.10.8 A company of repute manufactures four varieties of a product, namely, A, B, C, and D. If the company manufactures only one variety, the monthly production can be either 5,000 of A, or 10,000 of B or 15,000 of C or 30,000 of D. From the following information, you are required to find the profit or loss made on each variety, showing direct cost, works cost and total cost:

	A	*B*	*C*	*D*
Actual production in a month	675	1,800	4,050	9,450
Direct wages	₹3,000	₹5,500	₹7,500	₹21,000
Direct materials cost	3,500	6,500	9,000	27,500
Sales price per unit	30	20	15	12

Overhead expenses for the month are ₹81,000. Selling and distribution cost is to be calculated at 10 per cent of works cost. Overhead expenses are to be allocated to each variety on the basis of units produced.

Solution

Statement of Costs and Profits for Products A, B, C, and D

Particulars	*Products*				*Total*
	A	B	C	D	
Direct wages	₹3,000	₹5,500	₹7,500	₹21,000	₹37,000
Direct materials	3,500	6,500	9,000	27,500	46,500
Prime/Direct cost	6,500	12,000	16,500	48,500	83,500
Add factory overheads (see working notes)	12,150	16,200	24,300	28,350	81,000
Work cost	18,650	28,200	40,800	76,850	1,64,500
Add selling and distribution cost	1,865	2,820	4,080	7,685	16,450
Total cost	20,515	31,020	44,880	84,535	1,80,950
Profit/(Loss)	(265)	4,980	15,870	28,865	49,450
Sales revenue	20,250	36,000	60,750	1,13,400	2,30,400

Working Note

Determination of factory overheads: Production in equivalent units expressed as follows: A, = 5,000 units or B, 10,000 units or C, 15,000 units or D, 30,000 units. Alternatively: 1 unit of A = 2 units of B (10,000 ÷ 5,000); 3 units of C (15,000 ÷ 5,000); 6 units of D (30,000 ÷ 5,000). A: B: C: D = 1:2:3:6. The overhead allocation should be determined by applying weights in the reverse order, that is 6:3:2:1 (A:B:C:D).

Products	*Production (units)*	*Weight*	*Total weighted value*	*Overheads allocated*	
A	675	6	4,050	[(₹81,000 × 4,050) ÷ 27,000] =	₹12,150
B	1,800	3	5,400	[(₹81,000 × 5,400) ÷ 27,000] =	16,200
C	4,050	2	8,100	[(₹81,000 × 8,100) ÷ 27,000] =	24,300
D	9,450	1	9,450	[(₹81,000 × 9,450) ÷ 27,000] =	28,350
			27,000		81,000

P.10.9 The Margos Company Ltd has just completed operations for the current quarter. The company's assistant accountant (who is very inexperienced) prepared the following statement of profit and loss for the quarter activities:

Sales		₹32,00,000
Operating expenses:		
Insurance	₹40,000	
Gas, electricity and water	1,00,000	
Direct labour cost	6,00,000	
Indirect labour cost	1,20,000	
Depreciation on factory equipment	1,60,000	
Raw materials purchased during the year	12,00,000	
Rent	4,00,000	
Selling and administration overheads	3,20,000	29,40,000
Net profit		2,60,000

You have been asked to assist the company in preparing a correct statement of profit and loss for the quarter. The following additional information is available:

1. The company is a manufacturing firm that produces a product for sale to outside customers.
2. 80 per cent of the rent paid applies to factory operations and the remainder to selling and administrative activities.
3. No raw materials were on hand on April 1 (beginning of quarter). However, raw materials of the value of ₹1,50,000 purchased during the year were still on hand on June 30. The remainder was used in production during the quarter.
4. 70 per cent of the insurance and 90 per cent of the gas, electricity and water charges paid apply to factory operations; the remainder apply to selling and administrative activities.
5. Work-in-progress and finished goods inventories were:

	April 1	*June 30*
Work-in-progress	₹4,20,000	₹4,80,000
Finished goods	5,40,000	4,00,000

You are required to prepare:

(a) A statement of cost of goods manufactured in the current year, and

(b) A corrected profit and loss account for the year ended March 31.

Solution

(a) *Statement of Cost of Goods Manufactured for the Quarter ending June 30:*

Particulars		*Amount*
Direct material used		
Direct material purchases	₹12,00,000	
Less closing stock	1,50,000	₹10,50,000
Direct labour		6,00,000
Prime cost		16,50,000
Add factory overheads		
Indirect labour	1,20,000	
Rent (₹4,00,000 × 0.80)	3,20,000	
Insurance (₹40,000 × 0.70)	28,000	
Gas, electricity and water (0.90 × ₹1,00,000)	90,000	
Depreciation on factory equipment	1,60,000	7,18,000
Gross works cost		23,68,000
Add opening work-in-process		4,20,000
Less closing work-in-process		(4,80,000)
Cost of goods manufactured		23,08,000

Profit and Loss A/C for the Quarter Ended June 30

Particulars	*Dr Amount*		*Particulars*	*Cr Amount*
To cost of goods sold			By sales	₹32,00,000
Opening stock	₹5,40,000			
Add cost of goods manufactured (a)	23,08,000			
Less closing stock	(4,00,000)	₹24,48,000		
To administrative and selling expenses:				
Selling and administrative overheads	3,20,000			
Rent (0.20 × ₹4,00,000)	80,000			
Insurance (0.30 × ₹40,000)	12,000			
Gas, electricity and water (0.10 × ₹1,00,000)	10,000	4,22,000		
To profit		3,30,000		
		32,00,000		32,00,000

P. 10.10 From the following data calculate the cost per km of a vehicle.

Value of vehicle	₹15,000,00
Road license for the year	36,000
Insurance charges per year	24,000
Garage rent per year	30,000
Driver's and conductor wages per month	10,000
Cost of diesel per litre	40
Proportional charge for tyre and maintenance per km	2
Estimated life (kms)	1,50,000
Estimated annual mileage (kms)	30,000
Petrol consumption (kms/litre)	8

Solution

Operating Cost Statement to Determine Cost per km

Particulars	*Total annual cost of 6,000 kms*	*Cost per km*
(A) Standing charges:		
Road licence fee for the year	₹36,000	₹1.20
Insurance charges for the year	24,000	0.80
Garage rent per year	30,000	1.00
Driver's wages per year (₹10,000 × 12)	1,20,000	4.00
Total	2,10,000	7.00
(B) Running charges:		
Depreciation of vehicle (₹15,00,000 × 30,000) ÷ 1,50,000	3,00,000	10.00
Cost of diesel (₹40 × 30,000) ÷ 8	1,50,000	5.00
Tyre and maintenance	60,000	2.00
Total	5,10,000	17.00
(C) Total running cost per km (A+B)	7,20,000	24.00

P. 10.11 The Delhi Bus Company Ltd. operates a number of buses in Delhi city. The firm's buses make 200 trips per week with an average distance of 50 kms. Fares are ₹1.0 per km per passenger and each bus can carry 40 passengers. The firm has the following cost structure.

Driver's pay, ₹2,000 per week per driver	₹40,000
Conductors' pay, ₹1,500 per week per conductor	30,000
Other salaries and wages per week	30,000
Depreciation and maintenance of buses	50,000
Petrol, diesel and variable costs (per bus per km)	10

Determine the firm's weekly income if it operates with its buses on an average 75 per cent utilisation.

SOLUTION

Statement of Operating Cost and Profit for a week (3,00,000 passenger–kms)

Particulars		Amount
(A) Revenue (3,00,000 × ₹1)		₹3,00,000
(B) Operating costs		
(a) Standing charges:		
Driver's pay	₹40,000	
Conductor's pay	30,000	
Other salaries and wages	30,000	
Total	1,00,000	
(b) Running costs:		
Depreciation and maintenance	50,000	
Petrol, diesel and other variable costs (₹10 × 10,000 kms)[@]	1,00,000	
Total	1,50,000	
(c) Total costs (a + b)		2,50,000
(C) Profit (A – B)		50,000

[@](200 Trips × 50 Kms)

Determination of passenger–kms= (Trips × kms × passengers capacity) × 0.75 = (200 × 50 × 40) × 0.75 = 3,00,000 kms

P. 10.12 Iron ore is transported from two mines, A and B and unloaded at plots in a railway station. A is at a distance of 10 kms and B is at a distance of 15 kms from the railway plots. A fleet of lorries of 5-tonne carrying capacity is used for transport of ore from mines. Records reveal that lorries average a speed of 30 kms per hour when running and regularly take 10 minutes to unload at the railhead. At mine A, loading time averages 30 minutes per load while at mine B, loading time averages 20 minutes per load.

Drivers wages, depreciation, insurance, and taxes are found to cost ₹90 per hour of operating. Fuel, oil, tyres, repairs and maintenance cost ₹12 per km. Draw up a statement showing the per tonne–km cost of carrying iron ore from each mine.

SOLUTION

Operating Cost Statement determining Cost per tonne–km of carrying iron ore from two mines, A and B

Particulars	Mine A	Mine B
1 Distance from railway station (one way) (kms)	10	15
2 Distance from railway station (kms) (both ways or length of journey per trip)	20	30
3 Speed of lorries (kms per hour)	30	30
4 Time taken per trip (2) ÷ (3) (minutes)	40	60
5 Loading time at mines (minutes)	30	20
6 Unloading time at railway station (minutes)	10	10
7 Total time taken per trip (4 + 5 + 6)	80	90
8 Driver's wages, depreciation, insurance and taxes (per hour ₹)	90	90
9 Driver's wages, depreciation insurance etc. per trip	120*	135**
10 Fuel, oil, tyres, repairs and maintenance cost (₹per km)	12	12
11 Fuel oil, tyres, repairs, etc. per trip (2) x (10)	240	360
12 Total cost (9 + 11)	360	495
13 Total tonne–kms (Kms x capacity)	50	75
14 Cost per tonne–km (12 ÷13) (₹)	7.2	6.6

* = (80 × ₹90) ÷ 60 = ₹120

** = (90 × ₹90) ÷ 60 = ₹135

P. 10.13 A practising chartered accountant now spends ₹10 per km on taxi fare for his client's work. He is considering two other alternatives: the purchase of a new small car or an old big car. The estimated costs figure are:

Particulars	New small car	Big old car
Purchase price	₹3,50,000	₹2,00,000
Sale price of car after 5 years	1,90,000	1,20,000
Repairs and servicing per year	10,000	12,000
Taxes and insurance per year	17,000	7,000
Diesel price per litre	40	40
Diesel consumption (kms/litre)	10	7

He estimates that he covers 10,000 kms annually. Which of these alternatives will be cheaper? If his practice expands and he has to cover 19,000 kms per annum, what should be his decision?

SOLUTION

Comparative Operating Cost Statement

Particulars	Total cost			
	10,000 kms per year		19,000 kms per year	
	New small car	Big old car	New small car	Big old car
(A) Standing charges:				
Taxes and insurance per year	₹17,000	₹7,000	₹17,000	₹7,000
(B) Running charges:				
Repair and servicing per year	10,000	12,000	10,000	12,000
Depreciation per year (purchase price – salvage value) ÷ 5	32,000	16,000	32,000	16,000
Cost of Diesel	40,000	57,143	76,000	1,08,571
Total	82,000	85,143	1,18,000	1,36,571
(C) Total operating cost (A+B)	99,000	92,143	1,35,000	1,43,571

Conclusions: **(i)** Buying the big old car would be cheaper at 10,000 kms. **(ii)** Buying the new small car would be cheaper at 19,000 kms. However, it is important to recognise the interest cost. The new small car requires a cash outlay of ₹1,50,000 over and above the big old car. Assuming 10 per cent interest, the total cost of the new small car would be ₹1,35,000 + ₹15,000 (₹1,50,000 × 0.10) = ₹1,50,000 and the decision then would be different.

P. 10.14 A transport company supplies the following details in respect of a truck of 5 tonne capacity.

Cost of truck	₹18,00,000
Diesel, oil, grease (per trip each way)	1,200
Repairs and maintenance (per month)	30,000
Driver's (monthly) wages	12,000
Cleaner–cum–attendant's wages (monthly)	6,000
Insurance (per year)	1,80,000
Road licence (per year)	72,000
General supervision charges (per year)	1,44,000
Estimated life (years)	10

The truck carries goods to and from the city covering a distance of 50 kms each way. While going to the city, freight is available for a full load of the truck and on its return journey it can fetch freight only up to 20 per cent of its capacity. Truck has no salvage value at year-end 10.

On the assumption that the truck runs on an average 25 days a month, you are required to determine the following: **(i)** operating cost per tonne–km, **(ii)** rate per tonne per trip that the company should charge if profit of 100 per cent on cost is to be earned, and **(iii)** what price would you charge if one wants to engage the truck for one day for a trip to the city and back?

SOLUTION

Operating Cost Statement to determine Cost per km

Particulars	*Total cost per month of 7,500 tonne–kms*	*Cost per tonne–km*
(A) Standing charges		
Driver's wages	₹12,000	₹1.6
Cleaner–cum–attendant's wages	6,000	0.8
Insurance (₹1,80,000 ÷ 12)	15,000	2.0
Road licence (₹72,000 ÷ 12)	6,000	0.8
General supervision (₹1,44,000 ÷ 12)	12,000	1.6
Total	51,000	6.8
(B) Running charges		
Depreciation (₹18,00,000 ÷ (12 × 10)	15,000	2.0
Diesel, oil, grease (₹1,200 × 50 trips that is, 2 trips daily for 25 days)	60,000	8.0
Repairs and maintenance	30,000	4.0
Total	1,05,000	14.0
(C) Total cost per tonne–km (A+B)	1,56,000	20.8

WORKING NOTES

(i) *Determination of tonne–km per month:*	
Trip to city: 50 kms × 5 tonnes capacity × 25 days	6,250
Return back from city: 50 kms × 25 days × 1 tonne	1,250
	7,500

(*Contd.*)

(Contd.)

(ii)	Determination of freight rate:	
	Cost per tonne	₹20.8
	Add desired profit 100 per cent of cost	20.8
	Freight rate per tonne km	41.6
(iii)	*Quotation price:*	
	Freight tonne–km in both trips (250 + 50)	300
	Multiplied by freight rate per tonne–km	₹41.6
		12,480

P. 10.15 A cement manufacturing company is facing the problem of transportation of limestone from its quarry. The quarry is situated 25 kms away and the only means of transport available is the roadways. The company has received quotations from some of the local transporters at ₹325, ₹340 and ₹350 per tonne of limestone transported, with an escalation clause in respect of diesel/oil costs. The quantity of limestone to be transported per month is 24,000 tonnes. While examining the feasibility of departmental transport the following facts come to be recgonised.

1. Two types of trucks are available in the market, namely, 10–tonners and 8–tonners.
2. Details of operating costs for the trucks are:

	10–tonners	8–tonners
Purchase price	₹25,00,000	₹20,00,000
Estimated useful life (years)	5	5
Residual value	4,00,000	2,00,000
Km per litre of diesel (kms)	3	4
Estimated repairs and maintenance cost per truck per month	20,000	16,000
Vehicle and road tax per quarter	6,000	6,000

3. Cost of diesel per litre, ₹45.
4. Cost of finance for purchase of trucks, 12 per cent per annum.
5. Each vehicle can run 5 trips (up and down) each day and can run on an average 24 days each month.
6. Drivers will have to be recruited according to the number of trucks to be purchased. In addition, one extra driver for every 5 vehicles will be required for the entire fleet. Each driver will cost ₹8,000 per month.
7. An additional transport supervisor would be required at a cost of ₹15,000 per month.
8. Yet another possibility is to hire sufficient number of trucks (10–tonners only) from a transport company at the rate of ₹50,000 per month per truck. The transport company bears repair and maintenance costs as well as the vehicle and road tax. The cement company has to bear the cost of drivers, supervisor and other operational costs.

You are required to advise the company on an appropriate choice among the above alternatives, considering also the option of entrusting the job to the transport operators.

Solution

Statement of Operating Costs under Alternative Means of Transporting Limestone

	Purchase of trucks		Hiring of 10–tonners
Details of costs	*10–tonners*	*8–tonners*	
1 Repairs and maintenance per month	₹20,000	₹16,000	—
2 Vehicle and road tax per month	2,000	2,000	—

(Contd.)

(*Contd.*)

3 Cost of diesel per month (see working note 1)	90,000	67,500	₹90,000
4 Depreciation cost per month (see working note 2)	35,000	30,000	—
5 Finance cost per month (see working note 3)	25,000	20,000	—
6 Hiring charges per month	—	—	50,000
7 Supervisor's salary	15,000	15,000	15,000
8 Salary of drivers (see working note 5)	1,92,000	2,40,000	1,92,000
9 Total cost per truck per month [total (1) to (6)]	3,79,000	3,90,500	3,47,000
10 Number of trucks needed (see working note 4)	20	25	20
11 Total cost of entire fleet [(9) × (10) + (8) + (7)]	75,80,000	97,62,500	69,40,000
12 Cost per tonne limestone transported (11 ÷ 24,000)	315.83	406.77	289.16

The company is advised to hire 20 (10–tonner) trucks as it would involve the lowest cost per tonne of limestone transported. There is no question of entrusting the job to local transporters as their charges are higher, that is, ₹325, ₹340 and ₹350.

Working Notes

Particulars	*10–tonners*	*8–tonners*
1 Cost of diesel per month		
Distance to be covered per trip (kms)	50	50
(x) Number of trips	5	5
Total distance per day (kms)	250	250
(x) Number of days	24	24
Total distance per month (kms)	6,000	6,000
÷ Km covered per litre of diesel	3	4
Total diesel consumption (litres)	2,000	1,500
x Rate per litre	₹45	₹45
	90,000	67,500
2 *Depreciation cost per month*		
Purchase price	₹25,00,000	₹20,00,000
Less residual value	4,00,000	2,00,000
Depreciation cost	21,00,000	18,00,000
÷ Life (in months)	60	60
Depreciation per month	35,000	30,000
3 *Finance cost per year*	3,00,000*	2,40,000**
Finance cost per month [(3) ÷ 12]	25,000	20,000
4 *Number of trucks required*		
(a) Limestone to be transported (tonnes)	24,000	24,000
(b) Limestone transported in 24 days (tonnes)	1,200@	960@@
Number of trucks required (a ÷ b)	20	25
5 Number of drivers (regular)	20	25
Number of drivers (extra)	4	5
Total number of drivers	24	30
x Salary per driver per month	₹8,000	₹8,000
Total salary bill	1,92,000	2,40,000

* (₹25,00,000 × 0.12), ** (₹20,00,000 × 0.12)
@(5 × 10 × 24), @@ (5 × 8 × 24)

P. 10.16 Shankar has been promised a contract to run a tourist car on a 20-kms long route for the chief executive of a multinational firm. He buys a car costing ₹3,00,000. The annual cost of insurance and taxes are ₹9,000 and ₹2,400 respectively. He has to pay ₹500 per month for a garage where he keeps the car when it is not in use. The annual repair costs are estimated at ₹8,000. The car is estimated to have a life of 10 years, at the end of which the scrap value is likely to be ₹50,000.

He hires a driver who is to be paid ₹6,000 per month and 10 per cent of the takings as commission. Other incidental expenses are estimated at ₹2,000 per month.

Diesel and oil cost ₹500 per 100 kms. The car will make 4 round trips every day. Assuming that a profit of 15 per cent on takings is desired and that the car will be on the road for 25 days on an average per month, what should Shankar charge per round trip?

SOLUTION

Operating Cost Statement Showing Determination of Charges per Round Trip

Particulars	*Total amount*
(i) Standing charges per month	
Insurance (₹9,000 ÷ 12)	₹750
Taxes (₹2,400 ÷ 12)	200
Garage charges	500
Driver's salary	6,000
Incidental expenses	1,300
	8,750
(ii) Running charges per month	
Repairs cost (₹8,000 ÷ 12)	666.67
Diesel and oil (20 kms × 2 × 4 round trips × 25 days × ₹5 per km)	20,000.00
Depreciation (₹3,00,000 – ₹50,000) ÷ 120 months	2,083.33
	22,750
(iii) Total operating cost (i + ii) excluding commission	31,500
(iv) Driver's commission (*see working notes*)	4,200
(v) Desired profit (*see working notes*)	6,300
(vi) Total charges per 100 trips (25 days × 4 round trips)	42,000
(vii) Charges per round trip (₹42,000 ÷ 100)	420

WORKING NOTES

1. *Determination of takings per month*
   Let 'X' be the sum of total takings per month.
   Driver's commission is 10% of X = 0.10 X
   Desired profit 15% of X = 0.15 X
   Total takings per month = Total cost + Driver's commission + Desired profit
   X = ₹31,500 + 0.10 X + 0.15 X
   X – 0.10X – 0.15 X = ₹31,500, or, 0.75 X = ₹31,500
   X = ₹42,000 i.e. (₹31,500/0.75)
2. *Driver's commission* = 0.10 × ₹42,000 = ₹4,200
3. *Desired profit* = 0.15 × ₹42,000 = ₹6,300

P 10.17 From the following data relating to two different vehicles A and B, compute the cost running kilometer:

Particulars	*A*	*B*
Kilometers run (annual)	15,000	6,000
Cost of vehicles	₹5,00,000	₹3,00,000

(*Contd.*)

(*Contd.*)

Road license (annual)	9,250	8,000
Insurance (annual)	7,000	4,000
Garage rent (annual)	6,000	5,000
Driver wages per hour	20	20
Cost of diesel per litre	40	40
Kilometers run per litre	20	15
Repair charges per kilometer	1.65	2.00
Tyre cost per kilometer	2.00	2.00
Estimated life of the vehicle (kilometers)	1,00,000	75,000
Vehicle run per hour (kilometers)	20	20

SOLUTION

Operating Cost Statement showing Cost per Running km of Vehicles A and B

Particulars	*Total Cost*	
	Vehicle A	*Vehicle B*
(i) Standing charges per year:		
Road license	9,250	8,000
Insurance	7,000	4,000
Garage rent	6,000	5,000
	22,250	17,000
(ii) Running charges per year:		
Depreciation (₹5,00,000 ÷ 1,00,000 kms) ÷ 15,000	75,000	—
(₹3,00,000 ÷ 75,000 kms) × 6,000	—	24,000
Driver wages (15,000 km ÷ 20 kms) × ₹20 per hour	15,000	—
(6,000km ÷ 20 kms) ₹20 per hour	—	6,000
Diesel cost (15,000 km ÷ 20 kms) × ₹40 per litre	30,000	
(6,000 km ÷ 15 kms) × ₹40 per litre		16,000
Repair Charges (15,000 kms × ₹1.65)	24,750	
(6000 kms × ₹2.00)	12,000	
Tyre cost (15,000 kms × ₹2.00)	30,000	
(6,000 kms × ₹2.00)		12,000
	1,74,750	70,000
(iii) Total charges (i + ii)	1,97,000	87,000
(iv) Total kilometers run	15,000	6,000
(v) Cost per running km (iii ÷ iv)	13.13	14.50

P 10.18 A lorry starts with a load of 20 tonnes of goods from station A. It unloads 8 tonnes at station B and rest of goods at station C. It reaches back directly to station A after getting reloaded with 16 tonnes of goods at station C. The distance between A to B , B to C and then from C to A are 80 kms, 120 kms and 160 kms respective. Compute 'Absolute tonnes-kms' and 'Commercial tonnes-kms'.

SOLUTION

(a) *Determination of Absolute Tonnes-kms*

(Number of tonnes added × Distance in kms):		
From Station A to B	(20 tonnes × 80 kms)	1,600
From Station B to C	(12 tonnes × 120 kms)	1,440
From Station C to A	(16 tonnes × 160 kms)	2,560
Total tonnes-kms		5,600

(b) Determination of Commercial Tonne-kms

Average load × Total kms travelled
[(20 + 12 + 16)/3] × 30 kms = 5,760 tonnes-km

EXERCISES

10.1 Fill in the following blanks:

(i) Unit costing is used in industries which are engaged in manufacturing ________.

(ii) Unit cost is computed dividing ____________ by the number of units produced.

(iii) Cost unit for cement industry is ____________.

(iv) Cost unit for paint manufacturing is ____________.

(v) Cost unit for brick making is ____________.

(vi) ____________ is the statement that provides a detailed and systematic presentation of all elements of costs and profit.

(vii) Cost of sales is equal to cost of goods sold plus ____________.

(viii) Sum of prime cost and ____________ is factory cost (gross).

(ix) Cost unit for electricity organization is ____________.

(x) Cost unit for transport undertakings is ____________.

(**Answers: (i)** homogeneous product, **(ii)** total cost, **(iii)** per tonne, **(iv)** per litre, **(v)** 1,000 bricks made, **(vi)** cost sheet, **(vii)** selling overheads, **(viii)** factory overheads, **(ix)** kilowatt-hours, **(x)** passenger-km/tonne-km.)

10.2 Define unit costing. Name the industries to which this type of costing is most appropriate.

10.3 "Cost sheet and production account differ in presentation only." Elucidate the statement.

10.4 How would you deal with the following items in a cost sheet (i) Wastage and scrap; (ii) By-products; (iii) Rectification cost of defective work; (iv) Work-in-process valued at prime cost or factory cost; (v) Carriage on purchase.

10.5 What is operating costing? Describe the type of industries in which such a system would be suitable.

10.6 Why is operating costing called service costing? Describe in brief the cost accumulating procedure under operating costing.

10.7 "Classification of total costs into fixed and variable costs and determination of cost unit are the two essential pre-requisites of operating costing." Explain the statement with suitable illustrations.

10.8 Describe in brief the usefulness of operating costing with the help of suitable illustrations.

10.9 Mr Gopal furnishes the following data relating to the manufacture of a standard product during the month of April:

Raw materials consumed	₹15,000
Direct labour charges	9,000
Machine-hours worked	900
Machine-hour rate	5
Administrative overheads (per cent on works cost)	20
Selling overheads per unit	0.50
Units produced	17,100
Units sold at ₹4 per unit	16,000

You are required to prepare a cost sheet from the above, showing:

(a) The cost per unit,

(b) Profit per unit sold and profit for the period.

10.10 Gem Ltd is manufacturing refrigerators and the following details are furnished in respect of its factory operation for the year ended March 31:

Work-in-process, April 1 at prime cost	₹51,000	
Manufacturing expenses	15,000	₹66,000
Work-in-process, March 31 at prime cost	45,000	
Manufacturing expenses	9,000	54,000
Stock of raw materials, April 1		2,25,000
Purchase of raw materials		4,77,000
Direct labour		1,71,000
Manufacturing expenses		84,000
Stock of raw materials on March 31		2,04,000

On the basis of the above data, prepare a statement showing the cost of production. Also, indicate separately the amount of manufacturing expenses, which enter into the cost of production.

10.11 The following particulars are extracted from the works and other relevant sources in respect of A and Company Ltd:

1. Estimated materials cost of the job is ₹50,000 and the direct labour cost is likely to be ₹10,000.
2. In the machine shop, it will require machining by a German machine for 20 hours and a Japanese machine for 6 hours.
3. The machine-hour rates for the German and Japanese machines are ₹100 and ₹150 respectively.
4. The direct wages in all other shops last year amounted to ₹8,00,000 as against ₹4,80,000 factory overheads.
5. Last year, the factory cost of all jobs amounted to ₹25,00,000 against ₹3,75,000 office expenses.

Make out a quotation with 20 per cent profit on the selling price.

10.12 The working results of a section of an industrial organisation engaged in the production and sale of a machine X for the current year with estimates for the next year are furnished below:

Particulars	*Current year*	*Next year*
1. Raw materials	₹150	₹200
2. Spares and purchased parts	250	300
3. Indirect materials and consumables	120	160
4. Factory power	100	120
5. Direct labour cost	400	440
6. Factory overheads	330	400
Factory cost	1,350	1,620
7. Selling and administrative expenses	350	400
Cost of sales	1,700	2,020
8. Profit per machine	300	380
Selling price	2,000	2,400

Profit on sale of 2,500 machines: ₹7,50,000 (current year) and ₹9,50,000 (next year). It is proposed to produce only 2,000 machines next year and sell the same at ₹2,500 per unit. The statement may be recast taking into consideration the following costs:

(a) Spares and purchased parts would cost ₹320 per unit next year.

(b) Use of electric generating sets due to power cuts would cost ₹150 per machine instead of ₹120.

(c) Lay-off wages, and so on would increase labour costs per machine by ₹20 more than the estimated amount.

(d) Variable expenses under factory overheads will increase by ₹10 per machine. This head for both the years includes a sum of ₹3,70,000 which is fixed.

(e) The apportionment of selling and administrative expenses for this section will be reduced by ₹1,49,000 for the next year.

10.13 The following details have been obtained from the cost records of Coment Paints Limited for the month of September:

Stock of raw materials as on September 1	₹75,000
Stock of raw materials as on September 30	91,500
Direct wages	52,500
Indirect wages	2,750
Sales	2,11,000
Work-in-process on September 1	28,000
Work-in-process on September 30	35,000
Purchase of raw materials	66,000
Factory rent, rates and power	15,000
Depreciation of plant and machinery	3,500
Expenses on purchases	1,500
Carriage outwards	2,500
Advertising	3,500
Office rent and taxes	2,500
Traveller's wages and commission	6,500
Stock of finished goods on September 1	54,000
Stock of finished goods on September 30	31,000

Prepare a production account giving the maximum possible break-up of costs and profits for the month of September.

10.14 From the following particulars, make out a monthly cost sheet of Coke and By-product Ltd.

Coal used	5,000 tonnes, ₹12.50 per tonne
Coke produced and sold	3,505 tonnes, selling price ₹24 per tonne
Tar produced	200 tonnes, ₹48 per tonne
Sulphur, etc.	50 tonnes, ₹180 per tonne
Benzol, etc.	48 tonnes @ ₹75 per tonne
Raw materials used	₹ 3,900
Wages paid	9,600
Repairs and renewals	9,000
Salary and general charges	5,000

Show the percentage of coke produced to the weight of coal used.

10.15 The managing director of a small undertaking consults you as to the minimum price at which he can sell the output of one of the departments of the company which is intended for mass production in future. The company's record shows the following particulars for this department for the previous year:

Production and sales (units)	100
Materials	₹13,000
Direct labour	7,000
Direct charges	1,000
Works oncost	7,000
Office oncost	2,800
Selling oncost	3,200
Profit	5,000
	39,000

You ascertain that 40 per cent of the work oncost fluctuates directly with production and 70 per cent of selling oncost fluctuates with sales. It is anticipated that the department would produce 500 units per annum, the direct labour charges will be reduced by 20 per cent, while fixed work oncost charges will increase by ₹3,000. Office oncost and fixed selling oncost are anticipated to show increase of 25 per cent but otherwise no changes are expected.

Prepare a statement for submission to your client.

10.16 A factory has received an order for three different types of casting, weighing 18, 45, and 27 tonnes respectively; 10 per cent of the raw materials used are wasted in manufacturing and are sold as scrap for 20 per cent of their cost price.

The cost of raw materials is ₹250 per tonne, the respective wages for the three types of casting are ₹4,000, ₹10,500 and ₹5,500 respectively. The costs of the moulds for the three different types of castings are ₹400, ₹500 and ₹300 respectively.

If the factory overhead charges are 40 per cent of the wages in each case, determine the cost of each type of casting.

10.17 Mr Rohit has a small furniture factory. He specialises in the manufacture of small dining tables of standard size of which he can make 15,000 in a year. The cost per table worked out as under for the previous year when he made and sold 10,000 tables:

Materials	₹30
Labour	10
Overhead (fixed), recovered @ 50 per cent of material cost	15
Total cost	55

Prices are fixed by adding a standard margin of 10 per cent to the total cost arrived at above. In the current year, due to fall in the cost of materials, total cost worked out as under:

Materials	₹20
Labour	10
Overheads recovered @ 50 per cent of material cost	10
	40

Mrs Rohit maintained his standard margin of of 10 per cent on the cost of sales. Sales were at the previous year's level. You are asked to:

(i) Determine profit or loss for the current year.

(ii) Compute the price which should be charged in the current year to yield the same profit or loss as in previous year.

10.18 Mumbai Transport Ltd operates a fleet of lorries. The following information relates to lorry 10 for the month of June:

Days available	26
Days operated	22
Total kms covered	1,600
Total trips made	28
Total tonnage carried	3,000

Operating costs (June): Petrol, oil, and grease, ₹9,600; Wages - driver, ₹10,000, attendant, ₹6,000 and mechanic, ₹6,000. *Maintenance costs* (estimated for the year): ₹9,600. *Fixed costs* (estimated for the year): Insurance, ₹9,600, Road tax, ₹3,600 and miscellaneous, ₹2,400. *Capital cost,* ₹7,26,000; Residual value estimated to be ₹1,20,000 with an effective life of 5 years. *Administration and other overheads* for the year, ₹1,20,000.

Prepare operating cost statement determining cost per km operated.

10.19 An entrepreneur own a bus which runs from Delhi to Agra and back for 25 days in a month. The distance from Delhi to Agra is 170 kms. The bus completes the trip from Delhi to Agra and back on the same day. Calculate the fare the entrepreneur should charge a passenger if he wants to earn a profit of 33.33 per cent on cost. The following information is further available:

Cost of bus	₹30,00,000
Salary of driver per month	10,500
Salary of conductor per month	7,000
Salary of part-time accountant per month	8,500
Insurance per annum	33,600
Diesel consumption 4 kms. per litre costing	30
Local taxes per annum	12,000
Lubricant oil per 100 kms	40
Repairs and maintenance per annum	20,000
Licence fee per annum	36,925
Normal capacity (person)	50
Depreciation rate per annum	20

The bus usually runs full up to 90 per cent of its capacity (50 passengers) both ways. Interest is payable on the cost of bus at 10 per cent per annum.

10.20 A factory which uses a large amount of coal is situated between two collieries, X and Y, with both being at a distance of 5 and 10 kms, respectively, from the factory. A fleet or lorries of 5 tonnes carrying capacity is used for collecting coal from the pitheads. The lorries average a speed of 20 kilometres per hour when running and generally take 10 minutes to unload in the factory premises. At colliery X, loading time averages 30 minutes per load, while at colliery Y it is 20 minutes per load.

Driver's wages, licences, insurance, depreciation, garage, and similar charges cost `60 per hour operated. Fuel, oil, tyres repairs and similar charges cost `6 per km run.

Draw up a statement showing the cost per-tonne-kilometre of carrying coal from each colliery. If the coal is of same quality and price at pithead, which of the collieries should the company prefer to make purchases?

10.21 Union Transport Company Ltd supplies the following details in respect of a truck of a 5-tonne capacity:

Cost of truck	₹18,00,000
Estimated life (years)	10
Diesel, oil grease, etc. per trip each way	450
Repairs and maintenance per month	10,000
Driver's wages per month	10,000
Cleaner's wages per month	5,000
Insurance per year	24,000
Tax per year	12,000
General supervision charges per year	84,000

The truck carries goods to and from the city covering a distance of 50 kms each way.

On outward trip, freight is available up to the full capacity and on return trip, 20 per cent of capacity. Assume that the truck runs on an average of 25 days a month. Work out:

(a) Operating cost per tonne-km, and

(b) Rate per tonne per trip that the company should charge if a profit of 50 per cent on freight is to be earned.

10.22 Mr Ahuja runs a tempo service in the town and has two vehicles. He furnishes you the following data from which you are to compute the cost per running mile.

Particulars	Vehicle A	Vehicle B
Cost of vehicle	₹5,00,000	₹3,00,000
Road licence per year	7,000	7,500
Supervision and salary (yearly)	66,000	48,000
Driver's wages per hour	40	40
Cost of fuel per litre	42	42
Repairs and maintenance per mile	3.0	4.0
Tyre cost per mile	2.00	2.00
Garage rent per year	18,000	10,000
Insurance premium yearly	9,000	7,000
Km run per litre	6	5
Km run during the year	15,000	6,000
Estimated life of vehicles (kms)	1,00,000	75,000

Charge interest at 10 per cent per annum on the cost of vehicle. The vehicles run 20 kms. per hour on an average.

10.23 A transport company is running 4 buses between two towns which are 50 kms apart. Seating capacity of each bus is 40 passengers. The following particulars were obtained from their books for April month of the current year:

Wages of drivers and conductors	₹1,20,000
Salaries to office staff	50,000
Diesel and other oil	2,00,000
Repairs and maintenance	40,000
Taxes and insurance	80,000
Depreciation	1,30,000
Interest and other charges	1,00,000
	7,20,000

Actual passengers carried were 75 per cent of the seating capacity. All the four buses run on all days of the month. Each bus made one round trip per day. Find out the cost per passenger km.

10.24 From the following particulars, calculate the cost per running kilometer of a vehicle:

Cost of vehicle	₹25,00,000
Road licence fee for the year	75,000
Driver's and conductor wages per hour	100
Cost fuel per litre	40
Repairs per kilometer	1.50
Tyre cost per kilometer	2.00
Garage rent per year	1,32,500
Insurance per year	85,000
Kilometers run per litre	6
Kilometers run during the year	15,000
Estimated life of vehicles (kms)	1,00,000
Charge interest at 10 per cent on the cost of vehicle	
The vehicle runs 20 kms per hour on an average.	

ANSWERS [Comprehensive solutions to all numerical review questions are available on the companion website: http://www.mhhe.com/khan_jain_ma6e]

10.9 **(a)** Cost ₹2 per unit;
(b) Profit for the period, ₹24,000.

10.10 Cost of production ₹7,65,000. Manufacturing expenses included in cost of production, ₹90,000

10.11 Quotation price, ₹99,043.75

10.12 Cost of sales per machine, ₹2,162.50; Profit per machine, ₹337.50

10.13 Prime cost ₹1,03,500; Work cost, ₹1,17,750; Cost of goods sold ₹1,43,250; Cost of sales ₹1,55,750; Profit ₹55,250

10.14 Cost of production, ₹67,800; Profit ₹16,320

10.15 Total cost ₹1,35,100; selling price ₹1,54,900

10.16 Cost of casting per tonne: A, ₹606.55; B, ₹610; C, ₹568.52

10.17 **(a)** Profit ₹55,000
(b) Selling price ₹50.50

10.18 ₹33.625

10.19 ₹104.72 or ₹105

10.20 Colliery X should be preferred. Carrying cost per tonne ₹26 (X) and ₹42 (Y)

10.21 **(a)** ₹9.67
(b) ₹19.34

10.22 ₹29.0 (Vehicle A) and ₹37.4 (Vehicle B)

10.23 ₹2.0

10.24 ₹75.83

11

Chapter

Variable Costing and Absorption (Full) Costing

Learning Objectives

1. Discuss comparison of variable costing and full (absorption) costing from the view point of income determination
2. Outline the merits and demerits of variable costing

INTRODUCTION

Variable costing and absorption costing are not systems of costing such as process, operating, batch or job costing. Variable costing is a technique in which only variable costs are taken into account for purposes of product costing, inventory valuation and other allied important management decisions. In absorption costing, total costs are taken into account for these purposes. Thus, the variable costing technique is in marked contrast to the orthodox costing system known as 'full/absorption/traditional/conventional costing'. The material point of difference between the two techniques of costing is that the 'full' costing method 'absorbs' all costs necessary to produce the product and have it in a saleable form, while the variable costing technique recognises only variable costs as production costs. Thus, direct material, direct labour and variable overheads constitute the only relevant costs in variable costing whereas the full/absorption costing technique recognises fixed overheads also as a product cost in addition to material, labour and variable overheads. Hence, conceptually these two techniques differ in only one respect: fixed manufacturing overheads are included in product cost under absorption costing; they are excluded under variable costing.

Variable costing is a technique in which only variable costs are taken into account for product costing, inventory valuation and other allied management decisions.

Absorption costing takes into account total costs.

The two techniques of costing are, however, not mutually exclusive and are complementary in character. Income statements for external reporting and for tax purposes are to be on a full costing basis.[1] The usefulness of variable costing is that, it helps management in arriving at profit-maximising decisions in certain situations. It is for this reason that variable costing becomes more useful for internal reporting purposes. Thus, both techniques are significant. Which costing technique is to be employed depends on the purpose.

Section 1 presents a comparison of variable and absorption costing from the point of view of income determination. The merits and demerits of variable costing are listed in Section 2. The chapter concludes with the main points.

VARIABLE AND ABSORPTION COSTING: A COMPARISON

Variable costing is employed under the assumption that a certain investment in facilities and other productive factors is required before products can be manufactured. For instance, a factory building is to be hired for which rent is to be paid, plant is to be installed on which there will be a depreciation charge, factory insurance payment, property taxes, salary of plant manager and such other expenses have to be initially and subsequently incurred each year in the manufacturing business. Hence, the fixed costs resulting from this investment are not product costs but period cost. These costs must be incurred in order to have a manufacturing establishment and they will recur each year. Logically, therefore, "the fixed costs of manufacturing should be expensed each year and not carried as part of the cost of an inventory."[2] In other words, the principle underlying variable costs is that fixed manufacturing overhead are not inventoriable costs; they are period costs and must be matched against the revenue of that year. In contrast to this, absorption costing indicates that the manufacturing fixed overheads are inventoriable costs; they are the product costs and must be matched against the revenue of the year in which sales are made. Format 11.2 shows the flow of costs in an absorption costing system. The cost flow pattern for variable costing in shown in Format 11.1.

Format 11.1 Income Statement (Variable Costing)

		Amount
Sales revenue (Units sold × selling price)		. . . . .
Less: Variable costs (production costs):		
Direct material cost	. . . . .	
Direct labour cost	. . . . .	
Variable manufacturing overheads	. . . . .	
Total cost of good manufactured	. . . . .	
Plus: Cost of inventory in the beginning of the year (Units × variable cost)	. . . . .	
Less: Cost of inventory at the end of the year (Units × variable cost)	(. . . . .)	
Cost of goods manufactured and sold		(. . . . .)
Contribution (manufacturing)		. . . . .
Less: Variable non-production costs:		
Selling and distribution costs		
Administrative costs	. . . . .	(. . . . .)
Other costs (specify)	. . . . .	. . . . .
Contribution (final)	. . . . .	
Less: Fixed costs:		
Fixed production costs	. . . . .	
Fixed non-production costs (specify individual items)	. . . . .	(. . . . .)
Net income before income taxes		
Less: Income taxes		(. . . . .)
Net income after income taxes		

Format 11.2 Income Statement (Absorption Costing)

		Amount
Sales revenue (Number of units sold × selling price)		—
Less: Total costs of manufacturing:		
Direct material cost	—	
Direct labour cost	—	
Variable manufacturing overhead	—	
Fixed manufacturing overhead	—	
Total cost of goods manufactured		—
Plus: Cost of inventory in the beginning of the year (Units × total cost)		—
Less: Cost of inventory at the end of the year (Units × total cost)	( )	
Cost of goods manufactured and sold		( )
Gross margin (manufacturing) (unadjusted)		
Adjustment for capacity variance (+Favourable –Unfavourable)		(±)
Gross margin (adjusted)		
Less: Non-production costs:		
Selling and distribution costs		
Administrative costs	—	
Other costs (specify)	—	
Net income before income taxes	—	( )
Less: Income taxes		( )
Net income after taxes		

Note: If the firm's operating capacity is different from the normal capacity, there will be capacity variance.

The adjustment for such a variance is to be made before determining the gross margin. If capacity variance is favourable, the amount is to be deducted from the total costs of goods manufactured and sold; the amount is added to the cost if capacity variance is unfavourable.

Everything is common in both the formats except that fixed manufacturing overheads form part of production costs with 'full' costing whereas it is non-production cost is the case of variable costing. It is also important to note that the treatment of overheads other than manufacturing, namely, selling and administrative, is the same under both the techniques, full or variable.

The justification of the use of variable costing *vis-à-vis* absorption costing is based on two important factors:

1. Fixed costs relate to a particular period of time and should, therefore, be charged to that period only and to no other.
2. There is no method which is capable of apportioning fixed manufacturing costs to products. In the full costing method, fixed overheads are recovered from production by some agreed recovery method. This recovery can never be accurate and may even sometimes be misleading. Further, fixed overheads (such as rates and insurance), are predominantly concerned with time rather than volume of output and so should be recovered during the current period and not carried forward to burden the next.[3]

The differences between the two costing techniques can be better highlighted by showing the procedure of income statement preparation under the two costing concepts/techniques.

In variable costing, as explained earlier, product costs should include only the variable factory costs, and the fixed (period) costs should be charged to the revenue of the accounting period. The excess of sales revenue (SR) over variable costs (VC) is known as contribution (C) utilised towards the recovery of *first* fixed expenses (FC/period costs) and, second, to contribute to profits. On the other hand, absorption costing is based on the principle that all the manufacturing costs (direct, variable, as well as non-variable costs) should be charged to the production of a given period and fixed manufacturing overheads are charged to the products by using a pre-determined rate, designated as the standard fixed overhead rate (SFOR) of recovery. This rate is elaborated in a later chapter in detail and is usually determined with reference to budgeted fixed manufacturing overheads and the hours of operation at a normal level of production. The SFOR is determined by dividing the former amount with the latter amount. The products are assigned a standard charge for fixed overheads. If the plant operates above or below its normal capacity, the fixed manufacturing overheads will be over/under-absorbed; the over/under-absorbed overhead amount is designated as the capacity variance and is written off to operations for the year.

From the above principles of absorption costing, it follows that profits are affected not only by the sales volume, selling price, cost of production, but also by the quantity of units produced during the period. Accordingly, a firm may produce goods regardless of sales, and still the profit and loss account may reflect profit earned, whereas in reality there is simply a piling up of stocks of inventory in the factory godowns. The hypothetical/typical case for such a situation is that a firm has produced more than its normal capacity and, therefore, over-absorbed its actual fixed overheads. The firm, in spite of not making sales of even a single unit, will show gross margin to the extent of over-absorption of the fixed manufacturing overheads. Example 11.1 illustrates this point.

EXAMPLE 11.1

Hypothetical Ltd furnishes the following information from its cost records for the first quarter of the current year:

Normal production (units)	1,000
Actual production (units)	1,100
Actual overheads per quarter at normal production	₹4,000
Other expenses per quarter	300
Standard fixed overhead rate per unit	4
Variable costs per unit	6
Sales volume (selling price is ₹14)	Nil

Prepare the income statement under absorption and variable costings.

SOLUTION

The income statements are shown in Tables 11.1 and 11.2 respectively.

Table 11.1 Income Statement (Absorption Costing)

Particulars		*Amount*
Sales revenue		Nil
Less: *Total cost of manufacturing:*		
Variable costs (1,100 × ₹6)	₹6,600	
Fixed overheads (1,100 × ₹4)	4,400	
	11,000	
Less: Cost of inventory at the end of the year (1,100 × ₹10)	11,000	Nil
Cost of goods manufactured and sold		
Gross margin (unadjusted)		Nil
Capacity variance (favourable) (over-absorbed, 100 × ₹4)		₹400
Gross margin (adjusted)		400
Less: Other expenses		300
Net income before taxes		100

Table 11.2 Income Statement (Variable Costing)

Particulars		*Amount*
Sales revenue		Nil
Less: Variable costs (production costs) (1,100 × ₹6)	₹6,600	
Less: Cost of inventory at the end of the year (1,100 × ₹6)	6,600	
Cost of goods manufactured and sold		Nil
Contribution		Nil
Less: Fixed costs:		
Fixed overheads	4,000	
Other expenses	300	₹(4,300)
Net income before taxes (loss)		(4,300)

There is a marked difference in the profit results under the two methods: absorption costing shows net profit of ₹100, while a loss of ₹4,300 is reported under variable costing. This result is ascribed to the fact that under absorption costing, the fixed manufacturing overheads are inventoriable, whereas in variable costing inventory is valued only at variable costs. In Example 11.1, inventory is valued at ₹11,000 in absorption costing, while its valuation is ₹6,600 in variable costing. This is how the difference of ₹4,400 is accounted for.

From the above, it may be deduced that changes in inventory will influence reported income under the two costing techniques because under variable costing, fixed costs are deducted in the period in which they are incurred whereas under absorption costing, a portion of fixed costs is carried over with inventory. The reported net income, thus, differs under the two methods. When production exceeds sales, fixed cost absorption is more in full costing compared to variable costing and, therefore, to that extent, income/profits under absorption costing are more. The results are reversed when sales exceed production. Profits would be identical under the two methods, if production coincides with sales. Example 11.2 clearly brings out these differences.

EXAMPLE 11.2

Hypothetical Ltd furnishes the following information for its three different periods:

Particulars	*Year 1*	*Year 2*	*Year 3*
Production (units)	*10,000*	*10,000*	*10,000*
Sales (units)	10,000	5,000	15,000

Sales price per unit, ₹12
Variable cost per unit, ₹6
Fixed costs per year (at normal capacity of 10,000 units), ₹40,000
Standard fixed overhead rate: ₹4 per unit.
Show the profit under variable and absorption costing in different years.

SOLUTION

The profit is shown in Table 11.3.

Table 11.3 Income Statements for the Years Ended 1, 2, 3

Particulars	*Absorption Costing*	*Variable Costing*
	Year 1 (Production = Sales)	
Sales (10,000 × ₹12)	₹1,20,000	₹1,20,000
Less: Cost of goods manufactured		
Variable costs (10,000 × ₹6)	60,000	60,000
Fixed costs (10,000 × ₹4)	40,000	

(Contd.)

(*Contd.*)

Cost of goods manufactured and sold	1,00,000	60,000
Gross margin	20,000	—
Contribution	—	60,000
Less: Fixed costs	—	40,000
Net income before taxes	20,000	20,000
	Year 2 (Production > Sales)	
Sales (5,000 × ₹12)	60,000	60,000
Less: Cost of goods manufactured		
Variable costs (10,000 × ₹6)	60,000	60,000
Fixed costs (10,000 × ₹4)	40,000	—
Total cost of goods manufactured	1,00,000	60,000
Less: Cost of inventory at the end of the year		
(5,000 × ₹10)	(50,000)	
(5,000 × ₹6)		(30,000)
Cost goods manufactured and sold	50,000	30,000
Gross margin	10,000	—
Contribution	—	30,000
Less: Fixed costs	—	40,000
Net income (loss)	10,000	(10,000)
	Year 3 (Sales > Production)	
Sales (15,000 × ₹12)	1,80,000	1,80,000
Less: Cost of goods manufactured:		
Variable costs (10,000 × ₹6)	60,000	60,000
Fixed costs (10,00 × ₹4)	40,000	—
Total cost of goods manufactured	1,00,000	60,000
Plus: Cost of inventory in the year's beginning		
(5,000 × ₹10)	50,000	
(5,000 × ₹6)		30,000
Cost of goods manufactured and sold	1,50,000	90,000
Gross margin	30,000	—
Contribution	—	90,000
Less: Fixed costs	—	40,000
Net income	30,000	50,000

Summary of Results

Year 1: Net income is identical in both the methods.
Year 2: Absorption costing shows more profit than variable costing.
Year 3: Variable costing shows more profit than absorption costing.
All Years Combined: The total net income will be the same under either costing method because the total production and sales are equal (30,000 units).

Reasons for the Differences In year 1, the results of net income are identical because the equality of production and sales does not affect the level of inventory on hand. All goods produced have been sold and, thus, all fixed costs of production are charged to the income statement under absorption costing as well as variable costing.

In year 2, when sales are less than production, there is an increase in the level of inventory on hand. Under absorption costing, the increase in inventory carries proportionate fixed costs (to be spent next year) which means that fixed costs charged to revenue are less under absorption costing than under variable costing. Thus, the net income reported under variable costing is less than under absorption costing. The amount of ₹20,000 is equivalent to 5,000 units of inventory multiplied by ₹4 (standard fixed overhead rate).

In year 3, when sales exceed production, there is a decrease in the level of inventory on hand. Under absorption costing, the inventory of year 2 would carry a part of fixed costs (₹20,000). Thus, under absorption costing fixed costs charged against the revenue of the current year will be higher by ₹20,000 compared to variable costing. Hence, the additional fixed costs of ₹20,000 under full costing makes the net income revealed by variable costing more by this amount.

The fact that fixed costs move along with inventory signifies that the fixed costs will be released as part of goods sold in a later year(s) when sales are in excess of production. Hence, profits will not necessarily increase with increase in sales revenue. In fact, the profits will decrease if the effect of shifting fixed costs from one year to another as a part of inventory cost is more than the increased contribution to be derived from increased sales.[4]

The situation visualised above is by no means imaginary. For obvious reasons, the management will be bewildered by the decrease in profits with increased sales volume when no change whatsoever has occurred in selling prices and costs. In general, profits are expected to increase with increase in sales volume. Consider Example 11.3.

EXAMPLE 11.3

Hypothetical Ltd had the following relevant information for years 1 and 2:

Standard variable costs per unit		₹6
Sales price per unit		10
Fixed manufacturing overhead (at normal capacity of 1,50,000 units)		3,00,000
Selling and administrative expenses		
Fixed		1,30,000
Variable (per cent of sales)		5
Production volume: units	Year 1	1,70,000
	2	1,40,000
Sales volume:	1	1,40,000
	2	1,60,000

There was no inventory at the beginning of year 1. Income tax rate is 35 per cent.

REQUIRED: **1.** Prepare income statements for the two years under absorption costing and variable costing.

2. Show a reconciliation of the difference in net income for the two years (1 and 2) taken together.

SOLUTION

Table 11.4 Income Statement (Absorption Costing) for the Years 1 and 2

Particulars	*Year 1*	*Year 2*
Number of units produced	1,70,000	1,40,000
Number of units sold	1,40,000	1,60,000
Sales revenue	₹14,00,000	₹16,00,000
Less: Cost of manufacturing:		
Standard variable cost (₹6 per unit)	10,20,000	8,40,000
Fixed cost (₹2 per unit)	3,40,000	2,80,000
Total standard cost of manufacturing (₹8 per unit)	13,60,000	11,20,000
Plus: Cost of inventory (beginning)	—	2,40,000
Less: Cost of inventory (ending)	(2,40,000)	(80,000)
Cost of goods manufactured and sold (at standard absorption cost)	11,20,000	12,80,000

(*Contd.*)

(Contd.)

Gross margin manufacturing (unadjusted)	2,80,000	3,20,000
± Capacity variance	40,000 (F)	20,000 (A)
Gross margin (adjusted)	3,20,000	3,00,000
Less: Non-production costs:		
Selling and administrative expenses	2,00,000	2,10,000
Net income before taxes	1,20,000	90,000
Less: Income taxes (0.35)	42,000	31,500
Net income after taxes	78,000	58,500

F = Favourable, A = Adverse

Table 11.5 Income Statement (Variable Costing) for the Years 1 and 2

Particulars	*Year 1*	*Year 2*
Number of units produced	1,70,000	1,40,000
Number of units sold	1,40,000	1,60,000
Sales revenue	₹14,00,000	₹16,00,000
Less: Variable costs:		
Standard variable cost @ ₹6 per unit	10,20,000	8,40,000
+ Cost of inventory at standard cost (beginning)	Nil	1,80,000
– Cost of inventory at standard cost (ending)	(1,80,000)	(60,000)
Standard cost of goods manufactured and sold	8,40,000	9,60,000
@ of ₹6 per unit sold	8,40,000	9,60,000
Contribution (manufacturing)	5,60,000	6,40,000
Less: Variable non-production costs:		
Selling and administrative expenses	70,000	80,000
Contribution (final)	4,90,000	5,60,000
Less: Fixed costs:		
Fixed overheads	3,00,000	3,00,000
Selling and administrative expenses	1,30,000	1,30,000
Net income before taxes	60,000	1,30,000
Less: Taxes (0.35)	21,000	45,500
Net income after taxes	39,000	84,500

The income statement under absorption costing shows that the company earned less profit in year 2 compared to year 1 inspite of 20,000 more units sold in year 2 and there was no decrease either in selling price or increase in cost (both fixed and variable). Ordinarily, profits are expected to increase with increase in sales volume.

The income statement constructed on a variable costing basis shows, that the contribution has increased in year 2 as result of selling 20,000 more units. The profits are in tune with sales volume when the variable costing technique is adopted.

VARIABLE AND ABSORPTION COSTING: RECONCILIATION

The difference in results given by the above two methods can be explained in terms of: (i) The standard fixed overhead rate (SFOR); and (ii) The change in the inventories that has taken place during the period under consideration. Table 11.6 provides a complete explanation of the differences in results.

Table 11.6 Reconciliation Statement of Net Income Before Taxes under Absorption Costing and Variable Costing

Particulars	*Year 1*	*Year 2*	*Combined*
Net income before taxes as per:			
Absorption costing	₹1,20,000	₹90,000	₹2,10,000
Variable costing	60,000	1,30,000	1,90,000
Difference (to be explained)	60,000	(40,000)	20,000
(a) Standard fixed overhead rate	2	2	2
Change in inventory units:			
Opening inventory	Nil	30,000	—
Ending inventory	30,000	10,000	10,000
(b) Change in inventory	30,000	(20,000)	10,000
(c) Increase (decrease) difference in net income is explained by the product of (a) × (b)	60,000	(40,000)	20,000

Likewise, an increase in net income before taxes under variable costing by ₹70,000 in year 2 compared to year 1 can be explained in the form of a reconciliation statement (Table 11.7 and Table 11.8).

Table 11.7 Reconciliation Statement (Variable Costing)

Particulars	*Amount*
Increase in sales revenue in year 2 (20,000 × ₹10)	₹2,00,000
Less: Increased manufacturing variable cost in year 2 (20,000 × ₹6)	1,20,000
Increased contribution (20,000 × ₹4)	80,000
Less: Increased selling and administrative costs (0.05 × ₹2,00,000)	10,000
Increased contribution (final)	70,000

Table 11.8 Reconciliation Statement (Absorption Costing)

Particulars	*Amount*
Increased contribution (already explained in variable costing reconciliation statement)	₹70,000
Less: Fixed costs of year 1 on 30,000 units at the rate of ₹2 per unit shifted to year 2 (decreases year 1 cost)	(60,000)
Fixed costs of year 1 shifted to year 2 (increases year 2 cost)	(60,000)
Add: Fixed cost of year 2 on 10,000 units at the rate of ₹2 per unit shifted to year 3 (decreases year 2 cost)	20,000
Increase in costs caused by shift in fixed cost	1,00,000
Net decrease in net income before income taxes	(30,000)

Emphasis on Production or Sales Example 11.3 shows that variable costing focuses on sales, while the emphasis of absorption costing is on production. In profit making organisations, sales are generally regarded more important than production because out of sales all expenses are to be met and profits earned. It is very difficult to believe that profits can increase with more production without being sold. Therefore, a variable costing report on profits earned by the firm is more logical than an absorption costing report based on production. "However differences attributable to a lack of balance between sales and production are not revealed by variable costing. Sales activity may be overemphasised at the expense of production. In reality, profits depend upon both sales and production."[5]

Still another noteworthy feature of income determination under the two costing methods relates to total profits across time periods. A reference to Example 11.2 shows that the total net income for three years is ₹60,000 under both the methods.

In most industries, production will tend to equal sales over a long period of time. Therefore, over the long run, the two methods will produce similar results. Any controversy between the advocates of absorption costing and variable costing, in terms of income determination, is a matter of timing in the matching of fixed costs with revenues.[6]

As a logical sequel to the above, if a company follows the practice of preparing interim income statements quarterly/half-yearly to take stock of the firm's profits and if the demand for inventories and internal financial statements for its product is seasonal, profits will tend to fluctuate widely. This aspect should be recognised by management while studying income statements constructed on the principle of variable costing.

As stated earlier, the controversy between the two methods is futile. The controversy can be examined from two perspectives: external financial statements prepared for investors and internal financial statements for the use of management. The absorption costing method is adopted for the first purpose. The second purpose is best served by variable costing. This conclusion will be further reinforced by the discussion that follows which overwhelmingly demonstrates that the marginal contribution approach of variable costing is an important tool of profit planning and cost control. Thus, the choice of either method of costing is based upon a particular situation rather than on the innate superiority of one over the other.

ADVANTAGES AND LIMITATIONS OF VARIABLE COSTING

Advantages

We now briefly outline the advantages of variable costing:

1. In contrast to absorption costing, there is no problem of allocating and absorbing fixed overheads in variable costing as all fixed costs are considered period costs and written off against the total contribution of that period.
2. There is no complication of over-absorption of factory overheads or even their under-absorption as in the case of absorption costing. It may be recalled that the income under absorption costing is to be adjusted upwards for favourable capacity variance (over-absorption is to be adjusted upwards when the actual production exceeds the normal capacity) and downwards for unfavourable capacity variance (under-absorption of factory overheads when the actual production is less than the normal capacity). This aspect makes the income statement under absorption costing more difficult to prepare and understand than the income statement based on variable costing.
3. Management usually finds it easier to understand a variable income statement than one prepared on the basis of absorption costing. This is so because the former statements show profit responding more to changing sales levels than the combination of sales and production levels inasmuch as income statements prepared on the basis of absorption costing may show less profits with increased sales volume, though the cost and selling prices remain unchanged. Thus, the variable costing technique provides a measure of income, which is more accurate than under absorption costing. In fact, in situations of favourable capacity variance, absorption costing with no sales will show profits.
4. The impact of fixed costs on profits is emphasised because the total amount of such cost for the period appears in the income statement.

5. The process of bifurcation of costs into fixed and variable is of immense practical utility in cost control. There is a close nexus between variable costs and the controllable costs classification. This relationship assists the control function. It is imperative for effective cost control that responsibility of cost control must be with those who make cost-incurring decisions. This is possible through variable costing as it recognises the diverse behaviour of costs in relation to volume and/or time; only variable costs are charged to production, while the period costs which the management decides upon are not charged to production and so the foreman is not accountable for depreciation, insurance, property taxes, rent and such other fixed costs over which he has no control. Fixed costs for this reason are controllable only at the highest level of management. On the other hand, variable costs are incurred by all levels of management and by operators. The responsibility for variable costs can be traced with a substantial degree of certainty and, thus, allow the necessary control to be exercised. Thus, variable costing delineates responsibility clearly and assists management in the control function.

   In marked contrast, variable and fixed costs are treated alike under absorption costing, though they require different types of treatment for facilitating control. In this system, variable costs are clubbed with fixed costs, which are not controllable at the departmental level. From the above, it follows that variable costing is in alignment with responsibility accounting and, thus, facilitates management by exception.
6. Variable costs are relevant inputs for correct decision-making in many situations. Without variable costs data, management is likely to take wrong decisions affecting the profitability of the company. In recent years, there is an increasing acceptance among industries to use variable costing as a tool of profit planning.
7. Variable costing ties on with such effective plans for cost control as standard costs and flexible budgets. In fact, the flexible budget is an aspect of variable costing and many companies, thus, use variable costing methods for this purpose without recognising them as much.[7]

Limitations

The users of variable costing should, however, guard against its limitations both as regards income measurement and as a tool of profit planning:

1. Segregation of total cost into fixed and variable elements is a difficult task, particularly in the case of semi-variable costs. In such situations, resort to arbitrary classification may have to be made.
2. Variable costing carries the potential danger of encouraging a short-sighted approach to profit planning at the cost of a long-term view. There is the danger of too many sales being made at a price slightly higher than variable costs, possibly resulting in losses or very low profits. Management should not lose sight of the fact that profits will not result unless all the costs have been recovered; it should recognise that in the ultimate analysis fixed costs are also to be recovered from the selling price only. Management is likely to gather a very wrong impression of recovering only variable costs from the selling price.
3. Variable costing carries the danger of misinterpretation particularly where products require high investment outlay and the variable cost may constitute a small proportion of total cost of a product. The total contribution yield may be insufficient to warrant such an outlay. "In a manufacturing plant that is highly automated, the amount of variable cost may be small and this situation magnifies the problem of applying the technique."[8]
4. Focusing attention on the contribution margin and the possible non-recognition of fixed cost by management may be dangerous.

5. There is a difficulty in applying the technique to industries where large stocks of work-in-progress are locked up, particularly in contracting firms. If overheads were not included in the closing value of work-in-progress for each year of the contract, there would be losses, while at the end of the contract, when revenue is received, there would be a large profit. The fluctuations in profits in partly evened out by valuing work-in-progress at the total cost plus some element of profit."[9]

To sum up, it can be said that in principle there is no conflict between variable costing and absorption costing as regards accounting of costs. Both are equally important–variable costing for internal reporting and absorption costing for external users. Being so, management should recognise the importance of variable costing in profit planning (in specific situations) and cost control in general. The most useful contribution of variable costing is that it helps management in vital decision-making, particularly in dealing with problems, which require short-term decisions where fixed costs do not count.

REFERENCES

1. C.T. Horngren, Introduction to Management Accounting, (Prentice-Hall, Englewood Cliffs, N.J., 1978), p. 455.
2. C.L. Moore and R.K. Jaedicke, Management Accounting, (South Western Publishing Company, Ohio, 1972), p. 401.
3. J.L. Brown and L.R. Howard, Principles and Practice of Management Accounting, (English Language Book Society, London, 1969), p. 270.
4. C.L. Moore and R.K. Jaedicke, op. cit., p. 406.
5. Ibid, p. 408.
6. D.T. Decoster and E.L. Schafer, Management Accounting–A Decision Emphasis, (John Wiley and Sons, New York, 1976), p. 200.
7. National Association of Accountants, Research Series No. 23, New York, quoted in C.L. Moore and R.K. Jaedicke, op. cit., p. 410.
8. Norman Thornton, Management Accounting, (Allied Publishers, Bombay, 1979), p. 259.
9. J.L. Brown and L.R. Howard, op. cit., p. 287.

SUMMARY

- Variable costing is a technique in which only variable costs are considered for product costing, inventory valuation and other allied management decisions. It is, thus, in marked contrast to the orthodox costing system known as full costing, absorption costing, traditional costing, conventional costing and so on.
- The material point of difference between these two techniques is that the full costing method 'absorbs' all costs necessary to produce the product and have it in a saleable form, while variable costing recognises only variable cost as production and selling cost. In operational terms, the two techniques differ in one respect: fixed manufacturing overheads are excluded from product cost under variable costing but are included as a part of product cost under absorption costing.
- Nevertheless, they are not mutually exclusive; rather they are complementary in nature. Income statements for external reporting and for income-tax purposes are to be prepared on a full costing basis. The usefulness of variable costing is that it helps management to arrive at profit-maximising decisions in certain situations. It is for this reason that variable costing is more useful for internal reporting. Thus, both techniques are important and which technique is to be employed depends upon the purpose and the circumstances.

- The principle underlying variable costing is that the fixed manufacturing overheads are not inventoriable costs; they are period costs and must be matched against the revenue for the period. In contrast, absorption costing indicates that the manufacturing overheads are inventoriable costs; they are product costs and must be matched against the revenue for the year in which sales are made. The preparation of the income statement, therefore, in the case of variable costing is different from absorption costing. The concept of variable costs (separation of fixed costs from variable costs) is, however, not only useful in income measurement but is also very significant in managerial decision-making.
- The core of variable costing is the contribution margin. Contribution margin is the difference between sales revenue and variable costs. It is out of the contribution that the fixed costs are met and the excess of contribution over fixed costs represents the profit. The contribution approach is useful for decision-making.

SOLVED PROBLEMS

P.11.1 The Hind General Corporation Ltd produces a product, which has the following costs:
Variable manufacturing costs: ₹4 per unit
Fixed manufacturing costs: ₹2,00,000 per year
The normal capacity is set at 2,00,000 units
There are no work-in-process inventories

Last year, the company produced 2,00,000 units and sold 90 per cent at a price of ₹7 per unit. In the current year, the company produced 2,10,000 units and sold 2,15,000 units at the same price.

Prepare income statement for both the years based on (a) absorption costing, and (b) variable costing.

SOLUTION

Income Statement for the Previous Year and Current Year (Absorption Costing) of Hind General Corporation Ltd

Particulars	*Previous year*	*Current year*
Production (units)	2,00,000	2,10,000
Sales (units)	1,80,000	2,15,000
Opening inventory (units)	—	20,000
Closing inventory (units)	20,000	15,000
Sales revenue @ ₹7 per unit	₹12,60,000	₹15,05,000
Less production costs:		
Variable manufacturing costs@ ₹4 per unit	8,00,000	8,40,000
Fixed manufacturing costs @ ₹1 per unit (₹2,00,000 ÷ 2,00,000 normal capacity in units)	2,00,000	2,10,000
Total production cost of the current year	10,00,000	10,50,000
Add cost of inventory at the beginning of the year @ ₹5 per unit	—	1,00,000
Less cost of inventory at the end of the year @ ₹5 per unit	(1,00,000)	(75,000)
Cost of goods sold	9,00,000	10,75,000
Gross margin (unadjusted)	3,60,000	4,30,000
Add favourable capacity variance in the current year (10,000 × ₹1)	—	10,000
Gross margin (adjusted)/net income	3,60,000	4,40,000

Income Statements of the Previous Year and Current Year (Variable Costing)

Particulars	*Previous year*	*Current year*
Production (units)	2,00,000	2,10,000
Sales (units)	1,80,000	2,15,000
Opening inventory (units)	—	20,000
Closing inventory (units)	20,000	15,000
Sales revenue @ ₹7 per unit	₹12,60,000	₹15,05,000
Less production costs:		
Variable manufacturing costs @ ₹4 per unit	8,00,000	8,40,000
Add cost of inventory @ ₹4 per unit	—	80,000
Less cost of inventory @ ₹4 per unit at the end of the year	(80,000)	(60,000)
Cost of goods sold	7,20,000	8,60,000
Contribution (manufacturing and final)	5,40,000	6,45,000
Less non-production costs	(2,00,000)	(2,00,000)
Net income	3,40,000	4,45,000

P.11.2 Aggarwal Industries Ltd has a standard variable manufacturing cost of ₹8 per unit produced. Fixed production costs are ₹1,10,000 per month (for standard volume of 11,000 units per month) and fixed selling and administrative expenses are ₹70,000 per month. The firm begins January with no inventories and had the following activity in January, February and March:

	January	*February*	*March*
Production (units)	12,000	10,000	11,000
Sales (units)	10,000	11,000	11,000

The selling price was ₹30 per unit in each month.

You are required to prepare monthly income statements using both variable and absorption costing methods. You are also required to account for the difference, if any, in the results reported under the two methods.

SOLUTION

Comparative Income Statements (from January to March) of Aggarwal Industries Ltd Under Absorption and Variable Costing Methods

Particulars	*January*		*February*		*March*	
	Absorption	*Variable*	*Absorption*	*Variable*	*Absorption*	*Variable*
Production (units)	12,000	12,000	10,000	10,000	11,000	11,000
Sales (units)	10,000	10,000	11,000	11,000	11,000	11,000
Sales revenue	₹3,00,000	₹3,00,000	₹3,30,000	₹3,30,000	₹3,30,000	₹3,30,000
Less production costs:						
Variable manufacturing cost @ ₹8 per unit	96,000	96,000	80,000	80,000	88,000	88,000
Fixed manufacturing overheads @ ₹10 per unit (₹1,100,000 ÷ 11,000)	1,20,000	—	1,00,000	—	1,10,000	—
Plus cost of opening inventory	—	—	36,000	16,000	18,000	8,000
Less cost of closing inventory	(36,000)	(16,000)	(18,000)	(8,000)	(18,000)	(8,000)
Cost of goods produced and sold	1,80,000	80,000	1,98,000	88,000	1,98,000	88,000

(*Contd.*)

(Contd.)

Gross margin unadjusted/ Contribution	1,20,000	2,20,000	1,32,000	2,42,000	1,32,000	2,42,000
Add capacity variance favourable (less unfavourable) @ ₹10 per unit	10,000	—	(10,000)	—	—	—
Gross margin adjusted/ Contribution	1,30,000	2,20,000	1,22,000	2,42,000	1,32,000	2,42,000
Less non-production costs:						
Fixed manufacturing costs	—	(1,10,000)	—	(1,10,000)	—	(1,10,000)
Fixed selling and administrative expenses	(70,000)	(70,000)	(70,000)	(70,000)	(70,000)	(70,000)
Net income	60,000	40,000	52,000	62,000	62,000	62,000

Reconciliation Statement of Income (January - March)

Particulars	Net income January	February	March
Absorption costing	₹60,000	₹52,000	₹62,000
Variable costing	40,000	62,000	62,000
Difference to be explained: increase (decrease) in profits of absorption costing *vis-à-vis* variable costing	20,000	(10,000)	—
(a) Inventory units			
Opening inventory	—	2,000	1,000
Closing inventory	2,000	1,000	1,000
Increase (decrease) in inventory	2,000	(1,000)	—
(b) Standard fixed overhead rate per unit (₹)	10	10	—
(c) Change in net income [(a) × (b)]	20,000	(10,000)	—

P.11.3 S.K. Industries Ltd produced and sold 1,50,000 plastics buckets. Each bucket was sold at a price of ₹20. The variable costs were ₹14 per bucket and fixed manufacturing costs were ₹3,00,000 per annum. The company's normal production capacity is 1,50,000 plastic buckets.

1. You are required to prepare income statements under absorption costing and variable costing methods and comment on the results.
2. What would be the effect on income under the two different costing methods in the following situations: **(a)** Buckets produced and sold, 1,40,000 and **(b)** Buckets produced and sold, 1,60,000.

SOLUTION

Income Statement (Absorption and Variable Costing Methods)

Particulars	Absorption costing	Variable costing
Production and sales (units)	1,50,000	1,50,000
Sales revenue	₹30,00,000	₹30,00,000
Less production costs:		
Variable costs @ ₹14 per unit	21,00,000	21,00,000
Fixed overheads @ ₹2 per unit (₹3,00,000 ÷ 1,50,000 normal capacity)	3,00,000	—
Total cost of production/cost of goods sold	24,00,000	21,00,000
Income/Contribution	6,00,000	9,00,000
Less non-production costs:	—	—
Fixed manufacturing costs	—	3,00,000
Income	6,00,000	6,00,000

Incomes are the same under both the costing methods, for production is equivalent to sales (1,50,000 units). Differences in net income arise only when production varies from sales.

Income Statements under Variable and Absorption Costing Systems, Assuming Production and Sales: **(a)** 1,40,000 units, **(b)** 1,60,000 units:

Particulars	*(a) 1,40,000 units*		*(b) 1,60,000 units*	
	Absorption	*Variable*	*Absorption*	*Variable*
Sales revenue @ ₹20 per unit	₹28,00,000	₹28,00,000	₹32,00,000	₹32,00,000
Less production costs:				
Variable costs @ ₹14 per unit	19,60,000	19,60,000	22,40,000	22,40,000
Fixed overheads @ ₹2 per unit	2,80,000	—	3,20,000	—
Cost of goods produced and sold	22,40,000	19,60,000	25,60,000	22,40,000
Gross margin (adjusted)/Contribution	5,60,000	8,40,000	6,40,000	9,60,000
Less capacity variance: Unfavourable and add capacity variance favourable @ ₹2 per unit (10,000 units)	(20,000)	—	20,000	—
Gross margin (adjusted)/Contribution	5,40,000	8,40,000	6,60,000	9,60,000
Less non-production costs:				
Fixed manufacturing costs	—	3,00,000	—	3,00,000
Net income	5,40,000	5,40,000	6,60,000	6,60,000

Net incomes again are the same under both costing systems, as production is equal to sales in both situations. The fact whether production is equal to normal capacity or not, does not have any impact whatsoever on the net income. Here, production of 1,40,000 units as well as 1,60,000 units is different from 1,50,000, the normal level of production.

P.11.4 The Seers Can Company Ltd has two plants, one in Mumbai, and the other in Kolkata. The physical characteristics of the plants are similar and the results of the operations of both plants are compared each month in order to judge the performance of the two managements. The April income statements of the two plants were as follows:

Particulars	*Mumbai plant*	*Kolkata plant*
Sales	₹18,00,000	₹18,00,000
Less: Manufacturing cost of sales	12,60,000	13,60,000
Selling and administrative expenses	4,40,000	4,40,000
Net income	1,00,000	—

Each plant sells its product for the same price. During the month of April, each plant sold and shipped 3,00,000 cans. The production for the month at the two plants was as follows:

Particulars	*Mumbai plant*	*Kolkata plant*
Opening stock (number of cans)	1,00,000	1,00,000
Production during the month	4,00,00,000	3,00,00,000
	4,01,00,000	3,01,00,000
Cans shipped during the month	3,00,00,000	3,00,00,000
Closing stock	1,01,00,000	1,00,000

The Mumbai plant built up its stock in April in anticipation of the canning season, which begins in May on the West Coast. The East Coast canning season begins in the middle of June.

The standard cost sheet for the type of can sold in April discloses the following information for both plants:

	Cost per 1,000 cans
Direct material	₹25
Direct labour	5
Variable overheads	2
Fixed overheads	10
	42

For each plant, the manufacturing fixed costs budgeted for the month were ₹4,00,000. There were no spending or efficiency variances. All selling and administrative expenses were of a fixed nature.

Prepare revised income statements for the two plants, using variable costing. Explain the difference in income between the two plants.

SOLUTION

Income Statement (Variable Costing) for the Month Ending April

Particulars	*Mumbai plant*	*Kolkata plant*
Production (cans)	4,00,00,000	3,00,00,000
Sales (cans)	3,00,00,000	3,00,00,000
Sales revenue	₹18,00,000	₹18,00,000
Less: production costs:		
Direct material	10,00,000	7,50,000
Direct labour	2,00,000	1,50,000
Variable overheads	80,000	60,000
Total cost of production	12,80,000	9,60,000
Add cost of opening inventory(at standard cost)	3,200	3,200
Less closing inventory (at standard cost)	(3,23,200)	(3,200)
Cost of cans produced and sold	9,60,000	9,60,000
Contribution	8,40,000	8,40,000
Less: non-production costs:		
Fixed overheads	4,00,000	4,00,000
Selling and administrative expenses	4,40,000	4,40,000
Net income	Nil	Nil

Difference in income statements of the two plants on the basis of variable costing is nil. There would be a difference when a comparison is made of income statements for the Bombay plant on the basis of variable costing and absorption costing. The following reconciliation statement will explain the difference.

Reconciliation Statement of Income for Mumbai Plant for the Month of April

Net income:	
Absorption costing	₹1,00,000
Variable costing	Nil
Difference to be explained:	1,00,000
(a) Standard fixed overhead rate ₹10 (per 1,000 cans)	
(b) Change in inventory units:	
Opening inventory	1,00,000
Closing inventory	1,01,00,000
Change in inventory (increase)	1,00,00,000
(c) Difference in net income [(a) × (b)]	1,00,000

The Bombay plant produced 4,00,00,000 cans and, therefore, could absorb the entire amount of fixed overheads of ₹4,00,000 @ ₹10 per 1,000 cans. The Calcutta plant operated at below its normal capacity, as only 3,00,00,000 cans were produced.

There is a capacity variance unfavourable to the extent of ₹1,00,000 (fixed overheads were under-absorbed by ₹1,00,000). This also explains the difference in the net income between the two plants even on an absorption costing basis.

P.11.5 For several months the top management of a company has been puzzled by fluctuations in the income as reported by the accountant. The results for February, March and April as reported are as follows:

Particulars	*February*	*March*	*April*
Sales	₹18,00,000	₹18,00,000	₹9,00,000
Less: Manufacturing cost of sales	16,60,000	13,60,000	4,30,000
Selling and administrative expenses	4,40,000	4,40,000	4,40,000
Total	21,00,000	18,00,000	8,70,000
Net income (loss)	(3,00,000)	—	30,000

There has been no change in sales price during the three month period. During the months of February and March, the plant sold 3,00,00,000 units. In April, it sold 1,50,00,000 units.

The production for the three months was as follows:

Particulars	*February*	*March*	*April*
Opening inventory (units)	3,01,00,000	1,00,000	1,00,000
Production during the month	—	3,00,00,000	6,00,00,000
	3,01,00,000	3,01,00,000	6,01,00,000
Units sold	3,00,00,000	3,00,00,000	1,50,00,000
Closing inventory	1,00,000	1,00,000	4,51,00,000

The standard cost for the type of the units sold discloses the following information:

	Cost per 1,000 units
Direct material and labour	30
Overheads: Variable	2
Fixed	10
	42

The fixed manufacturing costs budgeted for each of the months were ₹4,00,000. There were no spending or efficiency variances during the three months. All selling and administrative expenses were of a fixed nature.

You are required to prepare comparative income statements for the three months, using variable costing.

SOLUTION

Income Statement for February, March and April (Variable Costing)

Particulars	*February*	*March*	*April*
Production (units)	Nil	3,00,00,000	6,00,00,000
Sales (units)	3,00,00,000	3,00,00,000	1,50,00,000
Sales revenue	₹18,00,000	₹18,00,000	₹9,00,000
Less: production costs:			
Standard variable cost (@) ₹32 per 1,000) Nil	9,60,000	19,20,000	
Add: opening inventory	9,63,200	3,200	3,200
Less: opening inventory	(3,200)	(3,200)	(14,43,200)
Cost of goods produced and sold	9,60,000	9,60,000	4,80,000
Contribution (manufacturing)	8,40,000	8,40,000	4,20,000
Less: non-production costs:			
Fixed overheads	4,00,000	4,00,000	4,00,000
Selling and administrative expenditure	4,40,000	4,40,000	4,40,000
Net income (loss)	Nil	Nil	(4,20,000)

P.11.6 As the chief financial analyst of a company, you have been asked by the chief executive to explain the differences between two income statements prepared for his consideration: one was prepared by the controller and the other by the sales manager. Both used the same data from operations.

Particulars	*Statement A*	*Statement B*
Sales (30,000 units)	₹30,00,000	₹30,00,000
Cost of goods sold:		
Opening inventory	—	—
Production costs	18,00,000	27,00,000
Less: closing inventory	(6,00,000)	(9,00,000)
Total	12,00,000	18,00,000
Gross profit	18,00,000	12,00,000
Less: other costs	(15,00,000)	(6,00,000)
Income	3,00,000	6,00,000

The only variable costs of production are ₹40 per unit.

(i) Determine which statement was prepared using variable costing and which using absorption costing. Explain how do you know it?

(ii) Determine: **(a)** fixed production costs; **(b)** selling and administrative costs; **(c)** production in units; and (d) cost per unit of inventory for both statements.

Solution

1. Statement A was prepared using variable costing and statement B using absorption costing. This can be determined in several ways: **(a)** Production costs are less in statement A because fixed costs are excluded, **(b)** Similarly, value of inventory is less in statement A because inventory is valued only at variable cost and fixed costs are excluded, **(c)** Other costs (non-production costs) are higher in statement A because of inclusion of fixed costs which are charged against the income of the same year.

2. (a) *Determination of fixed production costs:*

Production cost (absorption costing)	₹27,00,000
Production cost (variable costing)	18,00,000
Difference represents fixed production costs	9,00,000

(b) *Determination of selling and administrative costs*

Other costs	15,00,000
Less fixed production costs	9,00,000
Selling and administrative costs	6,00,000

(c) *Production (in units) Statement A*

1. Cost of goods sold (30,000 units)	₹12,00,000
2. Variable cost per unit (₹12,00,000 ÷ 30,000)	40
3. Total production cost (variable)	18,00,000
4. Production in units (₹18,00,000 ÷ ₹40)	45,000

(d) *Cost Per Unit of Inventory*

Particulars	*Variable costing basis*	*Absorption costing basis*
1. Closing inventory	₹6,00,000	₹9,00,000
2. Closing inventory (units) (45,000 — 30,000)	15,000	15,000
3. Cost per unit (1) ÷ (2)	40	60

P.11.7 Following is the income statement of Jain Tubes Company Ltd prepared on the basis of absorption costing:

Sales		₹4,70,000
Cost of goods sold:		
Opening inventory (variable costs, ₹42,000)	₹70,000	
Current production cost	2,56,000	
	3,26,000	
Less: closing inventory (variable costs, ₹31,200)	(52,000)	2,74,000
Gross margin (manufacturing) (unadjusted)		1,96,000
Less capacity variance (unfavourable)		32,000
Gross margin (adjusted)		1,64,000
Less: selling and distribution cost		20,000
Administrative cost		22,000
Net income before taxes		1,22,000

Additional Information

(a) The fixed manufacturing overheads are absorbed at a standard rate per unit of product.
(b) Total fixed cost of the current year (budgeted as well as actual) is ₹1,34,400.
(c) All units in inventory at the end of the year were manufactured during the year.
(d) Prepare an income statement on variable costing basis.

SOLUTION

Income Statement (Variable Costing Basis)

Particulars	*Amount*
Sales revenue	₹4,70,000
Less cost of goods sold:	
Variable manufacturing cost (current production) (Working note)	1,53,600
Add cost of opening inventory	42,000
Less cost of closing inventory	(31,200)
Total	1,64,400
Contribution (manufacturing and final)	3,05,600
Less non-production costs:	
Fixed manufacturing costs	(1,34,400)
Selling and distribution costs	(20,000)
Administrative costs	(22,000)
Net income before taxes	1,29,200

WORKING NOTES

Current production costs (absorption costing)		₹2,56,000
Less fixed overheads absorbed:		
Total fixed overheads	₹1,34,400	
Less unfavourable capacity variance (representing un-absorbed fixed overheads)	32,000	(1,02,400)
Current production costs (variable)		1,53,600

P.11.8 Mr Mukesh, The Chief Accountant of the Standard Glass Manufacturing Company Ltd has prepared the following income statement on traditional costing basis for three quarters of the current year.

Particulars	*Quarter 1*	*Quarter 2*	*Quarter 3*
Sales revenue	₹5,25,000	₹4,50,000	₹5,25,000
Less total current cost of manufacturing goods	4,55,000	5,20,000	3,90,000
Add cost of opening inventory	Nil	Nil	1,30,000

(*Contd.*)

(Contd.)

Less cost of closing inventory	Nil	(1,30,000)	(65,000)
Cost of goods produced and sold	4,55,000	3,90,000	4,55,000
Gross margin (unadjusted)	70,000	60,000	70,000
Less capacity variance	15,000	Nil	30,000
Gross margin (adjusted)	55,000	60,000	40,000
Selling and administrative expenses	20,000	20,000	20,000
Net income before taxes	35,000	40,000	20,000
Less income taxes (0.35)	12,250	14,000	7,000
Net income after taxes	22,750	26,000	10,000

(a) *Additional information:*

Units produced	35,000	40,000	30,000
Units sold	35,000	30,000	35,000

(b) Standard fixed manufacturing overhead rate is ₹3 per unit.

The management of the company is surprised at the results of the second quarter. It believes there must be some mistake in the income statement.

You are required to explain the income differences to the management by revising the statements on variable costing basis.

SOLUTION

Income Statements for Three Quarters of Current Year on Variable Costing Basis

Particulars	*Quarter* 1	2	3
Units produced	35,000	40,000	30,000
Units sold	35,000	30,000	35,000
Opening inventory (units)	—	—	10,000
Closing inventory (units)	—	10,000	5,000
Sales revenue	₹5,25,000	₹4,50,000	₹5,25,000
Less: manufacturing variable costs of goods sold (see working note)	3,50,000	4,00,000	3,00,000
Add cost of opening inventory @ ₹10 per unit	—	—	1,00,000
Less cost of closing inventory	—	(1,00,000)	(50,000)
Cost of goods sold	3,50,000	3,00,000	3,50,000
Contribution (final)	1,75,000	1,50,000	1,75,000
Less non-production costs:			
Fixed manufacturing overheads	(1,20,000)	(1,20,000)	(1,20,000)
Fixed selling overheads	(20,000)	(20,000)	(20,000)
Net income before income taxes	35,000	10,000	35,000
Less income taxes (0.35)	(12,250)	(3,500)	(12,250)
Net income after taxes	22,750	6,500	22,750

WORKING NOTES

1. Determination of variable costs:

Total cost of goods manufactured (including fixed overheads)	4,55,000	5,20,000	3,90,000
Less fixed overheads @ ₹3 per unit	(1,05,000)	(1,20,000)	(90,000)
Variable costs	3,50,000	4,00,000	3,00,000

2. Fixed manufacturing overhead (Fixed costs absorbed + Capacity variance) = ₹1,05,000 + ₹15,000
= ₹1,20,000.

P.11.9 The Chief Executive of PS Ltd, is puzzled by the income statements of the two most recent months–April and May, because sales increased in May and yet profits declined. He asks you to explain the results:

Income Statement

Particulars	April	May
Sales (₹20 per unit)	₹2,00,000	₹2,50,000
Standard cost of sales	1,20,000	1,50,000
Standard gross profit	80,000	1,00,000
Capacity variance favourable (unfavourable)	8,000	(16,000)
Selling and administrative expenses	20,000	20,000
Income	68,000	64,000

The standard fixed cost per unit is ₹8, based on normal production capacity of 12,000 units per month. You are required to

1. Determine production in each month.
2. Explain the results to the chief executive.
3. Prepare income statements based on variable costing.

SOLUTION

1. *Determination of Volume of Production:*

Particulars	April	May
(a) Capacity variance representing actual production Production is more (less) than normal production	₹8,000	₹(16,000)
(b) Standard fixed cost per unit	8	8
(c) Production more (less) than normal [(a) ÷ (b)]	1,000	(2,000)
(d) Normal production	12,000	12,000
(e) Actual production [(d) ± (c)]	13,000	10,000

2. Explanation: The Chief Executive should be advised that the income statements have been prepared on the basis of absorption costing in which the size of profit is influenced, inter-alia, by the level of production. Since production was more in April, so were the profits. The true picture will emerge only when income statements are prepared on a variable costing basis.

3. Income Statement Based on Variable Costing

Particulars	April	May
Production (units)	13,000	10,000
Sales (units) [sales revenue ÷ ₹20]	10,000	12,500
Opening inventory (units)	—	3,000
Closing inventory (units)	3,000	500
Sales revenue	₹2,00,000	₹2,50,000
Less cost of goods sold:		
Variable manufacturing cost @ ₹4 per unit	52,000	40,000
Plus cost of opening inventory @ ₹4 per unit		12,000
Less cost of closing inventory	(12,000)	(2,000)
Total cost of goods sold	40,000	50,000
Contribution (final)	1,60,000	2,00,000
Less non-production costs:		
Fixed overheads (12,000 × ₹8)	(96,000)	(96,000)
Selling and administrative expenses	(20,000)	(20,000)
Profit	44,000	84,000

WORKING NOTE

Determination of variable costs	*April*	*May*
Total standard cost of sales	₹1,20,000	₹1,50,000
Less fixed overheads @ ₹8 per unit:		
April (10,000 × ₹8)	(80,000)	
May (12,500 × ₹8)	(1,00,000)	
Variable costs (balancing figure)	40,000	50,000

P.11.10 Aggarwal Industries Ltd has taken a loan from a large bank. Among the provisions of the loan agreement are that: **(a)** the current ratio must be at least 300 per cent and that **(b)** the ratio of total debt to shareholders' equity must not be higher than 75 per cent. The balance sheet of the firm for the current year is as follows:

Liabilities	*Amount*	*Assets*	*Amount*
Equity capital	₹15,20,000	Inventory (40,000 units at variable cost)	₹4,00,000
12 % Long term bank loan	6,00,000	Cash and debtors	9,20,000
Current liabilities	4,00,000	Fixed assets (net)	12,00,000
	25,20,000		25,20,000

The budgeted income statement for next year is as follows:

Sales (1,00,000 units)		₹20,00,000
Less variable production costs		10,00,000
Contribution (manufacturing)		10,00,000
Less other variable costs (variable with sales)		1,00,000
Contribution (final)		9,00,000
Less fixed costs		
Manufacturing	₹6,00,000	
Other costs	1,00,000	7,00,000
Profit		2,00,000

Budgeted production is 1,00,000 units. The chief accountant of the firm anticipates substantial expenditure for fixed assets and intends to obtain a new loan to help finance these expenditures. For the purpose, he is negotiating with a bank. To complete the requisite papers, he projects the following proforma balance sheet for March, next year:

Liabilities	*Amount*	*Assets*	*Amount*
Equity capital	₹15,20,000	Inventory and receivables	₹8,00,000
Profit and loss A/c	2,00,000	Inventory (40,000 units at variable cost)	4,00,000
12% Long-term bank loan	9,20,000	Fixed assets (net)	19,20,000
Current liabilities	4,80,000		
	31,20,000		31,20,000

He sees that the firm will be in default on both provisions of the loan agreement. To resolve the problem, he lists the following points:

1. To work at normal capacity of 1,50,000 units.

2. The firm could perhaps benefit if absorption costing were used.

You are required to do the following:

(a) Recast the income statement and balance sheet using absorption costing, taking the normal capacity of 1,50,000 units as the basis for absorption of fixed manufacturing overheads.

(b) Assume that all increased production costs are paid in cash. Is the firm safe within limits of the loan agreement?

(c) Is the firm better off using absorption costing?

SOLUTION

(1) *Budgeted Income Statement for the Next Year (Absorption Costing Basis)*

Particulars	*Amount*
Sales (1,00,000 units)	₹20,00,000
Less production costs	
Variable cost of current production @ ₹10 per unit	15,00,000
Fixed overheads @ ₹4 per unit (₹6,00,000 ÷ 1,50,000)	6,00,000
Total current production cost	21,00,000
Add opening inventory @ ₹10 per unit	4,00,000
Less closing inventory @ ₹14 per unit	(12,60,000)
Cost of goods sold	12,40,000
Gross margin	7,60,000
Less non-production costs:	
Variable (with sales)	1,00,000
Fixed	1,00,000
Net income	5,60,000

Proforma Balance Sheet

Liabilities	*Amount*	*Assets*		*Amount*
Equity capital	₹15,20,000	Inventory (90,000 units		
Profit and loss A/c	5,60,000	@ ₹14 per unit)		₹12,60,000
12% Long term bank loan	9,20,000	Cash and receivables	₹8,00,000	
Current liabilities	4,80,000	*Less* added variable cost of 50,000 units at ₹10 per unit	5,00,000	3,00,000
		Total current assets		15,60,000
		Fixed assets (net)		19,20,000
	34,80,000			34,80,000

2. Current ratio (₹15,60,000 ÷ ₹4,80,000) × 100 = 325 per cent; Debt-equity ratio (₹14,00,000 ÷ ₹20,80,000) × 100 = 67.3 per cent. Yes, the firm is within safe limits of the loan agreement.

3. The use of absorption costing enables the firm to get the loan and, therefore, is very useful. However, the firm's situation is not good economically. Cash is reduced by ₹5,00,000, which may have an adverse impact on its ability to meet its current liabilities as reflected in the acid-test ratio (62.5 per cent as against the standard form of 100 per cent). The firm is required to carry a large volume of inventory (90,000 units, 90 per cent of the budgeted sales) adding to the expenses of the firm as carrying of inventory involves cost.

REVIEW QUESTIONS

RQ.11.1 Indicate whether the following statements are 'true' or 'false'.

(i) Variable costing and absorption costing techniques are similar to job and process costing.

(ii) Direct materials, direct labour and variable overheads constitute the only relevant cost in variable costing.

(iii) While variable costing is useful for tax purposes, absorption costing is useful for internal reporting purposes.

(iv) Fixed manufacturing costs are considered product costs in absorption costing.

(v) Fixed manufacturing costs are period costs in the context of variable costing.

(vi) Like fixed manufacturing costs, selling and administrative costs are also treated differently in variable costing compared to absorption costing.

(vii) Fixed manufacturing costs form part of closing inventory both in variable costing and full costing methods.

(viii) Variable costing focuses on sales whereas the emphasis of full costing is on production.

(ix) Both variable costing and full costing methods provide the same results in terms of profit or loss when production (in units) is equal to sales (in units).

(x) Capacity variance concept is applicable in variable costing as well as in absorption costing.

[Answer: (i) False, (ii) True, (iii) False, (iv) True, (v) True, (vi) False, (vii) False, (viii) True, (ix) True, (x) False.]

RQ.11.2 If a company sells more units than it produces, would the profits reported by absorption costing tend to be higher or lower than the profits reported by variable costing? Why?

RQ.11.3 What advantages are gained by separating fixed expenses from variable expenses? It has been said that the statement "fluctuating overheads are those which vary with output" is an unjustifiable simplification. How would you qualify the statement? How would your qualification affect your treatment of fluctuating overheads when compiling costs?

RQ.11.4 Distinguish between marginal costing and absorption costing. Also, examine their relative appropriateness.

RQ.11.5 "Direct costing produces income statements that are a more accurate reflection of the true profit fluctuations than the income statements produced by absorption costing." State briefly why you either agree or disagree with this statement.

RQ.11.6 "It is said that an income statement prepared by the variable costing procedure is more helpful to management than an income statement prepared by the absorption cost method." Do you agree? Discuss with the help of a suitable illustration.

RQ.11.7 Standard unit costs are given for the production of a spray attachment manufactured by Carson Products Company Ltd:

Direct materials	₹16
Direct labour	15
Variable manufacturing overheads	12
Fixed manufacturing overheads	30

At normal operating capacity, 2,00,000 units of product should be manufactured. Variable selling and administrative expenses amount to ₹5 per unit, and the fixed selling and administrative expenses amount to ₹7,50,000 a year. Income taxes are estimated at 40 per cent of net income before taxes.

Production and sales data are as follows:

Inventory on hand, April 1, year 1	28,000
Number of units produced in year 1	2,00,000
Number of units sold in year 1	1,60,000
Number of units produced in year 2	1,50,000
Number of units sold in year 2	1,80,000

In both years, each spray attachment was sold for ₹105. Prepare income statements for the two years by the absorption costing method. Also, prepare income statement for the two years by the variable costing method.

RQ.11.8 The following data relate to Strong Company Limited for three years:

	Year 1	*Year 2*	*Year 3*
Units produced	1,00,000	80,000	70,000
Units sold	60,000	90,000	1,00,000
Unit selling price	₹5	₹5	₹5
Unit variable manufacturing cost	2	2	2
Unit variable selling and administrative cost	0.50	0.50	0.50
Total fixed manufacturing cost		₹1,00,000	
Total fixed selling and administrative expenses		50,000	
Normal capacity (units)		1,00,000	
Inventory at the beginning of year 1		Nil	

You are required to prepare income statements for three years individually and collectively under absorption costing and variable costing methods, assuming that actual costs are in conformity with budgeted costs. You are also required to account for difference, if any, in the result report under the two methods.

RQ.11.9 The manager of Royal Industries Ltd. is confused by the income statement he has received from his accountant. He is particularly concerned that his return on sales declined much more than sales in February as compared to January.

Income Statement

Particulars	*January*	*February*
Sales revenue	₹4,50,000	₹3,75,000
Cost of sales	1,80,000	1,50,000
Gross profit	2,70,000	2,25,000
Operating expenses:		
Rent	6,000	6,000
Salaries, wages, commissions	1,57,500	1,42,500
Property insurance, taxes, etc.	4,500	4,500
Supplies	9,000	7,500
Miscellaneous	29,500	29,500
Total	2,06,500	1,90,000
Operating profit	63,500	35,000
Return on sales (per cent)	14.11	9.33

The manager informs you that in salaries, wages, and commissions, the accountant included the salaries of several clerks and himself. All salesmen work on commissions @ 20 per cent of sales. Expenses on account of supplies vary directly with sales. For various reasons, sales in February were expected to decline by ₹75,000. But he had expected income of ₹52,912.50 on sales of ₹3,75,000 @ 14.11 per cent.

You are required to explain the income differences to the manager by using contribution based income statement.

ANSWERS **[Comprehensive solutions to all numerical review questions are available on the companion website: http://www.mhhe.com/khan_jain_cost2e]**

RQ11.7 Absorption costing profit: ₹21,42,000 (year 1), ₹15,66,000 (year 2); Variable costing profit: ₹14,22,000 (year 1), ₹21,06,000 (year 2).

RQ11.8 Absorption costing profit: ₹40,000 (year 1), ₹65,600 (year 2). ₹70,000 (year 3), ₹1,75,000 (years 1-3); Variable costing profit: Zero (year 1), ₹75,000 (year 2), ₹1,00,000 (years 3), ₹1,75,000 (years 1-3).

RQ11.9 Profit: ₹63,500, January; ₹35,000, February.

12 Chapter

Uniform Costing and Inter-Firm Comparison

Learning Objectives

1. Examine meaning, scope and merits of uniform costing.
2. Understand the basic elements of inter-firm comparison.

INTRODUCTION

This chapter discusses uniform costing and the related aspect/its natural outcome—inter-firm comparison. While uniform costing is explained in Section 1, Section 2 examines inter-firm comparison. The main points are summarised in the last section.

UNIFORM COSTING

Meaning and Scope

The principles and methods adopted for the accumulation, analysis, apportionment, and allocation of costs vary so widely between firms that comparison of cost is difficult and unrealistic. Uniform costing attempts to establish uniform methods so that meaningful comparison of performance between firms can be made to their mutual advantage.

Uniform costing refers to the use of the same costing principles/practices by several understandings. It is, however, not a distinct/separate method of cost accounting. It is only a particular technique that applies the usual cost accounting methods like the job or process costing, standard costs, budgetary control and variable costing. The main feature of uniform costing is that whatever be the method of costing used, it is applied uniformly in: (a) A single enterprise having a number of branches/units each of which may be a separate manufacturing unit; (b) A number of concerns in the same industry bound together through a trade association or otherwise, and (c) Industries which are similar in nature, such as gas and electricity, various types of transport, and cotton, jute and woollen textiles.[1]

The cost structures obtaining in the various member units which decide to have a uniform system of cost accounting vary widely, and even in cases where the units manufacture identical products/ are engaged in common processes, the individual cost (items) may be different. In applying the uniform costing, therefore, a fundamental requirement is to locate such differences and overcome/eliminate, as far as practicable, the causes giving rise to such differences.

Causes/Reasons for Differences The causes for such differences may be: (a) Size and organisational set up, (b) Methods of production, and (c) Methods/principles of cost accounting applied.

Size and Organisational Set-Up In a small firm, several functions are combined and performed by a single individual, whereas, in a big concern, the work may be broken down into a number of elements/components each of which being performed by a number of individuals. The difficulty in operating uniform costing for companies that differ widely in regard to size and type of business may, to some extent, be overcome by arranging the various units in a number of size/type ranges and applying different uniform systems for each such type.

Methods of Production The use of different types of machines/plant/equipment, degree of mechanisation, differences in material mix, and sequence/nature of operations/processes are mainly responsible for the differences in costs.

Methods and Principles of Cost Accounting Applied The largest degree of differences pertain to the methods and principles of cost accounting applied in terms of: (i) Different methods of treatment of expenditure of buying, storage, and issue of materials, (ii) Pricing of issues of stores/materials, (iii) Payment to workers, (iv) Basis of classification/absorption of overheads, (v) Calculation of depreciation, and so on.

Scope for Standardisation There is no system of uniform costing that may fit in all circumstances. The system should be tailored to the needs of each individual case. The extent of uniformity in the various aspects of cost accounting depends primarily on its purpose such as: (i) Fixation of prices of common products and (ii) Comparison of performance of various cost centres, and so on. The essential points on which uniformity is normally required include, *inter alia*, the following:[2]

- Methods of cost accounting, for example, job costing, process costing or a variant of one/both of these
- Accounting classification including code
- Content of each account
- Methods of defining costs:
  - — Direct materials
  - — Direct labour
  - — Direct expenses
  - — Overhead costs
    1. Factory
    2. Selling
    3. Distribution
    4. Administration
    5. Research and development
- Methods of recovering depreciation
- Methods of allocating/apportioning overhead costs to cost centres and jobs/products
- Materials control including the issue pricing and valuation of stock
- Methods of recording accounting data, for example, integrated accounting system
- Reports and statements for planning and control
- System of remunerating labour

In brief, all aspects must receive attention to make comparison of results possible between different businesses. The latter may be in the same trade—most uniform costing systems are designed for this purpose.

Uniform Cost Manual Where a uniform costing is introduced, there must be a uniform cost manual, containing instructions to be followed in connection with cost ascertainment and cost control. The manual represents the formal evidence of the cost plan recommended and is of immense help in guiding the implementing firms to organise their cost accounting system for correct implementation of uniform principles. A typical uniform cost manual contains the following information:[3]

Introduction This includes the following:

- Statement of objectives/purpose of the system
- Scope of the system
- Advantages to be derived (elaborated in a subsequent section)
- Educating the management to appreciate the system
- Ideas on selling the system to the management and the extent of cooperation expected from the member units.

Organisation This includes:

- Stages in which the system is to be introduced
- Organisation for developing and operating the system, that is, whether the system is to be installed and operated by a body of cost accountants drawn from the various units within the industry, or by outside cost consultants.

Accounting Systems and Plans These include the following:

- General principles of accounting adopted
- Nature of coding system
- Terminology to be used
- Classification and description of accounts (a complete chart giving details) explaining the nature of transactions booked to each.

Cost Accounting System

- Methods of costing used (job, process, and so on)
- Techniques of costing used (standard, and so on).
- Relationship between cost and financial accounting
- System of integration of accounts
- Financial period
- Items to be included/excluded in/from costs
- Classification of departments (production, service, and so on).
- Material cost: Treatment of handling and storage costs; scrap, defective work, waste, and losses; pricing of materials issues; classification of direct/indirect materials, and so on.
- Labour cost: Classification of direct and indirect wages; treatment of idle time, overtime and shift allowances; treatment of labour-related costs such as dearness allowance and leave pay.
- Overheads: Classification, collection, apportionment and allocation of overheads to production, finished goods and cost of sales; methods of allocation and apportionment of service department expenses to production departments; calculation of depreciation; method of revaluation; administration and selling/distribution expenses overheads.

Presentation of Information Proper presentation of data is essential and the manual should include detailed instructions regarding:

- Forms and contents of statements to be prepared and dates of submission
- Reports to shareholders
- Reports to management
- Operations/production costs

- Cost ratios
- Other financial ratios
- Supplementary information.

Miscellaneous Information The other matters which should be dealt with in the manual are:
- Items to be excluded from the cost accounts
- Uniformity in the treatment of depreciation, interest on capital, wastages, scraps, by-products, and so on.

Advantages and Disadvantages/Limitations

The participating firms derive some advantages from the use of uniform cost accounting. The establishment and operation of any form of uniform costing system is attended with many problems too.

Advantages The benefits accruing to the participating concerns from the use of uniform costing are as listed below:[4]

1. Greater operating efficiency arising from
   - A more extensive and thorough understanding of all costs.
   - A competitive spirit introduced by comparison of costs with the costs of other businesses/average for the industry.
2. Facilitates the establishment of realistic pricing policies.
3. Establishment of the best methods and principles/techniques of costing.
4. Through the central/trade organisation the provision of information which assists in formulating policy, carrying out plans, controlling internally, and facilitating the making of plans to meet competition.
5. The advantages associated with inter-firm comparison (elaborated in next section).

Disadvantages/Limitations The limitations of uniform costing in terms of problems/difficulties in establishment and operation of such a system are summarised below:[5]

1. Standardisation of definitions and methods is difficult to achieve/accomplish.
2. Even when it is achieved, there is bound to be great difficulty in fitting the methods advocated by the system into the framework for each individual business unit. Many differences exist between firms such as age of plant, geographical location, availability of labour, cash and other vital ingredients of successful production, and the degree of mechanisation.
3. Many companies may not disclose the figures as they fear that the confidential information will be disclosed to the competitors.

A natural outcome of uniform costing systems is inter-firm comparison. These depend very much upon the acceptance of standard terms, definitions and methods of cost accounting which form the cornerstone of any system of inter-firm comparison.

INTER-FIRM COMPARISONS

Meaning and Need

Inter-firm Comparison is a tool to control and compare the performance of an industry with that of competitors to increase efficiency and profits.

Inter-firm comparison is the technique by which the performances, deficiencies, costs, and profits of various concerns in an industry are analysed on a voluntary basis by exchange of information, and a relative comparison is made. It is a tool for control by comparing own performance with those of competitors to increase efficiency and maximise profits. As a tool of control, inter-firm comparison differs from other control techniques such as standard costing and budgetary control. The latter techniques use standards/budgets set within the firm which are based on knowledge, skill, and experience with reference to conditions prevailing inside the firm. Such standards of performance are generally suitable for internal control. The inter-firm comparison technique *enables* performance appraisal in relation to competitors in the industry.

Inter-firm comparison should be made between comparable units. Enterprises in the same line of business/industry provide ideal comparable data though differences in size, methods of production/distribution, use of plants/equipments, and operations in different areas present some difficulty in making strict comparisons. A reasonable extent of comparability may be achieved in such cases by sub-classifying the firms into a number of groups based on size, location, capital employed, and so on. Nevertheless, inter-firm comparisons can be made in respect of firms in different industries in spite of the fact that individual cost items may not be comparable. Such comparison may be made in terms of certain ratios such as profit to capital employed, operating profit to operating assets, different types of costs to total sales, and so on.

Purpose/Scope

The main purpose of inter-firm comparison is the improvement of efficiency by showing the management the present achievements and possible weaknesses. Many problems may be overcome through the assistance of inter-firm comparisons. More usually, attention is focussed on weaknesses. Three special problems receive attention: (i) Adequacy of profit, (ii) Efficiency in selling, and (iii) Production efficiency. Extensive use is made of financial/cost ratios. These are selected with great care bearing in mind the problem being faced. The relevant ratios are listed in Exhibit 12.1 to illustrate their significance in inter-firm comparison.

Adequacy of Profit This is measured by the size of profit in relation to capital employed (called "primary ratios"[6]). If the earning power of a firm is less than that of a similar concern, there are some factor(s) which are not operating efficiently. These are isolated by means of other types of ratios. There are: (a) Supporting ratios, (b) General explanatory ratios, and (c) Specific explanatory ratios. All the ratios for a manufacturing firm are listed in Exhibit 12.1.

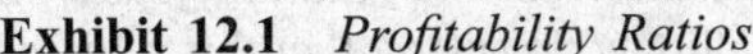
Exhibit 12.1 *Profitability Ratios*

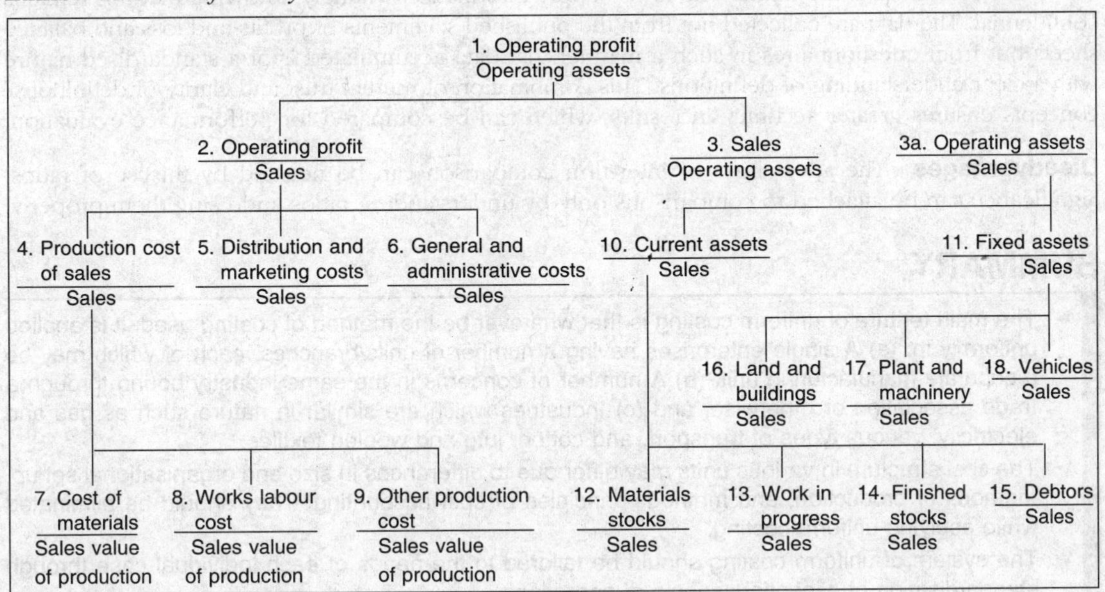

Efficiency in Selling The size of total sales to operating profits and to assets employed are key ratios. These are the supporting ratios in the profit earning structure. The sales to operating assets ratio (size of sales) can be analysed further by the following ratios:

1. Sales to fixed assets
2. Sales to current assets analysed into:
   (a) Stock turnover
   (b) Turnover of debtors

or (a) Sales to material stock
   (b) Sales to work-in-process
   (c) Sales to finished goods stock
   (d) Sales to debtors

Production Efficiency The factory cost of sales, sub-divided into: (i) Direct material, (ii) Direct labour, and (iii) Production overheads and related to sales value of production indicates the relative size of these three elements of cost. Comparison with other firm's figures or with its own preceding periods' figures would reveal a possible source of inefficiency, for example, labour utilisation or machine utilisation. A detailed analysis and investigation can then follow.

Advantages/Disadvantages

Advantages The advantages of using ratios are outside the scope of present book.[7] The advantages of inter-firm comparison based on ratios are briefly outlined below.

Weaknesses Revealed One of the most important benefits is the fact that weaknesses, if any, are revealed. Management is in consequence put on guard which would lead to remedial action.

A corollary of this advantage is the indication of the trend of sales, profits and costs as shown by the ratios.

Voluntary Basis A further advantage of inter-firm comparison comes from the voluntary basis on which the comparisons are made. The firms supply information willingly, knowing that this remains confidential. The data are collected not from the published statements of profits and loss and balance sheets but from questionnaires in such a manner that data accumulated is of a standardised nature with a clear understanding of definitions. This combination of mutual trust and clarity of definitions/concepts ensures greater accuracy in results, which can be compared for performance evaluation.

Disadvantages The advantages of inter-firm comparison can be negated by misuse of ratios. Significance can be attached to comparisons only by understanding ratios and using them properly.

SUMMARY

- The main feature of uniform costing is that whatever be the method of costing used, it is applied uniformly in: (a) A single enterprises having a number of units/branches, each of which may be a separate manufacturing unit, (b) A number of concerns in the same industry bound through a trade association or otherwise, and (c) Industries which are similar in nature such as gas and electricity, various types of transport, and cotton, jute and woolen textiles.
- The cost structure in various units may differ due to differences in size and organisational set up, methods of production, and methods/principles of cost accounting. They should be eliminated while applying uniform costing.
- The system of uniform costing should be tailored to the needs of each individual case through standardisation of essential aspects of operations.

- A uniform cost manual containing instructions to be followed in connection with cost ascertainment and cost control is used where uniform costing is introduced.
- The inter-firm comparison is a natural outcome of uniform costing. It is a tool for control by comparing own performance with those of competitors to increase efficiency and maximise profits.
- Many problems/weaknesses may be overcome through assistance of inter-firm comparison, namely, adequacy of profit, efficiency in selling, and production efficiency.
- Extensive use is made of cost/financial ratios. A scheme of inter-firm comparison combines the advantages of uniform costing system and the benefits arising out of the use of ratios.

REFERENCES

1. Prasad, N.K., *Principles and Practice of Cost Accounting*, Book Syndicate Private Ltd, (Calcutta, 1981), p. 700.
2. Batty, J., *Management Accountancy*, Macdonald and Evans (London, 1970), p. 443.
3. *Op. cit.*, p. 703.
4. *Op. cit.*, p. 444.
5. *Ibid*, p. 444.
6. *Ibid*, pp. 446-449.
7. Khan, M. Y. and P. K. Jain, Management Accounting, TMH (New Delhi, 2013), Chater 6.

EXERCISES

12.1 Indicate whether the following statements are true or false:

(i) Uniform costing is a costing method similar to job and process.

(ii) The primary objective of uniform costing is to facilitate meaningful inter-firm comparison of performance.

(iii) The system of uniform costing should be tailored to the needs of each individual case through standardization of essential aspects of operations.

(iv) It is not necessary to have a uniform cost manual for implementing uniform costing system.

(v) Meaningful inter-firm comparison can be made between any two firms, based on the cost ratios.

(vi) Inter-firm comparison should be made between comparable units.

(vii) Financial/Cost ratios are used extensively for useful inter-firm comparison.

(**Answers: (i)** False, **(ii)** True, **(iii)** True, **(iv)** False, **(v)** False, **(vi)** True, **(vii)** True)

12.2 Explain the objectives of uniform costing and outline the main causes of differences in costs between undertakings within the same industry.

12.3 What matters are found in a cost manual in a system of uniform costing?

12.4 What are the advantages of uniform costing?

12.5 What are the purposes of inter-firm comparison?

12.6 Briefly outline advantages and disadvantages of inter-firm comparison.

12.7 "A scheme of inter-firm comparison combines the advantages of uniform costing system and the benefits arising out of the use of ratios." Elaborate.

Reconciliation and Integration

Learning Objectives

1. Examine the need for, and the procedure involved in, reconciliation of financial and cost accounts.
2. Discuss the major considerations in the installation of integrated accounts.

INTRODUCTION

The objective of this chapter is to illustrate the reconciliation of financial and cost accounts and their integration. The need for, and the procedure involved in, reconciling the financial and cost account, is outlined in Section 1. The preparation of integrated accounts is shown in Section 2. The main points are summarised in Section 3.

RECONCILIATION OF FINANCIAL AND COST ACCOUNTS

When manufacturing firms maintain a separate cost accounting system, the profit or loss shown by such cost books may not agree with the corresponding profit or loss revealed by the financial accounting system. This disparity in financial results is caused by the use of different cost accumulating procedures in the two systems. For instance, financial books record *all* items of expenses, namely, factory, administrative, selling, and so on, on *actual cost* basis, while in general, in cost books, such expenses/overheads are charged to production on standard or budgeted cost basis. Likewise, the stock valuation procedure normally adopted in cost books is different from financial books. Moreover, certain items of expenditure and income are recorded only in one set of books. Therefore, there is need to reconcile the results shown by the cost and financial books. This reconciliation establishes arithmetical accuracy of both sets of books on the one hand, and explains factors causing differences in profit (losses) of these two books, on the other.

Reasons for Disagreement

The differences in results of cost and financial books can be attributed to the following reasons:

Transactions Included in One Set of Books Only Some transactions are recorded exclusively either in the financial accounts/books or in the cost accounts. Following is the list of items recorded only in financial accounts/books:

Items Recorded in Financial Accounts/Books Such items relate to (i) Appropriation of profits, (ii) Financial charges and (iii) Financial income.

Items Relating to the Appropriation of Profit Include the Following:

(i) Amounts transferred to different accumulated profit reserves, such as general reserve, dividend equalisation reserve, and so on.
(ii) Dividends paid to, or proposed for, preference shareholders and equity shareholders.
(iii) The extent of the amount of bonus shares issued to equity shareholders and appropriated out of the current year's profit and loss appropriation account.
(iv) Creation of additional provision for depreciation on plant and machinery and other fixed assets as well as the additional provision for bad and doubtful debts on sundry debtors.
(v) The sum transferred to Debenture Redemption Fund Account for the purpose of repayment of debentures or any other sum transferred to any other such account created for the purpose of discharge of long-term liability.

Items Exclusively Related to Financial Charges Pertain to the Following:

(i) Losses on sale of fixed assets such as plant and machinery or loss due to discarding or scrapping of plant.
(ii) Loss on sale of trade investments.
(iii) Amortisation of expenditure in respect of items, such as goodwill, preliminary expenses, expenses relating to capital issues, namely, underwriting commission, brokerage fees, legal charges, and so on.
(iv) Interest paid on debentures, long-tem loans, bank loans, owner's contributions, and so on, if interest is ignored in cost books.
(v) Damages payable.
(vi) Penalties payable.
(vii) Office transfer expenses.
(viii) Writing off the extraordinary abnormal losses of the past year(s) in instalments over a period of time.
(ix) Taxes paid.
(x) Capital expenditures such as payment of stamp duties and transfer fees paid on the purchase of shares treated as revenue expenses.

Transitions Exclusively Related to Financial Incomes Cover the Following Transactions:

(i) Profit from sale of fixed assets such as land, building, patents and, less often, from plant and equipment.
(ii) Profits accruing from disposition of trade investments.
(iii) Transfer fees received on issuing and registering transfer of shares.
(iv) Interest received on investments made outside the firm, namely, banks, inter-corporate loans and debentures, deposits made with financial institutions.
(v) Dividend received from shares of other companies.
(vi) Rent received or receivable from properties.
(vii) Appreciation of fixed assets (non-current assets).

Items Exclusively in the Purview of Cost Accounts The following notional charges are usually considered in cost accounts/books only.

1. Notional rent of premises if owned by the firm itself.
2. Notional interest on owner's capital contributions.
3. Sometimes it may so happen that a certain fixed asset, say, plant and machinery may have been fully depreciated so far as the book value is concerned, but it may be still in continuous use in the production department in view of its physical conditions and, hence, depreciation continues to be charged in cost books.

Treatment of Indirect Expenses/Overheads As stated earlier, the *actual expenses* incurred is the basis for treating overheads in financial accounts. In cost accounting, overheads are charged to production on the basis of some predetermined rate based on any of the following methods, namely, output, machine-hours, labour-hours percentage of the material cost, labour cost and prime cost. Reflecting the different basis of treatment, the overheads charged in cost books would either exceed or fall short of overheads recorded and shown in financial accounts, resulting in over-absorption or under-absorption of overheads. Over-absorption of overheads implies that actual expenses recovered and recorded in cost books are more compared to the financial accounts. As a result, the profit shown by cost books would naturally be less than that shown in the financial books. In the case of under-absorption of overheads, the expenses recovered and charged in cost accounts would be less than the amount charged in financial accounts, showing high profits in cost accounts compared to the financial books of accounts.

In Cost accounting overheads are charged to production on the basis of some predetermined rate based on output machine-hours, labour-hours percentage of material cost, labour cost and prime cost.

Different Bases of Inventory Valuation The basis of inventory valuation may be different in cost and financial records.

Raw Materials Inventory In cost books, materials issued to various jobs/production centres are charged on the basis of any of methods used for the purpose of pricing of the issue of materials, that is, LIFO, FIFO, weighted average, inflated price, standard cost, and so on. The raw material inventory is shown in financial accounting on the basis of *cost or market price, whichever is lower.*

Work-in-process (W.I.P.) Inventory In cost accounts, the work-in-process inventory is valued on the basis of work cost, prime cost or cost of production. But in financial accounts, the basis of valuation is the cost of production.

Finished Goods Inventory The lower of the cost or the market price is normally the guiding criterion for valuing closing stock in financial accounts, whereas it may be valued for cost accounting purposes at prime cost or factory cost only.

Different Bases of Depreciation There are a number of methods of charging depreciation in financial accounts, for example, straight line and diminishing balance methods. On the other hand, in cost books, machine-hour rate or output basis are normally recognised as the ideal methods of charging depreciation.

Abnormal Losses and Gains The complete disregard of abnormal losses and gains in cost books can be yet another source of differences in profits of these two sets of books.

Procedure for Reconciliation

For the above reasons, the financial results shown by the two sets of books would be different from each other. The reconciliation of the financial results shown by the two systems of accounting is done in the form of a reconciliation statement or memorandum reconciliation account. Their formats are given in Exhibits 13.1 and 13.2 respectively.

Exhibit 13.1 *Reconciliation Statement: Cost and Financial Profits*

Particulars	*Plus items*	*Minus items*
Profit (Loss) as per cost books		
Less expenses reducing profit in financial books but not recorded in cost books:		

(Contd.)

(Contd.)

Interest paid on loans	
Dividends paid to shareholders	
Taxes paid on profit	
Transfer to general or specific reserves	
Amortisation of deferred revenue expenditure	
Damages and penalties payable	
Add incomes augmenting profits in financial books not credited in cost books:	
Interest and dividend received	
Transfer fees received	
Profit on sale of fixed assets	
Less overheads under-absorbed or not recorded in cost accounts:	
Factory overheads (Actual overheads-Absorbed overheads)	
Administrative overheads (Actual-Absorbed)	
Selling and distribution overheads (Actual-Absorbed)	—
Add overheads over-absorbed in cost accounts:	
Factory overheads (Absorbed overheads-Actual overheads)	
Administrative overheads (Absorbed-Actual)	
Selling and distribution overheads (Absorbed-Actual)	—
Less under-valuation of opening inventories and over-valuation of closing inventories in cost books causing cost profits to increase:	
Raw materials	
Work-in-process	
Finished goods	—
Add over-valuation of opening inventories and under-valuation of closing inventories in cost books causing cost profits to decrease:	
Raw materials	
Work-in-process	
Finished goods	—
Less under-recovery of depreciation in cost books (Depreciation in financial accounts – Depreciation in cost accounts)	—
Add over-charge of depreciation in cost books (Depreciation in cost accounts – Depreciation in financial accounts)	—
Profits (Loss) as per financial accounts	

If profits as per financial accounts are taken as the starting point, items added in Exhibit 13.1 would be subtracted and items deducted would be added and the profits (loss) arrived at would be profits as revealed by cost accounts.

Exhibit 13.2 *Memorandum Reconciliation Account*

Particulars	*Amount*	*Particulars*	*Amount*
1. Expenses not included *in cost books:*		1. Profit as per cost accounts	
Interest paid on loans		2. Incomes not credited in cost *accounts:*	
Dividends paid to shareholders		Dividends and interest received	
Taxes paid on profits		Transfer fees received	
Transfer to general or specific reserves		Profit on sale of fixed assets	
Amortisation of deferred revenue Expenditure		3. Overheads over-absorbed in cost accounts	
Damages and penalties payable		4. Over-valuation of opening inventories	
2. Overheads under-absorbed or not recorded in cost accounts		5. Under-valuation of closing inventories	
3. Under-valuation of opening inventories		6. Over-absorption of depreciation in cost books	
4. Over-valuation of closing inventories			
5. Under-recovery of depreciation in cost books			
6. Profit as per financial accounts			

EXAMPLE 13.1

The following figures are extracted from the financial accounts of Selwel Ltd for the current year ending March 31.

Sales (20,000 units)		₹50,00,000
Materials		20,00,000
Wages		10,00,000
Factory overheads		9,00,000
Administrative overheads		5,20,000
Selling and distribution overheads		3,60,000
Finished goods (1,230 units)		3,00,000
Work-in-process:		
Materials	₹60,000	
Labour	40,000	
Factory overheads	40,000	1,40,000
Goodwill written off		4,00,000
Interest paid on capital		40,000

In the costing records, factory overhead is charged at 100 per cent of wages, administration overhead at 10 per cent of factory cost and selling and distribution overhead at the rate of ₹20 per unit sold.

Prepare a statement, reconciling the profit as per cost records with the profit as per financial records.

SOLUTION

Financial Profit and Loss Account for the Current Year Ending March

Particulars	*Dr Amount*	*Particulars*		*Cr Amount*
To materials	₹20,00,000	By sales (20,000 units)		₹50,00,000
To wages	10,00,000	By finished goods (1,230 units)		3,00,000
To factory overheads	9,00,000	*By work-in-process*		
To administrative overheads	5,20,000	Materials	₹60,000	
To selling and distribution		Labour	40,000	
overheads	3,60,000	Overheads	40,000	1,40,000
To goodwill written off	4,00,000			
To interest paid on capital	40,000			
To net profit	2,20,000			
	54,40,000			54,40,000

Costing Profit and Loss Account for the Current Year Ending March

Particulars	*Dr Amount*	*Particulars*	*Cr Amount*
To materials	₹20,00,000	By sales revenue	
To wages	10,00,000	(20,000 units × 250)	₹50,00,000
Prime cost	30,00,000		
To factory overheads			
(@ 100 per cent of wages)	10,00,000		
Gross works cost	40,00,000		
Less closing work-in-process	(1,40,000)		
Net works cost	38,60,000		
To administrative overheads			
(@ 10 per cent of factory cost)	3,86,000		

(Contd.)

(Contd.)

Cost of production (21,230 units @ ₹200 per unit)	42,46,000	
Less closing stock (1,230 units @ ₹ 200 per unit)	(2,46,000)	
Cost of goods sold	40,00,000	
To selling and distribution overheads [@ ₹20 per unit (20,000 × ₹20)]	4,00,000	
Cost of sales	44,00,000	
To net profit	6,00,000	
Sales	50,00,000	50,00,000

It is assumed that closing finished goods inventory is valued at total cost of production in the cost books.

Reconciliation Statement: Cost and Financial Profits

Particulars		*Plus items*	*Minus items*
Profit as per cost records		₹6,00,000	
Add over-absorption of factory overheads in cost records (₹10,00,000 – ₹9,00,000)		1,00,000	
Less under-absorption of administration overheads in cost records (₹5,20,000 – ₹3,86,000)			₹1,34,000
Add over-absorption of selling and distribution overheads in cost records (₹4,00,000 – ₹3,60,000)		40,000	
Add under-valuation of finished goods in cost records (₹3,00,000 – ₹2,46,000)		54,000	
Less expenses not charged in cost books:			
Goodwill written off	₹4,00,000		
Interest paid on capital	40,000		4,40,000
		7,94,000	5,74,000
Profit as per financial books			2,20,000

INTEGRATED ACCOUNTS

The preceding discussion has shown that there is a need for a reconciliation statement when separate sets of cost and financial records are made. The need for such a statement can be dispensed with if only *one* set of books is maintained to serve both financial and costing purposes. Such a system of accounts in which only one set of books is maintained to record both cost and financial transactions is referred to as integrated/integral accounts.

Integrated accounts mean no need of reconciliation statement; only one set of books maintained to record both cost and financial transactions.

Since under the integrated system of accounts only one set of books is maintained, there is considerable economy both in costs and clerical work in terms of time and efforts. Moreover, the accounting function is considerably simplified, paving the way for a more efficient control system of accounting. Such a system enhances the speed of accounting work and, hence, also facilitates the reporting function of accounting.

Installation of Integrated Accounts System

The installation of the integrated accounts system involves consideration of the following principles:

Degree of Integration The first and foremost thing to be decided in the integrated accounting system is the degree/extent of integration, that is, whether the whole accounting system is to be integrated or the integration is to be done partially up to the stage of prime cost or factory cost.

Number of Control Accounts Theoretically speaking, a single control account covering all items relating to the costing department can serve the purpose. However, it would be operationally better and more convenient from the point of view of control, if separate control accounts are opened for each of the elements of cost, namely:

(a) Stores control account (for materials).
(b) Wages control account.
(c) Factory overhead control account.
(d) Administrative overhead control account.
(e) Selling and distribution overhead control account.
(f) For more details, the last three control accounts dealing with indirect overheads can be further sub-divided into fixed and variable expenses.
(g) If a firm has more than one factory, it is desirable to open a complete series of control accounts for each.
(h) Work-in-process control account (to take care of incomplete manufactured units).
(i) Finished stock control account (to record the finished goods).
(j) Sales ledger control account/sundry debtors control account (to tally the balance of this account with the summary of the balance of individual debtors account of sales ledger).
(k) Bought ledger control account/sundry creditors control account (for the purpose of tallying the balance of this account with the individual aggregate balances of each creditors in the purchase ledger).
(l) *Assets account:* A separate individual account should be created for each asset, namely, plant and equipment, furniture, building, cash and bank balances, and so on. All these accounts are prepared on the basis of the financial accounting principles.
(m) *Cost of sales account:* This account would represent the cost of goods sold during the period. The accounting procedure of dealing with this is explained later.
(n) Share capital account.
(o) Debentures account.
(p) Other long-term loans account.
(q) Reserves and surplus account.
(r) Any other liability account.
(s) *Pre-payment and outstanding expenses accounts:* Adjustment should be made in respect of all outstanding and accrued expenses by debiting the relevant expense account (say, wages control, factory overhead control, administrative and selling overheads control accounts) and crediting the corresponding expense suspense account (say, wages control suspense account, factory overhead control suspense account, and so on). The accounting procedure would be reversed for pre-payments of expenses. These adjustments would enable each expense control account to be representative of the charges for the given period. At the time of making payment in future, the relevant cost suspense account would be debited and pre-payments would be adjusted by transferring to the relevant cost control account in the subsequent period.

EXAMPLE 13.2 *(Treatment of Pre-payment and Outstanding Expenses)*

Journalise the following transactions under the integrated accounting system for a manufacturing firm:

(i) Accrued wages	₹50,000
(ii) Unexpired insurance of the factory premises	2,000
(iii) Depreciation of plant and equipment	20,000

SOLUTION

Journal Entries

(i) Wages control A/c	.. Dr	₹50,000	
To wages control suspense A/c			₹50,000
(Being accrued wages recorded)			
(ii) Factory overhead control suspense A/c	...Dr	2,000	
To factory overhead control A/c			2,000
(Being unexpired insurance recorded to reduce factory overheads of the current year)			
(iii) Factory overhead control A/c	....Dr	20,000	
To plant and equipment			20,000
(Being depreciation on plant and equipment charged to factory overhead control A/c)			

In the subsequent period, the first two transactions would be journalised in the following way:

(i) *Payment for accrued wages*			
Wages control suspense A/c	...Dr	50,000	
To Bank			50,000
(ii) *Transferring unexpired insurance expense to the current year's expenses:*			
Factory overhead control A/c	...Dr	2,000	
To factory overhead control suspense A/c			2,000

Cost Compilation at Regular Intervals Full details of items relating to raw materials, direct labour and various overheads available in corresponding stores ledger control account (for each of the elements of overheads) is made available at convenient intervals for the purposes of judging the internal position.

Transaction Relating to Financial Expenses and Appropriations Financial expense items such as interest on capital, writing off deferred revenue expenditure and appropriations items such as transfer to general or specific reserves, dividends paid, are dealt with as per the conventional principles of financial accounting.

Closure of Nominal Accounts At periodical intervals, say, a month or quarter, all nominal accounts would be closed by transferring to profit and loss account. The following points deserve special attention in this context:

(a) Cost of sales account would be prepared separately. This account would represent profit earned equivalent to the difference of sales revenue and cost of sales. The amount of profit so arrived at would be transferred to profit and loss account by passing the following journal entry

Cost of sales A/c ...Dr

To profit and loss A/c

In the case of loss, the entry would be reversed. Exhibit 13.3 shows the procedure of determining cost of sales.

Exhibit 13.3 *Cost of Sales A/c*

To finished stock ledger control A/c (cost of goods sold)	——	By sales ledger control A/c (sales made)	——
To selling and distribution overheads control A/c		By profit and loss A/c (loss)	
To profit and loss A/c (profit)			

(b) Items relating to financial expenses, over- and under-absorption of any type of overheads, abnormal losses and gains will be recorded in the profit and loss account. The format of profit and loss account is given in Exhibit 13.4.

Exhibit 13.4 *Profit and Loss Account*

To cost of sales (losses transferred from)	—	By cost of sales (profits transferred from)	—
For absorption or under-absorption of overheads:		*For over-absorption of overheads:*	
To factory overheads control A/c	—	By factory overheads control A/c	—
To administrative overheads control A/c	—	To administrative overheads control A/c	—
To selling overheads control A/c	—	By selling overheads control A/c	—
To abnormal losses (specify)	—	By abnormal gains (specify)	—
To financial expenses (specify)	—	By non-operating gains (specify)	—
To appropriations (specify)	—	By losses (current year)	—
To profit (current period)	—		

Personal and Real Accounts Personal and real accounts will be carried to the balance sheet.

EXAMPLE 13.3 *(Accounting Procedure under Integrated Accounts)*
From the following information of a newly commenced manufacturing unit of Royal Industries Ltd., for the first quarter ending March 31, pass journal entries and prepare important ledger accounts, assuming that the cost and financial accounts are integrated:

Purchases of raw materials on credit	₹3,00,000
Wages paid	2,00,000
Indirect wages included in the wages paid	20,000
Direct materials issued to production	2,70,000
Factory expenses incurred	1,30,000
Factory expenses charged to production	1,55,000
Office and administrative expenses incurred	75,000
Office and administrative expenses charged to production	70,000
Selling and distribution overheads incurred	60,000
Selling and distribution overheads charged to sales	60,000
Credit sales during the period	8,00,000
Receipts from debtors	7,00,000
Paid to creditors	2,50,000
Finished product at cost	6,50,000
Closing stock of finished product	50,000
Interest paid	30,000

Assume that over- and under-absorption of overheads are straight-way carried to the profit and loss account. Also, determine the profit earned during the period.

SOLUTION

Journal Entries for the Quarter Ending March 31

Particulars		*Dr Amount*	*Cr Amount*
Stores ledger control A/c	Dr	₹3,00,000	
To bought ledger control A/c			₹3,00,000
(Being raw materials purchased on credit)			

(*Contd.*)

(*Contd.*)

Wages control A/c	Dr	₹2,00,000	
To cash			₹2,00,000
(Being wages paid as per the payroll)			
Work-in-process ledger control A/c	Dr	1,80,000	
Factory overhead control A/c	Dr	20,000	
To wages control A/c			2,00,000
(Being the allocation of wages between production and factory overhead)			
Work-in-process ledger control A/c	Dr	2,70,000	
To stores ledger control A/c			2,70,000
(Being materials issued for production)			
Factory overhead control A/c	Dr	1,30,000	
To cash/bank			1,30,000
(Being factory overheads incurred and paid)			
Work-in-process ledger control A/c	Dr	1,55,000	
To factory overheads control A/c			1,55,000
(Being factory overheads charged to production)			
Office and administrative overheads control A/c	Dr	75,000	
To bank			75,000
(Being payment made for office overheads)			
Work-in-process ledger control A/c	Dr	70,000	
To office and administrative overhead control A/c			70,000
(Being office and administrative overheads charged to production)			
Selling and distribution overhead control A/c	Dr	60,000	
To bank			60,000
(Being payment made of selling overheads)			
Cost of sales A/c	Dr	60,000	
To selling and distribution overheads control A/c			60,000
(Being selling overheads charged to cost of sales account)			
Sales ledger control A/c	Dr	8,00,000	
To cost of sales A/c			8,00,000
(Being sales made of finished output on credit)			
Bank A/c	Dr	7,00,000	
To sales ledger control A/c			7,00,000
(Being cash received from debtors)			
Bought ledger control A/c	Dr	2,50,000	
To bank A/c			2,50,000
(Being payment made to creditors)			
Finished stock ledger control A/c	Dr	6,50,000	
To work-in-process ledger control A/c			6,50,000
(Cost of finished output transferred to stock ledger control account)			
Interest A/c	Dr	30,000	
To bank A/c			30,000
(Being interest paid)			
Profit and loss A/c	Dr	30,000	
To interest A/c			30,000
(Being interest transferred to profit and loss A/c)			

(*Contd.*)

(*Contd.*)

Cost of sales A/c	Dr	₹6,00,000	
To finished stock ledger control A/c			₹6,00,000
(Cost of finished output sold transferred to cost of sales)			
Profit and loss A/c	Dr	5,000	
To office and administrative overheads control A/c			5,000
(Being under-absorption of office overheads transferred to profit and loss account)			
Factory overhead control A/c	Dr	5,000	
To profit and loss A/c			5,000
(Being over-absorption of factory overheads transferred to profit and loss) A/c			
Cost of sales A/c	Dr	1,40,000	
To profit and loss A/c			1,40,000
(Profit on sales transferred to profit and loss A/c)			

Stores Ledger Control A/c

To bought ledger control A/c	₹3,00,000	By work-in-progress ledger control A/c	₹2,70,000
		By balance c/d	30,000
	3,00,000		3,00,000

Work-in-Process Ledger Control A/c

To wages control A/c (direct wages)	₹1,80,000	By stock ledger control A/c (finished output transferred)	₹6,50,000
To stores ledger control A/c (materials)	2,70,000	By balance c/d	25,000
To factory overheads control A/c (factory expenses charged to production)	1,55,000		
To office and administrative overhead control A/c (office expenses charged to production)	70,000		
	6,75,000		6,75,000

Wages Control A/c

To cash	₹2,00,000	By work-in-process control A/c	₹1,80,000
		By factory overheads control A/c	20,000
	2,00,000		2,00,000

Factory Overhead Control A/c

To wages control A/c (indirect wages)	₹20,000	By work-in-process ledger control A/c (charged to production)	₹1,55,000
To cash (expenses)	1,30,000		
To profit and loss A/c (over-recovery of factory overheads)	5,000		
	1,55,000		1,55,000

Office and Administrative Overhead Control A/c

To bank	₹75,000	By work-in-process ledger control A/c (charged to production)	₹70,000
		By profit and loss A/c (under-absorption of overheads)	5,000
	75,000		75,000

Selling and Distribution Overhead Control A/c

To bank	₹60,000	By cost of sales A/c	₹60,000

Cost of Sales A/c

To finished stock ledger control A/c	₹6,00,000	By sales ledger control A/c	₹8,00,000
To selling and distribution overhead control A/c	60,000		
To profit and loss A/c	1,40,000		
	8,00,000		8,00,000

Sales Ledger Control A/c

To cost of sales A/c	₹8,00,000	By bank	₹7,00,000
		By balance c/d	1,00,000
	8,00,000		8,00,000

Bought Ledger Control A/c

To bank A/c	₹2,50,000	By stores ledger control A/c	₹3,00,000
To balance c/d	50,000		
	3,00,000		3,00,000

Finished Stock Ledger Control A/c

To work-in-process ledger control A/c	₹6,50,000	By cost of sales A/c	₹6,00,000
		By balance c/d	50,000
	6,50,000		6,50,000

Profit and Loss A/c

To interest	₹30,000	By factory overhead control A/c (over-recovery of overheads)	₹5,000
To office and administrative overheads control A/c (under-recovery)	5,000	By cost of sales	1,40,000
To balance c/d (profit of the quarter carried to the next quarter)	1,10,000		
	1,45,000		1,45,000

Integrated Accounts and Standard Cost Accounting

When the firm is following the standard costing system for recording costs, the integrated accounting system can be suitably modified to incorporate the same. The accounting procedure is similar to the one described before, except that there would be an additional entry in respect of variance account in the journal when actual costs differ from the standard costs. The relevant variance account (material, labour, overhead) would be debited if the actual costs are more than the standard costs and *vice-versa*.

EXAMPLE 13.4 *(Treatment of Standard Costing Under Integrated Account)*
Journalise the following transactions under the integrated accounting system of a firm.

(i) Raw materials purchased at ₹1,10,000 (standard cost is ₹1,00,000).
(ii) Wages paid, ₹1,90,000 (standard cost is ₹1,95,000).
(iii) Actual sales are ₹5,00,000 as against budget sales of ₹5,20,000.

SOLUTION
Journal Entries

(i) Stores ledger control A/c	Dr	₹1,00,000	
Material variance A/c	Dr	10,000	
To bought ledger control A/c			₹1,10,000
(Being purchase of materials and material variance recorded)			
(ii) Wage control A/c	Dr	1,95,000	
To wages variance A/c			5,000
To bank A/c			1,90,000
(Being wages paid and wage variance recorded)			
(iii) Sales ledger control A/c	Dr	5,00,000	
Sales variance A/c	Dr	20,000	
To cost of sales A/c			5,20,000
(Being actual sales and sales variance recorded)			

All favourable and unfavourable variances would be transferred to the profit and loss account. The journal entry for transferring favourable variance(s) would be to debit the specific variance(s) account and credit the profit and loss account; and for adverse variances, the journal entry recorded would be just the reverse. Thus, the profit and loss account would be more comprehensive as it would include unfavourable variances as well as favourable variances also.

SUMMARY

- The two systems of accounting, namely, financial and cost, maintained by a firm may show different operating results which should be reconciled to establish arithmetical accuracy of both types of records as also to identify the factors responsible for such differences.
- The main reasons for the difference in the results as revealed by financial and cost accounts are related to different cost accumulating procedures, such as, the inclusion of certain transactions in only one set of records, treatment of overheads, different bases of inventory valuation and depreciation, and treatment of abnormal losses and gains.
- The divergence in the financial results is reconciled in the form of either a reconciliation statement or a memorandum reconciliation account, taking the result shown by either of them as the starting point.
- There would be no need to reconcile the two sets of accounts if integrated accounts are maintained.
- In a system of integrated accounts, only one set of books is maintained to record both cost and financial transactions.
- Integrated system of accounting requires the preparation of control accounts, such as stores, wages, factory overheads, administrative, selling and distribution, work-in-process, finished goods, sales ledger, bought ledger, assets account, cost of sales and pre-payment and outstanding expenses.
- The integrated accounts can also be modified to incorporate standard cost accounting.

PRACTICAL PROBLEMS

P.13.1 In reconciliation between cost and financial accounts, one of the areas of difference is the different methods of stock valuation. State with reasons, in each of the following circumstances, whether costing profit will be higher or lower than financial profit:

Items of stock	*Cost valuation*	*Financial valuation*
1. Raw material (opening)	₹50,000	₹60,000
2. Finished stock (opening)	60,000	50,000
3. Work-in-process (closing)	60,000	50,000
4. Finished stock (closing)	50,000	60,000

SOLUTION

1. Since the opening raw material inventory is under-valued by ₹10,000 in cost records, the profits shown by the costing profit and loss account would be *higher* by ₹10,000 *vis-à-vis* financial profits.
2. Since the opening finished goods inventory is *over-valued* by ₹10,000 in cost records, profit would be *lower* by the same amount compared to financial profits.
3. Since the closing work-in-process is *over-valued* in cost records by ₹10,000, its profits would naturally be *higher* by ₹10,000 compared to financial profits.
4. Since the closing finished stock inventory is *under-valued* in cost records, its profit would be *lower* by ₹10,000 *vis-à-vis* financial records.

P.13.2 From the following prepare a reconciliation statement.

Net profits as per financial records	₹1,28,755
Net profit as per costing records	1,72,400
Works overhead under-recovered in costing records	3,120
Administrative overheads recovered in excess in cost records	1,700
Depreciation charged in financial records	11,200
Depreciation recovered in costing records	12,500
Interest received but not included in costing records	8,000
Obsolescence loss charged in financial records	5,700
Income tax provided in financial books	40,300
Bank interest credited in financial books	750
Stores adjustments (credited in financial books)	475
Depreciation of stock charged in financial books	6,750

SOLUTION

Reconciliation Statement: Cost and Financial Profits (Costing Profit as Base)

Particulars		*Plus items*	*Minus items*
Net profit as per costing records		₹1,72,400	
Less works overhead under-recovered in costing records			₹3,120
Add administrative overheads over-absorbed in cost books		1,700	
Add depreciation charged in excess in cost books (₹12,500-₹11,200)		1,300	
Add incomes not credited in cost books:			
Interest received	₹8,000		
Bank interest	750		
Stores adjustment (credit)	475	9,225	
Less expenses not charged in cost books:			
Obsolescence loss	5,700		
Income tax	40,300		
Depreciation of stock	6,750		52,750
		1,84,625	55,870
Net profit as per financial books			1,28,755

Reconciliation Statement: Cost and Financial Profits (Financial Profit as Base)

Particulars		Plus items	Minus items
Net profit as per financial books		₹1,28,755	
Add works overhead over-recovered in financial books		3,120	
Less administrative overheads under-absorbed in financial books			₹1,700
Less depreciation under-charged in financial books (₹12,500 – ₹11,200)			1,300
Less incomes credited only in financial books:			
Interest received	₹8,000		
Bank interest	750		
Stores adjustment (credit)	475		9,225
Add expenses charged only in financial books:			
Obsolescence loss	5,700		
Income tax	40,300		
Depreciation of stock	6,750	52,750	
		1,84,625	12,225
Net profit as per cost books			1,72,400

P.13.3 Given below is the trading and profit and loss account of Savera Plastics Ltd for the quarter ending June 30.

Particulars	Dr Amount	Particulars	Cr Amount
To direct materials consumed	₹9,00,000	By sales (2,50,000 units)	₹22,50,000
To direct wages	6,00,000		
To factory expenses	3,60,000		
To office expenses	1,20,000		
To selling and distribution expenses	2,40,000		
To net profit	30,000		
	22,50,000		22,50,000

The normal output (per quarter) of the factory is 2,00,000 units. Factory overheads (per quarter) are fixed upto ₹1,80,000 and office expenses (for quarter) are fixed for practical purposes. Selling and distribution expenses (per quarter) are fixed to the extent of ₹1,50,000; the rest are variable.

You are required to prepare a statement of cost and profit as per cost records, and reconcile the profit so determined with that of the financial books.

Solution

Statement of Cost and Profit for the Quarter Ending June 30

Particulars		Amount
Direct materials		₹9,00,000
Direct wages		6,00,000
Prime cost		15,00,000
Add factory overheads:		
Fixed overheads (₹1,80,000/₹2,00,000) × ₹2,50,000	₹2,25,000	
Variable overheads (₹3,60,000 – ₹1,80,000)	1,80,000	4,05,000
Factory cost		19,05,000
Add office expenses (₹1,20,000/₹2,00,000) × ₹2,50,000		1,50,000
Cost of production (2,50,000 units)		20,55,000
Add selling and distribution expenses:		
Fixed (₹1,50,000/₹2,00,000) × ₹2,50,000	1,87,500	
Variable (₹2,40,000 – ₹1,50,000)	90,000	2,77,500
Cost of sales		23,32,500
Profit (Loss)		(82,500)
Sales revenue (2,50,000 × ₹9)		22,50,000

Reconciliation Statement: Cost and Financial Profits

Particulars	*Plus items*	*Minus items*
Loss as per cost books		₹82,500
Add factory expenses over-absorbed in cost books (₹4,05,000 – ₹3,60,000)	₹45,000	
Add office expenses over-absorbed in cost books (₹1,50,000 – ₹1,20,000)	30,000	
Add selling and distribution expenses over-absorbed in cost books (₹2,77,500 – ₹2,40,000)	37,500	
	1,12,500	82,500
Profit as per financial books	30,000	

P.13.4 From the following data prepare reconciliation statement:

Profit as per cost accounts	₹1,45,500
Works overheads under-recovered	9,500
Administrative overheads under-recovered	22,750
Selling overheads over-recovered	19,500
Overvaluation of opening stock in cost accounts	15,000
Overvaluation of closing stock in cost accounts	7,500
Interest earned during the year	3,750
Rent received during the year	27,000
Bad debts written off during the year	9,000
Preliminary expenses written off during the year	18,000

Solution

Reconciliation Statement

Particulars	*Plus items*	*Minus items*
Profit as per cost account	₹1,45,500	
Add: Over-recovery of selling overheads	19,500	
Overvaluation of opening stock	15,000	
Income excluded from cost accounts		
—Interest earned	3,750	
—Rent received	27,000	
Less: Under-recoverey of work overheads		9,500
Under-recovery of administrative overheads		22,750
Over-valuation of closing stock		7,500
Expenses excluded from cost accounts		
—Bad debts		9,000
—Preliminary expenses		18,000
	2,10,750	66,750
Profit as per financial accounts		1,44,000

P.13.5 During the year, a company's profits have been estimated by the costing system to be ₹23,063, whereas final accounts prepared by the auditors disclose profits of ₹16,624. Given the following information, you are required to prepare a reconciliation statement showing clearly the reasons for the difference.

Profit and Loss Account for the Year Ended March 31.

To opening stock	₹2,47,179		By sales	₹3,46,500
Add purchases	82,154			
	3,29,333			
Less closing stock	(75,121)	₹2,54,212		
To direct wages		23,133		
To factory expenses		20,826		
To gross profit c/d		48,329		
		3,46,500		3,46,500
To administration expenditure		9,845	Gross profit b/d	48,329
To selling expenses		22,176	By sundry income	316
To net profit		16,624		
		48,645		48,645

The costing records show:

(i) A stock ledger closing balance of ₹78,197.
(ii) A direct wage absorption account with a closing balance of ₹24,867.
(iii) A factory overheads absorption account with a closing balance of ₹19,714.
(iv) Administrative expenses calculated at 3 per cent of the selling price.
(v) Selling prices include 5 per cent for selling expenses.
(vi) No mention of sundry income.

SOLUTION

Reconciliation Statement; Cost and Financial Profits (Cost Book Profit as Base)

Particulars	*Plus items*	*Minus items*
Profit as per cost books	₹23,063	
Less closing stock over-valued in cost books (₹78,197 – ₹75,121)		₹3,076
Add wages over-absorbed in cost books (₹24,867 – ₹23,133)	1,734	
Less factory overheads under-absorbed in cost books (₹20,826 – ₹19,714)		1,112
Add administration expenses over-observed in cost books (₹10,395 – ₹9,845)	550	
Less selling expenses under-absorbed in cost books (₹22,176 – ₹17,325)		4,851
Add sundry income not credited in cost books	316	
	25,663	9,039
Profit as per financial books		16,624

P.13.6 Small Company Limited furnishes the following summary of trading and profit and loss account for the current quarter ending March 31.

To raw materials	₹1,39,600	By sales (12,000 units)		₹4,80,000
To direct wages	76,200	By finished stock (200 units)		8,000
To production overheads	42,600	By work-in-process		
To selling and distribution overheads	42,700	Materials	₹28,200	
To administration overheads	39,100	Wages	11,796	
To preliminary expenses written off	2,200	Production overheads	7,999	47,995
To goodwill written off	2,501	By interest on securities (gross)		6,000
To dividend (net)	3,000			
To income-tax	4,100			
To net profit	1,89,994			
	5,41,995			5,41,995

The company manufactures a standard unit. The scrutiny of cost records for the same period shows that—

(i) Factory overheads have been allocated to production at 20 per cent on prime cost.
(ii) Administration overheads have been charged at ₹3 per unit on units produced.
(iii) Selling and distribution expenses have been charged at ₹4 per unit on units sold.

You are required to prepare a statement of cost, to work out profit as per cost accounts, and to reconcile the same with that shown in the financial accounts.

SOLUTION

Statement of Costs and Profit for the Quarter Ended March 31

Particulars		Amount
Materials consumed		₹1,39,600
Direct wages		76,200
Prime cost		2,15,800
Add factory overheads @ 20 per cent of prime cost		43,160
Gross works cost		2,58,960
Less closing work-in-process inventory:		
Materials	₹28,200	
Wages	11,796	
Production overheads	7,999	47,995
Works cost (Net)		2,10,965
Add administrative overheads (12,200 units × ₹3)		36,600
Cost of production(12,200 units @ ₹20.29 per unit)		2,47,565
Less closing stock (200 units × ₹20.29)		4,058
Cost of goods sold		2,43,507
Add selling and distribution overheads@ ₹4 per unit (12,000 × ₹4)		48,000
Cost of sales		2,91,507
Profit (balancing figure)		1,88,493
Sales (12,000 units × ₹40)		4,80,000

Assumptions

1. Work-in-process is assumed to have been valued on financial books basis. It is logical, too, as the work-in-process is valued at factory cost as per costing principles.
2. Finished goods have been valued at the total cost of production. This has been done because the cost records shown that administration overheads have been charged @ ₹3 per unit on units produced.

Reconciliation Statement: Cost and Financial Profits (Cost Books Profit as Basis)

Particulars		Plus items	Minus items
Profit as per cost books		₹1,88,493	
Add production overheads over-absorbed in cost records (₹43,160 – ₹42,600)		560	
Less administration overheads under-absorbed in cost records (₹39,100 – ₹36,600)			₹2,500
Add selling overheads over-absorbed in cost records (₹48,000 – ₹42,700)		5,300	
Add closing stock under-valued in cost records (₹8,000 – ₹4,058)		3,942	
Less expenses not recorded in cost books:			
Preliminary expenses written-off	₹2,200		
Goodwill written-off	2,501		
Dividend (net)	3,000		
Income tax	4,100		11,801

(Contd.)

(*Contd.*)

Add interest on securities not recorded as revenue income in cost books	6,000	
	2,04,295	14,301
Profit as per financial profit and loss account		1,89,994

P.13.7 From the following information provided by Royal Associates, prepare financial profit and loss account and reconciliation statement.

Statement of Costs and Profit for the Current Year

Raw materials consumed:		
Opening inventory	₹59,000	
Add purchases	3,73,000	
Less closing inventory	(64,000)	₹3,68,000
Direct wages		5,96,000
Prime cost		9,64,000
Add works overheads		3,57,600
Less closing inventory of work-in-process		(25,600)
Factory cost		12,96,000
Add administration overheads		2,16,000
Cost of production (9,000 units)		15,12,000
Less closing stock of finished goods (1,400 units)		(2,35,200)
Cost of goods sold (7,600 units)		12,76,800
Add selling overheads (0.20 × total sales)		3,64,800
Cost of sales		16,41,600
Profit		1,82,400
Sales		18,24,000

Additional information:

1. Bad debts not charged in cost books	₹35,000
2. Work overheads under-absorbed in cost books	23,900
3. Administration overheads under-absorbed in cost books	29,000
4. Interest received on investments	13,600
5. Selling and distribution overheads over-recovered	36,800
6. There is a uniform basis of valuing work-in-process and finished goods inventory in both financial and cost books	

Solution

Trading and Profit and Loss Account for the Current Year Ending

Particulars		*Dr Amount*	*Particulars*	*Cr Amount*
To opening stock of raw materials	₹59,000		By sales	₹18,24,000
Add purchases	3,73,000		By closing inventory	
Less closing inventory	(64,000)	₹3,68,000	Work-in-process	25,600
To direct wages		5,96,000	Finished goods	2,35,200
To work overheads (₹3,57,600 + ₹23,900)		3,81,500		
To gross profit c/d		7,39,300		
		20,84,800		20,84,800

(*Contd.*)

(*Contd.*)

To administration expenses (₹2,16,000 + ₹29,000)	2,45,000	By gross profit	7,39,300
		By interest on investment	13,600
To selling and distribution expenses (₹3,64,800 – ₹36,800)	3,28,000		
To bad debts written-off	35,000		
To net profit	1,44,900		
	7,52,900		7,52,900

Reconciliation Statement: Cost and Financial Profits (Cost Books Profit as Base)

Particulars	*Plus items*	*Minus items*
Profit as per cost records	₹1,82,400	
Less works overheads under-absorbed in cost books		₹23,900
Less administrative overheads under-absorbed in cost books		29,000
Add selling and distribution overheads over-recovered in cost books	36,800	
Less bad debts not charged in cost books		35,000
Add interest on investment not credited in cost books	13,600	
	2,32,800	87,900
Profit as per financial books		1,44,900

P.13.8 Trading and profit and loss account of XY (P) Ltd for the year ending March 31 (as prepared by the head office accounts department) is summarised as follows:

To stock, April 1	₹60,000	By sales	₹1,30,000
To purchases	82,000	By stock, March, 31	80,000
To wages	40,000		
To works expenses	1,800		
To gross profit c/d	26,200		
	2,10,000		2,10,000
To salaries	8,000	By gross profit b/d	26,200
To rent and rates	4,000	By rent received	6,000
To selling expenses	5,600	By dividend (gross)	20,000
To administration expenses	4,200		
To profit	30,400		
	52,200		52,200

The following information was also supplied:

Particulars	*April 1*	*March 31*
1. *Stock:*		
Manufactured units	₹24,000	₹20,000
Purchased units	14,000	44,000
Raw materials	22,000	16,000
	60,000	80,000
2. *Purchases:*		
Purchased units	54,000	
Raw materials	28,000	
	82,000	
3. *Wages:*		
Direct wages	30,000	
Indirect wages	8,000	
Clerical wages (sales)	2,000	
	40,000	

(*Contd.*)

(*Contd.*)

4. *Salaries:*	
Works supervision	2,200
Sales department	4,000
Administration	1,800
	8,000
5. *Rent and rates:*	
Works	2,000
Sales office	400
Let property	1,600
	4,000

Other particulars:

1. Purchased units 3,000 and manufactured units 10,000 were sold at the rate of ₹10 each.
2. Units purchased at ₹8 each. Units produced by the company were valued at ₹8 each.
3. Administration expenditure—two-third to be charged to works supervision and one-third to sales supervision.
4. Dividend was on trade investments.

You are required to prepare a costing profit and loss account for the year ending March 31 for submission to the higher management. Also prepare cost and financial profit reconciliation.

Solution

Costing Profit and Loss Account for the Year Ending March 31

Particulars		*Dr Amount*	*Particulars*	*Cr Amount*
To direct materials consumed:			By prime cost c/d	₹64,000
Opening stock	₹22,000			
Add purchases	28,000			
Less closing stock	(16,000)	₹34,000		
To wages (direct)		30,000		
		64,000		64,000
To prime cost b/d		64,000	By factory cost b/d	80,800
To factory overheads:				
Works expenses	₹1,800			
Indirect wages	8,000			
Salaries	2,200			
Rent and rates	2,000			
Administrative expenses	2,800	16,800		
		80,800		80,800
To factory cost b/d		80,800	By cost of production c/d	82,600
To *administrative overheads:*				
Salaries		1,800		
		82,600		82,600
To cost of production b/d		82,600		
To *opening stock:*			*By closing stock:*	
Manufactured units	₹24,000		Manufactured units	20,000
Purchased units	14,000	38,000	Purchased units	44,000
To purchases (from outside)		54,000	By cost of goods sold c/d	1,10,600
		1,74,600		1,74,600
To cost of goods sold b/d		1,10,600	By sales	1,30,000
To clerical wages (sales)		2,000		
To salaries (sales department)		4,000		

(*Contd.*)

To rent and rates (sales)	400		
To selling expenses	5,600		
To administrative expenses (1/3 × ₹4,200)	1,400		
To profit and loss A/c	6,000		
	1,30,000		1,30,000

Reconciliation Statement: Cost and Financial Profits (cost records profits as base)

Particulars		*Plus items*	*Minus items*
Profit as per cost books		₹6,000	
Add income not credited in cost books:			
Rent received	₹6,000		
Dividends (gross)	20,000	26,000	
Less expenses not charged in cost books:			
Rent and rates for property let out		32,000	₹1,600
Profits as per financial books			1,600
			30,400

P.13.9 From the following profit and loss account, draw up a memorandum reconciliation account.

Profit and Loss Account for the Year Ending

Particulars	*Amount*	*Particulars*	*Amount*
To office salaries	₹11,282	By gross profit	₹54,648
To office expenses	6,514	By dividend received	400
To salesmen's salaries	4,922	By interest on bank deposits	150
To sales expenses	9,304		
To distribution expenses	2,990		
To loss on sale of machinery	1,950		
To fines	200		
To discount on debentures	100		
To net profit	17,936		
	55,198		55,198
To income tax	8,000	By net profit	17,936
To reserve	1,000		
To dividend	4,000		
To balance c/d	4,936		
	17,936		17,936

The cost accountant of the company has ascertained a profit of ₹19,636 as per his books

SOLUTION

Memorandum Reconciliation Account

Particulars		*Particulars*	
To revenue transactions not Included in cost books:		By profit as per financial books	₹4,936
Dividend received	₹400	*By expenses transactions not included in cost books:*	
Interest on bank deposit	150	Loss on sale of machinery	1,950
To profit as per cost books	19,636	Fines	200
		Discount on debentures	100
		Income tax	8,000
		Reserve	1,000
		Dividends	4,000
	20,186		20,186

P.13.10 The following balances appeared on February 28 in the books of a company which has an integral system accounting.

Particulars	*Dr*	*Cr*
Capital and reserves		₹6,00,000
Creditors and accruals		1,76,000
Fixed assets	₹2,80,000	
Raw materials in store and process	1,60,000	
Direct wages in process	40,000	
Factory overheads in process (at standard cost)	20,000	
Finished stock	1,80,000	
Debtors	2,00,000	
Cash at bank	20,000	
Budgeted sales		11,70,000
Sales variances	24,000	
Standard factory cost of sales	9,86,000	
Material variance		10,000
Direct wages variance	14,000	
Factory overhead variance	4,000	
Administration and selling expenses	28,000	
	19,56,000	19,56,000

The following transactions took place during March:

1. Budgeted sales	₹2,10,000
2. Actual sales	1,96,000
3. Cash received from debtors	1,90,000
4. Cash paid to creditors	1,26,000
5. Cash paid (direct wages)	46,000
6. Raw materials purchased (actual cost)	80,000
7. Excess materials issued (at standard cost)	2,000
8. Factory expenses incurred	34,000
9. Administration and selling expenses incurred	6,000
10. Output finished (at standard cost):	
Materials	1,00,000
Direct wages	52,000
Factory overheads	26,000
11. Standard factory cost of actual sales	1,64,000
12. Standard cost of materials purchased	84,000
13. Closing valuation of work-in-process accounts (which are debited at actual and credited at standard):	
Direct wages (at standard)	30,000
Factory overheads (at standard)	26,000

You are required to (a) pass journal entries, (b) prepare ledger accounts, (c) prepare profit and loss for the period ending March 31 and balance sheet as on that date.

SOLUTION

(a) *Journal Entries (for March)*

Particulars		*Dr Amount*	*Cr Amount*
Sales ledger control A/c	...Dr	₹1,96,000	
Sales variance A/c	...Dr	14,000	
To budgeted sales A/c			₹2,10,000
(Being the amounts of actual sales and sales variance recorded)			
Bank A/c	...Dr	1,90,000	
To sales ledger control A/c			1,90,000
(Being the receipts from debtors recorded)			
Bought ledger control A/c	...Dr	1,26,000	
To bank			1,26,000
(Being payment made to creditors)			
Wages control A/c	...Dr	46,000	
To bank			46,000
(Being wages paid to direct labourers)			
Stores ledger control A/c	...Dr	84,000	
To bought ledger control A/c			80,000
To material variances A/c			4,000
(Being raw materials and material variances recorded)			
Finished stock ledger control A/c	...Dr	1,00,000	
Material variance A/c	...Dr	2,000	
To stores ledger control A/c			1,02,000
(Being raw materials issued at standard cost and variances recorded)			
Factory overheads control A/c	...Dr	34,000	
To bank			34,000
(Being factory overheads paid)			
Administrative and selling overheads control A/c	...Dr	6,000	
To bank			6,000
(Being administration and selling overheads paid)			
Finished stock ledger control A/c	...Dr	52,000	
Wages variance A/c	...Dr	4,000	
To wages control A/c			56,000
(Being wages charged to finished goods and variance of ₹4,000, that is, ₹56,000 – 52,000 recorded)			
Finished stock ledger control A/c	...Dr	26,000	
Factory overhead variance A/c	...Dr	2,000	
To wages control A/c			28,000
(Being factory overheads charged to production and unfavourable variance of ₹2,000 i.e., ₹20,000 + 34,000 – ₹26,000 – 26,000 recorded)			
Cost of sales A/c	...Dr	1,64,000	
To finished stock ledger control A/C			1,64,000
(Being standard cost of sales recorded)			

(*Contd.*)

(*Contd.*)

Profit and loss A/c	...Dr	12,46,000	
To cost of sales A/c			11,50,000
To sales variance A/c			38,000
To wages variance A/c			18,000
To factory overhead variance A/c			6,000
To administration and selling overhead control A/c			34,000
(Being various nominal accounts closed by transferring to profit and loss account)			
Budgeted sales A/c	...Dr	13,80,000	
Materials variance A/c	...Dr	12,000	
To profit and loss A/c			13,92,000
(Being budgeted sales and material variance favourable transferred to profit and loss A/c)			
Profit and loss A/c	...Dr	1,46,000	
To capital and reserve A/c			1,46,000
(Being profit transferred to capital and reserve)			

(b) *Ledger Accounts*

Sales Ledger Control or Debtors A/c

Particulars	*Amount*	*Particulars*	*Amount*
To balance b/d	₹2,00,000	By bank	₹1,90,000
To budgeted sales A/c	1,96,000	By balance c/d	2,06,000
	3,96,000		3,96,000
To balance b/d	2,06,000		

Sales Variance A/c

To balance b/d	₹24,000	By profit and loss A/c (transferred)	₹38,000
To budgeted sales A/c	14,000		
	38,000		38,000

Budgeted Sales A/c

To profit and loss A/c (transferred)	₹13,80,000	By balance b/d	₹11,70,000
		By sales ledger control A/c	1,96,000
		By sales variance A/c	14,000
	13,80,000		13,80,000

Bought Ledger Control or Creditors and Accruals A/c

To bank	₹1,26,000	By balance b/d	₹1,76,000
To balance c/d	1,30,000	By stores ledger control A/c	80,000
	2,56,000		2,56,000
		By balance b/d	1,30,000

Wages Control or Direct Wages in Process A/c

To balance b/d	₹40,000	By finished goods ledger control A/c	₹52,000
To bank	46,000	By wages variance A/c	4,000
		By balance c/d	30,000
	86,000		86,000

Stores Ledger Control or Raw Materials in Stores and Spares A/c

To balance b/d	₹1,60,000	By finished stock ledger control A/c	₹1,00,000
To bought ledger control A/c	80,000	By material variance A/c	2,000
To material variance A/c	4,000	By balance c/d	1,42,000
	2,44,000		2,44,000
To balance b/d	1,42,000		

Material Variance A/c

To stores ledger control A/c	₹2,000	By balance b/d	₹10,000
To profit and loss A/c (transfer)	12,000	By stores ledger control A/c	4,000
	14,000		14,000

Finished Stock Ledger Control A/c

To balance b/d	₹1,80,000	By cost of sales A/c	₹1,64,000
To stores ledger control A/c	1,00,000	By balance c/d	1,94,000
To wages control A/c	52,000		
To factory overhead A/c	26,000		
	3,58,000		3,58,000
To balance b/d	1,94,000		

Factory Overhead Control or in Process A/c

To balance b/d	₹20,000	By finished stock ledger control A/c	₹26,000
To bank	34,000	By factory overhead variance A/c	2,000
		By balance c/d	26,000
	54,000		54,000
To balance b/d	26,000		

Administration and Selling Overhead Control A/c

To balance b/d	₹28,000	By profit and loss A/c (transfer)	₹34,000
To wages control A/c	6,000		
	34,000		34,000

Direct Wages Variance A/c

To balance b/d	₹14,000	By profit and loss A/c (transfer)	₹18,000
To wages control A/c	4,000		
	18,000		18,000

Factory Overhead Variance A/c

To balance b/d	₹4,000	By profit and loss A/c (transfer)	₹6,000
To factory overhead A/c	2,000		
	6,000		6,000

Cost of Sales A/c

To balance b/d	₹9,86,000	By profit and loss A/c(transfer)	₹11,50,000
To finished stock ledger control A/c	1,64,000		
	11,50,000		11,50,000

Bank A/c

To balance b/d	₹20,000	By bought ledger control A/c	₹1,26,000
To sales ledger control A/c	1,90,000	By wages control A/c	46,000
To balance c/d	2,000	By factory overheads control A/c	34,000
		By administration & selling overheads control A/c	6,000
	2,12,000		2,12,000
		By balance b/d (overdraft)	2,000

Profit and Loss A/c (for the period ending March 31)

To cost of sales A/c	₹11,50,000	By budgeted sales A/c	₹13,80,000
To sales variance A/c	38,000	By materials variance A/c	12,000
To wages variance A/c	18,000		
To factory overhead variance A/c	6,000		
To administration and selling overheads control A/c	34,000		
To net profit (current year)	1,46,000		
	13,92,000		13,92,000

Capital and Reserves A/c

To balance c/d	₹7,46,000	By balance b/d	₹6,00,000
		By profit and loss A/c (current year's profits)	1,46,000
	7,46,000		7,46,000
		By balance b/d	7,46,000

Fixed Assets A/c

To balance b/d	₹2,80,000	By balance c/d	₹2,80,000
	2,80,000		2,80,000
To balance b/d	2,80,000		

Balance Sheet as on March 31

Liabilities	*Amount*	*Assets*	*Amount*
Capital and reserves	₹7,46,000	Fixed assets	₹2,80,000
Creditors and accruals	1,30,000	Finished stock	1,94,000
Bank overdraft	2,000	Materials in process	1,42,000
		Wages in process	30,000
		Factory overheads in process	26,000
		Debtors	2,06,000
	8,78,000		8,78,000

EXERCISES

13.1 Indicate whether the following statements are true or false:

(i) Profit (Loss) as per cost books is the identical sum shown by financial accounts.

(ii) It is normal for the two systems of accounting (financial and cost) maintained by a manufacturing firm to exhibit varying operating results.

(iii) It is necessary to have profit (loss) as per cost records as the starting point to prepare reconciliation statement to reconcile profits (loss) with financial accounts.

(iv) It is necessary to have profit (loss) as per financial accounts as the starting point to prepare reconciliation statement to reconcile profit (loss) as per cost records.

(v) Reconciliation statement can be prepared by taking profit (loss) shown by either cost or financial records as the starting point.

(vi) Overheads under-absorbed in cost books cause decrease in profits (increase in losses) in cost books compared to financial books.

(vii) Under-valuation of closing inventories cause cost profits to decrease compared to financial books.

(viii) Reconciliation statement is not required when only one set of books is maintained to serve both financial and cost purposes.

(ix) Integrated accounts entail more costs compared to maintaining sets of cost and financial records.

(x) Integrated system of accounts is more economical compared to maintenance of cost as well as financial records.

(**Answers:** **(i)** False, **(ii)** True, **(iii)** False, **(iv)** False, **(v)** True, **(vi)** False, **(vii)** True, **(viii)** True, **(ix)** False, **(x)** True)

13.2(a) Why is it necessary to reconcile cost and financial accounts?

13.2(b) A manufacturing firm prepares profit and loss account in cost books as well as in financial books. But the profits shown by the two books do not agree. Explain the reasons for the difference in profits as per the two sets of books. Would you recommend the reconciliation of the two profits? If yes, why?

13.3 At the end of an accounting period, it is found that the profit shown by the financial accounts falls considerably short of the profits according to the cost accounts. Indicate how the discrepancy may have arisen.

13.4 Mention major items of expenses or income, which will appear in financial accounts but will not normally appear in cost accounts.

13.5 What do you understand by integrated accounts? State the advantages of integrated accounts. State in brief the procedure of installing such a system in a newly started manufacturing firm.

13.6 From the following particulars prepare: (a) A statement of cost of manufacturing for the year ended; (b) A statement of profit as per cost accounts; (c) Profit and loss account in the financial books; and (d) Show to what you would attribute the difference in the profit as shown by (b) and (c).

Opening stock	₹1,44,000
Opening stock of finished articles	2,88,000
Purchase of raw materials	8,64,000
Stock of raw materials at the end	2,16,000
Stock of finished articles at the end	72,000
Wages	3,60,000

Calculating factory oncost at 20 per cent on prime cost; office overheads at 80 per cent on factory on cost; actual works expenses amounted to ₹2,27,150 and actual office expenses amounted to ₹1,85,950. The selling price was fixed at 20 per cent above the cost price.

13.7 A company's trading and profit and loss account was as follows:

To purchases	₹25,210	By sales (50,000 units	
Less closing stock	4,080	@ ₹1.50 each)	₹75,000
	21,130	By discount received	260
To direct wages	10,500	By profit on sale of land	2,340
To works expenses	12,130		
To selling expenses	7,100		

(Contd.)

(Contd.)

To administration expenses	5,340	
To depreciation	1,100	
To net profit	20,300	
	77,600	77,600

The profit as per cost accounts was only ₹19,770. Reconcile the financial and cost profits using the following information:

1. Cost accounts valued closing stock at ₹4,280.
2. The work expenses in the cost accounts were taken at 100 per cent of direct wages.
3. Selling and administrative expenses were charged in the cost accounts at 10 per cent of sales and ₹0.10 per unit respectively.
4. Depreciation in the cost accounts was ₹800.

13.8 From the accounts of Shanker and Company Ltd, manufacturing, trading and profit and loss accounts are reproduced below:

Particulars	*Dr Amount*	*Particulars*	*Cr Amount*
To raw materials:		*By work-in-process:*	
Opening stock	₹29,500	Material	₹4,000
Purchases	1,86,500	Wages	5,500
To wages	2,98,000	Works expenses	3,300
To works expenses	1,90,750	By cost of goods manufactured	6,59,950
		By closing stock of raw materials	32,000
	7,04,750		7,04,750
To cost of goods sold	6,59,950	By sales (7,600 units)	9,12,000
To administrative expenses	1,22,500	By finished stock (1,400 units)	1,17,600
To selling and distribution expenses	1,64,000	By interest on investments	6,800
To bad debts written-off	17,500		
To net profit (transferred to appropriation account)	72,450		
	10,36,400		10,36,400

The following information is also available:

1. Accrued wages of ₹17,000 included in wages.
2. Works expenses are allocated to production at 60 per cent of direct labour cost.
3. Administrative expenses are allocated at ₹12 per unit of production.
4. Selling and distribution expenses are allocated so as to work out at 20 per cent of selling price.

Prepare a costing profit and loss account and statement of reconciliation between the two accounts (cost and financial).

13.9 From the following summary trading and profit and loss account, which appears in the financial accounts of S.M. Industries Limited, and the additional information given, you are required to prepare a detailed statement reconciling the profit of ₹3,02,850 as disclosed by the financial accounts with the figure of ₹2,74,625 shown by the cost books.

Summary Trading Profit/Loss Account for the Year Ended March 31, current year

Particulars		*Dr Amount*	*Particulars*	*Cr Amount*
To opening stock	₹25,000		By sales revenue	₹15,75,000
Add purchases	6,75,000			
	7,00,000			

(Contd.)

(*Contd.*)

Less closing stock	(42,500)	₹6,57,500		
To direct wages		2,12,500		
To factory overheads:				
Indirect wages	₹12,300			
Heat and power	34,200			
Miscellaneous	6,000			
Depreciation	61,000	1,13,500		
To gross profit c/d		5,91,500		
		15,75,000		15,75,000
To selling expenses:				
Advertising	₹45,000		By gross profit b/d	5,91,500
Salaries	95,000			
Bad debts	4,000		By dividend income	18,750
Sundry	27,100	1,71,100		
To administration expenses:				
Salaries	₹82,000			
Printing and stationary	15,000			
Audit fee	2,000			
General	9,950			
		1,08,950		
To financial expenses:				
Debenture interest	₹20,000			
Bank interest	3,000			
Hire purchase interest	4,350	27,350		
To net profit		3,02,850		
		6,10,250		6,10,250

Additional information:

1. In the cost accounts (a) works overhead, excluding depreciation, is charged at a rate of ₹0.25 per unit produced; (b) selling overhead is charged at a rate of 12 per cent of sales turnover; (c) administration expenses are charged at a fixed sum of ₹1,25,000 per annum. Included in this is an allowance of ₹15,000 to cover all financial income and expenditure.
2. Depreciation in the financial accounts is calculated on a straight line basis but in the cost accounts there is a fixed annual charge equivalent to half of the straight line calculation plus a running charge of ₹0.125 per unit produced.
3. The company owns the business premises but in the cost accounts, in addition to the items mentioned above, there is a notional charge of ₹2,500 per annum for rent.
4. Items of a non-revenue nature are not included in the cost accounts.
5. In the cost accounts, stock is valued at direct cost (material and labour) but in the financial accounts it includes an allowance for overhead.
6. Opening stock consists of 5,000 units valued as:

Materials	₹15,500
Labour	5,500
Overheads	4,000
	25,000

Closing stock consists of 8,000 units valued as:

Materials	₹26,500
Labour	8,500
Overheads	7,500
	42,500

Sales were 2,10,000 units @ ₹7.50 per unit.

13.10 Prepare the under-noted statements, from the particulars given below:

1. Statement of cost of manufacture and percentage of each items of cost to total cost, calculating factory overheads at 25 per cent of prime cost, and office overhead at 75 per cent of factory overheads.
2. Statement of profit as per cost accounts.
3. Profit and loss account.
4. A reconciliation statement.

Opening stock:	
Raw materials	₹8,000
Finished articles	16,000
Purchase of raw materials	48,000
Wages	20,000
Office expenses	12,200
Works expenses	15,500
Sales	1,30,000
Closing stock:	
Raw materials	12,000
Finished articles	4,000

Profit is fixed at 20 per cent on selling price.

13.11 A radio manufacturing company, which commended business on April 1, supplies you with the following information and asks you to prepare a statement showing the profit per radio sold. Wages and materials are to be charged at actual cost, works expenses at 75 per cent on wages and office expenses at 30 per cent on works cost. You are also required to prepare a statement reconciling the profit as shown by the cost accounts with the profit as shown by the profit and loss account for the current year.

There were no radio sets in stock or in course of manufacture on March 31, and the number of radio sets sold during the year was 540. The particulars given are as under:

Materials per set	₹240
Wages per set	80
Selling price per set	600

Prepare the necessary statement showing the actual profit for the year, if the works expenses were ₹32,160 and the office expenses, ₹61,800.

13.12 From the following particulars, pass the journal entries in an integrated accounting system:

1. Issued materials, ₹3,00,000 of which ₹2,80,000 (standard, ₹2,40,000) is direct material.
2. Net wages paid, ₹70,000, deductions being ₹12,000 (standard, ₹75,000)
3. Gross salaries payable for the period are ₹26,000 (standard, ₹25,000), deductions, ₹2,000.
4. Sales (credit), ₹8,00,000.
5. Discount allowed, ₹5,000.
6. Salaries and wage allocation: ₹60,000 direct (standard, ₹62,000) and out of the balance 50 per cent production, 30 per cent administration and 20 per cent selling and distribution overheads.

13.13 Journalise the following transactions assuming that the cost and financial records are integrated:

Raw materials purchased	₹2,00,000
Direct materials issued to production	1,50,000
Wages paid (30 per cent indirect)	1,20,000
Wages charged to production	95,000
Manufacturing expenses incurred	84,000
Manufacturing overhead charged to production	92,000
Selling and distribution costs	20,000

(Contd.)

(Contd.)

Finished product (at cost)	2,00,000
Sales	2,90,000
Closing stock	Nil
Receipts from debtors	69,000
Payment to creditors	1,10,000

13.14 At the beginning of the current financial year, the following list of balances was extracted from the integrated accounts of a manufacturing company.

Debtors	₹1,80,000
Creditors	1,15,000
Cash	54,000
Fixed assets at cost	3,50,000
Raw materials at standard	85,000
Finished goods at standard	50,000
Work-in-process at standard	90,000
Depreciation-fixed assets	95,000
Investments	20,000
Ordinary share capital	5,00,000
Profit and loss—credit balance	1,19,000

The following information relates to transactions in the first quarter of the current financial year.

Particulars	*Actual*	*Standard*
Direct wages	₹22,000	₹21,000
Materials issued to production at standard prices	36,500	35,000
Purchase of raw materials, on credit	41,500	40,000
Factory overheads including indirect wages and ₹400, depreciation	20,100	
Factory overheads absorbed at 95 per cent normal capacity		19,000
Administration, selling and distribution expenses	13,000	
Sales on credit	97,600	1,00,000 (budgeted)

The cash transactions are as follows

Payments: Net wages, ₹26,500 (after subtracting ₹3,500)
Creditors, ₹70,000

Receipts: Debtors, ₹1,00,000

Overhead expenses (except wages) should be regarded as credit transactions.

At the end of the quarter, the following balances have been calculated on the basis of standard costs:

Work-in-process	₹95,000
Finished goods	48,000

Wages earned during the quarter have been paid.

The following adverse variances have been calculated and, along with the other variances to be ascertained, are to be charged against profit:

Overhead expenditure	₹100
Sales price	1,400
Labour rate	1,200

You are required to:

(a) Record the above information in integral form in the books of the company.

(b) Prepare for presentation to management the integral (i) profit and loss account for the quarter, and (ii) balance sheet at the end of the quarter.

13.15 From the following information write up the control accounts in the general ledger of a factory where cost and financial account are integrated and prepare a trial balance as on March 31 of the current year.

Ledger Balances as on April 1, Previous Year:

Share capital	₹1,50,000
Reserves	37,500
Sundry debtors	30,000
Plant and machinery	1,87,500
Sundry creditors	45,000
Bank (overdraft)	60,000
Raw materials	75,000

Transactions during the Year:

Raw material purchases	₹1,20,000
Raw material issued to production departments	1,50,000
Raw materials on hand (March 31)	39,000
Direct wages incurred	1,42,500
Direct wages charged to production	1,39,500
Production overhead incurred	1,31,250
Production overhead charged to production	1,39,500
Selling and distribution overhead	15,000
Finished stock (production at cost)	2,86,500
Finished stock (sales at selling price)	4,29,000
Payment to creditors	1,27,500
Receipts from debtors	4,50,000

ANSWERS

13.6 Profit as per cost book, ₹3,56,544; Profit as per financial books, ₹3,58,164.

13.7 Reconciliation statement will be prepared taking either of the profits (financial or cost) as the base.

13.8 Profit as per cost books, ₹91,200.

13.9 Reconciliation statement will be prepared taking either of the profits (financial or cost) as the base.

13.10 (a) ₹92,000 (47.83 per cent, 21.7 per cent, 17.4 per cent, 13 per cent);
(b) ₹26,000;
(c) ₹26,300.

13.11 Profit per radio ₹106; Actual profit, ₹57,240.

13.12 Journal entries are to be recorded

13.13 Various journal entries regarding purchase of raw materials, payment of wages, manufacturing expenses, and so on are to be recorded.

13.14 (i)Net profit, ₹7,500;
(ii)Balance sheet total, ₹7,37,000.

13.15 Sales ledger control account, bought ledger control account, stores ledger control account, finished stock ledger control account, factory overhead control account, administration and selling overhead control, and so on. are to be prepared.

14 Chapter

Volume-Cost-Profit Analysis

Learning Objectives

1. Explain break-even point and illustrate its determination both algebraically and graphically
2. Discuss break-even applications in determining sales to produce desired profits, additional sales volume to offset a reduction in selling price and so on
3. Understand cash break-even point and its applications.

INTRODUCTION

Profit planning is a function of the selling price of a unit of product, the variable cost of making and selling the product, the volume of product units sold, and, in the case of multi-product companies, sales-mix and, finally, the total fixed costs. The **volume-cost-profit (VCP) analysis** is a management accounting tool to show the relationship between these ingredients of profit planning. The entire gamut of profit planning is associated with VCP inter-relationships. A widely-used technique to study VCP relationships is break-even analysis.

Volume-cost-profit analysis shows the relationship among the various ingredients of profit planning, namely, unit sale price, variable cost, sales volume, sales mix and fixed cost.

A break-even analysis is concerned with the study of revenues and costs in relation to sales volume and, particularly, the determination of that volume of sales at which the firm's revenues and total costs will be exactly equal (or net income = zero). Thus, the break-even point (**BEP**) may be defined as a point at which the firm's total revenues are exactly equal to total costs, yielding zero income. The "no-profit, no-loss" point is a break-even point or a point at which losses cease and profits begin.

Break-even analysis, as a technique, seeks to provide answers to the following questions:

1. What sales volume is necessary to produce an *X* amount of operating profit?
2. What will the operating profit or loss at *X* sales volume be?
3. What profit will result from an *X* per cent increase in sales volume?
4. What is the additional sales volume required to make good an *X* per cent reduction in selling prices so as to maintain the current profit level?

5. What will the effect on operating profit be if the company's fixed costs have increased?
6. What will the effect on income be if the firm achieves a reduction in variable costs (say, material or direct labour)?
7. What is the required sales volume to cover the additional fixed charges from the proposed new project?
8. What will the effect on operating profit of the firm be if the sales mix is changed?
9. What will the effect on income be if there is an increase in fixed costs by an *X* amount due to new plant but will decrease the labour costs by *Y* amount per unit?
10. What sales volume is needed to achieve the budgeted profit?

BREAK-EVEN ANALYSIS

Break-even point is the sales volume at which revenue equals cost (i.e. no profit no loss).

A break-even analysis shows the relationship between the costs and profits with sales volume. The sales volume which equates total revenue with related costs and results in neither profit nor loss is called the **break-even volume or point (BEP)**. If all costs are assumed to be variable with sales volume, the BEP would be at zero sales. If all costs were fixed, profits would vary disproportionately with sales and the BEP would be at a point where total sales revenue equalled fixed costs. However, both are purely hypothetical situations. In actual practice, costs consist of both fixed and variable elements.

The BEP can be determined by two methods:

1. Algebraic methods: **(a)** Contribution margin approach and **(b)** Equation technique, and
2. Graphic presentation: **(a)** Break-even chart and **(b)** Profit volume graph.

Algebraic Methods

Contribution margin is the excess of unit sale price over unit variable cost.

Contribution Margin Approach The logic underlying the determination of the BEP under this approach can be stated by answering the following question: "How many ice-creams, having a unit cost of ₹20 and a selling price of ₹30, must a vendor sell in a fair to recover the ₹8,000 fees paid by him for getting a selling stall and additional cost of ₹4,000 to install the stall?" The answer can be determined dividing the fixed cost by the difference between the selling price (₹30) and cost price (₹20). Thus,

$$\text{BEP (units)} = \frac{\text{Fixed cost (Entry fees + Stall expenses)}}{\text{(Sales price − Unit variable cost)}} \qquad \textbf{(14.1)}$$

(₹8,000 + ₹4,000)/(₹30 – ₹20) = 1,200 units

Or,

$$\text{BEP (units)} = \frac{\text{Fixed costs}}{\text{Contribution margin } (CM) \text{ per unit}} \qquad \textbf{(14.2)}$$

Or,

BEP (amount)/BEP (Sales revenue)/*BESR* = BEP (units) × Selling price (*SP*) per unit
= 1,200 × ₹30 = ₹36,000 **(14.3)**

Or,

$$\text{BEP (amount)} = \frac{\text{Fixed costs}}{\text{Profit volume ratio (P/V ratio)}} \qquad \textbf{(14.4)}$$

$$\text{P/V ratio}^1 = \frac{\text{Contribution margin per unit}}{\text{Selling price per unit}} \quad (14.5)$$

$$\frac{₹1}{₹3} = \text{or } 33.33 \text{ per cent}$$

$$\text{BEP (amount)} = ₹12{,}000 \div 0.3333 = ₹36{,}000$$

From the P/V ratio, the variable cost to volume ratio (*V/V* ratio) can be easily derived:

$$V/V \text{ ratio} = 1 - \text{P/V ratio} \quad (14.6)$$

In the vendor's case, it is = 1–1/3 = 2/3 = 66.67 per cent

The *V/V* ratio, as the name suggests, establishes the relationship between variable costs (VC) and sales volume in amount. The direct method of its computation is:

$$\frac{\text{Variable cost}}{\text{Sales revenue}} = ₹20 \div ₹30 = 66.67 \text{ per cent} \quad (14.7)$$

Thus, P/V ratio + *V/V* ratio = 1 or 100 per cent

$$(1/3 + 2/3) = 1 \text{ (33.33 per cent + 66.67 per cent)} = 100 \text{ per cent} \quad (14.8)$$

Margin of Safety The excess of the actual sales revenue (ASR) over the break-even sales revenue (*BESR*) is known as the **margin of safety**. Symbolically, margin of safety = (ASR – BESR) **(14.9)**

Margin of safety is the excess of actual sales revenue over the break-even sales revenue.

When the margin of safety (amount) is divided by the actual sales (amount), the margin of safety ratio (*M/S* ratio) is obtained. Symbolically,

$$M/S \text{ ratio} = \frac{(\text{ASR} - \text{BESR})}{\text{ASR}} \quad (14.10)$$

The *M/S* ratio indicates the percentage by which the actual sales may be reduced before they fall below the break-even sales volume. It is important that there should be a reasonable margin of safety, lest a reduced level of activity should prove disastrous. The higher the margin of safety ratio, the better it is from the point of view of the company as it indicates that a "sizeable" sales volume can fall before the BEP is reached. This measure acquires special significance in depression/recession.

Assume in the vendor's case that sales is 2,000 units (₹60,000); margin of safety (₹60,000 – ₹36,000) = ₹24,000; and the *M/S* ratio is ₹24,000 ÷ ₹60,000 = 40 per cent.

The amount of profit can be directly determined with reference to the margin of safety and P/V ratio. Symbolically,

$$\text{Profit} = [\text{Margin of safety (amount)}] \times \text{P/V ratio} \quad (14.11)$$

$$\text{Or Profit} = [\text{Margin of safety (units)} \times CM \text{ per unit}] \quad (14.12)$$

In the vendor's case, profit = ₹24,000 × 0.3333 (33.33 per cent) = ₹8,000 or 800 × ₹10 = ₹8,000.

The reason is that once the total amount of fixed costs has been recovered, profits will increase by the difference of sales revenue and variable costs.

[1]A better term would be contribution to revenue ratio (*C/V*) as the numerator is the contribution margin (difference between the selling price and variable costs) and not profit. The *P/V* ratio in a strict sense of the term represents the relationship between profi and selling price only after the BEP, that is, when fixed costs have been recovered. Therefore, the *C/V* ratio is more appropriate term. In the text, both the terms have been used.

Equation Technique This is the most general form of analysis, which can be applied to any cost-volume-profit situation. It is based on an income equation: Sales revenue-Total costs = Net profit

Breaking up total costs into fixed and variable, Sales revenue – Fixed costs – Variable costs = Net profit. Or Sales revenue = Fixed costs + Variable costs + Net profit.

If *S* be the number of units required for break-even and sales revenue (*SP*) and variable costs (VC) are on per unit basis, the above equation can be written as follows:

$$SP\,(S) = \text{FC} + \text{VC}\,(S) + NI \quad \textbf{(14.13)}$$

Where SP = Selling price per unit

S = Number of units required to be sold to break-even

FC = Total fixed costs

VC = Variable costs per unit

NI = Net income (zero)

$$SP\,(S) = \text{FC} + \text{VC}\,(S) + \text{zero}$$

$$SP\,(S) - \text{VC}\,(S) = \text{FC}$$

or

$$S\,(SP - \text{VC}) = \text{FC}$$

$$S = \frac{\text{FC}}{SP - \text{VC}} \quad \textbf{(14.14)}$$

It can be seen that Eq. 14.14 is identical to Eq. 14.2 (contribution margin approach). Yet, it is *specially useful in situations in which unit price and unit variable costs are not clearly identifiable.*

Example 14.1

SV Ltd, a multi-product company, furnishes you the following data relating to the current year:

Particulars	*First half of the year*	*Second half of the year*
Sales	₹45,000	₹50,000
Total costs	40,000	43,000

Assuming that there is no change in prices and variable costs and that the fixed expenses are incurred equally in the two half-year periods, calculate for the year: (i) The profit-volume ratio, (ii) Fixed expenses, (iii) Break-even sales, and (iv) Percentage margin of safety.

Solution

Sales revenue – Total costs = Net profit

₹45,000 – ₹40,000 = ₹5,000 (first half)

₹50,000 – ₹43,000 = ₹7,000 (second half)

On a differential basis: Δ Sales revenue, ₹5,000 – Δ Total costs, ₹3,000 = Δ Total profit, ₹2,000

We know that only VC changes with a change in sales volume and, hence, change in total costs are equivalent to VC (₹3,000). Accordingly, the additional sales of ₹5,000 has earned a contribution margin of ₹2,000 [₹5,000 (*S*) – ₹3,000 (VC)].

P/V ratio = ₹2,000 ÷ ₹5,000 = 40 per cent

V/V ratio = 100 per cent – 40 per cent = 60 per cent

Accordingly, 60 per cent of the total costs are made up of variable costs and the balance represents the total fixed costs (FC).

Sales revenue = Fixed costs + Variable costs + Net profit

₹95,000 = FC + 0.60 × (₹95,000) + ₹12,000

₹95,000 = FC + ₹57,000 + ₹12,000

₹95,000 – ₹69,000 = FC or ₹26,000 = FC

BEP (amount) = ₹26,000 ÷ 0.40 = ₹65,000

Table 14.1 Verification

Particulars	Amount	Per cent
Break-even sales	₹65,000	100
Variable costs	39,000	60
Contribution	26,000	40
Fixed costs	26,000	40
Net income	Nil	Nil

$$M/S \text{ ratio} = \frac{(₹95{,}000 - ₹65{,}000)}{₹95{,}000} = 31.58 \text{ per cent}$$

Break-Even Analysis Applications

Sales Volume Required to Produce Desired Operating Profit One application of a BE analysis is to determine the required sales volume to generate a budgeted amount of profit. The required sales are given by Eq. 14.15.

$$(\text{Fixed expenses} + \text{Desired operating profit}) \div \text{P/V ratio} \qquad \textbf{(14.15)}$$

In Example 14.1, if the desired operating profit of *SV* Ltd is ₹13,000, required sales volume = (₹26,000 + ₹13,000)/0.40 = ₹97,500

A variant of the above approach is that the management may be interested in knowing the required sales volume to produce the desired profit after taxes. In this case, the analysis must be expanded slightly. Assume that *SV* Ltd wants a net income after taxes of ₹13,000 and that its current tax rate is 35 per cent, the net income after taxes is 65 per cent of the net income before taxes.

$$\text{Required sales volume} = \frac{\text{Fixed costs} + \left[\dfrac{\text{Desired income after taxes}}{1 - \text{tax rate}}\right]}{P/V \text{ ratio}} \qquad \textbf{(14.16)}$$

$$= \frac{₹\,26{,}000 + \left[\dfrac{₹\,13{,}000}{1 - 0.35}\right]}{0.40} = ₹\,1{,}15{,}000$$

Table 14.2 Verification

Sales volume	₹1,15,000
Less: Variable costs (0.60)	69,000
Contribution	46,000
Less: Fixed costs	26,000
Profits before taxes	20,000
Less: Taxes (0.35)	7,000
Profit after taxes	13,000

Operating Profit at a Given Level of Sales Volume [Actual Sales Revenue (ASR) – Break-even Sales Revenue (BESR)] × P/V ratio **(14.17)**

Effect on Operating Profit of a Given Increase in Sales Volume [Budgeted Sales Revenue (*BSR*) – BESR] × P/V ratio **(14.18)**

Suppose that *SV* Ltd forecasts 10 per cent increase in sales next year, the projected profit will be:

$$(₹1{,}04{,}500 - ₹65{,}000) \times 0.40 = ₹15{,}800$$

Additional Sales Volume Required to Offset a Reduction in Selling Price The sales manager on the basis of a market research/survey may report to the management that due to increased competition in the market and the liberal import policy of the government, the present price is relatively higher. He may advise reduction in prices to stay in competition.

Suppose that *SV* Ltd reduces its selling price from ₹10 a unit to ₹9. The sales volume needed to offset reduced selling price/maintain a present operating profit of ₹12,000 would be:

$$= \frac{\text{Desired profit } (P) + \text{Fixed expenses } (FC)}{\text{Revised } P/V \text{ ratio } (₹3/₹9)} = ₹(12{,}000 + ₹26{,}000) \div 0.3333 = ₹1{,}14{,}000$$

The required sales volume of ₹1,14,000 represents an increase of about 20 per cent over the present level. The management should explore new avenues of sales potential to maintain the existing amount of profit.

On the other hand, if the firm has the opportunity to increase the unit selling price of the product, the impact of increased sales price would be that the BEP will be reached sooner because an increase in the selling price will raise the contribution margin, assuming no change in the variable costs. An increased contribution margin will decrease the sales volume necessary to reach a desired goals.

Assume that the management of *SV* Ltd increases the selling price of its product from ₹10 to ₹12, the desired sales volume would be: $\frac{FC + P}{\text{Revised } P/V \text{ ratio}} = ₹38{,}000 \div 0.50\ (₹6 \div ₹12) = ₹76{,}000$

Effect of Changes in Fixed Costs A firm may be confronted with the situation of increasing fixed costs. An increase in the total budgeted fixed costs of a firm may be necessitated either by external factors, such as, an increase in property taxes, insurance rates, factory rent, and so on, or by a managerial decision of an increase in salaries of executives. More important than this in the latter category are expansion of the present plant capacity so as to cope with additional demand. The increase in the requirements of fixed costs would imply the computation of the following:

(a) Relative break-even points
(b) Required sales volume to earn the present profits
(c) Required sales volume to earn the same rate of profit on the proposed expansion programme as on the existing ones.

The effect of the increased FC*s* will be to raise the BEP of the firm. Assume the management of *SV* Ltd decides a major expansion programme of its existing production capacity. It is estimated that it will result in extra fixed costs of ₹8,000 on advertisement to boost sales volume and another ₹16,000 on account of new plant facility.

(a) *The relative BEPs will be:*

Present facilities = Fixed costs ÷ P/V ratio = ₹26,000/0.40 = ₹65,000

Proposed facilities = (Present FC*s* + Additional FC*s*) ÷ *P/V* ratio **(14.19)**

= (₹26,000 + ₹24,000)/0.40 = ₹1,25,000

It may be noted that increase in FC*s* (from ₹26,000 to ₹50,000) has caused disproportionate increase in the BEP (from ₹65,000 to ₹1,25,000).

(b) *The required sales volume to earn the present profit:*

[Present FC*s* + Additional FC*s* + Present profit (*NI*)] ÷ *P/V* ratio **(14.20)**

= [₹26,000 + ₹24,000 + ₹12,000] ÷ 0.40 = ₹1,55,000

(c) *The required sales volume to earn the present rate of profit on investment:*

(Present FC*s* + Additional FC*s* + Present return on investment + Return on new investment) *P/V* ratio **(14.21)**

Let us assume that the present investment is ₹1,00,000 and the new investment will involve an additional financial outlay of ₹60,000. The required sales volume will be (₹26,000 + ₹24,000 + ₹12,000+ ₹7,200 (0.12 × ₹60,000)/0.40 = ₹1,73,000

These computations may be reported in a summary form to the management as follows (Table 14.3).

Table 14.3 Effect of Changes in Fixed Costs

Particulars	*Present facilities*	*Prospective facilities*	*Increase*
Fixed costs	₹26,000	₹50,000	₹24,000
BEP sales volume	65,000	1,25,000	60,000
BEP sales volume (units)	6,500	12,500	6,000
Sales volume to earn existing profit	95,000	1,55,000	60,000
Sales volume in units to earn existing profit	9,500	15,500	6,000
Sales volume to earn existing ROI	95,000	1,73,000	78,000
Sales volume to earn existing ROI (in units)	9,500	17,300	7,800

Effect of Changes in Variable Costs Assuming an increase of VC by ₹1 a unit for *SV* Ltd, the new contribution margin will be: ₹3 (₹10 – ₹7) and the revised P/V ratio 0.30 that is, (₹3 ÷ ₹10).
Revised BEP = (₹26,000)/0.30 = ₹86,667
Desired sales volume to earn existing profit = ₹38,000/0.30 = ₹1,26,667

Assuming that variable costs of *SV* Ltd decline by ₹1 per unit, revised BEP = ₹26,000/0.50 = ₹52,000.

Desired sales volume to maintain existing profit = ₹38,000/0.50 = ₹76,000.

Effects of Multiple Changes So far we have assumed that a change takes place in one of the three variable affecting profits—cost, price and sales volume. In cases where more than one factor is affected, the BEP *analysis* can be applied as shown below:

$$\frac{FC + FC\text{ (new)} + \left[\dfrac{\text{Desired } EAT}{1 - \text{tax rate}}\right]}{[\text{Contribution margin per unit (New } SP - \text{New } VC)] \div \text{New selling price (New } SP)} \qquad \textbf{(14.22)}$$

Assuming the following set of new Figures for *SV* Ltd:

Particulars	*Existing data*	*New data*
Selling price per unit	₹10	₹11
Fixed costs	26,000	40,000
Variable cost per unit	6	5.50
Contribution margin per unit	4	5.50
Desired earnings after taxes (to maintain the existing ROI)	12,000	25,000
Tax rate	35 per cent	

Solution

Desired sales volume (on the basis of new data) [₹26,000 + ₹14,000 + (₹25,000 ÷ 0.65)] ÷ 0.50, that is (₹5.5 ÷ ₹11) = (₹78,461.5) ÷ 0.50 = ₹1,56,923

Desired sales volume on the basis of existing data = [₹26,000 + (₹12,000 ÷ 0.65)] ÷ 0.40 (₹4 ÷ ₹10) = ₹44,462 ÷ 0.40 = ₹1,11,154.

VCP Analysis and a Segment of the Business The fundamental approach of applying the VCP analysis to a segment of the business is the same as applying it to the business as a whole. The VCP approach "may be applied to problems relative to individual product lines, territories, methods of sale, channels of distribution or any particular segment of the business which is under scrutiny"[2]. In all these decisions, fixed costs and P/V ratio are the required inputs. Where fixed costs are inclusive of allocated costs also, in additional to direct costs, two BEPs may be determined.

EXAMPLE 14.2

SV Ltd has four sales divisions. The relevant data for its northern division is reproduced below:
Direct fixed costs, ₹10,000
P/V ratio, 0.40
Allocated fixed costs from head office, ₹5,000

The sales volume required to cover direct expenses would be: Direct fixed costs/ P/V ratio

$$= ₹10,000/0.40 = ₹25,000 \quad \textbf{(14.23)}$$

The total sales volume required to cover all fixed costs would be higher as shown by equation 14.24:

$$\frac{\text{Direct FCs + Allocated FCs}}{\text{P/V ratio}} \quad \textbf{(14.24)}$$

$$= (₹10,000 + ₹5,000) \div 0.40 = ₹37,500$$

Multi-product Firms (Sales-mix) So far, we have confined our discussion to a one-product company. However, many manufacturers make more than one type of product. The relative proportion of each product sold in the aggregate sales is known as the sales-mix. A change in the mix of products sold usually affects the weighted average P/V ratio and, hence, the BEP. Thus, when the products have different P/V ratios, changes in the sales-mix/product-mix will affect the BEP and the results from operation.

EXAMPLE 14.3

The Garware Paints Ltd presents to you the following income statement in a condensed form for the first quarter ending March 31:

Particulars	*Product*			*Total*
	X	*Y*	*Z*	
Sales	₹1,00,000	₹60,000	₹40,000	₹2,00,000
Variable costs	80,000	42,000	24,000	1,46,000
Contribution	20,000	18,000	16,000	54,000
Fixed costs				27,000
Net income				27,000
P/V ratio	0.20	0.30	0.40	0.27
Break-even sales				1,00,000
Sales-mix (per cent)	0.50	0.30	0.20	100

If ₹40,000 of the sales shown for Product *X* could be shifted equally to products *Y* and *Z*, the profit and the BEP would change as shown in Table 14.4.

Table 14.4 Break-even Point

Particulars	*Product*			*Total*
	X	*Y*	*Z*	
Sales	₹60,000	₹80,000	₹60,000	₹2,00,000
Less: Variable costs	48,000	56,000	36,000	1,40,000
Contribution	12,000	24,000	24,000	60,000
Less: Fixed costs				27,000
Net income				33,000
P/V ratio	0.20	0.30	0.40	0.30
BE sales				90,000
Sales-mix (per cent)	0.30	0.40	0.30	100

Example 14.3 shows that by increasing the mix of high P/V products (*Y* from 30 to 40 per cent, *Z* from 20 to 30 per cent) and decreasing the mix of a low P/V product (*X* from 50 to 30 per cent), the company can increase its overall profitability. In fact, it can further augment its total profits, if it can make, and the market can absorb, more quantities of *Y* and *Z*, say ₹1 lakh each (Table 14.5).

Table 14.5

Particulars	Product		Total
	Y	Z	
Sales	₹1,00,000	₹1,00,000	₹2,00,000
Less: Variable costs	70,000	60,000	1,30,000
Contribution	30,000	40,000	70,000
Less: Fixed costs			27,000
Net income			43,000
P/V ratio	0.30	0.40	0.35
BE sales			77,143
Sales-mix (per cent)	0.50	0.50	100

From the above, it can be generalised that, other things being equal, management should stress products with higher contribution margins. For individual product line income statements, fixed costs should not be allocated or apportioned.

Finally, it may be stressed that there is a need for a closer study of cost structures of individual product line/department within the same firm or of two different companies. It may be possible that the two departments/companies may have the same profits but very different cost structures. For instance, observe the Figures in Table 14.6 of two departments of *SV* Ltd.

Table 14.6

Particulars	Department X		Department Y	
	Amount	Per cent	Amount	Per cent
Sales revenue	₹1,00,000	(100)	₹1,00,000	(100)
Less: Variable costs	70,000	(70)	20,000	(20)
Contribution / P/V ratio	30,000	(30)	80,000	(80)
Less: Fixed costs	20,000		70,000	
Profit	10,000		10,000	
BEP (amount)	66,667		87,500	
Margin of safety (MS)	33,333		12,500	
Margin of safety ratio	0.3333		0.125	

Department *Y* is operating closer to the BEP than Department *X*. Department *Y* has a narrower margin of safety (12.5 per cent) compared to 33.33 per cent of *X*. The margin of safety ratio signifies that if the sales of *Y* decreases by more than 12.5 per cent, it will operate at a loss. In other words, the margin/cushion of safety is relatively smaller. *X* will not operate at a loss unless its sales volume drops by more than 33.33 per cent.

This type of profit analysis for two different companies is of special significance from the point of view of outside investor who want to invest in one of the two companies. Assuming companies *X* and *Y* in place of the departments *X* and *Y* in the above tabulation, Company *X* is certainly less risky than Company *Y*.

Graphic Presentation

Under the algebraic technique of break-even analysis, separate computations were needed to arrive at the above set of figures. The utility of the graphical technique is that such a set of figures can be determined without involving any separate calculations.

Break-Even Chart/Volume Cost Profit (VCP) Graph The **break even chart** is a graphic relationship between volume, costs and profits. It shows not only the BEP but also the effects of costs and revenue at varying levels of sales. The break-even chart can, therefore, be more appropriately called the volume-cost-profit graph (VCP graph).

Assumptions Regarding the VCP Graph are

1. Costs can be bifurcated into variable and fixed components.
2. Fixed costs will remain constant during the relevant volume range of graph.
3. Variable cost per unit will remain constant during the relevant volume range of graph.
4. Selling price per unit will remain constant irrespective of the quantity sold within the relevant range of the graph.
5. In the case of multi-product companies, in addition to the above four assumptions, it is assumed that the sales-mix remains constant.
6. Finally, production and sales volumes are equal.

The VCP graph may be prepared in a simple or elaborate manner. Figure 14.1 is an example of a simple and traditional form. In Figure 14.1, sales are shown on the horizontal axis; the vertical axis measures costs and revenues corresponding to varying volume of sales. Sales are expressed in terms of units, rupees and percentage level of activity. The VCP relationships portrayed in such a graph are valid only within the relevant range that underlies the construction of the graph. The importance of a relevant range should be recognised because in practice most firms will progressively reduce fixed costs as the volume tends to decrease towards zero activity. Similarly, fixed costs are to be increased beyond a certain volume. Accordingly, in Figure 14.1 the lower limit and upper limit of the VCP have been drawn.

The BEP lies at the point of intersection of the sales line and the total cost line. The vertical distance between the sales revenue and the total cost line measures the estimated net income (after the BEP) and the estimated net loss (before the BEP) at the related sales volume. The fixed cost line is parallel to the horizontal axis. The variable cost line is superimposed on the fixed cost line and moves upward uniformly with sales volume at the variable cost to volume ratio. This is the total cost line. The sales revenue line starts from the point of origin and moves upward uniformly with volume. The meeting point of the total cost line and sales line is the BEP. At this point, an angle is formed known as the angle of incidence. The management objective should be to have an angle of as large a size as possible because a high angle is a sign of a high rate of profit after the fixed costs have been covered; the narrower angle will signify that profits after the fixed costs have been covered; the narrower angle will signify that profits will increase at a lower rate after the BEP, showing that variable costs form a large part of cost of sales. Figure 14.1 is based on the following data relating to Hypothetical Ltd (Example 14.4).

EXAMPLE 14.4

Selling price per unit		₹10
Fixed costs		60,000
Variable costs per unit		5
Relevant range (units) : Lower limit		6,000
: Upper limit		20,000
Break-up of variable costs per unit:		
Direct material	₹2	
Direct labour	1.50	
Direct expenses	1	
Selling expenses	0.50	
Actual sales, 18,000 units (₹1,80,000)		
Plant capacity, 20,000 units (₹2,00,000)		
Tax rate, 50 per cent		

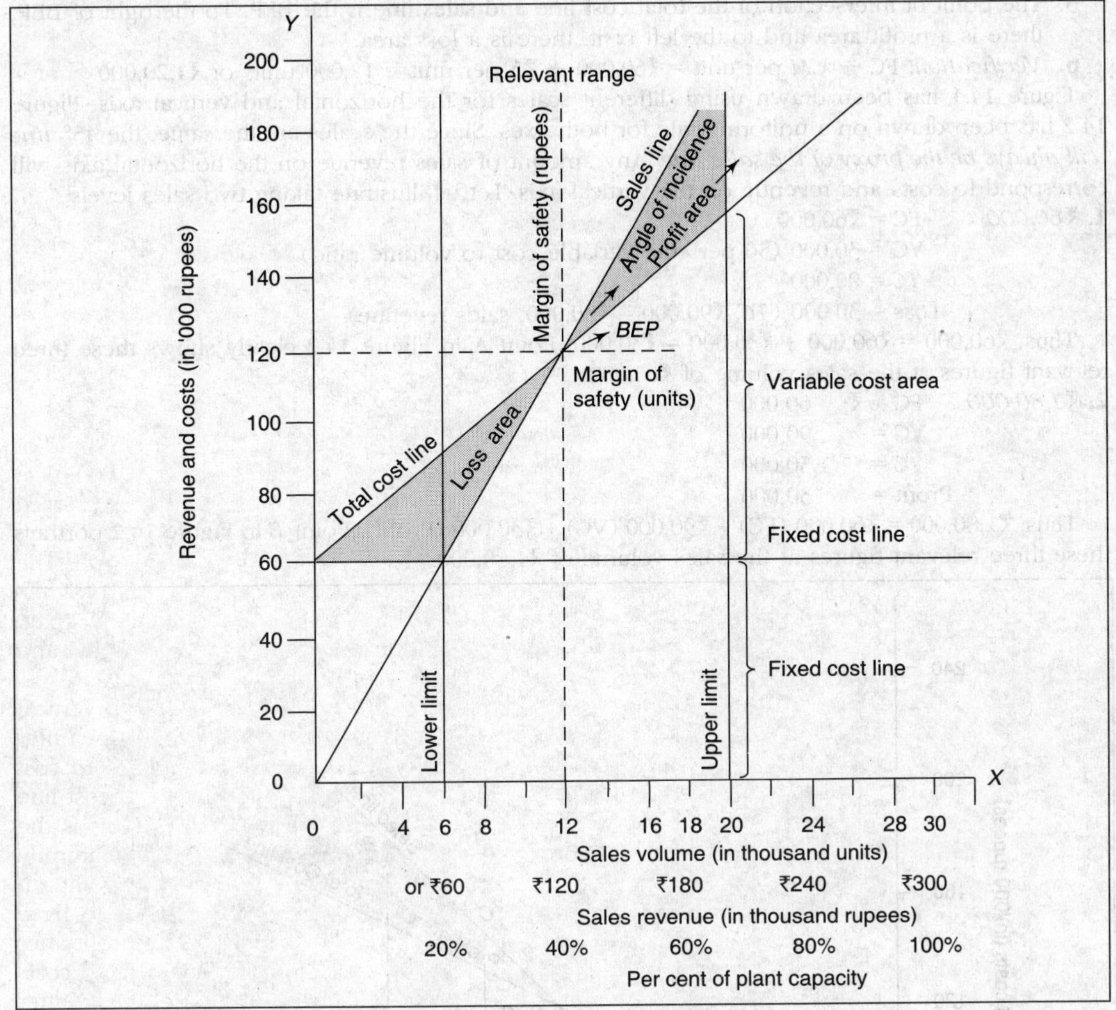

Figure 14.1 *Volume-Cost-Profit Graph, Different Scale*

Figure 14.1 has been drawn by using a sales line and a total cost line (including both fixed and variable costs). The steps involved in drawing the VCP graph are enumerated as follows:

1. Select an appropriate scale for sales volume on the horizontal axis, say, 2,000 units (₹20,000) per square, and plot the point for total sales revenues at relevant volume: 6,000 units × ₹10 = ₹60,000. Draw the sales line from the origin to ₹2,00,000 (the upper limit of the relevant range). Ensure that *all the points,* 0, ₹60,000 and ₹2,00,000 *fall in the same line.* This should be ensured for the total cost line also.
2. Select an appropriate scale for costs and sales revenues on the vertical axis, say, ₹10,000 per square. Draw the line showing ₹60,000 fixed cost parallel to the horizontal axis.
3. Determine the variable portion of costs at two volumes of scales (beginning and ending): 6,000 units × ₹5 = ₹30,000; 20,000 units × ₹5 = ₹1,00,000.
4. Variable costs are to be added to fixed costs (₹30,000 + ₹60,000 = ₹90,000). Plot the point at 6,000 units sales volume and ₹1,00,000 + ₹60,000 = ₹1,60,000. Point is to be plotted at 20,000 units sales volume. This obviously is the total cost line.

5. The point of intersection of the total cost line and sales line is the BEP. To the right of BEP, there is a profit area and to the left of it, there is a loss area.

6. *Verification*: FC ÷ *CM* per unit = ₹60,000 ÷ ₹5 per unit = 12,000 units or ₹1,20,000

Figure 14.1 has been drawn using different scales for the horizontal and vertical axis. Figure 14.2 has been drawn on a uniform scale for both axes. Since the scales are the same, the 45° *line will always be the proxy of the sales line.* Any amount of sales revenue on the horizontal axis will correspond to costs and revenue on the vertical axis. Let us illustrate taking two sales levels.

1. *₹60,000:*
FC = ₹60,000
VC = 30,000 (50 per cent variable cost to volume ratio)
TC = 90,000
Loss = 30,000 (*TC*, ₹90,000 – ₹30,000, sales revenue)

Thus, ₹60,000 = ₹60,000 + ₹30,000 – ₹30,000. Point A in Figure 14.2 clearly shows these three relevant figures at the sales volume of ₹60,000.

2. *₹1,80,000:*
FC = ₹ 60,000
VC = 90,000
TC = 1,50,000
Profit = 30,000

Thus, ₹1,80,000 = ₹60,000 (FC) + ₹90,000 (VC) + ₹30,000 (Profit). Point *B* in Figure 14.2 portrays these three relevant figures at the sales volume of ₹1,80,000.

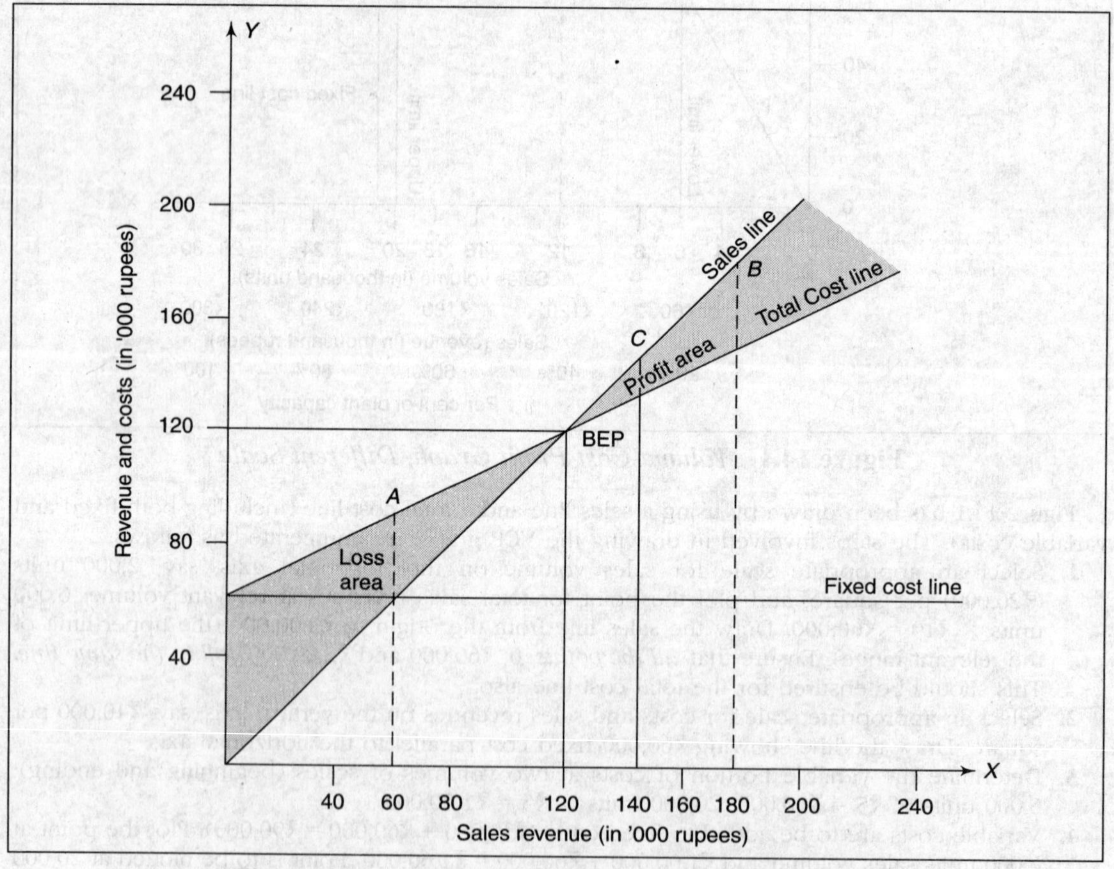

Figure 14.2 *Volume-Cost-Profit Graph, Same Scale*

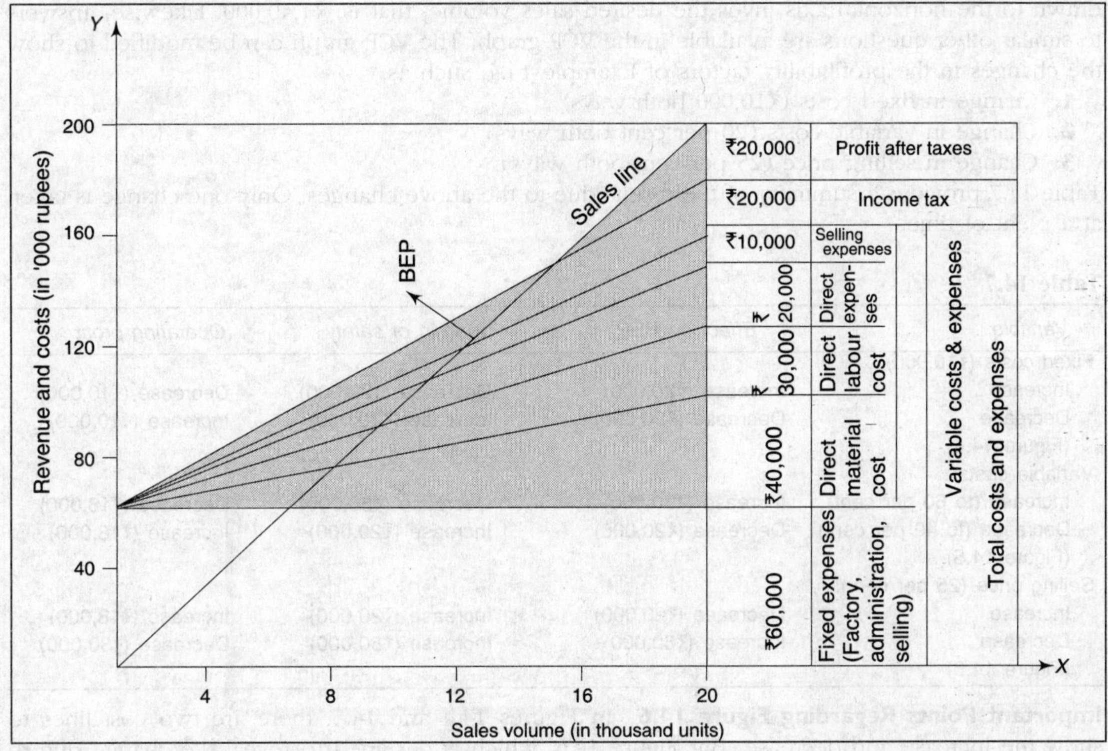

Figure 14.3 *Volume-Cost-Profit Graph, Cost-Wise*

The VCP graph in Figure 14.3 is drawn with the details of the individual segment of variable cost and is more informative. The steps involved in drawing the graph include an additional step of adding variable costs to the fixed cost. This is to be repeated four times for four different components: material, labour, direct expenses and selling expenses. In fact, fixed costs can also be further split-up into parts. Such a graph provides a bird's-eye view of the entire cost structure to the management. By drawing a line perpendicular from any volume (horizontal axis), the corresponding cost and profit variables can be ascertained on the vertical axis. For instance, at 20,000 unit level, following are the various cost figures, as shown by the VCP graph (line *A*).

Fixed costs	₹60,000
Variable costs:	
Material	40,000
Labour	30,000
Direct expenses	20,000
Selling expenses	10,000
Profit before taxes	40,000

VCP Applications Like the algebraic break-even applications, the VCP graph can also be applied to analyse the VCP relationship/profit planning. To illustrate, the company's management wants to know the sales volume, which will yield an operating profit of ₹10,000. As explained earlier, the vertical distance between the total cost line and the total sales line represents profit (one square is ₹10,000). At point *C*, one square distance is visible. Accordingly, from point C a perpendicular drawn to the horizontal axis gives the desired sales volume, that is, ₹1,40,000. Likewise, answers to similar other questions are available in the VCP graph. The VCP graph can be modified to show the changes in the profitability factors of Example 14.4, such as,

1. Change in fixed costs (₹10,000 both ways)
2. Change in variable costs (20 per cent both ways)
3. Change in selling price (25 per cent both ways).

Table 14.7 provides a summary of the results due to the above changes. Only one change is taken at a point of time.

Table 14.7

Variable	*Effect on BEP*	*Margin of safety*	*Operating profit*
Fixed costs (₹10,000):			
Increase	Increase (₹20,000)	Decrease (₹20,000)	Decrease (₹10,000)
Decrease	Decrease (₹20,000)	Increase (₹20,000)	Increase (₹10,000)
(Figure 14.4)			
Variable costs:			
Increase (to 60 per cent)	Increase (₹30,000)	Decrease (₹30,000)	Decrease (₹18,000)
Decrease (to 40 per cent)	Decrease (₹20,000)	Increase (₹20,000)	Increase (₹18,000)
(Figure 14.5)			
Selling price (25 per cent):			
Increase	Decrease (₹20,000)	Increase (₹20,000)	Increase (₹18,000)
Decrease	Increase (₹60,000)	Increase (₹60,000)	Decrease (₹30,000)
(Figure 14.6)			

Important Points Regarding Figure 14.6 In Figures 14.4 and 14.5, there are two cost lines to show the increase and decrease. But Figure 14.6, which is designed to reveal the change due to the selling price, has only one sales line (45°). The impact of change in the sales price is reflected indirectly in the variable cost line (which is merged with FC line and is represented by the total cost line). This is due to the fact that the *V/V* ratio which is an essential input for drawing the chart gets changed when the selling price is changed. In other words, Figure 14.6 is like Figure 14.5. The new *V/V* ratio has been determined as follows.

(i) When there is *an increase in selling price* by 25 per cent
Sales price (revised) = ₹5.50 (₹10 + 25 per cent) or 125 per cent (₹12.5 per unit)
Variable costs = ₹5 or 50 per cent (existing)
V/V Ratio = (₹5 ÷ ₹12.50) or (50 ÷ 125) or 40 per cent

(ii) When *there is a decrease in sales price* by 25 per cent
Sales price = ₹7.50 (₹10 – ₹2.50) or 75 per cent (₹7.5 per unit)
Variable costs = ₹5 or 50 pr cent (existing)
V/V Ratio = (₹5 ÷ ₹7.50) or (50 ÷ 75) or 66.67 per cent
Total cost line = ₹60,000 + 66.67 per cent sales

Since the *V/V* ratio assumes a fractional form, care has been taken to plot points at sales levels of ₹1,50,000 and ₹2,40,000 so that corresponding variable cost figures can be whole numbers, that is, ₹1,00,000 and ₹1,60,000 respectively.

Figure 14.7 portrays VCP relationships of a sales-mix for multi-product firm (Example 14.3).

The steps regarding the plotting of a sales line and fixed cost line are identical with those of a simple VCP graph concerning one product. An additional step pertains to the drawing of a variable cost line. For the purpose, the required input is the weighted average variable cost. In Example 14.3, it is 73 per cent (in an original sales mix of 5:3:2 for products *X*, *Y* and *Z* respectively). The figure 73 per cent is arrived at by deducting weighted P/V ratio from 100 (100 per cent–27 per cent, P/V ratio). For the revised sales-mix, it is 70 per cent (100 per cent–30 per cent).

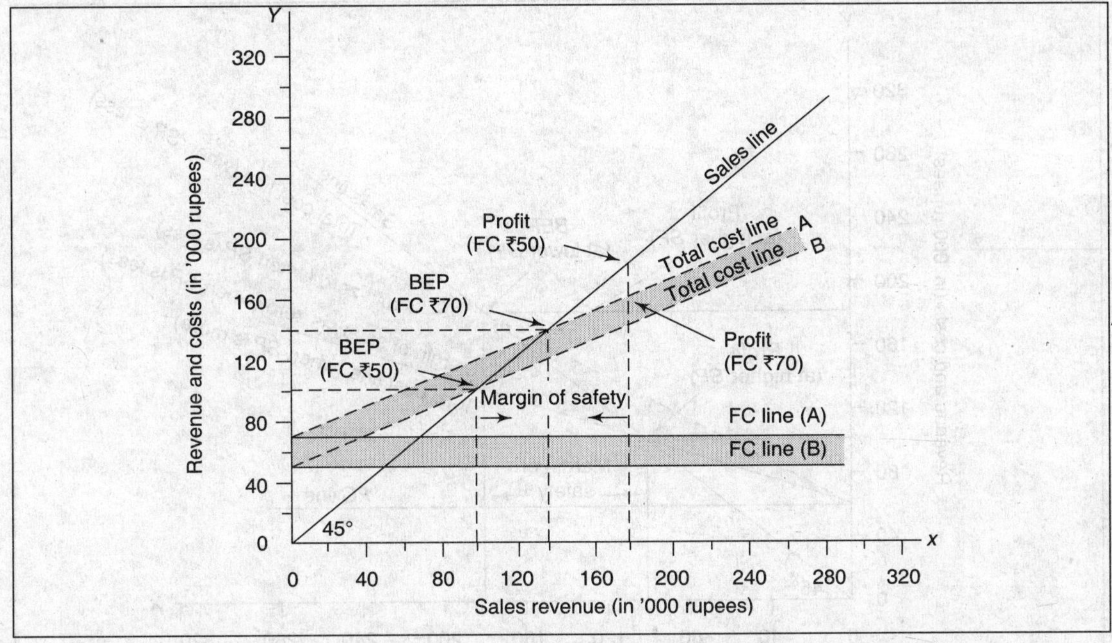

Figure 14.4 *Volume-Cost-Profit Graph, Change in Fixed Cost*

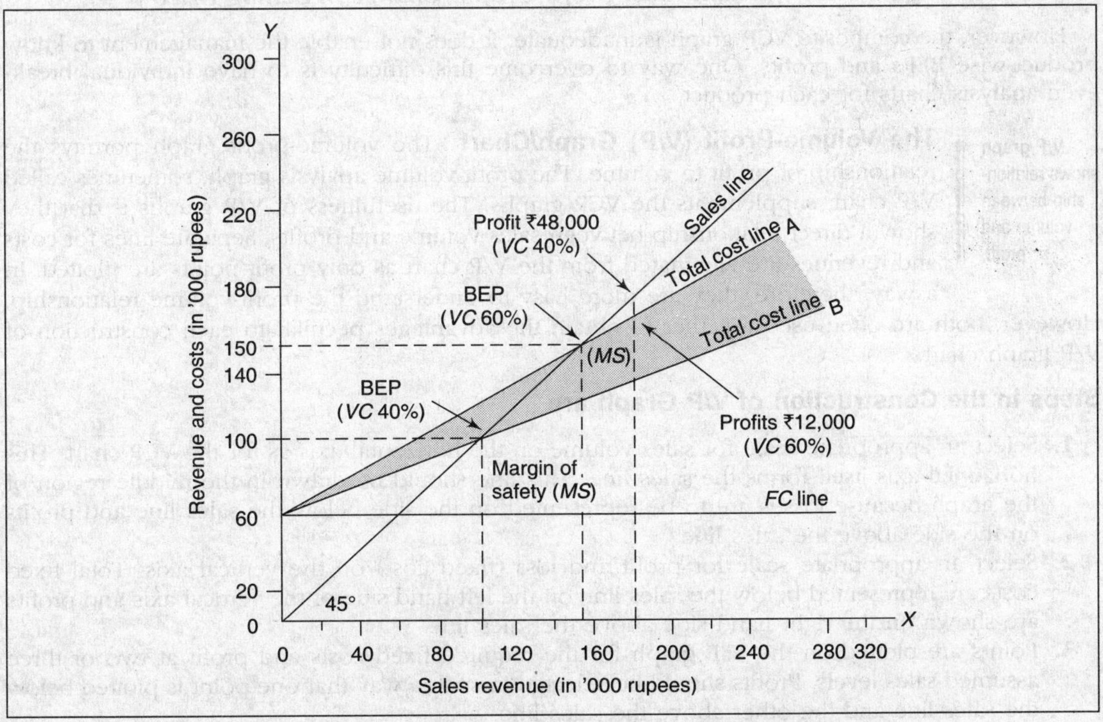

Figure 14.5 *Volume-Cost-Profit Graph, Change in Variable Cost*

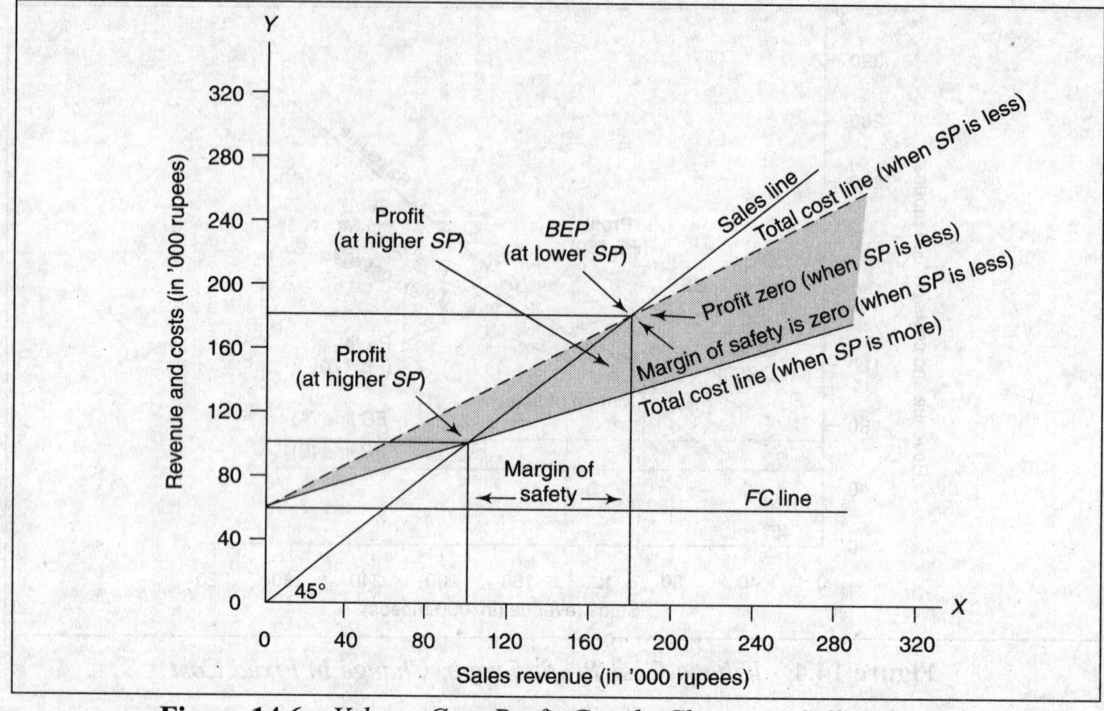

Figure 14.6 *Volume-Cost-Profit Graph, Change in Selling Price*

However, the composite VCP graph is inadequate, it does not enable the management to know product-wise BEPs and profits. One way to overcome this difficulty is to have individual break-even analysis charts for each product.

V/P graph shows relationship between volume and profit.

The Volume-Profit (V/P) Graph/Chart The volume-profit graph portrays the relationship of profit to volume. The profit-volume analysis graph, sometimes called V/P chart, supplements the VCP graphs. The usefulness of V/P graphs is that they show a direct relationship between sales volume and profits. Separate lines for costs and revenues are eliminated from the V/P chart as only profit points are plotted. In a way, therefore, they are more easy to understand the profit-volume relationship. However, both are often used together to obtain the advantages peculiar to each construction of V/P graph/chart.

Steps in the Construction of V/P Graph are

1. Select an appropriate scale for sales volume on the horizontal axis as for the VCP chart. This horizontal axis itself forms the sales line. This line should be drawn in the middle region of the graph because losses are to be represented on the side below the sales line and profits on the side above the sales line.
2. Select an appropriate scale for profit and loss (fixed cost) on the vertical axis. Total fixed costs are represented below the sales line on the left hand side of the vertical axis and profits are shown on the right hand side above the sales line.
3. Points are plotted on the V/P graph for the required fixed costs and profit at two or three assumed sales levels. Profits should be selected in such a way that one point is plotted below the sales line and the other above the sales line.

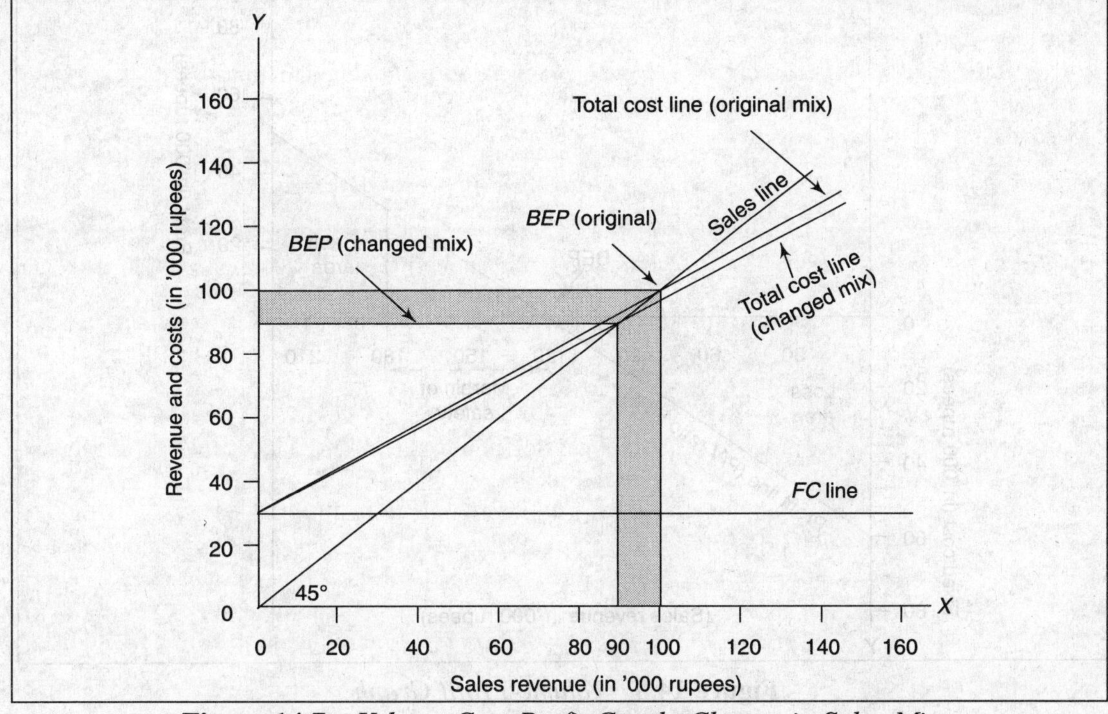

Figure 14.7 *Volume-Cost-Profit Graph, Change in Sales Mix*

4. Like the VCP graph, the origin of the curve (profit line) would be a point of total fixed cost (showing the entire amount as loss) at zero sales level.
5. Join the point of origin with two points developed as per step 3 by a diagonal line which crosses the sales line at the BEP.

Like the VCP graph, the V/P chart does not aim at projecting only the BEP. It contains a set of points where each point measures the quantum of profit/loss in relation to the sales volume. Using the figures of Example 14.4 (except the upper limit increased to 21,000 units), the V/P graph has been drawn in Figure 14.8. The chart visualises what changes will take place in the profit and loss pattern with changes in sales revenue.

For instance, let us suppose that the management for the next year projects a sales revenue of ₹2,10,000 (with no increase in fixed costs). The V/P chart readily shows that the amount of profit is ₹45,000, whereas in the VCP graph, the amount is to be determined.

Table 14.8 *Determination of Two Points for Figure 14.8 as per Step 3*

Particulars	*Point I*	*Point II*
Sales revenue	₹60,000	₹2,10,000
Less variable costs (0.50)	30,000	1,05,000
	30,000	1,05,000
Less fixed costs	60,000	60,000
Profit/(loss)	(30,000)	45,000

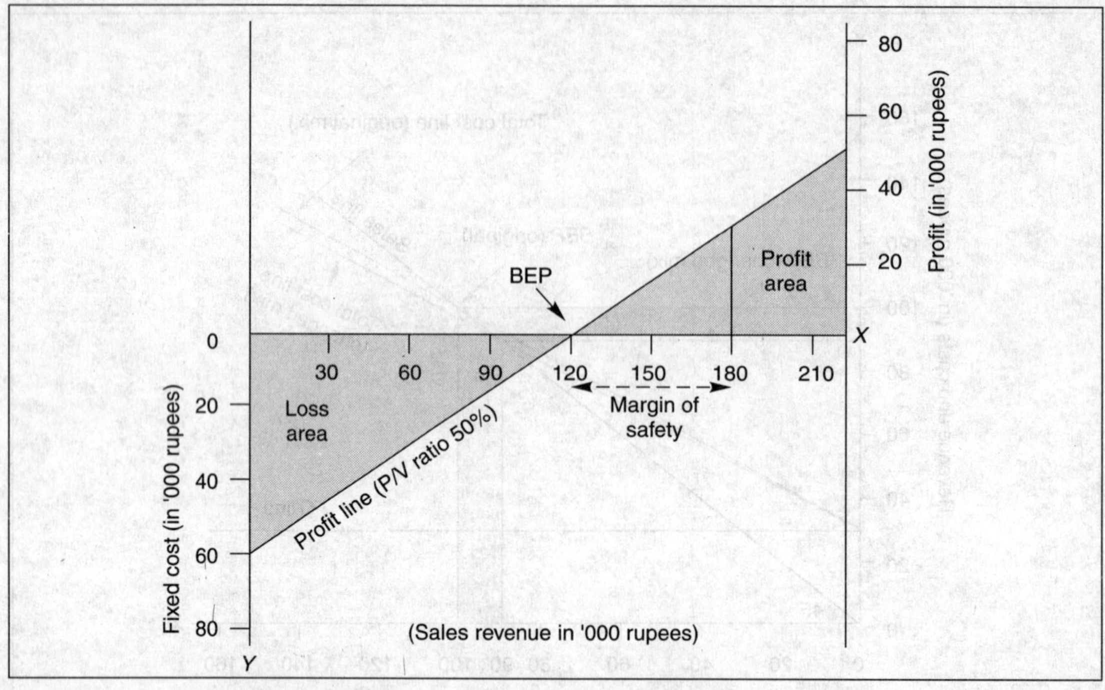

Figure 14.8 *Volume-Profit Graph*

Changes in Fixed Costs The proposed changes in FCs do not alter the P/V ratio. But they do affect both BEP and profits. An increase in the amount of FCs decreases profits above the BEP and increases losses below BEP; while the reverse holds true when there is a decrease in the amount of FCs.

In Example 14.4, with the proposed change of ₹10,000 (both ways) in fixed costs, the changes are summarised in Table 14.9.

Table 14.9 *Impact of Change in Fixed Costs on BEP, and Profit*

Particulars	*Fixed costs*		
	Increase (₹10,000)	*Original amount*	*Decrease (₹10,000)*
Sales revenue	₹1,80,000	₹1,80,000	₹1,80,000
Less variable costs	90,000	90,000	90,000
Contribution	90,000	90,000	90,000
Less fixed costs	70,000	60,000	50,000
Net income	20,000	30,000	40,000
Change in net income	(10,000)	N.A.	+ 10,000
BEP	1,40,000	1,20,000	1,00,000
Change in BEP	+ 20,000	N.A.	(20,000)
Margin of safety	40,000	60,000	80,000
Change in margin of safety	(20,000)	N.A.	+20,000
P/V ratio (per cent)	50	50	50

All the changes in Table 14.9 are clearly portrayed in Figure 14.9. Since the P/V ratio remains unchanged, the slope of the profit lines in Figure 14.9 remains the same. The only point of differ-

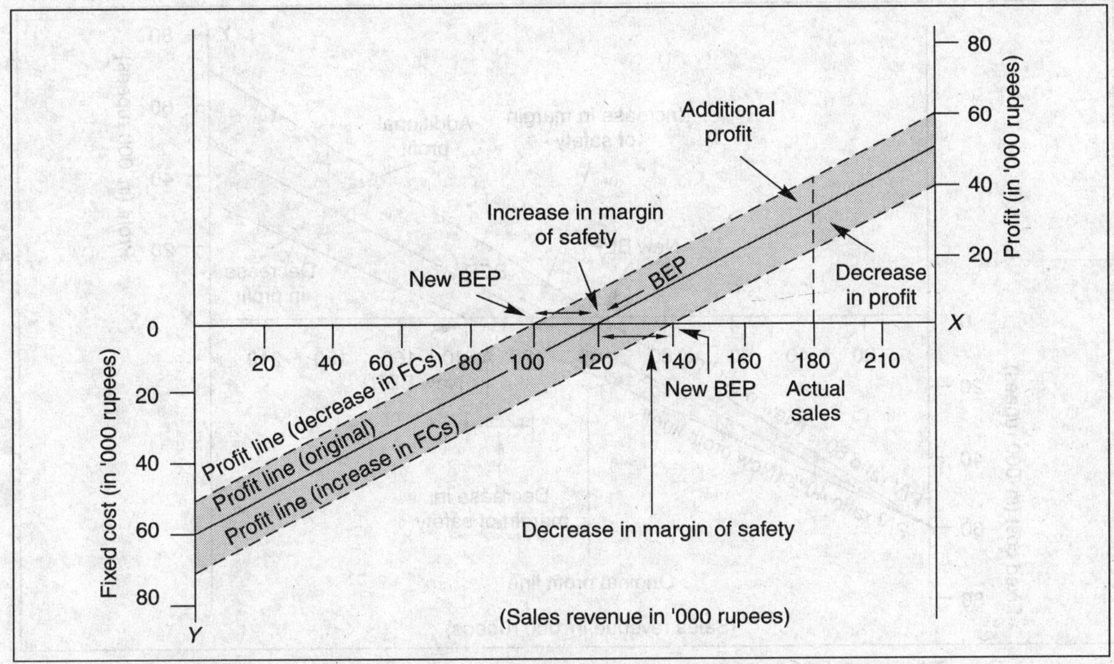

Figure 14.9 *Volume-Profit Graph, Change in Fixed Cost*

ence is that profit lines would originate at different points on the vertical axis. The procedure for determining the two points for the different profit lines is shown for Figure 14.9 in Table 14.10.

Table 14.10

Particulars	*Point I*		*Point II*	
Sales revenue	₹60,000		₹2,10,000	
Less variable costs	30,000		1,05,000	
Contribution	30,000		1,05,000	
Less fixed costs	(i) 50,000	(ii) ₹70,000	(i)50,000	(ii) ₹70,000
Profit/(loss)	(i) (20,000)	(ii) (40,000)	(i)55,000	(ii) 35,000

Changes in Variable Costs The proposed changes in variable costs change the P/V ratio, the BEP and the net income at any sales volume. Figure 14.10 is based on changes in the VC of 20 per cent (both sides) for data included in Example 14.4 Table 14.11 incorporates the results due to the proposed change.

Table 14.11 *Effecrt of Variable Cost on BEP and Margin of Safety*

	Variable costs		
Particulars	*Increase 20* per cent (*₹1* per unit)	*Original*	*Decrease 20 per cent* (*₹1* per unit)
Sales revenues	₹1,80,000	₹1,80,000	₹1,80,000
Less: variable costs	1,08,000	90,000	72,000

(*Contd.*)

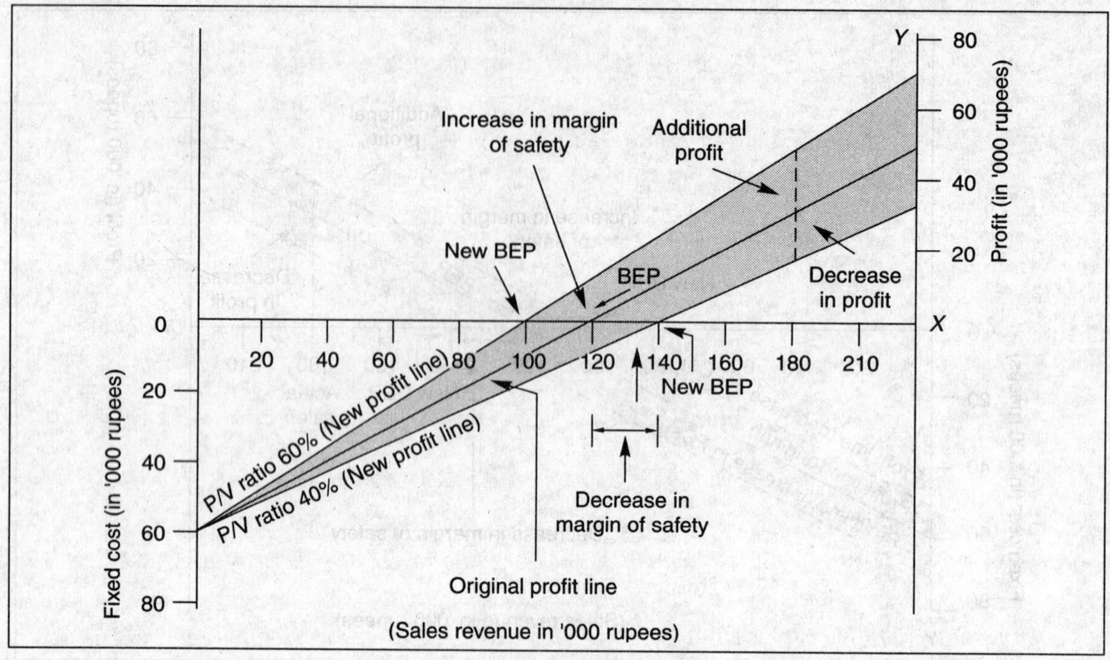

Figure 14.10 *Volume-Profit Graph, Change in Variable Cost*

(*Contd.*)

Contribution	72,000	60,000	1,08,000
Less: fixed costs	60,000	60,000	60,000
Net income	12,000	30,000	48,000
Changes in net income	(18,000)	—	+ 18,000
BEP	1,40,000	1,20,000	1,00,000
Change in BEP	+ 20,000	—	(20,000)
Margin of safety	40,000	60,000	80,000
Change in margin of safety	(20,000)	—	+ 20,000

V/P graph, product-wise shown in Fig. 14.11, is based on data used in Example 14.5.

Changes in Selling Prices The proposed changes in selling prices affect the P/V ratio, the BEP and the net income/loss. To illustrate how well a profit-volume chart lends itself to portraying different profit lines, data used in Example 14.4 are revised so as to incorporate 25 per cent change in the price per unit from the original price and have been plotted in a V/P graph (Figure 14.12). The change pertains to both increase and decrease in the selling price.

The revised profit line lies above the original profit line in the case of increase in the selling price and lies below the original profit line when there is a decrease in the selling price per unit. The originating point of all the three profit lines remains unchanged.

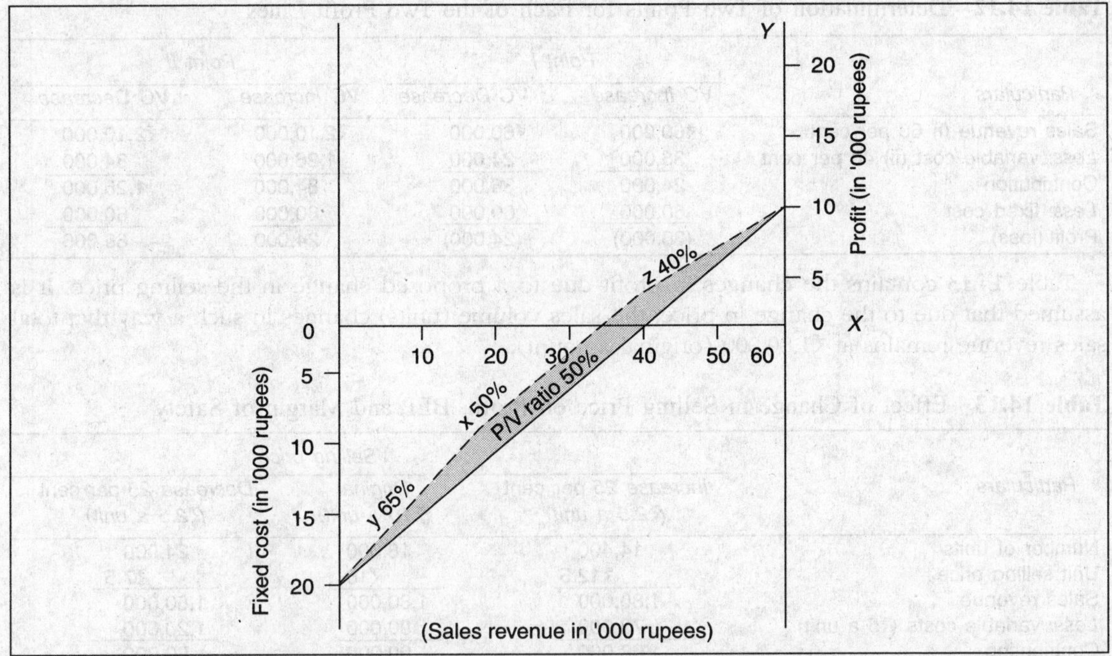

Figure 14.11 *Volume-profit Graph, Product-wise*

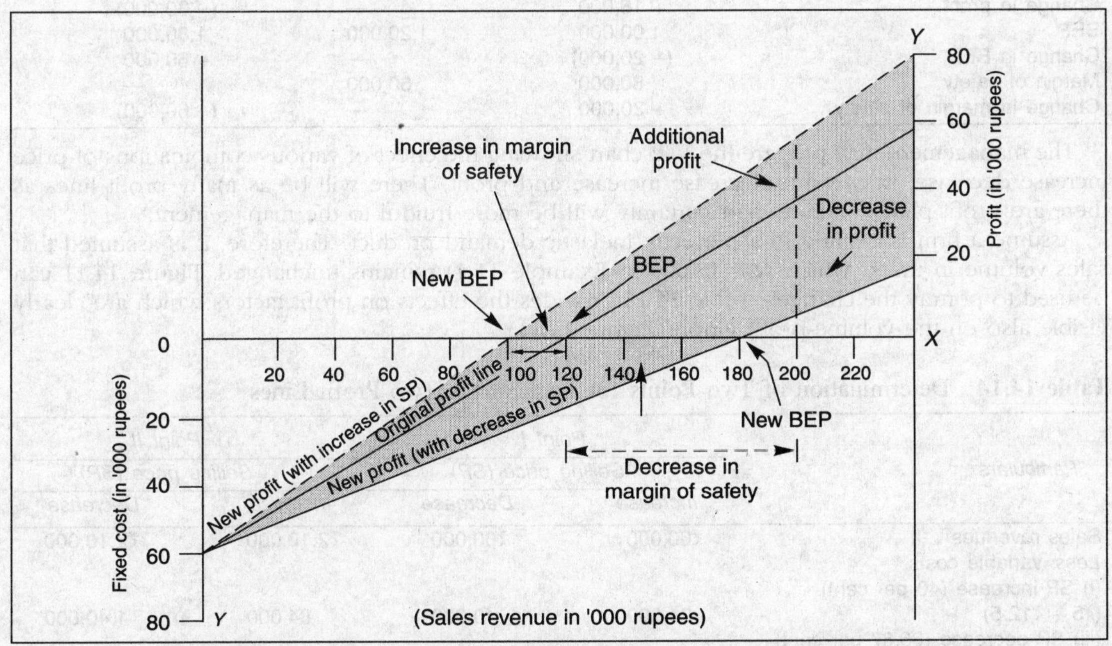

Figure 14.12 *Volume-profit Graph, Change in Selling Price*

Table 14.12 Determination of Two Points for Each of the Two Profit Lines

Particulars	*Point I*		*Point II*	
	VC Increase	*VC Decrease*	*VC Increase*	*VC Decrease*
Sales revenue (i) 60 per cent	₹60,000	₹60,000	₹2,10,000	₹2,10,000
Less: variable cost (ii) 40 per cent	36,000	24,000	1,26,000	84,000
Contribution	24,000	36,000	84,000	1,26,000
Less: fixed cost	60,000	60,000	80,000	60,000
Profit/(loss)	(36,000)	(24,000)	24,000	66,000

Table 14.13 contains the changes in profit due to a proposed change in the selling price. It is assumed that due to the change in price, the sales volume (units) changes in such a way that total sales revenue remains at ₹1,80,000 (original amount).

Table 14.13 Effect of Change in Selling Price on Profit, BEP and Margin of Safety

Particulars	*Selling price*		
	Increase 25 per cent (₹2.5 a unit)	*Original (₹10 a unit)*	*Decrease 25 per cent (₹2.5 a unit)*
Number of units	14,400	18,000	24,000
Unit selling price	₹12.5	₹10	₹7.5
Sales revenue	1,80,000	1,80,000	1,80,000
Less: variable costs (₹5 a unit)	72,000	90,000	1,20,000
Contribution	1,08,000	90,000	60,000
Less: fixed costs	60,000	60,000	60,000
Net profit/loss	48,000	30,000	—
Change in profit	+ 18,000	—	(– 30,000)
BEP	1,00,000	1,20,000	1,80,000
Change in BEP	(– 20,000)	—	+ 60,000
Margin of safety	80,000	60,000	—
Change in margin of safety	+ 20,000	—	(– 60,000)

The management may prepare the V/P chart showing the effect of various combinations of price increase/decrease, sales value decrease/increase and profit. There will be as many profit lines as there are profit plans. Such a chart certainly will be more fruitful to the management.

Assume a firm is dealing in a perfectly inelastic demand product. Therefore, it is assumed that sales volume in units (which was 18,000 in Example 11.4) remains unchanged. Figure 14.11 can be used to portray the changes. Table 14.15 provides the effects on profit factors which are clearly visible also on the volume-profit graph (Figure 14.11).

Table 14.14 Determination of Two Points for Each of the Two Profit Lines

Particulars	*Point I*		*Point II*	
	Selling price (SP)		*Selling price (SP)*	
	Increase	*Decrease*	*Increase*	*Decrease*
Sales revenues	₹60,000	₹60,000	₹2,10,000	₹2,10,000
Less: variable costs				
(i) SP increase (40 per cent)				
(₹5 ÷ ₹12.5)	24,000	40,000	84,000	1,40,000
(iii) SP decrease (66.67 per cent)				
(₹5 ÷ ₹7.5)				
Contribution	36,000	20,000	1,26,000	70,000
Less: fixed costs	60,000	60,000	60,000	60,000
Net profit (loss)	(24,000)	(40,000)	66,000	10,000

Table 14.15

Particulars	*Selling Price*		
	Increase 25% (₹2.5 a unit)	*Original (₹10 a unit)*	*Decrease 25% (₹2.5 a unit)*
Number of units	18,000	18,000	18,000
Unit selling price	₹12.5	₹10	₹7.5
Sales revenue	2,25,000	1,80,000	1,35,000
Less: variable costs (₹5 a unit)	90,000	90,000	90,000
Contribution	1,35,000	90,000	45,000
Less: fixed costs	60,000	60,000	60,000
Net profit/(loss)	75,000	30,000	(15,000)
Change in profit/(loss)	45,000	N.A.	(45,000)
BEP	1,00,000	1,20,000	1,80,000
Change in BEP	(-20,000)	N.A.	+60,000
Margin of safety	1,25,000	60,000	(45,000)
Change in margin of safety	(65,000)	N.A.	(1,05,000)

However, it may be noted that changes prominently shown relate to earlier data where sales volume remains at ₹1,80,000.

V/P Graph for Individual Products So far we have dealt with total sales and total profits for single-product firms. The virtue of the V/P graph is that it can be used to indicate the profit path of each product. It may be recalled here that the CVP chart fails to show such a relationship for individual products. The P/V chart portrays the cumulative effect of each product on the profit of the enterprise. The importance of such information is overwhelming from the point of view of the management because the management should know the figures showing not only the overall picture of P/V ratio but also the ratio for each product so that action can be taken to deal with any product(s) yielding a low P/V ratio. Low profit volume products can be replaced with more profit-yielding products.

EXAMPLE 14.5

Hypothetical Ltd company produces three products. The following are the results of one quarter.

Product	*Sales*	*Variable cost*
X	₹10,000	₹5,000
Y	20,000	7,000
Z	30,000	18,000

Fixed overheads: ₹20,000

SOLUTION

These results can be analysed as follows (Table 14.16).

Table 14.16

Product	*Sales revenue*	*Variable cost*	*Contribution margin*	*P/V ratio(%)*
X	₹10,000	₹5,000	₹5,000	50
Y	20,000	7,000	13,000	65
Z	30,000	18,000	12,000	40
	60,000	30,000	30,000	50
Less: fixed costs			20,000	
Net income			10,000	

BEP = FC ÷ PV ratio = ₹20,000 ÷ 0.50 = ₹40,000

Margin of safety = ₹20,000

Procedure for Drawing a V/P Graph (Figure 14.11)

1. Construct the P/V graph in the normal way as has been done for Figure 14.8, taking the weighted P/V ratio (Example 14.5) as 50 per cent of the profit line.
2. Arrange the given data in such a way that products are in order of descending P/V ratios. In Example 14.5, the sequence of products is Y, X and Z.
3. The profit yielding the highest P/V ratio is plotted first (product Y, 65 per cent PV ratio) and the product giving the lowest P/V ratio (product Z, P/V ratio, 40 per cent) is plotted last. The profit line for product Y begins at total fixed cost point of ₹20,000 and is drawn to the ₹7,000 point in the loss area directly below the sales volume of ₹20,000.
4. The plotting shows that ₹13,000 of the ₹20,000 fixed costs have been recovered.

   The profit path of Product X starts at a point where Y's path ends. X's contribution is ₹5,000 at the sales volume of ₹10,000. It implies that out of ₹7,000 unrecovered fixed costs (step 3), ₹5,000 has been recovered. Therefore, the point is to be plotted at ₹2,000 in the loss area directly below the sales volume of ₹30,000 [₹20,000 (Y) + ₹10,000 (X)].
5. The profit line for Product Z (having the lowest P/V ratio) starts at a point where the profit path for X ends. Z's contribution is ₹12,000 and its sales volume is ₹30,000. This indicates that not only has the uncovered fixed cost of ₹2,000 been recovered but there is a net profit of ₹10,000. Accordingly, its line starts in the loss area and ends in the profit area, crossing the sales line. The point is plotted at the profit figures of ₹10,000 directly below the sales revenue of ₹60,000 (₹20,000 Y + ₹10,000 X + ₹30,000 Z).

The plotting of the profit line for an individual product is a useful pictorial presentation from the point of view of management. If any of the products result in a loss and yields no contribution margin, its slope will be downward.

From Figure 14.11, it can be inferred that the larger the P/V ratio, the steeper is the profit path. Therefore, the management's objective should be to increase the P/V ratio, whenever it is possible to do so; where it cannot be increased, its endeavour should be to maintain it. The P/V ratio can be improved by increasing the selling price and decreasing the variable costs in the case of single-product companies. In the case of multiple-product companies, the additional factor can be the change in product-mix, as explained earlier.

Application of the P/V (C/V) Ratio

1. Determination of BEP = FC ÷ P/V ratio
2. Determination of profit at given/budgeted sales volume = (Actual sales – *BE* sales) × *P/V*ratio.
3. Determination of sales volume to earn budgeted profit = (FC + *DP*) ÷ P/V ratio
4. Determination of change in sales volume to maintain the current level of profit if there is (a) a change in sales price, (b) change in variable cost = (FC + *DP*) ÷ Revised P/V ratio.
5. Determination of the percentage of net profit with the help of margin of safety ratio = (P/V ratio × *MS* ratio) **(14.25)**

Cash Break-Even Point

Cash break-even point is total cash fixed cost divided by contribution margin per unit.

The VCP relationship can also be used to show the liquidity position of the firm. This is done through the computation of **cash break-even point** or cash break-even sales revenue (CBEP/CBESR). Algebraically:

$$CBEP = \frac{\text{Total cash fixed cost } (CFC)}{\text{Contribution margin per unit}} \quad \textbf{(14.26)}$$

$$CBESR = \frac{\text{Total cash fixed cost}}{P/V \text{ ratio}} \tag{14.27}$$

Graphically, the CBEP is determined at the point of intersection of total cash cost line and total sales line. The area to the left of the curve signifies cash losses and the area on the right side is indicative of cash profits.

Assuming for Example 14.4, the cash fixed cost to be ₹15,000, the CBESR using Equation 14.27 would be ₹30,000 = ₹15,000 ÷ 0.50

Figure 14.13 portrays the graphic presentation of the cash break-even sales revenue.

To conclude, the uses of break-even analysis, as a technique for profit planning, have been discussed in detail in this chapter. In brief, break-even analysis shows the interplay of profit factors, that is, cost, revenue and volume in a way, which assists management in choosing the best feasible alternative now and in the future. "The break-even system is at once an *X*-ray, exploratory and planning tool intended for frequent use and a proper cost-volume-profit analysis supported by the break-even chart can eliminate many of the time-consuming reports now being prepared at the company."[3]

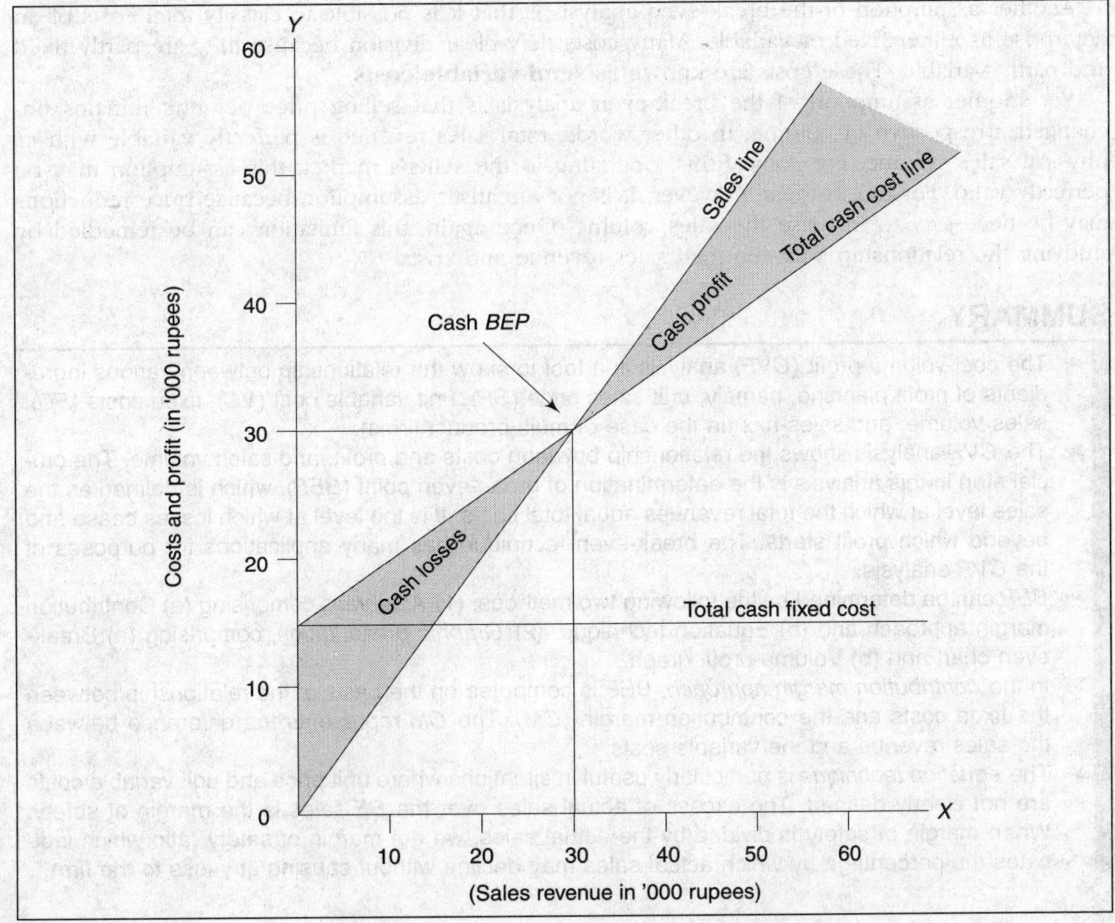

Figure 14.13 *Cash Break-even Point*

The graphs can be used to analyse the impact of various alternative proposals under consideration on the profit structure. Thus, the break-even system provides more readily understandable facts than conventional accounting or statistical data regarding the profit structure of the company.

However, it is important to recognise its limitations which originate from the given assumptions. The greater the deviation of actual facts from the given assumptions, the more imperfect, incorrect and invalid are the break-even calculations. These limitations limit the usefulness of the break-even chart and must be borne in mind by those who prepare or interpret the break-even chart. These limitations suggest that the validity of the break-even chart is in proportion to the validity of the assumptions. One of the assumptions of the break-even analysis is that an enterprise's cost are either perfectly variable or absolutely fixed over all ranges of operating volume. In other words, variable cost is a linear function of volume: fixed costs are assumed not to be affected by volume at all. In practice, these assumptions are not likely to be valid over all ranges of volume. Even within the relevant range of volume, there is a likelihood of some degree of imprecision and to that extent validity of the results is affected. For instance, variable costs are likely to increase as the firm approaches full capacity. The reason may be due to less efficient labour or costly overtime having been resorted to. This limitation can be overcome by studying the relationship between total costs and volume, non-linear, to correspond with economic reality.

Another assumption of the break-even analysis is that it is possible to classify total costs of an enterprise as either fixed or variable. Many costs defy clear division because they are partly fixed and partly variable. These costs are known as **semi-variable costs**.

Yet another assumption of the break-even analysis is that selling price per unit remains unchanged, irrespective of volume. In other words, total sales revenue is perfectly variable with its physical sales volume. For some firms, operating in the seller's market, this assumption may be perfectly valid. For most others, however, it is not a realistic assumption because price reductions may be necessary to increase the sales volume. Once again, this limitation can be remedied by studying the relationship between total sales revenue and costs.

SUMMARY

- The cost-volume-profit (*CVP*) analysis is a tool to show the relationship between various ingredients of profit planning, namely, unit sales price (*SP*), unit variable cost (*VC*), fixed costs (*FC*), sales volume, and sales-mix (in the case of multi-product firms).
- The *CVP* analysis shows the relationship between costs and profit, and sales volume. The crucial step in this analysis is the determination of break-even point (*BEP*), which is defined as the sales level at which the total revenues equal total costs. It is the level at which losses cease and beyond which profit starts. The break-even technique has many applications for purposes of the *CVP* analysis.
- *BEP* can be determined by the following two methods; (1) *Algebraic*, comprising (a) Contribution margin approach and (b) Equation technique. (2) *Graphic presentation*, comprising (a) Break-even chart and (b) Volume-profit graph.
- In the *contribution margin approach, BEP* is computed on the basis of the relationship between the fixed costs and the contribution margin (*CM*). The *CM* represents the difference between the sales revenue and the variable costs.
- The *equation technique* is particularly useful in situations where unit price and unit variable costs are not clearly defined. The excess of actual sales over the *BE* sales is the margin of safety. When margin of safety is divided by the actual sales, we get margin of safety ratio which indicates the percentage by which actual sales may decline without causing any loss to the firm.

➢ The break-even analysis is summarised below:

Contribution Margin Approach

(1) $BEP \text{ (units)} = \dfrac{\text{Fixed costs } (FC)}{\text{Unit sale price (SP)} - \text{Unit variable cost } (VC)}$

(2) $= \dfrac{\text{Total fixed costs}}{\text{Unit contribution margin } (CM)}$

(3) $BEP \text{ (amount)}/BESR = BEP \text{ (units)} \times SP$

(4) $= \dfrac{\text{Total fixed costs}}{\text{Contribution/Profit volume ratio } (C/V \text{ or } P/V \text{ ratio})}$

(5) $C/V\ (P/V) \text{ ratio} = \dfrac{CM}{SP} \times 100$

(6) $= \dfrac{\text{Total contribution } (TC)}{\text{Total sales revenue } (TSR)} \times 100$

(7) Variable cost to volume (V/V) ratio $= \dfrac{VC}{SP} \times 100$

(8) $= \dfrac{\text{Total variable costs } (TVC)}{TSR} \times 100$

(9) $= 1 - C/V\ (P/V) \text{ ratio}$

(10) In brief, $C/V(P/V)$ ratio + V/V ratio = 1 (100%)

(11) $BESR \text{ (multi-product firm)} = \dfrac{FC}{\text{Weighted } C/V \text{ ratio}} \times 100$

(12) $\text{Weighted } C/V \text{ ratio} = \dfrac{TC \text{ from all products}}{TSR \text{ from all products}} \times 100$

(13) $\text{Margin of safety } (MS) = TSR - BESR$

(14) $MS \text{ ratio} = \dfrac{TSR - BESR}{TSR} \times 100$

(15) $\text{Profit} = MS \text{ (rupees)} \times C/V(P/V) \text{ ratio}$

(16) $= MS \text{ (units)} \times CM$

Equation Technique

(17) $BESR = TFC + TVC + NI$ (zero profit)

➢ The break-even applications are summarised below:

1. (a) *Sales revenue required to earn desired operating profits (EBIT)*

$$= \frac{FC + \text{desired } EBIT}{C/V \text{ ratio}}$$

(b) *Sales revenue required to earn desired profits/earnings after taxes (EAT)*

$$= \frac{FC + (EAT/1 - \text{tax rate}, t)}{C/V \text{ ratio}}$$

2. *Operating profit at a given sales volume*

$$= (TSR - BESR) \times C/V \text{ ratio}$$

3. *Sales revenue to off-set reduction in sales price to maintain existing operating profits*

$$= \frac{FC + EBIT}{\text{Revised } C/V \text{ ratio}}$$

4. *Effect of changes in fixed costs*

(a) *The required sales revenue to maintain present operating profit*

$$= \frac{\text{Present } FC + \text{Additional } FC + \text{Present } EBIT}{C/V \text{ ratio}}$$

(b) *The required sales revenue to earn the present rate of return on investment*

Present F C + Additional FC + Present return on investment + Return on new investment

$$= \frac{\text{Present } FC + \text{Additional } FC + \text{Present return on investment} + \text{Return on new investment}}{C/V \text{ ratio}}$$

5. *Effect of changes in variable costs*

The required sales revenue to maintain existing operating profit

$$= \frac{FC + EBIT \text{ (Existing)}}{\text{Revised } C/V \text{ ratio}}$$

6. *Effect of multiple changes*

The required sales revenue to earn desired EAT

$$= \frac{FC + \text{Additional } FC + [\text{Desired } EAT/(1-t)]}{\text{Revised } C/V \text{ ratio}}$$

7. *Effect of change in sales-mix*

The desired sales revenue to maintain existing $EBIT$

$$= \frac{FC + EBIT}{\text{Revised Weighted } C/V \text{ ratio}}$$

$$\text{Revised weighted C/V ratio} = \frac{\text{Total contribution at revised mix}}{\text{Total sales revenue at revised mix}} \times 100$$

➢ The break-even chart is a graphic presentation of the relationship between costs, profits, and sales. It shows not only the break-even sales but also the estimated costs and profit at various levels of the sales revenue. It is, therefore, also referred to as volume-cost-profit (*VCP*) graph/chart.

➢ The volume-profit graph shows a direct relationship between sales revenue and profits.

REFERENCES

1. Wilson, J.D., "Practical Application of Cost-Volume-Profit Analysis" quoted by Anderson, D.L and D.L. Raun, *Information Analysis in Management Accounting* (John Wiley, New York, 1978), p 162.
2. Tuckker, S.A., *Break-Even System: A Tool for Profit Planning*, (Prentice Hall, Englewood Cliffs, N.J. 1963).

SOLVED PROBLEMS

P.14.1 From the following data, calculate the:

1. Break-even point expressed in terms of sale amount/revenue.
2. Number of units that must be sold to earn a profit of ₹60,000 per year.

Sales price (per unit)	₹20
Variable manufacturing cost per unit	11
Variable selling cost per unit	3
Fixed factory overheads (per year)	5,40,000
Fixed selling costs (per year)	2,52,000

SOLUTION

1. BEP *(amount)* = (Fixed factory overheads + Fixed selling costs)/P/V ratio (Sales price – Variable manufacturing cost – Variable selling cost) ÷ Sales price = (₹5,40,000 + ₹2,52,000)/0.30 (₹6 ÷ ₹20) = ₹26,40,000
2. *Desired sales volume (in units) to earn a profit of* ₹60,000 = (₹7,92,000 + ₹60,000)/ ₹6 (CM per unit) = ₹1,42,000 units

P.14.2 On investigation it was found that variable cost in *XYZ* Ltd is 80 per cent of the selling price. If the fixed expenses are ₹10,000, calculate the break-even sales of the company.

Another firm, IMN Company Ltd, having the same amount of fixed expenses, has its break-even point at a lower figure than that of *XYZ* Ltd. Comment on the causes.

SOLUTION

BEP (amount) = ₹10,000/ P/V ratio (100 per cent-Variable cost to volume ratio = 0.80)
= ₹10,000/0.20 = ₹50,000 (*XYZ* Ltd)

The lower break-even point of IMN Ltd *vis-à-vis XYZ* Ltd is due to its lower variable expenses to volume ratio, which in turn may be either due to its lower VC per unit or higher *SP* per unit, eventually yielding higher contribution margin and, hence, higher P/V ratio and lower BEP.

P.14.3 Two businesses, *AB* Ltd and *CD* Ltd, sell the same type of product in the same type of market. Their budgeted profit and loss accounts for the current year ending March 31, are as follows:

Particulars		*AB Ltd*		*CD Ltd*
Sales		₹150,000		₹1,50,000
Less: Variable costs	₹1,20,000		₹1,00,000	
Fixed costs	15,000	1,35,000	35,000	1,35,000
Net budgeted profit		15,000		15,000

You are required to:

1. Calculate the break-even points of each business; and
2. State which business is likely to earn greater profits in conditions of: (a) heavy demand for the product, (b) low demand for the product.

SOLUTION

1. BEP (amount) = Fixed cost/ P/V ratio; P/V ratio = Contribution/Sales revenuee
   BEP (AB Ltd) = ₹15,000/0.20 = ₹75,000
   P/V ratio = ₹30,000/ ₹1,50,000 = 20 per cent
   BEP (CD Ltd) = ₹35,000/0.3333 = ₹1,05,000
   P/V ratio = ₹50,000/ ₹1,50,000 = 33.33 per cent
2. Projected profit (heavy demand for the products):
   (a) CD Ltd is likely to earn larger profits in conditions of heavy demand of the product because its P/V ratio is higher than that of AB Ltd.
   (b) AB Ltd is likely to earn larger profits in condition of low demand of the product because its burden of fixed costs is much smaller than that of CD Ltd.

P.14.4 During the current year, *AB* Ltd showed a profit of ₹1,80,000 on a sale of ₹30,00,000. The variable expenses were ₹21,00,000.

You are required to work out:

1. The break-even sales at present

2. The break-even sale if variable costs increase by 5 per cent
3. The break-even sale to maintain the profit as at present, if the selling price is reduced by 5 per cent.

SOLUTION

₹30,00,000, Sales = ₹21,00,000, VC + FC + ₹1,80,000, profit or FC = ₹7,20,000

1. BEP = ₹7,20,000/ PV ratio = ₹7,20,000/0.30 = ₹24,00,000
   P/V ratio = ₹9,00,000/30,00,000 = 0.30
2. BEP (revised) = ₹7,20,000/0.265 = ₹27,16,981
   P/V ratio = ₹7,95,000/ ₹30,00,000 = 0.265
   ₹7,95,000 Contribution = (₹30,00,000 – ₹22,05,000, VC)
3. Revised P/V ratio with reduction in price

Sales revenue	₹28,50,000
Variable costs	21,00,000
Contribution	7,50,000

P/V ratio (₹7,50,000 ÷ ₹28,50,000) = 26.316 per cent
Desired sales volume = ₹9,00,000 (FC + *DP*)/0.26316 = ₹34,19,973

P.14.5 Calculate from the following data (i) the value of output at which the business breaks even; and (ii) the percentage of capacity at which it breaks even:

Particulars	*Budget based on 100 per cent capacity*	*Shut down expenditure*
Direct wages	₹2,09,964	
Direct materials	2,44,552	
Works expenses	88,292	₹93,528
Selling and distribution expenses	21,000	40,188
Administrative expenses	9,492	20,508
Net sales	8,40,000	

SOLUTION P/V RATIO

(i) *Net sales*		₹8,40,000
Less: Variable costs:		
Direct wages	₹2,09,964	
Direct materials	2,44,552	
Works expenses	88,292	
Selling and distribution expenses	21,000	
Administrative expenses	9,492	5,73,300
Contribution (C)		2,66,700
P/V ratio (C ÷ Sales) (per cent)		31.75

BEP (amount) = Fixed costs (shut down expenditure)/P/V ratio = ₹1,54,224/0.3175 = ₹4,85,744.88
(ii) Break-even sales/Sales at 100 per cent capacity = ₹4,85,744.88/₹8,40,000 = 57.83 per cent

P.14.6 The Soft-Flow Ink Ltd's income statement for the preceding year is presented below. Except as noted, the cost/revenue relationship for the coming year is expected to follow the same pattern as in the preceding year. Income statement for the year ending March 31 is as follows:

Sales (20,000 bottles @ ₹25 each)		₹5,00,000
Variable costs	₹3,00,000	
Fixed costs	1,00,000	4,00,000
Pre-tax profit		1,00,000
Less: Taxes (0.35)		35,000
Profit after tax		65,000

1. What is the break-even point in amount and units?
2. Suppose that a plant expansion will add ₹50,000 to fixed costs and increase capacity by 60 per cent. How many bottles would have to be sold after the addition to break-even?
3. At what level of sales will the company be able to maintain its present pre-tax profit position even after expansion?
4. The company's management feels that it should earn at least ₹10,000 (pre- tax per annum) on the new investment. What sales volume is required to enable the company to maintain existing profits and earn the minimum required return on new investments?
5. Suppose the plant operates at full capacity after the expansion, what profit after tax will be earned?

SOLUTION

1. BEP (amount) = ₹1,00,000/0.40 (₹2,00,000 ÷ ₹5,00,000) = ₹2,50,000
   BEP (units) = ₹1,00,000/₹10 = 10,000 units; CMPU = ₹25 – ₹15 VC = ₹10
2. BEP (increase in FC) = [₹1,00,000 + ₹50,000 (Additional FC)] ÷ ₹10 per unit = 15,000 units
3. Desired sales volume to maintain a pre- tax profit of ₹1,00,000 = [₹1,50,000 (FC) + ₹1,00,000] ÷ 0.40 = ₹6,25,000 (or 25,000 units)
4. Desired sales volume to earn a pre-tax profit of ₹1,10,000 (₹1,00,000 + ₹10,000) = [₹1,50,000 + ₹1,10,000]/0.40 = ₹6,50,000 (or 26,000 units)
5. Present capacity (assumed operating at 100 per cent capacity) (bottles)

Present capacity (assumed operating at 100 per cent capacity) (bottles)	20,000
Add: Additional capacity (60 per cent)	12,000
Total capacity (bottles)	32,000

Statement of Income (32,000 units)

Sales (32,000 bottles @ ₹25)	₹8,00,000
Less: Variable costs, 0.60 × (₹3,00,000 + ₹5,00,000)	4,80,000
Contribution	3,20,000
Less: Fixed costs	1,50,000
Pre-tax profits	1,70,000
Less: Income tax (0.35)	59,500
Profits after income tax	1,10,500

P.14.7 The following data are obtained from the records of a factory:

Sales (4,000 units @ ₹25 each)		₹1,00,000
Variable costs:		
Materials consumed	₹40,000	
Labour charges	20,000	
Variable overheads	10,000	
Fixed overheads	18,000	88,000
Net profit		12,000

Calculate:

1. Number of units by selling which the company will break-even.
2. Sales needed to earn a profit of 20 per cent on sales.
3. Extra units, which should be sold to obtain the present profit if it is proposed to reduce the selling price by 20 per cent and 25 per cent.
4. Selling price to be fixed to bring down its break-even point to 600 units under present conditions.

Solution

1. BEP (units), Fixed overheads = ₹18,000/CM per unit, ₹7.50 = 2,400 units

Determination of CM per Unit

Sales revenue (4,000 units)		₹1,00,000
Less: Variable costs		
Materials consumed	₹40,000	
Labour charges	20,000	
Variable overheads	10,000	70,000
Contribution (4,000 units)		30,000
CM per unit (₹30,000 ÷ 4,000)		7.5

2. (a) Sales revenue (SR) is a sum of total costs (TC) and total profits (TP) or (SR = TC + TP).
(b) TC can be split into FC and VC.
(c) VC will vary in direct proportion to SR.
(d) Accordingly, SR = FC + VC (SR) + TP (SR). Let us suppose, SR = 100 per cent; TC = 80 per cent; TP = 20 per cent; VC = 70 per cent (₹70,000/₹1,00,000); FC = ₹18,000

Substituting the values, we have,

100% SR = ₹18,000 + 0.70 SR + 0.20 SR

0.10 SR = ₹18,000

SR = ₹18,000/0.10 = ₹1,80,000

Verification

Sales revenue		₹1,80,000
Less: Variable cost (0.70)	₹1,26,000	
Less: Fixed overheads	18,000	1,44,000
Net profit		36,000
Net profit as percentage of sales revenue		20

3. Revised Contribution Margin per unit and Additional Units Required to maintain Profit of ₹12,000

Particulars	*Selling price reduced by*	
	20 per cent	*25 per cent*
Revised selling price	₹20.00	₹18.75
Less: Variable cost (0.70 × ₹25, original sales price)	17.50	17.50
Contribution	2.50	1.25
Desired sales volume (FC + NP) ÷ CM	30,000/2.50	30,000/1.25
Number of units required	12,000	24,000
Less: Existing number of units sold	4,000	4,000
Extra units to be sold to maintain a profit of ₹12,000	8,000	20,000

4. BEP = FC/CM per unit

CM per unit = FC/BEP = ₹18,000/600 units = ₹30

Sales price (per unit) = CM per unit + Variable cost per unit = ₹30 + ₹17.50 = ₹47.5

P.14.8 Calculate the break-even sales from the following data for a company producing three products:

Product	*Sales*	*Variable costs*
A	₹10,000	₹6,000
B	5,000	2,500
C	5,000	2,000
	20,000	10,500

Total fixed costs amount to ₹5,700.

SOLUTION

Determination of Weighted P/V Ratio

Product	Sales	Variable costs	Contribution
A	₹10,000	₹6,000	4,000
B	5,000	2,500	2,500
C	5,000	2,000	3,000
	20,000	10,500	9,500

Weighted P/V ratio = (Total contribution/Total sales) × 100 = (₹9,500/ ₹20,000) × 100 = 47.5 per cent
BEP = FC/Weighted P/V ratio = ₹5,700/0.475 = ₹12,000

P.14.9 *ABC* Ltd manufactures and sells four types of products under the brand names of *A*, *B*, *C* and *D*. The sales-mix in value comprises 33.33, 41.67, 16.67 and 8.33 per cents for products *A*, *B*, *C* and *D* respectively. The total budgeted sales (100 per cent) are ₹60,000 per month. Operating costs are: Variable costs as per cent of selling price: Product *A*, 60, *B*, 68, *C*, 80, and *D* 40. Fixed costs, ₹14,700 per month.

Calculate the break-even point for the products on an over-all basis.

SOLUTION

DETERMINATION OF WEIGHTED PV RATIO

Product	Sales revenue	(%)	Variable costs	(%)	Contribution	P/V ratio (%)
A	₹20,000	(33.33)	₹12,000	(60)	₹8,000	40
B	25,000	(41.67)	17,000	(68)	8,000	32
C	10,000	(16.67)	8,000	(80)	2,000	20
D	5,000	(8.33)	2,000	(40)	3,000	60
Total	60,000	(100)	39,000	(65)	21,000	35

BEP = Fixed costs/ Weighted P/V ratio = ₹14,700/0.35 = ₹42,000

Confirmation

Variable costs (0.65 × ₹42,000)	₹27,300
Fixed costs	14,700
Total costs	42,000
Total sales revenue	42,000

P.14.10 There are two similar plants under the same management. The management desires to merge these two plants. The following particulars are available:

	Factory I	Factory II
Capacity (%)	100	60
Sales (₹lakh)	300	120
Variable costs	220	90
Fixed costs	40	20

You are required to calculate: (a) What the break-even capacity of the merged plant would be, and (b) What the profitability on working at 75 per cent of the merged capacity would be?

SOLUTION

(a) Break-even Capacity

	Factory I (at 100% capacity)	Factory II (at 100% capacity)	Combined (at 100% capacity)
Sales (₹lakh)	300	200	500
Less: Variable costs	220	150	370
Contribution	80	50	130

Break-even (amount) = Fixed costs/Combined P/V ratio = ₹60 lakhs/0.26 = ₹230.769 lakh
0.26 = (₹130 lakh/₹500 lakh) × 100
Break-even point (per cent capacity) = (Break-even sales/Total capacity) × 100
= (₹230.8 lakh/ ₹500 lakh) × 100 = 46.15 per cent. The break-even capacity of the merged plant would be approximately 46.15 per cent.

(b) Income Statement at 75 per cent Merged Capacity

Sales (₹lakh)	375.00
Less: Variable costs (0.74 × ₹375)	277.50
Contribution	97.50
Less: Fixed costs	60.00
Net profit	37.50

Alternatively, (Actual sales – BE sales) × P/V ratio = (₹375 lakh – ₹230.769 lakh) × 0.26 = ₹37.50 lakh

P.14.11 The *XYZ* Ltd operates a chain of toy stores. The stores sell 10 different styles of toys with identical purchase costs and selling prices. The company is trying to determine the desirability of opening another store, which would have the following expense and revenue relationships per pair.

Variable data:	
Selling price	₹30.00
Cost of toy	19.50
Salesmen's commission	1.50
Total variable expenses	21.00
Annual fixed expenses:	
Rent	60,000
Salaries	2,00,000
Advertising	80,000
Other fixed expenses	20,000
	3,60,000

Required (consider each question independently):

1. What is the annual break-even point in sales amount and in unit sales?
2. If 35,000 toys are sold, what would the store's net income be?
3. If the store manager was paid ₹0.30 per pair commission, what would the annual break-even point be in sales amount and in unit sales?
4. Refer to the original data. If the store manager were paid ₹0.30 per toy as commission on each toy sold in excess of the break-even point, what would be the store's net income if 50,000 toys were sold?
5. Refer to the original data. If sales commissions were discontinued in favour of ₹81,000 increase in fixed salaries, what would the annual break-even point be in amount and in unit sales?
6. If the store wants to build up stocks by the end of the accounting period, will your analysis still hold good?

Solution

1. Selling price

Selling price	₹30
Less: Variable costs	21
CM per unit (pair)	9
P/V ratio (%)	30

BEP (amount) = ₹3,60,000/0.30 = ₹12,00,000

BEP (units) = ₹3,60,000/ CM per unit = ₹3,60,000/₹9 = ₹40,000 units

2. Income if 35,000 pairs of shoes are sold

Contribution (35,000 × ₹9)	₹3,15,000
Less: Fixed cost	3,60,000
Loss	(45,000)

3. Contribution is ₹8.70 (*less* by 30 paise commission paid to store manager): (₹30 – ₹21.30)
BEP (units) = ₹3,60,000/₹8.70 = 41,380 pairs
BEP (amount) = ₹3,60,000/0.29 = ₹12,41,379.30
P/V ratio = ₹8.70/₹30 = 29 per cent

4. CM per unit beyond the BEP × Margin of safety in units = Income
₹8.70 × 10,000 (50,000 – 40,000) = ₹87,000

5. Revised CM and P/V ratio

Sales price	₹30.00
Cost of shoes	19.50
CM	10.50
P/V ratio (%)	35

Fixed costs = ₹3,60,000 + ₹81,000 = ₹4,41,000
BEP (in units) = ₹4,41,000/₹10.50 = 42,000 units
BEP (amount) = ₹4,41,000/0.35 = ₹12,60,000
Alternatively, 42,000 × ₹30 = ₹12,60,000

6. No, the analysis will not hold true because in the volume-cost-profit relationship, it is assumed that production is equal to sales in the manufacturing firms or purchases are equal to sales in the case of trading firms.

P.14.12 Market Well Ltd manufactures filing cabinets. For the current year, the company expects to sell 4,000 cabinets involving a loss of ₹2,00,000. Only 40 per cent of the plant's normal capacity is being utilised during the current year. The fixed costs for the year are ₹10,00,000 and fully variable costs are 60 per cent of sales value.

You are required to

1. Calculate the break-even point;
2. Calculate the profit if the company operates at 70 per cent of its normal capacity;
3. Calculate the sales required to achieve a profit of ₹60,00,000;
4. Calculate the revised break-even point if the existing selling prices are decreased by 10 per cent, the total fixed and variable expenses remaining the same.

SOLUTION

1. BEP (amount) = FC/ PV ratio = ₹10,00,000/0.40 = ₹25,00,000
2. Determination of the Existing Sales Volume and Sales Price per Cabinet

Sales revenue	X
Less: Variable cost (0.60)	0.6 X
Contribution	(X – 0.6X)
Less: Fixed costs	₹10,00,000
Loss (given)	2,00,000

0.4 X – ₹10,00,000 = (– ₹2,00,000)
0.4 X = ₹8,00,000
X = 20,00,000 (sales revenue)
Sales price per cabinet = ₹20,00,000/4,000 cabinets = ₹500
Number of cabinets sold at 70 per cent capacity = 7,000 = (4,000 × 70/40)

Projected Income Statement at 70 per cent Capacity

Sales revenue (7,000 × ₹500)	₹35,00,000
Less: Variable cost (0.60)	21,00,000
Contribution	14,00,000
Less: Fixed costs	10,00,000
Profit	4,00,000

Alternatively, (Expected sales revenue – Break-even sales revenue) × P/V ratio or (Margin of safety) × P/V ratio = (₹35,00,000 – ₹25,00,000) × 0.40 = ₹4,00,000

3. Desired sales volume to earn a profit of ₹60,00,000 = (FC + ₹60,00,000)/0.40 = (₹10,00,000 + ₹60,00,000)/0.40 = ₹1,75,00,000

4. Break-even Point (Revised) at Reduced Selling Price by 10 per cent

Sales price	₹450
Less: Variable cost (0.60 × ₹500)	300
CM	150
P/V ratio (₹150/₹450) (%)	33.33
BEP ₹(10,00,000/0.3333)	30,00,000

P.14.13 The question as to which products to stress in order to obtain the most profitable sales-mix has always been of prime importance to businessmen. The amount of profit contribution, or the difference between the selling price and the variable costs, tells how much each product is contributing to fixed costs and profit in the present sales-mix. This information assists management in forming an opinion as to which products will add to profits if sales of these units can be increased.

Direct cost data can be utilised in this type of analysis when management seeks an answer to the question: "Which product shall we push"?

Data	*Product A*	*Product B*
Selling price	₹126.00	₹55.00
Variable cost	96.20	41.80
Fixed costs	20.70	6.50
Units per hour	45	70

1. What is the amount of net profit for each product?
2. What is the percentage of profit to selling price for each product?
3. What is the amount of profit contribution towards fixed cost and the profit for each product?
4. What is the profit contribution ratio?
5. What is the profit contribution per hour for each product?
6. If one allocates: (a) 200 hours to Product *A* and 100 hours to Product *B* or (b) 100 hours to Product *A* and 200 hours to Product B, which of the two courses is more profitable?

SOLUTION

1. Net Profit for Products *A* and *B*

Particulars	*A*	*B*
Selling price	₹126.00	₹55.00
Less: Costs:		
Variable	96.20	41.80
Fixed	20.70	6.50
Net profit	9.10	6.70

	A	B
2. Percentage of profit to selling price = (Net profit × 100) ÷ Selling price	7.22	12.18
3. Profit contribution (Selling price-Variable costs)	29.80	13.20
4. P/V ratio (%)	23.65	24
5. (Profit contribution per unit × Units produced per hour)		
Product *A* : ₹29.8 × 45	1,341	
B : ₹13.2 × 70		924

6. Statement of Profit Contribution

Particulars	*Alternative (a)*	*Alternative (b)*
Product A (Profit contribution per hour × Hours)	₹1,341 × 200 (a) 2,68,200	₹1,341 × 100 (a) 1,34,100
Product B (Profit contribution per hour × Hours)	924 × 100 (b) 92,400	924 × 200 (b) 1,84,800
Total profit contribution [(a) + (b)]	3,60,600	3,18,900

Alternative (a) of allocating 200 hours to Product *A* and 100 hours to Product *B* is the more profitable course as it yields higher contribution.

P.14.14 A.T. Ltd operating at 80 per cent level of activity furnishes the following information:

Particulars	*Products*		
	A	*B*	*C*
Selling price/units	₹10	₹12	₹20
Profit as percentage on selling price	25	33.33	20
Units produced and sold	10,000	15,000	5,000
Fixed costs	40,000	45,000	25,000

During the year, the variable costs are expected to increase by 10 per cent. There will, however, be no change in fixed costs, the selling prices and the units to be produced and sold. The sales potential for each of the products is unlimited.

(i) You are required to prepare a statement showing the P/V ratio, break-even point and margin of safety for each product and for the company as a whole.

(ii) The company intends to increase the production of only one of the three products to reach the full capacity level by utilising the spare capacity available. Assuming that all the three products take the same machine time, advise with reasons, which of the three products should be produced so that the overall profitability is the maximum.

Solution

(i) Statement showing BEP, Margin of Safety and P/V Ratio of A.T. Ltd for Year 1 and 2

Particulars	*Year 1*				*Year 2*			
	A	*B*	*C*	*All combined*	*A*	*B*	*C*	*All combined*
Units produced and sold	10,000	15,000	5,000	30,000	10,000	15,000	5,000	30,000
Selling price per unit	₹10	₹12	₹20	₹12.666	₹10	₹12	₹20	₹12.666
Sales revenue	1,00,000	1,80,000	1,00,000	3,80,000	1,00,000	1,80,000	1,00,000	3,80,000
Less: Variable costs (see working notes)	35,000	75,000	55,000	1,65,000	38,500	82,500	60,500	1,81,500
Contribution	65,000	1,05,000	45,000	2,15,000	61,500	97,500	39,500	1,98,500
Less: Fixed costs	40,000	45,000	25,000	1,10,000	40,000	45,000	25,000	1,10,000
Operating profit	25,000	60,000	20,000	1,05,000	21,500	52,500	14,500	88,500
P/V ratio (%)	65	58.33	45	56.58	61.5	54.17	39.5	52.24
BEP				1,94,419				2,10,580
Margin of safety				1,85,581				1,69,420

WORKING NOTES

A ₹1,00,000 = 40,000 FC + ₹25,000 profit (0.25 × ₹1,00,000) + VC, that is, ₹35,000.
B ₹1,80,000 = 45,000 FC + ₹60,000 profit (0.3333 × ₹1,80,000) + VC, that is, ₹75,000.
C ₹1,00,000 = 25,000 FC + ₹20,000 profit (0.20 × ₹1,00,000) + VC, that is, ₹55,000.

(ii) Product *C* should be produced to utilise the *SP* are capacity of 20 per cent as its marginal contribution per unit is maximum as shown below:

Particulars	*A*	*B*	*C*
Sales price	₹10	₹12	₹20
Less: Variable cost per unit	3.5	5.0	11
CM	6.5	7.0	9.0

P.14.15 Hansa Ltd manufacturing a single product is facing severe competition in selling it at ₹50 per unit. The company is operating at 60 per cent level of activity at which level sales are ₹12,00,000; variable costs are ₹30 per unit; semi-variable costs may be considerd fixed at ₹90,000 when output is nil and the variable element is ₹250 for each additional 1 per cent level of activity; fixed costs are ₹1,50,000 at the present level of activity, but if a level of activity of 80 per cent or above is reached, these costs are expected to increase by ₹50,000.

To cope with the competition, the management of the company is considering a proposal to reduce the selling price by 5 per cent. You are required to prepare a statement showing the operating profit at levels of activity of 60 per cent, 70 per cent and 82 per cent, assuming that:

1. The selling price remains at ₹50; and
2. The selling price is reduced by 5 per cent.

Show also the number of units, which will be required to be sold to maintain the present profits if the company decides to reduce the selling price of the product 5 by per cent.

SOLUTION

Statement Showing Operating Profit (Flexible Budgets)

Particulars	*Percentage of capacity*					
	60		*70*		*82*	
	Old selling price	*New selling price*	*Old selling price*	*New selling price*	*Old selling price*	*New selling price*
Units	24,000	24,000	28,000	28,000	32,800	32,800
Sales price	₹50	₹47.50	₹50	₹47.50	₹50	₹47.50
Sales revenue	12,00,000	11,40,000	14,00,000	13,30,000	16,40,000	15,58,000
Less:	*Costs:*					
Variable costs	7,20,000	7,20,000	8,40,000	8,40,000	9,84,000	9,84,000
Semi-variable costs	1,05,000	1,05,000	1,07,500	1,07,500	1,10,500	1,10,500
Fixed costs	1,50,000	1,50,000	1,50,000	1,50,000	2,00,000	2,00,000
Total costs	9,75,000	9,75,000	10,97,500	10,97,500	12,94,500	12,94,500
Operating profit	2,25,000	1,65,000	3,02,500	2,32,500	3,45,500	2,63,500

Sales volume required to maintain present level of profit: (Fixed costs + Profit)/CM per unit = (₹1,50,000 + 90,000 + 2,25,000)/₹16.875 = 27,556 units

WORKING NOTE

Selling price		₹47.50
Less: Variable cost	₹30.00	
Semi variable cost (variable element)	0.625	30.625
CM per unit		16.875

P.14.16 From the cost records of a company for a specific period, for product X, the information given in the first column can be ignored since it is only one of the several projections of an assistant accountant, but it may be useful to you.

	This period actual	*One of the future projections*
Sales (units)	10,000	20,000
Profit (loss)	₹(10,000)	₹10,000
Fixed costs	30,000	30,000
Variable cost per unit	8	8

On the basis of the first column, determine

1. What increased sales volume is required to cover an additional attractive packaging cost of ₹0.50 per unit, to increase the sales, at the existing sales price, to yield zero profit?
2. What increased sales volume in required at the present sale price, to cover an additional publicity expense of ₹5,000 for that period, while yielding a profit of ₹5,000.
3. What increased sale volume is required to reach a profit of ₹4,000 while reducing the selling price by 3 per cent per unit?

SOLUTION

1. *Sales volume required to yield zero profit*: = Fixed costs/ CM per unit = ₹30,000/₹1.50 = 20,000 units
   Sales volume required = 20,000 units (₹2,00,000)
   Existing sales volume = 10,000 units (₹1,00,000)
   Difference represents increase in sales volume required to make zero profit = 10,000 units (₹1,00,000)
2. *Assuming situation (2) independent of (1)*: Sales volume required to earn a profit of ₹5,000 = [₹30,000 + ₹5,000 (publicity expenses) + ₹5,000 (profit)]/₹2 = 20,000 units (₹2,00,000); 10,000 units (₹1,00,000) is the increased sales volume required.
3. *Assuming (3) to be independent of situations (1) and (2)*: Desired sales volume to earn a profit of ₹4,000 = (₹30,000 + ₹4,000)/ (₹9.70 – 8) = 20,000 units (or ₹1,94,000). Increased sales volume required is 10,000 units.

WORKING NOTE

Determination of total sales revenue and selling price per unit:
Total sales revenue = Total costs – Loss
Total costs = FC + (VC per unit × Sales in units)
₹80,000 = ₹30,000 + (₹8 × 10,000)
Total sales revenue = ₹1,10,000 – ₹10,000 = ₹1,00,000
SP per unit = ₹1,00,000/10,000 = ₹10

P.14.17 The ABC Ltd operates a restaurant with recreational facilities. The manager of the complex having 100 rooms, has asked your assistance in planning the coming year's operations. He is particularly concerned about the level of profits the firm is likely to earn.

Your conversation with the manager shows that he expects occupancy to be 70 per cent during the 200-day season that it is open. All rooms would be rented for ₹500 per day for any number of persons. On an average, two persons occupy a room. This is the past experience, which the manager believes is an accurate guide to the future. He further informs you that each person staying in the hotel spends ₹125 per day in the shops (also owned by the company) and ₹250 in the restaurant. There are no charges for the use of recreational facilities.

Cost data are:

Particulars	*Variable cost to volume ratio*	
	Shop	*Restaurant*
Cost of goods sold	50	25
Supplies	5	15
Others	5	10

For the hotel, the variable costs are ₹100 per day per occupied room, for cleaning, laundry, and utilities. Total fixed costs for the complex are ₹60,00,000 per year.

You are required to do the following:

1. Prepare an income statement for the coming year based on the information given.
2. The manager believes that if room rent were reduced to ₹400 per day, the occupancy would increase to 90 per cent. Will you endorse his suggestion of reducing the rent rates?

SOLUTION

1. *Income Statement*

Sales revenues:		
Hotel rooms (100 × 200 × 0.70 × ₹500)	₹70,00,000	
Shops (100 × 200 × 0.70 × 2 × ₹125)	35,00,000	
Restaurant (100 × 200 × 0.70 × 2 × ₹250)	70,00,000	
		₹1,75,00,000
Less: variable costs		
Hotel rooms (100 × 200 × 0.70 × ₹100)	14,00,000	
Shops (₹35,00,000 × 0.60, that is, 0.50 + 0.10)	21,00,000	
Restaurant (₹70,00,000 × 0.50 that is, 0.25 + 0.15 + 0.10)	35,00,000	70,00,000
Contribution		1,05,00,000
Less: fixed costs		60,00,000
Profit		45,00,000

2. *Income Statement (If Room Rents are Reduced)*

Sales revenue		
Hotel room (100 × 200 × 0.90 × ₹400)	₹72,00,000	
Shops (100 × 200 × 0.90 × 2 × ₹125)	45,00,000	
Restaurant (100 × 200 × 0.90 × 2 × ₹250)	90,00,000	₹2,07,00,000
Less: variable costs		
Hotel rooms (100 × 200 × 0.90 × ₹100)	18,00,000	
Shops (₹45,00,000 × 0.60)	27,00,000	
Restaurant (₹90,00,000 × 0.50)	45,00,000	90,00,000
Contribution		1,17,00,000
Less: fixed costs		60,00,000
Profit		57,00,000

Yes, we endorse the manager's suggestion to reduce the room rent as it augments profit.

P.14.18 After a study of cost-volume relationships, the Kaling Tubes Company Ltd concluded that its costs for any given volume of sales could be expressed as ₹1,00,000 for fixed costs plus variable costs equal to 60 per cent of sales. The company's range of volume was from zero to ₹8,00,000 of sales.

Prepare a graph, which will illustrate this cost-volume relationship. Also draw a proper sales line to the graph to form a break-even chart. Determine the break-even point.

A competitor operating a plant of the same size as Kaling also has fixed cost of approximately ₹1,00,000 per year, but his break-even point is ₹3,00,000 of sales. What may be the probable causes of the difference between the break- even points of the Kaling Company Ltd and its competitor?

SOLUTION

Since selling price per unit is not given, it is necessary to draw the cost-volume graph on the same scale so that a 45° line can be the proxy of the sales line.

Determination of Two Points for Drawing the Total Cost Line

Sales revenue	FC	VC	*TC*
₹1,00,000	₹1,00,000	₹60,000	₹1,60,000
8,00,000	1,00,000	4,80,000	5,80,000

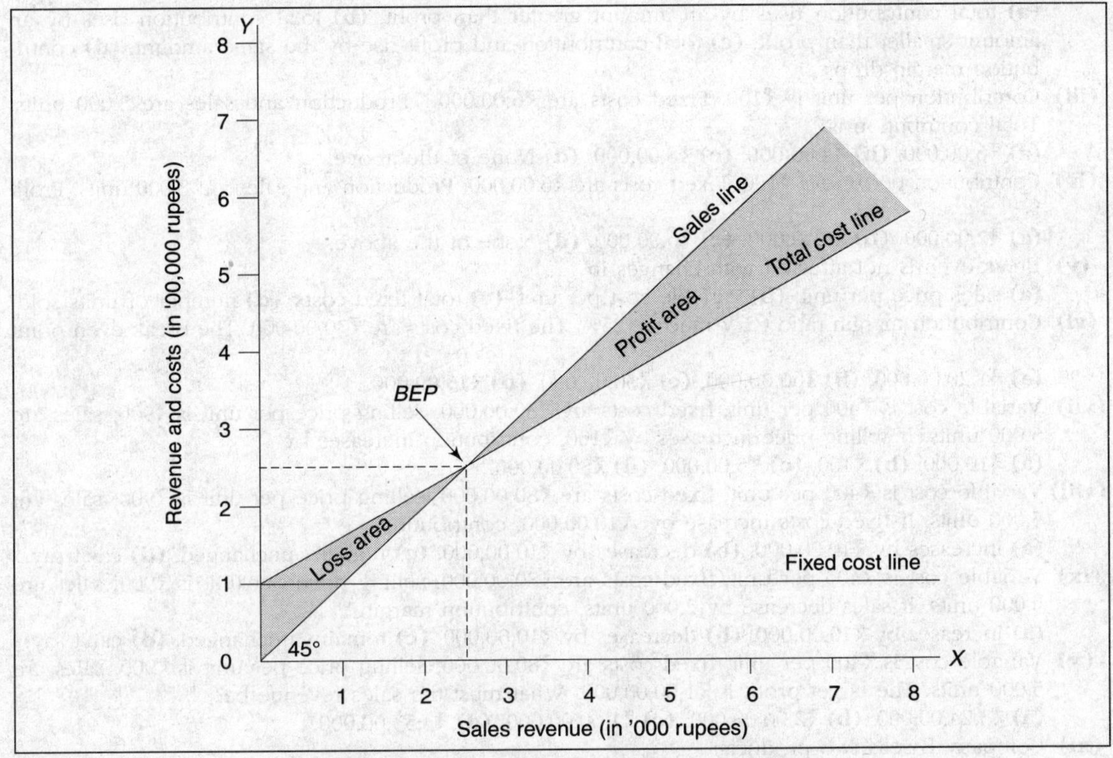

Figure 14.14 *Volume-Cost-Profit Graph*

The point of intersection of the TC line and sales line is BEP (₹2,50,000).
Verification: FC/P/V ratio = ₹1,00,000/0.40 = ₹2,50,000
Possible causes for the differences in BEP:

1. The competitors are having a higher variable cost to volume ratio than the Kaling Tubes Ltd. It is 66.67 per cent for the competitors, assuming the selling price per unit for both the firms is same.
   BEP = FC/ P/V ratio = ₹3,00,000 = ₹1,00,000 P/V ratio
   P/V ratio = ₹1,00,000/ ₹3,00,000 = 33.33 per cent
2. The competitors are having lower sales price per unit. Their prices per units are 6.67 per cent lower than those of the Kaling Tubes Ltd as shown below:
   BEP = ₹1,00,000/(0.9333-0.60) = ₹1,00,000/0.3333 = ₹3,00,000
3. Partly due to higher variable cost to volume ratio or partly due to lower selling price, the sum of the difference is 6.67 per cent.

REVIEW QUESTIONS

RQ.14.1 In the following multiple choice questions, select the correct answers.

(i) The margin of safety for a firm in a very volatile market is 5 per cent. Which of the following is true?
(a) The margin of safety is probably too high, **(b)** The margin of safety is probably too low, **(c)** The margin of safety is adequate, **(d)** We can't tell.

(ii) Contribution per unit is ₹100. Fixed costs are ₹6,00,000. Production and sales are 8,000 units. When sales rise

(a) total contribution rises by an amount greater than profit, **(b)** total contribution rises by an amount smaller than profit, **(c)** total contribution and profit rise by the same amount, **(d)** contribution margin drops.

(iii) Contribution per unit is ₹100. Fixed costs are ₹6,00,000. Production and sales are 8,000 units. Total contribution is
(a) ₹6,00,000, **(b)** ₹4,00,000, **(c)** ₹8,00,000, **(d)** None of the above.

(iv) Contribution per unit is ₹100. Fixed costs are ₹6,00,000. Production and sales are 8,000 units. Profit is
(a) ₹2,00,000, **(b)** ₹6,00,000, **(c)** ₹6,00,000, **(d)** None of the above.

(v) Break-even is not affected with changes in
(a) sales price per unit, **(b)** variable cost per unit, **(c)** total fixed costs, **(d)** number of units sold.

(vi) Contribution margin ratio (C/V ratio) is 25%. The fixed costs are ₹30,00,000. The break even point is
(a) ₹1,20,00,000, **(b)** ₹60,00,000, **(c)** ₹30,00,000, **(d)** ₹15,00,000.

(vii) Variable cost is ₹400 per unit, fixed costs are ₹80,00,000, selling price per unit is ₹900, sales are 5,000 units. If selling price increases by ₹100, contribution increases by
(a) ₹10,000, **(b)** ₹100, **(c)** ₹5,00,000, **(d)** ₹80,00,000.

(viii) Variable cost is ₹400 per unit, fixed costs are ₹80,00,000, selling price per unit is ₹900, sales are 5,000 units. If fixed costs increase by ₹10,00,000, contribution
(a) increases by ₹10,00,000, **(b)** decreases by ₹10,00,000, **(c)** remains unchanged, **(d)** can't say.

(ix) Variable cost is ₹400 per unit, fixed costs are ₹80,00,000, selling price per unit is ₹900, sales are 5,000 units. If sales decrease by 2,000 units, contribution margin
(a) increases by ₹10,00,000, **(b)** decreases by ₹10,00,000, **(c)** remains unchanged, **(d)** can't say.

(x) Variable cost is ₹400 per unit, fixed costs are ₹80,00,000, selling price per unit is ₹900, sales are 5,000 units. The target profit is ₹1,00,00,000. What must the sales revenue be?
(a) ₹3,24,00,000, **(b)** ₹2,00,00,000, **(c)** ₹1,60,00,000, **(d)** ₹3,53,00,000.

(xi) Company B sells two products:
Product A: [Contribution margin ratio = 20%, Sales = ₹100,000]
Product B: [Contribution margin ratio = 40%, Sales = ₹200,000]
If actual sales were (A) ₹200,000 and (B) ₹100,000, total contribution would:
(a) increase by ₹20,000, **(b)** decrease by ₹20,000, **(c)** increase by ₹40,000, **(d)** decrease by ₹40,000

(xii) Company B sells two products:
Product A: [Contribution margin ratio = 20%, Sales = ₹100,000]
Product B: [Contribution margin ratio = 40%, Sales = ₹200,000]
If actual sales were (A) ₹200,000 and (B) ₹100,000, fixed costs are ₹50,000. The break-even point in sales revenue would be
(a) ₹175,000, **(b)** ₹200,000, **(c)** ₹150,000, **(d)** ₹187,970.

(xiii) One of the following is not an assumption that underlies CVP analysis.
(a) Fixed costs per unit will remain the same throughout the relevant range. **(b)** Variable cost per unit will increase as sales increases. **(c)** Variable costs have a linear relationship with sales. **(d)** Selling price is constant throughout the relevant range.

(xiv) Which is the correct equation that calculates P (profit before tax)
Assume, Selling Price per unit = ₹S, Variable Cost per unit = ₹V, Number of units sold = U units and Total Fixed costs = ₹F.
(a) P = SV – F, **(b)** P = U (S – V) – F, **(c)** P = FS – V, **(d)** P = S (V – S).

(xv) The break-even point is 10,000 units, sales are 12,000 units. The margin of safety expressed in percentage is:
(a) 16.67%, **(b)** 80%, **(c)** 120%, **(d)** 20%.

[Answers: (i) b (ii) c (iii) c (iv) a (v) d (vi) a (vii) c (viii) c (ix) b (x) a (xi) b (xii) d (xiii) b (xiv) b (xv) a.]

RQ.14.2 Define break-even analysis and outline its uses and applications.

RQ.14.3 (a) Discus the importance of the following in relation to break-even analysis:

(1) Break-even point
(2) Margin of safety
(3) Contribution
(4) Profit volume ratio.

(b) Write a short note on the angle of incidence in a break-even chart.

RQ.14.4 Explain the significance and objective of a break-even chart and state the factors which would cause the break-even point to change.

RQ.14.5 "The effect of a price increase is always to increase the P/V ratio, to bring down the break-even point and to widen the margin of safety." Discuss.

RQ.14.6 A "break-even chart must be used with intelligent discrimination, with an adequate grasp of assumptions underlying the technique surrounding its practical application." Elucidate the statement giving illustrations.

RQ.14.7 Draw a break-even chart with a few illustrative figures. Explain the VCP relationship. How would a change in selling price affect the above?

RQ.14.8 The "volume-cost-profit relationships provide management with a simplified framework for organising its thinking on a number of problems." Discuss.

RQ.14.9 Explain the limitations of a break-even analysis.

RQ.14.10 What is cash break-even point? Draw a cash break-even chart with hypothetical figures.

RQ.14.11 Asian Industries Ltd. specialises in the manufacture of small capacity motors. The cost structure of a motor is as under: Material, ₹50; Labour, ₹80; Variable overheads, 75 per cent of labour cost. Fixed overheads of the company amount to ₹2.40 lakh per annum. The sale price of the motor is ₹230 each.

(a) Determine the number of motors that have to be manufactured and sold in a year in order to break-even.
(b) How many motors have to be made and sold to make a profit of ₹1 lakh per year?
(c) If the sale price is reduced by ₹15 each, how many motors have to be sold to break-even?

RQ.14.12 You are given the following information:

Output and sales (10,000 units)	₹2,00,000
Variable costs per unit	12
Fixed cost	40,000

It is proposed to reduce the selling price by 10 per cent.

(a) Calculate present and future profit–volume ratio
(b) Calculate present and future break–even points and
(c) Compute the sales volume to maintain the profit at the present level

RQ.14.13 From the following information, find (a) BEP in rupees, and **(b)** number of units to be sold to earn a net income of 10% of sales:

Selling price	₹20 per unit
Variable cost	12 per unit
Fixed cost	₹2,40,000

RQ.14.14 For two periods sales and profits were as under

	Period I	*Period II*
Sales	₹4,00,000	₹5,00,000
Profit	1,00,000	1,40,000

Find **(a)** BESR, **(b)** Sales for a profit of ₹2,00,000, **(c)** Profit when sales are ₹6,00,000, and **(d)** Margin of safety when profit is ₹50,000.

RQ.14.15 Two companies P Ltd. and Q Ltd. producing and selling similar products forecasted their Profits and Loss a/c for the next year, which is as follows:

	P Ltd.		*Q Ltd.*	
Sales		₹3,00,000		₹3,00,000
Less: Variable Cost	₹2,00,000		₹2,25,000	
Fixed Expenses	50,000	2,50,000	25,000	2,50,000
Estimated Profit		50,000		50,000

Calculate:
(a) P/V ratio, break-even point, and margin of safety for both the companies. **(b)** Sales required to earn a profit of ₹30,000 for both companies. **(c)** Under the following situations, which company will show better results (i) Increase in sales (ii) Decrease in sales.

RQ.14.16 An analysis of costs of Sullivan Manufacturing Company gives the following information. You are required to determine

(a) Break-even sales volume

(b) Profit at the budgeted sales of ₹18,50,000.

Cost elements	*Variable costs (Percentage of sales)*	*Fixed costs*
Direct materials	32.8	
Director labour	28.4	
Factory overheads	12.6	₹1,89,900
Distribution overheads	4.1	58,400
Administrative overheads	1.1	66,700

RQ.14.17 PQR Ltd. has furnished the following data for the two years:

	Year I	*Year II*
Sales	₹8,00,000	?
Profit/volume ratio (P/V ratio) (%)	50	37.5
Margin of safety sales as a % of total sales	40	21.875

There has been substantial savings in the fixed cost in the year 2 due to the restructuring process. The company could maintain its sales quantity level of year 1 in year 2 by reducing selling price.

You are required to calculate the following:

(i) Sales for year 2

(ii) Fixed cost for year 2

(iii) Break-even sales for year 2

RQ.14.18 For two consecutive years, sales and losses were as follows:

Particulars	*Year 1*	*Year 2*
Sales revenue	₹10,00,000	₹15,00,000
Loss	2,00,000	50,000

Determine break-even sales.

RQ.14.19 The Taylor Company Ltd. produces two products, A and B. Expected data for the first year of operations is:

	A	*B*
Expected sales (units)	8,000	12,000
Selling price	₹45	₹55
Variable costs	30	35

Total fixed costs are expected to be ₹3,60,000 for the year.

You are required to answer the following:

(i) If sales, prices, and costs are as expected, what will be the operating income and the break-even volume in sales revenue?

(ii) Assume that prices and costs were as expected, but Taylor sold 12,000 units of A and 8,000 units of B. Recalculate the operating income and the break-even volume in sales revenue.

RQ.14.20 The per tyre price structure of a cycle made by the Cycle Company Ltd. is as follows:

Material	₹60
Labour	20
Variable overheads	20
	100
Fixed overheads	50
Profit	50
Selling price	200

This is based on the manufacture of 1 lakh tyres per annum.

The company expects that due to competition, they will have to reduce selling price, but they want to keep the total profit intact. What level of production will have to be reached, that is, how many tyres will have to be made to get the same amount of profits, if: (a) the selling price is reduced by 10 per cent, (b) the selling price is reduced by 20 per cent?

RQ.14.21 (a) From the following data of a manufacturing unit, find out (i) sales to break-even and (ii) sales to earn a profit of ₹8,000.

Sales (8,000 units @ ₹10)	₹80,000
Variable expenses	64,000
Contribution	16,000
Fixed expenses	24,000
Loss	(8,000)

(b) The following information is available for companies A and B.

	Company A		Company B	
Units produced and sold		40,000		40,000
Revenue		₹80,000		₹80,000
Variable costs	₹20,000		₹60,000	
Fixed costs	50,000	70,000	10,000	70,000
Net operating income		10,000		10,000

(i) What is the break-even point for each company?

(ii) How would you explain the difference that you observe between these companies' break-even points?

RQ.14.22 A company has an opening stock of 6,000 units of output. The production planned for the current period is 24,000 units and expected sales for the current period amount to 28,000 units. The selling price per unit of output is ₹10. Variable cost per unit is expected to be ₹6 per unit while it was only ₹5 per unit during the previous period. What is the break-even volume for the current period if the total fixed costs for the current period are ₹86,000? Assume that the first-in first-out system is followed.

RQ.14.23 Two manufacturing companies, having the following operating details, decide to merge:

	Company 1	Company 2
Capacity utilization (%)	90	60
Sales (₹lakh)	540	300
Variable costs (₹lakh)	396	225
Fixed costs (₹lakh)	80	50

Assuming that the merger goes through, calculate:

(i) Break-even sales of the merged plant and the capacity utilisation at that stage.

(ii) Profitability of the merged plant at 80 per cent capacity utilisation.

(iii) Sales turnover of the merged plant to earn a profit of ₹75 lakh.

(iv) When the merged plant is working at a capacity to earn a profit of ₹75 lakh, what percentage increase in selling price is required to sustain an increase of 5 per cent in fixed overheads?

RQ.14.24 A, B, and C are three similar plants under the same management who wants to merge them for better operation. The details are as under:

Plant	*A*	*B*	*C*
Capacity operated (%)	100	70	50
Turnover (₹lakh)	300	280	150
Variable costs	200	210	75
Fixed costs	70	50	62

You have to find out: (i) the capacity of the merged plant for breaking event, (ii) the profit at 75 per cent capacity of the merged plant, and (iii) the turnover from the merged plant to give a profit of ₹28 lakh.

RQ.14.25 Cookwell Ltd. manufactures pressure cookers with the selling price being ₹300 per unit. Currently the capacity utilisation is 60 per cent with a sales turnover of ₹18 lakh. The company proposes to reduce the selling price by 20 per cent but desires to maintain the same profit position by increasing the output. Assuming that all the increased output could be made and sold, determine the level at which the company should operate to achieve the desired objective.

The following data is further available:

(i) Variable costs per unit, ₹60.

(ii) Semi-variable costs (including a variable element of ₹10 per unit), ₹1,80,000.

(iii) Fixed costs, ₹3,00,000 will remain constant up to 80 per cent level. Beyond this an additional amount of ₹60,000 will be incurred.

RQ.14.26 Small Ltd. has been offered a choice to buy one out of two machines, 'A' and 'B'. You are required to compute:

(a) Break-even point for each of the machines.

(b) The level of sales at which both machines would earn equal profit.

(c) The range of sales at which one is more profitable than the other.

The relevant data is given below:

	Machines	
	A	*B*
Annual output in units	10,000	10,000
Fixed costs	₹30,000	₹16,000
Profit at above level of production	30,000	24,000

The market price of the product is expected to be ₹10 per unit.

RQ.14.27 Kalyan University conducts a special course on "Computer Applications" for a month during summer. For this, it invites applications from graduates. An entrance test is taken of the candidates and based on the same, a final selection of hundred candidates is made. The entrance test consists of four objective type examinations and is spread over four days with one examination per day. Each candidate is charged a fee of ₹50 for appearing in the entrance text. The following data relates to the past two years:

Statement of net revenue from the entrance text for the course on "Computer Applications"

	Year 1	Year 2
Gross revenue (fees collected)	₹1,00,000	₹1,50,000
Costs		
Valuation	40,000	60,000
Question booklets	20,000	30,000
Hall rent at ₹2,000 per day	8,000	8,000
Honorarium to chief administrator	6,000	6,000
Supervision charges (one supervisor for every 100 candidates at the rate of ₹50 per day)	4,000	6,000
General administration expenses	6,000	6,000
Total costs	84,000	1,16,000
Net revenue	16,000	34,000

You are required to compute **(a)** the budgeted net revenue if 4,000 candidates are expected to take up the entrance test next year, **(b)** the break-even number of candidates, and **(c)** the number of candidates to be enrolled if the net income desired is ₹20,000.

RQ.14.28 Bharat Company Ltd. is at present operating at 60 per cent capacity, producing at the rate of 10,000 units a month, a single product selling for ₹9 a unit. The current year's results are as follows:

Sales (1,20,000 units @ ₹9)		₹10,80,000
Cost of sales		
Direct material	₹1,80,000	
Direct labour	3,60,000	
Variable overheads	90,000	
Fixed overheads	1,35,000	7,65,000
Gross profit		3,15,000
Selling expenses		
Fixed	₹50,000	
Variable	36,000	22,000
Administration expenses: fixed		22,000
		2,07,000

Although this firm is operating at a relatively high net profit rate of almost 20 per cent on sales even at a plant capacity of 60 per cent; it is a fact that if the price per unit could be reduced by 20 per cent the volume of sales would increase to 1,80,000 units per year with an increase in the fixed manufacturing overheads of ₹9,000 per year. If sales price could be reduced by $33^1/_3$ per cent, the volume of sales would increase to a full capacity of 2,00,000 units with increase in excess of the 60 per cent level as follows: fixed manufacturing overheads, ₹11,000; fixed selling expenses, ₹2,000; and fixed administrative expenses, ₹6,000.

You are required to prepare **(i)** a comparative statement showing the net income under the three alternative profit-volume relationships, and **(ii)** compute the break-even sales point in each case.

RQ.14.29 The following information is furnished to you with regard to a manufacturing concern for its operations during year 1.

Direct material	₹1,75,000
Direct labour	50,000
Fixed overheads	55,000
Semi-variable overheads	70,000
Variable overheads	65,000
Sales (at ₹800 per unit)	4,00,000

It was estimated that, at *the existing level of capacity utilisation,* half the semi-variable overheads were in the nature of fixed overheads, whereas variable overheads accounted for the other half.

You are required to make necessary calculations to answer the following queries:

(i) At what level of output is the break-even point likely to be reached during the year 2, if there is no change in the price level?

(ii) What price per unit should be quoted in respect of a tender to be executed during year 3 if fixed costs are likely to go up by 10 per cent, variable costs by 20 per cent, and a 12 per cent profit margin is sought to be attained on the total cost?

RQ.14.30 A company is considering expansion. Fixed costs amount to ₹4,20,000 and are expected to increase by 1,25,000 when plant expansion is completed. The present plant capacity is 80,000 units a year. Capacity will increase by 50 per cent with expansion. Variable costs are currently ₹6.80 per unit and are expected to go down by ₹0.40 per unit with the expansion. The current selling price is ₹16 per unit and is expected to remain the same under each alternative. What are the break-even points under each alternative? Which alternative is better, and why?

RQ.14.31 The sales of Forma Ltd. in the first half of the current year amounted to ₹2,70,000 and profit earned was ₹7,200. The sales in the second half year registered an increase and amounted to ₹3,42,000. The profit earned was ₹20,700 in that half year. Assuming no change in fixed cost, calculate **(i)** the *P/V* ratio, **(ii)** the amount of profit when sales are ₹2,16,000, and **(iii)** the amount of sales required to earn a profit of ₹36,000.

RQ.14.32 The following particulars are given: current unit price, ₹1,000; unit variable cost, ₹500; fixed costs, ₹30 lakh.

The following two suggestions are under the consideration of the management of an industrial company: **(a)** 10 per cent reduction in price to yield an increase in sales volume from 6,600 to 7,900 units **(b)** 10 per cent increase in price with decrease in volume of sales from 6,600 to 5,700 units.

Prepare a statement comparing gross revenue, profit contribution and *P/V* ratio of these two alternatives with the present results. Which suggestion would you recommend?

RQ.14.33 Reprographics Ltd. manufactures a document-reproducing machine which has a variable cost structure as follows:

Material	₹40
Labour	10
Overheads	4
Selling price	90

Sales during the current year are expected to be ₹13,50,000 and fixed overheads, ₹1,40,000.

Under a wage agreement, an increase of 10 per cent is payable to all direct workers from the beginning of the forthcoming year, while the material costs are expected to increase by 7.5 per cent, variable overhead costs by 5 percent, and fixed overhead costs by 3 per cent.

You are required to calculate: **(a)** the new selling price if the current profit/volume ratio is to be maintained, and **(b)** the quantity to be sold during the forthcoming year to yield the same amount of profit as the current year, assuming the selling price is to remain at ₹90.

RQ.14.34 The cost structure (%) of an article with a selling price of ₹45,000 is as follows:

Direct material	50
Direct labour	20
Overheads	30

An increase of 15 per cent in the cost of material and of 25 per cent in the cost of labour is anticipated. These increased costs in relation to the present selling price would cause a 25 per cent decrease in the amount of present profit per article.

You are required **(a)** to prepare a statement of profit per article at present and **(b)** the revised selling price to produce the same percentage of profit to sales as before.

ANSWERS **[Comprehensive solutions to all numerical review questions are available on the companion website: http://www.mhhe.com/khan_jain_cost2e]**

RQ.14.11 **(a)** BEP 6,000 motors, **(b)** 8,500 motors, **(c)** 9,600 motors

RQ.14.12 **(a)** P/V ratio 40% and $33\frac{1}{3}$, **(b)** BEP 5,000 and 6,667 units, **(c)** ₹2,40,000

RQ.14.13 **(a)** BESR ₹6,00,000, **(b)** 40,000 units

RQ.14.14 **(a)** BESR ₹1,50,000, **(b)** ₹6,50,000, **(c)** ₹1,80,000, **(d)** ₹1,25,000

RQ.14.15 **(a)** P Ltd.: P/V ratio $33\frac{1}{3}$%, BESR ₹1,50,000, Margin of safety ₹1,50,000; Q Ltd.: P/V ratio 25%, BESR ₹1,00,000, Margin of safety ₹2,00,000 **(b)** P (₹2,40,000), Q (₹2,20,000) **(c)** **(i)** Company P **(ii)** Company Q

RQ.14.16 **(a)** BESR ₹15,00,000 **(b)** ₹73,500

RQ.14.17 **(i)** ₹6,40,000 **(ii)** ₹1,87,500 **(iii)** ₹5,00,000

RQ.14.18 BESR ₹16,66,667

RQ.14.19 **(i)** BESR ₹10,20,000, operating income is zero **(ii)** BESR ₹10,37,647, operating loss ₹20,000

RQ.14.20 **(a)** 1,25,000 cycles, **(b)** 1,66,667 cycles

RQ.14.21 **(a)** **(i)** BESR ₹1,20,000 **(ii)** ₹1,60,000
(b) **(i)** BSER ₹66,667 (Company A), ₹40,000 (Company B)
(ii) Fixed costs of Company A are higher than those of Company B

RQ.14.22 BEP = 20,000 units

RQ.14.23 **(i)** ₹25.9 lakh, **(ii)** ₹93 lakh, **(iii)** ₹791.23 lakh, **(iv)** 0.82%

RQ.14.24 **(i)** 52%, **(ii)** ₹80.5 lakh, **(iii)** ₹600 lakh

RQ.14.25 84.7% level of capacity

RQ.14.26 **(a)** BEP 5,000 units (Machine A), 4000 units (Machine B) **(b)** 7,000 units **(c)** 4,000 – 6,999 (B will be more profitable) for 7,000 units and above (A will be more profitable)

RQ.14.27 **(a)** ₹52,000 **(b)** 1,111 **(c)** 2,230

RQ.14.28 **(i)** Net income ₹2,07,000 (Existing), ₹81,000 (Reduction in price by 20%), loss ₹1,36,000 (Reduction in price by $33\frac{1}{3}$%) **(ii)** BESR ₹5,40,000 (Existing), ₹9,42,546 (Reduction in price by 20%) ₹30,13,333 (Reduction in price by $33\frac{1}{3}$%).

RQ.14.29 **(i)** 600 units **(ii)** ₹1,095.36

RQ.14.30 BEP 45,653 (Pre-expansion), BEP 56,771 (Post-expansion)
Net income ₹3,16,000 (Pre-expansion), ₹6,07,000 (Post-expansion)

RQ.14.31 **(i)** P/V ratio 18.75% **(ii)** Net loss ₹2,925 (6 months), ₹46,350 (12 months) **(iii)** ₹6,55,200

RQ.14.32 Increase in selling price is recommended.

RQ.14.33 **(a)** ₹97 **(b)** 17,114 units

RQ.14.34 **(a)** Profit ₹15,000 **(b)** ₹50,625

CASES

14.C.1 Thandak Desert Coolers (VCP Analysis) Mr Coolguy of 'Thandak' desert coolers enjoys a monopoly in his local market catering to around 10,000 customers every year. His friend Mr Imandar Singh of 'Zordar' pumps supplies him good quality pumps at very reasonable rates (₹400 per pump). The year 2012 was not a good year for Mr. Coolguy. He lost his good friend Mr Imandar in a road accident. He also lost most of his savings in share market scam. The Sun God did not bless him with a hot summer and the sales were expected to fall by 20 per cent. To make the matter worse, the new head of 'Zordar' pumps, Mr Opportunist Singh increased the price of pumps by 30 per cent.

Mr Coolguy asked his chief accountant, Mr Calculator Singh, to show the current financial data and the projected financial data if the supply from Zordar pumps were to be maintained. Mr Calculator Singh came out with the following reports.

Cost Data

The cost data is divided into two parts: fixed cost and variable cost. The fixed and the variable components of the mixed costs are separated. The variable costs are divided into three major categories: direct material cost, direct labour costs and the variable overheads. The division of all the cost data is tabulated, for 10,000 units as well as 8,000 units, as follows:

(I) **Present Scenario (10,000 units)**

Item	*Fixed cost*	*Variable cost and expenses*		
		Direct material	*Direct labour*	*Variable overheads*
Labour	₹12,10,000		₹20,00,000	
Steel sheets		₹60,00,000		
Electricity	35,000			₹1,00,000
Depreciation	15,06,620			
Pumps (@ 400 per unit)		40,00,000		
Khus		9,00,000		
Tubes		5,00,000		
Wires		50,000		
Fan		14,50,000		
Telephone	4,580			4,60,000
Rent (office)	1,20,000			
Office expenses	22,000			3,46,000
Bank charges	18,000			
Insurance	35,000			
Repair and maintenance	25,000			2,40,000
Recruitment				64,000
Travel				3,80,000
Conveyance	16,800			1,90,000
Post, courier and parcel	7,000			1,70,000
Miscellaneous				1,50,000
Total	30,00,000	129,00,000	20,00,000	21,00,000

(II) **Future Scenario if Pumps are Bought from Zordar Pumps (8,000 units)**

Item	*Fixed cost*	*Variable cost and expenses*		
		Direct material	*Direct labour*	*Variable overheads*
Labour	₹12,10,000		₹16,00,000	
Steel sheets		₹48,00,000		
Electricity	35,000			₹80,000
Depreciation	15,06,620			
Pumps (@ 520 per unit)		41,60,000		
Khus		7,20,000		
Tubes		4,00,000		
Wires		40,000		
Fan		11,60,000		
Telephone	4,580			3,68,000
Rent (office)	1,20,000			
Office expenses	22,000			3,46,000
Bank charges	18,000			
Insurance	35,000			
Repair and maintenance	25,000			2,76,800
Recruitment				51,200

(*Contd.*)

(*Contd.*)

Travel				3,04,000
Conveyance	16,800			1,52,000
Post, courier and parcel	7,000			1,36,000
Miscellaneous				1,20,000
Total	30,00,000	112,80,000	16,00,000	18,34,000

(III) Comparative Analysis of Both Scenarios

Item	*10,000 units*	*8,000 units*
Sales revenue @ ₹2,500 per unit	₹250,00,000	₹200,00,000
Less: Variable costs		
Direct material	129,00,000	112,80,000
Direct labour	20,00,000	16,00,000
Variable overheads	21,00,000	18,34,000
Total contribution	80,00,000	52,86,000
Less: Total fixed costs	30,00,000	30,00,000
Operating profits	50,00,000	22,86,000

After going through the report Mr Coolguy realised that his profits would drop by ₹27.14 lakh if he continued to purchase pumps from Zordar pumps and sales drop to 8,000 units. Since there were no other pump manufacturers in the market, the only alternative for Mr Coolguy was to manufacture the pumps indigenously. But he had lost most of his money and for manufacturing pumps he needed to expand his factory and purchase a new machinery (overall ₹5 lakh more was needed). Raw material for pumps would be needed which would cost ₹300 per unit. Additional labour would be required to make the pumps, thus increasing the labour costs to ₹250 per unit. The making of pumps would also draw more electricity etc. thereby increasing the variable overhead costs. The banks were not willing to finance him. Mr Lalchi Singh, the loan shark, saw opportunity to make money and offered to loan money to Mr Coolguy for a period of one year at the rate of more than 20 per cent, the loan to be paid in two instalments of, ₹3 lakh each, the first one is to be made in the first six months and the second instalment at the end of the year. The interest would be paid at the end of the year. If Mr Coolguy fails to pay back the interest and the principal on the due date, Mr Lalchi would be entitled to auction off the factory and get back his sum. Mr Coolguy now has to decide whether to accept the offer or not.

Mr Coolguy asked Mr Calculator to find out the implications of the above mentioned factors on the profits and whether he would be able to satisfy Mr Lalchi's conditions. Mr Calculator came out with the following reports:

(IV) Cost if Loan is Taken for Production of Pumps

Item	*Fixed cost*	*Variable cost and expenses*		
		Direct material	*Direct labour*	*Variable overheads*
Labour	₹12,10,000		₹20,00,000	
Steel sheets		₹48,00,000		
Electricity	35,000			₹360,000
Depreciation	15,06,620			
Khus		7,20,000		
Tubes		4,00,000		
Wires		40,000		
Fan		11,60,000		
Telephone	4,580			3,68,000
Rent (office)	1,20,000			
Office expenses	22,000			3,46,000

(*Contd.*)

(*Contd.*)

Bank charges	18,000			
Insurance	35,000			
Repair and maintenance	25,000			2,76,800
Recruitment				51,200
Travel				3,04,000
Conveyance	16,800			1,52,000
Post, courier and parcel	7,000			1,36,000
Machinery	5,00,000			
Miscellaneous				1,20,000
Pump shaft		800,000		
Pump wires		400,000		
Pump cylinder		10,00,000		
Lubrication and insulation		200,000		
Total	3500,000	95,20,000	20,00,000	21,14,000

(V) **Projected Profit when Pumps are Produced**

Sales revenue @ ₹2,500 per unit (8,000 units)	₹200,00,000
Less: Variable costs	
Direct material	95,20,000
Direct labour	20,00,000
Variable overheads	21,14,000
Total contribution	63,66,000
Less: Fixed costs	35,00,000
Operating profit	28,66,000
Less: Interest + Principal	6,00,000
EBT	22,20,000

Contribution per unit = ₹63,66,000/8,000 = ₹795.75

BEP (units) = Total fixed cost/contribution margin per unit

= ₹41,00,000/795.75 = 5,152 units

Attributing no fixed cost in the first six months so as to pay the first instalment comfortably:

Number of units to be sold in the first six months = ₹300,000/contribution margin per unit

= ₹300,000/₹795.75 = 377 units

Number of units to be sold in the next six months = ₹38,00,000/₹795.75 = 4,775 units

Attributing half the fixed costs in the first six months:

Number of units to be sold in the first six months = ₹20,50,000/₹795.75 = 2,576 units

Number of units to be sold in the next six months = ₹20,50,000/₹795.75 = 2,576 units

Mr Calculator's Inference:

Manufacturing pumps indigenously would eat away the profits by another ₹66,000. There is also an inherent risk of default of the first instalment to Mr Lalchi as it would not be possible to sell even 377 units in the off season. There is no reason why Mr Coolguy should go ahead with the idea of indigenous pumps.

After seeing the income statement and break-even analysis, Mr Coolguy decided not to take the loan but since his son, Mr Cooldude (doing MBA from IIT Delhi) had come home for a few days. He thought it wise to take his opinion too.

Cooldude came up with a radically different opinion. He suggested that since the machinery was meant for long-term use, it would not be prudent to charge its cost in the current year itself. It would be better to amortise the cost over a period of five years. He suggested to amortise ₹1 lakh per year (assuming no sale value at the end of 5 years). This gave a different picture altogether.

(VI) Cost Estimate (Revised)

Item	*Fixed cost*	*Variable cost and expenses for 8,000 units*		
		Direct material	*Direct labour*	*Variable overhead*
Labour	₹12,10,000		₹20,00,000	
Steel sheets		₹48,00,000		
Electricity	35,000			₹360,000
Depreciation	15,06,620			
Khus		7,20,000		
Tubes		4,00,000		
Wires		40,000		
Fan		11,60,000		
Telephone	4,580			3,68,000
Rent (office)	1,20,000			
Office expenses	22,000			3,46,000
Bank charges	18,000			
Insurance	35,000			
Repair and maintenance	25,000			2,76,800
Recruitment				51,200
Travel				3,04,000
Conveyance	16,800			1,52,000
Post, courier and parcel	7,000			1,36,000
Miscellaneous				1,20,000
Depreciation on machinery	100,000			
Interest	1,00,000			
Pump shaft		800,000		
Pump wires		400,000		
Pump cylinder		10,00,000		
Lubrication and insulation		200,000		
Total	32,00,000	95,20,000	20,00,000	21,14,000

(VII) Projected Profits (Revised)

Sales revenue @ ₹2,500 per unit	₹200,00,000
Less: Variable costs	
Direct material	96,00,000
Direct labour	20,00,000
Variable overheads	20,34,000
Total contribution	63,66,000
Less: Fixed costs	32,00,000
EBIT	31,66,000

Cooldude then explained his father that charging the entire cost of the machine in the current year leads to the reduction in profits of the current year. Such purchases (capital expenditures) should be amortised over a period of time. Besides, payment of loan is not an expense. It is expense only to the extent of interest paid. Thus, what seemed to be a decrease in profit by ₹66,000 was actually an increase by ₹8,80,000.

At this juncture, Mr Coolguy became very enthusiastic about taking the loan. Cooldude then warned his father that Mr. Lalchi might have set up a trap for him as it was the beginning of February. Generally, desert coolers are not bought in these months. It would be difficult to sell even a modest target of 377 units (not taking the fixed costs into account in the first six months) in these months. However, by offering heavy off-season discount (up to 20 per cent) the sales can be pushed up significantly. Proper advertising should be done so as to inform the people that the discount would be available only for a short-term. As Thandak has a monopoly in the region, the people would like to cash on this opportunity, and the sales would go up. The discount should be discontinued as soon as the cash position (with respect to the first payment of instalment) is reached.

New selling price = ₹2,000

Revise contribution per unit = ₹295.75

₹3,00,000/₹295.75 = 1,014 units.

As soon as 1,014 units are sold the discount should be discontinued.

(VIII) **Projected Profits with Change in Selling Price**

Total contribution = 1,014* ₹295.75 + (8,000 − 1014)* ₹795.75	₹58,59,000
Less: Fixed costs	32,00,000
EBIT	26,59,000

Thus, the proposition of Mr Lalchi is not devoid of connivance. In order to pay the first instalment of ₹3 lakh to Mr Lalchi, Mr Coolguy would have to forego a substantial profit.

Recommendations

- Mr Coolguy should not take the loan this year.
- A mild summer one year is usually a harbinger of a scorching summer in the following year, in the city of Mr Coolguy. The demand for desert coolers is likely to shoot up the next year. It would not be prudent then to keep up purchasing pumps from Mr Opportunity Singh.
- Investment for making pumps should me made next year's winter from the profits of this year's summer.

14.C.2 (Break-even Point) Sybergrid Solutions is a Web Publishing firm involved in the design and hosting of websites for corporates and business houses. As the initial investment required to start web publishing is low, several new entrants have entered/are planning to enter this business. There are also some established players who are willing to operate at low margins. Website publishing is highly competitive coupled with low market demand.

A website consists of a number of web pages. On average, any website would be made up of 50 web pages. The costs, revenues and time are calculated on the basis of production of one web page, that is 1 unit = 1 web page (selling as ₹1,000).

Besides, Biplab Saha, the owner of Sybergrid Solutions, there are three permanent employees—a visualiser who does the conceptualising and designing the graphics, a DTP operator to enter data and make the design on the computer and an office boy. One contract programmer is also hired as and when Sybegrid gets an order for developing a website. The total hours available in a month are (7.5 × 25 × 3) 564 hours. The annual capacity is (564 × 12) 6,768 hours. The total man-hours per web page to make 1 web page are 8 hours consisting of 3 hours each taken by visualiser and owner/entrepreneur and 2 hours by the DTP operator.

The monthly man-power expenses are as follows: (i) Owner/entrepreneur, ₹12,000 (ii) Visualiser, ₹5,000, (iii) DTP operator, ₹4,000 and (iv) Office boy, ₹1,500.

The investments and operational expenses are summarised below:

Capital cost:		
Computers (2)	₹80,000	
Printer (1)	12,000	
Scanner (1)	35,000	
Internet connection per annum	15,000	₹1,42,500
Fixed cost per month:		
Rent	3,000	
Telephone	600	
Electricity	1,000	

(*Contd.*)

(*Contd.*)

Floppy disk, stationery and office expenses	500	
Books	250	
Magazines/newspapers	150	
Conveyance	1,000	6,500

The variable costs are given below:

Cost	*Rate*	*Time taken per web page*
Additional labour	₹30/hr	1 hour
Telephone	1.5/minute	10 minutes
Electricity	₹20 per web page	

These costs are classified into fixed and variable in Exhibit 1.

Exhibit 1 Fixed and Variable Costs

Cost element	*Fixed cost (annual)*	*Variable cost per 100 web page*		
		Direct labour	*Direct expenses*	*Selling expenses*
Labour:		₹3,000		
Owner/entrepreneur	₹1,44,000			
Visualiser	60,000			
DTP operator	48,000			
Office boy	18,000			
	2,70,000			
Rent	36,000			
Telephone	7,200		₹1,500	
Electricity	12,000		2,000	
Internet connection	15,000			
Floppy disks, stationery and office expenses	6,000		1,000	₹200
Depreciation (10%)*	12,700			
Interest (13%)**	16,500			
Conveyance	12,000			500
Magazine/newspapers	1,800			
Books	3,000			
Total	3,92,000	3,000	4,500	700

*₹1,27,000 (₹80,000 + ₹12,000 + ₹35,000) × 0.10

**₹1,27,000 × 0.13 (This is the opportunity cost of interest lost on owners funds used to buy computer, scanner and printer).

REQUIRED:

(a) Compute break-even sales revenue to establish viability of business.
(b) Compute number of orders to make operating profit of ₹15,000 per month.
(c) Determine sales volume required to offset reduction in sale price from ₹1,000 to ₹700 to maintain operating profit of ₹15,000 per month.
(d) Determine selling price at which Sybergrid would not suffer cash losses.

Solution

(a) Viability of business:

- Breakeven point (amount): Fixed cost ÷ CV ratio = ₹3,92,000 ÷ 0.918@ = ₹4,27,015
  @Sales price, ₹1,000 – ₹82, variable cost per unit (₹8,200 ÷ 100) = ₹918 ÷ ₹1,000 = 91.8% = 0.981
- Break-even point (units) = ₹4,27,015 ÷ ₹1,000 = 427 pages
  Number of orders for website to break-even in one year = 427 pages ÷ 50 pages for an order on website = 8.54 (9) orders.

  Man-hours required = 398 × 8 = 3,184
  Total capacity = 6,278 man-hours
  Capacity utilisation = 6,278 ÷ 3,184 = 50%

(b) Number of orders to get a desired profit of ₹15,000 per month (₹1,80,000 annual)
= [Fixed expenses + Desired profit] ÷ C/V ratio
= (₹3,92,000 + ₹1,80,000] ÷ 0.918 = ₹6,23,094 ÷ ₹1,000 = 623 pages
Number of website sale to make classified profit = 623 pages ÷ 50 pages = 12.46(13) orders per year to get the desired profit of ₹15,000 per month

(c) Additional sales volume required to offset a reduction in selling price from ₹1,000 to ₹700
Contribution (₹700 – ₹82) = ₹618 (revised)
C/V ratio = 88.29%
Sales volume to offset reduced selling price = [Desired profit + Fixed expenses] ÷ Revised C/V ratio
= ₹5,72,000 ÷ 0.8829 = ₹6,47,865 ÷ 100 = 648 web pages to be sold
Number of orders per year = 648 pages ÷ 50 pages = 13 orders

(d) Lowest selling price at which Sybergrid would not suffer cash losses.
Cash fixed cost = ₹3,92,000 – ₹12,700 Depreciation = ₹3,79,300
Desired Contribution per page = ₹3,79,300/427 BEP = ₹888.29
Desired selling price per page = Desired contribution (₹888.29) per page + Variable cost (₹82) per page
= ₹970.29
Thus, the minimum price per web page should be ₹970.29 to avoid any cash losses.

14.C.3 (Break-even Analysis) Amit Behki is an automobile engineer. After graduating from the IIT-Delhi, he is planning to set up an automobile service station in NOIDA. The Amit Automobile Service Station (AASS) would carry out three activities: (i) free services of new vehicles under warranty, (ii) paid services including changing of parts and (ii) denting and painting of cars/vehicles.

The land on which the AASS would be set up, the estimated cost of which is ₹44,00,000 is owned by his family. A feasibility analysis conducted by Amit has revealed that the initial fixed cost of setting up of the AASS would be as detailed in Exhibit 1.

Exhibit 1 Initial Fixed Cost Estimates

Item/Description	*Amount*
Salary and wages	₹1,57,776
Staff welfare	6,852
Repair and maintenance	32,166
Conveyance	11,184
Printing/stationery	2,816
General expenses	1,539
Consumable stores (LUBES)	3,656

(*Contd.*)

(Contd.)

Postage/Telephone	8,948
Professional fee	15,000
Electricity	18,000
Local taxes	10,000
	2,67,937

The feasibility analysis also estimates the revenues and operating cost associated with the three workshop activities as detailed below:

Free Service of New Vehicles The service charges would be reimbursed by the Vehicle Dealer. The average reimbursement for the first, second and third services would be ₹233 per vehicle.

The variable costs related to the various service jobs performed by the cleaners/washers in servicing the vehicles are estimated as shown below.

• Detergents	₹20
• Diesel	18
• Cloth	20
• Polish	20
• Grease	30
• Stationery	5
• Customer hospitality (cold drink)	20
	133

Paid Services The variable costs would be the same as in the case of free servicing. An additional cost on parts changed would average ₹1,000 per vehicle.

The per vehicle average revenue would be ₹275. There would also be a 10 per cent margin on the parts changed.

Denting and Painting The lumpsum charged for full painting averages ₹8,000 per vehicle. The variable costs per vehicle are also shown below:

(i) Labour (painter) cost		₹1,500
(ii) Material costs:		
— Cleanser (4 litres × ₹26)	₹104	
— Additive solvent (8 litres × ₹126)	1,008	
— Putty	450	
— Paint (4 litres × ₹350)	1,400	
— Sheet metal	110	
— Sand paper	100	
— M-seal	350	
— Carbide for welding gas (8 × ₹32)	256	
— Welding rod	60	
— Files (2 × ₹375)	150	
— Rubbing and polish	200	
— Rubber seal compound	150	
— Nut bolts	100	4,438
		5,938

REQUIRED:

(a) If Amit wants the AASS to break-even in the first year, compute the breakeven (i) in units (number of cars)and (ii) in amount for all the three services offered?

(b) If Amit wants to earn a monthly surplus of ₹10,000, what would be the answer to (i) and (ii)?

Solution

(a) (i) Computation of break-even (in units) for free services, paid services and denting and painting

Free Service: Fixed cost ÷ Contribution margin per car = ₹2,67,937 ÷ ₹100 (₹233 – ₹133) = 2,680 vehicles ÷ 312 days (26 days in a month x 12 months) = 9 vehicles daily

Paid Services: ₹2,67,937 ÷ ₹242 [₹275 + ₹100(0.10 × ₹1,000) – ₹133 or ₹1,275 – ₹1,033] = 1,108 vehicles ÷ 312 days = 4 vehicles daily

Denting and Painting: ₹2,67,937 ÷ ₹2,062 [₹8,000 – ₹5,938] = 130 vehicles ÷ 12 = 11 vehicles per month

(a) (ii) Computation of break-even (amount)

Free Services: Fixed cost ÷ VC ratio = ₹2,67,937 ÷ 0.4292 (contribution margin, ₹100 ÷ ₹233, operating revenue) = ₹6,24,271

Paid Services: ₹2,67,937 ÷ 0.1898 (₹242 ÷ ₹1,275) = ₹14,11,681

Denting and Painting: ₹267,937 ÷ 0.25775 (₹2,067 ÷ ₹8,000) = ₹10,39,523

(b) (i) Computation of break (units) to earn a monthly surplus of ₹10,000 (annual surplus, ₹1,20,000)

Free Services: (Fixed cost, ₹2,67,937 + Desired surplus, ₹1,20,000) ÷ ₹100 = 3,880 vehicles per annum ÷ 312 days = 12 vehicles per day

Paid Services: (₹2,67,937 + ₹1,20,000) ÷ ₹242 = 1,603 vehicles ÷ 312 = 6 cars daily

Denting and Painting: (₹2,67,937 + ₹1,20,000) ÷ ₹2,062= 188 vehicles per year ÷ 12 = 16 vehicles monthly.

(b) (ii) Break-even (amount)

Free Services:(₹2,67,937 + ₹1,20,000) ÷ 0.4292 = ₹9,03,861

Paid Services:(₹2,67,937 + ₹1,20,000) ÷ 0.1898 = ₹20,43,925

Denting and Painting: (₹2,67,937 + ₹1,20,000) ÷ 0.25775 = ₹15,05,090.

14.C.4 (Break-even Analysis) Mr. Sharma has been manufacturing wooden table tops of sewing machines in Ajmer district of Rajasthan for the last 20 years. He supplies these wooden tables tops to various sewing machine table stand manufacturers and also sells them in the open market. Mr. Sharma had also started a foundry unit 20 years ago with one partner but this unit was closed and sold due to large losses and dispute with the partner after two years. Meanwhile, he earned good profit and reputation in manufacturing wooden table tops and visited various sewing machines table stand manufacturing units in the country. Based on his rich experience in this market, and in order to expand his business, he decided to manufacture sewing machine table stand himself under the 'GAUTAM' brand. For this, he decided to set up a new foundry unit to manufacture various table stand cast parts required in sewing machine table in addition to the existing wooden top manufacturing unit.

To fulfill his wish, Mr. Sharma purchased agricultural land 20 kilometers away from city in close proximity of Rajasthan Industrial Credit Corporation (RICCO) industrial area and later on converted it into industrial land for setting up the new casting unit. He designed the factory layout, cupola, heating furnace and also purchased required machinery and tools for casting within six months based on his experience. The unit started production in April, 2009.

Although Mr. Sharma is very sincere and hard working, he does not have any formal education in engineering and finance. His administrative staff is also not well educated. He is worried about his new casting unit because of his lack of formal knowledge in engineering and finance and due to his past failure.

Therefore, Mr. Sharma asked his son-in-law, Nitin Tiwari, who is faculty member in the Mechanical Engineering Department of Government Engineering College, Ajmer, to assist him. Nitin is an expert in design engineering and could not help much in this regard, but to maintain his rapport with his father-in-law, he decided to take help from one colleague, Mr. Devendra Choudhary, who has his post-graduation in Industrial Engineering and also has experience in financial management.

Mr. Choudhary readily agreed to help in order to get hands-on experience in this new and small casting unit. He visited Mr. Sharma and his company with Nitin in October, 2009 and gathered various cost data for break-even analysis.

Cost Data: Mr. Choudhary segregated cost data provided by Mr. Sharma into the following three categories:

Fixed Cost (at Normal Capacity of 60,000 Table Stands per Year)

Cupola	₹4,00,000
Expected life of cupola (years)	7
Temporary building shed	12,00,000
Expected life (years)	7
Heating furnace cost	2,00,000
Cost of Diesel Generator (DG) set	1,75,000
Cost of power connection	3,50,000
Monthly salary of permanent staff	35,000
Annual maintenance cost	2,00,000
Minimum monthly electricity bill	3,000
Minimum monthly telephone bill	3,000
Cost of patterns per year	30,000
Cost of machine block (air compressor sand blasting, lathe, grinding, drilling etc.)	13,25,000
Other annual costs which are fixed in nature (moulding boxes and crucibles)	14,429

The average economic life of plants in the casting industry is seven years. Annual fixed cost = (Cupola + Temporary building shed + Heating furnace cost + DG set + Cost of power connection + Cost of Machine block) = ₹36.4 lakh ÷ 7 = ₹5.2 lakh + (Annual maintenance cost + Cost of patterns + Others) + (Salaries of permanent staff per month + Minimum monthly electricity bill + Minimum monthly telephone bill) × 12 = ₹12,56,429.

Variable Cost

Direct material cost for charging cupola once:	
Coal	₹18,620
Cast iron scrap	45,000
Flux	150
Others	1,280
Less scrap @ 5%	2,250
Total	62,800
Direct labour cost for producing finished goods for above cupola discharge	20,000
Cost of machining, blasting, painting, heating, packaging for all other products produced during a charge of cupola	12,000
Other variable overheads	3,000
Total variable cost for charging cupola once	97,800
Number of table stands manufactured from above discharge of cupola	600
Variable cost per table stand (₹97,800 ÷ 600)	163

Mixed Cost

Month	*Total units produced (X)*	*Total mixed cost (Y)*	*XY*	*X^2*
April	1,134	7,90,890	89,68,69,260	12,85,956
May	1,584	9,61,488	152,29,96,992	25,09,056
June	2,171	12,18,672	264,57,36,912	47,13,241
July	2,353	13,13,455	309,05,59,615	55,36,609
August	1,672	10,50,232	175,59,87,904	27,95,584
September	3,458	20,91,612	723,27,94,296	1,19,57,764
October	4,856	29,13,600	1,414,84,41,600	2,35,80,736
	17,228	1,03,39,949	3,129,33,86,579	5,23,78,946

Segregation of mixed cost into fixed and variable cost using method of least square.

The basic straight line regression equation is

$$Y = a + b X$$

Where Y = Total mixed cost

a = Fixed cost element of mixed cost

b = Variable cost element of mixed cost

X = Total units produced per month

Two linear equations are:

$$\Sigma Y = na + b\Sigma X$$

$$\Sigma XY = a\Sigma X + b\Sigma X^2$$

Substituting the values from table of mixed cost gives

$$1{,}03{,}39{,}949 = 7a + 17{,}228b \quad (1)$$

$$3{,}129{,}33{,}86{,}579 = 17{,}228a + 5{,}23{,}78{,}946b \quad (2)$$

Solving equations 1 and 2 gives

a = 35,408 (fixed cost)

b = 586 (variable cost)

Total annual fixed cost = ₹12,56,429 + (₹35,408 × 12) = ₹16,81,325

Total variable cost per table stand = ₹163 + ₹586 = ₹749.

Break-even Analysis

Sales price per unit = ₹850 (excluding 4% VAT and CST)

Contribution margin per unit (CMPU) =Sales price per unit – Variable cost per unit = ₹101

C/V Ratio = Contribution margin per unit (CMPU) ÷ Sales price per unit

= 11.88 per cent

V/V Ratio = 100 per cent – C/V Ratio = 88.12 per cent

BEP (in units) = Total annual fixed cost ÷ Contribution margin per unit (CMPU)

= 16,81,325 ÷ ₹101 = 16,647 units

BESR = Total annual fixed cost ÷ C/V Ratio

= 16,81,325 ÷ 0.1188 = ₹1,41,52,567

Cash Break-even Point (in units) = (Total annual fixed cost – Depreciation/Amortisation) ÷ CMPU
= (₹16,81,325 – ₹5,20,000) ÷ 101 = 11,498 units

CBESR = (Total cash annual fixed cost = ₹11,61,325) ÷ C/V ratio
= ₹97,75,463

Margin of Safety (in units) = Actual/estimated sales – BEP (in units) = 35,000 – 16,647 = 18,353

Projected EBT = Margin of safety (₹) =18,353 × ₹101 = ₹18,53,653

Margin of Safety Ratio = (Margin of Safety ÷ Actual/Estimated sales) x 100 = 52.44 per cent

Desired sales volume (in units) to earn EBT of ₹10,00,000
= (Total annual fixed cost + Desired EBT) ÷ CMPU
= (₹16,81,325 + ₹10,00,000) ÷ ₹101 = 26,548

Confirmation

Total sales revenue (26,548 × ₹850)	2,25,65,800
Less variable cost (26,548 × ₹749)	1,98,84,452
Total contribution	26,81,348
Less total fixed cost	16,81,325
EBT/EAT	10,00,023

Sensitivity Analysis

(a) BEP (in units) if variable cost increase by 5 per cent due to inflation:

Revised variable cost = ₹749 × 1.05 = ₹787

Revised CMPU = ₹850 – ₹787 = ₹63

Revised BEP (in units) = Total annual fixed cost ÷ revised CMPU = ₹16,81,325 ÷ ₹63
= ₹26,688

(b) BEP (in units) if variable cost increases by 10 per cent due to inflation:

Revised variable cost = ₹749 × 1.10 = ₹824

Revised CMPU = ₹850 – ₹824 = ₹26

Revised BEP (in units) = Total annual fixed cost ÷ revised CMPU = ₹16,81,325 ÷ ₹26 = 64,666.

COMMENTS: The company will incur losses if variable cost increases by 10 per cent because of inflation even though it produces at its normal capacity, that is, 5,000 table stands per month.

14.C.5 (Break-even Analysis) Mr. Deepu Narayan is the proprietor of DoorStep Delivery Company (DDC) which deals in logistics transfer between two cities, Aravalibad and Nilgiribad. In each of these two cities, Deepu has opened a small warehouse cum-office which incurs him the following costs: (a) Office rent: ₹25,000 per month for each office, (b) Insurance: ₹40,000 per year for all the trucks, (c) Miscellaneous expenses: ₹5,000 per month and (d) Annual depreciation: ₹40,000 per truck.

He runs a fleet of 5 trucks, which run to and from the two cities covering a round the trip distance of 1,000 kms. He charges ₹11,000 per trip. The trucks cover the round trip in four days. A truck can do a maximum number of 80 trips a year and the following are the costs involved: (a) Fuel costs per km: ₹4, (b) Wear/tear cost per km: ₹0.2 and (c) Annual maintenance charges: ₹60,000. Every round trip involves paying ₹200 as toll tax at the border toll booth and ₹300 as food expenses to the truck staff. At both the cities loading and unloading of cargo is needed. This activity is outsourced to hired labourers who charge him ₹400 per loading/unloading of truck.

Deepu has also hired the following staff for operating his trucks and manning his warehouse/office(s): (1) Supervisor for each office @ ₹5,000 per month, (2) Driver for each truck @ ₹5,000 per month, and (3) Cleaner for each truck @ ₹2,000 per month.

Before the start of the financial year 2009-10, the economy went into recession. The company is not sure about the number of delivery orders that would be received in the coming financial year. But due to existing goodwill the company got proposals for annual contracts, at the current prices from two firms – Kaanch Manufacturers Limited (KML) dealing in glass products and Taj Mahal Marble (TM) dealing in different varieties of marble floorings. Both the companies agreed to provide DoorStep Delivery orders equivalent to 100 per cent (i.e. 400 round trips) of the company. However, the cost structure of the company has changesd due to the following factors:

- Accepting proposal from KML would lead to additional protective packaging cost of ₹2,00,000 per year which has been outsourced to Surakasha Packaging.
- Accepting proposal from TM would lead to rise in fuel costs by ₹0.6 per km because of additional freight weight. Also, wear and tear charges would be double.

REQUIRED:

(i) Compute the original BEP, BESR and EAT at 100 per cent capacity utilisation, assuming 35 per cent tax.

(ii) Due to uncertainty in future demand, the DoorStep Delivery Company is keen on accepting one of the above two proposals. Suggest which proposal the company should go for. Calculate BEP and BSER for the selected proposal.

(iii) After the first 6 month period, there is increase in the fuel prices by ₹0.80 per km. Also, the toll tax was abolished. Calculate the revised BEP, BESR and EAT.

SOLUTION

(i) Computation of BEP/BESR/EAT

Sales revenue = (₹11,000/round trip × 400 round trips)	₹44,00,000
Less: Variable costs:	
Fuel costs: (₹4 × 1,000 × 400)	16,00,000
Wear and tear costs (₹0.2 × 1,000 × 400)	80,000
Toll tax (₹200 × 400)	80,000
Food expenses for truck staff (₹300 × 400)	1,20,000
Loading and unloading charges (2 × 400 Trips × ₹400)	3,20,000
	22,00,000
Fixed costs:	
Salaries for supervisors (2 × ₹5,000 × 12)	1,20,000
Salaries for truck drivers (5 × ₹5,000 × 12)	3,00,000
Salaries for cleaners (5 × ₹2,000 × 12)	1,20,000
Rent (2 × ₹25,000 × 12)	6,00,000
Annual maintenance charges	60,000
Insurance	40,000
Miscellaneous (electricity etc.)	60,000
Annual depreciation for 5 trucks (5 × ₹40,000)	2,00,000
	15,00,000

(Contd.)

(Contd.)

Earnings before taxes [₹44,00,000 – (₹22,00,000 + ₹15,00,000)]	7,00,000
EAT (at 35 per cent tax) = [₹7,00,000 (1 – 0.35)]	4,55,000
Selling price per unit (SP of one round trip)	11,000
Variable cost per unit for 400 trips (₹22,000 ÷ 400)	5,500
Contribution margin per unit [CMPU = SP – VCPU) = ₹11,000 – ₹5,500)	5,500
Contribution to volume ratio = ₹5,500 ÷ ₹11,000 = 50 per cent	
Break even point for the year 2009-2010 (Fixed cost ÷ CMPU = ₹15,00,00 ÷ ₹5,500) = 273 roundtrips	
Cash BEP (₹13,00,000 ÷ ₹5,500) = 236 roundtrips	
Break even sales revenue for the year 2008-2009 = Fixed Cost ÷ CV ratio (₹15,00,000 ÷ 0.05) = ₹30,00,000	
Cash BESR (₹13,00,000 ÷ 0.5) = ₹26,00,000	

(ii) Computation of BE and BESR

(a) Accepting Proposal From Kaanch Manufacturers Ltd:	
Sales revenue (₹11,000 × 400 roundtrips)	₹44,00,000
Less Variable costs:	
Fuel costs (₹4 × 1,000 × 400)	16,00,000
Wear and tear costs (₹0.2 × 1,000 × 400)	80,000
Toll tax (₹200 × 400)	80,000
Food expenses for truck staff (₹300 × 400)	1,20,000
Loading and unloading charges (2 × 400 × ₹400)	3,20,000
	22,00,000
Fixed costs:	
Salaries for supervisors (2 × ₹5,000 × 12)	1,20,000
Salaries for truck drivers (5 × ₹5,000 × 12)	3,00,000
Salaries for cleaners (5 × ₹2,000 × 12)	1,20,000
Rent (2 × ₹25,000 × 12)	6,00,000
Annual maintenance charges	60,000
Insurance	40,000
Miscellaneous (electricity etc)	60,000
Annual depreciation for 5 trucks (5 × ₹40,000)	2,00,000
Annual payment to Suraksha Packages	2,00,000
	17,00,000
Earnings before taxes [₹44,00,000 – (₹22,00,000 + ₹17,00,000)	5,00,000
EAT (at 35% tax) (₹5,00,000 (1 – 0.35)	3,25,000
(b) Accepting Proposal From Tajmahal Marbles	
Sales revenue (11000/round trip × 400 roundtrips	44,00,000
Less: Variable costs:	
Total fuel cost (₹4.6 × 1,000 × 400)	18,40,000
Wear and tear costs (₹0.4 × 1,000 × 400)	1,60,000
Toll tax (₹200 × 400)	80,000
Food expenses for truck staff (₹300 × 400)	1,20,000
Loading and unloading charges (2 × 400 × ₹400)	3,20,000
	25,20,000

(Contd.)

(*Contd.*)	
Fixed costs:	
Salaries for supervisors (2 × ₹5,000 × 12)	1,20,000
Salaries for truck drivers (5 × ₹5,000 × 12)	3,00,000
Salaries for cleaners (5 × ₹2,000 × 12)	1,20,000
Rent (2 × ₹25,000 × 12)	6,00,000
Annual maintenance charges	60,000
Insurance	40,000
Miscellaneous (electricity etc)	60,000
Annual depreciation for 5 trucks (5 × ₹40,000)	2,00,000
	15,00,000
Earnings before taxes [₹44,00,000 – (₹25,20,000 + ₹15,00,000)	3,80,000
EAT (at 35% tax) ₹3,80,000 (1 – 0.35)	2,47,000
BEP = (₹17,00,000 ÷ ₹5,500) = 310 roundtrips	
BESR (17,00,000 ÷ 0.5) = ₹34,00,000	
Cash BEP (₹15,00,000 ÷ ₹5,500) = 273 units	
Cash BESR (₹15,00,000 ÷ 0.5) = ₹30,00,000	

Therefore, DoorStep Delivery Service should accept the proposal from Kaanch Manufacturers as the EAT is more.

(iii) Computation of Revised BEP/BESR/EAT

Total sales revenue for the first 6 months (200 × ₹11,000)	₹22,00,000
Total fixed cost recovered for the first 6 months (CMPU × No. of trips in 6 month) (₹5,500 × 200)	11,00,000
Total fixed costs left to be recovered (₹17,00,000 – ₹11,00,000)	6,00,000
Due to changes in variable costs, new CPMU would change:	
Existing variable cost per trip	5,500
Add, Petrol charges (₹0.8 × 1,000)	800
Less toll charges abolished	(200)
New variable cost per trip	6,100
New CMPU per trip (₹11,000 – ₹6,100)	4,900
New C/V ratio (₹4,900 ÷ ₹11,000) = 0.45	
Therefore, number of trips to recover fixed cost (₹6,00,000 ÷ ₹4,900) = 122	
Sales revenue to recover fixed cost (₹6,00,000 ÷ 0.45) = ₹13,33,333	
Therefore, new BEP (200 + 123) = 323 trips	
Number of trips to recover ₹4,00,000 (excluding depreciation) (₹4,00,000 ÷ 4,900) = 82	
Cash BEP (200 + 82) = 282 roundtrips	
New BESR (₹22,00,000 + ₹13,33,333)	35,33,000
Cash BESR	33,33,000
Total contribution margin for first six months	11,00,000
Total contribution margin for next six months	9,80,000
Total contribution margin for the year	20,80,000
Less fixed costs	17,00,000
Earnings before taxes (₹20.8 – ₹17)	3,80,000
Less corporate taxes (@ 35%)	1,33,000
Earnings After Taxes (EAT)	2,47,000
Depreciation charged	2,00,000
Therefore Cash profit after taxes	4,47,000

Summary

1. The original BEP, BESR and EAT at 35 per cent tax rate is 273 roundtrips, ₹30,00,000 and ₹4,55,000 respectively.
2. DoorStep Delviery Service should accept the proposal of Kaanch Manufacturers with a BEP of 310 roundtrips and a BESR of ₹34,00,000.
3. Revised BEP is 323 round trips and BESR is ₹35,33,000 and EAT ₹2,47,000.

Budgeting

Learning Objectives

1. Understand the planning process
2. Explain the definition, meaning and purpose of a budget
3. Discuss types of budgets and illustrate their preparation.

INTRODUCTION

Budgets are an important tool of profit planning. The purpose of this chapter is to present a general view of budgeting as a device of planning and illustrate the preparation of various types of budgets. Section 1 of the chapter provides a brief account of the planning process *vis-à-vis* budgeting. Section 2 elaborates on the meaning of a budget and the purpose of budgeting. The important types of budgets are discussed and illustrated in Section 3. The major points are summarised in the last Section.

PLANNING PROCESS

Budgeting, as a tool of planning, is closely related to the broader system of planning in an organistion. **Planning** involves the specification of the basic objectives that the organisation will pursue and the fundamental policies that will guide it. In operational terms, it involves four stages: (i) Objectives (ii) Goals (iii) Strategies, and (iv) Plans/Budgets.

Planning involves specifications of basic objectives and fundamental policies.

Objectives

The first stage in the planning and control system is setting the **objectives** which are defined as the *broad and long-range desired state or position in the future.* They are motivational or directional in nature and are expressed in qualitative terms. Examples of fundamental objectives are identification of the line of business, customer satisfaction, employee welfare, and so on. Thus, they are the basic policies.

Objectives are broad and long-range desired state or position in future.

Goals are quantitative targets to be achieved in specified period.

Goals

The second stage in the planning process is specifying the **goals**. The term goal, as an element in planning, represents targets, specific in quantitative terms, to be achieved in a specific period of time. The timing of introducing new products, purchase of new plant and machinery and expected rate of return are examples of time and quantity-oriented goals.

Strategies represent specific course of action to achieve goals.

Strategies

The next step involves laying down the strategies. **Strategies** denote specific methods/courses of action to achieve the goals, for instance, promotion of sales through price reduction or aggressive advertisement, financial alternatives, and so on.

Plans/Budgets

The final step is the preparation of budgets/profit plans. Basically, budgeting is the periodic planning to implement the alternatives during a particular fiscal period, usually one year. It converts, in other words, goals and strategies into annual operating plans.

BUDGET—DEFINITION, MEANING AND PURPOSE

A budget is defined as a 'comprehensive and coordinated plan, expressed in financial terms, for the operations and resources of an enterprise for some specified period in the future.'[1] According to this definition, the essential elements of a budget are: (i) Plan, (ii) Operations and resources, (iii) Financial terms, (iv) Specified future period, (v) Comprehensiveness, and (vi) Coordination.

Plan

The first ingredient of a budget is its plan. The term 'plan' with reference to budgeting has a *specific connotation.* It includes two aspects which have a bearing on the operations of an enterprise. One set of factors, which determine a firm's future operations are wholly external and beyond its control. Included in this category of factors are general business conditions, government policy and size and composition of population. The second set of factors affecting future activities are within the firm's control and discretion, that is, they are internal. The promotional programmes and manufacturing processes are illustration of these factors. Budgeting, as a plan, covers both these aspects. In other words, budgeting not only suggests what should happen but should also make things happen.[2] In brief, a budget (plan) is an expression partly of what the management expects to happen and partly of what the management intends to happen.

Operations and Resources

A budget is a mechanism to plan for the firm's operations and resources. The operations are reflected in revenues and expenses. This means that a budget should quantify the revenues to be realised from products/services and the expenses to be incurred on goods/services used in generating revenues.

The plan also covers the resources of the firm. The planning of resources means the planning of the various assets and the sources of capital to finance these assets. The assets could be fixed assets as well as current assets.

Financial Terms

Budgets are prepared in financial terms, that is, in terms of monetary value such as the rupee, dollar, and so on. The reason is that the monetary unit is a common denominator. The various activities and operations are expressed in different units, for example, material in terms of weight, labour in terms of number/man-hours, sales in terms of territories, advertisement in terms of magazine space, and so on. If they have to be integrated in a plan, they must be expressed in comparable units of measurement. Monetary units provide such a measure.

Specified Future Period

A budget relates to a specified period of time, usually one year. If it is not related to a time horizon, it will be meaningless. Planning merely for a given amount of, say, sales/profits will not constitute a budget unless a time dimension is added, that is, the budget sales/profit is planned to be achieved in a predetermined time framework.

Comprehensiveness

A budget is comprehensive in that all the activities and operations of an organisation are included in it. It covers the organisation as a whole and not only some segments. The *modus operandi* is that budgets are prepared for each segment/facet/activity/division of an organisation. These are integrated into an overall budget for the entire organisation. The overall budget is referred to as the **master budget**.

Master budget is the overall budget for the entire organisation.

Coordination

Budgets are prepared for the different components/segments/divisions/facets/activities of an organisation so as to take care of the situations and problems of each component. The budgets for each of the components are prepared in harmony with each another. This is called coordination.

Budgets—Purpose

As a tool, budgets serve as a guide to the conduct of operations and a basis for evaluating actual results. The main objectives of budgeting are: (i) Explicit statement of expectations, (ii) Communication, (iii) Coordination, and (iv) Expectations as a framework for judging performance.[3]

Explicit Statement of Expectations One purpose of budgeting is to state expectations in formal terms so that most of the underlying assumptions may be identified. A firm has the basic objective of optimising long-run profit. Its long-range goals also include survival, consumer satisfaction, employee welfare, personal power and prestige, and so on. These long-range objectives can be achieved in successive phases over a period of time. In other words, long-range objectives have to be split into short-term operational plans. Thus, a budget can be said to be a device to express goals which are sought to be achieved in a short period of time. In other words, it is a means to establish congruence between short-term goals and the long-term objectives of the firm. Therefore, budgets formulate targets of expected performance. The advantage is that by laying down targets, budgets contain an explicit statement of expectations. These targets help direct their operations, identify problems, help motivate lower-level employees and clarify the relationship between current activities and future policies.[4] Another implication is that budgets explicitly state the underlying assumptions and goal and/or the means of attaining it. To illustrate, if the sales target (projected sales) for any given period is ₹5,00,000, the budget will not only indicate this figure but will also give details about the assumed prices, quantity, sales efforts, and so on. This explicit statement of assumption is one of the most important contributions of budgeting for managerial planning and control.

However, a budget does not lay down a statement of expectations in rigid terms. Budgets, as observed earlier, are based on factors which are either uncertain or are beyond the control of management. Some of these are economic, social and business conditions; supply and demand; competition; consumer taste; technological innovations; and so on. A budget should be modified when necessary in the light of the changes in the factors/assumptions on which the original estimates were based.

Communication Another purpose of budgeting is to communicate or inform others of the goals and methods selected by top management. Since budgeting deals with fundamental policies and objectives, it is prepared by top management. A formal budget by itself will not ensure that a firm's operations will be automatically geared to the achievement of the goals set in the budget. For this to happen, the managers and lower-level employees have to understand the goals and support them and coordinate their efforts to attain them. In other words, the employees should be aware well in advance of the level of performance expected of them. It is for this reason that a budget is viewed as a means of communicating to the employees the level of performance expected of them so that the goals set out in the budget can be accomplished.

Coordination Yet another purpose of budgeting is coordination. The term 'coordination' refers to the operation of all departments of an organisation in such a way that there is no bottleneck or imbalance. In other words, coordination implies a harmonious relationship between various departments to ensure smooth and uninterrupted operation of each of them. If an organisation is to achieve its long-run goals, coordination in the activities of all its departments is necessary. If there is no coordination, imbalances will be created which will hinder smooth operation and stand in the way of the accomplishment of the goals of the budgets.

To illustrate, one type of imbalance may be between the manufacturing/production and sales departments. The manufacturing department may be producing goods, which the sales department may not be able to sell. Conversely, the sales department may like the production department to produce goods which the production department is incapable of producing. Another example of lack of coordination is the purchasing-manufacturing imbalance when the production schedule is not related to the raw material purchases. Further, the production schedule may not be based on the capability of employees and capacity of plant and machinery.

In view of the above, coordination is a major function of budgeting. Budgets should be drafted in such a way that the operations of the various departments are related to each other for the achievement of the overall goal. Apart from the interdepartmental reconciliation, budgets also provide for flexibility to accommodate plans and operations to unexpected situations.

Expectations as a Framework for Judging Performance Finally, a budget establishes expectations as a framework for judging employee performance. A budget, as observed earlier, defines the goals, the means of implementing them and the level of performance by the employees. The extent to which employees have succeeded in the task assigned to them, can be judged on the basis of a comparison of the actual performance/achievement with the budget. If the actual performance equals or exceeds the budgeted level, it may be termed satisfactory, otherwise not. Thus, a budget can serve as a yardstick to judge employee performance or as a control device.

To conclude, budgeting, as a tool of planning and control, serves as a guide to conduct operations and a basis for evaluating actual results. Actual results can be judged satisfactory or unsatisfactory in the light of the relevant budgeted data and also in the light of changes in conditions. However, a budget should not be regarded as a rigid requirement of performance. Many of the factors upon which a budget is based are beyond the control of management and all of them are uncertain. The budget should, therefore, be regarded as a plan, not an immutable commitment of performance; it is a means of control, but not a straitjacket on operations.[5] In view of its significance as a managerial tool, the preparation of a budget is illustrated in the pages that follows.

PREPARATION/TYPES OF BUDGETS

It may be recalled that a budget with reference to planning and control refers to a comprehensive and coordinated budget generally known as master budget. In operational terms, a comprehensive or overall budget has several components. A master budget normally consists of three types of budgets: **(i)** Operating budgets, **(ii)** Financial budgets, and **(iii)** Special decision budgets. Another classification of a master budget is: **(i)** Fixed/static budget and **(ii)** Flexible/variable/sliding budget. In the discussions that follow we illustrate the preparation of the various components of a master budget, namely, operating and financial budgets. The mechanics of the preparation of a flexible budget is also discussed.

Operating Budgets

Operating budgets relate to the physical activities/operations of a firm such as sales, production, purchasing, debtors collection and creditors payment schedules. In specific terms, an **operating budget** has the following components:

Operating budgets relate to physical activities/operations such as sales, production, and so on.

1. Sales budget,
2. Production budget,
3. Purchase budget,
4. Direct labour budget,
5. Manufacturing expenses budget, and
6. Administrative and selling expenses budget, and so on.

Financial Budgets

Financial budgets are concerned with expected cash receipts/disbursements, financial position and results of operations. In other words, a financial budget has the following components:

Financial budgets are concerned with expected cash flows, financial position and result of operations.

1. Budgeted income statement,
2. Budgeted statement of retained earnings,
3. Cash budget, and
4. Budgeted balance sheet.

Cash Budget The principal aim of the cash budget, as a tool of planning, is to ascertain whether, at any time, there is likely to be an excess or shortage of cash. The preparation of a cash budget involves various steps.

The *first* element of a cash budget is the selection of the period of time to be covered by the budget. Alternatively, it is referred to as the 'planning horizon'. The planning horizon means the *time span* and the sub-periods within that time span over which the cash flows are to be projected. There is no hard and fast rule. The period coverage of a cash budget will differ from firm to firm depending upon its nature and the degree of accuracy with which the estimates can be made. As a general rule, the period selected should be neither too long nor too short. If it is too long, it is likely that the estimates will be upset as we cannot visualise them at the time of the preparation of the budget. If on the other hand, the time span is too small, the disadvantage are: **(i)** Failure to take into account important events which lie just beyond the period covered by the budget; **(ii)** Heavy workload in preparation; and **(iii)** Abnormal factors that may be operative.

The planning horizon of a cash budget should be determined in the light of the circumstances and requirements of a particular case. For instance, if the flows are expected to be stable and dependable, such a firm may prepare a cash budget covering a long period, say, a year and divide it into quarterly intervals. In the case of a firm whose flows are uncertain, a quarterly budget divided into monthly intervals may be appropriate. Where flows are affected by seasonal variations, monthly sub-divided into weekly or even daily budgets may be necessary. If the flows are subject to extreme fluctuations, a daily budget may be called for. The idea behind sub-dividing the budget period into smaller intervals is to highlight the movement of cash from one sub-period to another. The sub-division will provide information on the fluctuations in the cash reservoir level during the time span covered by the budget.

The *second* element of the cash budget is the factors that have a bearing on cash flows. The items included in the cash budget are the cash items only, non-cash items such as *depreciation* are excluded.[6] The factors that generate cash flow are generally divided, for purposes of constructing a cash budget, into two broad categories: **(a)** Operating and **(b)** Financial. This two-fold classification of cash budget items is based on their 'nature'. While the former category includes cash flows generated by the operations of the firms and are known as the 'operating cash flows,' the latter consist of the 'financial cash flows.' The major components of the two types of cash flows are outlined below.

Operating Cash Flows The main operating factors/items which generate cash outlfows and inflows over the time span of a cash budget are tabulated in Exhibit 15.1.

Exhibit 15.1 Operating Cash Flow Items

Cash inflows/Receipts	*Cash outflows/Disbursements*
1. Cash sales	1. Accounts payable/Payable payments
2. Collection of accounts receivable	2. Purchase of raw materials
3. Disposal of fixed assets	3. Wages and salary (pay roll)
	4. Factory expenses
	5. Administrative and selling expenses
	6. Maintenance expenses
	7. Purchase of fixed assets

Among the operating factors affecting cash flows, the collection of accounts receivable (inflows) and accounts payable (outflows) are the most important. The terms of credit and the speed with which the customers pay would determine the lag between the creation of the accounts receivable and their collection. Also, discounts and allowances for early payments, return from customers and bad debts affect the cash inflows. Similarly, accounts payable relating to credit purchases are affected by the purchase terms.

Financial Cash Flows The major financial factors/items affecting generation of cash flows are depicted in Exhibit 15.2.

Exhibit 15.2 Financial Cash Flow Items

Cash inflows/Receipts	*Cash outflows/Payments*
1. Loans/borrowings	1. Income tax/tax payments
2. Sale of securities	2. Redemption of loan
3. Interest received	3. Re-purchase of shares
4. Dividend received	4. Interest paid
5. Rent received	5. Dividends paid
6. Refund of tax	
7. Issues of new shares and securities	

After the time span of the cash budget has been decided upon and pertinent operating and financial factors have been identified, the final step is the construction of the cash budget.

The preparation of the master budget is illustrated in Example 15.1.

EXAMPLE 15.1

The following data relate to Hypothetical Limited:

Balance Sheet as at March 31, Current Year

Liabilities	*Amount*	*Assets*		*Amount*
Accounts payable (all for March purchases)	₹40,000	Cash		₹3,00,000
Taxes payable (all for March income)	25,000	Accounts receivable (all from March sales)		2,50,000
Share capital	11,00,000	Inventories:		
Retained earnings	10,26,800	Raw materials (9,600 kgs × ₹3)		28,800
		Finished goods (1,800 units × ₹35)		63,000
		Fixed assets:		
		Cost	₹20,00,000	
		Less: Accumulated depreciation	(4,50,000)	15,50,000
	21,91,800			21,91,800

2. *Sales forecasts:* Assume the marketing department has developed the following sales forecast for the first quarter of the next year and the selling price of ₹50 per unit.

Month	*Units sales*
April	9,000
May	12,000
June	16,000

3. The management desires closing inventory to equal 20 per cent of the following month's sales.
4. The manufacturing costs are as follows:

Direct materials: (5 kgs × ₹3) (per unit)	₹15
Direct labour	5
Variable overheads	9
Total fixed overheads (per annum)	7,20,000

5. Normal capacity is 1,20,000 units per annum. Assume absorption costing basis.
6. Each unit of final product requires 5 kgs of raw materials. Assume management desires closing raw material inventory to equal 20 per cent of the following month's requirements of production.
7. Assume fixed selling and administrative expenses are ₹20,000 per month and variable selling and administrative expenses are ₹5 per unit sold.
8. All sales are on account. Payment received within 10 days from the date of sale are subject to a 2 per cent cash discount. In the past, 60 per cent of the sales were collected during the month of sale and 40 per cent are collected during the following month. Of collections during the month of sale, 50 per cent are collected during the discount period. Accounts receivable are recorded at the gross amount and cash discounts are treated as a reduction in arriving at net sales during the month they are taken.
9. Tax rate is 35 per cent.
10. Additional information:
    (a) All purchases are on account. Two-thirds are paid for in the month of purchase and one-third, in the following month.
    (b) Fixed manufacturing costs include depreciation of ₹20,000 per month.
    (c) Taxes are paid in the following month.
    (d) All other costs and/or expenses are paid during the month in which incurred.

From the foregoing information prepare a master budget for the month of April only.

SOLUTION

1. Production Budget

Particulars	April	May
Sales (units)	9,000	12,000
Add: Desired closing inventory (0.20 × next month's sales)	2,400	3,200
Total finished goods requirement	11,400	15,200
Less: Opening inventory	(1,800)	(2,400)
Required production (units)	9,600	12,800

2. Manufacturing Cost Budget

Particulars	April
Required production (units)	9,600
Direct material cost (5 kgs × ₹3 per kg)	× ₹15
Total direct material cost	₹1,44,000
Total direct labour cost (₹5 per unit)	48,000
Total variable overhead cost (₹9 per unit)	86,400
Total variable manufacturing costs	2,78,400
All fixed manufacturing overheads (₹7,20,000 ÷ 12 months)	60,000
Total manufacturing cost	3,38,400

3. Purchase Budget (Raw Materials)

Particulars	April	May
Production requirement (units)	9,600	12,800
Raw material required for production @ 5 kgs per unit (kgs)	48,000	64,000
Add: Desired closing inventory (0.20 × May requirements)	12,800	
Total requirements	60,800	
Less: Opening inventory	(9,600)	
Purchase requirement	51,200	
Purchase requirement (amount @ ₹3 per kg)	₹1,53,600	

4. Selling and Administrative Expenses Budget

Particulars	April
Units sales	9,000
Variable costs @ ₹5 per unit	₹45,000
Fixed costs	20,000
Total selling and administrative expenses	65,000

5. Cost of Goods Sold Budget

Particulars		April
Units sold		9,000
Cost per unit		
Variable	₹29	
Fixed (₹60,000 ÷ 10,000 units)	6	× ₹35
Total cost		3,15,000

6. Budgeted Income Statement for the Month of April

Gross sales (9,000 × ₹50)	₹4,50,000
Less: Cash discount (₹4,50,000 × 0.6 × 0.5 × 0.02)	2,700

(Contd.)

(*Contd.*)

Net sales	4,47,300
Less: Cost of goods sold	3,15,000
Gross margin (unadjusted)	1,32,300
Less: Capacity variance unfavourable (400 units × ₹6)	2,400
Gross margin (adjusted)	1,29,900
Less: Selling and administrative expenses	65,000
Earnings before taxes	64,900
Less: Taxes (0.35)	22,715
Earning after taxes	42,185

7. Budgeted Statement of Retained Earnings

Opening balance	₹10,26,800
Add: Earnings after taxes	42,185
Closing balance	10,68,985

8. Cash Budget (April)

Opening balance			₹3,00,000	
Cash inflows:				
Collection from debtors:				
March sales		₹2,50,000		
April sales (gross) (₹4,50,000 × 0.60)	₹2,70,000			
Less: Cash discount (₹2,70,000 × 0.5 × 0.02)	2,700	2,67,300	5,17,300	₹8,17,300
Cash outflows:				
Payment to creditors:				
For March purchases		40,000		
For April purchases (₹1,53,600 × 2/3)		1,02,400	1,42,400	
Direct labour			48,000	
Variable manufacturing overhead			86,400	
Fixed manufacturing overhead		60,000		
Less: Depreciation		(20,000)	40,000	
Variable selling and administrative overheads			45,000	
Fixed selling and administrative overheads			20,000	
Taxes			25,000	4,06,800
Closing balance				4,10,500

9. Pro forma Balance Sheet as at March 31, Next Year

Liabilities	*Amount*	*Assets*		*Amount*
Accounts payable (₹40,000 + ₹1,53,600 – ₹1,42,400)	₹51,200	Cash		₹4,10,500
Taxes payable (₹25,000 + ₹22,715 – ₹25,000)	22,715	Accounts receivable (₹4,50,000 × 0.40)		1,80,000
Share capital	11,00,000	Inventories:		
Retained earnings	10,68,985	Raw material (12,800 × ₹3)	₹38,400	
		Finished goods (2,400 × ₹35)	84,000	1,22,400
		Fixed assets:		
		Cost	20,00,000	
		Less: Accumulated depreciation	(4,70,000)	15,30,000
	22,42,900			22,42,900

Special Decision Budgets

The third category of budgets are special decision budgets. They relate to inventory levels, break-even analysis, and so on. These are discussed comprehensively in other chapters of this volume.[7]

Flexible Budgets

The discussion of the **master budget** and its components in the preceding section was based on the assumption of fixed level of activity. In other words, the budgets were related to a specific level of operation implying thereby that a firm can accurately and precisely forecast the level of its behaviour/operations in a given period of time. If the business environment is capable of accurate prediction, this approach to budgeting is likely to yield dependable results. If, however, changes take place during the budget period, the budget will serve no useful purpose. Such a budget is technically referred to as a fixed/static budget. In other words, budgets prepared at a single level of activity, with no prospect of modification in the light of the changed circumstances, are fixed or static budgets. The alternative to fixed budgets are **flexible/variable/sliding budgets**. The term 'flexible' is the most apt description of the essential features/characteristics of these budgets and is used here to refer to such budgets.

Flexible budget estimates costs at several levels of activity.

A **flexible budget** estimates costs at several levels of activity. The merit of a flexible budget is that instead of one estimate it contains several estimates/plans in different assumed circumstances. Since business activities cannot be accurately predicted as the business conditions/environment are uncertain, it is a useful tool in real business situations, that is, an unpredictable environment. In view of its significance as a more realistic basis of budgeting, the setting up of a flexible budget is demonstrated in the discussions that follow.

It may at the outset be noted that the construction of a flexible budget is similar to that of a fixed budget except in one respect. While the fixed budget is based on costs and other business operations/activities at one level, the flexible budget considers several alternatives/levels/volumes of activity. The term 'volume/level' of activity refers to the usage of capacity. In other words, volume/level of activity signifies the percentage use of capacity. The term 'capacity' means the *installed capacity* of plant and personnel, that is, the fixed amount invested in these. For instance, if a plant when fully operated can produce 5,000 units, its capacity is 5,000 units of production. Assuming 2,500 units of production in a given period, the volume/level of activity is 50 per cent.

Thus, the essence of a flexible budget is the presentation of estimated cost data in a manner that permits their determination at various levels of volume. This means that all costs must be identified as to how they behave with a change in volume—whether they vary or remain fixed. The conceptual framework of flexible budgeting, therefore, relates to: **(i)** Measure of volume and **(ii)** Cost behaviour identified with change in volume.

Measure of Volume The volume measure selected for any given department/firm should be that quantity which displays the greatest degree of correlation with those costs that vary with the level of operating activity. Different departments may use different measures of volume. In the first place, the measure of volume may be expressed in terms of the activity or factor that causes costs to vary, for example, labour costs vary on the basis of number of hours worked, material costs vary due to quantity of materials consumed. Secondly, the volume measure should be related to factors controllable by management, that is, number of hours worked, the quantity of materials consumed and number of machine hours operated. Further, the activity chosen as a unit of measure should be one that is not greatly affected by factors other than volume, that is, quantity more useful than cost as indicator of volume. In brief, volume should be expressed in terms of some unit of input, such as direct labour hours, direct labour cost or machine hours. The measure applied in any particular case will depend on the peculiarities. For instance, in the light machinery department, direct labour hours may be an appropriate measure. But for the heavy machinery department, machine hours may be the best indicator of cost behaviour.

Cost Behaviour with Change in Volume Three different types of cost behaviour can be visualised with changes in volume/level of activity: **(i)** Fixed costs, **(ii)** Variable costs, and **(iii)** Mixed costs.

Fixed Costs The fixed costs are associated with inputs that do not fluctuate in response to changes in the total activity or output of the firm, within relevant range for a given budget period. They may also be called *non-variable costs.* They are normally fixed for a relevant range of volume but fluctuate beyond that range. Moreover, fixed costs are to be analysed in relation to a given period of time; they are subject to change over a period of time.

Fixed costs are fixed for a relevant range of volume for a given budget period.

Fixed costs may be: **(i)** Committed and **(ii)** Discretionary. Fixed costs that are associated with the acquisition of capacity-producing assets are known as the committed fixed costs. The identifying characteristic of a committed cost is that its occurrence as well as amount are predetermined and can be altered only by another major decision to reverse or amend the earlier commitment. Also known as *managed costs,* discretionary costs result from management decisions. They are incurred as well as reduced at the discretion of the management.

Each of the two types of fixed costs has a different implication for the budgetary process. Committed fixed costs can be budgeted on the basis of past commitment. Discretionary fixed cost, on the other hand, can be budgeted on the basis of inquiry from the decision-makers/management.

Variable Costs The variable costs are costs that are assumed to fluctuate in direct proportion to production activity/sales activity/some other measure of volume within relevant range for a given budget period. The level of variable costs at any volume can be estimated easily if the relationship between costs and volume is shown.

Variable costs fluctuate in direct proportion to activity/volume within relevant range for a given budget period.

Mixed Costs The mixed costs are composed of both fixed and variable elements. The fixed part of mixed costs often represents a cost of capacity, while the variable element is influenced by changed in activity. For budgeting purposes, mixed costs must be broken down into their fixed and variable components/segments. Once this is done, the amount of fixed costs and the rate at which total variable costs change in proportion to total changes in output/volume can be worked out. That is, the fixed costs remain constant regardless of activity, but the variable portion is assumed to change in direct proportion to change in labour hours, labour costs, machine hours, material costs/material quantity, and so on.

Mixed costs are composed of both fixed and variable elements.

The main elements in the construction of a flexible budget have been outlined above. To summarise, a flexible budget, in a sense, is a series of fixed budgets and an increase or decrease (any change) in the level/volume of activity must be reflected in it. Each expense in each department/segment is to be categorised into fixed, variable and mixed components. A budget may be first prepared at the expected level of activity, say, 100 per cent of capacity. Additional columns may then be added for costs below and above 100 per cent, say, 90 per cent and 110 per cent.

Hypothetical flexible budgets corresponding to the procedure described above for two departments of a firm: Maintenance and Manufacture, are illustrated in Tables 15.1 and 15.2.

Table 15.1 Hypothetical Ltd—Flexible Budget (Maintenance Department)

Volume (labour-hours)	*400*	*450*	*500*	*550*	*600*
Variable costs:					
Labour	₹6,000	₹6,750	₹7,500	₹8,250	₹9,000
Material	2,400	2,700	3,000	3,300	3,600
Others	800	900	1,000	1,100	1,200
Mixed costs:					
Labour	2,300	2,400	2,500	2,600	2,700
Maintenance	1,400	1,450	1,500	1,550	1,600
Other supplies	2,500	2,750	3,000	3,250	3,500
Discretionary fixed costs:					
Training	1,500	2,000	2,000	2,000	2,500
Experimental methods	3,500	4,000	4,000	4,000	4,500
Committed fixed costs:					
Depreciation	5,000	5,000	5,000	5,000	5,000
Rent, lease cost	3,500	3,500	3,500	3,500	3,500
Total	28,900	31,450	33,000	34,550	37,100

Table 15.2 Hypothetical Ltd—Flexible Budget (Manufacturing Department)

Volume(machine-hours)	*50*	*60*	*70*	*80*	*90*
Variable costs:					
Power	₹500	₹600	₹700	₹800	₹900
Helpers	250	300	350	400	450
Discretionary fixed costs:					
Training	800	900	900	900	1,000
Tools	200	200	200	300	300
Committed fixed costs:					
Depreciation	1,200	1,200	1,200	1,200	1,200
Rent	1,000	1,000	1,000	1,000	1,000
Total	3,950	4,200	4,350	4,600	4,850

Modified Flexible Budgets From the preceding discussion it should be clear that flexible budgets, as a tool of planning and control, are superior to fixed budgets. The major weaknesses of static budgets are their inability to: **(i)** Disclose the potential variability of various estimates used in preparing the budget and **(ii)** Indicate the range within which costs can be expected to fall. They are not useful, therefore, in an uncertain and unpredictable environment. Flexible budgets are better in that they present estimates of costs at different level/volume of activity. But their one limitation is that they do not explicitly consider the relative probability that any particular volume or cost will be achieved.[8] This limitation can be overcome by using a modified flexible budget, which will include columns for different levels of estimates—most likely, optimistic and pessimistic. The hypothetical modified flexible budget is shown in Table 15.3.

Table 15.3 Hypothetical Ltd—Modified Flexible Budget (Manufacturing Department)

	Pessimistic	*Most likely*	*Optimistic*
Volume (labour-hours)	*425*	*500*	*585*
Variable costs:			
Labour	₹6,375	₹7,500	₹8,775
Materials	2,650	3,000	3,510
Others	850	1,000	1,170
Mixed costs:			
Labour	2,350	2,500	3,425
Maintenance	1,425	1,500	1,585
Other supplies	2,625	3,000	2,670
Discretionary fixed costs:			
Training	1,750	2,000	2,250
Experimental methods	3,750	4,000	4,250
Committed fixed costs:			
Depreciation	5,000	5,000	5,000
Rent, etc.	3,500	3,500	3,500
Total	30,275	33,000	36,135

SUMMARY

- Budgeting is a tool of planning. Planning involves specification of the basic objectives that the organisation will pursue and the fundamental policies that will guide it. In operational terms, it involves four steps: **(i)** Objectives defined as the broad and long-range desired state/position of the firm, **(ii)** Specified goals-targets in quantitative terms to be achieved in a specified period of time, **(iii)** Strategies or specific methods/course of action to achieve these goals, and **(iv)** Budgets to convert goals and strategies into annual operating plans.
- A budget is defined as a comprehensive and coordinated plan, expressed in financial terms, for the operations and resources of an enterprise for some specified period in the future. The essential elements of a budget are: **(i)** Plan, **(ii)** Financial terms, **(iii)** Operations and resources, **(iv)** Specific future period, **(v)** Comprehensive coverage, and **(vi)** Coordination. As a tool, a budget serves as a guide to conduct operations and a basis for evaluating actual results. The main objectives of budgeting are: **(i)** Explicit statement of expectations, **(ii)** Communicati(*Contd.*)on, **(iii)** Coordination, and **(iv)** Expectations as a framework for judging performance.
- The overall budget is known as the master budget. It has the following components: **(i)** Sales budget, **(ii)** Production budget, **(iii)** Purchase budget, **(iv)** Direct labour budget, **(v)** Manufacturing expenses budget, **(vi)** Administrative and selling expenses budget, **(vii)** Budgeted income statement, **(viii)** Cash budget, and **(ix)** Budgeted balance sheet.
- The cash budget is a device to help a firm to plan for and control the use of cash. It is a statement showing the estimated cash inflows and cash outflows over the planning period. The principal aim of the cash budget, as a tool to predict cash flows over a period of time, is to ascertain whether there is likely to be excess/shortage of cash at any time.
- The preparation of a cash budget involves several steps. The first element of a cash budget is the selection of the period of the budget, that is, the planning horizon. The planning horizon of a cash budget should be determined in the light of the circumstances and requirements of a particular case. The second element of the cash budget is the selection/identification of the factors that have a bearing on cash flows. The factors that generate cash are generally divided into two broad categories: **(i)** Operating and **(ii)** Financial. The first category includes cash flows

from the operations of the firm, for example, sales, collections of receivables and so on. The second category of cash flows comprise collections and payment of financial nature, for example, borrowings, dividends paid, taxes paid and so on.

- Budgets prepared at a single level of activity, with no prospect of modification in the light of changed circumstances, are referred to as fixed budgets.
- The alternative to fixed budgets are flexible/variable/sliding budgets. The term 'flexible' is an apt description of the essential features of these budgets. A flexible budget estimates costs at several levels of activity. Its merit is that instead of one estimate, it contains several estimates/plans in different assumed circumstances. It is a useful tool in real world situations, that is, unpredictable environment. A flexible budget, in a sense, is a series of fixed budgets and any increase/decrease in the level/volume of activity must be reflected in it. The conceptual framework of flexible budgeting relates to: **(i)** Measure of volume and **(ii)** Cost behaviour with change in volume. Each expense in each department/segment is to be categorised into fixed, variable and mixed components. A budget may first be prepared at the expected level of activity, say, 100 per cent capacity. Additional columns may then be added for costs below and above, 90 per cent and 110 per cent capacity and so on.
- Flexible budgets, as a tool of planning and control, are superior to fixed budgets. The major weaknesses of fixed budgets are their inability to: **(i)** Show the potential variability of various estimates used in the preparation of the budget, and **(ii)** Indicate the range within which costs may be expected to vary. They are, therefore, not useful in an uncertain and unpredictable environment. Flexible budgets present estimates at different levels of activity, and are more useful.
- Flexible budgets suffer from one limitation in that they do not explicitly consider the relative probability of a particular volume/cost being achieved. This limitation can be overcome by using a modified flexible budget which will include columns for different levels of estimates: most likely, optimistic and pessimistic.

REFERENCES

1. J M Fremgen, *Accounting for Managerial Analysis,* (Richard D. Irwin, Homewood, Illinois, 1976), p 150.
2. *Ibid.,* p 151.
3. R M Copeland and P E Dascher, *Managerial Accounting,* (John Wiley and Sons, New York, 1978), p 35.
4. *Ibid.,* p 34.
5. Fremgen, *op cit.,* p 153.
6. It should, however, be noted that depreciation will be relevant to the computation of taxes.
7. Break-even analysis is discussed in Chapter 16 and inventory in Chapter 8.
8. Copeland and Dascher, *op cit.,* p 86.

SOLVED PROBLEMS

P.15.1 Your company manufacturers two products, A and B. A forecast of the units to be sold in the first seven months of the year is given below:

Month	*Product A*	*Product B*
January	1,000	2,800
February	1,200	2,800
March	1,600	2,400
April	2,000	2,000
May	2,400	1,600
June	2,400	1,600
July	2,000	1,800

It is anticipated that (a) there will be no work-in-process at the end of any month, and (b) finished units equal to half the sale for the next month will be in stock at the end of each month (including the previous December).

Budgeted production and production costs for the whole year are as follows:

Particulars	*Product A*	*Product B*
Product (units)	22,000	24,000
Per unit direct material	₹12.50	₹19.00
Per unit direct labour	4.50	7.00
Total factory overhead (apportioned)	66,000	96,000

Prepare for the six months period ending June 30 (i) (a) production budget for each month, and (ii) a summarised production cost budget.

Solution

(i) **Production Budget of Products A and B (units) for six months (January to June)**

Month	*Sales*		*Planned inventory*				*Budget production*	
			closing		*opening*		*(Col. 2 + 4 − 6)*	*(Col. 3 + 5 − 7)*
	A	*B*	*A*	*B*	*A*	*B*	*A*	*B*
1	*2*	*3*	*4*	*5*	*6*	*7*	*8*	*9*
January	1,000	2,800	600	1,400	500	1,400	1,100	2,800
February	1,200	2,800	800	1,200	600	1,400	1,400	2,600
March	1,600	2,400	1,000	1,000	800	1,200	1,800	2,200
April	2,000	2,000	1,200	800	1,000	1,000	2,200	1,800
May	2,400	1,600	1,200	800	1,200	800	2,400	1,600
June	2,400	1,600	1,000	900	1,200	800	2,200	1,700

(ii) **Cost of Production Budget for six months from January to June of Products A and B**

Particulars	*Product A*			*Product B*			*Total cost*
	Cost per Particulars	*Number of units unit*	*Total cost produced*	*Cost per*	*Number of units unit*	*Total produced*	*(A + B)*
Variable costs:							
Direct material	₹12.50	11,100	₹1,38,750	₹19	12,700	₹2,41,300	₹3,80,050
Direct labour	4.50	11,100	49,950	7	12,700	88,900	1,38,850
Fixed costs:							
Factory overheads apportioned at the rate of ₹3 (A) and ₹4 (B)	3.00	11,100	33,300	4	12,700	50,800	84,100
	20.00	11,100	2,22,000	30	12,700	3,81,000	6,03,000

P.15.2 The Delhi Electrical Supply Company Ltd has a business of supplying electrical goods to various government and non-government companies. The controller, in collaboration with the economist, has developed the following equation that, he says, will forecast sales quite well, based on past pattern of behaviour: monthly sales (amount) = ₹1,00,000 + (₹2,000 x orders received in prior month).

The sales manager is confused and seeks your advice. He presents you with the following data regarding actual and forecast numbers of orders. The forecasts have generally been quite accurate.

August (actual)	200
September (forecast)	300
October	450
November	700
December	650

It is the first week of September, the sales manager would like the forecasts of sales and income for as many months as you can prepare. The cost accountant informs you that costs of goods sold, which are all fixed costs, amount to ₹2,00,000 per month.

You are required to prepare the budgeted income statement for as many months as you can.

SOLUTION

Budgeted Income Statement of Delhi Electric Supply Company Ltd

Particulars	*September*	*October*	*November*	*December*	*January*
Sales:					
Fixed component	₹1,00,000	₹1,00,000	₹1,00,000	₹1,00,000	₹1,00,000
Variable component (₹2,000 × orders received in previous months)	4,00,000	6,00,000	9,00,000	14,00,000	13,00,000
Total sales	5,00,000	7,00,000	10,00,000	15,00,000	14,00,000
Less: Cost of goods sold (0.50 × of sales)	2,50,000	3,50,000	5,00,000	7,50,000	7,00,000
Contribution (manufacturing)	2,50,000	3,50,000	5,00,000	7,50,000	7,00,000
Less: Other variable costs (0.20 × sales)	50,000	70,000	1,00,000	1,50,000	1,40,000
Contribution (final)	2,00,000	2,80,000	4,00,000	6,00,000	5,60,000
Less: Fixed costs	2,00,000	2,00,000	2,00,000	2,00,000	2,00,000
Income	—	80,000	2,00,000	4,00,000	3,60,000

P.15.3 The administrator of Delhi Nursing Home has sought your assistance in preparing the budget for the next year. The nursing home obtains its revenues through charges for use of a hospital room and charges for use of the operating theatre. The use of basic room depends on whether the patient undergoes surgery during the stay in the nursing home. The following estimated data is provided for your guidance:

Patients requiring	*Number of patients expected*	*Average stay (days)*	*Percentage occupancy of rooms*		
			Private	*Semi-private*	*Ward*
Medical attention only	1,000	6	10	50	40
Surgical attention	1,200	12	20	70	10

The basic room charges are ₹1,000, ₹600 and ₹200 for private, semi-private and wards respectively.

Charges for use of the operating theatre depend on the length of the operation and the number of persons required to perform it. The charges are ₹50 per man-minute. (A 'man-minute' is one person for one minute). If an operation requires 4 persons for 60 minutes, the charges would be 240 minutes at ₹50 per minute = ₹12,000). Based on past experience, the following is a breakdown of the types of operations to be performed:

Type of operation	*Number*	*Minutes per operation*	*Number of persons required*
Minor	600	60	3
Major	500	120	6

You are required to do the following:

1. Prepare a budgeted revenue statement of room charges by type of patient and type of room;
2. Prepare of budgeted revenue statement of operating theatre charges by type of operation.

SOLUTION

1. Budgeted Revenue Statement (Room Charges)

Type of patient	*Total patient-days*	*Type of room* Private		*Semi-private*		*Ward*		*Total (₹)*
Medical attention (1,000 × 6)	6,000	600	(0.10)	3,000	(0.50)	2,400	(0.40)	
Multiplied by room rate		₹1,000		₹600		₹200		
Revenues (a)		6,00,000		18,00,000		4,80,000		28,80,000
Surgical (1,200 × 12)	14,400	2,880	(0.20)	10,080	(0.70)	1,440	(0.10)	
Multiplied by room rates		× ₹1,000		× ₹600		× ₹200		
Revenues (b)		28,80,000		60,48,000		2,88,000		92,16,000
Total revenue (a + b)		34,80,000		78,48,000		7,68,000		1,20,96,000

2. Budgeted revenue statement (Operating Theatre Charges)

Type of operation	*Man-minutes (Average number of minutes × persons)*	*Number of operations*	*Total man-minutes (Col. 2 × 3)*	*Total revenue (Col. 4 × ₹50)*
1	2	3	4	5
Minor	60 × 3 = 180	600	1,08,000	₹54,00,000
Major	120 × 6 = 720	500	3,60,000	1,80,00,000
Total revenue				2,34,00,000

P.15.4 The GEC Ltd manufacturers pumps used in coolers. The firm has developed a forecasting tool that has been successful in predicting sales for the company: Sales = 10,000 + (0.25 × coolers sold). The coming year's cooler sales are expected to be 2,00,000.

The pump contains material costing ₹50. Direct labour is ₹60 per unit and variable manufacturing overhead is ₹40 per pump. Besides the variable manufacturing costs, there are commissions to sales people of 10 per cent of sales amount. The pump sells for ₹250 per unit. Fixed costs of manufacturing are ₹10,00,000 per year and fixed selling and administrative expenses are ₹5,00,000 per year. Both are incurred evenly over the year.

Sales are seasonal, and about 75 per cent are in the April-September period which begins from April 1. The sales forecast by months, as percentages of yearly sales, are given below:

April	10
May	15
June	20
July	15
August	8
September	7
October	5
November	3

The company has a policy of keeping inventory of finished product equal to the budgeted sales for the following two months. Materials are purchased and delivered daily and no inventory is kept. The inventory of finished product on March 31 is expected to be 15,500 units.

You are required to prepare a:

(i) Budgeted income statement for the coming year
(ii) Budgeted income statement for the first six months of the year.
(iii) Production budget by months for the first six months, in unit.

SOLUTION

(i) and **(ii)** Budgeted Income Statement

Particulars	*Six months*	*Year*
Sales (units)	45,000	60,000
Sales price per unit	₹250	₹250
Total sales revenue	1,12,50,000	1,50,00,000
Less: Variable costs:		
Materials (₹60 per unit)	22,50,000	30,00,000
Labour (₹50 per unit)	27,00,000	36,00,000
Overheads (₹40 per unit)	18,00,000	24,00,000
Contribution (manufacturing)	45,00,000	60,00,000
Less: Sales commission (0.10 × sales)	11,25,000	15,00,000
Contribution (final)	33,75,000	45,00,000
Less: Fixed costs		
Manufacturing	5,00,000	10,00,000
Selling and administrative	2,50,000	5,00,000
Income	26,25,000	30,00,000

(iii) Production Budget (units)

Month	*Sales*	*Planned inventory*		*Required production (Col. 2 + 3 − 4)*
		Closing	*Opening*	
1	2	3	4	5
April	6,000	21,000	15,500	11,500
May	9,000	21,000	21,000	9,000
June	12,000	13,800	21,000	4,800
July	9,000	9,000	13,800	4,200
August	4,800	7,200	9,000	3,000
September	4,200	4,800	7,200	1,800

WORKING NOTES

(i) Sales forecasts for the coming year = 10,000 + (0.25 × 2,00,000) = 60,000 units

Sales forecasts by month (units):

April (0.10)	6,000	
May (0.15)	9,000	
June (0.20)	12,000	
July (0.15)	9,000	
August (0.08)	4,800	
September (0.07)	4,200	= 45,000 units (75 per cent)
October (0.05)	3,000	
November (0.03)	1,800	

P. 15.5 The cost of an article at the capacity level of 5,000 units is given under A below. For a variation of 25 per cent in capacity above or below this level, the individual expenses vary as indicated under B below:

Particulars	*A*	*B (per cent)*
Material cost	₹2,50,000	100 (variable)
Labour cost	1,50,000	100 (variable)
Power	12,500	80 (semi-variable)
Repairs and maintenance	20,000	75 (semi-variable)
Stores	10,000	100 (variable)
Inspection	5,000	20 (semi-variable)

(Contd.)

(*Contd.*)

Administration overheads	50,000	25 (semi-variable)
Selling overheads	30,000	50 (semi-variable)
Depreciation	1,00,000	100 (fixed)
Total	6,27,500	
Cost per unit	125.50	

Prepare the production cost budget at 4,000 units and 6,000 units.

SOLUTION

Production Cost (Flexible) Budget

Particulars	*4,000 units*	*6,000 units*
Material cost (variable)	₹2,00,000	₹3,00,000
Labour cost (variable)	1,20,000	1,80,000
Stores (variable)	8,000	12,000
Power (semi-variable)	10,500	14,500
Repairs and maintenance (semi-variable)	17,000	23,000
Inspection (semi-variable)	4,800	5,200
Administration overheads (semi-variable)	47,500	52,500
Selling overheads (semi-variable)	27,000	33,000
Depreciation (fixed)	1,00,000	1,00,000
Total	5,34,800	7,20,200
Cost per unit	133.70	120.00

P.15.6 The following data relate to the working of a small factory at Wardha for the current quarter:

Capacity worked, 50 per cent		
Fixed costs:		
Salaries	₹84,000	
Rent and rates	56,000	
Depreciation	70,000	
Other administrative expenses	80,000	₹2,90,000
Variable costs:		
Materials	2,40,000	
Labour	2,56,000	
Other expenses	38,000	5,34,000

Possible sales at various levels of working are:

Capacity (per cent)	Sales
60	₹9,50,000
75	11,50,000
90	13,75,000
100	15,25,000

Prepare a flexible budget and show the forecast of profit at 60, 75, 90, and 100 per cent capacity operations.

SOLUTION

Flexible Budget

Percentage of capacity worked	*60*	*75*	*90*	*100*
Sales revenue	₹9,50,000	₹11,50,000	₹13,75,000	₹15,25,000
Less: Costs:				
Variable costs:				
Materials	2,88,000	3,60,000	4,32,000	4,80,000
Labour	3,07,200	3,84,000	4,60,800	5,12,000
Other expenses	45,600	57,000	68,400	76,000
(A) Total variable cost	6,40,800	8,01,000	9,61,200	10,68,000

(*Contd.*)

(*Contd.*)

Fixed costs:				
Salaries	84,000	84,000	84,000	84,000
Rent and rates	56,000	56,000	56,000	56,000
Depreciation	70,000	70,000	70,000	70,000
Other administrative expenses	80,000	80,000	80,000	80,000
(B) Total fixed cost	2,90,000	2,90,000	2,90,000	2,90,000
Total cost **(A + B)**	9,30,800	10,91,000	12,51,200	13,58,000
Forecast profits	19,200	59,000	1,23,800	1,67,000

P.15.7 A company is drawing its production plan for the next year in respect of two of its products 'Gamma' and 'Delta'. The company's policy is not to carry any closing work-in-process (WIP) at the end of any month. However, its policy is to hold a closing stock of finished goods at 50 per cent of the anticipated quantity of sales of the succeeding month. For the next year, the company's budgeted production is 20,000 units of 'Gamma' and 25,000 units of 'Delta'. The following is the estimated cost data:

Particulars	*Gamma*	*Delta*
Direct material per unit	₹50	₹80
Direct labour per unit	20	80
Other manufacturing expenses apportionable to each type of product based on production	2,00,000	3,75,000

The estimated units to be sold in the first 7 months of the next year are as under:

Particulars	*April*	*May*	*June*	*July*	*August*	*September*	*October*
Gamma	900	1100	1400	1800	2200	2200	1800
Delta	2900	2900	2500	2100	1700	1700	1900

You are required to

(a) Prepare a production budget showing month-wise number of units to be manufactured:

(b) Present a summarised production cost budget for the half-year ending September 30.

SOLUTION

(a) Production Budget (Units) for the half year ending September 30

Particulars	*April*	*May*	*June*	*July*	*August*	*September*	*Total*
Product—Gamma:							
Budgeted sales	900	1,100	1,400	1,800	2,200	2,200	9,600
Add: Closing stock	550	700	900	1,100	1,100	900	900
	1,450	1,800	2,300	2,900	3,300	3,100	10,500
Less: Opening stock	450	550	700	900	1,100	1,100	450
Budgeted production	1,000	1,250	1,600	2,000	2,200	2,000	10,050
Product—Delta:							
Budgeted sales	2,900	2,900	2,500	2,100	1,700	1,700	13,800
Add: Closing stock	1,450	1,250	1,050	850	850	950	950
	4,350	4,150	3,550	2,950	2,550	2,650	14,750
Less: Opening stock	1,450	1,450	1,250	1,050	850	850	1,450
Budgeted production	2,900	2,700	2,300	1,900	1,700	1,800	13,300

(b) Cost Budget for the half year ending September 30

Particulars (units)	*Gamma (10,050 units)*		*Delta (13,300 units)*	
	Total	*Per unit*	*Total*	*Per unit*
Direct material	₹5,02,500	₹50	₹10,64,000	₹80
Direct labour	2,01,000	20	3,99,000	30
Other manufacturing expenses[1]	1,00,500	10	1,99,500	15
	8,04,000	80	16,62,500	125

[1]Other manufacturing expenses are apportioned on the basis of production.

	Gamma	Delta
1. Units to be produced	20,000	25,000
2. Other manufacturing expenses	₹2,00,000	₹3,75,000
3. Per unit (2 ÷ 1)	10	15

P.15.8 From the following particulars of Hypothetical Ltd, prepare a cash budget (₹in lakh):

	May	*June*	*July*	*August*	*September*	*October*	*November*	*December*	*January*
1. Sales (net of cash discounts)	10	10	20	30	40	20	20	10	10
2. Purchases	7	14	21	28	14	14	7	7	—
3. Wages and salaries	—	—	1.50	2	2.50	1.50	1.50	1	—
4. Rent	—	—	0.50	0.50	0.50	0.50	0.50	0.50	—
5. Other expenses	—	—	0.20	0.30	0.40	0.20	0.20	0.10	—
6. Taxes	—	—	—	—	—	4	—	4	—
7. Payment for plant construction	—	—	—	—	—	10	—	—	—

All sales are made on terms that allow a cash discount for payment within 20 days; if the discount is not taken, full payment may be made in 40 days. However, the experience has been that on 20 per cent of sales, payment is made during the month in which sales are made; on 70 per cent of the sales, payment is made during the second month and on the balance 10 per cent of sales, payment is made during the third month.

Materials amount to 70 per cent of sales and are bought in the month before the firm expects to sell the finished goods. Its purchase terms permit the company to delay payment for one month. The firm has to pay tax of ₹4 lakh on September 15 and on December 15.

Assume the firm needs to keep a minimum cash balance of ₹5 lakh in hand at all times. It is assumed to have an opening cash balance of ₹6 lakh on July 1.

Estimate the firm's requirements of cash for the period from July to December.

Solution

Cash Budget (*₹ in lakh*)

Particulars	*July*	*August*	*September*	*October*	*November*	*December*
1. Cash inflows:						
Collections						
(a) during month of sales (0.20)	4	6	8	4	4	2
(b) during second month (0.70)	7	14	21	28	14	14
(c) during third month (0.10)	1	1	2	3	4	2
Total	12	21	31	35	22	18
2. Cash outflows:						
(a) Purchases (one month lag)	14	21	28	14	14	7
(b) Wages and salary	1.5	2	2.5	1.5	1.5	1
(c) Rent	0.5	0.5	0.5	0.5	0.5	0.5
(d) Other expenses	0.2	0.3	0.4	0.2	0.2	0.1
(e) Taxes	—	—	4	—	—	4
(f) Payment for plant construction	—	—	—	10	—	—
Total	16.2	23.8	35.4	26.2	16.2	12.6
(C) Net cash receipt/outflow (A – B)	(4.2)	(2.8)	(4.4)	8.8	5.8	5.4
Cash at start of month*	6	5	5	5	5	9.2
Less desired level of cash	(5)	(5)	(5)	(5)	(5)	(5)
Borrowings (cumulative)	3.2	6	10.4	1.6	—	—
Surplus cash (cumulative)	—	—	—	—	4.2	9.6

*Cash at the beginning plus net receipts/less payments. It is equal to the cash at the end.

P. 15.9 From the following particulars of a firm, prepare a cash budget fort the six months, January-June:

1. *Balance Sheet as on December 31*

Liabilities		Assets		
Share capital	₹40,00,000	Cash		₹16,00,000
Reserves	60,00,000	Accounts receivables		10,00,000
		Inventory		49,00,000
		Fixed assets	₹30,00,000	
		Less depreciation	5,00,000	25,00,000
	1,00,00,000			1,00,00,000

2. *Sales Forecast*

January	₹20,00,000	April	₹60,00,000
February	40,00,000	May	90,00,000
March	50,00,000	June	50,00,000
		July	10,00,000

3. *Salary Expenses*

January	₹3,00,000	April	₹9,00,000
February	5,00,000	May	11,00,000
March	7,00,000	June	6,00,000

4. Monthly selling and distribution expenses are expected to be 10 per cent of sales. Depreciation charges are 1 per cent per month.

5. The firm operates on the following terms:

(a) Sales are on a 30-day basis. But payments are not received until the following month.

(b) All purchases of the firm are in cash.

(c) The firm purchases enough inventory each month to cover 125 per cent of the following month's sales. The firm has a policy of maintaining 20 per cent gross profit margin on sales.

(d) A minimum cash balance of ₹10 lakh is maintained.

6. Additional information: New equipment purchased for ₹5 lakh is scheduled for delivery on March 1 against payment.

SOLUTION

Cash Budget (₹ *lakh*)

Particulars	*January*	*February*	*March*	*April*	*May*	*June*
1. Cash inflows:						
Collections:						
During month following sale	₹10	₹20	₹40	₹50	₹60	₹90
2. Cash outflows:						
1. Purchases	40	50	60	90	50	10
2. Selling and distribution expenses	2	4	5	6	9	5
3. Salary expenses	3	5	7	9	11	6
4. Payment for new equipment	—	—	5	—	—	—
Total	45	59	77	105	70	21
3. *Net cash receipts or (payments)*	(35)	(39)	(37)	(55)	(10)	69
Cash at the start of month	10	10	10	10	10	10
Less: desired level of cash	(10)	(10)	(10)	(10)	(10)	(10)
Borrowings (cumulative)	35	74	111	166	176	107

P.15.10 The following information is available in respect of a firm:

1. *Balance Sheet as on August 1* (₹ *thousand*)

Liabilities	*Amount*	*Assets*		*Amount*
Accrued wages	₹600	Cash		₹5,100
Capital	59,200	Accounts receivable		14,700
Other liabilities	2,000	Inventory		26,000
		Fixed assets	₹20,000	
		Less depreciation	4,000	16,000
	61,800			61,800

2. *Assume:*

(a) Sales are 40 per cent against cash, 60 per cent on credit.
(b) Of the credit sales, 75 per cent are collected in the first month following sales and 25 per cent in the second month following sales.
(c) All inventory purchases are paid for during the month in which they are made.
(d) A basic inventory of ₹1 crore (cost) is constantly maintained and the firm follows a policy of purchasing enough additional inventory each month to cover 1.25 times the following month's sales. Its gross profit margin is 20 per cent on sales.
(e) A minimum cash balance of ₹20 lakh is to be maintained by the firm.
(f) "Accrued wages" and "other current liabilities" remain unchanged.

3. *Past Sales:* (₹ *thousand*)

June	₹18,000
July	20,000

4. *Sales Budget:* (₹ *thousand*)

August	₹20,000	November	₹40,000
September	26,000	December	50,000
October	24,000	January	18,000
	February	16,000	

5. *Monthly Expenses:*

(a) Wages and Salaries: (₹ *thousand*)

August	₹1,400	November	₹2,000
September	1,600	December	3,000
October	1,600	January	1,400

(b) Rent: ₹4 lakh per month
(c) Depreciation: ₹1.5 lakh per month
(d) Other expenses: 1 per cent of sales

Required: Indicate the maximum amount of necessary borrowings.

Solution

Cash Budget (*Amount in* ₹ *thousand*)

Particulars	*August*	*September*	*October*	*November*	*December*	*January*
(A) Cash inflows (collections):						
(i) Cash sales	₹8,000	₹10,400	₹9,600	₹16,000	₹20,000	₹7,200
(ii) Collection from debtors (2nd month of sales)	9,000	9,000	11,700	10,800	18,000	22,500

(*Contd.*)

(*Contd.*)

(iii) Collection from debtors (3rd month of sales)	2,700	3,000	3,000	3,900	3,900	6,000
Total	19,700	22,400	24,300	30,700	41,900	35,700
(B) *Cash outflows*:						
(i) Wages and salaries	1,400	1,600	1,600	2,000	3,000	1,400
(ii) Rent	400	400	400	400	400	400
(iii) Other expenses	200	260	240	400	500	180
(iv) Payment for purchases	26,000	24,000	40,000	50,000	18,000	16,000
Total	28,000	26,260	42,240	52,800	21,900	17,980
(C) Net cash receipts (deficit) (A-B)	(8,300)	(3,860)	(17,940)	(22,100)	20,000	17,720
Cash at start of month	5,100	2,000	2,000	2,000	2,000	2,000
Less: desired level of cash	(2,000)	(2,000)	(2,000)	(2,000)	(2,000)	(2,000)
Borrowings (cumulative)	(5,200)	(9,060)	(27,000)	(49,100)	(29,100)	(11,380)

P.15.11 The following quarterly results are expected by XYZ Ltd next year (₹in thousands)

	Quarter 1	2	3	4
Sales	7,500	10,500	18,000	10,500
Cash payments:				
Production costs	7,000	10,000	8,000	8,500
Selling, administrative and other costs	1,000	2,000	2,900	1,600
Purchases of plant and other fixed assets	100	1,100	2,100	2,100

Debtors at the end of a quarter are one-third of sales for the quarter. The opening balance of debtors is ₹30,00,000. Cash in hand at the beginning of the year is ₹6,50,000 and the desired minimum balance is ₹5,00,000. Borrowings are made in multiples of ₹10,000 at the beginning of the quarter in which need will occur and are repaid at the end of the quarter. Interest charges may be ignored..

You are required to prepare:

(i) Cash budget by quarters for the year, and

(ii) State the amount of loan outstanding at he end of the year.

SOLUTION

(i) *Cash Budget, Next Year (Quarter-wise)* (*Amount in '000 ₹*)

Particulars	*Quarter* 1	2	3	4	*Total*
(A) Cash inflows					
Collection from debtors					
(i) From prior quarter (1/3 of sales)	₹3,000	₹2,500	₹3,500	₹6,000	₹15,000
(ii) From current quarter (2/3 of sales)	5,000	7,000	12,000	7,000	31,000
Total cash receipts	8,000	9,500	15,500	13,000	46,000
(B) Cash outflows					
Production costs	7,000	10,000	8,000	8,500	33,500
Selling, administrative and other costs	1,000	2,000	2,900	1,600	7,500
Plant and other fixed assets purchase	100	1,100	2,100	2,100	5,400
Total cash payments	8,100	13,100	13,000	12,200	46,400

(*Contd.*)

(*Contd.*)

(C) Surplus/(deficit)	(100)	(3,600)	2,500	800	(400)
Opening balance	650	550	500	500	650
Closing balance (indicated)	550	3,050	3,000	1,300	250
Borrowings required (deficit minimum cash required)	—	3,550	—	—	3,550
(Repayments) made (balance minimum cash required)	—	—	(2,500)	(800)	(3,300)
Closing balance (actually now estimated)	550	500	500	500	500

(ii) Loan outstanding is ₹35,50,000 – ₹33,00,000 = ₹2,50,000

P.15.12 The following data pertain to a shop. The owner has made the following sales forecasts for the first five months of the coming year.

January	₹40,00,000
February	45,00,000
March	55,00,000
April	60,00,000
May	50,00,000

Other data are as follows:

1. Debtors' and creditors' balances at the beginning of the year are ₹30 lakh and ₹14 lakh, respectively. The balances of other relevant assets and liabilities are: Cash balance, ₹7.5 lakh; Stock, ₹51 lakh; Accrued sales commission, ₹3.5 lakh.
2. 40 per cent sales are on cash basis. Credit sales are collected in the following month.
3. Cost of sales is 60 per cent of sales.
4. The only other variable cost is a 5 per cent commission to sales agents. Sales commission is paid in the month after it is earned, that is, the time-lag is one month.
5. Inventory (stock) is kept equal to sales requirements for the next two months' budgeted sales.
6. Trade creditors are paid in the month following purchases.
7. Fixed costs are ₹5 lakh per month, including ₹2 lakh depreciation.

You are required to prepare a cash budget for each of the first three months of the coming year.

Solution

Cash Budget for Coming Year (Month-wise)

Particulars	*Month*		
	January	*February*	*March*
(A) Cash inflows			
Cash sales (0.40 × total sales)	₹16,00,000	₹18,00,000	₹22,00,000
Collection from debtors (one month after sale)	30,00,000	24,00,000	27,00,000
Total cash receipts	46,00,000	42,00,000	49,00,000
(B) Cash outflows			
Paid to trade creditors for purchase (working notes)	14,00,000	33,00,000	36,00,000
Sales commission (0.05 × previous month's sales)	3,50,000	2,00,000	2,25,000
Fixed costs (₹5,000 – ₹2,000 depreciation)	3,00,000	3,00,000	3,00,000
Total cash payments	20,50,000	38,00,000	41,25,000
(C) Surplus/(deficit) (A) – (B)	25,50,000	4,00,000	7,75,000
Opening balance	7,50,000	33,00,000	37,00,000
Closing balance (indicated)	33,00,000	37,00,000	44,75,000

WORKING NOTES

Purchase Budget

Desired closing inventory (at cost price)	₹60,00,000	₹69,00,000	₹66,00,000
Plus cost of goods sold (current month)	24,00,000	27,00,000	33,00,000
Total requirements	84,00,000	96,00,000	99,00,000
Less opening inventory	51,00,000	60,00,000	69,00,000
Purchases	33,00,000	36,00,000	30,00,000

REVIEW QUESTIONS

RQ.15.1 Fill in the following blanks:

(i) Overall budget is also known as ________.
(ii) Budgets prepared at the single level of activity are referred to as ________.
(iii) ________ estimates costs at several levels of activity.
(iv) For most of the business firms, ________ is key budget.
(v) Budgets are an important tool of ________.
(vi) Minimum desired cash balance concept is useful in the preparation of ________ budget.
(vii) Cash budget is a tool of ________ financial planning.
(viii) Factors generating cash are categorized into two broad categories, namely, ________.
(ix) The primary objective of cash budget is to ascertain whether there is likely to be ________ of cash at any time.
(x) Sales and production budgets are ________ budgets.

[Answers: (i) master budget, (ii) fixed budgets, (iii) flexible budget, (iv) sales budget, (v) profit planning, (vi) cash budget, (vii) short-term, (viii) operating and financial, (ix) excess/shortage, (x) operating.]

RQ.15.2 Are you in agreement with the view that budgeting should better be called 'profit planning and control'?

RQ.15.3 'If sales forecast is subject to error, then, there is no purpose of budgeting.' Do you agree? Also explain how a flexible budget can be used by management to help control costs.

RQ.15.4 In what respects does the production budget contribute to managerial (I) planning, (ii) coordination, and (iii) control.

RQ.15.5 Write a note on the advantages and limitations of budgeting.

RQ.15.6 Why do responsible people in an organisation tend to accept budgetary control in theory but resist in practice? Explain.

RQ.15.7 Define budgetary control and discuss the objectives of introducing a budgetary control system in your own organisation.

RQ.15.8 What do you understand by the terms budget and budgetary control? What are the advantages of budgetary control?

RQ.15.9 A manufacturing company operating a system of budgetary control finds that their production capacity during the year varies between 75 per cent and 90 per cent as against the budgeted capacity of 80 per cent for the year. It has been suggested that a system of flexible budgets should be introduced to effectively control costs. Outline the steps you would take to implement this suggestion keeping in mind that the management would still require periodic comparison with their overall budget during the year.

RQ.15.10 'Budgeting is profit planning.' Elaborate this statement. What accounting devices would you use where output varies?

RQ.15.11 ABC Company Ltd. expects the following sales by months in units for the first six months of next year.

January	5,400	April	5,700
February	5,700	May	6,000
March	7,500	June	4,500

The company has a policy of maintaining an inventory equal to budgeted sales for the following two months. The beginning inventory reflects this policy. Each unit costs ₹10.

You are required to prepare purchases budget for as many months as you can both in units and rupees. Also explain why you had to stop where you did.

RQ.15.12 Readymade Textiles Ltd. makes and sells baby suits. It has brisk sales in the October-December period as shown by the following sales budget (in units):

July	5,000	October	8,000
August	5,000	November	10,000
September	5,500	December	12,500

The firm's normal inventory policy has been to have a two months' supply of finished product on hand. The production manager has criticised the policy because it requires wide swings in production, which adds to costs. He estimates that unit-variable manufacturing cost is ₹2 higher than normal for each unit produced in excess of 9,000 units per month. The finance manager also supports the production manager on this. He estimates that it costs the firm ₹1 per unit in ending inventory, consisting of insurance, financing, and handling costs. He stresses that these costs are variable.

All the managers agree that the firm should have 22,500 units on hand by the end of October. The production manager wants to spread the required production equally over the four months.

(i) Prepare a production budget for July-October following the firm's current policy. Inventory on July 1 is 10,000 units.

(ii) Prepare a production budget using the production manager's preference.

(iii) Determine which budget gives lower costs.

RQ.15.13 The Royal Industries Ltd. has prepared its annual sales forecast, expecting to achieve sales of ₹30,00,000 next year. The controller is uncertain about the pattern of sales to be expected by month and asks you to prepare a monthly budget of sales. The following sales data pertain to the year, which is considered to be representative of a normal year.

Month	*Sales*	*Month*	*Sales*
January	₹1,10,000	July	₹2,60,000
February	1,15,000	August	3,30,000
March	1,00,000	September	3,40,000
April	1,40,000	October	3,50,000
May	1,80,000	November	2,00,000
June	2,25,000	December	1,50,000

Prepare a monthly sales budget for the coming year on the basis of the above data.

RQ.15.14 Lookahead Ltd. produces and sells a single product. Sales budget for the current calendar year by quarter is as under:

Quarter	Units to be sold
I	12,000
II	15,000
III	16,500
IV	18,000

The year is expected to open with an inventory of 4,000 units of finished product and close with an inventory of 6,500 units. Production is customarily scheduled to provide for two-thirds of the current quarter's sales demand plus one-third of the following quarter's demand. The standard cost details for one unit of the product is as follows:

Direct material, 1 lb @ Rs 5 paise per lb

Direct labour, 12 minutes @ ₹30 per hour

Variable overheads, 12 minutes @ ₹7.5 per hour

Fixed overheads, Rs 1,80,000are to be shared equally among 4 quarters.

(i) Prepare a production budget, by quarters, showing the number of units to be produced and the total costs of direct material, direct labour, variable overheads, and fixed overheads.

(ii) If the budgeted selling price per unit is ₹17, what would be the budgeted profit for the year as a whole?

(iii) In which quarter of the year is the company expected to break-even?

RQ.15.15 ABC Ltd. manufactures cakes in three varieties—A, B, and C—each requiring similar material, labour, and production facilities. The trading results of the firm for current year ending March are as under:

Particulars	*A*	*B*	*C*	*Total*
Sales	₹21,44,000	₹17,20,000	₹10,40,000	₹49,04,000
Variable costs:				
Material	5,36,000	5,16,000	4,16,000	14,68,000
Wages	4,28,800	2,58,000	3,36,000	10,22,800
Overheads	4,28,800	2,58,000	3,36,000	10,22,800
Total	13,93,600	10,32,000	10,88,000	35,13,600
contribution	7,50,400	6,88,000	(48,000)	13,90,400
Fixed overheads				8,70,400
Profit				5,20,000

The cake of variety C, despite best efforts, does not yield the desirable margin and thus the firm has decided to discontinue its production. However, the other two varieties, A and B, have good potential to grow and the market can easily absorb the increased production. The firm has, therefore, decided to raise the production of these varieties by diverting the labour and production facilities engaged in production of variety C.

In accordance with this, it is decided, effective April 1, to transfer two-thirds of the labour engaged in variety C to variety A and the remaining one-third to variety B, thus totally discontinuing production of variety C.

The following data for the next year beginning April is also available:

(a) Total direct wage bill for the next year would be at the same level as for the last year ending March.

(b) Similarly, the variable costs per unit of production and the selling price are to be assumed unchanged in the forthcoming year beginning April.

(c) Fixed overheads would increase by ₹55,200.

You are required:

(a) To prepare the budget for next year beginning April in the same format as given above

(b) To analyse and compare the budget for the year beginning April with that of the previous year and highlight main features, and

(c) To advise the management on comparative profitability if two-thirds of the workers engaged in C are transferred to B instead of A and the remaining one-third are engaged in A instead of B. Give detailed reasoning for your advice.

RQ.15.16 Prepare a flexible budget at 60, 80, and 100 per cent capacities from the following information:

(a) Fixed expenses	₹1,49,500
(b) Semi-variable expenses at 50% capacity	89,500
(c) Variable expenses at 50% capacity	2,67,000

Semi-variable expenses remained constant between 40 and 70 per cent capacity, increase by 10 per cent between 70 and 85 per cent capacity and by 15 per cent between 85 and 100 per cent capacity. Sales at 60 per cent capacity are ₹5,10,000, at 80 per cent capacity ₹6,80,000, and at 100 per cent capacity ₹8,50,000 (Assume that all products are sold).

RQ.15.17 The demand for output of a certain company is very elastic and a modern plant recently installed is capable of greatly increased production. Output at present is 80,000 units per year, and 5 lakh units are estimated to be within the capacity of the new plant. The present selling price per unit is ₹15.

The need for flexible budgeting is recognised and six alternative levels of output, in addition to the present level, are contemplated. Six equal increments in annual output level, up to a maximum of 5,00,000 units, would involve corresponding reductions of ₹1 each in unit price to ₹9 per unit at the maximum output.

The present variable costs amount to ₹4,00,000. Fixed costs which at present amount to ₹2,00,000 are not expected to increase for any of the six alternative output levels contemplated. Semi-fixed cost are expected to vary from the present annual figure of ₹2,30,000 to ₹3,20,000, the upward steps being to ₹2,60,000 at 2,20,000 units, ₹2,80,000 at 3,60,000 units, and ₹3,20,000 at 5,00,000 units. The costs classified as variable at the six projected levels of output are calculated to be as follows:

₹7,50,000	₹11,00,000	₹15,00,000
17,50,000	20,50,000	25,00,000

Prepare the flexible budget and identify the volume which should be set for the budgeted output.

RQ.15.18 Prepare a flexible budget from the following data made available in respect of a half-yearly period and forecast the working results at 70, 85, and 100 per cents of capacity when the respective sales are ₹50 lakh, ₹60 lakh, and ₹85 lakh. While fixed expenses remain constant, semi-variable expenses are constant between 55 and 75 per cent of capacity, increasing by 10 per cent between 75 and 90 per cent of capacity and by 20 per cent between 90 and 100 per cent of capacity. The expenses at 60 per cent capacity are as follows: *(Amount in lakh of rupees)*

Semi-variable:	Maintenance and repairs	1.25
	Indirect labour	5.00
	Sales department expenses	1.50
	Sundry overheads	1.25
Variable:	Material	12.00
	Labour	13.00
	Other expenses	2.00
Fixed:	Wages and salaries	4.20
	Rent, rates and taxes	2.80
	Depreciation	3.50
	Sundry overheads	4.50
		51.00

RQ.15.19 Messers Up-to-date Ltd. has instructed you to prepare a cash budget for October to December from the following particulars:

(i) *Cash and bank balance as on October* 1, ₹20,000.

(ii) *Actual and budgeted sales*:

June (actual)	₹60,000	October (budgeted)	₹80,000
July	65,000	November	82,000
August	70,000	December	89,000
September	75,000		

(iii) *Purchases: actual and budgeted*:

June	₹36,000	October	₹48,000
July	40,000	November	40,000
August	48,000	December	50,000
September	45,000		

(iv) *Salaries and other expenses: actual and budgeted:*

Month	Wages	Expenses
August (actual)	₹15,000	₹5,000
September	15,000	6,000
October (budgeted)	18,000	6,000
November	18,000	8,000
December	20,000	8,000

(v) Special points:
(a) Advance income tax, ₹5,000 in November.
(b) Plant, ₹10,000 in October.

(vi) ₹300 rent payable in advance.

(vii) 10 per cent of purchases and sales are on cash terms.

(viii) Time lag:
(a) Credit sales, 2 months
(b) Credit purchases, 1 month
(c) Salaries, two weeks
(d) Expenses, one week

RQ.15.20 ABC Ltd. produces a single product that sells for ₹75 per unit. Cost data are:

(a) Variable manufacturing costs, ₹35 per unit.

(b) Variable selling and administrative expenses, ₹5 per unit.

(c) Fixed manufacturing costs requiring cash, ₹2,50,000 per month. Fixed selling and administrative expenses, ₹2,00,000 per month, all requiring cash. Depreciation, ₹60,000 per month.

Other relevant data are:

(d) The firm has a policy of maintaining a two-month's supply of finished products. The opening inventory (January 1) is 42,000 units.

(e) The firm does not hold raw materials inventory and purchases raw materials as needed. The cost of raw materials is included in the variable manufacturing cost of ₹35.

(f) The firm has a practice of making all sales on credit, collecting 30 per cent in the month of sale and the balance in the following month. There are no bad debts and overdue accounts. The opening debtors' balance is ₹7,00,000.

(g) The firm pays all manufacturing costs in the month of production.

(h) The firm pays four-fifths of selling and administrative expenses in the month of incurrence and the balance one-fifth is paid in the following month. On January 1, the firm owed ₹30,000 for December expenses.

(i) The minimum desired cash balance is ₹80,000, which is also the amount the firm has on January 1. Borrowings are possible and can be made in multiples of ₹10,000. It must borrow at the beginning of a month and repay at the end if sufficient cash is available. The interest rate is 10 per cent and the firm pays interest when it repays loans or portions of them.

(j) The sales budget for the first six months in units is: January, 20,000; February, 26,000; March, 30,000; April, 32,000; May, 30,000; June, 28,000.

You are required to prepare an individual monthly cash budget for the first three months of the year, and also a consolidated budget for the same period.

ANSWERS **[Comprehensive solutions to all numerical review questions are available on the companion website: http://www.mhhe.com/khan_jain_cost2e]**

RQ.15.11 Purchase budget: January ₹75,000 (7,500 units), February ₹57,000 (5,700 units), March ₹60,000 (6,000 units), April ₹45,000 (4,500 units).

Budgeting beyond April is not possible as the data for July and August is not available.

RQ.15.12 **(i)** Product budget: July 5,500 units, August 8,000 units, September 10,000 units, October 12,500 units
(ii) Monthly production of 9,000 units
(iii) Current budget provides lower costs.

RQ.15.13 January (₹1,32,000), Feb. (₹1,38,000), March (₹1,20,000), April (₹1,68,000), May (₹2,16,000), June (₹2,70,000), July (₹3,12,000), August (₹3,96,000), September (₹4,08,000), October (₹4,20,000), November (₹2,40,000), December (₹1,80,000)

RQ.15.14 **(i)** Production budget: Quarter I (13,000 units), Quarter II (15,500 units), Quarter III (17,000 units), Quarter IV (18,500 units)
Total cost: Quarter I (₹2,07,500), Quarter II (₹2,38,750), Quarter III (₹2,57,500), Quarter IV (₹2,76,250)
(ii) Budgeted profit ₹96,750
(iii) Quarter III.

RQ.15.15 **(a)** Budgeted profit ₹12,03,467
(b) There is a significant increase in the important financial parameters. Profits ₹12,03,467 (next year).
(c) Profits would be higher at ₹13,06,133.

RQ.15.16 Flexible budget: At 60% (Loss ₹49,400), At 80% (Profit ₹4,850), At 100% (₹63,575).

RQ.15.17 4,30,000 units is the desired volume; at this volume the company has maximum budgeted income, ₹17,70,000.

RQ.15.18 Budgeted loss at ₹5.5 lakh (at 70%), loss ₹3.15 lakh (at 85%), profit ₹14.20 lakh (at 100%).

RQ.15.19 Cash balance: October-end ₹12,900, November-end ₹10,600, December-end ₹23,200.

RQ.15.20 Borrowings: January ₹6,00,000, February ₹60,000; Repayments: March ₹3,80,000 plus interest ₹9,500; March-end balance ₹85,500.

CASES

C.15.1 (Profit Planning) Sound Future Communications Limited (SFCL) is planning profit for the current year. The Chairman and Managing Director of the Company, Mr Wise has asked the Accounts and Finance Department to prepare the budget outlining the implications of achieving the profit goal of ₹7 lakh. The Budgeting Department has compiled the information related to its operating and financing activities as detailed in schedules I to VIII.

I. **Balance Sheet as at March 31 of the Current Year**

Liabilities	*Amount*	*Assets*		*Amount*
Share capital	₹31,77,428	Fixed assets	₹48,00,000	
Retained earnings	18,96,400	*Less:* Accumulated		
Creditors	44,000	depreciation	(12,00,000)	₹36,00,000
Taxes payable	74,000	Inventories:		
		Direct materials	1,35,828	
		Finished goods	1,60,000	2,95,828
		Debtors	11,20,000	
		Less: Provision for		
		bad debts	(64,000)	10,56,000
		Cash		2,40,000
	51,91,828			51,91,828

Notes: (i) Debtors include ₹1,60,000 from the third quarter sales of ₹20,00,000 and ₹9,60,000 from fourth quarter sales of ₹12,00,000; (ii) Direct materials include 6,300 kgs of material A @ ₹5.88 per kg and 12,600 kgs of material B @ ₹7.84 per kg; and (iii) Finished goods include 4,000 units @ ₹40 per unit.

II. *Budget assumptions*

(i) Selling price, ₹60 per unit

(ii) Quarterly sales forecast (units)

Quarter	Next year	Year following next year
First	20,000	30,000
Second	30,000	
Third	40,000	
Fourth	20,000	

III. *Inventory policy*

–Finished goods: 20 per cent of the following quarter's requirements at the end of each quarter.

–Raw materials: 30 per cent of the following quarter's requirements at the end of each quarter.

– The firm wishes to have 9,200 kgs of each type of direct material on hand at March 31 of the next year.

IV. *Manufacturing cost per unit*

Direct materials:		
1 kg of A @ ₹5.88	₹5.88	
2 kgs of B @ ₹7.84	15.68	₹21.56
Direct labour: 0.5 × direct labour-hour @ ₹8		4.00
Overheads:		
Variable (0.5 × direct labour-hour @ ₹12)	6.00	
Fixed (₹8,44,000 per year/Normal level of activity, 1,00,000 units)	8.44	14.44
Total		40.00

The quarterly fixed manufacturing costs of ₹2,11,000 include depreciation totaling ₹50,000. All production variances are written off as an adjustment to the cost of goods sold in the period in which they occurred. The firm follows absorption costing method for income determination.

V. *Selling and administrative costs*:

Commission and distribution, ₹6 per unit sold

Advertising, ₹10,000 per quarter

Administrative, ₹20,000 per quarter.

VI. *Cash disbursement policy*: Raw materials are purchased on terms of 2/10, net/30. Discount is always taken and purchases are recorded at net; 90 per cent of the purchases are paid for in the quarter of purchase and remainder are paid for in the following quarter. The list prices of materials A and B are ₹6 per kg and ₹8 per kg respectively. With the exception of income taxes, which are paid during the following quarter, all other payments are made when incurred.

VII. *Cash collection experience*: 20 per cent sales are for cash and 80 per cent are on credit. The terms of sales are 2/10, net/60 days. However, for payments, the sales are billed to customers on the first day of the following quarter; 50 per cent of the credit sales are collected during the discount period and another 40 per cent are received after the discount period but during the quarter in which the billing is done; 7.5 per cent are received during the following quarter and 2.5 per cent are bad debts. These accounts are written off at the end of the 2nd quarter following the sales. A provision of 2 per cent of sales is made for bad debts at the time of sales. Sales discounts are recorded as a deduction from sales in the quarter the discounts are taken. Based on prior experience, this deduction equals 0.8 per cent of the previous quarter's sales (0.8 × 0.5 × 0.02).

VIII. *Other information:*

–Income tax rate is 50 per cent.

–Cash dividends amount to ₹80,000 at the end of quarter 2 and quarter 4.

–At the end of the 4th quarter, equipment costing ₹6,00,000 was purchased.

Prepare a comprehensive, quarter-wise, budget to show the projected income of SFCL for the year.

SOLUTION

Quarter-wise Sales Forecast Schedule

Quarter	*First*	*Second*	*Third*	*Fourth*	*Total*
Units sales	20,000	30,000	40,000	20,000	1,10,000
Unit sale price	× ₹60	× ₹60	× ₹60	× ₹60	× ₹60
Sales revenue	12,00,000	18,00,000	24,00,000	12,00,000	66,00,000

Production Budget (Units)

Quarter	*First*	*Second*	*Third*	*Fourth*	*Total*
Sales	20,000	30,000	40,000	20,000	1,10,000
Add: Desired closing inventory (0.20 × next quarter)	6,000	8,000	4,000	6,000	6,000
Total finished goods requirement	26,000	38,000	44,000	26,000	1,16,000
Less: Opening Inventory	4,000	6,000	8,000	4,000	4,000
Required production	22,000	32,000	36,000	22,000	1,12,000

Quarterly Manufacturing Cost Budget

Quarter	*First*	*Second*	*Third*	*Fourth*	*Total*
Required production (units)	22,000	32,000	36,000	22,000	1,12,000
Variable costs:					
A (₹5.88 per unit)	₹1,29,360	₹1,88,160	₹2,11,680	₹1,29,360	₹6,58,560
B (₹15.68 per unit)	3,44,960	5,01,760	5,64,480	3,44,960	17,56,160
Direct labour (₹4 per unit)	88,000	1,28,000	1,44,000	88,000	4,48,000
Overheads (₹6 per unit)	1,32,000	1,92,000	2,16,000	1,32,000	6,72,000
	6,94,320	10,09,920	11,36,160	6,94,320	35,34,720
Fixed costs:					
Depreciation	50,000	50,000	50,000	50,000	2,00,000
Other overheads	1,61,000	1,61,000	1,61,000	1,61,000	6,44,000
	2,11,000	2,11,000	2,11,000	2,11,000	8,44,000
Total costs	9,05,000	12,20,920	13,47,160	9,05,320	43,78,720
Budgeted fixed costs	2,11,000	2,11,000	2,11,000	2,11,000	8,44,000
Less: Fixed costs charged (@₹8.44 per unit)	1,85,680	2,70,080	3,03,840	1,85,680	9,45,280
Capacity variance	25,320 (Unfavourable)*	59,080 (Favourable)**	92,840 (Favourable)	25,320 (Unfavourable)	1,01,280 (Favourable)

*Under-recovery/under-absorption of fixed costs;

**Over-recovery/over-absorption of fixed costs.

Quarterly Purchase Budget of Raw Materials

Quarter	*First*	*Second*	*Third*	*Fourth*	*Total*
Material (A):					
Production requirement (in units)	22,000	32,000	36,000	22,000	1,12,000
Raw material required @ 1 kg per unit	22,000	32,000	36,000	22,000	1,12,000

(*Contd.*)

(*Contd.*)

Add: Desired ending inventory (30 per cent of the next quarter's requirement)	9,600	10,800	6,600	9,200	9,200
Total requirement	31,600	42,800	42,600	31,200	1,21,200
Less: Opening inventory	6,300	9,600	10,800	6,600	6,300
Purchase requirement (kgs)	25,300	33,200	31,800	24,600	1,14,900
Purchase cost (@ ₹5.88 per kg)	₹1,48,764	₹1,95,216	₹1,86,984	₹1,44,648	₹6,75,612
Material (B):					
Raw material required @ 2 kg per unit)	44,000	64,000	72,000	44,000	2,24,000
Add: Desired ending inventory (30 per cent of the next quarter's requirement)	19,200	21,600	13,200	9,200	9,200
Total requirements	63,200	85,600	85,200	53,200	2,33,200
Less: Opening inventory	12,600	19,200	21,600	13,200	12,600
Purchase requirement (kgs)	50,600	66,400	63,600	40,000	2,20,600
Purchase cost (@ ₹7.84 per kg)	₹3,96,704	₹5,20,576	₹4,98,624	₹3,13,600	₹17,29,504
Total purchase cost **(A + B)**	5,45,468	7,15,792	6,85,608	4,58,248	24,05,116

Quarterly Selling and Administrative Expenses Budget

Quarter	*First*	*Second*	*Third*	*Fourth*	*Total*
Units sales	20,000	30,000	40,000	20,000	1,10,000
Variable costs:					
Commission and distribution (₹6 per unit)	₹1,20,000	₹1,80,000	₹2,40,000	₹1,20,000	₹6,60,000
Fixed costs:					
Advertising	10,000	10,000	10,000	10,000	40,000
Administrative	20,000	20,000	20,000	20,000	80,000
	30,000	30,000	30,000	30,000	1,20,000
Total	1,50,000	2,10,000	2,70,000	1,50,000	7,80,000

Qarterly Budgeted Income Statement (Absorption Costing)

Quarter	*First*	*Second*	*Third*	*Fourth*	*Total*
Sales revenue	₹12,00,000	₹18,00,000	₹24,00,000	₹12,00,000	₹66,00,000
Less: Provision for bad and doubtful debts (0.02 × sales)	24,000	36,000	48,000	24,000	1,32,000
Less: Sales discount (0.8 × previous quarter's sales)	9,600	9,600	14,400	19,200	52,800
Net sales	11,66,400	17,54,400	23,37,600	11,56,800	64,15,200
Less: Cost of goods sold (@ ₹40 per unit)	8,00,000	12,00,000	16,00,000	8,00,000	44,00,000
Gross margin (unadjusted)	3,66,400	5,54,400	7,37,600	3,56,800	20,15,200

(*Contd.*)

(Contd.)

Add: Capacity variance favourable					
Less: Unfavourable	(25,320)	59,080	92,840	(25,320)	1,01,280
Gross margin (adjusted)	3,41,080	6,13,480	8,30,440	3,31,480	21,16,480
Less: Selling and administrative costs	1,50,000	2,10,000	2,70,000	1,50,000	7,80,000
Earnings before taxes	1,91,080	4,03,480	5,60,440	1,81,480	13,36,480
Less: Taxes (0.50)	95,540	2,01,740	2,80,220	90,740	6,68,240
Earnings after taxes	95,540	2,01,740	2,80,220	90,740	6,68,240

Quarterly Budgeted Statement of Retained Earnings

Quarter	*First*	*Second*	*Third*	*Fourth*	*Total*
Opening balance	₹18,96,400	₹19,91,940	₹21,13,680	₹23,93,900	₹18,96,400
Add: Earnings after taxes	95,540	2,01,740	2,80,220	90,740	6,68,240
Closing balance	19,91,940	21,93,680	23,93,900	24,84,640	25,64,640
Less: Dividends paid	—	80,000	—	80,000	1,60,640
Closing balance	19,91,940	21,13,680	23,93,900	24,04,640	24,04,640

Quarterly Schedule Relating to Collection from Debtors

Quarter	*First*	*Second*	*Third*	*Fourth*	*Total*
Opening balance	₹11,20,000	₹10,56,000	₹15,36,000	₹20,64,000	₹11,20,000
Add: Credit sales	9,60,000	14,40,000	19,20,000	9,60,000	52,80,000
Total amount due	20,80,000	24,96,000	34,56,000	30,24,000	64,00,000
Less: Collection:					
(i) During discount period (0.50 × prior quarter credit sales)	4,80,000	4,80,000	7,20,000	9,60,000	26,40,000
(ii) After discount period (0.40 × prior quarter credit sales)	3,84,000	3,84,000	5,76,000	7,68,000	21,12,000
(0.075 × 2nd prior quarter credit sales)	1,20,000	72,000	72,000	1,08,000	3,72,000
Written-off bad debts (0.025 × credit sales of 2nd prior quarter credit sales)	40,000	24,000	24,000	36,000	1,24,000
Closing balance	10,56,000	15,36,000	20,64,000	11,52,000	11,52,000

Quarterly Schedule Relating to Payment to Creditors

Particulars	*First*	*Second*	*Third*	*Fourth*	*Total*
Opening balance	₹44,000	₹54,546.80	₹71,579.20	₹68,560.80	₹44,000
Add: Credit purchases (net of discount)	5,45,468	7,15,792.00	6,85,608.00	4,58,248	24,05,116
Total amount payable	5,89,468	7,70,338.80	7,57,187.20	5,26,808,80	24,49,116
Less: Payments:					
(i) During the same quarter (0.90)	4,90,921.20	6,44,212.80	6,17,047.20	4,12,423.20	21,64,604.4
(ii) For the prior quarter (0.10)	44,000.00	54,546.80	71,579.20	68,560.80	2,38,686.8
Closing balance	54,546.80	71,579.20	68,560.80	45,824.80	45,824.8

Quarterly Cash Budget

Particulars	First	Second	Third	Fourth	Total
Cash inflows:					
Cash sales (0.20)	₹2,40,000	₹3,60,000	₹4,80,000	₹2,40,000	₹13,20,000
Collection from debtors:					
Credit sales subject to discount (0.50)	4,80,000	4,80,000	7,20,000	9,60,000	26,40,000
Less: Discount (0.02)	9,600	9,600	14,400	19,200	52,800
Net amount	4,70,400	4,70,400	7,05,600	9,40,800	25,87,200
0.40 × prior quarter credit sales	3,84,000	3,84,000	5,76,000	7,68,000	21,12,000
0.075 × 2nd prior quarter sales	1,20,000	72,000	72,000	1,08,000	3,72,000
Total collections from debtors	9,74,400	9,26,400	13,53,600	18,16,800	50,71,200
Total cash inflows	12,14,400	12,86,400	18,33,600	20,56,800	63,91,200
Cash outflows:					
Payment to creditors	₹5,34,921.20	₹6,98,759.60	₹6,88,626.40	₹4,80,984.00	₹24,03,291.20
Direct labour	88,000	1,28,000.00	1,44,000	88,000	4,48,000.00
Variable overheads	1,32,000	1,92,000	2,16,000	1,32,000	6,72,000.00
Fixed overheads	1,61,000	1,61,000	1,61,000	1,61,000	6,44,000.00
Selling and administrative overheads	1,50,000	2,10,000	2,70,000	1,50,000	7,80,000.00
Income taxes	74,000	95,540	2,01,740	2,80,220	6,51,500.00
Dividends	—	80,000	—	80,000	1,60,000.00
Equipment	—	—	—	6,00,000	6,00,000.00
Total cash outflows	11,39,921.20	15,65,299.60	16,81,366.40	19,72,204	63,58,791.20
Net cash inflows	74,478.80	(2,78,899.60)	1,52,233.6	84,596.00	32,408.8
Opening balance	2,40,000.00	3,14,478.80	35,579.2	1,87,812.80	2,40,000.0
Closing balance	3,14,478.80	35,579.20	1,87,812.80	2,72,408.80	2,72,408.8

Budgeted Balance Sheet as at March 31, Next Year

Liabilities	Amount	Assets		Amount
Share capital	₹31,77,428	Fixed assets	₹54,00,000	
Retained earnings	24,04,640	*Less:* Accumulated depreciation	14,00,000	₹40,00,000
Creditors	45,824.80	Inventories:		
Taxes payable	90,740	Direct material (Material A, 9,200 × ₹5.88) (Material B, 9,200 × ₹7.84)	1,26,224	
		Finished goods (6,000 × ₹40)	2,40,000	3,66,224
		Debtors	11,52,000	
		Less: Allowances for bad debts (₹64,000 + ₹1,32,000 – ₹1,24,000)	72,000	10,80,000
		Cash		2,72,408.80
	57,18,632.8			57,18,632.8

16 Chapter

Standard Costs and Quality Costs

Learning Objectives

1. Understand the meaning of standard costs
2. Discuss the ways to establish cost standards
3. Explain the main components of standard costs
4. Examine and illustrate quality costs

INTRODUCTION

As observed earlier, management accounting is concerned with financial information for the use of management. It enables decision-making about the firm on behalf of the outside parties as well as *for* the firm for purposes of internal management. In particular, the availability of relevant information is a prerequisite for effective planning and control. The term "planning" refers to what a firm wishes to achieve and the actions to be taken to achieve the desired objectives. Control is the process of ensuring that action conform to plans. In other words, control as a management function, means that once a course of action has been decided, operational decisions and activities of management should coincide with the plans. This implies that management needs some criterion for judging the results of operating decisions. Cost data constitute an important element of the financial information to accomplish it. One approach to ensure that operations are in conformity with plans is to compare the actual performance with some standard. A widely-used technique is "standard cost" and variance analysis. The objective of this chapter is to discuss this control concept. In other words, standard cost is considered here as a criterion to measure performance. While Sections 1-3 cover meaning of standards, their establishment and components, quality costs are covered in Section 4. The main points are summarised in Section 5.

MEANING OF STANDARDS

Standards are performance expectations.[1] In other words, standards may be defined as measured quantities which should be attained in connection with some particular operation or activity. Stated in terms of a test of efficiency, a standard is a precise measure of what should occur if the performance is efficient. For example, a certain number of words per minute is a standard for an efficient steno-typist; a certain percentage of marks may be a standard to qualify in a certain examination

Standard is a precise measure of what should occur if performance is efficient.

or to obtain a certain grade, say A, or a division, say first, and so on. In other words, when we say that the standard for a typist is, say, 80 words per minute, what is meant is that a particular typist is considered efficient depending on his typing speed per minute *vis-à-vis* 80 words per minute. If he attains, or exceeds this level, his performance will be rated satisfactory, if not, he has to improve if the goals of the organisation are to be achieved. Thus, in a sense, a standard describes an approach to implement and achieve the goals of the firm. The standards are generally set by management in accordance with the best judgement. However, standards can be set only for repetitive tasks, that is, for work which is repeated again and again; standards cannot be set for tasks which are not performed regularly and continuously.

Thus defined, standards are different from another criterion to evaluate performance, namely, budgets. Budgets, as a tool of planning and control, have already been discussed in an earlier chapter of this book. One difference between standards and budgets is to be found in their scope of activity. While a budget relates to an entire activity or operation, the standard presents the same information on a per unit basis. For instance, the cost of material to produce 1,000 units is ₹5,000. In terms of budget, the cost of materials is expected to be ₹5,000. The standard would express it as ₹5 per unit. Secondly, budgets and standards are set by different persons. Usually, a budget committee prepares the budgets; the standards are generally established by management accountants in consultation with engineers, management, and so on. Moreover, functionally, budgets are used for planning and coordination purposes, whereas standards are primarily used as a control device.

Standard cost is a criterion/ measure of acceptable cost performance.

Standard cost may, therefore, be defined as a criterion or measure of acceptable cost performance. That is to say, whether the cost incurred by a firm is reasonable or not, can be judged in relation to the standard costs. Standard costs may be: **(i)** Ideal, **(ii)** Expected, and **(iii)** Normal/attainable. The ideal standard cost refers to estimates of costs under ideal or perfect conditions. The assumption would be that there would be no waste, no scrap, no idle items, no machine breakdown, and so on. Such a standard, obviously, cannot be achieved in real world situations.

The expected standard cost is based upon the most likely attainable result. Technically, it means what *can* happen and not what *should* happen. It is really not a standard in the real sense of the term as there is no inherent element of efficiency, which is the basic consideration underlying standard costs.

Normal standard costs are costs which are attainable if operations/activities are efficient.

Normal standards or currently attainable standards assume normal conditions as opposed to perfect conditions in the sense that normal wastage, normal breakdown and normal mistakes are visualised as part of the operations. Therefore, such standard costs may be defined as costs which are attainable but their achievement requires that operations and activities are efficient.[2] *For our purpose, standard costs invariably refer to the normal standard costs.*

ESTABLISHING COST STANDARDS

The effectiveness of standard cost, as a tool, will ultimately depend upon how the standards themselves have been established. Care, therefore, must be taken to set up standards which consider all relevant facts such as the employees, their abilities and aspirations and their degree of control over operations, and so on. There are several ways to devise standards: **(i)** Engineering estimates, **(ii)** Observed behaviour, **(iii)** Predicted behaviour, and **(iv)** Desired behaviour. The standard cost in a particular situation may be based on two or more of these techniques.

Engineering Estimates

One basis of setting up cost standards is engineering estimates. Technically, a standardised relationship between, say, a given unit of output and given units of input (say, raw materials) can be estimated fairly accurately depending upon the specifications of the machinery. On the basis of such technical specifications, cost standards can be set. Thus, cost standards according to the engineering estimates are based on what can be accomplished.

Observed Behaviour

Another technique to establish cost standards is past experience. Here, the approach is to treat the achievements of the past as standards for the future. If the processes and procedures of the past have not changed and are likely to operate in future also, this can provide a reliable guide for the future. If, however, changes occur in the processes and procedures, observed behaviour (what happened in the past) can certainly not provide a reliable basis for setting cost standards.

Predicted Behaviour

It is also likely that certain changes, such as technological, may be in the offing. These are likely to have a bearing on the cost estimates. In such cases, what is most likely to happen, that is, predicted behaviour in terms of adjustment to the historical standard cost, can be used to set cost standards.

Desired Behaviour

Desired behaviour can also affect standard cost. The term "desired behaviour" means what management desires. The desire of the management may be based on the experience of similar concerns or the industry as a whole. This basis will bring the cost standards of the company in line with those of the industry as a whole.

In brief, while several techniques are available to establish cost standards, it is basically based on management's judgement. In setting up of standards, management should be careful. Standards should be set at a level at which they are attainable with reasonable efforts. If they are too strict and too high, they may be difficult to achieve, leading to all-round demoralisation. If, on the other hand, cost standards are set low, there may not be sufficient motivation to achieve them.

COMPONENTS OF STANDARD COST

Standard costs are costs that should be reasonably incurred in the manufacture of a product.

From the preceding discussion standard costs may be defined as costs that should be reasonably incurred in the manufacturer of a product.[3] The main components of standard costs are: **(i)** Standard direct material cost, **(ii)** Standard direct labour cost, and **(iii)** Manufacturing overheads.

Standard Direct Material Cost

The standard direct material cost of a product is based upon price and quantity standards. In operational terms,

$$\text{Standard direct material cost} = \text{Price standards of direct material} \times \text{Quantity standard of direct material} \quad \mathbf{(16.1)}$$

Direct Materials Price Standard

One of the most important items of cost is the cost of direct materials used in the manufacture of goods. To exercise control over the cost, therefore, an important element of cost control is the price paid for the purchase of materials. In other words, one important dimension of materials cost control is that the price paid should be reasonable. Hence, the need for a materials price standard which is defined as the price which should be paid for particular direct raw material under the most favourable possible conditions. What is the most *favourbale possible condition* will differ from firm to firm depending upon the circumstances of each case. Therefore, material price standards should be set for each firm and not for the industry as a whole.

The standard material price should include all the components of the amount which is to be spent to acquire a particular material. To illustrate, in the first place, assuming the same quality of goods, the standard should be set on the basis of the lowest price. If, however, the supplier who is prepared to sell the material at the lowest cost, is not able to deliver them when needed, or he is not dependable, there will be no real saving to the firm. In such cases, differences in quality and/or in service may justify the setting up of the price standard on the basis of the higher price to be charged by the more reliable suppliers. Secondly, a firm has to incur freight charges on the purchase of raw materials which affect the cost of the materials. Since freight charges normally vary with the distance between the buyer and the supplier, while setting a material price standard, the firm should consider purchasing from the closest possible supplier, other things being equal. A related aspect is that in the case of purchase through imports, additional cost is involved in the form of import duties. These have to be taken into account while fixing standard price. Thirdly, discounts available on the purchase of materials are also relevant to the fixation of price standards. The discounts fall into two categories: **(i)** Quantity discounts which are granted for purchase in relatively large doses; **(ii)** Cash discounts which are granted for prompt payment. The effect of discounts is lower costs and, hence, lower price standards. The setting up of a materials price standard is illustrated in Example 16.1.

EXAMPLE 16.1

Hypothetical Ltd, on the basis of investigation of alternative sources of supply, decides to purchase raw materials from the most advantageous supplier—ABC Ltd which quotes a list price of ₹1,820 per tonne, exclusive of freight charges. It also offers a quantity discount @ ₹70 per tonne for orders exceeding 20 tonnes. It also allows 2 per cent cash discount for payment within 15 days. Moreover, freight charges are likely to be ₹1,700 per carload (20 tonnes of materials) and payable directly to the carrier. Compute the standard materials price for Hypothetical Ltd.

SOLUTION

Computation of Standard Materials Price

1. List price (per tonne)	₹1,820
2. *Less* quantity discount (per tonne)	70
Car load price	1,750
3. *Less* cash discount (0.02)	35
	1,715
4. *Add* freight charges (₹1,700 ÷ 20 tonnes)	85
Standard price per tonne	1,800

This standard price provides a basis for planning future material costs and for controlling current costs by providing a criterion against which actual prices paid may be evaluated.

Materials Quantity (Usage) Standard The quantity of the materials used is the second factor affecting cost of material. In order to standardise cost of materials, therefore, the quantity of materials used for the production of a particular product should also be standardised. The standards of the quantity of consumption of raw materials is referred to as materials quantity standards or materials usage standards. Such standards can be determined on the basis of two factors: **(i)** The necessary input-output relationship between materials and products and also upon observation of actual experience, **(ii)** The inherent loss of materials in the production processes owing to factors such as weight losses due to scrapping and smoothing, shrinkage and evaporation, and so on. Consider Example 16.2.

EXAMPLE 16.2

Hypothetical Ltd of Example 16.1 produces a single product by using steel. Each finished product weighs 380 kgs. Past experience coupled with careful engineering studies show that a loss of 5 per cent occurs in the weight of the input material in the production process. What is the standard material usage per unit?

SOLUTION

Computation of Standard Materials Usage Per Unit

Weight of finished product (kgs)	380
Allowance for normal loss in the production process (0.05)	20
Standard material usage	400

Two points in this connection are notable. First, there will be different quantity standards for different materials; and different standards may apply to the usage of a single material in different products/departments. Second, the material quantity standard does not provide for loss of materials due to: **(1)** Careless handling, **(2)** Damage to units in process, and **(3)** Other undesirable circumstances. In fact, the material usage standard is intended to eliminate such types of material losses.

Total Material Cost Standard The total material cost standard is computed by multiplying price standards by quantity standards. This is illustrated in Example 16.3.

EXAMPLE 16.3

Continuing the case of Hypothetical Ltd of **Examples 16.1** and **16.2**, the standard price is ₹1,800 per tonne; the standard quantity is 420 kgs per finished units of product. Compute the total standard material cost.

SOLUTION

Standard material cost = (Standard usage × Standard price per kg)
Standard price per kg = ₹1,800/ 2,000 = ₹0.9
Standard material cost = ₹0.9 × 400 = ₹360

Standard Direct Labour Cost

The second component of total standard cost is direct standard labour cost. It is calculated by multiplying Labour rate standards by Labour time standards.

Labour Rate/Price Standards The payment to labour for carrying on production is wages, which is paid either on a time basis (monthly, weekly, daily) or on a piece basis (per piece of production). The use of the term "labour rate/ price standard" is conventionally limited to wage rates standard only, that is, in case of time wage payment only. The wage rate standards are normally either a matter of company policy, or more often, the result of negotiations between management and union. Moreover, in most cases, there will be several different wage rates depending upon the degree of skill, the element of danger, seniority of workers, and so on. Thus, labour rate standards are quite different from material price standards. They are not entirely under the control of management. To illustrate, assume that Hypothetical Ltd has two production departments. In the first, the current standard wage rate is ₹48 per hour. In the second, the standard wage rate is ₹50 per hour. This has to be related to the labour time standard to work out the total labour standard.

Labour time standards is the amount of time which a particular operation should take.

Labour Time Standards The quantity (amount) of labour is measured in terms of time devoted to the completion of a particular operation. Therefore, labour time standards may be defined as the amount of time which a particular operation should take. They are normally established on the basis of observation of actual operations and a critical evaluation of whether or not those operations are being performed as efficiently as is feasible.[4] A fairly familiar and popular example are time and motion studies. It is on the basis of these that labour time standards are generally set. They should, of course, include provision for a reasonable amount of time lost simply because human beings are not mechanical devices and cannot utilise every single moment on the job for actual production. However, no allowance is made while setting standards for prolonged periods of illness or for incompetence.

Assuming that engineering studies in Hypothetical Ltd show that in one of its departments one unit of output should be produced in one-fourth of an hour, whereas in the other department it is one-half of an hour, the total labour time standard is three quarter-hour.

Total Labour Cost Standard The total labour cost standard is equal to labour rate standard multiplied by labour time standard. For Hypothetical Ltd the total labour cost standard would be:

(a) For Department 1 : ₹48 × 1/4 hour	=	₹12
(b) For Department 2 : ₹50 × 1/2 hour	=	25
(c) Total = (a + b)		37

Overheads Standards

The third component of cost standard is overheads. There is a basic difference between overheads standard and material and labour standards. It has been shown in the preceding sections that the standard material and labour costs are based upon price and quantity standards. The logic underlying this is that a functional relationship exists between the number of units of a product and the quantities of material and labour required as also the fact that each material has its standard price and each worker his standard wage rate. In sharp contrast, no such functional relationships exists between the units produced and total overheads cost. Even that portion of manufacturing overhead which varies with the volume of production cannot be directly related to production in the same way as direct material and direct labour. Therefore, the determination of overhead standard is different from that of direct materials and labour.

For these reasons, standard costs for overheads are generally based on budget and not upon standards. Operationally, they are determined essentially in the same way as normal manufacturing overhead rates which are covered in another chapter of this book. The overheads are, for purposes of planning and control, classified into: **(i)** Variable, and **(ii)** Fixed. The standard variable rate is set directly per unit of volume just as a normal variable rate. The volume measure is some measure of input, such as direct labour cost or hours. The determination of the standard fixed overhead is slightly different from that of the normal fixed overhead. This difference lies in the volume at which they are set. Normal fixed rates, illustrated in an earlier chapter in this book, are set at the budgeted volume for the budget period. Standard fixed rates, on the other hand, are usually set at some volume representative of the firm's operations over a longer period than a single budget period.

The volume level most commonly selected for setting standard manufacturing overheads rates is normal volume. The more logical and feasible concept of normal volume is the preferred rate of operating capacity. Each firm identifies a particular rate, or level of capacity/activity at which it would most like to operate its plants. Logically, this is the level at which the mix of productive inputs is optimal and the total manufacturing cost per unit is minimum. Such a concept of normal volume is consistent with the notion of standard cost—cost that should be incurred under efficient operating conditions. It is estimated that the preferred level of operating capacity is at or near 90 per cent of full capacity.[5]

EXAMPLE 16.4

Assume that Hypothetical Ltd uses direct labour-hours as the basis to allocate overheads to production. The variable overhead is budgeted at ₹160 per direct labour-hour in Department 1. The fixed manufacturing overhead is budgeted at a total of ₹16,00,000 per year and normal production volume has been established at 40,000 direct labour-hour per year. In Department 2, variable manufacturing overhead is budgeted at ₹100 per direct labour-hour and fixed overhead at ₹12,00,000 per year. Normal production volume is 80,000 labour-hours per year. Compute the standard overhead rates.

SOLUTION

Computation of Standard Overhead Rates

	Department 1	*Department 2*
1. Standard fixed overhead rate per Labour-hour (Fixed overheads ÷ Normal production volume)	₹40 (₹16,00,000/40,000)	₹15 (₹12,00,000/80,000)
2. Variable overhead per unit (Standard labour time × Variable overhead)	40 (1/4 hour × ₹160)	50 (1/2 hour × ₹100)
3. Fixed overhead per unit (Standard labour time × Standard fixed overhead rate)	10 (1/4 hour × ₹40)	7.5 (1/2 hour × ₹15)

Standard Cost Sheet

A summarised view of total standard cost is presented in the form of a standard cost sheet or standard cost card. The information about Hypothetical Ltd is presented in Table 16.1.

Table 16.1 Hypothetical Limited—Standard Cost Sheet

(a) Direct materials (400 kgs × ₹0.9)		₹360.00
(b) Direct labour:		
Department 1	₹12	
Department 2	25	37.00
(c) Variable manufacturing overhead:		
Department 1	40	
Department 2	50	90.00
(d) Fixed manufacturing overhead:		
Department 1	10	
Department 2	7.5	17.50
		504.50

QUALITY COSTS

To satisfy the customers needs for good quality products and short delivery times, it is necessary to find cost effective ways to continuously improve the quality of products and to shorten delivery times. **Quality is the total features and characteristics of a product/service made/performed according to specifications to satisfy customers at the time of purchase and during use.** Focussing on the quality of a product will generally build expertise in producing it, lower costs of making it, create higher satisfaction for using it and generate higher future revenues for the company selling it[6]. There are two basic aspects of quality: First, quality of design in terms of how closely the characteristics of a product/service

Quality is the total features and characteristics of a product/service made/performed according to specifications to satisfy customers at the time of purchase and during use.

meet the needs/wants of customers. Failure of a bank to provide online services is an example of a quality-of-design failure. Second, conformance quality in the sense of the performance of a product/service relative to its design/specifications. Deposit of a customer's cheque into the wrong account by a bank is an example of failure on conformance quality. To ensure that performance will achieve customer satisfaction, companies must first design products to satisfy customers through quality of design. They must then meet design specifications through conformance quality.

Costs of Quality/Quality Costs

Cost of Quality are the costs incurred to prevent, or the cost arising as a result of, producing a low-quality product.

The costs of quality are the costs incurred to prevent, or the cost arising as a result of, producing a low-quality product. These include any costs in excess of those that would have been incurred if goods were manufactured/ service provided exactly right at the first time.[7] These costs typically are categorised into four groups, described below.

Prevention costs are incurred to prevent defects and other quality problems/ to preclude the production of goods that do not conform to specifications.

Prevention Costs Such costs *are incurred to prevent defects and other quality problems/* to preclude the production of goods that do not conform to specifications. Examples of these costs are: design engineering, process engineering, supplier evaluation, preventive equipment maintenance, quality training, new materials used to manufacture products and so on. In a sense, they are "good quality" costs in the sense that they represent activities that often significantly reduce costs in the other three categories of quality costs.[8]

Quality appraisal costs are incurred to detect which individual unit of a product does not conform to specifications

Quality Appraisal (Detection) Costs Such costs are incurred to detect which individual unit of a product does not conform to specifications. Examples of these costs are inspection, testing and other activities designed to find problems before goods are delivered to customers.

Internal Failure Costs These costs are incurred as a result of the appraisal activities. These are incurred on a defective product before it is despatched to customers. Examples of such costs are spoilage, rework, scrap, breakdown maintenance, manufacturing/process engineering on internal failure and other activities to "make things better" before a product is delivered.

External failure costs are costs of making things right when a quality problem has occurred after the product has been delivered to the customer

External Failure Costs These are costs of making things right when a quality problem has occurred after the product has been delivered to the customer. Examples of this category of quality cost are refunds, warranty costs in terms of both repairs and replacements, product liability costs and the costs of repeating a service that was not performed properly at first time. Included in this category of costs is also the cost of lost future business resulting from dissatisfied customers.

Unlike product costs, the quality costs often are estimates based on special studies rather than the output of routine accounting system. Such costs are charged to the specific product that caused them to be incurred.

Quality Costs Illustrated

The cost of quality of design is mainly in the form of the opportunity cost of sales lost from not producing a product that consumers want. It is very difficult to measure the financial cost of design quality objectively.

We illustrate below the computation of quality costs in terms of cost of conformance quality. We use step-wise activity-based costing approach (**discussed in Chapter 7**) here to determine the cost of quality.

Step 1: Identify the Chosen Product Assume the product is 20,000 photocopying machines of Modi Xerox Ltd. The revenues and operating income from the sale of 20,000 machines are ₹70 crore and ₹6 crore respectively in 2007.

Step 2: Select Cost-Allocation Base for Allocating Indirect Costs of Quality The activities that result in quality costs are listed in Exhibit 16.1 (Column 1).

Step 3: Identify Indirect Costs Associated with Each Cost-Allocation Base These are the total costs computed by multiplying the rate per hour (**Column 2 for Exhibit 16.1**) and quantity (**Column 3 of Exhibit 16.1**) on each of the cost-of-quality activities.

Step 4: Compute the Rate Per Unit of Each Cost Allocation Base Used to Allocate Indirect Costs of Quality to Product For each activity, the total costs (**computed in Step 3**) are divided by the total quantity of the cost allocation base (calculated in Step 2) to compute the rate per unit of each cost allocation base. **Column 2 of Exhibit 16.1 shows these rates.**

Step 5: Compute the Indirect Costs of Quality Allocated to the Product These are shown in Column 4 of Exhibit 16.1.

Step 6: Compute the Total Costs of Quality by Adding All Costs of Quality Assigned to the Product This is **shown in Column 5** of Exhibit 16.1.

Exhibit 16.1 Analysis of Activity-based Cost of Quality of Photocopying Machines of Modi Xerox Ltd.

Cost of Quality Activities	*Allocation Base/Cost Driver*			*Percentage of revenue*
	Rate	*Quantity*	*Total costs [(2) × (3)]*	*[(4) ÷ ₹70 crore] %*
(1)	*(2)*	*(3)*	*(4)*	*(5)*
Prevention Costs:				
Design Engineering	₹400 per hour	20,000 hours	₹80,00,000	1.1%
Process Engineering	300 per hour	22,500 hours	67,50,000	1.0
Total			1,47,50,000	2.1
Appraisal Costs:				
Inspection	200 per hour	1,20,000 hours	2,40,00,000	3.4
Total			2,40,00,000	3.4
Internal Failure Costs:				
Rework	500 per hour	50,000 hours	2,50,00,000	3.6
Total			2,50,00,000	3.6
External Failure Costs:				
Customer support	250 per hour	6,000 hours	15,00,000	0.2
Transportation	1,200 per hour	1,500 hours	18,00,000	0.3
Warranty repair	550 per hour	60,000 hours	3,30,00,000	4.7
Total			3,63,00,000	5.2
Total Cost of Quality			10,00,50,000	14.3

Non-Financial Measures of Quality and Customer Satisfaction

Financial measures of quality, discussed earlier, focus on the start-run. To evaluate how well their actual performance satisfies customer needs, companies supplement financial measures with non-financial measures of quality of design and conformance quality. Non-financial measures indicate the future needs and preferences of customer as well as specific areas that need improvement. They are, in a sense, indicator of future long-term performance. The non-financial measures of customer satisfaction, *inter-alia,* include the following:[9]

- Market research information on customer preferences/satisfaction with specific product features.
- Number of defective units delivered to customers as percentage of total units delivered.
- Number of customer complaints.
- Percentage of products that fail soon/often.
- Delivery delays in terms of differences between the scheduled delivery date and the date requested by the customers.
- On-time delivery rate (i.e. percentage of delivery made on/before the scheduled delivery date).
- Surveys to measure customer satisfaction.

Management should monitor whether there is improvement or deterioration over time. Any improvement may be indicative of strong operating income in future whereas deterioration may indicate weak operating income.

SUMMARY

- ➢ Standard costs represent a control technique. In a sense, they are a target, which the management attempts to achieve. The control process involves a comparison of the actual performance with the standards set by management. The extent of success would be revealed by the relationship between the actual and the standard. If the actual performance coincides with the target, the performance can be said to be satisfactory. In case of divergence or deviations, management would have to analyse the causes. These deviations are technically referred to as "variance". Therefore, variance analysis is an important control concept related to standard costs. In other words, the variances which basically represent performance deviations are a significant element of the information base of an effective control system. The next two chapters discuss cost and revenue variances.
- ➢ Costs of quality are costs incurred to prevent or the cost arising as a result of, producing a low quality product. Such costs are categorised into prevention costs, quality appraisal (detection) costs, internal failure costs and external failure costs.
- ➢ Prevention costs are incurred to prevent defects and other quality problems/to preclude the production of goods that do not conform to specifications. Quality appraisal costs are incurred to detect which individual unit of a product does not conform to specifications. Internal failure costs are incurred on defective products before they are delivered to customers. External failure costs are costs of making things right when a quality problem has occurred after the product has been delivered to the customer.
- ➢ Financial measures of quality focus on the short-run. Non-financial measures indicate the future needs and preferences of customers as well as the specific areas that need improvement.

REFERENCES

1. R.M. Copeland and P.E. Dashcher, *Management Accounting,* (John Wiley and Sons, New York, 1978), p. 382.
2. D.T. Decoster and E.L. Schafer, *Management Accounting,* (John Wiley and Sons, New York, 1979), p. 204

3. J.M. Fremgen, *Accounting for Managerial Analysis,* (Richard D. Irwin, Homewood, Illinois, 1976), p. 237.
4. *Ibid.*, p. 233.
5. *Ibid.*, p. 239.
6. Horngren, C. T., *Cost Accounting,* Pearson (2004), p.654.
7. *Ibid,* p. 655.
8. Anthony, R. N., *Accounting: Text and Cases,* TMH (2005), p. 560.
9. Horngren, *Op. Cit,* p.661.

REVIEW QUESTIONS

RQ.16.1 Indicate whether the following statements are 'true' or 'false'.

(i) Standard costs are the measures of acceptable cost performance.
(ii) Standards should be tight to be an effective tool of cost control
(iii) Standards are used for planning and coordination purposes.
(iv) Standards should be current and attainable with reasonable efforts.
(v) Standard material price is based only on the cost price at which materials can be procured by the purchase manager.
(vi) Material quantity standard should also provide for normal loss of materials in the production process.
(vii) Labour time standards are generally set on the basis of motion and time studies.
(viii) Standard fixed overhead rate is based on budgeted output.
(ix) Overhead standards are set like material and labour standards.
(x) Standard direct labour cost is summation of labour rate standard and labour time standard.

[Answers: (i) True, (ii) False, (iii) False, (iv) True, (v) False, (vi) True, (vii) True, (viii) False, (ix) False, (x) False.]

RQ.16.2 (a) What are the points of similarity and points of difference between budgets and standard costs?

(b) What are the several types of standards and what are the assumptions on which these standards are based?

RQ.16.3 What is "standard costing" and how would you distinguish it from "budgetary control?"

RQ.16.4 Write short notes on the following:

(a) Standard costing as tool of management control.
(b) Control through standard costs.

RQ.16.5 How do standards and standard costs facilitate managerial planning and control?

RQ.16.6 What factors should be considered in setting a: **(a)** Materials price standard; **(b)** Materials usage standard; **(c)** Labour rate standard; and **(d)** Labour time standard?

RQ.16.7 What is the nature of the fundamental difference between standard costs for direct materials and labour and standard manufacturing overhead costs?

RQ.16.8 Define quality and explain the two aspects of quality.

RQ.16.9 Define quality costs. Explain the main categories of these costs.

RQ.16.10 Explain briefly the non-financial measures of quality and customer satisfaction.

Variance Analysis: Cost Variances

Learning Objectives

1. Explain the nature of cost variances
2. Discuss material variances and the factors responsible for various types of material variances
3. Illustrate the various types of labour variances and the reasons for such variances
4. Analyse variable and fixed manufacturing overhead costs separately as well as jointly
5. Understand the methods of analyzing overhead variances jointly
6. Illustrate how to incorporate standard costs in the accounting records

INTRODUCTION

Chapter 16 introduced an important control concept-standard costs. The object of this chapter is to illustrate the use of standard costs for purposes of planning and control of costs in a manufacturing concern. This objective is achieved by the process of comparison of actual costs (AC) incurred with the pre-determined standard costs (SC) and then seeking the reasons for the variances, if any. *Variance represents the difference between AC and SC.* If AC is less than SC, this is a sign of efficiency and the difference is termed as "favourable" variance (F). If the AC is more than SC, this is a sign of inefficiency and the difference is designated as "unfavourable"/"adverse" variance (U/A). Favourable variance is also sometimes referred to as "positive variance" while unfavourable variance is called "negative variance". The words favourable/positive and unfavourable/negative are merely indicative of the direction of variance from the SC. They need not necessarily be good or bad from the point of view of the firm. Such a qualitative evaluation can be made only after the underlying cause of the variance has been determined. And, above all, the answer will depend on the type of standards set by the firm. If standards are properly set in that they are reasonable and accurate and are revised from time to time in the light of changed circumstances, deviations would be true deviations. However, if standards are not properly set, conclusions drawn—favourable or unfavourable—will

> **Variance** is the difference between actual cost and standard cost.

be distorted. A still more serious situation would occur, when guided by such a wrong conclusion, futile efforts would be initiated by the management to correct the "not - incorrect operation."

Given the fact that standards are properly set (currently attainable), variances would serve as useful tool in the implementation of the concept of "management by exception" in that variances keep the management informed about the erratic and out-of-line behaviour of the business. The basic rule of management by exception is to concentrate on operations and segments of an enterprise that deviate from target performance and not to spend much time reviewing satisfactory performances. Further, both favourable and unfavourable variances deserve attention. An unfavourable variance suggests a condition that may require correction. A favourable variance may suggest an opportunity that management can exploit.[1]

Variances, as a control device, are calculated to assign/fix responsibility for deviations from the SC and, thus, to control the cost. For purposes of control, variances are classified as controllable and uncontrollable cost variances.

If a variance can be traced with the responsibility of a particular individual, it is said to be a "controllable" variance. If variance stems from causes beyond the control of responsible individuals, it is said to be "uncontrollable". Thus, uncontrollable variance arises when the responsibility for the variance cannot be attributed to any individual in an organisation. For instance, the increase in the price of materials and increase in the wage rates are commonly referred to as un/non-controllable variances, whereas excessive usage of materials in production, more than standard hours taken by labourers in production, are examples of controllable variances. This distinction of variances into controllable and uncontrollable is extremely important. Controllable variances are carefully analysed and reported to the management to enable it to pursue corrective action, and, thus, facilitate the implementation of the principle of management by exception.

As already observed, variances relate to costs of manufacturing enterprises. The three elements of the costs of such enterprises are: (i) Material (ii) Labour and (iii) Overheads. A complete list of the different types of variances is given in Figures 17.1 and 17.2. Sections 1–3 cover the cost variances associated with materials, labour and overheads respectively. The accounting for standard costs is illustrated in Section 4. The summary is given in Section 5.

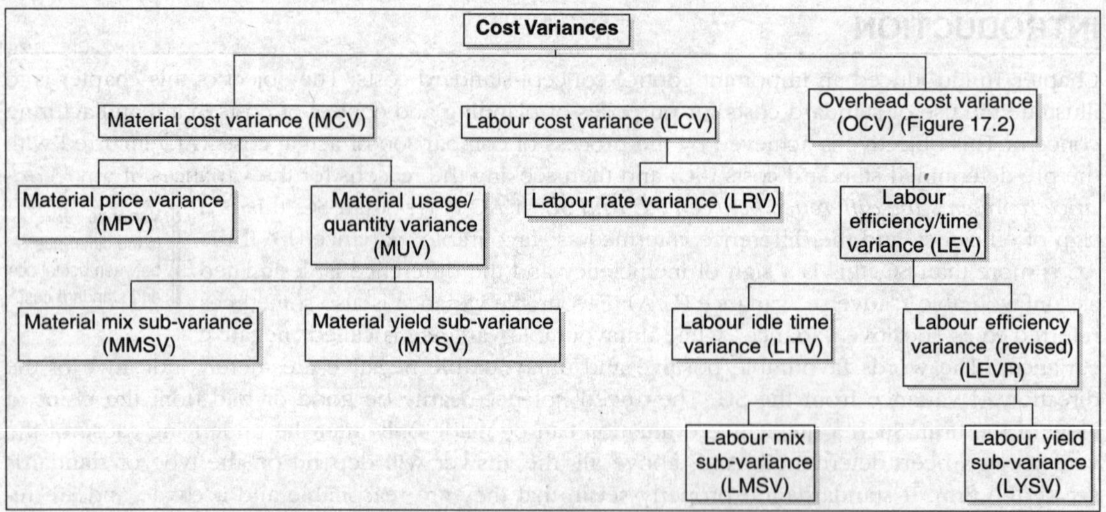

Figure 17.1 *Material and Labour Cost Variances*

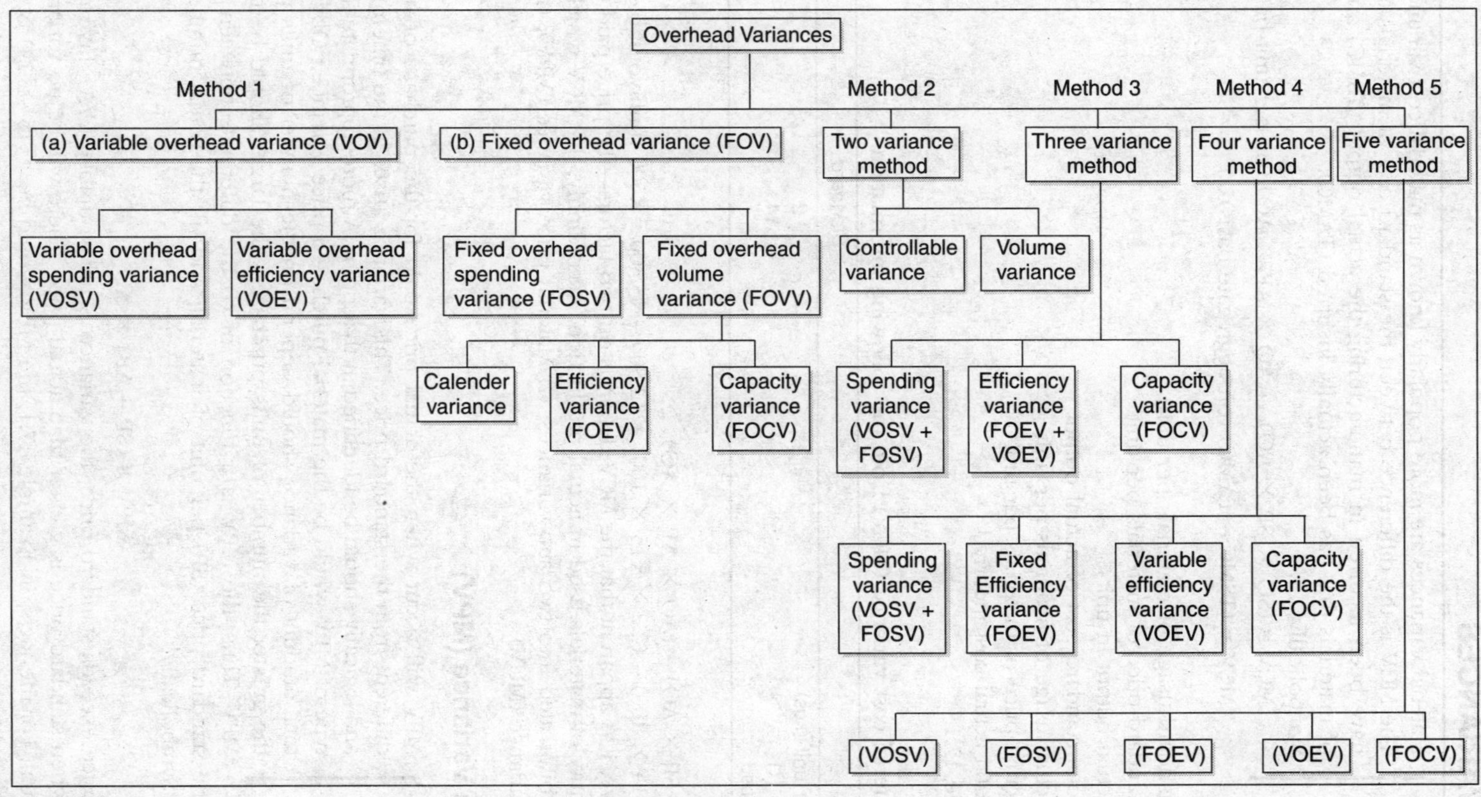

Figure 17.2 *Overhead Variances*

MATERIAL VARIANCES

Material cost variance is the difference between the standard cost of materials and the cost of materials actually incurred.

Material variances are more popularly known as material cost variances (MCV). The MCV is the difference between the standard cost of materials that should have been incurred in manufacturing the actual output (TSMC) and the cost of materials that has been actually incurred (TAMC).

Symbolically,

$$MCV = (SQ \times SP \times AO) - (AQ \times AP \times AO) \text{ (on per unit basis)} \quad \textbf{(17.1)}$$

$$MCV = (TSMC - TAMC) \text{ (on aggregate basis)} \quad \textbf{(17.2)}$$

Where,

SQ = Standard usage of materials per unit
SP = Standard price of materials per unit
AO = Actual output in units
TSMC = Total standard cost of actual output
AQ = Actual usage of materials per unit
AP = Actual price of materials per unit
TAMC = Total actual cost incurred

Consider Example 17.1.

EXAMPLE 17.1

Compute the material cost variance (MCV) from the following information.

Particulars	*Standard*	*Actual*
Material usage per unit (kgs)	2	2.2
Price per kilogram (₹)	14	15
Actual units produced		100

SOLUTION

MCV = (SQ × SP × AO) – (AQ × AP × AO)
= (2 × ₹14 × 100) – (2.2 × ₹15 × 100) = ₹2,800 – ₹3,300 = ₹500 (unfavourable/Adverse)

From the above, it is apparent that the MCV depends on two factors—the price paid for materials, and the quantity of materials used in actual production. Accordingly, the MCV which is a total variance can be bifurcated into two sub-variances: (i) Material price variance (MPV); (ii) Material usage/quantity variance (MUV).

Material Price Variance (MPV)

Material price variance is the difference between the actual price paid for purchase of materials and the standard price.

MPV will occur when the actual price paid for the purchase of materials is different from the standard price. This variance arises at the time of purchase and logically should be identified at that point. A more appropriate title for this type of MPV would be the material purchased price variance.[2] Obviously, the total amount of variance should depend on the number of units purchased; the greater the number of units purchased, the larger should be the size of MPV. Thus, the MPV is a function of (i) the difference between the actual price (AP) and the standard price (SP) per unit of material; and (ii) the actual number of units purchased (AQ). Symbolically,

$$MPV = (SP - AP) \times AQ \quad \textbf{(17.3)}$$

When actual price exceeds standard price, the variance is unfavourable (U/A); favourable variance (F) results when standard price is greater than actual price. There will be no variance if both the prices are equal. For the facts, in Example 17.1, the MPV would be: (₹15 – ₹14) × 220 kgs = ₹220 (unfavourable/A)

Factors Responsible for MPV There may be many causal factors for the MPV. Some of them may be acting favourably while others unfavourably. An illustrative list of the factors having a bearing on MPV is given below:

1. Changes in the basic price of materials due to inflation.
2. Excess transport charges, that is, freight on goods purchased which are normally considered as part of the cost of purchases.
3. Change in the pattern of amount of taxes and customs duties.
4. Increased excise duty on goods purchased and, hence, a higher price charged by the suppliers of their products.
5. In situations of material shortages, the price charged by, and paid to, the suppliers may be higher than the normal price.
6. Purchases may not have been made from the most desirable supplier or favourable market.
7. Not availing of cash discounts due to inadequate cash resources, while such discounts were well taken into account while determining the standard price.
8. Failure to take advantage of off-season low price.
9. Sudden change in the production volume, forcing the purchase manager to buy uneconomic quantities.
10. Change in standard quality or specifications of materials resulting in different prices being paid.
11. Use of substitute material having a different unit price from the standard.
12. Failure to purchase in the pre-estimated lot size resulting in a loss of trade discount.

Responsibility for MPV Material price variance is mainly the responsibility of the purchase officers who are in charge of making the entire purchases of the firm. Normally, they are required to prepare a statement which analyses the reasons for the variances. From the factors enumerated above, it is very clear that the purchase department may not be always held responsible for paying higher or lower than the standard price; the responsibility for some of the factors may rest with persons other than purchasing officers. For instance, the responsibility of a sudden change in production schedule rests with the production manager. Likewise, a general price increase falls beyond the jurisdiction of purchase officers. The purchases of smaller quantities depriving the benefit of trade discount and making late payment resulting in foregoing cash discount on account of lack of finances with the firm are not factors for which they are accountable. For example, the average market price of the materials purchased by a firm has increased by 10 per cent (on account of additional excise duty imposed on the manufacturer supplying the material to the firm) from the firm's standard price, and the MPV is unfavourable by 7 per cent. The situation implies efficient purchasing practices whereas simple computation would yield the opposite conclusion of ineffective/inefficient purchasing practices. On the contrary, the purchase manager might succeed in achieving a favourable material price variance by purchasing from an unreliable supplier, but consequent delivery delays may be fatal to the firm in that it may cause partial shutdown of production facilities, having an adverse impact on meeting customer's orders in time. Such a variance is favourable only in name and clearly not in effect.

Obviously, it would be naive to automatically assign all results directly to the purchasing department without a detailed analysis. It is logical, therefore, to attribute a segment of material price variance to a department(s) other than purchasing. For example, if a foreman of a production department fails to notify purchase requisitions of materials in time, an emergency order may become imperative to make available the required supplies so as to avert a production stoppage, entailing higher price being paid and perhaps also higher freight charges. Clearly, the production department is responsible for the creation of such a variance. From the *operational* viewpoint, however, it can be said that the causes rest with the purchase officer and it is his responsibility to explain unusual circumstances.

Material Usage/Quantity Variance (MUV)

Material usage variance occurs when actual usage of materials differs from standard usage.

The second component of MCV, material quantity/usage variance (MUV), measures how well the materials in production are utilised. This variance occurs when actual usage of material differs from standard usage. The data for actual usage of materials is collected from a summary of materials issue reports during the relevant period, while the standard quantity of materials in production would simply be the product of standard quantity of materials required for each unit of product and the number of units produced during the period. Since the MPV has already taken into account price differences, the MUV ignores such differences and the difference of quantities is multiplied by the standard price per unit. Symbolically

$$\text{MUV} = [(\text{SQ} \times \text{AO}) - (\text{AQ} \times \text{AO})] \times \text{SP} \qquad \textbf{(17.4)}$$

For Example 17.1, the MUV would be: = [(2 × 100) – (2.2 × 100)] × ₹14 = ₹280 (unvarouable).

Since the actual consumption of materials is more than the standard quantity required for producing 100 units of output, the MUV is unfavourable.

Factors Responsible for MUV There may be several reasons for a material quantity variance. The important ones are listed below:

1. Carelessness in the use of materials handled by workers and other production personnel.
2. Poor or improper machine adjustment.
3. Substitution of sub-standard or defective materials causing excessive materials consumption.
4. Change in product specification or design requiring usage different from the standard.
5. Inefficient and inadequate inspection of raw materials.
6. Theft of the materials due to poor janitorial services.
7. Wastage due to inefficient production methods or unskilled/untrained employees.
8. Substitution of higher quality materials than the standard leading to lower usage of materials.
9. Improvement in the production process and extra care taken by the workers in carrying out their jobs.
10. Pilferage, wastage and spoilage due to poor stock-keeping function.
11. Defective tools, machines, plant and equipment coupled with their improper maintenance leading to frequent breakdowns and more usage of raw materials.
12. Actual mix of materials being different from the standard mix.
13. Actual yield being different from the standard yield.

Responsibility for MUV The overall responsibility for this variance lies with the production personnel. However, this should not be allowed to become a general premise as in the case of MPV. For instance, the principal cause of a favourable MUV should be the substitution of above-standard materials which result in less waste than what was anticipated when the standard quantity was set. But the purchase of above-standard materials is certainly likely to contribute to an unfavourable material price variance as the higher quality materials would cost more. "Both variances would have been unavoidable, if the materials specified in developing the standard costs were not available, and the purchasing agent bought what he could".[3] From a practical viewpoint, for such a variance, production personnel do not deserve any appreciation and purchasing personnel any criticism. Likewise, the changes in product specifications may cause either favourable or unfavourable usage variances for which the only solution is to change the material usage standard. These examples tend to show that mere arithmetical computation of MUV or for that matter of any variance is not enough. It is the investigation into the causes of variances, which is more fruitful/useful from the point of control.

Graphical Presentation of Material Variances

In Figure 17.3, total MCV (unfavourable) or ₹500 is partly the result of the high material prices and partly the result of more quantities used.

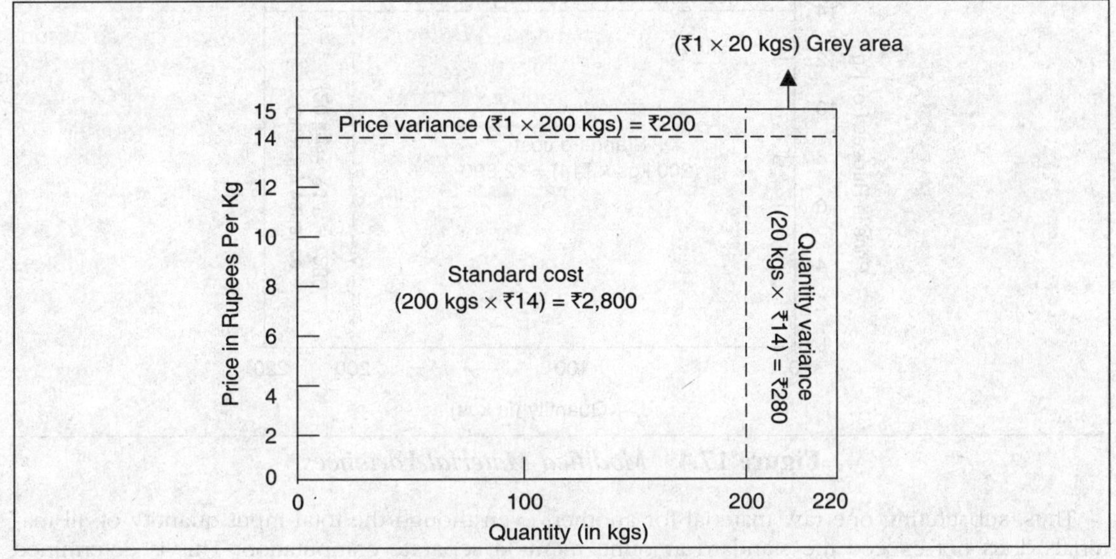

Figure 17.3 *Material Variances*

Clearly, at least ₹200 of the variance is a material price variance and ₹280 is the material usage variance. But the remaining ₹20 is what is called as a "grey area"[4]. It is an inextricable combination of the influence of both a high rate and more material used. But it will be just logical if ₹20 variance is clubbed with material price variance because the production personnel cannot be held responsible for the high prices paid by the purchase department. Moreover, it is the responsibility of the purchase manager to make the materials available at standard rates to the production department and, therefore, Figure 17.3 needs modification in terms of clubbing the grey area with price variance. The modification is shown in Figure 17.4.

It is in this context that the conventional variance analysis, which includes the joint price-efficiency variance as a part of an overall price variance, is said to be logically deficient. Further, the efficiency variance is considered more important than the price variance as the manager can exert more direct influence over the efficiency variance. It is also felt that joint-price efficiency variance is less likely to cause arguments if it is buried in the price variance.[5]

The MUV can be further subdivided into **(i)** Material mix sub-variance and **(ii)** Material yield sub-variance.

Material Mix Sub-Variance (MMSV) It is possible that a product may use more than one type/grade of raw materials or combination of materials. This combination is called the material mix. In such a situation, it may be possible to alter the mix of materials used from the pre-determined standard mix (ratio) set, the reasons being non-availability or inadequate supply of one or more types of raw material, or the price of a particular type of material may have gone up making it uneconomical in the given price situations of its finished product: the availability of a new substitute for one or more types of raw materials already being used either because they are cheaper and/or better in quality.

Material mix sub-variance is the difference between the standard mix and the actual mix input/quantities of all grades of material actually used and their corresponding standard price.

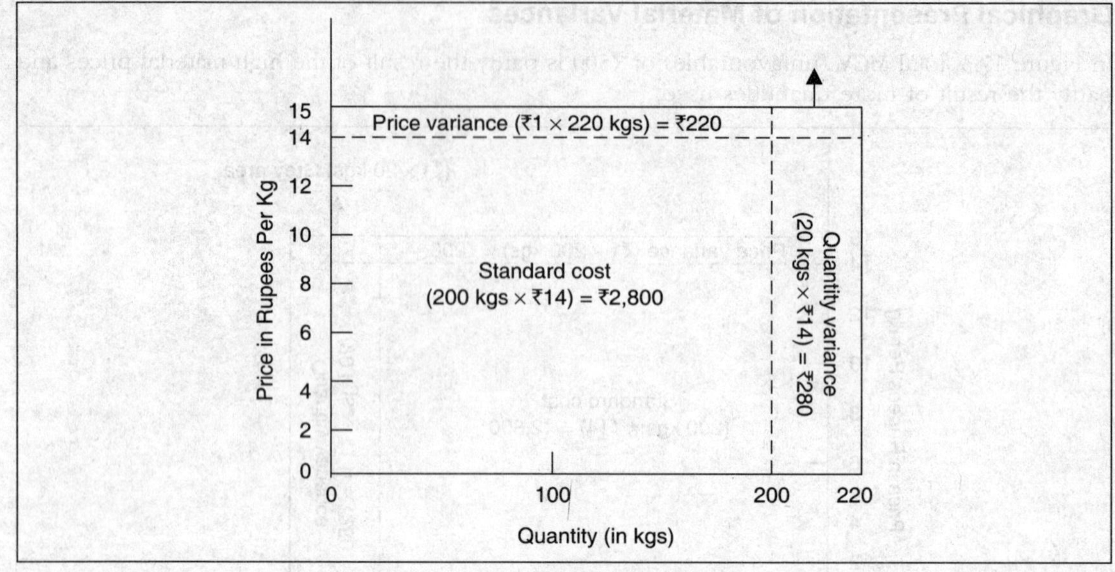

Figure 17.4 *Modified Material Variances*

Thus, substituting one raw material for another, even though the total input quantity of all materials does not exceed the standard amount, merits a separate computation. This is determined by a material mix variance. It may be stressed that the material mix variance is not an additional variance; it is a sub-variance of material usage/quantity variance and, therefore, it is more appropriately designated as material mix sub-variance (MMSV). Thus, the MMSV is a function of the difference between the standard mix and the actual mix input/quantities of all grades of materials actually used and their corresponding standard prices. Such a variance is to be calculated for each type of material. Symbolically,

MMSV = (Standard mix of actual total quantity of material used) – (Actual mix of actual quantity of material used) × SR

For the sake of abbreviation, standard mix may be referred to as revised standard quantity (RSQ) and actual mix (AM). Accordingly,

$$\text{MMSV} = (\text{RSQ} - \text{AQ}) \times \text{SR} \qquad \textbf{(17.5)}$$

Example 17.2

A manufacturing company uses the following standard mix of their compound in one batch of its production line:

50 kgs of material X at the standard price of ₹20.
30 kgs of material Y at the standard price of ₹30.
20 kgs of material Z at the standard price of ₹40.

The actual mix was as follows:

60 kgs of material X
40 kgs of material Y
10 kgs of material Z.

Determine the MMSV.

Solution

The determination of MMSV involves the following steps:

1. Standard proportion (mix) of materials X, Y and Z (5:3:2) or (50:30:20).

2. Actual total quantity used, 110.
3. Standard mix of actual quantity used (RSQ) by using the following criterion:
(Total actual quantity used) × (Standard proportion of each type of material) **(17.6)**

Where
X = 110 kgs × 5/10 = 55 kgs
Y = 110 kgs × 3/10 = 33 kgs
Z = 110 kgs × 2/10 = 22 kgs

MMSV = (RSQ – AQ) × SP
X (55 – 60) × ₹20 = ₹100 (unfavourable)
Y (33 – 40) × ₹30 = ₹210 (unfavourable)
Z (22 – 10) × ₹40 = ₹480 (favourable)
Net MMSV = ₹170 (favourable)

Example 17.2 demonstrates that MUV is unfavourable as the total usage (110 kgs) exceeds the actual usage (100 kgs) but the MMSV is favourable. This may be indicative of general production inefficiencies.

MMSV will occur only when there is a difference between standard material mix ratio and actual material mix ratio. It has no relation with actual material consumption. There may be a higher or lower amount of material usage from the standard but there will be no MMSV if standard mix matches with actual mix. This is illustrated in Table 17.1.

Table 17.1 Material Mix Sub-variance

Type of materials	*Combination of materials (kgs)*			
	Standard	*Actuals (in different situations)*		
		(1)	*(2)*	*(3)*
X	50	45	55	45
Y	30	27	33	36
Z	20	18	22	19
	100	90	110	100

In situations (1) and (2), there will be no MMSV as the proportion of the AQ used is in tune with standard proportion or RSQ and AQ are the same. To take situation (1) for illustration purposes: (RSQ – AQ) × SR

X = 90 × 5/10 = (45 – 45) × ₹20 = Nil
Y = 90 × 3/10 = (27 – 27) × ₹30 = Nil
Z = 90 × 2/10 = (18 – 18) × ₹40 = Nil

In situation (3), though there is no material usage variance, there is MMSV:

X = (50 – 45) × ₹20 = ₹100 (favourable)
Y = (30 – 36) × ₹30 = ₹180 (unfavourable)
Z = (20 – 19) × ₹40 = ₹ 40 (favourable)
Net MMSV = ₹ 40 (unfavourable)

Thus, the MMSV is a consequence of relative rather than absolute differentials in materials usage.

The computation of the MMSV is a useful exercise in that it reveals information that might otherwise be concealed. It shows separately the effect of varying the mix of materials on the material cost variance. Above all, the substantial deviations from the standard product mix may adversely affect the quality of the product.

In Example 17.2, the unfavourable MUV is ₹100, as shown by the following calculations:

MUV = (SQ – AQ) × SR
X = (50 kgs – 60 kgs) × ₹20 = ₹200 (unfavourable)

Y = (30 kgs – 40 kgs) × ₹30 = ₹300 (unfavourable)
Z = (20 kgs – 10 kgs) × ₹40 = ₹400 (favourable)
Net MUV = ₹100 (unfavourable)

Taking away the MMSV (₹170 favourable), there is a balance of ₹270 (unfavourable) to be explained. Obviously, this figure represents excess usage. The materials usage variance (revised) should reveal the excess usage (₹270), as shown in Table 17.2.

Table 17.2 Material usage Variance

Material	*SQ*	*AQ*	*SP*	*Total SC*
A	50	60	₹20	₹1,000
B	30	40	30	900
C	20	10	40	800
	100	110	27	2,700

MUV (revised) = (AQ – SQ) × Weighted average SP = (110 – 100) × ₹27 = ₹270 (unfavourable)
Weighted average standard price = Total SC/Total SQ = ₹2,700/100 = ₹27. Thus,

MUV = MMSV + MUV (revised) **(17.7)**

Material Yield Sub-Variance (MYSV) The material usage variance (revised) can be more appropriately designated as material yield sub-variance (MYSV). Excess or under material usage from the standard clearly reflects that actual production (yield) is more or less than standard production (yield) expected out of the actual materials input. "The world 'yield' denotes 'output', but this facts is not always directly recognised in the calculations used to ascertain the sub-variance. Often inputs of materials for a specific output are considered."[6] In other words, if the actual material usage is more than the standard, the yield variance would be negative or unfavourable. On the other hand, if standard material quantity exceeds the actual usage, the yield is favourable in that actual production is more than standard production.

In Example 17.2, on the basis of inputs, the yield sub-variance would be given by the following formula: (Actual input-Standard input) × Weighted average standard input price = (110 – 100) × ₹2.7 = ₹27 (unfavourable)

Keeping in view the meaning of yield as production, it will be more logical to determine MYSY on the basis of ouputs, that is, standard and actual production (yield). It is determined as follows:

MYSV = (Standard yield – Actual yield) × Standard material cost per unit of finished output **(17.8)**

Alternatively, MYSV = (Standard loss of final product in units – Actual loss of final product of units) × Standard material cost unit of finished output **(17.9)**

The concept of MYSV is particularly useful in the case of process industries like sugar, chemicals, and so on where a certain specified yield is expected from a given input of materials.

Example 17.3

In a chemical manufacturing company, 80 per cent is the standard yield expected of actual inputs; 50 units of inputs are introduced in the process and actual final production achieved is 38 units. The standard price per unit of input is ₹8. Determine the material yield sub-variance by various methods.

Solution

(a) *Output basis:*

(i) (Standard yield – Actual yield) × Standard material cost per unit of finished output
= [40 (0.80 × 50) – 38] × ₹10 (₹8 × 100/80) = ₹20 (unfavourable)

(ii) (Standard loss – Actual loss) × (Standard material per unit of finished output)
= (10 – 12) × ₹10 = ₹20 (unfavourable).

(b) *Input basis:*
(Actual input – Standard input) × Standard input price = [50 – 47.5 (38 × 10)/8] × ₹8 = ₹20 (unfavourable)

It is important to note that in the case of the output basis of determining the MYSV, the multiplying factor is standard yield price which is higher than standard input price. This is because the actual input required to produce one unit of final output would be higher. Therefore, loss or gain in the actual output from the standard should be at the standard yield price.

In the case of the input basis, the excess or lower consumption of materials for obvious reasons should be valued at the standard input price. In the case of products making use of more than one type of raw material, the multiplying factor should be the weighted average standard input price. Both the methods would give identical results.

LABOUR VARIANCES

Labour variance is popularly known as labour cost variance. Labour, unlike materials, cannot be stored. Therefore, the purchase and usage of labour services go hand in hand. However, labour cost variance (LCV) is computed like material cost variance. It is the difference between the standard labour costs and the actual labour costs of the period.

Labour cost variance is the difference between the standard labour costs and the actual labour costs.

Symbolically,

LCV = (SH × SR × AO) – (AH × AR × AO) (on per unit basis) **(17.10)**
LCV = (TSLC – TALC) (on aggregative basis) **(17.11)**

Where

SH = Standard labour hours required per unit
SR = Standard wage rate per hour
AO = Actual output achieved during the period
AH = Actual labour hours spent per unit
AR = Actual wage rate per hour
TSLC = Total standard labour cost of actual output
TALC = Total actual labour cost of actual output

EXAMPLE 17.4
From the following information, compute the labour cost variance (LCV).

Particulars	*Standard*	*Actual*
Labour-hours per unit	4	5
Wage rate (₹)	25	30
Units produced		100

SOLUTION

LCV = [(SH × SR × AO) – (AH × AR × AO)]
= (4 × ₹25 × 100) – (5 × ₹30 × 100) = ₹5,000 (₹10,000 – ₹15,000) (unfavourable/A)

It is useful to mention here that the treatment of labour variances, in large measure, parallels material variances. The LCV can be divided into: **(i)** Labour rate variance and **(ii)** Labour efficiency variance.

Labour/Wage Rate Variance (LRV)

This arises when there is a difference between the actual wage rate paid and the pre-determined standard wage rate. The LRV ignores the question of whether the actual labour-hours worked during the period were more or less than the

Labour rate variance is the difference between the actual wage rate and the standard wage rate.

standard labour-hours required to complete the work; it is concerned only with actual worked hours. Thus, the LRV is a function of the difference between the actual wage rate (AR) and the standard wage rate (SR) and the actual total labour-hours worked. Symbolically,

$$\text{LRV} = (\text{SR} - \text{AR}) \times \text{AH} \times \text{AO} \qquad \textbf{(17.12)}$$

In Example 17.4, LRV = (₹25 – ₹30) × 5 × 100 = ₹2,500 (unfavourable)

It is important to note here that if the mode of wage payment is on a product basis, the LRV would be equal to the difference between the standard piece wage rate and the actual piece wage rate multiplied by the actual units produced during a period. The LRV should be determined for each grade of labour, namely, skilled, semi-skilled and unskilled separately.

Factors Responsible for LRV The labour rate variance can be traced to a variety of causes. The important of these are enumerated below:

1. Change in the basic wage structure or in piece work rate not yet reflected in the standard wage rage.
2. Employing a worker-mix (explained later) different from the standard-mix which was originally planned. For instance, less skilled workers may be employed in place of skilled workers planned in the standard wage rate. Conversely, work which used to be performed by lower paid employees may have been assigned to the more skilled workers. In either case, a wage rate which is different from the standard wage rate will be paid.
3. To meet the demand of urgent orders, workers may have been asked to work overtime. The overtime rates may be higher than the standard wage rate, causing a variance to result.
4. During a recession period of lower demand and output, the lower paid unskilled labourers may have been laid off and their task assigned to higher paid skilled labourers. Skilled labourers are to be paid at a higher wage rate as compared to unskilled labourers.
5. Casual and temporary workers employed to meet seasonal demands or some special urgent job orders, are paid at the rates different from the standard.

Responsibility for LRV From the reasons outlined above, it is very clear that the LRV, often, will be an uncontrollable variance for rates are usually determined by supply and demand conditions in the labour market, wage awards by Wage Tribunals/Boards, and so on. The departmental executives may be held responsible only for that portion of the LRV which arises due to employment of wrong grades of labour. It does not mean that the LRV is of no significance to the management. Being largely uncontrollable in nature, the management should revise the wage rate standard for future periods.

Labour Efficiency Variance (LEV)

Labour efficiency variance is a function of the difference between the hours workers should have consumed in actual production and the actual hours worked and the standard wage rate.

This is similar to the material usage variance. The time required by the labour force is an index of its efficiency. Accordingly, the variance which seeks to isolate the impact of working greater or lesser number of hours than the standard hours in production is called the labour efficiency variance (LEV) or labour time variance. Like material usage variance, LEV is concerned only with the standard wage rate. Thus, LEV is a function of the difference between the hours workers should have consumed in actual production and the actual hours worked and the standard wage rate. Symbolically,

$$\text{LEV} = [(\text{SH} \times \text{AO}) - (\text{AH} \times \text{AO})] \times \text{SR} \qquad \textbf{(17.13)}$$

In Example 17.4, LEV will be: [(4 × 100) – (5 × 100)] × ₹25 = ₹2,500 (unfavourable)

However, if the method of piece wages payment is followed in the organisation, there will be no labour efficiency variance.

Reasons for LEV The chief causes giving rise to LEV are outlined as follows:

1. Lack of congenial working conditions adversely affecting the efficient working of the labour force. Examples of poor working conditions are inadequate or excessive heating, lighting and ventilation.
2. Failure to maintain machinery, equipment and tools in proper working condition or workers having to work with old and defective machines and tools which have frequent breakdowns.
3. Use of sub-standard raw materials, or higher standard raw materials requiring more or less time than the standard.
4. Inefficient organisation leading to delays in routing work, materials, tools and instructions.
5. Incompetent supervision or more strict supervision than required.
6. Work on new machines, equipment or tools in a factory requiring less time than provided for, but the standard remains unrevised.
7. Basic inefficiency of workers due to inadequate training, incorrect instructions and worker's dissatisfaction owing to low morale and lack of motivation.
8. Change in the quality control standards.
9. Increase in labour turnover.
10. Gang composition (labour-mix) being different from the standard.

This variance is of prime significance to the production managers. It is the best indication of labour efficiency. Hence, its causes should be carefully thought over and reported so that prompt action can be initiated to overcome the cause. This variance, unlike LRV, is largely controllable in nature, is more amenable to managerial action and management's prompt action can lead to large savings. To overcome an unfavourable LEV, management's endeavour should be to provide a conducive environment in terms of the introduction of new equipment or tools and their proper maintenance, proper lighting and ventilation facilities, and so on. These measures will help in improving the general efficiency of the workers.

The labour efficiency variance can be sub-divided into **(a)** Idle time variance; **(b)** Labour revised efficiency variance consisting of **(i)** Labour mix sub-variance and **(ii)** Labour yield sub-variance.

Idle Time Variance This variance represents that segment of the LEV which arises due to the standard cost of those actual hours for which the workers have been paid but during which they remain idle due to non-availability of raw materials, breakdown of machines, failure of power and such other abnormal circumstances. This variance, by definition, is unfavourable and is calculated as follows:

$$\text{(Idle time in hours} \times \text{Standard wage rate)} \quad \textbf{(17.14)}$$

Therefore, it will be more coherent to compute the true labour efficiency variance after making an adjustment for this factor. In the absence of that, the LEV is likely to be misunderstood. The management may regard the labour force inefficient which in fact may not be the case. In other words, employees will be blamed for inefficiency when the true cause may have been beyond their control, such as breakdown in power supply, and so on. To demonstrate the point, assume in Example 17.4 that the number of idle time hours during the period was 110. The idle time variance would be unfavourable by ₹2,750 (110 hours × ₹25). The workers, in fact, actually worked only for 390 hours, the standard hours allowed for which were 400. Clearly, the workers are more efficient and not inefficient. The earlier conclusion has just got reversed. The revised LEV is ₹250 favourable [(390 hours – 400 hours) × ₹25]. Thus, it is useful to segregate idle time variance from the total LEV:

Idle time variance	₹2,750 (unfavourable)
Labour efficiency variance (revised)	250 (favourable)
Total labour efficiency variance	2,500 (unfavourable)

This form of presentation of reporting LEV is certainly more useful to the management for controlling future costs and initiating control action compared to the single figure of the total LEV of ₹2,500.

Labour revised efficiency variance is a function of the difference between the actual labour mix and the standard labour mix and the standard wage rate.

Labour Revised Efficiency Variance Sometimes a change in the grade of labour employed on an operation has to be made from the standard labour-mix due to shortage of one grade of labour during a certain period. The variance which isolates the impact of such a change in gang composition (labour-mix) on the labour cost variance is designated as the labour-mix variance or gang composition variance. Like the material mix sub-variance (MMSV), this variance is a function of the difference between the actual labour-mix and standard labour-mix and the standard wage rate. Symbolically,

LEV = [Standard mix of actual labour hours worked (RSH) – Actual mix of actual hours worked (AH)] × SR **(17.15)**

EXAMPLE 17.5

The standard labour – mix for producing 100 units a of product is:

4 skilled men @ ₹30 per hour for 20 hours

6 unskilled men @ ₹20 per hour for 20 hours

But due to shortage of skilled men, more unskilled men were employed to produce 100 units. Actual hours paid for were:

2 skilled men @ ₹40 per hour for 25 hours

10 unskilled men @ ₹25 per hour for 25 hours.

Compute the labour mix variance.

SOLUTION

The data can be presented as follows:

Category of workers	*Standard*					*Actual*				
	Number	*Hours*	*Total hours*	*SR (₹)*	*TSLC (₹)*	*Number*	*Hours*	*Total hours*	*AR (₹)*	*TALC (₹)*
Skilled	4	20	80	30	2,400	2	25	50	40	2,000
Unskilled	6	20	120	20	2,400	10	25	250	25	6,250
Total			200	24	4,800			300	27.50	8,250

LCV = TSLC – TALC = ₹4,800 – ₹8,250 = ₹3,450 (unfavourable)

(a) LRV = (SR – AR) × AH)

(i) Skilled = (₹30 – ₹40) × 50 = ₹500 (unfavourable)

(ii) Unskilled = (₹20 – ₹25) × 250 = ₹1,250 (unfavourable)

Total LRV = ₹1,750 (unfavourable)

(b) LEV = (SH – AH) × SR

(i) Skilled = (80 – 50) × ₹30 = ₹900 (favourable)

(ii) Unskilled = (120 – 250) × ₹20 = ₹2,600 (unfavourble)

Total LEV = ₹1,700 (unfavourable)

Total LEV can be split into: **(a)** Labour mix sub-variance, and **(b)** Labour yield sub-varinace

Labour Mix Sub-Variance To determine the labour mix sub-variance (LMSV), we are required to calculate the values of revised standard hours for two grades of labour. The revised standard hours for skilled and unskilled labourers respectively would be: Actual total hours × Proportion of skilled hours to the total standard hours.

$$= \frac{300 \times 80}{200} = 120 \text{ hours (skilled)}$$

$$= \frac{300 \times 120}{200} = 180 \text{ hours (unskilled)}$$

LMSV = (RSH – AH) × SR

(i) Skilled = (120 – 50) × ₹30 = ₹2,100 (favourble)

(ii) Unskilled = (180 – 250) × ₹20 = ₹1,400 (unfavourble)

Total LMSV = ₹ 700 (favourable)

The residual LEV should be ₹2,400 (unfavourable).

Labour Yield Sub-Variance Like the material yield sub-variance, it is determined after taking away the materials mix sub-variance. The basis of computation of labour yield sub-variance (LYSV) would be to find out how many more or less than the total absolute standard hours (and not their break-up) are used in making the actual production (here 100 units). Here, the number of standard hours required are 200; the actual hours worked are 300. The difference is to be multiplied by the weighted average standard rate. Symbolically.

LYSV = (TSHs – TAHs) × Weighted average SR = (200 – 300) × ₹24 = ₹2,400 (unfavourable)

The above method of determining the LYSV is based on the input basis. The LYSV like the MYSV can be determined on the output basis also. The formula is:

(Standard yield in units expected from the actual hours worked-Actual yield) × Standard labour cost per unit **(17.16)**

= (150 – 100) × ₹48 = ₹2,400 (unfavourable)

In 300 hours, the standard yield should be 150 units because in 200 hours, the expected yield is 100 units.

LEV = LMSV = ₹ 700 (favourable)

LYSV = ₹2,400 (unfavourble)

= ₹1,700 (unfavourable)

This information indicates to the management that on account of employing more unskilled labourers, the LMSV turned out to be favourable. But it had an adverse bearing on the overall efficiency as the actual hours used were considerably larger than standard hours required to complete the work.

It is important to note that the two labour sub-variances—LMSV and LYSV—are parts of LEV adjusted for idle time variance. Total LEV has three sub-variances. To illustrate, assume idle time hours are 30. The revised values of various labour variances would be as follows:

LCV = (As in Example 17.5) = ₹3,450 (unfavourable)

LRV = ₹1,750 (unfavourable)

TLEV = ₹1,700 (unfavourable)

Labour idle time variance:

Skilled: (5 hours × ₹30) = ₹150

Unskilled: (25 hours × ₹20) = ₹500

₹650 (unfavourable)

The other two sub-variances will be based on the remaining working hours (300 – 30) = 270 hours.

$$\text{RSH: Skilled} = 270 \times \frac{80}{200} = 108 \text{ hours}$$

$$\text{Unskilled} = 270 \times \frac{120}{200} = 162 \text{ hours}$$

LMSV = (RSHs – AHs) × SR

Skilled = (108 – 45) × ₹30 = ₹1,890 (favourable)
Unskilled = (162 – 225) × ₹20 = ₹1,260 (unfavourable)
Total LMSV = ₹ 630 (favourable)

Note It is assumed that actual idle hours were in the ratio of 1:5 (50 : 250, actual hours worked).
LYSV = (200 – 270) × ₹24 = ₹1,680 (unfavourable)

OVERHEAD VARIANCES

At the outset, it may be noted that unlike direct materials and labour, the manufacturing overhead is not entirely variable with the level of production. Therefore, standard costs for factory overheads are based upon budgets and not on standards. Being so, the analysis concerning manufacturing overhead variances is materially different from that of variances relating to materials and labour. However, like material and labour variances, manufacturing overhead/factory overhead/overhead/ variance is the difference between the actual overhead cost incurred and standard overhead cost charged to production. For the purpose of determining the latter amount, the distinction between variable and fixed manufacturing overhead costs is very significant. In fact, one method of analysing factory overhead variance is to study separately variable overhead variances and fixed overhead variances. Alternatively, they can be analysed jointly. Both types of analyses are presented in this Section.

Variable Overhead Variances (VOV)

Variable overhead cost variance is the difference between the actual and standard variable overhead costs for actual output.

These are also called variable overhead cost variances (VOCV). In fact, the VOCV parallels the material and labour cost variances. The reason is that variable overheads by definition should change with production volume. Therefore, the standard variable overhead cost (SVOC) per unit will be uniform, production volume notwithstanding. Thus, the VOCV is the difference between the actual and standard variable overhead costs for actual output. Symbolically,

VOCV = (SVOC × AO) – (AVOC × AO) (on unit basis) **(17.17)**

VOCV = TSVOC – TAVOC (on aggregative basis) **(17.18)**

Where

SVOC = Standard variable overhead cost per unit
AVOC = Actual variable overhead cost per unit (Total variable overheads incurred ÷ Actual output in units)
TAVOC = Total standard variable overhead costs to achieve actual production.
TAVOC = Total actual variable overhead costs incurred

Example 17.6

The following is an extract of some relevant data of Hypothetical Ltd relating to its variable factory overheads.

Standard hours allowed (per unit)	2
Standard variable overhead costs allowed per direct labour-hour	₹30
Actual production (units)	80
Actual direct labour-hours	165
Actual variable overheads incurred	₹5,180

Determine the VOCV.

Solution

VOCV = (₹60* × 80) – ₹5,180 = ₹4,800 – ₹5,180 = ₹380 (unfavourable)
*₹60 = (SHs × SVOC per hour) = 2 × ₹30

₹38 (unfavourable) VOCV can be either due to overspending over the standard budget or due to more hours taken by the workers from the standard hours allowed. Accordingly, VOCV can be split up into two sub-variances: (a) Variable factory overhead efficiency variance (VFOEV); **(b)** Variable factory overhead spending variance (VFOSV).

Variable Factory Overhead Efficinecy Variance (VFOEV) The VFOEV is the function of the difference between the standard hours and actual hours and the standard variable factory overhead rate per hour (SVFOR). Symbolically,

VFOEV = [(AO × SHs per unit) – AHs] × SVFOR **(17.19)**

= (80 × 2 – 165) × ₹30 = ₹150 (unfavourable)

Variable factory overhead efficiency variance is the function of the difference between the standard hours and actual hours and the standard variable factory overhead rate per hour.

The variance is adverse because the actual hours (AHs) have exceeded the standard hours (SHs). The company wasted ₹150 on overheads because the workers were not efficient. It may be recalled that VFOEV is like the labour efficiency variance inasmuch as the formula is the same with the obvious difference of the multiplying factor. Therefore, *the actual factors for the variable factory overheads efficiency would be identical with the causes for labour efficiency variance.* For this reason, some firms club together the labour efficiency and variable factory overhead efficiency variances.[7] The formula for this variance would require modification only in terms of the multiplying factor as shown below:

[(AO × SHs per unit) – AHs] × [SVFOR + Standard wage rate per hour] **(17.20)**

The above formula will be valid only if the company employs direct labour-hours as the basis of measuring cost variability. In the case of machine-hours, the formula would be:

VFOEA = [(Actual output × Standard machine-hours per unit) – (Actual machine hours × Standard variable factor overhead rate)] **(17.21)**

The causes for such variances include lack of repairs and maintenance of tools, plant, machinery and equipment, causing more frequent break-down.

Variable Factory Overhead Spending Variance (VFOSV) The VFOSV is the difference between the actual overhead costs incurred and the amount that the flexible budget indicates should have been incurred for the actual production volume. To determine the standard costs, actual hours should be taken into account because the actual amount spent would be in relation to the actual hours worked. Thus, the standard hours are irrelevant. Symbolically,

Variable factory overhead spending variance is the difference between the actual and budgeted overhead costs for actual production

VFOSV = (Actual hours worked) × (Standard variable overhead rate per hour) – (Actual variable factory overhead costs) **(17.22)**

= (165 × ₹30) – ₹5,180 = ₹230 (unfavourable)

Thus VFOV = VFOEV + VFOSV: ₹380 = ₹150 + ₹230 (all unfavourable) **(17.23)**

Fixed Factory Overhead Variances (FFOV)

The treatment of FFOV is significantly different from that of VFOV. The reason is that fixed factory overheads do not vary with production volume. A proper understanding of the FFOV requires prior understanding of various concepts of production volume. The concept of under-absorption or over-absorption of fixed overheads is already explained in an earlier chapter. In brief, it can be stated here that fixed overheads are absorbed (charged to the production) at a pre-determined standard fixed overhead rate (SFOR). This SFOR is determined by dividing the budgeted fixed overheads by some production volume. So far as the amount of budgeted fixed overheads is concerned, it does not pose any problem whatsoever as the relevant figure can be seen from the budget. However, production volume is subject to different interpretations, that is, whether it should be normal volume, budgeted volume or actual volume. Normal volume refers to that level of production which can be achieved on the basis of the available plant capacity and other facilities in the factory. Budgeted volume signifies the level of production envisaged for the current budget period. Actual volume indicates actual production. It is rare, if ever, when all these three production volumes will be identical. Obviously, the amount of SFOR per unit (per hour, if production volume is expressed in hours), will depend on what production volume constitutes the denominator for the purpose.

Example 17.7

The budgeted fixed overheads of a company for a period are ₹4,00,000 and the normal production volume, budgeted volume and actual volume are 20,000, 16,000 and 10,000 units respectively. Compute the SFOR for different volumes.

Solution

The SFOR will be ₹20 per unit, (₹4,00,000 ÷ 20,000 units) on a normal volume basis; ₹25 (on a budgeted volume basis); and ₹40 (on the actual production basis).

Clearly, there will be different value of FFOV under the three different situations. The National Association of Accountants, USA, has advocated normal volume as the basis of determining SFOR. The interpretation of the term "normal level" should be determined in advance and should be applied consistently. Normal level should be related to the basis of normal capacity, that is, ability to produce, ability to sell or both along with the number of years, for example, 3, 4, 5 and 6 years to be taken as normal period.[8] Where normal volume is not shown, budgeted volume should be used.

The standard fixed overheads charged to production (absorbed overheads) will be given by the following formula: (Number of units produced × SFOR) **(17.24)**

SFOR = Budgeted fixed overheads/Normal level of activity

In Example 17.7, the standard fixed overhead cost is: 10,000 × ₹20 = ₹2,00,000

The costs unabsorbed are ₹2,00,000 = (₹4,00,000 actual fixed overheads – ₹2,00,000 charged to production). From the above the following may be deduced:

1. If the actual level of activity corresponds to the normal level of activity (referred to above as normal volume), there will be no unabsorbed fixed overhead costs. There will be no volume variances, as actual production corresponds to normal production. But the occurrence of such a case is only a theoretical possibility.
2. When the actual level of activity is less that the normal activity, the volume variance is unfavourable in that the entire amount of fixed overheads cannot be charged to production.
3. When the actual level of activity exceeds the normal activity, the volume variance is favourable as it amounts to better than expected utilisation of facilities.

There is no such volume variance for variable overheads. Thus, volume variance is the unique or special feature of fixed overhead variances which distinguishes it from other variances.

Fixed Overhead Cost Variance (FOCV) This variance represents the difference between the actual fixed overhead cost incurred and the standard fixed overheads charged to production. Symbolically,

FOCV = TAFOC – (SFOR per unit × AO) **(17.25)**

In the case of hours basis: FOSV = TAFOC – (SFOR per hour × SHs per unit × AO) **(17.26)**

Where

TAFOC = Total actual factory overhead cost incurred

SFOR = Standard fixed overhead rate

Example 17.8

The following data relate to the fixed overheads of a company for a week:

1. Actual fixed overheads incurred, ₹5,300.

2. Budgeted fixed overheads, ₹5,000
3. Normal level of activity for the period, 100 units or 200 hours
4. Standard hours allowed, 2 hours per unit
5. Actual production, 90 units
6. Actual hours worked, 190 hours

Determine the fixed overhead variances.

Solution

FOCV = ₹5,300 – (₹50 × 90) = ₹800 (unfavourable)

SFOR = ₹5,000 ÷ 100 units = ₹50 per unit

Alternatively (on hourly basis): FOCV = ₹5,300 – (₹25 × 2 × 90) = ₹800 (unfavourable)

SFOR = ₹5,000 ÷ 200 hours = ₹25 per hour

The FOCV (₹800) can be split into three sub-variances: **(i)** Fixed factory overhead spending variance, **(ii)** Fixed factory overhead efficiency variance and **(iii)** Volume variance.

Fixed Factory Overhead Spending Variance (FOSV) This variance is the difference between the planned level of fixed overheads expenditure and the actual level of fixed overheads incurred. Symbolically.

FOSV = (Actual fixed overhead costs) – (Budgeted fixed costs) **(17.27)**
= ₹5,300 – ₹5,000 = ₹300 (unfavourable)

The causal factors for the FOSV are at least as many as there are distinct cost items. The budget provides a certain amount per period for each fixed cost item. These budgeted amounts are based upon expected prices, consumption rates of various fixed items and a variety of other operating conditions. Any one or combination of these budget expectations may prove to be inaccurate. For instance, indirect materials may be more costly than budgeted; rise in property tax rates, power charges, insurance, factory rent and such other fixed items. To have a meaningful analysis of spending variance (as also variable overheads), we must take into account individual cost items. It is likely to be a non-controllable variance.

Fixed Overhead Efficiency Variance (FOEV) Like other efficiency variances, this variance is based on the actual hours and standard hours. Symbolically,

FOEV = [(AO × SHs per unit) – AHs] × SFOR (per hour) **(17.28)**
= (90 × 2 – 190) × ₹25 = ₹250 (unfavourable)

Volume Variance As mentioned earlier, volume variance pertains only to the fixed overheads and is not applicable to variable overheads. Therefore, the volume variance is not pre-fixed with "fixed-overheads".

The volume variance is concerned with the difference between normal hours and actual hours multiplied by the SFOR. In Example, 17.8,

Volume variance = (SHs – AHs) × SFOR = (200 – 190) × ₹25 = ₹250 (unfavourable)

It may be noted that the actual hours worked is less than the standard hours and still the variance is unfavourable, while in the case of efficiency variance such a variance is considered favourable. The reason for this difference is that in the case of efficiency variance the interest is to determine the standards hours required to achieve actual production and then to compare with actual hours. But the volume variance is concerned with the hours worked irrespective of the output achieved. In operational terms, volume variance, here, indicates that the plant has not been used up to its full capacity: In brief,

FOCV = FOSV + FOEV + Volume variance **(17.29)**
= ₹800 (unfavourable) = ₹300 (unfavourable) + ₹250 (unfavourable) + ₹250 (unfavourable)

It is important to mention here that volume variance should be determined on the basis of hours, otherwise it will not be a true indicator of excess or under-utilisation of plant's capacity. Moreover, if computed, on a units basis, it will submerge in it the fixed overhead efficiency variance. Management will not be supplied with the figure of the FOEV—a variance figure of utmost interest to management from the point of view of controlling future costs. Therefore, it will be another serious shortcoming of measuring volume variance on a unit basis. Thus, an hourly approach is recommended for determining FOCV[9].

In Example 17.8, volume variance on a unit basis will be ₹500 (unfavourable) as follows:

(Normal produciton – Actual produciton) × SFOR per unit **(17.30)**

= (100 units – 90 units) × ₹50 = ₹500 (unfavourable)

Causes Volume variance is attributed solely to the fact that the SFOR is computed at the normal level of activity and is then applied to production at some other volume. The fundamental nature of fixed costs, of course, is that they are some specified amount per period of time, regardless of operating volume. Thus, while a fixed manufacturing overhead rate per unit of volume may be required for cost accounting purposes, it detracts from the true nature of fixed costs. The volume variance, in other words, is a "man-made" variance.[10] As such, it is of no significance to management for purposes of planning and control. If budgeted production volume were not equal to normal volume (and it often would not be), a volume variance would be anticipated at the start of the period. Hence, it would signal no exception requiring management's attention.

What is of more significance to the management is the difference between the budgeted output and the actual output. This variance may be caused by shifts in demand for products, labour problems, strikes and lockouts, material shortages, poor product quality due to high labour turnover affecting sales and, therefore, production, and so on. Some of these factors are controllable by management while others are not.

Volume variance (output basis) in order to be used to the management should be split up into sub-variances. The important sub-variances are: **(i)** Fixed overhead efficiency variance (explained above); **(ii)** Calendar variance; **(iii)** Capacity variance.

Calendar Variance This variance should be calculated only when the actual number of working days are more or less than the standard number of working days scheduled for that period. This may be the result of unexpected public holidays being declared. If working days worked are more, the plant capacity will be greater in the sense that there is an increase in the number of hours (volume). The calendar variance will be favourable. Likewise, if the work is done for a lesser number of working days, the plant capacity will be reduced and so also the number of hours actually available for production. Obviously, the calendar variance will be unfavourable. Therefore, in order to compute the correct capacity variance, it will be necessary to adjust the budgeted hours available for production.

The calendar variance can be computed by the following formula:

[Number of standard working days (SD) – Number of actual working days (AD)] ×
Standard fixed overheads per day (SFOD)

Standard fixed overheads per day = Total budgeted fixed overheads ÷ Standard number of working days. Symbolically,

(SD – AD) × SFOD **(17.31)**

Capacity Variance The terms "capacity" and "volume variances" are indiscriminately used in common practice. But in view of the fact that we are calculating efficiency and calendar variances separately, capacity variance here would be sub-variance of volume variance.

Since the difference between actual and standard hours has already been taken care of by the overhead efficiency variance, the capacity variance will not be concerned with this difference. The capacity variance will be the function of the difference between the budgeted hours available on the basis of actual working days (budgeted hours per day × actual days worked) and the actual hours worked multiplied by the standard fixed overhead rate per hour:

(Budgeted hours on the basis of actual days worked – Actual hours worked) × SFOR per hour **(17.32)**

We now take a comprehensive example to calculate all overhead variances — variable and fixed (Example 17.9).

EXAMPLE 17.9

The following figures are extracted from the books of a company:

Particulars	*Budget*	*Actual*
Output (units)	6,000	6,500
Hours	3,000	3,300
Overhead cost—fixed	₹1,20,000	₹1,25,000
Variable overheads	60,000	66,500
Number of days	25	27

Compute and analyse the overhead variances.

SOLUTION

Total overhead variance (TOV) = [Actual overheads costs – Standard costs charged to production (standard hours for actual production) × TSOR per hour] = ₹1,91,500 – ₹1,95,000 or (3,250 × ₹60) = ₹3,500 (favourable)

Standard fixed overhead rate (SFOR) = ₹1,20,000 ÷ 3,000 = ₹40 per hour

SFOR (per unit) = ₹1,20,000 ÷ 6,000 = ₹20 per unit

Standard hours per unit = 3,000 hours ÷ 60,000 hours = 30 minutes

Standard variable overhead (SVOR) rate = ₹60,000 ÷ 3,000 = ₹20 per hour

SVOR (per unit) = ₹60,000/6,000 = ₹10 per unit

Total standard overhead rate (TSOR) = ₹1,80,000 ÷ 3,000 = ₹60 per hour

TSOR (per unit) = ₹1,80,000 ÷ 6,000 = ₹30 per unit

TOV can be split into (A) Variable overhead cost variance (VOV), and (B) Fixed overhead cost variance (FOV):

(A) VOV = Actual variable overhead costs – Standard variable costs charged to production = ₹66,500 – (3,250 standard hours × ₹20) = ₹65,000 = ₹1,500 (adverse)

There are two sub-variances of VOV:

(i) *Variable overhead spending variance*: *Actual variable overhead costs incurred – Standard variable overhead costs at actual hours* = ₹66,500 – (3,300 hours × ₹20) – ₹66,000 = ₹500 (adverse)

(ii) *Variable overhead efficiency variance*: (*Standard hours required for actual output – Actual hours worked for actual output*) × *Standard variable overhead rate per hour* = (3,250 – 3,300) × ₹20 = ₹1,000 (adverse)

(B) *Fixed overhead cost variance (FOV)*: (*Actual fixed overhead costs incurred – Standard fixed overhead charged to production*) = ₹1,25,000 – (3,250 standard hours × ₹40 = ₹1,30,000) = ₹5,000 (favourable)

There are two sub-variances of FOV:

(i) *Fixed overhead budget/spending variance*: (Actual fixed overhead costs incurred – Budgeted fixed overhead) = ₹1,25,000 – ₹1,20,000 = ₹5,000 (adverse)

(ii) *Volume variance*: [3,000 – (6,500 × 1/2 hour)] × ₹40 = 250 hours × ₹40 = ₹10,000 (favourable) Volume variance has three sub-parts:

(a) *Calendar variance*: (Number of scheduled working days – Number of actual working days) × Standard fixed overhead rate per day = (25-27) × ₹4,800 = ₹9,600 (favourable)

(b) *Fixed overhead efficiency variance*: (Standard hours allowed for actual production – Actual hours worked) × SFOR per hour = (3,250 – 3,300) × ₹40 = ₹2,000 (adverse)

(c) *Capacity variance*: (Budgeted hours on the basis of actual days worked – Actual hours worked) × Standard fixed overhead per hour or [Budgeted hours per day × Actual days worked] – (Actual hours worked) × SFOR = [(120 × 27) = 3,240 – 3,300] × ₹40 = ₹2,400 (favourable)

CONFIRMATION: Figure 17.5 provides a confirmation of the above calculations.

Figure 17.5 indicates that spending and efficiency variances relate to both variable and fixed overheads. The volume variance is entirely for fixed overheads. Instead of showing the first two variances separately, they are clubbed together. For instance, there can be one overhead spending variance (fixed overhead spending variance + variable overhead spending variance). Likewise, there can be only one overhead efficiency variance.

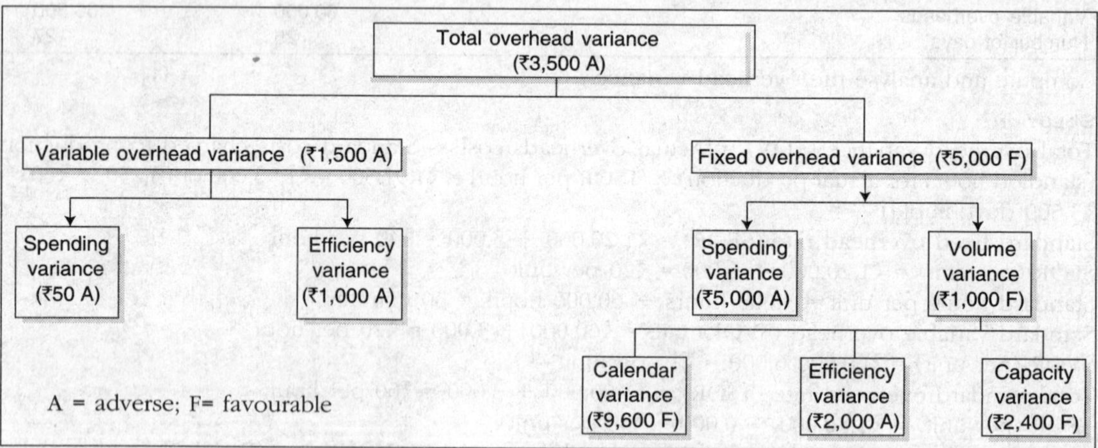

Figure 17.5 *Overhead Variances*

Joint Basis of Overhead Analysis

On the basis of the number of variances calculated, there are four methods of analysing overhead variances:

1. Two-variance method;
2. Three-variance method;
3. Four-variance method;
4. Five-variance method.

Two-Variance Method When production volume is measured in units of output and not in units of input (hours), the two separate manufacturing overhead variances can be calculated, viz. **(i)** controllable variance, and **(ii)** volume variance.

Controllable Variance is the difference between the actual expenditure and the budgeted expenditure at the actual level of production. Budgeted expenditure is determined as follows:

Budgeted fixed overheads (not affected by production volume) + Variable overheads (Actual units produced × Standard variable overhead cost per unit).

Volume Variance is the difference between the standard fixed manufacturing overhead cost charged to production and the budgeted fixed manufacturing overhead cost. In other words, volume variance indicates the unabsorbed or over-absorbed amount of fixed cost. It is the function of the difference between the normal capacity and the actual capacity and the standard fixed overhead rate per unit of output. It is computed as follows:

(Normal capacity in units – Actual production in units) × Standard fixed overhead rate per unit **(17.33)**

The two-variance method has a serious shortcoming, in that it does not reveal the efficiency variance. It identifies only spending and volume variances.

Three-Variance Method The limitation of the two-variance method is overcome by the three-variance method which identifies efficiency variance separately. Under this method, production volume is expressed in units of hours. There are three sub-variances of total overhead cost variance: **(i)** Expenditure/Spending variance; **(ii)** Efficiency variance; and **(iii)** Capacity variance.

Expenditure Variance This measures the difference between the actual overhead costs incurred and the budgeted overhead costs that should be incurred at actual hours. Thus, this variance measures the correct efficiency or inefficiency in spending because the variable overheads will vary with the number of actual hours worked rather than the standard. Therefore, if the actual hours worked are more or less than the standard, the actual amount payable will be more or less than the standard. Obviously, it will be illogical to compute spending variance on the basis of standard hours. It is for this reason that spending variance under this method is computed at actual hours. The formula is:
Actual overhead costs incurred – Budgeted overhead costs at actual hours **(17.34)**

Budgeted Overhead Cost

Fixed overheads (not affect by hours)	....
+ Variable overheads (Actual Hours × Standard variable overhead rate per hour)	....

Any change in the level of actual spending in respect of one or the other items of the expenses which constitute the total overhead cost results in expenditure variance.

Overhead Efficiency Variance This is that portion of the overhead variance which is due to the difference between actual hours used for the output achieved and the standard hours allowed multiplied by standard overhead rate. The formula is:

(SHs – AHs) × SOR **(17.35)**

Capacity Variance This is that segment of overhead variance which arises due to the difference between the normal capacity available in hours, and the actual hours worked multiplied by the standard fixed overhead rate. The formula is:

[Normal capacity in hours, NHs – AHs] × SFOR **(17.36)**

Four-Variance Method Under this method four sub-variances are computed: **(i)** Spending variance, **(ii)** Capacity variance, **(iii)** Fixed efficiency variance, and **(iv)** Variable efficiency variance.

Five-Variance Method The *modus operandi* of determining efficiency and capacity variances is the same as in the three-variance method. A notable feature is that, spending variance is bifurcated into two sub-parts: fixed overhead spending variance and variable overhead spending variance. These variances have already been discussed when we discussed fixed and variable overheads separately.

Example 17.10 illustrates the computation of overhead variance under all the above methods.

Example 17.10

SK Industries Ltd uses a standard cost system. The budget relating to overheads for the month of

January of the current year is as follows:

Normal capacity: 22,000 direct labour-hours, or 11,000 production units

Budgeted overheads at normal (100%) capacity:
- Fixed expenses, ₹3,30,000 or ₹15 per hour
- Variable expenses, ₹2,20,000 or ₹10 per hour
- Standard overhead rate, ₹25 per hour
- Standard overhead rate, ₹50 per unit

For the month of January, actual facts were:
- Actual hours worked, 21,000
- Standard hours allowed for actual production of 10,900 units, 21,800
- Actual overheads incurred, ₹5,47,000 (Fixed ₹3,34,900 + Variable ₹2,12,100)

Compute the overhead variances under the various methods.

Solution

Total overhead variance = (Actual overheads incurred – Standard overhead cost charged to production) = ₹5,47,000 – (21,800 SHs × ₹25, SOR per hour = ₹5,45,000) = ₹2,000 (unfavourable)

1. *Two-variance method*

(a) Controllable variance: Actual overheads incurred – Budgeted overheads at actual production = ₹5,47,000 – ₹5,48,000* = ₹1,000 (favourable)

* Fixed overheads	₹3,30,000
+ Variable overheads (10,900 × ₹20)	2,18,000
	5,48,000

(b) Volume variance: (Normal capacity in units – Actual production) × SFOR per unit = (11,000 – 10,900) × ₹30 = ₹3,000 (unfavourable)

Alternatively, (Normal capacity in hours – Standard hours allowed for actual production) × SFOR per unit = (22,000 – 21,800) × ₹15 = ₹3,000 (unfavourable)

Summary:

(a) Controllable variance	= ₹1,000 (favourable)
(b) Volume variance	3,000 (unfavourable)
Total overhead variance	2,000 (unfavourable)

2. *Three-variance method*

(a) Spending variance = Actual overheads incurred – Budgeted overheads at AHs = (₹5,47,000 – ₹5,40,000*) = ₹7,000 (unfavourable)

*Budgeted overheads costs – Fixed overheads	₹3,30,000
+ Variable overheads (AHs × SVOR per hour)	2,10,000
	5,40,000

(b) Efficiency variance = (SHs – AHs) × SOR per hour (21,800 – 21,000) × ₹25 = ₹20,000 (favourable)

(c) Capacity variance = (SHs – AHs) × SFOR per hour = (22,000 – 21,000) × ₹15 = ₹15,000 (unfavourable)

Summary:

(a) Spending variance	₹7,000 (unfavourable)
(b) Efficiency variance	20,000 (favourable)
(c) Capacity variance	15,000 (unfavourable)
Total overhead variance	2,000 (unfavourable)

3. *Four-variance method:*

(a) Spending variance	₹7,000 (unfavourable)
Efficiency variance:	
(b) Fixed = (SHs – AHs) × SFOR	
= (21,800 – 21,000) × ₹15	12,000 (favourable)
(c) Variable = (21,800 – 21,000) × ₹10	8,000 (favourable)
(d) Capacity variance	15,000 (unfavourable)
Total overhead variance	2,000 (unfavourable)

4. *Five-variance method:*

(a) Fixed spending variance (₹3,34,900 – ₹3,30,000)	₹4,900 (unfavourable)
(b) Variable spending variance ($AVOR_{PH}$ – $SVOR_{PH}$) × AH (₹10.10 – ₹10.00) × 21,000	2,100 (unfavourable)
(c) Fixed efficiency variance	12,000 (favourable)
(d) Variable efficiency variance	8,000 (favourable)
(e) Capacity variance	15,000 (unfavourable)
Total overhead variance	2,000 (unfavourable)

STANDARD COST ACCOUNTING

The preceding discussions have shown that variance analysis is based on a comparison of standard and actual data. The availability of standard data is, therefore, a prerequisite of variance analysis. This section dwells on the methods of incorporating standard costs in the accounting records.

Standard costs should be considered as costs which pass through the cost accumulation procedure into financial statements. There are three methods of incorporating standard costs in the costs accounting cycle: **(i)** single plan (full standard costing plan), **(ii)** partial plan, and **(iii)** dual plan. Of these, the first, namely, full standard costing plan is more appropriate for purposes of variance analysis, because debits and credits to the work-in-process account under this plan are made at standard costs only.

Under the single plan, the difference between standard and actual costs are debited or credited to the related variance account. Favourable variances are represented by credit balances as they reflect cost reductions or savings as compared with standard costs. Conversely, debit balances imply unfavourable variances as they represent excess costs.

The accounting procedure is similar to that of the actual cost system, the only difference being that there is an additional variance account that appears on the debit side in the case of excess actual cost, and on credit side in the case of lower actual costs, compared with standard costs. The accounting procedure of recording variances is illustrated below:

1. (a)	**(i)** *Purchase of materials* (AP > SP):	
	Materials Inventory A/c	Dr
	Materials Price Variance A/c	Dr
	To Suppliers/Cash	
	(ii) (AP < SP)	
	Materials Inventory A/c	Dr
	To Materials Price Variance A/c	
	To *Suppliers/Cash*	

The materials inventory account is debited, in all the cases, at the standard price of the units purchased. The liability in terms of the amount payable to the suppliers (in the case of credit purchases) is always at the actual cost, the difference being in the balance to be transferred to the materials price variance account.

(b) (i)	*Usage of materials:* (AQ > SQ)	
	Work-in-process A/c	Dr
	Materials Usage Variance A/c	Dr
	To Materials Inventory A/c	
(ii)	(SQ < AQ)	
	Work-in-process A/c	Dr
	To *Materials Inventory* A/c	
	To Materials Usage Variance A/c	
(iii)	(SQ = AQ)	
	Work-in-process A/c	Dr
	To Materials Inventory A/c	

The work-in-process account is debited for the standard quantity of materials to be consumed in producing the actual output at standard price. Materials inventory account, as already appearing at the standard price, will be credited by the product of actual quantities used and the standard price.

2. (a) (i)	*Accruals of direct labour* (AR > SR)	
	Direct labour payroll	Dr
	Labour rate variance	Dr
	To Accrued payroll	
(ii)	(SR < AR)	
	Direct labour payroll	Dr
	To Accrued payroll	
	To Labour rate variance	
(iii)	(SR = AR)	
	Direct labour payroll	Dr
	To Accrued payroll	

The direct labour payroll account is debited in all the cases at the standard wage rate (SR). The total amount debited would be equal to actual hours worked, multiplied by the SR per hour. The accrued payroll account will be credited with the actual amount payable to the workers. The labour rate variance accounts for this difference.

(b) (i)	*Actual hours used:* (AH > SH)	
	Work-in-process A/c	Dr
	Labour efficiency variance A/c	Dr
	To Direct labour payroll	
(ii)	(AH < SH)	
	Work-in-process A/c	Dr
	To Direct labour payroll	
	To Labour efficiency variance	
(iii)	(AH = SH)	
	Work-in-process A/c	Dr
	To Direct labour payroll	

The work-in-process account is debited for the standard hours in production at the standard wage rate. The direct labour payroll amount is determined by multiplying actual hours worked with standard wages rate. The difference between the two represents favourable or unfavourable labour efficiency variance.

3. *Manufacturing Overhead*

As outlined in the previous section, the treatment of manufacturing overhead is different and more typical compared to material and labour costs. Accordingly, the standard cost accounting procedure pertaining to overheads differs from that of material and labour. In fact, there is more than one way of determining overhead variances. (Details regarding the computation of variances have already been discussed).

EXAMPLE 17.11

Hypothetical Ltd furnishes you the following information

— Normal capacity: 12,000 hours
— Fixed expenses: ₹1,00,000
— Variable expenses (at normal capacity): ₹1,40,000
— Actual hours worked: 11,280
— Standard hours allowed for the work done: 11,400
— Actual factory overhead expenses: ₹2,31,750 (including variable overheads of ₹1,30,000)

Compute the factory overhead variances.

SOLUTION

The factory overhead variances can be computed by using the two-variance, three-variance, or four-variance methods. Accordingly, the entries have been framed under various methods.

(a) *Two-Variance Method*

(i) Actual factory overhead cost incurred:			
Factory overhead control A/c	Dr	₹2,31,750	
To Various accounts (details for each head is to be given separately)			₹2,31,750

It may be noted that the actual factory overhead costs are recorded under the standard costing system in the same way as under the actual cost system.

(ii) When overhead is applied to work-in-process:			
Work-in-process A/c	Dr	₹2,28,000	
To Factory overhead control A/c			₹2,28,000

The amount to be transferred to the work-in-process account is determined by the product of standard hours (SHs) required for actual output and standard overhead rate (SOR) per hour. Here, the standard overhead rate is ₹20, or [(₹1,00,000 + ₹1,40,000) ÷ 12,000 hours]. Accordingly, the amount is 11,400 hours × ₹20 = ₹2,28,000.

(iii) The factory overhead control account now has a debit balance of ₹3,750 which can be analysed and closed as follows:			
Volume variance A/c	Dr	₹5,000@	
To Controllable variance A/c			₹1,250
To Factory overhead control A/c			3,750

@ Volume variance = (NHs – SHs) × SOR = (12,000 – 11,400) × ₹100/12 = ₹5,000 (adverse)

Controllable variance = (AOC – Budgeted overhead cost at SH) = ₹2,31,750 – [₹1,00,000 (fixed) + (11,400 × 140/12) (variable) = ₹1,33,000 = ₹2,33,000] = ₹1,250 (favourable).

(b) *Three-Variance Method*

(i) For actual factory overhead:			
Factory overhead control A/c	Dr	₹2,31,750	
To Various accounts			₹2,31,750
(ii) When overhead is applied to work-in-process			
Work-in-process A/c	Dr	₹2,28,000	
To Factory overhead control A/c			₹2,28,000

(Contd.)

(*Contd.*)

(iii) The factory overhead control A/c now has a debit balance of ₹3,750, which can be broken up into the following three variance:			
Factory overhead spending variance A/c	Dr	₹150	
Idle capacity variance A/c		6,000	
To Factory overhead efficiency variance A/c			₹2,400
To Factory overhead control A/c			3,750

(c) *Four-Variance Method:* The first two entries for actual factory overhead, and the amount applied to work-in-process would be the same as under the three-variance method. There will be minor difference only in the last entry. The point of difference pertains to factory overhead efficiency variance. The amount will be bifurcated into fixed overhead efficiency variance and variable overhead efficiency variance. The fixed overhead efficiency variance would be: (120 hours) × SFOR, i.e. ₹100/12 = ₹1,000 (favourable)

The variable overhead efficiency variance would be: (120 hours) × SVOR, i.e. ₹140/12 = ₹1,400 (favourable)

The last entry for closing the factory overhead control account which has a debit balance of ₹375 would be:

Factory overhead spending variance A/c	Dr	₹150	
Idle capacity variance A/c	Dr	6,000	
To Variable factory overhead efficiency variance A/c			₹1,400
To Fixed factory overhead efficiency variance A/c			1,000
To Factory overhead control A/c			3,750

(d) *Five-Variance Method:* The distinguishing feature would pertain to spending variance. It will be subdivided into two parts, fixed and variable. Fixed spending variance = ₹1,00,000 – ₹1,01,750 = ₹1750 (adverse).

Variable spending variance = ₹1,31,600 – ₹1,30,000 = ₹1,600 (favourable). The entry would be,

Fixed overhead spending variance A/c	Dr	₹1,750	
Idle capacity variance A/c	Dr	6,000	
To Variable overhead spending variance A/c			₹1,600
To Variable overhead efficiency variance A/c			1,400
To Fixed overhead efficiency variance A/c			1,000
To Factory overhead control A/c			3,750

Standard Accounting Procedure for Completed Products

Under the single plan system, the work-in-process account is debited at standard costs only. Consequently, it will be standard costs of the completed units that will be transferred from that account to the finished product account. The required entry for the purpose is:

Finished product (at standard cost)	Dr
To Work-in-process (at standard costs)	
When goods are sold to customers the following two entries will be required:	
1. Debtors A/c	Dr
To Sales (at selling price)	
2. Cost of goods sold (at standard cost)	Dr
To Finished cost inventory (at standard cost)	

SUMMARY

- Variance analysis is a control technique. The control process involves comparison of actual costs *(AC)* with the standard costs (*SC*). Variances represent the difference between *AC* and *SC*. They basically relate to performance deviations. If *AC* is less than *SC*, it is a sign of efficiency and the difference is termed 'favourable'/'positive'. If it is more than *SC*, it is a sign of inefficiency and the difference is referred to as 'unfavourable'/'negative'.
- As controlling devices, variances help to assign responsibility for deviations and, thus, to control cost. For this purpose, they are classified as controllable and uncontrollable. If a variance can be traced with the responsibility of a particular segment, it is said to be controllable. If a variance arises from causes beyond the control of responsible individuals, it is said to be *uncontrollable.* This distinction is extremely important for managerial control.
- The cost variances relate to the costs of a manufacturing enterprise. The three elements of the costs of such an enterprise are: material, labour, and overheads.
- Material variances are summarised below:

Variance	*Formula*
(A) Material cost variance (*MCV*) (unit basis)	(*AQ* × *AO* × *AP*) – (*SQ* × *SP* × *AO*)
or MCV (aggregate basis)	*TAMC* – *TSMC*
(B) (i) Material purchase price variance	(*AP* – *SP*) × *AQ* purchased
(ii) Material price variance (*MPV*)	(*AP* – *SP*) × *AQ* issued
(C) Material usage/quality variance (*MUV*)	[(*AQ* × *AO*) – (*SQ* × *AO*)] × *SP*
(unit basis) *or MUV* (aggregate basis)	or (*TAMQ* – *TSMQ*) × *SP*
(i) Material-mix sub-variance (*MMSV*) and	(*RSQ* – *AQ*) × *SP*
(ii) Material-yield sub-variance (*MYSV*)	(*AY* – *SY*) × *SMC* per finished unit
(output basis) *or MYSV* (input basis)	(*TAMQ* – *TSMQ*) × Weighted average standard price per unit of material

Where,

AQ	Actual usage of material per unit
AO	Actual output in units
AP	Actual price of material per unit
SQ	Standard usage of material per unit
SP	Standard price of material per unit
TAMC	Total actual material costs incurred
TSMC	Total standard costs of actual output
TAMQ	Total actual quantity of material used
TSMQ	Total standard quantity of material required
RSQ	Revised standard quantity, i.e. standard mix/proportion of actual total quantity of material used
AY	Actual yield (actual finished output)
SY	Standard yield (expected output, given the actual input).

- Labour variances are summarised below:

Variance	*Formula*
(A) Labour cost variance (*LCV*), (unit basis)	[(*AH* × *AO* × *AR*) – (*SH* × *SR* × *AO*)]
or LCV (aggregate basis)	(*TALC* – *TSLC*)
(B) Labour/Wage rate variance (*LRV*)	(*AR* – *SR*) × *TAH* paid for
(C) Labour efficiency variance (*LEV*)	(*TAH* – *TSH*) × *SR* per hour
or	
(i) Labour idle time variance (*LIV*) *and*	(*IH*) × *SR* per hour
(ii) Labour efficiency variance revised (*LEV* revised)	(*TAHW* – *TSH*) × *SR* per hour

(*Contd.*)

(*Contd.*)

or	
Labour-mix sub-variance (*LMSV*)	(*RSH* – *AH*) × *SR* per hour
Labour-yield sub-variance (*LYSV*) (output basis)	(*AY* – *SY*) × Standard labour cost per finished unit
or LYSV (input basis)	(*TAH* – *TSH*) × Weighted average standard rate per hour

Where,

AH	Actual labour-hours spent per unit
AO	Actual output achieved in units
AR	Actual wage rate per hour
SH	Standard labour-hours required per unit
SR	Standard wage rate per hour
TALC	Total actual labour cost of actual output
TSLC	Total standard labour cost of actual output
TAH	Total actual labour-hours paid for
TSH	Total standard hours allowed for actual output
IH	Idle hours
TSHW	Total actual hours worked for production (*TAH* – *IH*)
RSH	Revised standard hours, i.e. standard proportion of actual hours used.

➢ Manufacturing Overheads Variances are summarised below:

Variance	*Formula*
(A) Variable overheads	
Variable overheads cost variance (*VOCV*)	[(*AH* × *AO* × *AVOR*) – (*SH* × *AO* × *SVOR*)
(unit basis) *or VOCV* (aggregate basis)	*TAVOC* – *TSVOC*
(a) Variable overheads spending variance (*VOSV*)	[*TAVOC* – (*TAH* × *SVOR*)]
(b) Variable overheads efficiency variance (*VOEV*)	(*TAH* – *TSH*) × *SVOR* per hour
For confirmation, *VOCV*	*VOEV* + *VOSV*
(B) *Fixed overheads*	
Fixed overheads cost variance (*FOCV*)	[*TAFOC* – (*SFOR* per unit × *AO*)]
(output basis) *or FOCV* (times basis)	[*TAFOC* – (*SFOR* per hour × *SH* × *AO*)]
(a) Fixed overheads spending variance (*FOSV*)	*TAFOC* – *BFOC*
(b) Volume variance (output basis) (*VV*)	[(*NO* – *AO*) × *SFOR* per unit]
or	
(i) Fixed overheads efficiency (*FOEV*)	[(*TAH* – *TSH*) × *SFOR* per hour]
(ii) Calender variance	(*AD* – *SD*) × SFOD
(iii) Capacity variance (*CV*)	[(*TAH* – *TNH*) × *SFOR* per hour]
For confirmation, *FOCY*	*FOSV* + *VV*
	or
	FOSV + *FOEV* + Calender variance + *CV*

The following may be used as an alternative to the above.

Overheads cost variance (*OCV*)	[*TAOC* – (*SOR* per unit × *AO*)]
or *OCV* (hours basis)	[*TAOC* – (*SOR* per hour × *SH* per unit × *AO*)]
(A) *Two-variance method*	
(i) Controllable expenditure variance	[*TAOC* – (*BFOC* + *SVOC* per unit × *AO*)]
(ii) Volume variance	(*NO* – *AO*) × *SFOR* per unit
(B) *Three-variance method*	
(i) Spending variance	[*TAOC* – (*BFOC* + *SVOC* per hour × TAH)]

(*Contd.*)

(*Contd.*)

(ii) Efficiency variance	[*TAH* – *TSH*) × *SOR* per hour]
(iii) Capacity variance	(*NH* – *TAH*) × *SFOR* per hour
(C) *Four-variance method*	
(i) Spending variance	As B(i) above
(ii) Variable efficiency variance	(*TAH* – *TSH*) × *SVOR* per hour
(iii) Fixed efficiency variance	(*TAH* – *TSH*) × *SFOR* per hour
(iv) Capacity variance	As B(iii) above
(D) *Five-variance method*	
(i) Fixed spending variance	*TAFOC* – *TBFOC*
(ii) Variable spending variance	$(AVOR_{PH} - SVOR_{PH}) \times TAH$
(iii) Variance efficiency variance	As C (ii) above
(iv) Fixed efficiency variance	As C (iii) above
(v) Capacity variance	As C (iv) above

Where,

AVOR Actual variable overheads (per hour or per unit, as the case may be)
SVOR Standard variable overheads (per hour or per unit, as the case may be)
TAVOC Total actual variable overheads incurred
TSVOC Total standard variable overhead costs
SFOR Standard fixed overheads rate (per unit or per hour, as the case may be)
TAFOC Total actual fixed overheads cost
BFOC Budgeted fixed overheads cost
NO Normal output in units
AD Actual days
SD Standard/budgeted days for which production was scheduled
SFOD Standard fixed overheads cost per day
TNH Total normal hours capacity
TAOC Total actual overheads cost (*TAVOC* + *TAFOC*)
SOR Standard overheads rate (per unit or per hour, as the case may be)

REFERENCES

1. J.M. Fremgen, *Accounting for Managerial Analysis*, (Richard D. Irwin, Homewood, Illinois, 1976), p. 250.
2. The assumption regarding this variance of MPV is that the quantity of raw material consumed is equal to the quantity of raw material purchased.
3. D.T. Decoster and E.L. Schafer, *Management Accounting—A Decision Empahsis*, (John Wiley, New York, 1976), p. 480.
4. R.N. Anthony, *Management Accounting, Text and Cases*, (Irwin, Georgetown, 1970), pp. 534-53.
5. C.T. Horngren, *Introduction to Management Accounting, (Prentice-Hall*, Englewood Cliffs, N.J., 1978), p. 193.
6. J. Batty, *Standard Costing*, (Macdonald and Evans, London, 1970), p. 68.
7. Decoster and Schaffer, *op. cit.* p. 484.
8. National Association of Accountants, "Accounting for Costing of Capacity" *N.A.A. Research Report No. 39* (New York, 1963), p. 64.
9. While the term 'volume' variance is sometimes used interchangeably with 'capacity variance, it is more appropriate to consider capacity variance, as a part of volume variance. The latter approach is adopted by us.
10. Fremgen, *op. cit.*, p. 265

SOLVED PROBLEMS

P.17.1 In a manufacturing process the following standards apply

Standard price : Raw material X @ ₹10 per kg
Raw material Y @ ₹50 per kg

Standard mix (by weight) : 75% X, 25% Y

Standard yield : (Weight of product as percentage of weight of raw material, 90%)

In a period, the actual costs, usages and output were as follows:

Used: 4,400 kgs, X costing ₹46,500
1,600 kgs, Y costing ₹78,500

Output: 5,670 kgs of products

The budget output for the period was 7,200 kgs.

Prepare a statement, showing how the material cost variance is built up, and give activity and yield percentages.

SOLUTION

Total input requirement = 5,670 kgs × 100/90 = 6,300 kgs

Raw material X = 4,725 kgs (0.75 × 6,300 kgs)
Y = 1,575 kgs (0.25 × 6,300 kgs)

	Standard			Actual		
Raw material	*(SQ)(kgs)*	*(SR)*	*(SC)*	*(AQ) (kgs)*	*(AR)*	*(AC)*
X	4,725	₹10	₹47,250	4,400	₹4,650/440	₹46,500
Y	1,575	50	78,750	1,600	7,850/160	78,500
Total	6,300	20	1,26,000	6,000	1,250/60	1,25,000

Material cost variance: (SC – AC) = (₹1,26,000 – ₹1,25,000) = ₹1,000 (favourable)

Material cost variance is built up of the following three sub-variances:

1. *Material price variance:* (SR – AR) × AQ = (SR × AQ) – (AR × AQ)

   Raw material X = (₹10 × 4,400) – ₹46,500 = ₹2,500 (adverse)
   Y = (₹50 × 1,600) – ₹78,500 = 1,500 (adverse)
   4,000 (adverse)

2. *Material mix variance* = (Standard mix of actual quantity used – Actual mix of actual quantity used) × SR

   Raw material X (0.75 × 6,000 = 4,500 – 4,400) × ₹10 = ₹1,000 (favourable)
   Y (0.25 × 6,000 = 1,500 – 1,600) × ₹50 5,000 (adverse)
   Total material mix variance 4,000 (adverse)

3. *Material yield variance:* (Standard yield – Actual yield) × SC per unit = (5,400 – 5,670) × ₹1,26,000/5,670 = ₹6,000 (favourable)

   Standard yield = 0.90 × 6,000 kgs = 5,400 kgs

   Alternatively, material yield variance, can be calculated on an input basis also: (Standard quantity of raw materials required to produce actual output – Actual quantity used for actual production) × Standard weighted average cost per kg = (6,300 – 6,000) × ₹20 = ₹6,000 (favourable).

   The material cost variance is built up of MPV, ₹1,000 (A), MMV, ₹4,000 (A), and MYV, ₹6,000 (F) = 1,000 (favourable).

$$\text{Activity percentage} = \frac{\text{Standard yield for actual input}}{\text{Budgeted output}} \times 100 = \frac{5{,}400}{7{,}200} \times 100 = 75 \text{ per cent}$$

$$\text{Yield percentage} = \frac{\text{Actual yield}}{\text{Standard yield}} \times 100 = \frac{5{,}670}{5{,}400} \times 100 = 105 \text{ per cent}$$

P.17.2 The standard material cost for 100 kgs of chemical D is made up of

Chemical A—30 kgs @ ₹40 per kg
Chemical B—40 kgs @ ₹50 per kg
Chemical C—80 kgs @ ₹60 per kg

In a batch, 500 kgs of chemical D were produced from a mix of:

Chemical A—140 kgs at a cost of ₹5,880
Chemical B—220 kgs at a cost of ₹10,560
Chemical C—440 kgs at a cost of ₹28,600

How do the yield, mix and the price factors contribute to the variance in the actual cost per 100 kgs of chemical D over the standard cost?

SOLUTION

Table Containing Actual Input Used for 100 kgs (500 kgs ÷ 5 = 100 kgs)

Chemical	*SQ (kgs)*	*SR*	*SC*	*AQ (kgs)*	*AR*	*AC*
A	30	₹40	₹1,200	28	₹42	₹1,176
B	40	50	2,000	44	48	2,112
C	80	60	4,800	88	65	5,720
	150	53.33	8,000	160	56.30	9,008

Material cost variance: (TSC – TAC) = (₹8,000 – ₹9,008) = ₹1,008 (adverse)

1. *Material price variance:* (SR – AR) × AQ
A: (₹40 – ₹42) × 28 kgs = ₹56 (adverse)
B: (₹50 – ₹48) × 44 kgs = 88 (favourable)
C: (₹60 – ₹65) × 88 kgs = 440 (adverse)
408 (adverse)

2. *Material mix variance:* (RSQ – AQ) × SR
A: 160 × 30/150 = (32 kgs – 28 kgs) × ₹40 = ₹160 (favourable)
B: 160 × 40/150 = (42.67 kgs – 44 kgs) × ₹50 = 66.67 (adverse)
C: 160 × 80/150 = (85.33 kgs – 88 kgs) × ₹60 = 160 (adverse)
66.70 (adverse)

3. *Material yield variance:* [Standard yield (SY) – Actual yield (AY) × SC per unit] = (106.667 – 100) × ₹80 = ₹533.30 A

Standard yield= Standard production expected from actual quantity used, that is, (160 kgs × 100)/150 kgs = 106.67 kgs

SC per unit = Total standard cost/Total standard output = ₹8,000/100 kgs = ₹80 per kg

Alternatively, material yield variance can be calculated on input basis also: (Total standard quality of raw material required to produce actual output – Actual quantity used for actual production) × Standard weighted average cost per kg = (150 kgs – 160 kgs) × ₹53.33 = ₹533.30 (adverse).

P.17.3 A foundry producing castings of a standard alloy uses standard costs. The standard mixture is as follows:

40 per cent material A at ₹3,000 per tonne
30 per cent material B at ₹1,000 per tonne
10 per cent material C at ₹4,200 per tonne
20 per cent scrap metal of this alloy.

It is expected that from each charge, there will be a 5 per cent loss in melt, 35 per cent will be returned to scrap stock (runners, heads, etc.) and 60 per cent will be good castings. Scrap is credited and charged at the standard average cost of the metal mixture. Scrap is credited and charged at the standard average cost of the metal mixture. In a certain period, the following materials are purchased and used:

380 tonnes material A at ₹3,100 per tonne
330 tonnes material B at ₹1,100 per tonne

90 tonnes material C at ₹4,200 per tonne
200 tonnes scrap metal at standard price.

From this material, 608 tonnes of good castings are produced and 340 tonnes of scrap metal are returned to scrap metal stock.

Prepare information for management showing standard metal costs, and variances from standard in respect of this period.

SOLUTION

The standard mixture of 608 tonnes of good casting will be as follows:

Since 60 tonnes of good castings require a standard mixture of 100 tonnes, 608 tonnes require = (608 × 100)/60 = 6,080/6 tonnes, the standard inputs of materials A, B, C and scrap would be 40 per cent, 30 per cent, 10 per cent, and 20 per cent of 6,080/6 tonnes, respectively.

The following table presents the above information:

Materials	*Standard*			*Actual*		
	SQ (tonnes)	*SR*	*SC*	*AQ (tonnes)*	*AR*	*AC*
Material A	1,216/3	₹3,000	₹12,16,000	380	₹3,100	₹11,78,000
B	304	1,000	3,04,000	330	1,100	3,63,000
C	608/6	4,200	4,25,600	90	4,200	3,78,000
Scrap metal	608/3	2,400	4,86,400	200	2,400	4,80,000
Total	6,080/6	2,400	24,32,000	1,000	2,399	23,99,000

Standard average price of scrap metal: Total standard cost of material A + B + C/Total quantity of material A, B, C = ₹19,45,600 ÷ 4,864/6 = ₹2,400

Total quantity of material A, B, C 4,864/6

Standard metal cost per tonne (₹24,32,000 ÷ 608) = ₹4,000

Material cost variance: (₹24,32,000 – ₹23,99,000) = ₹33,000 (favourable)

(A) *Material price variance:* (SR – AR) × AQ

Material	A (₹3,000 – ₹3,100) × 380	=	₹38,000 (adverse)
	B (₹1,000 – ₹1,100) × 330	=	33,000 (adverse)
	C (₹4,200 – ₹4,200) × 90	=	Nil
			71,000 (adverse)

(B) *Material usage variance:* (SQ – AQ) × SR

Material	A (1,216/3 tonnes – 380 tonnes) × ₹3,000	=	₹76,000 (favourable)
	B (304 tonnes – 330 tonnes) × ₹1,000	=	26,000 (adverse)
	C (608/6 tonnes – 90 tonnes) × ₹4,200	=	47,600 (favourable)
Scrap metal	(608/3 tonnes – 200 tonnes) × ₹2,400	=	6,400 (favourable)
			1,04,000 (favourable)

Material usage variance has two components:

(a) *Material mix variance:* (Standard mix of actual quantity used – Actual mix of actual quantity) × SR

Material	A (0.40 × 1,000 = 400 tonnes – 380 tonnes) × ₹3,000	=	₹60,000 (favourable)
	B (0.30 × 1,000 = 300 tonnes – 330 tonnes) × ₹1,000	=	30,000 (adverse)
	C (0.10 × 1,000 = 100 tonnes – 90 tonnes) × ₹4,200	=	42,000 (favourable)
Scrap metal	(0.20 × 1,000 = 200 tonnes – 200 tonnes) × ₹2,400		Nil
			72,000 (favourable)

(b) *Material yield variance:* (Standard yield – Actual yield) × SC per tonne
(600 tonnes – 608 tonnes) × ₹4,000 = ₹32,000 (favourable)

Total material cost variance = ₹71,000 (adverse) + ₹72,000 (favourable) + ₹32,000 (favourable)
= ₹33,000 (favourable).

P.17.4 Standard material for 100 kgs Chemical 456 is given below

Kgs		*Total*
45	of material A @ ₹20 per kg	₹900
40	of material B @ ₹40 per kg	1,600
25	of material C @ ₹60 per kg	1,500
110		
10	standard loss	
100		4,000

Actual production 2,000 units of Chemical 456 and actual material usage is as follows:

Material A	1,000 kgs @ ₹19 per kg	₹19,000
Material B	850 kgs @ ₹42 per kg	35,700
Material C	450 kgs @ ₹65 per kg	29,250
	2,300 kgs	83,950

Calculate the following: **(i)** Material cost variance, **(ii)** Material price variance, **(iii)** Material mixture variance, **(iv)** Material yield variance, and **(v)** Material usage variance.

SOLUTION

Standard material input required to produce 2,000 units of chemical 456

Material A: (45/100 × 2,000) = 900 kgs
B: (40/100 × 2,000) = 800 kgs
C: (25/100 × 2,000) = 500 kgs

	Standard			*Actual*		
Material	*SQ (kgs)*	*SR*	*SC*	*AQ (kgs)*	*AR*	*AC*
A	900	₹20	₹18,000	1,000	₹19	₹19,000
B	800	40	32,000	850	42	35,700
C	500	60	30,000	450	65	29,250
	2,200	36.30	80,000	2,300	36.5	83,950
	200 (standard loss)					
	2,000 (standard output)					
	₹40 SC per unit					

1. *Material cost variance:* (SC – AC): (₹80,000 – ₹83,950) = ₹3,950 (adverse)
2. *Material price variance:* (SR – AR) × AQ
   Material A: (₹20 – ₹19) × 1,000 kgs = ₹1,000 (favourable)
   B: (₹40 – ₹42) × 850 kgs = 1,700 (adverse)
   C: (₹60 – ₹65) × 450 kgs = 2,250 (adverse)
   2,950 (adverse)
3. *Material mix variance:* (RSQ – AQ) × SR
   Material A: [(2,300 × 45) ÷ 110) – 1,000 kgs] × ₹20= ₹1,181.80 (adverse)
   B: [(2,300 × 40) ÷ 110) – 850 kgs] × ₹40 = 545.50 (adverse)
   C: [(2,300 × 25) ÷ 110) – 450 kgs] × ₹60 = 4,363.60 (favourable)
   2,636.30 (favourable)
4. *Material yield variance:* (SY – AY) × SC per kg = [(2,300 × 100) ÷ 110) – 2,000 units] × ₹40
   = ₹3636.30 (adverse)
5. *Material usage variance:* (SQ – AQ) × SR
   Material A: (900 kgs – 1,000 kgs) × ₹20 = ₹2,000 (adverse)
   B: (800 kgs – 850 kgs) × ₹40 = 2,000 (adverse)
   C: (500 kgs – 450 kgs) × ₹60 = 3,000 (favourable)
   1,000 (adverse)

Alternatively,

Material mix variance	₹2,636.30 (favourable)
Plus, material yield variance	3,636.30 (adverse)
	1,000 (adverse)

P.17.5 From the data given below, calculate:

(a) Individual material price variance for the two materials, X and Y, assuming that the variances are calculated at the time of purchase;

(b) Individual material usage variances for material X and Y assuming that there was no work-in-progress, either at the commencement or at the end of the period.

Particulars	*Material X* Quantity (kg)	Value	*Material Y* Quantity (kg)	Value
Raw material purchases	2,000	₹40,000	5,000	₹62,500
Issued to work	2,150		3,950	
Work stock of material				
Opening	300		1,000	
Closing	200		1,250	
Standard price				
Material X – ₹19 per kg				
Material Y – ₹13 per kg				
Standard usage:				
	Material X		*Material Y*	
Product A	1 kg		1 kg	
Product B	0.5 kg		1 kg	
Output during the period				
Product A—1,130 units				
Product B—2,550 units				

SOLUTION

(a) *Material purchase price variance* = [Actual rate (AR) – Standard rate (SR)] × Actual quantity (AQ) purchased

Material X : [(AR × AQ) – (SR × AQ)] = [₹40,000 – (₹19 × 2,000)] = ₹40,000 – ₹38,000
= ₹2,000 (unfavourable)

Material Y = [₹62,500 – (₹13 × 5,000)] = ₹62,500 – ₹65,000 = ₹2,500 (unfavourable)

(b) *Material usage variance* = (Actual quantity used – Standard quantity) × SR

	Material X	*Material Y*
Actual quantity used:		
Opening stock (kgs)	300	1,000
Add issues to work	2,150	3,950
Less closing stock	(200)	(1,250)
	2,250	3,700
Standard usage:		
Product A	1,130	1,130
Product B	1,275	2,550
	2,405	3,680

Material X: (2,250 kgs – 2,405 kgs) × ₹19 = ₹2,945 (favourable)

Material Y: (3,700 kgs – 3,680 kgs) × ₹13 = ₹260 (favourable)

P.17.6 One kg of the product K requires two chemicals, A and B. The following are the details of the product K for the month of June.

(a) Standard mix of chemical A, 50 per cent and chemical B, 50 per cent

(b) Standard price per kg of chemical A, ₹120 and chemical B, ₹150

(Contd.)

(*Contd.*)

(c) Actual input of chemical B, 70 kgs
(d) Actual price per kg of chemical A, ₹150
(e) Standard normal loss,10 per cent of total output
(f) Material cost variance,total,₹6,500 adverse
(g) Material yield variance,total,₹1,350 adverse
(h) Actual output, 90 kgs

You are required to calculate: **(i)** Material mix variance(total), **(ii)** Material usage variance(total), **(iii)** Material price variance(total), **(iv)** Actual loss of actual input, **(v)** Actual input of chemical A, and **(vi)** Actual price per kg of chemical B.

SOLUTION

(i) *Material mix variance* = (Standard mix of actual quantity used – Actual mix) × Standard rate
A: [(110 kgs × 0.50 = 55kgs – 40 kgs)] × ₹120 = ₹1,800 (favourable)
B: [(110 kgs × 0.50 = 55kgs – 70 kgs)] × ₹150 = 2,250 (unfavourable)
450 (unfavourable)

(ii) *Material usage variance* = Material mix variance + Material yield variance = ₹450 (unfavourable) + ₹1,350 (unfavourable) = ₹1,800 (unfavourable)

(iii) *Material price variance* = (SR – AR) × AQ
A: (₹120 – ₹150) × 40 kgs = ₹1,200 (unfavourable)
B: (₹150 – ₹200) × 70 kgs = 3,500 (unfavourable)
4,700 (unfavourable)

(iv) *Actual loss of actual input* = (Actual input – Actual output) = 110 kgs – 90 kgs = 20 kgs

(v) *Actual input of chemical A,* = 40 kgs

(vi) *Actual price per kg of chemical B* = ₹200

WORKING NOTES

Standard material input and cost required to produce 90 kgs of product K

(a)

Chemical A	50 kgs @ ₹120 per kg	₹6,000
Chemical B	50 kgs @ ₹150 per kg	7,500
	100 kgs	13,500
Less standard normal loss	10 kgs	
Actual output	90 kgs	

(b) Standard rate per kg of product K = ₹13,500/90 kgs = ₹150

(c) Material yield variance = (SY – AY) × SR per kg of final product
₹1,350 U = (SY – 90 kgs) × ₹150
₹1,350 U = 150 SY – ₹13,500
₹1,350 U + ₹13,500 = 150 SY
₹14,850 = 150 SY or SY = ₹14,850/150 = 99 kgs

(d) Actual total input of A and B chemicals = 99 kgs × 100/90 = 110 kgs

(e) Actual inputs of chemical being 70 kgs, input of chemical A would be 40 kgs

(f) Actual costs of material used = Standard cost (₹13,500) + (unfavourable) material cost variance (₹6,500) = ₹20,000

(g)

Total cost of chemicals A and B	₹20,000
Less cost of chemical A (40 kgs × ₹150)	6,000
Costs of chemical B (70 kgs)	14,000
Cost of chemical B per kg (₹14,000/70 kgs)	200

P.17.7 From the data given below, calculate each of the three wage variances for the two departments:

Particulars	Department A	Department B
Actual gross wages	₹2,00,000	₹1,80,000
Standard hours produced	8,000	6,000
Standard rate per hour	₹30	₹35
Actual hours worked	8,200	5,800

SOLUTION

Labour cost variance: Actual wages paid – Standard wages charged to production (SH × SR)

Department A: ₹2,00,000 – (8,000 × ₹30) = ₹40,000 (favourable)

B: ₹1,80,000 – (6,000 × ₹35) = ₹30,000 (favourable)

Labour rate variance: (SR – AR) × Actual hours (AH) worked) or : (SR × AH) – (AR × AH)

Department A: (₹30 × 8,200) – ₹2,00,000 = ₹46,000 (favourable)

B: (₹35 × 5,800) – ₹1,80,000 = ₹23,000 (favourable)

Labour efficiency variance: (Standard hours produced – Actual hours worked) × Standard rate per hour

Department A: (8,000 – 8,200) × ₹30 = ₹6,000 (adverse)

B: (6,000 – 5,800) × ₹35 = ₹7,000 (favourable)

Confirmation

Particulars	Department A	Department B
Labour rate variance	₹46,000 (favourable)	₹23,000 (favourable)
Labour efficiency variance	6,000 (adverse)	7,000 (favourable)
Labour cost variance	40,000 (favourable)	30,000 (favourable)

P.17.8 The standard output of product EXE is 25 units per hour in the manufacturing department of a company, employing 100 workers. The standard wage rate per labour-hour is ₹60. In a 42-hour week, the department produced 1,040 units of EXE despite loss of 5 per cent of time paid due to abnormal reasons. The hourly wage rates actually paid were ₹62, ₹60, and ₹57, respectively, to 10,30 and 60 of the workers.

Compute relevant variances.

SOLUTION

Basic data:

1. *Standard man-hour per unit* Since 25 units are standard output when 100 workers are engaged for 1 hour, the standard man-hours per unit is 4.
2. *Standard data*

Standard man-hours for actual output	Rate per hour	Amount	Number of workers	Actual hours Col. 4 (×) 42	Idle time paid for	Effective hours	Rate per hour	Amount paid
(1)	(2)	(3)	(4)	(5)	(6)	(7)	(8)	(9) = (5× 8)
4,160*	₹60	₹2,49,600	10	4,200	21	399	₹62	₹26,040
			30	12,600	63	1,197	60	75,600
			60	25,200	126	2,394	57	1,43,640
		2,49,600		42,000	210	3,990		2,45,280

*1,040 units × 4 hours

Computation of variances:

Labour cost variance = (Standard labour cost – Actual labour cost) = (₹2,49,600 – ₹2,45,280)
= ₹4,320 (favourable)

Labour rate variance = (Standard rate per hour – Actual rate per hour) × Actual hours

(₹60 – ₹62) × 420 hours = ₹840 (adverse)

(₹60 – ₹60) × 1,260 hours = Nil

(₹60 – ₹57) × 2,520 hours = 7,560 (favourable)

6,720 (favourable)

Labour efficiency variance = (Standard man-hours – Actual production hours) × Standard rate per hour
= (4,160 hours – 3,990 hours) × ₹60 = ₹10,200 (favourable)

Labour idle variance = Standard rate per hour × Idle time = ₹60 × 210 hours = ₹12,600 (adverse)

Verification:

Labour cost variance = Labour rate variance + Labour efficiency variance + Labour idle time variance
₹4,320 (favourable) = ₹6,720 (favourable) + ₹10,200 (favourable) – ₹12,600 (adverse)

P.17.9 The standard labour, and the actual labour employment in a week for a job are as under:

Particulars	*Skilled workers*	*Semi-skilled workers*	*Unskilled workers*
(A) Standard number of workers in the gang	32	12	6
(B) Standard wage rate per hour	₹30	₹20	₹10
(C) Actual number of workers employed in the gang during the week	28	18	4
(D) Actual wage rate per hour	40	30	20

During the 40-hours working week, the gang produced 1,800 standard labour-hours of work. Calculate the: (1) Labour efficiency variance; (2) Labour mix variance; (3) Rate of wages variance; and (4) Total labour cost variance.

SOLUTION

Category of workers	*Number of workers*	*Number of hours*	*Total hours*	*Wage rate*	*Total wages*
			Standard		
Skilled	32	40	1,280	₹30	₹38,400
Semi-skilled	12	40	480	20	9,600
Unskilled	6	40	240	10	2,400
			2,000	25.20	50,400
			Actual		
Skilled	28	40	1,120	40	44,800
Semi-skilled	18	40	720	30	21,600
Unskilled	4	40	160	20	3,200
			2,000	34.80	69,600

1. *Labour efficiency variance:* (Standard labour-hours – Actual labour-hours) × Standard weighted average wage rate = (1,800 – 2,000) × ₹25.20 = ₹5,040 (adverse)
2. *Labour mix variance:* (Standard mix of actual hours worked – Actual mix of actual hours) × Standard wage rate

   Since standard total hours and actual total hours are the same (2,000 hours), there is no need to calculate a revised standard mix of actual hours.

   Accordingly,

   Skilled workers: (1,280 – 1,120) × ₹30 = ₹4,800 (favourable)
   Semi-skilled workers: (480 – 720) × ₹20 = 4,800 (adverse)
   Unskilled workers: (240 – 160) × ₹10 = 800 (favourable)
   Total labour mix variance = 800 (favourable)
3. *Rate of wages variance:* (SR – AR) × AH

   Skilled workers: (₹30 – ₹40) × 1,120 = ₹11,200 (adverse)
   Semi-skilled workers: (₹20 – ₹30) × 720 = 7,200 (adverse)
   Unskilled workers: (₹10 – ₹20) × 160 = 1,600 (adverse)
   Total labour rate variance = 20,000 (adverse)

4. *Total labour cost variance:* (Total standard labour cost at standard hours – Actual labour cost at actual hours)
   Standard labour cost = (Standard hours × Standard weighted average wage rate)
   = (1,800 × ₹25.20) = ₹45,360 – ₹69,600 = ₹24,240 (adverse)

P.17.10 A gang of workers normally consists of 30 highly skilled, 15 skilled, and 10 semi-skilled. They are paid standard hourly rates as under:

Highly skilled	₹80
Skilled	60
Semi-skilled	40

In a normal working week of 40 hours, the gang is expected to produce 2,000 units of output.

During the week ended December 31, the gang consisted of 40 highly skilled, 10 skilled, and 5 semi-skilled. The actual wages paid were at the rate of ₹70, ₹65 and ₹30, respectively. Four hours were lost due to abnormal idle time and 1,600 units were produced.

Calculate: **(i)** Wage variance; **(ii)** Wage rate variance; **(iii)** Labour efficiency variance; **(iv)** Gang composition variance (labour mix variance); and **(v)** Labour idle time variance.

Solution

1. *Wage variance:* (Standard labour cost of actual output – Actual labour cost) = ₹1,18,400 – ₹1,44,000 or (40 × ₹3,600) = ₹25,600 (adverse)

Standard cost = (Standard cost per gang-hour × Standard gang-hours required for actual output) = (₹3,700 × 32) = ₹1,18,400

Standard Labour Cost (SLC) per Gang-hour

Composition of gang	*Number*	*Rate*	*TSC*
Highly skilled	30	₹80	₹2,400
Skilled	15	60	900
Semi-skilled	10	40	400
Total SLC per gang hour			3,700

Standard gang-hours required: (Actual output ÷ Standard output per gang-hour) = 1,600/50 (2000 ÷ 40) = 32

Actual Labour Cost (ALC) per Gang-hour

Particulars	*Number*	*AR*	*Total AC*
Highly skilled	40	₹70	₹2,800
Skilled	10	65	650
Semi-skilled	5	30	150
Total ALC per gang hour			3,600

2. *Wage rate variance:* (Standard rate – Actual rate) × Actual hours paid for

Highly skilled:	(₹80 – ₹70) × 40 × 40	=	₹16,000 (favourable)
Skilled:	(₹60 – ₹65) × 10 × 40	=	2,000 (adverse)
Semi-skilled:	(₹40 – ₹30) × 5 × 40	=	2,000 (favourable)
			16,000 (favourable)

3. *Labour Efficiency Variance*

	Standard composition of gang		*Standard gang hours for actual production*		*Total standard hours required*		*Actual hours paid for*		*Standard wage rate per hour*	*Labour efficiency variance*
Highly skilled	(30	×	32	=	960	–	1,600)	×	₹80	= 51,200 (adverse)
Skilled	(15	×	32	=	480	–	400)	×	₹60	= 4,800 (favourable)
Semi-skilled	(10	×	32	=	320	–	200)	×	₹40	= 4,800 (favourable)
										41,600 (adverse)

4. *Labour idle time variance:* (Idle hours × Standard rate)

Highly skilled:	(40 × 4) × ₹80	=	₹12,800 (adverse)
Skilled:	(10 × 4) × ₹60	=	2,400 (adverse)
Semi-skilled	(5 × 4) × ₹40	=	800 (adverse)
			16,000 (adverse)

5. *Labour mix variances* (Gang composition variance): (Standard mix used for actual hours used in the production – Actual mix of actual hours) × SWR

Actual hours used = (Total actual hours – Idle time)

Highly skilled	(40 × 40)	1,600
Skilled	(10 × 40)	400
Semi-skilled	(5 × 40)	200
		2,200
Less: Idle time	(55 × 4)	220
Total actual hours		1,980

[Standard mix of actual hours		–	*Actual mix]*	×	*SWR*	=	*Labour mix variance*
Highly skilled:	(6/11 × 1,980) = 1,080	–	1,440 (40 × 36)	×	₹80	=	₹28,800 (adverse)
Skilled:	(3/11 × 1,980) = 540	–	360 (10 × 36)	×	₹60	=	10,800 (favourable)
Semi-skilled:	(2/11 × 1,980) = 360	–	180 (5 × 36)	×	₹40	=	7,200 (favourable)
	1,980		1,980				10,800 (adverse)

Labour efficiency variance (revised): (Standard gang-hours required for actual production – Actual gang hours used in production) × Standard wage rate per gang-hour = (32 – 36) × ₹3,700 = ₹14,800 (adverse).

Summary:

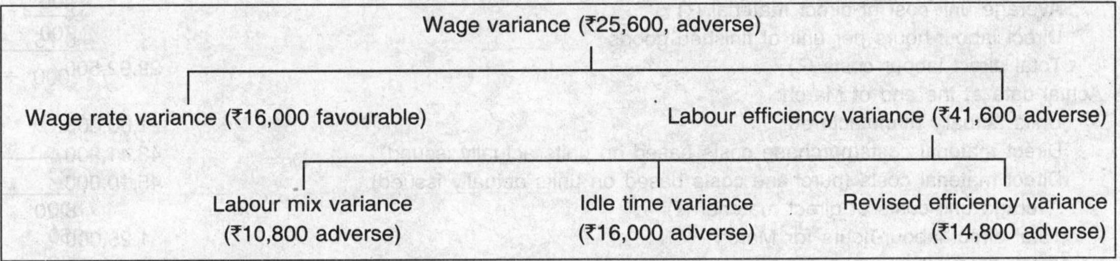

P.17.11 The Standard Supply Company Ltd produces a single article which goes through two operating departments. The standard cost card for this article indicated the following data:

	Standard time (hours)	*Standard rate*	*Total*
Department A	2.2	₹54	₹118.80
Department B	1.6	60	96.0

The production for the month of August is 1,000 units. The actual labour costs in the two departments were:

	Hours	*Cost*
Department A	2,000	₹1,29,080
Department B	1,800	1,02,000

Compute the labour cost, rate and efficiency variances.

SOLUTION

Department	*Standard time required to produce 1,000 units*	*Standard wage rate*	*Total standard wage bill*	*Actual time taken (hours)*	*Actual cost*
A	2,200 (1,000 × 2.2)	₹54	₹1,18,800	2,000	₹1,29,080
B	1,600 (1,000 × 1.6)	60	96,000	1,800	1,02,000
	3,800 (1,000 × 3.8)	56.5	2,14,800	3,800	2,31,080

Labour cost variance: (Total standard labour cost – Total actual labour cost) = (₹2,14,800 – ₹2,31,080) = ₹16,280 (adverse)

1. Labour rate variance

Department A : (₹54 × 2,000) – ₹1,29,080 = ₹21,080 (adverse)
Department B : (₹60 × 1,800) – ₹1,02,000 = 6,000 (favourable)
15,080 (adverse)

Labour efficiency variance

Department A : (2,200 hours – 2,000 hours) × ₹54 = ₹10,800 (favourable)
Department B : (1,600 hours – 1,800 hours) × ₹60 = 12,000 (adverse)
1,200 adverse

P.17.12 From the following data of ABC Ltd relating to the budgeted and actual performance for the month of March, compute direct material and direct labour cost variances.

Budgeted data for March:	
Units to be manufactured	1,50,000
Units of direct material required (based on standard rates)	4,95,000
Planned purchase for raw material (units)	5,40,000
Average unit cost of direct material (₹)	8
Direct labour-hours per unit of finished goods	0.75
Total direct labour costs (₹) ·	29,92,500
Actual data at the end of March:	
Units actually manufactured	1,60,000
Direct material costs(purchase costs based on units actually issued)	43,41,900
Direct material costs (purchase costs based on units actually issued)	45,10,000
Average unit costs of direct material (₹)	8.20
Total direct labour-hours for March	1,25,000
Total direct labour costs for March (₹)	33,75,000

SOLUTION

(i) *Material Cost Variance*

Actual material costs		₹43,41,900
Less standard material costs:		
Units actually manufactured	1,60,000	
(×) Direct raw material per unit (₹4,95,000/₹1,50,000)	× 3.3	
Total units of raw material	5,28,000	
(×) Standard unit cost of direct material	× ₹8	42,24,000
		1,17,900 (unfavourable)

(a) Material price variance (SR – AR) × AQ = (₹8 – ₹8.20) × 5,29,500 units* = ₹1,05,900 (unfavourable)
*5,29,500 units = ₹43,41,900/₹8.20 per unit

(b) Material usage variance (SQ – AQ) × AR = (5,28,000 – 5,29,500) × ₹8 = ₹12,000 (unfavourable)

(ii) *Labour Cost Variance*

Actual labour costs		₹33,75,000
Less standard labour costs:		
Units actually manufactured	1,60,000	
(x) Direct labour cost per unit	× ₹19.95	31,92,000
		1,83,000 (unfavourable)

(a) Labour rate variance: (SR – AR) × AH = (₹26.60@ × 1,25,000) – ₹33,75,000 = ₹50,000 (unfavourable) [@ ₹19.95 per unit/0.75 hour = ₹26.60 per hour]

(b) Labour efficiency variance: (SH – AH) × SR per hour = (1,60,000 × 0.75 = ₹1,20,000 hours – 1,25,000) × ₹26.6 = ₹1,33,000 (unfavourable)

P.17.13 A company manufacturing two products operates a standard costing system. The standard overhead content of each production in cost centre 101 is:

Product A, ₹240 (8 direct labour-hours @ ₹30 per hour)
Product B, ₹180 (6 direct labour-hours @ ₹30 per hour)

The rate of ₹30 per hour is arrived at as follows

Budgeted overheads, ₹57,000
Budgeted direct labour-hours, 1,900

For the month of October, the following data was recorded for cost centre 101:

Output of product A, 100 units
Output of product B, 200 units
No opening or closing stock
Actual direct labour-hours worked, 2,320
Actual overheads incurred, ₹64,000

1. You are required to calculate total overhead variance for the month of October.
2. Show its division into (a) Overhead expenditure variance, **(b)** Overhead capacity variance, (c) Overhead efficiency variance.

SOLUTION

1. *Total overhead variance:* (Actual overhead incurred – Standard overheads charged to production) = (₹64,000 – ₹60,000) = ₹4,000A

   Standard overheads charged to production:

Product A: (₹240 × 100)	=	₹24,000
B: (₹180 × 200)	=	36,000
		60,000

2. (a) *Overhead expenditure variance:* (Actual overheads – Budgeted overheads) = (₹64,000 – ₹57,000) = ₹7,000(A)

   (b) Overhead capacity variance: (NH – AH) × SOR = (1,900 – 2,320) × ₹30 = ₹12,600 (favourable)

   (c) Overhead efficiency variance: (Standard hours allowed for actual production – Actual hours used in production) × SOR = (2,000 hours* – 2,320 hours) × ₹30 = ₹9,600 (adverse)

   * Standard hours: Product A (100 units × 8) = 800
   B (200 units × 6) = 1,200
   2,000

P.17.14 The following data is given for Hypothetical Ltd.

Particulars	*Budget*	*Actuals*
Production (in units)	400	360
Man-hours to produce above	8000	7000
Variable overheads	₹1,00,000	₹91,500

The standard time to produce one unit of the product is 20 hours.

Calculate variable overhead variances, and give necessary journal entries to record the transactions.

SOLUTION

Basic data

1. Standard variable overhead rate (SVOR) per unit = ₹1,00,000/400 units = ₹250
2. Standard variable overhead rate (SVOR) per hour = ₹1,00,000/8,000 hours = ₹12.50
3. Variable overheads recovered = Actual output × SVOR per unit = 360 units × ₹250 = ₹90,000
4. Budgeted variable overhead = Actual hours worked × SVOR per hour = 7,000 hours × ₹12.50 = ₹87,500
5. Standard hours for actual output = Actual output × SH per unit = 360 units × 20 hours = 7,200 hours

Variances:

(i) *Variable overhead cost variance* = (Standard variable overheads – Actual variable overheads)
= ₹90,000 – ₹91,500 = ₹1,500 (adverse)

(ii) *Variable overhead expenditure variance*
= (Budgeted variable overheads at AH – Actual variable overheads)
= ₹87,500 – ₹91,500 = ₹4,000 (adverse)

(iii) *Variable overhead efficiency variance*
= (Standard hours for actual output – Actual hours) × SVOR per hour
= (7,200 – 7,000) × ₹12.50 = ₹2,500 (favourable)

Verification:

Variable overhead cost variance = ₹1,500 (adverse = Variable overhead efficiency variance + Variable overhead expenditure variance = ₹4,000 (adverse) + ₹2,500 (favourable)

Journal Entries

Variable overhead A/c	Dr	₹87,500	
Variable overhead expenditure variance	Dr	4,000	
To Creditors for expenses			₹91,500
Work-in-progress A/c	Dr	90,000	
To Variable overheads A/c			87,500
To Variable overhead efficiency variance A/c			2,500

P.17.15 Determine the various overhead variances from the following information

Actual hours worked, 6,200

Fixed overhead (8,00 hours normal capacity), ₹3,20,000

Actual production, 50 units

Standard man-hours per unit, 120

Standard overhead rate per standard man-hour, ₹100

Actual overheads incurred, ₹6,50,000

SOLUTION

Total overhead variance: (Actual overheads incurred – Standard overheads charged to production) = (₹6,50,000 – ₹6,00,000) = ₹50,000 (A)

Standard overheads = Units produced × Hours per unit × Standard overhead rate per hour)
= 50 × 120 × ₹100 = ₹6,00,000

1. *Two variance method*

(a) Expenditure variance = (Actual overheads – Budgeted overheads at standard hours)
= (₹6,50,000 – ₹6,80,000) = ₹30,000 (favourable)

Budgeted overheads:

Fixed overheads	₹3,20,000
Add variance overheads [6,000 standard hours (x) ₹60 standard variable overhead rate (₹100 TSOR – ₹40 SFOR, that is, ₹3,20,000 ÷ 8,000)]	3,60,000
	6,80,000

(b) Volume variance: (NH – SH) × SFOR per hour = (8,000 hours – 6,000 hours) × ₹40 = ₹80,000 (adverse)

2. *Three-variance method*

(a) Spending variance: (Actual overheads incurred – Budgeted overheads at actual hours) = (₹6,50,000 – ₹6,92,000) = ₹42,000 (favourable)

Budgeted overheads:

Fixed overheads	₹3,20,000
Plus variable overheads (6,200 hours × ₹60)	3,72,000
	6,92,000

(b) Efficiency variance: (SH – AH) × SOR per hour = (6,000 hours – 6,200 hours) × ₹100 = ₹20,000 (adverse)

(c) Capacity variance: (NH – AH) × SFOR per hour = (8,000 hours – 6,200 hours) × ₹40 = ₹72,000 (adverse).

3. *Four-variance method*:

(i) and **(iiii)** are the same as in the three-variance method. Efficiency variance will be split up into two sub-parts:

(a) Fixed overhead efficiency variance = (SH – AH) × SFOR = (6,000 hours – 6,200 hours) × ₹40 = ₹8,000 (adverse)

(b) Variable overhead efficiency variance = (SH – AH) × SVOR = (6,000 hours – 6,200 hours) × ₹60 = ₹12,000 (adverse)

P.17.16 XYZ Ltd forecasts its overhead expenditure for a period as under.

₹3,00,000 for 10,000 hours

₹2,75,000 for 9,000 hours

₹2,50,000 for 8,000 hours

The normal volume of activity is 10,000 hours. During a period, 8,750 hours were utilised for a total overhead expenditure of ₹2,87,500, of which fixed overheads totalled ₹52,500.

The utilisation of labour-hours should have been less by 5 per cent. How will you analyse the overhead variance?

Solution

1. Determination of variable overhead rate per hour (SVOR) = Change in overhead expenditure ÷ Change in hours = [₹50,000 (₹3,00,000 – ₹2,50,000)] ÷ 2,000 hours (10,000 – 8,000)] = ₹25 per hour

2. Fixed overheads

Total overheads at 10,000 hours	₹3,00,000
Less variable overheads (10,000 × ₹2.50)	2,50,000
Fixed overheads at normal capacity	50,000

3. Fixed overhead rate per hour (SFOR) = (₹50,000 ÷ 10,000 hours) = ₹5

4. Total overhead rate per hour (TSOR) = ₹30 (₹25 + ₹5)

Total overhead variance = Actual overheads incurred – Standard overheads charged to production = ₹2,87,500 – ₹2,49,375 = ₹38,125 (adverse)

Standard overheads:

Actual hours	8,750
Less 5% (more hours taken)	437.50
Standard hours	8,312.50
(x) TSOR per hour	₹30
	2,49,375

Four-variance method:

1. *Spending variance:* (Actual overheads incurred – Budgeted overheads at actual hours)
   = (₹2,87,500 – ₹2,68,750) = ₹18,750 (adverse)

   Budgeted overheads:

Fixed overheads	₹50,000
Plus variable overheads (8,750 hours × ₹25)	2,18,750
	2,68,750

2. *Fixed overhead efficiency variance:* (SH – AH) × SFOR = (8,312.5 hours – 8,750 hours) × ₹5 = ₹2,187.50 (adverse)
3. *Variable overhead efficiency variance:* (SH – AH) × SVOR = (8,312.5 hours – 8,750 hours) × ₹25 = ₹10,937.50 (adverse)
4. *Capacity variance:* (NH – AH) × SFOR = (10,000 hours – 8,750 hours) × ₹5 = ₹6,250 (adverse)

The spending variance can be bifurcated into two sub-variances:

1. **(a)** *Fixed overhead spending variance:* (₹52,500 – ₹50,000) = ₹2,500 (adverse)
   (b) *Variable overhead spending variance:* (₹2,35,000 – ₹2,18,750) = ₹16,250 (adverse)

P.17.17 Bharat Manufacturing Ltd manufactures the product DRYDRAP in standard batches of 100 units. A standard cost system is used. The standard costs for a batch are:

Raw materials, 60 kgs @ ₹5	₹300
Direct labour, 40 hours @ ₹25 per hour	1,000
Factory overhead, 40 hours @ ₹20 per hour	800
Total standard cost per batch for 100 units	2,100

Production for March amounted to 210 batches.

Relevant data are:

Normal capacity per month: 24,000 units
Direct labour cost (8,600 hours): ₹2,10,700
Actual factory overhead: ₹1,73,250
Fixed overhead for standard output: ₹72,000

The management has noted that actual costs per batch deviate from standard costs. Make a variance analysis of the factory overheads by using the two-variance, three-variance and four-variance methods for overheads.

Solution

Factory overhead variance: (Actual overheads costs – Standard overhead costs charged to production) = (₹1,73,250 – ₹1,68,000) = ₹5,250 (adverse)

Standard overhead costs charged to production: (Actual batches produced × Standard overhead cost per batch) = (210 × ₹800) = ₹1,68,000

Two-variance method:

1. *Controllable variance:* (Actual overhead costs – Budgeted overhead costs at actual production) = (₹1,73,250 – ₹1,77,000) = ₹3,750 (favourable)

Budgeted overhead costs:	Fixed overhead	₹72,000
	+ Variable overhead	1,05,000*
		1,77,000

   (Actual batches produced × Standard variable overhead cost per batch: 210 × ₹500)

*Factory overhead rate per batch	₹800
Less fixed factory overhead rate (₹72,000 ÷ 240)	300
Variable factory overhead rate	500

2. *Volume variance:* (Normal capacity in batches – Actual production in batches) = (240 – 210) × ₹300 = ₹9,000 (A)

Controllable variance + Volume variance = Total variance = ₹3,750F + ₹9,000 A = ₹5,250 (adverse)

Three-variance method:

1. *Spending variance:* (Actual overhead costs – Budgeted overhead costs at actual hours) = (₹1,73,250 – ₹1,79,500) = ₹6,250 (favourable)

Budgeted overhead costs:

Fixed overhead	₹72,000
+ Variable overhead	1,07,500*
	1,79,500

*(Actual hours used × Standard variable overhead rate per hour) = (8,600 × ₹12.50) = ₹1,07,500

2. *Efficiency variance:* (Actual batch production × Standard hours per batch) – (Actual hours worked × (Standard overhead rater per hours) = [(210 × 40) – 8,600] × ₹20 = 200 × ₹20 = ₹4,000 (adverse)
3. *Capacity variance:* (Normal capacity in hours – Actual hours worked) × Fixed standard overhead rate per hour = [9,600 (240 batches × 40) – 8,600] × ₹7.5 = 1,000 × ₹7.5 = ₹7,500 (adverse)

Confirmation: ₹6,250F + ₹4,000A + ₹7,500A = ₹5,250 (adverse)

Four-variance method:

Spending variance and capacity variance remain unchanged. Efficiency variance will be broken up into two parts: Fixed factory overhead efficiency variance, and Variable factory overhead efficiency variance.

1. *Fixed factory overhead efficiency variance:* (Actual batch production × Standard hours per batch) – (Actual hours worked × Fixed standard overhead rate per hour) = (210 × 40 – 8,600) × ₹7.5 = ₹1,500 (adverse)
2. *Variable factory overhead efficiency variance:* 200 × ₹12.5 = ₹2,500 (adverse)

₹6,250F + ₹1,500A + ₹2,500A + ₹7,500A = ₹5,250 A

P.17.18 From the following information compute: (i) Spending variance, (ii) Idle capacity variance, (iii) Efficiency variance.

Normal capacity, 12,000 hours

Fixed expenses, ₹10,00,000

Variable expenses (at normal capacity), ₹14,00,000

The plant worked for 11,280 actual hours, executing work for which 11,400 hours were allowed. Actual factory overhead expenses amounted to ₹23,17,500.

SOLUTION

(i) *Spending variance:* (Actual overhead costs – Budgeted overhead costs at actual hours) = (₹23,17,500 – ₹23,16,000) = ₹1,500 (adverse)

Budgeted overhead costs:

Fixed expenses	₹10,00,000
+ Variable expenses (11,280 hours × ₹1,400/12)	13,16,000
	23,16,000

(ii) *Idle capacity variance:* (Normal capacity in hours – Actual hours worked) × Standard fixed overhead rate per hour = (12,000 – 11,280) × ₹1,000/12 = ₹60,000 (adverse)

(iii) *Efficiency variance:* $(SH_s - AH_s)$ × SOR = (11,400 – 11,280) × ₹200 = ₹24,000 F

Total overhead variance = ₹1,500A + ₹60,000 A + ₹24,000 F = ₹37,500 (adverse)

Confirmation:

Factory overhead variance = (Actual overhead costs – Standard overhead cost charged to production)
= [₹23,17,500 – ₹22,80,000 or (11,400 standard hours × ₹200)]
= ₹37,500 (adverse).

P.17.19 For the month of April, you are given the following figures for a manufacturing firm:

Particulars	*Standard*	*Actual*
Number of units produced	15,000	8,000
Capacity (hours)	30,000	17,500
Variable overheads	₹30,00,000	₹15,00,000
Fixed overheads	45,00,000	46,30,000

Calculate expenditure variance and volume variance.

SOLUTION

SOR (per unit) = Total overheads/Units produced = ₹75,00,000/15,000 = ₹500
SOR (per hour) = Total overheads/Capacity hours = ₹75,00,000/30,000 = ₹250
Fixed SOR per unit = ₹45,00,000 ÷ 15,000 units = ₹300
Fixed SOR per hour = ₹45,00,000 ÷ 30,000 hours = 150
Variable SOR per unit = ₹30,00,000 ÷ 15,000 units = 200
Variable SOR per hour = ₹30,00,000 ÷ 30,000 hours = 100

Expenditure variance: (Actual overhead costs – Budgeted overhead costs at SH) = (₹61,30,000 – ₹61,00,000) = ₹30,000 (adverse)

Budgeted overhead costs:

Fixed overheads	₹45,00,000
Variable overheads (16,000 standard hours × ₹100)	16,00,000
	61,00,000

Volume variance: (Normal capacity in hours – Standard hours allowed for actual production) × Standard fixed overhead rate per hour = (30,000 – 16,000) × ₹150 = ₹21,00,000 (adverse)

Total overhead variance: ₹30,000 A + ₹21,00,000 A = ₹21,30,000 (adverse)

Confirmation: (Actual overhead costs – Standard overhead costs charged to production) = ₹61,30,000 – ₹40,00,000 = ₹21,30,000 (adverse)

Alternatively, the problem can be solved taking units produced as the basis for standard cost. For instance, *Expenditure variance:* (Actual overhead costs – Budgeted overhead costs, at actual production) = ₹61,30,000 – ₹61,00,000 = ₹30,000 (adverse).

Likewise, Volume variance would be, [normal capacity (in units) – Actual production] × Standard fixed overhead rate per unit = (15,000 – 8,000) × ₹300 = ₹21,00,000 (adverse).

P.17.20 A company's annual expenditure budget for the year was set at ₹48,00,000. Accordingly, monthly budget was taken at ₹4,00,000. Standard output for the year, on a 300 working days basis, was 3,00,000 units, and standard overhead recovery rate was fixed on this basis.

In February, there were 24 working days (28 days, less 4 Sunday). During this month production achieved was 23,000 units. Actual expenses in February totalled ₹4,10,000.

Calculate total overhead variance, budget, efficiency, volume and calendar variances.

SOLUTION

Summary of Overhead Expenditure for February (Budgeted and Actual)

	Budgeted	*Actual*
Overhead expenditure	₹4,00,000	₹4,10,000
Working days	25	24
Production	25,000	23,000

Overhead recovery rate = ₹16 per unit = ₹48,00,000/3,00,000 units

Total overhead variance: (Actual overhead cost incurred – Standard overhead charged to production) = ₹4,10,000 – (23,000 × ₹16) = ₹42,000 (adverse)

Budget variance: (Actual overhead cost – Budgeted overhead costs) = ₹4,10,000 – ₹4,00,000 = ₹10,000 (adverse)

Volume variance: (Budgeted output – Actual output) × SOR per unit = (25,000 – 23,000) × ₹16 = ₹32,000 (adverse)

Volume variance has two components:

Efficiency variance: [(Budgeted output per day × Actual working days) – Actual output] × SOR per unit (1,000 × 24 = 24,000 – 23,000) × ₹16 = ₹16,000 (adverse)

Calendar variance: (Number of scheduled working days – Actual working days) × SOR per day = (25 – 24) × ₹16,000 = ₹16,000 (adverse)

P.17.21 Eastern Manufacturers Ltd operates a standard costing system. In connection with the weekly cost report for the process X, you have been informed that:

1. The standard costs per hour of the process, based on a normal week of 40 hours work, are:

Wages	₹90
Variable expenses	25
Fixed expenses	125
	240

Standard output in units per hour, 20.

2. The following information has been recorded in respect of the process for one week:

Hours worked	36
Non-productive hours (awaiting work)	4
Total hours paid for	40
Output (units)	850
Actual wages paid	₹3,700
Actual variable expenses	1,200
Actual fixed expenses	5,000

You are required to compute the variances relating to process X for the week.

SOLUTION

1. *Labour cost variance:* (Actual labour costs – Standard labour costs charged to production) = (₹3,700 – ₹3,825) = ₹125 F

Standard labour cost: (Standard hours required for actual production × Standard wages rate per hour) = (42.5 hours) or (850 units/20) × ₹90 = ₹3,825

(a) Labour rate variance: (Standard wage rate per hour – Actual wage rate per hour) × Actual hours worked = (₹90 – ₹92.50) × 40 hours = ₹100 (adverse)

(b) Idle time variance: (Idle hours/non-productive hours) × Standard wage rate per hour) = 4 hours × ₹90 = ₹360 (adverse)

(c) Labour efficiency variance: [(Actual units produced × Standard hours per unit) – Actual hours worked] × Standard wage rate = [(850 × 1/20) – 36] × ₹90 = ₹585 F

Total labour cost variance: ₹100 A + ₹360 A + ₹585 F = ₹125 F

2. *Factory overhead variance:* (Actual overhead costs – Standard overhead costs charged to production) = [₹6,200 – ₹6,375 (₹7.5 × 850 units)] = ₹175 (favourable)

Two-variance method:

(a) Controllable variance: (Actual overhead costs – Budgeted overhead costs at standard hours) = (₹6,200 – ₹6,062.50) = ₹137.50 (adverse)

Budgeted overhead costs:

Fixed expenses (40 hours × ₹125)	=	₹5,000
Variable expenses (42.5 hours × ₹25)	=	1,062.50
		6,062.50

(b) Volume variance: (Normal capacity in hours – Standard hours) × Fixed overhead rate per hour (40 – 42.5) × ₹125 = ₹312.50 F

Total overhead variance = ₹137.50 A + ₹312.50 F = ₹175 (favourable)

P.17.22 From the following data, compute the following: (1) Total overhead variance, (2) Overhead expenditure variance, (3) Overhead volume variance, (4) Overhead calendar variance, (5) Overhead capacity variance, and (6) Overhead efficiency variance.

Particualrs		*Budgeted*		*Actual*
Production (units)		10,000		12,000
Production (hours)		5,000		6,100
Number of days		25		27
Overhead expenses:				
Fixed	₹3,00,000		₹3,70,000	
Variable	1,00,000	₹4,00,000	1,20,000	₹4,90,000

SOLUTION

1. *Total overhead variance:* (Actual overheads incurred – Standard overheads charged to production) = (₹4,90,000 – ₹4,80,000) = ₹10,000 (adverse)

   SOR:

Standard fixed overhead rate (₹3,00,000 ÷ 10,000 units)	₹30
+ Standard variable overhead rate (₹1,00,000 ÷ 10,000 units)	10
Standard overhead rate per unit	40
Standard overheads (12,000 units)	₹4,80,000
Standard overhead rate per hour (₹60 + ₹20)	80

2. *Overhead expenditure variance:* (Actual overheads incurred – Budgeted overheads at standard hours) = (₹4,90,000 – 4,20,000) = ₹70,000 (adverse)

   Budgeted overheads:

Fixed overheads	₹3,00,000
Plus variable overheads (6,000 standard hours × ₹20, SVOR per hour)	1,20,000
	4,20,000

3. *Overhead volume variance:* (Normal capacity in hours – Standard hours) × SFOR per hour = (5,000 hours – 6,000 hours) × ₹60 = ₹60,000 (favourable)
4. *Overhead calendar variance:* (Budgeted working days – Actual working days) × SFOR per day = (25-27) × ₹12,000, that is, (₹3,00,000 ÷ 25 days) = ₹24,000 (favourable)
5. *Overhead capacity variance:* (Normal capacity in hours on the basis of actual working days – Actual hours used) × SFOR per hour = (200 hours per day × 27 = 5,400 hours – 6,100 hours) × ₹60 = ₹42,000 (favourable)
6. *Overhead efficiency variance:* (SH – AH) × SOR per hour = (6,000 hours – 6,100 hours) × ₹60 = ₹6,000 (adverse)

P. 17.23 A chemical company produces a chemical which has a standard cost per 50 litres as follows:

Material	
15 litres of A @ ₹20	₹300
35 litres of B @ ₹2.5	87.50
Labour	
2 hours @ ₹20	40
Factory overhead	
Variable, 2 hours @ ₹75	150
Fixed, 2 hours @ ₹50	100
	677.50

Actual results for the current year are as follows:

Production completed	:	5,00,000 litres
Direct labour-hours	:	21,000 @ ₹22 per hour
Material usage	:	1,60,000 litres of A @ ₹20 per litre and 3,60,000 litres of B @ ₹2.5 per litre
Variable factory overhead	:	₹16,50,000
Fixed factory overhead	:	₹13,00,000
Normal capacity		25,000 direct labour-hours

Inventory data:

Opening: 25,000 litres, 100 per cent complete as to materials and 50 per cent complete as to labour and overheads.

Closing: 40,000 litres, 100 per cent complete as to materials, and 50 per cent complete as to labour and overheads.

Determine and analyse the following: (1) Material cost variances (2) Labour cost variances (3) Overhead cost variances.

SOLUTION

1. *Materials cost variances:* (Standard cost of 5,15,000 litres – Actual cost of 5,15,000 litres) = (₹39,91,250 – ₹41,00,000) = ₹1,08,750 (adverse)

Standard cost: (₹387.50 ÷ 50 litres = ₹7.75) × 5,15,000 litres	₹39,91,250
Actual cost:	
1,60,000 litres of A (×) ₹20	32,00,000
3,60,000 litres of B (×) ₹2.50	9,00,000
	41,00,000

5,15,000 litres = Production completed + Closing stock – Opening stock = 5,00,000 litres + 40,000 litres – 25,000 litres

(a) Materials price variance: = Nil

(b) Materials mix variance: (RSQ – AQ) × SR

Material A:	1,56,000 litres – 1,60,000] × ₹20	=	₹80,000 (adverse)
B:	3,64,000 litres – 3,60,000] × ₹2.50	=	10,000 (favourable)
			70,000 (adverse)

(c) Material yield variance: (SY – AY) × SMC per unit = (5,20,000 litres – 5,15,000) × ₹7.75 = ₹38,750 (adverse)

2. *Labour cost variance:* (Standard labour cost of 5,07,500 litres – Actual labour cost of 5,07,500 litres) = (₹4,06,000 – ₹4,62,000) = ₹56,000 (adverse)

Standard labour cost: (₹40 ÷ 50) × 5,07,500 litres = ₹4,06,000

(a) Labour rate variance: (SR – AR) × AH = (₹20 – ₹22) × 21,000 = ₹42,000 (adverse)

(b) Labour efficiency variance: (SH – AH) × SR = (20,300 hours – 21,000 hours) × ₹20 = ₹14,000 (adverse)

Standard hours = (5,07,500 ÷ 25) × 2 = 20,300 hours; 5,07,500 litres = 5,00,000 litres + 20,000 litres Closing, (0.50 × 40,000) – 12,500 litres, opening (0.50 × 25,000)

3. *Overhead cost variance:* (Actual overheads incurred – Standard overheads of 5,07,500 litres) = (₹29,50,000 – ₹25,37,500) = ₹4,12,500 (adverse)

Standard overheads: (₹250 ÷ 50) × 5,07,500 = ₹25,37,500

(a) Spending variance: (Actual overheads – Budgeted overhead at AH) = ₹29,50,000 – ₹28,25,000 = ₹1,25,000 (adverse)

Budgeted overheads:

Fixed overheads (25,000 hours × ₹50) (Assuming normal capacity as the basis of absorption of fixed overheads)	₹12,50,000
Plus variable overheads (21,000 hours × ₹75)	15,75,000
	28,25,000

(b) Variable overheads efficiency variance: (SH – AH) × SVOR = (20,300 hours – 21,000 hours) × ₹75 = ₹52,500 (adverse)

(c) Fixed overheads efficiency variance: (SH – AH) × SFOR = (20,300 hours – 21,000 hours) × ₹50 = ₹35,000 (adverse)

(d) Capacity variance: (NH – AH) × SFOR = (25,000 hours – 21,000 hours) × ₹50 = ₹2,00,000 (adverse)

P. 17.24 The Amindon Company Ltd produces a product with the following standard cost per unit:

Material	2 kgs at ₹50	₹100
Labour	5 hours at ₹20	100
Overheads	5 hours at ₹40	200
		400

The overhead rate for the year was determined on the basis of the following data:

Fixed overheads	₹25,00,000
Variable overheads	75,00,000
Expected output (units)	5,00,000

Actual data for the year was as follows:

1. Purchases 1,00,000 kgs of material at ₹49 per kg.
2. Labour was obtained at a price of ₹31 per hour.
3. Production completed, 37,500 units.
4. Labour-hours, 1,90,000.
5. Material used, 90,000 kgs.
6. Fixed overheads, ₹25,00,000.
7. Variable overheads, ₹58,90,000.

Inventories data: Opening, 1,000 units, 50 per cent complete as to material, labour and overhead.
Closing, 4,000 units, 75 per cent complete as to material, labour and overhead.

REQUIRED

1. Calculate material price variance at the point of purchase and issue,
2. Calculate labour variances,
3. Calculate fixed factory overhead variances, and
4. Calculate variable factory overheads variances.

SOLUTION

1.(a) *Material purchase price variance:* (SR – AR) × AQ purchased = (₹50 – ₹49) × 1,00,000 kgs = ₹1,00,000 (favourable)

(b) *Material price variance* (at the time of issue): (SR – AR) × AQ used = (₹50 – ₹49) × 90,000 kgs = ₹90,000 (favourable)

2. *Labour variance:*

Labour cost variance = (Standard labour cost of 40,000 units* – Actual labour cost) = [₹40,00,000 – 58,90,000] = ₹18,90,000 (adverse)

*Units produced during the year:

Production completed	37,500
Plus closing inventory (4,000 × 0.75)	3,000
Less opening (1,000 × 0.50)	500
	40,000

(a) Labour rate variance: (SR – AR) × AH = (₹20 – ₹31) × 1,90,000 = ₹20,90,000 (adverse)

(b) Labour efficiency variance: (SH – AH) × SR = [2,00,000 hours or (40,000 × 5) – 1,90,000 hours] × ₹20 = ₹2,00,000 (favourable)

3. *Fixed factory overhead variance:* (Actual fixed overhead incurred – Standard fixed overhead charged to production) = [₹25,00,000 – (40,000 units × ₹50, SFOR)] = ₹5,00,000 (adverse)

SFOR = Fixed overheads/Expected output = ₹25,00,000/50,000 units = ₹50 per unit
SFOR = ₹25,00,000/2,50,000 hours (50,000 × 5) = ₹10 per hour

(a) Spending variance: (Actual overheads – Budgeted overheads) = (₹25,00,000 – ₹25,00,000) = Nil
(b) Efficiency variance (SH – AH) × SOFR per hour = (2,00,000 hours – 1,90,000 hours) × ₹10
= ₹1,00,000 (favourable)
(c) Capacity variance: (NH – AH) × SFOR per hour = (2,50,000 hours – 1,90,000 hours) × ₹10
= ₹6,00,000 (adverse)

4. *Variable factory overheads variance:* (Actual variable overheads incurred – Standard variable overheads charged to production of 40,000 units) = ₹58,90,000 – (40,000 × ₹150, SVOR) = ₹1,10,000 (favourable)
SVOR = ₹75,00,000 ÷ 50,000 units = ₹150 per unit
SVOR = ₹75,00,000 ÷ 2,50,000 hours = ₹30 per hour

(i) Spending variance: (Actual variable overheads – Budgeted variable overheads at actual hours) = ₹58,90,000 – 57,00,000 = ₹1,90,000 (adverse)
(ii) Efficiency variance: (SH – AH) × SVOR (2,00,000 hours – 1,90,000 hours) × ₹30 = ₹3,00,000 (favourable)

REVIEW QUESTIONS

RQ.17.1 Indicate whether the following statements are true or false.

(i) Material price variance is an uncontrollable variance.
(ii) The purchase manager is held accountable for unfavourable material usage variance.
(iii) Material mix variance measures whether the proportion of total actual quantity of materials used is in conformity with the standard proportion specified.
(iv) Material mix variance is controllable variance.
(v) Labour efficiency variance is favourable when actual hours used are higher than standard hours-allowed.
(vi) Labour rate variance is the product of difference in wage rates (standard and actual) and total standard hours.
(vii) Normal loss of materials is considered while setting standard related to material quantity to be used in producing a product.
(viii) A product requires use of materials X, Y and Z in making a product (to be used in a standard proportion). Assume material quantity various is favourable, it implies material mix sub-variance for each material X, Y and Z will also be favourable.
(ix) Unfavourable fixed overhead spending variance implies that the firm is not working upto its full capacity.
(x) Variable overhead efficiency variance is the product of difference in hours (actual and standard) and standard variable overhead rate per hour.

[Answers: (i) True, (ii) False, (iii) True, (iv) False, (v) False, (vi) False, (vii) True, (viii) False, (ix) False, (x) True.]

RQ.17.2 Fill in the following blanks (in same cases choices are provided).

(i) Idle time variance is always ____________ variance (favourable/unfavourable).
(ii) For unfavourable material mix variance ____________ manager is held accountable.
(iii) Management should focus more on ____________ variances (efficiency/rate).
(iv) Efficiency variances by and large are ____________ variances (controllable/uncontrollable).
(v) If variable overhead efficiency is favourable, it also implies that ____________ will also be favourable.
(vi) Volume variance is sub-divided into fixed overhead efficiency variance and ____________.
(vii) Difference in quantity of material used is multiplied by ____________ to determine material quantity variance (actual price/standard price).
(viii) Rate variances, by and large, are ____________ variances (controllable/uncontrollable).
(ix) If actual labour hours used are more than normal capacity hours, capacity variance is said to be ____________. (favourable/unfavourable).
(x) Material yield variance is ____________ when standard yield is higher than actual yield (favourable/unfavouralbe).

[Answers: (i) unfavourable, (ii) production, (iii) efficiency, (iv) controllable, (v) labour efficiency and fixed overhead efficiency variances, (vi) capacity variance, (vii) standard price, (viii) uncontrollable, (ix) favourable, (x) unfavourable.]

RQ.17.3 What is the significance of the term "variance" relating to standard costing? What types of variances are computed for **(a)** materials, **(b)** labour, and **(c)** factory overheads?

RQ.17.4 What are the differences between two-variance and three-variance analysis of indirect manufacturing costs? What are the variances computed in each case, and how are they calculated?

RQ.17.5 "The presence of under-absorbed overheads reflects operating inefficiency." Discuss.

RQ.17.6 Distinguish between:

1. Labour rate variance and Labour efficiency variance.
2. Variable overheads and Fixed overheads.
3. Materials price variance and Materials usage variance.

RQ.17.7 State the significance and the method of computing the following:

1. Materials mix variance.
2. Variable overhead efficiency variance.
3. Fixed overhead efficiency variance.

RQ.17.8 From the following figures given to you, calculate material variances:

Particulars	*Material X*	*Material Y*
Standard price per kg.	₹240	₹320
Actual price paid per kg.	227.50	308
Actual quantity (kgs.)	16	13

The standard production for the period is 400 units, for which the standard quantity allowances for material are 30 kgs. of X and 25 kgs. of Y. Actual production for the period is 192 units.

RQ.17.9 A company produces a certain chemical, the standard material cost being:

40 per cent of material *X* at ₹20 per kg.

60 per cent of material *Y* at ₹30 per kg.

A standard loss of 10 per cent is expected in production. During one month, 171 kgs. of chemical was produced from the use of 90 kgs. of material *X* at ₹18 per kg. and 110 kgs. of material *Y* at ₹34 per kg. Calculate the following variances for the month: (i) materials price variance, (ii) materials mix variance, and (iii) materials yield variance.

RQ.17.10 A chemical company produces a petro-product, using the following proportion of material:

Particulars	*(kgs.)*	*Cost per kg.*	*Amount*
Material A	50	₹50	₹2,500
Material B	40	60	2,400
Material C	60	30	1,800
	150		6,700
Standard shrinkage ($33\frac{1}{3}$%)	50	—	—
Net weight and costs	100	67	6,700

A recent production-run yielding 100 kgs. output required an input of:

Particulars	*(kgs.)*	*Per kgs.*	*Amount*
Material A	40	₹52	₹2,080
Material B	55	60	3,300
Material C	65	26	1,690
	160		7,070

Calculate materials price, mix, and yield variances.

RQ.17.11 The Standard Supply Company Ltd. produces a single article, which goes through two operating departments. The standard card for this article indicated the following data:

	Standard time (hours)	*Standard rate*	*Total*
Department A	2.2	₹54	₹118.80
Department B	1.6	60	96

The production for the month of August is 1,000 units. The actual labour costs in the two departments were:

	Hours	*Cost*
Department A	2,000	₹1,29,080
Department B	1,800	1,02,000

What are the labour cost and labour efficiency variances?

RQ.17.12 Using the following information, calculate each of the three labour variances for each department:

	Department X	*Department Y*
Gross wages (direct)	₹2,80,800	₹1,93,700
Standard hours worked	8,640	6,015
Standard rate per hour	30	34
Actual hours worked	8,200	6,395

RQ.17.13 A gang of workers normally consists of 10 skilled, 5 semi-skilled and 5 unskilled, paid at standard hourly rates of ₹40, ₹30 and ₹20, respectively. In a normal working week of 40 hours, the gang is expected to produce 1,000 units of output.

In a certain week, the gang consisted of 13 skilled, 4 semi-skilled and 3 unskilled, 72 hours were worked, actual wages paid amounted to ₹25,000, and 1,000 units of output were produced.

Present the information in respect of labour cost variance arising during this period.

RQ.17.14 The standard overhead rate per unit of product is as follows: Variable, ₹20 + Fixed (₹30,000 ÷ 3,000), ₹100 = ₹120.

Standard time for producing each unit of output is 10 hours. During a period, the following actual data is available:

Hours worked, 27,000; Output, 2,600 units.

Overheads = Variable, ₹50,000 + Fixed, ₹2,80,000 = ₹3,30,000.

Calculate different overheads variances, including efficiency variance and capacity variance.

RQ.17.15 From the following information, compute the various variances:

Standard:	
Materials quantity	1 kg per unit
Materials price	₹14 per kg
Direct labour-hours	1.5 hours per unit
Labour rate	₹30 per unit
Overheads	₹10 per standard direct labour-hour
Capacity	5,000 units
Actual:	
Materials purchased	10,000 kgs
Material price	₹15 per kg
Materials used	5,400 kgs
Direct labour hours	8,000
Labour rate	₹3,150 per hour
Overheads	₹88,000
Units produced	5,000

RQ.17.16 Calculate overhead variances for the following data.

Items	*Budgeted*	*Actual*
Number of working days	20	22
Man-hours per day	8,000	8,400
Output per man-hour (units)	1	0.9
Overhead cost	₹16,00,000	₹16,80,000

RQ.17.17 In Department X, the following data is submitted for the week ended February 20:

Standard output for 40 hours per week (units)	1,400
Standard fixed overhead	₹14,000
Actual output (units)	1,200
Actual hours worked	32
Actual fixed overhead	₹15,000

Calculate the relevant overhead variance.

RQ.17.18 From the following data for a factory for the month of January, compute overhead variances under the four-way analysis:

	Standard	*Actual*
Number of units produced	15,000	8,000
Capacity (hours)	30,000	17,000
Variable overheads	₹3,00,000	₹1,55,000
Fixed overheads	4,50,000	4,60,000

ANSWERS

[Comprehensive solutions to all numerical review questions are available on the companion website: http://www.mhhe.com/khan_jain_cost2e]

17.8 MCV, ₹348 U, MPV, ₹356 F, MUV, ₹718.55 U, MMV, ₹14.54 F.

17.9 **(a)** ₹260 U,
(b) ₹100 F,
(c) ₹260 U,

17.10 MPV, ₹180 F, MMV, ₹103.30 U, MYV, ₹446.90 U.

17.11 LCV, ₹16,280 U, LRV, ₹15,080 U, LEV, ₹1,200.

17.12 Department X (Labour variances): Cost, ₹21,600 U, Rate, ₹34,800 U, Efficiency, ₹13,200 F. Department Y: Cost, ₹10,810 F, Rate, ₹23,730 F, Efficiency, ₹12,920 U.

17.13 TLCV = ₹1,000 F, LEV = ₹24,400 U (LMSV ₹3,600 U + LESV ₹20,800 U), LRV = ₹25,400 F.

17.14 **(a)** TOCV = ₹18,000 U;
(b) VOSV = ₹4,000 F,
VOEV = ₹2,000 U, and
TVOCV = ₹2,000 F
(c) FOSV = ₹20,000 F,
FOEV = ₹10,000 U, CV ₹ 30,000 U = TFOCV ₹20,000 U

17.15 Material: Cost variance, ₹11,000 U, MPV, ₹5,400 U, MUV, ₹5,600 U; Labour: Cost variance, ₹27,000 U, LRV, ₹12,000 U, LEV, ₹15,000 U; Overhead: Cost variance, ₹13,000 U, Spending variance, ₹8,000 U, Efficiency variance, ₹5,000 U.

17.16 Total overhead variance, ₹16,800 U, spending, ₹80,000 U, volume, ₹63,200 F (Calendar ₹16,000 F, Efficiency, ₹1,84,800 U, Capacity, ₹88,000 F).

17.17 Total fixed overhead variance, ₹3,000 U: Spending, ₹1,000 U, Efficiency, ₹800 F, Capacity, ₹2800 U.

17.18 Total overhead variance, ₹2,15,000 U: Spending, ₹5,000 F, Variance efficiency, ₹10,000 U, Fixed efficiency, ₹15,000 U, Capacity, ₹1,95,000 U.

18 Chapter

Variance Analysis: Revenue and Profit Variances

Learning Objectives

1. Discuss sales variances and their causes
2. Illustrate the various profit variances
3. Understand reconciliation of actual profit and budgeted profit
4. Explain the method of reporting variances
5. Examine the methods for disposing off variances

INTRODUCTION

The preceding chapter has dealt with the determination and analysis of variances relating to three major elements of manufacturing cost, namely, materials, labour and factory overheads. Outside the manufacturing areas, standard costs and variances are usually not incorporated in the accounts, but are determined by supplemental analysis.[1] For this reason, variances relating to selling and administrative costs were not discussed in the preceding chapter. In this chapter, attention is directed to the determination and analysis of revenue variances. Section 1 deals with sales variances, followed by profit variances. A comprehensive illustration has been attempted to cover all revenue and expenses variances, to provide a summary to management, of all variances responsible for deviations in actual profit as compared to budgeted profit. To be more specific, effort will be made to reconcile actual profit with budgeted profit. Sections 2 and 3 deal with variance reporting and disposition of variances respectively. The main points are summarised in the last Section.

SALES VARIANCES

The principal sales variances are sales revenue variances. They are divided into **(a)** Sales price variance, **(b)** Sale volume variance sub-divided into **(i)** Sales mix sub-variance, and **(ii)** Sale volume sub-variance.

Sales revenue variance is the difference between the standard sale value and the actual sale value

Sales Revenue Variance

Like material cost variance, sales revenue variance (SRV) is the aggregate variance or net variance. It is determined by the difference between the standard sales value (SSV) and actual sales value (ASV). The formula may be abbreviated as follows:

$$SRV = SSV - ASV \text{ (unfavourable)} \quad \textbf{(18.1)}$$

$$SRV = ASV - SSV \text{ (favourable)} \quad \textbf{(18.2)}$$

The chief causes responsible for SRV may be one or more of the following:

1. Actual sales prices are more or less than budgeted sales price (Sales price variance).
2. Actual sales volume is larger or smaller than budgeted sales volume (Sales volume variance).
3. Actual sales-mix is different from the standard sales-mix originally envisaged in the budget (Sales-mix variance). Such a variance will result only in the case of multi-product manufacturing and selling companies.
4. Actual sales allowance is more or less than the budgeted/standard allowance.

Sales Price Variance The sales price variance (SPV) is a sub-variance of SRV. This variance, like material price variance, is obtained by the difference between actual selling price (ASP) and standard selling price (SSP) multiplied by actual units (AQ) sold. Like the SRV, the SPV formula can be abbreviated as follows:

$$SPV = (ASP - SSP) \times AQ \text{ (favourable)} \quad \textbf{(18.3)}$$

$$SPV = (SSP - ASP) \times AQ \text{ (unfavourable)} \quad \textbf{(18.4)}$$

The possible reasons for unfavourable sales price variance are as follows:

1. Unforeseen market competitive conditions forcing the organisation to cut its planned sales price.
2. Management decisions to try new marketing strategies in terms of changing the channel of distribution from retailers followed hitherto to wholesalers.
3. Management decisions to tap new markets, and decisions to offer products at lower than standard prices. This may particularly hold true for export markets, and large tenders from reputed business units, or government departments having prospects of a perpetual source of demand in the future.
4. Latitude allowed to individual sales managers or sales people in quoting prices.[2]

In the case of multi-product firms, the SPV is to be determined for each line of the product sold.

Sales Volume Variance Sales volume variance (SVV) emanates from the difference in the actual product units sold and the planned sales of product units. The formula for determining SVV can be stated as follows:

$$SVV = [(\text{Actual volume (AQ)} - \text{Standard volume (SQ)}] \times \text{Standard selling price (favourable)} \quad \textbf{(18.5)}$$

$$SVV = (SQ - AQ) \times \text{Standard selling price (unfavourable)} \quad \textbf{(18.6)}$$

The following reasons[3] can contribute to SVV:

1. Unexpected competition,
2. Ineffective sales promotion,
3. Ineffective advertising,
4. Customers meeting adverse business conditions, thus, unable to take their usual order, and
5. Lack of proper supervision and control of salesmen.

To have a complete picture, sales volume variance should be determined for each line of the product sold.

In the case of a single-product firm, SPV and SVV together will account for total SRV. However, in the case of multi-product firms, it is necessary to have a break-up of sales volume variance into two sub-variances: **(1)** Sales mix sub-variance, and **(2)** Sales volume sub-variance.

Sales Mix Sub-Variance Sales mix sub-variance, or sales-mix variance (SMV) originates when the actual sales-mix deviates from the standard sales-mix. SMV will be present only when the proportion of actual units sold differs from the standard proportion. Therefore, this variance does not bear any relationship whatsoever with the sales volume variance. It may be quite possible that actual total quantity sold varies very significantly from the planned sales quantity. Yet, there is no SMV. Likewise, there is a possibility of a reverse situation also. Consider Examples 18.1 and 18.2.

EXAMPLE 18.1 *(No Sales Mix Variance)*

The following is a summary statement of budgeted and actual sales (for January) of ABC Ltd:

Products	*Budgeted (units)*	*Actual (units)*	*Budgeted selling price*
A	5,000	4,000	₹40
B	4,000	3,200	50
C	1,000	800	100
	10,000	8,000	

Determine sales-mix variance.

SOLUTION

Sales mix variance (SMV) = [Standard mix of actual quantity sold (RSQ) – Actual mix of actual quantity sold (AQ)] × Standard selling price **(18.7)**

The respective standard proportion of products, A, B, and C is 5:4:1 [5,000 (A), 4,000 (B), 1,000 (C)]. The RSQ of products A, B and C would be:

A : 8,000 × 5/10 = 4,000 units
B : 8,000 × 4/10 = 3,200 units
C : 8,000 × 1/10 = 800 units

Incorporating the calculated values in Equation (18.7), we have

SMV = (RSQ – AQ) × Standard selling price
A : (4,000 – 4,000) × ₹40 = Nil
B : (3,200 – 3,200) × ₹50 = Nil
C : (800 – 800) × ₹100 = Nil

The entire variance pertains to sales volume sub-variance.

EXAMPLE 18.2 *(No Sales Volume Sub-Variance)*

The following is a summarised sales report of XYZ Ltd:

Products	*Budgeted sales (units)*	*Actual sales (units)*	*Budgeted selling price*
X	5,000	4,200	₹40
Y	4,000	4,500	50
Z	1,000	1,300	100
	10,000	10,000	

Determine the sales-mix variance.

SOLUTION

Sales mix variance SMV = (RSQ – AQ) × Selling price

X : (5,000 – 4,200) × ₹40 = ₹32,000 (unfavourable)
Y : (4,000 – 4,500) × ₹50 = 25,000 (favourable)
Z : (1,000 – 1,300) × ₹100 = 30,000 (favourable)
Net SMV 23,000 (favourable)

There is no sales volume sub-variance as total units sold are identical with the total budgeted sales units. Thus, the sales-mix variance alone accounts for the entire sales volume variance.

The net SMV is likely to be favourable, when in actual sales there is a larger proportion of such products which have higher selling prices, as compared to their corresponding standard proportions. When there is a larger proportion of lower selling price products in the actual units sold, the emerging net SMV is likely to be unfavourable. However, it is important to note that in net SMV some product(s) will have favourable SMV, while other(s) will have unfavourable SMV. For instance, in Example 18.2, sales-mix variances for products Y and Z are favourable while, for product X, are unfavourable. For products, X, Y, and Z individually all SMV cannot be either favourable or unfavourable. Some of them will be favourable, while other(s) will be unfavourable.

Sales Volume Sub-Variance Sales volume sub-variance (SVSV) is the second part of sales volume variance. Like material yield variance, it is based on the *aggregate* figures of budgeted sales and actual sales, the difference so obtained being multiplied by average selling price. The following are the formulae for determining sales volume sub-variance:

SVSV (favourable) = [Total actual units sold – Total budgeted unit sales]
× Average standard selling price **(18.8)**

SVSV (unfavourable) = [Total budgeted unit sales – Total actual units sold]
× Average standard selling price **(18.9)**

Consider Example 18.3.

EXAMPLE 18.3

Hypothetical Ltd budgets to sell in the first quarter of the current year, 500 units of product X at ₹30 per unit, 400 units of product Y at ₹20 per unit, and 100 units of product Z at ₹50 per unit. During the quarter, actual sales were as follows:

— 400 units of product X at ₹40 per unit.
— 500 units of product Y at ₹10 per unit.
— 50 units of product Z at ₹40 per unit.

You are required to determine all sales variances.

SOLUTION

Determination of Sales Variances (SRV)

Product	Standard			Actual		
	Quantity (SQ) (units)	Price (SSP)	Total sales	Quantity (AQ) (units)	Price (ASP)	Total sales
X	500	₹30	₹15,000	400	₹40	₹16,000
Y	400	20	8,000	500	10	5,000
Z	100	50	5,000	50	40	2,000
	1,000	28	28,000	950		23,000

SRV = (TSV – ASV) = ₹28,000 – ₹23,000 = ₹5,000 (unfavourable)

SPV = (ASP – SSP) × AQ

X: (₹40 – ₹30) × 400 units = ₹4,000 (favourable)
Y: (₹10 – ₹20) × 500 units = 5,000 (unfavourable)
Z: (₹40 – ₹50) × 50 units = 500 (unfavourable)
Total SVP = 1,500 (unfavourable)

SVV = (AQ – SQ) × Standard selling price

X: (400 – 500) × ₹30 = ₹3,000 (unfavourable)
Y: (500 – 400) × ₹20 = 2,000 (favourable)
Z: (50 – 100) × ₹50 = 2,500 (unfavourable)
Total SVV = 3,500 (unfavourable)

There are two sub-parts of SVV:

(i) *Sales-mix variance:* (SMV) = (RSQ – AQ) × Standard selling price

X: [475 (950 × 5/10) – 400] × ₹30 = ₹2,250 (unfavourable)
Y: [380 (950 × 4/10) – 500] × ₹20 = 2,400 (favourable)
Z: [95 (950 × 1/10) – 50] × ₹50 = 2,250 (unfavourable)
= 2,100 (unfavourable)

(ii) *Sales volume sub-variance:* SVSV = [Total budgeted sales of all products – Total actual units sold] × Average standard selling price = (1,000 – 950) × ₹28 = ₹1,400 (unfavourable)

Confirmation: SRV = ₹5,000 (unfavourable) consisting of:

(i) SPV = ₹1,500 (unfavourable)
(ii) SMV = 2,100 (unfavourable)
(iii) SVSV = 1,400 (unfavourable)

PROFIT VARIANCES

Sales variances are significant as they have a direct bearing on profits earned by the organisation. In fact, sales variances can be used as the basis of determining profit variance.

Profit variance = Sales revenue variance – Standard cost of sales of products not sold (The formula will hold true when there are no cost variances).

The importance of the determination of profit variance lies in the fact that it helps management to take the necessary remedial actions to achieve its profit target. It enables management to assign responsibility to the heads of various responsibility *centres.* In fact, it may provoke management to probe into the matter by looking into the sales performance territory-wise, or market-channel-wise. Above all, it permits scrutiny of the performance of individual sales managers.

The principal profit variance is *overall profit variance.* It is divided into: **(a)** Sales price variance, **(b)** Sales volume variance sub-divided in to **(i)** Sales mix sub-variance, **(ii)** Sales volume sub-variance, and **(c)** Cost variance.

Except cost variance, there is no difference between the various sales variances and profit variances as, their names as well as break-up are identical. Such variances have, therefore, not been discussed here. Nevertheless, it is important to note the changes in the formulae in respect of those profit variances which differ from selling variances.

Overall Profit Variance

Standard/budgeted profit – Actual profit (unfavourable)
Actual profit – Standard/budgeted profit (favourable)
Standard profit can be determined in either of the following ways:

(i) *Profit Basis:* Number of budgeted units sold for each product × Standard profit per unit of the concerned product **(18.10)**

(ii) *Cost Basis:* Under both the methods = [Standard sales revenue of budgeted sales of each product – Standard cost of budgeted sales of each product] **(18.11)**

In the case of multi-product firms, a product-wise break-up should be made.

The calculation of actual profit is simple, that is, (Actual quantity sold × Actual profit per unit) or (Actual sales revenue – Actual costs incurred).

Sales Price Variance The formula is the same (18.3) as the difference in selling prices directly affects the profits or losses of the firm.

Sales Volume Variance The formula, from the point of view of determining profit variance, needs minor modification. The amended formula is:

(AQ – SQ) × Standard profit per unit (favourable) **(18.12)**

(SQ – AQ) × Standard profit per unit (unfavourable) **(18.13)**

Sales Mix Variance and Sales Volume Sub-Variances The expression, standard price, would be substituted for standard profit and average standard profit respectively.

Sales mix variance = (RSQ – AQ) × Standard profit per unit **(18.14)**

Sales volume sub-variance = [Total budgeted sales – Total actual sales] × Average standard profit **(18.15)**

Cost Variances As the name suggests, the cost variance will result when actual costs differ from standard costs. Since the previous chapter has already enumerated the various cost variances in detail, reference to their calculations can be made from that chapter. In brief, cost variances can be determined by the following formula:

(Standard cost – Actual cost) × Actual quantity sold (favourable) **(18.16)**

(Actual cost – Standard cost) × Actual quantity sold (unfavourable) **(18.17)**

The computation of profit variances is illustrated in Example 18.4.

Example 18.4

In Example 18.3 of Hypothetical Ltd, assume that standard costs of products X, Y, and Z respectively are ₹20, ₹10 and ₹30. Further, assume that actual costs are in line with budgeted costs.

You are required to determine the profit variances.

Solution

Computation of Profit

Products	*Standard*			*Actual*		
	SQ (units)	*Profit per unit (SP)*	*Total profit*	*AQ (units)*	*Profit per unit (AP)*	*Total profit*
X	500	₹10	₹5,000	400	₹20	₹8000
Y	400	10	4,000	500	0	Nil
Z	100	20	2,000	50	10	500
	1,000	11	11,000	950		8,500

Standard selling price – Standard costs = Standard profit

X: (₹30 – ₹20) = ₹10 per unit

Y: (₹20 – ₹10) = ₹10 per unit

Z: (₹50 – ₹30) = ₹20 per unit

Overall profit variance: Budgeted profit – Actual profit = ₹11,000 – ₹8,500 = ₹2,500 (unfavourable)

(i) Sales price variance: ₹1,500 (unfavourable) (See solution to Example 18.3)

(ii) Sales volume variance: (SQ – AQ) × SP per unit

X (500 – 400) × ₹10	=	₹1,000 (unfavourable)
Y (400 – 500) × ₹10	=	1,000 (favourable)
Z (100 – 50) × ₹20	=	1,000 (unfavourable)
Total	=	1,000 (unfavourable)

(a) Sales mix sub-variance: (RS Q – AQ) × SP per unit

X (475 – 400) × ₹10	=	₹750 (unfavourable)
Y (380 – 500) × ₹10	=	1,200 (favourable)
Z (95 – 50) × ₹20	=	900 (unfavourable)
Total	=	450 (unfavourable)

(b) *Sales volume sub-variance:* [Total budgeted sales of all production – Total actual units sold] × Average standard profit per unit = (1,000 – 950) × ₹11 = ₹550 (unfavourable)

Confirmation: Overall profit variance = ₹2,500 (unfavourable). It consists of (i) Sales price variance, ₹1,500 (unfavourable), (ii) Sales mix variance, ₹450 (unfavourable), and (iii) Sales volume sub-variance, ₹550 (unfavourable)

Alternatively, overall profit variance:

Sales revenue variance	₹5,000 (unfavourable)
Less standard cost of sales of products not sold:	
100 units of X at ₹20	2,000 (unfavourable)
100 units of Y at ₹10	1,000 (favourable)
50 units of Z at ₹30	1,500 (unfavourable)
Profit variance	2,500 (unfavourable)

So far, we have assumed that there are no cost variances. Let us now incorporate cost variances also to complete the discussion on profit variance.

Assuming that the actual cost per unit of products X, Y and Z are ₹22, ₹8 and ₹28 respectively as against ₹20, ₹10 and ₹30 assumed earlier, the effects of cost variances on profit variances are shown below:

Determination of actual profit: (AP – AC) = AP × AQ = Total profit

X (₹40 – ₹22) = ₹18 × 400	=	₹7,200
Y (₹10 – ₹8) = ₹2 × 500	=	1,000
Z (₹40 – ₹28) = ₹12 × 50	=	600
Total		8,800

Overall profit variance:

Standard profit =	₹11,000
Actual profit	8,800
	2,200 (unfavourable)

Cost variance: (SC – AC) × AQ

X (₹20 – ₹22) × 400	=	₹800 (unfavourable)
Y (₹10 – ₹8) × 500	=	1,000 (favourable)
Z (₹30 – ₹28) × 50	=	100 (favourable)
Total		300 (favourable)

Confirmation: Overall variance given in solution to Example 18.4 =₹2,500 (unfavourable)
Less cost variance 300 (favourable)
Total profit variance 2,200 (unfavourable)

ACTUAL PROFIT AND BUDGETED PROFIT: RECONCILIATION

As stated earlier, the primary objective of variance analysis is to enable management to know the responsibility centres which can be held accountable for various variances. In operational terms, management should be informed about various cost and revenue variances so that it may know the various reasons why actual profits have differed from the budgeted profits. For control purposes, the information regarding the profit earned by the firm on the basis of historical cost recording will not be as relevant as the information on the basis of standard cost. For this reason, an income statement depicting actual costs and standard costs and variances along with their causes is of greater value to management *vis-à-vis* a historical income statement. Such a statement, as can be seen from the following proforma income statement (**Format 18.1**) and subsequent example, clearly highlights inefficiencies causing lower profits, and also efficient factors (like labour efficiency) adding to more profits. In brief, such information will be of immense practical utility to management in controlling cost.

Format 18.1 Proforma Income Statement (Reconciliation)

	Favourable	Unfavourable	
Budgeted sales revenue:			
Sales variance adjustment (Product-wise details may be given):			
Sales price variance			
Sales mix variance			
Sales volume sub-variance			(+) or (–) as the case may be
Actual sales revenue:			
Less: standard cost in units sold:			
Material (direct)	....		
Labour (direct)	....		
Other direct expenses (if any)	....		
Variable overheads (main details may be given)			
Fixed overhead (main details may be given.	....	....	
Budgeted profit			
Cost variances:			
Material			
Price variance			
Yield variance			
Mix variance			
Labour variances:			
Rate variance			
Mix variance			
Efficiency variance			
Idle time variance			
Variable overhead variances:			
Spending variance			
Efficiency variance			
Fixed overhead variances:			
Spending variance			
Efficiency variance			

Capacity variance		
Calendar variance		(+) or (–) as the case may be
Actual profit		

It may be noted that transactions relating to taxation, interest and dividends do not form a part of this income statement because these items are non-controllable costs.

Consider Example 18.5.

EXAMPLE 18.5

The income statement of Modern Electricals Ltd for the first quarter of the current year is given as follows:

Sales revenue (18,000 units)		₹ 72,00,000
Less: cost of goods sold:		
Direct materials	₹43,28,000	
Direct labour	11,66,000	
Other direct expenses	3,04,000	
Factory overheads	4,40,000	
Administrative and selling expenses	3,20,000	65,58,000
Net profit		6,42,000

The standard output and sales for the period was 20,000 units and the standard cost and profit per unit is as under:

Direct material (3 units at the rate of ₹75)	₹225
Direct labour (3 hours at the rate of ₹20)	60
Other direct expenses	15
Factory overheads:	
Fixed overheads	15
Variable	10
Administrative and selling charges (fixed)	15
Total standard cost	340
Standard profit	40
Selling price (standard)/(budgeted)	380

Labour was paid at the rate of ₹22 per hour and material prices were ₹80 per unit. Factory overheads (actual) include ₹2,80,000, fixed, and the balance amount represents variable. There was no inventory at the beginning or at the end of the year. The company employs labour-hour rate as the basis of absorption of fixed overheads.

You are required to:

1. Calculate, cost, sales, and profit variances.
2. Prepare a reconciliation statement of profit variances with as many details as possible.

SOLUTION

Elements of cost	*Standard*			*Actual*		
	Input (units/hours)	*Rate*	*Total cost*	*Input (units/hours)*	*Rate*	*Total cost*
Direct materials	54,000	₹75	₹40,50,000	54,100	₹80	₹43,28,000
Direct labour	54,000	20	10,80,000	53,000	22	11,66,000
Other direct expenses	18,000	15	2,70,000	N.A.	N.A.	3,04,000

(Contd.)

(*Contd.*)

Factory overheads:						
Fixed	54,000	5.0	2,70,000	53,000	Not required	2,80,000
Variable	54,000	₹10/3	1,80,000	53,000	Not required	1,60,000
Administrative and selling charges	18,000	15	2,70,000	18,000	Not required	3,20,000
			61,20,000			65,58,000

(A) *Total cost variance:* TSC – TAC = (₹61,20,000 – ₹65,58,000) = ₹4,38,000 (unfavourable)

1. Material cost variance: SMC – AMC = (₹40,50,000 – ₹43,28,000) = ₹2,78,000 (unfavourable)

(a) *Material price variance:* (SR – AR) × AQ = (₹75 – ₹80) × 54,100 = ₹2,70,500 (unfavourable)

(b) *Material usage variance:* (AQ – SQ) × SR = (54,100 – 54,000) × ₹75 = ₹7,500 (unfavourable)

2. Labour cost variance: SLC – ALC = ₹10,80,000 – ₹11,66,000 = ₹86,000 (unfavourable)

(a) *Labour rate variance*: (SR – AR) × AH = (₹20 – ₹22) × 53,000 = ₹1,06,000 (unfavourable)

(b) *Labour efficiency variance*: (SH – AH) × SR = (54,000 – 53,000) × ₹20 = ₹20,000 (favourable)

3. Direct expense variance*:* Standard expenses – Actual expenses = ₹2,70,000 – ₹3,04,000 = ₹34,000 (unfavourable)

4. Fixed overhead variance*:* (Actual fixed overheads incurred – Standard fixed overheads charged to production) = (₹2,80,000 – ₹2,70,000) = ₹10,000 (unfavourable)

(a) *Fixed overhead spending variance*: Budgeted overheads – Actual overheads = [₹3,00,000 or (20,000 × ₹15) = ₹2,80,000] = ₹20,000 (favourable)

(b) *Fixed overhead efficiency variance*:(SH – AH) × Standard fixed overhead rate per hour = (54,000 – 53,000) × ₹5 = ₹5,000 (favourable)

(c) *Capacity variance*: (Normal capacity in hours – Actual hours utilised) × Standard fixed overhead rate per hour = (60,000 – 53,000) × ₹5 = ₹35,000 (unfavourable)

5. Variable overhead variance: SOC – AOC = (₹1,80,000 – ₹1,60,000) = ₹20,000 (favourable)

(a) *Variable overhead spending variance*: Actual overheads-Standard overhead cost at actual hours = (₹1,60,000 – ₹1,76,666.67) = ₹16,666.67 (favourable)

(b) *Variable overhead efficiency variance*: (SH – AH) × Standard variable overhead rate per hour = (54,000 – 53,000) × ₹10/3 = ₹3333.33 (favourable)

6. (A) Administrative and selling charges*:* Standard cost – Actual cost = (₹2,70,000 – ₹3,20,000) = ₹50,000 (unfavourable)

(a) *Administrative overhead spending variance*: Budgeted overheads–Actual overheads = (₹3,00,000 – ₹3,20,000) = ₹20,000 (unfavourable)

(b) *Capacity variance:* (Normal output and sales – Actual output and sales) × Standard overhead rate per unit = (20,000 – 18,000) × ₹15 = ₹30,000 (unfavourable)

(B) *Sales revenue variance (SRV):* Budgeted sales – Actual sales
₹76,00,000 – ₹72,00,000 = ₹4,00,000 (unfavourable)

(a) *Sales price variance (SPV):* (ASP – SSP) × AQ = (₹400 – ₹380) × 18,000 = ₹3,60,000 (favourable)

(b) *Sales volume variance (SVV):* (SQ – AQ) × SSP = (20,000 – 18,000) × ₹380 = ₹7,60,000 (unfavourable)

(C) *Profit Variance:*

Standard profit – Actual profit (₹8,00,000 – ₹6,42,000) = ₹1,58,000 (unfavourable)

(a) *Sales price variance:* ₹3,60,000 (favourable) (calculated above)

(b) *Sales volume variance*: = (SQ – AQ) × Standard profit per unit
= (20,000–18,000) × ₹40 = ₹80,000 (unfavourable)

(c) *Cost variance* already calculated = ₹4,38,000 (unfavourable)

Profit Reconciliation Statement (taking sales as basis)

Particulars				*Amount*
Budgeted sales revenue (20,000 × ₹380)				₹76,00,000
Sales revenue variance:		*Favourable*	*Unfavourable*	
Sales price variance		₹3,60,000		
Sales volume variance			(₹7,60,000)	(4,00,000)
Actual sales revenue				72,00,000
Less: standard cost of 18,000 units sold:				
Direct materials			40,50,000	
Direct labour			10,80,000	
Other direct expenses			2,70,000	
Factory overheads:	Fixed		2,70,000	
	Variable		1,80,000	
Administrative and selling charges			2,70,000	61,20,000
Budgeted net profit				10,80,000
Cost variances:				
Material price variance			2,70,500	
Material usage variance			7,500	
Labour rate variance			1,06,000	
Labour efficiency variance		20,000		
Direct expenses variance			34,000	
Fixed overhead spending variance		20,000		
Fixed overhead efficiency variance		5,000		
Capacity variance			35,000	
Variable overhead spending variance		16,666.67		
Variable overhead efficiency variance		3333.33		
Administrative overhead spending variance			20,000	
Capacity variance			30,000	4,38,000
Actual profit				6,42,000

The profit reconciliation statement shows that cost variances are primarily responsible for distorting the profit picture. Within cost variances, efficiency variances, in general, are favourable. Price variance pertaining to material and labour account for a substantial portion of unfavourable cost variance. It may be possible that material prices may have gone up in the market and so the labour rate, warranting upward revision of their standard rates. The favourable sales price variance further confirms the necessity for the same. The fact that whatever is produced is sold indicates that idle capacity variance is a reflection of the inefficiency of the production department. The production manager should be called for explanation, and efforts should be made to overcome all production hurdles in future to ensure normal production.

VARIANCE REPORTING

Basically, variances can be favourable or unfavourable. While it is true that unfavourable variances call for management attention, favourable variances should not be completely ignored, the reason being that favourable variances do not always necessarily mean efficient performance. For instance, a favourable labour efficiency variance may result not merely from more efficient means of producing output, but may also be at the cost of the quality of the product. Similarly, material price variance may arise due to the use of sub-standard material acquired at a lower price although, the fact that the variance is favourable may *prima facie* be indicative of economical procurement at lower prices.

The unfavourable variances also are not necessarily due to inefficient performance. To illustrate, an unfavourable material price variance may have been caused by the purchase of better quality than the budgeted ones. The recruitment of better skilled and trained workers may lead to an unfavourable labour rate variance.

In view of these possibilities, favourable and unfavourable variances should not be taken at their face value; there is rather a need for indepth analysis and investigation by management. The degree of investigation will depend upon: **(i)** The nature of variance—controllable or uncontrollable and **(ii)** The significance in terms of its magnitude and frequency of occurrence.

Controllable variances are variances that are controllable at the level of various responsibility centres.

The controllable variances are those that are controllable at the level of the various responsibility centres. Examples of such variances are material usage variance, labour efficiency, and overhead efficiency variances. The variances that are generally not controllable include material price variance, labour rate variance, and fixed and variable spending variances. The solution to uncontrollable variances in most situations is a revision of the relevant standards. Controllable variances merit management attention and should be properly reported.

The second factor having a bearing on the degree of investigation is the amount and frequency of occurrence of the variances. The larger the amount of variance, the more significant it is to the management. Moreover, the likelihood of a variance recurring is of still greater significance to management. Thus, if the variance is both large and persistent, management should analyse it in detail to identify the probable causes. Whether a variance is large enough will vary from firm to firm, and within the same firm from one operation to another. One possible approach to determine whether the size of the variance is significant, is the establishment of arbitrary limits based on managerial judgement. A better alternative would be to look at the trend of past variances. If, for example, in the past, a particular operation has frequently generated variances of say, 10 per cent, this 10 percent can be used to determine whether the size of a variance in that operation is significant or not. This 10 per cent variance represents the cut-off or tolerance limit for purposes of determining the significance of a variance of a particular size. Moreover, the variance should also be viewed in the light of the *tightness* of the underlying standards. If the standards are tight, a higher tolerance limit may be set. If the standards are attainable, a lower tolerance limit may be more appropriate.

The variances can be expressed either in absolute figures or in relative figures. The relative figures are usually shown in the form of ratios. The key ratios relating to the variances are listed below:

$$\text{Material price variance ratio} = \frac{\text{Actual price}}{\text{Standard price}} \quad (18.18)$$

$$\text{Material usage variance ratio} = \frac{\text{Actual quantity}}{\text{Standard quantity required for actual output}} \quad (18.19)$$

$$\text{Material yield ratio} = \frac{\text{Actual output (yield)}}{\text{Standard yield from actual output}} \quad (18.20)$$

$$\text{Material cost variance ratio} = [\text{Material price variance ratio} \times \text{Material usage variance ratio}] \quad (18.21)$$

$$\text{Labour rate variance ratio} = \frac{\text{Actual wage rate}}{\text{Standard wage rate}} \quad (18.22)$$

$$\text{Labour efficiency variance ratio} = \frac{\text{Actual hours}}{\text{Standard hours required for actual production}} \quad (18.23)$$

$$\text{Labour cost variance ratio} = \text{Labour rate variance ratio} \times \text{Labour efficiency variance ratio} \quad (18.24)$$

$$\text{Overhead expenditure variance ratio} = \frac{\text{Actual overheads incurred}}{\text{Budgeted overheads required for actual output, that is, Fixed overheads + [Actual output} \times \text{Variable overhead rate per unit]}} \quad \textbf{(18.25)}$$

$$\text{Volume (capacity) variance ratio or overhead utilisation ratio} = \frac{\text{Actual production}}{\text{Normal production}} \quad \textbf{(18.26)}$$

A good management reporting system requires that top management should be furnished with such other ratios also which gauge the overall performance of the business firm from the point of view of assessing its utilisation of capacity, labour, material and other resources. Some significant ratios for the purpose are enumerated below:

$$\text{Efficiency ratio} = \frac{\text{Standard hours required for actual production}}{\text{Actual hours worked}} \times 100 \quad \textbf{(18.27)}$$

$$\text{Activity ratio} = \frac{\text{Standard hours required for actual output}}{\text{Budgeted standard hours}} \times 100 \quad \textbf{(18.28)}$$

$$\text{Capacity usage ratio} = \frac{\text{Budgeted hours}}{\text{Normal capacity hours}} \times 100 \quad \textbf{(18.29)}$$

$$\text{Capacity utilisation ratio} = \frac{\text{Actual hours worked}}{\text{Budgeted hours}} \times 100 \quad \textbf{(18.30)}$$

The capacity utilisation, activity and efficiency of ratios are illustrated in Example 18.6.

EXAMPLE 18.6

Product X takes 5 hours to make and Y requires 10 hours. In a month of 25 effective days of 8 hours a day, 1,000 units of X and 600 units of Y were produced. ABC Ltd employs 50 workers in the production department. The budgeted hours are 1,02,000 for the year. Calculate capacity utilisation ratio, activity ratio and efficiency ratio.

SOLUTION

Computation of Ratios

$$\text{Capacity utilisation ratio} = \frac{\text{Actual hours work ed*}}{\text{Budgeted hours}} \times 100 = \frac{1,20,000}{1,02,000} \times 100 = 117.65 \text{ per cent}$$

*Actual hours worked in a year = Working hours per day × Number of workers × Number of effective days in a year × 12 months = (8 × 50 × 25 × 12) = 1,20,000 hours

$$\text{Activity ratio} = \frac{\text{Standard hours required for actual production}}{\text{Budgeted standard hours}} \times 100 = \frac{1,32,000}{1,02,000} \times 100 = 129.41 \text{ per cent}$$

Standard hours required (yearly basis) = Standard hours required to produce a unit × Number of units produced per year

Product X = (5 × 1,000 × 12) =	60,000
Product Y = (10 × 600 × 12) =	72,000
	1,32,000

$$\text{Efficiency ratio} = \frac{\text{Standard hours required for actual production}}{\text{Actual hours worked}} \times 100 = \frac{1,32,000}{1,20,000} \times 100 = 110 \text{ per cent}$$

Once the tolerance limits, namely, upper control limit and lower control limit, have been determined, significant variance can be reported in two forms: **(i)** In graphic form and **(ii)** In a tabular format.

The graphic method/control chart is the effective method of reporting significant variances. Figure 18.1 presents the control chart.

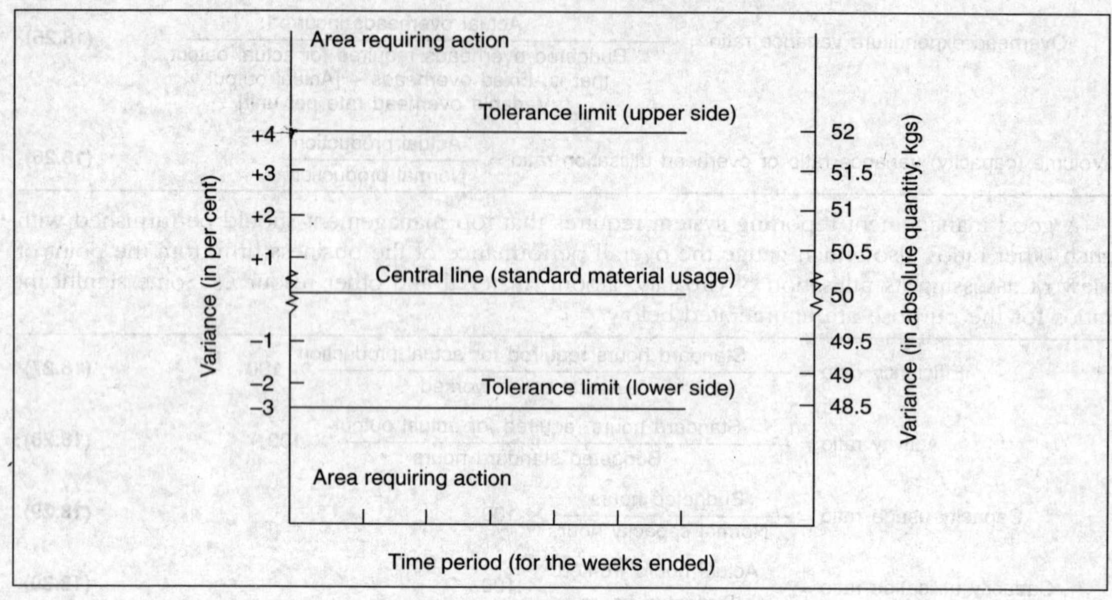

Figure 18.1 *Control Chart*

It is a graphic report of the materials usage variance in a production department over a period of about 1.5 months. It exhibits variances as percentages of standard quantity required. The central line represents standard material usage required per unit. On both sides of this line, there are tolerance limits: 4 per cent on the upper side and 3 per cent on the lower side. It is significant to observe that tolerance excess usage (4 per cent of standard) is greater than the tolerance variance below standard (3 per cent). It may be needed to maintain the product quality, in the sense that, if material consumption falls below the minimum, it may so adversely effect the product quality that the products may be rejected when put to a quality test. From Figure 18.1, it is apparent that management is not required to initiate any control action as the actual observations at different times are within control limits.

The immense utility of graphs, for the purpose of understanding broad relationships and trends notwithstanding, they tend to be less precise and informative than tabulations. Therefore, to fill up the gap and to provide the full information to the top management, the tabulation method of variance reporting is appropriate. Under this method, there are four columns: **(i)** Standard cost, **(ii)** Actual cost, **(iii)** Variance, and **(iv)** Those variances that exceed the required cut-off point. The last column would require management attention. Example 18.7 presents information on a tabular basis of the production department of a company for six weeks.

Example 18.7

Week	*Standard cost of material allowed for actual output*	*Actual cost*	*Variance: Favourable (F)/ Adverse (A)*	*Relative amount (per cent)*
1	₹3,000	₹3,015	₹15 A	0.5
2	2,400	2,496	96 A	4.0
3	2,400	2,280	120 F	5.0
4	3,300	3,311	11 A	0.3
5	3,000	3,030	30 A	1.0
6	2,400	2,424	24 A	1.0

Suppose further that tolerance limits are 3 per cent of standard; the variance for consecutive weeks, 2 and 3 require investigation. In practice, these variances may either be circled or written in different colours or may be separately shown in one more column added to the above presentation.

Steps involved in variance reporting

1. Determine whether the variance is significant.
2. If it is, investigate to discover the events, which caused the variance.
3. Depending on the cause, take action to change future operating conditions, or to re-plan with a resulting change in the standard, or budget so that this variance will not recur from the same cause in the future unless the corrective action was ineffective.

DISPOSITION OF VARIANCES

Cost variances may be disposed off by following either of the following two methods: (i) They may be transferred to the current year's income statement; or (ii) They may be considered as cost of the product and, thus, can be allocated to work-in-process, finished goods and cost of goods sold. In fact, the scientific procedure is to judge each variance individually and then to make a decision based on the nature of the cause of the variance. Therefore, there is no question of exclusive adoption of one or another. Both are complementary in character. For instance, unfavourable material price variance caused by a permanent increase in the prices of raw materials should be considered as a part of the cost of the product, and accordingly should be allocated to product cost. On the other hand, idle capacity variance caused by operating 1,000 direct labour-hours instead of 2,000 normal direct labour-hours per fortnight should be written off against the current year's revenues, as they represent losses caused by inactivity; these are cost of inefficiencies and it would be illogical to consider them as a part of the cost of product. We now illustrate the methods of disposition of variance.

Transfer to Current Period's Income Statement

Under this method, the profit and loss account of the concerned period is debited for unfavourable variances and credited for favourable variances. In the profit and loss account, the net effect of all variances is adjusted to the gross profit figure. If the net variance is favourable, it is added to the gross profit computed at standard costs. The structure of the income statement is illustrated in Format 18.2:

Format 18.2 Variance-adjusted Income Statement

	Debit balances (unfavourable)	Credit balances (favourable)	
Sales revenue			
Less cost of goods sold (at standard cost)			
Gross profit (at standard cost)			
Adjustment for various variances:			
Material usage variance			
Labour rate variance			
Spending variance			
Capacity variance			
Material price variance			
Labour efficiency variance			
Fixed overhead efficiency variance			
Variable overhead efficiency variance			
Net variance			
Gross profit (adjusted)			
Less other expenses			....
Net profit			

This method is theoretically sound and practically satisfactory for disposing of variances if standards are *current and attainable* because, variances are valid indicators of departures from cost levels that should have been attained otherwise.

Allocating Variance as Part of the Cost of Goods Sold and Inventories

If standards are tight or loose and do not reflect *currently attainable cost levels,* the standards are not reasonably representative of what costs ought to be. The treatment of charging off net variances to current revenues may result in an overstatement or understatement of the current period's net income. In other words, inventories and cost of goods sold would tend to be incorrectly overvalued or undervalued. In such a case, it is appropriate to adjust work-in-process, finished goods inventory and cost of goods sold figures to actual costs by allocating the manufacturing variances among them. The amount allocated to each of these accounts (work-in-process, finished goods inventory and cost of goods sold inventory), would be determined by the relative proportion of standard cost in each amount, to the total amount of that standard cost charged to production during the period as illustrated in Example 18.8.

EXAMPLE 18.8

Accounts	Materials		Labour		Factory overhead	
	Amount	Per cent	Amount	Per cent	Amount	Per cent
Work-in-process	₹2,000	20	₹1,000	20	₹6,000	40
Finished goods inventory	3,000	30	1,000	20	1,500	10
Cost of goods sold	5,000	50	3,000	60	7,500	50
Total standard cost	10,000	100	5,000	100	15,000	100
Total actual cost	11,000		6,000		17,000	

Material price variance	₹1,000 (unfavourable)
Labour efficiency variance	1,000 (unfavourable)
Controllable variance	500 (favourable)
Volume variance	2,500 (unfavourable)

Show the allocation of the variances.

SOLUTION

Allocation of Variances

Name of the variance	Total amount	Work-in-process	Finished goods inventory	Cost of goods sold
Materials price variance	₹1,000 (U)	₹200	₹300	₹500
Labour efficiency variance	1,000 (U)	200	200	600
Controllable variance	1,500 (F)	(200)	(50)	(250)
Volume variance	2,500 (U)	1,000	250	1,250
Total	4,000	1,200	700	2,100

Further, supposing that sales revenue is ₹25,000, the income statement of hypothetical company would appear as follows:

Income Statement (Method I)

Sales revenue	₹25,000
Cost of goods sold [standard adjusted to actual (₹15,500 + ₹2,100)]	17,600
Gross profit (actual)	7,400
Less other expenses (assumed)	1,900
Net profit	5,500

Income Statement (Method II)

	Debit balances	Credit balances	
Sales revenue			₹ 25,000
Cost of goods sold (standard cost)			15,500
Gross profit (standard)			9,500
Adjusted for variances:			
Material price variance	₹1,000		
Labour efficiency variance	1,000		
Controllable variance:		₹500	
Volume variance	2,500		
Net debit variance	(4,500)	500	(4,000)
Gross profit (adjusted)			5,500
Less other expenses			1,900
Net profit			3,600

The net profit under the second method is more by ₹1,900 (₹5,500 – ₹3,600). The difference is attributable to the following:

Cost added to:

Work-in-process	₹1,200
Finished goods inventory	700
	1,900

In Example 18.8, it is assumed that there is no material inventory. In practice, the situation is not likely to be so. In such a situation, the material price variance would partly be allocated to materials inventory, and the balance in the three accounts in the manner shown above.

SUMMARY

- The second major category of variances consists of (i) Sales variances and (ii) Profit variances.
- Sales Variances are summarised below:

Variance	Formula
Sales revenue variance (*SRV*) (unit basis)	[(*AQ* × *ASP*) – (*BQ* × SSP)]
or *SRV* (aggregate basis)	*TASR* – *TBSR*/*TSSR*
(a) Sales price variance (*SPV*)	(*ASP* – *SSP*) × *AQ* sold
(b) Sales volume variance (*SVV*)	(*TAQ* – *TBQ*) × *SSP* per unit
or	
(i) Sales mixture sub-variance (*SMSV*)	(*RSQ* – *AQ*) × *SSP*
and	
(ii) Sales quantity sub-variance (*SQSV*)	(*TAQ* – *TBQ*) × Weighted average *SSP*

Where,

AQ	Actual units sold
ASP	Actual selling price per unit
BQ	Budgeted sales in units
SSP	Standard (budgeted) selling price per unit
TASR	Total actual sales revenue
TBSR	Total budgeted/standard sales revenue
TAQ	Total actual sales in units
TBQ	Total budgeted sales in units
RSQ	Revised standard quantity, i.e. standard mix of actual units sold

- Profit variances are summarised below:

Variance	*Formula*
Profit variance (unit basis)	[(*AP* × *AO*) – (*BP* × *AO*)]
or Profit variance (aggregate basis)	*TAP* – *TBP*
or	
(A) Sales price variance	(*ASP* – *SSP*) × *AQ* sold
(B) Sales volume variance	(*TAQ* – *TBQ*) × BP per unit
or	
(i) Sales mixture sub-variance	(*RSQ* – *AQ*) × *BP* per unit
(ii) Sales quantity sub-variance	(*TAQ* – *TBQ*) × Weighted average budgeted profit per unit
(C) Cost variance	(*AC* – *SC*) × *AQ* sold

Where,

AP Actual profit per unit
BP Budgeted/standard profit per unit
TAP Total actual profit
TBP Total budgeted profit
TAQ Total actual units sold
TBQ Total budgeted sales in units
AC Actual cost per unit
SC Standing/budgeted cost per unit

- The primary aim of variance analysis is to enable the management to assign responsibility for the deviations. For purposes of managerial control, an income statement depicting actual costs and standard costs and variances along with their causes is prepared. This is referred to as proforma income statement (reconciliation) to reconcile the actual profits and budgeted profits.
- Another aspect of variance analysis is variance reporting. The variances can be reported either in absolute figures or in relative figures in terms of ratios. The key ratios relating to variances are: (i) Material price variance ratio, (ii) Material usage variance ratio, (iii) Material yield variance ratio, (iv) Material cost variance ratio, (v) Labour rate variance ratio, (vi) Labour efficiency variance ratio, (vii) Labour cost variance ratio, (viii) Overhead expenditure variance ratio, (x) Efficiency ratio, (xi) Activity ratio, and (xii) Capacity usage/Utilisation ratio.
- Finally, cost variances may be disposed of in either of two ways: (i) They may be transferred to the current year's income statement, or (ii) They may be considered as cost of the product, and allocated as part of cost of goods sold and inventory.

REFERENCES

1. C.L. Moore and Robert K., Jaedicke, *Managerial Accounting*, (South West Publishing Co, Ohio, 1972), p. 378.
2. Jack Gray and Kenneth S. Johnston, Accounting and Management Action, (McGraw Hill, New York, 1977), p. 653.
3. J. Batty, *Standard Costing*, (Macdonald and Evans Ltd, London, 1970), p. 263.

SOLVED PROBLEMS

P.18.1 The budgeted and the actual sales for a month in respect of three products are given below:

Budgeted sales:

Product	*Quantity*	*Price*	*Value*
A	1,000	₹5	₹5,000
B	750	10	7,500
C	500	15	7,500
	2,250		20,000

Actuals sales:

Product	Quantity	Price	Value
A	1,200	₹6	₹7,200
B	700	9	6,300
C	600	14	8,400
	2,500		21,900

Calculate sales variances.

SOLUTION

Budgeted Sales

	Budgeted			Actual			Actual quantity
Product	Quantity	Price	Value	Quantity	Price	Value	× Budgeted price
A	1,000	₹5	₹5,000	1,200	₹6	₹7,200	₹6,000
B	750	10	7,500	700	9	6,300	7,000
C	500	15	7,500	600	14	8,400	9,000
	2,250		20,000	2,500		21,900	22,000

Sales variances:

1. *Sales revenue variances* = Actual sales – Budgeted sales = ₹(21,900 – 20,000) = 1,900 (favourable)
2. *Sales volume variances* = (Actual quantity – Budgeted quantity) × Budgeted selling price per unit
   A : (1,200 – 1,000) × ₹5 = ₹1,000 (favourable)
   B : (700 – 750) × ₹10 = 500 (adverse)
   C : (600 – 500) × ₹15 = 1,500 (favourable)
   2,000 (favourable)
3. *Sales price variance* = (Actual price – Budgeted price) × Actual quantity
   A : (₹6 – ₹5) × 1,200 = 1,200 (favourable)
   B : (₹9 – ₹10) × 700 = 700 (adverse)
   C : (₹14 – ₹15) × 600 = 600 (adverse)
   100 (adverse)

Sales volume variance has the following two components:

4. *Sales mix variance* = (Standard mix of AQ sold – Actual mix) × Budgeted selling price per unit
   A : (2,500 × 4/9 = 1111.11 – 1,200) × ₹5 = ₹444 (favourable)
   B : (2,500 × 3/0 = 833.33 – 700) × ₹10 = 1,333 (unfavourable)
   C : (2,500 × 2/9 = 555.56 – 600) × ₹15 = 667 (favourable)
   222 (unfavourable)
5. *Sales volume sub-variance* = (Total budgeted unit sales – Total actual units sold) × Average budgeted selling price
   = (2,250 – 2,500) × ₹20,000/2,250 = ₹2,222 (favourable)

P.18.2 Royal Industries Ltd provides the following data regarding actual and budgeted sales, costs and profit for a month of the current year:

Budgeted data

Product	Quantity (units)	Selling price per unit	Sales value	Cost per unit	Total cost	Standard profit (SP) per unit	Total profit
A	4,000	₹15	₹60,000	₹7.50	₹30,000	₹7.50	₹30,000
B	4,800	25	1,20,000	12.50	60,000	12.50	60,000
C	7,200	40	2,88,000	20.00	1,44,000	20.00	1,44,000
	16,000	29.25	4,68,000		2,34,000		2,34,000

Actual data

A	3,600	15	54,000	7.50	27,000	7.50	27,000
B	4,000	26	1,04,000	13.00	52,000	13.00	52,000
C	6,400	37.50	2,40,000	20.00	1,28,000	17.50	1,12,000
	14,000		3,98,000		2,07,000		1,91,000

Compute sales and profit variances.

Solution

(A) Sales variances (*SRV*): (Budgeted sales-Actual sales)=(₹4,68,000–₹3,98,000) = ₹70,000 (adverse/unfavourable)

1. *Sales price variance* (SPV) : (SSP – ASP) × AQ

Product			
	A: (₹15 – ₹15) × 3,600 units	=	Nil
	B: (₹25 – ₹26) × 4,000 units	=	₹4,000 (favourable)
	C: (₹40 – ₹37.50) × 6,400 units	=	16,000 (adverse)
			12,000 (adverse)

2. *Sale mix sub-variance* (SMSV): (RSQ – AQ) × SSP

Product		
	A: (3,500 units – 3,600 units) × ₹15 =	₹1,500 (favourable)
	B: (4,200 units – 4,000 units) × ₹25 =	5,000 (adverse)
	C: (6,300 units – 6,400 units) × ₹40 =	4,000 (favourable)
		500 (favourable)

*Standard proportion is 4,000: 4,800: 7,200 for products A, B and C, that is, ₹5: 6: 9 or 5/20, 6/20, 9/20 (of 14,000 units sold) respectively.

3. *Sales volume sub-variance (SVSV):* [Total budgeted sales of all products – Total actual sales of all products] × Weighted standard selling price = (16,000 units – 14,000 units) × ₹29.25 = ₹58,500 (adverse)
4. *Sales volume variance (overall):* (SQ – AQ) × SSP

Product		
	A: (4,000 units – 3,600 units) × ₹15 =	₹6,000 (adverse)
	B: (4,800 units – 4,000 units) × ₹25	20,000 (adverse)
	C: (7,200 units – 6,400 units) × ₹40	32,000 (adverse)
		58,000 (adverse)

Confirmation: SPV, ₹12,000 (A) + SMSV, ₹500 (F) + SVSV, ₹58,500 (A) = ₹70,000 (adverse)

(B) *Profit variance (overall):* (Budgeted profit–Actual profit) = (₹2,34,000 – ₹1,91,000) = ₹43,000 (adverse)

1. *Sales price variance:* ₹12,000 (adverse) (calculated above)
2. *Sales mix sub–variance* (*SMSV*): (RS Q – AQ) × SP per unit

Product			
	A (3,500 units – 3,600 units) × ₹7.50	=	₹750 (favourable)
	B (4,200 units – 4,000 units) × ₹12.50	=	2,500 (adverse)
	C (6,300 units – 6,400 units) × ₹20.00	=	2,000 (favourable)
			250 (favourable)

3. *Sales volume sub-variance (SVSV):* [Total budgeted sales of all products-Total actual sales of all products] × Weighted standard profit per unit = (16,000 units-14,000 units) × ₹14,625=₹29,250 (adverse)
4. *Cost variance:* (SC –AC) × AQ sold

Product			
	A : (₹7.50 – ₹7.50) × 3,600 units	=	Nil
	B : (₹12.50 – ₹13) × 4,000 units	=	₹2,000 (adverse)
	C : (₹20 – ₹20) × 6,400 units	=	Nil
			2,000 (adverse)

Confirmation: (i) ₹12,000 (A) + (ii) ₹250 (F) + (iii) ₹29,250 (A) + (iv) ₹2,000 (A) = ₹43,000 (A)

P.18.3 The accounting department of SIL Ltd, has furnished the following information to its management for the first quarter of the current year:

Standard cost and profit sheet per unit:	
Materials cost (2 kgs @ ₹50)	₹100
Wages (direct, 1 hour @ ₹20 per hour)	20
Variable overhead (1 hour @ ₹20 per hour)	20
Fixed overheads (normal capacity 10,000 buckets per quarter): 1 hour @ ₹40 per hour	40
Total standard cost	180
Standard profit per unit	20
Standard price per unit	200
Budgeted sales: 10,000 units per quarter.	
Actual cost, production and sales data:	
Materials purchased and consumed, 16,500 kgs @ ₹48 per kg	7,92,000
Wages: 9,000 hours @ ₹16 per hour	1,44,000
Variable overheads	1,62,000
Fixed overheads	3,80,000
Actual sales (₹210 per unit)	16,80,000
Actual production (units)	8,000

You are required to:
1. Calculate cost, sales and profit variances.
2. Prepare a reconciliation statement of profit variances with as many details as possible.

SOLUTION

Elements of cost	*Standard*			*Actual*		
	Input (kgs/hours)	*Rate*	*Total cost*	*Input (kgs/hours)*	*Rate*	*Total cost*
Material	16,000	₹50	₹8,00,000	16,500	₹48	₹7,92,000
Wages	8,000	20	1,60,000	9,000	16	1,44,000
Variable overheads	8,000	20	1,60,000	9,000	18	1,62,000
Fixed overheads	8,000	40	3,20,000*	9,000	Not required	3,80,000
			14,40,000			14,78,000

*₹3,20,000 is the standard cost of fixed overheads charged to production.

(A) *Total cost variance:* (Actual cost of 8,000 units – Standard cost of 8,000 units) = (₹14,78,000 – ₹14,40,000) = ₹38,000 (adverse).

1. Material cost variance: (SMC – AMC) = (₹8,00,000 – ₹7,92,000) = ₹8,000 (favourable)
   (a) Material price variance: (SR – AR) × AQ = (₹50 – ₹48) × 16,500 kgs = ₹33,000 (favourable)
   (b) Material usage variance: (SQ – AQ) × SR = (16,000 – 16,500) × ₹50 = ₹25,000 (adverse)
2. Labour cost variance: (SLC – ALC) = (₹1,60,000 – 1,44,000) = ₹16,000 (favourable)
   (a) Labour rate variance: (SR – AR) × AH = (₹20 – ₹16) × 9,000 = ₹36,000 (favourable)
   (b) Labour efficiency variance: (SH – AH) × SR per hour = (8,000 – 9,000) × ₹20 = ₹20,000 (adverse)
3. Variable overhead variance: (SVOC – AVOC) = (₹1,60,000 – 1,62,000) = ₹2,000 (adverse)
   (a) Variable overhead spending variance: (Actual overhead cost incurred – Standard overhead cost at actual hours) = (₹1,62,000 – ₹1,80,000) = ₹18,000 (favourable)
   (b) Variable overhead efficiency: (SH – AH) × Standard VOR per hour = (8,000 – 9,000) × ₹20 = ₹20,000 (adverse)
4. Fixed overhead variance: (Actual fixed overhead spent – Standard fixed overhead charged to production)

   = [₹3,80,000 – ₹3,20,000] = ₹60,000 (adverse)

(a) Fixed overhead spending variance: (Budgeted overhead–Actual overhead)
= [₹4,00,000 – ₹3,80,000]
= ₹20,000 (favourable)

(b) Fixed overhead efficiency variance: (SH–AH) × Standard FOR per hour = (8,000 – 9,000) × ₹40
= ₹40,000 (adverse)

(c) Capacity variance:(Normal capacity in hours–Actual hours utilised) × Standard FOR per hour
= (10,000 – 9,000) × ₹40 = ₹40,000 (adverse)

(B) *Sales variance (sales revenue variance):* (Budgeted sales – Actual sales) = [₹20,00,000 – ₹16,80,000]
= ₹3,20,000 (adverse)

(a) Sales price variance (SPV): (ASP – SSP) × AQ = (₹210 – ₹200) × 8,000 = ₹80,000 (favourable)

(b) Sales volume variance: (SQ – AQ) × SSP = (10,000 – 8,000) × ₹200 = ₹4,00,000 (adverse)

(c) Profit variance: (Standard profit – Actual profit) = ₹2,00,000 – ₹2,02,000* = ₹2,000 (favourable)

*Statement Showing Actual Profit

Actual sales revenue		₹16,80,000
Less: actual costs:		
Materials	₹7,92,000	
Wages	1,44,000	
Variable overheads	1,62,000	
Fixed overheads	3,80,000	14,78,000
Actual profit		2,02,000

1. *Sales price variance* = ₹80,000 (favourable: already calculated)
2. *Sales volume variance* =(SQ–AQ) × Standard profit per bucket = (10,000–8,000) × ₹20
= ₹40,000 (adverse)
3. *Cost variance* = (SC – AC) = ₹14,40,000 – ₹14,78,000 = ₹38,000 (adverse)

(C) *Statement of Reconciliation of Actual Profit with Budgeted Profit*

	Favourable	*Adverse*	
Budgeted profit			₹2,00,000
(a) Sales variances:			
Sales price	₹80,000		
Sales volume		₹40,000	
(b) Cost variances:			
Material price	33,000		
Material usage		25,000	
Labour rate	36,000		
Labour efficiency		20,000	
Variable overhead spending	18,000		
Variable overhead efficiency		20,000	
Fixed overhead spending	20,000		
Fixed overhead efficiency		40,000	
Capacity		40,000	
	1,87,000	(1,85,000)	2,000
Actual net profit			2,02,000

Alternatively: Profit Reconciliation Statement (taking Sales as Basis)

	Favourable	*Adverse*	
Budgeted sales revenue (10,000 × ₹200)			₹20,00,000
Sales revenue variance:			
Sales price	₹80,000		
Sales volume		(₹4,00,000)	(3,20,000)
Actual sales revenue			16,80,000

(Contd.)

(Contd.)

Less: standard cost of 8,000 buckets sold:			
Material	8,00,000		
Labour	1,60,000		
Variable overheads	1,60,000		
Fixed overheads	3,20,000		14,40,000
Standard net profit			2,40,000
Cost variance:			
Material price	33,000		
Material usage		25,000	
Labour rate	36,000		
Labour efficiency		20,000	
Variable overhead spending	18,000		
Variable overhead efficiency		20,000	
Spending fixed overhead	20,000		
Fixed overhead efficiency		40,000	
Capacity variance		40,000	
	1,07,000	(1,45,000)	(38,000)
Actual net profit			2,02,000

P.18.4 At the end of the current year, the cost accounting department of SK Industries Ltd has furnished the following summary of labour and material variances to its management:

Materials price variance	₹15,68,000 (Dr)
Materials usage variance	49,600 (Dr)
Labour rate variance (skilled labour)	3,84,000 (Dr)
Labour efficiency variance (skilled labour)	13,32,000 (Dr)

Mr Harishanker, the managing director of the company, finds it difficult to understand why the variances are so large. During the year, the company operated at 96,000 direct labour-hours and produced 4,80,000 units.

The standard cost sheet per unit is as follows:

Direct materials (2 units @ ₹12.4)	₹24.80
Direct labour (7.5 minutes @ ₹74 per hour)	9.25

The management is informed that materials can now be purchased only at ₹14 a unit. The material consumed during the period is 9,64,000 units.

The new wage rates of skilled labourers as per the new agreement with their trade union is ₹82. It is also brought to the notice of the management that only 5 units of product can be produced per labour–hour.

You are required to (i) Set up a more realistic schedule of standard unit costs for materials and labour, and (ii) Recompute the variances according to the new schedule.

Solution

(A) Statement showing standard cost per unit	
Material cost (2 units @ ₹14 a unit)	₹28
Direct labour cost (12 minutes @ ₹82 per hour)	16.40
Standard cost per unit (total)	44.40
(B) 1. *Material price variance (revised).* It would be less by ₹1.6 per unit of raw materials consumed.	
(a) Material price (standard revised)	14
Less material price (existing standard)	12.40
	1.60

(Contd.)

(*Contd.*)

(b) × units produced	9,64,000
	15,42,400
(c) Existing MPV (adverse)	15,68,000
(d) Material price variance (unfavourable)	25,600
2. *Material usage variance (revised)*	
(Standard usage – Actual usage) × ₹1.6 = (9,60,000 units – 9,64,000) × ₹1.6	6,400
Existing MUV (adverse)	49,600
MUV (adverse)	56,000
3. *Labour rate variance (revised)*	
Direct labour rate per hour (revised standard)	82
Less direct labour rate per hour (existing standard)	74
	8
(×) Direct labour hours used	96,000
	7,68,000
Existing labour rate variance (adverse)	3,84,000
Labour rate variance (favourable)	3,84,000

4. *Labour efficiency variance (revised)* = (SH – AH) × SR per hour
= (96,000 – 96,000) × ₹82 = Nil

P.18.5 ABC Ltd follows standard costing system. The standard output for a period is 20,000 units and the standard cost and profit per unit are as under:

Direct material (3 units @ ₹15)	₹45
Direct labour, unskilled (3 hours @ ₹10)	30
Direct expenses	5
Factory overheads: Variable	2.5
Fixed	3.0
Administrative overheads	3.0
Total cost	88.50
Profit	11.50
Selling price (fixed by the Government)	100.00

The actual production and sales for a period was 14,400 units. There has been no price revision by the government during the period.

The following are the variances worked out at the end of the period:

	Favourable	Adverse
Direct material:		
Price		₹42,500
Usage	₹10,500	
Direct labour:		
Rate		40,000
Efficiency	32,000	
Factory overheads:		
Variable expenditure	4,000	
Fixed expenditure	4,000	
Fixed volume		16,800
Administrative overheads:		
Expenditure		4,000
Volume		16,800

You are required to: (i) Ascertain the details of actual costs and prepare a profit and loss statement for the period showing the actual profit/loss (show workings clearly), (ii) Reconcile the actual profit with the standard profit.

SOLUTION

(i) *Statement Showing Determination of Actual Cost*

Type of cost	*Standard cost (14,400 units)*	*Variances (F)*	*Variances (A)*	*Actual cost [Add (A) Less(F)]*
Direct material	₹6,48,000	₹10,500	₹42,500	₹6,80,000
Direct labour	4,32,000	32,000	40,000	4,40,000
Factory overhead:				
Variable expenditure	36,000	4,000		32,000
Fixed expenditure and volume	43,200	4,000	16,800	56,000
Administrative overheads:				
Expenditure and volume	43,200		4,000	
			16,800	64,000

Profit and Loss Statement

Sales revenue (14,400 units × ₹100)			₹14,40,000
Less costs			
Direct material		₹6,80,000	
Direct labour		4,40,000	
Direct expenses (assumed to have no variance)		72,000	
Factory overheads:			
Variable	₹32,000		
Fixed	56,000	88,000	
Administrative overheads		64,000	13,44,000
Actual profit			96,000
Standard profit (20,000 units × ₹11.50)			2,30,000

Sales variances:

Sales price variance: (SR – AR) × AQ = (₹100 – ₹100) × 14,400 = Nil

Sales volume variance: (SQ – AQ) × SP per unit = (5,600 units × ₹11.50) = ₹64,400 (adverse)

Statement of Reconciliation of Actual Profit with Budgeted Profit

	Favourable	*Adverse*	
Budgeted profit			₹2,30,000
Sales volume		₹64,400	
Material price variance		42,500	
Material usage variance	₹10,500		
Labour rate variance		40,000	
Labour efficiency variance	32,000		
Factory overheads			
Expenditure variance (variable)	4,000		
Expenditure variance (fixed)	4,000		
Volume (fixed)		16,800	
Administrative overheads:			
Expenditure		4,000	
Volume		16,800	
	50,500	(1,84,500)	(1,34,000)
Actual profit			96,000

P.18.6 You are appointed cost accountant of Zed Ltd. Given below is the company's operating report for the month of March:

		Standard and variances	Actual
Sales (budgeted)		₹18,000	
Variance due to			
Volume of orders		1,000	
Selling prices		400	₹19,400
Profit (budgeted)		3,800	
Variance due to			
Sales volume		240	
Sales price		400	4,440
Production cost variances			
Labour	—rate	(250)	
	—efficiency	(100)	(350)
Material	—price	150	
	—usage	(60)	90
Overhead	—expenditure (fixed)	100	
	—variable	(250)	
	—efficiency	200	
	—capacity	100	150
Operating profit			4,330

Your assistant provides the following information about sales and costs for the month of April:

Product	Budgeted units	Sales value	Actual units	Sales value
A	250	₹10,000	280	₹10,800
B	200	6,000	190	5,500
C	150	3,000	180	3,500
		19,000		19,800

Product	Standard selling prices per unit	Standard product costs per unit
A	₹40	₹31
B	30	25
C	20	15

Labour:	
Standard labour cost per hour	₹ 0.90
Budgeted hours	4,000
Actual clocked hours	4,400
Standard hours produced	4,500
Actual labour costs	4,260
Material:	
Standard costs of material actually used	5,230
Standard costs of material allowed	5,330
Actual costs of material used	5,430
Overheads:	
Budgeted rates of overheads recovery per Labour-hour	
Fixed	0.50
Variable	1.00
Total	1.50

(*Contd.*)

(*Contd.*)

Actual overhead costs	
Fixed	2,000
Variable	4,300
Total	6,300

Prepare the operating statement for the month of April in the same form as for the month of March.

SOLUTION

Operating Statement for the Month of April

Particulars			Standard and variance	Actual
Sales (budgeted)			₹19,000	
Add favourable (F) variances and				
Less unfavourable (U) variances				
Volume of orders (1) (i)			1,500 (F)	
Selling prices 1 (ii)			700 (U)	₹19,800
Profit (budgeted)				
(BQ × Standard profit per unit)				
(250 × ₹9)		₹2,250		
(200 × ₹5)		1,000		
(150 × ₹5)		750	4,000	
Variance due to				
Sales volume	(2) (i)		370 (F)	
Sales price	(2) (ii)		700 (U)	3,670
Production cost variances				
Labour-rate (3) (i)			300 (U)	
—efficiency	(3) (ii)		90 (F)	210 (U)
Material —price	(4) (i)		200 (U)	
—usage	(4) (ii)		100 (F)	100 (U)
Overhead —expenditure (fixed)	(5) (i)		Nil	
—variable	(5) (ii)		100 (F)	
—efficiency	(5) (iii)		150 (F)	
—capacity	(5) (iv)		200 (F)	450 (F)
Operating profit				3,810

WORKING NOTES

Determination of variances

1. *Sales variances* due to

(i) Volume of orders measured by sales quantity variance = (Budgeted sales in units – Actual sales in units) × Budgeted selling price per unit

A : (250 – 280) × ₹40 =	₹1,200 (favourable)
B : (200 – 190) × ₹30 =	300 (unfavourable)
C : (150 – 180) × ₹20 =	600 (favourable)
	1,500 (favourable)

Selling prices measured by sales price variance = (Budgeted selling price – Actual selling price) × actual quantity

or, [(Budgeted selling price × AQ) – (Actual selling price × AQ)]

A : (₹40 × 280 = ₹11,200) – ₹10,800	=	₹400 (unfavourable)
B : (₹30 × 190 = ₹5,700) – ₹5,500	=	200 (unfavourable)
C : (₹20 × 180 = ₹3,600) – ₹3,500	=	100 (unfavourable)
		700 (unfavourable)

2. *Profit variance* due to
   (i) Sales volume = (Budgeted sales in units – Actual sales in units) × Budgeted profit per unit
   A : (250 – 280) × ₹9 = ₹270 (favourable)
   B : (200 – 190) × ₹5 = 50 (unfavourable)
   C : (150 – 180) × ₹5 = 150 (favaourable)
   370 (favourable)
   (ii)Sales price = ₹700 (unfavourable) (calculated in part 1)
3. *Labour cost variance*
   (i) Labour rates variances (Standard wage rate – Actual wage rate) × Actual hours or,
   [(Standard wage rate × AH) – (Actual wage rate × AH)] = [(₹0.90 × 4,400 = ₹3,960) – (₹4,260)]
   = ₹300 (unfavourable)
   (ii) Labour efficiency variance = (SH – AH) × SR = (4,500 – 4,400) × 0.90 = ₹90 (favourable)
4. *Material cost variance*
   (i) Material price variance = (SR – AR) × AQ or [(SR × AQ) – (AR × AQ)]
   = ₹5,230 – ₹5,430 = ₹200 (unfavourable)
   (ii) Material usage variance= (SQ – AQ) 3 SR or [(SQ × SR) – (AQ × SR)]
   = ₹5,330 – ₹5,230 = ₹100 (favourable)
5. *Overhead costs variance*
   (i) Fixed expenditure variance = Budgeted fixed overheads – Actual fixed overheads
   = (₹0.50 × 4,000 = ₹2,000 – ₹2,000) = Nil
   (ii) Variable expenditure variance = (Budgeted variable overheads at AH – Actual variable overheads)
   = (₹1 × 4,400 = ₹4,400 – ₹4,300) = ₹100 (favourable)
   (iii) Efficiency variance = (SH – AH) × Standard overheads rate per hour
   = (4,500 – 4,400) × ₹1.50 = ₹150 (favourable)
   (iv) Capacity variance = (Budgeted/normal capacity hours–Actual hours) × Standard fixed overhead rate per hour
   = (4,000 – 4,400) × ₹0.50 = ₹200 (favourable)

P.18.7 The managers of Garware Company Ltd, which manufactures paints, were disappointed at the shortfall in profits for the current year as shown below:

Income Statement for the Current Year (*₹ in lakh*)

Particulars	Budgeted	Actual
Units sales (in lakh of litres)	5	5.4
Sales revenue	60.00	61.02
Variable manufacturing costs:		
Materials	10.00	10.90
Direct labour	7.50	8.50
Variable overheads	2.50	2.60
Total variable costs	20.00	22.00
Contribution	40.00	39.02
Fixed costs:		
Manufacturing	25.00	25.40
Selling and administrative	10.00	9.95
Total fixed costs	35.00	35.35
Profit before tax	5.00	3.67

The President of the company asks you to make an analysis in detail showing why the results fell short of the budgeted profits. Production equalled sales during the period under reference.

SOLUTION

Profit variance (overall): (Budgeted profit–Actual profit) = (₹5 lakh–₹3.67 lakh) = ₹1.33 lakh (adverse)

1. *Sales price variances:* (SSP–ASP) × AQ sold = (₹12–₹11.30) × ₹5.4 lakh = ₹3.78 lakh (adverse)
2. *Sales volume variance:* (SQ – AQ) × SP per unit = (5 lakh – 5.4 lakh) × ₹1 = ₹0.4 lakh (favourable)
3. *Cost variances:*
   (a) Materials (SMC – AMC) × AQ or (SMC × AQ) – (AMC × AQ) = (₹2 per unit × 5.4 lakh) – ₹10.9 lakh = ₹0.1 lakh (adverse)
   (b) Direct labour (SLC – ALC) × AQ or [(SLC × AQ) – (ALC × AQ)] = (₹1.50 per unit × 5.4 lakh) – ₹5.4 lakh) – ₹8.5 lakh = ₹0.4 lakh (adverse)
   (c) Variable overheads (SVOR – AVOR) × AQ or (AVOR × AQ) – (AVOR × AQ) = (₹0.50 per unit × 5.4 lakh) – ₹2.6 lakh = ₹0.1 lakh (favourable)
   (d) Fixed overheads variance: (Actual overheads – Standard overheads charged to production) = [(₹35.35 lakh (5.4 lakh units × ₹7 SFOR per unit)] = ₹2.45 lakh (favourable)
      (i) Spending variance: (Actual overheads–Budgeted overheads) = (₹35.35 lakh – ₹35.0 lakh) = ₹0.35 lakh (adverse)
      (ii) Capacity variance: (Budgeted capacity – Actual capacity) × SFOR = (5 lakh units – 5.4 lakh) × ₹7 = ₹2.8 lakh (favourable)

Reconciliation Statement of Budgeted Profits with Actual Profits *(₹ in lakh)*

Particulars	Variances: Favourable	Variances: Adverse	Amount
Budgeted profit			5.00
Sales price variance		3.78	
Sales volume variance	0.4		
Material variance		0.10	
Direct labour variance		0.40	
Variable overheads variance	0.1		
Fixed overheads variances:			
Spending variance		0.35	
Capacity variance	2.8		
Total	3.3	(4.63)	(1.33)
Actual profit			3.67

P.18.8 A department in a factory working 40-hours a week can employ upto maximum of 30 employees. In a budget period of 4 weeks, it is expected that 4,000 labour-hours will be worked and that production will equal 5,000 standard hours.

At the end of the period, it is found that 3,600 labour-hours have actually been used and production amounts to 4,000 standard hours.

Present figures to management to illustrate the efficiency, activity and capacity usage. Show where there is scope for improvement and how improvement may be effected.

SOLUTION

Efficiency ratio = (Standard hours for actual production/Actual hours) × 100 = (4,000/3,600) × 100 = 111.11 per cent

Activity ratio = (Standard hour for actual output/Budgeted standard hours) × 100 = (4,000/5,000) × 100 = 80 per cent

Capacity usage ratio = (Actual hours worked/Budgeted hours) × 100 = 3,600/4,000) × 100 = 90 per cent

There is need for increasing the use of idle capacity (represented by less then 100 per cent activity and capacity utilisation ratios). This can be effected by increasing production.

REVIEW QUESTIONS

RQ.18.1 Indicate whether the following statements are 'True' or 'False'.

(i) Profit variance is explained by total cost variance and total sales variance.

(ii) Profit variance is explained by total cost variance, sales price variance and sales volume variance.

(iii) Sales mix variance originates when the proportion of actual units sold differs from the standard proportion.

(iv) The basis of determining sales volume variance is the same whether it is a part of profit variance or sales variance.

(v) The basis of determining sales volume variance differs when it is a part of profit variance and when it is a part of sales variance.

(vi) If profit variance is unfavourable, it implies that its all sub-variances are also unfavourable.

(vii) A good management reporting system requires that significant variances only should be reported.

(viii) Tabular format is the more effective method of reporting variances than control chart.

(ix) Cost variances can be disposed off by following either of the two methods. The firm has an option of exclusive adoption of one or another.

(x) Variances can be disposed off by transferring to profit and loss account. This method is appropriate if standards are current and attainable.

[Answers: (i) False, (ii) True, (iii) True, (iv) False, (v) True, (vi) False, (vii) True, (viii) True, (ix) False, (x) True.]

RQ.18.2 Fill in the following blanks.

(i) __________ chart is an effective method of reporting significant variances.

(ii) There are two methods of disposing off cost variances: first is they may be transferred to profit and loss account and the second method requires them to be considered as __________.

(iii) Efficiency ratio is determined dividing __________ by actual hours worked.

(iv) Capacity utilization ratio is determined dividing actual hours worked by __________.

(v) Material yield ratios is based on actual yield and __________.

(vi) Volume variance ratio shows the relationship between actual production and __________.

(vii) Material cost variance ratio is the product of material price variance ratio and __________.

(viii) Control chart is primarily based on __________.

(ix) __________ is prepared to reconcile actual profit and budgeted profits.

(x) Profit variance is difference between actual profit and __________.

[Answers: (i) Control, (ii) cost of product, (iii) standard hours required for actual production, (iv) budgeted hours, (v) standard yield, (vi) Normal production, (vii) material usage variance ratio, (viii) tolerance limits, (ix) Profit reconciliation statement, (x) budgeted profit.]

RQ.18.3 Describe the procedure of determining sales and profit variances. Are they similar in certain respects?

RQ.18.4 "Variances are not an end in themselves." In the light of the above statement, explain briefly what you understand by variances control and responsibility?

RQ.18.5 Comment on the following statements:

1. "Variances should not be viewed in isolation."
2. "Profit reconciliation statement is an important statement from the point of view of management."
3. "Management should not be guided by the designated variances—favourable or unfavourable."

RQ.18.6 In what ways is variance analysis helpful to management?

RQ.18.7 Certain ratios are very important in connection with budgetary control and standard costing. What are these ratios? State the application of such ratios.

RQ.18.8 What are the two approaches to disposing off variances? Which will be preferred, when, and why? Take suitable examples to support your viewpoint.

RQ.18.9 Write short notes on:

1. Tolerance limits
2. Significant and non-significant variances
3. Graphic and tabular presentation of variances
4. Disposal of variances.

RQ.18.10 From the following details, reconcile the budgeted sales with actual sales and standard profit with actual profit in terms of variances:

Products	*Budgeted*			*Actual*		
	Quantity (units)	*Selling price*	*Cost*	*Quantity (units)*	*Selling price*	*Cost*
Product A	4,000	₹24	₹14	4,500	₹22	₹15
Product B	6,000	18	12	3,000	20	11

RQ.18.11 PH Ltd. furnishes the following information relating to budgeted sales and actual sales for April.

	Product	*Sales quantity (units)*	*Selling price per unit*
Budgeted	A	1,200	₹15
	B	800	20
	C	2,000	40
Actual sales	A	880	18
	B	880	20
	C	2,640	38

Calculate the following variances:

(1) Sales quantity variance,
(2) Sales mix variance,
(3) Sales price variance, and
(4) Total sales variance.

RQ.18.12 From the following budgeted and actual figures, calculate and present the variances in respect of profit on sales and cost of sales.

Budget:	Sales, 2,000 units @ ₹15 each	₹30,000
	Cost of sales @ ₹12 each	24,000
	Profit	6,000
Actual:	Sales, 1,900 units @ ₹14 each	26,000
	Cost of sales @ ₹10 each	19,000
	Profit	7,600

RQ.18.13 From the following data for a particular period, compute sales and profit variances:

Budgeted sales:	X, 3,000 units @ ₹20 (standard cost ₹12)
	Y, 2,000 units @ ₹10 (standard cost ₹6)
Actual sales:	X, 4,000 units @ ₹18 each
	Y, 2,500 units @ ₹11 each

RQ.18.14 From the following information, calculate the various sales variances.

Product	*Standard*		*Actual*	
	Quantity	*Price*	*Quantity*	*Price*
X	15,000	₹5.00	18,000	₹5.10
Y	9,000	8.00	10,000	7.00
Z	6,000	10.00	5,000	9.50

ANSWERS [Comprehensive solutions to all numerical review questions are available on the companion website: http://www.mhhe.com/khan_jain_cost2e]

RQ.18.10 SPV, ₹3,000 (A); SMV, ₹9,000 (F); SVSV, ₹51,000 (A); Total sales variance, ₹45,000 (A). Profit variance, ₹17,500 (A); SPV, ₹3,000 (A); SMV, ₹6,000 (F); SVSV, ₹19,000 (A); Cost variance, ₹1,500 (A).

RQ.18.11 **(i)**SQV, ₹11,400 (F);
(ii) SMV, ₹11,000 (F);
(iii) SPV, ₹2,640 (A);
(iv) Total sales variance, ₹19,760 (F).

RQ.18.12 **(a)**Total sales variance ₹3,400 (A); SPV, ₹1,900 (A); SVV, ₹1,500 (A)
(c) Cost of sales variance, ₹3,800 (F).
(d) Overall profit variance, ₹1,600 (F): SPV, ₹1,900 (A), SVV, ₹3,000 (A), Cost variance, ₹3,800 (F).

RQ.18.13 Total sales variance, ₹19,500 (F): SPV, ₹5,500 (A); SMV, ₹1,000 (F); SVV, ₹24,000 (F)
Total profit variance, ₹4,500 (F): SPV, ₹5,500 (A); SMV, ₹400 (F); SVV, ₹9,600 (F).

RQ.18.14 Total sales variance, ₹2,300 (F): SPV, ₹10,700 A; SMV, ₹7,700 A; SVV, ₹20,700 (F).

CASES

18.C.1 (Profit Variance Analysis) Supreme Ltd. is an auto-parts manufacturing company. Supreme has shown consistently profitable performance over the last 8 years. However, in the last quarter of the current year, Supreme's net profits and net sales dipped by 20 per cent and 25 per cent respectively.

The CEO of Supreme, Saurabh Bharat, directed the Controller, Sumantra Chatterjee, to present an account of the budgeted and actual performance of the company for the current month. Sumantra Chatterjee, with the help of the Chief Cost Accountant, presented the relevant cost/profit data summarised in Exhibit 1.

Exhibit 1 Cost/Profit Data for October

Standard Data:		
1. Material cost (per unit):		
Material A (5 kgs @ ₹50/kg)	₹250	
B (3 kgs @ ₹70/kg)	210	
C (2 kgs @ ₹105/kg)	210	₹670
2. Labour cost (per unit):		
Department X (6 hours × ₹20/hr)	120	
Department Y (4 hours × ₹25/hr)	100	220
3. Variable overheads per unit (10 hours × ₹10/hr)		100
4. Fixed overheads per unit (10 hours × ₹8/hr)		80
	1,070	
5. Unit sale price		1,400
6. Budgeted sales (units)		4,000
7. Normal capacity (units)		5,000
8. Budgeted fixed overheads (₹)		4,00,000
Actual Data:		
1. Material cost (total):		
Material A (24,500 kgs @ ₹48/kg)	11,76,000	
B (10,500 kgs @ ₹72/kg)	7,56,000	
C (3,500 kgs @ ₹105/kg)	3,67,500	22,99,500
2. Labour cost (total):		
Department X (28,000 hours @ ₹18/hr)	5,04,000	
Y (10,500 hours @ ₹27/hr)	2,83,500	7,87,500

(Contd.)

(*Contd.*)

3. Vehicles overheads (38,500 hours @ ₹11/hr)	4,23,500
4. Fixed overheads	4,20,000
5. Sales (units)	3,500
6. Unit sale price (₹)	1,350

Based on the above, the Controller prepared a comparative profit statement to present to the CEO (Exhibit 2)

Exhibit 2 Profit Calculations—Budgeted and Actual

Budgeted Profit:			
Budgeted profit per unit, ₹330 × Budged sales, 4,000 units			₹13,20,000
Actual Profit:			
Sales (₹1,350 × 3,500 units)			47,25,000
Less costs:			
Material costs:			
Material A	₹11,76,000		
B	7,56,000		
C	3,67,500	22,99,500	
Labour costs:			
Department X	5,04,000		
Y	2,83,500	7,87,500	
Variable overheads		4,23,500	
Fixed overheads		4,20,000	39,30,500
Profit			7,94,500

REQUIRED:

Prepare a detailed variance analysis and highlight the remedial measures that Supreme should take to remedy the situation arising out of declining profitability and sales in recent months and fix responsibility for the variances.

SOLUTION

Total Profit Variance = ₹(13,20,000 budgeted – ₹7,94,500 actual) = ₹5,25,500 (unfavourable)

(A) Sales Price Variance = (₹1,350 budgeted – ₹1,400 actual) × 3,500 = ₹1,75,000 (unfavourable)

(B) Sales Quantity Variance (3,500 actual – 4,000 budgeted) × ₹330 = ₹1,65,000 (unfavourable)

(C) Total Cost Variance (₹39,30,500 actual – ₹37,45,000 budgeted) = ₹1,85,500 (unfavourable)

(a) Total Actual Material Cost and Total Standard Material Cost of 3,500 Units

Raw	*Actual*			*Standard*		
Material	*AQ (kgs)*	*AP*	*TAMC*	*SQ (kgs)*	*SP*	*TSMC*
A	24,500	₹48	₹11,76,000	17,500	₹50	₹8,75,000
B	10,500	72	7,56,000	10,500	70	7,35,000
C	3,500	105	3,67,500	7,000	105	7,35,000
Total	38,500		22,99,500	35,000		23,45,000

AQ = actual quantity SP = standard price

AP = actual price TAMC = total actual material cost

SQ = standard quantity TSMC = total standard material cost

Total Material Cost Variance (TMCV) = (₹22,99,500 – ₹23,45,000) = ₹45,500 (favourable)

TMCV is sub-divided into the following 3 sub-variances:

- Material Price Variance

Material A (₹48 – ₹50) × 24,500 kgs = ₹49,000 (favourable)
B (₹72 – ₹70) × 10,500 kgs = 21,000 (unfavourable)
C (₹105 – ₹105) × 3,500 kgs = Nil
28,000 (favourable)

- Material Mix Sub Variance

Material A (24,500 – 19,250) kgs × ₹50 = ₹2,62,500 (unfavourable)
B (10,500 – 11,550) kgs × ₹70 = 73,500 (favourable)
C (3,500 – 77,000) kgs × ₹105 = 4,41,000 (favourable)
2,52,000 (favourable)

- Material Yield Sub Variance (MYSV)

Standard yield = 38,500/(5 + 3 + 2) = 3,850 units
Standard material cost per kg of finished production = (5 kgs × ₹50 + 3kgs × ₹70 + 2 kgs × 105)
= ₹670
MYSV = (3,500 – 3,850) kgs × ₹670 = ₹2,34,500 (unfavourable)

(b) Labour Cost Variance

Total Actual Labour Cost and Total Standard Labour Cost of 3,500 Units Department-wise

Department	*Actual*			*Standard*		
	TAH	*AR*	*TALC*	*TSH*	*SR*	*TSLC*
X	28,000	₹18	₹5,04,000	21,000	₹20	₹4,20,000
Y	10,500	27	2,83,500	14,000	25	3,50,000
Total	38,500		7,87,500	35,000		7,70,000

TAH = total actual hour SR = standard rate
AR = actual rate TALC = total actual labour cost
TSH total standard hours TSLC = total standard labour cost

Total Labour Cost Variance (TLCV) = (₹7,87,500 – ₹7,70,000) = ₹17,500 (unfavourable)

TLCV is sub divided into 2 sub-variances:

- Labour Rate Variance

Department X (₹18 – ₹20) × 28,000 hours = ₹56,000 (favourable)
Y (₹27 – ₹25) × 10,500 hours = 21,000 (unfavourable)
₹35,000 (favourable)

- Labour Efficiency Variance (LEV)

Department X (28,000 hrs – 21,000 hrs) × ₹20 = ₹1,40,000 (unfavourable)
Y (10,500 hrs – 14,000 hrs) × 25 = 87,500 (favourable)
52,500 (unfavourable)

LEV can be further subdivided into two sub-variances:

(1) Labour Mix Sub Variance

Department X (28,000 hrs – 23,100 hrs) × ₹20 = ₹98,000 (unfavourable)
Y (10,500 hrs – 15,500 hrs) × 25 = 1,22,500 (favourable)
24,500 (unfavourable)

(2) Labour Yield Sub Variance (LYSV)

Standard yield = 38,500/(6 + 4) = 3,850 units
Standard rate per unit = (₹6 × 20 + 4 × ₹25) = ₹220
LYSV = (3,500 – 3,850) × ₹220 = ₹77,000 (unfavourable)

(c) Total Variable Overhead Cost Variance (TVOCV) = (₹4,23,500 – ₹3,50,000) = ₹73,500 (unfavourable)
TVOCV is further subdivided into the following 2 sub-variances:

- Variable Overhead Spending Variance
  (₹11 – ₹10) × 38,500 = ₹38,500 (unfavourable)
- Variable Overhead Efficiency Variance
  (38,500 – 35,000) × ₹10 = ₹35,000 (unfavourable)

(d) Total Fixed Overhead Cost Variance (TFOCV) = (₹4,20,000 – ₹2,80,000) = ₹1,40,000 (unfavourable)
TFOCV is further subdivided into the following 3 sub-variances:

- Fixed Overhead Spending Variance = (₹4,20,000 – ₹4,00,000) = ₹20,000 (unfavourable)
- Fixed Overhead Efficiency Variance = (38,500 – 35,000) × ₹8 = ₹28,000 (unfavourable)
- Capacity Variance = (38,500 hrs – 50,000 hrs) × ₹8 = ₹92,000 (unfavourable)

Statement of Reconciliation of Actual Profit with Budgeted Total Profit

Budgeted Profits		₹13,20,000
Add Favourable Variances:		
Material Price Variance	₹28,000	
Material Mix Sub Variance	2,52,000	
Labour Rate Variance	35,000	
Labour Mix SubVariance	24,500	3,39,500
Less Unfavourable Variance:		
Sales Price Variance	₹1,75,000	
Sales Quantity Variance	1,65,000	
Material Yield Sub Variance	2,34,500	
Labour shield Sub Variance	77,000	
Variable Overhead Spending Variance	38,500	
Variable Overhead Efficiency Variance	35,000	
Fixed Overhead Spending Variance	20,000	
Fixed Overhead Efficiency Variance	28,000	
Capacity Variance	92,000	(8,65,000)
Actual Profit		7,94,500

Summary: Unfavourable Variance

Controllable	*Responsibility*
Sales Quantity Variance	Sales manager
Material Yield Sub Variance	Production manager
Labour Yield Sub Variance	Production manager
Variable Overhead Efficiency Variance	Production manager
Fixed Overhead Efficiency Variance	Production manager

18.C.2 (Profit Variance Analysis) Mughal Pharmaceuticals manufactures and sells prickly heat powder under the brand Shower to Towel. The standard cost sheet per carton (100 packs of 200 grams each) of Shower to Towel powder is given in Exhibit 1.

Exhibit 1 Cost and Price Data

Standard Cost:		
1. Materials:		
Boric acid (1 kg @ ₹250 per kg)	₹250	
Zinc oxide (3 kgs @ ₹200 per kg)	600	
Perfumed talc base (16 kgs @ ₹75 per kg)	1,200	₹2,050
2. Labour cost (5 hours @ ₹20 per hour)		100
3. Variable overheads (5 hours @ ₹40 per hour)		200

(Contd.)

(*Contd.*)

4. Fixed overheads (5 hours @ ₹100 per hour)		500
		2,850
Standard price per carton		4,000
Budgeted sales volume (cartons in the current quarter)		6,000
Normal capacity (cartons per quarter)		6,000
Actual Cost for First Quarter, Current Year:		
1. Materials purchased/consumed:		
Boric acid (4,730 kgs @ ₹240 per kg)	₹11,35,200	
Zinc oxide (14,450 kgs @ ₹210 per kg)	30,34,500	
Perfumed talc base (81,350 kgs @ ₹78 per kg)	63,45,300	1,05,15,000
2. Labour cost (25,000 hours @ ₹22)		5,61,000
3. Variable overheads (25,500 hours @ ₹42)		10,71,000
4. Fixed overheads (30,000 hours @ ₹101)		30,60,000
		1,52,07,000
Actual production/sales (5,000 cartons @ ₹4,000 per carton)		2,00,00,000
Idle hours		850

The profit statement for the quarter is given in Exhibit 2.

Exhibit 2 Profit Statement for the Quarter

Budgeted Profit:			
6,000 cartons × ₹1,150 (sales price ₹4,000 – ₹2,850, cost)			₹69,00,000
Actual Profit:			
Sales (₹4,000 × 5,000 cartons)		₹2,00,00,000	
Less costs:			
Material cost	₹1,05,15,000		
Labour cost	5,61,000		
Variable overheads	10,71,000		
Fixed overheads	30,60,000	1,52,07,000	47,93,000
(Budgeted profit – Actual profit)			21,07,000

Mr Akbar, the CEO of Mughal Pharmaceuticals is unable to make out where the problem was in the business that could account for the reduction in profits in the current quarter.

REQUIRED

Prepare a detailed variance analysis to identify the causes for the decline in profit for the consideration of the CEO.

SOLUTION

Total Profit Variance = Total Actual Profit – Total Budgeted Profit
= ₹47,93,000 – ₹69,00,000 = ₹21,07,000 (unvarouable). This variance is caused due to the following three sub-variances:

(1) Total Quantity Variance: [Actual Quantity (AQ) – Budgeted Quantity (BQ) × Standard profit per unit
= (5,000 AQ – 6,000 BQ) × ₹1,150 = ₹11,50,00 (unvarouable)

(2) Sales Price Variance = [Actual Price (AP) – Budgeted Price (BP) × AQ sold
= (₹4,000 – ₹4,000) × 5,000 = 0.

(3) Total Cost Variance = [Total Actual Cost (AC) – Total Standard Cost (SC)]
= (₹1,52,07,000 – ₹1,42,50,000) = ₹9,57,000 (unvarouable)

Total cost variance is further sub-divided into various sub-cost variances (material, labour and overheads):

(A) Total Material Cost Variance = Total actual material cost – Total standard material cost = ₹1,05,15,000 – 1,02,50,000 = ₹2,65,000 (unfavourable)

(a) Material Price Variance = (Actual price – standard price) × Actual quantity

Boric acid (₹240 – ₹250) ×	4,730 kgs	₹47,300 (favourable)
Zinc oxide (₹210 – ₹200) ×	14,450 kgs	1,44,500 (unvarouable)
Perfumed talc base (₹78 – ₹75) ×	81,350 kgs	2,44,050 (unvarouable)
Total	1,00,530 kgs	3,41,250 (unfavourable)

(b) Mix Variance = (Standard mix of actual quantity – actual mix) × Standard price

Boric acid [(1,00,530 × 1/20) – 4,730] × ₹250	=	₹74,125 (favourable)
Zinc oxide [(1,00,530 × 3/20) – 14,450] × ₹200	=	1,25,900 (favourable)
Perfumed talc base [(1,00,530 × 16/20) – 81,350] × ₹75	=	69,450 (unvarouable)
Total		1,30,575 (favourable)

(c) Material Yield Variance = (Standard Yield – Actual Yield) × Standard material cost per unit = (5,026.5* – 5,000) × ₹2,050 = ₹54,325 (unfavourable)

*(1,00,530 kg mix should yield 1,00,530/20 = 5,026.5 cartons)

(B) Total Labour Cost Variance = Total actual labour cost – Total standard labour cost = ₹5,61,000 – ₹5,00,000 = ₹61,000 (unfavourable)

(a) Labour efficiency variance = (Actual hours – Standard hours) × Standard rate per hour) = (25,500 – 25,000) × ₹20 = ₹10,000 (favourable)

(i) Idle time variance = (Idle hours x Standard cost per hour) = 850 × ₹20 = ₹17,000 (unfavourable)

(ii) Revised labour efficiency variance = (Actual hours worked – Standard hours) × Standard rate per hour = (24,650 – 25,000) × ₹20 = ₹7,000 (favourble)

(b) Labour rate variance = (Actual rate – Standard rate) × Actual hours paid = (₹22 – ₹20) × 25,500 = ₹51,000 (unfavourable)

(C) Total variable overhead cost variance = Total actual variable cost – Total Standard variable overhead cost = ₹10,71,000 – ₹10,00,000 = ₹71,000 (unfavourable)

(a) Variable overhead efficiency variance = (Actual hours – Standard hours) × Standard variable overhead rate per hour = (25,500 – 25,000) × ₹40 = ₹20,000 (unfavourable)

(b) Variable overhead rate variance = (Actual rate – Standard rate) × Actual hours = (Total actual variable overheads – (Standard rate × Actual hours) = ₹10,71,000 – (₹40 × 25,500) = ₹51,000 (unfavourable)

(D) Total fixed overhead cost variance = Total actual fixed overhead cost – Total standard fixed overhead cost = ₹30,60,000 – ₹25,00,000 = ₹5,60,000 (unfavourable)

(a) Fixed overhead efficiency variance = (Actual hours – Standard hours) × Standard overhead rate per hour = (25,500 – 25,000) × ₹100 = ₹50,000 (unfavourable)

(b) Fixed overhead spending variance = (Total actual fixed overhead cost – Total budgeted fixed overhead cost) = ₹30,60,000 – ₹30,00,000 = ₹60,000 (unfavourble)

(c) Capacity variance = (Normal hours – Actual hours) × Standard overhead rate per hour = (30,000 – 25,500) × ₹100 = 4,50,000 (unfavourable).

Causes for Variances

1. The significant reduction in profit was mainly due to the discrepancies caused by the maintenance and the production departments.
2. Maintenance department should be attributed the major share of reduction in the profits. The capacity variance is ₹5,60,000 and could be due to breakdown in the machinery last month. The idle labour hours

might also have been due to the same factor for the efficiency variance of the labour is favourable. An explanation is required from the manager of the department.

3. Production manager has much more digressed from the normal course of his business by not only purchasing materials at the higher rate (causing material cost variance unfavourable) but also by changing the product-mix to get positive mix variance. He has used more quantity of cheaper talc base material and less of costlier Boric acid material. This can bring hazard to the future sales of the powder for it is a mix sensitive product. An explanation should be called from him.

18.C.3 (Cost Variance Analysis) HydeSign Leathers Ltd. manufactures leather jackets in Ludhiana. The company has witnessed steady increase in business and profits. Hyde Sign sells jackets to exporters and design houses. It makes leather jackets in three sizes: small, medium and large, medium being the most popular size in terms of demand followed by large and small. Each size of leather jacket takes the same amount of labour-hours and has the same variable and fixed overheads. The material cost and quality is also the same for each jacket size. The only difference is in the amount of material (i.e. leather, lining cloth and accessories) each size of jacket takes.

The standard cost sheet for the three sizes of leather jackets is given in Exhibit 1.

Exhibit 1 Standard Cost Sheet For Jackets (Capacity: 20,000 jackets)

Particulars	*Small Jackets (Budgeted Sales 4,000 jackets)*	*Medium jackets (Budgeted Sales 10,000 jackets)*	*Large jackets (Budgeted Sales 6,000 jackets)*
1. Materials:			
Leather: (4 meters × ₹400)	₹1,600		
(5 meters × ₹400)		₹2,000	
(6.5 meters × ₹400)			₹2,600
Lining cloth: (4 meters × ₹50)	200		
(5 meters × ₹50)		250	
(7 meters × ₹50)			350
Accessories	100	100	100
Total	1,900	2,350	3,050
2. Labour cost (5 hours × ₹30)	150	150	150
3. Variable overheads (5 hours × ₹40)	200	200	200
4. Fixed overheads (5 hours × ₹60)	300	300	300
Total cost	2,550	3,000	3,700
5. Unit sales price	3,000	3,500	4,200
6. Profit per unit	450	500	500

The actual cost sheet for the most current year is given in Exhibit 2.

Exhibit 2 Actual Total Cost Sheet (Production: 20,000 jackets)

	Small jackets (4,000 units)	*Medium jackets (10,000 units)*	*Large jackets (6,000 units)*
1. Material cost:			
Leather: (4 meters × ₹390 × 4,000)	₹62,40,000		
(5 meters × ₹390 × 10,000)		₹1,95,00,000	
(6.5 meters × ₹390 × 6,000)			₹1,52,10,000
Lining cloth: (4 meters × ₹55 × 4,000)	8,80,000		
(5 meters × ₹55 × 10,000)		27,50,000	
(6.5 meters × ₹55 × 6,000)			23,10,000

(*Contd.*)

(*Contd.*)

Accessories	4,80,000	12,00,000	7,20,000
	76,00,000	2,34,50,000	1,82,40,000
2. Labour cost: (22,000 hours × ₹30.50)	6,71,000		
(55,000 hours × ₹30.50)		16,77,500	
(33,000 hours × ₹30.50			10,06,500
3. Variable overheads	9,90,000	24,75,000	14,85,000
4. Fixed overheads (5 hours × ₹60)	13,20,000	33,00,000	19,80,000
	1,05,81,000	3,09,02,500	2,27,11,500

The total budget profit and actual profit are shown in Exhibit 3.

Exhibit 3 Budgeted and Actual Profits

Budgeted Profit:			
Small jackets	(4,000 × ₹450)	₹18,00,000	
Medium	(10,000 × ₹500)	50,00,000	
Large	(6,000 × ₹50)	30,00,000	₹98,00,000
Actual Profit:			
Sales:			
Small	(4,000 × ₹3,000)	₹1,20,00,000	
Medium	(10,000 × ₹3,500)	3,50,00,000	
Large	(6,000 × ₹4,200)	2,52,00,000	₹7,22,00,000
Less Costs:			
Material (₹76,00,000 + ₹2,34,50,000 + ₹1,82,40,000)		₹4,92,90,000	
Labour (₹6,71,000 + ₹16,77,500 + ₹10,06,500)		33,55,000	
Variable overheads (₹9,90,000 + ₹24,75,000 + ₹14,85,000)		49,50,000	
Fixed overheads (₹13,20,000 + ₹33,00,000 + ₹19,90,000)		66,00,000	6,41,95,000
Profit			80,05,000

The CEO of Hyde Sign, Kalpana Singh, is unable to figure out why profits have declined. She asks the CFO, Tarun Soneja, to carry out a detail analysis of the reasons for drop in profit.

Required

Compute the various cost variances to identify the causes and suggest remedial measures.

Solution

Total Profit Variance = Total Actual Profit – Total Budgeted Profit
= ₹80,05,000 – ₹98,00,000 = ₹17,95,000 (unfavourable)

Sales price variance = Nil

Sales Quantity Variance = (Actual Quantity 20,000 – Budgeted Quantity 20,000) × Standard Profit per Unit = Nil

Total cost variance = Total actual costs – Total budgeted costs
= ₹6,41,95,000 – ₹6,24,00,000 = ₹17,95,000 (unfavourable)

Total Cost Sub-Variance is further sub-divided into various sub-cost variances:

Total Material Cost Variance = Total Actual Material Cost – Total Standard Material Cost
= ₹4,92,90,000 - ₹4,94,00,000 = ₹1,10,000 (favourable)

Material Price Variance = (Actual Price – Standard Price) × Actual Quantity

Leather (₹390 – ₹400) × 3,10,000 meters	₹31,00,000 (favourable)
Lining Cloth (₹55 – ₹50) × 3,20,000 meters	16,00,000 (unfavourable)
Accessories (₹120 – ₹100) × 20,000 jackets	4,00,000 (unfavourable)
	11,00,000 (favourable)

Total Labour Cost Variance = Total Actual Labour Cost – Total Labour Cost
= ₹33,55,000 – 30,00,000 = ₹3,55,000 (unfavourable)

Labour Efficiency Variance = (Actual Hours – Standard Hours) × Standard Rate Per Hour
= (1,10,000 – 1,00,000) × ₹30 = ₹3,00,000 (unfavourable)

Labour Rate Variance = (Actual Rate – Standard Rate) × Actual Hours Paid
= (₹30.5 – ₹30) × 1,10,000 = ₹55,000 (unfavourable)

Total Variable Overhead Cost Variance
= Total Actual Variable Overhead Cost – Total Standard Variable Overhead Cost
= ₹49,50,000 – ₹40,00,000 = ₹9,50,000 (unfavourable)

Variable Overhead Efficiency Variance
= (Actual Hours – Standard Hours) × Standard Overhead Variable Overhead Rate Per Hour
= (1,10,000 – 1,00,000) × ₹40 = ₹4,00,000 (unfavourable)

Variable Overhead Rate Variance = (Actual Rate – Standard Rate) × Actual Hours
= (₹45 – ₹40) × 1,10,000 = ₹5,50,000 (unfavourable)

Total Fixed Overhead Variance = Total Actual Fixed Overhead – Total Standard Fixed Overhead
= ₹66,00,000 – ₹60,00,000 = ₹6,00,000 (unfavourable)

Fixed Overhead Efficiency Variance = (Actual hours – Standard hours) × Standard overhead rate per hour
= (1,10,000 – 1,00,000) × ₹60 = ₹6,00,000 (unfavourable)

Fixed Overhead Spending Variance = Total Actual Fixed Overhead Cost – Total Budgeted Fixed Overhead Cost
= ₹66,00,000 – ₹60,00,000 = ₹6,00,000 (unfavourable)

Capacity Variance = (Normal Hours – Actual Hours) × Standard Fixed Overhead Rate Per Hour
= (1,00,000 – 1,10,000) × ₹60 = ₹6,00,000 (favourable).

Reasons for Drop in Profits: The dip in profits (₹17,95,000) is mainly due to increase in production costs as sales variance is nil. An important contributory factor in substantially higher production cost is the increase in labour cost as reflected in labour efficiency variance. The unfavourable labour efficiency variance is the result of increase in number of hours taken to produce each jacket by half-hour as well as increase in labour costs by ₹0.50 per hour. The variable overheads have also increased due to increase in the number of hours of production.

The responsibility for these variance should rest with the heads of the production and personnel departments. The sales department should be commended for achieving the budgeted sales volume and revenue.

Responsibility Accounting

Learning Objectives

1. Understand the meaning, objectives and structure of responsibility accounting as divisional performance measurement.
2. Analyse and evaluate cost centre as a responsibility centre.
3. Illustrate and evaluate profit centre as a responsibility centre.
4. Explain as well as evaluate investment centre as a responsibility centre.

INTRODUCTION

As observed earlier, one of the uses of management accounting is managerial control. Among the control techniques, "responsibility accounting" occupies considerable significance. While the other control devices are applicable to the organisation as a whole, responsibility accounting represents a method of measuring the performance of various divisions of an organisation. The term "division" with reference to responsibility accounting is used in a general sense to **include any logical segment/component/sub-component of an organisation**. Defined in this way, it includes a division, a department, a branch office, a service centre, a product-line, a channel of distribution, a class of customers, and so on. The test to identify a division is that the operating performance is separately identifiable and measurable in some way that is of practical significance to management[1]. The purpose of the present chapter is to describe the organisational structure in which the management control process through responsibility accounting takes place. Section 1 briefly discusses the meaning and structure of responsibility accounting as divisional performance measurement followed by its objectives. Section 2 provides an in-depth analysis of the structure-responsibility centres. The coverage includes illustration as well as evaluation of the three centres, namely, cost, profit, and investment. Finally, Section 3 summaries the main points.

Division includes any logical segment/component/sub-component of an organisation.

MEANING AND OBJECTIVES

Responsibility accounting is a device to measure divisional performance.

Meaning

"Responsibility accounting collects and reports planned and actual accounting information about the inputs and outputs of responsibility centres."[2] From this description one may deduce the following features of responsibility accounting: (i) Inputs and outputs (ii) Planned and actual and (iii) Responsibility centres.

Inputs and Outputs Responsibility accounting is based on information relating to inputs and outputs. The resources used are called inputs. The resources used by an organisation are essentially physical in nature, such as quantity of materials consumed, hours of labour, and so on. For managerial control, these heterogeneous physical resources are converted into a common denominator—monetary measure. When physical resources are expressed in monetary terms, they are called "cost". Thus, inputs are expressed as cost. Similarly, outputs are measured in monetary terms as "revenues". In other words, responsibility accounting is *based on cost and revenue data for financial information.*

Planned and Actual The financial information included is both actual and planned. For planning and control, it not only contains historical information about cost/revenues, but also estimated future cost angd revenue data.

Responsibility Centres Responsibility accounting focuses on responsibility centres. A responsibility centre is a sub-unit of an organisation under the control of a manager who is responsible for the activities of that responsibility centre. A small firm can possibly be managed by an individual or a small group of individuals. However, for effective control, a large firm is divided into meaningful segments/departments. Each sub-unit has certain activities to perform and its manager is assigned the responsibility/authority to carry out those activities. These sub-units of an enterprise, for the purpose of control, are called responsibility centres/divisions. The responsibility centre can be a big unit, such as a production department or division, or a small unit such as the cash section of the accounting department. The important criterion for creating a responsibility centre is that the *unit of the organisation should be separable and identifiable for operating purposes and its performances measurement should be possible.*

Responsibility centre is the unit of an organisation that is separable and identifiable for operating purposes and its performance measurement should be possible

For control purposes, responsibility centres are generally categorised into: **(i)** Cost centres, **(ii)** Profit centres, and **(iii)** Investment centres. While these are discussed in detail in the next section of this chapter, a simplified view of responsibility centres (based on cost) in illustrated in Example 19.1.

EXAMPLE 19.1

The following information is available relating to the cost of production of the Hypothetical Ltd:

(₹ in lakh)

Cost item	*Amount*
Direct material	₹400
Direct labour	260
Overheads	280
Total	940

It may be assumed that the firm has four departments—two production and two service. Assuming an imaginary division of the cost between the four departments (responsibility centres), show the cost allocation.

SOLUTION

The allocation of the costs to the four responsibility centres is illustrated in Table 19.1.

Table 19.1 Allocation of Costs to Responsibility Centres

		Responsibility Centres (Departments) (₹ in lakh)			
	Total	*A*	*B*	*C*	*D*
Direct material	₹400	₹360	₹40	₹—	₹—
Direct labour	260	80	180	—	—
	660	440	220	—	—
Overheads:					
Supervision	76	14	18	16	28
Indirect labour	132	12	16	42	62
Supplies	24	10	8	2	4
Other costs	48	6	16	10	16
	280	42	58	70	110
Total	940	482	278	70	110

Thus, responsibility accounting is a method for dividing the organisation structure into various responsibility centres to measure the performance of each of the responsibility centres. In other words, *responsibility accounting is a device to measure divisional performance.*

Objectives

The objective of divisional performance measurement may be classified into three basic categories: (i) To determine the contribution of a division to the total organisation, (ii) To provide basis for evaluation of quality of performance, and (iii) To motivate, consistent with the basic goals of the organisation.

Determination of Contribution of a Division The performance of a responsibility centre can be measured in terms of its *efficiency* and/or in terms of its *effectiveness.* Efficiency measures the relationship of inputs to outputs; and the relationship between output and the goals of the organisation is called effectiveness. Efficiency is a relative term: the lower the consumption of resources (input) to turn out a given amount of output, the greater is the efficiency. A particular responsibility centre may be found more/less efficient if the cost of production in a month is lower/higher than in one preceding/following month. Similarly, in comparison to another centre, it may be more/less efficient. In brief, an efficient responsibility centre is one that does whatever it does with the lowest consumption of resources[3].

Efficient responsibility centre is one which does what it does with the lowest consumption of resources.

Effectiveness is related to the goals of the organisation. Applied to responsibility accounting, it implies how well a responsibility centre contributes to the goals of the organisation. If a centre is not able to contribute what is expected of it, it is not effective. In determining the contribution of each responsibility centre to the organisation as a whole, both efficiency and effectiveness are relevant, that is, a responsibility centre should be both efficient and effective.

Evaluation of Quality of Performance Responsibility accounting is used to measure the performance of managers and it, therefore, influences the way the managers behave. In discussing responsibility accounting, we must take behavioural considerations into account. It is for this reason that responsibility accounting contains a discussion of how managers are influenced by the nature of accounting information they receive.

Could a valid distinction be made between the performance of a division as an entity and the personal performance of a divisional manager? The two may not be distinguishable in the long run.

In the short term, however, a very useful and necessary distinction may be made. It is conceivable that a division may not have made a satisfactory contribution to the goals of the organisation. Yet the manager may be judged to have discharged his responsibility very well.

Motivation Consistent with Organisational Goals As observed earlier, any performance measurement system can be expected to influence the behaviour of the managers affected by it. Divisional performance measurement (responsibility accounting) should be designed in such a way that, in seeking to achieve their own goals, divisional managers will simultaneously work to achieve the goals of the firm. This is called "goal congruence."[4] This can be ensured through a system of incentives, for example, bonus for good performance, and so on.

In brief, responsibility accounting as a control device aims at measuring the performance of the various responsibility centres or divisions of an organisation. It may be noted that *it is measurement and not evaluation of performance.* In other words, responsibility accounting focuses on *what and not how well the performance is.*

TYPES OF RESPONSIBILITY CENTRES

For purposes of measuring financial performance, the divisions of a firm may be classified according to the type of financial data used in the measurement of performance. Three basic classes of divisions can be identified on these grounds: Expense/cost centre, Profit centre, and Investment centre.

Expense/Cost Centres

Expense/cost centre is a segment of an organisation whose financial performance is measured in terms of cost.

An expense centre is a responsibility centre in which inputs, but not outputs, are measured in monetary terms.[5] It has been pointed out earlier that responsibility accounting is based on financial information relating to inputs (cost) and outputs (revenues). In an expense centre of responsibility, the accounting system records only the cost incurred in/by the centre/division/unit but the revenues earned (output) are excluded. Stated differently, an expense centre is a segment whose financial performance is measured in terms of cost. Since the performance of an expense centre is measured by the financial measure of input (cost) only, an essential requirements is that the cost of operating the division be directly traceable to it. This means that the relevant costs are the *incremental or avoidable* cost of operating that division.[6] The incremental cost would include both variable and fixed costs but would exclude costs common to several divisions and allocated among them on some arbitrary basis.

From the viewpoint of the measurement of performance of the divisional manager, the implication of the expense centre is that his performance will be judged on the basis of the cost incurred in his department/division; what is done in the division (output/revenue) will be of no consequence. The analysis of performance is restricted to the consumption of resources in the division, and there is no reference to what the division has achieved as a consequence of consuming those resources. In other words, the performance measure in an expense centre is the efficiency of operation in that centre in terms of the quantity of inputs used in producing some given output. The *modus operandi* is to compare actual inputs to some pre-determined level that represents efficient utilisation (planned/budgeted/standard). The variance between the actual and the budget/standard/plan would be indicative of the efficiency of the division/divisional manager.

Suitability What is the suitability of cost as an index of performance? The expense centre can be employed in three situations.

In the first place, in several cases, the output (revenue) of a responsibility centre cannot be reliably measured in financial terms. Included in this category are centres such as legal departments, accounting departments, public relations departments and the personnel departments. Each of these centres/divisions has a conceptually identifiable output—legal advice (legal department), good public relations (public relations department), reliable accounting reports (accounting department), and better qualified personnel (personnel department). Their outputs cannot obviously be expressed in monetary terms. The only measurable performance measure is their efficiency in the use of inputs. Thus, such divisions can be evaluated only as expense centres. In brief, *cost is a suitable measure of performance in staff units/divisions.*

Secondly, if a production centre/unit/segment is producing one single product, its performance can be measured as expense centre in terms of *efficiency* and *effectiveness.* Although, the output cannot be expressed in monetary terms, the number of units produced can reasonably represent output. The cost per unit of the product would be indicative of the efficiency of department. A comparison of the actual number of units produced of a single product with the units produced in some previous period would measure divisional effectiveness.

Thirdly, an expense centre can also be suitably employed to measure performance if the responsibility of the departmental manager is to produce a stated quantity of outputs at the lowest feasible cost.[7]

Limitations However, in general, an expense centre is not a useful basis of measuring performance of responsibility centres. This is mainly because it ignores output (revenues) measured in financial terms. A common feature of production departments is that they are multi-product units. There must be some common basis to aggregate the dissimilar products to arrive at the overall output of the department/responsibility centre. If this is not done, the efficiency and effectiveness of the responsibility centre cannot be measured. Monetary measure represents the common denominator to measure the overall output of the responsibility centre producing multi-products. The implication is, that to arrive at the overall output, the different products have to be expressed in financial terms. This is a limitation of the expense centre. The profit centre provides a solution to this problem.

Cost Centre Evaluation Cost centre evaluation techniques include variance analysis, job order system, process costing system. These methods can be applied directly to the particular manufacturing department, product-line, marketing function, or other segments. These cost control techniques have already been discussed extensively earlier in this book. These techniques can, however, be used in profit centre/investment centre evaluation also.

Profit Centres

"A profit centre is a responsibility centre in which inputs are measured in terms of expenses and outputs are measured in terms of revenues."[8] Both the elements of accounting information—cost (input) and revenues (output) are considered. In other words, in a profit centre, the measure of performance is broader than in an expense centre because in an expense centre the accounting system measures only one element (cost), whereas in a profit centre both the elements (cost as well as revenue) are measured in monetary terms. The difference between revenues and costs is profit. Stated operationally, the profit centre is a division/sub-unit of an organisation in which financial performance is measured on the basis of profit, that is, revenues less costs. While the cost figures are the same as used in expense centres, the term "revenue" with reference to responsibility accounting is used in a different sense. It may be recalled that the generally accepted principle of accounting is to recognise revenue only when sales are made to outside customers. For purposes of profit centre performance, revenue represents a monetary measure of the output of a profit centre in a given accounting period whether or not the firm actually realises the revenue in that period. *The test is that a department has output (goods and services) which are amenable to monetary measurement.*

Profit centre is a segment of an organisation in which financial performance is measured on the basis of profit.

Since in a profit centre there are financial measures of the output as well as of the input, it is possible to measure the effectiveness and efficiency of performance in financial terms. Profit analysis can be used as a basis for evaluating the performance of a division as an entity and/or for evaluating the performance of a divisional manager. A profit centre requires all of the data needed in an expense centre as well as additional data regarding revenues. Therefore, management can determine whether the division was efficient in the utilisation of resources and, whether the division was effective in attaining its objectives. This objective is presumably to earn a *satisfactory* "profit". The criterion for a satisfactory profit may be budgeted profit/past profit in the division/profits of other similar divisions/some combination of two or more of these. "Profit", as a performance measure, is based on revenues and expenses directly traceable to the division and avoidable if the division were closed down. This concept of divisional profit is referred to as "profit contribution," as it is the amount of profit contributed directly by the division. It might also be described as "incremental profit" or the additional profit earned solely as a result of operations of the division. Further, divisional profits are before taxes, the reason being that taxes are assessed on the basis of the income of the entire company and they may be regarded as similar to common costs and excluded from the calculation of the divisional profit.

Divisional profit/profit contribution is the amount of profit contributed by the division.

There is the yet another element in the computation of profit as performance measurement for a profit centre. This relates to the types of profit centres. A profit centre, for example, a product division, uses inputs (cost) and produces output (revenues). Such a profit centre is very like an independent firm. It is called a "natural profit centre". The alternative to the natural profit centre is the "constructive profit centre."[9] It is not a natural profit centre but it may be made to appear as one. An example is the computer centre or data processing department. It makes use of inputs (cost) but it produces no revenues (output) as it renders computer services to other departments and does not sell its products/services. This is logically an expense centre. However, the management has an alternative to owning and operating a computer: to purchase computer time from a data processing service. The management will compare the two alternatives and select one which involves a lower cost. *The cost avoided is the revenue to the firm by owing a computer. This is constructive profit. Divisional profit data can be used to evaluate the performance of the division/divisional manager in the case of natural profit centres alone.*

Natural profit centre is a division which uses costs and produces revenues like an independent firm.

In brief, the relevant profit to form the basis of performance measurement of a profit centre is the *before-tax incremental/contribution profit/margin of a natural profit centre.* The profits of all the divisions thus calculated will not necessarily be equal to the profit of the entire firm. The divergence would arise from the fact that costs not attributable to any single division are excluded from the computation of the profit of the organisation as a whole. It may, therefore, be concluded *that divisional profit is a unique concept, designed to serve specific managerial needs.*

Advantages A profit centre, as a responsibility centre, is of considerable significance in measuring the performance of divisions/divisional managers. Three aspects deserve special mention.

In the first place, profit, defined as the differences between revenues and costs/expenses, is a combined measure of both effectiveness and efficiency. It provides a powerful tool for measuring how well the profit centre/manager of the profit centre has performed.

Secondly, a profit centre resembles a business in miniature. Like a separate firm, its profits are calculated. The performance of the managers is measured by profit. Therefore, they will be motivated to take decisions about inputs and outputs in such a way that the profit of a profit centre is maximised. In other words, managers can be expected to behave as if they were running their own business. For this reason, the profit centre is a good training ground for general management responsibility.

Thirdly, the profit centre is closely related to the organisational principle of decentralisation; profit centres make decentralised organisation possible. Top management can safely delegate the authority to the divisional managers because the profit centre reports provide adequate information about how well the operating managers are doing their jobs.[10]

In brief, profit centres provide a broader and more inclusive measurement of performance than the expense centres. If managers are responsible for both revenue and expense aspects of performance (profit centre), the contribution of each manager to the goal of the entire organisation is easier to measure than when no single manager is responsible for both revenues and expenses (expense centres).

Limitations The profit centre approach also encounters certain problems. These relate to: **(i)** Criterion for profit centres, **(ii)** Measurement of expenses, and **(iii)** Transfer prices.

Criteria for Profit Centres One problem with profit centre is that it cannot be used for all responsibility centres. The criteria to use profit centre as a responsibility centre includes the consideration of the following points: **(i)** Extra record-keeping is involved to measure input and output in monetary terms; **(ii)** When a responsibility centre is required by management to provide service to other responsibility centres, the service department (for example, internal audit) should not be a profit department; **(iii)** Unless the divisional managers of responsibility centres have reasonable authority to decide on the quality/quantity of outputs or on the relations of output to costs, a profit centre will be of little use as a control device; **(iv)** If the output of a product/division is fairly homogeneous (for example, cement), a profit centre may not offer substantial advantage, however, an expense centre may do so; **(v)** There may be friction between profit centres due to the spirit of intense competition. Moreover, it may generate too much interest in short run profit to the detriment of long-term results. The operational implication is that unless these problems are overcome, the profit centre technique would not serve its purpose and should, therefore, not be used.

Measurement of Expenses Another problem with profit centres may relate to the measurement of certain types of expenses which have to be included in the computation of profit centres. There is a scope for difference of opinion relating to the treatment of those expenses which relate to the organisation as a whole. In view of the special nature of divisional profits, such expenses should not be considered since, they are not the responsibility of the division/divisional manager. That such expenses are not the responsibility of the division is another way of saying that they cannot be traceable/attributable to it and should be ignored in working out the profit of the division as a profit centre.

Transfer Prices The measurement of profit in a profit centre type of responsibility accounting is also complicated by the problem of transfer prices. A transfer price is a price used to measure the value of goods/services furnished by a profit centre to other responsibility centres within a company.[11] In other words, when internal exchange of goods and services take place between the different divisions of a firm, they have to be expressed in monetary terms. The monetary amount for these inter-divisional exchanges/transfers is called the transfer price. The determination of an appropriate transfer price is one of the major problems of profit centres. The implication of the transfer price is that for the selling division (the division whose goods/services are being transferred) it is a source of revenue, whereas, for the buying division (the division which is receiving/acquiring the goods/services) it is an element of cost. It will, therefore, have a significant bearing on the revenues, costs, and profits of responsibility centres. Hence, the need for correct determination of transfer prices. The determination is, however, complicated because a wide variety of alternative methods are available. We, therefore, first discuss the basic types of transfer prices. Transfer price policies to indicate the circumstances in which different types of transfer prices are suitable are also examined.

Transfer price is the monetary amount of inter-divisional exchanges/transfer of goods and services.

In order to assess the validity and acceptability of different transfer pricing methods, three criteria are generally used. In the first place, the transfer price should be objectively determinable. Secondly, it should be equal to the value of the intermediate products being transferred, that is, the transfer price should reward/compensate the transferring division and charge the buying/acquiring division in keeping with the value of the functions performed and/or the value of the product exchanged. Finally, it should be compatible with the policy that maximises attainment of company goals and evaluation of segment performance.

Types of Transfer Prices There are two general approaches to the determination of a transfer price: **(i)** Cost-based; and **(ii)** Market-based. Based on these, there are six basic types of transfer prices: **(a)** Cost, **(b)** Cost plus a normal mark-up, **(c)** Incremental cost, **(d)** Market price, **(e)** Negotiated price, and **(f)** Dual (two-way) prices.

Cost Price According to this, transfer price is equal to the cost price. This means the goods/services transferred will be priced on the basis of the selling division's unit cost of production. The cost could be either actual cost of production or, where available, standard cost of production.

The merit of this method is simplicity and convenience because all the required information is available in the cost accounting records. But it is inappropriate for profit centre analysis. The reason is that transfer prices based on cost would distort the profit figures. For the selling division, the profit figures would be an underestimate as it will not earn any profit on goods/services sold to the sister divisions. The profit figures for the purchasing department would be inflated to the extent the cost of purchases of goods would be lower because there is no element of profit for the selling divisions. If profit figures are distorted, the profit centre analysis would not be of much value.

Cost Plus a Normal Mark-up This type of transfer price is an improvement over the first category. It includes, besides unit cost of production, some profit margin or normal mark-up. Thus, the price received/paid by the selling and the purchasing departments respectively will contain an element of profit. There are two ways in which the normal mark-up/profit margin is determined. First, the management of the firm may set a target profit. Alternatively, the normal mark-up may be equivalent to the profit margin that a competing firm might reasonably be expected to realise. If the second basis is adopted, the transfer price will approximate a market value. Depending upon its closeness to the real market value, it may be useful for profit centre analysis. But if the basis is the managerial pre-determined target, the mark-up is an artificial margin dictated by policy.[12] Therefore, its validity as performance measurement of a division/divisional manager, is open to question. On the whole, therefore, this type of transfer price has no unique value of its own for profit centre analysis.

Incremental Cost Yet another basis of transfer prices is the incremental cost in the selling division. Depending upon the circumstances, incremental cost can be computed in two ways. The first situation may be such that the entire production of the selling division is transferred to the sister divisions, and there are no independent outside customers for the goods. In that case, incremental cost includes all variable costs plus any fixed costs directly and exclusively attributable to the internal transfer/internal divisional transfer. Transfer pricing at incremental cost defined in this sense is inconsistent with the objectives of measuring divisional profit as performance measurement.

An alternative market situation arises when there may be outside customers for the goods and the division is unable to produce the full demand (from the outside customers as well as sister divisions). The incremental cost to the selling division in that case would be the revenue lost on sales to outside customers that must be foregone to make the internal transfer to a sister division. Then, the incremental cost would equal the market price for those goods/services. This version of the incremental cost data could be useful for profit centre analysis. The incremental cost data related to the internal production costs is not of much analytical value.

Market Price Another approach to transfer pricing is the market price based approach. There are three ways to arrive at the market price.

First, through the prevailing market price if there is an active market for the goods/services transferred between divisions. The prevailing price would require adjustment for discounts as well as for certain selling costs that are not involved in inter-divisional exchange. The merits of this basis of transfer price are: **(i)** Market prices represent the alternatives to the divisions. That is to say, if the selling division sells the goods to outside customers, or if the buying division purchases the goods from outside suppliers, the market price will be the basis. **(ii)** They are neither arbitrary nor artificial, rather they reflect the collective values of several buyers/sellers. In operational terms, a market price-based approach implies that the selling division will receive equal to what it would get by selling the goods to outside customers, while the purchasing division will pay what it would pay to outside suppliers. Yet, both the selling and the buying divisions would derive some special benefits. The advantages to the selling division include: **(a)** No risk of bad debt on sales to sister divisions, and **(b)** No direct promotional expenses on sale to a sister division. The special benefit to the buying department will be in the form of assured delivery schedules and full customer service. Therefore, where divisions have the alternative to buy/sell to/from the open market, they would prefer to buy from/sell to the sister division.

Secondly, in cases where easily identified market prices are not available, costs plus a normal profit margin can be a reasonable approximation of the market price.

Finally, in situations in which market price is not readily available, bids from several different manufactures can form the basis. The low bid may be taken as the market price and used for internal transfer pricing. This alternative of market price suffers from two limitations: either spurious bids would be submitted by the bidders, or bids will not be submitted. This is likely because the bidders would come to know that the firm does not intend buying the goods but, will only use the bid for internal pricing.

Negotiated Price The inter-divisional exchange pricing can also be based on a price mutually agreed upon by the buying as well as the selling departments, through negotiation. The advantage of this approach is that it will lead to a transfer price mutually advantageous to both, the divisions as well as the entire organisation. The limitation is that it can be applied only in situations in which the selling division has a choice of customers and the purchasing division has a choice of suppliers.

Dual (Two-Way) Prices According to this method of transfer pricing for segment performance evaluation, the transferring division is credited with one price but the acquiring division is charged at different price. The merit of this method is that it eliminates the possibility of conflict caused by a single transfer price, in which case one segment receives relatively less contribution of profit because the price setting process entitles the segment to receive relatively more.

The price to be charged to the acquiring division should be based on what it costs the firm as a whole to produce and distribute the intermediate product internally under normal conditions. The appropriate transfer prices are *incremental costs* in non-recurring situations, and *full standard costs* for long-run continuous situations. These prices reflect the effective cost of the resources consumed by the firm and by the segment. For this reason, this is an appropriate basis for evaluating the performance of the user of those resources. The transferring division, on the other hand, should receive the market price for the intermediate product. If no market price exists, a negotiated price based on the market price of the final product should be used to approximate the net realisable value of intermediate product. This price represents the best possible assessment of the exchange value of the intermediate product.[13]

The use of dual prices would lead to a divergence between the segment profits and the total profits of the company. But it should not stand in the way of the use of this method because, the transfer price is intended only for purposes of segment performance evaluation and not for decision-making.

Transfer Price Policies Transfer price policies refer to the selection of policies/methods that would govern the calculations of such prices under various circumstances. The concern of transfer price policies is with developing a transfer pricing system that allows: **(i)** A measure of performance to reflect the use of resources by a division and **(ii)** The optimal allocation of the firms' resources.[14] In other words, suitable transfer prices should be related to: **(a)** Management performance assessment and **(b)** Decision-optimisation.

Management Performance The best transfer price for measuring management performance is the one that reflects the price in an open, competitive market. These market prices are the best measure of revenue for the selling division, and of cost for the purchasing division. For market prices to have maximum effectiveness in management performance measurement, both the buying and the selling divisions must be able to act independently, that is, the selling division must have a choice of customer and the purchasing department must have a choice of suppliers.

If, however, a market price for the goods/services is not readily available, negotiated prices may be used to determine the transfer price. This price is negotiated between the buying and the selling units.

In circumstances where there are no competitive market prices and a negotiated transfer price cannot be established, the firm cannot set up profit centres. It can use cost centres for management performance measurement. By using standard cost as the transfer prices for cost centres, the selling divisions are encouraged to have good control.

Decision-Optimisation The ideal transfer price for management decision-making is the price that would be used by a firm if it were not divided into units/divisions. In other words, for decision-making purposes, the transfer price should reflect the opportunity cost of the goods/services transferred between divisons.[15] This is so, because an optimal allocation of resources takes place only if the goods/services are priced on transfer at the opportunity cost that would be incurred to obtain the goods/services elsewhere, when they are needed. The best measure of opportunity cost is the open market price, if available. In case, market prices are not readily available, the top management may prescribe a transfer price. Alternatively, a negotiated price between divisions with arbitration, if necessary, by top management, reflecting the corporate objectives, and coordination of the activities of all the divisions, may be taken to be the opportunity cost. One widely-used approach treats the incremental costs of the selling division as the transfer price. The advantage of this is that if price/standard costs are used, the inefficiency of the selling division will not be *ipso facto* passed on to the buying division.

To conclude, the question of appropriate transfer prices for the two functions of management—performance measurement, and decision-optimisation does not have any easy answer. There is no single measure of transfer price that can fit all circumstances. The firm must give serious consideration to its goals and objectives in using transfer prices before adopting a particular measure. Another possibility is to use a dual pricing system. Such a basis of transfer pricing removes some of the deficiencies and conflicts that would, otherwise, be present in segment performance evaluation. It also permits a more objective assessment of segments as individual entities.

Profit Centre Evaluation[16] Profit centre evaluation requires an income statement approach. The conventional income statement format can be recast to highlight the various sub-categories. These sub-categories are arranged according to the criteria of **(i)** variability, **(ii)** controllability, and **(iii)** attributability. The controllable concept implies that the performance attributes should be controllable by the division/responsibility centre. The attributability concept refers to the outcomes/performance characteristics that are directly associated with, or directly traceable to the existence and operations of a segment. According to the variability attribute, costs that are neither directly controllable by a particular segment, nor attributable to it, are excluded from the measurement of divisional performance. Included in this category of costs are administrative salaries, property taxes, depreciation, and so on. The main sub-categories that might be included in a typical segmented income statements are: **(1)** Sales and other major revenues, **(2)** Controllable variable costs, **(3)** Controllable contribution margin, **(4)** Controllable fixed costs, **(5)** Controllable segment margin, **(6)** Attributable segment costs, **(7)** Segment profit contribution, **(8)** Common firm-wide cost, and **(9)** Segment net income.

Sales and Other Major Revenues Sales earned by a particular segment are usually easy to identify and measure when these are made to outside customers only, or, market transactions determine the amount of sales or the products/services sold by one division as distinct from those of other divisions. However, there may be some difficulty in estimating the revenue of a segment due to the problems associated with transfer pricing.

To evaluate a segment's sales revenues, they must be compared with other performance measures such as: **(i)** Prior period sales of the same segment, **(ii)** Sales volumes of a comparable department of the same firm, **(iii)** Sales of other companies in the same industry, and **(iv)** The division's pre-determined budgeted sales volume. These comparisons may be made in terms of total amount, physical volume, rates of change, or deviations from budgeted amounts. Only short-run sales data should not be used as a basis for divisional performance measurement. Trend and comparative measures are more useful for this purpose.

Controllable Variable Costs All the costs in this group are directly controllable by the divisional managers and vary according to the division's activity levels, namely, the division's variable cost of goods sold, and variable administrative and marketing costs. These can be usually measured objectively except when transfer prices for individual acquisitions are involved. These costs should be evaluated using variance analysis, trend analysis, variable cost to sales ratio analysis, comparison with other segments of the same firm and with similar segments of other companies in the same industry.

Controllable variable costs are costs directly controllable by the divisional managers at a given activity level.

Controllable Contribution Margin Sales revenue minus controllable variable cost equals the division's controllable contribution margin. It measures the profitability of the sales of a department. It can be used to evaluate the ability of a division to sustain itself, to make a contribution to costs of other divisions, common costs of the firm and profits of the organisation. The evaluation would primarily be based on variance analysis.

Controllable Fixed Costs The controllable fixed costs are those fixed costs of a period that are directly and exclusively related to the decisions of the management of a division. Such costs are, for example, divisional rental charges for equipment and property, executives' salaries, advertising costs, and so on. Such costs should be compared with budgeted fixed costs to evaluate performance.

Controllable Segment Margin The excess of controllable contribution margin over controllable fixed costs is the controllable segment margin. This should be compared with the previous period's results and pre-determined budgeted amounts.

Attributable segment costs include all costs uncontrollable by a divisional manager.

Attributable Segment Costs Included in such costs are all those costs which are not controllable by a divisional manager and which could have been avoided had the decision been withdrawn. Examples of such costs are the divisional manager's salary, depreciation, rent, insurance on facilities used exclusively by the division but acquired as a results of decision made at higher management levels, and interest charges on debt that was incurred specifically to support the operations of a division but which was decided upon outside the division. Obviously, these costs are not directly controllable by the divisional manager. Yet, they should be considered in overall segment performance through comparison with the budgeted amounts and with the division's results for the prior period.

Segment Profit Contribution The segment profit contribution is the difference between the controllable segment margin and the attributable segment costs. Variance analysis, percentage analysis of individual costs and revenues, and trend and time period analysis can be used to evaluate the various components of segment profit contribution. Comparison can also be made with industry or product line standards.

Common firm-wide costs are costs incurred for the firm as a whole which should be proportionately recovered from the revenues of the segments.

Common Firm-Wide Costs The common firm-wide costs are incurred for the firm as a whole. Such costs do not relate to any specific segment. Nevertheless, they have to be proportionately recovered from the revenues of these segments to calculate the profit of the firm. The share of each segment will naturally depend on the method applied to allocate these common costs to various segments. If the allocation method is inappropriate, it may distort the profitability of a segment. Hence, the need for a proper objective and scientific method of apportioning common costs. In the short-run, however, such allocated cost may not be relevant for performance evaluation of a segment as the division may have a positive controllable contribution margin, but may show losses due to the share of allocated common costs. In the long run, segments must collectively generate sufficient contribution to the total profit to allow the recovery of the firm-wide costs and the achievement of corporate profit goals. It is, however, difficult to decide how much of the common costs of the firm should be borne by each division to justify its long-term existence.

Segment Net Income The last sub-category of the segment income statement is the segment net income, which is equal to the difference between the segment profit contribution minus the allocated common firm-wide cost. However, this measure should be used with caution as a criterion for evaluation in view of the problems associated with apportionment of the firm's common costs.

We now illustrate the profit centre evaluation in Example 19.2.

Example 19.2

The Hypothetical Ltd employs a budgetary control system and measures performance on segmented basis of its product line divisions, A and B. The budgeted and actual sales figures for the month of March are as follows:

Division	*Unit sales*		*Sales revenue*	
	Budgeted	*Actual*	*Budgeted*	*Actual*
A	20,000	24,000	₹2,00,000	₹2,40,000
B	40,000	40,000	2,00,000	2,40,000

The standard unit controllable variable costs are ₹4 for product line A and ₹2 for product line B. The company's budgeted controllable fixed costs for the month are ₹20,000 each for products A and B, whereas the actuals amounted to ₹22,000 for product A and ₹26,000 for product B . The attributable segment costs are: For product A, ₹40,000 (budgeted) and ₹44,000 (actual), and for product B, ₹60,000 (budgeted) and ₹64,000 (actual).

Assume that these costs represent all manufacturing costs and no opening and closing inventories. Actual variable manufacturing costs during March were ₹84,000 and ₹96,000 for divisions A and B respectively. The common firm-wide costs are assumed to be ₹48,000 to be apportioned on the basis of segment sales revenue.

From the above, prepare a performance evaluation report, if the Hypothetical Ltd employs profit centre basis of divisional performance measurement.

SOLUTION

Since, the basis of divisional performance measurement is the profit centre, the performance evaluation report should be compiled in the form of a segment income statement. These are illustrated sequence-wise in Table 19.2.

Table 19.2 Performance Evaluation Report

(Figures in '000)

	Product Line A			*Product Line B*			*Total*		
Particulars	*Budget*	*Actual*	*Variance*	*Budget*	*Actual*	*Variance*	*Budget*	*Actual*	*Variance*
Sales revenue	₹200	₹240	₹40F	₹200	₹240	₹40F	₹400	₹480	₹80F
Less controllable variable costs	80	84	4A	80	96	16A	160	180	20A
Controllable contribution margins	120	156	36F	120	144	24F	240	300	60F
Less controllable fixed costs	20	22	2A	20	26	6A	40	48	8A
Controllable segment margin	100	134	34F	100	118	18F	200	252	52F
Less attributable segment costs	40	44	4A	60	64	4A	100	108	8A
Segment profit contribution	60	90	30F	40	54	14F	100	144	44F
Less common firm-wide costs	24	24	—	24	24	—	48	48	—
Net income	36	66	30F	16	30	14F	52	96	44F

*F = Favourable, A = Adverse.

Uses of Profit Centre The profit centre, as a measurement of performance, can be used: **(i)** For evaluation and ranking of profit centres and **(ii)** As a basis for decisions to modify operations of profit centres.

Evaluation and Ranking of Profit Centres Profit centres may be evaluated on the basis of their performance in relation to the various types of profit goals. As observed in the preceding discussion, the various profits goals with reference to profit centre performance are, controllable contribution margin, controllable segment margin, segment profit contribution, contribution margin ratio, segment profit contribution rate, and so on. In evaluating profit centres, it has to be seen whether individual segments have achieved their objectives and ranking given to the comparative performance of segments. Table 19.3 exhibits comparative performance based on segment profit contribution.

Table 19.3 Income Statement for the Quarter Ended March 31

	Divisions			*Total*
Particulars	*A*	*B*	*C*	
Sales	₹6,00,000	₹8,00,000	₹10,00,000	₹24,00,000
Less controllable variable costs	2,00,000	4,00,000	6,00,000	12,00,000
Controllable contribution margin	4,00,000	4,00,000	4,00,000	12,00,000
Less direct fixed costs	1,00,000	2,00,000	1,00,000	4,00,000
Controllable segment margin	3,00,000	2,00,000	3,00,000	8,00,000
Less attributable segment costs	1,40,000	2,40,000	80,000	4,60,000
Segment Profit contribution	1,60,000	(40,000)	2,20,000	3,40,000
Less firm-wide cost	—	—	—	1,40,000
Corporate net income	—	—	—	2,00,000

Based on their segment profit contribution, the three divisions would be ranked (1) C, (2) A, and (3) B. The negative segment profit contribution for division B shows its inability to recover all of its fixed and attributable costs. However, it does not follow automatically that it should be closed down. In order to decide whether to continue or discontinue division B, it is necessary to know whether all these fixed and attributable costs are avoidable. If not, the division should continue as its closure would cause a larger deficit than ₹40,000.

Further, since the three divisions show significant differences in sales value, contribution margin ratios, fixed costs, and attributable costs, ranking them on the basis of segment profit contribution would seem to be unfair. A better alternative would be a comparison between actual and budgeted segment profit contribution.

Performance evaluation in terms of other variables such as product lines, sales territories, wholesale and retail distribution channel, and so on is an alternative to segment reporting based on division.

Assume for Table 19.3 that the sales of the three divisions, territory-wise, are as follows:

Division	*Northern territory*	*Southern territory*	*Total*
A	₹2,40,000	₹3,60,000	₹6,00,000
B	4,00,000	4,00,000	8,00,000
C	6,00,000	4,00,000	10,00,000
	12,40,000	11,60,000	24,00,000

Costs were directly identified with sales territories as follows:

	Northern territory	*Southern territory*	*Total*
Direct fixed costs	₹1,00,000	₹2,00,000	₹3,00,000
Attributable costs	1,40,000	2,40,000	3,80,000

Due to re-classification of the basis from divisions to territory, the remaining costs totalling ₹3,20,000 must be classified as common firm-wide costs. The income statement segmented on a sales-territory basis is presented in Table 19.4.

Table 19.4 Territory-wise Segmented Income Statement for the Quarter Ended March 31

Particulars	*Northern Sales Territory*	*Southern Sales Territory*	*Total*
Sales	₹12,40,000	₹11,60,000	₹24,00,000
Less controllable costs	6,40,000	5,60,000	12,00,000
Controllable segment margin	6,00,000	6,00,000	12,00,000
Less direct fixed costs	1,00,000	2,00,000	3,00,000
Controllable segment margin	5,00,000	4,00,000	9,00,000
Less attributable segment costs	1,40,000	2,40,000	3,80,000
Segment Profit contribution	3,60,000	1,60,000	5,20,000
Less firm-wide costs			3,20,000
Corporate net income			2,00,000

To summarise the discussion relating to alternative measures of profit centre performance, various indicators are appropriate depending on the purpose of analysis and the time period involved. For short-run evaluation, for instance, assuming that direct fixed costs and attributable costs do not vary with changes in segment activity level, *controllable contribution margin* is an appropriate measure. *Controllable segment margin* is a suitable measure of the long-run use of resources by segment managers. *Segment profit contribution* is the preferable long-term measure of a segment's ability to sustain itself as a separate company sub-unit. Profit centres should not be judged solely on the basis of their ability to maximise their sales revenues; to do so may lead to production and sale of products that generate higher sales revenues but a smaller profit contribution.

Decisions to Modify Operations of Profit Centres Apart from evaluation for ranking of profit centres, another use of profit centre performance assessment is that it guides decisions to modify operations of the profit centres. The modification in operations of profit centres comprises expansion, contraction, addition, or closure. The decision criterion in such cases would be the incremental effect on the overall profits of the company. In the short-run, assuming all attributable segment costs as constant, expansion or contraction in a profit centre's operations will affect the controllable contribution margin. In the long run, account will also have to be taken of changes in direct fixed costs and/or attributable segment costs. The decision whether to add or discontinue the entire segment will depend on the effect this may have on the segment profit contribution provided the decision does not affect the common firm-wide costs or the profit performance of other segments.

Investment Centres

Investment centre is a responsibility centre whose performance is measured in relation to revenues/profits and the assets employed in the division.

The third type of responsibility centre is an investment centre. It is defined as a responsibility centre in which inputs are measured in terms of cost/expenses and outputs are measured in terms of revenues and in which assets employed are also measured[17]. In other words, investment centres consider not only cost and revenues but also the assets used in the division. As a responsibility centre, the performance of a unit would be measured in relation to the revenues/profits and the assets employed in a division. The essence of investment centre analysis is the relationship between the profits and the assets that are used to generate those profits. It may, therefore, be said to be an extension of the profit centre in that it covers all the elements relevant to the measurement of the overall performance of a firm/its various divisions. In point of fact, an investment centre is essentially a profit centre. It is for this reason that it is sometimes said that there is no distinction between investment centres and profit centres, and the term "profit centre" is used to apply to both. Since, however, the investment centre is one step above a profit centre in terms of the additional financial data (assets), it should best be treated as a separate responsibility centre.

The investment centre analysis can be used as a basis for evaluating the contribution of a division as an entity as also the performance of a divisional manager. The measure of performance in an investment centre is based on the relationship between the profits/income, and the amount of assets employed in generating the profits. There are two ways to relate income to assets: **(i)** Return on investment and **(ii)** Residual income.

Segment return on investment is the segment profit contribution divided by the segment assets/resources.

Return on Investment (ROI) Analysis With reference to responsibility accounting, the ROI will be the segment return on investment (SROI). Symbolically,

$$\text{SROI} = \text{Segment profit contribution (SPC)} \div \text{Segment resources/assets (SR/SA)} \quad \textbf{(19.1)}$$

The SROI can be used both for operating performance measurement, and managerial evaluation. Accordingly, there are two variations of segment return on investments, namely,

$$\text{SROI} = \text{SPC before interest} \div \text{Segment total assets} \quad \textbf{(19.2)}$$

$$\text{SROI (net)} = \text{SPC after interest} \div \text{Segment net assets} \quad \textbf{(19.3)}$$

The SROI is useful in evaluating the total earning power of all assets directly employed by a segment regardless of how they are financed. The net SROI is a better indicator of a division's ability to generate profit contributions in excess of the direct cost of financing its operations.

Alternatively, the SROI can be viewed as the product of two components, namely, segment profit contribution margin, and segment assets turnover. Symbolically,

$$\text{SROI} = \frac{\text{Segment profit contribution (SPC)}}{\text{Segment salts revenue}} \times \frac{\text{Segment salts revenue}}{\text{Segment assets}} \quad \textbf{(19.4)}$$

Advantages There are several advantages in using ROI to measure divisional performance. In the first place, ROI is the generally accepted measure of overall performance. As a measure of divisional performance, it is consistent with a firm-wise rate of return analysis. It is also compatible with the common sense view that investments are made to achieve the goal of a desired rate of return.

Secondly, ROI analysis is a relative, and not absolute measure. It is, in fact, a ratio/percentage. It, therefore, serves as a common denominator so that a comparison can be made between the performance of different divisions. By enabling an interdivisional comparison, ROI is of great practical significance.

Thirdly, ROI is conceptually easy to understand and interpret.

Finally, ROI analysis can provide incentive for optimum utilisation of the assets of a firm. In operational terms, it encourages divisional managers to obtain/retain assets that provide satisfactory return on investment and to discard/dispose off assets that are not giving acceptable returns.

Limitations The ROI analysis is conceptually sound and appealing, as a performance measure. Nevertheless, it suffers from certain operational limitations: **(i)** Determination of investment base and **(ii)** Determination of net income.

Investment base is the measurement of the value of divisional investment.

Investment Base One operational problem with the ROI analysis relates to the determination of the investment base. One significant element in the ROI analysis is the assets/investment employed in the generation of net income/profits. The determination/measurement of the value of investments is referred to as "investment base". The measurement of the divisional investment base requires: **(i)** A precise definition of all elements that should be included and **(ii)** The value that should be assigned to them. There are, however, operational problems in respect of each of these aspects in that there are alternatives available which imply different practices. This is so because the measurement of investments/assets is not standardised. The problems of measuring investment in assets in connection with the investment centre analysis fall into two categories: **(i)** Problems of allocation/apportionment and **(ii)** Problems of valuation.

Allocation Problems These arise out of the possibility of different treatment of assets that are pooled/shared among the different divisions. The most common of such assets are cash, receivables, and inventories. How should such assets be allocated among different divisions? One alternative is to ignore them while working out the investment base of a division, the underlying principle being that only those assets which are exclusively used/directly traceable to a division should be included. Alternatively, the common/jointly shared assets should be allocated to the benefiting divisions for the proper measurement of their individual investments. Apart from the theoretical differences as to whether such assets should be allocated or not, there is a more difficult problem of identification of assets with separate divisions and reasonable allocation.

The second aspect of the allocational problem relates to the treatment of assets that are currently idle. If such assets are excluded as they presumably do not generate income, the ROI would be actually a return on capital employed rather than on the total investments/assets/available invested capital. This approach would tend to raise the ROI. This will not, however, reveal how efficiently assets have been used, the basic objective of ROI analysis. The presence of idle assets is suggestive of inefficient utilisation of resources. Its inclusion/exclusion would affect the ROI.

Valuation Problems Apart from the problem allocation/traceability of items of assets, the measurement of investment base is complicated by the difficulty of assigning values to the assets of a division. There are variety of methods to value assets for purpose of ROI analysis. They include: **(i)** Book value, **(ii)** Gross book value (original costs), and **(iii)** Current replacement cost.

Book Value The most readily available method of valuation of assets, defined as the original cost less accumulated depreciation, is probably the least useful measure owing to an inherent weakness. Due to the declining investment base as a result of depreciation charge, the carrying value of assets declines. If the net income of the division remains constant, or does not decline as rapidly as the book value of the division's assets, the divisional ROI would show improving performance as the assets become more worn-out and obsolete. Since continued use of obsolete resources due to a low investment base would inflate ROI, the division's productive capacity would ultimately decline.

Gross Book Value Which is the original cost without any deduction for depreciation, provides a partial solution to the defect in ROI analysis based on book values. If earnings are constant, this approach will give a constant ROI over the years. A variation of this approach is to use a method of depreciation with increasing charges over the life of the assets. It will result in a constant ROI, as each year a lower income is related to a smaller asset base. While this approach thus avoids the problem of meaningless rise in the ROI as time passes, it is not a measure of the current economic value of the assets involved.

Replacement Cost Basis Provides the best measure of current performance. Its weakness, however, is that replacement cost is difficult to determine and may require subjective assessment.

In brief, in arriving at the value of the assets that generate income for ROI analysis, several alternative approaches/practices are available/possible. That several approaches can be adopted is another way of saying that the measurement of the investment base is problematic.

Net Income The second element in the computation of ROI is the net income/profit of a responsibility centre. The determination of divisional net income also involves some problems.

First, as an extension of the profit centre, *the investment centre analysis encounters all the problems of the profit centre analysis.*

In addition, there are some special problems of income measurement as a rate of return is to be calculated. These relate to the treatment of **(a)** tax **(b)** interest. These items are outside the control of the divisional managers. Should they be considered in calculating the divisional income? According to the incremental approach, since these items do not fall in the areas of responsibility of a division, that is, they are not controllable by the division, they are to be excluded. Further, should depreciation be based on historical cost or replacement cost? If replacement cost is the basis of asset valuation, depreciation should also be based upon replacement cost. Moreover, since the ROI measures current operating performance, non-recurring items such as extraordinary gains and losses should be excluded. Thus, items having a bearing on net income can be treated in different ways. This creates problems in the measurement of net income for ROI analysis.

Segment Residual Income An alternative measure of financial performance in an investment centre is segment *residual income.* The preceding discussion clearly shows that the SROI suffers from serious limitations. Essentially, it is a relative measure, that is, a ratio or rate of return. This is so because net profit is related to investments which encounter several problems. The segment residual income alternative to measure divisional performance avoids some of the problems associated with the SROI analysis.

Segment residual income is the difference betwen the actual operating income of a division and the required expected income.

Residual income is the amount that remains after deducting an "implied" interest charge from operating income. The implied interest charge reflects an opportunity cost. The basis of the interest charge is the amount of assets in each investment centre. The rate of interest charge is equal to the minimum rate on investment specified by top management as part of the corporate strategic plan. Operationally, the management of the firm lays down an amount of interest charge as a compensation for providing the original investment to a division. The difference between the actual operating income of a division and the required/expected income is segment residual income.

Symbolically,

$$SRI = SPC - (SROI \times SR) \quad \textbf{(19.5)}$$

where,

SRI = Segment residual income
SPC = Segment profit contribution
SROI = Desired segment ROI
SR = Segment resources

To illustrate, assume the budgeted investment of a firm is ₹10 lakh. Assume further, a budgeted net income of ₹2 lakh. The required rate of return (cost of capital) may be assumed to be 15 per cent. The residual income of the division would be:

Divisional income	₹2,00,000
Required income (0.15 × ₹10 lakh)	(1,50,000)
Segment residual income	50,000

Merits The residual income approach has some merits.

A principal advantage is that it encourages capital investment any time a divisional manager can earn more than the required/cut-off rate. The amount of the residual income indicates the investment centre's ability to earn more than a normal profit on the amount of capital that it uses. Any new investment will increase the residual income if it yields an income higher than the required/ cut-off percentage.

A second advantage is that it allows different rates of return for different divisions/assets, for example, higher rates for risky and lower for less risky/certain.

Limitations Residual income as performance measure overcomes some of the shortcomings of ROI analysis. But it is not a perfect measure. It has certain limitations. First, most of the problems in measuring the divisional income and divisional investment base are also present in the measurement of residual income. There is an additional problem of selecting/specifying a fair and equitable measure of the required/cut-off percentage (that is, the cost of capital).

SUMMARY

- Segment profit contribution is the best direct measure of profit performance attributable to, and controllable by a segment. Segment net income may also be a useful measure as it emphasises the long-run ability of a segment to contribute to the profits of an organisation. Segment profit contribution and segment net income may be used for **(i)** evaluating segment performance in relation to pre-determined objectives, **(ii)** competitive ranking of segments, **(iii)** decisions relating to the expansion, contractions, additions or discontinuation of segments.
- Although the profit centre basis is superior to expense centre, as a criterion for divisional performance measurement, this approach suffers from certain operational problems. These relate to criteria for profit centres, measurement of expenses and transfer prices. Of the three, transfer price is a critical aspect of profit centre performance evaluation. The choice of transfer pricing system has to reconcile the requirements of managerial decision-making, on the one hand, and performance evaluation, on the other. Alternative transfer prices for performance evaluation include market-based prices, cost-based prices, cost plus normal mark-up, incremental cost, negotiated prices and dual prices. All of these lack one or more of the desired transfer pricing criteria of **(i)** objectivity, **(ii)** equivalence to the value of change, and **(iii)** compatibility

of decision-making with the goals of the segment and those of the organisation as a whole. The market price of a product, that is, equivalent to the intermediate product, being transferred between segments, is by and large, the most suitable for segment performance evaluation although it has limited value for decision-making purposes.

➢ The investment centre approach is an extension of the profit centre approach. The measure of performance in an investment centre is based on the relationship between the segment profit contribution and segment assets. There are two ways to relate segment profit contribution to segment resources: segment rate of return on investment and segment residual income.

The computation of segment rate of return on investment (*SROI*) is summarised below:

(1) $$SROI = \frac{\text{Segment profit contribution } (SPC)}{\text{Segment resources/assets } (SR/SA)} \times 100$$

(2) $$SROI = \frac{(SPC)}{\text{Segment sales revenue}} \times \frac{\text{Segment sales revenue}}{\text{Segment assets}}$$

(3) $$SROI \text{ (operating)} = \frac{SPC \text{ before interest}}{\text{Segment total assets}} \times 100$$

(4) $$SROI \text{ (net)} = \frac{SPC \text{ After interest}}{\text{Segment net assets}} \times 100$$

(5) Segment residual income (*SRI*) is = $SRI = SPC - (SROI \times SR)$

➢ The segment *ROI*, as a measure of divisional performance, has the merit of being a generally accepted measure consistent with firm-wise rate of return analysis. It is, moreover, a relative measure. It is conceptually easy to understand and interpret, and it can provide incentive for optimal utilisation of the resources of the firm. In spite of its conceptual soundness and appeal, it suffers from certain operational problems. These are: **(i)** determination of the segment investment base, and **(ii)** determination of the segment contribution. The problem of measuring segment resources are basically problems of allocation and valuation. The determination of contribution margin is associated with the problem of transfer pricing and the treatment of tax and interest.

➢ An alternative measure of financial performance in an investment centre is the segment residual income. The main advantage of this approach is that it encourages capital investment any time a divisional manager can earn more than a required rate of return. It also allows different rates of return for different divisions and, thus, is consistent with the decision-criterion in capital budgeting. Thus, it overcomes some of the shortcomings of the *SROI* analysis.

➢ In brief, among the approaches to measure performance in investment centre analysis, segment residual income is conceptually superior but segment *ROI* is more widely-used.

➢ Responsibility accounting, as a control device, is relevant to divisional performance measurement, whereas the other control devices are applicable to the organisation as a whole. The objectives of divisional performance measurement are: 1. To determine the contribution that a division makes to the organisation as a whole. 2. To provide a basis for evaluating the quality of the divisional managers' performance. 3. To motivate the divisional manager to operate his division in line with the basic goals of the organisation.

➢ Responsibility accounting focuses on responsibility centres. A responsibility centre is a sub-unit of an organisation under the control of a manager, who is responsible for the activities of that responsibility centre. The important criterion for creating responsibility centres is that the unit of the organisation should be separable and identifiable for operating purposes and evaluation of its performance. For the purpose of measuring divisional performance, the responsibility centres are divided into: **(1)** Expense centres, **(2)** Profit centres, and **(3)** Investment centres. The *modus operandi* of responsibility accounting is the comparison of budgeted and actual performance.

> ➢ An expense centre is a segment whose financial performance is measured in terms of cost. The analysis of performance is restricted to the use of resources in the division; what has been achieved as a consequence of consuming those resources is not considered. The suitability of cost, as an index of performance, and, therefore, of expense centres as divisional performance measure, is relevant in situations in which the revenue of a responsibility centre cannot be reliably measured, or the segment produces one single product, or, if the divisional manager is to produce a stated quantity of output at the lowest feasible cost. The cost centres evaluation techniques include variance analysis and job and process costing systems. However, in general, an expense centre is not a useful basis for measuring the performance of responsibility centres.
>
> ➢ The profit centre is that division of an organisation in which financial performance is measured on the basis of profit (revenue-expenses). With reference to responsibility accounting, a profit related performance criterion must be developed to suit the requirements of the divisional performance measurement. The traditional income statement format can be modified to provide a criterion for profit centre performance. The key categories in the revised income statement are: **(i)** Controllable contribution margin, **(ii)** Segment contribution margin, **(iii)** Segment profit contribution, and **(iv)** Segment net income.

REFERENCES

1. J.M. Fremgen, *Accounting for Managerial Analysis,* (Richard D. Irwin, Homewood, Illinois, 1976), p. 328.
2. R.N. Anthony and G.A. Welsch, *Management Accounting,* (Richard D. Irwin, Homewood, Illinois, 1977), p. 403.
3. *Ibid.*, p. 406.
4. Fremgen, *op. cit.*, p. 329.
5. Anthony and Welsch, *op. cit.*, p. 407.
6. Fremgen, *op. cit.*, p. 331.
7. Anthony and Welsh, *op. cit.*, p. 407.
8. *Ibid.*, p. 408
9. Fremgen, *op. cit.*, p. 334.
10. Anthony and Welsch, *op. cit.*, p. 411
11. *Ibid.*, p. 413
12. Fremgen, *op. cit.*, p. 343.
13. Chartfield, M. and Neilson, Denis, Cost Accounting, (Harcourt Brace Jovanovich, New York), 1983, p. 987.
14. D.T. Decoster and E.L. Schafer, Management Accounting, (John Wiley and Sons, New York, 1979), p. 426.
15. *Ibid.*, p. 427.
16. Based on Chatfield, M. Neilson, D., *Cost Accounting,* Harcourt Braces Jovanoich, Inc., New York), 1983.
17. Anthony and Welsch, op. cit., p. 417.

SOLVED PROBLEMS

P.19.1 ABC Ltd operates a number of divisions located in different regions. Division A incurred losses in the first quarter of the current year. Relevant revenue and cost data pertaining to this division are as follows:

Sales revenue	₹6,50,000
Controllable variable costs	3,50,000
Controllable fixed costs	2,00,000
Attributable segment costs	50,000
Common firm-wide costs allocated to division A	60,000
Loss	(10,000)

You are required: **(i)** To prepare a performance evaluation report of division A in the proper format and **(ii)** Advise the management whether its operations should be continued or shut down.

SOLUTION

(i) Performance Evaluation Report of Division A

Particulars	*Amount*
Sales revenue	₹6,50,000
Less controllable variable costs	3,50,000
Controllable contribution margin	3,00,000
Less controllable fixed costs	2,00,000
Controllable segment margin	1,00,000
Less attributable segment costs	50,000
Segment profit contribution	50,000
Less common firm-wide costs	60,000
Loss	(10,000)

(ii) In the short-run, division A justifies its existence as it generates a positive segment profit contribution (₹50,000), regardless of its share of firm-wide costs. Of course, in the long-run, division A must collectively generate sufficient total profit contribution to allow the recovery of all firm-wide costs and the achievement of corporate profit goals.

P.19.2 The Hypothetical Ltd has the following total operating results for the first half of current year:

Sales revenue	₹56,00,000
Less variable costs	37,20,000
Contribution	18,80,000
Less fixed costs	10,00,000
Net income	8,80,000

The following additional information concerning the performance of each of the firm's three operating departments has been provided:

	Departments		
	A	*B*	*C*
Sales revenue	₹24,00,000	₹20,00,000	₹12,00,000
Variable costs	16,80,000	12,00,000	8,40,000
Direct fixed costs	3,20,000	2,80,000	2,00,000

1. Rank the three departments on the basis of their proportionate measure of relative profitability.
2. A proposal to increase advertising expenses by ₹1,23,200 is expected to generate a 10 per cent increase in sales in all three departments. Analyse the effect of this proposal on the firm as a whole and on each department. Assume that the cost of advertising will be allocated to divisions according to each division's percentage to sales, and is to be considered as an attributable fixed cost of each department.

SOLUTION

1. *Performance Evaluation Report*

Particulars	*Departments* A	B	C	*Total*
Sales revenue	₹24,00,000	₹20,00,000	₹12,00,000	₹56,00,000
Less controllable variable costs	16,80,000	12,00,000	8,40,000	37,20,000
Controllable contribution margin	7,20,000	8,00,000	3,60,000	18,80,000
Less controllable/direct fixed costs	3,20,000	2,80,000	2,00,000	8,00,000
Segment profit contribution	4,00,000	5,20,000	1,60,000	10,80,000
Less common firm-wide costs				2,00,000
Net income				8,80,000
Segment profit contribution as per cent of sales revenue	16.67	26	13.33	
Ranking	2	1	3	

2. *Performance Evaluation Report (Impact of Advertisement Cost Analysed)*

Particulars	*Departments* A	B	C	*Total*
Sales revenue	₹26,40,000	₹22,00,000	₹13,20,000	₹61,60,000
Less controllable variable cost	18,48,000	13,20,000	9,24,000	40,92,000
Controllable contribution margin	7,92,000	8,80,000	3,96,000	20,68,000
Less direct fixed costs (existing)	3,20,000	2,80,000	2,00,000	8,00,000
Less advertising costs (allocated on the basis of sales ratio, additional)	52,800	44,000	26,400	1,23,200
Segment profit contribution	4,19,200	5,56,000	1,69,600	11,44,800
Less common firm-wide costs				2,00,000
Net income				9,44,800
Segment profit contribution as per cent of sales	15.88	25.27	12.85	
Ranking	2	1	3	

Although there has been a decline in segment profit contribution as percentages of sales for all the three departments, total segment profit contribution as a sequel to advertisement campaign, has shown a rise. As a result, the firm's net income has increased from ₹8,80,000 to ₹9,44,800.

P. 19.3 The current year's operating results of the three divisions (A, B, and C) of Hypothetical Ltd are given below:

(Amount in '000 ₹)

	Divisions A	B	C
Sales revenue	400	400	2,000
Less expenses	360	200	1,800
Segment profit contribution	40	200	200
Segment assets	200	800	4,000

Determine the rate of return for the three divisions and rank these divisions assuming that the firm follows investment centre basis of performance evaluation.

SOLUTION

Segment Rates of Return of A, B and C Divisions of Hypothetical Ltd *(Amount in '000' ₹)*

Particulars	Divisions A	Divisions B	Divisions C
1. Sales revenue	400	400	2,000
2. *Less* expenses	360	200	1,800
3. Segment profit contribution	40	200	200
4. Segment assets	200	800	4,000
5. Return on sales [(3) ÷ (1)] (per cent)	10	50	10
6. Asset turnover rate [(1) ÷ (4)] (times)	2	0.5	0.5
7. Segment rate of return (per cent)	20	25	5

In absolute terms, segment profit contributions are similar (₹2,00,000) for divisions B and C. However, in relative terms, B's performance is far better than that of division C, the respective figures for return on sales being 50 and 10 per cents. Segment rate of return of division B is also much higher (25 per cent) than that of C (5 per cent).

Although A and C both have 10 per cent rate of return on sales, A earned a 20 per cent return on investment compared to C's 5 per cent because asset turnover rate of A is 2 whereas that of C is only 0.5.

Based on their segment rate of return, the three divisions would be ranked B (1), A (2) and C (3).

P. 19.4 A.N. Vinod, the chief accounts officer of XYZ Ltd, has set a number of transfer prices to be used by service departments within the firm, all of which used to be cost centres. One is for typing services. The charge is ₹100 per hour which is based on total budgeted hours of available service and total budgeted costs for the typing service pool. The manager of one of the operating departments, a profit centre, has obtained a price of ₹70 per hour of typists' time from an outside agency. The task will take about 100 hours. The manager informs A.N. Vinod and B.C. Mehta, the manager of the typing service cost centre, of the outside price. In turn, he was informed that he could avail of the outside facility if he so desired, but the price set internally would not be lowered from the existing rate of ₹100 per hour.

Comment on the position taken by the managers. Budgeted costs for a pool are about 75 per cent fixed. Make your recommendations.

SOLUTION

The outside typing facility should be availed of by the operating department to improve its performance.

Judging the problem from the point of view of the manager of typing cost centre, it does not really matter for him if the operating manager seeks typing facilities from outside. This is so because efficiency of cost centre is to be evaluated by reference to budgeted costs which remain unaffected by the operating manager seeking outside services.

Looking at the problem from the angle of the firm as a whole, the operating managers' suggestion may not be a profitable proposition as the variable cost saved is ₹25 per hour and incremental variable costs will be ₹70 per hour, entailing a loss of ₹45 per hour (total loss being ₹4,500 for 100 hours). However, such a conclusion would not hold good if typists were overburdened and working at full capacity. If that were the case, *in the short run*, it would pay the firm if the operating manager makes use of 'outside' typing facilities. If the typing cost centre is operating below capacity, it would be in the interest of the firm to set the transfer price equal/below the outside market to discourage managers to go outside for typing facilities.

P.19.5 Hypothetical Ltd, a large-sized well established manufacturing enterprise has set up most of its service departments as artificial profit centres. The firm rents a computer for a fixed fee of ₹15,000 per month which is charged to the manager of the computer centre. The manager, in turn, charges operating units for use of the computer at ₹200 per hour. One of the operating managers, has an acquaintance in a data processing service company that charges only ₹150 per hour for *similar* type of computer services that the manager rents.

The managers in the firm are free to buy services inside or outside the firm. The operating manager told the manager of the computer centre either to reduce his price to ₹150 per hour or he would use the outside firm.

REQUIRED:

(i) Suppose that the operating department uses 20 hours of computer time per month and the firm has idle capacity. What would your recommendation be regarding lowering price from the point of view of the firm?

(ii) If the firm's computer is overloaded and demand exceeds the total time available in a month, what would your recommendation be regarding lowering price?

SOLUTION

(i) It would be profitable for the firm to lower the transfer price to ₹150 because the computer costs are fixed and there is idle capacity. The firm will lose ₹3,000 (20 hours × ₹150) if the operating department opts for outside computer services.

(ii) If the computer is overloaded at ₹200 per hour, it might be completely swamped at ₹150, with an increased in turnaround time, leading to possible dissatisfaction on the part of the users. Moreover, if the time is a critical factor for information desired, the company may suffer on account of delayed decisions.

Apart from *qualitative* factors, in monetary terms also, when business can be obtained at ₹200 per hour, there is no need of lowering the transfer price to ₹150. The department will lose 20 hours at ₹200 and gain them back at ₹150. However, it should be ensured that it does not lead to mass following from other departments rendering the capacity of the computer centre idle in future.

P.19.6 The sales manager of Bombay Textiles Ltd is judged by the total sales. Exceeding the sales budget is considered good performance. The sales budget and cost data for the current quarter are shown below:

	Products			Total
Particulars	Sarees	Long-cloth	Bedsheets	
Sales budget	₹4,50,000	₹9,00,000	₹16,50,000	₹30,00,000
Variable costs	(2,25,000)	(4,05,000)	(4,95,000)	(11,25,000)
Contribution	2,25,000	4,95,000	11,55,000	18,75,000
Actual sales	15,00,000	12,00,000	6,00,000	33,00,000

Actual prices were equal to budgeted prices and variable costs incurred were as budgeted per unit.

REQUIRED:

(i) Did the sales manager perform well? Support your answer with calculations.

(ii) Suggest better performance measurement criterion to be used by the firm.

SOLUTION

Performance Evaluation Report

	Products			Total
Particulars	Sarees	Long-cloth	Bedsheets	
Sales	₹15,00,000	₹12,00,000	₹6,00,000	₹33,00,000
Less variable costs:				
(50 per cent of sarees)	(7,50,000)			
(45 per cent of long cloth)		(5,40,000)		
(30 per cent of bedsheets)			(1,80,000)	
(44.54 per cent of total sales)				(14,70,000)
Contribution	7,50,000	6,60,000	4,20,000	18,30,000
Contribution margin ratio (per cent)	50	55	70	55.45

(i) Apparently, the sales manager seems to have performed well as the actual sales exceeded budgeted sales by ₹3,00,000, but the actual contribution is ₹45,000 lower than budgeted. This has happened because of the unfavourable change in the sales-mix, the most profitable product (bedsheets) has the least sales volume and the relatively less profitable products have much higher sales volume. As a sequel to such a change, the weighted average contribution margin based on planned mix which was 62.5 per cent (₹18,75,000 ÷ ₹30,00,000) has decreased to 55.45 per cent. In real terms, the sales manager did not perform better than planned.

(ii) The use of total sales, without reference to relative profitability of sales of different products, is unwise. It may not be possible to sell high-profit yielding products in budgeted volumes. If it is so, the sales manager could concentrate on low-profit yielding products, which may be more easily sold.

The performance of the sales manager should better be judged by the following criterion: Sales revenue less *(i) budgeted variable costs of production and (ii) actual selling costs.*

In the present system of transferring product at actual costs, the production department passes on its inefficiencies to the sales department, which should not be responsible for such costs. The sales manager should be charged with actual selling costs as he is responsible for incurrence of such costs and, above all, such costs are controllable at his level.

P.19.7 The following is the profit plan prepared for ABC Ltd for the current year ending March 31 (₹ in lakh):

Particulars	*Product line*			*Total*
	X	*Y*	*Z*	
Sales revenue	1,000	600	400	2,000
Controllable variable cost to make and sell	500	360	280	1,140
Controllable contribution margin	500	240	120	860
Common firm-wide costs (fixed)	—	—	—	660
				200

The income statement for the current year ended March 31 showed the following (₹ in lakh):

Particulars	*Product line*			*Total*
	X	*Y*	*Z*	
Sales	660	660	880	2,200
Less special discounts	20	—	—	20
	640	660	880	2,180
Controllable variable costs to make and sell	332	400	620	1,352
Controllable contribution margin	308	260	260	828
Common firm-wide costs (fixed)				670
Profit				158

Two steps were taken to increase the sales of product line X: **(a)** Special discounts were granted on large orders and **(b)** An additional appropriation of ₹6 lakh was approved for advertising and sales promotion. Selling prices did not change in the current year.

You are required to prepare an analysis of the changes in net income that would be helpful in fixing responsibility, using the contribution approach.

SOLUTION

Statement Showing Analysis of Changes in Income (₹in lakh)

Particulars		*Decrease*	*Increase*
Increase in contribution [(₹200 lakh sales revenue × 0.43, per cent weighted contribution to volume ratio, that is, ₹860 ÷ ₹2,000)]			86
Decrease in contribution due to special discounts		20	
Decrease in contribution due to unfavourable sales-mix:			
Budgeted contribution (₹2,200 × 0.43)	946		

(*Contd.*)

(Contd.)

Less actual contribution (See working note)			
Product X: (₹660 × 0.50)	330		
Y: (₹660 × 0.40)	264		
Z: (₹880 × 0.30)	264	858	
Total			88
Decrease in contribution due to increase in variable cost:			
Actual variable costs		1,352	
Less budgeted variable costs			
Product X: (₹660 × 0.50)	330		
Y: (₹660 × 0.60)	396		
Z: (₹880 × 0.70)	616	1,342	10
			118	86
Decrease in contribution (net)		32	
Increase in advertisement cost		6	
Increase in other common firm-wide costs (fixed)		4	
Decrease in income (net)		42	

WORKING NOTES

	Contribution ratio (per cent)		*Variable cost ratio (per cent)*
Product	X: (₹500 ÷ ₹1,000)	= 50	50
	Y: (₹240 ÷ ₹600)	= 40	60
	Z: (₹120 ÷ ₹400)	= 30	70

P.19.8 Home Comforts Ltd deals in three products, Ace, Nice, and Grace and these are sold directly through salesmen in three zones, Prime, Extension, and Outreach. The responsibility for sales promotion rests with the headquarters and so does the overall control of distribution and sales. Cost of sales as per cent of sales are: Ace, 85; Nice, 80; Grace, 75. Details of sales and selling and distribution expenses for the year are as follows:

Zones	*Products*	*Sales*	*Selling and distribution expenses allocated direct*
Prime zone	Ace	₹9,00,000	₹63,990
	Nice	9,00,000	84,465
	Grace	4,50,000	47,160
		22,50,000	1,95,615
Extension zone	Ace	6,75,000	46,710
	Nice	4,50,000	47,700
	Grace	2,25,000	23,940
		13,50,000	1,18,350
Outreach zone	Ace	2,25,000	18,900
	Nice	1,80,000	15,165
	Grace	4,95,000	66,375
		9,00,000	1,00,440

Selling and distribution expenses at headquarters are as follows:

Office expenses	₹94,500
Advertisement	1,35,000
Other expenses	1,21,500

Advertisement costs are allocated to zones and products on the basis of sales. Office expenses and other expenses are apportioned equally to the zones or the products, while computing the profit or loss for the zones or the products, as the case may be.

Prepare a comparative profit and loss statement, presenting zonal performance as distinct from product performance.

SOLUTION

Comparative Profit and Loss Statement (Evaluating Zonal Performance)

Particulars	*Zones*			*Total*
	Prime	*Extension*	*Outreach*	
Sales revenue	₹22,50,000	₹13,50,000	₹9,00,000	₹45,00,000
Less cost of sales:				
Ace (0.85)	7,65,000	5,73,750	1,91,250	15,30,000
Nice (0.80)	7,20,000	3,60,000	1,44,000	12,24,000
Grace (0.75)	3,37,500	1,68,750	3,71,250	8,77,500
Total	18,22,500	11,02,500	7,06,500	36,31,500
Gross profit/margin	4,27,500	2,47,500	1,93,500	8,68,500
Less selling and distribution expenses:				
Direct costs (allocated)	1,95,615	1,18,350	1,00,440	4,14,405
Advertisement (apportioned in sales ratio: 225: 135: 90)	67,500	40,500	27,000	1,35,000
Office expenses (apportioned equally)	31,500	31,500	31,500	94,500
Other expenses (equally)	40,500	40,500	40,500	1,21,500
Total selling and distribution costs	3,35,115	2,30,850	1,99,440	7,65,405
Net profit (loss)	92,385	16,650	(5,940)	1,03,095

P.19.9 Alfa Ltd has two divisions, A and B. A division is currently operating at full capacity. It has been asked to supply its product to division B. Division A sells its product to its regular customers for ₹30 each. Division B (currently operating at 50 per cent capacity) is willing to pay ₹20 each for the component produced by division A (this represents the full absorption cost per component at division A). The components will be used by division B in supplementing its main product to conform to the need of special order. As per the contract terms of sale, the buyer calls for reimbursement of full cost to division B, plus 10 per cent.

Division A has a variable cost of ₹17 per component. The cost per unit of division B subsequent to the buying part from division A is estimated as follows:

Purchased parts—outside vendors	₹90
Purchased part—division A	20
Other variable costs	50
Fixed overheads and administration	40
	200

The company uses return on investment in the measurement of divisional and division manager's performance.

REQUIRED:

(a) As manager of division A, would you recommend sales of your output to division B at the stipulated price of ₹20?

(b) Would it be in the over-all interest of the company for division A to sell its output to division B?

(c) Suggest an alternative transfer price and show how could it lead to goal congruence?

SOLUTION

(a) As manager of division A, I would not recommend sales at ₹20 per unit to division B. The division is already operating at its full capacity and the market is presumably absorbing all its output at ₹30 per unit. The internal transfer made to division B, hence, would reduce its profit (by ₹10 per unit) as well as the ROI.

(b) *Decision Analysis (Whether to Transfer Part from Division A to Division B at ₹20 per unit or Not).*

Particulars	Sold externally	Transferred to division B
Sale price (division A)	₹30	
Sale price (division B) (₹200 + 10 per cent)		₹220
Less relevant/incremental cost:		
For part of division A	17	17
Purchased parts from outside	—	90
Other variable costs	—	50
Profit per unit	13	63

Yes, it will be the over-all interest of the company that the transfer takes place as it would augment the firm's profit by ₹50 per unit.

(c) Dual price basis of effecting transfer is the most appropriate. In this case, the relevant transfer price will be ₹30 (sale) so far as division A is concerned, and ₹20 (purchase) so far as division B is concerned. It will keep the profits of division A unaffected and will facilitate the utilisation of the idle capacity of division B, as also increase its profit:

Sale price (₹200 + 10 per cent)	₹220
Less costs (₹90 + ₹20 + ₹50)	160
	60

P.19.10 The Royal Industries Ltd has two divisions, A and B. Division A manufactures product X which it sells in an outside market as well as to division B, which processes it to manufacture Z. The manager of division B has expressed the opinion that the transfer price is too high.

The two divisional managers are about to enter into discussions to resolve the conflict, and the manager of division A wants you to supply him with some information prior to the discussions.

Division A has been selling 40,000 units to outsiders and 10,000 units to division B, all at ₹20 per unit. It is not anticipated that these demands will change. The variable cost is ₹12 per unit and the fixed costs are ₹2 lakh.

The manager of division A anticipates that division B will want a transfer price of ₹18. If he does not sell to division B, ₹30,000 of fixed costs and ₹1,75,000 of assets can be avoided. The manager of division A would have no control over the proceeds from the sale of the assets and is judged primarily on his rate of return. The firm's existing assets are of ₹8 lakh.

(a) Should the manager of division A transfer its products at ₹18 to division B?

(b) What is the lowest price that the division A should accept? Support your decision with detailed calculations.

SOLUTION

(a) *Comparative Statement of Profit of Division A*

Particulars	Alternative situations		
	Sell at ₹20	Transfer at ₹18	Do not transfer
Sales revenue:			
Market sales (40,000 units × ₹20)	₹8,00,000	₹8,00,000	₹8,00,000
Transfer to division B (10,000 units)	2,00,000	1,80,000	—
Total (a)	10,00,000	9,80,000	8,00,000
Variable costs (₹12 per unit)	6,00,000	6,00,000	4,80,000
Fixed costs	2,00,000	2,00,000	1,70,000
Total (b)	8,00,000	8,00,000	6,50,000
Total profit (a – b)	2,00,000	1,80,000	1,50,000
Total assets	8,00,000	8,00,000	6,25,000
SROI (per cent)	25	22.5	24

The manager of division A should not agree to sell at ₹18 per unit as it lowers down its rate of return—the index of his evaluation.

(b) The lowest transfer price acceptable to division A is one which maintains its rate of return of 24 per cent (the possible SROI without selling to division B):

$$\frac{\text{Toal sales revenue} - \text{Total cost}}{\text{Total assets}} = \frac{\text{Rs } 8{,}00{,}000 + 10{,}000X - \text{Rs } 8{,}00{,}000}{\text{Rs } 8{,}00{,}000} = 0.24$$

Where X = transfer price per unit
10,000 X = ₹1,92,000
X = ₹19.20
The lowest transfer price acceptable to division A is ₹19.20 per unit.

P.19.11 The AB Ltd has two divisions, X and Y. One of the parts produced by division X is used in the manufacture of a product that is assembled at division Y. The part is not unique and there is a readily defined market such that X can sell outside the firm and Y can buy from outside. The following information is descriptive of the normal expectations of division X:

Capacity to produce the part (units)	1,25,000
External sales at ₹100 per unit (units)	1,00,000
Transfer to division Y (units)	25,000
Costs:	
Variable manufacturing cost per unit	₹34
Variable selling costs (on external sales only but not incurred on internal transfers)	2
Fixed manufacturing cost (based on 1,25,000 units)	6
Fixed selling cost (based on 1,00,000 units)	1

The division Y presents the following data on the assumption of a volume of 25,000 units (one part is needed for each unit of its own production):

Variable manufacturing cost per unit (exclusive of transfer price or outside purchase price)	₹100
Variable selling expenses per unit	6
Fixed manufacturing cost	10
Fixed selling expenses	4
Selling price of finished product	240

REQUIRED:

(i) If division X could sell 1,25,000 units at ₹100 each in the outside market, what transfer price would the company management prefer in order to provide proper motivation to division Y?

(ii) As management accountant, would you advise division Y to buy at the transfer price determined in part (i)?

(iii) Assume the situation and the transfer price determined in part (i). If the selling price dropped to ₹200, should Y buy at that price? Would this be desirable from the point of the firm? Why?

(iv) Assume that division X's product did not have an outside demand in excess of 1,00,000 units and its total fixed manufacturing cost could be reduced by 10 per cent, if the volume of production were reduced by 10 per cent, if the volume of production were reduced to 1,00,000 units, what is the appropriate transfer price?

(v) Suppose that X division's maximum outside demand is 1,10,000 units at ₹100, and there is no other usage for the capacity. What transfer price(s) should the company management prefer?

(vi) Suppose the unit selling price of Y's product is ₹180; one of its customers is also a customer of division X; division Y refuses to buy the part from the outside market at ₹100 since the selling price of ₹180 would not be high enough to even cover the variable costs. If division X does not lower the transfer price, division Y will not sell to this customer who, in turn, will probably cancel the usual order of 50,000 units to division X; there is no other demand for the product and no other usage of X's capacity; fixed costs would not change at either division. What is the lowest transfer price that the division X would be well advised to accept? Support your recommendation with computations.

SOLUTION

(i) *Determination of Transfer Price*

(a) Variable manufacturing cost of division X		₹84
(b) Opportunity cost (in terms of contribution foregone by transfer to division Y):		
Selling price	₹100	
Less total variable costs to make and sell (₹84 + ₹2)	86	14
Transfer price		98

(ii) *Statement of Contribution Per Unit—Division Y*

Selling price		₹240
Less variable costs:		
Manufacturing cost (division Y)	₹100	
Transfer price from division X	98	
Variable selling expenses	6	204
Contribution margin per unit		36

Yes, division Y is advised to buy from division X.

(iii) At ₹200 selling price per unit, division Y will not be able to earn a positive contribution:

Selling price	₹200
Less variable costs (part ii)	204
Negative contribution	(4)

No, division Y should not buy at that price. Yes, it would be desirable from the standpoint of the firm also due to higher contribution on external sales:

Comparative Income Statement of the Firm

	Sell externally	*Transfer to Y*
Selling price per unit	₹100	₹200
Out-of-pocket-costs:		
Division X	86	84
Division Y	—	106
Contribution margin	14	10

(iv) *Appropriate Transfer Price Per Unit*

Variable cost	₹84
Plus opportunity cost (in terms of reduction of fixed manufacturing cost by 10 per cent) (see working note 1)	3
	87

(v) Transfer Price

Units	*Transfers price*
15,000 units (working note 2)	₹84
10,000 units (part ii)	98

(vi) Determination of Transfer Price

Variable cost of production of 25,000 units (25,000 units × ₹84)	₹21,00,000
Less opportunity cost of lost sales (working note 3)	7,00,000
Lowest transfer price of 25,000 units	14,00,000
Transfer price per unit (₹14,00,000 ÷ 25,000 units)	56

WORKING NOTES

1.

Present cost of manufacturing (1,25,000 × ₹6)	₹7,50,000
Less budgeted costs (0.90 × ₹7,50,000)	6,75,000
Fixed cost of manufacturing 25,000 units	75,000
Opportunity cost per unit (₹75,000 ÷ 25,000 units)	3

2. For 15,000 units [1,25,000 units capacity (1,10,000 units market can absorb)], the opportunity cost is zero. The transfer price should, therefore, be equal to the variable cost, that is, ₹84.

3. *Opportunity cost of losing sale of 50,000 units*

Sales revenues (50,000 units × ₹100)	₹50,00,000
Less variable manufacturing and selling costs (50,000 units × ₹86)	43,00,000
	7,00,000

REVIEW QUESTIONS

RQ.19.1 Fill in the following blanks. In some cases choices are provided.

(i) Responsibility accounting focuses on ________.

(ii) ________ is a sub-unit of an organisation under the control of a manager who is responsible for its activities.

(iii) Responsibility centres are: ________.

(iv) A sub unit of an organisation whose financial performance is measured in terms of cost is referred to as ________.

(v) Division of an organisation in which financial performance is measured on the basis of revenues-expenses is known as ________.

(vi) ________ is a price used to measure the value of goods/services furnished by a profit centre to other responsibility centres within a firm.

(vii) Controllable segment margin = Sales revenue (–) Controllable variable costs (–) ________.

(viii) Segment profit contribution = Controllable segment margin (–) ________.

(ix) That method of transfer pricing in which the transferring division is credited with one price and acquiring division is charged with different price is known as ________.

(x) ________ considers not only costs and revenues but also the assets used in the division.

(xi) Segment ROI = Segment profit contribution/________.

(xii) Segment residual income = Segment profit contribution - (Segment assets × ________).

(xiii) Corporate/firm's net income = S segment profit contribution from all divisions of a firm (–) ________.

(xiv) Fixed costs that are directly and exclusively related to the decisions of the management of a division are referred to as ________.

(xv) Sales revenue (–) controllable variable costs = ________.

[Answers: (i) responsibility centres, (ii) responsibility centre, (iii) (a) expenses, (b) profit and (c) investment, (iv) expense centre, (v) profit centre, (vi) transfer price, (vii) controllable fixed costs, (viii) attributable segment costs, (ix) dual prices, (x) investment centre, (xi) segment assets, (xii) desired segment ROI, (xiii) firm-wide costs, (xiv) controllable fixed costs, (xv) controllable contribution margin.]

RQ.19.2 What is responsibility accounting? Discuss its significance in divisional performance measurement.

RQ.19.3 Define an expense centre. What is the suitability of the measure of performance in an expense centre?

RQ.19.4 What kind of performance is measured in profit centres? What are the criteria for evaluating that performance?

RQ.19.5 What is transfer prices? What are the different types of transfer prices? Under what circumstances is each type of transfer price appropriate and useful?

RQ.19.6 Define residual profit. Discuss its suitability as a performance measure.

RQ.19.7 "ROI is the best measure of overall performance." Do you agree?

RQ.19.8 Briefly differentiate expense centres, profit centres and investment centres. Identify the basic characteristics of each.

RQ.19.9 Why is ROI classified as a composite performance measure? Explain its significance.

RQ.19.10 "Responsibility accounting consists in accumulation and reporting of costs by levels of responsibility within an organisation." Offer your observations on the above statement.

RQ.19.11 "In addition to full cost accounting and differential accounting, a third type of accounting information is used in the management control process." (Anthony and Reece). What is this third type of accounting information called? What are its functions and how is it useful to management?

RQ.19.12 "What management does, or at least what it attempts to do, is to control the action of the people who are responsible for incurring costs." Comment.

RQ.19.13 "An important management function is that of assuring that activities of members of the organisation help to accomplish the organisation's goals."

RQ.19.14 "The management control process involves human beings, from those in the lowest responsibility centres of the organisational hierarchy up to and including each member of top management." Discuss.

RQ.19.15 Explain why a decision centre should be treated as a profit centre rather than as a cost centre.

RQ.19.16 Explain briefly the elements of profits centre performance.

RQ.19.17 What problems exist with regard to firm-wide common costs when segments are treated and evaluated as profit centres? What are the alternative treatments available?

RQ.19.18 Why must profit centres be evaluated and/or ranked? What problems arise when undue emphasis is placed on the comparison of segment profit performance?

RQ.19.19 Explain why an incremental approach is most useful in making decisions that involve possible modifications to the operations of segments of the profit centres.

RQ.19.20 What are the potential merits of a dual (two-way) transfer pricing system? What are its limitations?

RQ.19.21 "Transfer prices must always be equal to externally determined market prices of comparative products or services." Comment fully.

RQ.19.22 The ABC Ltd. has three divisions, A, B, and C. For the current year, the following data were reported:

Particulars	*Divisions*		
	A	*B*	*C*
Sales revenue	₹4,00,000	?	?
Profit	40,000	₹3,20,000	?
Investment	2,00,000	?	₹10,00,000
Investment turnover	?	4	?
Margin of profit on sales	?	?	0.15
SROI	?	0.2	?
Segment profits using 10 per cent cost of capital	?	?	1,01,000

(a) Complete the table.

(b) Rank the divisions in terms of their effective use of resources in capturing the market.

RQ.19.23 The home appliances division of Benjamin Industries Ltd. now shows a profit of 5 per cent on sales of ₹12 lakh. An investment of ₹4,00,000 is needed to finance these sales. The management of the firm in considering the following two alternative plans for improving operations submitted by two employees, E_1 and E_2:

(a) E_1 believes that the sales volume can be doubled by greater promotional effort. It would lower the profit rate to 4 per cent of sales and require an additional investment of ₹1,00,000.

(b) E_2 favours eliminating some unprofitable appliances and improving efficiency by adding ₹2,00,000 in capital equipment. This alternative would decrease sales volume by 10 per cent but improve the profit rate to 7 per cent of sales.

You are required to determine: **(a)** The company's current rate of return on investment in the division, **(b)** The anticipated rates of return under the alternatives suggested by E_1 and E_2, and **(c)** Which plan, if any, will you recommend?

RQ.19.24 Alfa Ltd. has two decentralised divisions, D_1 and D_2. D_1 has always purchased certain units from D_2 at ₹300 per unit. As D_2 plans to raise the price to ₹400 per unit, D_1 desires to purchase these units from outside suppliers for ₹300 per unit. The costs of D_2 are as follows:

Variable cost per unit	₹250
Annual fixed costs	50,000
Annual production for D_1 (units)	1,000

If D_1 buys from an outside supplier, the facilities D_2 uses to manufacture these units would remain idle.

From the viewpoint of the company as a whole, should D_1 purchase from D_2 at ₹400 per unit, or from outside at ₹300 per unit?

RQ.19.25 Hypothetical Ltd. has two divisions, A and B, which are operated as profit centres. Division A has been selling a part of its production to division B at ₹200 per unit. Annual output of division A is 10,000 units; sales are made as follows:

Division B	4,000 units
Outside companies	6,000 units

Units costs in division A are as follows:

Fixed	₹75
Variable	100
	175

Division B has found that it can negotiate a contract to buy from an outside supplier at ₹150 per unit. Should division B be allowed to purchase from outside? In the light of its implications, can you suggest an alternative?

RQ.19.26 Avon Ltd. with two manufacturing divisions is organised on profit centre basis. Division A is the only source for the supply of a component that is used in division B in the manufacture of a product, KLIM. One such part is used in each unit of the product, KLIM. As the demand for the product is not steady, division B can obtain orders for increased quantities only by spending more on sales promotion and by reducing the selling prices. The manager of division B has accordingly prepared the following forecast of sales quantities and selling prices:

Sales units per day	*Average selling price per unit*
1,000	₹52.50
2,000	39.80
3,000	33.00
4,000	27.80
5,000	24.00
6,000	20.10

The manufacturing cost of KLIM in division B is ₹37,500 for the first 1,000 units and ₹7,500 per 1,000 units in excess of 1,000 units.

Division A incurs total cost of ₹15,000 per day for an output upto 1,000 components, and the total costs will increase by ₹9,000 per day for every additional 1,000 components manufactured. The manager of division A states that the operating results of his division will be optimised if the transfer price of component is set at ₹12 per unit, and he has accordingly set the aforesaid transfer price for his supplies of the component to division A.

Required:

(a) Prepare a schedule showing the profitability at each level of output for division A and division B.

(b) Find the profitability of the company as a whole at the output level at which

(i) Division A's net profit is maximum

(ii) Division B's net profit is maximum.

(c) If the company is not organised on profit centre basis, what level of output will be chosen to yield the maximum profit?

RQ.19.27 The installed capacity of XYZ Ltd. is 50,000 units per month. Sales normally permit operations at 80 per cent of this capacity. At normal capacity, indirect manufacturing overheads total ₹3,60,000.

During the month of April of the current year, sales demand was above normal and 45,000 units were manufactured and sold. Indirect manufacturing costs of the order of ₹3,87,000 were recorded.

An argument has ensued between the plant superintendent and the production supervisor. The supervisor claims credit for reducing unit cost. The superintendent contends that waste and inefficiency have crept into the plant, as reflected in cost increases.

The chief executive of the company cannot follow the superintendent's reasoning and has called you to settle the argument.

The analysis of the company's costs shows that fixed indirect manufacturing costs are ₹2,00,000 per month. The company has the practice of recovering these costs from the normal capacity.

You are required to prepare a report for the chief executive of the company to help him in rewarding the right man/or assigning responsibility for poor performance.

ANSWERS **[Comprehensive solutions to all numerical review questions are available on the companion website: http://www.mhhe.com/khan_jain_cost2e]**

RQ.19.22 **(i)** Sales revenue: B, ₹8,00,000; C, ₹13,40,000
(ii) Profit: C, ₹2,01,000
(iii) Investment: B, ₹2,00,000
(iv) Investment turnover: A, 2; C, 1.34
(v) Margin of profit on sales: A, 0.1; B, 0.05
(vi) SROI: A, 0.20; C. 0.201
(vii) Segment profit: A, ₹20,000; B, ₹3,00,000.

RQ.19.23 **(a)** 15 per cent
(b) (i) 19.2 per cent
(ii) 12.6 per cent
(c) E_1 plan.

RQ.19.24 Should buy from D_2.

RQ.19.25 Division B should continue to buy form division A. Dual (two-way) price could be an alternative.

RQ.19.26 **(a)** (i) ₹(3,000), Nil, ₹3,000, ₹6,000, ₹9,000, and ₹10,000
(ii) ₹3,000, ₹10,600, ₹10,500, ₹3,200, (₹7,500) and (₹26,400)
(b) (i) ₹(14,400) loss
(ii) ₹10,600.
Maximum profit (₹13,500) at the level of 3,000 units produced and sold.

RQ.19.27 The contention of the superintendent in correct.

Short-run Decision Analysis

Learning Objectives

1. Describe the analytical framework for short-term decisions in terms of relevant data, that is, differential costs and revenues
2. Illustrate the application of differential costs/revenues in various decision situations such as special orders, disposing of inventories, loss leaders, sell now or process further, make or buy, elimination of products/divisions/department, short-term use of scarce resources, and operate or shut down.
3. Explain target costing.

INTRODUCTION

The main purpose of this chapter is two-fold: **(i)** To describe the framework of analysis for short-term decisions, and **(ii)** Its application for such decision-making. Section 1 of the chapter sets out the analytical framework in terms of the data requirement, that is, the differential/incremental costs and revenues. Section 2 deals with the application of the framework in different situations. Target costing is explained in Section 3. The last Section summarises the main points.

ANALYTICAL FRAMEWORK

Decision-making involves the act of selecting one course of action from among various feasible alternatives available. Short-term decisions are of a special nature. The type of information required for decision-making depends on the decision situation under consideration. The information required for such decisions is called '*relevant data*.' The relevant data refers to decision-making elements required to meet the needs of specific situations. The conventional accounting data would not serve the purpose. They have to be altered/modified in terms of addition/deletion to tailor the historical costs to the requirements of decision-making.

Relevant data are decision-making elements required to meet the needs of specific situations.

The first element of the relevant data is that it is future-oriented, that is, it relates to a future period. The underlying consideration is that these decisions imply some future activity. In other

Future costs are costs expected to happen under an assumed set of conditions.

words, while historical cost represents what has happened under existing conditions, the future costs refer to what is expected to happen under an assumed set of conditions. They are special purpose costs that are applicable only to the situations for which they are constructed. They do not have universal applicability.

The second component of the analytical framework of short-term decision-making is that is is primarily quantitative (tangible). Factors having a bearing on decision-making can be either qualitative (intangible)—defined as factors which are not amenable to precise and direct measurement, or quantitative—which can be expressed in numerical terms. It is true that quantitative factors do influence decision-making, for example, the management of a company may decide to manufacture certain components even though it costs less to buy them from outside, in view of a long-term policy of avoiding dependence on outside suppliers. Yet, these are not of operational significance because they cannot be included in accounting information.

Thus, short-term decision-making is based on quantifiable, future accounting information. This is derived from the alteration of the historical cost data. The modification is based on the following cost concepts. A detailed discussion of these concepts was made in an earlier chapter. They are briefly recapitulated here.

Relevant Costs

Relevant costs are costs which would change as a result of the decision.

These are the costs which would change as a result of the decision under consideration, whereas *irrelevant costs* are those which would remain unaffected by the decision. Therefore, only relevant costs would be included in the analytical framework.

Opportunity Costs

Opportunity costs are monetary benefits foregone for not pursuing the alternative course.

Another costs concept relevant to the short-term decision-making is the opportunity/imputed costs. When a decision to follow one course of action is made, the opportunity to pursue some other course is foregone. The monetary benefits that would accrue from taking the alternative course are sacrificed and these benefits, if measurable, should be added to the costs of the decision.

Sunk Costs (Committed Costs)

Sunk costs are costs already incurred.

Such costs are historical costs that are irrevocable in a given situation. They are the costs that have been incurred by a decision that was made in the past and cannot be changed by any decision that would be made in the future. They are, therefore, irrelevant in decision-making and have to be deleted from the historical costs.

Avoidable/Escapable/Discretionary Costs

Avoidable costs are costs that can be avoided in future as a result of managerial choice.

These costs can be avoided in the future as a result of managerial choices because management can choose not to incur them. Avoidable costs are relevant costs when particulars decision-alternatives are compared.

Incremental/Differential Costs

Differential costs include variable costs and additional fixed costs resulting from particular decision.

These costs are also useful in planning and decision-making. They provide a device for testing the profitability of increased output, and give a better measure than the average cost. Defined in this sense, incremental costs differ from variable costs. The former is a comprehensive term, which includes, besides variable costs, additional fixed costs resulting from a particulars decision, whereas, the latter is comprised of variable costs only. The difference between incremental/differential costs and revenues is the incremental/differential contribution. Format 20.1 shows the procedure of computing incremental contribution. The incremental contribution so computed is the basis of short-term decision-making.

Format 20.1 Incremental Contribution

Incremental revenues (product-wise)	____
Add cost savings (specify items)	____
Total incremental revenues	____
Less lost contribution (product-wise)	____
Less incremental costs (specify items)	____
Incremental contribution	____

DECISION-SITUATIONS

This Section demonstrates the application of incremental/differential costs and revenue data for decision-making in the following situations:

1. Sales volume related
2. Sell or further process
3. Make or buy
4. Product lines/divisions/departments
5. Short-term use of scarce resources
6. Joint outputs of common processing operations
7. Operate or shut-down

Sales Volume Related Decisions

Such decisions cover: **(i)** Acceptance of special/extra sales orders, **(ii)** Disposing of inventories, and **(iii)** Loss leaders.

Special Orders One decision-situation relates to increase in sales volume outside the normal marketing pattern. Typical examples of such types of sales are acceptance of special orders, one-time quantity sale, and sales to foreign customers. If such special sales do not affect the normal sales, the accept-reject decision would be based on the incremental contribution. In case, the special sale would affect the future sales volume and/or selling price, the opportunity cost in terms of lost revenue will also be relevant to the decision-making. This is illustrated in Example 20.1

EXAMPLE 20.1 *(PRICING SPECIAL ORDERS)*
Assume that Royal Industries Ltd has excess capacity. The normal plant capacity is 3,00,000 units per year and current production is 2,00,000 units. There is no alternative use for the idle facilities. The company receives an offer from a foreign customer to buy 1,00,000 units at ₹10 a unit. The regular market price is ₹14 a unit. The current manufacturing and selling costs are:

Particulars	*Per unit*	*Total*
Total variable cost:		
Direct labour	₹2	₹4,00,000
Direct material	3	6,00,000
Variable overheads	2	4,00,000
Manufacturing cost	7	14,00,000
Variable selling cost	1	2,00,000
	8	16,00,000
Fixed overheads:		
Manufacturing	2.50	5,00,000
Selling	0.50	1,00,000
Total cost	11.00	22,00,000

(a) Should the offer be accepted assuming that shipment charges of ₹50,000 are to be borne by the seller? There will be a special packing of the products which will involve packing cost of ₹0.25 per unit. Being an export order, the management is convinced of the fact that the regular market price of ₹14 a unit will not be affected;

(b) Assume that the order is from a local supplier and, therefore, should the order be accepted, all products in future are to be offered at the special order price.

Solution

The decision analysis in situations (a) and (b) is depicted in Tables 20.1 and 20.2.

Table 20.1 (a) Decision Analysis

Particulars	*Without special order*	*Amount*	*With special order*	*Amount*
Sales	(2,00,000 × ₹14)	₹28,00,000	(2,00,0000 × ₹14)	₹28,00,000
			(1,00,000 × ₹10)	10,00,000
		28,00,000		38,00,000
Less incremental costs:				
Direct labour	(2,00,000 × ₹2)	4,00,000	(3,00,000 × ₹2)	6,00,000
Direct material	(2,00,000 × ₹3)	6,00,000	(3,00,000 × ₹3)	9,00,000
Variable overheads	(2,00,000 × ₹2)	4,00,000	(3,00,000 × ₹2)	6,00,000
Packing costs	—	—	(1,00,000 × ₹0.25)	25,000
Selling costs	(2,00,000 × ₹1)	2,00,000	(2,00,000 × ₹1)	2,00,000
Shipment costs	—	—		50,000
Contribution		12,00,000		14,25,000

The incremental contribution is 2,25,000 and, therefore, the order should be accepted.

Table 20.2 (b) Decision Analysis

Particulars		*Amount*
Sales (3,00,000 × ₹10)		₹30,00,000
Less relevant costs:		
Manufacturing variable costs (3,00,000 × ₹7)	₹21,00,000	
Packing costs (1,00,000 × ₹0.25)	25,000	
Variable selling costs (2,00,000 × ₹1)	2,00,000	
Shipment costs	50,000	23,75,000
Contribution		6,25,000

Since the contribution has declined, the order from the local supplier should not be accepted.

Disposing of Inventories Pricing decisions must consider the relative marketability of inventories. Due to damage/obsolescence or lack of demand, inventory may not be saleable through normal marketing channels or under normal operating conditions. In such cases, incremental analysis is appropriate for decision-making as all prior costs of producing/acquiring inventory are sunk costs and, therefore, irrelevant to the decisions. Example 20.2 illustrates the point.

Example 20.2 *(Disposal of Inventories)*

ABC Ltd has on hand 5,000 units of a product that cannot be sold through regular sales. These were produced at a total cost of ₹1,50,000, and would normally have been sold for ₹40 per unit. Three alternatives are being considered:

(i) Sell the items as scrap for ₹2 per unit.

(ii) Repackage at a cost of ₹20,000, and sell them at ₹8 per unit.

(iii) Dispose them off at the city dump at removal cost of ₹2,500.

Which alternative should be accepted?

SOLUTION

Table 20.3 exhibits the decision analysis.

Table 20.3 Decision Analysis

Particulars	*Alternatives* (I) Sell as scrap	(II) Repackage and sell	(III) Disposal
Sales revenue	₹10,000	₹40,000	—
Less costs:			
Repackage cost	—	20,000	—
Removal cost	—	—	2,500
Contribution (Loss)	10,000	20,000	(2,500)

Alternative II should be accepted.

Loss Leaders Sometimes an item may be deliberately priced so low that the firm has to suffer loss in the expectation that additional sales will be generated which will offset the loss. Such sales are referred to as loss leaders.[1] Consider Example 20.3.

Loss leaders are sales deliberately priced to suffer loss to be offset by additional sales in future.

EXAMPLE 20.3

The contribution margin of Hypothetical Ltd is 50 per cent. Its regular monthly gross sales average ₹4,00,000. Monthly fixed costs are ₹1,00,000. To increase the sales, the firm plans to sell a special product at ₹8 each. If 10,000 units of this item can be purchased for ₹12 per unit, determine the increase in the sales revenue of the normally priced items to make the promotion worthwhile.

SOLUTION

Table 20.4 Decision Analysis

Particulars	*Amount*
Incremental revenue	₹80,000
Less incremental costs	1,20,000
(Incremental loss)	(40,000)
Desired increase in sales revenue = Loss (₹40,000)/ C/V ratio (0.50)	80,000

The interpretation of ₹80,000 is that the increase in the sales revenue exceeding this amount will justify the promotional campaign.

Sell Now or Process Further Decisions

Short-term incremental analysis also applies to *sell or process further* decision-situations. As already discussed in an earlier chapter, when an item of production passes through various processes, it is saleable at different stages/points, that is, at various physical stages of production. In deciding at what stage to sell the product, the two critical variables are: (i) Identification of sunk costs and (ii) Calculation of incremental returns at various sales alternatives. All costs, whether fixed or variable, incurred before the sell or process further point, should be treated as sunk, and therefore, irrelevant costs. The incremental return relevant to the decision is the difference between the costs that are incurred beyond the decision point and the revenues. If, however, the fixed resources would remain idle as a result of not processing the product further, and if they could be diverted to some other use, *opportunity cost* would also become relevant to the decision analysis. Such decisions are illustrated in Examples 20.4 and 20.5.

EXAMPLE 20.4 *(ADDITIONAL PROCESSING-SINGLE PRODUCT)*
Avon Ltd manufactures a single product, which it sells to firms which process it further before sale. The normal quarterly operating volume for the company is 50,000 units produced and sold. The relevant cost data are as follows:

Selling price		₹100
Standard costs:		
Direct materials	₹30	
Direct labour	15	
Variable manufacturing overheads	10	
Fixed manufacturing overheads (₹2,50,000 per quarter)	5	
Variable selling overheads	10	
Fixed selling expenses (₹1,25,000 per quarter)	2.5	72.50
Standard profit per unit		27.50

The company management is considering the possibility of further processing it itself, necessary for the operation to sell directly to the customers. The management estimates that the product can be sold @ ₹140 per unit after further processing. The following are the estimates of the additional costs of processing 50,000 units:

Direct labour (per unit)	₹10
Variable manufacturing overheads (per unit)	5
Variable selling costs (per unit)	2
Additional fixed manufacturing overheads per quarter	1,00,000
Additional sales expenses per quarter	50,000

You are required to decide whether further processing should be done or not.

SOLUTION
Table 20.5 presents the decision analysis.

Table 20.5 Decision Analysis

Particulars	*Without further processing*		*With further processing*		*Incremental revenues and costs*	
	Per unit	*Total*	*Per unit*	*Total*	*Per unit*	*Total*
Sales	₹100	₹50,00,000	₹140	₹70,00,000	₹40	₹20,00,000
Less incremental costs:						
Direct material	30	15,00,000	30	15,00,000	0.0	—
Direct labour	15	7,50,000	25	12,50,000	10	5,00,000
Manufacturing overheads	10	5,00,000	17*	8,50,000	7*	3,50,000
Selling overheads	10	5,00,000	13*	6,50,000	3*	1,50,000
Contribution	35	17,50,000	55	27,50,000	20	10,00,000

* including additional fixed overheads.

Since further processing would result in a greater contribution, the new proposal would be more profitable and should be accepted.

EXAMPLE 20.5 *(SELL OR PROCESS FURTHER—MULTIPLE PRODUCTS)*
Hypothetical Ltd produces three products, A, B and C. One type of raw material is used for all these products. The raw material enters the process in Department 1 of the factory. Department 1 separates materials for products A, B and C. During the quarter, material worth ₹4,00,000 was issued to Department 1. Other direct costs of operating Department 1 were ₹2,00,000. The output of products from Department 1 was: A, 10,000 units; B, 5,000 units ; and C, 2,000 units.

Products A, B and C can be sold after being processed from Department 1 (split-off point) at prices of ₹60, ₹30 and ₹20, respectively. After the split-off, product A could be processed further in Department 2. With additional processing cost of ₹50,000, this product can be sold for ₹70 per unit. After the split-off, product B could be processed further in Department 3 for ₹30,000 additional cost, and will then fetch ₹35 per unit. Product C is not suitable for further processing and has to be sold at the point of split-off. What action should the management take?

SOLUTION

Table 20.6 presents the decision analysis.

Table 20.6 Decision Analysis

Particulars	*Product A*			*Product B*		
	Sell now	*Process further*	*Incremental revenues and costs*	*Sell now*	*Process further*	*Incremental revenues and costs*
Sales	₹6,00,000	₹7,00,000	₹1,00,000	₹1,50,000	₹1,75,000	₹25,000
Less separable costs	—	50,000	50,000	—	30,000	30,000
Contribution	6,00,000	6,50,000	50,000	1,50,000	1,45000	(5,000)

Table 20.6 shows that it is profitable to process product A further because it yields an incremental contribution of ₹50,000. The decision is based on the assumption that there is no other opportunity cost for using the facilities of Departments 2 and 3. The management is advised to process product A further and sell product B as it is.

Make or Buy Decisions

Many firms have to choose between manufacturing certain components themselves or acquiring them from outside suppliers. Incremental analysis provides solution to this kind of decision-problems too. The relevant input information is the committed/avoidable costs if the firm has adequate idle capacity to make the components, because the firm would not be required to incur fixed costs to produce the components. If, however, there is need to enlarge the capacity of existing plant, or the existing capacity of the plant is diverted for the production of the components, opportunity cost in terms of lost contribution will be relevant to the decision analysis. Examples 20.6 and 20.7 illustrate the make or buy decision involving avoidable committed costs and opportunity cost.

Committed costs are costs if a firm has idle capacity.

EXAMPLE 20.6 *(MAKE OR BUY DECISION)*

The Philips Company Ltd produces most of its tube parts in its own plant. The company is at present considering the feasibility of buying a part from an outside supplier for ₹4.5 per part. If this were done, monthly costs would increase by ₹5,000.

The part under consideration is manufactured in Department 1 along with numerous other parts. On account of discontinuing the production of this part, Department 1 would have somewhat reduced operations. The average monthly usage production of this part is 20,000 units. The costs of producing this part on per unit basis are as follows:

Material	₹1.80
Labour (half-hour)	2.40
Fixed overheads	0.80
Total costs	5.00

The company follows the practice of applying manufacturing overheads on the basis of direct labour-hours. Normal production volume in Department 1 is 1,50,000 hours per month, and current actual production is at about the same level. Discontinuation of production of this part would cause an unfavourable volume variance of ₹16,000 per month in this department.

How would you advise the management in this regard?

SOLUTION

Table 20.7 presents the decision analysis.

Table 20.7 Decision Analysis

Particulars	*Make costs*		*Buy cost*	
	Total	*Per unit*	*Total*	*Per unit*
Relevant costs:				
Materials	₹36,000	₹1.80	—	—
Labour	48,000	2.40	—	—
Purchasing cost	—	—	₹90,000	₹4.50
Additional cost of purchasing from outside	—	—	5,000	0.25
	84,000	4.20	95,000	4.75
Differential costs	11,000 per month			
favouring making of the parts		0.55 per unit		

The company should continue the practice of producing the part in Department 1.

WORKING NOTES

(i) Unfavourable volume variance of ₹16,000 (10,000 hours required in producing 20,000 parts @ ₹1.60 per hours) indicates that there is no alternative use of the facilities, and they would remain idle if part production is discontinued. Therefore, they are irrelevant costs.

EXAMPLE 20.7 *(MAKE OR BUY DECISION)*

The ABC Company Ltd produces most of its own parts and components. The standard wage rate in the parts department is ₹30 per hour. Variable manufacturing overheads is applied at a standard rate of ₹20 per labour-hour and fixed manufacturing overheads are charged at a standard rate of ₹25 per hour.

For its current years's output, the company will require a new part. This part can be made in the parts department without any expansion of existing facilities. Nevertheless, it would be necessary to increase the cost of product testing and inspection by ₹50,000 per month. Estimated labour time for the new part is half an hour per unit. Raw materials cost has been estimated at ₹60 per unit.

The alternative choice before the company is to purchase part from an outside supplier at ₹90 per unit. The company has estimated that it will need 2,00,000 new parts during the current years.

Advise the company whether it would be more economical to buy or make the new parts. Would your answer be different if the requirement of new parts was only 1,00,000 parts?

SOLUTION

The decision analysis is presented in Table 20.8.

Table 20.8 (i) Decision Analysis: 2,00,000 units

Particulars	Make costs Total	Make costs Per unit	Buy costs Total	Buy costs Per unit
Raw material	₹1,20,00,000	₹60	—	—
Direct wages	30,00,000	15	—	—
Variable overheads	20,00,000	10	—	—
Additional fixed costs:				
Product testing and inspection (₹50,000 × 12)	6,00,000	3	—	—
Purchase costs	—	—	₹1,80,00,000	₹90
Total costs	1,76,00,000	88	1,80,00,000	90
Differential costs favouring the decision of making the component ₹4,00,000 total, ₹2 per component				

The company is advised to make the new part.

(ii) Decision Analysis: 1,00,000 units:

Raw material	₹60,00,000	₹60	—	—
Direct wages	15,00,000	15	—	—
Variable overheads	10,00,000	10	—	—
Fixed costs	6,00,000	6	—	—
Purchase costs	—	—	₹90,00,000	₹90
Total costs	91,00,000	91	90,00,000	90

If the requirement of the new part is 1,00,000 units, the company would be well advised to buy from an outside supplier. Buy costs are ₹90 per unit, compared to make costs of ₹91 per unit.

Addition/Elimination of Product Lines/Divisions/Shifts/Departments

When a firm is divided into multiple sales outlets, product lines, divisions, departments (segments), it may have to evaluate their individual performances to decide whether or not to continue operations of each of these segments or add a new segment. The decision criterion would be the *segment margin.* The segment margin equals segment's contribution margin less fixed costs that are directly traceable to that segment. Examples 20.8 and 20.9 illustrate such decisions.

Segment margin equals segments contribution margin less fixed costs directly traceable to the segment.

Example 20.8 *(Addition of Second Shift)*

Ulfa Ltd produces a single product in its plant. This product sells for ₹100 per unit. The standard production cost per unit is as follows:

Raw materials (0.5 kg @ ₹80 per kg)	₹40
Direct labour (0.2 hour @ ₹50 per kg)	10
Variable manufacturing overheads	10
Fixed manufacturing overheads	20
	80

The plant is currently operating at full capacity of 1,00,000 units per years on a single shift. This output is inadequate to meet the projected sales demand, and the sales manager has estimated that the firm will lose sales of 40,000 units next years if the capacity is not expanded

Plant capacity could be doubled by adding a second shift. This would require additional out-of-pocket fixed manufacturing overhead costs of ₹10,00,000 annually. Also, a night work wage premium equal to 25 per cent of the standard wage would have to be paid during the second shift. However, if annual production volume were 1,30,000 units or more, the company could take advantage of 2 per cent quantity discount on its raw material purchases.

You are required to advise whether it would be profitable to add the second shift in order to obtain the sales volume of 40,000 units per year?

SOLUTION

Table 20.9 presents the decision analysis.

Table 20.9 Decision Analysis

Particulars	*Profit without expansion*	*Profits with expansion*
Sales revenue	₹1,00,00,000	₹1,40,00,000
Less variable costs:		
Raw materials	40,00,000	54,88,000@
Direct labour	10,00,000	15,00,000@@
Variable manufacturing overhead	10,00,000	14,00,000
Contribution	40,00,000	56,12,000
Less fixed costs (₹1,00,000 × 20)	20,00,000	30,00,000
Net income	20,00,000	26,12,000

@(₹39.20 × 1,40,000 units)

@@ (₹10,00,000 + (40,000 units × 0.2 hour × ₹62.50 per hour = ₹5,00,000) = ₹15,00,000

Yes, it would be profitable to add the second shift as it would increase profits by ₹6,12,000.

EXAMPLE 20.9 (*ELIMINATION OF A PRODUCT LINE*)

Avon Garments Ltd manufactures readymade garments and uses its cut-pieces of cloth to manufacture dolls. The following statement of cost has been prepared:

Particulars	*Readymade garments*	*Dolls*	*Total*
Direct material	₹80,000	₹6,000	₹86,000
Direct labour	13,000	1,200	14,200
Variable overheads	17,000	2,800	19,800
Fixed overheads	24,000	3,000	27,000
Total cost	1,34,000	13,000	1,47,000
Sales	1,70,000	12,000	1,82,000
Profit (loss)	36,000	(1,000)	35,000

The cut-pieces used in dolls have a scrap value of ₹1,000 if sold in the market. As there is a loss of ₹1,000 in the manufacturing of dolls, it is suggested to discontinue their manufacture. Advise the management.

SOLUTION

Table 20.10 presents the decision analysis.

Table 20.10 Decision Analysis

Particulars	*Production of dolls*	*Non-production of dolls*
Sales revenue	₹12,000	—
Scrap value of cut-pieces	—	₹1,000
Less avoidable costs		
Direct material	6,000	
Direct labour	1,200	
Variable overheads	2,800	
Differential revenue	2,000	1,000

The management is advised that the differential revenue favours continuation of production of dolls.

Short-term Use of Scarce Resources

Incremental analysis can also be used to allocate resources that are limited in quantity (key factors). The key factor refers to scarce resource which may be raw material, skilled labour or machine capacity. If the machine capacity is inadequate to permit manufacture of all products, the most profitable course of action is to use the available machine capacity/hours to make the products which contribute the maximum contribution margin per machine hour. If materials are in short supply, the management should produce according to the largest contribution margin per input of material. Thus, the contribution per unit of the key factor of production is to be determined and the products ranked according to the descending order of contribution per unit of key factor. This will maximise the total contribution of the firm. Consider Example 20.10.

EXAMPLE 20.10 *(USE OF SCARCE RESOURCES)*

Precision Engineers Pvt. Ltd are producing to specific orders. Their factory capacity is limited by one major machine forming a critical cost centre through which all products pass. The factory normally works for 250 days in a year on 24 hours, 3 shifts a day, and 5 days a week basis. The maximum achievable capacity is 80 per cent, corresponding to the average level of activity in the critical cost centre. The operating results summarised for management in previous year are as follows (₹ in lakh):

Sales		₹48
Less costs:		
Materials	₹18.00	
Labour-variable costs	5.75	
Factory-variable costs	6.25	
Factory-fixed costs	3.00	
Selling and administration costs	10.00	43
Profit		5

The average profitability experienced during the previous years is being maintained during the current year also.

The company has an opportunity of taking any one of two large contracts either of which will substitute for a large amount of current production without affecting the hourly variable production costs. Details of the contracts are:

Particulars	*Contract X*	*Contract Y*
Material cost per unit	₹375	₹1,750
Machine-hours (critical cost centre) per unit	2	3
Contract price per unit	1,500	3,750
Extra selling expenses per unit	25	50

Prepare a report for the managing director making your recommendations as to which of the two contracts should be preferred.

SOLUTION

Table 20.11 Decision Analysis

Particulars	*Contract X* 2,400 units (4,800 ÷ 2)		*Contract Y* 1,600 units (4,800 ÷ 3)	
	Per unit	*Total*	*Per unit*	*Total*
Contract price	₹1,500	₹36,00,000	₹3,750	₹60,00,000
Less incremental costs:				
Material costs	375	9,00,000	1,750	28,00,000
Other variable production cost	500	12,00,000	750	12,00,000
Additional selling expenses	25	60,000	50	80,000
Contribution	600	14,40,000	1,200	19,20,000
Contribution per machine-hour (key factor)	300*		400**	
Less fixed costs:				
Factory overheads		3,00,000		3,00,000
Selling and administration (assumed)		10,00,000		10,00,000
Profit		1,40,000		6,20,000
Present profit			5,00,000	

*(₹600 ÷ 2); **(₹1,200 ÷ 3)

The managing director is advised to accept contract Y, as its contribution margin per machine-hour as well as profit is higher.

WORKING NOTES

1. Machine-hours available = (Working days × 24 hours) = 250 × 24 = 6,000 hours
   Operating capacity available = 0.80 × 6,000 hours = 4,800 hours
2. Variable production costs (other than materials) per hour: (₹5,75,000 + ₹6,25,000) ÷ 4,800 hours = ₹250 per hour.
3. It is assumed that the company, at present, is operating at its maximum achievable capacity, that is, 4,800 hours. In operational terms, the variable production costs (labour and other variable costs) are at the level of 4,800 hours.
4. The company would be in a position to sell all the units of Y contract.
5. Selling and administration overheads are assumed to be fixed.

Joint Outputs of Common Processing Operations

A decision-situation faced by the management is whether to sell joint outputs at the split-off point or process them further. The decision-criterion should be to choose the alternative, which will maximise the total contribution of the various joint products to the common processing costs. As the common processing costs before the split-off point are sunk costs, that have already been incurred to create the joint products, they are irrelevant and will not be considered in decision-making. The only relevant costs will be the additional common processing costs. Example 20.11 illustrates the point. A related short-term decision involves selecting an alternative processing plan for joint products when the proportions of the outputs (sales-mix) from the common processing costs can be varied (Example 20.12).

EXAMPLE 20.11 *(SELL AT SPLIT-OFF POINT OR BEYOND)*

The Premier Chemicals Ltd manufactures two chemical solvents, A and B, in fixed proportions of 1: 2 respectively. During one month, 60,000 litres were produced and common processing costs of ₹2,40,000 were incurred. A and B solvents could be sold in their present form for ₹6 and ₹8 per litre respectively. However, solvent A can be sold as A-Plus for ₹8 per litre by adding an extra ingredient costing ₹1.50 per litre. Solvent B can be sold as Super-B for ₹12 per litre if it is reprocessed at an additional cost for ₹4 per litre plus an additional ₹40,000 per month for hiring a special filtering machine with a capacity of 40,000 litres per month.

Should the solvents be sold at the split-off point or be processed further?

SOLUTION

Table 20.12 Decision Analysis

Particulars	*Solvents*	
	A	*B*
Incremental revenue	₹40,000	₹1,60,000
Less incremental cost:		
Manufacturing costs	30,000	1,60,000
Less hiring costs	—	40,000
Contribution (loss)	10,000	(40,000)

Therefore, solvent A should be processed further and solvent B should be sold at the split-off point.

EXAMPLE 20.12 *(DIFFERENT MIX OF JOINT OUTPUTS)*

Royal Industries Ltd manufactures three different plastic products from a single raw material and by a common process.

Budgeted data for the coming years are presented below. The production costs identified with the individual products are only the separate processing costs incurred after the split-off point.

Particulars	Products			Joint cost
	A	B	C	
Output (units)	45,000	30,000	15,000	
Selling price per unit	₹6	₹12	₹18	
Production units:				
Direct material	—	—		3,00,000
Direct labour	24,000	36,000	30,000	1,50,000
Variable manufacturing overheads	12,000	18,000	12,000	48,000
Fixed manufacturing overheads	18,000	30,000	24,000	96,000

The sales manager has suggested the following sales-mix of products A, 30,000; B, 40,000; and C, 20,000 involving additional joint processing costs of ₹1,00,000.

Comment on the economic feasibility of the proposed mix.

Solution

Table 20.13 Decision Analysis

Particulars		Present sales mix	Proposed sales mix	Incremental revenues and cost
Sales revenue	A	₹2,70,000	₹1,80,000	₹(90,000)
	B	3,60,000	4,80,000	1,20,000
	C	2,70,000	3,60,000	90,000
Total		9,00,000	10,20,000	1,20,000
Less incremental costs:				
Joint processing cost		4,98,000	5,98,000	(1,00,000)
Direct labour		90,000	90,000	—
Manufacturing overheads		42,000	42,000	—
Contribution		2,70,000	2,90,000	20,000

The proposed mix is economically desirable.

Operate or Shut Down

Shut-down point is a point at which losses from continued operations are equal to the shut-down costs.

The decision criterion in such a situation will be based on the comparison of the shut-down losses and the losses associated with continuing operations. In case, shut-down losses are more than the losses from continuing operations, it would be beneficial for the firm to continue its business operations. In case, shut down losses are less than the losses from continued operations, it would be profitable for the firm to shut-down its operations. Thus, the shut-down point may be defined as a point at which losses from continued operations are equal to the shutdown costs. The concept is illustrated in Example 20.13.

Example 20.13 *(Operate or Shut Down)*

The annual budget of ABC Ltd at 60 per cent and 80 per cent level of performance is as under (₹in thousands):

Particulars	60 per cent	80 per cent
Direct material	360	480
Direct labour	480	640
Production overheads	252	276
Administrative overheads	124	132
Selling and distribution overheads	136	148
Total	1,352	1,676

The company is experiencing difficulties in selling its products and is at present operating at 50 per cent capacity level.

The sales revenue for the year is estimated at ₹9,90,000. The directors are seriously considering suspending operations till the market picks up.

Market research undertaken by the company reveals that in about 12 months, the sales will pick up and the company can comfortably operate at 75 per cent level of performance and earn a sales income of ₹18 lakh in that year.

The sales personnel of the company do not want to suspend operations for fear of adverse reactions in the market, but the directors want to decide the issue purely on financial considerations.

If the manufacturing and other operations of the company are suspended for a year, it is estimated that:

1. The present fixed cost could be reduced to ₹2,20,000 per annum.
2. The settlement cost of personnel not required would amount to ₹1,50,000.
3. The maintenance of plant has to go on and that would cost ₹20,000 per annum.
4. On resuming operations, the expenditure connected with reopening after shut down would amount to ₹80,000.

Submit a report to the directors, and indicate therein, based on purely financial considerations, whether it would be advisable to suspend the company's operation in the current year.

SOLUTION

Table 20.14 Decision Analysis

Particulars		*Operate the factory*	*Shut-down the factory*
Sales revenue		₹9,90,000	—
Less variable costs			
Direct material		3,00,000	—
Direct labour		4,00,000	—
Variable overheads: (see working notes)			
Production	(₹72,000 ÷ 60) × 50	60,000	—
Administration	(₹24,000 ÷ 60) × 50	20,000	—
Selling and distribution	(₹36,000 ÷ 60) × 50	30,000	—
Contribution		1,80,000	—
Less fixed costs:			
Production	₹1,80,000		
Administration	1,00,000		
Selling and distribution	1,00,000	3,80,000	₹2,20,000
Settlement costs (personnel)		—	1,50,000
Maintenance of plant		—	20,000
Overhauling costs		—	80,000
Net income (loss)		(2,00,000)	(4,70,000)

It is not advisable for the company to suspend operations as shut-down loss is higher than the loss associated with continued operation of the plant.

WORKING NOTES

Segregation of various total overheads costs into fixed and variable components:

Nature of overhead cost	*Budgeted expenditure at various capacity levels*		*Difference at 20 per cent capacity level showing variable expenses*	*1 per cent capacity difference*	*Total*	
	60 per cent	*80 per cent*			*Variable overheads (60 per cent)*	*Fixed overheads*
Production	₹2,52,000	₹2,76,000	₹24,000	₹1,200	₹72,000	₹1,80,000
Administration	1,24,000	1,32,000	8,000	400	24,000	1,00,000
Selling and distribution	1,36,000	1,48,000	12,000	600	36,000	1,00,000

TARGET COSTING

Manufacturing companies are always searching for ways to cut costs. Unfortunately, once a product is designed, that is, its features are specified, detailed engineering plans are made and manufacturing of the product is ready to commence, it is very difficult to make changes that will reduce costs. It is estimated that 80 per cent of the production-related expenses are committed once the process begins.[2] These committed resources cannot be changed later without great cost to the company. The primary reason for this state of affairs is that product features drive costs. Consider the case of Maharaja Home Appliance Ltd. (MHA). The MHA is considering bringing a new coffeemaker to the market designed with an automatic grinder, a water filter and a stainless steel carafe that keeps coffee warm for five hours. The cost of manufacturing the coffee pot will be largely determined by these features. It will be very difficult to reduce the cost once the production of the coffee pot starts. In fact, costs related to purchase of equipment to produce the grinders, the filters and the carafes are sunk costs/investments and cannot be changed.

Target costing provides a solution to the above problem/difficulty. It is **an integrated approach to determining product features, product price, product cost and product design that helps ensure a company will earn reasonable profit on new products.**[3]

Target costing is an integrated approach to determine product features, product price, product costs and product design that helps ensure a company will earn reasonable profit on new products.

Target Costing Process

Target costing is a business process aimed at the earliest stages of new product and service development before creation and design of production methods. It is a process driven by the customer, focused on design and encompassing the entire life of the product. The objective is to create for the company a production process that provides adequate profits.

The target costing process begins with the customer. The desire of customers about functionality, quality and price drive the analysis. Having a clear understanding of customer need is critical. There are likely to be functional requirements to meet customer needs. Moreover, the customer may be unwilling to trade off functional requirements for lower price/quality. Knowing customer requirements also means understanding competitor offerings. Consumers do not operate in a vacuum. They demand product characteristic based on what is available in the market. If a competitor offers a higher-quality product with a similar functionality at a lower price, then companies attempt to reengineer their processes to meet that competition.[4]

Components of Target Costing Process The *desired target cost* is the cost of the resources that should be consumed to create a product that can be sold at a target price. **A target price is the estimated price for a product/service that potential customers will pay.** This estimate is based on an understanding of customers' perceived value for a product and how competitors will price competing products. A company's sales and marketing organisation, through close contact and interaction with customers, is usually in the best position to identify customer's needs and their perceived value for a product. Companies also conduct market research studies about product features that customer want and the prices they are willing to pay for these features. Understanding what customers value is a key aspect of being customer focussed.

Target cost is the cost of the resources that should be consumed to create a product that can be sold at a target price.

Target price is the estimated price for a product/service that potential customers will pay.

Target price, calculated using information from customers and competitors, forms the basis for target cost. Target cost per unit is the target price minus target operating income per unit. Target operating income per unit is the operating

Target operating income per unit is the operating income that a company aims to earn per unit of a product/service sold.

Target cost per unit is the estimated long-run cost per unit of a product/service that enables the company to achieve its target operating income per unit when selling at the target price.

income that a company aims to earn per unit of a product/service sold. Target cost per unit is the estimated long-run cost per unit of a product/service that enables the company to achieve its target operating income per unit when selling at the target price. Target cost per unit is often lower than the existing full cost per unit of the product. It is only a target that the company must aim for. To achieve target cost per unit and target operating cost per unit, the company must reduce the cost of making its products. The basic target cost formula is as follows:

Target Cost = Target price – Profit margin.

To illustrate, assume that Maharaja Home Appliances, given the features of its new coffee maker, can sell 50,000 units per year for ₹2,000 each. Assume further that Maharaja wants a profit margin of 30 per cent or, alternatively, a profit of ₹600. The target cost is ₹1,400 (₹2,000 – ₹600). Maharaja Home Appliances should design a product that can be produced at ₹1,400 or less. If it cannot be produced for ₹1,400 per unit, Maharaja will reconsider features and price. For example, it may decide to slightly lower its price and go with a plastic carafe as opposed to more expensive stainless steel carafe.

The components of the target costing process are exhibited in Figure 20.1.[5] There are four components of target costing process: (i) planning and market analysis, (ii) development, (iii) production design and (iv) production and continuous improvement. The first two components lead to an expected target price. The latter two stages are where the achievement of the target cost occurs.

Planning and Market Analysis Significant resources are consumed in planning and market analysis. At this stage, the customer **niche** is identified and thoroughly documented.

Concept Development This stage focuses on product feasibility studies. Development involves a cycle of testing and reformulating the product to understand customer requirements.

Production Design and Value Engineering This phase follows the establishment of the product concept in the development phase engineering and experienced production personnel use **value engineering** to determine the least costly combination of resources to create a product desired by the customers.

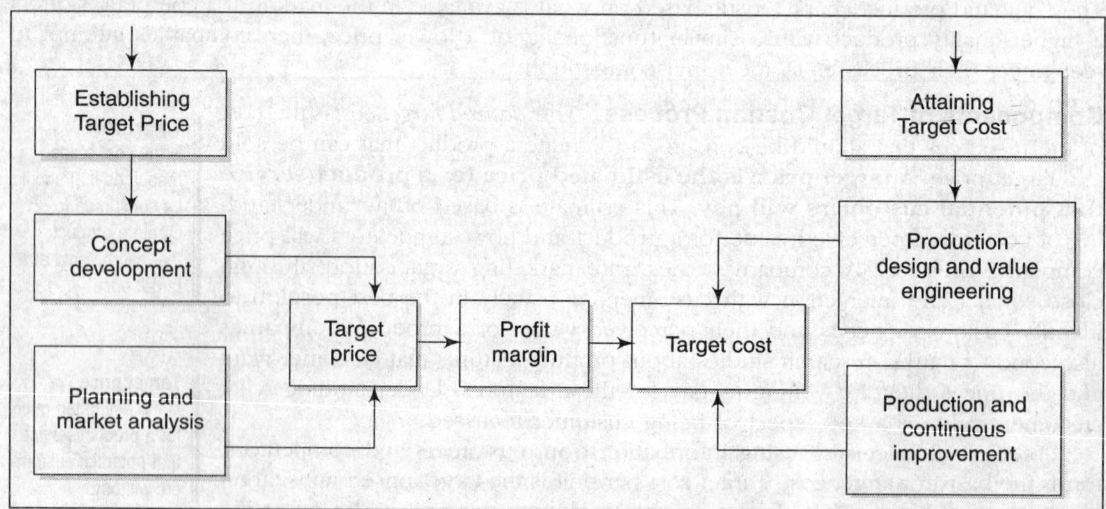

Figure 20.1 *Target Costing Process*

Production and Continuous Improvement Finally, production begins and a continuous process is used to attain the target costs.

Target Costing Illustrated

We illustrate the step-wise target pricing and target costing below.

Assume HCL Ltd. manufactures two brands of personnel computers (PCs): Deskpoint and Provalue. Deskpoint is HLL's top-of-the-line product, a Pentium 4 chip-based PC. Provalue is a less powerful Pentium chip-based machine. The HLL currently produces 1,50,000 units of Provalue. The per unit sale price of Provalue is ₹10,000. The full cost of Provalue is ₹1,35,00,00,000 consisting of manufacturing cost of ₹102,00,00,000 and operating cost of ₹33,00,00,000.

Step 1: Develop a Product That Satisfies Needs of Potential Customers Marketing research indicates that customers do not value Provalue's extra features such as special audio features and designs that accommodate upgrades that can make the PC run faster and perform calculations more quickly. They want HLL to redesign Provalue into a no-frills PC and sell it at a much lower price. The HLL is, accordingly, planning design modification for Provalue.

Step 2: Choose a Target Price The HLL expects its competitors to lower the price of PCs that compete against Provalue by 15 per cent. The management of HLL wants to respond aggressively by reducing Provalue's price by 20 per cent from ₹10,000 to ₹8,000 per unit. At this lower price, marketing manager of HLL forecasts an increase in annual sales from 1,50,000 to 2,00,000 units.

Step 3: Derive a Target Cost Per Unit (Target Price – Target Operating Income) The management of HLL wants a 10 per cent target operating income on sales revenues.
Total target revenues = ₹8,000 per unit × 2,00,000 units = ₹160,00,00,000.
Total target operating income = 0.10 × ₹160,00,00,000 = ₹16,00,00,000
Target operating income per unit = ₹16,00,00,000 × 2,00,000 units = ₹800 per unit
Target cost per unit = Target price per unit – Target operating income per unit = ₹8,000 – ₹800 = ₹7,200
Total full costs of Provalue = ₹135,00,00,000
Current full per unit cost of Provalue = ₹1,35,00,00,000 ÷ 1,50,000 units = ₹9,000 per unit

The target cost value of Provalue of ₹7,200 is well below its existing ₹9,000 unit cost. The HLL's goal is to reduce its unit cost by ₹1,800. The cost reduction efforts should be extended to all parts of the chain value – from R&D to customer service including seeking lower prices from suppliers of materials and components.

Step 4: Perform Value Engineering to Achieve Target Cost Value engineering is a systematic evaluation of all aspects of value chain business functions with the objective of reducing costs while satisfying customer needs. It can result in improvements in product design, changes in materials specifications and modification in process methods. **A detailed account of value engineering is, however, beyond the scope of our discussion.**

SUMMARY

- Cost data collected under conventional accounting principles do not serve the purpose for short-term decision-making. They have to be specially tailored to the requirements of specific decisions. Which costs are relevant depends on the decision under consideration. Decision-making involves choosing between different courses of action. The tailoring of the data in line with the decision-situations requires the application of different concepts, which are not in consonance with the generally accepted accounting principles for external reporting purposes. All costs must, of course, be covered in the long-run, otherwise a firm will not survive. Nevertheless, in the short-run, some costs can be ignored.

➢ The cost concepts which are relevant to short-term decision-making are opportunity cost, sunk costs, avoidable costs, and incremental/differential costs. Only costs that have a bearing on the decision are applicable to the choice between alternatives. *Decision-making costs are the relevant costs*, defined as the future costs that will change with the decision. The major short-term choices relate to: Sales volume related decisions, Sell or further process decisions, Make or buy decisions, Addition/elimination of product lines/decisions/departments, Short-term use of scarce resources, Joint outputs of common processing operations, and Operate or shut-down decisions.

➢ The general format of differential contribution, as a framework for short-term decision-making is summarised below:

Particulars		*Amount*
(I) Incremental revenues (product-wise)		—
Add cost savings (specify items)		—
Total incremental revenues		—
(II) *Less incremental costs*		
Increase in existing fixed costs	—	
Increase in variable costs	—	
Less decrease in contribution of existing products (specify each product) due to reduction in sales		—
Less opportunity cost foregone (say, by using equipment/space which was earlier leased/rented out)		—
Incremental (decrease in) contribution/profits		—

➢ Incremental analysis for acceptance of special order is summarised below

Particulars		*Amount*
Increase in sales revenue		—
Less incremental costs of executing sales order		
Direct material	—	
Direct labour	—	
Variable manufacturing overheads	—	
Freight costs (if to be incurred by seller)	—	
Production set-up costs	—	
Additional fixed costs (if any)	—	—
Incremental profits		—

➢ Decision analysis for further processing is summarised below:

Particulars	*Without further processing*		*With further processing*		*Incremental revenues/costs*	
	Per unit	*Total*	*Per unit*	*Total*	*Per unit*	*Total*
Sales revenue						
Less costs						
Direct material						
Direct labour						
Variable overheads						
Manufacturing						
Administrative						
Selling						
Fixed overheads (if incremental)						
Income (loss)						

➢ Make or buy Decision is summarised below:

Particulars	*Make costs*	*Buy costs*
Direct material	—	
Direct labour	—	
Power	—	
Other variable overheads	—	
Avoidable fixed overheads	—	
Buying costs		—
Freight costs		—
Indirect labour (receiving, inspecting and handling of the purchased parts)		—

➢ Decision analysis (operate or shut-down plant) is summarised below:

Particulars	*Operate plant*	*Shut down plant*
Sales revenue		
Less variable costs		
Direct material	—	
Direct Labour	—	
Variable overheads		
Manufacturing	—	
Administration	—	
Selling	—	
Contribution		
Less fixed costs		
Manufacturing	—	—
Administration	—	—
Selling	—	—
Other costs		
Settlement cost (personnel)		—
Other closing down costs		—
Maintenance of plant		—
Overhauling costs		—
Net profit (loss)		

➢ Target costing is an integrated approach to determining product features, product price, product cost and product design that helps ensure a company will earn reasonable profit on new products.

➢ Target cost is the cost of resources that should be consumed to create a product that can be sold at a target price.

➢ Target price is the estimated price for a product/service that potential customers will pay.

➢ There are four components of target costing process: planning and market analysis, development, production design and production and continuous improvement.

REFERENCES

1. Chartifield, M. and Neilson, Denis, Cost Accounting (New York, Harcourt Brace Jovanovich, Inc.), 1983, p. 389.
2. William, J. R., *Financial and Managerial Accounting,* TMH, 2004, p. 783.
3. Jiambaloo, J., *Managerial Accounting,* John Wiley, NY, 2004, p. 278.
4. William, J. R., *Op. Cit,* p.783.
5. *Ibid,* p 784.

SOLVED PROBLEMS

P.20.1 (a) Standard Sports Ltd produces high quality balls. It has received an offer from a sports store to buy 10,000 balls at ₹10 per ball. The store would sell the ball for ₹13 each which is ₹5 less than is normally charged by dealers selling the company's product. It is promised by the owner of the store that he would not disclose the maker's name.

The company can produce 1,00,000 balls per year. Planned results for the coming years without considering the order from the store are as follows:

Sales (80,000 balls @ 12 per ball)	₹9,60,000
Cost of goods sold (80,000 balls @ 7 per ball)	5,60,000
Gross profit	4,00,000
Selling and administrative expenses (all fixed)	2,50,000
Income	1,50,000

Cost of goods sold contains variable cost of ₹5 per ball. It is estimated that variable cost of printing the name on the ball is ₹0.25 per ball.

You are required to advise whether the company should accept the offer or not. Will your answer change if the seller's name is to appear on the ball to be sold by the store?

SOLUTION

Incremental Analysis (Accept Special Offer or Not)

Particulars	*Amount*
Increase in sales revenue (10,000 × ₹10)	₹1,00,000
Less variable costs (₹4.75 × 10,000)	47,500
Incremental profit	52,500

The offer should be accepted. The firm has enough capacity to make the balls and the incremental revenues exceed the incremental cost.

The answer *may* or *may not* change, but the factors that must be considered is whether regular sales would be affected if customers come to know that they could buy the balls at ₹13 instead of ₹18 per ball. It may be contended that the maximum loss might be 10,000 balls, the number that the store would sell, as a result of which planned sales would decrease by 10,000 balls to 70,000. In that case, the firm would suffer a loss of ₹20,000 by accepting the offer. Sales revenue of 10,000 balls @ 12 per ball was 1,20,000. Instead of selling to the store, the company would get ₹1,00,000 (10,000 × ₹10). Moreover, there could be some ill will among customers affecting, thus, future sales

(b) The Vittetaw Company Ltd, a maker of a variety of metal and plastic products, is in the midst of a business downturn and is saddled with many idle facilities. The National Hospital Supply Company Ltd has approached Vittetaw Ltd to produce 3,00,000 nonslide serving trays. National will pay ₹12 for each.

Vittetaw predicts that its variable costs will be ₹13 each. However, its fixed cost, which has been averaging ₹10 per unit on a variety of other products, will now be spread over twice as much volume. The managing director commented, "Sure, we will lose ₹1 each on the variable costs, but we will gain ₹5 per unit by spreading our fixed costs. Therefore, we should take the offer because it represents an advantage of ₹4 per unit."

Do you agree with the managing director? Why? Suppose the regular business had a current volume of 3,00,000 units, sales of ₹60,00,000, variable costs of ₹39,00,000 and fixed costs of ₹30,00,000. Show your workings of operating income or loss without acceptance of the bid and with acceptance of the bid.

SOLUTION

We do not agree with the managing director's comment. As a result of accepting the bid, the firm would be incurring an additional loss of ₹3,00,000 because incremental revenue is ₹12 per unit while additional variable costs will be ₹13 per unit. The managing director's comment is based on the wrong premise of spreading of fixed costs. Fixed costs (₹30,00,000) in absolute figures will remain unchanged whether the order is accepted or not. Therefore, consideration of fixed costs is an irrelevant factor here, as shown in the following operating income statement:

Contribution Based Income Statement With and Without Acceptance of the Bid of Vittetaw Company

Particulars	*Income (loss) if*	
	bid is accepted	*bid is not accepted*
Sales revenue		
Regular sales (3,00,000 × ₹20)	₹60,00,000	₹60,00,000
Bid sales (3,00,000 × ₹12)	36,00,000	—
Total	96,00,000	60,00,000
Less: variable costs @ ₹13 per unit	78,00,000	39,00,000
Contribution	18,00,000	21,00,000
Less: fixed costs	30,00,000	30,00,000
Operating loss	(12,00,000)	(9,00,000)

P.20.2 The Sick Instruments Company Ltd (SICL) manufacturers calculators under the brand 'PURANA', using old technology. It was selling them at ₹500 each. The normal capacity of SICL is 10,000 calculators. Due to the availability of calculators based on new technologies, the SICL's sales are adversaly affected. There is a pile-up of inventories of 1,000 units of PURANA calculators at a cost of ₹250 each and 2,000 units of raw materials at ₹100 per unit, production of one calculator requiring one unit of raw materials. The calculators can now fetch only 10 per cent of cost as salvage value and the raw materials which have become obsolete could be sold as a scrap for ₹20,000.

Meanwhile, the SICL receives an offer from Sellwell Marketing Company Ltd (SWML) to buy 5,000 PURANA calculators at ₹200 each with a 20 per cent commission on sales. The cost associated with the production of 5,000 units is estimated as shown below:

- — Existing total labour cost, ₹1,20,000
- — Fixed cost, ₹4,50,000
- — Additional labour cost, ₹40,000
- — Current price of materials, ₹125
- — Additional overheads, ₹50,000

The chief accountant computes the cost per calculator for the offer as given below:

Raw material cost:		
Existing raw material cost @ ₹100 × 2,000 units	₹2,00,000	
Additional new raw material cost @ ₹125 × 2,000 units	2,50,000	₹4,50,000
Labour cost:		
Existing total labour cost	1,20,000	
Additional labour cost	40,000	1,60,000
Overhead cost:		
Fixed overhead costs	4,50,000	
Additional overhead charges	50,000	5,00,000
Finished goods:		
'PURANA' Calculators (@ ₹250 × 1000 units)		2,50,000
Commission: (@ 0.20 × ₹200 × 5,000)		2,00,000
Total costs		15,60,000
Cost per calculator (₹15,60,000 ÷ 5,000)		312

With the above calculations, the chief accountant suggests the Managing Director not to accept the offer as it would result in a loss of ₹112 per calculator and pushing the cumulative losses further. Should the SWML's offer be accepted?

SOLUTION

Incremental Analysis (whether to Accept the Offer of Selling PURANA Calculators or Not)

Incremental sales revenue: (5,000 units of PURANA calculators × ₹200)		₹10,00,000
Incremental costs:		
Incremental raw materials (new) (2,000 units @ ₹125 per unit)	₹2,50,000	
Incremental labour cost	40,000	
Incremental overheads	50,000	
Commission (0.20 × 5,000 units × ₹200)	2,00,000	
Opportunity cost of raw material scrap value	20,000	
Calculator salvage value (0.10 × 1,000 × ₹250)	25,000	5,85,000
Incremental profit		4,15,000

Recommendation SICL should accept the offer of SWML as it reduces losses.

P.20.3 Snowhite Ltd makes readymade shirts (of one male size). Revenue and cost data relating to the coming years are given below:

Sales (9,000 shirts @ ₹1,000 per shirt)	₹90,00,000
Cost of sales	64,00,000
Gross profit	26,00,000
Selling and administrative expenses	15,00,000
Income	11,00,000

The firm has a capacity to make 10,000 shirts per year. The fixed costs included in the cost of goods sold are ₹10,00,000. The only variable selling, general and administrative expenses are: 4 per cent sales commission, and ₹20 per shirt paid to the designer.

A chain store manager has approached the sales manager of Snowhite Ltd offering to by 1,000 shirts at ₹700 per shirt. The sales manager believes that accepting this offer would result in a loss because the average cost of a shirt is higher than ₹700. He feels that a loss would still result, even if sales commission would not be paid on the sales order. The designer has agreed to waive 50 per cent of his fee on any number of shirts sold to such a store.

(i) Tender you advice to the sales manager of Snowhite Ltd.

(ii) Suppose that the order was for 2,500 instead of 1,000 shirts, what would be your advice?

(iii) Assuming the same facts as in part (ii), what is the lowest price that the firm would accept and still earn ₹11,00,000?

SOLUTION

(i) *Incremental Analysis Approach (Accept Special Offer or Not : 1,000 shirts)*

Particulars		*Amount*
Increase in sales revenue (1,000 × ₹700)		₹7,00,000
Less incremental costs:		
Variable cost (1,000 × ₹600)*	₹6,00,000	
Designer's fees (1,000 × ₹10)	10,000	6,10,000
Incremental profit		90,000

*(₹64,00,000 – ₹10,00,000) ÷ 9,000

The sales manager is advised to accept the offer as it yields additional income of 90,000.

(ii) Special offer: 2,500 shirts

Additional contribution (2,500 × ₹90)	₹2,25,000
Less lost profit contribution (1,500 × ₹340) on regular sales of 1,500 units (regular sales would be 9,000 – 1,500 = 7,500 shirts) @ 340 per unit arrived as follows:	5,10,000
Decrease in contribution	(2,85,000)

Selling price	₹1,000
Less: variable making cost	600
Sales commission	40
Designer's fees	20
	340

The firm's income would be less by ₹2,85,000. The sales manager should not accept this offer.

(iii) Computation of the lowest price

Sales price (offered)	₹700
Add additional contribution required to be earned so that profit level is maintained:	
₹2,85,000 from 2,500 units to be sold: increase in sales price per shirt is (₹2,85,000 ÷ 2,500)	114
The lowest price for accepting the offer of 2,500 shirts	814

P.20.4 Sound Well Music Company Ltd (SMC) manufactures cassette record players. It is operating at full capacity of 10,000 units annually with a sales price of ₹3,000 per unit. The cost data are: **(i)** Raw materials, ₹900 per unit, **(ii)** Direct labour, ₹400 per unit, **(iii)** Variable overheads, ₹300 per unit, and **(iv)** Fixed cost, ₹60,00,000.

While the SMC was planning to expand its operations, Audiocon Ltd launched a new competitive product: HiFi CD player at ₹3,500 per unit. To meet the competition from this new product, the SMC has under consideration two alternatives: **(i)** Reduce the price of the cassette player to ₹2,499 **(ii)** Add new features to the product by further processing and sell for ₹3,700.

The further processing of the product would involve the following.

— Raw materials cost, ₹600 per unit;
— Labour charges, ₹300 per unit;
— Additional variable overheads, ₹300 per unit; and
— Additional fixed costs, ₹40,00,000.

As a consultant, what course of action would you recommend the SMC to follow?

SOLUTION

Decision Analysis (Whether to Sell cassette record players as they are, or Process them Further) (₹in lakh)

Particulars	*Sell now*	*Process further*
Sales revenue	₹249.90	₹370
Less variable costs:		
Raw material	90.00	150
Direct labour	40.00	70
Variable overheads	30.00	60
Contribution	89.90	90
Less fixed overheads	60.00	100
Net profit (loss)	29.90	(10)

Recommendation The SMC is advised to sell cassette record players at ₹2,499 (without undergoing any further processing)

P.20.5 A cycle tyre manufacturing company (engaged in producing tyres for cycles of kids) has been approached by a large shopkeeper to buy 10,000 tyres at ₹32 each. Delivery must be made within 30 days. The production capacity of the company is 64,000 units per month and there is inventory of 2,000 tyres on hand. Expected sales at regular prices for the coming month are 60,000 tyres. It is estimated by the sales manager that about 50 per cent of sales lost during the month would be made up in later months. Price and cost data per unit are as follows:

Selling price		₹48
Variable costs:		
Production	₹24	
Selling	6	30
Profit contribution		18

The variable selling costs on the special order would be ₹1 per unit.

(i) Determine whether the offer should be accepted by the firm or not.

(ii) Determine the lowest price that the company could charge on the special order and not reduce its income.

(iii) Suppose now that the shopkeeper offers to buy 8,000 tyres per month at ₹32 per tyre. The offer would be for an entire year. Expected sales are 60,000 tyres per month without accepting the special order. Assuming further that there is no beginning inventory and that sales lost during the year would not be made up in the following year, determine whether the offer should be accepted, and determine the lowest price that the company could accept.

SOLUTION

(i) *Decision Analysis (Acceptance of Special Offer or Not: 10,000 Tyres)*

Particulars	*Special order*	*Loss in regular sales*	*Effect*
Units sold (loss in regular sales)	10,000	(2,000)*	
(x) Contribution margin per tyre: Special order (₹32 – ₹24 – ₹1)	7	18	
Total contribution	₹70,000	₹(36,000)	+ ₹34,000

The company is advised to accept the offer.

WORKING NOTES

**Regular Unit Sales Lost*:

Inventory	2,000
Production	64,000
Available production	66,000
Special order	10,000
Available for regular sales	56,000
Expected regular sales	60,000
Sales lost	4,000
Less 50 per cent recovery in the following month	2,000
Net lost sale	(2,000)

(ii) *Statement Showing the Determination of the Lowest Price*

Profit contribution lost on regular sales	₹36,000
÷ Units of special order	10,000
Required contribution margin per tyre	3.60
Add variable cost @ ₹25 per unit	25.00
Lowest price	28.60

(iii) *Decision-making (new terms)*

Particulars	*Contribution margin per month*		
	Special order	*Regular sales*	*Effect*
Units sold (loss in regular sales)	8,000	(4,000) @	
(x) Contribution margin per unit	₹7	₹18	
Total contribution gained (lost)	56,000	(72,000)	(16,000)

@ (60,000 units – 56,000 units)

The special order would reduce income by ₹16,000 per month.

Lowest Price Per Unit

Profit contribution lost on regular sales	₹72,000
(÷) Number of units of special order	8,000
Required contribution per tyre	9
Add variable costs @ 25 per unit	25
	34

P.20.6 Young Orchids Ltd (YOL) is a shoe manufacturing company that started business two years back. Their target group of customers are kids below the age of five. Its production capacity is 6,500 pairs of shoes per month and there is inventory of 200 pairs of shoes on hand. Expected sales at regular prices for the coming month are 6,000 pairs of shoes. Price and cost data per unit are as follows:

Selling price		₹500
Variable costs:		
Production	₹240	
Selling	60	300
Profit contribution		200

The OYL has received an order from a store to buy 1,000 pairs at ₹350 each. The variable selling costs on the special order would be ₹10 per unit. The delivery is to be made within 30 days.

(i) Should young Orchids go for the offer or reject it straight away?

(ii) What should be the lowest price that the YOL should charge on the special order and not reduce its income?

(iii) Suppose now that the shopkeeper offers to buy 800 pairs per month at ₹350 per pair. The offer would be for an entire year. Expected sales are 6,000 pairs per month without accepting the special order. Assuming further that there is no beginning inventory, determine whether the offer should be accepted by YOL.

Solution

(i) *Analysis Whether to Accept Store Order of Supplying 1,000 Pairs of Shoes or Not*

Contribution earned (₹350 – ₹240 – ₹10) × 1,000 units	₹1,00,000
Less contribution foregone on lost sales (₹200 × 300 units*)	60,000
Increase in contribution	40,000

*(Inventory, 200 units + Production, 6,500 units – Present offer, 1,000 units = 5,700 units available for regular sales; Existing sales, 6,000 units – 5,700 units available for sale = 300 units)

Recommendation As contribution is positive, the company is advised to accept the store order.

(ii) *Statement Showing the Lowest Price*

Contribution lost on regular sales	₹60,000
Divided by number of units of store order	(÷) 1,000
Desired contribution to be recovered per unit	60
Add variable cost (₹240 + ₹10)	250
Lowest price	310

(iii) *Analysis Whether to Accept Store Order of Supplying 800 Pairs of Shoes Per Month or Not*

Contribution earned (₹100 × 800 units)	₹80,000
Less contribution foregone on lost sales (₹200 × 300 units)**	60,000
Increase in contribution	20,000

**6,500 units produced – Present offer, 800 units = 5,700 units available for regular sales; Existing sales 6,000 units – 5,700 units available for sale = 300 units.

Recommendation Offer should be accepted as it augments contribution by ₹20,000 per month. Between the two, this offer is better as it augments profit by ₹2,40,000 in a year (₹20,000 × 12 months), vis-avis, ₹40,000 one time increase in earlier offer.

P.20.7 Baluja Shoes Ltd which has a chain of shoe shops throughout the country has two shops in Madras of which Shop I makes a profit and Shop II makes a loss. The following is the summarised profit and loss account of shop II for the current month ended March 31:

Sales	₹6,00,000
Cost of sales	4,92,000
Gross profit	1,08,000

(Contd.)

(Contd.)

Expenses:		
Commission to salesmen	₹6,000	
Manager's salary	12,000	
Head office expenses	10,500	
Motor van expenses:		
Fixed (allocated)	6,900	
Variable (allocated)	2,400	
Other items (like rent, insurance, salesmen's salaries)	1,09,950	1,47,750
Loss for the year		(39,750)

The commission to salesmen is a fixed percentage on turnover. There is a common manager for the two shops and his salary is equally shared by the two shops. The motor van is also common to the two shops. Its fixed expenses are shared equally by the two shops but the running expenses are apportioned on the basis of the turnover.

Prepare a report explaining the financial implication of the closing down Shop II, assuming that 20 per cent of its turnover will be gained by Shop I without that shop needing any additional staff.

SOLUTION

Differential Cost and Revenue Statement (Operate or Shut-down Shop II)

Particulars	*Operate Shop II*	*Shut down Shop II*	*Differential costs and revenues (decrease)*
Sales revenue	₹6,00,000	₹1,20,000	₹(4,80,000)
Less variable costs:			
Cost of sales	4,92,000	98,400	(3,93,600)
Salesmen's commission	6,000	1,200	(4,800)
Motor van expenses	2,400	480	(1,920)
Contribution	99,600	19,920	(79,680)
Less common fixed costs:			
Manager's salary	12,000	12,000	—
Head office expenses	10,500	10,500	—
Motor van expenses	6,900	6,900	—
Less avoidable fixed costs:			
Other items (like rent, insurance, salary of salesman, etc. which no longer will be incurred)	1,09,650	—	(1,09,650)
Loss	(39,450)	(9,480)	(29,970)

Shop II should be shut down as it will lead to cost savings of ₹29,970 per month.

P. 20.8 A company manufactures three products. The respective details are:

Particulars	*A*	*B*	*C*
Capacity engaged (per cent)	20	40	40
Units produced	2,000	5,000	6,000
Cost per unit:			
Material cost	20	32	36
Wages	10	12	16
Variable overheads	7	9	11
Fixed overheads	6	9	10
Total	43	62	73
Selling price per unit	40	75	85
Profit (loss) per unit	(3)	13	12

The management proposes to discontinue line A as for the last few years it has been showing losses. Future prospects of the other two lines being good, it is intended to utilise the disengaged capacity in line A, in line B and, C equally. Expected per cent rise in prices and costs are:

	B	C
Material	10	10
Wages	5	5
Selling price	2	5

Fixed overheads shall remain the same. You are required to prepare a statement of projected profitability and advise the management as to whether the scheme may be adopted.

SOLUTION

Statement of Projected Profitability with Products B and C only

Particulars		*Products* B	*Products* C	*Combined*
Capacity engaged (per cent)		50	50	100
Units produced		6,250	7,500	
Selling price		₹76.50	₹89.25	—
Sales revenue		4,78,125	6,69,375	₹11,47,500
Less variable costs:				
Material cost:				
B: ₹35.20 per unit		2,20,000		2,20,000
C: ₹39.60 per unit			2,97,000	2,97,000
Wages:				
B: ₹12.60		78,750		78,750
C: ₹16.80			1,26,000	1,26,000
Variable overheads:				
B: ₹9		56,250		56,250
C: ₹11			82,500	82,500
Total		3,55,000	5,05,500	8,60,500
Contribution		1,23,125	1,63,875	2,87,000
Less: fixed overheads:				
A: 2,000 × ₹6 =	₹12,000			
B: 5,000 × ₹9 =	45,000			
C: 6,000 × ₹10 =	60,000			1,17,000
Net profit				1,70,000

Statement of Profitability with Products A, B and C (summary form)

Particulars	*Products* A	*Products* B	*Products* C	*Combined*
Capacity engaged (%)	20	40	40	100
Units produced	2,000	5,000	6,000	—
Sales revenue	₹80,000	₹3,82,500	₹5,35,500	₹9,98,000
Less variable costs (new)	74,000	2,84,000	4,04,400	7,62,400
Contribution	6,000	98,500	1,31,100	2,35,600
Less fixed costs				1,17,000
Net profit				1,18,600

Assumptions

(i) Selling price per unit as well as variable cost per unit pertaining to product A does not increase.

(ii) Profitability statement with products A, B and C taken together is prepared on the basis of revised cost data, as variable costs as well as selling prices in respect of products B and C will increase, irrespective of the fact whether product A is dropped or not. The only point of difference is the number of units produced.

P.20.9 The following costs and other data apply to two component parts used by Bajaj Electricals Ltd:

Particulars	Part X	Part Y
Direct material	₹8.0	₹160.0
Direct labour	20.0	94.0
Overheads	80.0	40.0
Unit cost	108.0	294.0
Units needed per year	6,000	8,000
Machine-hours per unit	2	1
Unit cost, if purchased	100	300

The company hitherto has been manufacturing all its required components. However, in the current years, only 14,000 hours of otherwise idle machine time can be devoted to the production of components. Accordingly, some of the parts must be purchased from outside suppliers. In producing parts, overhead is applied at ₹40 per machine-hour. Fixed capacity costs, which will not be affected by any make or buy decision, represent 70 per cent of the applied overhead.

REQUIRED

1. Assuming that the 14,000 hours of available machine time are to be scheduled so that the company realises maximum potential cost savings, determine the relevant production cost that should be considered in the decision to schedule machine time.
2. Compute the number of units that Bajaj Electricals Ltd should produce if it allocates the machine time on the basis of the potential cost savings per machine-hour.

SOLUTION

The relevant production costs are: direct material, direct labour, overheads (to the extent of 30 per cent), and buying costs. Scheduling of machine time will be governed by cost savings per machine-hour. This is shown in the following calculations.

	Part X		Part Y	
Particulars	Total	Per unit	Total	Per unit
(A) Buying cost	₹6,00,000	₹100	₹24,00,000	₹300
(B) Making cost:				
Direct material	48,000	8	12,80,000	160
Direct labour	1,20,000	20	7,52,000	94
Overheads (30 per cent assumed variable)	1,44,000	24	96,000	12
Total (making)	3,12,000	52	21,28,000	266
Cost savings[@]	2,88,000	48	2,72,000	34
Machine-hour per unit		2		1
Cost savings per machine-hour		24		34

[@]Excess buy costs payable are equal to cost savings.

Since cost savings per machine-hour are more in the case of product Y, the company should allocate 8,000 hours in producing 8,000 parts of Y and the remaining 6,000 hours should be utilised for producing 3,000 parts of X.

P.20.10 Perfect Product Ltd is currently buying a component from a local supplier at 15 each. The supply is tending to be irregular. Two proposals are under consideration:

(i) Buy and instal a semi-automatic machine for manufacturing this component, which would involve an annual fixed cost of ₹9 lakh and a variable cost of ₹6 per manufactured component.

(ii) Buy and instal an automatic machine for manufacturing this component, incurring an annual fixed cost of ₹15 lakh and a variable cost of ₹5 per manufactured component. Determine with necessary computation:

1. The annual volume required in each case to justify the switchover from "outside purchase" to "own manufacture."

2. The annual volume required to justify selection of the automatic machine instead of semi-automatic machine.
3. If the annual requirement for the coming year is expected to be 5,00,000 units and the volume is expected to increase rapidly thereafter, would you recommended the automatic or semi-automatic machine? Justify your recommendation.

Solution

1. Volume required to justify own manufacture of a component = Fixed costs (incremental)/(Buying cost per unit – Variable cost per unit):
   (a) Semi-automatic machine = ₹9,00,000 ÷ (₹15 – ₹6) = 1,00,000 units
   (b) Automatic machine = ₹15,00,000 ÷ (₹15 – ₹5) = 1,50,000 units
2. 1,50,000 units as shown in (1) b.
3. *Production Cost Statement*

Particulars	Automatic machine	Semi-automatic machine
Number of units	5,00,000	5,00,000
Variable cost per unit	₹5	₹6
Total variable cost	25,00,000	30,00,000
Plus fixed cost	15,00,000	9,00,000
Total cost	40,00,000	39,00,000
Per unit cost	8	7.8

At the expected volume of 5,00,000 units, calculations suggest that the semi-automatic machine should be bought. However, as the demand is expected to increase rapidly after one year, from the long-term point of view, purchase of the automatic machine is recommended as cost per unit would be equal to 6,00,000 units as shown below:

Production Cost Statement (6,00,000 units)

Particulars	Automatic machine	Semi-automatic machine
Total variable cost	₹30,00,000	₹36,00,000
Plus fixed cost	15,00,000	9,00,000
Total cost	45,00,000	45,00,000
Cost per unit	7.50	7.50

Clearly, at the production volume of greater than 6,00,000 units, total cost per unit would be lower with the automatic machine compared to the semi-automatic machine.

P.20.11 Farishta Company Ltd's old equipment for making sub-assemblies is worn-out. The company is considering two courses of action: (a) Completely replacing the old equipment with a new equipment, (b) Buying sub-assemblies from a reliable outside supplier who has quoted a unit price of ₹10 on a 7-year contract for a minimum of 50,000 units per year.

Production was 60,000 units in each of the past two years. Future needs for the next 7 years are not expected to fluctuate beyond 50,000 to 70,000 units per year. Cost records for the past 2 years reveal the following unit costs of manufacturing the sub-assemblies:

Direct material	₹2.50
Direct labour	4.00
Variable overheads	1.00
Fixed overheads (including ₹1.0 for depreciation and ₹1.0 for supervision and other direct departmental fixed overhead)	2.50
	10.00

The new equipment will cost ₹18,80,000, will last 7 years, and will have a disposal value of ₹2,00,000. The current disposal value of the old equipment is ₹1,00,000. The salesman for the new equipment has summarised his position as follows: The increase in machine speed will reduce direct labour and variable overhead by ₹3.50 per unit. Consider last year's experience of one of our major competitors with identical equipment. They produced 1,00,000 units under operating conditions very comparable to us and showed the following unit costs:

Direct material	₹2.50
Direct labour	1.00
Variable overheads	0.50
Fixed overhead, including ₹2.40, depreciation	4.00
	8.00

You are required to compare the alternative on a: **(i)** Total cost basis **(ii)** Per unit basis for annual needs of 60,000 units. Which alternative seems more attractive? (Assume that any idle facilities cannot be put to alternative use, and also assume that ₹0.5 of the old Farishta unit cost is allocated fixed overhead that will be unaffected by the decision). Ignore interest and tax cost.

SOLUTION

Differential Cost Statement Regarding Making or Buying a Component (60,000 units)

	Make with a machine		*Buying from outside supplier*	
Particulars	*Per unit*	*Total*	*Per unit*	*Total*
Direct material	₹2.50	1,50,000	—	—
Direct labour	1.00	60,000	—	—
Variable overheads	0.50	30,000	—	—
Relevant fixed overheads:				
Depreciation (₹2,40,000[@] ÷ 60,000 units)	4.00	2,40,000	—	—
Supervision cost	1.00	60,000	—	—
Irrelevant fixed overheads:				
Allocated costs	N.A.	N.A.	—	—
Purchase costs	—	—	10	6,00,000
	9.00	5,40,000	10	6,00,000
Differential costs (favourable for making)			1.0	60,000

[@](₹18,80,000 – ₹2,00,000)/7 years = ₹2,40,000

P.20.12 Hypothetical Ltd produces two products, X and Y. As per the existing operations, raw materials are processed in Department 1, and the two products are separated at the end of this processing. For every unit of product X, 3 units of Y are obtained. X is then finished in Department 2 and Y in Department 3. Budgeted operating data for year 1 are as follows:

	Departments		
Particulars	*1*	*2*	*3*
Units produced and sold:			
Product X	1,00,000	1,00,000	
Product Y	3,00,000		3,00,000
Costs incurred:			
Direct materials	₹6,00,000		
Direct labour	3,20,000	₹1,20,000	₹1,60,000
Variable manufacturing overheads	80,000	40,000	80,000
Fixed manufacturing overheads	3,60,000	1,00,000	1,40,000

All costs are directly traceable to the individual departments. At present, X is sold for ₹10 per unit and Y for ₹5 per unit. Both products are also readily saleable at the completion of processing in Department 1—product X for ₹8 per unit and product Y for ₹3 per unit.

You are required to advise the company whether each product should be sold after final completion or at the split-off point.

SOLUTION

Incremental Profit Analysis (Sell Now or Process Further)

Particulars	Product X			Product Y		
	Sell now	*Process in Department 2*	*Differential (costs) and revenue*	*Sell now*	*Process in Department 2*	*Differential (costs) and revenue*
Sales revenue	₹8,00,000	₹10,00,000	₹2,00,000	₹9,00,000	₹15,00,000	₹6,00,000
Less: costs:						
Departments 2 and 3						
Direct labour	—	1,20,000	(1,20,000)	—	1,60,000	(1,60,000)
Variable manufacturing overheads	—	40,000	(40,000)	—	80,000	(80,000)
Contribution (incremental)			40,000			3,60,000
Less: fixed costs: (direct/avoidable)	—	1,00,000	(1,00,000)	—	1,40,000	(1,40,000)
Production margin (incremental) (Profit/loss)			(60,000)			2,20,000

Product X should be sold after the split-off point (that is after processing in Department 1). Product Y should be sold after final completion (that is after processing in Department 3).

Note (i) Costs of Department 1 are joint costs and, therefore, irrelevant for the decision-making.
(ii) Fixed costs are avoidable costs and, therefore, relevant costs.

P.20.13 The XYZ Ltd produces a single product which passes through three successive departments, X, Y and Z. Following are the budgeted annual production costs for an output of 30,000 units which is considered to be the normal volume.

Particulars	Departments		
	X	Y	Z
Direct materials	₹66,000	₹23,000	—
Direct labour	42,000	54,000	₹25,000
Variable manufacturing overheads	21,000	27,000	13,500
Fixed manufacturing overheads (15 per cent of direct labour)	63,000	81,000	37,500
	1,92,000	1,85,000	76,000

The marketing manager of the company has informed the management that it can purchase a semi-finished product at a price of ₹5, delivered. Department Y can directly use this product instead of the basic raw material processed in Department X. However, direct labour and variable manufacturing overhead costs in Department Y would be 5 per cent more because of changes in operations necessitated by the introduction of the semi-finished product into the departments.

You are required to advise the company on the basis of short-run profitability whether it should purchase the semi-finished product or continue its existing practice of producing in Department X.

SOLUTION

Decision Analysis (Make or Buy Semi-finished Product, 30,000 units)

Particulars	Make costs (Department X)		Costs if purchased from outside supplier	
	Total	Per unit	Total	Per unit
Direct materials	₹66,000	₹2.20	—	—
Direct labour	42,000	1.40	—	—
Variable manufacturing overheads	21,000	0.70	—	—
Purchasing costs	—	—	₹1,50,000	₹5.00

(Contd.)

(*Contd.*)

Additional out-of-pocket costs if semi-finished *product is processed in Department Y*:				
Direct labour (₹54,000 × 0.05)	—	—	2,700	0.09
Variable manufacturing overheads (₹27,000 × 0.05)	—	—	1,350	0.045
Total cost	1,29,000	4.30	1,54,050	5.135

Differential costs favouring making of the product in Department X, ₹25,050, total and ₹0.835 per unit. The company should continue its existing practice of producing it in Department X.

Assumptions **1.** There is no alternative use of facilities released from Department X.

2. Fixed costs are committed costs and unavoidable.

P.20.14 A company produces three products on the same plant. Fixed costs are applied to products based on the number of direct labour-hours required to make the product. The rate of application is based on budgeted fixed costs of ₹60,00,000 and budgeted direct labour-hours of 1,00,000. Per unit data for the three products are as follows.

Particulars	*P*	*R*	*S*
Selling price	₹800	₹340	₹450
Production costs, including applied fixed costs based on predetermined rate	750	280	400
Direct labour-hours required per unit of product	5	2.5	1

You are required to do the following:

1. Determine variable production costs per unit for each product.

2. Assuming that variable costs of production are the only variably costs, determine which product yields: (a) the highest contribution margin per unit, (b) the highest contribution margin percentage, and (c) the highest contribution margin per direct labour-hour.

3. If the firm asks you which product should be given more emphasis, what will be your answer?

SOLUTION

1. *Determination of Variable Costs*

Particulars	*P*	*R*	*S*
Total costs per unit	₹750	₹280	₹400
Less fixed costs included @ ₹6 per labour-hour (₹60,00,000 ÷ 1,00,000)			
P: (₹60 × 5)	300		
R: (₹60 × 2.5)		150	
S: (₹60 × 1)			60
Variable costs per unit	450	130	340
2. Selling price per unit	800	340	450
Less variable costs per unit	450	130	340
(a) Contribution margin per unit	350	210	110
(b) Contribution margin percentage	43.75	61.76	24.44
(c) Direct labour hours	5	2.5	1.0
(d) Contribution margin per direct labour-hour [(a) ÷ labour hours]	70	84	110

3. The answer depends on the purpose for which the firm wants the information. Product P has the highest marginal contribution on a unit basis, product R on percentage basis and product S on labour-hour basis. Thus, if labour force is a scarce (key) factor and sales is no problem, product S should be given the maximum emphasis. If labour is not a key factor and promotion is expected to increase unit sales (of any product by the same amount), the per rupee spent emphasis should go to product P. Product R is the best if sales are expected to increase equally from the promotion campaign.

P.20.15 In a factory producing two different kinds of articles, the limiting factor is availability of material but the same material is used in both articles.

Particulars	*Product A*	*Product B*
Cost per unit		
Materials	₹15	₹10.00
Labour	6	4.50
Overheads: Variable	2	1.00
Fixed	6	4.50
Total	29	20.00
Selling price per unit (net)	35	24.50

The demand during each period for the two products is 10,000 units of A and 8,000 units of B.

It is also considered desirable that, should demand be there, the firm should be willing to meet at least half the demand stated above in all circumstances. The total availability of materials for some time will be restricted to the quantity available for ₹1,20,000 only.

State how the available raw materials should be utilised.

Solution

Statement Showing Utilisation of Raw Materials (Key Factor) With Given Constraints of Producing Minimum Number of Products, A and B.

Particulars	*Product A*	*Product B*
Selling price unit	₹35.00	₹24.50
Less variable costs		
Materials	15.00	10.00
Labour	6.00	4.50
Variable overheads	2.00	1.00
Total variable costs	23.00	15.50
Contribution margin	12.00	9.00
Contribution margin per rupee of material used		
(₹12 ÷ ₹15)	0.80	
(₹9 ÷ ₹10)		0.90
Value of raw material consumed		
(5,000 × ₹15)	75,000	
(4,000 × ₹10)		40,000
Units produced	5,000	4,000
Raw material left (₹1,20,000 – ₹75,000 – ₹40,000) = ₹5,000 to be used in producing product B as its contribution margin is higher. Number of units of B produced (₹5,000 ÷ ₹10, consumption of raw material per unit)	—	500
Desired production (units)	5,000	4,500
Utilisation of raw material (₹)	75,000	45,000

P.20.16 During a year, a manufacturing company has produced and sold 3 products: Product A—20,000 units, Product B—14,000 units and Product C—10,000 units.

The following further information is per unit also available:

Particulars	*A*	*B*	*C*
Variable costs	₹100	₹180	₹160
Time taken (hours)	2.5	3.0	2.5
List price	200	300	400
Fixed cost (total)		₹20,00,000	

The list prices of the products are subject to a uniform trade discount of 10 per cent. Due to labour shortage, the available working hours for the next year are estimated to be only 90,000. Suggest a suitable sales-mix for the next year:

1. When there is enough demand for all the products.
2. When the potential demand is 18,000 units for product A, 10,000 units for product B and 12,000 units for product C.

SOLUTION

1. *Optimal Sales-mix (No Demand Constraint)*

Particulars	*Product*		
	A	*B*	*C*
Effective selling price (list price-trade discount)	₹180	₹270	₹360
Less: Variable cost	100	180	160
Contribution margin (per unit)	80	90	200
Time (key factor) per unit (hours)	2.5	3.0	2.5
Contribution margin per hour	32	30	80

Given no market constraint, the manufacturing company should concentrate on production of C because its contribution margin per hour is maximum, (₹80 per hour); 36,000 units of product C can be produced

= Estimated working hours ÷ Hours required per unit = 90,000 ÷ 2.5 = 36,000 units

2. *Optimal Sales-mix (With Demand Constraints)*

Particulars	*Products*		
	C	*A*	*B*
Contribution margin per hour	₹80	₹32	₹30

Optimal sales-mix with demand constraint should be decided on the basis of descending contribution margin per hour of the various products. Accordingly, as many units of product C should be produced as can be sold, followed by A and B: Time taken per unit × Demand (units) = Total time consumed (hours)

Product C (2.5 hours × 12,000) = 30,000
A (2.5 hours × 18,000) = 45,000
B (3 hours × 5,000) = 15,000

Note: After producing C and A, only 15,000 hours are available for product B. Thus, the suitable sales-mix for the next year is C: 12,000 units; A: 18,000 units; and B: 5,000 units.

P.20.17 The following particulars are extracted from the records of a company:

Particulars	*Product A*	*Product B*
Sales	₹1,000	₹1,200
Material cost	100	150
Direct wage cost	150	100
Direct expenses	50	60
Overhead expenses:		
Fixed	50	100
Variable	150	200
Machine-hours used	3	2
Consumption of materials (kgs)	2	3
Direct wages per hour	₹50	

Comment on the profitability of each product when:

(i) Total sales potential in units is limited.

(ii) Total sales potential in value is limited.

(iii) Raw material is in short supply.

(iv) Production capacity (in terms of machine hours) is the limiting factor.

2. Assuming raw material as the key factor, the availability of which is 10,000 kgs., and the maximum sales potential of each product is 3,500 units, find out the product-mix which will yield the maximum profit.

SOLUTION

1. (i) *Statement of Profitability for Products A and B:*

Particulars	*Product A*	*Product B*
Sales price per unit	₹1,000	₹1,200
Less: Variable costs:		
Material cost	100	150
Direct wage cost	150	100
Direct expenses	50	60
Overheads	150	200
Total	450	510
Contribution margin	550	690

Product B will be more profitable because its contribution margin is higher.

(ii) Total sales potential in value is limited: P/V ratio = (Contribution margin/sales) × 100

A = (₹550/₹100) × 100 = 55 per cent

B = (₹690/₹120) × 100 = 57.5 per cent

Product B is more profitable because it has a higher P/V ratio.

(iii) Raw material is the key factor: Contribution margin per kg of raw material used = Contribution margin per unit/Consumption of materials (kgs)

A = ₹550/2 kgs = ₹275

B = ₹690/3 kgs = ₹230

Product A is more profitable.

(iv) Machine hour is the key factor: Contribution margin per machine hour:

A = ₹550/3 = ₹183.33

B = ₹690/2 = ₹345.00

Product B is more profitable.

2. The optimal product-mix with raw materials and sales as key factors should be on the basis of descending contribution margin per kg. Accordingly, the company should produce 3,500 units of product A and the unused materials should be used to produce B.

Materials consumed per unit × Demand of units = Total consumed used

Product A (2 kgs × 3,500) = 7,000 kgs

Product B (3 kgs × 1,000) = 3,000 kgs

Statement of Profit

Particulars	*Product A*	*Product B*	*Combined*
Sales revenue	₹35,00,000	₹12,00,000	₹47,00,000
Less: Variable costs	15,75,000	5,10,000	20,85,000
Contribution	19,25,000	6,90,000	26,15,000
Less: Fixed costs	1,75,000	1,00,000	2,75,000
Net income	17,50,000	5,90,000	23,40,000

It is assumed that actual fixed costs are equivalent to the amount absorbed.

P.20.18 The Managing Director of XYZ Ltd, which manufactures three products, X, Y and Z, wants your advice on the production-mix of the company. He has furnished you the following data:

	Product X	Product Y	Product Z
Direct materials	₹400	₹300	₹200
Variable overheads	20	50	30

Direct labour:

Department	Rate per hour	Hours	Hours	Hours
1	₹10	6	10	5
2	20	6	15	11

Data from current budget:			
Production (number of units per year)	5,000	6,000	10,000
Selling price per unit	₹780	₹1,000	₹600
Fixed overheads		₹20,00,000	
Forecast by the sales department of the maximum possible sales during the next year (number of units)	6,000	8,000	12,000

Note **The type of labour required by Department 1 is in short supply and it is not possible to increase the manpower of this department beyond its present level.**

You are required to present a statement to the managing director of the company, showing the most profitable mix of the products to be made and sold. The statement should give the following formation:

1. The profit expected on the current budgeted production, and
2. The profit which could be expected if the most profitable mixture was produced.

SOLUTION

1. *Statement Showing Profit on the Current Budgeted Production*

Particulars	Products			Total
	X	Y	Z	
Sale revenue	₹39,00,000	₹60,00,000	₹60,00,000	₹1,59,00,000
Less: Variable costs:				
Direct materials	20,00,000	18,00,000	20,00,000	58,00,000
Direct labour:				
Department 1	3,00,000	6,00,000	5,00,000	14,00,000
Department 2	6,00,000	18,00,000	22,00,000	46,00,000
Variable overheads	1,00,000	3,00,000	3,00,000	7,00,000
Total	30,00,000	45,00,000	50,00,000	1,25,00,000
Contribution	9,00,000	15,00,000	10,00,000	34,00,000
Less: Fixed costs				20,00,000
Net profit				14,00,000

2. Optimal product-mix is to be decided by determining contribution margin per hour of Department 1 (key factor).

Product X = ₹9 lakh/5,000 = ₹180/6 hours = ₹30 per hour

Product Y = ₹15 lakh/6,000 = ₹250/10 hours = ₹25 per hour

Product Z = ₹10 lakh/10,000 = ₹100/5 hours = ₹20 per hour

Optimal Product-mix:

Product	*Time taken of Department 1 per unit*	× *Expected sales in units*	= *Total hours spent*
X	(6 hours	× 6,000)	= 36,000
Y	(10 hours	× 8,000)	= 80,000
Z@	(5 hours	× 4,800)	= 24,000
			1,40,000

@ Total existing capacity (in hours) product:

X	(6 hours	× 5,000 units)	30,000
Y	(10 hours	× 6,000 units)	60,000
Z	(5 hours	× 10,000 units)	50,000
			1,40,000

Statement of Profit at Optimal Product-mix:

Particulars	*Products*			*Total*
	X	*Y*	*Z*	
Sales revenue	₹46,80,000	₹80,00,000	₹28,80,000	₹1,55,60,000
Less: Variable costs:				
Direct materials	24,00,000	24,00,000	9,60,000	57,60,000
Direct labour:				
Department 1	3,60,000	8,00,000	2,40,000	14,00,000
2	7,20,000	24,00,000	10,56,000	41,76,000
Variable overheads	1,20,000	4,00,000	1,44,000	6,64,000
Total	36,00,000	60,00,000	24,00,000	1,20,00,000
Contribution	10,80,000	20,00,000	4,80,000	35,60,000
Less: Fixed cost				20,00,000
Net profit				15,60,000

P. 20.19 On the basis of following information, determine the product-mix to give the highest attainable profit rate:

Material per unit (kgs)	20	12	30
Machine-hours per unit	3	5	4
Selling price per unit	₹2,500	₹2,000	₹4,000
Maximum possible sales (units)	1,500	1,000	750

Machine-hours for production are available up to 9,200 maximum at a cost of ₹100 per hour and 50,000 kgs of raw material @ ₹100 per kg can be obtained.

SOLUTION

Determination of Contribution Margin Per Key Factor

Particulars	*Products*		
	A	*B*	*C*
Selling price per unit	₹2,500	₹2,000	₹4,000
Less relevant costs:			
Material	2,000	1,200	3,000
Machine charges	300	500	400
Contribution margin (CM)	200	300	600
Key factors: Material (kgs)	20	12	30
CM per kg	10	25	20
Key factor: Machine-hours	3	5	4
CM per kg per hour	₹3.33	5.0	5.0

Since contribution margin per key factor is the same for products B and C, the priority in determining product-mix would be maximum possible production of B and C and the left-over inputs used in product A.

Statement Indicating Product-mix

Product	Maximum production possible	Use of inputs		Inputs left		Actual product mix
		Materials (kgs)	Machine-hours	Materials (kgs)	Machine-hours	
B	1,000	12,000	5,000	38,000	4,200	1,000
C	750	22,500	3,000	15,500	1,200	750
A	1,500	8,000	1,200	7,500	—	400

Product-mix as shown in the last column would give the highest profit

P.20.20 XY Ltd. is manufacturing three household products A, B and C, and selling them in a competitive market. Details of current demand, selling price and cost structure are given below:

Particulars	A	B	C
Expected demand (units)	10,000	12,000	20,000
Selling price per unit (₹)	20	16	10
Variable cost per unit (₹)			
Direct materials (₹10/kg.)	6	4	2
Direct labour (₹15/hr.)	3	3	1.50
Variable overheads	2	1	1
Fixed overhead per unit (₹)	5	4	2

The company is frequently affected by acute scarcity of raw material and high labour turnover. During the next period, it is expected to have one of the following situations:

(a) Raw materials available will be only 12,100 kgs.

(b) Direct labour-hours available will be only 5,000 hours.

(c) It may be possible to increase sales of any one product by 25 per cent without any additional fixed costs but by spending ₹20,000 on advertisement. There will be no shortage of materials or labour.

Suggest the best production plan in each case and the resultant profit that the company would earn according to your suggestion.

SOLUTION

Determination of Profitability Ranking in Various Situations

Particulars	Products		
	A	B	C
Selling price per unit	₹20	₹16	₹10
Less variable costs per unit:			
Direct material	6	4	2.00
Direct labour	3	3	1.50
Variable overheads	2	1	1.00
Total variable cost per unit	11	8	4.5
Contribution per unit	9	8	5.5
C/V ratio	45% (rank 3)	50% (Rank 2)	55% (Rank 1)
Ranking with raw material as key factor:			
Raw material used per unit			
(Raw material cost)/(Price per kg)	0.6 kg	0.4 kg	0.2 kg
Contribution per kg of raw material	₹15 (Rank 3)	₹20 (Rank 2)	₹27.50 (Rank 1)
Ranking with labour as key factor	111	11	1
Labour hours required per unit			
(Labour cost/Wages per hour)	1/5	1/5	1/10
Contribution per labour-hour	₹45 (Rank 2)	₹40 (Rank 3)	₹55 (Rank 1)

Situation (a): Optimal Production Plan when Raw Material Available is 12,100 kgs

Product	Number of units	Raw material required (kgs)	Contribution per unit	Total contribution
C	20,000	4,000	₹5.50	₹1,10,000
B	12,000	4,800	8.00	96,000
A	5,500@	3,300	9.00	49,500
		12,100		2,55,500
Less fixed costs				1,38,000@@
Net profit				1,17,500

@3300 ÷ 0.06 kg = 5500 units

@@ *Determination of fixed costs:*

A 10,000 × ₹5	= ₹	50,000
B 12,000 × ₹4	=	48,000
C 20,000 × ₹2	=	40,000
		1,38,000

Situation (b): Optimal Production Plan when Labour-Hours Available is 5,000 Hours

Product	Number of units	Labour-hours required	Contribution per unit	Total contribution
C	20,000	2,000	₹5.50	₹1,10,000
A	12,000	2,000	9.00	90,000
B	5,000@	1,000	8.00	40,000
		5,000		2,40,000
Less, fixed costs				1,38,000
Net profit				1,02,000

@ 1,000 hours ÷ 1/5 = 5,000 units

Situation (C): Since there is no shortage of material and labour, ranking will be based on C/V ratio. Accordingly, production of C product with highest C/V ratio will be increased by 5,000 units (0.25 × 20,000).

Statement of Profit at Optimal Production Plan

Product	Number of units	Contribution per unit	Total contribution
A	10,000	₹9.00	₹90,000
B	12,000	8.00	96,000
C	25,000	5.50	1,37,500
			3,23,500
Less fixed cost		₹1,38,000	
Additional advertisement expenditure		20,000	1,58,000
Net profit			1,65,500

P.20.21 The following particulars are taken from the records of a company engaged in manufacturing two products, A and B, from a certain material:

Particulars	Product A (Per unit)	Product B (Per unit)
Sales	₹2,500	₹5,000
Material cost (₹50 per kg)	500	1,250
Direct labour (₹30 per hour)	750	1,500
Variable overhead	250	500
Total fixed overheads:	₹10,00,000	

Comment on the profitability of each product when:

(i) Total sales in value is limited.

(ii) Raw materials is in short supply.

(iii) Production capacity (in terms of direct labour hours) is the limiting factor.

(iv) Total availability of raw materials is 20,000 kgs. and maximum sales potential of each product is 1,000 units. Find the product mix to yield maximum profits.

SOLUTION

(i) Contribution Per Unit

Particulars		*Product A*		*Product B*
Sales		₹2,500		₹5,000
Less variable costs				
Material	₹500		₹1,250	
Labour	750		1,500	
Overheads	250	1,500	500	3,250
Contribution per unit		1,000		1,750
P/V ratio/C/V ratio (%)		40		35
Raw material required per unit (kgs).		10@		25@@
Contribution per kg of raw material		100		70
Labour-hours per unit		25(x)		50(xx)
Contribution per hour of labour		40		35

@₹500/₹50 = 10 kgs; @@ ₹1,250/₹50 = 25 kgs
(x) ₹750/₹30 = 25 hours (xx) ₹1,500/₹30 = 50 hours

(i) *Profitability when total sales in value is limited*
Since P/V ratio of product A (40 per cent) is more than that of product B (35 per cent) producing and selling of product A will be more profitable.

(ii) *Profitability when raw material is in short supply*
Since contribution per kg of raw material is higher is case of product A (₹100) than product B (₹70), producing and selling of product A will be more profitable in the case of short supply of raw material.

(iii) *Profitability when production capacity is limited*
Since contribution per direct labour hour is higher in case of product A (₹40) than that of product B (₹35), producing and selling of product A will be more profitable.

(iv) Statement of Product Mix to Yield Maximum Profit when Raw Material Supply is Limited to 20,000 kgs

Product	*Units*	*Raw material consumed*	*Contribution per unit*	*Total contribution*	*Fixed cost*	*Profit*
A	1,000	10,000*	₹1,000	₹10,00,000	—	
B	400**	10,000	1,750	7,00,000	—	
				17,00,000	₹10,00,000	₹7,00,000

* 1,000 × 10 = 10,000 kgs; ** 10,000 ÷ 25 kgs = 400 units

P.20.22 When Alps Ltd operates at normal capacity, it manufactures 2,00,000 units of product per year. The unit cost of manufacturing at normal capacity is as follows:

Direct materials	₹7.80
Direct labour	2.10
Variable overheads	2.50
Fixed overheads	4.00
Product cost (per unit)	16.40
Selling price	21.00

During the next 3 months, only 10,000 units can be purchased and sold. Management plans to shut down the plant, estimating that the fixed manufacturing overheads can be reduced to ₹74,000 for the quarter when the plant is not operating; the fixed overhead costs are incurred at a uniform rate throughout the year. Additional costs of plant shutdown for the 3 months are estimated at ₹14,000.

You are required to answer:

(a) Should the plant be shut down for 3 months? Show computations.

(b) What is the shutdown point for the 3 months in units of product?

SOLUTION

(a) *Decision Analysis (Shut-down Plant)*

Particulars		*Operate plant*	*Shutdown plant*
(i) *Estimated revenue* (10,000 × ₹21)		₹2,10,000	—
(ii) *Estimated variable cost:*			
Direct materials	₹7.80		
Direct labour	2.10		
Variable overheads	2.50		
	12.40	(1,24,000)	—
(iii) Estimated contribution		86,000	—
Less fixed costs		(2,00,000)	(74,000)
Shut-down costs		—	(14,000)
Net profit (loss)		(1,14,000)	(88,000)

The plant should be shut down for 3 months as the loss is ₹88,000 only, while operating the plant would entail a greater loss (₹1,14,000).

(b) The shut-down point = [Fixed cost when plant is operating – Shut-down costs when plant is not operating] ÷ Contribution margin per unit = (₹2,00,000 – ₹88,000) ÷ ₹8.60 = 13,023 units

P.20.23 Alfa Engineering Works Ltd had the following annual budget for the current year ending March 31:

Product capacity	*60 per cent*	*80 per cent*
Costs: (₹in lakh)		
Direct material	9.60	12.80
Direct labour	7.20	9.60
Factory expenses	7.56	8.04
Administrative expenses	3.72	3.88
Selling and distribution expenses	4.08	4.32
Total	32.16	38.64
Profit	4.86	10.72
Sales	37.02	49.36

Owing to adverse trading conditions, the company has been operating during April-June of this years at 40 per cent capacity realising budgeted selling prices.

Owing to acute competition, it has become inevitable to reduce prices by 25 per cent even to maintain the sales at the existing level. The directors are considering whether or not their factory should be closed down until the trade recession has passed. A market research consultant has advised that in about a years' time there is every indication that sales will increase to 75 per cent of normal capacity and that the revenues to be produced for a full year at that volume could be expected to be ₹40 lakh.

If the directors decide to close down the factory for a year it is estimated that

(a) The present fixed costs would be reduced to ₹6 lakh per annum;
(b) Closing down costs (redundancy payments, etc.) would amount to ₹2 lakh;
(c) Necessary maintenance of plant would cost ₹50,000 per annum; and
(d) On re-operating the factory, the cost of overhauling the plant, training and engagement of new personnel would amount to ₹80,000.

Prepare a report for the directors, making you recommendations.

SOLUTION

Decision Analysis (continue or shut-down the factory) (₹in lakh)

Particulars	*Operate*	*Shut-down*	*Differential revenues and costs*
Sales revenue	18.51	—	18.51
Costs:			
Direct material	6.40	—	(6.40)
Direct labour	4.80	—	(4.80)

(Contd.)

(Contd.)

Factory expenses (variable)	0.96	—	(0.96)
Factory expenses (fixed)	6.12	6.00	(0.12)
Administrative expenses (variable)	0.32	—	(0.32)
Administrative expenses (fixed)	3.24	—	(3.24)
Selling and distribution expenses (variable)	0.48	—	(0.48)
Selling and distribution expenses (fixed)	3.36	—	(3.36)
Closing down costs:			
Redundancy payments	—	2.00	2.00
Maintenance of plant	—	0.50	0.50
Overhauling costs	—	0.80	0.80
Total costs	25.68	9.30	(16.38)
Differential revenues favouring the decision to operate the plant			2.13

The directors are advised to operate the plant.

P.20.24 Infotech Ltd is a leading software company with clientele overseas. It received an order from Double Standard Railway Network Inc of America to develop software for their railway networks on payment of ₹35,00,000. The software was to consist of 100 programmes and was to be done in four stages. The stage-wise expenditures as calculated by Infotech Ltd is detailed below;

Stage	*Expenditure per programme*	*Duration (months)*
Preparation of high level design	₹5,000	2
Preparation of low level design	4,000	1
Coding (programming)	3,000	2
Testing	1,000	1
Total	13,000	6

The project was started in a rented place, the monthly rent being ₹1,00,000. Infotech Ltd acquired 10 new terminals at a cost of ₹50,000 each, besides a server for ₹1,00,000. Other fixed costs for the project were estimated at ₹1,00,000.

At the completion stage of coding, Double Standard Railway Network cancelled the order in the aftermath of the American sanctions following the nuclear test—Pokharan II.

According to information available with Infotech's office in Paris, Opportunist Consultants are ready to buy the software for ₹10,00,000 if the testing stage is completed. The office also reports that Anglesent Railway Company (ARC) in France wants the software for their operations for ₹34,00,000. The cost and other parameters of the alternative proposal are:

- The required software will consist of 150 programmes.
- The project will take 4 months to complete.
- The ARC will send 2 managers to assist Infotech to modify the 100 programmes already written to suit their requirements. They will stay for 5 days in India and the daily cost of their stay would be ₹20,000. Their air fare will be borne by ARC.
- The modification of softwares will involved additional cost of ₹500 per programme and a fixed cost of ₹50,000.
- The ARC has agreed to give 2 years maintenance contract to Infotech for ₹2,00,000. The maintenance cost worked out by Infotech is ₹1,00,000.
- The cost incurred in connection with the visit of a manager of Infotech to negotiate the deal is ₹1,00,000.

Should Infotech Ltd accept the offer to sell the software to ARC? Why?

SOLUTION

Incremental Analysis (whether to accept the offer from ARC or not)

Incremental revenue:		
From software	₹34,00,000	
From maintenance	2,00,000	₹36,00,000

(Contd.)

(*Contd.*)

Less incremental costs:		
Preparation of high level design (₹5,000 × 50)	2,50,000	
Preparation of low level design (₹4,000 × 50)	2,00,000	
Coding/Programming (₹3,000 × 50)	1,50,000	
Testing (₹1,000 × 150)	1,50,000	
Office rent (₹1,00,000 × 4)	4,00,000	
Additional fixed cost	50,000	
Cost of modification of existing programmes	50,000	
Expenditure on managers from ARC (₹20,000 × 5)	1,00,000	
Maintenance cost	1,00,000	
Opportunity cost/Net selling cost to Opportunist		
Consultants (₹10,00,000 – ₹1,00,000, cost of testing)	9,00,000	23,50,000
Incremental profit		12,50,000

Recommendation The offer should be accepted as it yields incremental profit of ₹12,50,000.

WORKING NOTES

The following costs since already incurred have been ignored:

Preparation of high level design (₹5,000 × 100 programmes)	₹5,00,000
Preparation of low level design (₹4,000 × 100)	4,00,000
Coding (₹3,000 × 100)	3,00,000
Office rent (₹1,00,000 × 5 months)	5,00,000
Hardware cost:	
Terminals (10 × ₹50,000)	5,00,000
Server	1,00,000
Other fixed costs	1,00,000
Cost incurred on manager's visit	1,00,000
	25,00,000

P.20.25 Uttam Computers Ltd (UCL) provides assembled computers to retail outlets as well as network support to small/medium business organisations. Anticipating boom in demand after the reduced import duty, UCL assembled 50 computers in advance to meet demand. The specifications of the computer were as follows:

Parts	*Specifications*	*Cost*
(a) Computer Kit		
• Mother board	Universal serial bus	₹5,000
• Microprocessor chip	133 MHz chip XL of Megahurts	5,000
• Floppy drive	1.44 MB	1,500
• Hard disk	1.2 GB Ultra	4,000
• VGA card	1 MB VRAM	1,500
• RAM	16 MB SDRAM	2,500
(b) Multimedia Kit		
• CD Rom	32 X Drive	3,500
• Sound Card	Surround sound wave blaster	1,700
• Speaker	100 W PMPO (< 1% distortion)	800
(c) Cabinet With digital display and SMPS	1,500	
(d) Keyboard	105 keys membrane	500
(e) Monitor 1024 × 768 pixels	8,000	
(f) Mouse 3 Button mouse	500	
(g) Cables	—	200
(h) Labour and packaging	—	500
(i) Software	OEM pack "Khirki 98"	500
		37,200

The current market price is ₹40,000 per computer. Pending the sales of the computers, Megahurts, the microprocessor chip manufacturing company, introduced a new upgraded version of its existing chip XL. The new chip—Chip XXL (266 MHz)—is 100 per cent faster than chip XL and also includes enhanced multimedia technology. Costing ₹7,000, it is compatible with all other parts except that it needs a new kind of mother board priced at ₹5,000. The price of computers with new chip and motherboard is quoted at ₹42,000.

The introduction of the new chip XXL has led to a decrease in demand for computers fitted with old chip and mother board as a result of which quoted market price declined to ₹35,000.

The UCM was contemplating to replace the old chips/mother board by new ones. The replacement would involve additional labour and packing cost of ₹5,000. It can sell the old chip/mother board in the grey market which is ready to absorb them for ₹5,000.

It was about this time that another alternative emerged. The Bright Futures School (BFS) has agreed to buy 45 Uttam computers with old chip/mother board for its computer lab. Aware as it is of the new chips, the BFS stipulates as follows:

- It will buy 45 computers at ₹1,000 less than the quoted price of ₹40,000.
- It will like to receive free of cost network support for its lab and installation. For network support, each of the 45 computers will require a LAN (Local Area Network) card which are priced at ₹2,000 each. In addition, the network would require about 50 feet of cables @ ₹20 per foot as well as 3 signal boosters/hubs with price of ₹3,000 per piece. Also, the installation cost of the network and server software and accessories will amount to ₹15,000.

If the BFS's offer is accepted, the remaining 5 computers can be sold for ₹35,000 each.

The UCL seeks your advice as to which course of action to choose: **(i)** Replace old chip/mother board with new ones or **(ii)** Accept BFS's offer. Give your recommendations together with the reasons.

SOLUTION

Incremental Analysis (whether to Replace Old Chip and Mother Board with New Ones)

Incremental sales revenues:		
(a) Sale of 50 computers @ ₹42,000 per computer	₹21,00,000	
(b) Salvage value of 50 old chips and motherboard @ ₹5,000 combined	2,50,000	₹23,50,000
Incremental costs:		
(a) Cost of 50 Chip XXL @ ₹7,000 per chip	3,50,000	
(b) Cost of 50 new motherboards @ ₹5,000 per unit	2,50,000	
(c) Additional labour and packaging cost	5,000	
(d) Opportunity cost of selling at reduced price of ₹35,000	17,50,000	23,55,000
Incremental loss		(5,000)

Incremental Analysis (whether to Accept Bright Futures Offer)

Incremental sales revenue:		
Sale of 45 computers @ ₹39,000 per computer	₹17,55,000	
Sale of 5 computers @ ₹35,000 per computer	1,75,000	₹19,30,000
Incremental costs		
Network additions		
3 network signal boosters/hubs @ ₹3,000 per piece	9,000	
45 LAN cards @ ₹2,000 per card	90,000	
Cabling 50 feet @ ₹20 per foot	1,000	
Server accessories and software	15,000	
Opportunity cost of selling at reduced price (₹35,000 × 50)	17,50,000	18,65,000
Profits		65,000

Recommendations The UCL is advised to accept the offer of BFS. It is financially profitable. Also, the company would be increasing its clientele domain from business organization to educational institutions. In addition, it would also generate some revenues from after sales service/maintenance contracts with the school.

REVIEW QUESTIONS

RQ.20.1 Indicate whether the following statements are true or false.

(i) Costs incurred in selecting a site for construction of a factory are sunk costs.
(ii) Existing fixed costs are relevant costs for decision-making.
(iii) A firm is engaged in production of multiple products. One of its products incurs losses. Without any further cost analysis, the production of the said product should be discontinued.
(iv) Avoidable costs are irrelevant costs for decision-making.
(v) Incremental costs consist of variable costs only.
(vi) Committed costs are like sunk costs and therefore irrelevant costs for decision-making.
(vii) All future costs are relevant costs.
(viii) A branch of business segment that shows negative operating income should be shut-down.
(ix) Variable costs are always relevant and fixed costs are always irrelevant.
(x) Opportunity costs are out-of-pocket cash costs.

[Answers: (i) True, (ii) False, (iii) False, (iv) False, (v) False, (vi) True, (vii) True, (viii) False, (ix) False, (x) False.]

RQ.20.2 Fill in the following blanks (in some cases choices are provided).

(i) ____________ analysis is appropriate technique for short-term decisions.
(ii) Sales made at loss in expectation of additional sales in future are referred to as ____________.
(iii) Resources that are limited in quantity are known as ____________.
(iv) Maximising ____________ should be the basis for determining optimal product mix when input resources are scarce.
(v) Common processing costs in the case of joint products are ____________.
(vi) All those costs which affect the decision are known as ____________.
(vii) Sunk costs are ____________ costs.
(viii) Only ____________ fixed costs are reckoned in decision-making.
(ix) In the case of analysing special order decisions, it is assumed that the existing sale price charged by the firm is ____________.

[Answers: (i) incremental, (ii) loss leaders, (iii) key factors, (iv) contribution margin per unit of key factor, (v) sunk costs, (vi) relevant costs, (vii) committed, (viii) incremental, (ix) not affected.]

RQ.20.3 What decision criteria are appropriate for short-run decisions? Outline the format used for such decisions.

RQ.20.4 Differentiate between 'sunk' and 'avoidable' costs. What is the relevance of such a distinction for short-run decisions?

RQ.20.5 What is an opportunity cost? When do opportunity costs affect short-run decisions? What accounting problems do opportunity costs involve?

RQ.20.6 In disposing of inventory that has already been manufactured, what costs should be considered when the product is: **(i)** Still marketable in a normal way and **(ii)** Obsolete, damaged or out of fashion?

RQ.20.7 Explain the role of **(i)** Committed, **(ii)** Sunk, **(iii)** Avoidable, and **(iv)** Opportunity costs in make-or-buy decisions?

RQ.20.8 When the discontinuation of a product line, division, or department is being considered, what relevant data are useful in short-run situations?

RQ.20.9 What comparisons should be made in deciding whether or not to accept a one-time order at a price different from the regular sales price?

RQ.20.10 Explain the role of: **(i)** Incremental revenues and **(ii)** Subsequent processing cost in sell-or-process-further decisions.

RQ.20.11 Briefly explain the target costing process.

RQ.20.12 Write brief note on the components of target costing process.

RQ.20.13 Explain: **(i)** Target costing, **(ii)** Target pricing.

RQ.20.14 Electric Manufacturing Company Ltd. is engaged in producing a variety of precision instruments and other specialised electric components. The company is presently following a policy of pricing all of its products at 150 per cent of the total variable costs to produce and sell them. Because of the specialised nature of these products, this has proved to be a useful pricing policy.

Recently, the Government invited tender for 1,000 electric components to be used at the TV station. The company's management is exploring the possibility of the firm entering into a Government contract. The management accountant has prepared the following cost estimates for the purpose:

Direct materials	₹8,00,000
Direct labour	5,50,000
Variable overheads	2,25,000
Fixed manufacturing overheads	3,00,000
Production set-up costs	1,25,000
Special tools and dyes (no salvage value after use)	3,00,000
Total costs	23,00,000
Unit cost (Rs 23,00,000 ÷ 1,000 units):	2,300

The Government requires delivery of all 1,000 units within one year. In order to meet that schedule, the company would have to forego a regular sales order of value of ₹22,50,000.

You are required to state the lowest price the company could bid on the contract for the components without sacrificing short-run profit. State your assumptions, if any.

RQ.20.15 Uniform Product Company Ltd. produces a single product. Its maximum annual production capacity is 4,80,000 labour-hours. Currently, it is producing at an annual rate of 3,75,000 labour-hours. Normal volume (the basis of absorption of fixed overhead) is 4,50,000 hours.

The company has received an offer of 70,000 such units at a special price of ₹120 per unit. The regular selling price is ₹150 per unit. The standard cost sheet for one unit of the product is as follows:

Direct materials (2 kgs @ ₹25)	₹50
Direct labour (1.5 hours @ ₹20)	30
Variable overheads (1.5 hours @ ₹20)	30
Fixed overheads (1.5 hours @ ₹10)	15
	125

In the short run, would it be profitable to accept the offer?

RQ.20.16 X Ltd., having an installed capacity of 1,00,000 units of a product, is currently operating at 70 per cent utilisation. At current levels of input prices, the FOB unit cost (after taking credit for applicable export incentives) works out as follows:

Capacity utilisation (per cent)	*FOB unit costs*
70	₹97
80	92
90	87
100	82

The company has received 3 foreign offers from different sources: A, 5,000 units at ₹55 per unit FOB; B, 10,000 units at ₹52 per unit FOB; and C, 10,000 units at ₹51 per unit FOB. Advise the company as to whether any, or all, export orders should be accepted or not.

RQ.20.17 A factory is divided into three departments, D1, D2 and D3, in each of which the capacity available during the 3 months (January 1 to March 31) is 2,000 hours. The fixed and variable overhead expenses budgeted for each department for this period are as follows:

Department	*Fixed*	*Variable per hour*
D1	₹20,000	₹35
D2	25,000	25
D3	70,000	30

On January 1, 2 orders (O_1 and O_2) were received for each of which a selling price of ₹6,00,000 can be charged and on each of which prime costs are expected to be ₹2,50,000. The use which the two orders would make of factory capacity differs and is expected to be as follows:

Department	*O_1 (hours)*	*O_2 (hours)*
D1	1,000	2,000
D2	400	600
D3	2,000	1,000

You are required to state which of the two orders (if any) should be accepted, and to show the calculations on which your opinion is based.

RQ.20.18 Kerala Engineering Ltd., manufactures and markets three products: X, Y, and Z in varying proportions during a year. Based upon past experience and future market expectations, the management accountant of the company provides the followed information for the current year:

Product	*Price per unit*	*Variable cost per unit*	*Possible sale*	
			Mix 1	*Mix 2*
X	30	12	6,00,000	3,00,000
Y	40	20	3,00,000	2,00,000
Z	25	15	1,00,000	5,00,000

The fixed costs during the year are estimated at ₹2,64,000. Which product-mix would you adopt?

RQ.20.19 Vinak Ltd., which produces three products, furnishes you the following data for the current year.

Particulars	*Products*		
	A	*B*	*C*
Selling price per unit	₹100	₹75	₹50
Profit volume ratio (per cent)	10	20	40
Maximum sales potential (units)	40,000	25,000	10,000
Raw material content as percentage of variable costs (per cent)	50	50	50

The fixed expenses are estimated at ₹6,80,000. The company uses a single raw material in all the three products. Raw material is in short supply and the company has a quota for the supply of raw materials of the value of ₹18,00,000 for the current year for the manufacture of its products to meet its sales demand.

You are required to:

1. Set a product-mix which will give a maximum overall profit keeping the short supply of raw materials in view.
2. Compute the maximum profit.

RQ.20.20 Three different product lines are sold by M/s Mercury Mills Ltd. Product A contributes 20 per cent of its revenue to fixed costs and profits. Product B contributes 10 per cent, and Product C contributes 50 per cent. The products sell for the following prices: Product A, ₹80; Product B, ₹20; Product C, ₹30.

The company earned a net profit of ₹5,00,000 before income tax last year by selling 50,000 units of Product A, 1,50,000 units of Product B, and 60,000 units of Product C. The sales manager believes that the profit picture can be improved by eliminating product B and concentrating the sales efforts on products A and C. He sees an opportunity to increase the sales of products A to 70,000 units, but admits that product C will probably sell at the same amount next year.

Prepare a projected profit and loss statement using sales manager's assumption. Do you agree with him? Explain what would cause the profit to increase or decrease, as the case may be.

RQ.20.21 You are the cost accountant of a manufacturing company. The top management seeks your assistance in arriving at a decision whether to continue manufacturing a part or to buy it from an outside supplier. The part is a component used in several of the company's finished products.

The following data have been arrived at on the basis of cost records and further investigation:

1. The annual requirement is 40,000 units.
2. The lowest list price quotation from a supplier was ₹27.50 per unit.
3. Following are the total costs incurred last year, when 40,000 parts were produced in Department A of the company:

Materials	₹12,00,000
Labour	15,00,000
Indirect labour	4,00,000
Light and heat	80,000
Power	1,20,000
Depreciation	7,00,000
Property taxes and insurance	70,000
Miscellaneous	1,50,000

4. The following proportions (percentages) of the variable costs in Department A could be avoided if production of parts was discontinued: Materials, 35; Direct labour, 40; Power, 25.
5. If parts are purchased from an outside supplier, average freight cost is ₹0.50 per unit. Also, indirect labour in Department A would increase by ₹30,000 annually because of receiving, inspecting and handling of the purchased parts.

On the basis of the above information, advise management on the commercial feasibility of the proposed plan.

RQ.20.22 XYZ Company Ltd. buys crude vegetable oil. The refining of this oil results in four products, A, B, C, and D. The cost of oil refined in the current year was ₹2,76,000, and the refining department has total processing costs of ₹7,00,000. The output and sales for the four products were as follows:

Product	*Output (gallons)*	*Sales*	*Additional processing cost after split-off*
A	5,00,000	₹11,50,000	₹3,00,000
B	10,000	1,00,000	60,000
C	5,000	40,000	—
D	9,000	3,00,000	10,000

REQUIRED

(i) Assume that the net realisable value at split-off is used for allocating joint costs. What is the net income for products, A, B, C, and D? Joint costs total ₹9,76,000.

(ii) The company had been tempted to sell out at split-off directly to other processors. If that alternative had been selected, sales per galloon would have been: A, ₹150; B, ₹5; C, ₹8 and D, ₹30. The company expects to operate at the same level of output and sales in the forthcoming year. Could the company increase net income by altering processing decisions? If so, what would the expected overall net income be? Which products should be processed further and which should be sold at split-off? Assume that all costs incurred after split-off are variable.

RQ.20.23 The management of a company considers that product Y, one of its three main lines, is not as profitable as the other two, with the result that no particular efforts are being made to push its sales. The selling prices and costs of the products are:

Product	*Selling price*	*Direct material*	*Direct labour*		
			Department A	*Department B*	*Department C*
X	₹68	₹10	₹8	₹2	₹2
Y	58	6	2	8	2
Z	64	8	2	2	8

Overhead rates on each department per rupee of direct labour are as follows:

	Department A	Department B	Department C
Variable overhead	1.20	0.40	1.00
Fixed overhead	1.20	2.00	1.40
	2.40	2.40	2.40

What advice would you give to the management about the profitability of product Y? Give reasons.

RQ.20.24 A confectioner markets three products all of which require sugar. His average monthly sales, cost of sales and sugar consumption are as follows:

	Products			Total
	X	Y	Z	
Sales	₹1,00,000	₹1,20,000	₹80,000	₹3,00,000
Cost of sales (variable)	60,000	80,000	56,000	1,96,000
Sugar requirement (kgs)	500	800	240	1,540

Due to the Government restrictions, his sugar quota has been reduced to 1,405 kgs per month. Suggest a suitable sales mix which would give the company maximum profit under the given circumstances.

RQ.20.25 A company has asked for your assistance in determining the most profitable sales and product mix of its products for current year. The company manufactures a line of toys. The sales department has provided you with the following budget data:

Toy	Estimated demand (units)	Selling price per toy
A	60,000	₹14.50
B	1,00,000	7.90
C	70,000	16.60
D	45,000	25.20
E	2,20,000	6.00

The cost account has developed the following additional data from the accounting files.

1. Standard direct production cost per unit are as follows:

Toy	Materials	Labour
A	₹4.10	₹5.00
B	2.10	2.50
C	5.50	6.00
D	10.00	8.00
E	1.90	1.50

2. The standard wage rate of ₹10 per hour is expected to continue unchanged throughout the year. The plant has an effective production capacity of 1,51,000 labour-hours per year on a single shift. The current equipment can be used to produce any and all of the toys.
3. Variable manufacturing overhead is budgeted at ₹3 per direct labour-hour. Total fixed manufacturing overhead is planned at ₹7,20,000.

You are required to:

(i) Prepare a schedule that will be most useful to management in planning the product-mix. Determine the amount of net income at such a product-mix.

(ii) Is the present effective capacity on a single shift adequate to meet the estimated sales demand in current year? If not, what will the optimal product-mix be to keep producing within the limits of a single shift?

ANSWERS

[Comprehensive solutions to all numerical review questions are available on the companion website: http://www.mhhe.com/khan_jain_cost2e]

RQ.20.14 ₹27,50,000 lowest price; no sales value of special tools after their use, interest costs are ignored.

RQ.20.15 Yes, profitable to accept the order; increase in profits by ₹7,00,000.

RQ.20.16 Accept all export orders; increase in profits by ₹3,05,000.

RQ.20.17 Accept both the order; order O_1 will increase profits by ₹2,45,000 and O_2 by ₹2,35,000.

RQ.20.18 Net income, ₹2,86,000 (sales-mix 1), ₹2,16,000 (sales-mix 2).

RQ.20.19 **(i)** Product A, 20,000 units; Product B, 25,000 units; Product C, 10,000 units.
(ii) ₹95,000.

RQ.20.20 Profit, ₹5,20,000. Yes.

RQ.20.21 Continue to make the parts; purchases from outside supplier will increase costs by ₹1,00,000.

RQ.20.22 **(i)** Net income for product A is ₹1,70,000; product B, ₹8,000; product C, ₹8,000; and product D, ₹58,000.
(ii) Net income would decrease by altering processing decisions by ₹1,10,000 (from ₹2,44,000 to ₹1,34,000). Products A and D should be processed further; incremental profits are ₹1,00,000 and ₹20,000 respectively; unprofitable to process product B as it decreases profits by ₹10,000.

RQ.20.23 Product Y is profitable; contribution margin per unit is ₹32.40; continue its production.

RQ.20.24 Sales mix for products Z, X and Y is ₹80,000, ₹1,00,000 and ₹99,750 respectively. It is assumed that sales of individual products cannot be increased beyond ₹1,00,000 (product X), ₹1,20,000 (product Y) and ₹80,000 (product Z).

RQ.20.25 **(i)** Contribution margin per hour (key factor) is ₹7.8 (A); ₹10.20 (B), ₹5.50; (C), ₹6.00 (D); and ₹14.33 (E). Net income is ₹6,06,500.
(ii) No.

CASES

20.C.1 (Acceptance of Special Orders) M/s Precision Company Ltd (PCL) is in the business of making **Fingertrips**' brand calculators. Fingertrips brand of calculators has a good reputation among students, office staff and college faculty for its quality and price. Its current market price is ₹310 per calculator. Its unit cost structure is given in Exhibit 1.

Exhibit 1 Cost Structure of Fingertrips Calculators

Direct material cost	₹150
Direct labour cost	40
Variable overheads (including printing cost, ₹2 and packaging cost, ₹5)	40
Allocated fixed overheads	50
Total	280

The PCL was started three years ago. A market research had estimated a demand for 1,80,000 calculator annually. The PCL was set up with an installed capacity of 2,00,000 calculators. But even after 3 years the annual demand for Fingertrip calculators stood at 1,50,000 units. The CEO of PCL, Bharm Dharan, was concerned about its future prospects. Meanwhile, he got an export order from Dutch Exim Ltd (DEL), Netherlands, for 1,00,000 calculators at ₹260 per calculator.

DEL is in the business of marketing stationery to schools and offices and has planned to start selling calculators as well. It would import the Fingetrip brand calculators but put its own brand name and would also take care of packaging to suit the local market requirements. Initially, it is one-year contract renewable depending on market conditions.

The CEO of PCL is interested in the order as it would help in utilising the spare capacity of 50,000 units. The marketing manager of PCL, Sonal Agarwal, supports the proposal because the calculator would be sold in Netherlands under a different brand name, and the sale of Fignertrip calculators in the local market would not be adversely affected.

According to John Mathew, production manager, to increase the production capacity by 50,000 units, a new machine, similar to the one being currently used, would have to be acquired. Two alternative machines are available in the market. The first machine could be leased at an annual cost of ₹25 lakh. The maintenance cost per year is estimated to be ₹2 lakh. The second machine uses a new technology. It can be leased for an yearly rental of ₹30 lakh. However, the maintenance cost would be ₹1.5 lakh per year. The new technology-based machine would also reduce the labour cost and variable overhead cost by ₹5 and ₹2 per calculator respectively.

The CEO asks the finance manager to carry out a financial analysis of the alternatives.

REQUIRED

Based on the financial analysis, what recommendation would you, as the finance manger, make to the CEO of PCL?

SOLUTION

Financial (Incremental) Analysis of Export Order with Old Technology Machine

Increment revenues (₹260 × 1,00,000 calculators)		₹2,60,00,000
Less:		
• Direct material cost (₹150 × 1,00,000)	₹150,00,000	
• Direct labour cost (₹40 × 1,00,000)	40,00,000	
• Variable overheads (₹33@ × 1,00,000)	33,00,000	
• Lease rent	25,00,000	
• Maintenance cost	2,00,000	2,50,00,000
Incremental profits		10,00,000

@[₹40 – (₹2 printing cost – ₹5 packaging cost)]

Financial Analysis of Export Order With New Technology Machine

Increment revenues (₹260 × 1,00,000)		₹2,60,00,000
Less:		
• Direct material cost (₹150 × 1,00,000)	₹1,50,00,000	
• Direct labour cost [(₹40 × 50,000) + (₹35 × 50,000)]	37,50,000	
• Variable overheads [(₹33 × 50,000) + (₹31 × 50,000)]	32,00,000	
• Lease rent	30,00,000	
• Maintenance cost	1,50,000	2,51,00,000
Incremental profits		9,00,000

RECOMMENDATION The CEO should accept the export order. To increase the production capacity to meet the order, he should lease the old-technology machine as the incremental profits are higher.

20.C.2 (Shut-down Decision) M/S Janta Watch Company (JWC) manufacturers electronic watches in its manufacturing plant at Noida. It has not been doing well recently due to old technology and lack of effort in research and development. Moreover, due to the recent Free Trade Agreement between India and Thailand, chip electronic watches manufactured in Thailand and China are flooding the Indian market. As a result, the JWC is currently running only at its 50 per cent capacity. When the market conditions were good, JWC used to operate at full capacity of 4,00,000 watches per annum. The cost structure of JWC per watch is given in Exhibit 1.

Exhibit 1 Cost Structure of Janta Watches Per Watch

Direct material cost	₹30
Direct labour cost	8
Variable manufacturing overheads	12
Variable administrative overheads	10
	60

The unit sale price of Janta Watches is ₹100. The imported watches are available at a much lower price. JWC is consequently incurring huge losses. Meanwhile, a Japanese firm, Citizen Watch Company (CWC) has offered a new technology to JWC to compete with the imported watches. But due to some contractual obligations, the CWC would be able to handover the technology to JWC after one year.

The Chief Operating Officer of JWC, Sheshadri Chatterjee, has proposed a shutdown of operations for one year and its reopening after the new technology would be available. The CFO, Yogendra Dhabi, is not in favour of the one-year shutdown. The shutdown costs estimated by him are given in Exhibit 2.

Exhibit 2 One-year Shutdown Costs of JWC

Fixed costs (present, ₹90,00,000)	₹24,00,000
Settlement costs of personnel laid-off	6,00,000
Shut-down cost of plant	1,00,000
Reopening cost after 1 year	2,00,000
Total	33,00,000

REQUIRED In view of the conflicting opinion of the COO and the CFO, what course of action should the CEO of JWC take?

SOLUTION

Financial Analysis of CFO's proposal (Operate Plant)

Sales revenue [₹100 × 2,00,000 units (4,00,000 × 0.50)		₹2,00,00,000
Less Variable costs:		
Direct material costs (₹30 × 2,00,000)	₹60,00,000	
Direct labour cost (₹8 × 2,00,000)	16,00,000	
Manufacturing overheads (₹12 × 2,00,000)	24,00,000	
Administrative overheads (₹10 × 2,00,000)	20,00,000	1,20,00,000
Total contribution		80,00,000
Less fixed costs		90,00,000
Loss		(10,00,000)

Decision: As against a loss of ₹10,00,000 when the plant is operated, the shutdown cost (Exhibit 2) is ₹33,00,000. So the incremental cost of shutdown is ₹23,00,000. The CEO of JWC would be well advised to continue operating the Noida plant for one year, pending the introduction of new Japanese technology. In addition to the financial loss, the shutdown would also have implications in terms of adverse effect on reputation/distribution system, hampering of production line, theft of spare parts, unauthorised encroachment and so on.

20.C.3 (Shut-down Decision) Monte Carlo (MC) manufactures winter wear. For the coming season MC is planning to expand its product line by adding a new jacket as a follow-up to a market research conducted on its behalf involving an expenditure of ₹20,000. A committee comprising the finance manager, production manager, marketing manager and human resources manager has, after proper analysis, concluded as follows:

- The demand in the coming season would be for 10,000 jackets.
- The requirement of a special material which would have no other use would cost ₹100 per meter.

- There would be need for additional skilled and unskilled labour. Since there is a shortage of skilled labour, MC would have to reduce the production of one of its products, namely, pullovers, by 10,000 units, the unit contribution of pullovers being ₹10. The skilled labour will also require special training of 15 days in tune with the requirement of the new product at an estimated cost of ₹50,000.
- A new machine would have to be purchased at an estimated cost of ₹1,00,000, with a salvage value of ₹10,000 after producing 10,000 jackets.
- The cost, sales and profit data are developed by the cost accountants are summarised in Exhibit 1.

Exhibit 1 Cost Sheet

Material cost (2 meteres × ₹50)	₹100
Skilled labour (₹75 × 1 hour)	75
Market research (₹20,000 ÷ 10,000)	2
Training expenses (₹50,000 ÷ 10,000)	5
Unskilled labour (1 hour × ₹45)	45
Allocated fixed overheads	30
Additional allocated fixed costs	10
Salary of sales personnel	5
Sales commission	5
Advertisement	5
Total cost per unit	282
Profit per unit	8
Sales price per unit	290

- The skilled labour will require compensation @ 50 per cent of their regular wages for the entire remaining units if the production of jackets is discontinued at any stage.
- Raw material would be purchased in advance to avoid price rises and avail of purchase discounts.
- Advertising before launching the product will cost ₹50,000. The existing sales force would be used on commission basis to sell the new product.

To cope with the seasonal demand of jackets, production started immediately after a green signal from the CEO, Alok Dixit. After producing 5,000 jackets, the marketing department advertised the product. While collecting orders, the sales force found that other players have also entered the market. It was not possible to sell the jackets at the ₹290 quoted price. The marketing manager was able to find 5 wholesalers in different cities, each of whom was ready to purchase a lot of 2,000 jackets each for ₹260 per jacket. They were ready to acquire jackets in two equal lots, one right now and another after one month. The production system of MC is capable of producing 5,000 jackets every month.

If, however, production is stopped after producing the first 5,000 jackets, the machine purchased for the purpose can be sold for ₹15,000.

REQUIRED

The CEO of MC is confronted with the situation whether to discontinue further production of 5,000 jackets. What advise would you give him?

20.C.4 (Product Decision) Amrita Agro Ltd. (AAL) has since 1990 been manufacturing and marketing *vanaspati ghee*, cheese and chips under the brand names Gagan Vanastpai Ghee, Gagan Cheese and Gagan Chips. The AAL's performance has been satisfactory and it had consolidated its position in the market over the years. However, in recent months, Gagan Chips has been incurring losses. The product-wise income statement of AAL for the most recent month is summaried in Exhibit 1.

Exhibit 1 Product-wise Income Statement of AAL for Most Recent Month

Particulars	Gagan Vanaspati	Gagan Cheese	Gagan Chips	Total
Sales revenues	₹2,00,000	₹80,000	₹12,000	₹2,92,000
Less variable costs	80,000	50,000	5,000	1,35,000
Contribution margin	1,20,000	30,000	7,000	1,57,000
Less fixed costs for product line	10,000	5,000	4,000	19,000
Segment/product margin	1,10,000	25,000	3,000	1,38,000
Less firm-related fixed costs	10,000	8,000	4,000	22,000
Net income	1,00,000	17,000	(1,000)	1,16,000

The CEO of AAL, Komila Punia, and the Joint CEO, Annapurna Alladi, are concerned about the profitability of Gagan Chips.

REQUIRED:

Should Gagan Chips be dropped?

SOLUTION

Financial Analysis (Income Statement of AAL Without Gagan Chips)

Sales (₹2,00,000 + ₹80,000)	₹2,80,000
Less variable costs (₹80,000 + ₹50,000)	1,30,000
Contribution margin	1,50,000
Less product-line fixed costs	15,000
Product margin	1,35,000
Less firm-related fixed costs	22,000
Net income	1,13,000

Decision: Dropping of product line Gagan Chips would result in decline in profits of AAL. Its production should continue.

20.C.5 (Product-Mix) Assume for **22.C.4** the price and cost data per unit summarised in Exhibit 1.

Exhibit 1 Unit Sale Price and Cost of AAL

	Gagan Ghee	Gagan Cheese	Gagan Chips
Sales price per unit	₹40	₹25	₹15
Direct material cost per unit	6	3	3
Direct labour cost per unit	20	16	8
Variable overheads per unit	4	2	1

The projected output for a month is *ghee* 7,000 units, cheese 4,000 units and chips 10,000 units. Due to employee turnover in recent months, AAL is now left with only 350 workers. They work 24 days in a month and 8 hours per day. The direct wage rate is ₹4 per hour.

REQUIRED:

Determine the optimal product mix for AAL.

SOLUTION

Ranking In Order of Profitability of Products of AAL

	Gagan Ghee		Gagan Cheese		Gagan Chips	
1. Sales price per unit		₹40		₹25		₹15
2. Less variable cost per unit:						
• Direct material	₹6		₹3		₹3	
• Direct labour	20		16		8	
• Variable overheads	4	30	2	21	1	12

(*Contd.*)

(Contd.)

3. Contribution margin per unit	10	4	3
4. Direct labour hours (DLH) [Direct labour cost ÷ ₹4]	5	4	2
5. Contribution margin per DL hour (3 ÷ 4)	2	1	1.5
6. Rank (in order of profitability)	1	3	2

Statement Showing Utilisation of DLH Yielding Optimal Product-mix

Total direct labour-hours available: (350 workers × 25 days × 8 hours)		70,000
Direct labour-hours required to produce:		
• Gagan Ghee (7,000 × 5)	35,000	
• Gagan Chips (10,000 × 2)	20,000	55,000
DLHs available for Gagan Cheese		15,000
Units of cheese that can be produced (15,000 ÷ 4)		3,750

Income Statement for the Most Current Month of AAL

Particulars	*Gagan Ghee*	*Gagan Cheese*	*Gagan Chips*	*Total*
1. Units sold	7,000	3,750	10,000	
2. Unit sale price	₹40	₹25	₹15	
3. Sales revenue (1 × 2)	2,80,000	93,750	1,50,000	₹5,23,750
4. Variable costs per unit	30	21	12	
5. Total variable costs (1 × 4)	2,10,000	78,750	1,20,000	4,08,750
6. Contribution (3 – 5)	70,000	15,000	30,000	1,15,000
7. Total fixed costs				50,000
8. Net income				65,000

Decision: The optimal product-mix is: Gagan Ghee, 7,000; Gagan Cheese, 3,750; and Gagan Chips 10,000.

20.C.6 (Product Decisin) Apeksha Jain is the CEO of Nanak Milk Company Ltd. (NMCL). The NMCL has been in milk supply business over 20 years and has developed a good distribution channel for its business. Apeksha has invested in new technologies for pasteurising milk as a result of which milk stays fresh for 60 hours even after packaging. The milk is sold in special **PET** bottles which are bought from Avon Bottling Company Ltd for ₹0.50 per 500 ml (0.50 litre) bottle. The bottle are "take home" type, that is, the buyer takes away the bottle and need not return after consumption of milk. Keeping the brand reputation and Government regulations in view, NMCL has standing instructions to distributors to crush the unsold bottles after 2 days. The monthly production of milk by NMCL is 20,00,000 bottles and on average 80,000 bottles have to be crushed.

The cost (all variable) of a milk bottle is ₹9 comprising of procurement cost, ₹5.50, other variable cost, ₹3, and bottling cost ₹0.50. Total fixed costs amount to ₹1,20,00,000. The sale price of a bottle of milk is ₹12.

Due to competition from Mother Dairy, the sales of NMCL are declining having an adverse effect on its profitability. The CEO directs Adheer Upadhayay, CFO, to seek the opinion of Smart Consultants about the course of action to meet the situation. Smart Consultants have suggested the following alternatives:

Alternative I: Reduce production/supply by 50,000 bottles.

Alternative II: Make *paneer* from the unsold milk. The recalling costs of unsold (80,000) bottles to the factory would be ₹3 per bottle. The recalled bottles can be reused after washing. Milk from 4 bottles can be used to make 1 packet (200 gms) of *paneer* which can be sold at ₹35 per packet. All the *paneer* packets can be sold. The monthly incremental costs of manufacturing and selling *paneer* packets are as follows: **(a)** Labour cost, 20,000; **(b)** Overheads, ₹40,000; and **(c)** Selling costs, ₹30,000. The technology and machinery needed to make *paneer* is available with the NMCL.

REQUIRED: What course of actions should Apeksha Jain choose?

SOLUTION

Financial (Cost Savings) Analysis (To Decrease Production/Sale of Milk by 50,000 Bottles)

Total savings in variable cost (50,000 bottles × ₹9)	₹4,50,000
Loss of incremental profits (₹3 x 50,000 bottles)	1,50,000
	3,00,000

Financial Analysis (To Enter into *Paneer* Production)

Incremental sales (80,000 × 0.25 × ₹35)	₹7,00,000	
Savings in bottling cost (80,000 × 0.50)	40,000	₹7,40,000
Less incremental costs:		
• Labour costs	20,000	
• Overheads	40,000	
• Selling costs	30,000	
• Recalling costs (80,000 × ₹3)	2,40,000	3,30,000
		4,10,000

Decision: Apeksha Jain, the CEO of Nanak Milk Company should go for making *paneer*.

20.C.7 Supreme Construction Company (SCC) Ltd (Acceptance of Special Order) The SCC, a reputed construction firm, has won a contract for constructing 1,000 three-bedroom flats for a real estate firm, Dream Homes Limited. It has quoted a very competitive rate which is ₹17,00,000 per flat. The flats are to be completed in one year. The work is in progress at site. The SCC has submitted the bid price of ₹17,00,000 per flat on the basis of following analysis:

Cost Statement

Fixed Costs:\		
Office cost		₹10,00,000
Cost of concrete batching plant, tower crane and other equipments		20,00,00,000
Cost of shuttering		6,00,000
Cost of sample flat		9,00,000
Salary of permanent staff:		
Junior engineers (6 × ₹20,000 per month)	₹14,40,000	
Sr. engineers (3 × ₹40,000 per month)	14,40,000	
Project manager (₹90,000 per month)	10,80,000	
Clerks (2 × ₹10,000 each per month)	2,40,000	42,00,000
Total fixed cost		20,67,00,000
Variable Cost per flat:		
Raw material	8,50,000	
Labour cost	4,00,000	
Other variable costs	2,00,000	14,50,000
Total variable cost (1,000 flats × ₹14,50,000)		145,00,00,000

Income Statement

Sales revenue	₹170,00,00,000
Less: Total cost	165,67,00,000
Profit before taxes	4,33,00,000
Tax @ 35 per cent	1,51,55,000
Earnings after taxes (EAT)	2,81,45,000

The Dream Homes Limited (DHL) is selling the flats at ₹23,00,000 per flat which it has already booked fully through pre-launch. The cost of land incurred by Dream Homes is ₹2,00,000 per flat. It is earning a profit of ₹4,00,000 after paying ₹17,00,000 per flat to the SCC.

The DHL has another adjacent site where it wants to launch phase-II of its scheme consisting of 600 three-bedroom flats. However, due to recession in the market and demand for affordable housing, DHL is not able to sell its flats at its previous price of ₹23,00,000. The DHL's marketing team has assessed that they can get a maximum price of ₹21,00,000 per flat now. Therefore, it has given an offer of constructing 600 flats to the SCC at ₹16,00,000 per flat.

The technical team of the SCC has informed the CEO of the SCC, Himanshu Pandey, that they can complete the additional requirement of 600 flats in remaining six months with the same batching and equipments. However, they will require three more junior engineers and additional shuttering material costing ₹2,00,000. The CEO is contemplating whether to reject this offer as cost per flat is already ₹16,56,700 and the technical team has additional requirement of ₹5,60,000. He has asked his finance manager, Neeraj Bodra, to give his opinion.

REQUIRED: What advice should the finance manager give to the CEO of the SCC? Why?

SOLUTION

The finance manager after going through the costs involved presented the following incremental analysis to the CEO:

Sales revenue (₹16,00,000 × 600)	₹96,00,00,000
Incremental cost: Total variable cost (₹14,50,000 × 600)	87,00,00,000
Additional cost salary of 3 junior engineers (3 × ₹20,000 × 6)	3,60,000
Additional shuttering material	2,00,000
Incremental profit	8,94,40,000

As the SCC is expected to earn incremental profit of ₹8,94,40,000, the CEO should accept the offer.

20.C.8 (Special Order) Mr. Bharat Bhushan is the owner of a small manufacturing firm, Twinkle Light, which is into manufacturing of night lamps. Predicting a great demand for Diwali lights, he started producing the same as he had a confirmed order of 1,000 units from a buyer at ₹70 per unit; and who has paid a non-refundable advance of ₹5,000. To produce these lamps, he has to employ two additional workers, each at ₹300 per day. Also, he has to take on rent a machine which is used to make covers for fancy lights for ₹15,000 per month. He has also to purchase some consumables like lubricant oil, etc., for ₹2,000.

He started producing 50 units per day. Eight days after starting production, he received a call from the buyer expressing his inability to buy all the 1,000 units since the market price of Diwali lights had fallen due to unexpectedly high import of cheaper Chinese lights. However, he was wiling to buy the units made up to that time at ₹40 per unit. If Mr. Bharat decides to sell the units produced during the eight days, he would have to pay to each labour ₹1,000 as compensation charges. The scrap value of the remaining raw material is ₹2,000. He also has an offer from a buyer who is ready to buy completed 1,000 units at ₹30 per unit. The buyer would accept the complete order or nothing at all. What should Mr. Bharat Bhushan do now?

SOLUTION

(1) Determination of Incremental Sale Revenue if Units Made in 8 days are Sold @ ₹40

Sales (400 units × ₹40)	₹16,000
Less advance payment	(5,000)
Payment to be received from the buyer	11,000
Scrap value of raw materials	2,000
Total	13,000
Less incremental costs: Compensation to labour (₹1,000 × 2)	2,000
Incremental profit (decrease in loss)	11,000

Income Statement:

Costs already incurred:	
Machine rent	₹15,000
Consumables	2,000
Material cost	30,000
Labour cost (2 workers × ₹300 × 8 days)	4,800
Labour compensation (2 workers × ₹1,000)	2,000
Total cost	53,800
Sales revenue	11,000
Advanced payment received	5,000
Sale of raw material	2,000
Total revenues	18,000
Loss	(35,800)

(2) Determination of Incremental Profit if an Offer to Supply 1,000 units @ ₹30 is Accepted

Sale (1,000 units x ₹30)	₹30,000
Labour compensation saved	2,000
Less incremental costs:	
Wages of labour (₹300 × 2 × 12)	(7,200)
Raw material opportunity cost	(2,000)
Incremental profit/Decrease in loss	22,800

Income Statement

Machine rent	₹15,000
Consumables	2,000
Material cost	30,000
Labour cost (2 workers × ₹300 × 20 days)	12,000
Total cost	59,000
Sales revenue (1,000 units × ₹30)	30,000
Advanced payment received	5,000
Total revenues	35,000
Loss	(24,000)

RECOMMENDATION There is a decrease in loss of ₹11,800 (₹35,800 – ₹24,000) when the decision to sell the complete order at ₹30 is taken. Therefore, Mr. Bharat Bhushan should accept the offer from the second buyer.

20.C.9 (Special Order) Telshodan Ltd (TL) is in the business of refining and marketing of petroleum products. The company imports crude oil and refines in its refinery situated at Panvel near Mumbai. There are three finished products after refining, namely, petrol, diesel and lube oil. It sells the finished product to registered dealers in India. As the dealers take delivery of the finished products from the refinery, there is no transportation cost for Telshodhan Limited.

Presently, TL has capacity of 15 MMTPA (million metric ton per annum) crude refining. It is operating presently at a capacity of 11.5 MMTPA crude refining. Normally, 5 per cent of the input is lost during the process of refining. The normal mix of the total finished product contains 38 per cent of petrol, 50 per cent of diesel and 12 per cent lube oil.

The crude oil currently costs ₹290 crore per MMT, the labour cost is ₹30 crore per MMT and other variable cost (including maintenance cost) is ₹40 crore per MMT for crude oil processing. The current selling price of finished products are ₹540 crore, ₹310 crore and ₹680 crore per MMT for petrol, diesel and lube oil, respectively. It is expected that the cost of crude oil is not going to vary in the coming year and the price of finished products are also likely to remain constant.

Telshodhan Limited got a fresh order of 1.9 MMT of petrol, 2.5 MMT of diesel and 0.6 MTM of lube oil for ₹510 crore, ₹290 crore and ₹630 crore per MMT for petrol, diesel and lube oil, respectively, from Telvikreta Limited. If the TL buys the finished products from another refining company, Telzone Limited, it will have to pay ₹508 crore, ₹287 crore and ₹628 crore per MMT for petrol, diesel and lube oil, respectively. It will also involve an additional safe packaging (because petroleum products are highly inflammable and require proper safety precautions in packaging) and transportation cost (to deliver up to the tankers of Telshodhan Ltd in specially designed safe transporting tankers) of ₹35 crore per MMT of finished products.

Mr. Sanjay Khanna, the MD of Telshodhan Limited, convened a meeting of managers from the finance, production, marketing and technical departments of the company to discuss the proposal so as to take a final decision on the new order by Televikreta Ltd. The following additional facts emerged in the meeting:

- ➢ As the machines are working at a capacity of 11.5 MMTPA, the unused capacity of 3.5 MMTPA is available for further production.
- ➢ As it is an opportunity to expand the market, the company should not lose the order. However, the production department is not ready to refine more than their maximum capacity, that is, 15 MMTPA.
- ➢ The technical department is agreeable to increase the capacity by 2 MMTPA. It will require setting up an additional vessel in whole volume capacity like 1, 2, 3 MMTPA and not in fraction like 1.5, 2.3 and so on to meet additional demand of Televikreta Ltd. This will require an additional fixed cost of ₹50 crore.
- ➢ The labour cost and other variable cost for crude oil processing will remain the same, that is, ₹30 crore and ₹40 crore per MMT, respectively.

On the basis of above information and other relevant financial aspects, the finance manager, Virendra Rathi, was then asked to submit a report on the alternatives available to carry out the offer/proposal, namely:

1. Increase the processing capacity of crude oil by 2 MMTPA to 17 MMTPA
2. Utilise the full capacity of existing refinery and outsource the additional volume of finished products from Telzone Ltd.

The data compiled by Virendra Rathi, in consultation with Bikrant Singh, the Controller of Accounts, for the purpose of the analysis of the two alternatives is summarised below.

Alternative 1: Increase the Processing Capacity of Crude Oil from 15 MMTPA to 17 MMTPA

Computation of Incremental Profit

Particulars	*Amount (₹crore)*	*Total Amount (₹crore)*
Increase in Sales Revenue:		
1.9 MMTPA of petrol (1.9 × ₹510)	969.0	
2.5 MMTPA of diesel (2.5 × ₹290)	725.0	
0.6 MMTPA of petrol (0.6 × ₹630)	378.0	2,072.0
Less Incremental Cost:		
Additional material cost (5.263[@] × ₹290)	1,526.27	
Additional labour cost (5.263 × ₹30)	157.89	
Additional variable overheads (5.263 × ₹40)	210.52	
Additional fixed cost for setting up of an additional vessel	50.00	1,944.68
Incremental Profit (₹2,072.0 – ₹1,944.68)		127.32

[@]The volume crude oil required for 5.0 MMTPA finished product (as 5 per cent crude is lost in processing) = (5.0/0.95) MMTPA = 5.263 MMTPA.

Alternative 2: Buy Additional Requirement of Finished Products From Telzone Limited.

Computation of Incremental Profit (₹crore)

Increase in Sales Revenue:		
1.9 MMTPA of petrol (1.9 × ₹510)	₹969.0	
2.5 MMTPA of diesel (2.5 × ₹290)	725.0	
0.6 MMTPA of petrol (0.6 × ₹630)	378.0	₹2,072.0
Less Incremental Cost:		
Additional material cost (3.5 × ₹290)	1,015.0	
Additional labour cost (3.5 × ₹30)	105.0	
Additional variable overheads (3.5 × ₹40)	140.0	
Additional cost of purchase of finished petrol (0.636 × ₹508)	323.09	
Additional cost of purchase of finished diesel (0.837 × ₹287)	240.22	
Additional cost of purchase of finished lube oil (0.202 × ₹628)	126.9	
Additional cost of packaging and transporting of finished products (1.675 × ₹35)	58.62	2,008.83
Incremental Profit (₹2072.0 – ₹2008.79)		63.17

Summary: The report of the finance manager shows that alternative 1 is better than alternative 2 as the incremental profit is more but in the second alternative the capacity of refining crude oil of Telshodhan Limited will increase from 15 MMTPA to 17 MMTPA and the dependence on another supplier to execute additional order will be avoided. So, it is better for Telshodhan Ltd to go for expansion to meet the order of Telvikreta Ltd.

WORKING NOTES

1. By processing 3.5 MMTPA crude in own refinery, 3.325 MMTPA finished products will be manufactured in the following quantities:

Quantity of petrol produced (0.38 × 3.325) MTTPA	= 1.264 MMTPA
Quantity of diesel produced (0.50 × 3.325) MTTPA	= 1.663 MMTPA
Quantity of lube oil produced (0.12 × 3.325) MTTPA	= 0.399 MMTPA

2. Quantity of finished products required purchasing from Telzone Limited

Quantity of petrol to be purchased (1.900 – 1.264) MMTPA	= 0.636 MMTPA
Quantity of diesel to be purchased (2.500 – 1.663) MMTPA	= 0.837 MMTPA
Quantity of petrol to be purchased (0.600 – 0.398) MMTPA	= 0.202 MMTPA

Total finished product volume to be purchased from Telzone Limited = (0.636 + 0.837 + 0.202) = 1.675 MMTPA. The packaging and transportation cost will be applicable on this volume.

20.C.10 (Product Mix) BASF is planning to introduce three new products in the market, namely, Relugan RE, Relugan RF and Relugan FS. The budgeted annual production of the three chemicals agreed upon by the top management comprising of Sachin Wasuja and Nikhil Pathak in discussion with the production manager, Malay Khasnavis, is 12,000, 16,000 and 20,000 kg, respectively. The sale price of each of the products as decided by the top management is ₹90, ₹120 and ₹60 per kg of the respective products. The fixed overheads associated with the manufacturing of these three products are found to be ₹5,00,000 per annum. The sales department, however, is very enthusiastic about the products and is predicting the sales to be at least 25 per cent higher than the budgeted production level. The BASF has a policy of pricing their products three times of the direct material consumed. It has observed that in manufacturing a product, the major costs incurred are the direct material and the direct labour costs which account for 80 per cent of the total variable costs. There are two departments within the company, namely, (i) the production department and (ii) the spray drying department, through which the products are manufactured into its final form. The cost of labour in the production department is ₹2 per hour and in the spray department is ₹1 per hour. One kg of Relugan RE takes 8 and 4 hours in the production and spray drying departments, respectively. Corresponding time taken by Relugan RF is 10 hours in each department and by Relugan FS are 4 and 6 hours in each of the departments, respectively. The spray drying department employs skilled labour set which is in short supply. So, the spray drying department is not in a position to enhance its capacity.

REQUIRED: The BASF management has furnished the above information to its financial advisor, Mr. Rajeev Khandelwal, and has sought his advice on the product-mix profitability of the project.

SOLUTION

Statement Showing Profit on Current Budgeted Production

Particulars	*Products*							
	Relugan RE		*Relugan RF*		*Relugan FS*		*Total*	
Sales revenue		₹10,80,000		₹19,20,000		₹,12,00,000		₹,42,00,000
Less: Variable costs:								
Direct materials	₹3,60,000		₹6,40,000		₹4,00,000		₹14,00,000	
Direct labour:								
Production Department	1,92,000		3,20,000		1,60,000		6,72,000	
Spray Drying Department	48,000		1,60,000		1,20,000		3,28,000	
Overheads	1,50,000	7,50,000	2,80,000	14,00,000	1,70,000	8,50,000	6,00,000	30,00,000
Contribution		3,30,000		5,20,000		3,50,000		12,00,000
Less: Fixed Costs								5,00,000
Operating profit								7,00,000

Statement Showing Profit on Production of Optimal Product Mix

Particulars	*Products*							
	Relugan RE		*Relugan RF*		*Relugan FS*		*Total*	
Sales revenue		₹13,50,000		₹24,00,000		₹, 6,80,000		₹, 44,30,000
Less: Variable costs:								
Direct materials	₹, 4,50,000		₹, 8,00,000		₹2,26,700		₹14,76,700	
Direct labour:								
Production Department	2,40,000		4,00,000		90,600		7,30,600	
Spray Drying Department	60,000		2,00,000		68,000		3,28,000	
Overheads	1,87,500	9,37,500	3,50,000	17,50,000	96,300	4,81,600	6,33,800	31,69,100
Contribution		4,12,500		6,50,000		1,98,400		12,60,900
Less: Fixed Costs								5,00,000
Operating profit								7,60,900

WORKING NOTES

The labour hours in the Spray Drying Department are limited because we are not in a position to hire additional workforce to increase the labour hours to maximise our profit. So, we need to alter our product mix in such a manner so that there is a maximum contribution margin per hour used of Spray Drying Department. This, In turn, would maximise operating profits of the firm.

Total labour hours available in the Spray Drying Department = (4 × 12,000) + (10 × 16,000) + (6 × 20,000) = 3,28,000

Contribution margin per hour of the Spray Drying Department:

Relugan RE = ₹3,30,000 ÷ (12,000 × 4) = ₹6.875

Relugan RF = ₹5,20,000 ÷ (16,000 × 10) = 3.250

Relugan FS = ₹3,50,000 ÷ (20,000 × 6) = 2.917

Relugan RE having the highest contribution margin amongst all the three products should be given the highest priority in production followed by Relugan RF and Relugan FS, respectively. So, Relugan RE needs to be produced as per the full requirement of 15,000 kg, and in the same way Relugan RF needs to be produced 20,000 kgs.

Total labour hour consumed in production of the required quantity of Relugan RE and Relugan RF = (4 × 15,000) + (10 × 20,000) = 2,60,000

Remaining labour hours in the Treatment Department = 3,28,000 – 2.60,000 = 68,000.

Number of units of Relugan FS that can be produced = 68,000 ÷ 6 = 11,333.

20.C.11 (Shutdown Vs Operate Plant) ABJ Computer Services Private Limited was established in 1998 on the Build-Market-Retail Model of HP Inc of the USA. Its founder Managing Director is Mr. Ankur Sood who is conservative in his approach in dealing with financial details of his company. Mr. Ankur Sood has worked very hard for establishing the ABJ Computers and since the company was doing well he was satisfied with his efforts. ABJ's crown jewel is its manufacturing plant which is renowned for its efficiency in India and abroad. It manufactures various models of computers catering to the needs of the modern consumer. India being a low penetration market, the MD of the ABJ Computers, focussed on the US for its growth and has since enjoyed a large share of the market in the US It has established itself as a household brand image/equity.

Markets in the US have been under serious strain in recent times due to the Subprime crisis and the orders for computers are drying up fast. The situation is tense for Mr. Ankur Sood whose company is in throes due to this financial crisis. Like a silver lining to the cloud, Mr. Ankur Sood received an order for 15,800 computers for four different models of computers for the month of October 2009. Mr Sood who is a big supplier and usually deals with order size greater than 2,00,000 and above is reasonably disappointed and rejects the order on the following grounds:

- His company is a big company and will not supply such a small order.
- This order size would entail considerable costs on the machines and labour used since Mr. Sood feels that the marginal costs for large orders keep on reducing as the order size grows larger than 2,00,000.
- His company would not be able to recover the additional expenses entailed in processing such a small order.
- The crisis would lead to a further drop in the rates of computers and since the company is not hedging the price of the order it doesn't make sense to accept such a small order.

Mr. Ankur Sood discusses the order with his finance director, Balamurgan, and the marketing director, Jitendra Kumar. He also tells them about his decision of not taking the order and asks them about his opinion. He asks the finance director to examine the order more closely and advise him in regard to the acceptance of the order. In the light of the order schedule for October 2009 and the costing for the four computers, the following facts emerge.

(i) Break-up of Fixed Costs

Administration Cost:	
Office expenses	₹55,00,000
Electricity	18,00,000
Salary	3,09,00,000
Manufacturing Cost:	
Factory insurance	24,00,000
Factory rent	1,50,00,000
Indirect labour cost	53,00,000
Workflow standardisation	1,40,00,000
Selling Cost:	
Warehousing and storage	2,60,00,000
Transportation	56,00,000
Distribution and logistics	1,70,00,000
Total	12,35,00,000

The finance director estimates that approximately ₹1,00,00,000 would be incurred as additional fixed costs on account of maintenance of machines and production set-up costs in case the company decides to accept the order.

(ii) Estimated Variable Costs Per Unit Produced

Part Name	*Destktop*	*Server*	*Laptop*	*Tablet*
Hard disk	₹2,500	₹50,000	₹4,000	₹6,000
RAM	3,000	10,000	5,000	7,000
Graphics card	500	N/A	1,500	2,500
TFT screen	10,000	N/A	15,000	30,000
Motherboard	4,000	15,000	8,000	10,000
Keyboard	1,000	N/A	3,000	4,000
Mouse	250	N/A	N/A	N/A
Processor	6,000	25,000	15,000	20,000
Touchpad	N/A	N/A	2,000	2,000
Battery	N/A	N/A	1,000	2,000
UPS	2,000	5,000	N/A	N/A
Direct labour	300	500	800	1,000
Variable Overheads:				
Manufacturing	80	160	260	320
Administration	40	40	90	90
Selling	60	100	130	190
Total Variable Cost Per Unit	29,730	1,05,800	55,780	85,100

(iii) Order Schedules for October as Detailed Out in Purchase Books

Product	*Number of Units*	*Selling Price/Unit*
Desktop	6,500	₹35,000
Server	1,800	1,25,000
Laptop	5,000	64,000
Tablet	2,500	92,000

The finance director then performs an incremental analysis to analyse the situation and judge whether to accept the order or shut down the plant in the month of October.

Decision Analysis Whether to Accept the Order or Not

Product	*Number of units*	*Selling price per unit*	*Total revenue*
Incremental sales revenue:			
Desktop	6,500	₹35,000	22,75,00,000
Server	1,800	1,25,000	22,50,00,000
Laptop	5,000	64,000	32,00,00,000
Tablet	2,500	92,000	23,00,00,000
Total	15,800		100,25,00,000
Incremental cost:			
Desktop	6,500	₹29,730	₹19,32,45,000
Server	1,800	1,05,800	19,04,40,000
Laptop	5,000	55,780	27,89,00,000
Tablet	2,500	85,100	21,27,50,000
Additional fixed cost			1,00,00,000
Total			88,53,35,000
Incremental profit (₹10,025,00,000 – ₹88,53,35,000)			11,71,65,000

Decision Analysis: Shut Down or Operate Plant

Particulars	*Operate*	*Shutdown*
Estimated Revenue	₹100,25,00,000	
Less Variable Cost	87,53,35,000	
Contribution	12,71,65,000	
Less Fixed Cost	12,35,00,000	₹12,35,00,000
Less Additional fixed cost	1,00,00,000	
Net profit (loss)	(63,35,000)	(12,35,00,000)

RECOMMENDATION After carrying all the analyses, the finance director submits his report to the MD which is as under:

- ABJ Computers should accept the order in October as the incremental profit (which is the decrease in loss) is ₹11,58,65,000.
- By operating the plant the company is reducing the losses from ₹12,35,00,000 (if plant is shut down in October) to ₹63,35,000 if the company continues with the small order in hand.

Select Bibliography

Anderson, D.L. and D.L. Raun, *Information Analysis in Management Accounting* (Santa Barbara, John Wiley), 1978.

Anderson, W.T., C.A. Moyer and A.R. Wyatt, (Ed.), *Accounting: Basic Financial, Cost and Control Concepts* (New York John Wiley), 1965.

Anthony, R.N., *Management Accounting—Text and Cases* (Illinois, Irwin), 1970.

———, *Accounting: Text and Cases* (New Delhi, Tata McGraw-Hill), 1995

——— and G.A. Welsch, *Fundamentals of Management Accounting*, (Illinois, Irwin), 1981.

Baxter, W.T. and S. Davidson (Eds.), *Studies in Accounting, (London, England Institute of Chartered Accountants)*, 1977.

Bierman, H., Jr. and A.R. Drebin, *Management Accounting*, (New York, Macmillan), 1976.

Boer, G., *Direct Cost and Contribution Accounting*, (London, John Wiley), 1974.

Brown, R.G., *Decision Rules for Inventory Management*, (New York, Holt, Rinehart and Winston), 1963.

Bruns, W.J. and D.T. Decoster, *Accounting and Its Behavioural Implications*, (New York, McGraw-Hill), 1969.

Chatfield, M. and D. Neilson, *Cost Accounting*, (New York, Harcourt Brace Jovanovich, Inc.) 1983.

Copeland, R.M. and P.E. Dascher, *Management Accounting*, (New York, John Wiley), 1978.

Crowningshield, G.R. and K.A. Gorman, *Cost Accounting: Principles and Managerial Applications*, (Boston, Houghton Mifflin Company), 1979.

Cushing, B.E., *Accounting Information Systems and Business Organisation*, (London, Addison Wesley), 1978.

Dearden, J., *Cost Accounting and Financial Control Systems*, (California, Addison-Wesley Pub. Co.), 1976.

Decoster, D.T. and E.L. Schafer, *Management Accounting: A Decision Emphasis*, (New York, John Wiley), 1979.

Garrison, R.H. and Eric Noreen, *Managerial Accounting*, (New York, McGraw-Hill), 1997.

Gibbs, G., *Accounting for Management Decisions*, (Scranton, International Textbook), 1968.

Gordon, M.J. and G. Shillinglow, *Accounting: A Management Approach*, (Illinois, Irwin), 1974.

Hartley, R.V., *Cost and Managerial Accounting*, (Boston, Allyn and Bacon, Inc.), 1983.

Horngren, C.T., *Accounting for Management Control*, (New Jersey, Prentice-Hall), 1978.

———, *Cost Accounting: A Managerial Emphasis*, (New Delhi, Prentice-Hall), 1997.

Horngren, C.T. and G.L. Sundlem, *Introduction to Management Accounting,* (New Delhi, Prentice-Hall), 1990.

Institute of Chartered Accountants, *Standard Costing: An Introduction to the Accounting Processes,* (London), 1956.

Laidler, E., *Variance Accounting,* (London, Mcmillan), 1976.

Matz, A. and M.F. Usry, *Cost Accounting: Planning and Control,* (Ohio, South Western Publishing Company), 1976.

Maner, M.W., *Cost Accounting,* (New York, McGraw-Hill), 1997.

Meigs, R.F., *Accounting: The Basis for Business Decisions,* (McGraw-Hill, New York), 1996.

Metcalf, R.W. and P.L. Titard, *Principles of Accounting,* (Philadelphia, W.B. Saunder), 1976.

Moore, C.L. and R.K., Jaedicke, *Managerial Accounting,* (New York, South Western Publishing Company), 1976.

Morse, D., Managerial Accounting, (New York, McGraw-Hill), 1997.

Moscove, S.A. *et. al., Cost Accounting-with Managerial Applications* (Boston, Houghton Mifflin Company), 1985.

Moriarity, S. and C.P. Allen, *Cost Accounting* (New York, Haper and Row), 1984.

National Association of Accountants, *Statement on Management Accounting Practices,* (New York, NAA), 1971.

———, *Managing the Cash Flow,* 1974.

———, *Developing and Reporting of Variances,* 1962.

———, *Direct Costing,* 1953.

———, *Separating and Using Costs as Fixed and Variable, 1960.*

———, *Applications of Direct Costing,* 1961.

———, *Cost-Volume-Profit Relationships,* 1962.

———, *Accounting for Costs of Capacity,* 1963.

———, *Product Costs for Pricing Purposes,* 1953.

———, *Analysis of Non-manufacturing Costs for Managerial Decisions,* 1951.

Pierce, G.J., *Measurement of Capital Employed* (London, Business Books), 1972.

Rayburn, L.G., *Principles of Cost Accounting: Managerial Applications,* (Homewood, Illinois, Irwin), 1983.

Shillinglow, G., *Managerial Cost Accounting,* (Illinois, Irwin), 1977.

———, *Cost Accounting: Analysis and Control,* (Illinois, Irwin), 1967.

Thacker, R.J., *Introduction to Modern Accounting,* (New Jersey, Prentice-Hall), 1977.

——— and R.L. Smith, *Modern Management Accounting,* (Reston, Reston Publishing Company), 1977.

Tracy, J.F., *Fundamentals of Management Accounting,* (New York, John Wiley), 1976.

Willsmore, A.W., *Accounting for Management Control,* (London, Pitman), 1971.

Zimmerman, J., *Accounting for Decision Making and Control,* (New York, McGraw-Hill), 1997.

Index